THE HANDYMAN'S GUIDE

THE HANDYMAN'S GUIDE

Essential Woodworking Tools and Techniques

PAUL N. HASLUCK

SKYHORSE PUBLISHING

Skyhorse Publishing books may be purchased in bulk at special discounts for sales promotion, corporate gifts, fund-raising, or educational purposes. Special editions can also be created to specifications. For details, contact the Special Sales Department, Skyhorse Publishing, 307 West 36th Street, 11th Floor, New York, NY 10018 or info@skyhorsepublishing.com.

Skyhorse® and Skyhorse Publishing® are registered trademarks of Skyhorse Publishing, Inc.®, a Delaware corporation.

www.skyhorsepublishing.com

10 9 8 7 6 5 4 3 2 1

Library of Congress Cataloging-in-Publication Data is available on file.

ISBN: 978-1-60239-173-4

Printed in the United States of America

PREFACE.

THE HANDYMAN'S BOOK is a practical work on practical handicraft in wood, and it is published in the confident belief that it is by far the most exhaustive book on the subject hitherto produced.

The book is intended for all those who would handle tools, and who, by the use of them, wish to furnish the home and to profit their pockets. The treatment adopted throughout is simple and practical, and there has been a consistent endeavour to combine accurate information with clear and definite instruction, anything that did not further this object having been excluded. The amateur's restricted requirements have been carefully studied; still the contents make a direct appeal to the professional craftsman in carpentry, joinery, and cabinet work, to whom this book will be invaluable for ready reference, containing as it does a large and varied collection of workmanlike designs for a multitude of articles of use in the homestead, garden, workshop, office, and home. This book will be found especially useful to colonists and persons in out-of-the-way places, as it teems with practical hints and details that must be of the utmost worth to those whose very existence often depends on their ability to use woodworking tools.

Woodworkers' tools, materials, and processes are treated of in a manner that is both simple and explicit. The seven chapters on tools are in themselves a comprehensive treatise in which the shape, construction, manipulation, care and maintenance of all approved hand tools used in present-day woodworking are profitably discussed and described and clearly illustrated. The processes explained include all the more general operations of setting out work, cutting, planing, sawing, boring, jointing, etc., as well as some that are more special in character, such as turning and veneering, and in every case the process is explained step by step, plain instruction being rendered the more explicit by the lavish use of illustrations.

Mere amateurism and faddishness have been avoided. The tools and processes described are those found in daily use in the workshop. The expert and well-informed reader will, of course, make due allowance for the great variations of trade practice in different localities. Throughout this book actual practice is recorded, and mere discussion of theory has been excluded, except where it is an essential preliminary to understanding the principles underlying a method, a process, or the action of a tool. The examples of construction have been adapted from existing articles, and the columns of WORK and BUILDING WORLD, two weekly journals it is my fortune to edit, have been drawn on

PREFACE.

freely. In most cases the method of doing the work is described by the actual maker, who often is the designer as well; but the matter has been, where thought desirable, re-arranged, altered, and in some cases re-written, in accordance with the general plan of the book and with the endeavour to present the information in the clearest possible manner, and to adopt a simple and consistent style throughout.

Wood is the material chiefly used in the construction of the articles described in this book, and the section relating to it exhausts the subject as far as it is of practical interest to the handicraft woodworker. Enough of botany is introduced to make intelligible the process of seasoning; converting is sufficiently explained; and, to assist the inexperienced person in judging and selecting wood, the many varieties of commercial timber are plainly described.

The thousand and one examples of woodwork, here treated where necessary in minute detail, are arranged as far as possible so as to form a graded course, ranging in domestic furniture from a simple paste-board to a chiffonier or bedstead, in office furniture from a paper rack to a pedestal writing-desk, and in homestead and garden appurtenances from a chicken-run to a greenhouse. Chapters on outdoor rustic carpentry, gates, rough fencing, etc., are also given; and the wide range indicated affords ample scope for a most extensive variety of examples in practical handicraft in wood.

The book contains more than 2,500 illustrations, many of which have been specially photographed by myself. Neither trouble nor expense has been spared in making them really helpful, and an examination of the pages will show their value. Fully two-thirds of their number portray in detail articles that can be made by the handyman who has systematically pursued the graded course of study set out in this book. Of the remaining illustrations—more than 500 show woodworkers' tools and appliances; and in this connection special acknowledgment must be made to Messrs. Marples & Sons, Sheffield; Messrs. Melhuish, Sons & Co., London; Messrs. C. Nurse & Co., London; Messrs. Chas. Churchill & Co., Ltd., London; Mr. H. Hobday, Chatham; Messrs. O'Brien, Thomas & Co., London; and Messrs. Spear & Jackson, Sheffield, for their great help in kindly having lent electrotypes illustrating modern tools of approved design.

The eighteen-page index, containing between 3,000 and 4,000 entries, affords a means by which readers can easily find any item of information contained in the book.

P. N. HASLUCK.

CONTENTS.

CONTENTS.

WOODWORKING.

—◆◇◆—

INTRODUCTION.

THE SCOPE AND OBJECT OF THIS BOOK.

WOODWORKING is intended to treat fully upon mechanical handicraft, to show what to do and how to do it, to include the tools, materials, and processes, and to be supplemented with a full selection of varied examples of work. The tools will be described and illustrated, and their peculiar features and adaptability will be discussed. The materials will be examined and the characteristics of different varieties will be mentioned, and the suitability of each explained. The processes incidental to woodworking, such as preparing stuff, setting out work, making joints, etc., will be detailed. Specimens of handicraft work in wood will be minutely portrayed in working drawings, beginning with simple work involving but slight skill to execute, and advancing to complex work developing the highest dexterity. The contents of the book range from the rudimentary teaching that will show the tyro how to hold tools to the construction of high-class examples that will interest the adept craftsman.

WHAT IS A TOOL?

A tool may be considered to be any implement used for performing or facilitating mechanical operations, or for enabling man to change the form of material; but perhaps the second definition is too restrictive, and if it is adopted, certain so-called tools will be found to be mere contrivances. According to it a chisel or a hammer is a tool; but the boxing of a chisel or a

plane and the handle of a hammer are contrivances, for by them the modes of application and the power of the tools are extended and varied; and according to the second definition, a vice, a soldering bit, a nail, a square are not tools, but "contrivances" only. This is the opinion of Mr. A. Rigg, M.A., as expressed in Cantor Lectures delivered before the Society of Arts. According to the lecturer, it is hardly possible to draw a distinction between a tool and a machine. Whilst the former is more simple than the latter, they so merge into one another that it is difficult to determine where one ends and the other begins. For example, a lathe is a handicraft tool, and yet in its highly developed form it is a very complicated machine. It was one of the earliest devices to be erased from the list of tools and promoted to a place amongst machines.

TOOLS AS HUMAN BENEFACTORS.

It may be said that tools increase and vary human power, economise human time, and convert substances apparently the most common and worthless into valuable and useful products. Without tools the hand would be nearly powerless; add to it a hammer and a cutting instrument, and its capacity is increased many fold. Rollers as a means of moving heavy blocks of stone were a contrivance which very largely extended the powers of men; the application of grease to bearings and surfaces enabled man to utilise a much larger portion of his power; whoever first pointed a strip of bone or shell, and made an eye in it, gave to man as a tool an invention far exceeding in importance and value anything yet accomplished by heat or electricity ; and whoever first applied a barb to a spear and a hook, introduced a contrivance of inestimable importance.

TOOLS USED IN PREHISTORIC TIMES.

Aristotle (384—322 B.C.) made the first known attempt at determining the place which man should occupy in a general zoological classification. He selected as the distinguishing characteristic of man, regarded for this purpose alone, that man was ".a tool-making animal," and he could not find any other group of animals who made special implements and used them as man does tools. This view of man is accepted generally, and in recent times the inferences from it are wider and more extended than Aristotle could have anticipated, antiquarians now admitting that wherever on the earth tools are found, there men must once have dwelt. The first traces of tools are said to be met with in the post-tertiary strata, and the inference is, that man's existence may be placed so far back that centuries seem insignificant periods of time. Sir Charles Lyell speculates that at least two hundred thousand years have passed since implements were formed ; these implements are found in the respective geological strata, not in isolation, but in groups which are silent evidences of facts long precedent to all human traditions. History, at all reliable, written in a known language, and in intelligible alphabetical characters, does not carry further back than the days of Herodotus ("the father of history"), born between 490 and 480 B.C. In a scheme of geological strata, the strata found above the tertiary are divided into three classes—the post-glacial, prehistoric, and historic ; in the post-glacial there are not any traces of handicraft work ; in the prehistoric, there are found remains of canoes made of trees, of dwellings erected on piles, implements made of flint and stone, and fragments of charred wood. For the present purpose these are three

"ages": in the first one tools were of stone, and this is again subdivided into two periods, the palæolithic or ancient stone period, when the stone tools were left with rude and rough exteriors, and the neolithic or recent, when there was somewhat of an external finish or polish on the tools. In the second age bronze tools are found, and also those of pure copper, these latter tools being so rare that they are comprehended in the term bronze. In the third age tools are of iron, and form an introduction to the present age. These ages are not markedly distinct, and it is probable that whilst in one part of the world men were using bronze, in another they were using iron. It is known that in times to which even geologists might hesitate to apply the term "recent," the smelting of copper and of tin was known, and the combining of these metals to form a bronze as hard as any made and used at the present time was also practised. An analysis of these ancient bronze implements shows that the copper is alloyed with from 5 to 10 per cent. of tin. Analysis of Egyptian bronze implements gives 94·0 copper, 5·9 tin, and 0·1 iron.

TOOLS USED BY SAVAGE RACES.

Another source of information materially helps in supplying inferential, if not actual, knowledge with regard to the first formed tools. The traditions and customs of a people are preserved and repeated, generation after generation, by savage and isolated races of men. Hence amongst savage tribes and roving barbarians may be found at this day tools altogether different in form from those amongst civilised people. Such tools may be, and probably are, derived from ancestors of geological antiquity. In the Pacific Islands, in North America, Australia, Africa, and elsewhere, there are races who know not the use of metals, and whose implements correspond exactly with those found mixed with the fossil remains of extinct animals. Herodotus mentions that flint knives were used in Egypt in embalming, and such knives are found in the tombs, and were employed long after bronze and other metals were general. There is thus a connection between the tools used in prehistoric times and those of savage races. The handicraft contrivances and skill of the untutored are not to be despised, and much is owing to uneducated men of clear thought, cunning resource, singular ingenuity, and much handicraft skill. It is well known that even in our own times the earliest germs of many most important inventions and discoveries have their origin in the suggestions of hard-working but illiterate artisans.

Tools used in Ancient Egypt.

To pass from the earliest suggestions of bronze implements to the first unquestionable period of metal tools, the forms and modes of using which are so clearly shown pictorially, Egyptian history must be considered. The paintings and sculptures of ancient Egypt and Herculaneum show very clearly the tools which were then in use, and an amazing amount of information has thus been preserved. The subject cannot be gone into here, but it may be said that the tools and contrivances used in the building of the early pyramids are not known. The erection of these early pyramids is placed about 2120 B.C., that is, about a century before Abraham arrived in Egypt, and (1902 + 2120) 4,022 years ago. There are no hieroglyphics on these, and they do not carry their history as the tombs do. In a tomb at Thebes have been found a case of tools and a tool basket, belonging to a cabinet maker, these now being in the British Museum ; the tools, etc., are : Bass of palm fibres, neatly plaited, with cover ; bell-shaped wooden mallets or hammers, such as are used by masons at the present day ; bronze nails ; a skin pouch for holding small tools and nails ; a horn for oil for sharpening tools, such as now is used in a country wheelwright's shop ; drill bow, drill spindle, and drill cap ; chisels ; hatchet heads ; adzes, knives, and chisels with wooden handles. On one bronze hatchet, and one bronze adze, and one bronze saw is the name Thothmes III. of eighteenth dynasty, 1453 B.C. These therefore were in use (1902 + 1450) 3,352 years ago. And on other blades of axes is the name of Ata, an officer in the time of the sixth dynasty. In addition to these, the Egyptian cabinet maker had in his bass rasps, a plummet, and a hone. Sufficient has now been said, it is thought, to convince the reader of the antiquity of many commonly used tools.

Classification of Tools.

Tools may be classed according to their functions and modes of action, as follows : (1) Geometrical tools for laying off and testing work : such tools are rules, straightedges, gauges, etc. (2) Tools for holding and supporting work : such tools are benches, vices, stools, etc. (3) Paring or shaving tools, such as chisels, spokeshaves, planes, etc. (4) Saws. (5) Percussion or impelling tools, such as hammers, mallets, screwdrivers and (combined with cutting) hatchets, axes, adzes, etc. (6) Boring tools, such as gimlets, brace-bits, etc. (7) Abrading and scraping tools, such as rasps, scrapers, glasspaper, and implements such as whetstones, etc., for sharpening edged tools. These tools and their functions will be described in much the same order as the above.

GEOMETRICAL TOOLS.

TOOLS FOR MARKING AND SCRIBING.

THE simplest of these is the lead pencil, which is of a flat oval section sharpened to a chisel edge; if sharpened to a point, the pencil wears away quickly and is capable of marking a fine, solid line for only a few minutes together. There is a greater body

Fig. 1.—Chisel-end Marking Awl.

of lead in the chisel edge, which therefore lasts some time before requiring to be re-sharpened. Steel scribing and marking tools are illustrated by Figs. 1 to 3. The chisel end marking awl (Fig. 1) and the striking knife (Fig. 2) are used for all purposes of scribing and marking smooth work, where an indented line answers the purpose better than a black line, the scratch providing a good starting point for edge tools. It is advisable to use a pencil for rough surfaces. A home-made striking knife (Fig. 3) commonly used in workshops is ground down from an old table knife.

STRAIGHT-EDGE.

A straight-edge 15 ft. long, 6 in. wide, and 1¼ in. thick is large enough for all practical purposes of the joiner, mason, bricklayer, engineer, millwright, etc. The best

Fig. 2.—Striking Knife and Marking Awl.

material is pine, it being the least affected (permanently) by change of temperature or weather. The pine board must be cut from a straight-grown tree, as a board from a crooked trunk will not keep parallel and straight for any length of time, owing to the grain crossing and recrossing its (thick-

ness) edge. Straight-edges are made from all parts of boards cut from whole logs, but they cannot be relied upon to keep perfectly straight and true for any length of time. A strip that has been made without regard to the position it had in the whole tree will have to be trued up occasionally, and it therefore can never be relied upon unless tested each time it is required to be used, which is a great annoyance.

TESTING STRAIGHT-EDGE.

To test the truth of a straight-edge having the above measurements, get a clean board 1 ft. longer and about 7 in. or 8 in. wide. Lay the straight strip at about the centre of the board, and with a sharp pencil draw a line on the board along the trued edge

Fig. 3.—Home-made Striking Knife.

of the strip, keeping the side close to the board, and making the line as fine as possible. Now turn the strip over, placing the edge on the other side of the line, and if the trued edge is perfectly straight the line also will appear so. If the line is wavy, the edge must be planed until only one line is made when marked and tested from each side; mark a fresh line for each test, otherwise there will be confusion and inaccuracy. One edge now being perfectly true, proceed with the other edge. Set a sharp gauge to the required width, and mark the second edge lightly on each side of the rule, working the gauge from the true edge; then the wood is planed off to the gauge marks, and the second edge tested as to its being true with the first one, using the pencil line, as before. A still more delicate test than the gauge line for parallelism is by the use of a pair of callipers. The points of the callipers are drawn along the edges, and if they are perfectly parallel there will be no easy or hard places, the presence of which might possibly not be detected by the pencil line. If the edges will stand both these tests, the strip is perfectly straight and parallel.

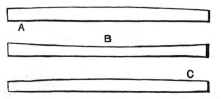

Fig. 4.—Whitworth method of Testing Straight-edges.

WHITWORTH METHOD OF TESTING STRAIGHT-EDGES.

Sir J. Whitworth's famous method of trueing engineers' straight-edges should interest the woodworker. Three straight-edges are prepared singly, and each is brought to a moderate state of accuracy; two of them, A and B (Fig. 4), are compared with each other by placing them edge to edge, and any irregularities found are removed, the process being repeated until A and B fit each other perfectly. The third straight-edge, C, now is compared with both A and B, and when it fits perfectly

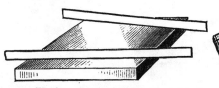

Fig. 5.—Testing Surface with Straight-edges.

both these two, then there is no doubt whatever that the three are straight, approximating to the truth in proportion to the labour that has been spent upon them. Why this is so is obvious when it is remembered that though A may be rounded instead of being straight, and B may be hollow sufficiently to make them fit each other perfectly, yet it is impossible for C

to fit both the rounded and the hollow straight-edge.

TESTING SURFACES WITH STRAIGHT-EDGES.

How surfaces are tested for winding with straight-edges is shown by Fig. 5, from which it is obvious that if the work has warped ever so slightly a true straight-edge

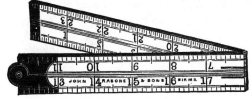

Fig. 6.—Two-ft. Four-fold Rule.

must disclose the fact, as it could not then lie flat on its edge across the work. If the board is in winding, each straight-edge will magnify the error. If the winding is wavy, the edges will touch at certain points, and in other places light will be seen between them and the work. Taking a sight from one straight-edge to the other is another test.

RULES.

A 2-ft. four-fold boxwood rule (Fig. 6) is

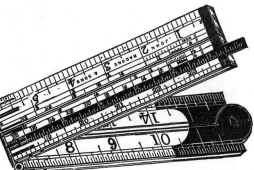

Fig. 7.—Rule with Brass Slide.

the best for the all-round purposes of the joiner; and for those who can use the slide rule, the tool shown by Fig. 7 would be handy. A simple 2-ft. two-fold rule (Fig. 8) is cheaper, but it is the greatest economy to buy the best tools, and for that reason perhaps the rule with double arch joints shown by Fig. 9, though costing more than twice as much as the one illustrated by Fig. 6, will be found the best and cheapest in the end. The average worker will find a simple rule preferable to an elaborate one. Fig. 10 shows a combined rule and spirit level, the rule joint also being set out to serve as a protractor. This tool may prove useful in

greater will be the slant) each 2-in. mark must denote a one-sixth part of the width. Say a board anything less than 24 in. in length or width is to be divided into eight parts ; then as 3 in. is one-eighth of 2 ft., use a 2-ft. rule in the same manner as before, and mark off at every 3 in.

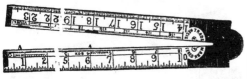

Fig. 8.—Two-ft. Two-fold Rule.

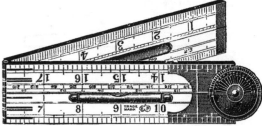

Fig. 10.—Rule with Spirit Level.

special circumstances, but its use as a spirit level is not recommended, it being preferable to have rule and level two quite distinct tools.

SQUARES AND BEVELS.

The woodworker constantly uses squares for setting out and testing work, as will be described in detail later. The simplest is the try square (Fig. 12), which has a stock of rosewood or ebony. In the square shown by Fig. 13, the stock is so shaped that it is of service in setting out and testing

DIVIDING A BOARD WITH A RULE.

A reliable method of dividing a board of any given width into any number of parts is illustrated by Fig. 11. Suppose a board 9 in. wide is to be cut into six equal parts ; place the 1-ft. rule so that its ends touch the opposite edges of board, as shown in

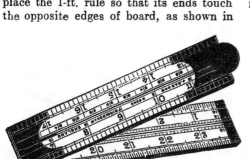

Fig. 9.—Rule with Double Arch Joints.

Fig. 11.—Dividing Board with Rule.

Fig. 11 ; draw a line right across, and upon this line mark off from the rule every 2 in., as 2, 4, 6, etc. Remove the rule, and draw lines parallel with the edge of the board, intersecting with the marks upon the oblique line, thus obtaining six parts, each really 1½ in. wide. The principle of this is simple : 2 in. is the one-sixth part of 1 ft., and whatever be the slant of the rule across the board (and the narrower the board the

mitres, a proper mitre square which has an ebony stock being shown by Fig. 14. Another combination try and mitre square is shown by Fig. 15, and this has an iron stock, hollowed out to lower its weight to that of a wooden one. This is a useful and cheap tool, very unlikely to get out of truth. A patent adjustable try square is illustrated by Fig. 16. The set screw clamps the blade in the stock just where it may be most convenient for such awkward work as putting

Fig. 12.—Try square.

butts, locks, and other fittings on doors and windows. The graduated blade is very useful. The sliding bevel is a handy appliance for setting off angles in duplicate, as by means of the set screw the blade can

A carpenter's try-square that is thought to be untrue may be tested in the following way. Get a piece of board whose edge has been proved to be quite straight, apply the

Fig. 14.—Mitre Square.

square as shown at A (Fig. 19), and draw a line; then turn the square as at B, and if it is true the blade should fit the line; if it is less than a right angle it will be as shown at C D (Fig. 19), and if more than a right

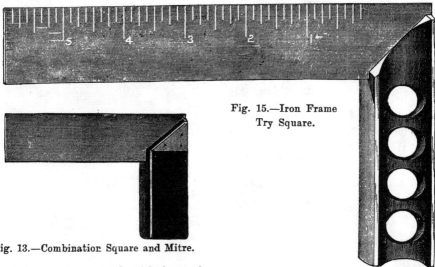

Fig. 15.—Iron Frame Try Square.

Fig. 13.—Combination Square and Mitre.

be made to assume any angle with the stock. Fig. 17 shows a bevel with a simple ebony stock, and Fig. 18 one with an ebony stock framed in brass, this protection keeping the edges true for an almost unlimited period. The joiner's steel square is a mere right angle of steel, sometimes nickel plated, graduated in inches, $\frac{1}{4}$ in., and $\frac{1}{8}$ in. Squares with other graduations can be obtained.

angle the defect will be as indicated at E F (Fig. 19). If the blade has moved or has been knocked out of truth through a fall, it should be knocked back into its proper position, and, when true, the rivets should be tightened by careful hammering. If the blade is too fast in the stock to be knocked back, the blade must be filed true.

Crenelated Squares.

A crenelated square has a tongue in which there is a series of crenelations or notches at the graduations. It is especially useful in marking off mortises, etc., though it is available for all other ordinary applications. Three sides of a piece of timber can be set

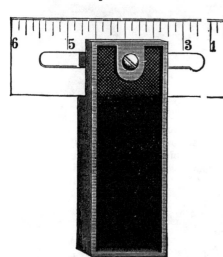

Fig. 16.—Adjustable Try Square.

out without moving the work. To use this square, say in marking out a mortise or tenon, take it in the left hand and lay its tongue upon the surface of the work, as in Fig. 20. The lower end of the main arm is lowered for 2 in. or so from the surface to

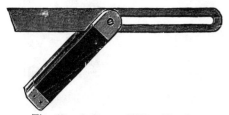

Fig. 17.—Ordinary Sliding Bevel.

get a better purchase, and then an awl, held in the right hand, is placed in a notch at the correct distance from the edge to mark the left-hand edge of the mortise or left-hand face of tenon as the case may be. Then push the square forward, pressing it down gently upon the work, and one mark will have been made. Replace the square, and with the awl in another notch at the thickness of the tenon or width of the mortise

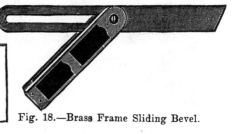

Fig. 18.—Brass Frame Sliding Bevel.

make a second mark. Horizontals are drawn by means of the smooth edge of the tongue (see Fig. 20).

Marking Work for Sawing.

The chalk line, pencil and rule, and scribe are variously used for the marking of the lines by which the saw is guided. The first-named is used for long pieces of timber, the second for ordinary and roughly

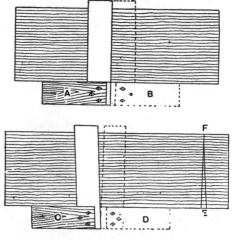

Fig. 19.—Testing Try Squares in Truth.

approximate work, the third for the most accurate sawing. Lining off a plank or board for ripping, when rough on the edges, is commonly done with a straight-edge or chalk line. If square-edged it can be done by the rule and pencil, as explained in

Fig. 21 The rule is held in the left hand, measuring off on the board the breadth to be ripped, and the forefinger placed against the edge to act as fence. The pencil is

Fig. 20.—Marking Mortise with Crenelated Square.

held in the right hand to the end of the rule on the board. Both hands are then moved simultaneously, and the required line is traced backward or forward, as may be desired. Lines for cross-cutting, when square

across or at right angles to the edge, are readily obtained by the square, keeping its blade flat on the board or plank and its stock hard to the edge (see Fig. 22). For

lines at an angle of 45° to the edge use the mitre square (see Fig. 23), and for other angles, set and apply the bevel-stock in the same way (see Fig. 24). For this and similar purposes the bevel-stock differs from the square only in having the blade

Fig. 22.—Squaring Line on Board.

movable, and capable of being adjusted at any desired angle with the stock by means of a screw. In the chalk line method of marking (see Fig. 25) a piece of fine cord is whitened with chalk, and being strained taut between two points whose

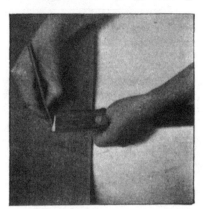

Fig. 21.—Lining Board with Rule and Pencil.

Fig. 23.—Marking Mitre Line on Board.

positions are marked to correspond with the terminations of the line of cut, the chalk line is lifted vertically at or near the centre, and, being suddenly released, chalks a perfectly straight and fine line upon the timber, and furnishes a correct guide to the saw. Lines are marked with the timber scribe in such cases as squaring the ends of planed stuff and in marking dovetails

Fig. 24.—Using Sliding Bevel.

and tenons. The saw may then be made to cut close outside the scribed line, allowing just sufficient margin of material to be removed with the plane ; or the saw may pass right along the scribed line, as in cutting

Fig. 25.—Using Chalk Line.

dovetails and tenons, no after-finish being required. In either case the scribed line is preferable to the pencil-marked one, because the cutting can be done much more accurately in the first case than in the latter.

Also, when the end of a piece of timber has to be squared with the plane, there is, besides the greater accuracy, much less risk of spalting or breaking out of the grain oc-

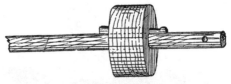

Fig. 26.—Pencil Gauge with Round Stem.

curring with scribed lines than with pencil-marked lines. In the case of planed ends, a careful workman will also contrive to saw extremely close to the scribed lines, in order to diminish as much as possible the labour of planing.

MARKING AND CUTTING GAUGES.

The carpenter draws a line at a short dis-

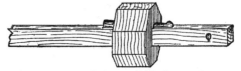

Fig. 27.—Pencil Gauge with Square Stem.

tance from, and parallel to, the edge of a board by means of a rule and pencil, the method being made clear by Fig. 21, p. 9. The use of the pencil or marking gauge would be found an advantage over this method. It will be seen from Figs. 26 and 27 that there are two ways of making the pencil gauge. It can be made of any hard

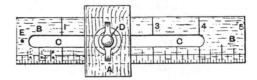

Fig. 28.—Rule Pencil and Cutting Gauge.

wood, preferably beech. The stem may be round (Fig. 26) or square (Fig. 27) in section, and the head may be round or octagonal. The head must slide up and down the stem easily, but without sideplay. The gauge may be made to use up odd pieces of lead pencil, and these should be sharpened (with a chisel) to a wedge-shaped point. Figs. 28 and 29 show a pencil gauge made from a broken rule fitted into a block so as to run easily, and secured

Fig. 29.—Section through Rule Gauge.

at any distance (as indicated by the rule's edge) by means of a thumbscrew. A is a block of birch, 1½ in. by 1 in. by 1 in., mortised so as to receive the rule. B is a

Fig. 30.—Improved Pencil Gauge.

5-in. length of an ordinary rule, with a slot c just large enough to admit the screw D, which is fixed in the block A. The thickness of the wood between the washer and

Fig. 31.—Ordinary Marking Gauge.

the rule should be only ⅛ in., to allow a little pliability. A cutting or scratch gauge may be made similarly by inserting a pin at E, exactly over the first $\frac{1}{16}$ in., that distance always being allowed for. Shop-bought marking and cutting gauges are

illustrated by Figs. 30 to 35. A beechwood pencil gauge is shown by Fig. 30, a marking gauge having a steel point by Fig. 31, an improved cutting gauge for scribing deep lines by Fig. 32, and mortise gauges for scribing mortise holes and tenons by Figs. 33 to 35. The mortise gauges are of ebony

Fig. 32.—Cutting Gauge.

and brass, the one illustrated by Fig. 35 having a stem of brass. The ordinary marking gauge is shown by Fig. 36, and the use of mortise gauges will come later.

Fig. 33.—Square Mortise Gauge.

PANEL GAUGES.

A panel gauge (Fig. 37) is used to mark a line parallel to the true edge of a panel, or of any piece of wood too wide for the ordinary gauge to take in. The stock (of which

Fig. 34.—Oval Mortise Gauge.

Figs. 38 to 42 give four alternative patterns) is of maple, beech, or similar wood. It is 1 in. thick, and has a ⅜-in. by ⅜-in. rebate at the bottom. A mortise is made for the stem to pass through, and another one at the side for the wedge. The edges of the stock are shown square, but it is an improvement to have them rounded. The wedge (Fig. 43) should be made of box-wood or ebony if possible, and is a bare $\frac{1}{4}$ in. thick. The taper of the mortise in the stock must be made to correspond with it.

Fig. 35.—Brass Stem Mortise Gauge.

The stem should be about 2 ft. 6 in. long, and may be made of a piece of straight-grained mahogany. It should fit the mortise, not too tightly, but so that it can be moved with the hands without tapping, and is held in position by the wedge when set. A piece is dovetailed in the end, as shown, to bring the marking point level with the bottom of the rebate. The stem may be made square if preferred, or if the rounded

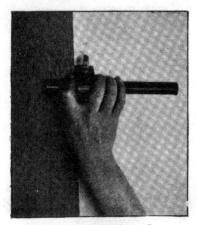

Fig. 36.—Using Marking Gauge.

mortise presents a difficulty. The stock should be well finished and nicely polished.

COMPASSES, DIVIDERS, AND CALLIPERS.

The joiner and cabinet worker have a multitude of uses for the above tools, which are of the simplest construction. The ordinary

form of wing compasses is shown by Fig. 44, in which the wing (the curved side projection) forms one with the left leg, whilst the right leg has a slot by means of which it slides up and down the wing, the set screw being tightened when the legs are to be fixed at a certain distance apart. For very accurate work, compasses with the sensitive adjustment at side, as shown in

Fig. 37.—Panel Gauge.

Fig. 45, are found to be useful. Compasses can be used very conveniently as simple dividers, but these cost very little. They are used for stepping off a number of equal distances, for transferring measurements, and for scribing. Callipers are used for measuring diameters of round pins, circular recesses, etc. ; for the former purpose outside

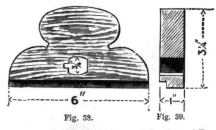

Fig. 38.　　　　　　　Fig. 39.

Figs. 38 and 39.—Elevation and Section of Panel Gauge Stock.

callipers (Fig. 46) and for the latter purpose inside callipers (Fig. 47) are used. Callipers are subject to great variation in shape, but those used in woodworking should be the simplest obtainable.

SHOOTING-BOARDS.

The shooting-board is used for trueing up the edges of square stuff. The ordinary shooting-board (Fig. 48) is made of two pieces of plank, the lower one wider than the other, to support the plane, and the upper to form a base on which to hold the wood. This sometimes is not altogether satisfactory, because the board

Fig. 40.—Stock of Panel Gauge.

is likely to warp, and the grain of the wood, being all in the same direction, renders the board likely to split at, or near, the place where the pieces are joined. The shooting-board shown by Figs. 49 to 53 is a desirable improvement. Fig. 49 shows the elevation, in which A is the board on

Fig. 41.—Stock of Panel Gauge.

which the work rests; B, the ledge or rail on which the plane moves; C being rails fixed to B, as shown in the other figures; D, the stop. Fig. 50 is a plan. Reference letters are the same in each figure. Fig. 51 shows the edge of B. Fig. 52 shows the frame on which A is fixed; the dotted lines

Fig. 42.—Stock of Panel Gauge.

indicate the tenons and wedges. Fig. 53 shows end of completed board. Each of the cross-rails also acts as a ledge to the upper

board, materially stiffening the whole; while advantage may be taken of the opportunity thus afforded to leave room for the powdery waste, produced in shooting the ends of the wood, to fall out of the way. A further improvement might be made by fix-

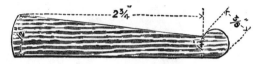

Fig. 43.—Wedge of Panel Gauge.

ing a narrow piece of plate glass along the path on which the plane is to travel, to reduce friction.

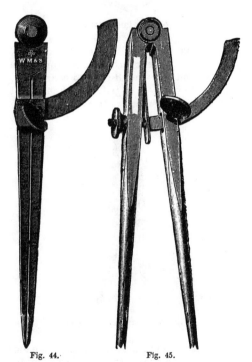

Fig. 44. Fig. 45.

Fig. 44.—Wing Compasses. Fig. 45.—Compasses with Sensitive Adjustment.

IMPROVED SHOOTING-BOARD GIVING OBLIQUE PLANING.

A prominent fault of shooting-boards, as generally constructed, is that the plane used on the board loses its edge very quickly, especially on thin wood and when dealing with material of uniform thickness.

Fig. 46.—Outside Callipers.

The reason for this is that only a small part of the edge of the plane-iron is in use, and the same small portion constantly. All who have used edged tools know that an oblique movement cuts sweeter than a

Fig. 47.—Inside Callipers.

direct and forward movement, the edge employed in the actual cutting having a greater width than the shaving removed. The same thing is observable in a rebate plane. A skew-mouth plane not only keeps better up to its work, but the shaving seems to be more smoothly removed, and the cut surface has a better finish. In order to obtain these advantages, the shooting-

board shown by Fig. 54 is offered. The planes used on a shooting-board should be sharpened squarely with a straight cutting edge; this is very important when shooting mitres, especially picture frames. If the iron of the plane is so sharpened, the distance between the surfaces on which rest the plane and the material worked upon need not exceed $\frac{3}{8}$ in.; nearly the

Fig. 48.—Shooting Board.

whole width of the plane-iron is then available for use. Supposing that a shooting-board is required to take advantage of the oblique cut and the employment of a larger part of the edge, the wood operated on may be taken to be not more than $\frac{3}{4}$ in. thick (for thicker work is more independent of a shooting-board): then the difference in level at the two ends of

Fig. 49.

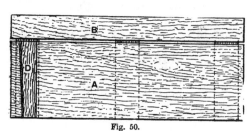

Fig. 50.

Figs. 49 and 50.—Elevation and Plan of Improved Shooting Board.

the shooting-board may be possibly as much as $1\frac{1}{2}$ in. This board (Fig. 54) is not drawn to scale, but may be made of any size suitable for the purpose for which the maker intends it, and it might be improved by making the incline adjustable with a pair of thumbscrews, or perhaps, preferably, by hingeing the two parts together at one end and employing a movable wedge and bolts at the other end for the purpose of adjustment.

APPLIANCES FOR MITRING.

The technical term mitre is applied usually to the angle between any two pieces of wood or moulding where they join or intersect, as in the case of a picture-frame.

Fig. 51.

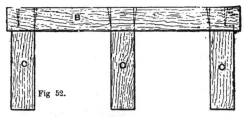

Fig 52.

Figs. 51 and 52.—Frame of Improved Shooting Board.

In this instance the joint would be a true mitre—that is to say, it would be 45°, or half the right angle (90°) formed by the two inner edges of the frame. Although the term mitre is generally understood to apply to a right angle, yet any angle, acute or obtuse, may be called a mitre.

The best form of mitre block is made from a piece of dry beech, about 16 in. long, 6 in. wide, and 3 in. thick. A rebate c is cut to about the size shown, care being taken that the angle is perfectly true. Lines A and B are set out to an angle of 45°, and they then are squared down the rebate and back of block. The lines are cut down with a tenon saw, and upon the accuracy of the sawing depends the value of the finished mitres. Fig. 56 is a section of the mitre block as commonly used by the joiner. This is merely two pieces of wood (deal, as a rule) planed up true and screwed or nailed

Fig. 53.—End Elevation of Improved Shooting Board.

together. This plan answers very well, as when it becomes worn and out of truth another can be made for a few pence. The block shown by Fig. 57 has a ledge on the bottom as shown; owing to the inward slant the work is more easily held.

MITRE BOX.

Fig. 58 shows a mitre box which answers the same purpose as the block. This is

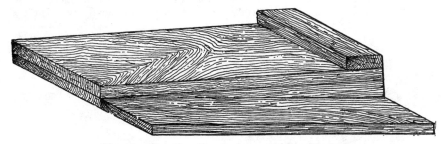

Fig. 54.—Shooting Board giving Oblique Planing.

MITRE BLOCKS.

There are various appliances employed in cutting mitres, the simplest being known as the mitre block. The work is laid upon the rebate c (Fig. 55), and the saw kerfs A B serve as a guide for the tenon saw.

made with three pieces of deal about 1 in. thick, nailed together at the bottom as shown. Mitre boxes for heavy work require a strengthening piece on top to hold together the sides (see Fig. 59), or even three pieces may be necessary (see Fig. 60);

both these illustrations show pieces of moulding in position for mitre-cutting.

Mitre Shooting Block.

Figs. 61 and 62 show a mitre shooting

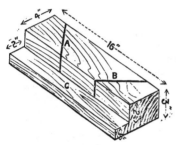

Fig. 55.—Mitre Sawing Block.

block for shooting or planing the edges of stuff sawn in the mitre block or box. In Fig. 61 the bottom piece is of dry red deal, 2 ft. 6 in. long, and rebated. The top piece

Fig. 56.—Section of Mitre Block.

must be made of some hard material, such as mahogany or beech, by preference. It is planed up perfectly true, and cut at the ends to a "true mitre" (45°); it is firmly screwed to the bottom piece. It is an im-

Fig. 57.—Inclined Mitre Sawing Block.

provement to fix ledger pieces across the bottom, to keep the board from warping. In Fig. 62 the bottom piece is of two separate boards as shown.

Combination Shooting-board.

Notwithstanding the large number of patented mitring machines in the market, skilled joiners, when any particularly good

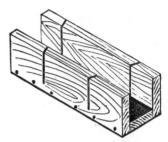

Fig. 58.—Mitre Box.

piece of work is in hand, still prefer to use the ordinary home made wooden shoot. The

Fig. 59.—Mitre Box with Strengthening Piece.

machines, whilst new and in good condition, are undoubtedly the more expeditious in use, but if carelessly handled they are

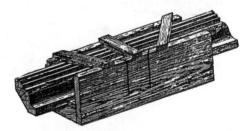

Fig. 60.—Mitre Box with Strengthening Pieces.

apt to get out of order, and then their work is far from satisfactory; whilst the wood shoot will stand a deal of rough usage, and is also easily repaired. Figs. 63 to 67 illustrate several improvements on the old form of shoot. A mitre-shoot, square-shoot, and joint-shoot are combined in the one board, which will prove very handy where these appliances are wanted only occasionally. The shoot consists of a top board of seasoned yellow deal 3 ft.

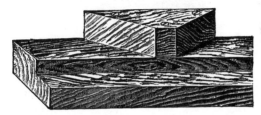

Fig. 61.—Mitre Shooting Block with Solid Base.

by 9 in. by 1¾ in., slot-screwed to an under-frame of teak, made up of the plane bed B, 3 ft. by 2¾ in. by 1½ in., into which are framed three cross rails 2¼ in. by 1 in. flush on the under-side. This frame is shown in plan and in section respectively in Figs. 65 and 66. In the centre of the top board is the mitre-block, a piece of dry oak 2 in. thick cut with two of its

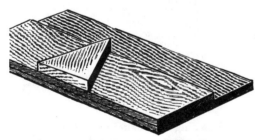

Fig. 62.—Mitre Shooting Block with made-up Base.

sides exactly square with each other, and at an angle of 45° with the third. This block, instead of being fixed in the usual way, is mounted on a pivot in its centre, as shown at B (Figs. 63 and 64), and is capable of adjustment either as a mitre-shoot, as shown in the full lines, or as a square-shoot, as indicated by the dotted lines in Fig. 63; it is firmly secured in either position by means of three ½-in. by 3-in. square-head screw bolts similar to Fig. 68. The grain of the block should run parallel with

2

the plane bed, then shrinkage will not alter its shape. The board is arranged

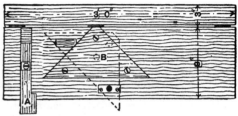

Fig. 63.—Combination Shooting Board.

for jointing by removing the mitre-block and working the boards against the adjustable stop A. This stop, which is shown in perspective also at Fig. 69, works in an undercut groove, and is secured in any required position by the screw bolt; the

Fig. 64.—End Elevation of Combination Board

projection at the end prevents the boards slipping whilst being planed.

DONKEY'S-EAR SHOOTING BLOCK.

A "donkey's-ear" is used for mitreing or bevelling the edges of wide but thin

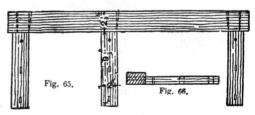

Figs. 65 and 66.—Frame of Combination Board.

material, with the cut at right angles to that adopted for stouter mouldings. Fig. 70 gives an idea of its form and construction. Fig. 71 shows another handy form of mitre-shoot for wide surfaces that have to be edge-mitred. This also is known as a "donkey's-ear," and it consists of a rest A for the material to be mitred, a bed B for the shooting plane, a guide c for the

Fig. 67.—Elevation of Combination Board.

plane, and a frame D for the purpose of elevating the appliance to a convenient height by fixing it in the bench-screw or to the tail of the bench. The rest A is made of a piece of deal 1 ft. 3 in. long, 4½ in. deep, and 3 in. thick, and has a

Fig. 68.—Screw-bolt.

rebate run along two of its edges (see the section), Fig. 72. The bed B should preferably be of teak, as this wood is of a greasy nature and does not cast. It should be about 2 ft. long, 3 in. wide, and 2 in. thick. The guides c are 1 in. thick, and project about ½ in. above the bed. The frame D is made up of 3-in. by 1-in. deal,

Fig. 69.—Adjustable Stop.

and tenoned through the bed with barefaced tenons, with shoulders towards the rest.

MITRE TEMPLATES.

Of constant use as an aid in cutting mitres is a mitre template, which is made from a piece of hard wood, in the form

shown by Fig. 73; it is usually about 4 in. long, 3 in. wide each way, and ½ in. thick.

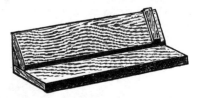

Fig. 70.—Donkey's-ear Shooting Block.

It is made by planing up true a square block of hard wood, cutting out a rebate B,

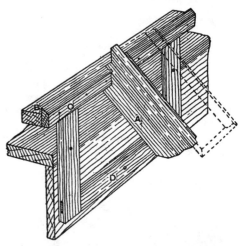

Fig. 71.—Donkey's-ear Block for Shooting Wide Surfaces.

and making a "true mitre" (45°) upon each end, as shown. If an ordinary cupboard

Fig. 72.—Rest of Donkey's-ear Block.

framing is examined at the junction of the rail with the jambs, it will be seen that each of the moulded edges has been mitred as shown in Fig. 74. To obtain this mitre, the template is used, as Fig. 75. Fig. 76 shows the template applied to the edge being

Fig. 73.—Mitre Template.

held by the left hand, whilst the right guides the chisel A.

Fig. 74.—Moulding with Mitred Joint.

Spirit Level.

The spirit level is used for determining the plane of the horizon, that is the plane forming a right angle to the vertical plane.

scale engraved on the glass tube or on a brass or steel rule fastened to the frame

Fig. 75.—Application of Mitre Template.

beside it, so as to mark the position of the bubble, the tube being so shaped that

Fig. 76.—Using Chisel with Mitre Template.

when the level is lying on a flat and horizontal surface the bubble occupies the centre of the tube. Many levels have pro-

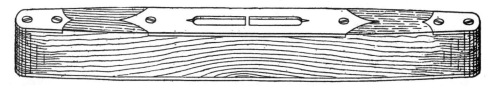

Fig. 77.—Spirit Level.

A frame firmly holds a closed glass tube nearly filled with anhydrous ether, or with

vision for altering the length of the bubble. Fig. 77 is a view of an ordinary spirit

Fig. 78.—Section of Spirit Level.

a mixture of ether and alcohol. Good spirit levels are provided with a graduated

level, and its construction is made quite clear by the sectional view, Fig. 78. In use the level is applied to the work twice, it being reversed at the second application, and the mean of the two indications then is adopted. Spirit levels are made in many sizes and shapes, but the method of construction always is the same. A serviceable tool is of the narrow shape, about 10 in. long, its greatest breadth being $1\frac{1}{16}$ in., and diminishing to $\frac{1}{2}$ in. at the ends. The frame is of any hard, tough wood, such as box, ebony, lignum-vitæ, birch, beech, walnut, or oak. At the back of the tube should be silvering, which shows up the bubble and enables side lights to be dispensed with. The tube is set in plaster-of-paris, and has a brass cover. Shop-bought spirit levels are constructed generally in ebony or rosewood, better qualities having a metal protection for the edges and faces. This protection preserves the truth of the instruments for a long time, and is very desirable. A serviceable American level has a mount entirely of steel, which is hexagonal in section, and has rounded ends. Another handy form is the one mounted wholly in brass; this has a revolving protector over the bulb opening, and there is provision for adjustment should the level after a time wear out of truth. A very convenient form of level is the one with a graduated screw slide, by means of which the fall per foot is shown at a glance.

HOLDING TOOLS.

BENCHES.

BEFORE any definite work can be done, a bench, or its substitute, must be obtained. For general manual work the ordinary bench in use by the joiner is, all things considered, the most serviceable; There are many good and suitable benches on the market, but the worker must not get one that is too low, and the height should be influenced by the kind of work it is intended to perform upon it. The smaller benches sold at the tool-shops are not high enough for an adult—from 33 to

Fig. 79.—Workman and Bench.

it should not be less than 6 ft. long, 2 ft. 6 in. high, and, say, 2 ft. 6 in. wide. It should be fitted with two wood bench screws and wood vice cheeks, one at each left-hand corner of the bench, to accommodate two workers. If possible, the bench should be so placed that light may fall directly upon both the ends—that is to say, the workers must face the windows. 34 in. for a man is excellent, 26 to 30 in. for boys. The worker will become accustomed to work at the ordinary bench height, but it is absurd to suppose that one height suits tall and short people equally. The worker should choose a bench of the height at which he has the most command over his tools. He should be able to do his work conveniently without

Fig. 80.—Bench with Side and Tail Vices.

just right for mere occasional use, but too low to work at for any length of time. A simple method of raising it slightly from the floor is to put a piece of quartering under each pair of legs. For heavy work the bench may have to be fixed to the quartering, and the quartering to the floor, for which purpose stout screws or screw bolts will answer. Fig. 79 shows the relative heights of worker and bench.

Various Kinds of Benches Described.

much necessity for stooping; but the height of the bench should not prevent his standing well over his work (see Fig. 79). It will thus be seen that some latitude is allowable, although no doubt something near ordinary bench height, somewhere about 2 ft. 6 in., is about the best. The height of an ordinary bench can .be altered easily by cutting the legs shorter or putting something under them. A height of 2 ft. 6 in. may be found

Fig. 80 is a general view of a simple bench with side and tail vices. This form is extremely useful for cabinet making and similar work, where it is desirable to hold pieces of material that may have to be planed, moulded, chamfered, mortised, grooved, etc., without using a bench knife or similar method of fixing. The material could be held between stops, one being inserted in one of the holes in the top of the bench and another in the hole made in the cheek of the tail vice. The following dimensions are, of course, only suggestive, and the bench may be made longer or shorter, narrower or wider, to meet requirements: Top, 5 ft. by 1 ft. 9 in., and 2 in. thick. Height, 2 ft. 7 in. Distance between legs, 3 ft. 2 in. lengthwise, and 1 ft. 3 in. sideways. Legs, 3 in. by 3 in. The whole may be constructed of hard wood, such as beech or birch, and in any case it will be best to have hard wood for all the parts forming the top, side cheeks, and cheeks of vices, these being the main parts of the bench; the framing of the legs, rails, etc., might be of red deal. A simple bench is illustrated by Fig. 81; this is suitable for general carpentry and joinery. The framework is of thoroughly seasoned dry spruce fir or red pine, and

Fig. 81.—Double Bench with Vice at each end.

the top of birch or yellow pine. This is a very serviceable bench for general utility. The folding bench illustrated by Fig. 82 will be found very suitable where a portable bench is required for occasional use only. It will be seen that when the bench is not in use, the screw, screw cheek, and runner can be taken out, the legs folded on to the wall, and the top and side folded and let down as indicated in Fig. 83. A more elaborate bench for cabinet work is shown by Fig. 84; it consists of two principal parts, the underneath framework and support, and the top. The former has two standards joined

Fig. 82.—Folding Bench in use.

by two bars. On the feet of the standards rests a board which serves to hold heavy tools and other articles. There is a rack for small tools, and underneath this a band, tacked at short intervals, for other tools. The front rail has holes on its top face 1 in. by ¾ in. for holding bench stops, whilst in the front face of the rail are round holes for holding other pins T, 1½ in. square at one end, but made round at the other end to fit tightly into the holes. The pin T and the block V (Fig. 84), screwed on the end of the movable jaw of the vice, serve to hold wood during the process of edge planing. Holes in the back rail receive pins W which are convenient for cramping up joints. A kitchen table bench is shown by Fig. 85. The end of the table employed is not the one containing the usual drawer. Two blocks of wood A B, 3 in. square, are attached to the table top by two cramps embedded in the ends of one of the pieces. Through mortise holes C C are inserted slats glued and wedged to block A, but running loosely in holes in B. S is a screw, and the

two parts of the bench serve the purpose also of vice cheeks; though if desired the two blocks can be screwed together solid.

BENCH STOPS.

The ordinary bench is provided with holes for the reception of stops, against which or between which work is held for planing, etc. These stops are of iron shaped as in Fig. 86, and have springs at

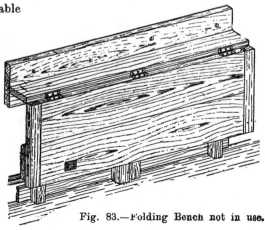

Fig. 83.—Folding Bench not in use.

their sides by means of which they are held tightly and at any required height 88. A long, light screw through the middle hole in the loose side will afford sufficient

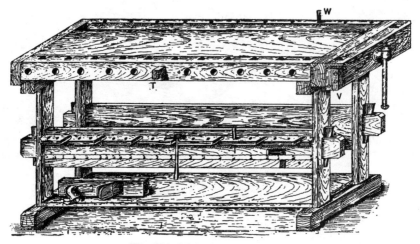

Fig. 84.—Cabinet-worker's Bench.

in the bench holes. An adjustable stop for screwing to the bench is shown by Fig. 87. For a temporary stop some workers drive a few nails into the bench end, leaving the heads projecting enough to hold the wood. A much better substitute can be made out of an ordinary butt hinge, one end of which should be filed into teeth so as to hold the adjustment for thin or thick stuff. When done with, the hinge can be taken up and put away.

COMMON BENCH SCREW VICE.

A common form of joiner's bench screw is shown in general view by Fig. 89; Fig. 90 is a view looking from the inside, sup-

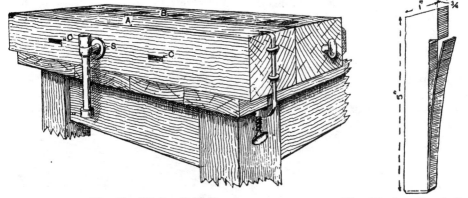

Fig. 85.—Kitchen Table Bench.

Fig. 86.—Iron Bench Stop.

wood better. This end should be left loose, and the other side screwed down tightly to the bench end as shown by Fig. posing the top, leg, and bearer of the bench to be removed, and Fig. 91 is a sectional view. D is the side or cheek of the bench to which the wooden nut A is screwed. The box B, which accurately fits the runner shown inside it, is fixed to the top rail connecting the legs, and to the top and side of the bench. Care is taken

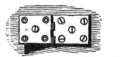

Fig. 87.—Adjustable Bench Stop.

to keep the runner at right angles to the vice cheeks. To fasten the vice outer cheek and screw together so that upon turn-

Fig. 88.—Hinge used as Bench Stop.

ing the latter the former will follow it, a groove E (Fig. 91) is cut. Then from the under edge of the cheek a mortise is made,

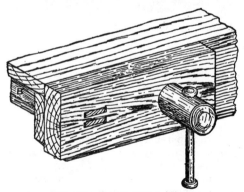

Fig. 89.—Bench Screw Vice.

and a hardwood key F is driven to fit fairly tight into the mortise, its end entering E. The screw cheek is usually about 1 ft. 9 in. long, 9 in. wide, and 2 in. to 3 in. thick. The runner is about 3 in. by 3 in. and 2 ft. long. The wooden screws and nuts can be bought ready made.

IMPROVED BENCH SCREW VICE.

The defects of the old-fashioned form of bench vice shown by Fig. 92 may be noted.

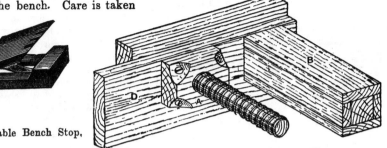

Fig. 90.—Inside View of Screw Vice.

Suppose it is required to hold a door rail whilst tenons are cut, a piece of stuff of the exact thickness of the rail has to be inserted between the jaw and the bench at the opposite end to that in which the door rail is put, and, should the piece inserted be a trifle thicker or thinner than the rail, difficulty will be experienced in tightening

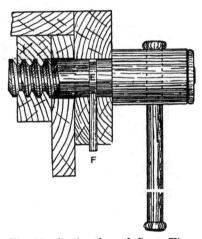

Fig. 91.—Section through Screw Vice.

the screw sufficiently to keep the rail rigid whilst cutting the tenon, and even then it will probably slip about and become loose. If it is required to plough, say, the edge of a mullion, when this is placed in the screw and tightened up the jaw tilts over as shown in Fig. 93 and grips the mullion hard on its two arrises; and in fixing it in the vice in order to plough the second edge, great care must be exercised to avoid splitting off pieces from the rail at each side of the groove, and thus disfiguring the work, and there are other disad-

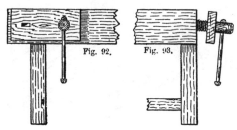

Figs. 92 and 93.—Ordinary Screw Vice and its Defect.

vantages. An improvement on the old form is suggested by Figs. 94 and 95. Instead of having the jaw horizontal, the idea is to adjust it in a raking position; it will then grip the work on both sides of the screw, instead of only on one side as formerly, thus avoiding the tilt; and this advantage is assured whether the work be placed in the vice vertically, horizontally, or obliquely. There is another good point in this arrangement—namely, the rail mortised into the jaw at its lower end may fit

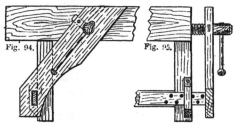

Figs. 94 and 95.—Improved Bench Vice.

rather loosely in the socket screwed on to the bench leg. Holes are bored through this rail at certain distances apart, and in any one of these a pin is inserted. This

pin answers the purpose of the blocks placed between the jaw and the bench when the vice is horizontal, with the advantage that, no matter in which of the holes the pin is placed, the vice will grip two or three thicknesses of stuff, thus avoiding the necessity of providing a new block every time work of a different thickness is put into the vice. With this newer form of vice the work can be held securely and satisfactorily by about a quarter turn of the screw. Iron vices for joiners can, of course, be obtained, and against these nothing is urged but their price, which is prohibitive to a great many. The arrangement here advocated is therefore confidently recommended as being at once inexpensive to construct and thoroughly efficient in use.

Fig. 96.—Instantaneous Grip Vice.

INSTANTANEOUS GRIP VICE.

An instantaneous grip vice is a very great improvement upon the wooden screw vice. Without any unscrewing it will take in anything, from a sheet of paper to a block 12 in. in thickness. Vices of this pattern apparently are not so widely known and used as they should be, and many a carpenter keeps to the old screw vice, although by the adoption of the parallel and instantaneous grip vice much time is saved, because this seizes and secures work instantly by the third of a turn of the hand, whereas with the old vice the jaws must be opened, perhaps with many a turn, to a sufficient extent, and then tightened with more turning, a contrast to the rapid and effectual action of the grip vice, whose rack can be thrown out of gear at once by an upward motion of the hand, and the front jaw pulled out, pressed against the wood, and then tightened in an immovable grip by a downward movement of the hand. The pattern shown in Fig. 96 is fixed to the bench from beneath as indicated, and the tops of the jaws are level with the surface of the bench; one-third of a turn of the handle releases the work. Like all the grip vices, its holding force is so great that if a long piece of wood be clutched by one end in the vice its weight will be powerless to alter its position in the vice in the smallest degree. There are but two working parts in the vice, the spiral H, and the short rack L.

Screw Vice for Kitchen Table.

The worker who may be obliged to dispense with the convenience of a regular bench may be glad to know of such a simple arrangement as that shown by Figs. 97 to 99 for fixing a screw vice to a kitchen table, the vice being detachable

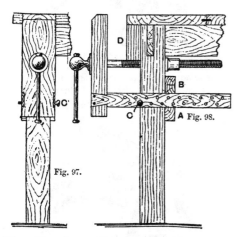

Figs. 97 and 98.—Kitchen Table Screw Vice.

for removal as required. The device illustrated does not cause the least degree of damage to the table. A hole is made in the table leg for the screw to pass through, the nut or box of which is fixed to the

back of the leg as shown. Two hardwood runners, 2 in. by ¾ in. by 1 ft. 8 in., should be made and dovetailed into the screw cheek, which is 2¼ in. thick, 1 ft. 3 in. long, and has its breadth regulated by the size of the leg. The distance between the

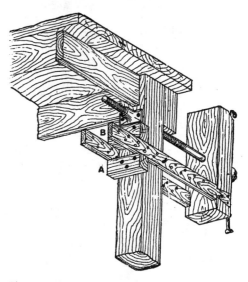

Fig. 99.—Side General View of Kitchen Table Vice.

runners should be the same as the thickness of the leg. The runners are kept in position by two blocks A and B, which are screwed to the back of the leg. An adjustable pin C, made from a piece of ½-in. round iron, will be required, and must be sufficiently long to pass through both runners. It will be advisable to screw a block D (Fig. 98) to the leg, the face of the block being flush with the front edge of the top.

Sawing Stools or Trestles.

Fig. 100 shows the kind of sawing stool in common use by carpenters, Fig. 101 being a side elevation, and Fig. 102 an end elevation. Suggestive sizes are figured on the drawings. The thickness of the material can, of course, be increased or decreased according to requirements. The simplest sawing stool, but the least reliable, is the one with three legs shown by Fig. 103, but this is of little service and almost useless. Better and more usual forms are shown by Figs. 104 and 105, these

Fig. 100.—Common Sawing Stool.

being about 20 in. high, firmly and stiffly made. In Fig. 104 all the parts are mortised and tenoned together, and strutted

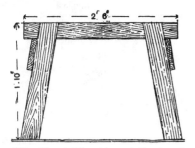

Fig. 101.—Front Elevation of Sawing Stool.

to give strength, but in Fig. 105 the legs are simply shouldered and bolted into the sides of the top. The cross stretchers are

Fig. 102.—End Elevation of Sawing Stool.

slightly shouldered back and screwed or bolted to the legs. Sometimes the carpenter uses the sawing horse, the ordinary form of which is shown in Fig. 106, but this is

more generally used for rough sawing, such as firewood, etc.

Fig. 103.—Three-legged Sawing Stool.

CRAMPS.

Cramps are used to hold work on the bench, to hold together work in course of

Fig. 104.—Braced Sawing Stool.

construction, to facilitate the making of articles in which tight and accurate joints are essential, to hold together glued joints

Fig. 105.—Bolted Sawing Stool.

until the glue is dry and hard, and for other purposes that suggest themselves. Their uses will be treated in detail as occasion requires, and in the meantime it will suffice to illustrate a few types commonly employed in workshops. A holdfast for temporarily securing work to the bench is shown by Fig. 107. This ranges in length from

Fig. 106.—Sawing Horse.

12 in. to 16 in. The old-fashioned holdfast cramp is illustrated by Fig. 108; this is entirely of wood, and the cheeks of the cramp range in length from 6 in.

Fig. 107.—Bench Holdfast.

screw, whilst Fig. 110 shows one of Hammer's G-cramps with instantaneous adjustment, this being an improved appliance of some merit. The screw merely is pushed

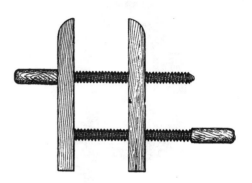

Fig. 108.—Wooden Holdfast Cramp.

until it is tight on the work held in the cramp, and a slight turn of the winged head then tightens up the screw sufficiently. The sliding pattern G-cramp is illustrated by Fig. 111, this possessing an advantage similar to, but not as great as, that of Hammer's

Fig. 109.—G-cramp.

to 16 in. Iron cramps are shown by Figs. 109 and 110, Fig. 109 being the ordinary G-cramp, of which different makes vary only in unimportant details; some, for instance, have a lever and screw instead of a thumb-cramp. Sash cramps and joiners' cramps (non-patent) resemble Fig. 112, a lengthening bar being supplied with them at an increase in price of, roughly, 60 to 80 per cent. There are several makes and many differences in detail, but Fig. 112 illustrates the type. There are a number of patent cramps for sashes and general joinery, of which

side view by Figs. 114 and 115, which are sufficiently explanatory when it is said that the cross pieces slide upon the side pieces.

Fig. 110.—Hammer's G-cramp.

Fig. 111.—Sliding G-cramp.

Crampton's appliance (Fig. 113) is sufficiently typical. The right-hand jaw can be set at any position on the rack. When the work has been inserted the right-hand jaw is pushed against it tightly, and the lever handle gives instantaneous adjustment. The joiner has a choice between a very great number of cramps. When jointing up thin stuff, if an ordinary

one sliding bar being made immovable by iron pins placed in holes in the side pieces. In cramping very thin stuff, place a weight upon it before finally tightening the hand screw.

ROPE AND BLOCK CRAMP.

Fig. 116 illustrates the method of cramping up boards with rope and blocks. The

Fig. 112.—Sash Cramp.

cramp is used, there is a great risk of the material buckling up, and the joint being broken. This risk is obviated largely by the use of the cramp shown in plan and

wood blocks A, about 4 in. long and 1½ in. square, are placed on the edges of the boards B, and a rope is passed round them twice and knotted. A small piece of wood is then placed between the two strands of rope and twisted round. This twisting draws the rope tighter on the blocks, thereing in width from 4 in. to 2 in. The boards E to be cramped are placed on the appliance, pieces D are laid against the

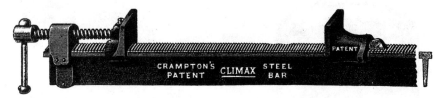

Fig. 113.—Crampton's Patent Cramp.

by cramping the boards together. Three of these sets would be sufficient to cramp a number of long boards.

WEDGE CRAMP.

A more serviceable cramp is illustrated by Fig. 117. A piece of wood A, about 2 ft.

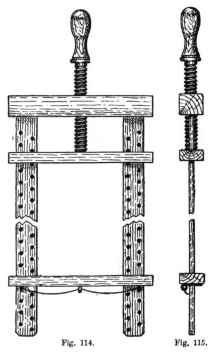

Fig. 114. Fig. 115.

Figs. 114 and 115.—Cramp for Thin Work.

9 in. long, 6 in. wide, by 1 in. thick, is planed up. On each end of this are fixed blocks B, 6 in. long, 1 in. thick, and taper-

edges of the boards to protect them, and the wedges c are then driven home.

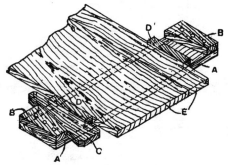

Fig. 116.—Rope and Block Cramp.

These wedges should be about 10 in. long, 1 in. thick, and tapering in width from 4 to 1½ in. The whole of this device should be made of hardwood, except the

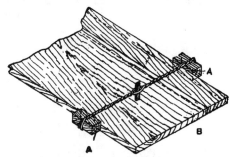

Fig. 117.—Wedge Cramp.

packing pieces D, which should be deal, so that if too much pressure is applied to the wedges any injury threatening the edges will be taken by the packing pieces rather than by the boards.

Fig. 118.—Dog, Round Section.

CRAMPING FLOOR BOARDS.

Floor boards are commonly cramped or tightened up by means of " dogs," of which

Fig. 119.—Dog, Square Section.

two forms are shown respectively by Figs. 118 and 119. The boards being already close together, the dog is inserted across, that is, at a right angle to the line of joint,

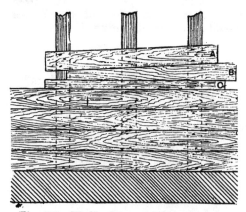

Fig. 120.—Wedge Cramp for Floor Boards.

one point being in one board and one in the other. The further in the dog is hammered, the closer are the boards cramped together.

Floor boards can be tightened up without the aid of a floor dog by the method shown at Fig. 120. The board next the wall

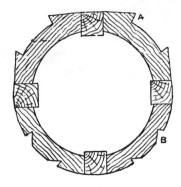

Fig. 121.—Circular Seat with Cut Cramping Pieces.

should be well secured to the joists, and then three or four boards can be laid down and tightened up by means of wedges, as shown. The following is the method of procedure:—Place a piece of quartering

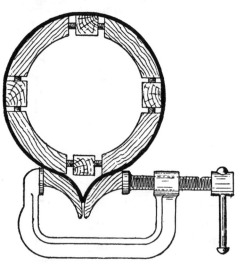

Fig. 122.—Circular Seat with Flexible Cramp.

about 2 in. by 3 in. next to the floor board, as at c. Cut a wedge, and place it as at B ; then nail down a piece of batten to the joists, as at A (both this and the wedge can be cut out of odd pieces of floor board). The wedge B should be driven with a large hammer or axe until the joints of the board are quite close.

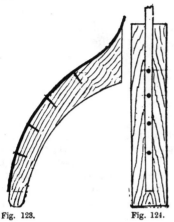

Fig. 123.   Fig. 124.

Figs. 123 and 124.—Wood Horn of Flexible Cramp.

CRAMPING CIRCULAR WORK.

There will now be explained away many of the difficulties in closing or cramping the joints in circular work, such as chair-seat frames, circular rims for loo tables, and

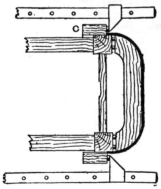

Fig. 125.—Flexible Cramp.

other circular work built up in segments, and the methods described also apply equally well to oval, semicircular, and other curved work. One method of closing with straight bar cramps is to provide

projecting cramping pieces A (Fig. 121). This is done when setting out the stuff, the cramp jaws embracing one cramping piece at each side of the leg, and the seat frame being dressed up afterwards. This method, however, entails a great waste of wood, and in marking out circular work it is of great economy to mark one piece

Fig. 126.—Screw-end Flexible Cramp.

with the other, which cannot be done with the method described above. Where the curved members act as stuffing rails to be covered by the upholstery, another method is to cut a piece out of the rails as shown at B, the cramp jaws in this case fitting in the notches, which are afterwards filled up by the pieces of wood being glued in again. But this method makes the frames very unsightly. The flexible cramp shown

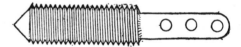

Fig. 127.—Screw of Flexible Cramp.

applied externally to a circular seat at Fig. 122 consists simply of a pair of beechwood horns (Figs. 123 and 124) about 8 in. long by 2 in. thick, to which a narrow band of hoop iron is attached by means of screws or rivets. This hoop passes round the seat frame, and pressure is brought to bear on the horns by a hand cramp or by an ordinary bar cramp. The cost of these cramps is small, and a variety of sizes will be found exceedingly useful. Another

3

flexible cramp is shown at Fig. 125, the horns in this case being replaced by rectangular pieces of hardwood. The cramp is shown as applied to a curved couch end, the pressure being applied by a bar cramp

tightening up the nuts. This kind of cramp applies to almost any kind of irregularly shaped work.

PINCERS.

Pincers are very familiar tools used for

Fig. 128.—Lancashire Pincers.

at each side. This kind of cramp is useful for semicircular work, such as bowfront chairs, curved pediments, bell-shaped backs, etc. Fig. 126 illustrates a flexible cramp which is self-contained, the hoop iron band being riveted to steel or brass

extracting and beheading nails, and for other purposes where a form of hand vice is wanted for momentary use. There is but little variety in their shape, and they range in size from 5 in. to 9 in. Usually one handle ends in a small cone (see Fig. 128) or

Fig. 129.—Tower Pincers.

ends, which are threaded (see Fig. 127) to receive winged nuts. They pass through a stiff bar of hardwood, which keeps them in position, the cramping being done by

ball (see Fig. 129), and the other in a claw for levering out nails, etc. Fig. 128 shows Lancashire pincers, and Fig. 129 Tower pincers.

PARING AND SHAVING TOOLS.

THE ACTION OF A PARING CHISEL.

BEFORE describing edge tools and their uses, it will be well to discuss the action of such typical tools as the chisel and knife ; though the latter is not generally found amongst woodworkers' ordinary tools. It is desirable to examine the manner in which the power applied to a chisel is used, and for simplicity's sake it is better to conceive the cut as being made upon some homogeneous material, such as lead. Taking first the ordinary method of paring, in which the face of the chisel is in contact with the mass of the material, Fig. 130 shows the force A that impels the chisel ; B is the resistance of the material to the crushing action of the edge of the chisel ; C is the reaction of the paring to the pressure exerted by the bevel of the chisel ; and D is the reaction of the body of the material to the pressure exerted to the face of the chisel. To obtain a proper conception of the actual cutting edge, it must be borne in mind that the edge of even so delicately sharpened a blade as a razor presents a jagged, rough appearance when viewed through a microscope, and theoretical or mathematical conception of an edge is never attained in practice. It is the greater or less approximation to it—or, in other words, the sharpness or bluntness of the chisel—that determines the amount of the force B (Fig. 130). The passage of a thin parallel blade with a square edge through, say, a bar of soap is obtained entirely by the crushing and displacement of the material, and the thinner the blade the less the resistance, and therefore the smaller the force required. The edge of the chisel must be regarded as such a blade of exceeding thinness ; but to allow the passage of the chisel blade, which has considerable thickness, the paring must be bent

aside as it advances. In setting out the force B, the frictional resistance to the advance of the chisel may be included. In its resistance to being bent aside, the paring acts as a very short cantilever ; so it is evident that the bending force which produces the reaction C increases rapidly as the paring becomes thicker.

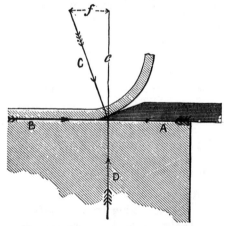

Fig. 130.—Direct Paring with Chisel.

ANGLES OF CUTTING EDGES.

Whatever the amount of the force required to bend the paring, it is clear that the smaller the angle at which the chisel is sharpened the smaller will be the horizontal component f (Fig. 130), and, consequently, the smaller will be the thrust required to make the cut. This shows the advantage of sharpening at a small angle ; for, if the angle be greater than is necessary, the extra force required is wasted in bending the paring to a sharper curve. To avoid complication, the sharpening of the chisel is shown as one bevel, instead of the two produced by the successive actions of grindstone and oilstone (see p. 39). When the oilstone bevel is very small, the reaction c may be regarded as taking place (in cutting wood, at any rate) between the grindstone bevel and the paring; but when the oilstone bevel is very wide, reaction takes

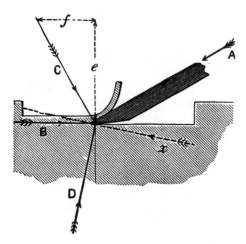

Fig. 131.—Inclined Paring with Chisel.

place chiefly between the latter bevel and the paring; and since it has a greater angle than the grindstone bevel, more force is required in using the chisel. Hence it is desirable to grind the chisel frequently.

ROUGHNESS OF CUT SURFACES.

Sometimes in cutting wood the surface left is found to be extremely rough, even though the chisel be as sharp as it is possible to make it. This is due to the crushing stress having been too great to be confined to the immediate neighbourhood of the cutting edge, so that it has disturbed the material for some little distance round it. This difficulty is overcome, practically, by giving a compound motion to the chisel, drawing it sideways as well as thrusting it forward. In this way the jaggedness—which always exists, however unapparent—of the edge acts like a saw upon the fibres, and thus relieves the crushing stress, with the result that in making the cut less force is expended. The benefit of this action is more pronounced in the case of the knife than in that of the chisel, as the former permits of a freer sideways motion.

USING CHISEL BEVEL DOWNWARDS.

When obstacles render it necessary to use the chisel as in Fig. 131, an increased effort is required to make the cut. The vertical component e now is opposed by the resistance to crushing of the amount of material covered by the oilstone bevel. Since this is small, the material will be considerably compressed; and if the oilstone bevel be thrust along whilst it is held in a horizontal position, the crushing of the material as the bevel moves will add a downward-acting vertical component to the motion, and so the paring will increase in thickness and the surface will not be cut horizontally. To prevent this, the chisel must be so inclined that the oilstone bevel takes the direction x, and thus the downward motion due to the crushing is exactly balanced by the upward motion due to the direction x. But this crushing cannot take place without absorbing work; so that a

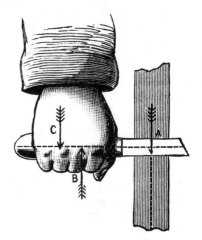

Fig. 132.—Equilibrium of Forces in using Knife.

paring of given thickness requires much more force when produced in this way than with the method shown by Fig. 130. An additional reason why more force is required is that only the horizontal component of A is now available for actually cutting, whilst the vertical component of A goes to increase the force acting against D, and therefore increases the crushing action. Moreover, the component *f* is greater, owing to the increased angle of the cutting edge. The double-bent tools used by the carver have the oilstone bevel merged into the grindstone bevel, so as to give an extended bearing surface, and therefore produce less crushing, and so require a smaller expenditure of power.

THE ACTION OF A KNIFE.

So far as the actual cutting is concerned, the action of the knife is very similar to that of the chisel indicated in Fig. 130; but in the manner in which the force A is applied to the tool an important difference exists. In Fig. 132 the force A is again shown; but in this case it is obtained by the muscular resistance to the forces, B and C. Now, since C + A equals B (for it is a case of parallel forces, and the sum of the forces acting in one direction must equal the sum of those acting in the opposite direction), it is evident that B alone is greater than A.

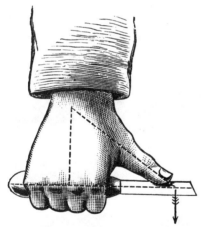

Fig. 133.—Thumb used as Strut in Cutting with Knife.

In the case of the chisel, the muscular effort is that required to produce the force A; but in the case of the knife, muscular effort equal to B + C has to be produced; and, of these forces, one alone is greater than A. Under these conditions, it is the advantage obtained by the sawing motion that enables the knife to compete with the chisel. When

the thumb is extended along the back of the knife, there is virtually a strutted cantilever (Fig. 133), and the strain on the muscles is then not so great. In almost every case,

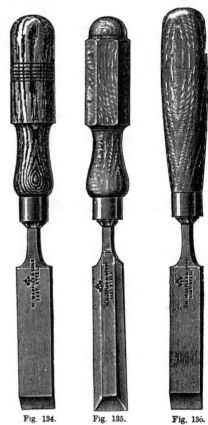

Fig. 134.   Fig. 135.   Fig. 136.
Figs. 134 to 136.—Firmer Chisels.

however, the use of the knife results in the maximum of effort and the minimum of effect, and as a workshop tool it cannot compete with the chisel, though experience has shown it to have many advantages from an educational standpoint.

CHISELS THAT ARE REQUISITE.

A few firmer chisels (Figs. 134 to 136) will be necessary. These are made in various sizes, ranging from about ⅛ in. to 1½ in. in width. As the whole set is not a necessity, a few of convenient size may be purchased, adding to them as occasion requires. The following sizes of chisels will

perhaps be found the most serviceable :
¼ in., ½ in., ¾ in., and 1 in. The firmer
chisel is used by both carpenter and joiner
for cutting away superfluous wood by thin

oilstone bevel should almost form one with
the grindstone bevel as shown ; otherwise
the resistance offered by the wood to an
obtuse oilstone facet not only adds to the

Fig. 137.—Long Paring Chisel.

chips. It is a strong chisel, with an iron
back and a steel face (the best are made of
cast steel) ; and it is used with the aid of a

labour, but causes the tool to slide away
from its work. A lock mortise chisel of
great strength is shown by Fig. 140.

Fig. 138.—Mortise Chisel.

mallet. It is more generally used than any
other for all kinds of hand chiselling—such
as paring, for purposes of fitting, etc. The

How Chisel Edges Should be Shaped.

Edge tools used in wood working are more

Fig. 139.—Sash Mortise Chisel.

stouter kinds, being strong enough to resist
the blow of a mallet, are also used for
broad and shallow mortises. A long par-

sensitive to ill-treatment than those used
for working metal, and of the latter those
which are operated by hand are relatively

Fig. 140.—Socket Lock Mortise Chisel.

ing chisel is shown by Fig. 137. Figs. 138
and 139 show a tool known as a mortise
chisel ; it is much stronger than the firmer
chisel, and is used only for mortising. The

more sensitive than those that are actuated
by machine, the reason being, of course,
that the more delicate the nature of the
work, the more readily is the action of

the tool felt. Many tools in daily use in factory machines are badly formed, so causing a great waste of power that could not be tolerated if they were hand worked, owing to the excess of energy required. In many cases, tools do not cut, or they cut badly, because the wedge form is impaired. The chisel, and all chisel-like tools, should be ground with one facet only, not with several. This applies alike to the chisel for wood working and that for metal cutting, to the gouge, the axe, adze, knife, razor, plane-iron, spokeshave, and others. The reason

Fig. 141.—Correctly Shaped Chisel Edge.

why it must be so in order to develop the full efficiency of these tools is apparent from the accompanying illustrations. Thus, comparing Figs. 141 and 142, which are slightly exaggerated for the purpose of illustration, the former shows how a chisel-like tool ought to be ground, the concavity of the facet exactly corresponding with the curve of the stone upon which it is ground. Such grinding requires some practice in the case of broad chisels and plane-irons, the tendency in unskilful hands being to

Fig. 142.—Incorrectly Shaped Chisel Edge.

produce a succession of facets like Fig. 142, due to the slipping up and down of the tool on the revolving stone. But the advantages of the form shown by Fig. 141 are very great. First, the necessity for regrinding is delayed much longer than in Fig. 142, where the facet is on the whole convex instead of concave. Fig. 141 approaches to the hollow razor form (Fig. 143), and for some little time the grinding angle and the sharpening angle will coincide ; after awhile it becomes necessary to tip the facet in

sharpening (see Fig. 144), and the sharpening angle is gradually rendered more obtuse until regrinding becomes necessary. But in Fig. 142 the sharpening angle is obtuse from

Fig. 143.—Section of Hollow-ground Razor.

the beginning, and regrinding soon is necessary. Moreover, since the angle is so obtuse, a greater expenditure of energy than in the former case is necessary to remove the shavings, there being less penetrative power. This is apparent from the dotted lines, which show the effective angles of the two by comparison. The endeavour, then, should be to preserve the wedge-like form of a tool edge as long as possible, the grinding of the hollow facet being regarded as of the greatest importance. Chisels are often

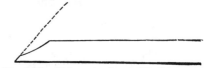

Fig. 144.—Obtuse Angle of Old Chisel Edge.

badly sharpened by tilting up the face for the purpose of turning back the wire edge. The result is that the face is like Fig. 145. This again detracts from the wedge form. Worse than that, it destroys the guidance afforded by a perfectly flat face, this being a very important point. The chisel must be tilted before it will cut, and there is no longer that contact of broad faces which is conducive to the guidance of the tool, and

Fig. 145.—Badly Sharpened Chisel Edge.

the difficulty of cutting surfaces and ends is much increased. No matter how flat the general area of the chisel face is, if there is a second facet, however narrow at the cutting edge, that determines the action of the tool. The tool angle is measured between that and the sharpened facet on the bevelled face. Of course, with all tools the labour of cutting is increased as the wedge form becomes impaired by legitimate wear, that is

Fig. 146.—Sharpening Chisel on Oilstone.

as their angles become more obtuse. When the amount of this is slight only, the tools need sharpening; but when, by repeated sharpening. the tool angle becomes very obtuse, grinding is necessary to remove material in greater quantity. The grinding and sharpening of chisels are operations practically identical with grinding and sharpening plane irons (see pp. 54 and 55). Fig. 146, however, shows the position in which the chisel is held on the oilstone.

GOUGES.
A few gouges also (Fig. 147) may be found

arcs of circles. Fig. 148 shows the sectional curves to which gouges are made.

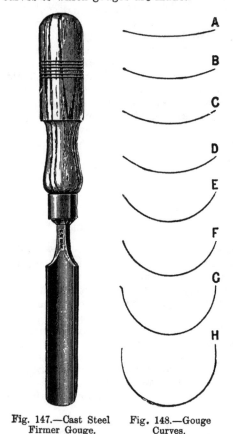

Fig. 147.—Cast Steel Firmer Gouge.

Fig. 148.—Gouge Curves.

DRAWING KNIFE.
The drawing or draw knife has its typical form illustrated by Fig. 149. It is used for

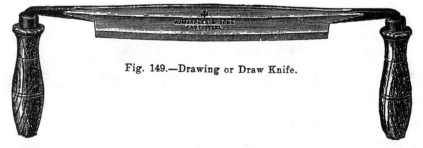

Fig. 149.—Drawing or Draw Knife.

useful. Their action is that of a chisel, but instead of being flat their sections form

roughing stuff to shape preparatory to working with finer tools.

SPOKESHAVES.

The spokeshave (Fig. 150) is made in various forms; the one illustrated is of box-

Fig. 150.—Wooden Spokeshave.

wood, and the simplest made; but this form is not recommended, many better kinds being made entirely of iron, with screws to regulate the cutting-iron. An iron spoke-

Fig. 151.—Iron Spokeshave.

shave is shown by Fig. 151. The beech-wood spokeshave shown by Fig. 152 has a metal plate in front of the blade, and that shown by Fig. 153 is regulatable by means

Fig. 152.—Plated Spokeshave.

on the thumbscrews. In principle, the spokeshave is merely a knife or chisel edge in a suitable two-handled holder. In use it may jump if the iron is loose;

Fig. 153.—Spokeshave with Regulatable Blade.

if the back part of iron touches before the cutting edge; if there is insufficient clearance for the shavings in the mouth; if the cutting edge of the iron is

worn to an obtuse angle and requires grinding; or if the face of shave is either too flat or too round; or the defects may simply be due to want of skill. With some kinds of ash it is very difficult to get a level surface with a spokeshave, and a compass plane should be used.

SHARPENING SPOKESHAVE BLADES.

It is somewhat trying to the hands of the operator to sharpen the short blades used in iron spokeshaves and small planes. The difficulty, however, may be readily overcome as follows: Procure a piece of hard wood about 10 in. or 1 ft. long, say 2 in. broad, and ½ in. thick. With a tenon saw make a cut across one end about 1 in. deep. The blunt blade being now inserted in this cut will be held sufficiently tight, and may be sharpened like an ordinary plane-iron (see pp. 54 and 55) with comparative ease and without fatigue to the hands. It will be found to be a slight advantage if one or both of the long edges at the end where the saw-cut has been made be chamfered, so as to admit of the short blade being held on the oilstone at the correct angle when pushed well into the cut. By means of such a holder the blades may also be conveniently held on the grindstone while being ground.

PLANES.

In workshop practice, planes are the tools chiefly used for smoothing the surface of

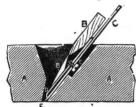

Fig. 154.—Section of Plane.

wood after it has been sawn to approximate size. In its simplest form, a plane is a chisel firmly fixed into a block of wood by which it is guided in its cut, and the amount of wood taken off in the form of a shaving is regulated to a nicety. In fact, such a simple tool actually is used sometimes, when a proper plane of the requisite shape and of a suitable size cannot be procured. To make the construction of an ordinary plane quite clear, a section of one is illustrated by Fig. 154, in which A shows the section of stock ; B, the wedge ; c, cutting iron ; D, back iron ; E, the screw for fastening irons together ; and F is the mouth through which the shavings pass upwards.

A plane is simply a copying tool, and a notch in the plane-iron at once proves that the pattern produced corresponds with the

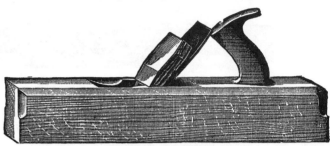

Fig. 155.—Jack Plane.

edge of the plane-iron, and all the imperfections of this edge will be copied on to the stuff. In all planing operations the edge of the tool is the pattern, which is copied in reverse on the wood. If a hollow is required to be produced on the wood, a tool is used with a round edge of exactly similar form to the hollow we wish produced. In machine planing the pattern is the edge of the tool, which produces a similar surface upon the wood.

DIRECTION OF GRAIN IN PLANES.

For flat planes such as jack, try, and smoothing planes, the grain must be straight and, of course, run lengthways of the tool. The wood is selected from a centre plank of beech as near to the bark as possible ; in all planes, the wood nearest the bark, that being the hardest part of the

Fig. 156.—Sunk Handle Jack Plane with Closed Toat.

wood, becomes the sole or working surface. The wood is seasoned thoroughly, and never is used until at least three years after cutting. Moulding planes mostly work on the spring, and need not have the grain so straight as flat planes. Hollows, rounds, trueing plane (Fig. 157) is almost exactly the same as that of the jack plane, but it is much longer, so as to produce truer

Fig. 157.—Trying Plane.

and rebate planes are exceptional, however, and should have the grain as straight as possible, because the rebate plane is cut right through, and is liable to cast or warp if not quite straight-grained ; and most of the hollows and rounds, being thin, are liable to cast also if not of straight, mild, and well-seasoned wood. Wood for plane making should be as free from knots as possible.

JACK AND TRYING PLANES.

The jack plane (Figs. 155 and 156) is the first applied to the wood after it has been sawn. This plane is always employed to remove the roughness of the work before finishing up with trying and smoothing planes. It is made up of five parts—namely, the stock (which should be 17 in. in length), the toat or handle, the wedge, the cutting iron or cutter (2⅜ in. broad), and back iron. Immediately behind the iron is a handle, which, in use, is grasped only by the right hand in planing fir ; but in heavy planing, and especially in hard wood, it is necessary to place the left hand across the front of the plane to press it down, to cause the iron to take hold of the wood. When using both hands to the plane, the left is placed with the four fingers lying across the top near the fore end, the thumb passing down the near side. Well-seasoned beech is a suitable wood for the stock. The construction of the trying or

surfaces. The following instructions on manipulating the jack plane apply equally well to the trying plane.

REMOVING AND REPLACING IRON IN JACK PLANE.

To remove the iron, the stock should be grasped by the left hand, with the thumb on the inside of the mouth, as shown by Fig. 158. The back of the plane may be rested against the body, whilst the front of the tool is gently knocked with the hammer (or mallet, by preference), which will loosen

Fig. 158.—Knocking out Iron of Jack Plane.

the wedge, and enable the iron to be withdrawn. Another method is to knock the front of it with face upwards smartly on the bench while holding wedge and iron in the left hand ; one blow is generally enough. The iron, it will now be observed, consists

Fig. 159.—Cutting Iron.   Fig. 160.—Cutting and Back Irons.

in reality of two parts ; the cutting iron is faced with good steel (see Figs. 159 and 160), and the back is of iron. Badger jack planes have irons as in Figs. 161 and 162. The back iron (see Figs. 160 and 162) screw fastens the irons tightly together, and it is for the purpose of regulating the thickness of shavings, as will be explained in a separate paragraph. To take the irons apart, place the wedge upon the bench, as at A (Fig. 163), and lay the iron screw uppermost upon it. Now loosen the screw with a screwdriver (do not take it out), and slide the back iron up until the head of screw will pass out at the hole made for the purpose. The unscrewing of a plane iron with a long driver is illustrated by Fig. 164. Sometimes a large screwdriver and a small hammer are required for unscrewing the iron and setting the plane ; but by a few minutes' work on the grind-

stone, the flat pene of a hammer can easily be ground so that it will serve as a screwdriver, thus answering both purposes. When the iron has been sharpened (see pp. 54 and 55), screw on the back iron in the same manner that it was taken off (see Fig. 163), and place it in the groove or mouth of the plane, keeping it in position with the thumb of the left hand, the fingers grasping the face, as at Fig. 158. Now insert the wedge, and lightly tap it with the hammer. Place the end of the plane upon the bench, and draw the top towards the worker ; now look down the face in the direction of the arrow, and the iron should be seen projecting about $\frac{1}{16}$ in. Should it be more, gently tap the head of the plane, again driving in the wedge tightly. The tool is now ready for

Fig. 161.—Badger Cutting Iron.   Fig. 162.—Badger Cutting and Back Irons.

use. The two irons should be screwed perfectly tight (see Fig. 165) ; if they are left as in Fig. 166 the plane will choke and no longer work. If the back iron is too close to the mouth of the plane, chattering may occur; to remedy it, slightly ease the front part of the mouth with a sharp chisel, to allow the shavings to pass through.

Fig. 163.—Unscrewing Plane Irons with Special Tools.

Chattering may be caused by the back iron not fitting close to the cutting iron, when shavings will get in and cause it to jump (see also p. 51).

ADJUSTING PLANE IRONS.

The manner of handling and adjusting the cutting iron is a most important consideration, especially when planing against the grain of a brittle wood, such as pitch pine. In planing wood that is cross-grained and liable to rip or tear up, the cutting iron

Fig 164.—Unscrewing Plane Irons with Long Screwdriver.

should be set very finely—that is, its edge should be quite close to the edge of the back iron (see Fig. 167), but for the jack plane it must be placed further back, as at

Fig. 165. The finer the shaving to be taken off the wood, the closer should it be set. When dressing a difficult wood against the grain, although the cutting edge may be in splendid condition and sharp as a razor,

Fig. 165.—Plane Irons Tightly Screwed.

the perfect condition and adjustment of the back iron is also an absolute necessity in order to leave a fine smooth surface. The finer the shaving the smoother will be the surface obtained; and if the edge of the back iron, as it is lying on the cutting blade, is in the least degree rough or does not press evenly and firmly on the whole width of the blade, the shaving will get in between and stop the work. However, it is easy to set the iron too fine, especially when jack-planing soft, straight-grained stuff like

Fig. 166.—Plane Irons Loosely Screwed.

pine, which perhaps wants considerably reducing.

SMOOTHING PLANES.

This plane, as its name implies, is for the purpose of smoothing the work to form a finished surface. After the drawing in, mortising, tenoning, dovetailing, etc., are done, and before the work is put together, all the parts that cannot afterwards be operated upon are finished with this plane. For fine or other soft woods it is 9 in. long, having an iron $2\frac{1}{4}$ in. wide on the cutting face. The stock of this plane has the sole and top parallel, but the sides are curved, making the two ends narrower than the centre. The wooden smoothing plane (Figs. 168 and 169) has not a toat or

Fig. 167.—Adjusted Plane Irons.

handle, but the iron plane has a toat; for general usefulness, however, the plane made of beech cannot be excelled. This plane is specially shaped with a view to the extreme handiness indispensable to a tool that has to contend with varying directions of grain in the wood. Hard woods, particularly the more ornamental kinds, often are troublesome to clean off, and however well the smoothing plane is used, much must still be left to the scraper. The conditions of successful work with the smoothing plane will repay study, since practical experience of those conditions will tend to the more skilful handling of the larger planes. The sole of the plane should be flat; tested in any direction with a straight-edge the result should be agreement, but in the case of the iron-fronted plane (Fig. 169) the sole is curved lengthways. The cutting iron should rest on the sloping surface prepared for it without any rocking, touching all over the surfaces in contact. When the back iron is screwed on, the same condition should obtain. Hence the flexure caused by tightening the screw should be mainly taken by the back iron, whose object is to stiffen the cutting iron and not to distort it. If, therefore, the cutting iron, with the back iron affixed, is in winding, either the bed of the iron in the plane is bad or the plane must be fitted to suit the winding iron. A little further consideration will show that (1) the warping of a plane involves alteration of

Fig. 168.—Smoothing Plane.

the surface on which the iron rests; that (2) it is desirable both that this surface be flat and that the plane iron be flat on its back surface; and for these reasons it will be found (3) that "parallel irons"

are far superior in stiffness and accuracy to the ordinary plane iron. The wedge also must fit so well that the iron may rest immovable under ordinary working strains; but it is not fair to expect the wedge to force into agreement crooked irons and warped planes. It should never be

Fig. 169.—Iron-fronted Smoothing Plane.

necessary to drive the wedge so tightly that its withdrawal becomes difficult. As the function of the back iron is to stiffen the cutter and deflect the shaving, care must be taken to avoid breaking or bending the edge of the back iron. A gap into which a part of the shaving could get must not be allowed to remain, and rounding or under-cutting of the contact edge must not be permitted. The upper surface of the back iron is to be kept clean and smooth, so that the shaving may glide up its polished surface. The sharpened edge of the cutting iron must be a little convex, but only sufficiently in most cases to prevent the corners of the iron digging in. It is therefore necessary to sharpen the irons of all planes with some attention to the thickness of the shaving they will be required to remove, and to sharpen away a little from the corners of the iron accordingly, diminishing the convexity for trying and smoothing planes, but increasing it for jack planes, which are intended to be coarsely set. It might be thought that this convexity would produce hollows in the work, but it must be remembered that the iron is not used upright, but at an angle which will reduce the convexity about one-half. The aperture or mouth of the plane should be as narrow as possible, so as not to encourage tearing up. The passage of the shaving without hindrance is all that is desirable ; but the mouth should be so formed that it may be possible to bring the back iron edge very close to the cutting edge, and still allow the shaving to

Fig. 170.—Knocking out Iron of Smoothing Plane.

pass freely. However well the smoothing plane is set, sharpened, and used, the scraper and glass-paper are still required for finishing hard woods. The plane iron is knocked out in quite a different way from the jack plane. Hold the tool in the left

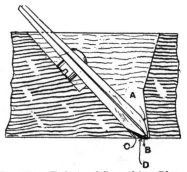

Fig. 171.—Defects of Smoothing Plane.

hand, as in Fig. 170, with the thumb on the inside of its mouth, and with a hammer held in the right hand tap the back until the wedge is loosened sufficiently to admit of the iron being withdrawn. Beginners, as a rule, will hammer away at the top

of the plane, as with the jack plane, but this is neither desirable nor necessary.

SMOOTHING PLANE WORKING BADLY.

Any of the following defects may prevent a smoothing plane working properly, causing it to tear up the surface of the work. It may be close at A (Fig. 171), so as not to pass the shavings between the back iron and mouth, or, if very open at the same place, it would jump at the ends of a board being planed ; the back iron may not fit close to the cutting iron at B, which would cause shavings to pass between them, clogging the mouth ; the cutting edge may be thick as at D, when the black portion would have to be removed with the grindstone, the iron being finished on the oilstone, or it may not bed properly behind the cutting iron at C, which would cause the iron to chatter. In this case, the remedy is to glue a thin piece of card or leather on to make the back level as described on p. 51.

REBATE PLANES.

A rebate plane (Fig. 172) is made of beech, and is 9 in. long, its width varying considerably, but a useful size is about $1\frac{1}{2}$ in. The cutting iron extends the full width of the plane, thus enabling the angles of rebates to be cleaned up. A back iron is not used with this plane. To withdraw the iron of a rebate plane, it should be taken in the

Fig. 172.—Rebate Plane.

left hand, grasping the wedge and the iron firmly with the palm, as illustrated by Fig. 173 ; the wedge is then smartly struck with a hammer until removed ; in Fig. 173 A is a front and side view of the iron, and B is the wedge. In sharpening the iron upon the oilstone, take great care to keep the edge straight across. In replacing the iron, it should be adjusted so that, upon glancing down the face of the plane, it shows equally across its width; if this is not carefully attended to, a long corner may result.

Fig. 173.—Rebate Plane taken Apart.

OTHER VARIETIES OF PLANES.

The joiner and cabinet-maker have occasion to use many other kinds of planes, only few of which, however, require to be mentioned here. The bead plane illustrated by Fig. 174 is for the purpose of working the moulding known as a bead (this will be described later). Bead planes are made in sets, ranging from ⅛ in. to 1 in., in a set of eight. The router, or old woman's tooth (Fig. 175), is a kind of plane used for working out the bottoms of rectangular cavities; it is used for cutting cross grooves in timber to a certain depth, particularly

Fig. 174.—Bead Plane.

when the groove does not go the whole width of the stuff, as, for instance, with sinkings for treads and risers in strings. It has a broad sole, and its cutter projects the depth of the required sinking. The chariot plane (Fig. 176) is a plane used for

the small parts of the work which cannot be conveniently got at with the smoothing plane. Also it is used for planing end grain and cross-grain work; the iron being very near the toe of the stock also renders the plane very useful for chamfering and for

Fig. 175.—Router or Old Woman's Tooth Plane.

planing work recessed out of the solid. The best chariot planes are made of gunmetal, with a steel face. They are not used very much now. Chamfer planes are used for taking off sharp edges to form chamfers. There are great differences in their shapes, as may be seen from Figs. 177 to 179. Fig. 177 shows Preston's plane, Fig. 178 Melhuish's plane, and Fig. 179 Nurse's plane. A mitre shooting plane is illustrated by Fig. 180, and a plough or plough plane, a most important tool, whose use will be fully described later, is shown by Fig. 181.

HOW TO USE THE JACK PLANE.

In use, the jack plane is pressed down on

Fig. 176.—Chariot Plane.

the work and thrust forward with a steady but deliberate stroke (see Fig. 182), when, if in proper condition, it should take off a shaving nearly as wide as the iron and as long as the piece being planed. Keep the face of the plane well oiled just in front of the iron. Always work with the grain if possible (Fig. 183). A far thicker shaving can be taken off smoothly in this way than if worked as in Fig. 184, which requires more careful work with a more finely set plane. Do not use the plane at an uncomfortable

Fig. 177.—Preston's Chamfer Plane with Adjustable Fence.

height. When the board to be planed is in position, and the worker takes the jack plane in hand ready to begin, a line drawn through his elbow and wrist should be rather lower than higher at the wrist, though if the forearm is level it will do. Do not attempt to take off thick shavings at the outset, and do not be disappointed if a shaving is not taken off from end to end at the first trial. If the wood has any hollow in it, it will be impossible to do

Fig. 178.—Melhuish's Chamfer Plane with Adjustable Fence.

this, and even if it is perfectly straight the beginner will have great difficulty in doing it. Beginners always plane too much off the end near the bench stop, and are too apt to move the arm in the arc of a circle. These errors must be avoided by careful

4

practice. Try to plane the centre of the material rather than the margin, for if a good plane is in proper order it is impossible to make the wood much too hollow or concave ; whereas, however good the plane, careless use of it can and will

Fig. 179.—Nurse's Chamfer Plane.

make the work convex in every direction. Probably there is no better lesson than to try to face up—that is, level—two pieces of stuff so that they will, when brought together, be in mutual contact. This simple job will require much perseverance on the part of a beginner if it is to be done successfully. Good progress will not be made if the wood practised upon is too small ; little pieces are sure to be made convex in length by a beginner.

Fig. 180.—Mitre Shooting Plane.

Take a piece not less than 2 ft. long, though experience has shown that the best results in this exercise are obtained by using pieces of spruce 4 ft. long, $4\frac{1}{2}$ in. wide, and 3 in. thick ; this is too stiff to bend, and affords a good surface. When some facility has been obtained, the blade of a 12 in. square or a straight-edge should be employed to test the work. To take a

Fig. 181.—Handled Plough.

surface out of winding, get two straight-edges—say, 12 in. long, 1½ in. wide, and 1 in. thick, and see that they are parallel. Place these across the work, one at each end; then by viewing both, bringing the eye down to glance from one to the other, it will be seen whether the two are in one plane. If they do not appear to lie in one plane, the surface is in winding, and opposite corners must be reduced till satisfactory. (See also p. 5.)

How to Use the Smoothing Plane.

Fig. 185 shows the method of holding

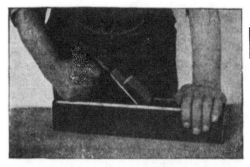

Fig. 182.—Holding Jack Plane.

the smoothing plane, the right hand grasping it firmly at the back, whilst the left hand steadies it in front. In starting,

the tool is applied to the fore-end of the board, and gradually worked backwards, thus taking out any marks previously used tools may have made. It should be held firmly, and lifted sharply at the end of stroke, or a mark will be left where the plane finished. The work is continued until the board presents a perfectly smooth surface, without marks of any kind. The left hand should frequently be passed across the face of the board, as any marks made by the plane can be readily detected in this manner. It may also with advantage be held so that the light passes across its surface from the side, thus showing up imperfect planing. Should there be too much iron out, a few blows with the hammer at the back of

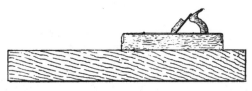

Fig. 183.—Planing with the Grain.

the plane will draw it back. Take care to tighten up the wedge again. A few drops of

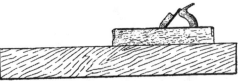

Fig. 184.—Planing against the Grain.

linseed oil applied to the face of the plane will facilitate the planing.

Planing Hollow.

A plane in operating on a rough piece of wood removes successive shavings from the more prominent parts, until a level surface is attained. The flatness attainable with the plane is greatly dependent on the skill of the workman. He must always try to plane hollow rather than round, for if a plane be flat and long in the stock, it is impossible, as has been stated, to give any appreciable concavity to a surface of moderate size. For this reason roughing-out planes, or jack planes, are made as long in the stock as possible without making them too heavy and inconvenient. Planes used for trueing are invariably called trying planes, and are used to correct the inequalities left by the jack. Very long ones go by the name of jointers, and are principally used for making long joints.

New Planes Becoming Choked.

New planes often are a source of trouble

Fig. 185.—Holding Smoothing Plane.

owing to the shavings getting fast in the mouth, the plane refusing to take any more until the wedge and iron have been removed, and all cleared out. The cause of this difficulty is that the mouth of the plane is too narrow (see Fig. 186). Sometimes workmen cut a little out with a chisel, but in many instances this results in spoiling the tool, because in a short time the bottom of the plane wears away, and consequently the mouth gets larger, subsequently getting so large as to require a piece to be planted in. The mouth of the plane can be kept open as long as needed by gluing a strip of soft leather, about ¾ in. wide, in the mouth of the plane under

the top end of the iron (see Fig. 187). When the plane bottom is sufficiently worn the leather can be removed and the iron put back into its original position. The

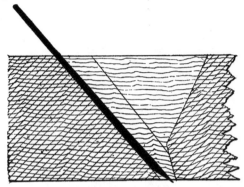

Fig. 186.—Plane with Narrow Mouth.

leather causes the iron to be more upright, and consequently there is a larger opening in the mouth (two thicknesses can be put under if necessary).

Remedying Worn Mouth of Plane.

Fig. 188 shows the section of a plane that has its mouth worn very open, through the plane having been shot and the iron

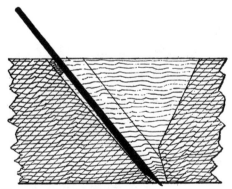

Fig. 187.—Leather Slip under Top of Plane Iron.

ground short. One method of remedying this defect is to let a piece of hardwood into the face; but the simplest and best plan is to glue a thin strip of wood or leather behind the iron at the bottom (Fig. 189). This gives the iron a sharper angle, closes the open mouth as much as desired, and, when a new and thicker iron is bought, the strip can be reduced or removed.

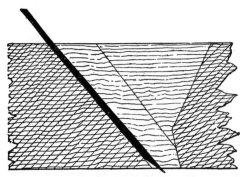

Fig. 188.—Plane with Wide Mouth.

Oiling Plane Stocks.

Plane stocks are oiled in order to improve them for working and to preserve the wood in perfect condition. A wooden smoothing plane is hardly regarded as complete until it has been saturated with linseed oil, a very common plan being to fill the hole with oil, after stopping it on the

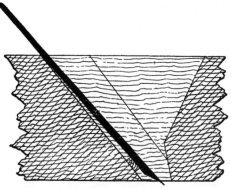

Fig. 189.—Leather Slip under Bottom of Plane Iron.

face, and leave it till absorbed. Planes that are too greasy to handle pleasantly will improve with time. This oiling, however, largely increases the weight of the plane; and a tool that has been soaked too long in the oil so as to be too heavy for convenient use should be placed in a moderately warm oven for a few hours to evaporate some of the oil. The oven must not be hot, or a number of shakes will be produced, and the plane will warp.

Pitch of Plane Cutting Iron.

To assist the reader to understand correctly the principles of plane-iron sharpening, the following information is given. The seat of the plane-iron is made at different angles, to give the pitch to suit different kinds of work. The four angles most in use are as follows:—Common pitch, in which the seat for the back of the iron is at an angle of 45° from the sole (this inclination is usually employed for all planes for soft wood); York pitch, which has an angle of 50°, and is adapted for use with mahogany and other hard, stringy woods; middle pitch or 55°, and half pitch or 60°, which are employed with moulding planes, the former being for soft wood and the latter for the harder kinds. Fig. 190 affords an idea of three angles, A giving the set of a half-pitched plane, B that of an ordinary plane, while C shows the inclination of an extra-pitched plane. The pitch or angle at which the cutter is set is of importance. There are three angles involved in this case: (1) The angle between the cutter and the surface of the work; this should be as small an angle as possible. It is obvious that if the surfaces of the cutter and the work were perfectly parallel, the cutter would glide over the surface without cutting, except under great pressure. By making the cutter edge rather than its whole surface touch the work, the tendency to cut and to continue the contact is secured. The angle, which may be called the clearance angle, or the back angle, should only be enough to secure this condition of contact. (2) The angle of the cutter itself. The more acute this angle the better, if only the material will stand the strain and face the work without losing its edge. (3) The front or remaining angle may be found by subtracting both (1) and (2) from 180°, if dealing with plane surfaces, and is available for the passing away of the waste material; in the case of the plane, however, this is limited, in order to provide means to prevent the shaving being torn up in advance of the cutting action. This provision is made by the front portion of the plane, and to be efficacious must be in contact with the work and as near the edge of the cutter as possible to allow waste to escape. A few experiments with a knife will show that for soft materials a slight angle is best. This involves a thin knife, and its side almost in contact with the material to be cut; but as harder things are tried the stiffness of the cutter, and the consequent angle, must be increased, not because it is merely desirable, but because it is absolutely necessary to have a stronger cutter. The more upright an iron is set, the less liable is it to tear up the wood in planing; but in the same

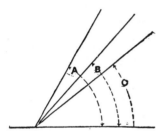

Fig. 190.—Three Pitch Angles for Planes.

degree the iron loses its edge more quickly, is more likely to jump and chatter, and is more laborious to work. In toothing planes the irons are set upright, and in "old woman's tooth planes" or routers nearly upright. In working with an upright iron, the action of the tool is that of scraping the work, while the more the iron is inclined the nearer it approaches the action of splitting the wood. For this reason an ordinary or extra-pitched plane is more liable to splinter up the surface of a piece of work; but this accident may be in great measure prevented by using a properly adjusted back iron. Moulding planes, rounds and hollows, bead planes, and others that work without a back-iron, are usually preferred set to the half-pitch angle; while for working on end-

grained stuff, extra-pitched tools, such as shoulder and bull-nosed planes, give the best results. In examining the side of a plane-iron, it is found to be made up of an iron back faced with steel. The steel,

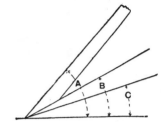

Fig. 191.—The Three Angles of a Plane Iron.

welded on to the iron and distinguished by its brighter colour and finer grain, acts as a cutting edge, the iron being required to give sufficient stiffness to prevent chattering. When newly ground and sharpened, a plane-iron has three angles, one due to the pitch, A (Fig. 191), one made by the grindstone, B, and one made by the oilstone, C. The angles A and B do not alter, but C gradually becomes more acute with sharpening on the oilstone, until it lines with the face of the plane, as in Fig. 192, when the iron refuses to cut properly, and requires grinding. The pitch angle A (Fig. 190) varies in planes by different makers, as described above.

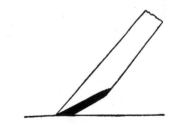

Fig. 192.—Plane Iron before and after Grinding.

GRINDING PLANE CUTTING IRONS.

As stated above, when a plane-iron has been sharpened on the oilstone a number of times the edge becomes thick as in Fig. 192, when the portion shown black in the drawing should be removed by the grindstone. Of course it might be taken off with the oilstone, but this would involve a waste of time, the more economical plan being to keep the oilstone simply for imparting a keen edge, and using the grindstone to take off the waste material at the back as occasion requires. The iron may be ground as follows: The worker should stand, if possible, with the grindstone revolving towards him. The stone should be well wetted, as a dry grindstone will heat the tool and spoil its temper. The back iron may be kept on the plane cutter and

Fig. 193.—Grinding Plane Iron.

set about ⅛ in. back. This allows of a firmer grip being taken of the iron, and forms a gauge for keeping the cutting edge square, if it should be required. Fig. 193 shows the method of holding the tool on the stone; it should first be held towards the top, and the iron gradually lowered towards the worker until the bevel of the iron fits the stone, which may be felt by the additional force required to keep the tool in position. The grinding should be stopped just before the cutting edge is reached, unless it is required to remove a gap, or the iron is out of square. Some grind the iron until there is a wire edge $\frac{1}{16}$ in.

long attached to the cutting edge, and as this has to be removed with the oilstone, that much of the iron is wasted, leaving

Fig. 194.—Tool-grinding Rest.

the tool at the finish exactly the same as if the grinding had been stopped just before it reached the edge. The iron should not be ground too thin, or it will chatter. On the other hand, if too thick, it will soon require grinding again. If the angle is made about three times as long as the iron is thick, it will give a good working result. A mechanical appliance for maintaining the plane iron at a certain angle on the grindstone is illustrated by Fig. 194, which is self-explanatory.

SHARPENING PLANE CUTTING IRONS ON THE OILSTONE.

A good oilstone, capable of putting a keen edge on the tool, is a necessity to

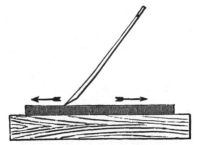

Fig. 195.—Plane Iron on Oilstone.

all woodworkers. Washita, Nova Scotia, and other fast cutting stones are useful for removing waste metal when the iron is thick; but it is seldom that one of these stones can be trusted to leave a keen edge on the tool. Turkey stones are the only

Fig. 196.—Sharpening Plane Iron.

stones that have the two good qualities combined of cutting quickly and leaving a good edge. Charnley Forest oilstones are slow cutters, but they are to be relied on for leaving a good keen edge. It is necessary that the oilstone should be kept perfectly level, or it will not be possible to

Fig. 197.—Finishing Plane Iron on Oilstone.

get a true edge. The stone should also be free from grit, or the iron will be gapped in sharpening, and will leave ridges

on the planed work. (Fuller particulars of the varieties of oilstones will be given later.) In sharpening the iron after it has been newly ground, the hands should be kept low to make the bevel correspond

Fig. 198.—Properly Sharpened Plane Iron.

nearly with that made by the grindstone. As time goes on, when the iron is resharpened the hands are kept a little higher upon each occasion (see Fig. 195), until it becomes thick, as in Fig. 192, then it must be again put upon the grindstone. Some workers find it convenient to use two oilstones—one as a quick cutter, to some extent superseding the grindstone, the other for finishing the edge. In using the oilstone, first put a few drops of good oil upon the stone, and grasp the iron as in Fig. 196; the right hand is at the top, and the thumb and fourth finger pass under. Place the whole of the fingers of the left hand upon the iron, with the thumb at the back, as seen. Now put the cutting edge (previously ground to a bevel) upon the stone in an oblique direction, as shown in Fig. 196, bearing in mind the previous remarks on the necessary inclination. The iron should now be rubbed up and down the stone, pressing it down with both hands. If the edge had been examined before placing it upon the stone, it would have been found to show a fine white line. The object of sharpening is to remove this, which must be done by rubbing on an oilstone. Having accomplished this, turn the iron face down upon the stone, and rub it lightly a few times (see Fig. 197). The iron

Fig. 199.—Badly Sharpened Plane Iron.

should now have the appearances indicated by Fig. 198. If the face of the iron has not been kept perfectly flat, it would appear as Fig. 199, and would be of no use as a cutting iron. If the iron has been rubbed too long, a wire edge will appear and utterly spoil the cutting properties of the iron unless removed. This may readily be done by rubbing the iron alternately upon each side until the wire edge falls off.

Fig. 200.—Fully Rounded Plane Iron.

When the iron is judged to be sufficiently sharp, it should be cleaned, whetted on the left hand, and its edge tried for keenness. Some try the edge by passing the thumb gently across it, but its sharpness may be judged by looking directly at it. In a sharp tool the edge is not visible to the naked eye, while, if the iron should be blunt, the edge will be plainly perceptible as a bright line.

Fig. 201.—Slightly Rounded Plane Iron.

EDGES OF PLANE CUTTING IRONS.

The edge of a cutting iron should be ground and sharpened to suit the tool in which it is to be used. If this is not done, the plane marks will be visible when the work is finished especially with polished or varnished surfaces. For a single-iron jack plane the edge should be rounded as in Fig. 200 ; for an ordinary jack plane the iron should be slightly rounded, as in Fig.

Fig. 202.—Plane Iron with Rounded Corners.

201 ; while for smoothing, panel, and trying planes the edge should be straight, but with just the corners rounded slightly to prevent their marking the work, as shown in Fig. 202. Trying planes, shooting planes, as well as rebate planes, badger jack

planes, and rebating jack planes, should be sharpened with the edge straight. When a smoothing or panel plane is sharpened to the proper shape, and a board skilfully planed with it, no ridges will be perceptible to the touch if the hand is passed across it from side to side.

Fig. 203.—Plane Irons with Thin Cutter Between.

DEFECTIVE BACK IRONS IN PLANES.

If a plane does not work properly the fault often may be with the back iron. If the back iron does not fit perfectly close across the full width of the plane, the shavings get between it and the cutting iron and clog the mouth of the plane. The remedy is to fit the edge of the back iron to the face of the cutting iron. This may be done either with a file or by bending it over a piece of round iron with a hammer. A defect often found in back irons is that of slipping over the edge of the cutting iron when the screw is tightened to hold the two together, thus destroying the edge. This sometimes may be remedied by roughing the top end of the back iron

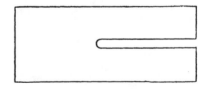

Fig. 204.—Steel Cutter for Improved Plane Iron.

where it fits on the top of the cutting iron, by placing it on a flat file and then hammering it ; or the screw may be tightened with the back iron some distance back from the edge, and afterwards gently hammered to its proper position.

IMPROVEMENTS IN PLANE CUTTING IRONS.

Much time is lost in grinding and sharpening plane irons of the thickness to which they are made at the present time. It is only the thin steel face of the iron that requires a keen edge; yet to obtain

iron; Fig. 203 shows the back and fore iron, between the two being the thin steel cutter, shown separately by Fig. 204.

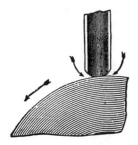

Fig. 205.—Grinding Gouge.

this a waste of time is incurred, owing to the amount of metal that must be removed at the back of the edge. Now if a thin

Fig. 206.—Grinding Gouge.

steel cutter could be introduced to place between the two irons, it would do away with the grindstone altogether for sharpening planes. This idea is not by any means new, and it has been practically carried

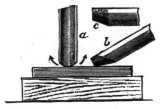

Fig. 207.—Sharpening Gouge on Oilstone.

out, both with hand and machine tools, with marked success. Fig. 203 shows this principle applied to an ordinary plane

Fig. 208.—Sharpening Gouge with Oilstone Slip.

Cutters of this description could be produced at half the cost of ordinary plane irons, if made in any quantity. Grinding a plane iron is a dirty job, even under the

Fig. 209.—Two Pieces of Wood Scribed Together.

most favourable circumstances, and it is thought that a cutter that does away with it is bound to meet with success.

GRINDING AND SHARPENING GOUGES.

A chisel edge is the same shape as the edge of a plane iron, and is produced in

Fig. 210.—Scribed Piece of Wood.

the same way, and there is no need to treat chisels separately here. Information, however, on keeping gouges in order may be welcome. They seldom require grinding, but this, when necessary, must be done with great care, as the bevel must follow the curve of the tool to ensure good work. Fig. 205 shows the gouge applied to the stone; it must be constantly turned backwards and forwards, as shown by the arrows. Fig. 206 illustrates the manner of

Fig. 211.—Scribed Piece of Wood.

holding the tool whilst grinding. The same rule as regards turning the gouge applies when sharpening it upon the oilstone; this is shown by the arrows at *a* (Fig. 207); if it were held like a chisel, as *b*, a good result would never be obtained—that is, the sweep of the tool would not be correct, as shown at *c*. After rubbing upon the flat stone, it may be necessary for some purposes to sharpen the gouge from the inside. This is done by means of an oilstone slip. The tool is held in the left hand, *b*, as in Fig. 208, and the slip, held in the right hand, is rubbed up and down the

gouge, taking care to keep the slip pressed quite flat against the groove, so as not to turn the edge. The reason for having the

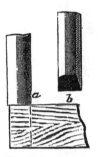

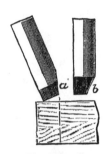

Fig. 212.—Gouge ground Inside.

Fig. 213.—Gouge ground Outside.

gouge edge so sharpened for ordinary use is evident from the following explanation of the use of a gouge sharpened the reverse way; that is, with the bevel inside the groove. Fig. 209 shows two pieces of wood fitted or scribed together. Figs. 210 and 211 are the piece marked (A) removed, the more plainly to illustrate the application of the gouge. At Fig. 212 is seen a scribing gouge *b*, showing by a section that it is ground on the inside, thus enabling it to cut straight down, as *a*; this is impossible with the ordinary gouge ground upon the outside, as Fig. 213 plainly shows.

HAND SAWS.

THE SAW AS A TOOL.

THE saw cannot be classified with any other tool. The hammer is a tool for consolidating material; the splitting axe, although usually regarded as an edge tool, is generally a hammer with a wedge pane, and is used for dividing material in the line of the fibres. The true edge tool in its most elementary form is the chisel, and by various added contrivances the chisel becomes the shears and the plane; but saws, which are to be discussed in this chapter, differ from all these. They can scarcely be called derivatives from these, unless the knife be regarded as the connecting link; for sometimes it is used as a chisel and at other times as a saw. All these tools, including the knife, cut or work in the direction of the grain or fibre, but the saw is essentially a tool for use across or at right angles to this fibre, although custom and convenience have arranged the saw for use with the fibre. Even then it is only because the fibres are not straight and parallel. When they are so, as in lath wood, then the saw is not employed. It is true that in such work as the felling of timber the axe is used across the grain, and therefore at right angles to the length of the fibre; yet if the action of the forester be observed, it will be seen that the direction of his blow is not that of the line of separation. He goes at his work indirectly when using the axe, directly when using the saw. These and the following remarks on the theory of the saw's action and application are taken from Rigg's Cantor Lectures, to which reference has been made already.

PRINCIPLES OF THE SAW'S ACTION.

For the purpose of separating a bundle of fibres, an edge drawn across will cut the surface fibres only; this is insufficient, for a saw is required to separate fibres below a surface. This separation must be a cutting (not a tearing) action. Looking at the work of a single cutting edge, it will be noticed that, although the continuity of the fibre is destroyed, the separated ends are still interlaced amongst the other fibres. To obtain a piece removable as by a small narrow chisel, it will be requisite to make a second cut parallel to the first. This being done, there is the short piece, retained in position by adhesion only, which must be removed, for the room it occupies is that in which the back of the cutting edge must move. To slide, as it were, a narrow chisel along and cut it out is more simple in sug-

Fig. 214.—Diagram showing Principle of Saw's Cutting Action.

gestion than in execution; for instance, the absence of any guide would cause great difficulty. To draw a pointed cutting edge along the same deepening line needs a very steady hand and eye. To increase the number of cutting edges, and form, as it were, a linear sequence of them, may give a partial guidance. Instead of having two parallel cutters these cutters may be externally parallel but internally oblique to the line of cut, as shown in the sectional and exaggerated view of saw teeth (Fig. 214), in which the portions of wood A B D and E C D have been removed by the gradual penetration of the oblique arms; not only have they been cut, but they have been carried forward and backward and removed, leaving a clear space behind them of the width A E. But a portion within the oblique arms is left, this consisting of particles of woody fibre adhering to each other only by the glutinous or gummy matter of the timber, and not cohering. If the breadth A E is not too large, the whole of the heap would be rubbed away by the power exerted by the workman, and both power and material are economised by narrowing A E. The resultant saw kerf is shown in section by Fig. 215. The active portion of a saw has three edges, of

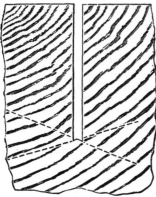

Fig. 215.—Saw Kerf.

which the lower or horizontal one only is operative, for the tool rides upon the fibres and divides them, and the sloping parts remove the hillock. To act thus, the lower edges would be required to be sharpened at A and E, so as to clear a way for the metal to follow. The resistance to the downward pressure, required to cause the cutting segments to penetrate vertically, is the breadth of the tooth, for it rides upon a number of fibres and divides them by sliding over; the complete action requires not only downward pressure for the cut, but also horizontal pressure for the motion, the latter both in the advance and withdrawal of the tool. These two pressures being at right angles do not aid each other, and will require the use of the workman's two hands. The compounding of these pressures will give freedom to at least one hand. For the present, assume that the two pressures to be compounded are equal, then the simple operation is to employ one pressure making (say) an angle of 45° with

the horizontal line of thrust. If the tool becomes a single-handed one, and relies for its operation upon thrust or tension in one direction only (say thrust), then cutting edges on the back portions of the teeth are useless, and had better be removed.

ACTION OF CROSS-CUTTING SAW.

Taking the ordinary cross-cutting single-handed saw, the forward thrust is intended to separate the fibres, by removing a small piece by two parallel cuts. For example, if o o (Fig. 216) be a fibre, then the action of the saw must be to cut clean out the piece a b, so making a space (a b) wider than the steel of which the saw is made. The cleaner the parallel cuts a d, b c are, the better. Now this clean cut is to be made by the tooth advancing towards the fibre. If the tooth come on in axe fashion, there is a direct thrust of a sharp edge; and though a wedge-like action may be the best for separating fibre adhering to fibre, it is quite out of place in the cross-cutting of a single fibre, in which cohesion has to be destroyed. There must be a cutting action, that is, the drawing of an edge across the mark for separation; besides this drawing action there also is pressure. Now, in soft timber, and with a saw having teeth only moderately sharp, this pressure tends to force the fibres into closer contact, to squeeze

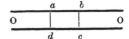

Fig. 216.—Wood Fibre Divided by Saw.

them amongst each other, to solidify the timber, and increase the difficulty in cutting. Two actions are here, pressure and thrust. The pressure must be very light indeed; if otherwise, the point of the tooth will gather up more fibres than the strength of the workman can separate; indeed, as a rule, in the cross-cutting of broad timber, and when all the saw teeth are in action, pressure is not required, the average weight of the saw-blade sufficing for the picking up of the fibres. Whatever may be the form of the teeth, the small piece a, b, c, d (Fig. 216), has to be removed so as to leave the ends from which it is taken as smooth and clean-cut as possible ; therefore the cutting edge must be on the outside of the tooth. This

in the shape of what in America are called "gums" and in England "throats," in which the teeth may be said to be set.

Fig. 217.—Hand Saw Handle.

being so, it follows that the act of severing a fibre will be attended with compression, and thus condensed it will be forced up into

Fig. 220.—Hand Saw Handle.

Saws cannot work easily unless as much care is bestowed upon the throats or gums as is given to the teeth.

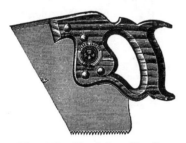

Fig. 218.—Hand Saw Handle.

the space between the teeth. This space must be so formed as to allow the condensed piece to drop freely away as soon as the

Fig. 221.—Hand Saw Handle.

THICKNESS AND STRENGTH OF SAW BLADES.

A saw must in one dimension (that of thickness of blade at least) be very thin, and that

Fig. 219.—Hand Saw Handle.

tooth passes from the timber, or the saw will become choked, and its proper action cease. In large saws this is provided for

Fig. 222.—Hand Saw Handle.

part cannot be strengthened by means of ribs. When a strengthening bar is introduced at the back as in tenon saws (see

Fig. 244, p. 66), the depth of cut is limited. If a light saw blade be pressed against an object or hooked on one, then tension causes

Fig. 223.—Three Rip Saw Teeth Points to Inch.

this straight blade to be more and more strengthened. On the other hand, if the saw blade be pressed forward by thrust, the weakness of the blade is apparent from the bending. Now, formed as saw teeth are, either to cut in both directions or in the forward direction only, there is always one direction in which the work to be done is accomplished by a

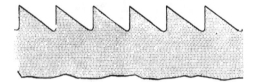

Fig. 224.—Three and a half Rip Saw Teeth Points to Inch.

thrust upon this thin metal. Clearly the metal will bend. If, however, the teeth cut in the direction of tension only, the work tends to preserve the straightness of blade, and upon this an important quality and use of the tool depend. That this tension system can be efficient with a very narrow blade is clear from the extensive use of

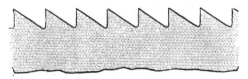

Fig. 225.—Four Rip Saw Teeth Points to Inch.

band saws. There is, however, a property in the breadth of the blade which applies equally to the tension and thrust systems—it is the guide principle. The breadth of

the blade operates by touching the sides of the gateway opened by the teeth. When it is desired to dispense with a straight guide for sawing purposes, it is done by narrowing

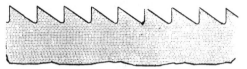

Fig. 226.—Four and a half Rip Saw Teeth Points to Inch.

the blade as in lock saws, keyhole saws, tension frame saws, etc.

POSITION AND SHAPE OF SAW HANDLES.

In thrust saws the hand and arm of the workman occupy a definite position, and the line of pressure on the saw is thus very much determined by the inclination of the handle to the line of teeth prolonged backwards. If the handle be placed at such an

Fig. 227.—Five Rip Saw Teeth Points to Inch.

angle that a large part of the resolved thrust be perpendicular to the line of teeth, then the bite may be greater than the other resolved portion of the power can overcome. At another angle the bite may be very little, and although the saw thus constructed would move easily it would work sweetly, but slowly. The construction is suitable

Fig. 228.—Five and a half Rip Saw Teeth Points to Inch.

for saws with fine teeth and for clear cuttings. With regard to single-handed saws only, whatever may be the other conditions required, most handles have curved hook projections, shown in Figs. 217 to 224, p. 61 which show a variety of shapes in hand saw handles. These projections are connected

Fig. 229.—Twelve Cross-cut Saw Teeth Points to Inch.

with the pressure of the sawyer on the teeth. If, in sawing, the hand bears upon the upper hook, then an increased pressure is given to

Fig. 230.—Eleven Cross-cut Saw Teeth Points to Inch.

the forward teeth ; if upon the lower hook the pressure on the saw teeth is released, and there is consequent ease in sawing.

Fig. 231.—Ten Cross-cut Saw Teeth Points to Inch.

The angle at which direct thrust ought to act upon the line of teeth in the saws is obviously very different. Each material

Fig. 232.—Nine Cross-cut Saw Teeth Points to Inch.

may be said to have its own proper angle, and in some saws provision is made by two set screws opposite the hooks for varying

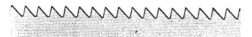

Fig. 233.—Eight Cross-cut Saw Teeth Points to Inch.

the intersection of the line of thrust with the line of teeth. In the biggest one-man saw used in handicraft—a tool quite 4 ft.

long—the upper hook of the handle is wanting (see Fig. 222), because under any circum-

Fig. 234.—Seven Cross-cut Saw Teeth Points to Inch.

stances the weight of the saw is more than sufficient, and therefore it is not requisite that any resolved portion of the workman's energy should be compounded with this.

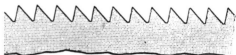

Fig. 235.—Six Cross-cut Saw Teeth Points to Inch.

But the lower hook must be retained, that the weight of the saw may be taken from the work. For these reasons the line of direct thrust is nearly parallel with that of

Fig. 236.—Five Cross-cut Saw Teeth Points to Inch.

the teeth. There appears to be much inconsistency in the placing as well as in the formation of saw handles, and this is the case particularly with saws for cutting metal.

Fig. 237.—Four Cross-cut Saw Teeth Points to Inch.

PITCH, ETC., OF SAW TEETH.

The coarseness and fineness of saws are estimated by the number of teeth points in an inch. Figs. 223 to 237 show (to full scale) a variety of sizes. By the saw-maker's term "pitch" is meant the inclina-

in the ordinary two-handled saw used for the cross-cutting of timber and some varieties of soft stone. The forms, however, of

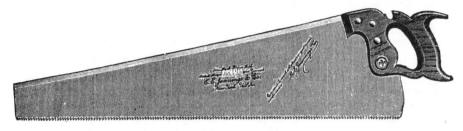

Fig. 238.—Straight Back Hand Saw.

tion of the face of the teeth up which the shaving ascends. Clearly if the saw is to cut when drawn in both directions, the slope of the teeth from the points must be the same on both sides; indeed,

teeth to cut in both directions are sometimes more varied. In cross-cutting timber with a one-handled saw, the action is either tension or thrust—one of these only. The only reason why both are not adopted seems

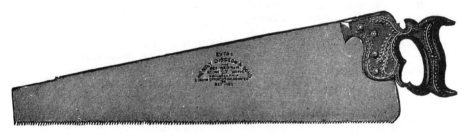

Fig. 239.—Hand Saw with Nibbed Back.

this may be considered the primitive form of saw teeth, and derived as the saw is said to have been from the backbone of a fish, it is the form that would be suggested. To use in the most perfect manner a saw

to be that very different muscular motions and postures of the body would then be introduced, and experience may have shown that these are more fatiguing than the alternate pressure and relaxation which take

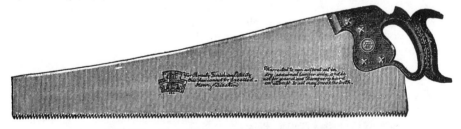

Fig. 240.—Skew Back or Hollow Back Hand Saw.

with such teeth would require that the action at each end should be the same; hence, these are the forms of teeth generally met

place in the ordinary process of hand-sawing. Now, if the cut is in the thrust only, then the form of the back of the tooth must be the very reverse of that of the front, for it ought to slide past the wood, and not separate the fibres. In this case the back

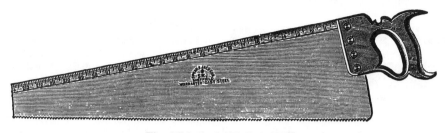

Fig. 241.—Saw with Rule Edge.

of the tooth may be sloped away, as shown later, or it may be shaped otherwise. The faces of the teeth are no longer bound to be formed in reference to an equality at

half-moon tooth, gullet tooth, briar tooth; also upright pitch, flat pitch, slight pitch. The customary shape has the face of the

tooth at right angles to the line of the teeth. The backs of the teeth are, therefore, sloped according to the distance between the teeth and the coarseness or fineness of

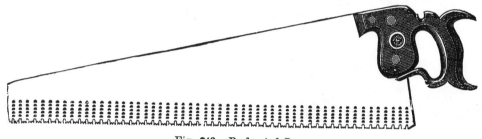

Fig. 242.—Perforated Saw.

the back. Indeed, with the liberty thus accorded, there has arisen an amount of fancy in the forms of teeth, which fancy has developed into prejudice and fashion.

the saw. This is called ordinary, or hand-saw pitch. (The substance of this paragraph and of the five that precede it is derived from Rigg's Cantor Lectures.)

Fig. 243.—One-man Two-handled Saw.

Names dependent either upon uses or forms are given to these, and thus they are distinguished in the tool trade; some of these names are: Peg tooth, M tooth,

VARIETIES OF HAND SAWS AND THEIR USES.

The ordinary wood-worker has some six or eight saws, comprising the rip, cross-cut, hand, panel, tenon, dovetail, bow or turn-ing, and keyhole. The hand saw type in-cludes the hand saw proper, the ripping, half-ripping, and panel saws, all of similar

Fig. 244.—Tenon Saw.

outline, but differing in dimensions, and in form and size of teeth. There is no sharp distinction between these tools, as they merge one into the other; yet at the ex-tremes it would be impossible to substitute the ripping and panel saws one for the other. The hand saw, however, which is a kind of compromise between extremes, is used in-discriminately for all purposes. Repre-

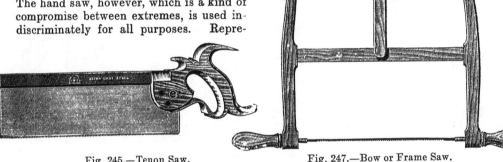

Fig. 245.—Tenon Saw.

sentative hand saws are illustrated by Figs. 238 to 243. Fig. 238 shows a saw with straight back; Fig. 239 shows a saw with nibbed back; Fig. 240 is a skew back or round back saw which runs without any "set"; it is of extremely high temper.

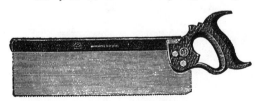

Fig. 246.—Tenon Saw.

Fig. 241 shows a hand saw with its back edge graduated as a rule. Fig. 242 is a per-forated saw with American shaped teeth, and Fig. 243 is a "one-man" two-handled

saw, the extra handle being removable at will. The typical hand saw is from 24 in. to 28 in. long, being measured on the blade, which corresponds with the maxi-mum range of thrust of which the arm is capable. Its blade is as thin as possible consistent with sufficient strength to pre-vent the saw buckling under thrust. The blade tapers in length, a form which is also best calculated to withstand thrusting stress without unduly increasing the mass of metal. The handle completely encloses the hand, so that muscular effort is not required to keep the hand from slipping away from its proper grasp. The teeth are bent to right and left alternately, while their out-line is angular—the cutting angle being so

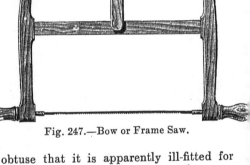

Fig. 247.—Bow or Frame Saw.

obtuse that it is apparently ill-fitted for dividing fibres. Lastly, the teeth are so sharpened that their outer points first enter the wood, and the fibre is divided by a gradually incisive kind of action. Not one of these points can be neglected with im-punity, for they all conduce to the proper operation of the hand saw. Six teeth to the inch are very suitable for a hand saw. This tool is used for the coarser kinds of work, sawing off stuff—especially large stuff —and for use on buildings, trimming joists and cutting rafters, halving plates together, and other rough jobs; it is not much re-quired in a shop. As a good general tool in a shop, or for fixing work in the interior of a house, a panel saw is much to be pre-ferred. This is a saw about 2 in. or 3 in. shorter, and much narrower, thinner, and lighter than the hand saw. If a panel saw is once taken to for general work, the hand saw will not be much used, except for heavy work. For cutting along the grain

Fig. 248.—Compass Saw.

(technically known as ripping) is used the rip saw, as by means of its large teeth the work may be accomplished more quickly than with the hand saw. The blade is about 28 in. long, and there are three teeth to the inch, these being sharpened square across the blade, and set very much forward. For cutting shoulders, the tenon saw is used,

Fig. 249.—Compass Saw.

owing to the teeth being finer, thus producing the clean cut which is so desirable for this purpose. Figs. 244 to 246 show three tenon saws, which differ only very slightly from one another. The common tenon saw has more or less both of set and rake, according to the material upon which it is chiefly used. Usually it is set and sharpened in a medium or average style for general bench

tenon to the 6-in. or 8-in. dovetail, the teeth in the latter case being so fine that the thinnest wood and the most delicate joints can be cut without risk of tearing up the grain. As to the proper saws to be used for cutting the parts of joinery, there can be no hard-and-fast rules laid down. A tenon may be so large that it may be formed by cutting with the

Fig. 250.—Compass Saw.

grain with the rip saw and across the grain with a panel saw, or so small that a dovetail saw is of ample size for both purposes. Again, a dovetail joint may easily be large enough to warrant the use of a tenon saw, and yet not be so large as dovetails are sometimes required. It is of importance to learn to use the saw so as to require as little as possible the aid of chisels to pare

Fig. 251.—Compass Saw.

the tenons, etc. It is far more economical of time to cut the work properly at first rather than to trust to the use of chisels to reduce tenons too stout, dovetails too big,

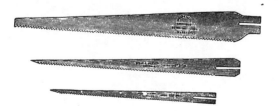

Fig. 252.—Set of Interchangeable Saws.

use. But according to the character of the work mainly done, the size of the saw selected is from the 12-in. or 14-in.

sockets too small, or mortises too narrow; and attention is directed to instructions given on p. 83 on the proper use of the saw.

The bow saw, turning saw, or frame saw (Fig. 247) is invaluable for cutting out curved work either with or across the grain ; for a similar purpose is used the compass or lock saw, of which Figs. 248 to 251 show four kinds. A nest or set of interchangeable

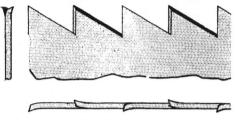

Fig. 253.—Rip Saw Teeth.

saws (Fig. 252) is a boon to the occasional worker.

Varieties of Saw Teeth.

Many workmen think that so long as the tooth of a saw has a sharp edge the shape of the tooth is a matter of small importance, and as a result of this ignorance or indifference they are always in trouble with their saws, and their work becomes much more laborious than if proper attention had been paid to the shape of the teeth. Substances of different texture cannot be cut advantageously with the same tool ; in fact, the tool must be adapted to the work if the best all-round results are to be produced. Fig. 253 illustrates a form of tooth suitable for an ordinary hand rip saw. The

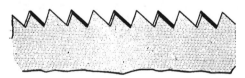

Fig. 254.—Cross-cut Saw Teeth.

tooth points number about four to the inch, and the front of the tooth is upright, that is, at an angle of 90°. The face of the tooth should be filed to an angle of 85° to 87°, or 3° to 5° from the square. Some experts contend that the teeth of a rip saw should be filed dead square. The object in filing them a little on the bevel is that the teeth

may cut more freely and easily when they have become a bit dull, there being then what is termed a little clearance cut in the teeth. In nearly all timber there is, it is

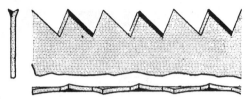

Fig. 255.—Cross-cut Saw Teeth for Hard Wood.

well known, a certain amount of fibre to be cut either directly or obliquely across, and teeth that are filed square will not, whether they are sharp or dull, divide this fibre so easily as teeth that have a slight bevel. Fig. 254 shows a suitable tooth for a hand-saw used for cross-cutting soft wood. The tooth points in this saw may

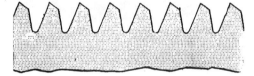

Fig. 256.—American Cross-cut Saw Teeth.

number five or six to the inch. The front of the tooth slopes at an angle of about 105°. The face of the tooth in sharpening should be filed to an angle of from 55° to 60°. The softer the timber that is to be cross-cut, the more acute should be the angle of the teeth, as the keener edge

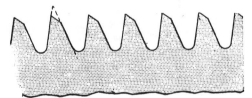

Fig. 257.—American Cross-cut Saw Teeth.

separates the fibres more easily. Fig. 255 shows a form of hand-saw tooth suitable for cross-cutting hard wood. The number of tooth points may be from six to eight to the inch, and the front of the tooth should slope at an angle of 110° to 115°, according to the hardness of the timber to be sawn. The face of this tooth should be

Fig. 258.—Saw Teeth filed hollow: Incorrect.

filed to an angle of 70° to 75°, because the cutting edge must be less acute owing to hard-wood fibres being more compact than those of soft wood. Another form of tooth in a one-way hard-wood cross-cut saw is shown by Fig. 256. If this form of tooth is properly sharpened, it will be found to cut much faster in hard wood than a tooth that cuts both ways. The front of this tooth, as illustrated, slopes at an angle of about 105°. If the wood to be cross-cut is dry and very hard, the teeth should slope at an angle of 110°, or even more. The tooth points of this saw should be about ⅝ in. from point to point, and the face of the tooth should be filed or ground, as the case may be, to an angle of about 70°. The teeth should be parallel with the back edge of the saw, which, in working, should be pulled and pushed perfectly straight.

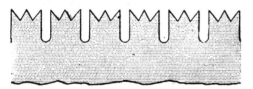

Fig. 259.—American Regulating Saw Teeth.

There is not much difference between Fig. 256 and Fig. 257, but the dotted lines in the latter figure show that the angle of the tooth is shaped correctly. By "hook" is meant the lead or rake the fronts of teeth have—that is, the distance the point of tooth overhangs the bottom of front of tooth. It will be noticed that in Fig. 258

the teeth are filed a little hollow in front and at the back. This is a great mistake, and several reasons could be assigned. One reason is that a correct angle cannot be determined (see dotted lines in Fig. 258). In shaping the teeth of a tenon saw it is wrong to make their cutting faces upright as shown in Fig. 253. This causes the saw

Fig. 260.—American Lightened Teeth.

to bind in the wood at the forward stroke. The front edges of the teeth being vertical, they bite too much. For a tenon saw to act freely, the front edges of the teeth should make angles of about 80°. There are several peculiar forms of American teeth, though they are no great improvement on the ordinary saw teeth. Figs. 259 and 260 represent American cross-cut saw teeth. Fig. 259 is termed the regulating tooth. By filing the centre tooth to an acute angle, it will be suitable for cutting soft wood; for cutting hard wood the teeth should be filed to a more obtuse angle. Fig. 260 is termed the lightened tooth. The sharpening should be much the same as Fig. 259 for different kinds of wood. A tooth that is least difficult to sharpen when filed to its proper cutting angle is found to be the best form of tooth. For general cross-cut-

Fig. 261.—American Peg Teeth.

ting the peg tooth (Fig. 261) is recommended. This is suitable for a soft wood cross-cut saw with two handles. The faces of this tooth, which cuts both ways, should

be filed to an angle of 50°, the space between
being 130°. When this form of tooth is used
in cutting hard wood it should be filed to
a more obtuse angle. If a saw is to cross-

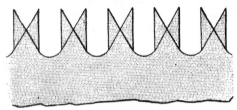

Fig. 262.—M-shaped Saw Teeth.

cut hard wood only, the gullet or one-way
cross-cut tooth (Fig. 256) is recommended.
This tooth will be found easy to sharpen,
and, if properly sharpened, will cut as fast
as any tooth, and faster than most. The
more upright the front of teeth (Fig. 257)

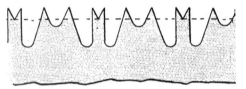

Fig. 263.—Disston Saw Teeth.

the faster the cut, but the more difficult
to work. The more they incline backward
the more easily they will work, but the
more slowly they cut. M-shaped teeth
(Fig. 262) are now largely used for cross-
cutting, chiefly in America, and as they
have cutting edges both back and front they

Fig. 264.—Teeth of Pit Saw.

will cut in both directions. Usually, they are
bevelled and set alternately, and they cut
rapidly if kept in good order. The teeth of
Disston's American saws (Fig. 263) have less
set than those in most English saws. Figs.
264 and 265 represent pit saw teeth. The

form of tooth shown by Fig. 264 may
answer fairly well for soft wood of ordinary
thickness, but for thick timber, and especially the harder kinds, such teeth will cause
jarring and bad work. Teeth as in Fig.
265 are the more suitable form. Of course,
with all saws, the harder the timber to be

Fig. 265.—Teeth of Pit Saw.

sawn the more obtuse the angles of the
saw teeth. The teeth in a saw cutting
hard wood should be about $\frac{5}{8}$ in. apart,
and for soft wood, $\frac{3}{4}$ in. For cross-cutting
logs with a two-handled saw, a saw with
teeth similar to Fig. 266, instead of
ordinary cross-cut teeth, can be recommended, as it is much quicker and cleaner
in cutting. These saws were invented and
are largely used in America. The cutting
is done by the single teeth, the double ones
acting as clearers, and being filed about
$\frac{1}{32}$ in. shorter than the scoring teeth. The
teeth are often formed on both edges of
the blade, and when one set are worn
down, they are knocked off, and the other
edge of the blade used. The saw is made
slightly curved ; the handles are reversible.
Fourteen gauge steel is used. This form
of saw is rapid and easy to work, and does
not bind in the cut ; at the same time com-

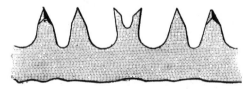

Fig. 266.—Teeth of Two-handled Cross-cut Saw.

paratively little set is required. It will
cut well both hard and soft wood.

SAW VICES.

For holding a saw during the process of
sharpening a saw vice will be required.

This is made in various forms, one of which is shown by Figs. 267 and 268. It can be made of any hard wood, such as oak or mahogany. It consists of two parts, hinged

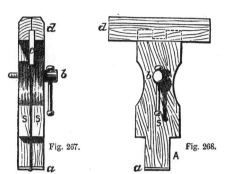

Fig. 267. Fig. 268.

Figs. 267 and 268.—Saw Vice.

together at the bottom *a*; an iron screw working in a plate or nut is placed in the centre *b* for the purpose of tightening up the jaws *d* between which the saw is placed. The piece cut out at *c* is to allow the back of a tenon saw to pass through. The jaws *d* should be about 12 in. by $2\frac{1}{2}$ in. by $1\frac{1}{2}$ in., and the sides s 15 in. by 6 in. by $1\frac{1}{2}$ in. These sides are fixed to the jaws by means of two small tenons, as shown by dotted lines, being glued to keep them in position. Fig. 269 shows a handy and cheap vice, which can

Fig. 269.—Saw Vice.

be fixed to any support by means of a screw-bolt and fly-nut passing through it. The movable jaw is acted upon by a similar bolt and fly-nut. Figs. 270 and 271 show

an improved saw vice, differing from ordinary vices only in the method of tightening up the jaws; Figs. 272 and 273 show plan and elevation of eccentric clamp

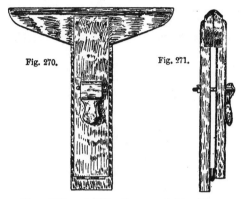

Fig. 270. Fig. 271.

Figs. 270 and 271.—Improved Saw Vice.

with rod and nuts. The rod is of $\frac{1}{4}$-in. round iron, screwed at each end (mild steel would be more suitable), the bends being made when the iron is heated red hot.

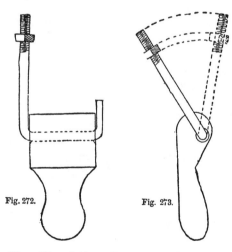

Fig. 272. Fig. 273.

Figs. 272 and 273.—Clamp of Improved Vice.

This clamp must be shaped out, and the protuberant part where it will tighten on the stock should be smooth and true. Two $\frac{5}{16}$-in. holes, which will be $6\frac{3}{4}$ in. down, are bored through both uprights to accommodate the ends of the rod, and collars may be let in flush at the back to tighten the nuts against. When the nuts are adjusted, a saw is instantly clamped by pressing the handle down as shown in Figs. 270 and 271. To release the saw, pull up the handle of the eccentric clamp or lever. The

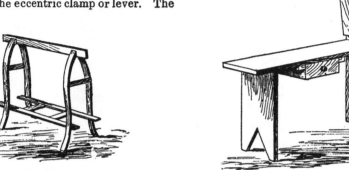

Fig. 274.—Saw Bench.

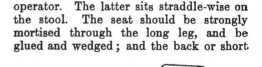

Fig. 275.—Portable Saw Vice.

position of the rod hole is as shown in the illustrations. It will add to the grip of the jaws to make the uprights slightly curved outwards in the middle, and a 2½-in. butt hinge will complete the vice. A strip of vulcanised rubber or leather fastened along the top inside edge of jaws will improve the grip.

SAW BENCH.

Fig. 274 represents a handy bench in which to fix a saw. The treadle-like frame at the bottom, when pressed upon by the feet, acts through the two upper

operator. The latter sits straddle-wise on the stool. The seat should be strongly mortised through the long leg, and be glued and wedged; and the back or short leg should be similarly mortised through the seat, unless the drawer shown—which is convenient for holding files—is omitted, when, as is frequently the case, the short leg may be hinged to fold up under the seat. In the latter case an iron stay—two would be better—must be provided to hold the leg rigid whilst the "horse" is in use. The movable jaw is simply a piece of wood hinged at the bottom to the long leg, and cramped up tightly against the other jaw by a fly-nut working on a screw, or by a screw as shown in the illustration. In order to keep the vice jaws from warping, strips

Fig. 276.—Triangular Saw File.

side pieces as fulcra upon the two gripping jaws.

PORTABLE SAW VICE AND BENCH.

A portable vice for use when sharpening hand saws is shown by Fig. 275. It consists, practically, of a low stool, with one leg fixed at the extreme end, and continued upwards to a height suitable for the

of oak, mahogany, or other hardwood should be screwed on the inside surface of each, as shown, and these, again, may be covered with sheet lead. As the wood of which the jaws are made will be almost sure to curve somewhat as it gets dry, care should be taken that the growth marks or annular rings take a course from the outside of each jaw towards the inside; the jaws will then have a tendency to become concave on their faces, and will at each end tightly grip a saw placed between them,

Fig. 277.—Double-ended Saw File and Handle.

and the tightening-up process will tend towards bringing together the central part of the jaw faces. If the wood is placed so that the annular rings have the opposite direction, the jaws will, in course of time,

the other end used. For sharpening American cross-cut saws the file shown by Fig. 278 is used, and for American rip

saws that shown by Fig. 279. Saw files are generally cut in three degrees of fineness, a second cut or smooth-cut

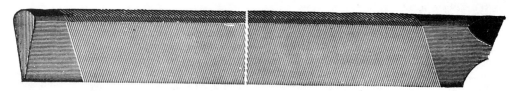

Fig. 278.—File for American Cross-cut Saws.

become convex, and difficulty will be experienced in holding a saw firmly.

SAW FILES.

The triangular file shown by Fig. 276

file being best for sharpening a hand saw. A file for sharpening saws must be of the very best quality. See that the teeth are cut perfectly even, and that the colour of the file is uniform. If it is of whitey-grey

Fig. 279.—File for American Rip Saws.

is the one usually adopted in sharpening English hand saws. Its size varies with that of the saw for which it is required. It is

colour throughout, it shows that the temper is uniform; but if it is mottled, the temper probably is uneven. For levelling

Fig. 280.—File for Topping Saw Teeth.

economical to use a double-ended saw file as shown by Fig. 277; when one end has become dull, the file may be reversed, and

down or topping saw teeth preparatory to sharpening, a flat file (Fig. 280) will be necessary.

ASCERTAINING ANGLE OF SAW TEETH.

To ascertain the angle of a saw tooth, draw a semicircle on cardboard, and mark off degrees to form a protractor (see Fig.

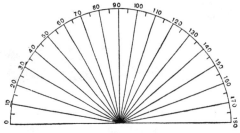

Fig. 281.—Protractor.

281). Place a 2-ft. rule on the horizontal line, and open the rule to the angle required. Draw a line D (Fig. 282) on the saw-plate; or, if the saw to be tested is a circular saw, place one part of the rule on the top of the bench table, and move the other part of the rule until it is in a line with the point of the centre tooth. If the front of the tooth corresponds with the bevel

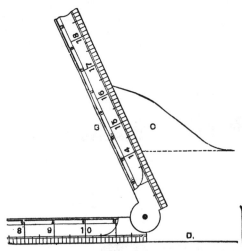

Fig. 282.—Ascertaining Angle of Saw Teeth.

of the rule, the rake or lead is correct. If the circular saw is a large one, and the rule is not long enough to reach the tooth from the table, place a parallel block of wood on the table, and put the rule on it, or draw a line on the plate, and place the

rule on the plate in a line with this line. This test applies to all hand saws mentioned in this chapter. Fig. 282 shows how to find the angle of a saw-tooth; B is the rule, C is the saw-tooth at an angle of about 65º, and

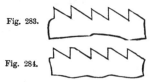

Fig. 283.

Fig. 284.

Figs. 283 and 284.—Unevenly Worn Teeth.

D is the line on the saw-plate, or on the top of the saw-table, as the case may be.

BEGINNING HAND SAW SHARPENING.

Before attempting to set and sharpen saws for actual work, the beginner should practise on an old saw or on a piece of saw blade which he cannot possibly spoil. If such a vice as shown by Figs. 267 and 268, p. 71, is used, fix the bottom of it A in the bench-vice, and then place the saw between its jaws with the teeth standing about ½ in. above. If the saw is placed further out of the block, the action of filing will cause it to vibrate, and very soon the teeth will be stripped off the file. The teeth of an old saw will probably appear as in Figs. 283 and 284, that is to say, the teeth will be

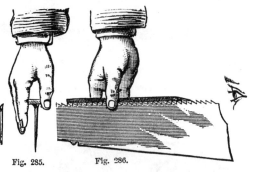

Fig. 285.　　　　　Fig. 286.

Figs. 285 and 286.—Topping Saw Teeth.

uneven and some may be longer than others. With the saw in this condition only some of the teeth can be at work, therefore they all must be brought to one common level.

To accomplish this the flat file (Fig. 280, p. 73) is passed down the saw's edge, or top of teeth, two or three times in succession, in the manner shown at Figs. 285 and 286,

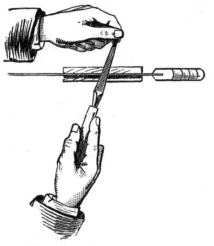

Fig. 287.—Filing Saw Teeth.

the former being an end view, and the latter a front view. It may now be seen by looking down the edge, as shown in Fig. 286, whether all are level. If the tooth points are not in line, those which are below the rest will not work. Hence, in sharpening, as in setting, perfect uniformity is essential to the best results. This process of filing down the teeth is called topping.

Sharpening Hand Saws.

The teeth at both point and butt of a hand saw should be very slightly smaller

Fig. 288.—Filing Saw Teeth.

than those in the middle, as it is at the last-named point where the greatest force is exerted in every down stroke. But it is absolutely necessary that the set is the

same from point to butt of every saw, whether rip or cross-cut. The middle of the cutting edge of a cross-cut saw should be slightly rounded, being highest at about

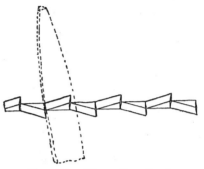

Fig. 289.—Filing Saw Teeth.

the middle. The saw being still in the saw vice, insert the file in a handle, and grasp it with the right hand, taking the point of file in the left, as shown in Fig. 287. Place the file against the face of that tooth nearest the handle that inclines away from the worker, holding the file at an angle with the blade of saw as shown in Fig. 287. Then lower the right hand to about the angle shown in Fig. 288 (which shows the left hand removed). The file should be held obliquely across the saw blade, as in Figs. 289 and 290, the point end of the file being inclined towards the saw handle as

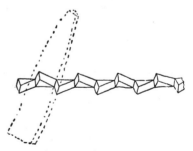

Fig. 290.—Filing Saw Teeth.

illustrated by Fig. 287. Gently push the file forwards, lifting it at the end of stroke, returning it, and again pushing it, until the point of the tooth has a keen edge. Repeat this upon each alternate tooth until all upon one side are sharpened. Afterwards turn the saw in its vice and sharpen the teeth upon the other side in the same manner. Be careful not to press the file

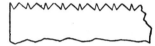

Fig. 291.—Badly Sharpened Tenon Saw Teeth.

against the back of the tooth, or unevenness will surely result. It may occasionally happen that when touched with the file, the saw may be found to be too hard. To soften it, remove the handle, and "blaze" by smearing the blade with a mixture of wax, suet, and oil, and heating over a fire till the mixture ignites. But this is not a method for the beginner, who would certainly spoil the saw. Keep all saws slightly rounding on the edge. The rip saw and hand saw can have a quarter of an inch rounding with advantage. To do this the points of the teeth must be frequently filed down, and the heel and the point filed away. There are always several teeth at the heel and at the point that do little work; those in the middle portion do most, and consequently wear away fastest. All saws, except circulars, have a constant tendency to get hollow, and this must be prevented; and the only way to prevent it is to file the teeth down by passing a partly-worn file along the edges, till it touches every tooth. Then, in filing the teeth, take care only just to take out this bright mark—not one touch more, or that tooth gets low and does not work; if some teeth are filed away even a little too much, the saw might just as well be that number of teeth fewer, as they do no work. A saw in thoroughly good order is so sharpened that each tooth does a share, and no one tooth more than the others.

Sharpening Tenon Saws.

Sharpening tenon saws is practically the same as sharpening hand saws. It may happen, however, that some of the teeth

will be much larger than others, this being due to the file not having been held at the same angle in sharpening each tooth. Fig. 291 shows the saw teeth improperly sharpened, the front of the large teeth inclining much more than the front of the small teeth. If the teeth on one range are found to be filed smaller than those on the other, file the back of the smaller teeth to a more acute angle, keeping the file at the same time well against the front of the other tooth at the bottom; and see, before the filing is finished, that the front of the next tooth has been filed up to its point, as it is the front, not the back, of the tooth that does the cutting. To regulate the teeth of the saw, file every tooth in succession, shooting the file straight across the teeth. After filing all the teeth from one side, turn the saw and file as before from the other side. When the teeth are fairly regular and to the form of Fig. 292, top them by laying a second-cut topping file on their points and pass the file along over the teeth from heel to point of the saw. This will bring the teeth uniform in length. Now file every alternate tooth, first on one side and then on the other side of the saw, as shown in Fig. 293. Hold the file as nearly as possible to the same angle in each case, as it is on this filing that the regularity of the teeth depends. When all the flat places caused by the file when topping the teeth disappear, cease filing, as any further filing may cause low teeth, which tend to make the saw run out of truth, and to destroy sweet cutting.

Flat-jointing Saws.

After a saw has been sharpened, it should be carefully laid flat on its side and

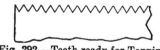

Fig. 292.—Teeth ready for Topping.

the teeth rubbed down with a whetstone or smooth file to remove any feather edge that may be left by the file in sharpening.

This gives a larger and better cutting edge to the saw. If the points only of the teeth are allowed to do the work, the action is a scratching and not a cutting one.

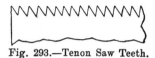

Fig. 293.—Tenon Saw Teeth.

Obtaining Uniform Tooth Bevels and Angles.

One of the great difficulties in hand sharpening is to get the bevels of the teeth exactly alike. A number of mechanical arrangements to guide the saw and effect this object have been tried with more or less success. In one of the best of these devices a circular casting is divided and indexed from its centre each way, giving bevels for each side of the saw, or square across. The file is fitted into a guide, and is held by a set-screw. The index shows the pitch at which the file is set, and a rod passes through holes in a graduating ring and guides the file. The frame upon which the ring is held slides in grooves cut on each side of the vice in which the saw in fixed; a table connected with the guide is arranged and indexed so as to give the required bevel and pitch for the kind of saw to be filed, and it is only necessary to set the ring for the bevel, and the indicator for the pitch, and the apparatus is ready for use. As the filing is proceeded with from tooth to tooth, the frame follows, giving to each tooth on one side of the saw the same bevel, pitch, and size as on the other, thus leaving the saw, when filing is finished, with the teeth all uniform in size, pitch, and bevel, so that each tooth will do its share of cutting equally with the others, thus turning out more and better quality of work with less expenditure of energy. An old-fashioned way of getting the right angle of a tooth of a hand saw in filing is shown by Fig. 294. A hand saw blade is narrowest in width at the point, and broadest at the butt; and the slope of the back, compared with the line of teeth, is almost always uniform for all saws;

and if a square be placed against this back, a tooth may be filed whose cutting edge is perfectly in line with the edge of the square. All the teeth being thus filed and afterwards set, a saw which will answer general purposes is produced, and one which will suit the worker who has but one hand saw. It will cross-cut soft woods and rip hard woods, thus being a kind of half-rip. Moreover, this square may be used as a gauge, the teeth not necessarily being filed as shown; and if the rake or lead be very much, an adjustable bevel may be used.

Time Wasted by Badly Sharpened Saws.

It should be borne in mind that the workman who can saw squarely to a line is at least two hours a week ahead of one who, either because his saws are in bad order or because he has never got out of the bad habit of sawing out of square, cannot do it. It may be partly, or altogether, the fault of the saw. If one row of teeth is longer than the other, the longer side must of necessity advance faster than the shorter, and constantly tend to force the saw away from the line. The user, in his endeavour, by main force, to compel the saw to follow the line—that is, by twisting that part of the saw which is for the time being above the wood—cannot yet force the bottom half of the saw, which has to follow the direction given to it by the set of the teeth, and consequently

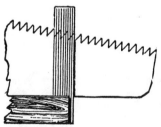

Fig. 294.—Obtaining Correct Bevel of Saw Teeth.

the saw is said to "run." This continues, and the amount it runs from a square cut is doubled, so that, if the stuff has to be planed square and the saw runs only $\frac{1}{8}$ in. in 2 in., this implies that $\frac{1}{4}$ in. has to be planed away before the edges can be got to fit the square. This wastes both time and material.

"Set" of Saw Teeth.

The theoretical aspect of this matter

Fig. 295.—Saw-set with Blunt End.

has been dealt with already. After the saw is filed, and all the teeth made as uniform as possible in shape, length, and gullet, comes the important operation of setting the teeth so as to afford a ready clearance for the saw-blade. The "set" consists of the setting over, or bending, of each alternate tooth to one side. The set should be as little as circumstances will allow, on account of the amount of labour it entails in working the saw. For dry, hard, thin wood cut length-ways, a very little will suffice; but for soft, wet, thick, or resinous material, a larger amount of set is necessary to free the saw. This is easily understood when it is remembered that the set causes the kerf, or groove made by the teeth, to be slightly greater than the thickness of the plate, so that the broad surfaces of the latter shall move through the wood with the least possible amount of friction. The blades of the best saws are thinned slightly towards the back, but this does not obviate the necessity for setting. Some idea of the set of a hand saw can be obtained from Figs. 289 and 290, p. 75, which however, somewhat exaggerate the amount of set. No

Fig. 296.—Saw-set with Pointed End.

more set should be given to a saw than is absolutely required, as the more the set the greater the power required to work, and the greater the loss of wood. A saw should have only just enough set to clear itself; if it has too much it is not properly guided by

the kerf; it wastes too much wood, and does not cut smooth or easy. If the setting is not uniform, power will be wasted. The longest teeth, having the greatest set, are rapidly worn down, and the work turned out is scored and rough, and at the same time

Fig. 297.—Saw-set with Gauge.

the saw will run from the straight line to the side on which there is most set. If a saw is properly and uniformly set, the teeth should form an angular groove, easily seen when held up to the light and looked at from point to heel.

Spring-setting Saw Teeth.

Two kinds of setting are used for hand saws—namely, spring-setting and hammer-setting. In the former the teeth are bent from the line by a saw-set; in the latter they are set over by a blow from a hammer. First, spring-setting will be described. For this purpose is used a saw-set (Fig. 295), which is made of steel, and has a series of graduated notches cut into each edge. Figs. 295 and 296 show the ordinary kind of saw-set, whilst the one illustrated by Fig. 297 has a gauge attached to it. To use a saw-set, the back of saw is held in the left hand (as A, Fig. 298), or it is gripped in a

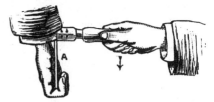

Fig. 298.—Setting Saw held in Hand.

vice (see Fig. 299), and the handle of the saw-set is taken in the right hand. Then select a notch that easily fits over the tooth, and proceed very carefully to bend alternate teeth towards the body by pressing the handle downwards. Care must be taken to make the pressure equal upon each tooth, or they will be set out of line. The top of the tooth only must be bent, as a (Fig. 300). Should the whole of the tooth be bent, b, it is very likely to break out. Having set the teeth upon each side, glance down the edge to see if the set is true and regular.

all the teeth can readily be set to one line, and when the contrivance is fixed it is impossible to overset a tooth; and should the saw be found to bind at any particular point,

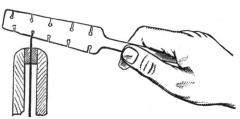

Fig. 299.—Setting Saw held in Vice.

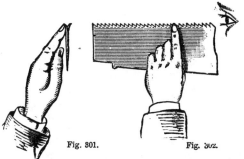

Figs. 301 and 302.—Testing Set of Saw Teeth.

The forefinger may be run down the blade at the same time to mark any irregularity, which may be at once corrected by bending the faulty tooth in the desired direction. Figs. 301 and 302 fully illustrate this, Fig. 301 being an end view. Care should be taken to pull the tooth over only a very little; it is far easier to give it a little more than to take some off, and with the slighter amount of bending there is less likelihood of breaking off the teeth. A rip saw requires but very little set; a hand saw about a fourth of its own thickness on each side. After setting a saw, lay it flat on a board, then take a file without its handle and slide it down the sides of the teeth, taking care that it leans towards the back of the saw. This will regulate the set, and if a tooth or two is bent over a little

the teeth can, with this contrivance, be set into line, and any excessive friction reduced. Fig. 303 illustrates such a set, adapted for setting hand, circular, mill, or band saws. Its operation will be readily understood: Hold the saw c with the teeth upwards; adjust the die B (Fig. 303), by means of the screw A in the end of the set, so that the angle on the die B will come near the root of the tooth on a fine saw; on a coarse saw, the angle of the die should strike the tooth about two-thirds down from the point. Set the guard E on the under side of the set forward to about $\frac{3}{16}$ in. from the die B; then let the set hang loose on the saw. The space between the tooth and the die will then show the amount of set that is being given to the saw. To in-

Fig. 300.—Set of Saw Teeth.

too much, it will file off the excess. After this, pass the oilstone down the same way as the file.

PATENT SAW-SETS.

Several excellent contrivances are now made for spring-setting, so arranged that

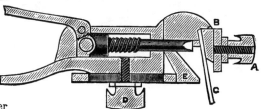

Fig. 303.—Patent Saw-set in Use.

crease the set, move the guard E still closer to the die; to decrease the set, move the guard back. Many other excellent saw-sets may be obtained at a moderate price.

HAMMER-SETTING SAW TEETH.

The teeth of a hand saw may be hammer-set by securing in a vice a small setting iron, about 6 in. or 7 in. long, shown in end view

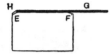

Fig. 304.—Setting Iron.

by Fig. 304. This iron is bevelled at E and F. The saw, of which G is a section, is laid flat on the iron, and tooth H struck with the pene of a small hammer (see Fig. 305), the operator striking every alternate tooth from one side, then every alternate tooth from the other side of the saw plate. Fig. 304 shows bevel E to be somewhat greater than bevel F; the larger teeth are set on bevel E, and the smaller teeth on bevel F. Instead of the block shown by Fig. 304, that illustrated in section by Fig. 306, p. 81, can be employed, but the beginner will prefer the former, as it determines the amount of set. Another device is a steel plate about 6 in. long, with one edge turned over, as at

lightly striking it with the hammer, which bends the tooth to the bevel of plate, as at d (Fig. 308). Another shape of hammer is illustrated by Fig. 309, p. 82, in which pene J is used for setting the coarser teeth and pene K for the finer teeth. Fig. 310 shows a hammer for setting two-handled cross-cut saws, the teeth of which are set in a similar manner to that just described. Fig. 311 shows an end view of the anvil or setting iron, which is larger than that used for a hand saw, and the bevel is longer. L is a section of the saw, and the tooth M comes over the bevel N; every alternate tooth is struck with the poll O of the hammer shown in Fig. 310. Great care is necessary in hammering; never strike the blade of the saw, or it will buckle; this buckling sometimes happens with spring-setting, but in most cases the saw will go back again when setting the opposite side. Saws that are set by the blow of a hammer or punch are apt to be more irregular than spring-set saws; the operation should therefore be very carefully done, and the teeth constantly tried with a gauge or straight-edge, to see that all the teeth are exactly in line. Hammer-set teeth stand well up to their

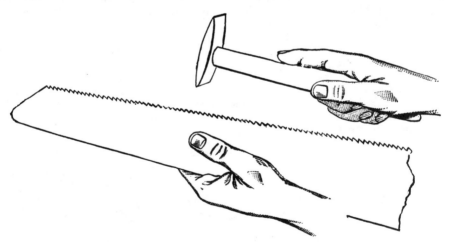

Fig. 305.—Hammer-setting Saw Teeth.

a (Fig. 307); the other edge b is placed in the vice, and the saw c is then laid upon it as shown, being held in position with the left hand. The tooth is then bent over by

work in cross-grained and knotty wood, whilst spring-set teeth are more inclined to dodge the knots. Some saws have part of the teeth spring-set and part hammer-set, but the difficulty of keeping them exactly uniform neutralises any advantages the plan may possess. Saw teeth are very apt to fracture if given unnecessary set; that is, by trying to get the set from the whole length of the tooth. In connection with this, Disston says that a saw that is easily filed and set is easily made dull, but he dares not make saws as hard as he would like to, until a better method of setting is adopted by the average mechanic, who instead of getting the whole of the set out of the tooth, tries to get part of it from the body of the plate; and, of course, as soon as he gets below the root of the tooth, the saw plate is distorted and strained. This causes a full-tempered saw blade to crack, and ultimately the saw will break at this point.

GRIMSHAW ON SELECTING HAND SAWS.

Hand saws are made of various lengths and thicknesses, and with different degrees of fineness of teeth, to suit the several kinds of work to be done by them. It is important to bear this fact in mind when purchasing, and not to expect that a saw selected indiscriminately can be used for anything and everything. Grimshaw says that a good hand saw should be springy and elastic. It should spring regularly in proportion to its width and gauge; that is, the point should spring more than the heel, and hence the curve should not be a perfect arc of a circle. If the blade is too thick for the size of the teeth, the saw will work stiffly. If the blade is not evenly and smoothly

Fig. 306.—Setting-block in Vice Jaws.

ground, it will work hard and tend to spring. The thinner the gauge and the narrower the blade, the more need for perfectly uniform and smooth grinding. The cutting edge

6

should have a convex curve, to adapt it to the natural rocking motion of the hand and arm. A soft saw is not economical; it costs more in a year for files and filing than a

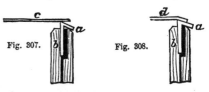

Figs. 307 and 308.—Hammer-setting Teeth on Plate.

hard one, dulls sooner, works harder, and does not last so long. A saw that will take a few more minutes and a little harder work to sharpen will keep its edge and its set longer than one which can be put in order quickly, and it will work better in knots and hard wood.

HODGSON ON SELECTING HAND SAWS.

Hodgson made a number of experiments on saws to test their qualities, and arrived at the following conclusions: (1) A saw with a thick blade is, in nine cases out of ten, of inferior quality, and is more apt to break than a thin-bladed saw; it requires more set, will not stand an edge nearly so long as a thin one, is more difficult to file, and, cutting a wide kerf, is more tiring to use. (2) Saws hung in plain beech handles, with the rivets flush, are lighter, easier to handle, less liable to receive injury, occupy less space in the tool-chest, and can be placed with other saws without dulling the teeth of the latter by abrasion on the rivets. (3) Blades that are dark in colour, and have a clear, bell-like ring when struck with the ball of the finger, appear to be of better stuff than those of a light iron-grey colour; and he noticed, in proof of this, that the thinner the blade the darker was the colour, and that saws of this description were less liable to buckle or twist. (4) American-made saws, as a rule, are better hung than English ones. (5) Polished blades cut more freely and much more easily than blades left in the rough, and are less liable to rust. (6) Saws that when held by the handle and struck on the point with the hand ring clear and without tremor, will be found to be securely handled ; saws that when struck on the point of the blade tremble and jar in the handle never give satisfaction.

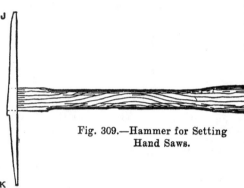

Fig. 309.—Hammer for Setting Hand Saws.

DISSTON ON SELECTING HAND SAWS.

The following are some of Disston's notes on purchasing saws : In selecting a hand saw, see that it hangs right ; grasp it by the handle and hold it in position for working, and then try if the handle fits the hand properly. These are points of great importance. Many saw handles are made of green wood ; they soon shrink and become loose, the screws standing above the wood. An unseasoned handle is liable to warp and make the saw untrue. Next try the blade by springing it ; then see that it bends evenly from point to butt in proportion as the width of the saw varies. If the blade be too heavy in comparison with the teeth, the saw will never give satisfaction, because it will require much more power to use it. A narrow true saw is better than a wide true saw— there is less danger of dragging or creating friction. The thinner the saw blade is, the

OTHER POINTS IN SAW SELECTION.

Another very important point to be noticed when purchasing a hand saw is to see that after its blade has been fully bent it springs back perfectly straight. A soft saw will not, as a rule, spring back like this, nor will a saw of uneven temper. A serious defect in some saws should here be mentioned. Very often one or more silvery-grey spots may be seen in the saw plate, generally at the tooth edge. Such a spot indicates a hard or, as it is often termed, a rash place. In setting

Fig. 311.—Large Setting Iron.

the teeth they will often break at these places, and sometimes a piece of the plate breaks out. Should a piece break out halfway between the heel and point, the saw becomes useless until the teeth are recut ; and to recut with a file requires some

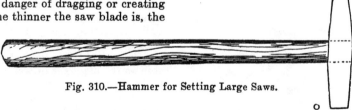

Fig. 310.—Hammer for Setting Large Saws.

better. Always try a saw before buying it. See that it is well set and sharpened, and has its toothed edge rounding ; hold it so that the light strikes it fairly, and any imperfections in grinding or hammering are at once detected.

practice. It will be wise, therefore, when choosing a hand saw to select one free from such blemishes. In selecting a saw, for whatever purpose, do not be tempted by a low first cost, as this is no criterion as to its ultimate cheapness. What is required is a blade made of the very best quality of steel, combining, as far as may be, flexibility and toughness with a sufficient degree of hardness to allow of the steel carrying a good cutting edge. A saw bearing the name of a maker of repute should, and usually does, give satisfaction. The handle should be comfortable to the grasp and made out of thoroughly seasoned wood. Beech handles, with countersunk rivets, are preferred by many. A thin and narrow saw is preferable to a thick and wide one, but care must be taken, however, not to select too thin a blade, and that the saw is stiff in work, as, should it buckle, it may give a great deal of trouble. If the saw has been hammer-set—in contradistinction to spring-set—without fracture to the teeth, it is a very fair test as to the quality of the steel. The blade should ring clearly when struck with the finger, and when sprung over by hand it should not jar in the handle. Finally, if possible, try the saw on a piece of difficult cutting wood, and see how it behaves : if it cuts fast and clean with a moderate expenditure of power, it is what is required. Increment teeth have of late come more into use—that is, the point of the saw is arranged with finer teeth than the heel—and are liked by many workers, as the fine teeth begin the cut smoothly, and the coarse teeth prevent the saw clogging.

DIMENSIONS OF SAWS.

The table below gives length in inches, breadth in inches at heel and at point, thickness according to the Birmingham wire gauge, and teeth to the inch, of a typical rip saw, fine rip saw, hand saw, cut-off saw, panel saw, and fine panel saw.

Names.	Length in Inches.	Breadth at Heel.	Breadth at Point.	Gauge or Thickness.	Teeth to Inch.
Rip saw	28-30	8	3	19 T	3½
Fine rip saw :...	26-28	7½	2½	20 T	4
Hand saw ...	24-26	6-7	2½	20	5½-5
Cut-off saw ...	24-26	6-7	2½	20	6
Panel saw ...	20-24	5-6	2-2½	20 E	7
Fine panel saw	20-24	5-6	2-2½	20 E	8

In the table, T denotes tight to the gauge, and E easy to the gauge. These gauges are the thickness that the saws should be on the tooth edge, as all saws should be thinner on the back edge.

HOW TO USE A SAW.

The correct method of sawing will now be described, and some common faults in sawing pointed out, with notes on how to avoid them. The beginner has to find out or be shown the best methods, and to practise them ; then proficiency and confidence will be gradually gained, and good workmanship will follow. Bad habits, once acquired, are, of course, to be overcome only

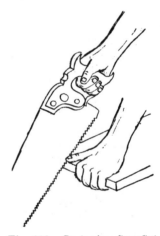

Fig. 312.—Beginning Saw Cut.

by perseverance ; but the pains taken will enable the workman to economise his energy, to get better results in both quantity and quality, and to reduce considerably the wear and tear of his tools. A common fault with beginners is that they do not take sufficient care at the commencement of the cut or kerf. The first part of a cut is most important, because if that is not made square through the wood it is afterwards a very difficult matter to get the cut square without twisting the saw, and perhaps spoiling it. Begin sawing by placing the left thumb (see Fig. 312) or forefinger to the line, so as to guide the saw at the commencement of the kerf, then take a few gentle and careful strokes, making sure that the saw enters.

the wood at right angles. Move the left hand to a more secure position, as indicated in the later figures (Figs. 314 to 316). Then, using nearly the whole length of the saw, take care not to draw it right out of the kerf, or it may be damaged by striking against the work at the return stroke ; see that each stroke is regular ; and allow a slight pause between each stroke to enable the worker to regain energy for each downward (working) stroke. Short, jerky, and quick strokes must be avoided, for they rapidly produce fatigue, and result in bad work. Do not force the saw : that is, do not press too hard at each downward stroke, as this fault not only leads to fatigue, but also strains the saw. Occasionally test the saw in the cut with a square to see whether it is perpendicular to the surface of the wood (see Fig. 313). The general position to be assumed in sawing is shown in Figs. 314 to 316. As far as practicable, the saw blade, marked line. and saw-cut, the eyes, shoulder, elbow,

Fig. 313.—Testing Saw with Square.

and hand, should be in one plane, much as shown in Fig. 316, which also shows the

head to be over the saw, so that the operator is able to see that the saw-blade is out of

Fig. 314.—Correct Position when Sawing.

winding with, and in the same plane as, the line ; this is a very important point. A faulty position for hand sawing is to have the head not over the saw, but some distance to the left of it; consequently the saw leans to the left, and cuts out of the perpendicular. This fault is usually combined with another, namely, getting too far behind the tool, which attitude does not allow the operator to compare the saw with the line, because he is not able to keep his head over it, and he is also prevented from having such full command over the saw as he would have by adopting the attitude illustrated at Fig. 315, where the position is one of much greater freedom, giving at the same time much more power over the saw, with less exertion. By holding the saw in a more vertical position (as illustrated at Fig. 315), there are fewer teeth in contact with the wood at one time, and hence there is less resistance than when the saw is made to slant more nearly to the horizontal. The defect noted is that known as "laying" the saw. With thick

Fig. 315.—Ripping Plank, Front View.

stuff it is a good plan to square the lines down each end and line out each side, and then, during the process of sawing, to turn the wood over occasionally, and thus saw from both sides. When, however, it is desired to saw the wood entirely from one side, the blade should be tested now and again with a square, to see whether the saw is at right angles to the surface of the wood (see Fig. 313). After sawing down a foot or two, it will be found desirable to open the cut a little by inserting a screwdriver or wedge, so as to reduce the friction between the sides of the kerf and the sawblade. Do not open the saw-kerf wide, as this tends to split the wood, and to cause the saw to wobble, thus increasing the difficulty of following the line. It is desirable to lubricate the blade with a little oil.

Sawing Wet Wood.

In attempting to cut down a piece of wet plank with a hand saw, great labour and difficulty will be met, and the difficulty will

be much increased if the cut is made across the grain—that is, transversely to the direction of the fibres. If the stuff is very thick, the saw blade will stick fast in its kerf. There are two reasons why the saw sticks in soft wet wood. One is that the kerf is not wide enough, and the other that the sawdust cannot get away quickly enough. Hence the remedy is to increase the set and to enlarge the spacing of the saw teeth, which means an increase of the space between the centres of the teeth, with a consequent increase in the sizes of the teeth themselves. In attempting to use the same saw on thin and hard wood, trouble of another kind will be met. The teeth will catch in the wood, the saw will sway too loosely and freely in the kerf, and, if cut across the grain, the timber will become broken or spalted out.

Straightening Buckled Hand Saw.

A piece of iron with a flat, smooth surface, such as an anvil, or even a flat iron, will

Fig. 316.—Ripping Plank, End View.

be required for straightening a bent or buckled hand saw. If a flat iron is used, it could be held firmly in a vice or a bench screw. Place the saw, with the convex side upwards, on the surface of the iron or anvil,

Fig. 317.—Hand Saw Buckled Lengthways.

and then hammer, but do not deal heavy blows. After every two or three strokes with the hammer the saw blade should be examined to see the effects. The surface of the hammer should be very slightly spherical, so as to prevent the possibility of leaving hammer marks on the blade. Much care

Fig. 318.—Buckled Hand Saw.

and practice are required for hammering a saw properly. The plate of a hand saw being thin, requires a much lighter blow than steel of stout gauge. If the blows given are too heavy, they will indent and stretch the plate, and in consequence a bad state will be made worse. Fig. 317 represents a saw undulating, or wavy, lengthways of the plate at L, and bent or seamy across the

Fig. 319.—Buckled Hand Saw.

plate at C. It will be seen that at L the blows are delivered across the plate, and at C lengthways of plate, using for the purpose a cross-pened hammer. Figs. 318 and 319 represent a saw that has a bend at the edge; in this case the cross-pened hammer should be used on the convex side, as at B (Fig. 318), and on the concave side, as at B (Fig. 318), and on the concave side, as at B (Fig. 319), after which it should be struck very lightly with a dog-head hammer, as indicated by round marks on both sides. In-

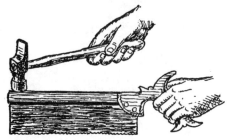

Fig. 320.—Straightening Buckled Tenon Saw.

stead of the cross-pened hammer, the carpenter's ordinary hammer will answer if the pene is ground a little convex.

STRAIGHTENING BUCKLED TENON SAW.

If a tenon saw or dovetail saw is buckled only slightly, a light tap or two on the end of the back with a hammer, as shown in Fig. 320, should bring the blade true. If this fails, take the back right off, and hammer it so that the edges of the slit fit

Fig. 321.—Replacing Tenon Saw in Back.

tightly together. Keep the slit perfectly straight. Next hammer the buckled part of the blade on a flat and smooth iron surface. Then enter the blade into the slit of the back, as shown by Fig. 321, and gradually drive down by striking the teeth with a flat wooden striker; driving it not more than about ¼ in. into the back.

TOOLS OF PERCUSSION AND IMPULSION.

HAMMERS AND IMPACT.

THE most important tool among those implied by the chapter heading is the hand hammer, and at the same time it is the most simple. The hammer may be regarded as a weight at one end of a rod. Speaking generally, the effect is produced by allowing the weight head to fall through a space, and then come in contact with the material to be influenced by the blow. Perhaps the objects to be accomplished by the blows of hammers are more varied than those to be effected by any other single tool. It is doubtful whether any handicraftsman carries through any branch of his trade without using some kind of hammer. This may be anything, from the heavy two-handed maul to the smallest tapping hammers of the jeweller and watch-maker, file-maker, and diamond-splitter. It may be well to discuss the manner in which the power of a hammer actually is developed. The development of power, according to Rigg's Cantor Lectures, takes place at the instant of contact of the moving hammer with the struck body. Such contacts as those of hammers belong to the department of mechanical philosophy called " impact." Impact is pressure of short duration—so short that, compared with the time in which the velocity on the impinging body is being acquired, it is inappreciable; similarly the space passed through by the hammer-head after impact is almost inappreciable when compared with the space passed through before impact. It may assist the worker to realise the source as well as the magnitude of the power of a hammer, if the following simple experiment be tried. Attempt to drive a nail vertically into a horizontal piece of timber by the statical effect of the simple pressure of a load on the head of the nail, the load being placed on the head gently, and measure the depth to which the nail is thus moved. Again, let the same nail, under the same circumstances, be driven to the same depth by the impact of the hammer-head, then it may for the present purpose be said that the load placed on the nail is a representative statical measure of the impact of the hammer. This is a representative and an approximately accurate method for comparing the effects of hammers under all ordinary circumstances, though the method is not faultless.

HISTORY OF THE HAMMER.

The hammer is the most ancient of tools, and in all parts of the world and amongst all people hammers are in use. Even the name hammer seems to have a prehistoric origin, for it is common to all the northern languages. There is no tool more simple and more useful than the primitive or handicraft hammer. Indeed, so simple has it been esteemed that it does not possess any literature. The only mechanical tools for external use with which man is provided by nature are the hammer, a compound vice, and a scratching or scraping tool. These are in the hand; and none of the various compound tools introduced from time to time has surpassed in comprehensiveness of variety these three in one. However, as a hammer only can it now be discussed. Whilst for impact upon a substance softer than itself the fist can deal an appreciable blow, yet upon one harder than itself the reaction of the substance transfers the blow to the flesh and bone, and as a hammer the fist then is useless. Hence, amongst prehistoric contrivances, perhaps the first to be invented was the stone hammer-head, shaped, it may be supposed, by the action of water, and so rounded as to fit the hand. These stones are called by antiquarians " mauls," and they were probably held in the hollow of the hand, and used on objects which otherwise could not have been broken. Mauls represent the original hammer. It may be assumed that occa-

When held in the hollow of the hand, the resistance was met by (say) a depth of tissue of about three-quarters of an inch, but when it was grasped round its middle the

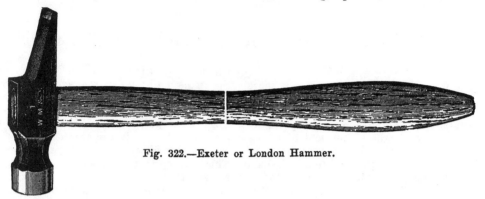

Fig. 322.—Exeter or London Hammer.

sionally the mauls proved too heavy, but more frequently too light; and obviously on very heavy work the holding of the stone in the hollow of the hand, and striking blows with it, caused a reaction which was mainly met by the muscular action of the back of the hand and of the thinnest section of the wrist; this would be not only fatiguing, but injurious, and it may have been that such effects led

resistance was met by a depth of tissue of about three inches. Hence, whilst mechanically (owing to the mass of stone) and muscularly (owing to the position of the hand in reference to the direction of the blow) the maul in this second stage was a decided improvement upon the first, yet it must be admitted that experience would soon suggest that even thus there was wanting sufficient energy to overcome resist-

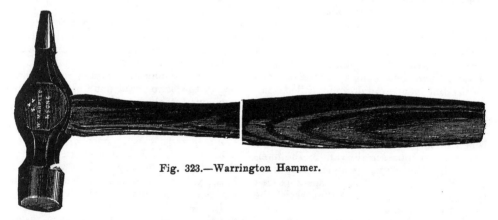

Fig. 323.—Warrington Hammer.

to the invention of double-ended mauls, which were held by the middle. A blow given by one of these is counteracted not only by the increased mass of material, but by the changed position of the hand and wrist in relation to the direction of the blow.

ances, and that the double-headed maul might be improved. This, at any rate, will be admitted by anyone who has been obliged to use a stone in the hand as a hammer. Even the prehistoric races knew that whilst the hand possessed inimitable contrivances for grasping, and the arm for rapid motions, both jointly failed in giving the maul the power that often would be required. Ingenuity so far busied itself as to lash withes round such mauls as were found suitable—much after the manner in which present day blacksmiths lash withes round the heads of cutting and punching tools and swages. There are traces of even a higher advance, for what seem stone mauls, or hammers, are found with holes through them, suitable for handles, and holes are, in some instances, coned, and as well adapted for hammer handles as the best-made metal tools of these days. One such stone hammer-head was found in the river Thames, and is now in the British Museum. In this, the double-coned hole for the attachment and wedging-up of a

claw pattern (Fig. 324). The first two are the most usual ones in the workshop, but the last is very convenient for many kinds of handiwork. The substance of the hammer-heads is iron, but the faces and penes are of steel. It is desirable to obtain two hammers, one weighing from 1 lb. to $1\frac{1}{2}$ lb., and the other from $\frac{1}{2}$ lb. to $\frac{3}{4}$ lb. A heavy hammer applied lightly and skilfully leaves fewer marks and does less damage than a light hammer necessarily applied with great force.

FASTENING HAMMER-HEADS TO SHAFTS.

The most simple, and the most generally trustworthy, method of fastening a hammer-head on a shaft is by means of a hard wood or metal wedge driven into a slit in the handle after the head has been put on (see

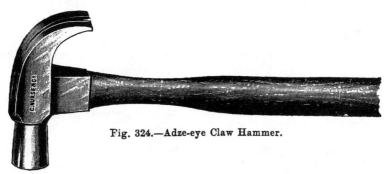

Fig. 324.—Adze-eye Claw Hammer.

handle is formed admirably, and the shape of the hammer is worthy of much commendation. How the ancients fixed a handle in a double-coned hole in a stone maul is more than is known now, but antiquarians surmise that having found the branch of a tree about the size of the smallest part of the eye of the maul, the stone was hung on it, and after a few years the growth of the tree fixed the handle in the maul, and then the branch was separated by a sharp stone implement, thus producing a hammer in which the shaft formed a perfect fit with the head.

SELECTING HAMMERS.

The woodworker has the choice between two or three shapes of hammer-head. There is the Exeter or London pattern (Fig. 322), the Warrington (Fig. 323), and the adze-eye

the sectional view, Fig. 325). If a hammer-head gets loose after wedging, it can be permanently tightened by driving in a few short, stout nails beside the wedge. The reason is that a nail will force its way into the handle, which may be sufficiently dense to resist the hardest wedge. Soaking in water is another common method of tightening the head. There are many ways of wedging the heads of hammers in place, all more or less satisfactory, but for wooden wedges one of the best methods is to bore with a bradawl two sloping holes (Fig. 326), as at A and B (Fig. 327), through the outer end of the handle and the wedge, after the latter has been driven tightly into the handle. Then drive into each a strong wire nail, and file it off close. Even if the wooden handle or the wedge itself shrinks somewhat, it is almost impossible for the latter to work loose and fall out, and so allow the hammer-head or other similar tool to fly off while being used. Another method is to make with a sharp chisel two or more cuts on each side of a

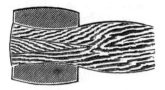

Fig. 325.—Wedged-on Hammer Head.

red hot iron wedge (see Fig. 328), so as to raise the surface into something like teeth on a very coarse single-cut file; then drive in the wedge as tightly as possible. Another method is as follows:—Having fitted the hammer-head upon the handle

Fig. 326.　　　　Fig. 327.

Figs. 326 and 327.—Fastening on Hammer Head with Nailed Wedge.

to the line A B (Fig. 329), take the head off again. Bore a hole at C C through the shaft about ⅜ in. above the line A B, and groove each side of the shaft from the hole to the top. Put a piece of steel wire through the hole, and turn it up

Fig. 328.—Iron Wedge.

in the grooves, letting it project as at D D (Fig. 329). Put on the hammer-head down to the line A B. Drive in a wedge w (Fig. 330), fold the wire to lap over the wedge from

each side; this prevents the wedge from coming out. The head may work itself loose a little in time; if so, steep it in water a few minutes, and it will be firm again.

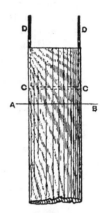

Fig. 329.—Fastening on Hammer Head with Wired Wedge.

It is doubtful if this method holds as well as the nailed wedge.

MALLETS.

Mallets are used by the woodworker for driving wood chisels, for knocking light framing together, and for other purposes where the use of a steel-faced hammer would leave unsightly marks and probably damage both tools and material. Suitable mallets are illustrated by Figs. 331 and 332. The first of these shows the ordinary mortised beech "square" mallet; a convenient size for this head is from 4 in. to 6 in. long, and about half as thick. The square handle is slightly rounded to suit the hand. Perhaps a more convenient tool is the American

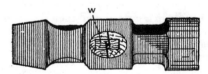

Fig. 330.—Hammer Head with Wired Wedge.

pattern shown by Fig. 332, in which all the sharp edges are chamfered off, and the handle is round and easier to grasp. In some kinds of American mallets the handle screws into the head. English mallets are of beech, and American ones of hickory or lignum vitæ. The round mallet that is bound or cored with iron is not recommended for joiners' use. If the sides of a

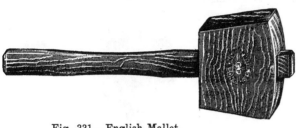

Fig. 331.—English Mallet.

wooden mallet are slightly convex, there will be less risk of damaging the work when knocking it together. The mallet itself is, in both form and material, a very old tool. Those figured on the tombs of Egypt might have been drawn from present day stonemasons' mallets, they are so like them. The Egyptian mallets—or hammers, as they would be called now—are indented in a deep circular ring, as though used all round against the very jagged head of a metal chisel.

AXES AND HATCHETS.

These are both percussion and cutting tools, as they combine the offices of the

Fig. 332.—American Mallet.

hammer and chisel. The distinction between axes and hatchets is that axes are used with the two hands, and have long handles, and may be swung as sledge hammers. Hatchets are used with one hand;

they have short handles, are much lighter and thinner than axes, and are employed more in the trimming than in the felling of timber. Both narrow and broad axes are employed in forestry, the woodman's choice

Fig. 333.—Kent Axe Head.

being affected by the size of the timber and the character of the fibre. A hatchet is handled with the centre of gravity nearer the cutting edge than an axe. A few types of axe heads are here illustrated. Fig. 333 shows the Kent or English pattern, Fig. 334 the Scotch pattern, and Fig. 335 the Suffolk pattern ; Fig. 336 shows the Kent or English pattern of felling axe. The handle used with these generally is of the shape shown

Fig. 334.—Scotch Axe Head.

by Fig. 337. The well-known American wedge-shape axe-head is illustrated by Fig. 338. Of hatchets, Fig. 339 illustrates the Kent or English pattern, and Fig. 340 the Canada or American pattern.

The Cutting Edge of an Axe.

The cutting edge is nearly always convex, as shown in all the types illustrated. The junction of the light and dark shading in many of the illustrations denotes the extent

Fig. 335.—Suffolk Axe Head.

of the bevel. The object of having a curved cutting edge is not only to prevent the jar and damage which might be done by the too sudden stoppage of the rapid motion of the heavy head in separating a group of fibres, but also to facilitate that separation by attacking these fibres in succession. For, assuming the axe falls square on its work in the direction of the fibres, a convex edge will first separate two fibres, and in doing this it will release a portion of the bond which holds adjoining fibres. An edge thus convex, progressing at each side of the convexity which first strikes the wood, facilitates the entrance of successive portions from the middle outwards. If the edge had been straight and fallen parallel to itself upon the end of the wood, none of this pre-

but not always, has equally inclined sides. Assume that one face only is inclined, and that the plane of the other is continuous to the edge; now in striking a blow, it is obvious that the plane in the line of the fibres cannot cause any separation of these fibres,

Fig. 336.—Kent Felling Axe Head.

but at the other side of the axe the slope entering the wood will separate the fibres on its own side. For some work, the axe with unequally inclined faces may be preferable, for instance in chopping the projecting corners from a square log in preparing it for the lathe; this tool (Fig. 341) would do the work with greater ease to the workman, and with a higher finish than would the common hatchet with equally inclined sides. Coach-

Fig. 337.—Handle of Felling Axe.

liminary preparation would have taken place; on the contrary, in all probability there would have been in some parts a progressive condensation of fibres, and to that extent an increase in the difficulty of the work. The wedge-form of axe generally,

makers have much of this class of hatchet-paring work to do, and the tool they use is bevelled on one side only; under where the handle enters the eye in a coachmaker's axe (see Fig. 341) is a projection rising towards the handle; on this the finger of the workman rests in order to steady the blade in its entrance into the timber in the plane of the straight part of the blade, and to counteract the tendency of the wedge side pressing the hatchet out of its true plane. Carpenters for work across the fibre. The axe is simply a wedge, and therefore arranged to cleave rather than to cut the wood. Now, a calculation of the *pressure* necessary to thrust forward a wedge, and the *impact*

Fig. 338.—American Axe Head.

Fig. 339.—Kent Hatchet.

and joiners may perhaps profit from a brief study of this tool used in a branch of wood-working different from their own. It is very evident, in using an axe, that different conditions of edge are requisite. There is much less resistance to the entrance of the edge when the blow is given in the direction of the fibre than when the blow is across that fibre. So great, indeed, may this difference become, that, whilst in the one direction the edge of the axe continues sound and efficient, yet a few blows on the same timber at right angles to this direction seriously

necessary to cause the same wedge to enter the same depth, would explain why (regarded as a wedge only) the handle proves an important adjunct to the arm of the workman. This may be tested with an ordinary-handled hatchet on a soft straight-grained wood, or with a small axe with a straight and not a curved edge. Let it rest upon a lump of moderately soft clay; add

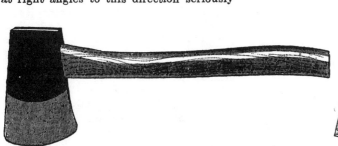

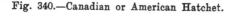
Fig. 340.—Canadian or American Hatchet.   Fig. 341.—Coachmaker's Side Axe Head.

damages the edge. These remarks apply only to axes and hatchets used in dividing materials, and not to those used in merely preparing surfaces. The mode in which the axe is used will explain why it is unsuited

weights until it has sunk to any desired depth, then take the axe by the head, and by pressure force the axe to the same depth. Next hold the axe by the handle, first at, say, 1 ft. from the head, then at 2 ft., then, perhaps, at 3 ft., and give blows which seem of equal intensity, and mark the depth. Thus a practical testimony to the value of a handle will be shown by the respective depths.

How to Use an Axe.

The motions of the hands on the handle of an axe are similar to those of a workman on that of a sledge-hammer. The handle of a

Fig. 342.—English Adze.

properly fitted axe (Fig. 337) is curved, that of a sledge-hammer is straight. For present consideration this curvature may be ignored, although it plays an important part in the using of an axe with success and ease. If the almost unconscious motions of a workman skilled in the use of an axe be observed, it will be noticed that whilst the hand furthest from the axe-head grasps the handle continuously and as it were fixedly at the same or nearly the same part, the other hand, or the one nearest to the head, frequently moves. Assume that the

axe has just been brought down with a blow and entered between the fibres of the wood. In this position it may be regarded as wedged in the wood—held, in fact, by the pressure of the fibres against the sides of the axe. From this fixity it is released usually by action on or near the head. For this purpose the workman slides his hand along the handle, and availing himself (if need be) of the oval form of the handle after it has passed through the eye of the metal, he releases the head. The axe has now to be raised to give another stroke; for this purpose his hand remains near to the head, so causing the length of the path of his hand and that of the axe-head to be nearly the same. The effect of this is to require but a minimum of power to be exerted by the muscles in raising the axe; whereas, if the hand had remained near the end of the handle most distant from the head, the raising of the axe-head would have been done at a mechanical disadvantage. Remembering that the power exerted to raise a body is in the adverse ratio of the spaces passed through by the body, and the point of application of the power, it may thus be obvious how great a strain will be on the muscles if the axe-head be raised by the hands at the opposite extremity of the handle. Reverse the problem. Assume the head of an ordinary axe, the handle being in the plane of the axe-blade, to be raised until the handle is vertical. Now the left hand is at the extremity of the handle, the right hand is very near to the axe-head, and the blow is about to be given. The requirement in this case is that there should be concentrated at the axe-head all the force or power possible; hence it is not desirable to ease the descent; far from it, indeed. Consequently, whilst with the hand nearest to the head (as it is when the axe reaches its highest elevation) the workman momentarily forces forward the axe, availing himself of the leverage now formed by regarding the left hand as the fulcrum of motion, he gives an impulse, and this impelling force is continued until he is conscious that the speed of the axe in its descent is greater than muscular efforts can maintain. To permit gravity to have free play the workman then withdraws the hand nearest to the head, and sliding it along the handle, brings it close to the left hand, which is at the extremity of the handle ; thus the head comes down upon the work with all the energy which a combination of muscular action and gravity can effect.   The process is repeated by the right

Fig. 343.—Scotch Adze.

hand sliding along the handle, and releasing as well as raising the head.

Axe Handles.

The form of the axe handle deserves notice, differing as it does from that of the sledge-hammer.   In the latter it is round or nearly so, in the axe it is oval, the thin end of the oval being on the underside, and more than this the longer axis of the oval increases as the handle approaches the head. till at its entrance into the head it may be double what it is at the other ex-

tremity.   It often has also a projection at the extremity of the handle.   The increasing thickness near the head gives strength where needed as the axe is being driven in. There is, too, this further difference—in a sledge-hammer more or less recoil has to be provided for, and the handle does this ; in the axe no recoil should take place.   The entrance of the axe edge is, or ought to be, sufficient to retain it, and the whole of the energy resulting from muscular action and gravity should be utilised.   The curvature, too, of the handle is in marked contrast with the straight line of the sledge-hammer handle.   The object of this curvature is worthy of note.   The handle of an American forester's axe is very long and curved.   In sledge-hammer work the face is to be brought down flat, that is, as a rule, in a

Fig. 344.—American Adze.

horizontal plane, whereas the forester's axe has to be brought down at varying obliquities.   If, now, the hewer's hand had to be counteracting the influence of gravity, he would have much needless labour ; hence the care of a skilled forester in the balance of the axe-head and the curvature of the handle.

THE ADZE.

The variety in the shapes of adze-heads is very great, there being two or three kinds

Fig. 345.—Adze Handle.

used by each of the following :—Carpenters and joiners, ship carpenters, wheelwrights, and coopers. The carpenter knows three principal varieties, the English pattern (Fig. 342), Scotch pattern (Fig. 343), and American pattern (Fig. 344). The ash handles used with these may have either of the shapes illustrated by Figs. 345 and 346. The adze must be sharpened from the inside, and when its action is considered (see

Fig. 346.—Adze Handle.

next paragraph), it is clear that the curvature of the face of the adze-iron must be circular, or nearly so. The true curvature of the metal may be approximately deduced from considering the radius of the circle described by the workman's arms, and the handle of the adze. The edge of the adze

release chips of timber beneath which the adze is lightly embedded.

HOW TO USE AN ADZE.

The general method of using the adze is as follows :—The workman stands with one foot upon the wood in the line of the fibre, and thus assists in steadying the work. The long handle of the adze is curved so as to permit of an efficient blow being given, and the tool brought to a stop before the handle strikes any part of the workman's body ; it is caused to stop by the exhaustion of its impact energy in the fibres of wood. The adze is raised by both hands until nearly horizontal, and then not allowed simply to fall, but steadily driven downwards until the curved metal, with its broad and sharp edge, enters near to, if not below the sole of the workman's shoe, separating a large chip of wood from the mass ; the handle is rapidly raised, and the blows are repeated quickly, the workman gradually

Fig. 347.—Plain Handle London Screwdriver.

is slightly convex for the same reasons as influenced the curvature of the axe edge already alluded to (see p. 92). The curvature in the blade also serves (though partially) as a fulcrum, for, by slightly thrusting the handle from him, the workman may

drawing back his foot until the end flakes of wood are separated. The edge of an adze often is so keen as to cut through a horsehair pressed against it. It is not pleasant to contemplate an error of judgment or an unsteady blow, but practice brings great skill in the use of this tool. The Indian workman uses the adze for producing curved surfaces, and holds the tool so near its head that the hand touches the metal, the

defaced screw-head. The worker then must decide for himself what sizes will best suit his purposes. The principal patterns are illustrated here. Figs. 347 and 348 are the

Fig. 348.—Oval Handle London Screwdriver.

blows being delivered chiefly from the elbow.

SCREWDRIVERS.

A description of screwdrivers in this chapter may seem out of place, but as they are tools of impulsion, even as is the hammer, they may fitly be dealt with here. Two or three screwdrivers at least will be required,

London patterns, the former with handle of beech or boxwood, and the latter with an oval ebony handle. Cabinet screwdrivers are shown by Figs. 349 to 351, Fig. 349 having a plain beech handle, Fig. 350 an oval boxwood handle, and Fig. 351 a fluted or " firm-grip " boxwood handle. For special work, it is necessary to have a long spindle-blade screwdriver, as shown by Fig. 352.

Fig. 349.—Plain Handle Cabinet Screwdriver.

long and short, and with wide and narrow blade. For general work, a tool of medium length should be obtained, although there are on the one hand enthusiastic advocates of a short tool, and on the other hand of a long tool for any and every purpose. Any advantage gained by a short over a long tool, or the reverse, is one of advantage in special circumstances only, and not one of

The power gained by a screwdriver in turning a screw depends entirely on the diameter of its handle, quite irrespective of the length of its blade. Taking two screwdrivers having blades of the same length and breadth, but one A having a handle one-half again as broad as that of the other B, then A will turn the same size of screw as will B with exactly one-third less power ex-

Fig. 350.—Oval Handle Cabinet Screwdriver.

saved energy ; theoretically, the length does not enter into consideration at all, except when, in starting to extract a difficult screw, the driver is tilted from the upright, but this is at the risk of a broken tool edge and

pended ; it is purely a question of leverage, and quite independent of the length of the blade. Of course, in correctly proportioned screwdrivers the longer blades generally have the wider handles, but it is not always

7

so, and the increased length of the blade is usually disadvantageous except as already noted. An important point in working

ratchet in position for withdrawing a screw. The handle is 4 in. long, which gives it, theoretically, great mechanical power. Prac-

Fig. 351.—Fluted Handle Cabinet Screwdriver.

with large screws is to see that the point of the blade fills the entire width of the slot in the screw-head. A useful screwdriver is the one illustrated by Fig. 353. The handle is that of a gimlet, and can be separated from the blade, a great convenience for carrying, although the whole tool is only

tically, the advantage over the ordinary form is more than it is theoretically, as owing to the shape of the handle the power is better applied. Another very convenient form of screwdriver is shown in use by Fig. 354, and consists of a screwdriver bit (Fig. 355) used in an ordinary brace. It is chiefly

Fig. 352.—Spindle Blade Screwdriver.

6 in. long. In the handle are two hardened steel pawls acting on a ratchet, so that in driving a screw the right hand never moves

useful where many large or medium-sized screws are required to be driven. The power gained is considerable, owing to the

Fig. 353.—Gimlet-handled Screwdriver.

Fig. 354.—Brace Screwdriver in use.

off the handle, the left being thus at liberty to guide the screw. Reversing the handle on the tang of the blade puts the

length of lever afforded by the sweep of the brace, and it has the additional advantage that the entire weight of the workman can be applied to keep the driver in the screw-slot without decreasing his power of turning as in the ordinary pattern; it is also very speedy, as the turning is continuous. The ordinary screwdriver may be found in of brass and partly of wood. In using it the blade must be drawn out to its full length, and inserted in the slot of the screw, which is then driven home by pressure on the top of the handle (see Fig. 358), which by

Fig. 355.—Screwdriver Bit.

the way when screwing a lock on or off, inside the front of a drawer, as this is generally done with the drawer in position. The short screwdriver illustrated by Fig. 356 is well adapted for work of this description, and the handle being broad and flat is convenient to hold in the hand. Another short screwdriver is shown by Fig. 357, and this is designed especially for unscrewing plane irons, as shown on p. 45, Fig. 163.

Fig. 356.—Short Screwdriver.

AUTOMATIC SCREWDRIVERS.

The automatic screwdriver is made in variety, but the principle of all is much the

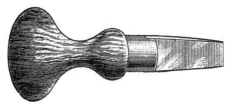

Fig. 357.—Plane Iron Screwdriver.

travelling down the spiral grooves in the spindle causes the blade to revolve. It is useful for rapidly driving a number of screws in a small space. If the blade is buried in its handle as far as may be, the tool can be used as any ordinary screwdriver for turning either forwards or backwards. A quick-action screwdriver (see Fig. 359) has a wooden handle of ordinary shape, into which slides a metal rod traversed from end to end by two spiral grooves—one right- and one left-handed—which receive an adjustable pin placed

Fig. 358.—Automatic Screwdriver in use.

just inside the handle-sheath. A moderately strong coiled spring forces the rod outwards from the handle when not under pressure. The outer end of the rod is provided with adjustable jaws in which to

same. The blade of the screwdriver, which is cylindrical throughout its length except for about 1 in. at the point, where it is flattened so as to enter the slot in the screw head, works in a hollow handle partly hold slot bits. A turn of the ferrule at the end of the handle tightens the rod and admits of its being used as an ordin- in a screw or after the preliminary loosening when taking it out, are given very rapidly by Archimedean action following

Fig. 359.—Millers Falls Automatic Screwdriver.

ary screwdriver, while the twists necessary before the final tightening when driving pressure of the handle in the direction of the tool's length.

BORING TOOLS.

THERE is a great variety of boring tools, and apart from the important question of size, there is that of suitability. Bradawls are well-known and useful tools for soft wood. The stem is cylindrical, and the chisel edge cuts the fibres, and the wedge-like form of the tool pushes them aside; used in end grain, it scrapes and pushes its way in, and, roughly though effectually, it makes a hole for a nail or a screw. The bradawl can be used for hard wood, but its special use is for soft wood, and its province is limited to comparatively small holes. In hard wood it has to be turned right and

when attempting to withdraw the bradawl from a piece of hard wood, handle and blade may come apart, the handle remaining in the operator's hand and the blade in the wood. In the brass-capped bradawl (Fig. 362) the end of the handle is so fitted into the brass cap replacing the ferrule that the blade is secured in the handle so firmly that they cannot come apart in the manner described above. When the handle of the ordinary awl parts from the blade, the latter is removed from the work by means of pincers, with the risk of bruising the work or perhaps breaking the bradawl in the hole. Therefore it is very necessary to guard against the bradawl coming apart,

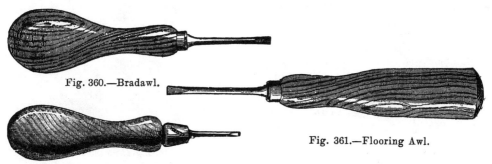

Fig. 360.—Bradawl.

Fig. 361.—Flooring Awl.

Fig. 362.—Brass-capped Bradawl.

left more freely than is necessary in soft wood, the edge acting more like a scraper in the harder material. The great limitation of the bradawl is that there is no provision for the waste material, and so it can be used for small holes only. The ordinary form of bradawl is shown by Fig. 360, and a larger kind, the flooring awl, by Fig. 361. These may have handles of ash, beech, or boxwood. The patent brass-capped bradawl (Fig. 362) is an improvement on the ordinary form. In the old bradawl the tang of the blade is driven into the handle, and a semblance of strength given to the tool by a brass or iron ferrule; but occasionally,

and so the following method should be adopted: First, the steel tang of the bradawl blade is to be softened at the extreme end by making it red-hot in a gas flame. When allowed to cool gradually it will be found to be softer and tougher than before. The softness is not to be confined to just the extreme end, but very great care should be taken not to draw the temper of the cutting part of the tool. Mark the length of the tang on the bradawl handle, and at $\frac{1}{8}$ in. from this mark towards the end where the shoulder of the awl comes, bore a hole at right angles, or nearly so, with the tang. The tang of a bradawl is usually, and should be always, oblong in section. Bend the tip of the tang slightly, and insert it in its handle. Now by judiciously driving a brad into the hole previously bored (see Fig. 363) the slight bending of the tang can be increased to form a hook, while the brad makes the bent end embed itself tightly

Fig. 363.—Fixing Bradawl Blade.

in the handle. Finally, the brad is filed off at both ends, and given one or two riveting blows (see Fig. 364). A bradawl so treated, if done well, will not come out of its handle, and will last until either blade or handle is broken. Care must be taken that the tang is driven only just past the hole bored for the brad, and the brad driven to increase the bending of the tang. For this purpose, when the bending is sufficiently started, it will be best to drive the blade home and then the brad; but if the tang is inserted too far when the brad is driven, instead of increasing the bend the brad will diminish it, and the desired effect will not be produced. The method of boring a hole with a bradawl is shown by Fig.

Fig. 364.—Bradawl with Fixed Blade.

365, the edge of the awl being across and not in line with the grain of the wood.

Gimlets and How to Sharpen Them.

The ordinary forms of this small but essential tool are the twist gimlet (Fig. 366) and the shell gimlet (Fig. 367); but other forms are the twist-nose or Swiss gimlet (Fig. 368) and the auger gimlet (Fig. 369).

Gimlets are found suitable to bore end grain as well as across the fibres; but in boring near the end of a narrow strip of wood, the pointed screw, drawing the tool rapidly into the compact wood, acts like a wedge, and splits the wood quickly. The way in which to hold a gimlet in use is shown by Fig. 370, p. 104. When a gimlet gets rather the worse for wear and slightly rusty, the shank (providing the handle is quite tight) can be sharpened and the tool made as fit for work as a new one. For sharpening a twist gimlet, fix a piece of oak, about $1\frac{1}{4}$ in. thick, in the vice, and make a hole, $\frac{3}{4}$ in. deep, in its top surface with the gimlet to be

Fig. 365.—Boring Hole with Bradawl.

sharpened. Fill the hole with flour emery and a few drops of oil, and then reinsert the gimlet and screw down well into the wood, until its point just shows on the other side. After working it backwards and forwards for a few minutes, supplying fresh emery and oil at intervals, it will be found, on withdrawing it from the hole, to be quite free from rust and perfectly sharpened. Another piece of wood, this time soft deal, is now taken, a hole bored as before, filled with fine dry flour emery (no oil), and the gimlet worked well into it, until, on being finally withdrawn, it should have a good polish, the edges of the spiral groove being sharp and capable of cutting a clean hole. Besides bringing the shank into good working order, the vigorous screwing backwards and forwards in the hard wood fully tests the strength and tightness of the handle, for after passing satisfactorily through that test it may be safely reckoned to stand any amount of ordinary wear. Though a gimlet is a comparatively unimportant tool, it by no means follows that it should not receive attention.

their proper action. To try for centreing the bit, fix the brace in a vice by the head or cap; then rotate the brace, and observe if the bit turns concentric. The brace and bits are used for boring holes for nails, screws, or pins, for cutting circular holes, such as the circles for coins in cabinets, or for bottles in chemical cabinets, or for test-tube stands, and for making circles to serve as ornamentation. Wood may also be cut away in roughing out carv-

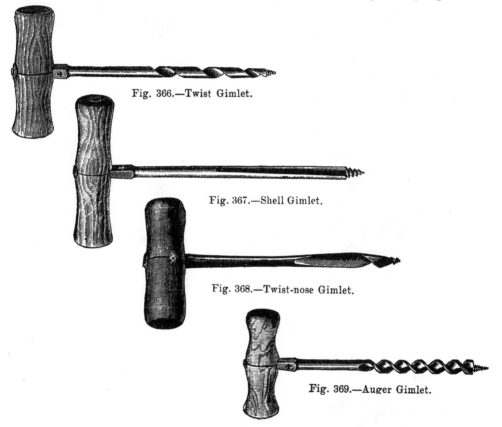

Fig. 366.—Twist Gimlet.

Fig. 367.—Shell Gimlet.

Fig. 368.—Twist-nose Gimlet.

Fig. 369.—Auger Gimlet.

THE BORING BRACE.

The brace supplies the most useful boring tool; from the variety of bits that can be used with it, it serves many purposes. It is better to buy the bits fitted to the brace, as they are more truly centred than those bought separate are likely to be, and the centreing of the bits is essential to

ing, frequently more quickly and certainly by the aid of a brace and bits than by any other means. Mortises are often better cut by first boring away the bulk of the wood; such a proceeding prevents splitting. The brace can be used to bore vertically or horizontally. The greatest force is obtained in the latter position, holding the cap with the left hand, and pressing with the stomach leaning against the tool. It is quite possible to break a brace by pressing on it too strongly. An iron one may

Fig. 370.—Using Gimlet.

Fig. 371.—Wooden Brace.

bend, and if bent the bit is made eccentric. To bore vertically, the work should be low,

so that the operator may lean over the top of the brace, and, holding the cap in the palm of one hand, press on the back of the hand with the right shoulder and turn with the other hand. Braces suitable for the woodworker's use are illustrated by Figs. 371 to 374. Fig. 371 shows the simplest type of wooden brace, a thoroughly well-made though somewhat expensive tool, but it must be remembered that its life is very long. The body of the brace is of beech,

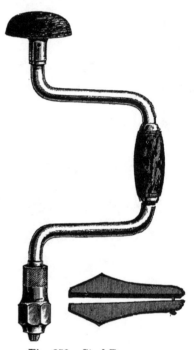

Fig. 372.—Steel Brace.

but the head, where there is constant friction and wear, is of lignum vitæ. Steel braces, much cheaper than wooden ones, are very largely used, and Fig. 372 is a type of them. The handle and head are of hard wood, and the body and jaws are of steel, the handle being strengthened with brass rings at the ends and the head turning on ball-bearings, as shown in Fig. 373. The form of the jaws is made quite clear; they are opened and closed by screwing the milled cnuck off or on respectively. Practically the same tool is shown by Fig. 373, with the addition, however, of a ratchet; by means of this it is not necessary to complete the revolutions of the sweep in awkward places where there is but little room in which to work. Having turned

Fig. 373.—Ratchet Brace.

the sweep as far as it will go in the same direction as clock hands move, it can be brought back without the bit being twisted out of the work. The simple steel brace illustrated by Fig. 374 has a tapered square hole for the reception of the bit, the thumbscrew serving to tighten the split end when the bit has been inserted.

Boring Bits.

Braces are sold separately, or fitted with twelve, eighteen, twenty-four, thirty-six, or forty-eight bits, the bits being either bright, black, or straw-coloured, the last being the most expensive, but not necessarily better for use than the black,

except that in bright bits any flaws are more easily detected. Bits, as a rule, do not require sharpening; if slightly notched they may be repaired with a sharp file. In boring with fine bits use a little grease, pull out the bit occasionally and remove the borings; if the bit gets fixed, take off the brace and pull out with pincers. All boring tools may be so much heated by use as to spoil their temper.

Shell- and Twist-type Bits.

Woodworkers use many shapes of boring bits. The pin-bit is like a gouge sharpened both inside and outside. As sold by the tool-dealers, it is sharpened only outside and obliquely, but it will be found that if

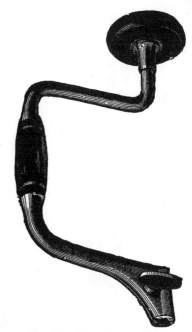

Fig. 374.—Thumbscrew Brace.

sharpened inside just a little and both the corners removed (when it becomes a shell-bit, Fig. 375), so that the contact with the wood takes place in the centre of the gouge-like end of the bit, its cutting is improved, while smoothing and polishing all over will allow the chips to escape more freely;

this condition is necessary in the working of every cutting tool. The shell bit is only suitable for boring at right angles to the fibre of the wood, the sharp gouge-like edge cutting freely; in a hole of considerable depth

hold tenons in their mortises, it is first-rate. When the sharp edge of the shell-bit is ground to a point, it forms what is called a dowel-bit, which is practically the same shape as a spoon-bit (see below), but has a wider stem. The spoon-bit (Fig. 376) resembles the shell-bit, but is pointed to somewhat resemble a tea-spoon, yet is more like the outline of a Gothic arch, the metal being hollowed out to form a cutting edge. This bit bores easily, freely, and well, will enter more exactly where the worker wishes, and is strong and cheap. The nose bit (Fig. 377) is of similar construction. Its cutting edge, from which it derives its name, is a part of the steel bent nearly to a right angle, and sharpened so that it forms a sort of chisel. To avoid catching, the corners are rounded off. For boring across the grain it is not dependable, generally entering half its diameter away from where it was started; but for boring the end-way of the grain the nose bit is efficient

and cheap. This bit also must be withdrawn now and then for the removal of chips, or it gets choked. In many ways superior to any of the foregoing is the half-twist

Fig. 375.
Shell Bit.

Fig. 376.
Spoon Bit.

Fig. 377.
Nose Bit.

Fig. 378.
Twist-nose Bit.

Fig. 379.
Hollow Taper Bit.

the chips have a tendency to remain; it is, however, an excellent bit for boring right through. For boring top and bottom laths for Venetian blinds, etc., and boring pins to

or Norwegian bit (Fig. 378), known also as the twist-nose bit. This tool screws itself into the wood, and the chips tend to rise out of the hole. It would not do to bore holes in narrow strips of wood, but for every other purpose it works well in either hard or soft wood any way of the grain. This bit is exactly the same shape as the twist-nose gimlet (Fig. 368). This completes the list of what may be termed shell- and twist-type bits. They vary from quite small bits to about ⅞ in. diameter, rarely even being made so large. They can all be obtained in a great variety of sizes, but exact size is not guaran- teed, the usual plan being to bore a hole and measure it rather than to measure the bit. A hollow taper bit used for enlarging holes is illustrated by Fig. 379.

between any of the following: Gedge's, Fig. 380; Scotch pattern, Fig. 381; Jennings', Fig. 382; single twist, Fig. 383;

Fig. 384.—Solid Nose Screw Bit.

Fig. 385.—Centre Bit with Pin.

Fig. 386.—Centre Bit with Screw.

and solid nose, Fig. 384. Gedge's and Jennings' are particularly good.

CENTRE BITS.

Centre bits are the most commonly used bits, and the ordinary form with pin is shown by Fig. 385, another form with screw being shown by Fig. 386. Centre bits are useful for boring large holes, and are much superior to shell-type bits in the important point of boring exactly where the hole is required; hence in fitting locks small centre bits are useful for keyholes. Centre bits of the kind referred to are the most useful for holes up to about ½ in. The centre bit consists of a piece of steel so shaped as to fulfil these three requirements—a centre, a circle-cutter (the "nicker"), and a chisel (the "router") to remove the core of the hole,

PATENT SCREW BITS.

The patent twisted bits having a screw centre (they are known as screw bits) are first-class, the only thing against them being the expense; they bore well in any wood and in any direction, relieving them-

Fig. 380.—Gedge's Twist Screw Bit.

Fig. 381.—Scotch Twist Screw Bit.

Fig. 382.—Jennings' Twist Screw Bit.

Fig. 383.—Single Twist Screw Bit.

selves of the chips and cutting true to dimension. Most of the patents have now expired, and there is not much to choose

and must be so formed as to act in the order named. In buying centre bits, bear in mind that the hole by no means agrees with the size of the bit; for instance, a $\frac{1}{2}$-in. bit bores a hole at least $\frac{9}{16}$ in. in diameter. The reason of this is that the pin is not quite in the centre, and so the circle cut is of larger diameter than the width of the tool. To gauge a centre bit, measure the distance between the nicker and centre of the pin, but not so as to get an oblique measurement. To be exact, bore a hole in

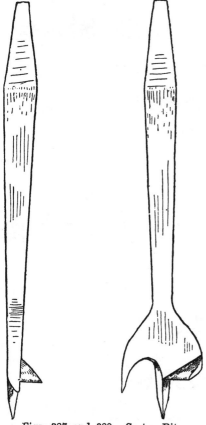

Figs. 387 and 388.—Centre Bit.

a piece of waste wood similar to the kind being worked on, and measure the diameter of this. Large centre bits have two, sometimes even three, nickers on one side, and these bits are expensive. If it is required to cut out of thin wood circles of greater diameter than 3 in., they may be cut by a tool like the knife of a cutting gauge, fixed to an arm that rotates on a pivot fixed on a block of wood, acting like beam compasses.

RECTIFYING CENTRE BITS.

It is intended to show here the chief faults commonly found in a new centre bit, and

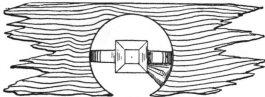

Fig. 389.—Plan of Centre Bit in use.

the best methods of rectifying them. Figs. 387 to 389 show a well-finished and properly

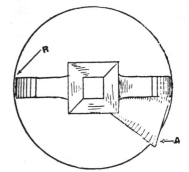

Fig. 390.—Faulty Router of Centre Bit.

made bit, in front elevation, side elevation, and plan respectively. The most common

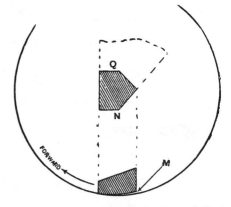

Fig. 391.—Section of Correctly Formed Centre Bit.

fault is shown at A (Fig. 390); the corner of the horizontal cutter or router operates outside the limits of the circle described by the vertical cutter or nicker. This produces a deep scoring round the inside of the hole, and generally gives the boring a ragged and unfinished appearance. It also puts unne-

the horizontal cutter is made to slant upwards in the direction shown by c d (Fig. 393), instead of downwards, as at b (Fig. 395). This defect is remedied by using a fine file and an oilstone slip, placing the bit

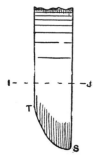

Fig. 392.—Centre Bit Nicker.

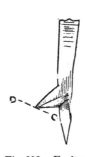

Fig. 393.—Faulty Centre Bit Router.

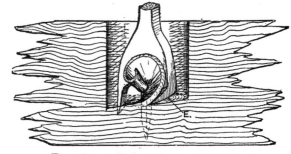

Fig. 396.—Action of Centre Bit in Good Condition.

cessary strain on the operator. The projection should be filed away until the outline of the lip corresponds with, and just clears, the inside of the hole, as shown in Fig. 389. The second fault to be noticed is that the outside of the nicker often is formed badly, having more clearance at the front side (R, Fig. 390) than at the back, this producing a continual wedging at the side of the bit. A correctly formed nicker should have, if anything, a little clearance at the back, as shown at M, Fig. 391, which is a section taken on the line I J (Fig. 392).

on the corner of the bench, as shown in Fig. 397. The slope at the bottom of the horizontal cutter e, Fig. 396, is the most important influence affecting the cutting power of the bit. It may be regulated so that, no matter what pressure bears upon the brace, the rate of advance in boring is

Fig. 394.— Badly Sharpened Nicker.

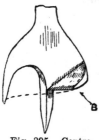

Fig. 395.—Centre Bit Cutters.

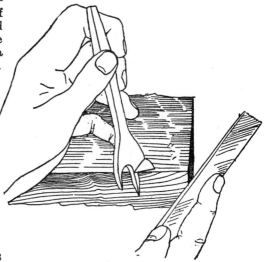

Fig. 397.—Sharpening Centre Bit Router.

Other minor faults are shown at Figs. 393 and 394. Often in finishing chisels, plane-irons, gouges, and other edged tools, the workman tops off the edge from the wrong side, possibly to prevent accident; the centre bit, too, suffers similarly. The edge of

uniform. In fact, owing to the want of a little attention here, much labour is often lost, in vain efforts on the part of the workman to make the bit cut faster. On the other hand, the angle of slope may be made so steep that the horizontal cutter will out-feed itself, and endeavour to expel from the hole more material than has been separ-

angle, or it will cause the edge to cut too deeply into the wood, and thus take off thick shavings and produce roughness. The correct angle for the under side of the horizontal cutter or router is regulated for the

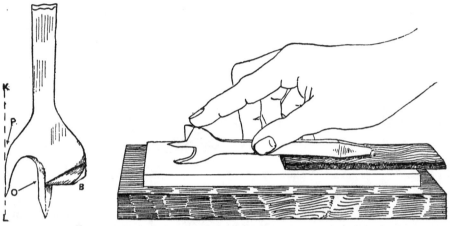

Fig. 398.—Centre Bit Cutters.   Fig. 399.—Sharpening Centre Bit Nicker.

ated from the main body of the wood by the vertical cutter. The hole is then ragged on the inside, and many of the fibres project from the sides, while in other places there are signs of fibres having been dragged and torn away. Frequently bits are not correct to the sizes stamped on them; often they are too large, for the reason already given. To remedy this, if the discrepancy is not more than $\frac{1}{32}$ in. to $\frac{1}{16}$ in., a little filing may be done at the side of the centre pin. If the bit is too large, the filing should be done on the side Q (Fig. 391); if too small, file on the side N. If too large by more than, say, $\frac{1}{16}$ in., the bit should be softened by heat and the vertical cutter closed up a little, the bit afterwards being re-tempered.

Sharpening Centre Bits.

Centre bits should be sharpened with a file and oilstone slip, the latter producing the finished edge. The nicker o (Fig. 398) must be sharpened from the inside only, and in such a manner that the leading part of the edge is highest, as indicated by s in Fig. 392. The router B (Fig. 398) should be sharpened mostly from the top side; the under side should not have too great an

most part by the length of the vertical cutter or nicker opposite to it. Its slant should be part of a spiral, which, when continued round the bit, would pass through the lower

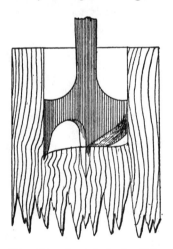

Fig. 400.—Special Centre Bit.

part (near the point) of the nicker, as shown by the dotted line in Fig. 395, and also in Fig. 396. Theoretically, this is quite correct, and under such conditions it would be quite impossible for a bit to overfeed itself. But besides the question of necessary clearance, there is a temptation to make the angle steeper, to help in drawing the bit forward. The length of the nicker and a little experiment will in each case soon determine the most desirable angle. The nicker, too, is occasionally topped off on the outside, as shown in Fig. 394. Faults of boring with a bit so formed are excessive strain on the operator, and a badly finished and more or less oval-shaped hole. The nicker should be, if not quite upright, very nearly so, right down to the point, as shown by the line K L in Fig. 398. This line is not quite parallel to the axis of the bit, being a little nearer to the axis at K than at L. Having sharpened the point of the nicker from the inside with a file and oilstone slip, take away any feather-edge that may have burred over to the outside by rubbing on the oilstone as shown in Fig. 399,

nicker, as seen from the side, is given by Fig. 392. In a new bit there is scarcely any curve, but just a straight slightly sloping edge; if it is correctly made and sharpened

Fig. 402.—Horizontal Boring with Brace.

there should be a keen edge from s round the curve to about T (Fig. 392). The length of this edge should equal, or slightly exceed, the depth of the thickest shaving the router is capable of removing.

How to Use the Centre Bit.

For boring holes across the grain with the centre bit, hold the board firmly on a piece of waste wood, then bore right through into the latter; or bore from the face of the board until just the point of the bit appears at the other side; then reverse the board, place the point in the hole, and finish boring. In boring, see that the chips rise out of the hole; when they do not, remove the bit and shake out the pieces, or the chips may wedge against the tool, and the bit will run to one side or be broken. Boring holes into the end grain of a piece of timber with a centre bit is an operation that sometimes gives trouble. In some woods little pieces of detached material persistently get wedged between the bit and the side of the hole, as at P (Fig. 398). Twist bits are best for this class of work, but when a series of exceptionally clean holes is required in the end grain, and when there is not sufficient room to take the brace and a long twist bit, the specially designed centre bit shown by Fig. 400 will give excellent results. It is made of ½-in. steel beaten out, turned up, and filed to the proper shape. The method

Fig. 401.—Vertical Boring with Brace.

which illustrates the safest way of doing this. To keep the back of the bit to the proper height while it is being rubbed, place on the stone a piece of wood whose thickness will depend upon the size of the bit to be sharpened. The proper shape of the

of holding the brace when boring vertically is shown by Fig. 401, and when boring horizontally by Fig. 402. The use of a hand drill, which for some purposes may be preferred to the ordinary brace, is illus-

Fig. 403.—Horizontal Boring with Hand Drill.

trated clearly by Figs. 403 and 404, the former showing horizontal boring, and the latter vertical boring. A method of getting

Fig. 404.—Vertical Boring with Hand Drill.

a true horizontal hole is shown by Fig. 405, a shaped support for the bit being held in the bench vice or in some other manner.

Expanding Centre Bits.

The advantages of a bit whose working size can be altered with ease are apparent,

and there are a number of such bits on the market. Fig. 406 shows one of the simplest, Anderson's, this being made in three sizes—$\frac{5}{16}$ in. to $\frac{9}{16}$ in., $\frac{9}{16}$ in. to 1 in., and 1 in. to 2 in. Fig. 407 shows Steers', this

Fig. 405.—Method of Obtaining Accurate Horizontal Boring.

being made in three sizes, $\frac{5}{8}$ in. to $1\frac{3}{4}$ in., $\frac{7}{8}$ in. to 3 in., and $\frac{7}{8}$ in. to 4 in., whilst extra cutters for other sizes can be obtained. Clark's patent bit (Fig. 408) is made in four sizes, $\frac{1}{2}$ in. to $1\frac{1}{2}$ in., and $\frac{7}{8}$ in. to 3 in., 4 in., and 5 in. respectively. Anderson's is a cheap bit, the two others being somewhat expensive, though only in first cost, and being thoroughly reliable they obviate the need of a great number of separate bits.

The Forstner Auger Bit.

The Forstner auger bit (Fig. 409) is a useful tool for smooth, round, oval, or

Fig. 406.—Anderson's Expanding Bit.

square boring, scroll and twist work. Its speciality is that it is guided by its periphery instead of its centre, and consequently it will bore any arc of a circle, and can be guided in any direction, regardless of grain or knots, leaving a true, polished, cylindrical hollow. It is a great improvement in wood-boring tools. Hitherto, with the exception of the shell bit, which has a gouge-like cutting edge, and is in some respects very defective, the centre bit has been the type of wood-boring tools, for hand use. Some of the twist auger bits are really improved centre bits, and have a screw point in common. All have also a well-polished groove, along which the chips can pass out and relieve the bit, permitting it to cut without the frequent

Fig. 407.—Steers' Expanding Bit.

withdrawal that some bits require. With these twist bits and the centre bits as exceptions, all the rest of the wood-worker's boring tools make a small hole first and gradually enlarge it, especially the spoon bits and the Norwegian twist-nose bits, so that to bore a comparatively large hole in a narrow strip of wood generally implies splitting it. Even the twist auger bits just

Fig. 408.—Clark's Expanding Bit.

mentioned are apt to do so by the wedge action of the taper screw. Then some bits bore well in only one way of the grain. Not one of them, however, is capable of boring a part only of a cylindrical hole, that is, they cannot form a semi-cylindrical groove on a piece of wood; every one of them has a tendency to split the wood, and some of them wander from the point at which

ordinary bits nearly always bore a hole larger than themselves, but the Forstner bit bores truly in the place in which it is set, and truly to the size of itself. It has no tendency to split the wood, and works entirely by the guidance of the cutter, which forms the periphery or circumference of the bit itself. Another cutter (or several, according to the size of the bit) is provided to remove the core, and the bottom of a hole bored by this peculiar bit is smooth and flat. The bit seems quite independent of

Fig. 409.—Forstner Auger Bit.

the grain of the wood, boring equally well at any angle. But for deep holes the bit must be withdrawn frequently, or the chips will collect round the shaft and make progress or withdrawal somewhat difficult.

AUGERS.

Augers bore well in the direction of the grain of the wood, which centre bits will not do in most woods, unless they have a screw in place of the pin (see Fig. 386, p. 107). Augers are made complete in themselves, and used to bore holes of considerable depth and size in wood. They consist of a steel rod, having a round eye at one end through which a round wooden handle fits at right angles; at the other end is a spiral twist of larger diameter, terminating in a conical screw with a sharp point; the edge of the spiral is a nicker which cuts the grain

Fig. 410.—Auger.

they are started. The Forstner bit, on the other hand, can be placed close to the edge, or even with part projecting considerably beyond the boundary of the wood, and, with a little care in starting, it will bore its hole or its groove cleanly and well. Then, too,

of the wood around the edge of the hole (see Fig. 410). When using an auger, most power is obtained by standing over the work and boring downwards; a little grease should be used with it. Screw bits replace large augers in cabinet work.

ABRADING AND SCRAPING TOOLS.

THE scraper illustrated by Fig. 411, and shown handled by Fig. 412, is an aid in producing surfaces more flat and regular than can be produced with the plane alone. Its use does not dispense with the plane;

Fig. 411.—Steel Scraper.

on the contrary, any surface on which the scraper is to be used must previously be planed as level and smooth as plane can make it. But the plane, in doing its work—no matter how sharp it may be, or how closely the back-iron is set up to the edge of the cutting iron, or how straight across the edge the cutting iron is sharpened—is liable to leave marks and ridges on the face of the work, which, on hard woods, are not effectively removed by the use of glasspaper alone. The scraper is used after the plane has finished its work, and previous to the final operation of glass-papering. In addition to the removal of the ridges left by the plane, the scraper is used for dressing up all kinds of cross-grained surfaces that occur in curly and figured solid and veneer woods; but as far as possible this use of the scraper should be avoided. Excessive dressing up of a cross-grained patch on a panel, a stile, or a table-top will most certainly show, and spoil the flatness and general appearance of the article when it is polished. As a rule, such excessive scraping is resorted to in conse-

quence of the plane having been sharpened and set badly, or of some other technical oversight or unskilful manipulation.

The Scraper Described.

The scraper is a thin and very hard steel plate, about 5 in. by 3 in., or $4\frac{1}{2}$ in. by $2\frac{1}{2}$ in., and slightly less than $\frac{1}{16}$ in. in thickness. The long edges are sharpened in a peculiar manner. Both of the long edges may be straight, as in Fig. 411 and at A B, Fig. 413, or one edge may have round corners of differing radii, as at C D. These corners are often useful in working up hollows and mouldings generally. The "straight" edge A B, it will be noticed, is not quite straight throughout its whole length. Near the ends the edge is gradually rounded off, to prevent the corners catching in the surface that is being operated on. In this respect, the commercial scraper (Fig. 411) is incorrectly shaped. The cutting power of a scraper depends upon, first, the quality and temper of the steel of which it is made; and, secondly, upon the proper formation

Fig. 412.—Handled Steel Scraper.

of the burr or feather along its edges. Also, the faces of the steel plate must be perfectly bright and free from rust marks or indentations of any kind. It is by no means an uncommon thing to find any rusty piece of sheet steel—a piece of an old hand-saw or try-square, for example—being used as a scraper. The smallest appreciation of how the scraper cuts would indicate how useless such material is for this particular purpose. On the other hand, scarcely anything better can be found for making a scraper than a piece of broken saw-blade, provided the sides of it are still polished and bright.

Fig. 413.—Correctly Shaped Steel Scraper.

The fact that the saw was broken may often be taken to indicate a greater hardness than usual in the blade, thus fitting it exactly for the purposes of a scraper. An ordinary saw-blade is not usually hard enough. Provided that there is enough elasticity to "give" in the operator's hands as it is being pushed along, the scraper should be nearly too hard for an ordinary file to touch. If it can be filed easily, then its edge will soon be gone. At the same time, if the steel is merely hard, without the desired amount of elasticity, the burr edge

—and as in practice it often is—a mere abrader of the surface. When in good working trim, the scraper should, if desired, take off shaving after shaving perfectly uniform in thickness, and nearly as wide as the cutting edge is long. But such a performance is rarely required of it, and never when the plane has previously done its work well. Too much emphasis cannot be laid on the fact that the proper duty of the scraper is not to make a surface, but to correct the irregularities on it. In explanation of the cutting action of the scraper, a diagrammatic figure is shown (Fig. 414). This illustration correctly illustrates the cutting principle, though it does not represent a true section of the scraper. In use, the scraper is held firmly in both hands and tilted forwards, away from the operator, until the cutting edge grips the surface of the wood, exactly as shown in Fig. 415. It is then kept steadily at this angle, and made to cut a fine shaving at each stroke as it is being pushed away from the operator in the direction from E to F (Fig. 415).

SHARPENING STEEL SCRAPERS.

The proper formation of the burr edge is of the greatest importance. Having pro-

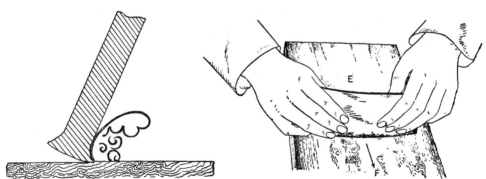

Fig. 414.—Diagram showing Action of Scraper.

Fig. 415.—Scraper in use.

will strip off as soon as it is applied to the work, leaving a coarse, jagged, and utterly useless edge behind.

WHY THE SCRAPER CUTS.

The correctly sharpened scraper is a real cutting tool, and not as its name suggests

cured a suitable piece of steel plate, a usual but not recommended method is as follows: The plate is laid down on the bench as shown in Fig. 416, the edge of the scraper projecting slightly beyond the edge of the bench. A narrow bradawl, gouge, or special sharpener (Fig. 417) then is laid on the scraper horizontally, and, with considerable pressure, is stroked backwards and forwards from end to end of the plate, G to H

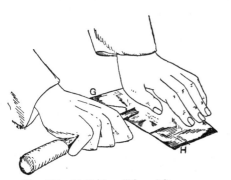

Fig. 416.—Polishing Sides of Scraper.

(Fig. 416). After about ten or a dozen strokes, the scraper is turned upside down and the other side treated in a similar way. This completes the first part of the sharpening. Next, the gouge is placed vertically against the edge of the scraper, as shown in Fig. 418, and stroked to and fro with about the same degree of pressure and firmness as in the previous operation, and for about the same number of times. Or else, for this second part of the sharpening, the scraper is placed on its corner on the bench, as illustrated in Fig. 419, and held firmly in the left hand, while the right hand deftly strokes a gouge, with a quick action and considerable pressure, once or twice in an upward direction, as from I to J in Fig. 419. The scraper is then tried on the work to determine its sharpness or otherwise; often this trial is very disappointing. If, by good fortune, a satisfactory edge has been made, that fact is just

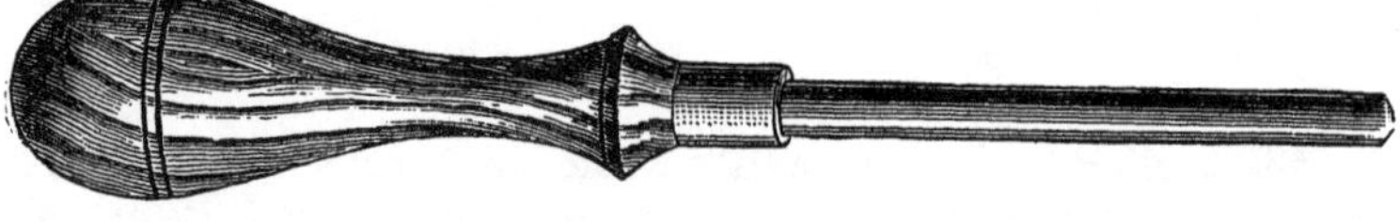

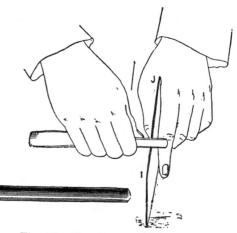

Fig. 417.—Scraper Sharpener.

as often due to the circumstances of chance as to the absolute skill of the workman. If the scraper fails to cut satisfactorily, it

is laid down on the bench and the two processes are repeated. The following is a better method of sharpening a scraper.

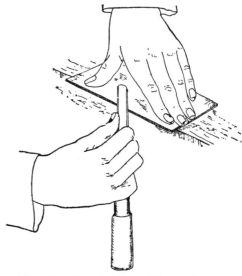

Fig. 418.—Forming Burr Edge on Scraper.

Grind the edge straight and square, and slope it up at the ends, as shown by A and B (Fig. 413). It should then be placed on

Fig. 419.—Forming Burr Edge on Scraper.

its edge on a fine-cutting oilstone, as shown in Fig. 420, and rubbed backwards and forwards until all traces of the grinding have disappeared. Then it should be laid flat on its side, still on the oilstone, as in Fig. 421, and rubbed until the sides are bright and polished all along the edges. If any false burr or feather-edge has been created in this last process, the scraper must be set up on its edge again, as in Fig. 420, and rubbed a little more, until two perfectly square and sharp corners appear all along the scraper. Now, if due care has really been taken in making the corners perfect and square, the scraper in this condition would produce shavings tolerably well on any hard wood ; but the shaving would be the result of abrasive and not of cutting action. It is purely a matter of choice if, at this stage, a smooth-backed gouge is passed to and fro over the side of the scraper, as in Fig. 416, with the object of imparting a still higher polish to the plate of steel at the places where the burr is to be formed. But the greatest care must be taken not to press too heavily, and also to maintain a perfectly level position with the gouge, while the polishing is being done. As stated, this polishing of the side is not really necessary, and the scraper would cut very well without its supposed assistance. Next, the scraper is placed on its corner on the bench,

over of the corner ; the gouge must be very lightly pressed, or it will cause the burr to curl up too much, and also it must be kept

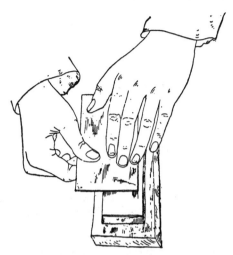

Fig. 421.—Squaring Scraper Edge on Oilstone.

nearly, though not quite, horizontal. With regard to resharpening the scraper, when this becomes necessary, the scraper must be placed upon the oilstone and rubbed up

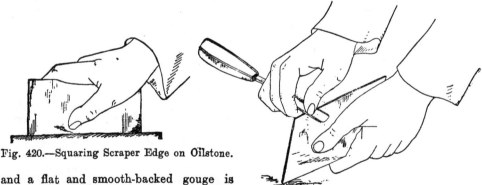

Fig. 420.—Squaring Scraper Edge on Oilstone.

Fig. 422.—Forming Burr Edge on Scraper.

and a flat and smooth-backed gouge is passed once—or at most twice—along the edge. The scraper during this operation may be held either as already shown in Fig. 419, or as is here recommended and shown in Fig. 422 ; or it may be fastened in the bench-vice. The aim in this particular action is the production of an exceedingly fine burr, scarcely enough to be called a burr at all, but a perfectly regular bending

again to perfectly square corners as previously described in connection with Figs. 420 and 421.

DEFECTIVE SHARPENING OF SCRAPERS.

A frequent mistake is to put too great pressure on the gouge, and to stroke too much, the burr thus produced being large, jagged, and too much bent over to enable the scraper to do its work at a comfortable inclination. Another is to give the gouge too much slant, as shown in

Fig. 423.—Wrong Method of Forming Burr Edge.

Fig. 423, this also necessitating excessive tilting over of the scraper when at work, as indicated in Fig. 424. In resharpening, many workmen, instead of rubbing the corners square upon the oilstone, simply lay the scraper on the bench, and, as already stated, stroke it over in both directions afresh. Figs. 425 to 427 illustrate the bad effect of this. If the scraper was sharpened well in the first instance, it will, when ready for resharpening, appear like the section at κ (Fig. 425). When the gouge is stroked heavily along it, the burr edge must either be closed against the side, as shown at Fig. 426, or be drawn out as at Fig. 427. If the former, then the difficulty of forming a new burr edge is very great; if the latter, then the original burr is merely bent outwards again when the gouge is applied to the edge of the scraper, and will invariably be found stripped off and broken,

Fig. 424.—Using Badly Sharpened Scraper.

if the edge is examined after the scraper has been applied to the work a second time. Scrapers for special work are illustrated by Figs. 428 and 429, and there are many other shapes.

GLASSPAPER.

Glasspaper is the chief abrading material used in woodworking, and consists of strong paper coated with powdered glass. In the

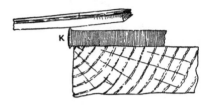

Fig. 425.—Wrong Method of Forming Burr Edge.

manufacture of glasspaper, first the glass is washed and sorted, and then broken very fine by stamps or other machinery. The glass chiefly used for best glasspaper is that from old port wine and stout bottles; this, when pulverised, is of a golden colour. The different grades of glasspaper are numbered from 3 to 0 (and even finer), and there are corresponding sieves to divide the various grades, or to "size," as it is technically called. These sieves are numbered from 140 to 30, the numbers representing the number of meshes per lineal inch; the finer sieves are covered with Swiss silk, the remainder with woven wire. In this part of the process considerable care must be exercised, as one large particle of glass on a sheet of fine paper would scratch the work upon which it was used, and would produce an uneven surface. The placing of the glass on paper requires considerable skill and experience. The workman has delivered to him plain paper in reams of 120 sheets, each sheet making four sheets of ordinary size. The appliances used are a copper holding 56 lb. of glue, a table, a bench on

Fig. 426.

Fig. 427.

Figs. 426 and 427.—Badly Sharpened Scrapers.

which the sheets are laid to cover them with glass, a hot plate for firing the sheets, a drying room, a cutting machine, and a press for packing and tying up. A ream or two of paper is placed on the table, and the top sheet is coated with glue by means of a brush resembling a boot-brush, but with longer hair. The sheet is lifted by two corners and laid on the bench, glue side uppermost; the bench has a border standing up some 7 in. or 8 in. high on three sides, with a narrow fillet in front. Powdered glass is simply thrown or scraped over the sheet, which then is raised from one side so that the superfluous glass runs off on to the

Fig. 428.—Special Steel Scraper.

bench and is used again. The sheet is then placed on the hot plate, a hollow, flat iron bench heated with steam; this causes the glue to boil up and thus securely fix the particles of glass on the paper. All this is done much more quickly than it can be described. After drying, the sheets are cut up and arranged in quires and reams

Fig. 429.—Special Steel Scraper.

ready for the market. Glasspaper has entirely replaced the old-fashioned sandpaper; this was made in the same way as glasspaper except that sharp, fine sand instead of glass was used.

How to Use Glasspaper.

For properly using glasspaper a rubber is needed. A piece of mahogany or clean pine, $5\frac{3}{4}$ in. by 3 in. by 1 in., shaped as in Fig. 430, answers well if a piece of sheet cork is glued on the face as shown. Fold a piece of glasspaper, 6 in. wide and about 10 in. long, into three, place it glass side

downwards, and put the face of the rubber on the middle division. Grasp the rubber so that the ends of the glasspaper are held firmly on its back and sides (see Fig. 431), and work then can be commenced.

Rasps.

The woodworker occasionally uses rasps, and these generally are half-round, though

Fig. 430.—Glasspaper Rubber.

sometimes flat. The wood rasp (Fig. 432) is coarser than the cabinet rasp (Fig. 433). Cabinet and wood rasps range from 4 in. to 14 in. in length, and at 12 in. and less the price is about 1d. per inch. The extra 2 in. in a 14-in. rasp adds nearly 50 per cent. to the price. Files also are used, but principally for keeping saws in order, and those necessary are mentioned on p. 73.

Fig. 431.—Using Glasspaper Rubber.

The Use of Grindstones.

When a plane iron, chisel, or other edge tool has been sharpened on the oilstone a number of times, the edge becomes thick. There is too much metal for the oilstone to remove, so the grindstone has to be employed. The grindstone is not a tool for producing a cutting edge, but one for removing a superfluous thickness of metal, yet in nine cases out of ten tools are ground right up to the edge, and often there is $\frac{1}{16}$ in. of wire edge to be removed by the oilstone, this being entirely waste. The grindstone should never be allowed to work quite up to the cutting edge of the tool unless it is to remove a gap.

SELECTING GRINDSTONES.

The grindstone, as a rule, is neglected except just when it is wanted for use ; conse-

Choose a stone of from 30 in. to 36 in. in diameter and $3\frac{1}{2}$ in. to 4 in. thick, of an even light grey colour, with a rough, gritty surface. Test it with the thumb-nail, and the stone should wear the nail down with a few rubs backwards and forwards and leave straight furrows on the nail; this shows a good free-cutting stone.

Fig. 432.—Half-round Wood Rasp.

quently, it is only with difficulty that tools can be ground on it at all. A good grindstone kept in proper order will save its own cost in twelve months. It should be selected of a light grey colour, even throughout. A dark streak through the centre, or a dark patch on one place, indicates that the stone is much harder at those places than elsewhere; consequently, it will wear away faster at the softer parts, and will never be truly round for long together. It will wear lumpy, and at the dark places the tool that is being ground will glide over easily, and directly afterwards catch hold of the softer stone suddenly, and most likely " dig in." A stone that shows flaws on the sides, such as little smooth places running into it with fine cracks showing away from the ends,

MOUNTING AND CARE OF GRINDSTONES

A grindstone mounted in a dwarf iron stand is shown by Fig. 434 ; this is one of the cheapest forms for the worker's use, but, of course, one mounted on a high iron or wooden stand with treadle, as in Fig. 435 or Fig. 436, is much more convenient. The home-worker who does not care to buy an expensively mounted stone may construct a strong frame on which to mount a grindstone of 4-in. by 3-in. stuff, with the legs well spread out and braced together about 6 in. from the ground. It is sometimes a great advantage when grinding a thick heavy iron or axe to be able to stand higher on one foot. Under the stone should be a box to hold water, in which the stone will

Fig. 433.—Half-round Cabinet Rasp.

should be rejected, as such a stone will not stand frosty weather ; a thick stone, also, is undesirable—one $3\frac{1}{2}$ in. or 4 in. wide on the face being ample—as it will tend to wear hollow, and from that cause always be faulty. A smooth stone with a bluish tint should be avoided, as it will work harder and smoother till it becomes like a glass bottle, and of no use at all for proper work.

be partly immersed. Some prefer a can fixed above to allow the water to drip on the stone. Too much has the disadvantage of splashing on the ground and over the legs and boots of the grinder. Others dislike the box below the stone, as the water always left in the box tends to soften that part of the stone which is immersed in it. This can be avoided by having the box loose and letting the two end pieces run up longer than the sides. Let these pieces be of the same width at the top as the rails in the ends of frame, and with a pair of butt hinges hang one end to the frame. Nail firmly to the other end of the box a leather strap, and punch half a dozen holes in it about 1 in. apart, the end with the holes projecting

Fig. 434.—Grindstone in Dwarf Iron Stand.

above the box, and screw a stout 2-in. screw centrally into the other end rail. By this means the box with the water can be raised whilst grinding, and, when finished with, it can be dropped down a couple of holes so as to clear the stone. Thus all the advantages of a box, without its drawbacks, can be secured. It can also be easily dropped right down to the ground for cleaning out, or in the event of any small tool falling into the box, as sometimes happens. Always grind wide tools near the edges, which will help to keep the stone slightly rounding on the face.

TRUEING GRINDSTONE.

When a stone gets worn out of the circle, say ½ in. to ¾ in., it should be trued up again, and this is best done when the stone is dry. To do this, get two old flat files, or two short pieces of flat bar iron and a piece of stout hoop iron about 18 in. long; firmly cramp the hoop iron between the other pieces, allowing the end to project about ¼ in., and with this turn the stone away. It is surprising how it will cut, and by turning the iron over occasionally a good cutting edge can be kept upon it. The expenditure of a few minutes occasionally will keep a stone in perfect order and make its

use a pleasure instead of a trouble. Another method, probably not so good, is to true a stone with a simple piece of hard steel, such as a worn-out file, this being held so that as the stone turns it scrapes against the parts that project further than the general surface. The file must be held resting close to the scraping end rigidly against a firm part of the framing of the grindstone stand. The tool is thus made to turn down the unevenness. The point to be attended to is to hold the tool quite firmly without any motion to and from the centre of the stone corresponding with its

Fig. 435.—Treadle Grindstone on Iron Stand.

rotation. The stone will yield to the steel more readily if well soaked in water before being treated.

SPEED OF GRINDSTONES.

There appears to be great differences in the speeds at which grindstones are run, but in England the speed of the face may be taken at from 800 ft. to 1,000 ft. per minute. Taking the higher of these values, the speed of a stone 1 ft. in diameter will be $\dfrac{1,000 \times 7}{22} = 318$ revolutions per minute.

The speed of a grindstone is calculated by the number of feet per minute which the periphery travels. To find the rate of speed at the periphery, multiply the diameter in inches by 3·1416 and divide by 12,

Fig. 436.—Treadle Grindstone on Wooden Stand.

then multiply by the number of revolutions, the product being the number of feet per minute which the stone is travelling. Example: A stone 24 in. in diameter, making 159 revolutions per minute, has a speed of 999 ft. (roughly 1,000 ft.) per minute $\left(\dfrac{24 \times 3·1416}{12} \times 159 = 999\right)$

The makers of Ohio and Huron grindstones state that the former should run at about 2,500 ft. per minute, and the latter somewhat higher.

CHARNLEY FOREST AND TURKEY OILSTONES.

The oilstones in most general use are four in number—the Charnley Forest, Turkey, Washita, and Arkansas. The Charnley Forest oilstone is an old-fashioned English variety, and a good one will last a lifetime. This stone is of a greenish-slate colour, sometimes with small red or brown spots. The lighter the colour of the stone, the more serviceable it will be. The softest and most even-grained stone should be selected, hardness being the most general defect. Stones of this variety may be good for some time, but if neglected, or if linseed oil is used, the stone will absorb the oil and become very hard, rendering a lot of rubbing necessary to sharpen a tool. A Charnley Forest oilstone may take a little more rubbing than other stones to get an edge, but it will be keen and fine, and as the stone wears slowly it seldom requires rubbing down. When two oilstones are used, a Charnley Forest stone is about the best for finishing the edge after it has been rubbed on a coarse cutting stone. The experience of many years suggests that the best stone a woodworker can select is a Charnley Forest stone, the edge produced by it enabling the woodworker to do the best work and more of it before the tool requires resharpening. Turkey stone is generally known as white, grey, and black, but its appearance is generally more or less of a mixture of brown and blue shades. It is of very close grain. Some Turkey oilstones are of a dark slate colour when oiled, with white veining and sometimes white spots. They give a keen, fine edge to tools, but wear very unevenly. In addition to this defect, they are the most brittle oilstones, great care being necessary to prevent a breakage when fitting them into a case, and a fall from the bench will generally result in cracking the stone, even after being boxed. The Turkey oilstone is a notoriously slow cutting stone; to most woodworkers its price is prohibitive.

AMERICAN OILSTONES.

The cheapest oilstone in the market at first cost is the Nova Scotia or Canada stone, which is brownish yellow in colour, and wears away rather quickly. They vary considerably in quality ; one may cut like a grindstone and leave about as good an edge, whilst another may be very hard, requiring a lot of rubbing to sharpen a tool. One between the two extremes should be chosen if possible. The Washita (Ouachita) stone is yellowish-grey in colour, and though it wears away quickly it does so much more regularly than Turkey stone. Some kinds are of a whitish-grey or light buff colour when oiled. The same remarks apply to these as to the Canada stones, but they are usually finer in grain and more even in texture, and for this reason are general favourites. These stones sharpen the tools quickly, but do not leave so good an edge as is obtained with the Charnley Forest stones, and they wear away more quickly. The edge produced by a Washita stone is generally of a " wire edge " description, and rapidly becomes dull. These and other soft stones soon get full of grooves and furrows if much used for sharpening narrow tools, small chisels, or other pointed instruments, for which a hard stone should be employed. Arkansas oilstone is a compact white stone something like Washita stone, but finer in grain. It wears well and cuts slowly, being largely used for finishing the fine edges of surgical instruments. Workers generally consider them to be the best oilstones in the market, but, unfortunately, they are very expensive.

SELECTING OILSTONES.

The choice of a suitable oilstone is one of the greatest difficulties that present themselves to the woodworker when selecting his tools. The degree of hardness is important, oilstones having a tendency to become harder after being in use for a time. Many of the American oilstones are manufactured from fine grit, cemented together. Generally they are even in grain,

but are often too coarse, and although they sharpen the tool quickly enough, the cutting edge is not sufficiently keen for woodworking, and should be finished on a stone of finer texture. Natural stones are often uneven in grain, but, with care in selection, they can be obtained far better and more lasting than artificial stones. If a natural stone is wetted, the grain will show up clearly, and if it is uneven, or if there are fossils embedded in the stone,

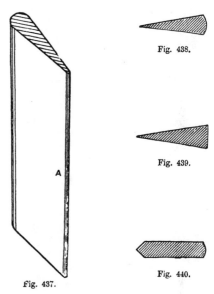

Fig. 438.

Fig. 439.

A

Fig. 440.

Fig. 437.

Figs. 437 to 440.—Oilstone Slips.

unequal wear will be the result, and it will be necessary to rub it down frequently. The colour also forms a guide to a slight extent ; if this is variable, the wear will probably be variable. In choosing an oilstone from a number of the same variety, the cutting properties can be judged by rubbing the surface with the thumb nail, but this is only a comparative test, as a rougher surface will always be found on new or freshly rubbed down stone than on one that has been in use for sharpening tools for some time. For this reason, sharpening a tool on a new stone is not a true test of its cutting properties. If a tool-dealer's catalogue is examined, several varieties of oilstone will be found enumerated in it, the prices of which may be anything from 6d. to 15s. In purchasing an ordinary tool, paying a good price generally procures a good article; but this is not so with oilstones, as bad ones are often to be found among high-priced articles.

SIZES AND SHAPES OF OILSTONES.

The usual dimensions of an oilstone, excepting the slips (or small stones for

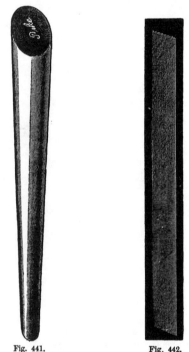

Fig. 441.   Fig. 442.

Figs. 441 and 442.—Oilstone Slips.

sharpening gouges, bead irons, etc.) are: length, about 8 in.; width, 2 in.; and thickness, 1 in. A wide stone should never be selected owing to the difficulty of making it wear evenly, and to the care required to keep the plane irons sharpened on it to the shape necessary to produce the best results. The most convenient width is 1½ in. A stone may be used by making the thickness side the working face; the tool should be moved across the stone from right to left and not always sharpened in the

same place. A small oilstone about 4 in. by 1¼ in. is useful for sharpening spokeshaves, and pieces of stone or slips of various sizes and shapes are required for gouges, beads, etc. These often have to be rubbed to a particular shape (by one of the methods to be described) to sharpen a tool for some special purpose. A slip as shown by Fig. 437 is used for sharpening router cutters, etc. It will soon wear out of shape, especially the part A, but the shape may be restored by rubbing the stone on a piece of sharp gritstone, using silver sand and water, though a grindstone, if handy, will be preferable. It will be found better for some purposes to use the side of the grindstone, if it be in good condition, rather than the edge. Here also water and a little fine sand will be found an advantage. For sharpening bead irons and gouges this conveniently shaped slip can be purchased at most tool shops; its suitability is apparent. Sections of commonly used oilstone slips are shown by Figs. 438 to 442.

CASING OR BOXING OILSTONES.

Oilstones may be purchased fitted in a case. To make the case obtain a piece of even-grained timber, fairly hard and tough, free from shakes, about 1½ in. longer, 1 in. wider, than the stone selected, and of about the same thickness. The wood should not absorb oil or break away at the ends. The most uneven side of the stone is placed centrally on the wood that forms the bottom of the case, and is marked round with a scriber. A centre-bit is then used to bore out as much as possible of the wood inside the line, the remainder being cut out with a mortise chisel, and boxed down with a router or old woman's tooth, finally cleaning out to about three-quarters of the depth of the stone. Another piece of wood slightly thinner is then boxed out in a similar manner to form the lid of the case. The bottom of the case should be eased round the edges with the chisel to enable the stone to drop in without pressure, which will leave sufficient space for the cement used to hold the stone in its place. A mixture of white- and red-lead is generally used for this purpose, but should be obtained in a powdered state and mixed with gold-size. If the ordinary tub lead is 'used, the stone will absorb the linseed oil and will be hardened. Another cement may be made by melting glue and mixing powdered red-lead with it to form a thick paste. This is put into the case whilst hot and the stone pressed into it, the surplus cement being forced up round the edges and cleaned off before setting. After the stone is firmly fixed with the cement, the lid may be fitted on and the case cleaned off true and square, when the plainness may be relieved by chamfering or moulding the top. A bead should be placed round the bottom edge of the lid to break the joint. By placing a block of wood at each end of the stone, a much longer stroke can be taken in sharpening, and the stone tends to wear much more evenly. It also prevents the chipping of the tool should it happen to slip over the ends of the stone while sharpening. It may be better to hinge the cover of the case, and secure it by means of a small brass hook and eye as illustrated in Fig. 443, or the cover may be similarly hinged and secured at the sides. The stone can then be picked up without the cover dropping off. It also prevents injury to the stone by the cover accidentally coming off either on the bench or in the tool basket or box. Figs. 444 and 445 show methods of finishing an oilstone case, and Fig. 446 is a section of a case with a less elaborate moulding. To give the stone a better bearing on the bench when a tool is being sharpened, the bottom of the case between the ends is cut away as shown in Figs. 443 to 445. In addition to this generally a couple of nails or steel points are driven in at one end and filed off to a point, leaving about $\frac{1}{8}$ in. below the bottom of the case (see A, Fig. 447). This gives the case a firm grip on the bench, but scratches it. A better plan is shown in section by Fig. 448. In this two small cylinders of india-rubber are glued into two centre-bit holes of about $\frac{1}{4}$ in. or $\frac{3}{8}$ in. diameter bored at one end of the case, one on each side. The pieces of rubber are cut to size with a knife previously dipped in water, but are

made about $\frac{1}{32}$ in. longer than the hole is deep, so as to project below the surface. They may be cemented in with thick knotting or shellac varnish. The friction of the rubber will effectually prevent the stone from slipping about when a tool is being sharpened, and the rubbers do not injure any surface upon which the case may

Fig. 443.—Oilstone in Plain Case.

be placed. An oilstone case should be well French polished, the polish being tinted with a little dragon's blood or other stain if preferred. It is much easier to keep the case clean if polished than when oiled.

OIL FOR USE WITH OILSTONES.

Oil is used not only for assisting the stone to produce a keen cutting edge, but as a lubricator to prevent the stone heating the tool, and to prevent the entrance into the stone of the metal particles rubbed off the edge of the tool whilst sharpening. The oil should not gum up or harden if left, or it will cause the stone to glaze. Either neat's-foot oil or sperm commonly is considered best for oilstone use, all others hardening the surface much more quickly. Good for the purpose is lard oil to which sufficient petroleum has been added to prevent it becoming thick in the can in cold weather. Sweet oil or vaseline thinned with petroleum makes a good sharpening oil, in fact, any oil of animal extraction mixed with mineral oil may be

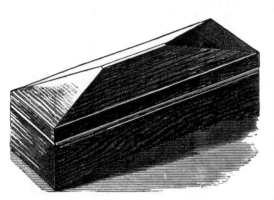

Fig. 444.—Oilstone Case.

used, but vegetable oils that are obtained from seeds and nuts and are used for making paint should be avoided. Sweet oil with the addition of about one-eighth of paraffin is used largely for quick-cutting stones. Petroleum, paraffin, etc., however, are not advised, the oil hardening the stone and destroying its cutting properties; where it is used for thinning oil no more than is necessary for the purpose should be added; however, if the stone becomes dirty or gummed up, a very small quantity of paraffin or turps may be used for cleansing purposes, but it should be wiped off as soon as possible. The oil may be kept for use in a small oil-can (Fig. 449). Soap has been recommended for the same purpose. The stone is wetted and rubbed with soap, and more water is applied until a lather forms. This dries, and when the stone is required for use it is merely necessary to wet it slightly.

Wiping Oilstone.

When a tool has been sharpened, the oilstone should be wiped and the cover put on or the lid closed to keep away the dust of the workshop, which is often charged

with particles of grit from glasspaper; if grit or other sharp particles lodge on the stone they will leave gaps in the next tool that is sharpened. An essential point is to preserve the original sharpness of the stone. A clean rag or cotton waste is preferable for wiping it after sharpening a tool, as shavings generally leave it dirty.

Oilstone Becoming Hard.

When an oilstone has been in use for some time its surface is apt to become hard, especially if certain oils—paraffin in particular—are used on it. The reason is that the pores of the stone are closed by the viscid or gummy oil, which contains particles of steel rubbed off in sharpening; when the stone is in this condition it is not touched by the tool, which rides upon a substance as hard as itself; therefore the stone fails to cut the tool. A mixture of oil and turpentine is often applied to hard stones to clean them and make them cut; for this purpose, also, they are sometimes boiled in soda water. Hard oilstones may be made to cut and give

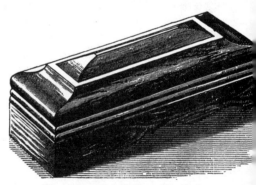

Fig. 445.—Oilstone Case, Moulded.

edges to tools by sprinkling a very little flour emery on them after the oil has been applied, but in this case it is the emery and not the stone that cuts.

Levelling and Rubbing Down Oilstones.

When an oilstone becomes uneven with wear it is necessary to level it. This may be done by glueing or tacking a sheet of glasspaper on a level board and rubbing the stone on the glasspaper. If the stone is of a very hard nature, emery cloth may be used. If the cloth is tacked down it can be taken up frequently and well

Fig. 446.—Section of Cased Oilstone.

shaken or beaten on the back to get rid of the oilstone dust, and so doing lengthens the life of the emery cloth. Another method is to use fine sand and water sprinkled on a level iron plate or sheet of glass, emery powder being used instead of the sand for hard stones. The face of the stone is rubbed on the metal or glass, the grit and water being replenished as required. This leaves a smooth and even surface. Some workmen level the stone with an old file, or hold it on the side of a revolving grindstone. The

Fig. 447.—Section of Oilstone Case showing Points.

" strickle " method, described below, has just the same effect as emery cloth has, with, however, more trouble. Some workers will use no other method, however. An emery strickle is used by carding engine minders in cotton and woollen mills, from whom they can be obtained. For the benefit of those who cannot get an old strickle, make a substitute as follows :

To (say) one gill of hot glue add about a dessert spoonful of ordinary glycerine, stirring well, and keep the mixture hot. Get a pine board 1 in. thick, from 4 in. to 6 in. wide, and any length up to about

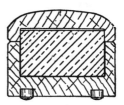

Fig. 448.—Section of Oilstone Case showing Rubbers.

2 ft., and having planed one surface true, and bored a $\frac{1}{2}$-in. or $\frac{5}{8}$-in. hole to hang it up by, lay it face upward upon a large sheet of paper. Coat the board with the hot glue, rubbing it in well and evenly with the brush, and at once cover quickly with a thick layer of coarse emery ; pat this down all over with the flat of the hand ; raise the board, shake off the superfluous emery, and give the board a smart rap or two on the bench or table top. Then put aside in a warm, dry place for twelve hours, and repeat the glueing, and

Fig. 449.—Bench Oilcan.

covering with emery on the top of the first coat. Rap off all the loose emery, and again put aside to dry. Finally, give the surface a thin coat of boiled oil (with or without the addition of a little black paint), taking care that the interstices between the emery grains are well filled. It will be dry in two or three days, and then will be found to be a most effective appliance for keeping oilstones level.

CUTTING AND MENDING OILSTONES.

Sometimes it is required to cut an oilstone into pieces, and this may be done by rubbing across it the edge of a sheet of soft iron or mild steel, using sand and water as required. Or instead, a piece of hoop iron (such as that used on casks) may be used with emery, either wet or dry, as the cutting agent; cutting is quicker when the emery is dry. Another method is to insert a piece of an old hand-saw into a wooden block and to rub the stone on this, the teeth being, of course, set uppermost. An uncased oilstone, if brittle, is easily broken by a sharp jar or fall, and the two pieces will be of but little use until mounted. Get a piece of well-seasoned mahogany for a case, and mortise it out so that both portions of the oilstone can be fitted in fairly tight. Then, with one of the cements previously described, bed both portions of the stone in the case, taking care to keep close the broken joint of the stone. Let the stone stand for a time to allow the cement to become set, after which the surface should be rubbed down with silver sand and water on a flat stone. If the stone is used with care the fracture will scarcely be detrimental.

EMERY OILSTONES.

Emery oilstones have been made for the last twenty-five years, but until quite lately they were too poor in quality to come into general use. The Whelden emery oilstone is manufactured from Turkish emery, one face being of fine and the other of medium coarse material. The coarser side is very fast cutting, and on it a 2-in. plane iron about $\frac{1}{32}$-in. thick at the edge has been sharpened to a fine cutting edge in three minutes, as against seventeen minutes on a good Washita stone and thirty-six minutes on an Arkansas stone. The coarse side leaves the tool in about the same condition as a good Washita stone, and the fine side in about the same condition as a fine Turkey or soft Arkansas, better than a Washita, but not so

fine as a good hard Arkansas. The emery oilstone has the advantage over any natural stone that it is quite uniform in texture, there being no hard or soft spots, cracks or fissures. They are not brittle, and can be dropped a reasonable distance without breaking. The stock size is the No. 10, which is 8 in. long, 2 in. wide, and 1 in. thick, but the makers advise the use of Nos. 12 and 15, the former being 8 in. long, $1\frac{3}{8}$ in. wide, and $1\frac{3}{8}$ in. thick, and the latter 2 in. wide and otherwise the same as No. 12. The lubricant used with these stones is water or paraffin, and therefore iron cases are preferable to wooden ones. All the usual shapes of slips, etc., are made in this emery stone.

OILSTONE SUBSTITUTES.

A very good substitute for an oilstone

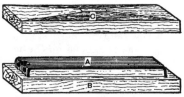

Fig. 450.—Oilstone Substitute.

is to be made very cheaply with zinc and emery. Get a piece of zinc about 8 in. by $2\frac{1}{2}$ in., and tack it at the corners to a flat piece of wood; then use a little flour emery and oil, and rub the tool on it as usual. Fig. 450 shows a cheap and efficient form of carpenter's hone, which is an excellent substitute for the oilstone. It consists of a strip of sheet zinc A, stretched over the wooden mount B, and screwed down at each end lengthways of the grain. To use the sharpener thus made it is necessary to sprinkle a little flour emery on the zinc, and moisten in the usual way with oil. For general purposes it will be found very handy, and will do the same work as the oilstone does in less time, but it will not leave the edge in quite such a finished condition as does a good oilstone. C, Fig. 450, shows a cover for the stone.

NAILS, SCREWS, AND GLUE.

NAILS.

A NAIL is a pin or slender piece of metal used for driving through or into wood or other material to hold separate pieces together; or part of the nail is left projecting so that things may be hung on it. It may be of iron, steel, etc., and may be wrought, cast, or cut; or it may be of wire. In former practice, nails were said to be 6-lb., 8-lb., etc., according as 1,000 of the variety weighed 6 lb., 8 lb., etc.; hence such now meaningless terms as sixpenny, eightpenny, and tenpenny nails, in which "penny" is a corruption of "pound." Nails consist of two parts, the head and the shank; and although they are mostly made of iron and steel, large numbers are also made of copper, zinc, etc. The varieties of nails number about 300, but the carpenter and joiner does not use many of these. Briefly the action of a nail is as follows. It is wedge-shaped so as to break through the fibres of the wood, and there it is held tightly by the elastic fibres, which endeavour to regain their original position, and so press tightly on the nail. The flattened out tops of nails known as the heads assist greatly in holding the nails in position, especially if there is any pulling strain at the opposite ends.

WHY A NAIL HOLDS.

A very simple experiment, to be made by anyone with a hammer and a few nails, will throw much light on the reason why a nail holds woodwork together. Take a piece of straight-grained deal, about 2 in. wide and 1 in. thick, and mark a line along the centre of one of the narrow sides; drive in various nails in a row, about 1 in. apart, and then split the piece down the middle line so as to expose the nails throughout their length. The smooth wire nails called French nails will be found to have penetrated the wood with very little disturbance of the surrounding fibres, and, as a consequence, they go in easily, and will draw out again with great facility. What hold they have is chiefly by friction from the compressed fibres reacting against the sides of the nails. On the other hand, a 3-in. floor brad, which has a flat square point, produces great disturbance in the fibres. Immediately under the point the fibres are crushed and pushed downwards, carrying others partly down with them so that they press against the sides, and at the same time point downwards. It will be observed that every little group of fibres is like a strut pushing against the nail, and preventing its withdrawal. This experiment may be varied indefinitely; and the effect of boring holes before driving the nails can be studied. The difference also between the holes produced by a gimlet, a sharp bradawl, and a blunt bradawl will be instructive.

HOLDING POWERS OF NAILS.

The holding powers of nails, of course, vary with the shape of the nails and the kind of wood into which they are driven. The following statements have been made as the result of tests carried out at Sibley College, Cornell University:—Cut nails are superior to wire nails in all positions, and if pointed they would be 30 per cent. more efficient in direct tension. The advantage of a wire nail is the sharp point; without a point it would have but one-half its ordinary holding power. The surface of the nail should be slightly rough, but not barbed; barbing decreases the efficiency of cut nails by about 32 per cent. Nails should be wedge-shaped in both directions when there are no special dangers of splitting. The length of nails to be used in tension should be about three times the thickness of the thinnest piece nailed. Nails usually hold about 50 per cent. more when driven perpendicularly to the grain than when parallel to it. When subjected to shock, nails have been found to hold less than one-twelfth the dead load they will stand when weight is applied gradually. Professor Soule has proved that, under all ordinary conditions, cut nails hold better than wire nails. Holding effect increases with the length of a nail, but not in proportions expressible by any simple formula. When a cut nail is properly pointed, its hold is increased by 33 per cent. Nails driven into certain woods, Californian redwood for example, will take a better hold the longer they are left in; the reverse happens with other woods, Douglas pine for instance. Deals, when nailed to a block, show about equal holding powers for equal areas of nail, whether a few thick nails or a greater number of thin nails are employed; the advantage is slightly in favour of the thick nails. Haupt, in his "Military Bridges," gives a table showing the holding power of wrought iron nails weighing 77 to the lb., and having a length of about 3 in. The nails were driven through a 1-in. board into a block from which it was dragged in a direction perpendicular to length of nails. Taking a pine plank nailed to a pine block, with eight nails to the square foot, the average breaking weight per nail was found to be 380 lb.; in oak the power was 415 lb.; with twelve nails per square foot the holding power was 542·5 lb.; and with six nails in pine 463·5 lb. The highest result was obtained for twelve nails per square foot in pine, the breaking weight being 612 lb. per nail. The average strength decreased with the increase of surface. In Bevan's experiments the force in pounds required to extract "threepenny" brads from dry Christiania deal, at right angles to grain of wood, was found to be 58 lb.; the force required to draw a wrought-iron "sixpenny" nail was 187 lb., the length forced into the wood being 1 in. The relative adhesion, when the nail is driven transversely and longitudinally, is in deal about 2 to 1.

To extract a common "sixpenny" nail from a depth of 1 in., in dry beech, across grain, required 167 lb.; in dry Christiania deal, across grain, 187 lb., and with grain 87 lb.; in elm the required force was 327 lb. across grain, and 257 lb. with grain; and in oak 507 lb. across grain. From Lieutenant Fraser's experiments, it would appear that the holding power of spike nails in fir is 460 lb. to 730 lb. per inch in length; while the adhesive power of "wood screws" 2 in. long and 22·1 diameter, at exterior of threads, 12 to the inch, driven into ½-in. board, was 790 lb. in hard wood, and about half that amount in soft wood.

Cut Clasp Nails.

Of the various kinds of nails commonly used in wood-working, the cut clasp (Fig. 451), machine-made from a sheet of iron, must rank first. These nails, if of a good brand, may be used for almost any purpose; being cut clean by the machine, they are not liable to split the work. The

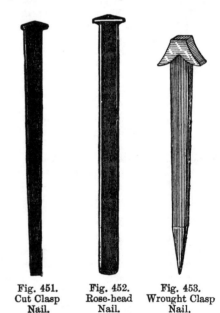

Fig. 451. Cut Clasp Nail.   Fig. 452. Rose-head Nail.   Fig. 453. Wrought Clasp Nail.

head is not very large, and when the nail has been inserted, should be punched just below the surface of the wood. Cut clasp nails are typical of many old-fashioned nails, which are, however, gradually being displaced by the newer serrated steel brads. A good nail of the same class is made from steel, very tough, and therefore

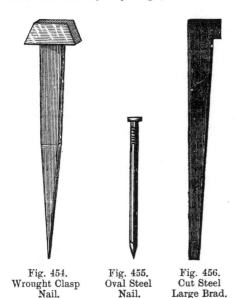

Fig. 454.
Wrought Clasp
Nail.

Fig. 455.
Oval Steel
Nail.

Fig. 456.
Cut Steel
Large Brad.

useful for many purposes, the increase in cost being very small. Cut clasp nails may be had of almost any size, from ¾ in. to 6 in. in length.

ROSE-HEAD NAILS.

The nails (Fig. 452) have a shank parallel in width, but tapered to a chisel point in thickness. They are made of tough wrought iron, being used principally for such work as field gates and fencing, where a strong nail is desirable. The usual sizes are 1¼ in., 1½ in., 2 in., 2½ in., and 3 in.

WROUGHT CLASP NAILS.

These nails are of wrought iron, and their shape is similar to that of the cut clasp, but the wrought nails are sharper pointed (Figs. 453 and 454). They are used principally in the construction of common ledged doors, as they will readily clinch. They are very strong, and the shape of the head gives it a better hold than that of the cut clasp nail. Owing to the fibrous nature of the metal of which it is made it

is much used where its projecting point is to be clinched on the reverse side of the piece of work.

OVAL STEEL NAILS.

The oval steel nail is shown by Fig. 455; it is nicely made, very tough, and less than any other kind splits the material into which it is driven. Near the head are slight shallow grooves round it, which greatly increase the holding power of the nail, and the flat head does not project so much as in the cut nails. The sharp points and oval shape of these nails make them very handy. The sizes in which these are made are as follow: ¾ in., 1 in., 1¼ in., 1½ in., 2 in., 2½ in., 3 in., 3½ in., 4 in., 5 in., and 6 in.

BRADS.

Of all nails used by the woodworker, the brad is perhaps the most useful. The cut steel large brad (Fig. 456) is used where there is but little strain, as in flooring for instance; the head projects on one side only. They do not make such large holes as cut nails, and, owing to the very slight bend at the point, they tend to draw gradually from an upright to a sloping position

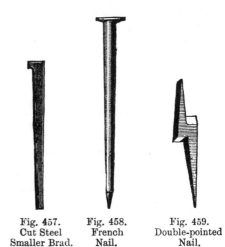

Fig. 457.
Cut Steel
Smaller Brad.

Fig. 458.
French
Nail.

Fig. 459.
Double-pointed
Nail.

as they are driven in. The holes for these nails should therefore be bored in a slightly inclined direction to counteract this erratic tendency. The cut steel small brad is of much the same shape (see Fig. 457), the ordinary sizes of this being ½ in. and upwards, the cut steel large brad ranging from 2 in. upwards.

FRENCH NAILS.

French nails (Fig. 458) are of round wire, pointed, either quite cylindrical or slightly tapered, the head being proportionately large and round and flat. They lie flat on the face of the wood, and do not need to be punched in. These nails are strong and tenacious, but their unsightly heads cause their use to be confined to rough work.

Fig. 460.—Driving in a Nail.

DOUBLE-POINTED NAIL.

A secret nail for dowelling and other purposes in wood-working is shown by Fig. 459; this is useful for jointing pieces of wood together edge to edge, for which purpose the ordinary wooden dowelling peg generally, or, more frequently, a French nail or wire nail with the head taken off and a rough point made with a file, is used; wire pins thus formed will, when used at intervals along a joint, hold pieces of wood together very well, and there will be considerable difficulty in forcing two pieces apart when thus connected. The double-pointed nail can be used in cabinet work and joinery, for closely and firmly jointing floor boards and parquetry work, in putting together shelving and pieces of wood

of narrow width to form the sides of boxes. For small work the nails are cut in four useful sizes—namely, ¾ in., 1 in., 1¼ in., and 1¾ in. The nail has a projection or hammer-head as shown, by which it can be driven home into one of the pieces to be jointed, the chisel edge or point readily penetrating the material; the piece to be attached is placed against the point projecting from the wood into which the lower half of the nail has been driven and blocked down. When used in connecting hard wood, holes for the points should first be made with a bradawl.

DRIVING IN NAILS.

It is surprising, considering the importance of the subject, how little is known generally of the art of nail-driving. Very many really creditable pieces of carpentry or joinery are ruined completely by the unskilful driving of the nails used in their construction. This result must follow if the correct method be not adopted. Many things must be considered before the nail is driven home, as will be seen from the following. In starting to insert a nail, it should be held between the thumb and the next two fingers of the left hand, and struck lightly with the hammer (see Fig. 460). In Fig. 461 A represents the side of a box and B one of the ends, to which the side is in the process of being nailed. It must be remembered that the nail is retained in position by cohesion and friction, and therefore it must be considered how to give full effect to these. The nails are being driven in an oblique direction; this is on account of their entering the end grain of the piece B, c d showing that they cut across the grain or fibres, thus rendering them less liable to draw out. Fig. 462 illustrates the manner in which the unskilled worker would probably drive them. A comparison of the nails at c d with the corresponding ones in Fig. 461 will at once show the former to be the better method. Fig. 463 illustrates the angle of a box turned round to show that the nail should be very carefully retained in an upright position with relation to the end, or as a result it will surely find its way out at one side or the other, as in Fig. 464. When driving nails near the end of the stuff.

as just described, a bradawl of suitable size should invariably be used, as this lessens not only the danger of the nail passing out at the side, but also that of splitting the material. Fig. 465 illustrates the manner

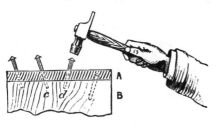

Fig. 461.—Nailing together a Box.

in which the bradawl should be used. It is grasped as seen, and firmly pressed into the wood with a motion of twisting—that is to say, turned first to the right and back again to the left in a succession of short half-turns until deep enough for the purpose. It is often driven with a hammer; but this is more with the object of saving time, and often results in the awl leaving the handle,

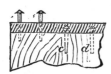

Fig. 462.—Incorrect Nailing.

and is not advocated. If the bradawl be driven into the board as at E (Fig. 465) it must of necessity split the wood; if the awl is driven as at D, it will cut its way without injury into the stuff. The nail is at times

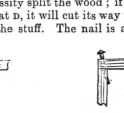

Fig. 463.
Side View of
Correct Nailing.

Fig. 464.
Careless
Nailing.

liable to twist or turn in the grain after starting; this must at once be rectified, or the board will be split. The hammer must be held as near the end of the handle as convenient, especially in driving large nails,

as greater power then is gained. The nail must be struck fairly upon the centre of its head, care being taken that the hammer does not glance off, as such an accident would probably both bend the nail and

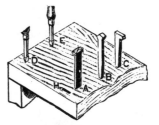

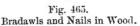

Fig. 465.
Bradawls and Nails in Wood.

Fig. 466.
Clinched Nails.

damage the work. All nails are more or less of a wedge form; as a consequence, nails of the clasp shape should be driven as B, C (Fig. 465), the width or side of nail being parallel to the grain of wood; but those that are chisel-pointed must be driven as at A (Fig. 465), that is, across the grain.

Fig. 467.
Square Nail Set
or Punch.

Fig. 468.
Round Nail Set
or Punch.

If A be driven in the manner shown at H, the wedge shape of the nail will split the board. Fig. 466 shows two pieces of wood nailed together, the nails being clinched at the back, as in making a ledged door. Of course, wrought nails must be used, A being a rose-head and B a clasp nail. As these nails are usually punched below the surface on both sides of the work, the clasp should be used where convenient, as a smaller hole is made at the back. For punching the nail head below the surface of the work, the steel set is used; a square set or "punch" is shown by Fig. 467, and a round one by Fig.

Fig. 469.—Using Nail Set or Punch.

468. The method of holding the set is made clear by Fig. 469.

WITHDRAWING NAILS.

Should the nail, in spite of all care, split the stuff or turn out at the side, it should be carefully withdrawn before the head has been driven too low, or withdrawal becomes difficult. To draw the nail, its head is carefully and tightly grasped with the pincers, as in Fig. 470, and the ends of the handle are then pressed down towards the face of the work; few nails can resist the force of this leverage. Should the nail be of the cut variety, care must be exercised, or it may break off. A piece of wood should be laid under the pincers as shown, or they may bruise the work.

SECRET NAILING.

Sometimes, after a piece of work is finished, some of the joints will spring, and it

will be necessary to secure them from the surface with nails. In a general way, the heads of these are punched in, and the holes stopped with beeswax and shellac coloured to match the wood; or, in the case of painted wood, putty would be used as a filling. The stopping may be carefully put in and cleaned off, but it can always be detected if the work is closely examined. The method of nailing shown in Fig. 471 has the advantage of perfectly concealing the nail head. An outside mitred corner is shown for the purpose of illustrating the method of nailing. A chip is raised by means of a narrow chisel or gouge, a hole bored underneath the chip, and the brad driven and punched in. The chip is then glued down over the head of the brad, and, when dry, is cleaned off. It will be readily seen that, as the chip is of the same colour and grain as the piece from which it was raised, the hole will not be visible. This method of nailing would apply equally well to a planted bead or moulding, or to any other purpose that may be required.

CLEANING RUSTY NAILS AND SCREWS.

The best way of brightening a quantity of nails that are very rusty is to dip the

Fig. 470.—Withdrawing Nail with Pincers.

nails in oil and put them in a bag with emery powder; by rapid friction some of the rust may be removed. Such articles should be kept in a dry place, when they would not rust. A tumbling drum often is used for cleaning rusty nails, etc. The apparatus consists of a barrel, with a door in it, which runs eccentrically on a spindle, the spindle being driven either by hand or steam. Into the drum are placed river sand, moistened with dilute sulphuric acid, and then the articles to be cleaned. When the drum is revolved the articles are continuously shifted, so that every part is polished. Screws that are too small for separate treatment may be cleaned as follows: Take, say, one pound of screws, and place them in a small box, such as a cigar box. Put a small quantity of oil on them and shake for a minute; then put a piece of cotton waste in the box, and repeat for a minute; finally put a handful of sawdust in the box and shake for another minute or so, and remove the sawdust by sifting it from the screws in a fine sieve. This treatment will be found effective. Larger quantities are apt to be ruined by being shaken together, the sharp corners, threads, and points rapidly disappearing.

History of Wood Screws.

The screw nail used for uniting woodwork is known as the "wood screw." This combines several of the most important principles of science and mechanics. As a mechanical power its basis is the inclined plane. Previous to the opening of the nineteenth century, iron, brass, and steel screws were but rarely used. During 1813, Penniman, in America, perfected machinery

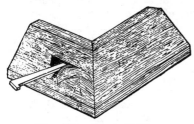

Fig. 471.—Secret Nailing.

for drawing wire suitable for screws of all kinds. During 1817, Dow and Treadwell, of Boston, made other improvements; their machine drew the wire from the reel, cut it

to the length required for each screw, headed the screw, cut the thread, and polished the screw. Meanwhile English manufacturers were also making improvements in the quality and finish of screws for woodwork, until these screws obtained, on both sides of the Atlantic, the commercial name of "wood screws," to distinguish them from those used to put together and operate machinery. But the wood screw had one

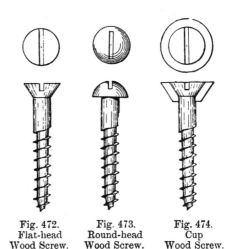

Fig. 472.
Flat-head
Wood Screw.

Fig. 473.
Round-head
Wood Screw.

Fig. 474.
Cup
Wood Screw.

obvious defect. The worker was compelled to use a bradawl, gimlet, brace and bits, or some similar implement to make a fairly large hole to give the screw an entrance, and this operation occupied so much time that many workmen chose well-finished nails in preference to screws. During 1841, however, Thomas J. Sloan invented the now familiar "gimlet point" wood screw, which, under the pressure of a good screwdriver in a workman's hand, entered any kind of wood as readily and with no more danger of splitting the wood than the entrance of a carefully handled bit or gimlet. From that time screws replaced wrought and annealed nails in all fixing where the hammer could not conveniently be used, or where jarring was to be avoided. It was soon demonstrated that the wood screw possessed ten times the compression and attractive strength of ordinary nails, especially in all pine and other soft and open grain woods.

The screw was found to be convenient for use in putting work together which was soon to be taken down, because its removal did not injure anything.

SHAPES OF WOOD SCREWS.

Screws, which, like nails, consist of two parts—head and shank—are made in almost endless variety, but the three following examples are sufficient for the present purpose. Fig. 472 is the most common, being made from iron, steel, or brass, according to the purpose for which it is to be used. Fig. 473 shows a round-headed screw.

Fig. 475.—Wood Bored ready for Screw.

These are usually japanned, being used principally in fixing bolts, locks, etc. Fig. 474 is a variety known as a cup screw, because it has a cup into which the head of the screw fits; this cup is let into the work flush with the surface, the screw being turned down through it. It will be noticed that the thread extends for only about two-thirds the length of the screw, this being all that is really requisite. Further threading would only weaken the lateral strength of the screw. The sizes in which wood screws are made are almost endless, but usually they range from $\frac{1}{4}$ in. to 6 in.

DRIVING IN SCREWS.

For starting the screw, a hole should be bored through the top piece sufficiently large to allow the screw to pass freely, as A (Fig. 475). This may be done with a gimlet, the top of the hole being enlarged with a gouge to receive the head of the screw, so that it may be a trifle below the surface. This is shown at B B (Fig. 475). The two pieces of wood should now be placed together, and a bradawl inserted in the bottom piece (as G), to help the screw in its course. Drive home the screw as follows: Take the screwdriver in the right hand, and guide its end into the cut on the head of the screw with the left hand. The handle should now be turned from left to right (or " clockwise "),

using both hands in the process, until the screw is driven as tightly down as possible. The method of holding the screwdriver is shown by Fig. 476, this, however, not showing the left hand, though this invariably must be employed. The practice of putting screws in the mouth just before using them is bad ; it causes the screws to rust and to be difficult to withdraw. Before inserting screws in woodwork, dip their points in grease. This assists both insertion and withdrawal, and keeps the screws free from rust. A small box to hold grease is a useful adjunct of the bench.

WITHDRAWING DIFFICULT SCREWS.

For one particular job, at any rate, the long screwdriver is more powerful than the short one, and that is the starting of stiff screws. Let D (Fig. 477) represent the screw, and D E the centre line of screw produced. Take a screwdriver, say of half the length of D E, and, for the sake of simplification, ignore the width of handle, and let the driver be represented by F. The leverage of the driver in starting the screw will depend upon the amount it may be safely canted from the vertical line. In Fig. 477 this is represented by F C. Now, the amount of safe canting will be the same for a long or short driver if the points are similar ; so a driver of twice the length of F is taken and represented by P. It will be seen at a glance that the leverage is now twice that of F ; for whereas in the first instance it is represented by F C, it is now represented by P E. So the greater power, whenever present, of a long driver depends on the canting of the tool from the screw centre line. Often an old screw is in so tight that it cannot be loosened by the screwdriver. The best plan then is to get a piece of bar iron, flat at the end, make it red hot, and place it on the head of the rusty screw ; remove the iron in two or three minutes, and then the screw can be drawn with the screwdriver as if it had only been recently inserted. The expansion of the screw by the heat breaks the rust contact previously existing between it and the wood. If these methods fail, the wood has to be bored out with a shell bit, the screw coming away with the core.

REMOVING BROKEN-IN SCREWS.

Many years ago screws were so badly made that coach-makers preferred to put countersunk clout nails in the hinges of carriage doors, as on extra strain the screws were apt to break off at the end of the threaded part; or if the head impinged a little more on one edge of the countersink than the other, the countersink of the hinge being iron recessed conically and un-yieldingly to the canted head, not at right angles to the countersunk face. The attempt to use a screw in hard wood had a like effect, but to a less degree. If the cone of the countersink were fainter in its angle than the cone of the screw head, the chances of a screw breaking would be lessened, as the neck of the cone of the screw head would take the bearing on one side of the hinge, or wood counter-sink. The screw (see Fig. 478) is bent out of straight at its weak part, and at every half-turn round it is bent back when the opposite side of the screw is turned to B, which, in effect, is the same as holding the thread part tightly, while the stem part A is crooked first one way then the other, the strain being augmented also by the tightening of the thread part producing a torsion strain on the weak part of the screw. A broken screw in the hinge of a heavy house door or of a carriage door was, and is, a serious matter. One plan, in the case of a carriage door, was to bore a larger hole from the other side of the pillar opposite the point of the screw, and punch the broken part through the hole; then plug up with a wood pin and glue, which needed a few hours to dry hard before it could be bored into for another screw. Another plan was to drive a clout nail in to fill the hole, beside the broken screw. Sometimes the head would be the trouble. If a blunt screwdriver were driven into the narrow slot, half the head would fly off; even impinging on the countersunk hole, more one side than the other, would cause the head to break half-side off. If the screw could not be got out, the remedy then was to leave it, and put in putty to hide the mischief; but if not quite tight it had to be got out somehow. To get out of a hole

a tight screw without a head was not an easy task, and would give much trouble at the present day, with all the many handy tools now available for any trouble-some jobs. It is understood easily then why countersunk clout nails were used in preference to screws in post-chaise and stage-coach work in many shops, and often in door hinges on oak door posts. A method of withdrawing a headless screw from a hole is to cut with a fine chisel the stem of the screw to the shape of a triangle; then fit on it a triangular steel pipe stem, like a short length of a padlock key, and make this square on the projecting part for an inch, and with an iron cramp force this key tightly on the broken screw; while holding it thus tightly, which prevents

Fig. 476.—Using Screwdriver.

it coming off, turn back the thread of the cramp with a wrench that fits the square, withdrawing the screw with it. It is a keen sense of touch, not eyesight, which determines the degree of pressure of the cramp screw, as the broken part is turned back far enough to enable a small hand vice to grip it, and turn it right out. It is believed that this device was first sug-gested by a workman named Crundle.

THE AMERICAN IMPROVED WOOD SCREW.

During the last sixty or seventy years

screws have been progressively improved, the chief improvements relating to the tougher iron used in the acute chisel edge of the thread, and, as has been mentioned, the screw tapering to a sharp point, with the thread right up to the tip. The American improved screw has a stem smaller in diameter than the thread part, so that the old evil of having to make a big hole in one piece, to prevent it becoming "stem-bound" and not drawing, is averted, though a smaller hole is used (Fig. 479). It is almost impossible for

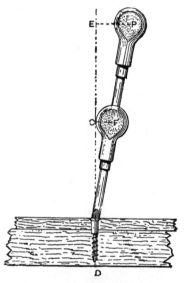

Fig. 477.—Advantage of Long over Short Screw-driver in withdrawing Difficult Screw.

the head of this screw to break half off, as the slot does not extend to the edge of the head, but is as a mortise in it, as the diagram shows. The cutting thread is exceptionally sharp. These screws are made of a mild steel of intense toughness, swaged and rolled cold. The cutting is done laterally, not longitudinally, the latter making a feeble thread. A big attempt, made about ten years ago, to introduce these screws into Great Britain failed, but under circumstances that threw no reflection upon the capabilities of the screw, which mechanically shows great talent in its invention.

What Glue is.

Glue, size, and gelatine are varieties of the same substance; they differ only in the quantity of moisture and of impurities which they contain. Glue contains so many impurities that it is unsuited for use other than as an adhesive for wood, paper, etc. Gelatine-yielding substances are legion, those in commercial use including the skins of all animals, tendons, intestines, bladders, bones, hoofs, and horns. In the preparation of ordinary glue, great use is made of the parings and cuttings of hides from tan-yards; tanned leather is useless for the purpose. Briefly, the process consists in boiling the animal matter and straining the product into coolers, where it thickens into a jelly. This is cut into sheets of suitable thickness and dried in the open air on frames of wire netting. Spring and autumn are the most suitable times for drying the glue, the frost of winter and the dry heat of summer having injurious effects. The size is not dried, but is sold just as it is cut from the coolers.

Manufacture of American Glue.

In making glue from shredded skins (chiefly those of rabbits), the processes at a large factory in America are as follow: 350 lb. of shredded skin and about 400 pailfuls of water are put into a suitable vat and boiled for two hours, the material being well stirred every fifteen or twenty minutes to prevent it settling. The liquid is then run off from the bottom of the vat and strained in a press, which may be about 4 ft. square, 3 ft. high, and made of wooden slats. The interior of the press is lined with bagging, and through this material the liquid is strained or pressed by means of a hydraulic jack. The hot strained liquid drops into a vat below, whence it is conducted by means of hose into barrels. In from eight to ten hours the stuff is cool, and has a skin formed on the top; in warm weather ice is laid on this skin to harden it; this is size. For making glue, the strained liquid is run into coolers, these being wooden troughs lined with zinc, and in twelve hours' time the material, then in the form of a jelly, is loosened from the trough by running a wire along it, the wire being bent to conform with the rectangular section of the trough. The block of jelly is cut up into cakes, and these are then sliced in an arrangement of fine wires stretched tightly across an iron frame about ½ in. apart; this frame is drawn through the jelly. The drying frames, upon which the slices of jelly are then placed, are about 5 ft. 6 in. long and 2 ft. wide, and are made of galvanised wire netting. The frames, when full, are placed in racks through which the air can circulate freely. It takes but a few days for the jelly to dry in a cool west wind; yet a system of artificial drying, by means of which the size becomes glue in but a few hours, is now being practised. In drying, the material shrinks to one-half its former bulk. The hard glue is now washed to remove dust, etc., and to produce a glazed appearance. In some factories the cakes of glue are cut up into small pieces by means of two rotary knives, each making 300 revolutions per minute. First the glue is passed between two 4-in. toothed rollers which hold it in position and draw it forward after each stroke of the knife.

MANUFACTURE OF ENGLISH GLUE.

In England the raw material, before being boiled, is limed; this treatment is not necessary in the case of hide cuttings from leather dressers and tanners, scrap from trotter-boilers, dry glue pieces and parchment cuttings, which are already limed. The liming is effected by soaking the material in milk of lime contained in pits. Afterwards it is necessary to remove or kill the lime by washing with water in vats or pits, or even in revolving drums. The lime in old glue pieces is killed sufficiently by the action of the atmospheric carbonic acid, the glue being spread out in trays so as to be more readily affected. In some works the washed materials are subjected to heavy pressure, but in others the boiling is proceeded with at once. The boilers or pans generally have each a capacity of several tons. A false bottom of bars keeps a clear space at the bottom. In the middle of the boiler is a removable vertical framework, and its object, like that of the false bottom, is partly to give free space, so that the boiling liquid can circulate thoroughly, and partly to simplify the straining of the liquid. The pans are heated by a fire beneath, by steam, or by the two together. In placing the materials in the pans, any horn "sloughs" that may be used are built up around the central framework, the rest of the material being then put in. During the boiling,

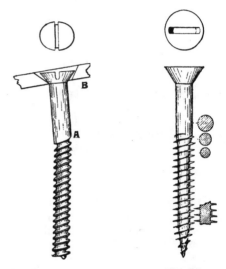

Fig. 478.
Defect of Old-fashioned
Wood Screw.

Fig. 479.
American Improved
Wood Screw.

intermittent stirring is necessary, and the fat which rises to the surface has to be skimmed off. The charge for the pans is in the proportion of twelve tons of fleshings to one ton of water. On the completion of the boiling the fire is put out, or the heat is otherwise removed; a time is allowed for partial settling and cooling, and the liquid is then drawn off through a wooden channel from the space beneath the false bottom. In this wooden channel are lumps of alum, and the liquid glue is conducted to cooling troughs, where it is allowed to cool and harden into a jelly or size. The succeeding processes by which the size becomes glue resemble those practised in America and previously noted. The methods outlined above admit of many variations, nearly every manufacturer adopting a system that in some particular differs from that adopted by his fellows.

Fig. 480.—Glue-pot and Brush.

Testing and Selecting Glue.

Glue should be of a bright brown or amber colour, free from specks or blotches, which are often caused by the non-removal of lime used in dressing the skins. It should be nearly transparent and with but little taste or smell. Black, opaque, unclean-looking glue is of no use. Very light-coloured glue is often fairly good and of medium price, but the bleaching to which it is subjected sometimes lowers its strength. For some purposes, such as gluing down thin, light-coloured veneers, it is very good, simply because it does not darken the tone of the wood, as the darker glue may do. Glue should be hard and moderately brittle, should not be readily affected by atmospheric damp, and should break sharply, with a glassy, shining appearance. If the glue shivers as easily as a piece of glass it is too brittle to be perfect, but at the same time it should not be tough and leathery. The appearance of the fractured edges also

is often a good indication, as is also the feel when it is held or rubbed between a moistened finger and thumb. Good glue will not give off an unpleasant smell after being prepared a few days; some of the commoner kinds are very bad in this respect, the odour from them being unbearable. Good glue will not dissolve in cold water, but will swell and assume the consistency of jelly. For this reason some recommend as a test that the glue should be weighed, soaked, and washed in cold water, then dried and weighed again. If there is a loss of weight it shows that some has been dissolved, and according to the difference the quality may be judged. If the water dissolves it as it soaks in, and penetrates for a slight depth only, there is something wrong. Roughly speaking, a glue which will absorb more water than another is the one that is preferable. Glue is sometimes tested by gluing two pieces of wood end to end. Two pieces of mahogany exhibited at Bethnal Green Museum were tried in this way, and parted under a strain of 504 lb. per square inch. If two pieces of dry red deal be properly glued together side to side, or end to end, the wood will break before the

Fig. 481.—Section through Glue-pot.

joint if the glue be of fair average quality. The adhesive power of glue is in proportion to its consistency and elasticity after it has been soaked in water for some hours and has absorbed many times its own weight of moisture. For the woodworker's purpose, Scotch glue is the best. In colour it is a clear, wholesome, ruddy brown, not a muddy-looking compound, nor yet refined to gelatine.

Preparing Glue.

Much depends upon the manner in which the glue is prepared. It does not suffice to place it in water, and at once bring to the boil, because this method produces a glue of but little strength. The proper way of preparing glue is first to break the cakes up small by wrapping in canvas and striking with a hammer. If the canvas is not used the

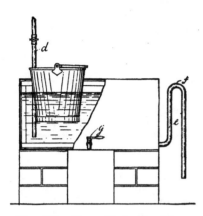

Fig. 482.—Steam Heater for Glue.

glue will fly into small fragments, many of which will be lost. Put the glue into a clean vessel and cover with clean cold water, allowing it to remain until the next day, when it will have absorbed some of the water and present the appearance of lumps of jelly. Pour off the surplus water, and place the glue in the inner vessel of a glue-pot and just cover with water, then keep the water boiling in the outer vessel for two or three hours. To test for thickness, dip the brush in, and if the glue just runs easily without breaking into drops it is fit for use. Some workmen are able to test the thickness by rubbing the liquid glue between the finger and thumb. A drop of suitably prepared glue, if placed on a cold surface, should quickly become a jelly. If too thin it will be some time in hardening sufficiently to be handled, and if it is so thick as to harden almost directly and be unworkable with the brush, more water must be added. The inner pot should never be placed on the fire, or the glue will burn and become worthless, the right temperature for heating being that of boiling water. Do not

boil the same glue more than twice—it loses its strength. If only a little is to be used at intervals, allow it after the first boiling to get cold and form a jelly; then pieces of the jelly may be cut off and heated as required. Thus a stock of reliable glue is always at hand.

WORKSHOP GLUE-POTS.

In the workshop different kinds of glue-pots are used according to the quantity required. For workshop use the ordinary glue-pot (Fig. 480) may be used. This has an outer and an inner vessel, as shown in the section (Fig. 481). In large workshops, where glue is used in quantity, and steam-pipes are laid on for heating purposes, a tank constructed as shown in Figs. 482 and 483 may be used. It is made of $\frac{1}{4}$-in. plate iron or steel, with four holes (c, Fig. 483) in the top, large enough to accommodate buckets or specially made glue-pots; d is a steam-pipe carried nearly to the bottom of the tank, and e is an overflow pipe to carry away the waste water produced by the condensation of the steam. A small hole must be provided at f, or the overflow pipe will syphon all the water out of the tank. A draw-off tap at g facilitates cleaning out, or supplies hot water. When required for use, the tank

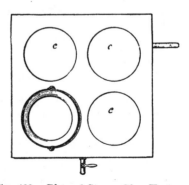

Fig. 483.—Plan of Steam Glue Heater.

is filled with water and the steam turned into it, which will cause the water to boil. If steam-pipes are not laid on, the glue-tank may be constructed as shown in Fig. 484, and heated with coal or waste wood.

HOUSEHOLD GLUE-POTS.

For home use the glue may be melted in a cup or tin placed in a saucepan of boiling water. A serviceable glue-pot is made as follows: Get a cocoa or mustard tin, and pierce two holes in it opposite each other, about 1 in. from the top; get

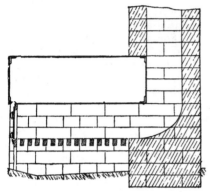

Fig. 484.—Heating Arrangement for Glue Tank.

about 8 in. of tinned wire and run it through the holes, the wire resting on the edges of the saucepan. *Another device:*—A disused golden syrup tin, about 4 in. by 4 in., is very suitable for the outer pot, as it has a ring round the top, inside, about ⅜ in. wide, on which the flange of the inner pot may rest. In each side of this tin, about 1 in. from the top, pierce a hole, and bend a piece of iron wire into a half circle, place the two ends into the holes in the tin, as shown in Fig. 485, and clinch them over inside. The inner pot may be made from a coffee tin, 3 in. in diameter by 6 in. deep. This, of course, is too deep, so, scribing a line right round the tin 3 in. from the bottom, cut from the top downwards a number of slits ¾ in. apart to the line. Bend all these pieces of tin, except one on each side, at the line to right angles with the sides of the tin, thus forming a flange about 3 in. wide. Cut down this flange to about 1 in. wide, and the two upstanding pieces to 1 in. high, rounding at the top. In each of these two pieces pierce a hole, and get another piece of iron wire, bent as before, but slightly shorter; put each end through the holes, clinch

over, and the pot is complete, the inner pot appearing something like Fig. 486. *Another device:*—Fig. 487 shows a 2-lb. syrup tin A, a condensed milk tin B, and pieces of wire C, and explains itself. If the water should boil over it cannot get into the glue, and, when using, the brush is wiped upon the wires C, and that does away with the accumulations of glue commonly seen on glue-pots. A different kind of inner pot is made as follows:—A 2⅛-in. round hole is made in the lid of a 2-lb. syrup tin, and the ring thus made is put over the top of a ¼-lb. round mustard tin, and soldered to it at the distance of ½ in. from the top of the tin. In running the solder round a small space may be missed to allow the steam to escape, or a hole may be made in a convenient place. The handle may be made by cutting off the screws of two screw-eyes, making holes in the sides of the syrup tin, and soldering them in. The lid of the mustard tin may be used to cover up the glue when not in use. *Another device:*—Take a piece of suitable wire A (Fig. 488), and make three loops B at equal distances, according to the size of the vessel used. This is placed at a convenient height on the vessel C, so that it well clears the bottom of the vessel D, in which it is placed. A piece

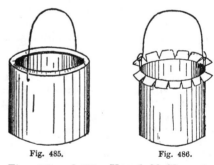

Fig. 485.　　　　　　Fig. 486.

Figs. 485 and 486.—Household Glue-pot.

of wire E is then placed over the top, the two ends being bent down to come between the wire circle A and the inner vessel C, preferably between two loops as shown. All is then twisted up till it grips the vessel quite tightly. The vessel C is then placed in the outer vessel, and the loops are turned down equally on all three sides, thus keeping it firmly in the centre, the two ends being bent flat against the inner vessel to be out of the way and to prevent the inner vessel floating. Of course, the

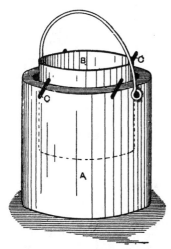

Fig. 487.—Household Glue-pot.

two ends could form the third loop if desired. The arrangement is made in a few minutes, and the inner vessel is not perforated at all. In the illustration one loop is not shown, it being at the back of vessel c. The wire E is for cleaning the brush, which may be put either in the centre or at one side.

GLUE BRUSHES.

A glue brush can be bought for a few pence. If the hairs are too long the brush must be tied to make them shorter as far as their action is concerned. Start by placing the twine as in Fig. 489, and then bind it tightly round the hair until the brush is sufficiently short; finish off by passing the end of the twine through the last two coils (see Fig. 490) and drawing tight, and then turn back the loose ends and secure each of them with a tack (see Fig. 491), to prevent the ends slipping down. The brush should not be put into glue until ready for use, and, when finished with, should be washed in hot water. The following is a method of keeping glue brushes in good condition. Fix a stout

wire across the pot in one of the ways already described. By pressing the brush against the wire to free it from superfluous glue, the sides of the pot will always be clean, the glue will heat quicker, and no material will be wasted. It is a good plan to cut away one side of a small-sized screw-eye to transform it into a hook, and put it into the handle just below the ferrule, or about 2 in. from the bristles; the hook holds the brush on the wire clear off the bottom of the pot. A brush left to rest upon the bottom of the pot quickly becomes too crooked to use. Fig. 492 illustrates a brush that has been spoilt in this way. The bristles refuse to stand in the proper position, and it is useless for particular work. The following is a method of improving the brush, though a tool in such condition can never be made to work thoroughly well. First remove the glue by washing, then hold the bristles in very hot water for a few minutes and refill the brush again with glue; get a strip of old rag, and, holding the brush as shown in Fig. 493, wind the material round the entire length of the hair, and secure the end by tying twine round

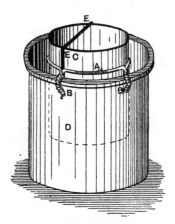

Fig. 488.—Household Glue-pot.

tightly. The bristles will now stand erect, and the brush is put aside and the binding allowed to dry hard on it; in the course of a day or two the brush may be held in hot water and the binding peeled off. Once doing is not enough if the tool is in a very bad state, but after the same process has been repeated several times it is usually in good workable condition. Glue brushes are so cheap, however, that it is doubtful whether the result is worth the trouble. An effective glue brush can be made out of a piece of common cane, and the cane brush is preferred by many competent and practical workers to any other. Take a piece of rattan cane about 8 in. long, cut away the flinty skin for an inch or so at one end, soak this end in boiling water for a minute or two, and then hammer this till the fibres are softened and loosened, the only care required being not to cut them off while hammering (see Fig. 494). Such a brush will last a long time—in fact, as long as there is any cane left from which to hammer out a fresh end.

METHOD OF GLUING.

Glue should be used as hot as possible and in a warm room. The pieces of wood to be joined should be warmed before being put together, and should be well fitted so as to get as little glue in the joint as possible ; the glue should be well rubbed in with a brush or by rubbing the two pieces of wood together, and the joint should be made close by clamping, tying, or rubbing, so as to squeeze out all superfluous glue (see pp. 183 to 185). When practicable, as it generally is, except

Fig. 489.   Fig. 490.   Fig. 491.

Figs. 489 to 491.—Shortening Hair of Glue
Brush by Tying.

in the case of large veneers, the glued pieces should be worked against each other with gradually increasing pressure, to expel any air between them, and to squeeze out as much of the glue as possible. On the extent to which this is managed much of the strength of the joint depends. The thinner the film of glue

between the pieces, the more firmly will they adhere ; nothing is gained by leaving a thick layer of glue. The quantity of glue in a joint should be so small that, if the two surfaces are true and bear uniformly on each other, its presence should be denoted only by the hair line which marks the joint. The joint should be made as quickly as possible, and after the pieces are fixed they should remain in a warm place for at least twelve hours. If a joint

Fig. 492.—Glue Brush with Bent Hair.

is broken after it has commenced to set, no amount of clamping will make a good job of it ; the glue must all be cleaned off and the joint made again. When the wood is porous it will be of advantage to size the surface with some very weak glue. This will fill up the grain and prevent the glue from sinking into the wood when the joint is made, but let this size be quite dry before gluing, or the effect will be to cool and dilute the glue. The methods of gluing on veneers are described fully later. Great care should be taken that dust, grease, or oil does not get on the surfaces to be joined, or the glue will not hold. Some woods are, however, of a greasy nature. Take teak for instance ; if the wood is not thoroughly dry the glue will not set on it, but will peel off. Wood of a greasy nature should not be used where glued joints are employed, or for veneering. A later chapter will deal comprehensively with gluing up joints, etc. (see pp. 183 to 185, and p. 187).

LIQUID GLUES.

Liquid glues, such as Le Page's and " Scoli," have become popular. The advantages of these liquid glues are that they are always ready for use, requiring no heat, and that they do not spoil by being exposed to the air, though they then become thick, simply from the evaporation of moisture. The remedy, of course, if this happens, is to add a little more water, but in practice, with ordinary care, this is seldom requisite, and is not desirable. In very cold weather a little warmth is necessary, but if kept in a warm room or placed near a fire for a time, liquid glue is soon fit for use. As already stated, it is not applied hot. For work requiring a colourless or almost colourless glue it is unsurpassed, and as it does not set so quickly as the ordinary kind, it is well adapted for marquetry and inlaid work generally. When it does set it possesses great tenacity if properly used, that is, thinly applied and well rubbed in. Although it is not better than best quality animal glue employed under the most favourable conditions, it is certainly superior to ordinary common glue which has not been made, mixed, and used with skill and care. At first sight it may seem expensive, but as a little of it goes a long way, and as it does not waste by keeping,

Fig. 493.—Improving Glue Brush.

it will be found, when required for occa-sional use only, to cost in the end but little, if any, more than the usual kind.

WATERPROOF GLUES.

A glue that is absolutely waterproof has yet to be discovered; and for the joints of work which are exposed to weather it is much better to use thick white-lead paint in place of glue. A damp-resisting glue may be made by soaking in water enough glue to make a pint when dissolved ready for use, and, after dissolving it as usual, but in as little water as possible, adding three tablespoonfuls of boiled linseed oil, keeping up the heat and constantly stirring the glue until the oil disappears, then adding and thoroughly incorporating a tablespoonful of whiting. Glue to which bichromate of potash has been added is, after exposure to strong light, rendered insoluble; and glue compounded with skim milk instead of water

Fig. 494.—Cane Brush for Glue.

resists damp better than ordinary glue, but a joint made with it will not stand for long in a wet situation. There are ready-made waterproof glues on the market. One kind is sold in cone-shaped tins which have spring bottoms like those of small oilcans. The hole in the top of the cone, the exit for the glue, is stopped with a pin, whose head is soldered to the tin with soft composition, which can be easily removed with a knife, to allow of the withdrawal of the pin, which must be replaced as soon as sufficient glue has been pressed out of the tin. Thus the glue can be applied without heating and without using a brush. After the glue is set, it will bear prolonged exposure to damp, or actual immersion in water for a long period. It is economical, because it can be used with-out the slightest waste.

TIMBER:

ITS GROWTH, SEASONING, CONVERSION, SELECTION, AND VARIETIES.

INTRODUCTION.

This chapter will deal comprehensively with timber, and is intended to supply just the information that will enable the handyman to select and purchase his material intelligently and profitably. The word timber is derived from a Teutonic root meaning "to build." Timber, therefore, is wood for constructional and general building purposes.

DIVISIONS OF PLANTS.

There are two great divisions of plants—flowering and non-flowering. Flowering plants are sub-divided into outward- and inward-growing plants. Outward-growing plants increase in bulk by outward additions—that is, by additions on the inner side of the bark, but outside and above the wood already formed. In inward-growing plants the addition of new matter takes place towards the centre of the stem. A cross-section of an exogenous or outward-growing plant shows the additions as concentric layers or "annual rings," each ring being popularly supposed to represent a year's growth. It is from trees of this type that the varieties of timber in general use are obtained. A similar examination of an endogenous or inward-growing plant, however, does not reveal a corresponding indication of growth, the bamboo, sugar cane, and palm being examples. It is evident, then, that for timber trees attention may be confined to the exogenous sub-division of the phanerogamous or flowering plants.

ORGANS OF TREES.

The organs engaged in the maintenance of the tree are the root, the stem or trunk, the branches (which are merely continua-tions of the stem or trunk), and the leaves ; these are termed vegetative organs. The organs concerned in the reproduction of the tree are the flowers and the fruit. The vegetative organs may be classed in two sets—one being the roots, and the other consisting of stem or trunk, branches, and leaves. All these organs, and indeed each part of every plant, are composed of minute bodies termed cells. A cell is simply an enclosed space, but its contents are of importance, the cell being a mere chamber in which the operation of growth is carried on. On microscopical examina-tion a single cell is found to be merely a little bladder or sac, round or oval in shape. The walls are composed of cellu-lose, a porous substance of which cotton-wool or pure blotting paper are familiar examples. The contents of living cells consist mainly of a jelly-like substance called protoplasm, which is the really liv-ing substance of a plant. A collection of cells united together is called a tissue.

TREE TISSUES.

Outward-growing trees have three kinds of tissue (cellular, woody, and vascular). Cellular tissue is composed of cells packed together and adhering in masses. In micro-scopical examination they present, in cross-section, a network of polygonal figures. Pores in the wall form the only communica-tion between the cells. This tissue is very brittle, and possesses little or no cohesion. Woody tissue is composed of bundles of slender, transparent fibres or tubes, taper-ing to each end, and generally understood to be merely long, compressed cells, com-munication being by invisible pores. This tissue possesses great strength and tenacity. Vascular tissue consists of small tubes or canals which transmit fluids necessary for the nourishment and growth of the plant. They are formed by the junction of cells with their ends opening into each other. When a fibre is coiled spirally on the inside of the walls, these tubes are termed spiral vessels. If the interior of the tubes be marked by separate rings of fibre, or present a dotted or netted appearance, the vessel is termed a duct. If a spiral vessel be stretched, and then suddenly released,

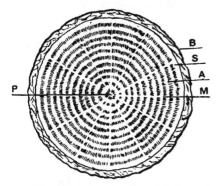

Fig. 495.—Cross-section of Oak.

the vessel will be sufficiently elastic to return to its former condition. A duct, on the other hand, would rupture. Spiral vessels are situated chiefly in the medullary sheath (to be explained later on) and sometimes in the roots.

TREE STRUCTURE.

The stem or trunk is the source of the greater quantity of useful timber. For the purpose of clearly seeing the various parts without microscopical aid, the cross-section of the oak (see Fig. 495) is selected. There are five parts to be considered—the pith P, formed of cellular tissue, is in the centre, and in the very early stage the whole process of growth is carried on in the pith until transferred to the annual rings. The pith ultimately shrivels up and dies. The medullary rays M are the thin white lines or radii which pierce the annual rings, and are composed of cellular tissue in the form of thin, hard, vertical plates, termed by carpenters the " silver grain." The annual rings A are circular layers of formed wood, composed of woody and vascular tissue intermingled. These rings change colour

a few years after being deposited, the altered wood being termed the heart wood. A complete annual ring of formed wood consists of one light and one dark layer, these being formed during spring and autumn respectively. The cells of the autumn layer are thicker walled and more compactly deposited than those of the spring layer. In tropical climates a year's growth cannot be exactly determined. The sapwood S (Fig. 495) is on the inner side of the bark and outside the heartwood. It is the last-formed layer of wood, and is generally light in colour, and the watery sap is supposed to ascend the tree chiefly through it. The bark B is the outer covering or skin of the tree, and really consists of two parts—the outer part, which is a layer of cellular tissue, and the inner part, which consists of woody and vascular tissue. It is generally understood that the sap, after being purified, descends the tree between the liber or inner bark and the alburnum or sapwood. A new ring of bark is formed every year, but it is not distinguishable like a new annual ring. The old bark stretches to allow of the addition of the new material ; but, when the limit to this stretching is passed, the old bark divides in clefts or fissures, peels off in plates, or tears in ribands.

EARLY GROWTH OF TREES.

In the shoot arising from the seed there is nothing but pith, a circular mass of cel-

Fig. 496.—Cross-section of Shoot.

lular tissue, surrounded by a thin bark, as shown by Fig. 496. In a few weeks a woody ring is interposed between the pith and the bark. This ring is composed of bundles, wedge-shaped in cross-section (Fig. 497), and composed of distinctive layers. The original constituent is the thin cambium layer C, the cells of which enlarge, divide, and sub-divide under the influence of heat and nutriment. It is by this property that a new ring is added to the tree every year. Above this layer is the liber layer L, and below, lying next the pith or centre of the tree, is the formed wood w. The first-

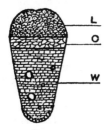

Fig. 497.—Cross-section of Bundle in Woody Ring.

formed layer of the woody ring is of vascular tissue, which envelops the pith, and is termed the "medullary sheath." On its outer side wood is deposited, consisting of woody and vascular tissue intermingled. The ring, being in sections, is not complete, thus forming the medullary rays. In Fig. 498 is seen the white cellular mass of the pith P crushed by the deposit of bundles of the woody ring v into thin white strips; these strips are the medullary rays M. Eventually each new woody ring becomes an "annual ring," the ring of bark is added to, the medullary rays are extended, and the plant is developed generally. One part, however, the medullary sheath, is an exception to this development, since no similar formation occurs in the further growth of the tree.

PLANT FOOD.

From the soil the root and its offshoots absorb sap, which ascends the tree until it reaches the leaves. This motion may be said to be caused chiefly by heat, since this increases the flow, while cold diminishes it. Thus the flow is rapid in spring, still more so in summer, while it gradually diminishes in autumn, and almost ceases in winter. Generally speaking, plants live on inorganic food alone. (Trees, of course, are only large plants.) The few exceptions are parasites, as, for example, the fungi that grow upon trees. The inorganic food comes partly from the soil and partly from the air. The soil food is absorbed into the tree through the roots as an exceedingly dilute solution of inorganic salts, not unlike ordinary drinking water, called the sap. The foods obtained from the air are gases, and consist principally of combined carbon and oxygen—carbon dioxide. This gas is taken in by the leaves and other green parts of the plant. As regards soil foods, the following are essential to almost every plant —hydrogen, oxygen, potassium, sodium, chlorine, calcium, sulphur, magnesium, phosphorus, and iron. If one or more of these be missing, the seedling does not thrive—the absence of iron, for instance, would soon be apparent by the white leaves, normally green, and so on; yet the soil food finally forms but a small proportion of the solid portions of the plant. In a piece of wood, for example, the solid material procured from the soil is represented by the fine white ashes left behind when the wood is burnt, and similarly with all other vegetable matter. The great bulk of every plant, and practically all wood substance, is made from materials which are obtained from the air, and which in burning are returned to the air. Only liquid matter can be taken up by the roots, for under greatest magnification they do not exhibit pores. The root ends of most timber

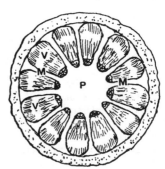

Fig. 498.—Section of Woody Ring.

trees are provided with a protecting layer or shield of firm cells, technically known as the root cap. Fig. 499 shows the section end of a young root split down lengthwise. The rootcap A to B is advanced very slowly and with many convolutions through the soil by the formation of new cells at the point A. The soil substances are made soluble by the action of rainwater, and by sulphuric, nitric, and other acids, which are constantly forming in the air and in the soil, and by the acid sap excreted by the roots themselves, this excretion being merely a local affair, and having nothing to do with the supposed "coming down" of the sap in winter. The absorption of the soluble matter is practically continuous throughout the life of any plant, whether annual or perennial, deciduous or evergreen. In the dormant winter period movement in the sap is scarcely, if at all, perceptible, but there are times when the sap travels upwards many feet in a day (Sachs observed particles of water [sap] rising in wood in the summer time for a distance of one metre [say, about 3 ft. 3 in.], or even more than that, in less than an hour); but there is no emission of "large quantities of sap" by the roots, during the autumn or winter, as is often supposed. The young leaves of a tree are not formed from or by the sap brought directly from the soil, and for a long time, at the beginning of each growing season, the food materials stored in the twigs, branches, stem, etc. (at the close of the previous year), are sufficient to meet the demands of all new growth.

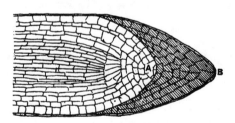

Fig. 499.—Tree Rootlet.

CRUDE SAP CIRCULATION IN TIMBER TREES.

The crude sap in its upward course passes through the sapwood, or alburnum, of the tree (see Figs. 500 and 501, G G). Assuming that the appearance of the leaves may be taken as a gauge of interference with the sap current, then several interesting experiments are possible in demonstrating what is the upward path of the sap. (1) If

a deep girdle of the bark is removed from a tree as at A (Fig. 500), the leaves are unaffected, and the tree will continue to grow for a number of years. The bark, therefore, is not essential in the upward flow. (2) If a section of the heartwood of such a

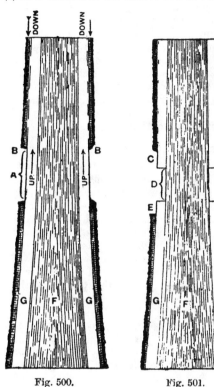

Fig. 500.
Tree with Girdle of
Bark Removed.

Fig. 501.
Tree with Girdle of
Sapwood and Bark
Removed.

girdled tree is taken away, the leaves are still unaffected, and the tree continues to grow. (3) If the outside of the exposed sapwood in such a tree is carefully scraped so that no remains of the cambium can possibly be present, it still grows. (4) If a young elder shoot, say two or three years old, is girdled as at A (Fig. 500), and a long section of the pith removed, the leaves still flourish. Clearly, then, these four elements, the bark, the cambium, the heartwood, and the pith, are not essential to the ascent of the sap. On the other hand, if a girdle of the sapwood, as well as of the bark, be removed, as shown at C, D, E in Fig. 501, then the leaves wither and the tree shortly dies. It is proved then that the crude sap, in its upward course, passes through the sapwood, or alburnum, of the tree. Further, a series of experiments, conducted in 1879, go to prove that the ascending current is not only confined to the sapwood, but that it is the spring portion only of the annual rings of the sapwood that is instrumental in conveying the sap, and that in many trees the current, in all probability, ascends in the form of so many isolated tubular layers of liquid, each layer quite disconnected from adjoining layers, internally and externally.

CHEMICAL CHANGES IN PLANT FOODS.

The crude sap taken in at the roots travels upwards undiminished through the stem and branches to the leaves. Entering the leaf-stalk by very minute channels, it is spread out and dispersed through the green layers of cells that lie just underneath the top surface of the leaf. Here, under the action of light and warmth, the bulk of the water is evaporated, and the dissolved nutrient salts remain behind to become the constituents of various compounds useful in the life of the plant. The water set free in the leaf emerges in a gaseous state from the under side, passing out through the millions of trap-doors (these are known as stomata) that are dotted all over its surface. At the same time other changes, no less important, are going on in respect to the gases imbibed from the air. The atoms of carbon dioxide are drawn into the working chambers (palisade cells) of the leaf, where the carbon is retained and united with the substances brought from the soil; while the oxygen is allowed to escape into the air again. All day long, and even far into the night, the leaf cells are receiving and transforming crude materials, the manufactured food comprising the returning current of sap.

CIRCULATION OF ELABORATED SAP.

In the same way that the crude sap was distributed, the elaborated article is collected again, but by another set of channels, this time of a looser, less woody char-

acter than those which served on its upward journey. The current, too, is no longer mobile, but is sluggish and heavy. Presently, however, it emerges into the trunk on its return journey, and proceeds up and down as required. This substance builds up all permanent parts of the stem, branches, roots, and all parts not completed out of the reserves of the previous year. But the translocation of new food in an upward direction is comparatively rare, and is confined principally to the extremities of branches and twigs. In the trunk, by virtue of its position, the current is invariably downwards. In the case of a tree having a section of bark removed in springtime by way of experiment, as at A (Fig. 500), no new wood is put on below the points B B, but all the upper parts of the trunk, and all the branches, are covered with a layer of new wood as usual. Where new shoots grow out of tree-stumps their substance is at first drawn entirely from reserves of food laid up in the stump, the protoplasm of the merismatic cells still being alive, and capable of dividing. Afterwards their own leaves afford the necessary nourishment. Merismatic cells are those that divide by the formation of internal partitions. Neither pith, sapwood, nor heartwood takes part in conveying the downward current of sap; trees having no heartwood—hollow at the centre—continue to put on new rings of wood from year to year and exhibit generally all the signs of a healthy life. The bark only is the downward conducting layer, and it has inner layers, commonly known as the liber, which are very fully equipped with peculiar vessels or tubes extending for long distances up and down the tree. These are called sieve-tubes, because of the little disc-like gratings that occur at intervals in their length. A good deal of the food (elaborated sap) passes down through these tubes, which have charge of the nitrogenous substances. The rest of the food travels by way of the adjoining parenchymatous tissue. From these it is further conveyed and distributed radially by means of the medullary rays, and utilised by the rays themselves or else stored in the wood. Where masses of parenchyma lie close together, the sap is able to pass tangentially from point to point, as well as up or down. Indeed, the parenchymatous tissue of the bark, of the medullary rays, and of the wood all over the plant, is in such intimate and continuous connection that unlimited facilities are afforded for the transit or storage of food material.

THE CAMBIUM LAYER.

Perhaps no part of the plant is less understood generally than the cambium, and yet no other part, except the flower or fruit, is of so much importance. It is situated just inside the bark, exactly where the wood finishes and the bark begins, and it follows the course of every branch and twig, and completely covers the tree like a huge many-pointed glove. This cambium is the great building layer from which is evolved the whole mass of wood and bark. It consists essentially of a single layer of cells that contain living, working protoplasm; but as a matter of fact the protoplasm rarely is confined to a single layer, but extends for a variable distance on each side of what may be termed the centre or plane of vitality. The protoplasm of the cambium is capable of dividing up and making new cells indefinitely out of the food substances brought to it. On each side of the actively dividing layer are to be found various types of cells in all stages of completion; those external to it become modified into the soft fibrous elements of the bark, while those on its inside develop in time into the hard lignified substance known as wood. During the growing period the position of the cambium is changed almost from day to day, and at such times it is constantly withdrawing into the more newly created cells. The range of the protoplasm on each side of the plane of activity varies from about two or three to six cells, the outermost of which—that is, those farthest away from the active layer, whether in the wood or in the bark—are nearing completion. From finished cells (except in parenchymatous tissue) the protoplasm is withdrawn altogether. Probably the food required is fed to the cambium by gentle lateral diffusion.

DIFFERENCE BETWEEN SPRING AND SUMMER WOOD.

With respect to the difference in the character of the spring- and summer-wood portions of the annual ring, a general notion exists (and some authorities state) that the pressure of the bark due to the increasing diameter of the tree is responsible for this difference. Pressure of the bark undoubtedly exists, but this appears quite insufficient to explain the simple differences seen in conifer woods, to say nothing of the immense structural differences that appear in all ring-porous woods.

FELLING TIMBER TREES.

The growth and structure of the tree from the botanist's standpoint having been discussed in sufficient detail, the more practical matters of felling and seasoning timber may now be dealt with. Timber is the term applied to the body, stem, or trunk of a tree. The best time for felling trees is when maturity is reached, and when they contain the least sap. The forester generally judges whether the tree is mature by the appearance of the foliage, the size of the tree, and other outward indications. If felling is delayed beyond the stage of maturity, the material deteriorates, becoming brittle and unyielding, whilst if the trees are cut very young the greater part is sapwood, and thus not at all durable as timber. The period at which each kind of timber tree attains maturity differs considerably; thus the oak may be perfect at any time between sixty and a hundred years, whilst the spruce and pine are generally cut between seventy and eighty years. It unfortunately happens, however, that the trees are cut as soon as they are a moderate size, without regard to age; this is the fault of most timber that now reaches the English ports. The sapwood, generally speaking, is very easily detected; in the case of deal it is often a blue colour, whilst that of oak is a dirty white. Midwinter is considered usually the most suitable period of the year for felling, and then there is hardly any flow of sap. If the tree is felled when the sap is flowing, the cells in course of formation are not sufficiently developed, or are not strong enough to resist decay. Autumn also is recommended, providing the sap is hardly circulating. Midsummer is also recommended, on the argument that when the leaves are fully expanded the sap has ceased to flow, and the extraneous vegetable matter intended for the leaves has

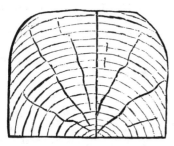

Fig. 502.—Log Cut " On the Quarter."

been expelled from the trunk by the common sap, leaving it free from that germinative principle which is readily excited by heat and moisture, and which, if the timber were cut while it remained, would subject it to rapid decay and to the ravages of worms. Perhaps the real reason why midsummer is a suitable time for felling trees is because the sap vessels are then in full activity, and the moisture of the tree is readily evaporated by the foliage, while the sap escapes from the wounds. As little sap as possible is wanted in the timber, and some persons are of opinion that in order to harden the sapwood the bark should be taken off in the spring before felling. The methods employed in felling trees vary according to circumstances. In ordinary cases, however, the trunk is severed close to the root, and then thrown or pulled down by means of ropes and other suitable apparatus. When special methods have to be adopted, they are usually modifications of this method. After the tree has been felled it is stripped of its branches and other appendages. By means of an adze the bark is chipped off until the trunk is converted roughly from a circular form to one square in cross-section, when it becomes a log.

SEASONING TIMBER.

Trees, when first cut down, are, of course unfit for immediate use. The timber is then full of the juices popularly known as sap, and the object of seasoning is to get rid of this sap. When properly carried out, seasoning adds considerably to the strength of timber ; in fact, it has been proved by experiment that if two pieces of equal size are cut from a green log, and one is broken at once and the other after being seasoned, the latter will bear twice as much weight before it breaks as the former. The so-called natural method of seasoning consists in stacking the timber in suitable piles and allowing the sap to dry up of its own accord. The timber, after felling, is placed in a dry position, so that the air may circulate freely round it. It should not be placed in the sun or wind, or it will crack and warp very much in drying. If the timber is roughly squared with the adze or axe, it will not split so much as if it were left in the round. If the trees are large, they may with advantage be cut " on the quarter," as in Fig. 502,

Fig. 503.—Timber Stacked on Edge.

after a period of drying in the whole state. A good plan is to set the timber upright, when it will dry much more rapidly. After remaining in the " quartered " state some time, it may be cut up into the desired size. The boards, as now cut, will require careful attention before being in a fit state to use.

They should be placed in drying-sheds, with the ends open to the air, avoiding, if possible, positions in which the wind will act directly upon them. The floor should be of some hard material, such as cement, and should be kept perfectly dry. Bearers about 4 ft. apart must be placed horizontally between the uprights, leaving a space between equal to the width of

Fig. 504.—Strip with Nail, to go between Boards.

the boards (Fig. 503). The boards are placed on edge with strips between them, a nail being driven into the top of each strip, as shown in Fig. 504, to prevent its falling downwards. An alternative arrangement is to place the boards one upon the other, with strips between the boards, taking care to place the strips one exactly over the other, as Fig. 505. The loss in conversion—that is when the wood is finally cut up for use—will greatly depend upon the method of stacking the logs and planks. Different varieties of timber require different methods of stacking. Some woods take much longer to season than others, and the loss by shrinkage is subject to a like variation. Stacks of timber should never be based directly on the soil ; the seasoning yard should be paved, or at least covered with a thick layer of ashes.

Loss of Moisture in Seasoning.

The trunk of a tree freshly cut down contains 50 per cent. by weight of water. The sapwood contains more than this percentage, the heartwood less. When the trunk is allowed to remain out of doors, more than half of this water will evaporate

in the first few months ; if the trunk is sawn into planks and stacked in an open yard, the water will be further reduced to 12 to 15 per cent. of the total weight ; if it is taken into an ordinary living-room, the amount of water in it will be brought down to 8 to 10 per cent. ; if it is put into a drying kiln having a temperature of from 150° to 180° F., only 2 to 4 per cent. of water will be left ; but though the temperature is raised to 300° F. (when chemical destruction begins to set in), water will still be given off. Immediately wood is taken out of a kiln of this description it begins to absorb moisture again. In a week it will have regained 5 to 6 per cent. moisture ; in a month or so its condition, if kept out of doors, will be normal again (that is, 12 per cent. of the whole weight will be due to moisture).

Stacking Deal for Seasoning.

The stacking of deal to season is usually done in the following way : A layer of planks is put on rough sleepers, the pieces being placed about 3 in. apart for 7-in. battens, and others in proportion. The

Fig. 505.—Timber Stacked on the Flat.

succeeding layer is arranged so that each plank rests its edges on the edges of two planks of the first layer, and covers the space between them. The third layer is placed exactly like the first, and the fourth like the second, and so on in alternate series until the whole have been stacked.

By this arrangement the air is allowed to circulate through the stack. To prevent the penetration of rain, the planks of the topmost layer are put close together and tilted up at one end by means of a plank standing on edge beneath them. Fig. 506 shows the arrangement of a stack of deals. If possible, the planks forming the roof should overlap by a foot or so those below. From eighteen months to two years is generally long enough for deal to be stored for outside work, and after that time the stacks should be carefully watched for signs of decay. Rot may be detected by the ends of the pieces showing a number of small red spots, or having the appearance of being dusted with flour. Sometimes (especially if the stacks have been laid on the bare ground) a fungoid growth will spread in fan-shaped layers of about the thickness of paper over the timber. Directly rot makes its appearance the stack should be pulled to pieces and each plank exposed to the air, and the wood should be used up without delay. Deals of inferior quality often show signs of decay at the edges in less than twelve months. When deal is required in the form of boards, the planks are cut up as economically as

Fig. 506.—Stack of Deals for Seasoning.

possible, and the resulting pieces are stacked in perches to season. Figs. 507 and 508 give two views of a perch for stacking boards. The pieces are put in alternately, one on each side, thus providing for a free circulation of air around each board. Some dealers stack the boards on each side alternately in pairs, thus keeping the inner faces of each pair cleaner for planing

up than when both sides are fully exposed. Boards cut from battens will generally clean up to $6\frac{3}{4}$ in. wide when seasoned; those from 9-in. deals to $8\frac{3}{4}$ in., and those from 11-in. to $10\frac{3}{8}$ in. White deal shrinks a little less than yellow in seasoning, but, besides being more liable to the attacks of rot, it shows a greater tendency to split and warp.

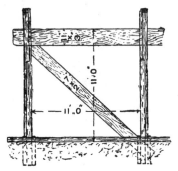

Fig. 507.—Perch for Seasoning Short Boards.

Seasoning Hardwoods.

Hardwoods require a much longer period to season than deal. Country timber merchants keep English hardwoods in the round for from one to three years after cutting down, and then saw them into planks of marketable thickness. These are stacked one on the other, with strips between them, the outside rounded pieces being put at the top to guard against the weather. The stacks are made in the open yard, and are left for a period varying from two to seven years, according to the size and class of material. This method, though effective, is rather wasteful, the exposure to sun and wind resulting in the formation of weather or surface shakes, which have to be removed when the timber is converted, and often involve a loss of $\frac{1}{2}$ in. or more from the surface of the board. The ends of the planks most exposed to sun and wind are liable to split. To prevent this, some timber dealers nail pieces of wood across the ends of the planks, or at any rate at the ends of those that have begun to split. This, however, is a very bad practice, for the nails on the outside edges of the plank prevent shrinking inwards, and keep the split open, the wood shrinking outwards on each side of it; and as an oak plank will sometimes shrink ¾ in. in seasoning, the split will open to that extent. A glance at Fig. 509 will help to explain this. A better plan is to give the ends of the planks a thick coating of paint, which will do much to prevent splitting. Young timber is more liable to fly when exposed than old. The best results with hardwoods are obtained when the seasoning is accomplished under shelter in a suitable drying shed, the only really essential conditions of which are—the provision of a weatherproof roof, protection from sun and high winds, a paved flooring, and free exposure to the air for each piece of timber to be seasoned. Fig. 510 shows a section through a timber-seasoning shed. It will be seen that the sides are made up of a wooden framework which is filled in with louvres.

—even in a dry shed—to produce dark bars across the boards at the strips. White woods should not be stacked with oak

Fig. 509.—Strip nailed to Plank End.

strips, as the gallic acid in that wood will combine with the sap from the pieces being seasoned, and produce weather-stains. Water charged with lime—such as lime-

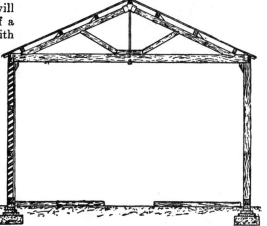

Fig. 508.—End View of Perch Board. Fig. 510.—Section through Timber-seasoning Shed.

Seasoning Fancy Woods.

Pine, mahogany, walnut, and other fancy woods should always be seasoned in a dry place. The first is liable to decay if exposed, and the others to become weatherstained. Sycamore, maple, and other white woods are often spoilt for polished work by being weather-stained with dark marks across each board where the strips have been placed for seasoning. Sycamore being a very delicate wood, it is a good plan to stack panels of this material on their edges, the strips between them being vertical; as when stacked one on the other, with strips between to season, the moisture from the sap is often sufficient

wash—leaves on mahogany a stain of a deep port-wine colour.

Time Required for Seasoning.

The following table has been compiled from practical observation by Mr. Laslett, and gives approximate times in months required for seasoning:—

			Oak.	Fir.
Balks more than 24 in. square require about			26	13
Balks less than 24 in. to 20 „	„		22	11
„ „ 20 „ „ 16 „	„		18	9
„ „ 16 „ „ 12 „	„		14	7
„ „ 12 „ „ 8 „	„		10	5
„ „ 8 „ „ 4 „	„		6	3

Planks require from half to two-thirds the above times, according to their thickness. This table has been largely quoted, but from independent observation it is thought that the time given is insufficient, unless the pieces are cut from fairly dry logs.   Oak

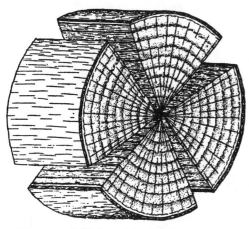

Fig. 511.—Splitting of Log whilst Drying.

planks 4 in. thick require from three to four years in the drying shed before they are fit for joiner's work; and. even then, if cut into smaller pieces, exposing a fresh surface to the air, the timber will shrink still further. All kinds of timber improve by being seasoned slowly; for this reason the place of storage should be cool, with just light enough for convenient handling. Galvanised iron roofs are not suitable for timber-storing sheds, as they become very hot in summer; but, on the other hand, when elevated on poles without sides or ends—with the exception of a few rough boards in the most exposed positions—simply to form a shelter, such roofs soon repay their cost.

SUSCEPTIBILITY OF SEASONED TIMBER.

There is a general impression that timber cannot be used too dry, and that the longer it is kept the better it will be when worked. This is a delusion. Timber should be used as soon as it is thoroughly seasoned, because from that moment it begins to deteriorate. There is, of course, a point at which seasoned timber ceases to shrink

any further; and when this point has been reached the wood will expand and contract with every change of temperature, and more especially with the alternations of dampness and dryness of the atmosphere. This susceptibility is utilised in the workshop; in bending panels to fit curves, for instance, one side of the board is damped and the other warmed, with the result that the damp side swells with the moisture while the other side contracts, causing the panel to bend to the required curve. Timber should never be seasoned in a warmer or drier place than that which it is destined to occupy in actual work; otherwise the expansibility of the material (unless, indeed, it has been duly provided for in planning the work) will probably lead to disaster. For instance, if a panelled door is made in hot weather, the panels being fitted in tightly, and then exposed to the weather, the panels will expand with the wet, and buckle, or will break the joints of the door. Supposing the panel to be 1 ft. long and $\frac{1}{2}$ in. thick; if the panel expands $\frac{1}{20}$ in. the pressure on the framing will be 30 cwt. Another familiar example

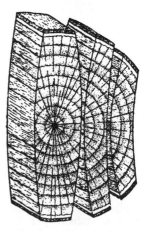

Fig. 512.—Warped Planks.

is a clamped board, which, if made of very dry timber, and put in a damp place, will swell beyond the clamps at each end. Some woods, it is well known, are much more sensitive than others to atmospheric changes. While, for instance, seasoned teak undergoes very little change, American pine expands and contracts considerably.

Shrinkage in Seasoning.

When logs are cut into planks for seasoning, the loss by shrinkage need be considered only so far as regards the final thickness, and an allowance of ¼ in. on thin and ⅜ in. on thick planks will usually be found sufficient; but when logs are cut into scantling that must finish to a given

Fig. 513.—Section of Distorted Plank.

size, the allowance to be made becomes a subject for careful calculation. Planks cut from the same tree always vary in the amount of loss by shrinkage. Some lose more in thickness than others. In others, again, the loss will be principally in width. In shrinking, timber always follows a certain regular course, a glance at which will now be necessary to a clear understanding of the notes that follow. The shrinkage always takes a circular direction around the tree; thus, if a log is left in the round to dry, the fibres of the outer rings will contract together, and clefts will open (see Fig. 511) to admit of this contraction. Or, take a log that has been cut into planks

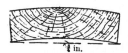

Fig. 514.—Section of Distorted Plank.

and stacked for seasoning; when dry, the planks will have the appearance shown at Fig. 512 (where, of course, the shrinkage is exaggerated). Fig. 513 shows a piece of American oak that was kept seasoning for seven years. It was originally cut square, but the shrinkage naturally took a direction parallel with the annual rings, and the plank contracted to the shape shown. Fig. 514 shows another plank from the same stack. In this the shrinkage, tak-

ing place in the same direction, has caused the timber to warp ¾ in. From these examples it may be gathered that in cutting scantling no fixed rules can be laid down governing the allowance to be made

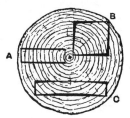

Fig. 515.—Diagram showing Shrinkage of Timber.

in order that it may measure a given size after shrinking, since the allowance must differ for each piece. For instance, in Fig. 515 the plank A will shrink in thickness; B will shrink diagonally, and be out of square when seasoned; while C will contract in width, and warp as shown by the inner line. In cutting up logs for seasoning, the heart of the tree should always,

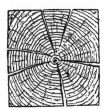

Fig. 516.—Log Split during Seasoning.

when possible, be cut through, because when a piece of wood has the heart left in, the sides are liable to split in seasoning, as shown in Fig. 516. The heart is also—with the exception of the sapwood—the first portion of the tree to decay. When a piece of scantling is required to be of such dimensions that it cannot be obtained without including the heart of the tree in its centre, the log, as some authorities recommend, is split down with the saw, and the two halves are turned over and bolted together again, so that the heart may be fully exposed to the air. It has been already noted that in shrinking some woods lose more than others. Of the timber in general use, probably teak shrinks the least and oak the most. Of the varieties of oak, the American oak shrinks the most, English oak the next, and Stettin oak the least. The following notes will give some idea of the relative losses of these three varieties after being stacked for seven years, the pieces of scantling forming the stack being cut originally to 11¼ in. wide by 4¾ in. thick. American oak (the worst pieces), 10⅝ in. by 4½ in. ; English oak, 10¾ in. by 4½ in. ; Stettin oak, 10⅞ in. full by 4⅝ in. In the same stack the English oak showed the greatest propensity for splitting, the American for warping and twisting, while the Stettin was the soundest of all. In seasoning, timber loses a

Fig. 517.—Position of Cut for Figured Board.

little of its length ; but this is of no consequence, the loss being practically covered by the allowance of a few inches for the dirty and shaky ends that it is usually necessary to cut off from planks taken from the seasoning stack. There is also a slight shrinkage radially from the centre to the outside, but, as has been shown, the shrinkage takes place principally in the circumference of the annual rings.

Seasoning Oak and Elm.

In seasoning oak timber, the best material is the most liable to split, the soft spongy kinds being remarkably free from this fault. Planks cut from young trees of either oak or ash are the better for being kept in a cool dark place, one on the other, without strips, for some time before being stacked, as they are very liable to split if exposed. In stacking elm, the strips, if used at all, should be thin and close together, as this wood twists and buckles a great deal in seasoning. The tendency with elm is to dry it too much. When this wood is overseasoned it loses its strength and turns to a dirty grey colour, and if, when in this condition, it be exposed to wet, it will soon rot.

Artificial Seasoning.

In the artificial seasoning processes the sap is dried up, either by keeping the logs in a heated room, burying them in hot sand, or forcing steam through the pores of the wood. In artificial drying, temperatures of 150° F. to 180° F. are usually employed, the wood being enclosed in specially constructed chambers in which a current of air is kept circulating by means of a blower fan. In this way pine and spruce lumber can be dried fresh from the saw, and is ready for use after allowing about four days per inch of thickness. But oak and other hardwoods should first be air-seasoned for about six months, or there will be " case-hardening " and " checking." Hardwood planks are kept in the kiln for six to ten days per inch of thickness, and are ready for use immediately on withdrawal. Other processes have been invented from time to time, such as extracting the sap by suction and substituting other matter ; but such methods, however efficient they might prove as substitutes for the natural method, are not likely to come into general use while the expense of handling remains greater than the cost of storing and keeping to season naturally. The great objection to artificially seasoned wood is the drying. Dried timber is inferior to naturally seasoned timber, as the drying process seems to take all the nature out of the wood, so that in working it the shavings break away in short pieces, and fine dust rises from the saw and other tools. This defect is known as "sleepiness." Dried timber, moreover, is always deficient in weight ; it follows, therefore, that weighing affords a ready means of testing quality. Artificial seasoning spoils the brightness of the wood, and is by many thought to often impair its durability as well as its elasticity.

WARPING OF UNSEASONED TIMBER.

The evil effects of using unseasoned timber are to be seen almost everywhere in the form of badly fitting doors and windows, floors with joints large enough for articles to fall through, cracked plaster, and many other defects The cause of timber shrinking is, of course, the gradual drying up of the sap or moisture that fills its cells. The warping is caused by irregular drying. The heartwood, being harder, shrinks less than the sapwood, and as a result boards cut as Fig. 514 will always assume the form shown. A board that is apparently dry curls up if placed close to a wall or flat upon the bench after planing. This may generally, however, be corrected by damping the hollow side and placing the board in the sun or before a fire, the "rounding side" being exposed to the warmth. In the case of mahogany, etc., the "hollow side" should be well damped, to stretch the fibres, and afterwards placed under pressure until dry. If very badly twisted, the board should be sawn down and jointed up with glue, to bring it back to its original state. When a thick board is twisted, or, to use a shop term, is "in winding," it is necessary to plane it true, or "take it out of winding," which process of course involves a loss of time and labour.

SECOND SEASONING.

Many woods require a second seasoning after they have been worked, and articles of joinery should be left some time to season before they are wedged up and finished. A board that appears to be thoroughly seasoned will often warp again when the surface has been dressed with the plane. However thoroughly a piece of timber may be seasoned, it will surely shrink more or less when cut down to a smaller size ; and whatever preliminary seasoning timber may have had, it should be reduced to something near the size it is intended to remain and then seasoned further. In constructive woodwork, the fact should always be taken into account that wood, however dry, is subject to this change. Patternmakers find that well-seasoned wood varies at the rate of one-tenth of an inch to the foot in width between the temperature of the pattern shop and that of the foundry. The best, cheapest, and most effective way to overcome this difficulty is by a framed construction using the wood lengthwise of the grain to keep the essential sizes or outline of the pattern, and leaving open joints so as to allow the wood freedom to expand or contract across the grain, and yet not affect the essential sizes.

FIGURE AND GRAIN.

Figure is a source of great annoyance to the worker who has not sufficient skill, or the proper tools, to clean up a "flowery"

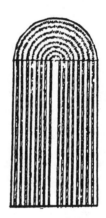

Fig. 518.—Straight Grain.

piece of wood without tearing up the grain. In some cases the logs are cut to show as much of the figure as possible, and the resulting boards are named and priced by the timber merchant accordingly. Figured oak is an example of this. It will be found that on the end of an oak log there is a series of circles, commencing at the centre and getting larger to the outside. These are called the annual rings, because one is added to the tree every year. The medullary rays, the lines radiating like a star from the centre to the outside, produce the figure, or silver grain as it is sometimes termed. To produce figured boards, the timber is cut slanting across the medullary rays as shown at A (Fig. 517, p. 158). A number of cabinet-making woods, such as mahogany, walnut, maple, ash, etc., are named and

Fig. 519.—Longitudinal Section through Annual Rings.

valued according to the figuring upon them, produced sometimes by knots, sometimes by wavy or cross grain, and sometimes, as already stated, by the manner of cutting. In Fig. 518, the grain is shown as straight lines, a result of cutting through the annual rings; but in Fig. 519 there is a figure, pairs of lines in the grain being shown converging to points. This is a common circumstance, these conical terminations determining the length of certain of the annual rings in that particular board. This will be understood when it is remembered that the trunk of a tree tapers from the root upward, and that the annual rings increase in length until the maximum height of the tree is reached. If the annual rings

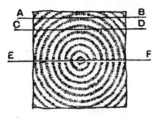

Fig. 520.—Methods of Converting Timber.

are closely deposited the wood is termed "close-grained," while widely deposited rings produce an open grain. The medul-

lary rays aid greatly in securing a grain of fine figure, as with the "silver grain" of oak. They are also well marked in beech, such as is used for planes.

Wainscot Oak.

Oak boards and planks that show prominently a good silver-grain figure are spoken of as wainscot stuff. The term is not now, as was formerly the case, restricted to the oak brought from any particular country. Russian wainscot, Austrian wainscot, English wainscot, and American wainscot are the principal kinds now in the market. Russian wainscot oak is brought over in flitches, Austrian stuff principally in plank

Fig. 521.—Methods of Converting Timber.

form. English wainscot also is mostly in plank, and American rift-sawn or quarter-sawn oak, as it is called, in plank and in board. To obtain the figure it is necessary that the faces of the planks and the boards coincide, as near as may be, with the direction of the medullary rays; the more nearly they do this, the higher is the class of wainscot produced (see Fig. 524, p. 162).

Terms Applied to Various Sizes of Timber.

Timber may be sawn into planks, boards, deals, battens, and scantlings. These terms are by no means very definitely applied. A plank, however, is generally of the same breadth as a board, but greater in thickness. A board is thinner, but wider than a deal, which, again, may be thicker than a plank. Battens are less both in breadth and thickness than deals, while scantling is simply a name given to miscellaneous smaller pieces of timber. According to one system, the sizes of these are as follow : The log is the name by which the tree

Fig. 522.—Method of Converting Timber.

is known after felling. Balk is the tree roughly squared. Plank is sawn timber, 11 in. or more in width, and from 2 in. to 6 in. thick. Deal is 9 in. wide, and not more than 4 in. thick. Batten is 7 in. wide, and not more than 3 in. thick. Board is any width, and not more than 2 in. thick. Quartering is the term applied to small sawn stuff, such as 3 in. by 2 in., 4 in. by 2 in., etc. The name does not apply to stuff above $4\frac{1}{2}$ in. wide. Stuff is a general term, applied to any sawn timber. In Quebec the following classification of planks, deals, and battens is observed : Planks, 11 in. by 2 in., or 11 in. by $1\frac{1}{2}$ in. ; deals, 9 in. by 3 in., or 9 in. by 2 in. ; and battens, 7 in. by 3 in., or 7 in. by 2 in.

CONVERTING OR CUTTING UP TIMBER.

Logs may be sawn in two ways : first, as indicated by the lines A B and C D, and secondly as shown by the line E F (Fig. 520). The lines A B and C D may be tangent or chord respectively of the annual rings, while E F is a diameter of the circular cross-section of the tree. Fig. 521 is another diagram illustrating the same principle. The first method aims at securing a beautiful grain or appearance in length section, and at securing timber of the greatest rectangular section. The second method, sawing radially as it is termed,

11

is intended to obtain the beautiful appearance of the medullary rays when cut obliquely. Converting logs and balks into scantlings, boards, battens, etc., is now done almost entirely by machinery, the same engine frequently working the saw, planing machine, mortising and dovetailing machine, etc. ; or a universal joiner is used, which performs many of the operations formerly executed by hand. Fig. 522 shows another method of converting, also not uncommon ; and in this the central piece, containing the pith, is comparatively weaker than the outer pieces. Fig. 523 shows four methods of cutting a quartered log into boards. Each method has some recommendation. The radial cuts shown at A give the best boards, but the waste of material is great. At B there is a compromise between the methods shown at A and C. The latter gives thick planks without waste. At D the quarter is cut into thinner boards without much waste. Fig. 524 shows the ideal system of wainscot cutting, where each board in the log is made to fall exactly on the lines of the medullary rays. This method of cutting is expensive, and necessarily involves much waste of material. In America, where the production of good wainscot stuff is now receiving special

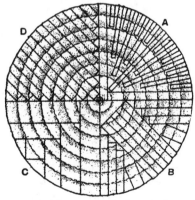

Fig. 523.—Different Methods of Converting Timber.

attention, the modified system shown in Fig. 525 appears to be most popular. The figure in the outer boards of each group is obviously not so good as it is in the centre ones. When the divergence between the line of the ray and the face of the board is greater than 15° the figure begins to be poor, and could hardly be described as wainscot (see Fig. 526).

Selecting Timber.

Timber should be selected bright and fresh in appearance, without variation of colour except that between the sapwood and the heartwood. Live knots, if not too big, are not objectionable except in ornamental work. Dead knots should be glued in before fixing the work, or knocked out altogether and their places filled with suitable plugs of wood. Where possible it is

species it may be. Generally the strongest and most durable will be that which has grown the slowest, as indicated by the narrowness of the annular rings. The cellular tissue, as seen in the medullary rays, when these are visible, should be hard and compact. The fibro-vascular part, which contains the woody fibre and the tubes for the circulation of sap, should unite firmly; a freshly cut surface should not be woolly, nor should the wood clog the teeth of the saw with loose fibres. The freshly cut surface should be firm and shiny. In specimens of the same species superior heaviness and darkness of colour are, in general, signs of extra strength and durability. Resinous woods having the least resin in their pores,

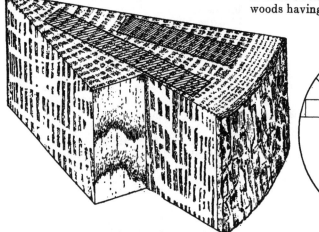

Fig. 524.—Cutting Wainscot Oak.

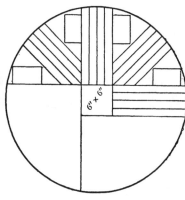

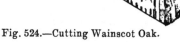

Fig. 525.—American Rift-sawing.

best to avoid them. Shakes must be avoided, and also gumming, if possible. Sapwood, since it is but partly formed wood, is unsuitable for use, especially in a moist situation. A characteristic of strength in timber is closeness and uniformity of the annual rings. The soundness of timber may be tested by placing the ear close to one end of the log, while another person delivers a succession of smart blows with a hammer upon the opposite end, when a continuance of the vibrations will indicate to an experienced ear the degree of soundness. If only a dull thud can be heard, the listener may be certain that the wood is not sound. Certain appearances are characteristic of good wood, of whatever

and non-resinous woods having the least sap in them, are generally the best.

General Defects in Timber.

The strength of timber is affected by numerous circumstances—as nature of soil; position; manner of felling; method of handling after felling; method of seasoning, over-drying having the effect of destroying its toughness; method of converting by the sawyer, who has to exercise considerable care and skill in cutting the logs to the best advantage to remove defects; the attacks of worms and other insects, whose injuries to the wood, though small when taken singly, will collectively prove a serious matter. There is a great variation in the strength of the same kinds of timber. A piece of oak may be found as soft and kind as deal, or a piece of ash as light and brittle as pine ; and practical skill is neces-

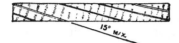

Fig. 526.—Inferior Wainscot Oak.

sary in distinguishing between the good qualities and the bad. Even the most skilful judges are sometimes deceived, especially with log timber. Often a tree apparently sound will, when cut up, be found to have defects rendering most of its timber of little value.

SHAKES IN TIMBER.

Shakes are splits, clefts, or cracks caused by the unequal contraction of the inner and outer portions of the tree, due to the loss

Fig. 527.—Shrinkage at Annual Rings.

of sap in seasoning, or to the drying-up, decay, or unequal shrinkage of the central portion of the tree. Shrinkage in wood takes place along the circumference of the annual rings, as shown by arrows in Fig. 527, the result being suggested by Fig. 528. If unequal, the shrinkage is confined to certain sections of the heartwood, these sections separating from the portions which do not shrink, and shakes are the openings left. In damp weather it is often a difficult matter to find the shakes, but if the board suspected be placed with its centre on the

Fig. 528.—Shrunken Wood.

corner of a bench, or on another board, and the edges pressed down with the hands, the shake will open sufficiently to make known its presence. Shakes of every description

are a great source of weakness. They are dangerous beyond calculation, because of their possible developments when the timber is loaded. Fig. 529 shows the joint at the head of the king post in a king-post roof truss ; in this joint the top of the post is under a shearing stress, and the result of a shake in the position shown at A can be readily imagined.

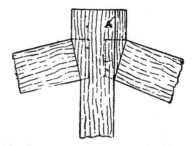

Fig. 529.—Joint at Head of King-post.

RING AND CUP SHAKES.

Ring shakes (Fig. 530) are caused by a separation of the annual rings, and may be attributed either to weak nourishment in the sap due to poor soil, or to the excessive bending and straightening of the tree when exposed to high winds. When the shakes occur at the outer portion of the tree, they may be caused by the expansion during hard frost of an unusually large quantity of sap.

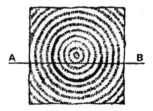

Fig. 530.—Ring Shake.

This sap, like water, expands while freezing, thus rupturing and separating the annual rings. Ring shake occurs generally near the root end, and is rarely so serious as either heart-shakes or star-shakes (described on p. 164). The most serious ring shakes extend the greater length of the tree, and as the two portions readily separate, the log is worthless for sawing into planks.

When the shake forms but a small portion of an arc, the larger portion of the tree is not affected by it, and may be cut into planks in the usual way. When a log with ring shake is cut as at A B (Fig. 530), the result is a cup shake in the plank, this name

Fig. 531.—Cup Shake.

arising from the shape of the detached portion (see Fig. 531).

HEART AND STAR SHAKES.

Heart shakes (Fig. 532), the commonest defect in timber, may be described as a split extending through the centre, and more or less across the whole diameter of the tree. If this shake or crack follows a straight course along the trunk, it is not so serious a defect as if it twists around spirally, as heart shakes sometimes do. If upon inspecting the opposite ends of a piece of timber the shake is seen to be twisted to any considerable extent, it is clear that the piece will waste in cutting up. A prevailing wind may cause a tree to twist in its growth, and such a tree would split in a spiral direction. Such trees are rarely cut into planks, but they are used as whole logs. Heart shake is a defect common to exogenous

Fig. 532.—Heart Shakes.

trees, but in some timber it is so insignificant that the inexperienced would fail to notice it. Star shake (Fig. 533) is another defect, similar to, but more serious than, heart shake; splits radiate from the centre to the circumference, and separate the

whole tree into so many pieces that sound planks cannot be cut from it. A freshly felled tree does not show the shakes, but they are made plain as soon as the log has dried somewhat. Heart and star shakes are supposed to be caused by the decay of the heart of the tree after it has reached the period of full growth. They may be also due to unequal shrinkage, caused by sudden changes of temperature, and possibly, as has been suggested, violent winds on the growing tree help to produce them.

WANDERING HEART, TWISTED FIBRES, CROOKS, ETC.

Sometimes, in the trunk of a tree that is fairly straight on the outside, the heart does not follow the outer lines of the trunk, but inclines first towards one side, then towards another, throughout the length of the log;

Fig. 533.—Star Shakes.

this defect is known as wandering heart. In trees rising in unsheltered positions, either on open ground or on the margins of woods, the growing fibres are apt to wind in a spiral direction from the base to the top of the trunk; and in a plank cut from a log taken from a tree having this defect, the fibres of the timber, instead of running from end to end, would cross the plank obliquely, as shown in Fig. 534; this defect is known as "twisted fibres." Some trees, notably pines and poplars, rear straight trunks independently of situation; but some others, deprived of the shelter of woods or copses, are apt to grow crooked trunks. Such crooks are often found in hedgerow oak and ash trees, and for certain purposes are an advantage rather than a defect. Planks cut from logs of this description should be used for cutting compass pieces. Cross grain is obtained by cutting a straight plank from a crooked or twisted log. If straight beams or scantlings are cut from trees showing any of these three peculiarities, the fibres will be, to a greater or less extent, cut across, producing cross-grained timber. In pieces of this descrip-

Fig. 534.—Log with "Twisted Fibres."

tion, the stresses are liable to be diverted from the direction intended by the designer of a piece of work, a compressive or tensile stress being, perhaps, converted into a shearing or splitting stress. Thus, cross-grained wood should not be used in any position where there is likely to be a strain upon it.

Upsets.

These are caused in felling the tree, or in removing the logs to the point of shipment. They have the appearance of a crack or shake across the grain of the wood, and, of course, weaken it. An upset has the same effect upon the strength of a piece of timber across the grain as a shake would have in the direction of the grain. An upset cannot be readily distinguished in a rough sawn log, but when the wood is planed a line may be seen across the grain, where the fibres have been crushed together, or in some cases torn asunder. In a piece of timber bearing a tensile stress, an upset has much the same effect on its strength as cutting the fibres asunder with a saw.

Knots.

Knots are of two kinds—live and dead. Live knots are those which are apparently part of the board in which they occur, and are due to the presence of a living branch when the tree was cut down. In some fancy woods their appearance is welcome, but in deal and pine they are always liable to exude resinous matter, sometimes months after a piece of work has been finished and painted. Dead knots are the inner portions of branches that were dead when the tree was felled. As a rule they are darker in colour than live knots, and are often surrounded by a black ring. If timber containing these is used, the knots should be knocked out with a hammer and glued back in position again. Knots are a source of weakness, especially in positions where the fibres must withstand a tensile stress. Where there is a direct compressive stress, live knots need not materially weaken the work, but to the full extent of their size dead knots will reduce the strength of a piece of timber in any position. For example, take the case of a beam supported and loaded as in Fig. 535. If this beam would safely bear a load of 10 cwt. when sound, a knot 1 in. in diameter, in the position shown at A, would weaken the beam to such an extent that its carrying capacity would be reduced to 8¼ cwt. On the other hand, a live knot at B, in the compressive half of the beam, would not weaken it appreciably. A vertical knot, 1 in. in diameter, in the position c (Fig. 535), would reduce the safe load on the beam to 7¼ cwt. From these figures it will be seen that the strength of a knotty beam depends to a great extent upon the position it may occupy; and knotty timber, if used at all, should be placed where the fibres are to withstand a tensile stress.

Sapwood.

Beneath the bark of all trees there is found a circle of wood—the sapwood—not so fully matured as that nearer the heart.

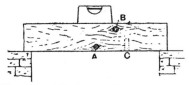

Fig. 535.—Weakening Effect of Knots.

In some timbers, such as hickory and elm, this sapwood may be easily distinguished by the difference in colour. In others, such as pine and deal, the variation in colour is not so noticeable unless the sapwood is stained with water, when it assumes a greenish hue. In ash trees the difference between the sapwood and the heart cannot usually be distinguished, but in old trees the heart becomes brown, and sometimes nearly black. It is one of the characteristics of the genus *Fraxinus* (ash family) that the formation of heartwood is long delayed. But if the trees are allowed to grow old enough, heartwood is eventually formed. American ash is one of the earliest to show signs of heartwood. It usually begins to form when the tree is from twenty to thirty years old. It is of a light brown colour, and does not follow the course of the annual rings, but crosses them backwards and forwards as an irregular central blotch. In English ash the heartwood is rarely seen. The trees are mostly cut down, or get bad in the middle, before it begins to show. It usually makes its appearance between the fortieth and fiftieth year. As in oak trees, soil influences the formation of the heartwood a good deal. Speaking generally, the sapwood of ash is tougher than the heartwood, yet not quite so hard. Oak trees contain a large amount of sapwood, it sometimes being as much as $2\frac{1}{2}$ in. or even more. This is lighter in colour than the inner portion of the tree, and will often rot away before the heartwood is thoroughly seasoned. The amount of sapwood present in a log is due partly to the nature of the soil and partly to the season of felling. Trees cut down in late spring, when the sap is rising, or in early autumn, when the sap is falling, show a large percentage of sapwood in the timber. The sapwood of hickory and elm is as strong as the heartwood, but is more liable to the attacks of insect pests. In examining worm-eaten pieces of these timbers, it is often found that most of the worms have penetrated to the heartwood, and have there stopped. The sapwood of oak, pine, walnut, and deal is weak, is liable to become worm-eaten and to rot away, and should always be cut off by the sawyer in converting the timber.

RIND GALLS.

These are caused by injury to the bark of a growing tree. If a piece of bark is removed from a growing tree, the sap, in forming the annual rings, freely escapes from the wound at first, but gradually a hard ring is formed round the hole, which in time will close, and as years go on will heal up, and the annual rings and the bark grow over the place, until, except for a swelling, the injured part is not visible from the outside. Logs that have been cut from a forked tree will have what is sometimes known as a rind gall, extending from 18 in. to 2 ft. from the top end in the centre of the log, caused by the two branches of the fork injuring each other's bark at the point of division. Rind galls have much the same effect upon the strength of wood as knots, that is, they break the continuity of the fibres.

ECCENTRIC PITH.

The pith at the end of a log may not be in the centre; when found very far off it, the fact has been attributed to the circumstance of one side of the tree having a more favourable exposure than the other.

EFFECT OF WET.

Wet timber is weaker than dry, and soaking in water affects its strength in the same manner as if it were used before being seasoned. For this reason a greater margin of safety should be allowed in designing a structure where any of the beams are liable to be loaded while wet.

DURABILITY OF WOOD.

Wood-substance, the material of which the cell walls in wood are built, is one of the most stable of organic compounds. Providing the wood—as oak, alder, birch, cedar, poplar, etc.—is free from specially injurious external influences, each species alike appears to last indefinitely, whereas most organic bodies, immediately life has ceased, begin to putrefy. The process of putrefaction goes on with greater or with less rapidity in exact ratio as the nitrogenous elements, which largely comprise the bodies, are present or absent. The durability of wood is due to the very small proportion of nitrogen—amounting to considerably less than one per cent. of the total bulk—in its composition. Wood is, therefore, not much subject to decay arising from internal weakness, or from chemical changes like those that occur during putrefaction; while senility (or decay from age) of any part of the wood-substance is practically unknown. The period of its life appears to be controlled solely by external influences.

DESTRUCTIVE INFLUENCES.

Failure, when failure occurs, is nearly always due to one of three causes, namely:—(1) External chemical influences; (2) mechanical, or physically disruptive, influences; and (3) the influence of a few of the larger and more voracious of the vegetable parasites. By chemical influence is meant the influence of the actions of corrosive liquids, vapours, or gases. This often occurs through the formation of sulphuric, nitric, and other acids, by the action of rainwater on various kinds of soil; and it also occurs by simple maceration. The wood is affected then just as pulpwood is affected in the digesters, preparatory to its use for paper manufacture: that is to say, the chemicals render soluble certain of the wood elements, the general organisation consequently being broken down. Certain kinds of combustion, or oxidation, also come under this heading, particularly that kind of eremacausis (or slow chemical combustion) to which the name wet rot has been applied (see next column). Mechanical influences imply abrasions and injuries caused by contact with other hard substances, or through the ravages of wood-boring insects, or from splits, shakes, sun-cracks, and other violences against its natural constitution, whether these are due to changes in locality, to changes in temperature, to moisture, or to any similar cause. The fungial parasites and their very destructive work are described on p. 168. Examples of ancient timber and woodwork that have not been subject to the separate or combined effects of these three influences are rare. The greatest sphere for the employment of wood lies within the radius of a few feet above or below the surface of the earth; but unfortunately, that is a situation in which the destructive influences are found here in their fullest activity—innumerable

natural chemical processes, attacks of insects, and injurious vegetable growths. Existing examples of very old timber, therefore, usually have been preserved in some way outside the scope of the influences named.

PRESERVATION.

Immunity from attack, under natural conditions, is possible usually in one of three possible ways. (1) The wood may be completely submerged in harmless liquids, usually water; (2) it may be buried in a dry soil not subject to extreme changes of temperature; and (3) it may be in ordinary atmospheres, but protected from the baneful influences mentioned above Wood is remarkably durable when exposed in the air, providing only it is kept dry, and kept safe from mechanical and chemical injuries. The fungi will not attack it in a dry condition. The amount of nitrogen in its composition is not sufficient to promote their growth, and moisture in both air and wood is essential to their life and well-being. Well-preserved, aged woodwork most often is found in very large buildings, where it mostly forms parts of roofs, high up from the ground, or otherwise removed from harmful influences. Usually, much of the ground surface in its vicinity is paved in some way, so that the injurious chemical exhalations of the soil are wholly obviated, or are reduced to a minimum; and usually it is found in an atmosphere not congenial to or in a situation inaccessible to depredatory insect life. In some cases, no doubt, the natural secretions of the wood are in no small measure an efficient protection.

WET ROT AND DRY ROT.

Both wet rot and dry rot weaken timber by destroying the toughness of its fibres Wet rot attacks either the growing tree or timber that is subject to alternate periods of wetness and dryness. Trees that are felled and left in the woods to become covered with dead leaves and undergrowth are subject to this disease, by which some timbers are rapidly destroyed. The sapwood of oak trees is very liable to be attacked, and logs left in the forests some time after felling will often be found with the sap converted into touchwood, but leaving the heartwood sound. In designing new work, the evil effects of dry rot have not generally to be taken into consideration, except so far as regards preventive measures against its development. It is due to a fungus-like growth, which speedily manifests itself in timber confined in a close, moist atmosphere ; and, in order to prevent its appearance, timber should never be placed in a position where a free circulation of air cannot be maintained. A confined, moist atmosphere, such as that found in the space under a floor that is not ventilated, is conducive to its development. Its presence may be detected by the material presenting a speckled appearance, being comparatively light in weight, and emitting a characteristic fusty smell. A floor joist attacked will sometimes have the appearance of being covered with a sheet of white paper. Care should be taken to avoid timber with any signs of dry rot, as the disease will spread at the first opportunity and do irreparable damage. Beams and joists built into walls are liable to be attacked by dry rot, and for this reason the ends of these should be put in so as to leave an air space on each side. Foxiness is a yellow or red tinge found in timber, and is due to the rotting of the fibres. Doatiness is a somewhat similar form of rot, but shows in speckled patches. It is found largely in ash, especially in American ash, also in birch poles and in beech, and is often produced, as are other forms of rot, by being packed in the close hold of a ship, or by being stacked for seasoning without sufficient care. The effect of rot upon timber is first to render it brittle, and in time to reduce the fibres to powder.

Worms in Timber.

Timber containing worm holes should be regarded with suspicion, as worms seldom attack timber that is not defective in some way or other. Beech, when used for furniture, is liable to the attacks of these pests. There are three branches of the beetle family that commit ravages in wood. The *Ptinus* and *Anobium* genera are chiefly responsible for the holes that appear in old furniture, roofs, and all interior woodwork. The *Lymoxylon* confines its operations mainly to oak timber that is kept in wood yards near the sea. This latter is a borer of comparatively recent introduction, and on account of its liking for the vicinity of the sea is generally known as the " dockyard borer." In their operations the three kinds behave exactly alike. First, the eggs of the mother beetle are deposited on or just under the surface of the wood, where they lie until the larvæ are hatched. The larva, when it is strong enough, begins to bore a passage deeper into the wood, filling up the tunnel as it goes with fine white wood powder. At a certain stage of its progress the usual transformation cocoon is made, and at the end of the resting period the changed insect emerges in the form of a small winged beetle. The remedies are : (1) Fumigation in a closed chamber with pungent and noxious fumes. (2) Steeping the articles affected in solutions of poisonous chemicals, such as bichloride of mercury, copper sulphate, chloride of calcium, iodide of potassium, etc. (3) The application by hand of various oils and spirits, as petroleum, benzine, chloroform, and alcohol. (4) The most recent recommendation is the use of a 15 per cent. solution of hydrogen peroxide well brushed over the wood. (5) A coating of asphaltum or coal tar is said to repel the teredo or ship worm, which attacks piles and other submerged wood.

Decay of Cabinet Woods.

The decay of cabinet woods used in the construction of furniture has a characteristic peculiarly its own, and is entirely distinct from that which is met with in timbers used in building construction. This decay takes various forms. If the timber decays to such an extent that it becomes practically useless for its purpose, and is full of moisture, it is said to be " rotten " ; if, on the other hand, the wood is dry and crumbling to the touch, the effect is called " dry rot." In cabinet woods decay is met with in another form. Portions of an article may be pierced with small holes of varying depths, large enough to admit pin-points ; generally they are most abundant at the bottom of the article, near the floor. On knocking against the wood, a very fine powder falls from these holes, and small white grubs, which on examination through a powerful glass closely resemble beetles, are occasionally found. They are known as weevils, and seem to thrive by burrowing into the heart of the wood ; and, strange to note, the harder the wood the more destructive the insect becomes ; oak, elm, birch, and walnut appear to be its special favourites. Thoroughly well-seasoned timber is rarely attacked. Wood that is cut and worked up green is most susceptible, for though such wood may be easily worked and appear dry on the outside, inwardly there is a notable percentage of moisture. Cabinet woods, when made up, are usually sealed up with French polish, or varnish, or size and colour, and the moisture is prevented from working outwards ; and as the articles most attacked are those standing on the floor and in living-rooms, the air is warmer as it gets higher. The warmth dries the top of the article more than the bottom, and the confined moisture, in endeavouring to find a vent, travels downwards, and is checked by the currents of cold air that pass along the floor as doors are opened, thus setting up a condition that encourages animal life. Hardwoods faced with plaster-of-Paris are peculiarly susceptible to this decay. For instance, the bases of harps, made of beech or oak, faced with plaster enrichments, will, if laid aside for years, be found much worm-eaten, the mischief in some cases extending half-way up the pole and belly or soundboard ; and it is generally found that old violins thus infested have been stored away for years in a case shut up away from light and air. Such articles should be moved occasionally, and exposed to light and air to prevent rot ; but if they are already badly infested, cut away the most infested portions and replace them with sound wood. Of course, no solution will add life and vitality to wood that is already decayed ; the utmost that can be done is, by destroying the grubs, to prevent further mischief. It should be noted that if an infested article is left undisturbed, the weevils will migrate to other articles in the same room. The

simplest way to kill the grubs is to saturate the articles well with benzoline, wood naphtha, turpentine, or liquid ammonia ; or a solution (1 oz. to 1 pt. of water) of bichloride of mercury (corrosive sublimate) can be injected into the holes, and will prove a more thorough remedy. Hydrogen peroxide has of late been very highly recommended, as noted in the previous paragraph. In any case, merely washing the surface with solutions is ineffective. It must be applied liberally, but this treatment is pretty certain to destroy the polished surface.

BUYING TIMBER.

When timber is to be used in large quantities, it is as a rule bought some considerable time (in many instances two years) before it is required for use, in order to complete seasoning, etc. There is the risk of loss by rot if the timber is not carefully stacked, or if it is stored in damp or unsuitable positions, and too much care cannot be taken in stacking timber when it has to be kept for any considerable time. The published tables that show the brands, stamped or otherwise, marked on the timber to denote its quality, place of origin, etc., will be of considerable use to the inexperienced buyer ; it is probable, however, that a practised hand relies more upon his own judgment than upon these marks and brands, though even to him the brands are not without their value. Other useful aids to the timber buyer are the specifications or lists issued by timber merchants. These lists give particulars of the several parcels of wood offered for sale, such as the port of shipment, the kind of timber, the brand or distinguishing mark, the number and length of the pieces, where stored in the docks, and sometimes the price. The following is an illustrative example : —

Ex "Abel" @ Holmsund.

CENTRE YARD SHEDS.

M.D.F.	110 pieces 28 ft. to 24 ft.	3 by 11
	30 pieces 23 ft. to 21 ft.	yellow.
	60 ·pieces 18 ft. to 16 ft.	
	30 pieces 9 ft. to 6 ft.	
	at per foot run	

Timber Standards.

Timber is reckoned and sold by several standards, but that in most general use is the Petersburg standard, in which 120 pieces of deal 11 in. by 1½ in. and 12 ft. long, and having a cubical content of 165 ft., is called one hundred deals. Timber is also sold by the load (which in squared timber is equal to 50 ft. cube), by the 120 pieces, and often by the running or lineal foot. In planks, 600 ft. superficial of 1-in. stuff, or 400 ft. of 1½-in., and so on, would be equal to a load. This difference in the mode of selling is somewhat perplexing to an inexperienced person, but some useful tables are published called "equation of deals," which show the relative cost of the Petersburg standard, the load, and the 120 12-ft. lengths of various sizes; thus, taking £10 per Petersburg standard as the rate, 120 12-ft. lengths of 9 in. by 3 in. would be £16 7s. 4d., and 120 12-ft. lengths of 6½ in. by 2½ in. would be £9 17s., and a load would be £3 0s. 8d. It sometimes happens that planks, deals, and battens of the more uncommon scantlings are proportionately cheaper than the sizes for which there is a greater demand. The standards described above are used almost wholly for what are generally called soft woods—such as fir, etc.—from Baltic ports. Hardwoods are usually sold by the foot superficial, and are mostly quoted as in the inch thickness; the average width affects the prices to some extent. Mahogany is generally to be had from ¼ in. in thickness up to several inches, and in widths varying on an average from 10 in. to, say, 23 in. or thereabouts. According to one timber price list consulted at random, prices are quoted for birch from ¼ in. to 1 in. thick, average widths 10 in. to 15 in.; teak ½ in. to 1½ in. thick, averaging 10 in. wide; American walnut from ¼ in. to 4 in. thick; and oak ¼ in. to 2 in. thick.

Cost of Sawing Timber.

As regards sawing, in the case of battens, deals, and planks, the charges are usually at per dozen cuts, and price varies according to the length and also to the depth— that is, whether to battens, deals, or planks. To saw a plank 3 in. wide into three boards, each 1 in. thick, would need two deep cuts, or into four boards would require three cuts, and so on. It need hardly be pointed out that owing to the waste the boards would not hold the full thickness; thus, supposing one deep cut to 3-in. stuff, the two resulting planks, if of equal thickness, would only be 1½ in. thick nominally. Flatting cuts for converting deals, etc., into quartering and small scantlings are generally charged at per 100 ft. run, according to the thickness. Arris or feather-edged cutting costs extra. The sawing of hardwood is much more costly than in the case of fir (soft wood), and is usually charged at per 100 ft. superficial. For details as to the sawing charges, one of the London sawing mills price lists could be consulted with advantage.

Short Ends of Timber.

It often happens that the timber dealers have a lot of 9 in. by 3 in. deals that are known as "short ends." These vary in length from 5 ft. to 8 ft., and have been cut from the best deals abroad, where they are too long for shipping. They may be purchased for about 2d. per foot, and the extra charge for sawing into boards will be ¼d. per foot. It is advisable to stock a few dozen deals cut to various sizes, such as ½-in., ¾-in., and 1-in. board, as they improve by keeping if properly stacked.

Hard and Soft Woods.

Timber is classed as hard or soft, and the main point of difference between the trees that produce these classes is that the soft-wooded tree has "needle" leaves— slim, narrow, and almost uniform in breadth—whilst the hardwood trees have broad leaves of various shapes. Again, some soft-wood trees carry cones, such trees being termed conifers. Resin, too, is more characteristic of soft than of hard wood. To the class of soft woods belong the pines, spruces, and firs, and the most common examples of these are yellow pine, white fir, pitch pine, and spruce or red fir. In the commoner hard woods are oak, beech, mahogany, ash, walnut, plane, elm, birch, and ebony. There are many varieties of timber, and information can be obtained regarding four hundred different specimens, while in Great Britain alone the number runs up to thirty-six. It is intended here to deal only with varieties to be met in the course of daily carpentry, joinery, and ordinary cabinet work.

WEYMOUTH OR YELLOW PINE.

Yellow pine is the product of five-leaved pine trees, which are few in number but

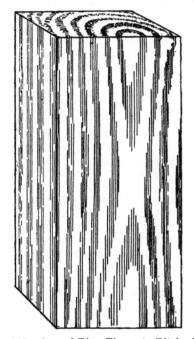

Fig. 536.—Annual Ring Figure in Pitch-pine.

widely scattered. They may be termed the aristocracy of the pine tribe. They are clean-looking, graceful, and slender-limbed trees. They sometimes grow to a very large size, approaching the dimensions of the gigantic redwood trees; but they never lose the superior refined look that is characteristic of their growth as seedlings and as young trees. The branching habit is more regular than in the three-leaved and four-leaved pines, and seldom breaks down or becomes otherwise interrupted. The leaves also are much more slender and grass-like than those of the two- or three-leaved pines. The wood is soft and light, and remarkable for its evenness of texture. The most familiar example is Weymouth pine, the yellow pine of cabinet makers, also called soft pine, pine, and American pine in this country, while in America it is known exclusively as white pine. The character of the wood afforded by the various five-leaved pines is nearly identical. The principal varieties are the Weymouth pine (*Pinus strobus*), a native of America; the Bhotan pine (*Pinus excelsa*), an Indian tree; and the sugar pine (*Pinus Lambertiana*). A hard-and-fast line cannot be drawn between this wood and spruce fir or white deal, described in the next paragraph but one.

BALTIC RED OR YELLOW DEAL.

This timber, produced by the Scotch fir, more properly called the Scots pine (*Pinus sylvestris*), is more largely used than any other kind. It is commonly known as Northern pine. It is imported into Great Britain from the shores of the Baltic, and from Norway and Sweden, in planks about 16 ft. long by 9 in. broad by 3 in. thick, known as deals; 7 in. broad by 2½ in. thick, known as battens; and 11 in. broad by 3 in. thick, known as planks. These are cut into boards, and stacked in perches to season, and the buyer is usually allowed to make a selection. Avoid knots, shakes, and sap. The last may be distinguished by its colour, which is generally of a greenish or brownish hue on one or both edges of the boards. Also examine the ends of the boards for rot. Yellow deal is of a honey-yellow colour, and timber from the same kind of tree, but slightly different in colour, is known in some parts of the country as red deal. It is useful for both inside and outside work.

SPRUCE FIR OR WHITE DEAL.

This wood is known as white deal, white fir, spruce fir, and spruce deal, and it is imported in planks named according to size, as in the case of yellow deal. It is produced by the *Picea excelsa*, which grows in the same districts as the *Pinus sylvestris*.

The same rules should be observed in the selection as for yellow deal, but spruce is more subject to dead knots. The knots are hard and glassy, and are usually at right angles with the surface. The boards are white in colour, and plane with a silky lustre. In planing, the wedge holding the plane-iron should be driven in tightly, as there is danger, when the cutter strikes a knot, of its being forced completely out of the plane. White deal is not so durable, and is more liable to warp than the yellow kind. The annual rings are distinct, and the autumn layer, containing less red matter than red or yellow deal, is not so deep in colour, being inclined to a brownish tint. A peculiar characteristic is that the sapwood can hardly be distinguished from the heartwood. White deal warps if unrestrained, and thus is unsuitable for independent joinery work such as doors, but shrinks very little, and is used frequently for panels. It retains its clean light colour.

PITCH-PINE.

Pitch-pine is a heavy resinous wood that comes from the Southern States of America, but chiefly from Georgia, Savannah, and Pensacola. It is beautifully figured, and was in general use a few years ago for the seats and fittings of public buildings. It is liable to split, shrinks very much, exudes resin, and if varnished soon loses its polish, as the resin of the wood seems to kill the varnish. In appearance it is light reddish-brown, very straight-grained, and highly resinous. It is strong, and difficult to work compared with other pines. The resin in it is troublesome in tooling. The wood is liable to shake and to shrink, but can be obtained in great lengths; it is used for heavy beams, stair material, doors, etc. It often has a beautifully figured grain, and offers a good example of strong annual ring figure (see Fig. 536, p. 171). The resinous quality renders it very durable, especially when exposed to water; if cut from trees that have been recently tapped, the durability and strength are greatly reduced. As these trees grow to a great height, and throw out their branches from the top, the wood is very free from knots.

Pitch-pine may be had in logs from 10 in. to 18 in. square, and from 20 ft. to over 40 ft. long. Being subject to shakes, it will be advantageous to obtain it in planks, which may be had from 3 in. to 5 in. thick, and from 10 in. to 15 in. wide. Pitch-pine commonly is supposed to be the produce of *Pinus resinosa*. The produce of the *Pinus rigida* is in some parts of the United States locally called pitch-pine, but it is not the same wood, it is thought, as is known in England by that name. Notwithstanding great variations of quality, the wood known in England as pitch-pine (but not so called in America) may be taken as the produce of the *Pinus australis*, American names for which are Southern pine, Georgia pine, yellow pine, hard pine, long-leaved pine. It grows over a vast tract of country, and its differences of quality may be attributed, as in the case of the Scotch fir, to the great variations in soil, climate, elevation, etc. But it is rarely found extending beyond 150 miles from the coast. Because it can be got in great lengths and is cheap, there is a considerable temptation to use it for long tie-beams of roofs; but the greatest care should be taken to ventilate it thoroughly in all parts, especially the ends, and if this be neglected it will soon decay. In a dry atmosphere it becomes after a time very brittle, and when it breaks from being subjected to cross strain (which a tie-beam is not, and a floor girder is), it breaks off short. Also, it may be noted that, if subjected to moist heat, as in a greenhouse, it has a very short life.

LARCH.

The timber of the larch is considered excellent, and it is not subject to knots, as are the other members of the pine family. The wood is used for house building in the region of its native habitat, the Alps, and is much prized on account of its non-liability to rot, even in damp places. English-grown larch is largely used in rural districts by wheelwrights and carpenters, and it is the kind of wood most commonly used for fencing, for which purposes it is said to exceed oak in durability. Larch shrinks considerably in drying. The larches are in some respects more allied to the cedars than to the pines, firs, or spruces. The leaves are very short and tiny, and grow in small tufts together, indefinite in number. This is also the habit of the cedars, but the larch is a deciduous tree (it annually sheds the whole of its leaves), while the cedars are evergreens. The cones of the larch are small compared with the cones of the trees already mentioned, and usually persist on the branches for some time after the annual shedding of the leaves. The three most important larches are the Siberian larch (*Larix davurica*), the European larch (*Larix europœa*), and the American larch or tamarack (*Larix pendula*).

DISTINGUISHING PINE FROM FIR WOOD.

The absolute distinction of the woods produced by the various pine trees is only possible by microscopic examination, and in many cases it is even then a matter of extreme difficulty. To furnish an example of what is implied, when viewed microscopically the Weymouth pine shows only one large pit in the parenchyma cells of the medullary ray that adjoins the vertical tracheides of the wood, while spruce exhibits three to five very small pits in the same cells. This is but one example of the structural differences that are only revealed by high magnification. The density, weight, colour, and arrangement of the annual rings are aids, but these do not by any means constitute a reliable basis of distinction. The firs do not furnish much valuable wood; as a rule the quality is poor, and the material looked upon with disfavour by all trades alike. The wood of the silver fir is perhaps best known, and furnishes a fair standard by which the value of other kinds may be estimated.

AMERICAN WHITEWOOD OR BASSWOOD.

Basswood is one of the many names applied to the wood of the *Liriodendron tulipifera*, which is a native of the eastern side of North America; it is a large tree with very luxuriant foliage, fond of low-lying districts and moist soil. In the London market the wood is better known as American poplar, yellow poplar, canary wood (on account of its colour, which in best qualities is a yellowy green, though some specimens are greenish-white), or American whitewood, and it would be described as such in the lists. In America it is known as whitewood, poplar, canoe-wood, and saddletree-wood. Basswood or "bass" is, however, the name by which it is best known in the English workshops. The white wooden articles for enamelling sold at fancy shops are made of this wood. The wood is soft, easily worked, straight in the grain, and of a remarkably uniform texture. For this latter quality probably it is not excelled by any known soft wood, and it also has the valuable property of taking glue well. It is readily obtainable in all ordinary lengths, and in widths of from 2 ft. to 3 ft. It is, however, rather liable to shrink, and sometimes to warp, but does not twist. In America the wood called basswood comes from a totally different tree—the *Tilia americana*, or American lime. This wood is harder and whiter than that of the *Liriodendron tulipifera*; it is of even texture, and not much liable to shrinkage. Both wood and tree are much like the ordinary lime of Europe—*Tilia europœa*.

CALIFORNIAN REDWOOD OR SEQUOIA.

This wood is produced by a Californian tree which grows to an enormous size. It is coarse-grained, soft, easily split and worked, and is used for backing furniture, for the sides and bottoms of drawers, and for temporary unpainted articles. It is not difficult to plane or saw, but is inclined to be very brittle. Because of this defect the wood is difficult to make smooth on the end grain. It is not suitable for polishing or painting, as the grain is liable to rise after the work is finished, giving a wavy appearance. Its light-red colour when first planed turns to a reddish brown with age.

CEDAR.

This is the product of species of the coniferous genus *Cedrus*, and of allied genera, growing in many parts of the world, but chiefly in America, though the most famed cedar tree is that of Lebanon, *Cedrus Libani*. The commercial varieties are coarse-grained, easily worked woods, much like Honduras mahogany in appearance, for which cedar is sometimes sold, but the latter may be easily distinguished by its smell. Cigar boxes are made of a kind of cedar. The wood of the cedar of Lebanon is very highly valued where procurable, but as a rule the trees are too rare to be much cut for timber. In India, however, the deodar cedar is plentiful, and its wood is used for general purposes.

MAHOGANY AND BAYWOOD.

Spanish, Honduras, and bay mahogany are all three produced by the true mahogany tree, *Swietenia mahagani*. The distinguishing names were originally given in reference to the localities from which the wood was principally shipped. Thus, Spanish mahogany came from Cuba and some other West Indian islands and ports belonging to Spain ; Honduras mahogany came from the province of Honduras in Central America—chiefly from the neighbourhood of the mouth of the Rio Hondo ; while baywood or bay mahogany was obtained from various places around the coast of the bay of Honduras. The mahogany procured from these three districts varied considerably in colour, in hardness, and in figure—the Spanish wood being much the best and the baywood the poorest. Now, of course, mahogany wood is obtained from many other districts and ports in Central America, as, for example, Tabasco, Minatitlan, Tecolutla, Panama, Costa Rica, and St. Domingo, but to the average woodworker in England only three grades still exist, namely, Spanish, Honduras, and baywood, chiefly because each of these three names has come to represent an arbitrary standard of quality, colour, and figure, regardless of the origin. Beyond saying that the baywood is the soft, light, straight-grained, and pinkish (nearly white) material, and that the Spanish is the dark, ruddy-brown, often cross-grained, and curly wood, no definite rule can be given ; observation will soon disclose the ordinary limits of each term. Some regard the chalky deposit in the pores of dark-coloured mahogany as conclusive evidence that the wood is of Spanish origin, but the occurrence of this substance is by no means an infallible test. Mahogany is one of the best cabinet-making woods imported, and although its use, perhaps, is rather unfashionable at the present time, it is superior to the cabinet woods that have replaced it. It has the advantage of being durable, takes a fine polish, and improves in colour with age. It has got into disrepute through being used for cheap veneered furniture, as veneers may be cut from it so thin that a large surface may be covered with them at a small cost. Baywood is soft and easily worked, and is largely used for carriage and other panels. It may be obtained in widths up to 2 ft. 6 in., but the price per foot is much higher for wide than for narrow boards. The variety known as Spanish mahogany is harder than the others, and is often beautifully figured : considerable skill is required in cleaning it up, so that it is hardly a suitable wood for a novice to handle. Mahogany unites with glue better than any other wood.

TEAK.

This comes from India and Burmah, and is the wood of the *Tectona grandis*. It is of a greenish-brown colour when freshly worked, but turns to a rich brown in a short time. It varies considerably in texture, some pieces being soft and others very hard. The pores are filled with a gritty substance, which quickly blunts the edges of tools. It is popularly considered to be of a greasy nature (a subject returned to later), so that glue will not adhere to it for any length of time. For this reason, it should not be used where glue is depended on for holding the work together. It shrinks little in seasoning, but is rather liable to split. Its great feature is its immense durability, irrespective of the most diverse external conditions. Kept under cover, it lasts from century to century without a sign of peculiar or of inherent decay. The exterior layers of the wood merely darken with age a little. Delicate carvings in teak hundreds of years old still exist, absolutely perfect in detail, the tool marks showing clear and glossy as if the work were quite new. Kept out of doors the wood whitens, and, after many years, the arrises or fine edges become slightly blurred, and lose their sharpness ; but here, again, there is no induced decay,—never anything of the nature of a fungus growth present, nor any deterioration arising from oxidation of the fibre pure and simple. Also, teak is unique in its immunity from the ravages of the white ant and the ship-worm. Neither the structure nor the com-position of teak is very exceptional. It is a ring-porous wood, having large vessels, round or slightly elliptical in outline, and a loose spongy parenchymatous structure in the immediate neighbourhood of the vessels. The medullary rays are small but numerous ; while the fibres have large in-ternal cavities, and, but for practical evi-dence to the contrary, they might well be taken to represent a wood of a decidedly soft nature. Some woodworkers object to teak, and assert that its oiliness clogs the

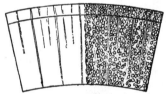

Fig. 537.—Section of Satin Walnut, highly magnified.

saw, splinters of it poison the fingers, the odour of the wood is disagreeable, and so on. But these and similar ills, imaginary or real, are not evident when once the work is fixed in position. There is scarcely another wood to be found possessing its peculiar qualities in regard to working across the grain, or chiselling the end grain, or sawing in either direction. As a set-off against the initial expense of this wood, its greater durability must be reckoned. The question may then be roughly limited to one of cost of labour ; and in respect to this, also, teak will oftentimes be found the cheaper material. The wood is supposed to be of an excep-tionally oily nature, but though to the hand it does indeed appear to feel oily, the impression is incorrect, there actually being less oil in teak than in almost any other wood ; an abundance of soft and free resin accounts largely for the oily touch.

A mineral substance often fills up the cracks and shakes in the wood, and occurs also in the hair-like vessels throughout the wood substance of the tree. It is a cry-stalline deposit, with acicular crystals that are readily soluble in dilute acids. Chemic-ally speaking, the deposit is a hydrocalcic orthophosphate, with about 11·4 per cent. of ammonio-magnesian phosphate.

BLACK WALNUT, SATIN WALNUT, ETC.

Walnut is more largely used for cabinet-making than any other wood. Black wal-nut, a North American variety (*Juglans nigra*), is that in most general use. The sapwood of this is whitish in colour, and must be all cut off, this often involving con-siderable loss. The timber is hard, but is not difficult to work. It cleans up to a smooth surface, and takes polish well. It is used for furniture generally. Satin wal-nut is much softer than black, and is lighter in colour. It planes with a silky appearance. It is a capital wood for carving, as it works with an even grain, and is not liable to split. English and Italian are varieties of walnut that are used for good work. Both are figured with a dark veining, the last-named variety being often beautifully marked. The wood which is, in England, called satin walnut is known in the Southern States of America as " red gum," and in the Northern States as " sweet gum." It is never referred to as " satin walnut," except in the towns ; but is sometimes called " bilsted," which is a Dutch name that has been given it. The tree which produces it is not in any way connected with the walnuts, *Juglans*, or any allied genus ; nor is it connected with satin wood, *Chloroxylon*, or with the trees that are usually called " gums "—the *Eucalypti* of Australia. It is the *Liquid-ambar Styraciflua*, of the genus *Nyssa*, under favourable conditions gum-yielding, and it is in this connection that it first was heard of. Under the microscope the wood is seen to be of the " diffuse-porous " kind : that is to say, the large vessels are not grouped at one side of the annual ring, as in oak or chestnut, but are distributed uniformly all over the end section. There are numerous fine medullary rays. Fibre-cells and parenchyma-cells are large and thin-walled, a fact which helps to explain why a hard wood is reported to be wanting in durability. The section in Fig. 537, p. 175, left partly blank and partly filled in with detail, includes the width of one annual ring and part of the next. It is somewhat highly magnified, the surface represented being in actual size about $\frac{1}{4}$ in. long and $\frac{1}{8}$ in. wide. Satin walnut is tough, of medium hardness, heavy, and fairly uniform and close in texture ; the plane leaves a fine glossy surface that polishes extremely well. There is a wide margin of white sapwood. The colour of the heartwood is ruddy-brown, streaked, in various ways, with grey, light yellow, dark brown, and iron splashes. The features of the marking do not usually run parallel to the sides of the board, nor do they follow the course of the annual rings. The general appearance is as if an acid of some kind had been irregularly splashed down the length of the board. In some boards the figure is very realistic, suggesting landscapes and seascapes, or the effect of a storm. The wood, however, has a bad reputation for warping and twisting, and this is its chief and almost only drawback ; but up to now only a poor class of material has been imported. Its use in England, while steadily on the increase, has hitherto been mostly confined to the cabinet, car-building, and shop-fitting trades, in each of which it is used to advantage. In cabinet-making it is used effectively with ash. It appears to stand very well after being worked up.

ASH.

The ash (*Fraxinus excelsior*) is a native of Europe and Asia. It grows very quickly, the young tree being the most valuable. The wood is fairly durable in a dry situation, but soon decays if exposed to the damp. It is the toughest of all British timber, and is useful where sudden shocks are to be expected. The wood often is beautifully marked, works fairly well, and will take a high polish. Pieces of milk-white colour are the best, those of a red-dish tinge, or dirty white, being deficient in toughness. In old trees the central portion becomes brown, often in veins and streaks, and pieces of this colour require careful selection, as they are liable to decay. The annual rings are very distinct. It has no larger septa. English ash is used by the wheelwright, and for tool-handles generally. American ash is that generally used by the cabinet-maker. It is straighter in grain and not so tough as English, and cleans up with a silky appearance. It often comes to this country " sleepy " (see p. 158) through being over-dried. Hungarian ash has a beautiful wavy grain, and generally is cut into veneers.

BEECH.

The beech (*Fagus sylvatica*) is common in Europe. There are two kinds, black and white. Beech is very durable if constantly wet, but mere dampness soon causes it to decay, and it is very subject to worms, as any old furniture will testify. Its colour is a light reddish-brown, being darker in the black variety. It is hard and tough, the grain is straight, and the larger septa are very fine, but, if cut obliquely, give an appearance similar to oak, though smaller. The annual rings are also very distinct. Planes and the handles of some woodworking tools are made of ash. Care should be taken that the outside of the tree is used as a wearing surface, the medullary rays (which are very prominent in beech) pointing towards the bottom. If the other sides are used as wearing surfaces the plane will wear more quickly and unevenly. Formerly beech was largely used by furniture-makers, but its liability to the attack of worms has thrown it into disrepute for this purpose. When it is so used it is veneered generally with a better wood.

BIRCH.

This is a hard, close-grained wood, the principal portion of which comes from America, where it is produced by many species of the genus *Betula*. Some pieces are nicely figured with a wavy grain. It is a fairly easy wood to work, and is used for cabinet-making.

SYCAMORE.

This is the wood of the *Acer pseudo-platanus*, a very common tree in England, thriving well near the sea-coast; it grows to a large size, and is durable if kept dry. The annual rings are not very distinct, and the larger septa are small and

Fig. 538.—Medullary Ray Figure in Oak.

close. It is easy to work, being of a uniform texture, and is creamy-white in colour. It is used principally for domestic articles and in wood-carving.

ELM.

The rough-leaved elm (*Ulmus campestris*) is the most durable of the many elm trees common in England. The tree is of slow growth, and is very durable in situations where wet is constant; the wood is used largely in boat-building. The colour is generally of a dark reddish-brown, the sapwood being a dirty white. It is very porous and cross-grained, having an unpleasant odour. It warps and shrinks very much in drying, but does not often split.

12

Larger septa are absent, and the wood is difficult to work.

OAK.

Several species of oak are very valuable as timber. The British oak (*Robur*) is found in all temperate parts of Europe, and grows to a very large size. The colour is a light fawn when newly cut, but it soon turns to a handsome brown. The grain is fairly straight, and usually the medullary rays are very beautifully marked. It is most valuable for all purposes where strength or hard wear is expected, no other timber standing so well. It is difficult to work. The larger transverse septa are very distinct. British oak is the most beautiful and lasting of native woods. It twists and shrinks a good deal in seasoning; and however dry a piece may be, if cut so as to expose a fresh surface it will shrink again. There are several varieties grown, but the best may be known by the acorns growing with long stems and singly. English oak is not a good timber for a beginner to take in hand. The sessile-fruited oak (*Sessiliflora*) also is a native of Europe, being found abundantly in the north of England. The wood is a darker colour than the *robur*, and the larger septa are fewer in number. It is very smooth and glossy, and resembles chestnut. It is also harder and heavier than the *robur*, and splits and warps very much in drying. The red oak (*Quercus rubra*) is found in Canada. It is so named from the leaves turning red before falling. It grows to a height of 90 ft. to 100 ft.; the wood is light, spongy, and not very durable. The wood of the English oak is very tough and cross-grained, and being very difficult to work, it does not take kindly to glue. The foreign oak works more easily. Oak also is obtainable in Asia and on the continent of America. Stettin oak is lighter in colour, straighter in grain, and not so well figured as the other varieties. Picture mouldings are often made of this timber. American oak is imported in logs, some of which often reach a length of 60 ft. The white variety is good tough timber, but the reddish coloured is poor. Austrian oak trees are generally remarkable for their tallness, straight growth, large dimensions, and comparative freedom from defects. The grain of the wood is very straight and regular. The pores of the spring layers run in very regular longitudinal streaks, almost at fixed intervals. The medullary rays are strongly marked, but are not so numerous as in some other varieties of oak, and on account of the straight growth of the tree they are more uniform in shape, running almost parallel to each other, but consequently are not so beautiful in appearance as the rays in woods of more irregular growth. The wood is often light in colour, but is generally inclined to a more reddish tint than other kinds of oak. It is one of the easiest of the oaks to work. It is not quite so heavy as English oak, and for outdoor work it is said to be less durable. Wainscot (see p. 161) is got by cutting up logs of oak (principally Russian) in a way that will expose the medullary plates, pith rays, or silver grain on the faces of all the boards. In other words, the faces of the boards are made to fall on the radial planes of the tree. Wainscot, properly sawn, involves a good deal of waste in conversion, and in practice it is usual to have only two boards in each quarter on the radii, the other boards being cut parallel to these. Then, by sawing boards off alternate faces of the quarter, nearly all the wood may be used up (see p. 161). Pollard oak is produced by lopping off the heads and branches, and otherwise tampering with oak trees for a number of years, as they grow. This treatment induces the denuded trunk to send out a great number of young shoots each year, and also brings about the formation of burrs, and other abnormal excrescences of the kind. The result of all is, that remarkable contortions of the fibres are produced, giving to this wood its singular beauty. Its chief use is in the form of veneer, but it is also used solid in the manufacture of knife and dagger handles, small cabinets, gloveboxes, etc.

FIGURE IN OAK.

In oak there are two distinct sets of rays —the large thick rays that produce the well-known figure, and thousands of smaller ones that are mostly too minute to be detected by the naked eye. Large rays only are shown in Fig. 538, p. 177, while in the microscopic enlargement shown by Fig. 539 a single large ray appears as a dark band on the left, the smaller rays also being shown dispersed over the field. (The view is taken looking from the outside in towards the centre of the tree. All details of the fibres and parenchyma are omitted for the sake of clearness.) Referring to the large ray, part only of its depth is shown. Its total height was between 300 and 400 cells. Its width averaged eighteen cells. Its length may have been 6 in. to 8 in., or perhaps a little more than that. Rays of this size are quite common in oak, and, as before stated, it is these alone that constitute the silver-grain figure in that wood. The brilliancy of figure and the colour contrast that are often observed in oak and other silver-grain woods are in the majority of cases due to differences in the character of the contents of the medullary ray cells, and of those cells that constitute the surrounding wood. Upon the contents of these cells light and exposure to the atmosphere produce marked effects. The rays often become darker at the edges, and present a "shot" appearance at their centres, making a well-defined figure upon the background of the general mass of wood. In other cases the medullary rays are naturally darker than the surrounding wood, having perhaps absorbed more colouring matter; but where no difference of colour exists the differentiated structure is alone sufficient to affect strongly the reflection of light; and whether the reflection is enhanced or retarded, the result is a marked contrast between the appearance of the rays and that of the wood in which they are embedded. English oak, beech, and sycamore are good examples of silver grain woods; comparing these three, the figure is largest and best in oak; but there are many woods scattered over the world that form a far superior figure to that seen in oak even. America possesses a few of these. Western plane wood, with its thousands of medium-sized rays, is doubtless familiar to all, and the figure in American oaks and alders rivals anything that can be found in European timbers.

HEMLOCK.

Hemlock often is used in the cheaper kinds of carpentry. It is indigenous to nearly all places which are favourable to the production of spruce and light pines. In dry situations, when the wood has been properly seasoned and carefully protected from the action of the sun, it may be considered as a fourth-rate wood. Its peculiar structure, tending to twist or split the grain, makes it entirely unreliable for large timbers where there is tensile or compressive stress anticipated. It decays quickly in damp situations, and if exposed in an

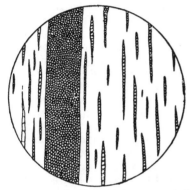

Fig. 539.—Oak Rays, highly magnified.

unseasoned state the heartwood cleaves from the surrounding wood by the action of either sun or wind. It is usually cut into small studding joists or common boards. Hemlock possesses one quality in common with oak and other hard woods, that is, the tenacity with which it adheres to a nail. An ordinary cut nail, if driven into the wood half its length, will part before it can be drawn out. This quality is one of its first recommendations for common or rough boarding, as it firmly holds the nails of shingling, slating, etc. Most of the wood dwelling-houses in America are covered in with well-seasoned hemlock shingles, which keep perfectly dry. The colour of this wood is a light brown. It shrinks in seasoning a little less than spruce, and loses one-fourth its weight.

CHESTNUT.

Chestnut is produced by the sweet or Spanish chestnut, *Castanea vesca*, growing in Western Asia, Southern Europe, and in the United States. It is of great value, and in many respects nearly identical with oak, which it resembles in colour, toughness, and solidity. It is a native of temperate regions, and is usually found growing side by side with the oak. For most purposes for which oak is used chestnut is of equal value. Some experience is required to distinguish between the two woods; but chestnut may always be known by the absence of distinct medullary rays at the ends of the planks; consequently it has no silver grain. The timber is also lighter in weight than oak, and the gallic acid, which will blacken oak sawdust when in contact with iron, is not found in chestnut. It is exceedingly durable, even in damp places, and in a variable atmosphere it may be found preferable to oak. For posts set in the ground it may be considered good for forty years. As in oak, the grain of the wood is compact, and that of young trees is very tough and flexible, but old wood is brittle, appearing sound without while within it is decayed and rotten. It has the particularly valuable quality that, when once seasoned, it is but slightly susceptible to shrinkage or swelling. Casks are made from it, as it does not give a disagreeable taste to liquids. The wood is very liable to split with nailing. It is used for inside fittings, many churches having the seats, etc., of this timber. Horse chestnut, the product of *Æsculus hippocastanum*, is practically worthless.

NEW WOODS.

Timber that is new to Great Britain is imported from time to time, some of the latest and handsomest varieties coming from Tasmania and New Zealand; but these hardly come within the scope of this work.

USES OF DIFFERENT WOODS.

Floor boards composed of Petersburg, Archangel, and Onega yellow deal (known in the north of England as red deal) are best for lower floors, as they wear well and are not so liable to be affected by any slight dampness. Christiania and Dram prepared boards of white deal form good upper floors. They are much in favour, owing to their keeping a clean, light colour, and not turning dark after being scrubbed, as yellow deal does. For the members of roof trusses and purlins the best timber is Riga, Memel, or Dantzic northern pine. Of these, the first mentioned is generally considered the best, on account of its cheapness, together with lightness, strength, and durability, as compared with oak, pitch-pine, etc. Good yellow deal is used for ordinary staircases, but for hard wear pitch-pine or teak would be more suitable for treads. For inside doors use Christiania white deal or the best Baltic yellow deal for the framing, and American yellow pine for the panels. In some parts of the United Kingdom American yellow pine is largely used for all parts of inside doors. External doors should be of yellow deal, as both pine and white deal are not so durable when exposed to the weather. Sills should be prepared of English oak, as they are subject to more wet than other parts. Linings, pulley stiles, sashes, etc., should be of the best yellow deal, owing to its durability for external work when painted; white deal and American pine are not sufficiently durable for such purposes. The best Christiania white deal is very suitable for ordinary joiners'

work. The following woods are very suitable for carpenters' work:—Riga, Memel, and Dantzic northern pine balk timber for roofs, large framing, and structural work generally. The best deals are also suitable for external joinery, being stronger and more durable than the next mentioned. Owing to their deficiency in strength and durability if exposed, white deal and American yellow and red pine are unsuitable for carpenters' work; but as these properties are not so essential for internal joinery, and as the better kinds are very free from knots and also straight in grain—partly owing to which they warp, shrink, and twist very little if properly seasoned—and are at the same time more easily worked than other coniferous woods, they have much to recommend them, and thus are frequently used for joiners' work. Pitch-pine is largely used for good carpenters' work, especially for heavy structures where great strength and durability are required. It is also much used both by the carpenter and the joiner for ornamental effects, on account of its beautifully distinct grain, which can be seen at a distance when wrought and varnished. It is probably on account of this characteristic that it has been so extensively used for such exposed parts as beams, and for the timbers of church and other roofs; also for fittings of churches and other public buildings.

JOINTS.

SHOOTING EDGES OF BOARDS.

Before even plain glued butt joints can be attempted, there are one or two processes, not yet described, with which the beginner must familiarise himself. The first of these is shooting edges—that is, planing the edges of boards until they are square and true.

indicates the bench top; c, vice; B, bench screw; K, head of screw; D, handle; A, stop; J, side of bench; H, leg; G, bearer; E, board; and P, the plane. For accurate work the shooting board is used; varieties of this appliance are illustrated and described on pp. 12 to 15. The work is placed on the bed of the shooting board, and a

Fig. 540.—Shooting Edge of Board.

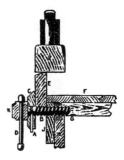

Fig. 541.—End View of Shooting Plane and Board.

Ordinary planing has already been discussed (see pp. 48 to 51). Insert a pin, made in the form of a hook, into one of the holes in the side of the bench, as at *a* (Fig. 540). The edge of the board B is then placed upon the hook, and the other end securely fastened in the bench vice, A. Fig. 540 shows this in front view, and Fig. 541 in end view. The edge is now planed first with the jack plane, and afterwards with the trying plane, until straight as viewed from the end, the edge being frequently tested with a square (as in Fig. 542). The trying plane is held in the manner shown in Fig. 540, the fingers of the left hand acting as a guide to keep it in position. The shavings should pass freely, as at *c*, and be taken off the whole length of board to finish. Fig. 541 shows the application of the jack plane to the edge of the board. In that illustration F

plane in good condition is shot along its edge, which is thus reduced to perfect truth.

GAUGING BOARD TO THICKNESS.

A board to be reduced in thickness has first to be gauged along its edges. Set the marking gauge with its tooth at a distance from the head equal to the thinnest part of the board, and, grasping it firmly, work it along the edges of the board in a succession of short, sharp strokes, keeping the head firmly pressed to the face side of the board. Having gauged the board, roughly chamfer the edges nearly down to the line, as A B (Fig. 543), E being the face side. Now plane away the stuff until level, as at F. This, though completing it so far as the trueness of its surface is concerned, may yet leave it in a very rough state. The grain may have been strong and ripped up, or the irons of the planes may not have been in perfect condition, thus leaving marks or ridges. These have to be cleaned off with the smoothing plane (see p. 50).

GLUED JOINTS.

The glued joint is adopted where it is desired to make a number of narrow

Fig. 542.—Testing Squareness of Shot Edge.

boards serve as one wide one. For instance, table-tops, panels of doors, and many other things, are made preferably by gluing up rather than by using one wide board. The plain glued butt joint, shown by Fig. 544, is serviceable enough for thin wood, say for anything under $\frac{1}{2}$ in. thick, and, in certain situations, suffices for material of any substance. When the wood is thick enough something better than a butt joint can be used. With thin stuff, however, this is the only joint available, as there is no room for tongues or dowels. The plain glued butt joint will be considered first; then the stronger and more serviceable dowelled joint, and that formed by ploughing and cross tongueing, will be dealt with. A properly glued butt joint ought to be stronger than the natural wood; that is to say, a board should split at any part rather than the joint, except perhaps in the case of some tough woods. With ordinary pine or bay

Fig. 543.—Board Chamfered and Planed to Thickness.

wood, if the fracture is along the joint, this proves that the workmanship or the glue is at fault. Under a severe strain a board often will give way, leaving the joint unbroken, it being actually stronger than the wood itself.

PREPARING BOARDS FOR JOINTING.

For first efforts at making a plain butt joint (Fig. 544) get two pieces of board, say about 2 ft. long, and not less than 1 in. thick. Plane up the board true and out of winding, always remembering to pencil the face mark upon the finished surface. Shoot the edges perfectly straight, true, and square, or at right angles to the face side; they should then be placed one upon the other (the bottom board to be in the bench vice), and a small straightedge (A,

Fig. 544.—Plain Glued Butt Joint.

Fig. 545) applied to the face to test the joint for " upright." It will often occur that the boards " tip," as shown. This will, of course, have to be rectified by shooting one or both edges. The boards being upright, the joint should be so placed that the light is thrown upon the back, when it is seen at once if the boards touch all along the joint. If they do not touch at one or two places, make a pencil mark upon the face where the bumps occur, and carefully take off a shaving at these points. The top board (A, Fig. 546) may then be

Fig. 545.—Testing Butt Joint.

taken in both hands, as shown, and gently rubbed along the other, and the feel will indicate if their edges are in good contact. Occasionally the edges touch at opposite corners, and then a little must be taken off each, the edge being in winding. The plane-iron for shooting joints should be very sharp and finely set, as this will add greatly to the ease with which a good joint can be made. In the case of very long joints, say from 6 ft. to 8 ft., some

Fig. 546.—Rubbing Edges of Board Together.

workmen allow the boards to touch at the ends, but not towards the centre ; if the space is but small no great harm will

Fig. 547.—Gluing Butt Joint, Side View.

result. They consider this space advisable for long pieces. To convey an idea of the hollowness of the edge towards the centre, assume two boards 5 ft. or 6 ft. long, with

edges perfectly true. Now with the plane remove a shaving or two, just the suspicion of one at its commencement, a few inches from the end of the board, till there is, when the boards are placed together, a perceptible space between them tapering from the centre to nothing near the ends. Even at the widest the space must be narrow enough to be closed by pressure of the cramps, within which the boards will be placed while the glue is setting.

BUTT JOINTING.

The glue should be about as thick as

Fig. 548.—Gluing Butt Joint, Front View.

cream—if thicker, hot water must be added from the outer pot. The glue being ready, place it upon the bench, with a block of wood under it (as A, Fig. 547). Next fasten the board D in the screw, as C, taking the other board E in the left hand, tipping it as shown. Fill the brush with really hot glue, and apply it to the edges, as shown at B. This will, perhaps, be better understood from Fig. 548, which is a front view. Put on plenty of glue ; but do not "paint" the joint, and do the work quickly. Take the board in both hands, as in Fig. 546, dropping the left hand until the fingers are over the joint (this is to ensure the boards being fair upon the face when finished), and rub

Fig. 549.—Cramp for Glued Joint.

the top board along to squeeze out all the glue possible, as upon this, to some extent, depends the success of the job. If it can be arranged, it is always better for two persons to rub the joint, one being at each end; after rubbing a few times the joint will seem to draw or stick; it may then be finished "fair" with the ends. Take care, in removing the hands, that the board is not moved, or the glue will have to be washed off, and the whole process repeated. One important point is to have the edges of the board warm, so that the glue does not chill as soon as applied, but remains

Fig. 550.—Cramp for Glued Joint.

liquid and sticky. They must not, however, be too hot, but there is not so much danger from this as from being too cold. If one board is held by the bench screw, it may happen that the glue has hardened on it, or at least is not in its most adhesive state when the other is put to it. There might be a slight film on its surface, and, of course, this prevents its adhering to the other piece as well as it might. Let this be sufficiently warm to melt the glue again, and the adherence should be perfect. The

Fig. 551.—Wedge Cramp for Glued Joint.

rubbing of the joint is of the utmost importance. Do not be content with simply pressing the glued edges together, but having brought them cleanly together, slide them slightly against each other, length-

wise, using as much pressure as convenient. This expels any air, as well as a good deal of the superfluous glue, the presence of which, were it suffered to remain, would be fatal to a good joint. It then only remains to cramp the two pieces together, and let them rest till the glue has thoroughly set, when the boards may be worked on as if there were no joint.

CRAMPING GLUED JOINTS.

Cramps for carpenters' and joiners' use are illustrated on pp. 28 to 33. In the case of plain glued joints, however, it is always better not to use cramps; but if the boards are thin, it is sometimes advisable to use one of the following devices, which may be constructed in a few minutes from

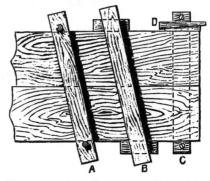

Fig. 552.—Three Cramps for Glued Joints.

any spare strips of wood. The device shown by Fig. 549 is made of two strips about 2 in. wide, with a ½-in. pin driven through at top and bottom. Fig. 550 shows one strip of like width and 1 in. thick, with a small block screwed on at top and bottom. Fig. 551 is made in the same manner as Fig. 550, more room being given at the top to allow a pair of folding wedges to be driven in. The face view of all these three cramps, lettered in their order, is given by Fig. 552, which illustrates the application of the strips to the joint. A and B are simply placed close to the board, and gently driven along until sufficiently tight. C has two folding wedges D driven as shown, this being perhaps the better method. After "gluing-up," the board must be carefully removed from the bench, and a strip of wood placed at an angle against the wall, or any available place, as shown at A, Fig. 553. The board should be carefully placed with the bottom D close to the

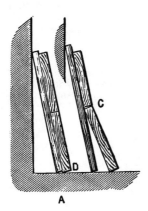

Fig. 553.—Supporting Fresh Glued Joint.

strip; otherwise the joint at C is spoilt. It will thus be seen that there are many little points to attend to in making a glued joint; but if care is taken in every detail, success is certain, and a good joint that will resist any reasonable strain will be obtained.

Bad and Good Glued Butt Joints.

Just to show distinctly what a good joint is, compare two joints of different quality. In one the line of the joint is seen quite easily for most of its length. It is a dark line, thicker in some places than in others, from end to end of the join. In some places it is interrupted for an inch or two, where all the glue seems to have been pressed out, and these places are the only ones at which the joint is thorough. Instead of being perfectly flat there is an angle at the joint; this may be very slight, but it is quite perceptible if a straightedge be laid across. On the perfectly jointed piece no line is discernible anywhere, but the grain of the wood is stopped short off along a certain imaginary line; the figure seems abruptly broken, not only on one side of this line, but on both. That is all there is to indicate the joint, and it is almost sure to stand the straightedge test.

Dowels.

Dowels are round wooden pins used in a common method of jointing up. They are hardly ever used in wood under $\frac{3}{4}$ in. thick. Usually they have a diameter of $\frac{3}{8}$ in., but beyond this being a generally convenient size there is no special reason for it. Whatever their diameter, it must be the same as that of the bit with which the dowel holes are bored. The dowels must fit tightly in if they are to be of any use. Where they are used in large quantities, the dowels are bought ready made, or, rather, the lengths from which the dowels can be cut when wanted are got. Almost any straight-grained, strong wood will do for dowels, but beech, birch, and oak are employed generally. Waste pieces of any strong wood may be used instead. The pieces are cut in sticks roughly rounded, and then hammered through the dowel plate. This removes any irregularities, and the screw beneath it forms a rough kind of groove or furrow in the stick as it passes through. The length of the sticks is not of much consequence, but, on account of their liability to break, 9 in. or 12 in. is long enough. If the dowels are not as dry as possible, they will shrink, and not retain their proper hold on the wood in which they are inserted.

Making Dowels.

For making dowels, prepare a dowel plate, as illustrated by Fig. 554. It consists of a piece of hardwood, such as oak or beech, 3 in. square and 10 in. long, in the

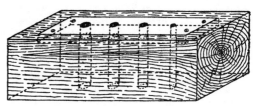

Fig. 554.—Dowel Plate.

top of which a $\frac{3}{8}$-in. steel plate, 2 in. wide, is let flush and screwed down. The plate is properly tempered and faced up with a file and emery; it is punched, when hot, with four holes of $\frac{7}{16}$ in., $\frac{3}{8}$ in., $\frac{5}{16}$ in., and $\frac{1}{4}$ in. diameter respectively, $1\frac{1}{2}$ in. apart; corresponding holes, a little larger, to clear the holes in the plate, are bored through the wood. Next provide a pin or dowel-board, consisting of a deal board $1\frac{1}{2}$ in. thick, 6 in. wide, and 12 in. long, on which are planted four wooden fillets as shown in Fig. 555. The first pair are $\frac{3}{4}$ in. wide, $\frac{1}{4}$ in. thick, and planted $\frac{5}{16}$ in. apart. The second pair are $\frac{3}{4}$ in. wide, $\frac{3}{8}$ in. thick, and planted $\frac{7}{16}$ in. apart. One fillet of each pair has a

dowel is inserted in two boards, half of it being in each one, the holes bored for its reception must be exactly placed. To do this is not difficult. The edges of the boards having been trued, place the boards on edge side by side, and hold them together in the bench screw or by any other suitable means. With the square mark off across the edges of both at intervals of from 8 in. to 12 in., more or less, according to circumstances. If the boards are then placed edge to edge, their lines must cor-

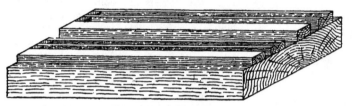

Fig. 555.—Dowel Board.

Fig. 556.—Section of Dowel.

V-groove worked in it, in which a stop is glued and sprigged at the farthest end, the square grooves also having stops glued and sprigged in between. The work can be started by ripping down squares of oak about 10 in. long to the size of the dowels required. Place each in its proper square groove on the pin board, and plane them down nearly flush with the tops of the fillets. Next place each in its proper V-groove, take off the arrises all round, and, with a mallet, drive the dowels through their proper holes in the dowel piece, which is placed over a hole in the bench. The blow must be dealt gently at first, and the dowel held perfectly upright. When driven through, place the dowels in the V-grooves again on the pin-board, and run a V along the dowel itself with a V-tool. It is not necessary that the groove should be very straight or very even, as it is only intended to form a vent for the superfluous glue when the dowel is driven home, although if it is omitted the work may be split. The section of the dowel when completed is shown at Fig. 556.

BORING DOWEL HOLES.

It is quite evident that as the pin or

respond. With a gauge set to about half the thickness of the wood, mark off a point on each of the lines. Each point, of course, gives the centre of a dowel hole. An ordinary centre bit may be used, but a

Fig. 557.—Dowelling Gauge.

twist bit is better, because it leaves a cleaner hole. A suitable gauge (Fig. 557) is made with a piece of deal 2 in. or 3 in. long, notched out at one end and having a steel point, driven in at a given distance, and sharpened up as a marking gauge. In marking off with the gauge, be careful to work from the same surface of the two boards, either from the face of both or from the back of both. Before preparing the edges, look at the surfaces of the boards. Both may be equally good, but often it is found that one side of a plank is better than the other, and the better one should form the visible side. The dowel holes should be bored to a uniform depth of, say, 1 in., and in practice it is generally advisable to bore them in pairs and not to make all those in one plank before beginning the other. To do this, of course, it is assumed that they are left in the bench screw and bored immediately after marking. In order to get all the holes the same depth, a simple contrivance can be used. To make this, get a piece of wood with a hole bored through its centre in the direction of the grain. The length of the wood is such that when the brace bit is passed through the hole the top of the wood is against the brace stock, and the portion of the bit projecting at the bottom is as long as the required dowel hole is deep. Other devices are obtainable at most tool shops. The holes may be bored fairly equal without the aid of special devices by noting the number of turns of the brace given to the first one, and making the other holes the same. The boring has a tendency, more or less marked according to the wood and the kind of bit used, to raise the wood round the holes, and it is sometimes advisable to run the plane over the edges afterwards.

Countersinking Dowel Holes.

The mouths of the holes must be widened with the reamer or rose bit to form a slight countersink, facilitating the insertion of the dowels, and forming a little space into which the surplus glue can run. This countersinking must be only very slight, in fact, barely more than necessary to remove sharp edges and any burr there may be from the bit used in boring the holes. The object of the dowel is to hold the boards together, and it is important, therefore, that as much as possible of the dowel should be in contact with the wood in which it is inserted. If the countersinking then is to the depth of $\frac{1}{4}$ in. or so, it is evident that this space is waste so far as regards the adherence of the dowel. Repeating the distance in the other plank, at once there is a space of $\frac{1}{2}$ in. which is practically wasted.

Rounding Ends of Dowels.

To facilitate the dowel entering the hole, it is usual either to round off the entering end or to hammer its edges just sufficiently to make it slightly blunt. Tools

for rounding the ends may be purchased. Fig. 558 shows a typical one known as a shaver. Both methods are practised, but hammering is to be preferred. Bad results do not follow if the rounding is not too great; only the edge must be removed, and it is neither advisable nor necessary to taper the pin, nor to give the end a hemispherical shape. Hammering the ends does not remove any of the wood, but compresses the fibres, so that to all intents and purposes the end of the dowel is tapered off; but it swells again under the action of the glue when it has been driven home, thus making a perfectly tight fit.

Fixing Dowelled Joint.

It is assumed that the two boards are ready for fixing together. Take a piece of

Fig. 558.—Dowel Shaver.

the dowel wood, whatever its length may be, and round one end in the way preferred. Then glue the inside of the hole. or dip the end of the dowel in glue. Dipping is a very general method, but must be regarded as slovenly; for applying the glue to the walls of the hole, use a small brush, or beat out the end of a piece of cane, or even use a stick a little less than the thickness of the dowel; this carries enough of the glue and disposes it easily in the hole. Do not fill the hole with glue, nor yet put in only a drop and leave the dowel to force it round. As quickly as convenient, so that the glue may not get set before it is done, hammer the dowel home. The reason for the V-groove in this now is apparent, for if there were no such channel the glue could not escape, and would be forced down to the bottom, and air would be imprisoned. This latter alone would give rise to a considerable risk of the board being split. Glue which may exude should not be allowed to set, or it would interfere with the close contact of the two boards. A small quantity will not matter if the joint is to be completed at once, and any there may be in the widened mouth of the hole may stop there. When the dowel is driven

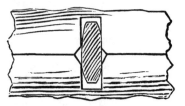

Fig. 559.—Dowelled Joint with Excessive Countersink and Rounding.

home, saw off the excess, leaving the projection from the wood as nearly as possible the exact length of the corresponding hole in the other piece. In practice, to be on the safe side, it is usual to cut a trifle short, for if the dowel is too long the edges of the two boards cannot come into close contact. All the holes are dowelled in the same manner in one of the boards, and the projecting ends rounded off by means of a file or special dowel rounder. Naturally hammering cannot be done so conveniently on the second end. Glue the edges of both pieces of wood, one of which, at least, should be warmed before doing so, and, of course, glue the holes which are not yet filled. All being ready, the boards are brought together and clamped up, when they should be left until the glue has set. Figs. 559 and 560 show sections of a dowel inserted in its hole; they are respectively incorrect and correct for the reasons made clear on p. 187. This is a strong form of joint, stronger than the plain butt, yet

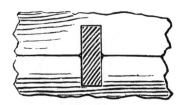

Fig. 560.—Dowelled Joint correctly made.

not so strong as the ploughed and tongued, described on p. 191.

REBATING.

The term "rebate" is applied to all rectangular recesses where cut upon the edge of the material, such as the recess in door-jambs into which the door shuts; also

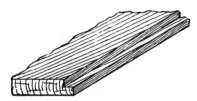

Fig. 561.—Portion of Rebated Board.

the space occupied by the glass and putty in window-sashes, picture-frames, and in numerous other examples. Rebates will occur in some of the joints to be dealt with in this chapter, as illustrated by many of the figures on p. 190. To work a rebate perfectly requires close attention to details and a certain amount of skill in the use of tools; this last comes by patience and perseverance. Fig. 561 shows a rebate cut upon the edge of a board. Suppose a rebate to be of square section and $\frac{1}{2}$ in. deep both ways. To work it, set the marking gauge to $\frac{1}{2}$ in., and run it along both face and edge of board, and place the board, face side up, upon the bench, as B (Fig. 562),

Fig. 562.—Use of Mallet and Chisel in Rebating.

taking care to keep the end quite close to the bench stop s, and drive a bench knife (a piece broken from an old table knife) into both board and bench, as shown at A (Fig. 562). The board now is firmly fixed to the bench. Hold the chisel firmly in the left hand, with the bevel at the back, as shown, and, inclining the handle slightly towards the worker, proceed carefully to cut a succession of notches from the front to back of the board, taking care not to cut beyond the lines on face or

Fig. 563.—Removing Chips in Rebating.

edge. If the chisel is held too loosely, it may slip through the hand, a nasty pinch resulting through the contact of the mallet with the hand on top of the handle. Having cut the notches, the chisel should be held bevel downwards in the right hand, as in Fig. 563, and, starting at the back, the chips may be carefully cleaned out, leaving the rebate B as shown in the section c (Fig. 563). If the grain of the wood is in the direction shown at a (Fig. 564), the notches should be cut in two directions as illustrated, or the result may be a notch too far below the line to be taken out, as shown by a (Fig. 565). If a knot should happen to be in the way, the same course must be followed with additional care ; or the knot, the wood having been cleaned out upon both sides of it, may be cut off with a tenon saw. The rebate now is roughly worked, and to finish it up the rebate plane (for description of this

Fig. 564.   Fig. 565.

Figs. 564 and 565.—Method of Chipping Awkwardly Grained Stuff.

see pp. 47 and 48) must be applied to both sides of the recess (see Fig. 566), using each side successively as the bed for the plane. The plane is held in much the same manner as the smoothing plane. Care must be taken to finish the two sides of the rebate at right angles to each other, and to work

exactly to the gauge lines, otherwise the rebate is sure to be uneven or worked in holes. It may happen that the iron has not worked exactly up to the angle of the rebate, leaving, as a result, a small ridge. This may be removed by means of a chisel, which should be run along both faces of the rebate, when the piece will be cut clean

Fig. 566.—Using Rebate Plane.

out. The joiner would use in rebating a tool known as a plough (see Fig. 181, p. 50), and the use of this is described on p. 191.

PARING.

It is often necessary to pare—that is, cut off clean—the end of a piece of stuff. To manage this, place any odd piece of board upon the bench, and upon it lay the work to be pared. Hold the chisel in the right hand, as at b (Fig. 567), with the bevel outwards. Steady it with the left hand, as shown, and apply pressure to the handle in the direction of the arrow ; also, if necessary, the right shoulder may be brought to assist in forcing the chisel downwards.

Fig. 567.—Paring with Chisel.

WORKING COVES OR HOLLOWS.

The working of beads and mouldings will be treated in detail later, but the working of a simple cove or hollow on the edge of a board may here be described. Run a line upon face and edge, as in rebating, and with a jack plane remove the stuff between the lines; this is termed chamfering. The

Fig. 568.—Rebated Joint.

gouge is then applied to the chamfer, being held in the same manner as the chisel at Fig. 563; the tips of the fingers of the left hand are also applied to the top of the gouge to steady it; the wrist is allowed to

Fig. 569.—Rebated and Filleted Joint.

rest upon the bench, as this will act as a guard against the tool slipping and spoiling the work. The chips should be taken out in short strokes of the tool, the whole length

Fig. 570.—Grooved and Tongued Joint.

of the cove being carefully finished with a sharp gouge.

REBATED, GROOVED AND TONGUED JOINTS.

Figs. 568 to 576 show nine joints that have much in common. The simple rebated

Fig. 571.—Rebated, Grooved and Tongued Joint.

joint (Fig. 568) is made by rebating the edges of two boards to half their depth, the edges being then brought together and the projections made to lap over each other. In the rebated and filleted joint (Fig. 569) the rebates are more shallow,

Fig. 572.—Ploughed and Cross-tongued Joint.

and instead of the projections lapping, the joint is made with fillets of fir or harder wood. This prevents the joint opening

from ultimate shrinkage, and the joint is thus suited to flooring, etc. The grooved and tongued, or ploughed and tongued joint (Fig. 570), also does not open on shrinkage, and is suitable for stopping light rays and the passage of air, dust, etc. The edge of one board has a rectangular groove

Fig. 573.—Dovetailed Slip Feather Joint.

ploughed in it, whilst the other board is rebated from both faces to form a fillet or tongue that fits in the groove. The rebated, grooved (ploughed), and tongued joint (Fig. 571) differs but little from the last, a groove and tongue being combined

Fig. 574.—Matched and Beaded Joint.

with a rebate. This is a good joint for flooring, and is known also as the grooved and rebated joint. The ploughed and cross-tongued joint (Fig. 572) is known also as the grooved and tongued, ploughed and feathered, or grooved and feathered joint.

Fig. 575.—Matched and V-grooved Joint.

The edges of the boards are grooved to correspond, and the tongue is of obliquely cut wood, or less commonly of iron. This is one of the most important joints used, and will be treated in detail. The dovetailed slip feather joint (Fig. 573) resembles the last, but the tongue or feather is dove-

Fig. 576.—Splay-rebated, Grooved and Tongued Joint.

tailed into each board, thus forming a very strong joint. The matched and beaded joint (Fig. 574), and the matched and V-grooved joint (Fig. 575) are practically the same as the grooved and tongued joint (Fig. 570), the working of the face of the boards near the joint being the only point of difference. Fig. 574 shows a quirked bead disguising the joint, which appears as a second quirk; this is a common method in matched-boarding. Fig. 575 shows a chamfer on each edge, the joint

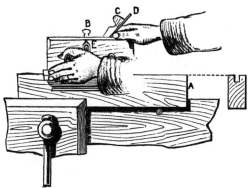

Fig. 577.—Ploughing Board, Front View.

complete showing a V-groove which disguises the line of jointing. The splay-rebated grooved and tongued joint (Fig. 576) is a somewhat uncommon joint, made by sinking a special groove in one edge and then chamfering as shown; a tongue and projection to correspond are worked on the other board.

Ploughed and Cross-tongued Joints.

The ploughed and cross-tongued joint (Fig. 572) may now be considered. It is probably stronger than either the plain or the dowelled joint, but as the latter is sufficient for ordinary purposes, and is more easily made, tongueing is not used much in cabinet work (only jointing up in order to get required width is here referred to). Still, there are occasions when it is more suitable than either of the others, as, for example, with pitch-pine boards. In making it, a groove is cut or ploughed along the edge of one or both of the planks to be joined, and the space so made is filled with a thin strip of wood. If both planks have been ploughed this strip is separately made, and half its width inserted in each (Fig. 572). When, however, only one has been prepared this way, the other is planed or rebated down from each side to leave a

projecting ridge, which fits in the ploughed groove; this is the joint shown by Fig. 570. The former is the stronger of the two, and is the one almost invariably used, and is generally preferred because only one plane other than the ordinary smoothing planes is required; while in the second form a pair, one for cutting the grooves and the other for the tongue, will be necessary. The best form is considered here; after this the other is simple.

Ploughing Grooves.

Grooves have to be ploughed in work for a variety of purposes; in doors, for instance, the framing has to be ploughed on its inner edges to receive the panels; and in jointing boards to obtain extra width, grooves have to be ploughed on their edges to receive the tongues or feathers. The plough (see Fig. 181, p. 50) is one of the most useful tools in the joiner's kit. It can be set to any required distance from the edge of the stuff, and also to any depth up to $\frac{7}{8}$ in. To obtain practice, fix some work in the bench vice, as A (Fig. 577), put the $\frac{5}{16}$ in. iron D in the plough, and drive in the wedge C; set the plough with the iron in the centre of the edge of the stuff, and set the guide (by means of the thumbscrew B) to $\frac{1}{2}$ in., this being the depth of groove; thus a groove fully $\frac{5}{16}$ in. wide and $\frac{1}{2}$ in. deep is to be cut. Hold the plough in both hands, as shown in the elevation Fig. 577,

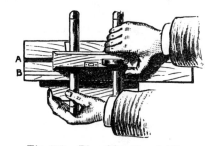

Fig. 578.—Ploughing Board, Plan.

and plan Fig. 578, and, standing within easy reach of the end of the stuff, proceed carefully to work the plane backwards and forwards until it will not go deeper. The distance from A to B (Fig. 579) will show the shape of the groove at this stage, C being the section of one end, and D of the other. Now take a step backwards, and repeat the process, taking out another section, as shown by dotted lines; proceed in like manner until the whole is done, finishing up by running the plough from end to end, to be

Fig. 579.—Diagrams of Ploughed Groove.

sure that the groove is of uniform depth. For jointing, the edges are shot perfectly true as for a plain joint, this being necessary in joints of all kinds. The plough plane must be set so that the iron cuts the groove about the middle of the edge of the plank. Those who possess a plough will have no difficulty in understanding how to regulate the fence, which, by being pressed or kept in contact with the surface of the wood, causes the iron to cut in the same straight line. It will thus be seen that in working a plough, two pressures, as they may be described, are required, one of them downwards and the other sideways during the whole of the forward thrust. If the iron is not set to cut exactly in the middle of the wood, bear in mind that the groove must be run equally on both pieces; the distance from the face being taken with due regard to the grooves corresponding when the edges are brought together. A little thought will show the necessity for this caution.

TONGUEING.

The work with the plough having been completed, the boards are ready for tongueing. There are two ways of doing this; one of them giving but little strength in the joint, and the other correct both theoretically and practically, and forming a really strong joint. As has been stated, the tongue is a strip or feather of wood glued in both the ploughed grooves. If this strip is cut so that the grain is coincident with that of the boards to be connected by it, it is evident that the strength cannot be so great as if the grain were at right angles with that of the board (see Fig. 580, in which A indicates boards, and B tongue or feather). In other words, the grain of the tongue must be end on to the bottom of the grooves. This is the key to the proper way of making the tongued and grooved joint. It is much easier to plane up a length of tongue with the grain than across it, and a moment's reflection will show that there is no occasion whatever for the tongue to be all in one piece, even if this were always possible, so that all that is necessary to do is to cut pieces of the required width and thickness from the end of any boards. The wood from which the tongue is cut is first prepared by planing to the right size. When prepared, the tongueings are to be fixed in with glue and the boards cramped together; but after what has been said in this chapter about this part of the operation, no further directions are needed. The three forms of jointing, namely, plain, dowelled, and tongued, which have been dealt with, are those principally in use in all kinds of joinery.

Fig. 580.—Ploughed and Cross-tongued Joint Apart.

SCREWED BUTT JOINT.

Figs. 581 to 583 illustrate a screwed butt joint that is both useful and novel, especially where the joint will be exposed to dampness likely to cause the glue to give way, as in w.c. seats and risers; also for fixing brackets to standards of over-mantels to carry the shelves, for gluing up shelves when time is short, as they can be cleaned off at once; and for church bench

Fig. 581.—Edges of Boards to be Screw Jointed.

heads, where it is necessary to joint to get the required width, and in many other ways it can be used to advantage. Fig. 581 shows a view of edges of boards, with screws fitted and mortises cut; Fig. 582, boards in position for jointing; Fig. 583, joint complete. The screw heads enter the holes bored for them, and then the boards

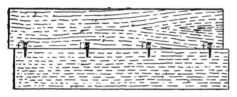

Fig. 582.—Screwed Butt Joint, Incomplete.

are merely slid together tightly to form a strong joint which can be taken apart easily.

SIMPLE NAILED JOINTS.

The simplest way to join wood at right angles is that adopted in making packing-cases (see Fig. 584); each piece is cut carefully, the ends planed true if necessary, and then merely nailed together. This method is only applicable to the roughest work, and needs no further attention, the

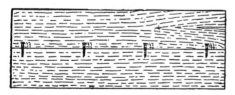

Fig. 583.—Screwed Butt Joint, Complete.

present object being to show how the angle joints in articles of furniture and in woodwork construction generally are formed. Taking the simple packing-case joint (Fig. 584) as an example, it is ob-

13

vious that if only the inside is to be seen, no objection on the score of unsightliness could be made, the only drawback to the nailed joint being its lack of strength.

Fig. 584.
Simplest Form of
Nailed Joint.

Fig. 585.
Nailed Lapped
Joint.

Seen, however, from the outside, the heads of the nails and the end grain of one of the boards are left exposed. Suppose, therefore, that for the corner of a simple cupboard a dovetailed joint is not deemed necessary, though a neater union than the packing-case presents is required. Fig. 585 shows what is meant, the top of the cupboard being cut in the form of a rebate, and the side nailed to it, the joint being covered afterwards by an applied moulding. Such a joint will be

Fig. 586.—Halved Joint.

superior to the packing-case joint both in strength and appearance, because the use of glue as well as nails becomes possible, and because of the increased surface given by the rebate, the strength of glued joints being very largely dependent upon the area of the surfaces in mutual contact.

HALVED JOINT.

The joints described in the following pages should be practised in the order

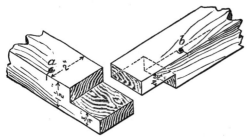

Fig. 587.—Halved Joint Apart.

in which they appear, by first constructing a working drawing, and then making the joint from it. The actual work should not be begun until a good working drawing has been made. Fig. 586 shows a simple halved joint, and Fig. 587 the parts of one with the halving at the other ends. This is of common use, and usually is adopted for connecting wall-plates of a roof at the angles. To make it, plane up true two pieces of wood, each, say, 9 in. by 2 in. by 1½ in. finished size, measured upon the side first planed, which is termed the face side ; draw a fancy mark, such as a tailed scroll (see *a*, *b*, in plan, Fig. 588), with the tail drawn to the edge ; upon the corresponding edge make a dash only (see *c*, in elevation, Fig. 589). In practice, these

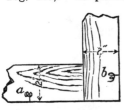

Fig. 588.—Plan of Halved Joint.

marks are omitted, all measurements, gauge marks, and squaring being made from the side upon which they occur. To begin the joint, square off one end of each piece, and from this, square over a line at a distance

equal to the width of the stuff (2 in.). This line denotes the shoulders, one piece having it upon the face, and the other upon the back. Set a marking gauge to half the thickness of material (¾ in.), and run along the sides and ends as far as the shoulder lines. Fix each piece alternately in the bench vice, and saw down in the outside of the piece that is to remain. If the saw-kerf is upon the wrong side—that is, the inside—of the line, the two pieces, upon being placed to-

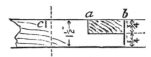

Fig. 589.—Elevation of Halved Joint.

gether, will not stand level or flush upon the surface, the saw-kerf having removed some of the substance. Having cut in these lines, form the shoulders by cutting across the grain with the tenon saw in each case to meet the end of the saw-kerf. This joint is usually nailed together, but when the joint is to be kept as a sample or model, it is not desirable to use a nail. A screw might be inserted from the back, where it will be out of sight, and may easily be withdrawn to allow of the joint being examined. This applies to many other joints.

HALF-LAP JOINT.

A halved joint that is commonly used

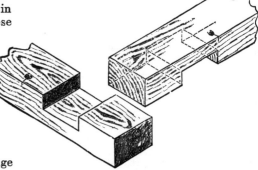

Fig. 590.—Half-lap Joint.

under the name "half-lap" is shown by Fig. 590. The difference between this and the previous joint is in the projecting ends ; these are a decided advantage, and render it serviceable and strong where circumstances allow of its use. It may be set out

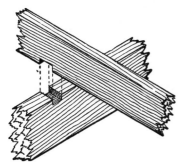

Fig. 591.—Notched Joint.

by placing one piece upon the other, taking care to keep the pieces at right angles, and marking each side with a striking-knife. The gauge is then set to half the thickness, and run along the edges between the square lines. The shoulders may be cut in with the tenon saw as far as gauge lines, and the stuff between should be cut out by means of chisel and mallet, and afterwards carefully pared down to the gauge marks upon both edges of the stuff.

NOTCHED JOINT.

One form of notched joint closely re-

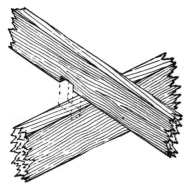

Fig. 592.—Notched Joint.

sembles the half-lap joint, but differs from it in the depth to which the notching is cut. In the half-lap one-half was cut out from each piece, the whole finishing flush

upon top and bottom ; in this joint, however, only one-quarter or one-eighth the depth of the material is cut away (see Fig. 591), or one piece may not even be notched at all (see Fig. 592). Fig. 593 shows another form of notched joint, and this is the kind often adopted at the top of a post carrying a piece of timber, such as a plate, etc.

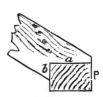

Fig. 593.
Notched Joint at
Top of Post.

Fig. 594.
Bird's-mouth
Joint.

BIRD'S-MOUTH JOINT.

The bird's-mouth joint is shown in end view by Fig. 594, an isometric sketch of it being shown by Fig. 595. Usually it is adopted at the foot or bottom of a rafter, where abutting against the wall-plate P (Fig. 594). This may be set out by means of the sliding bevel, a and b (Fig. 594) forming a right angle. The piece is cut out of the end with a tenon saw.

COGGED JOINT.

Fig. 596 illustrates a joint occasionally,

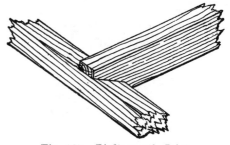

Fig. 595.—Bird's-mouth Joint.

employed to connect the tie-beam and wall-plate. The joint is again shown by Fig. 597. It is set out by first marking the width of the top piece B upon the bottom piece

A. The mortise gauge is set to one-third the width, and it is run between the lines upon the face side, denoted by the scroll or mark. Set a gauge to one-fourth the depth, and run along both of the sides, as at *a a*.

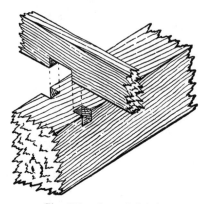

Fig. 596.—Cogged Joint.

The top piece has merely a groove cut upon it to correspond with the cog. The recesses *c c* may be cut out by means of mallet and chisel, care being taken to ensure all the angles being square. The groove in the top piece may be first run in with the tenon saw, removing the piece with a chisel of suitable width.

MITRED JOINT.

To form mitred joints the work is cut on

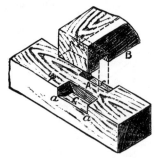

Fig. 597.—Cogged Joint.

mitre blocks or in mitre boxes (see pp. 15 and 16). Say a piece of moulding is to be mitred. Place the moulding A (Fig. 598) in the rebate B of the mitre block, and press

the thumb of the left hand (the fingers being upon the block) firmly upon it. Holding the tenon saw C in the right hand, place the blade in the kerf, and carefully cut the moulding, being sure to stop sawing when

Fig. 598.—Cutting Moulding in Mitre Block.

the piece is cut through, or the block will be damaged. Having cut one end, mark the desired length upon the moulding, and repeat the process in the other cut D, Figs. 59 and 60 (p. 16) show how moulding is cut in a mitre box. For accurate work the mitres must be shot. Place one of the pieces of moulding upon the mitre shooting block (Fig. 61, p. 17), as A (Fig. 599), with the end slightly projecting beyond, as seen. Press the left hand firmly upon it,

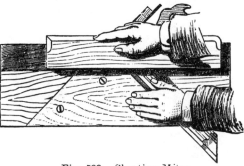

Fig. 599.—Shooting Mitre.

as in cutting the mitre. Turn the trying-plane upon its side in the rebate, and carefully work it across the mitre until true. To shoot the other end, the board must be turned round, the position of the hands being reversed, the right hand holding the moulding whilst the left hand works the plane. This position is shown in the photo-reproduction (Fig. 600) illustrating a differ-

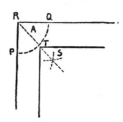

Fig. 600.—Shooting Mitre.

ent kind of shooting board, in which two strips replace the triangle.

SETTING OUT MITRES.

In Fig. 601 are shown two lines forming an angle of 90°; to obtain the angle of 45° between them, the mitre line, the angle A is bisected as follows. With R as centre, and any convenient radius, describe the arc P Q; with P and Q as centres, and any radius more than half the distance from P to Q, describe the intersecting arcs S; join R S, and this line will be the desired mitre. By drawing the two inner lines parallel with the others, and joining R T, the same results would be obtained. Fig.

Fig. 601.—Setting out True Mitre.

602 is an angle that often occurs in a bay window; and Fig. 603 shows the angle for the moulding in a piece of irregular fram-ing. The method is the same as in Fig. 601, the application being perfectly general,

and therefore requiring no explanation. Fig. 604 clearly shows the position of two mouldings if the mitre had been incorrectly drawn, as A B. They may form a right angle on the outside, and also fit close

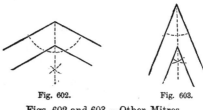

Fig. 602.   Fig. 603.

Figs. 602 and 603.—Other Mitres.

together at the mitre, but the various members, as indicated by the parallel lines in the diagrams, will not intersect, although

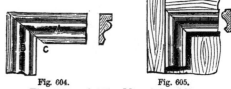

Fig. 604.   Fig. 605.

Figs. 604 and 605.—Mitred Mouldings.

A and B are of the same width. It will be good exercise to cut such a mitre. It is often desirable to place a small moulding

Fig. 606.—Shooting Mitre in Bench Vice.

on the panel of a piece of framing, as a door for instance, to relieve the square appearance. One corner of such an arrange-ment is shown at Fig. 605; in these small mouldings it is not the practice to shoot the mitres; any slight irregularity is corrected with the smoothing plane, the moulding being held in the bench vice, as in Fig. 606. Many patented machines are on the market for cutting mitres, some with and some without the aid of saw and plane, but all claiming almost automatic working and the impossibility of inaccurate work. There is no need, however, to describe them in detail here.

HOUSING OR HOUSED JOINT.

The housing joint (if joint it may be called) is available when one of the pieces of wood overhangs or projects beyond the face of the other. Fig. 607 illustrates the simplest form; the piece *a*, termed a sill or rail—as the case may be—is let bodily into the post or upright *b* to a depth of

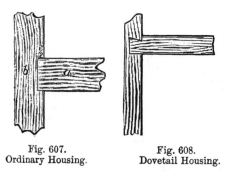

Fig. 607.
Ordinary Housing.

Fig. 608.
Dovetail Housing.

about ½ in.; it may be cut with the saw and cleared out by means of mallet and chisel, being nailed in position from the top and sides. Housing is formed by the ordinary joining of the back rail of a plinth or cornice; this is a mere housing joint with a block above and below. Fig. 608 shows the dovetail housing; this is not always available, because if the overhang of the top is but little the outer portion of the socket may break off, and if the width from back to front is considerable it is difficult to make a good fit; but for fixing the stiles to the top of a sideboard slab, hinged to fall down, it is a very useful mode of attachment.

MORTISE AND TENON JOINT.

The mortise and tenon joint is probably the most important joint used in wood-

working; it enters largely into the construction of all classes of joinery, such, for instance, as door-frames, doors, sashes, etc., and household furniture of all kinds. Great care is necessary upon the part of the learner to ensure that it is nicely fitted, and if careful attention is devoted to the

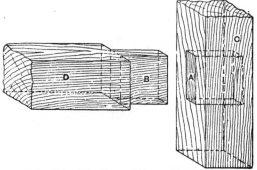

Fig. 609.—Mortise and Tenon Joint Apart.

details in working, few joints give greater satisfaction in the result, it being neat, strong, and durable. The simplest form of mortise and tenon is shown in the general view (Fig. 609), in which A is the mortise, in piece C, and B the tenon on piece D. Figs. 610 and 611 show plan and elevation of two pieces of wood framed together at

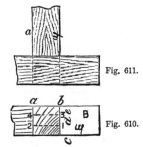

Fig. 611.

Fig. 610.

Figs. 610 and 611.—Plan and Elevation of Mortise and Tenon Joint.

right angles by means of a mortise and tenon; A indicates the upright, or stile, which in this case has the tenon cut upon its lower extremity, and which passes through the rail B. The stile is shown in section on the plan, *a b* showing its width, and the dotted lines *d* indicating the position of the tenon, and *c e* the shoulders.

As a general rule, the tenons are cut upon all rails, and the mortises in the stiles. Before attempting to make this joint, Figs. 610 and 611 and detail views of the separate

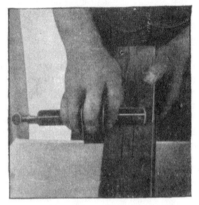

Fig. 612.—Using Mortise Gauge.

tenon should be drawn out to the full size of the material selected (say 9 in. long, 2 in. wide, and 1½ in. thick), to serve as working drawings. The importance of always working from drawings cannot be insisted upon too strongly.

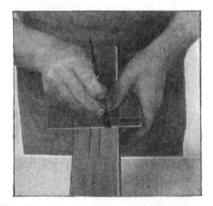

Fig. 613.—Squaring End Lines of Mortise.

SETTING OUT MORTISE AND TENON JOINT.

Plane up true two pieces of wood to the sizes given, allowing at least ⅛ in. extra in width and thickness for thicknessing; lay the rail as B (Fig. 610) upon the bench, having the face uppermost. At the desired distance from the end draw the line *b c*,

and make *b a* equal to the width (2 in.) of the piece on which the tenon is to be. Divide the line *b c* into three equal parts, making each just ½ in.; set the marking gauge to the first mark, and run it from 1 to 2; set another gauge to the second division, and run this from 3 to 4. The space between the dotted lines will presently be cut out; square the lines *a* and *b* down the side of the stuff, and also across the other face; now, taking care to work from the same side as indicated by a scroll (shown in Figs. 610 and 611), run the gauges along the other face as just described, thus setting out the mortise. As a general rule, the tenon is made one-third the thickness of material; in this case, the stuff being 1½ in. thick, the mortise has been set out as

Fig. 615.   Fig. 614.

Fig. 614.—Part Section of Tenon, showing Kerfs.
Fig. 615.—Sawing Tenon.

½ in. The width of the mortise, however, is varied occasionally to suit the width of the chisel employed, as these two always should agree. The mortise gauge (Figs. 33 to 35, pp. 11 and 12) is usually employed to gauge the mortise and tenon, it marking both lines at the same time. Its use is made quite clear by Fig. 612, the lines denoting the ends of the mortise being drawn with square and scriber as in Fig. 613. To set out the tenon, place the second piece on edge upon the bench, and from the end, as *c* to *d* (Fig. 614), mark off the depth of the mortise (in this case 2 in.). Square this line carefully down both sides with a striking-knife to indicate the shoulders; run the marking gauges along both sides, *e g* and *f h*, and also across the end, thus setting out the joint ; or do the work more quickly by using a mortise gauge.

CUTTING TENONS.

The process of tenon cutting is illustrated by Fig. 615. Fasten the work *a*

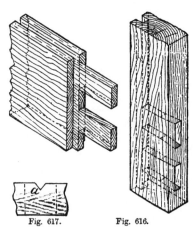

Fig. 617.   Fig. 616.

Fig. 616.—Double Tenon.   Fig. 617.—Nick for
Starting Mortise.

securely in the bench vice, and proceed to cut down on the outside of each gauge line with the hand-saw until the saw is level across from line to line on the edges, as *c d* shows. If the piece is large, the saw should be run in alternately from each edge until down to the lines, as this ensures the tenon being cut an equal thickness throughout. The saw-kerf should always be on the outside of the tenon, or else the tenon will be too small for the mortise. Fig. 614 shows in section the two kerfs cut in at *e g*, *f h*. The shoulders should now be cut square. Here again, the cut must be to the outside or right side of the line, so as to leave the knife-cut line to form the actual joint ; otherwise the saw-kerf reduces the length of the rail by the thickness of the kerf. Cut the shoulders of the tenon with a tenon saw.

MORTISING.

In cases where it is not necessary that the tenon should go through, particular care should be taken as to the direction of the mortise ; neglect of this would, in case

of narrow bars like sash bars, cause them to appear bent—in fact, would bend them. In making a door or similar article of joinery, the size of the mortise depends upon the size of the plough-groove (if any), the position depending on the size of any moulding that may be worked upon the stiles ; yet the cutting of the mortises is not to be left until these operations are accomplished. The mortises are best cut before either the groove is ploughed or the moulding worked, though of course the necessary allowances must be made. If on the inner edge of the stile a section of each rail in its right position is drawn, there will not be much likelihood of making any mistake in the planning of the mortises. Every groove, rebate, moulding, etc., should be drawn, and it would be well if a section of stiles, muntins, or bars were similarly drawn upon the rails ; this would at once give the shoulders, and suggest where either mitring or scribing is necessary. The plough groove is shown in Fig. 616, which illustrates a double tenon on the bottom rail of a 2-in. door, the mortises shown allowing for wedging. One other consideration ought to be mentioned, that is, that if the edges of the wood are

Fig. 618.—Cutting Mortise.

not square (and some workmen leave the outer edges to be planed to finished sizes after the work is glued up), the mortise may be made apparently true, perpendicular to the bench or mortise stool, and yet, because the work is not properly prepared, it may not be parallel to the face of the work as it should be. In making a small mortise the stile should be fastened tightly in the bench vice before starting work. To begin the mortise in the piece shown by

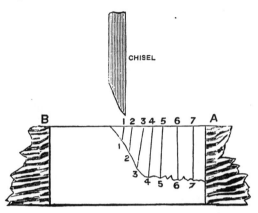

Fig. 619.—Diagram of Chisel Cuts in Mortising.

Fig. 610, cut out with the ½-in. chisel a small V-shaped piece in the centre, as *a*, Fig. 617; starting from this, proceed to cut a succession of chips, one about every ¼ in., taking care to drive the chisel deeper at each successive blow, as seen at Fig. 618, and as shown diagrammatically by Fig. 619, in which A and B are the ends of the mortise, and the numerals indicate the order of the cuts. Having now worked from the centre to the end of mortise *b* (Fig. 618), the chips may be cleared out in the manner shown at Fig. 620. Turn the chisel round so that its face *d* (Fig. 618) shall be the opposite way about, and again starting from *a*, cut the remaining portion of the mortise up to the line *c*. Now turn the stile over, and cut the mortise from the back edge in precisely the same manner until cut quite through. A (Fig. 618) shows the chisel in position, looking at its face, and B the mortise cut through. From lack of method beginners invariably make mortises somewhat larger than is required, and the core is an embarrassment to them. If the cuts are made in the above order on both sides of the nick which was first made, there will not be much core left when all the cuts have been made, and what there is will be in the middle, where it is most easily re-

moved. If the mortise is right through, it is better to use a core-driver than to pick out the core with a chisel or other tool; if it does not go right through, use a sharp chisel somewhat smaller than the mortise chisel.

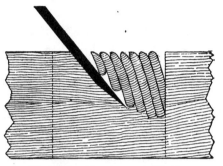

Fig. 620.—Clearing out Mortise.

WEDGED MORTISE AND TENON JOINT.

Mortises intended for tenons that pass through the stile usually have the outer portion enlarged for wedging, not of course in width, but in the length; this enlargement for the wedges ought to be a very gentle taper, because taper wedges hold better

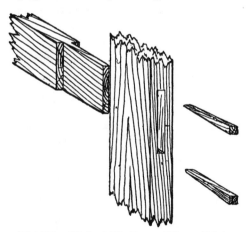

Fig. 621.—Wedged Mortise and Tenon Joint.

than abrupt ones. An engineer's key in a cog wheel may serve as an excellent example, or the wedge of a plane is about a correct angle for wedge of tenon; these wedges, when glued and driven, convert the tenon into a dovetail, and also give an opportunity for adjustment in putting together the work. A typical joint is shown by Fig. 621, whilst Fig. 622 shows a pair of single wedged tenons, commonly

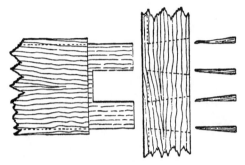

Fig. 622.—Pair of Single Wedged Tenons.

called double tenons. The proper dovetail tenon is shown by Fig. 623.

ATTITUDE OF WORKER IN MORTISING.

In mortising, as in every mechanical operation, attitude is of importance. It is common knowledge that a circular disc does not appear to be circular unless every portion of the outline is equally drawn from the eye ; a circle drawn on a piece of paper and viewed obliquely appears to

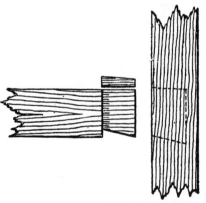

Fig. 623.—Dovetail Tenon.

be an ellipse. It is equally well known that any three points may be regarded as being in one plane, or in other words a plane surface (of suitable dimensions) may be made to touch any three points wher-

ever they may be placed. Apply these two facts to the operation of making a mortise. Let the centre line of the tool and the centre line of the mortise be drawn or

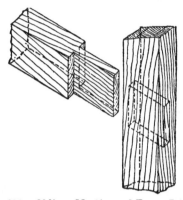

Fig. 624.—Oblique Mortise and Tenon Joint.

imagined ; both of these are in one vertical plane, and their intersection forms a right angle. When the tool is in a correct position to cut, the eye of the workman should be in the same plane as the two imaginary lines which have been supposed. To further make this clear, stretch a chalk line between two points ; at any point on the line stretch another to a point above, or preferably let a plumb-line cut the horizontal chalk line. When the operator is standing so that these two lines range in one line, he is in the true attitude to

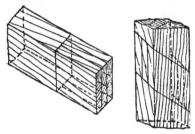

Fig. 625.—Setting out Oblique Mortise and Tenon Joint.

assume with respect to cutting a mortise. This important point must be realised, and may be clearly demonstrated by trying the following simple experiment. Take a piece of wood, draw on it a straight line, on this line stick a straight wire—a mattress needle or a long knitting pin will do ; light a lamp or a candle, and the needle will cast a shadow which by a little adjust-

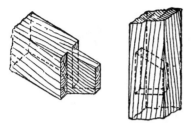

Fig. 626.—Oblique Mortise and Tenon Joint.

ment can be made to lie along the line ; the flame of the candle is now in the plane of both the lines ; if the wire is slanted out of the same vertical plane as the line, it will still be possible to make the shadow range, but in that case the light is not on or over the central line, as it ought to be. The beginner cannot rely on making a true mortise unless he can assume this position, in which he can see the direction of his chisel.

Boring instead of Chiselling Mortises.

The method given on p. 201 is the one adopted by carpenter, joiner, and cabinetmaker ; but many other woodworkers, as coach-builders, etc., do not make mortises in this manner. After marking out the mor-

beech, or other hard woods, saving a large amount of work with the mallet, but the beginner must exercise great care or he will pare away too much in finishing.

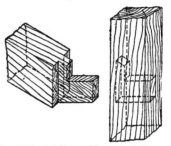

Fig. 628.—Oblique Haunched Tenon.

Oblique Mortise and Tenon Joints.

There are a few varieties of the oblique mortise and tenon joint. In each case they are first set out ready for sawing and mortising, and then prepared for fixing together. The mortise shown by Fig. 624 is rather difficult to make, as it goes obliquely through the wood ; it is set out as in Fig. 625. The joint shown by Fig. 626 would not be wedged, but fixed by gluing or pinning ; it is set out as in Fig. 627. Fig. 628 shows a haunched joint which can be wedged ; this is set out as in Fig. 629. In each case the parts are first prepared for sawing and mortising, and then

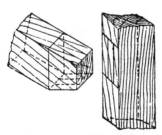

Fig. 627.—Setting out Oblique Mortise and Tenon Joint.

tises in the usual way, as much as possible of the timber is bored out from the centre of the mortise with brace and bit, and the rest is pared away with sharp chisels. This method is excellent for ash, oak,

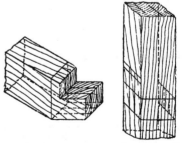

Fig. 629.—Setting out Oblique Haunched Tenon.

prepared for fixing together. A form of the oblique mortise and tenon joint which is often used in preference to the bridle-joint to connect the foot of principal rafter and tie-beam is shown by Figs. 630 and

631. In Fig. 631 the part at *a* is cut into one-eighth the depth of beam, a small mortise one-third the thickness being cut beyond the shoulder-line *a c*, as *d b* show; in Fig.

Fig. 630.—Oblique Mortise and Tenon Joint for Rafter and Tie-beam.

630, B is the beam, and C the principal rafter. No difficulty will be experienced in working this joint without further explanation.

DRAW-BORING.

Draw-boring is one of the easiest methods of tightening up permanently a mortise and tenon joint, the mode of procedure

Fig. 631.—Oblique Mortise.

being as follows. Bore a hole of suitable size through the side of the mortise, as A (Fig. 632); now drive in the tenon B, and inserting a bradawl in the hole A, mark the tenon as shown by the dotted hole. Remove the tenon and bore a hole in it a

its head being slightly larger than the hole, and tapering nicely off to a point. Drive it in the hole in the direction of arrow (see Fig. 634), which will draw the joint up

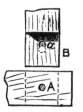

Fig. 632.—Tenon with Draw-bore.

to its place. It will be seen from Fig. 634 that the pin P must bear upon the hole bored in the rail at *a a*, and upon the opposite side of the hole in the tenon at *b*; as a result the pin, being tapered, must,

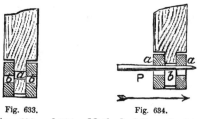

Fig. 633.   Fig. 634.

Figs. 633 and 634.—Method of Draw-boring.

upon being driven forward, draw the pieces of stuff tightly up to the shoulders. For permanent fastening, the pin is cut off flush. The draw-bore pin shown by Fig.

Fig. 635.—Draw-bore Pin.

trifle nearer the shoulder as at *a*, Fig. 632, and sectional view (Fig. 633). Care should be taken in this matter, because should the hole be farther away, instead of nearer, the joint will be drawn apart instead of together. Fig. 633 illustrates the joint with the shoulders slightly off, *a* being the hole in tenon, and *b b* in the mortise. Make a pin from a straight-grained piece of stuff,

635 is of steel in a boxwood handle; this draws the joint together, and then a wooden pin is substituted. The hole in the tenon should be bored only a slight distance nearer the shoulder, or the pin, after passing half-way through, will split, and force its way through at the back shoulder, effectually preventing the joint drawing up. Examples of this and all

other joints described should be faithfully worked out in any available material, such as red deal ; or if preferred, they may be worked to scale, say 1½ in. to a foot ; in this case a harder wood should be selected,

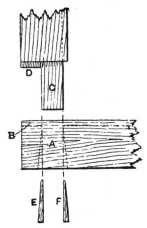

Fig. 636.—Haunched Tenon Joint.

such as bay wood, which may be bought cheaply.

HAUNCHED TENON JOINT.

The haunched tenon joint is illustrated by Fig. 636. This is the joint cut on the door rail which finishes flush with the end of the stile. The mortise is set out to the size at A, and the part B is cut in to a depth of ½ in. only. The tenon is shown at C,

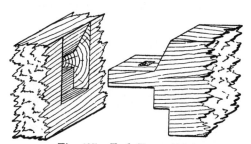

Fig. 637.—Tusk Tenon Joint.

the part D being known as the haunch ; the haunch is cut ½ in. long, to correspond with the depth in the stile. This joint should be well glued, and secured with two wedges E F, which are also glued and driven tightly home.

TUSK TENON JOINT.

Fig. 637 shows the tusk tenon joint, one of the most useful and well-designed joints it is possible to conceive for the purpose

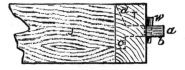

Fig. 638.—Elevation of Tusk Tenon.

to which it is adapted. On entering a building at a certain stage in the course of its construction, it may be seen that a clear space has been left between the joist and chimney-breast or fireplace ; several of the joists have been cut short, and another, called a trimmer, has been carried across at right angles to them. Into this trimmer the joists are fastened by means of a tusk tenon, which is cut in about half the thickness of joist. The tenon a (Fig. 638) is not so thick in proportion as in other tenon joints, the rule of one-third the thickness not applying here. A line taken along the centre of a piece of timber is termed its neutral axis, for the reason that if it is bent by a weight the axial fibres of the wood are not strained in any way ; therefore place the bottom edge of the tenon, as b (Fig. 638) in the centre of the trimmer T. The thickness of the tenon

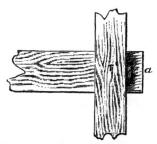

Fig. 639.—Plan of Tusk Tenon.

should be one-sixth the depth of the joist, the necessary strength being obtained by sinking a piece c below the tenon, and also a bevelled piece d above it. The sinking may be one-fifth the thickness of the joist, and its depth two-thirds that of the joist as measured from the top. A wedge w is inserted, as shown, to draw all tightly up to bearings. Fig. 638 is a side elevation and section of joint, and Fig. 639 is a plan.

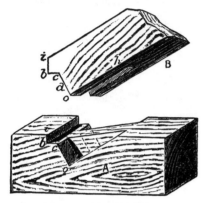

Fig. 640.—Bridle Joint.

A convenient size for the stuff would be about 9 in. by 3 in. by 2 in. Having planed up the wood, set the mortise gauge to the distances given above, and set out the mortise and tenon; next mark upon the face of the trimmer the parts c d, and the mortise and tenon may now be cut, the housings and shoulders being cut afterwards.

BRIDLE JOINT.

The bridle joint is shown by Fig. 640; it is applicable to the foot of a roof-truss. In practice A would be the tie-beam, and B the foot of the principal rafter. To make the joint, first carefully plane up two pieces of stuff to the following sizes: 9 in. by 3 in. by 2 in., and 6 in. by 2¼ in. by 2 in., respectively, or others bearing the same pro-

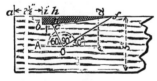

Fig. 641.—Setting out Bridle Joint.

portions. Upon the first piece (Fig. 641) mark off a distance of about 2½ in. from the end a. Square over a line upon the edge at this point and down both sides, as

from i to b. Set the marking gauge to 1 in., and run it along both sides, the head being worked upon the top edge, as b to c, which should also be 1 in., as shown. Set a gauge to one-half the depth of stuff, which must be 1½ in., as from d to e, and from the top edge (as before) run it along both sides, giving the dotted line A e. Sup-

Fig. 642.—Setting out Bridle Joint.

pose the rafter (B, Fig. 640) to be inclined at an angle of 30°. With the horizontal tie-beam A the angle o will be one of 90°, o c being struck square from the edge of rafter at h; it therefore follows that the outside or complementary angle will be

Fig. 643.—Setting out Bridle Joint.

one of 60°. Apply the 60° set-square to the centre line (A e, Fig. 641), moving it along until its edge cuts the point c on the line b c. Draw the line c o; turn the set-square over, and draw o f, cutting the top edge at f, as seen. Carefully repeat this upon the other side, which may easily be

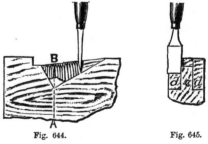

Fig. 644.   Fig. 645.

Figs. 644 and 645.—Cutting Bridle Joint.

done by squaring over the points i h f, and also the point o. The rafter (Fig. 642) may be set out by marking off points to correspond with those upon the tie-beam. The foregoing method of setting out the work direct upon the stuff has been adopted in order to show as forcibly as possible the disadvantage of not making a working drawing. In working from a drawing, all the angles can be taken with the sliding bevel, and marked direct upon the stuff, thus saving time and all chance of mistake.

Fig. 646.—Clearing out Bridle Joint.

The next step is to cut away the shaded portions shown in Figs. 641 and 642. This may be done with the tenon saw, carefully paring across the edge of the piece shown in Fig. 641 with a 1½ in. firmer chisel. Now scribe with the mortise gauge, set to one-third the thickness, as shown by Fig. 643, the distance between dotted lines giving the thickness of bridle or tenon. The gauge is now to be run along from *f* to *c*, Fig. 641, and *f o c* (Fig. 642). The joint is now set out. Turning the rafter upon its edge, it will be seen that a saw may readily be run into the lines between *f o* (Fig. 643), thus

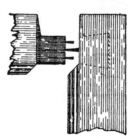

Fig. 647.—Foxtail Tenon Joint Apart.

cutting from *o* to the dotted line *c f* (Fig. 642). The piece between saw-kerfs can be removed by means of mallet and chisel. A bridle or tenon now has to be worked upon the tie-beam, Fig. 641, and the lines *f o*, *o c* will form the shoulders. This may be managed as previously described for ordinary mortise and tenon joints. Fig.

644 shows the process of cutting down upon each side of the bridle, Fig. 645 being a section upon A B, *c* indicating the bridle, and *d d* the parts to be removed. Fig. 646 illustrates the method of removing the chips or core; this is done roughly with the chisel used bevel downwards, finishing with a sharp chisel in the manner shown.

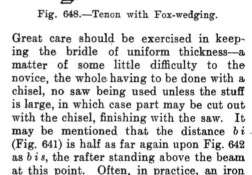

Fig. 648.—Tenon with Fox-wedging.

Great care should be exercised in keeping the bridle of uniform thickness—a matter of some little difficulty to the novice, the whole having to be done with a chisel, no saw being used unless the stuff is large, in which case part may be cut out with the chisel, finishing with the saw. It may be mentioned that the distance *b i* (Fig. 641) is half as far again upon Fig. 642 as *b i s*, the rafter standing above the beam at this point. Often, in practice, an iron strap is passed round the rafter and under

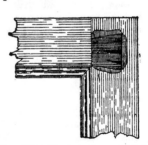

Fig. 649.—Foxtail Tenon Joint.

the beam in the direction of a right angle to the back of the rafter.

FOXTAIL TENON JOINT OR FOX-WEDGING.

This is a very strong form of mortise and tenon joint, largely used in cabinet work. Fig. 647 shows a part of a rail and the top portion of a stile. The wedges are shown inserted in the tenon ready to be driven home. Fig. 648 shows an enlarged view of the tenon ; the dotted lines represent how much the tenon will be spread out when inside the mortise. The sum of the thickest parts of the three wedges should be $\frac{3}{8}$ in., as that is the distance which the tenon spreads. The centre wedge should

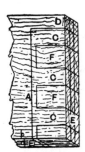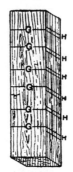

Fig. 650.—Setting Out
Plain Clamping.

Fig. 651.
Plain Clamp.

be $\frac{3}{16}$ in. in its thickest part and 1 in. in length, and each of the others a bare $\frac{1}{8}$ in. thick and $\frac{3}{4}$ in. long. The mortise, the shape of which is shown in dotted lines on the stile in Fig. 647, must be a shade deeper than the tenon is long ; that this is so must be ascertained before the wedges are inserted, or the shoulders may not come up when glued and driven home. Fig. 649 shows the same joint when finished ; a portion of the wood on the face is removed to show the interior.

Plain Clamping.

By clamping is meant the putting of a narrow piece of wood on the ends of a wider piece, the grain of one piece being at a right angle to that of the other; the narrow piece, or clamp, prevents the board from twisting or warping. There are three methods of clamping. One consists in merely nailing the clamps on, and is hardly worthy of the name. The second method—plain clamping—is shown by Figs. 650 and 651. Fig. 650 shows one end of the board to be clamped. After being planed up, the scribed line A—the shoulder mark—must be squared all round and at both ends, if they are both to be clamped.

Then, $\frac{1}{2}$ in. nearer the end, another line is pencilled. Set out the tenons c, having about $1\frac{1}{2}$ in. at each edge of board for haunching, as D. From D mark off about 2 in. for tenon at each edge, and then mark out the rest of the space into tenons according to width of board. The maximum distance between tenons should be 5 in., and should not be less than 3 in. It will be easy to get them somewhere between these two distances. Set the mortise gauge to the right size according to the thickness of board, and then make the lines E on the edges and ends of board as shown. Cut out the waste pieces between mortises, as at F, just as far as the pencil line, and cut the tenons and shoulders at A ; also cut out the haunchings at D, and then take the clamp (Fig. 651), and, laying it under the tenons c (Fig. 650), close up to shoulder A, and mark these on to the clamp, as at G (Fig. 651). Square these marks over on both edges ; then make wedging marks on the outside, as shown at H, and, also with the mortise gauge, the marks for thickness of mortises, as with the tenon in Fig. 650. The reason for leaving the $\frac{1}{2}$ in. to the right of A is to form a haunching right across for the reception of which a groove is made in

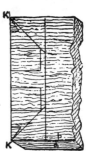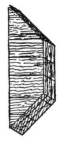

Fig. 652.—Setting Out
Mitre Clamping.

Fig. 653.
Mitre Clamp.

face edge of clamp the same width as mortises, and, of course, $\frac{1}{2}$ in. deep.

Mitre Clamping.

Plain clamping is the strongest method, but it will not do for good work, as the end grain of the clamp shows on the edge of the board. It is usual in better classes of work to adopt mitre clamping, shown in

Figs. 652 and 653. This is set out like the former, except that a mitre is formed at the ends of the clamp, as shown in Fig. 652. The clamp is made first, and the mitres

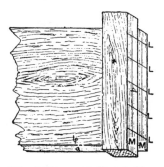

Fig. 654.—Setting out Dowel Clamping.

are then marked from it upon the board. When the mitres are cut and the tenons made, the clamp is placed in position on the tenons as before, and the marks made for the mortises. The haunchings are made just as in the first case, but they are allowed to go away to nothing, as shown at K (Fig. 652).

Fig. 655.—Jointed Boards with Heart Sides Alternating.

DOWEL CLAMPING.

The above mitre clamping is a very good criterion of a man's ability to use tools, and the difficulties of making a good job of it have led many to adopt the system of dowelling the clamp on. This is shown in Fig. 654, and is much easier to do, though it is questionable whether it is as strong. Fig. 654 shows plain dowel clamping, but mitre clamping is done in the same way. If plain clamping with dowels is

Fig. 656.—Jointed Boards with Heart Side all one way.

being done, all that is necessary is to plane the end of board straight and true and fit the clamp to it in the same way as when making a glue joint. Then

14

lay them face to face, as in Fig. 654, and square across the marks L at intervals of about 2 in. Then run a gauge-mark along at about the middle of the thickness, as at M. The dowel holes are bored with a bit where the marks cross one another. In mitre clamping with dowels a little more skill is necessary, the mitred clamp being fitted into the end of the board and then laid on, and the marks for dowels squared across the two as before. In this method no end grain shows. In the mitre clamping, as shown in Figs. 652 and 653, there are still the ends of tenons showing where they come through the clamp; but the dowelling does away with even these.

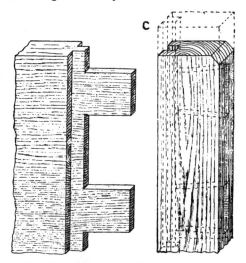

Fig. 657.—Clamp and Haunched Tenons.

MAKING CLAMPED BLACKBOARDS.

Blackboard construction affords good exercise in clamping. To produce a good blackboard it is necessary that only thoroughly seasoned timber be employed. The best yellow pine is the wood most frequently used, and boards should be selected from those planks which contain the heart of the tree; the further from the heart the planks are cut the more are they liable to warp and shrink. (This matter is dealt with in the previous chapter.) If it is inconvenient to obtain all heart boards, those as near as possible to the heart should be used. The heart sides of the boards should alternate as illustrated by Fig. 655. When the boards are jointed as shown in Fig. 656, the inevitable warping at the centre will cause the joint to break. This is often the cause

gauged as shown in Fig. 658, and the tenons cut down as far as the haunchings. The latter can be easily made by cutting the shoulders to their proper depth and then

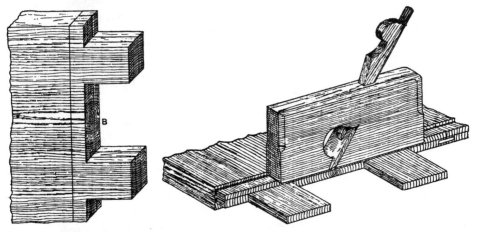

Fig. 658.—Setting out Haunched Tenons.

Fig. 659.—Planing Rebate.

of blackboards cracking. The surface of a board jointed as shown in Fig. 655 may not be flat, but at the same time cracks are much less likely to appear on it. There will also be no abrupt parts as is the case when the method of jointing illustrated by Fig. 656 is employed. The warping as illustrated is much exaggerated. The first thing to be done when making a clamped blackboard is to cut off the stuff and tongue together the edges of the boards as described on p. 191. The plough groove should be ½ in. deep and ⅛ in. wide. The clamps can now be planed up, set out, mortised and ploughed for haunchings (see Fig. 657). Of course, at this stage there should be a "horn" at each end of the clamps, as indicated by dotted lines at c (Fig. 657). When the joints are set, which probably will not be for at least twelve hours, the board should be trued up on one side and gauged to a thickness. The shoulder lines should be scribed, the tenons and haunchings set out, and the pieces of waste wood between the tenons sawn out. Cutting to the lines parallel to the shoulders (see B, Fig. 658) with a bow saw is preferable to mortising with a chisel. The tenons and haunchings should now be

forming the haunchings and roots of the tenons with a rebate plane as illustrated at Fig. 659. Of course, if preferred, some of this superfluous wood can be first pared

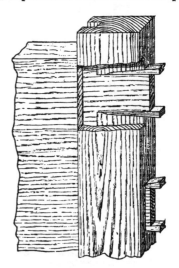

Fig. 660.—Wedged Clamp.

off with a chisel. This method will be found easier than sawing right down to the shoulder line and thus forming the haunchings with the saw, unless a circular saw is possessed, in which case they could be sawn down to the right depth at once. The clamps can now be tried on, and, when

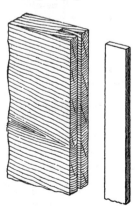

Fig. 661.—Clamped Blackboard.

fitted satisfactorily, they may be glued, cramped on, and the tenons wedged into the mortises as indicated at Figs. 660 and 661. When the glue has become thoroughly set, the surfaces can be trued off smooth. Now cut off the horns, mark to the exact sizes, shoot the edges, and take off the corners as shown by Fig. 661. Plane off the sharp arrises, and then finish the surfaces with fine glasspaper.

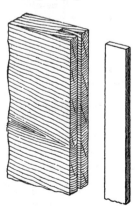

Fig. 662.—Iron Tongue and Groove.

Making Iron-tongued Blackboards.

The same methods of jointing up the boards, planing the surface, and getting it to a thickness are employed when making an iron-tongued blackboard. The board should be set out to size, the edges shot, and each end ploughed for the iron tongues as indicated in Fig. 662. The tongues are

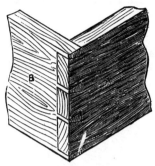

Fig. 663.—Dovetail Joint.

usually about $\frac{7}{8}$ in. by $\frac{3}{16}$ in. in section. A plough iron should be chosen which will make a groove slightly less wide than the thickness of the tongue, so as to allow the latter to just go in tight without splitting the wood. When the tongues are inserted, the finishing, which is very similar to that described for the clamped blackboard, may be proceeded with.

Dovetail Joint.

The dovetail joint is a very important one, entering as it does into the construction of so many articles made by the cabinet-maker and joiner. Where the

Fig. 664.—Dovetail Joint Apart.

dovetails are properly made, with only a slight bevel, the result is a strong joint; but a case will sometimes occur, especially on polished work, where the ordinary dovetail, as it exposes so much of the end grain of the wood, would be rather unsightly, and then it is desirable to conceal the end grain of the timber either by veneering over the dovetails or by secret dovetailing. There may be an objection to its use in outside carpentry owing to the shrinkage of the material, but this does not apply in joinery and cabinet work, as, for all interior purposes, the stuff is always used in as dry a condition as

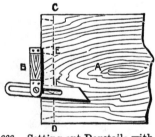

Fig. 665.—Gauging Shoulder Line in Dovetailing.

it is possible to obtain it. The dovetail joint is usually looked upon by the novice as a most difficult joint to make, and certainly it must not be expected that a perfect joint can result from first efforts, but with careful attention to the following instructions the job can soon be mastered.

SETTING OUT DOVETAIL JOINT.

The most common form of dovetail is employed usually at the angles of a box, as in Fig. 663. Dovetails or pins are made upon the ends, with corresponding sockets or mortises upon the front A and back B.

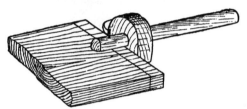

Fig. 666.—Setting out Dovetails with Bevel.

Fig. 664 is the same angle with the two pieces separated to show the working. To set out the dovetail sockets or mortises, first plane up the stuff true, and square the ends (suppose it to be 9 in. long, 6 in. wide, and

⅝ in. thick); next set a gauge to ⅝ in., and run it lightly across the front and back at each end, as shown by Fig. 665 and by the dotted line C D (Fig. 666). Now space off the width of board into as many

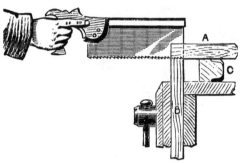

Fig. 667.—Marking Dovetails with Tenon Saw.

divisions as required, there being no rule as to number; but the nearer the dovetails and spaces between them correspond in size the stronger the joint will be—upon the principle of halving. The one point to guard against is making the dovetails too wide at the broad part, as this only tends to make them weak, on account of the tendency to split off at this point. The first attempt should be made upon rather large dovetails, say ½ in. at the wide end and ¼ in. at the narrow end. Therefore set them out to this size; it will be observed that at the ends C D there is only half a dovetail, this being the common practice. Divide the space equally between C D into three parts, thus making two dovetails. Set the bevel B to the desired angle, and mark off the sockets with a pencil, as shown.

Fig. 668.—Lines Squared over in Dovetailing.

Fix the piece in the bench vice, and cut down inside each line as far as the gauge line C D. Take one of the end pieces, and fix it in the vice with the end uppermost, as B (Fig. 667). Place the piece A (with the end "fair") upon B, blocking it up level with one of the planes turned upon its side, as C; take the dovetail saw (a small tenon saw) in the right hand, placing the left hand upon the work to steady it, and mark each dovetail by carefully placing the point of the saw in the cut already

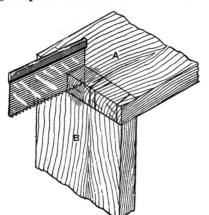

Fig. 669.—Marking Dovetails with Tenon Saw.

made and drawing it gently outwards. Now square these lines down the face of B, as shown at Fig. 668. Fig. 669 illustrates the foregoing operation in a manner that cannot fail to make it perfectly clear, the letters corresponding in all. In boxes the pins are generally cut on the ends and the sockets on the sides. Drawers have the pins on front and back, the rule being to have the bevelled parts so that they are in opposition to the greatest stress that comes upon the piece of work to which the joint is applied. The maximum strength

Fig. 670.—Weak Dovetails with Acute Angles.

would be gained by having the pins and sockets equal; but this is scarcely ever done. Small pins are used for the sake of appearance, but fairly large ones are preferable. In Fig. 664, p. 211, the outside

pins are about the same size as the others, but it is better to have them larger. The fit of the joint should not be too tight, or there is danger of part being split off, as shown at A, Fig. 670. As remarked

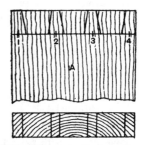

Fig. 671.—Dovetail Sockets Set out.

before, in all dovetailed joints the angle should be slight, and not acute (as shown in Fig. 670). When a novice makes his first attempt at dovetailing, he will probably, if not instructed otherwise, make the pins at too acute an angle; and, on first thought, one might suppose that acute-angled dovetails would make a strong joint, but on further consideration and practical trial it will be found that in putting an acute-angled dovetail together there is great danger of the wood on each side of the mortise splitting off, as shown at B B (Fig. 670). In good dovetailed work

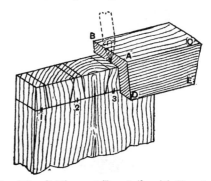

Fig. 672.—Setting out Dovetails with Template.

the angle is never made more acute than that shown in Fig. 664. For the sake of neatness in open dovetailing the pins are made small and spaced rather wide apart as a general rule, the result being a joint that is not so strong as would be the case if the pins were larger and spaced more closely together; but in secret dovetailing (to be described later), as the pins are concealed, they may be made fairly large, and with a space between each pin of about twice its width, or closer if desired.

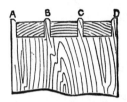

Fig. 673.—Dovetail Pins with Extra Length.

SETTING OUT DOVETAILS WITH TEMPLATE.

There are other ways of marking or setting out dovetails than that described above. In another good method a template is used. First set out the shoulder lines on each piece, and if the ends are shot true this may be done with a gauge. Mark off the centre of each socket, and then half the breadth of the sockets on each side as at A (Fig. 671). Make a template, as shown at Fig. 672, the edge A B being square to A C; A D and C E should be about 80° to

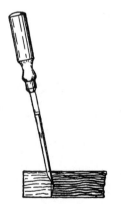

Fig. 674.—Undercutting in Dovetailing.

the edge A C. Then mark out the sockets with the template and a sharp pencil (or awl) as indicated in Fig. 672. Saw carefully in the waste parts; then place the socket piece on the pin piece, and mark

the shape of the latter by using the end of a saw placed in the sockets as already described.

Fig. 675.—Undercut Dovetails.

CUTTING DOVETAILS.

The joint having been set out, the spaces between the dovetails on the ends B (Fig. 664) should now be cut out; if the work in hand is large, they may first be roughly sawn out with a bow saw, afterwards laying them flat upon the bench, and finishing up to the gauge line with a sharp chisel, taking care to cut half-way through from each side. The sockets should next be carefully cut out with a bevelled edge chisel, the top and bottom pieces being cut out with the dovetail saw. Correctly speaking, the dovetails should be a trifle longer than the thickness of stuff, as A B C D (Fig. 673), the tops being slightly chamfered off with a chisel, to lessen the danger of their driving a piece off the front when driven home. In cleaning out the mortises and the spaces between the pins, the worker must first chop half-way through, then turn the board over, and finish from the other side, care being taken to hold the chisel upright, and not slanting as in Fig. 674, which causes undercutting, as shown in Fig. 675, which is some-

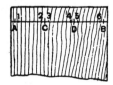

Fig. 676.—Marking off Dovetail Pins.

times done to ensure the joint fitting on the outside; then, although the joint may appear to be sound from the outside, there will be a space in the centre where the glue cannot hold the joint together. There is also danger of the wood on the inside of the mortise being split off when the work is put together. Another dodge that is sometimes employed by slipshod workmen is to make the pins about $\frac{1}{16}$ in. longer than required, and to rivet them over with the

Fig. 677.—Squaring Dovetail Pin.

hammer, thus filling up the spaces where, through careless workmanship, the pins do not fit the mortises—a practice sometimes known as "bishoping" the dovetails. Of course, where the joints are put together properly, this will not be required, and "bishoped" dovetails can easily be detected by the bruised appearance of the ends of the pins after the joint is cleaned off.

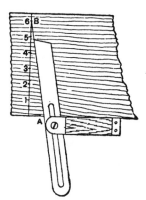

Fig. 678.—Obtaining Angle in Setting out Dovetails.

ALTERNATIVE METHOD OF SETTING OUT AND CUTTING DOVETAILS.

Below is described the method of setting out dovetail joints, the pins being made first, and the sockets marked from

them. This method is, perhaps, not quite so generally employed as that which is described on p. 212 of making the sockets first and marking the pins from them. Plane the wood up true to breadth and thickness, and get each piece to its proper

Fig. 679.—Using Bevel in Setting out Dovetails.

length by shooting all the ends quite square. This allows the dovetailing to be more easily and accurately set out than when the ends are left rough until after the joints are put together. Set a marking gauge equal to the thickness of the wood, and gauge a line all round from each end of each piece (see Fig. 665, p. 212). The operations for each of the four joints will be the same. Mark off the centre of each of the half pins, as A B (Fig. 676), and set off the centre of each of the other pins C D. In cases where there are a number of pins this can be accurately done by means of a pair of compasses. Half the thickness of the outside of the pins should now be marked off on each side as indicated at 1 2 3 4 5 and 6 (Fig. 676). The try-square can now be applied and the straight sides of the pins marked with a scribing awl as shown in Fig. 677. Set a bevel to an angle of about 1 in 6. To construct this angle, set off a square line on a piece of board and mark off 1 in., say, on the edge and 6 in. up the square line, and join by a line as shown by A B (Fig. 678). The bevel can now be set to this angle as shown, and applied to the end of the stuff, and the ends of the pins marked out as shown in Fig. 679. The next process will be to saw carefully just by the side of the line in the waste portion (E, Fig. 680), so as to leave the pins their exact size when the waste pieces are removed. It is a good plan to cut these waste pieces out with a bow saw a little from the line, and then to pare to

Fig. 680.—Saw Kerf in Waste Portion.

the shoulder line with a sharp chisel. The ends of the pins should then be accurately placed on the socket piece with their inside edges just to the shoulder line of the latter, and the shape of the pins carefully marked with a marking awl (see Fig. 681). The square edges of the sockets should next be marked out, using the square and marking awl as shown at Fig. 682. The sockets can then be sawn, cutting in the waste as shown at F (Fig. 683), and the waste pieces removed. The joint will then be finished.

Gluing Up Dovetail Joints.

When fitting a dovetail joint together, take the precaution to mark each piece, as then there is no danger of gluing the wrong pieces together. Glue the dovetails, and drive them into the front and back, forcing out as much glue as possible, and

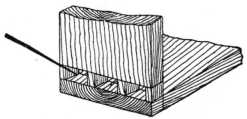

Fig. 681.—Using Dovetail Pins as Template.

lightly tap with a hammer the ends of projecting dovetails; this is not for the purpose of riveting over the ends, a practice already condemned, but for bringing the joint closer without using the nails

so often employed. If the dovetails are more than $\frac{1}{8}$ in. beyond the sides, they should be cut off before hammering, or the chances are that the dovetail will be broken off, or the side will split. The bot-

Fig. 682.—Using Square in Setting out Dovetails.

tom should next be nailed on, taking care to square the box before it is dry. Before attempting a box, two or more pieces of wood should be dovetailed together for practice, which will by no means be time thrown away.

Secret Lap Dovetail Joint.

In secret dovetailing, the pins and sockets are hidden on one or both faces, and the means to obtain this end are many and ingenious. The simplest of the secret dovetail joints is that shown by Fig. 684. The lap dovetail is so named because one piece runs over, or laps, the other. This class of dovetail is usually employed in drawer-making; the front of the drawer is about 1 in. thick, and the

Fig. 683.—Saw Kerf in Waste Portion.

sides are $\frac{5}{8}$ in. (See Fig. 685, where A indicates the side and B the front.) To set out the joint proceed as in making the common dovetail (see p. 212), with the exception of the front, in which the gauge is run down the ends of the drawer-front from the back, thus leaving the extra thickness, as seen, on the outside. The dovetails cannot, of course, be cut with a saw, beyond running it in across the angle, the spaces being carefully

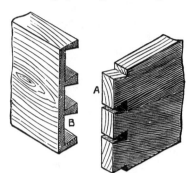

Fig. 684.—Secret Lap Dovetail.

cut out by means of a mallet and chisel. It will be seen from this that the dovetails do not show upon the front of the drawer when the latter is closed.

SECRET DOUBLE-LAP OR REBATED DOVETAIL JOINT.

In the joint shown by Fig. 684 only one side is concealed; but cases sometimes occur where it becomes desirable to hide the dovetails entirely. This may be accomplished by forming a lap on both the pieces of wood to be joined, as shown at A and B in Fig. 686. To make this joint, the ends are first planed true and square,

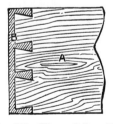

Fig. 685.—Side View of Lap Dovetail.

and the pins gauged, marked, and cleaned out, as at A (Fig. 686). The lap C, which may come to within about $\frac{1}{16}$ in. of the outside, is then cut on B (Fig. 686). The piece A is then placed on B, and the position of

the recesses marked with a sharp scriber. When these are cleaned out, the joint may be fitted together, care being taken that the pins are not too tight, nor sufficiently long to split off the lap. When this joint

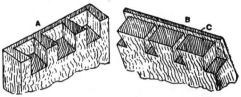

Fig. 686.—Double-lap or Rebated Dovetail.

is glued up and dry, the outer angle may be rounded off, as shown at Fig. 687, and a good strong corner will be the result, with very little end-grain timber showing.

SECRET LAP-MITRED DOVETAIL JOINT.

A lapped dovetail joint in part mitred is shown by Fig. 688; in this the end grain is almost concealed. The pin B is mitred, A being cut to correspond. This joint would be suitable for a workbox, the joint of the lid coming through B, so that it has the appearance of a mitred joint when the box is open. This is a good joint, and is more easily made than the mitred dovetail joint described later, which it equals in appearance if, after gluing up, the edge is rounded. In making this joint, first cut the pins, then the lap, and mark the sockets with the scriber or marking awl.

SECRET MITRED DOVETAIL.

This is really the true secret dovetail, but is seldom employed. except upon good

Fig. 687.—Side View of Double-lap Dovetail.

work, on account of the time taken in making it. If this joint is not carefully constructed, it will always be an eyesore; but the student is advised to make several, for the practice thus gained will be very valuable. This joint (Fig. 689) is the most difficult to put together. The top pin is mitred right across, for the sake of appearance. In making this joint, both parts

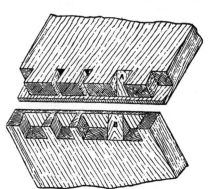

Fig. 688.—Lap-mitred Dovetail.

must have a lap or rebate cut on them, similar to the socket part of Fig. 688. Then the construction will be nearly the same, with the addition of mitring. To make this dovetail joint, first cut a small rebate (size according to thickness of stuff) upon each piece. Now proceed to cut the dovetails as upon the end of A (Fig. 689). Having done this, place it upright upon

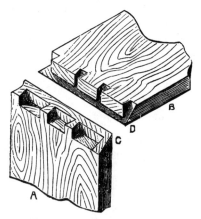

Fig. 689.—Mitred Dovetail.

the piece B, and mark out the sockets, carefully cutting them out with a chisel of suitable size. Set the bevel to an angle of 45° (a true mitre), and mark each piece upon the top edge, as A B, and carefully

cut right down each piece, thus forming a mitre beyond the dovetails, as plainly shown. The top dovetail is usually cut to a mitre for the sake of the superior appear-

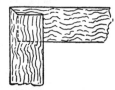

Fig. 690.—Side View of Mitred Dovetail.

ance, but the one at bottom may be left square, it being out of sight. Fig. 690 is a side view of the joint put together; at the other side the joint would show a mere mitre line. This class of work is usually done in hard wood, such as mahogany, the dovetails being made to fit somewhat

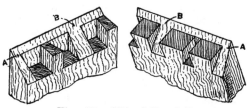

Fig. 691.—Mitred Dovetail.

tightly, to ensure the joint remaining firm when glued. In gluing up, some means of keeping the joints up, such as two small cramps, is advisable. When a box that has been secret-dovetailed together has to be cut into two pieces to form a body and lid, as in the case of a writing desk, the dovetails at the point where cut asunder

Fig. 692.—Side View of Mitred Dovetail.

may be mitred as shown at B B (Fig. 691); this gives a neat joint where exposed to view, as the mitre line shows on both the sides; the appearance at one side is indicated in Fig. 692.

Box Pin Joint.

The method of joining corners shown by Fig. 693 will not present any difficulty when dovetailing has been mastered. It

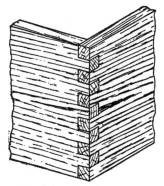

Fig. 693.—Box Pin Joint.

is easy to set out and cut, is strong and neat, and can be used for wood of any thickness from ⅛ in. upwards ; of course, it is not so strong as dovetailing. Each half should be cut accurately to obtain a close fit, and then a touch of glue will complete the joint. If the parts fit loosely, no amount of glue or nails will make a firm joint ; therefore a gauge must be used so that the pins and spaces can be accurately and quickly spaced. The correct proportions of the pins (as wide as they are thick) are shown in Fig. 693, but joints are sometimes made with the pins twice as

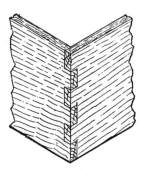

Fig. 694.—Box Pin Joint.

wide as the material is thick, as is shown by Fig. 694. The latter joint takes less time to cut, and is the one described here.

Zinc Gauge for Marking Box Joint.

For this gauge, square up the edges of a piece of stout sheet zinc 9 in. long by 1⅜ in. wide, and with dividers or compasses mark ½-in. spaces along one of the edges. Draw the line A B (Fig. 695) ½ in. from the top edge, and by means of a square and a scriber draw lines from the ½-in. marks down to this line, marking them alternately

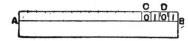

Fig. 695.—Gauge for Marking Box Pin Joint.

1 and 0, as shown. Cut the openings in which the saw is to be placed when marking off the joinings. Begin by making notches with a triangular file, as shown at c (Fig. 695). The zinc is then clamped in the vice in front of a piece of hard wood, and the cuts made down to the line A B with an iron- or brass-backed saw having fine teeth, both wood and zinc being cut at the same time. All the metal cut out by the saw must be taken from the pieces marked 0, as shown at D (Fig. 695); it is also shown in Fig. 696. When the sixteen cuts have been made, a line is drawn ¼ in.

Fig. 696.—Gauge for Marking Box Pin Joint.

from the top across three of the pieces marked 0, one near each end and one in the middle. The gauge is clamped in the vice to this line, and the part from the top to the line turned over square with a hammer and punch, as indicated at A (Fig. 696). A $\frac{1}{32}$ in. punch is now driven through each of the turned-over pieces while they are resting on a piece of soft wood, these holes preventing the gauge slipping endways when it is being used. The gauge, shown by Fig. 696, commences with a piece marked 1, and finishes with a piece marked 0. At c a small shoulder is made by cutting sixteen notches and removing the end piece marked 1. The lower corners of the gauge are also marked 1 and 2, as shown in Fig. 696.

SETTING OUT BOX JOINT WITH GAUGE.

To use the gauge made as above, the sides of the box or drawer are planed to size,

Fig. 697.—Setting out Box Pin Joint.

and after the ends are squared off a line is drawn as shown by the dotted lines A and B (Fig. 697), distant from the ends by $\frac{1}{16}$ in. more than the thickness of the wood to allow for cleaning off. The distance from the line A or B to a similar line at the other end of the same piece of wood will be the inside measure of the box or drawer. The sides are now placed in the position they are to occupy when completed, and marked 1 and 2 as shown by Fig. 697. They are then separated and fixed end up, one at a time, in a bench vice, in any suitable manner. The gauge is now laid on the wood with the end marked 1 level with the side of the wood marked 1, and held firmly. With a suitable saw, mark off the joinings by making a small cut on the front edge of the wood.

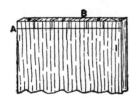

Fig. 698.—Box Pin Joint Set out.

If the saw makes a narrower cut than that in the gauge, care must be taken that the blade is held close to each side of the pieces marked 1. For a long piece of wood the gauge can be moved further along,

care being taken to place the saw in the last mark on the wood, and in a similar notch to that from which the last mark was made. For example, if the last cut made by the saw is from the left side of a piece marked 1, the saw must remain in the cut, and the gauge must be replaced so that the

Fig. 699.—Part of Box Pin Joint.

saw is again to the left of a piece marked 1. The other piece of wood is then similarly marked, the gauge being laid with the end marked 2 level with the side of the wood marked 2. Fine pencil lines should be drawn with a square from the saw cuts to the line at A (Fig. 698) and also across the top at B. The saw cuts can be continued down to the line A with the saw used for marking off, keeping it perfectly square. When all the kerfs have been cut, place the gauge as when marking off, or hold it in front, and mark the pins as shown at Fig. 698, opposite similar markings on the gauge. The wood is next turned in the vice so that the line at A is vertical, and the pins are carefully cut out along the line with a fret saw, as shown in Fig. 699.

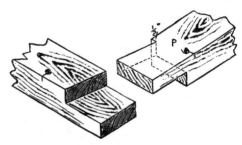

Fig. 700.—Dovetail Halved Joint.

For small work such as the sides of small drawers 2 in. or 3 in. deep, a light brass-back saw and a jeweller's saw frame will be found convenient in cutting down to form the pins.

The dovetail halved joint is objected to by some because when the piece carrying the tenon shrinks it will depend for its support on the screw, nail, or bolt, as the

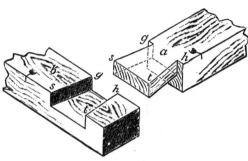

Fig. 701.—Dovetail Halved Joint.

case may be. Then the dovetail form will not be of assistance in strengthening it, but will be a source of weakness at the shoulder, and the more the joint is bevelled the weaker it will be. The simplest dovetail halved joint is on the ends of stuff as in Fig. 700. To make this, proceed as with the ordinary halved joint (see p. 194), but instead of cutting both shoulders square, the top one has a piece left on the inner edge which may be about ½ in., tapering to nothing, and a corresponding piece is cut away from the plate P, thus forming a kind of half-dovetail. Fig. 701 is another description of dovetail

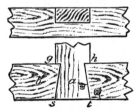

Fig. 702.—Plan and Elevation of Dovetail Halved Joint.

halving; this joint is only possible where it occurs at a distance from the end of material; Fig. 702 shows a plan and elevation of this joint when complete. First cut out half the thickness of the top piece

a (Fig. 701), in the same manner as for a common halved joint; then from the edges g h mark off ½ in., as shown. From these lines draw others to the points s t; the distance between s t is equal to the full width of stuff. Cut out these wedge-shape pieces, leaving the dovetail as shown. The dovetail should now be placed upon the other plate in the manner shown in plan (Fig. 702), which is lettered to correspond with Fig. 701. Having (with a square applied to the edge) seen that the pieces are at right angles, a striking knife may be run along the edges of dovetail, thus marking its shape upon the piece b. Run the half-thickness gauge upon both edges of b, and cut in the dovetail lines with a tenon saw, keeping it upon the inside of lines, so that

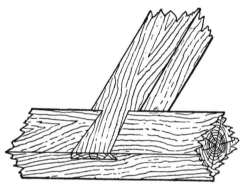

Fig. 703.—Dovetail Halving with Two Bevels.

the joint may fit fairly tight. The piece between may be removed by means of a mallet and chisel, working from both edges, and keeping the surface between the gauge lines as level as possible. The joint may now be knocked together. It must not be unduly tight; if this should occur, the joint must be fitted with a chisel. This must always be guarded against, as it shows bad workmanship. The dovetail should, if the job has been carefully done, fit at once off the saw. These two joints are little used in practice on account of the shrinkage of timber causing the dovetail to draw away at the shoulders; and this is a serious defect which, of course, renders the joint useless as a tie.

DOVETAIL HALVED JOINT WITH TWO BEVELS.

The dovetail halving with two bevels (Fig. 703) is of but little practical value, but

Fig. 704.—Part of Dovetail Bevelled Halving.

interesting as a puzzle joint. Fig. 703 is an isometric view of the dovetail joint showing the two bevels, and Figs. 704 and 705 are views of the joint apart. If the thickness of the wood is 1 in., mark down on the shoulder line half the thickness, and on the extreme end gauge it down about $\frac{3}{16}$ in. and connect these two points with a line. Shoulder it on the under side with the saw, and then cut the under side of the dovetail away to the line drawn. Draw the dovetail on the top, which gives the bevel. The lower edges of the dovetail are equal to the width of the stuff, and the bevel must be the same all through. The work should then have the appearance of Fig. 704. Fig. 705 shows the dovetailed rebate taken out of the cross-piece. The same gauge marks and the same bevels must be used for this, and. after it is cut out and faired the pin should slide in, getting a little tight as the shoulder comes up. When it has been finished properly, it should be glued up.

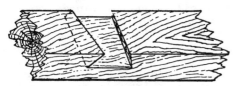

Fig. 705.—Counterpart of Dovetail Bevelled Halving.

HALF-MITRE JOINT.

The half-mitre joint is shown by Fig. 706. To form it, carefully plane up two pieces of wood, each 9 in. by 2 in. by 1½ in., or others of like proportions. Draw a square figure of any size, and join the

angles, either of the diameters giving a mitre or an angle of 45°. Set the bevel to one of these lines, and screw it fast; or the original mitre line might be set off with a combined mitre and square. It will be

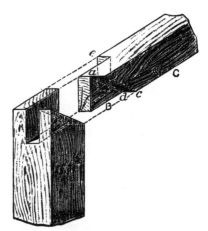

Fig. 706.—Half-mitre Joint apart.

noticed that it assumes somewhat the form of a mortise and tenon joint—the difference being in the mitre upon the face. First of all, square off stuff to the desired length, and mark off a distance from each end equal to the width of material—in this case it would be 2 in. (see $a\,b$, $b\,c$, Fig. 707). Take one of the pieces, and run the mortise gauge, previously set to one-third the thickness—that is, ½ in.—along the sides

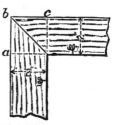

Fig. 707.—Side Elevation of Half-mitre Joint.

and end as far as the lines upon the edge, which indicate the width of the wood. Fix the piece in the bench-vice, and cut down on the inside of the gauge lines, as the piece between will afterwards be removed with mallet and chisel, thus forming a kind of open-end mortise, as at a (Fig. 708). Upon the side A (Fig. 708), apply the bevel, as from b to c, Fig. 709). The corner piece, $b c f$ (Fig. 709), must be cut off with a fine tenon saw, finishing nicely to the shoulder or mitre line with a plane. The first part of the joint is now complete, and is repre-

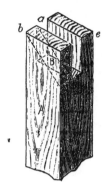

Fig. 708 —Open-end   Fig. 709.—Setting
Mortise.   out Half-mitre Joint.

sented by the left-hand part of Fig. 706. The second part of the joint is somewhat different, having upon the end a tenon instead of a mortise (see Fig. 706). In setting out this piece, the gauge may be applied in the same manner as before ; but it will be noticed that only one line is required upon the back edge, as the tenon is not cut right through, but only as far in as the line of mitre. The piece at the back of the tenon should be first cut out by running in the hand saw on the outside of line, afterwards cutting the shoulder e with the tenon saw. The piece should now be again fixed in the vice, in such a position that the mitre line is brought about horizontal. The saw may then be run in as from a to d (Fig. 706), afterwards removing the piece to form the mitre with saw and rebate plane as before. The joint should now be tried, and, if the job has been carefully done, it will not require fitting ; it may be drawn tightly together by draw-boring (described on p. 204). Fig. 710 shows the position of the draw-boring hole upon the tenon. If the foregoing joint has been applied to a square frame, two of the pieces should be worked with a mortise upon each end, and the other two must

therefore have a tenon. The frame also might be rebated and chamfered, thus giving additional practice.

ANGLE BRACKET.

The angle bracket is termed also a braced bracket or a gallows bracket, and it is

Fig. 710.—Draw-bore Hole of Half-mitre Joint.

made in various ways, but the form shown by Fig. 711 is certainly the best of all. It is commonly used to support a shelf, and often is made in the form of three or more brackets where the number of shelves requires it. In this case the upright A is extended in length, and the bearers C are tenoned into it, instead of being dovetailed as seen at d. The brace B often is notched at top and bottom, and fixed with nails. Fig. 712 shows the shape of the brace as prepared for fixing. Before attempting to make the joint, prepare a working drawing.

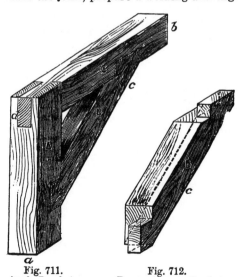

Fig. 711.   Fig. 712.
Angle Bracket.   Brace of Angle Bracket.

Draw the elevation (Fig. 713) and correctly mark all dimensions as shown, drawing the brace B at an angle of 45° ; next draw the plan (Fig. 714). Plane up true three pieces of stuff, each being an inch or so longer than the finished sizes, and upon the end of the bearer set out a dovetail to the sizes given at d in the plan. The tenon

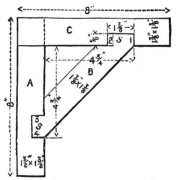

Fig. 713.—Elevation of Angle Bracket.

saw should now be run down on the outside of the lines as far as the shoulders, afterwards carefully cutting away the stuff on the outside of the dovetail, leaving it as seen at Fig. 714. The upright A should

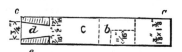

Fig. 714.—Plan of Angle Bracket.

now be squared off and fixed in the bench-vice, with its back edge facing the worker; place the dovetail d (Fig. 714) upon the squared end of the upright, now in position in the bench-vice, carefully keeping

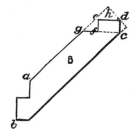

Fig. 715.—Elevation of Brace.

the pieces in a straight line, as from c to a (Fig. 714). Now mark the dovetail upon the end of the upright with a point or with the end of the saw. The lines thus made

upon the end should be carried down both edges of the upright to a distance equal to the bearer's depth—namely 1¼ in. Run the tenon saw down on the inside of these lines, afterwards removing the centre-piece by means of a mallet and chisel. Carefully

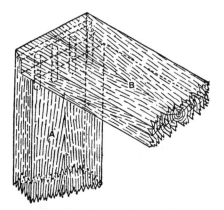

Fig. 716.—Dowelled Angle Joint.

fit the dovetail into the socket, and see that it is not too tight; place the bracket as now prepared upon its side on the bench, and test the angle with a square. Mark the distances 4¾ in., which denote the outside of brace (see Figs. 713 and 714), and also the spaces s s to the sizes given in the illustrations. Square over the lines 1 2 and 3 4 (Fig. 713) upon the edge of the stuff, and run a gauge, which has been set to one-half the thickness, between them: these lines are shown at b (Fig. 714). The spaces s s should now be removed with

Fig. 717.—Elevation of Dowelled Angle Joint.

mallet and chisel. Place the brace, of which Fig. 715 is a drawing, upon the bench, and lay the other portion of the bracket upon it, so that the front edge of the brace coincides with the points b c.

Mark the shoulder-line and bare-faced tenon with the striking-knife, and cut off the corners of the brace, starting at *e d* (Fig. 715); this removes the piece *h*. Run the gauge, before used, from *c* to *d*, and

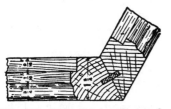

Fig. 718.—Mitred Joint, Tongued.

cut along this line as far as the shoulder *g c*. Now cut the shoulder, and afterwards cut out the pieces *g f e* and *c d*, thus leaving the brace as shown. The whole may now be knocked together and glued or screwed as may be desired. It may be mentioned that often the brace is cut first, marking the other portions of the bracket from it: this method should be adopted if found the more convenient.

DOWEL ANGLE JOINTS.

The making of flush dowel joints is described fully on pp. 185 to 188, and the information given there should be read before attempting the following. Secret dowelling is an alternative method to secret dovetailing of joining timber at right angles; although the effect, both in

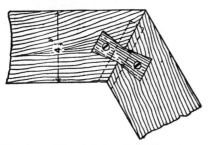

Fig. 719.—Mitred Joint, Dovetail Keyed.

appearance and durability, is equal to that resulting from the latter method, secret dowelling requires less skill and takes less time. The $\frac{1}{4}$-in. diameter dowels may be employed to join up the

15

corners of a fascia or box, say about 4 in. wide and 1 in. thick, as shown in Fig. 716. Having worked the rebates and mitres (the dotted lines denote that they can be lipped if preferred), take the gauge

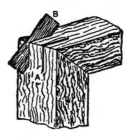

Fig. 720.—Mitred Joint, Veneer Keyed.

shown in Fig. 557, p. 186, the position of its marking point having been previously determined, and run a gauge line along the shoulder of the rebate. This should be exactly in the centre of the shoulder of the end grain piece A, Fig. 716, and at the same distance on the inside face of the other piece marked B. With a pair of compasses divide off the correct position of the dowel holes (let the outside ones be half the distance between the inside ones from the end), and with a brace and bit bore the holes perfectly upright. The depths of the holes bored in the piece A are not so important as those in pieces B, it being necessary to regulate those in the latter; otherwise they will project through the stuff. The

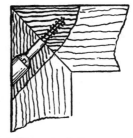

Fig. 721.—Mitred Joint, Screwed.

holes all being bored, take a stout splinter of wood, and, after dipping it in some good hot glue, work it into the dowel holes of the piece A, the dowels being carefully driven home and cut off to the necessary length. The holes in the piece B are glued in a similar manner. Glue the rebates and mitres quickly with a brush, and gently drive the work together. Test the work to see if it is square, and wipe off any superfluous glue with a shaving dipped in hot water. If these instructions are properly carried out, a very strong and satis-

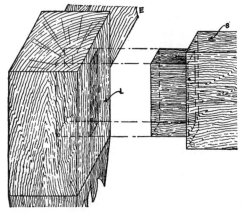

Fig. 722.—Simple Tenon in Table Framing.

factory joint will be produced. It will be noticed that in the side elevation (Fig. 717) the piece that corresponds with B in Fig. 716 shows a small cavity at the top of the dowel; this is left to absorb the superfluous glue at that end when the work is driven together.

KEYING MITRED JOINTS.

In some situations, a stronger means than glue is required for fixing mitred joints, and this is the case particularly when the work is to be exposed to a damp atmosphere. A cross-tongue, as shown in Fig. 718, greatly strengthens a glued joint, but the dovetail key, indicated in Fig. 719, makes a still stronger joint, which will suffice for most purposes. Small glued mitre joints, such as those in frames, etc., can be strengthened with keys of veneer. A saw kerf is made in the corner A (Fig. 720), and a piece of veneer B is then glued in, this being cut off flush when the glue is hard. Fig. 721 shows a way in which a countersunk screw is used, and this does not need description. After

the screw is inserted, the hole remaining may be stopped up.

DETACHABLE JOINTS IN TABLE FRAMINGS.

It is frequently necessary to construct plain tables, dressers, etc., of a size that renders them very awkward to move, and there is possibly some advantage to be gained by substituting for the usual mortising and tenoning shown in Fig. 722 the dovetailing shown in Fig. 723. In both of the figures L is the table leg, E the end rail, and S the side rail. The end rail is tenoned and dowelled as usual, but the side rail is dovetailed instead; and if the dovetail is cut a bare length, and the shoulders are cut slightly inwards, quite as good and secure jointing will be obtained without using dowels as can be obtained with a mortise. When the table top is screwed down, the whole will be secured together. Now, when wishing to move (perhaps through a narrow doorway or down a staircase), the screws are withdrawn and the top is removed; next, the side rails are

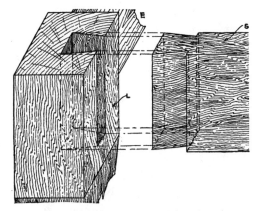

Fig. 723.—Dovetail Tenon in Table Framing.

tapped out of the legs, leaving the end rail and two legs in one piece, thus obtaining, instead of one cumbersome piece of furniture, five light and portable pieces. The whole can be put together again in a few minutes, and, if care is used, no damage will have been done to the dovetails.

EASY EXAMPLES OF WOODWORK.

THE OBJECT OF THIS CHAPTER.

THE reader, having made himself familiar with the shapes of tools and their uses, with the materials and various timbers used, and with the kinds of joints commonly employed for woodwork, may now be reasonably supposed to have sufficient skill to make many simple articles ; and this chapter will give designs of, and brief instructions for putting together, examples to which the information given in previous pages can be applied. Only those articles which do not require the use of special tools will here be dealt with, and the tools required will be only two or three saws, a hammer, two screwdrivers, brace

Fig. 724.—Position of " Middle Board " in Log.

and bits, two or three planes, spokeshave, a few chisels, etc. ; whilst the materials will for the most part be the more common woods, and nails, screws, and glue.

PARALLEL STRAIGHT-EDGE.

Information on selecting wood for making straight-edges is given on p. 4. The best board for making a 15-ft. straight-edge is the middle one of a straight tree (see Fig. 724). Cut the rule from either edge, as A B or C D. Fig. 725 shows how the grain will appear in this board, the end view showing the medullary rays running across the annular rings and parallel to the width. These rings are parallel in depth, and the medullary rays cross them at right angles ; therefore the rule will shrink not in length, but

in width or thickness only. The first thing to be done in truing up a piece of wood is to take one side out of winding. This is done by placing two winding sticks one across

Fig. 725.—Straight-edge.

each end, and looking over the top edge of one until the eye catches sight of the top edge of the other ; now move one stick about 2 ft. at a time nearer the other, looking over the top edges as before. Repeat this throughout the length, and if the two edges are parallel that proves that the surfaces on which they are placed are perfectly true. Winding may arise from the board having twisted since being sawn. Full information on testing surfaces with winding sticks or small straight-edges is given on p. 5. Having got a true surface, work from the face side in squaring the two edges. First shoot one edge, then place the stock of a square (whose blade must be longer than the width of the rule) on this

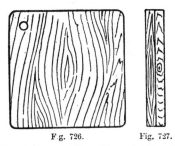

F.g. 726.   Fig. 727.

Figs. 726 and 727.—Chopping Board.

edge with the blade against the face side. If the edge is perfectly square with the face side all the length, it must be tested to see that it is perfectly straight. Then proceed as explained on p. 4.

CHOPPING BOARD.

A common chopping board (Fig. 726) may be made of beech, which can be got from

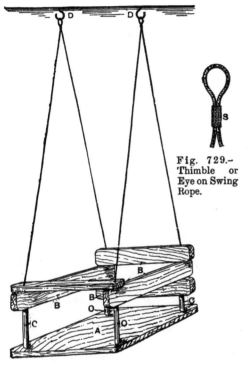

Fig. 729.—Thimble or Eye on Swing Rope.

Fig. 728.—Child's Swing.

the ends of an old orange-box. Knock out the ends carefully, and draw the nails; square both pieces, say, to 10 in. square, or more if the wood will allow. Plane one face of each piece flat and true, and with hot glue rub the two faces together, crossing the grain as shown in sectional view (Fig. 727), and place under pressure till the glue is properly set. This can be done in many ways—in a copying-press, by the use of cramps, or under weights. Do not begin gluing till everything is in readiness to bring pressure quickly to bear. If a press is used, have it in such a position that as little time as possible may be lost. The cramps should be tried, and adjusted so as to bring pressure to bear in the least possible time; and if there is no other means than weighting, have a flat surface

ready to place the work on, and weights ready. Above all, have the glue hot; good, lasting work can never be done properly with lukewarm glue. The work being properly set, release from pressure, plane both sides, square the edges, and bore a $\frac{5}{8}$-in. hole for hanging up; this is more convenient than a small hole and string. If made as described, the chopping board will stand any amount of rough usage, and will last for years.

CHILD'S SWING.

The child's swing shown by Fig. 728 is exceedingly easy to make, and is inexpensive. The materials required will be: One piece of hardwood, 15 in. square, for the seat, A (elm, oak, or birch will serve equally well if they are sound); five pieces of wood, B, 15 in. long by 2½ in. wide by ¾ in. thick (pine will be best for these, as it is easiest to work up); four pieces of ¾-in. brass tubing, C, two of them 2½ in. long, the other two 5 in.; six or seven yards of strong sashcord, two ceiling hooks D, and two thimbles or eyes (Fig. 729), which may be bought from any tent- or rick-cover maker. Plane up the seat and the five pieces of deal,

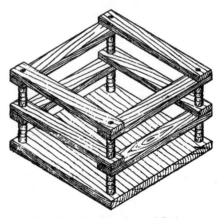

Fig. 730.—Another form of Swing.

the latter being as long as the seat is square; round off and spokeshave all the corners. Bore four ¼-in. or $\frac{5}{16}$ in. holes in the seat, one at each corner, about 1½ in. from the edge, and bore a hole through four pieces of the deal strips from edge to edge,

$1\frac{1}{2}$ in. from each end; this will be understood by reference to Fig. 728. The remaining piece of deal is for the front piece of swing; bore it through the flat side, the same distance from the ends as the others, the holes being ⅞ in. or more to allow of its being moved up the ropes (for the child to be placed in), and then brought down again, when it forms a barrier which prevents the child from falling out. The length of the sashcord will depend on the distance the swing is hung from the ceiling. Thread the sashcord through the strips and bottom piece as shown in Fig. 728, and tie a good knot underneath. Place the cord round the thimbles (Fig. 729), and tie round with a very strong string s. Fix the ceiling hooks

eight wooden spindles, 1 in. in diameter and 3 in. long, are bored from end to end with ⅜-in. holes to allow the lower ropes to slide through. These spindles can be bought very cheaply or turned very simply, full information on simple turning for woodworkers being given later. Ordinary cotton reels or spools are good substitutes for spindles. Eight cross-bars, 2 in. by ¾ in. by 15 in., bored near the ends with ⅜-in. holes, are strung on, four between the two sets of spindles and four above them. The cross-bars and spindles preferably are of beech, oak, or other hard wood, or they will be apt to split and lead to accident. Both in this and the former swing the seat-guard can be deepened by adding cross-bars, and

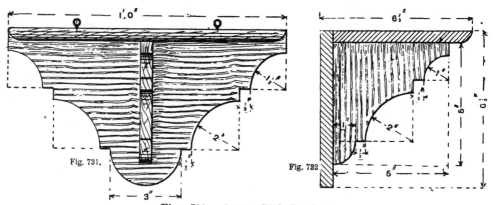

Figs. 731 and 732.—Wall Bracket.

into one of the upper floor joists, so that they do not hang merely by the plaster or lathing. The positions of the joists can be found without unnecessary damage by driving a knitting needle into the ceiling. The swing may be put out of the way, if near to a wall, by placing a ring underneath the bottom of the swing and hooking it on to a nail fixed in the wall. The pieces of deal may be painted, stained, or enamelled.

ANOTHER FORM OF SWING.

Another shape of simple swing, very easily constructed, is shown by Fig. 730. The seat is a piece of beech 1 in. thick and 15 in. by 15 in., with a hole ⅜ in. right through each corner. Four ropes are passed through these holes as before. The

there is plenty of scope for modifications of the designs.

WALL BRACKET.

The wall bracket shown by Figs. 731 and 732 may be made of ½-in. wood. Fig. 731 is a front view, and Fig. 732 shows the shape of the support, the shelf and back being in section. If the back is sawn with a fret-saw from a piece of wood 18 in. long and 7½ in. wide, there will be enough material left on which to repeat the part, and so get the back of another bracket. Similarly, by sawing the support from a piece 5 in. by 6 in., another support can be obtained economically. The support may be fixed to the back and to the shelf with fine nails or screws.

Another Wall Bracket.

Fig. 733 is the front elevation of a small wall bracket. It may be of ⅜-in. or ½-in.

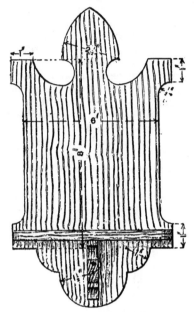

Fig. 733.—Wall Bracket.

wood, and a hole might be made in the back to take a small oval mirror. The ends of the shelf are rounded. Fig. 734 shows the shape of the support and the end of the shelf. Two screw eyes by which to hang the bracket are inserted in the top corners.

Simple Foot-stool.

A simple foot-stool is shown in elevation by Figs. 735 and 737 and in plan by Fig. 736. Prepare the legs shown in Fig. 737, and across these screw the braces B (Fig. 735) of 1¾-in. by ½-in. stuff. Take a piece of wood, 1 ft. by 7 in. by ½ in., plane true and round the edges, and screw it to the legs and side braces to make the top. It is desirable that the stool be painted and grained to match the other furniture of the kitchen.

Corner Shelves.

Fig. 738 shows the shape of the back of a set of corner shelves, while Fig. 739 is a horizontal section of the same on line x x (Fig. 738). Other designs are shown by

Figs. 740 and 741. The whole thing is 3 ft. 2 in. high by 1 ft. 9 in. wide. The material used should be ¾-in. pine. The dimensions and the number of the shelves, of course,

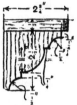

Fig. 734.—Wall Bracket Support.

can be varied. The side or back shown in Fig. 738 is the wider of the two, the fellow board having to fit against it at right angles, as shown in Fig. 739. The two are screwed together, and the angle at B is trimmed off so as to allow the work to go well into the corner. In each case there are three shelves, of which the largest is shown in Fig. 739, the others differing from it in size only. The sides of this, which fit against the back-boards, measure 14 in., and those of the smallest measure 4½ in. only. The back-boards have to be well finished—preferably ebonised and polished—but the shelves may be left comparatively rough, as they

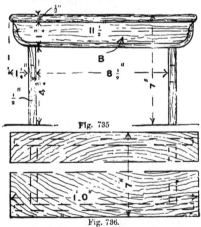

Figs. 735 and 736.—Elevation and Plan of Stool.

should be covered with cotton velvet, which makes a safer surface for the china, etc., than polished wood, and shows up the articles better. It is well to cover both sides of the shelves, but the under sides may be ebonised if preferred. The velvet can be simply stretched over, and tacked to the edges of the boards, the very small permanent tacks being as a rule hidden by thin

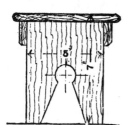

Fig. 737.—End Elevation of Stool.

strips of ebonised wood, fixed on with brass pins; or by strips of leather, attached with brass studs. The shelves are held in their places by screws driven through the backboards. Nails must not be used. In Figs. 740 and 741 both the back-boards and shelves are covered with velvet, and the outline is thus kept more simple. So long as the lines of a board are straight there is no difficulty about covering it by merely tacking down the edges; it is with curves that difficulties arise, especially when the curves are sharp. In Fig. 740 most of the curves are easy, yet, even with these,

fixing up, it will be sufficient if two holes for nails or screws be bored through each back-board. This will be found to give an ample provision for any weight of china.

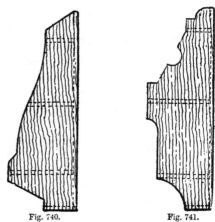

Fig. 740.   Fig. 741.

Figs. 740 and 741.—Alternative Elevation of Corner Shelves.

The more correct method is to plug the wall and to fix the back-boards to the plugs with round-headed brass screws; but a readier method will be simply to drive brass-headed nails into the joints of the brickwork, and this, for all ordinary purposes, will be found sufficient.

KITCHEN COAL-BOX.

A rough-and-ready coal-box for kitchen

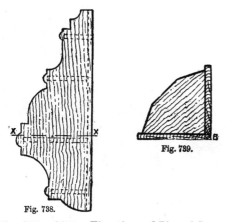

Fig. 738.

Figs. 738 and 739.—Elevation and Plan of Corner Shelves.

Fig. 739.

Fig. 742.—Kitchen Coal-box.

a neater finish may be gained by fastening down with glue rather than with tacks, and the edges will of course have to be snipped at convenient distances. With respect to

use is shown by Fig. 742. Get a suitable sound box or packing case, or put a box together fairly roughly. Then cut it as shown by dotted lines in Fig. 743. Cut a piece to fit the bevel part at bottom, and nail into position, and a piece of the lid to nail on top; Fig. 744, which is a side view, gives the position. The body of the coal-box is now complete. For the handle, nail or screw strips on each side as shown. Cut a piece of an old broomstick ½ in. longer than the width of the box. To prevent this split-

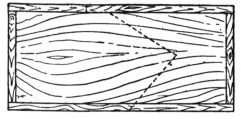

Fig. 743.—Coal-box before Cutting.

ting, with a large centre-bit bore circular recesses on the inner faces of the side strips before nailing them into position, these recesses being ¼ in. deep and just large enough to take the ends of the round handle. Now drive some good long screws through the side strips into the handle; or a piece of metal tube or stout bamboo may be used, but in this case the ends must be plugged so as to well hold the screws. Paint it any dark colour.

BICYCLE STAND.

A bicycle stand is shown in general view

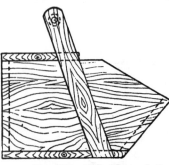

Fig. 744.—Side View of Coal-box.

by Fig. 745, a plan being represented by Fig. 746, front elevation by Fig. 747, and left end elevation by Fig. 748. If the stand is made of soft wood, stained and varnished, or of hard wood, polished, it has a neat appearance. A board 6 ft. long, 9 in. wide,

and about ⅞ in. thick, planed both sides, will be suitable, and on it the several pieces should be marked out according to the dimensions given in Figs. 746 to 748. For the curved parts use a bow saw and smooth the edges with a spokeshave. The appearance will be improved if the edges are rounded as indicated. The fixing is extremely simple; there are no tenons and mortises; the ends are merely squared and the pieces fixed together with 1¼-in. screws, not nails.

STRONG STOOL OR STAND.

A small stool that can be put to a variety of uses is illustrated by Fig. 749. It has many advantages over the common three-legged one. It is simple to make, will bear a very heavy load, and is not liable to turn over. It is useful as a foot-stool, or as a stand to support a great weight. The sizes given in Figs. 750 and 751 need not be followed exactly—the height may be adapted to the use to which the stool is to be put. Four stools made on this principle make excellent trestles or stands for erect-

Fig. 745.—Bicycle Stand.

ing heavy work of any description. Fig. 750 is the top of the stool, and Fig. 751 the side, the end resembling the side but being two thicknesses of the stuff shorter. To make the stool five pieces of board will be required—one piece for the top, two for the sides, and two for the ends. Whatever the size, the sides should be just double the thickness of the board longer

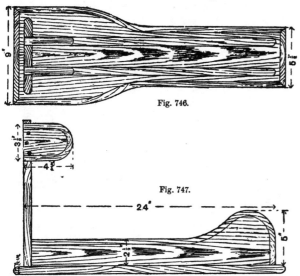

Fig. 746.

Fig. 747.

24"

Fig. 748.

Figs. 746 to 748.—Plan and Elevations of Bicycle Stand.

than the ends, as already noted, to give a square base. All that is necessary after cutting to size and planing up is simply to nail together. The nails must be driven at a slight angle, alternating right and left.

Folding Stand for Child's Cradle.

Figs. 752 and 753 are end and side views respectively of a folding stand for a cradle. To make the stand, get four pieces of sound

and planed to 1 in. by $\frac{5}{8}$ in., are required for the connecting bars, the ends of which are seen in Fig. 752. The two pieces forming each end are pivoted together by a brass bolt $2\frac{1}{2}$ in. long, with wing nut; the bars are fixed by light screws $1\frac{1}{4}$ in. long. To make the bars on which the cradle rests, heat one end of a piece of $\frac{1}{4}$-in. bar iron and form a ring on a stout screw eye. Bend the other end at right angles to fit into a corresponding eye, as seen in Fig. 752. When these bars are attached, the stand is complete.

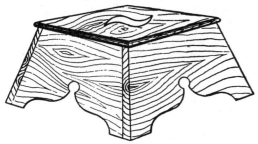

Fig. 749.—Strong Stool or Stand.

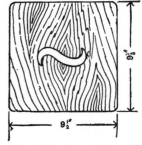

Fig. 750.—Top of Stool.

pine, ash, or oak, as preferred, 2 ft. 7 in. long, and plane them to $1\frac{1}{2}$ in. by $\frac{3}{4}$ in. These form the ends whose shape is shown in Fig. 752. Four pieces, 1 ft. 11 in. long

Newspaper Racks.

Fig. 754 shows a newspaper rack as it hangs against a wall by two brass plates screwed to the top back rail. The back frame consists of two end pillars connected by two flat straps jointed into the back of the pillars and fixed with screws. The front frame is similar, with a number of flat strips screwed vertically to the two rails at equal distances.

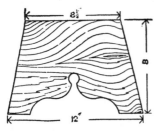

Fig. 751.—Side of Stool.

The flat strips may be pointed at one end and flat at the other, as shown, or rounded or pointed at both ends, or the ends may be cut to an ornamental shape. The two rails are connected together at the bottom, a **V**-shaped piece of wood being fastened between them by screws having the front rail at an angle as shown in the sectional view (Fig. 755). Another rack may be made on the same lines as this, having two pieces with the vertical strips, and fixing these, one on each side of the centre, on a square base made of four pieces of wood the re-

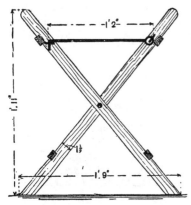

Fig. 752.—End View of Cradle Stand.

quired length and width, and dovetailed together at the corners. This will stand on a table or sideboard. Red deal, kauri, mahogany, oak, or any kind of wood may be used in making these racks.

PIPE RACK.

For the pipe rack shown in front elevation by Fig. 756, plan and part section by Fig. 757, and side elevation by Fig. 758, satin

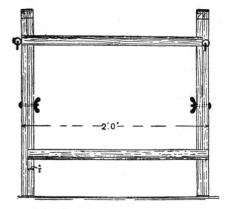

Fig. 753.—Front View of Cradle Stand.

walnut is suitable, as it is fairly tough, easy and clean to work, and of a good colour. All the parts except the shelf c are planed to a thickness of $\frac{5}{16}$ in. The shelf c requires a piece $13\frac{1}{2}$ in. by 2 in. by $1\frac{9}{16}$ in. (finished sizes). The size of the back part is $14\frac{1}{4}$ in. by $9\frac{3}{8}$ in. The other sizes may be easily obtained by means of a scale. A piece 2 ft. by $9\frac{1}{2}$ in. by $\frac{3}{8}$ in. is sufficient for all the

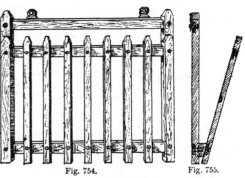

Fig. 754.   Fig. 755.

Figs. 754 and 755.—Newspaper Rack.

parts but c. When the wood is planed to thickness, the outlines are marked out, and pencil lines made on the back to show the positions of other parts. Each part is cut out by means of a bow saw, and the curved edges are worked to shape with spokeshave and chisels. The straight edges are best finished by using a plane and shooting board. Stopped housing joints (see p. 198) are used to join the smaller pieces together, as shown by the dotted lines in the illustration, and screws put in through the back fasten these to the back piece. Possible shrinkage of the back may be provided for in the following manner : Leave the vertical pieces D D unglued, and, instead of bedding their ends to the bottom of the housing, leave about $\frac{1}{16}$ in. of space at each between the two abutting pieces. Fasten D D to the

of the moulding which forms the shelf. A fine dovetail saw and a $\frac{1}{4}$-in. chisel will be necessary to do this. The width of each

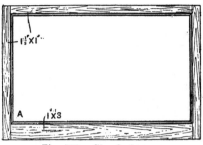

Fig. 759.—Simple Frame.

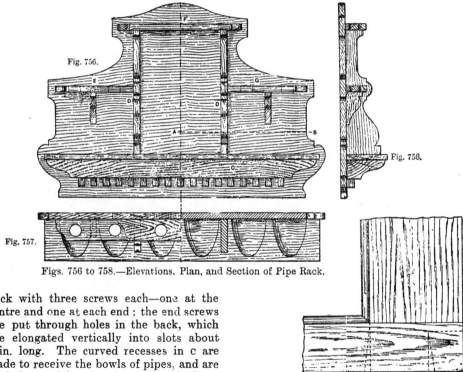

Figs. 756 to 758.—Elevations, Plan, and Section of Pipe Rack.

back with three screws each—one at the centre and one at each end : the end screws are put through holes in the back, which are elongated vertically into slots about $\frac{1}{4}$ in. long. The curved recesses in C are made to receive the bowls of pipes, and are made by straight cuts with a gouge inclined about 15° to the horizontal ; the bottom of the recess is shown by a slanting dotted line in the side elevation. One half of the plan is shown below the plane of section A B, to present a full view of these recesses. The dentils, as the small projections at the bottom are called, are not made of separate pieces, but are cut out of the lowest member

Fig. 760.—Haunched and Wedged Mortise and Tenon Joint.

dentil and space is $\frac{5}{16}$ in. The pieces E, F, and G have centre-bit holes through them to receive the stems of the pipes, and the centres of these must be in the same vertical planes as the centre lines of the recesses. The method of suspending the rack is not shown, as that is a matter which must depend upon circumstances; it may be screwed to woodwork, or two brass eye-

plates may be screwed on so that it may hang on the wall, or two holes may be bored for the same purpose; if so, they should be

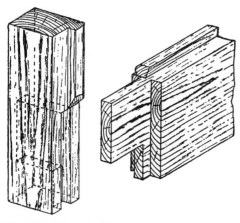

Fig. 761.—Haunched Mortise and Tenon Apart.

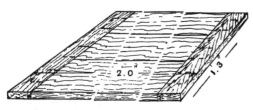

Fig. 762.—Simple Paste Board.

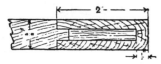

Fig. 763.—Pasteboard Clamping.

towards the ends and immediately under the pieces E and G. The illustrations are drawn to scale.

SIMPLE FRAME.

A simple frame which is intended for a wire blind, but which may have a great many other uses, is shown by Fig. 759. It is an exercise in making one of the joints

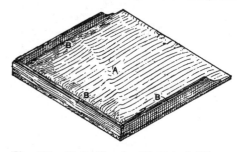

Fig. 764.—Paste Board with Raised Sides.

treated in the previous chapter. Fig. 760 is an elevation of the joint A (Fig. 759) to a larger scale. The tenon, mortise, haunch,

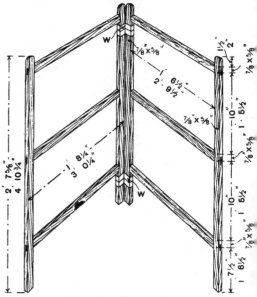

Fig. 765.—Clothes Horse.

and wedges are indicated by dotted lines. Fig. 761 shows the construction of the joint, the mitring of the head, which is stuck on the solid, and the rebate formed for the movable bead (the last-named is not shown). The beads should be about ½ in.

Simple Paste Board.

Fig. 762 is a view of a clamped paste board made from clean yellow pine. The following quantities of timber are required: 6 ft. by 5 in. by $\frac{5}{8}$ in., 2 ft. 8 in. by 2 in. by $\frac{5}{8}$ in., and 1 ft. 4 in. by 2 in. by 2 in. The paste board is made of three widths of timber, with reversed grain to equalise shrinkage. The boards are grooved, tongued, and glue-jointed together (see p. 191). The ends are tongued and tenoned to take a clamping piece (see p. 208) 2 in. wide (see Fig. 763), and the tenons are cut $\frac{1}{4}$ in., so as not to project through the clamp. Glue the ends on, and, when they are dry, plane and glasspaper the boards so as to clean off the joints.

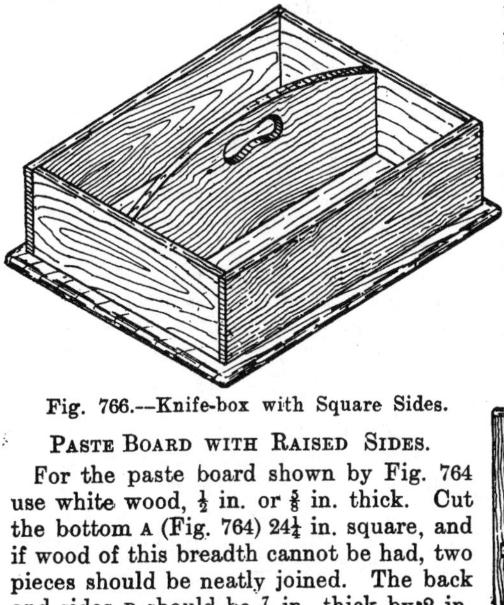

Fig. 766.--Knife-box with Square Sides.

Paste Board with Raised Sides.

For the paste board shown by Fig. 764 use white wood, $\frac{1}{2}$ in. or $\frac{5}{8}$ in. thick. Cut the bottom A (Fig. 764) $24\frac{1}{4}$ in. square, and if wood of this breadth cannot be had, two pieces should be neatly joined. The back and sides B should be $\frac{7}{8}$ in. thick by 2 in. broad, the former being 24 in. long, while the latter measures $22\frac{1}{2}$ in. Square the ends of the back and sides which have to be dovetailed, and shape the other ends of the sides as illustrated. Cut the dovetails in the sides and back and glue them together. Then plane the bottom smooth and round the corners at the front. When the frame is quite dry, plane the edges flush, and glue the bottom edges, fastening the frame to the bottom with 1-in. screws. Plane the projecting edges of the bottom flush with the frame, and round over or run a sash or ogee moulding on the top edge.

Clothes Horse.

A small horse for airing clothes is shown by Fig. 765. This should be of clean yellow pine, $\frac{7}{8}$ in. by $\frac{5}{8}$ in., planed to size, and with

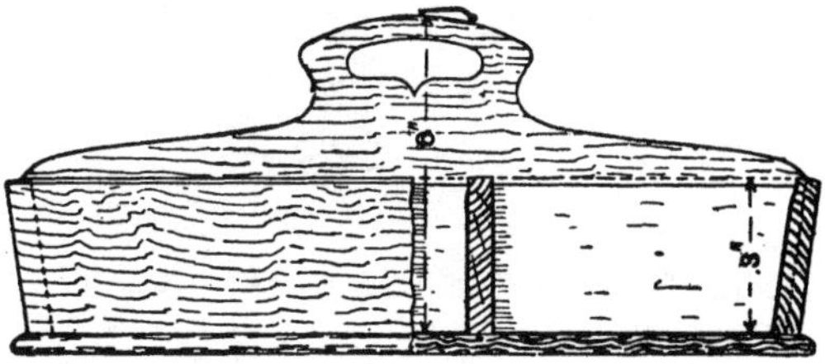

Fig. 767.—Knife-box with Splayed Sides.

the edges slightly chamfered. The material required is: Four pieces 2 ft. 8 in. by $\frac{7}{8}$ in. by $\frac{5}{8}$ in., and six pieces 1 ft. 9 in. by $\frac{7}{8}$ in. by $\frac{5}{8}$ in. When the framing is wedged, sandpaper it, and leave in the white. The cross rails are tenoned into the uprights, and the tenons wedged from the face edges. The tops of the uprights are rounded, and the two parts hinged together with strong webbing, tightly tacked. Two pieces of webbing are required for each hinge W (Fig. 765). The lower set of dimensions shown in Fig. 765 are for a larger horse made of $1\frac{3}{8}$-in. by $\frac{7}{8}$-in. uprights, with $1\frac{1}{4}$-in. by $\frac{5}{8}$-in. cross rails.

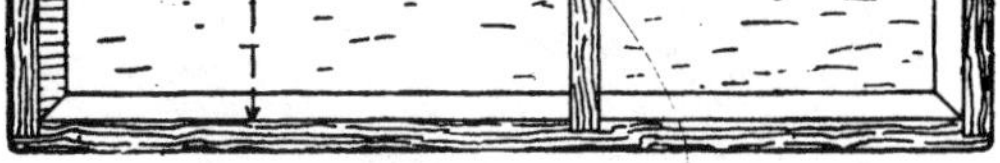

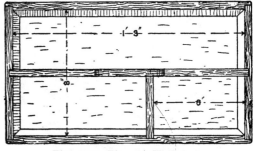

Fig. 768.—Plan of Knife-box.

Knife-box with Square Sides.

The simplest form of knife-box is shown by Fig. 766. It is made from $\frac{1}{2}$-in. wood. The stuff having been sawn and planed, it is only necessary to shoot the edges, then glue and nail the parts together, though the corners could be dovetailed if desired. Put the four sides together, and fit the middle division; but, before fixing, put in the finger-hole. The bottom should be nosed all round. The outside measurements are: Length 13 in., width 10 in., depth 4 in., ex-

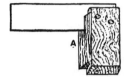

Fig. 769.—Square for Trying Angles.

treme height of middle piece 5 in. The bottom is 11 in. by 14 in.

KNIFE-BOXES WITH SPLAYED SIDES.

A better but more difficult knife-box is shown in part elevation and part cross sec-

Fig. 770.—Half-lap for Knife-box Corners.　　Fig. 771.—Edge of Baize Sunk in Bevelled Rebate.

tion by Fig. 767, a plan being given by Fig. 768. It may be made of mahogany or walnut, $\frac{1}{2}$ in. thick, which should be planed to $\frac{3}{8}$ in. The pieces forming the bottom and cross partitions should be

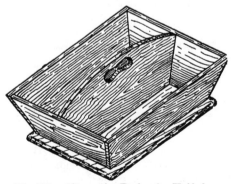

Fig. 772.—Alternative Design for Knife-box.

planed to $\frac{1}{4}$ in. and $\frac{5}{16}$ in. thick respectively. For the sides, two pieces 1 ft. $3\frac{3}{4}$ in. by 3 in.; and for the ends, two pieces $8\frac{5}{8}$ in.

by 3 in. will be required. Plane these and cut them off, giving a $\frac{3}{8}$-in. bevel in the depth of the sides and ends. These pieces will not be exactly true at the ends, but they may be planed to the correct bevel by

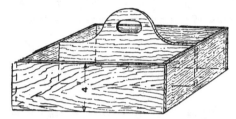

Fig. 773.—Box for Blacklead Brushes.

getting out a piece of wood to the same bevel as the sides, fixing it to the stock of the square, and then running a saw kerf in the top edge to fit on the blade of the square as at A in Fig. 769. In using this square, the bevelled piece of wood is placed against the face of the sides and the ends, the stock of the square being kept parallel with the top and the bottom edges. The corners of the box may be dovetailed or lapjointed; for the lap on one piece, see Fig. 770. The joint should be glued and secured with a few $\frac{3}{4}$-in. panel pins, the heads being punched in and stopped with beeswax and resin. Groove the ends for the long partition, and one side for the cross partition (see Fig. 768). The inside of the box should be lined with green baize, and to prevent the edges becoming loose, run a bevelled rebate about $\frac{3}{16}$ in. below the inside top edges of the sides and ends as at A (Fig. 771), and on both sides of the divisions, as indicated in the right-hand half of Fig. 767. The top

Fig. 774.—Joint of Sides and Bottom of Box.

edge of the baize is sunk into these rebates, thus preventing its being torn when articles are placed in the box. The sides and ends of the box are glued and pinned together, and a piece of stuff, 1 ft. $3\frac{3}{8}$ in. by 6 in., prepared for the centre division and handle, and marked to the shape shown in Fig. 767. The top can be cut with a pad or bow saw. The top edge should be rounded with a spokeshave, rasp, and glasspaper. The groove for the cross partition can next be made and the piece driven in, glued, and

Fig. 766, p. 237, except for the splayed sides, and it will not present any difficulty when the box shown by Fig. 767 has been made. The ends would be better dovetailed than butt-jointed.

BOX FOR BLACKLEAD BRUSHES.

A box in which to keep blacklead brushes is illustrated by Fig. 773. It is made of pine

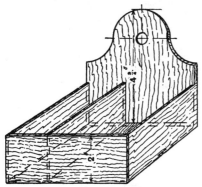

Fig. 775.—Soap Box.

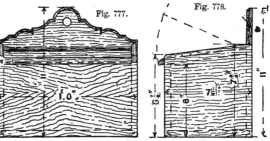

Figs. 777 and 778.—Elevations of Salt-box.

secured at both ends with panel pins; the cross partition is secured in the position shown in Fig. 768. When the glue is thoroughly dry, the under side may be levelled with a plane and the piece for the bottom prepared. This should be $\frac{3}{8}$ in longer and wider than the under side of the box, and rounded as shown in Fig. 767; it may be secured with a few $\frac{5}{8}$-in. No. 3 screws and a little glue. If the box is to be French-polished, the sides and the rounded edge of the bottom should be filled in with a rubber or two of polish before the bottom is fixed. In lining the box with green baize, use good hot glue, or a stiff flour paste with

or deal, and following is the quantity of material required: Two sides, 1 ft. 1½ in. by 4¼ in. by $\frac{3}{8}$ in.; two ends, 8½ in. by 4¼ in. by $\frac{3}{8}$ in.; one partition, 1 ft. 1 in. by 7 in. by $\frac{2}{8}$ in.; and the bottom, 1 ft. 1 in. by 8 in. by $\frac{1}{2}$ in. The sides and ends are nailed together, and the bottom is rebated and glued, as shown in Fig. 774, in which B is the bottom and S the side. The partition 7 in. deep in the centre of the box is grooved in each end about $\frac{1}{8}$ in. deep and nailed to the bottom, and is cut to form a handle as shown in Fig. 773. The outside of the box should be painted black, and then varnished, so that it can readily be cleaned; or black enamel can be used.

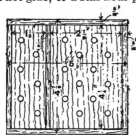

Fig. 776.—Soap-box Bottom.

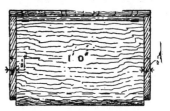

Fig. 779.—Plan of Salt-box.

a little powdered resin added. The top edge should be well rubbed into the rebate, as shown at A in Fig. 771. Another pattern of box is shown by Fig. 772; this resembles

SOAP BOX.

Fig. 775 shows a small soap box that can be made of any hard wood, of the following dimensions: Back, 4¾ in. by 5½ in. by

$\frac{5}{16}$ in. ; sides, 1 ft. 6 in. by 2 in. by $\frac{5}{16}$ in. ; front, 5½ in. by 2 in by $\frac{5}{16}$ in. ; partition, 5 in. by 2 in. by ¼ in. ; and bottom, 5½ in. by 5½ in. by $\frac{5}{16}$ in. The back has a circular top, and a hole hanging, as shown. The sides

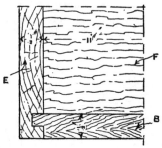

Fig. 780.—Salt-box Bottom Grooved into Side.

are nailed together and shouldered and nailed to the back. The ¼-in. thick partition divides off a part for a nail-brush. The bottom is nailed in and provided with drainage holes as shown in Fig. 776. Alternative methods of finishing the bottom are to nail it on the sides, with a ¼-in. rounded nosing projecting, or to replace the wood with a piece of perforated zinc.

SALT BOX.

A box for holding 12 lb. or 14 lb. of table salt is shown in front elevation by Fig. 777, in end elevation by Fig. 778, and in plan by Fig. 779. It may be made of mahogany or birch, which must be very dry, otherwise

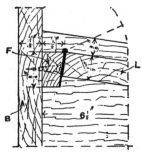

Fig. 781.—Hingeing of Salt-box Lid.

the salt will become discoloured. The following material is required: Back, 1 ft. 1 in. by 11¼ in. by ½ in. ; front, 1 ft. 1 in. by 6¼ in. by ½ in. ; lid, 1 ft. by 8½ in. by ½ in. ; bottom, 1 ft. 1 in. by 7½ in. by ½ in. ; two

ends, 7½ in. by 7½ in. by ½ in. ; and a fillet, 1 ft. by ¾ in. by ½ in. Plane the pieces to thickness, square the ends, and mark out the dovetailing for the vertical corners. The bottom is grooved in ¼ in. or $\frac{3}{16}$ in. deep and glued ; see Fig. 780, in which B is the bottom, E the end, and F the front. The back piece is 11 in. high to allow for a shaped top, shown in Fig. 777, the edges being finished with a deep chamfer. The lid is hinged to a fillet, ¾ in. by ½ in., screwed to the back (see Fig. 781, in which L is the lid, F the fillet, and B the back), and projects over the front ½ in. (see Fig. 782, in which F is the front, E the end, and L the lid). The ends, as shown in Fig. 778, project ⅜ in. above the lid, and have rounded edges at the top.

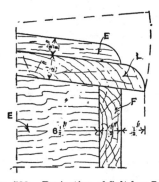

Fig. 782.—Projection of Salt-box Lid.

The interior of the box should be lined with stout white drawing paper, and the outside should be sized and varnished or polished.

NEWSPAPER BOX.

The newspaper box shown by Fig. 783 is easy to make and costs very little. The wood does not need planing up, as it is afterwards covered over with paper. The dimensions are given in Fig. 783. The back is made from ¼-in. stuff, and has a piece nailed across the top at the back to the depth of about 8 in., with the grain of the wood running crossways to the back to strengthen it. The back will have to be made from two pieces to give the required width, and must be well glued at the joint. When the box has been put together and nailed up, rub down all sharp edges with glasspaper. The box may then be decorated with coloured paper according to taste. Bore two holes in the back of the box, as in Fig. 783, thread a picture cord through them, and all that is then necessary for

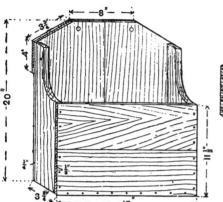

Fig. 783.—Newspaper Box.

hanging the rack up is simply a nail or hook made fast in the wall.

BRUSH AND COMB BOX.

The brush and comb box shown in Figs. 784 and 785 may be made of ⅜-in. wood. A piece 14 in. long and 8 in. wide will make the back and front. The point A (Fig. 784) will be 7 in. from one end, and by cutting out

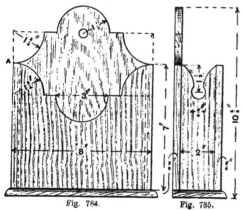

Figs. 784 and 785.—Brush and Comb Box.

with a fretsaw the back and front are shaped at one operation. No further instructions will be needed.

16

WINDOW BOX FOR FLOWERS.

Fig. 786 is a view of a window box for flowers. The wood should be about ¾ in.

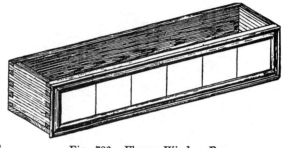

Fig. 786.—Flower Window Box.

or 1 in. thick, according to the size of the box; the angles should be dovetailed and nailed together as shown in the end view (Fig. 787). The bottom is simply nailed to the sides and ends. The appearance of the box is considerably improved by mitring and fixing a moulding round the front as shown; and tiles can be fitted to the front with bolection moulding, which is rebated as in the section (Fig. 788). Two or three wedge-shape strips should be nailed on the bottom as shown at A (Fig. 787); they require cutting to the splay of the sill; this allows of the box standing level. It is a good plan to coat thickly with lead paint all the joints and parts of the box that will be in contact before fixing them together, so

Fig. 787.—End of Window Box.

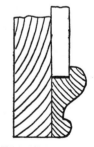

Fig. 788.—Section of Tile and Moulding.

as to resist the rotting effect of the moist earth which the box will afterwards contain.

WASHING TRAY.

Wooden vessels for holding water for washing and other purposes are much better

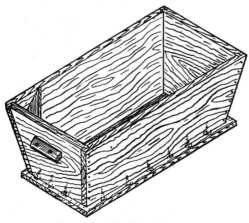

Fig. 789.—Washing Tray.

than metal ones, as they are less liable to be chemically affected by sodas and other chemicals, are more durable, and are more easily kept clean. Fig. 789 shows a wooden washing tray, which is not difficult to construct when marked out in a proper manner, and forms a useful exercise in woodwork. It is preferably made of white pine, 1 in. or 2 in. thick, according to the size of the utensil required; but good sound red or yellow deal, free from loose

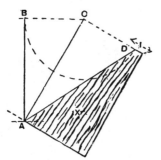

Fig. 790.—Setting out Angle of Sides of Washing Tray.

knots and sap, is an excellent substitute. All nails used for fastening the joints should be of copper, and where screws are required they should be of brass, thus avoiding rust,

which occurs with iron and steel. Iron and steel nails, however, may be used, provided the heads are puttied over. The sides and ends are grooved and tongued together

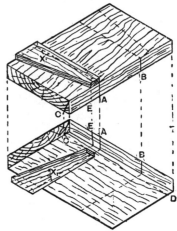

Fig. 791.—Applying Mould to Sides of Washing Tray.

at the angles, and as these joints are not at right angles to the faces, it is here that the difficulty of construction is experienced. This is overcome by properly setting out, one method of which is shown in Fig. 790, and another is described in connection with the next example. Draw an upright line; from A mark off at B the vertical depth of the vessel required; at right angles to A B draw B C, and draw A C at the desired slope for the sides and ends, which should be both the same. This angle will, of course,

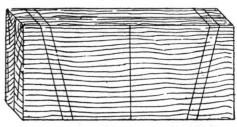

Fig. 792.—Setting out Angle of Sides of Washing Tray.

be the bevel of the bottom, and it is indicated in Fig. 790 by the angle bevel. To find the pitch of the angles, draw C D at right angles to B C, and make C D equal to

B C; through D draw a line A D, which is the pitch required. Make a thin wood mould as shown in Fig. 790 by the grained portion marked x. Having cut the material a little longer than the full length required, with the faces planed and edges straight and squared, mark it out as follows: Lay both sides together and both ends with their edges fair with each other and face to face; square the two lines marked A and B (Fig.

Fig. 793.—Section of Washing Tray Lift.

791) over the edges at equal distances from the ends, and 2 in. shorter than the finished internal length of the vessel at the bottom for the sides, and 1½ in. shorter for the ends; this is taken up again by the 1-in. end of the mould in application. Except in the case of the ends, ½ in. is allowed for tongues. Square these lines over both faces and mark the bevel (Fig. 790) for the bottom on the ends of each part, as shown in Fig. 791 at c, and draw on one face the line C D parallel to the edge as shown. The application of

groove the sides beyond the marks to bevel E, and shoot off the bottom edge to bevel C. Another method of obtaining the pitch of

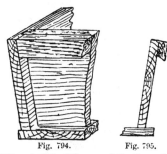

Fig. 794. Fig. 795.

Figs. 794 and 795.—View and Section of End of Washing Tray.

the sides is shown by Fig. 792; a centre line is squared across the sides and ends, and half the required width is set off from it at both top and bottom; then connect these marks as shown in Fig. 792. Fit the joints, make them tight, nail well, plane off the edges all round so that the bottom fits well, and put them all together without paper, paint, or white-lead. If brown paper is used in the joints the tray will certainly leak and, worse still, go rotten. Fix an oaken lift, of which Fig. 793 is a

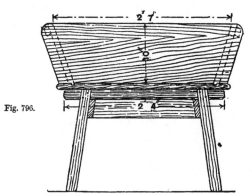

Fig. 796.

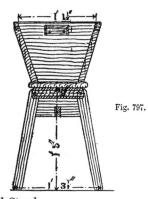

Fig. 797.

Figs. 796 and 797.—Washing Tray and Stand.

the mould x is distinctly illustrated, and does not need further explanation. When both sides are marked with the mould, join the marks over the edge as at E (Fig. 791), and cut and plane ends to these lines for the ends of the vessel, shouldering the tongues ¼ in. back to the same bevel as E;

section, at each end as in Fig. 789, and finish by fixing a piece of ½-in. stuff across one of the angles, as seen to the left in Fig. 789, so as to form a receptacle for soap or other articles. A little leakage may take place at first, but after the tray has held water for a short time the wood will swell and the joints will effectually close up. An improvement on the above is to trench the ends into the sides for the full thickness, as shown in Figs. 794 and 795, and to have the grip at the extreme top of the

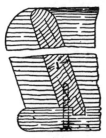

Fig. 798.—Section of End of Washing Tray.

ends running quite across as shown in Fig. 794, so that two hands can take hold if necessary.

A MORE SUBSTANTIAL WASHING TRAY.

Fig. 796 is the side elevation and Fig. 797 the end elevation of a wooden washing tray and stand of substantial construction. The depth and pitch of the sides are arranged so that they may be got out of 11-in. boards 1 in. thick, an easily procurable size.

to allow the latter to be housed-in solid; they should be fitted very tight, the housing being stopped $\frac{1}{2}$ in. down from the top. The lower edges of the sides and ends are tongued into a $\frac{1}{2}$-in. groove in the bottom $\frac{3}{8}$ in. deep (the tongue being square to the bottom, so that the latter may be ploughed from the edge and put on after the frame is made up (see Fig. 798). The screws must be kept outside the groove to prevent leakage. Having worked the tongues and fitted the housings, they may be at once put together plain, or coated with a mixture of equal parts of white- and red-lead, worked up in linseed oil to the consistency of rather thick paint. Nail them together with $2\frac{1}{2}$-in. copper or zinc clouts, dovetail fashion. Then rack the tray square and stand it on the

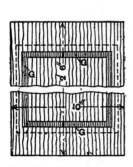

Fig. 799.—Grooved Bottom of Washing Tray.

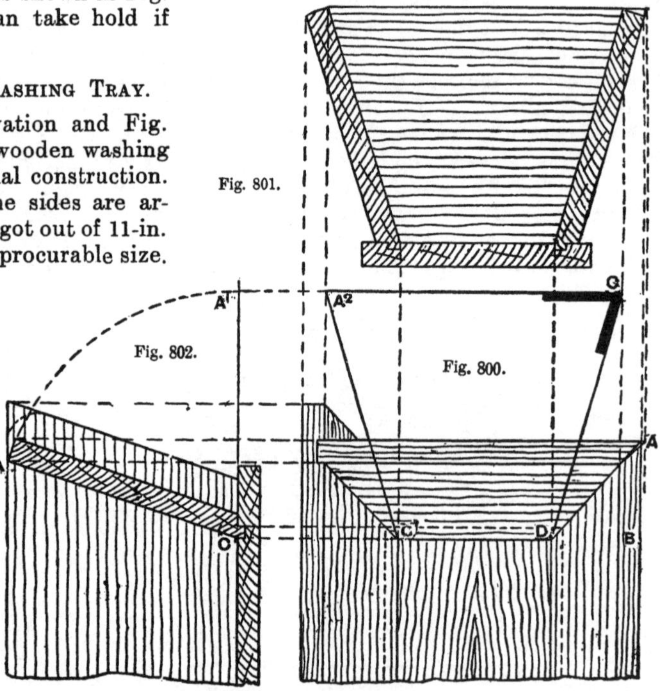

Figs. 800 to 802.—Obtaining Bevel for Washing Tray Sides and Ends.

The board should, for economy of material, be cut " in and out "—that is, the long edge of one piece following the short edge of another. The length may be varied to suit requirements, but in any case the sides should overhang the ends 1½ in. as shown,

bottom, mark around the inside of the tongue, and cut the groove in the bottom slightly smaller than the marks; the grooves will be stopped as shown at G (Fig. 799). The sides are secured in the grooves with brass screws. Round the edges of the tray with a spokeshave, and screw on two pieces, 1 in. by 4 in., at the ends, for hand grips or lifts.

OBTAINING BEVELS FOR WASHING TRAY.

The sides of the tray are inclined, and as

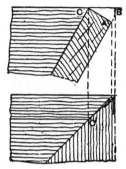

Fig. 803.—Setting out Bevel.

they are drawn on a plane not parallel to the plane of inclination, the bevel lines shown will not be the true bevels required for marking the shoulders and grooves; these must be discovered by turning one of the ends either into the vertical or into the horizontal plane. It is usual to do this on the ground plane or plan. The method is shown in Figs. 800 to 802, which are drawn to a slightly larger scale, to render the

line of the end) describe the arc A A¹. Produce the inside line of the bottom to meet it, and project the intersection A¹ into the plan; and between the projections of the top edges of the sides draw the line A² G (Fig. 800), representing the top edge of the end. Join A² and G to C¹ and D, the points of intersection of the lower edge of the end

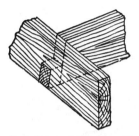

Fig. 805.—Rail Joint of Washing Tray Stand.

with the bottom, and A² G D C¹ will then be the true shape of the end between the inner surfaces of the sides and bottom; the common bevel is shown at G. This bevel, when applied from the top edges, will mark the housing in the sides, and also the end cuts, which are the extra amounts required for the sinkings to be allowed beyond the sight lines. Made as described, the edges cut will be square from the surface; but should

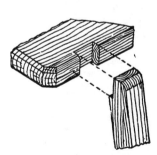

Fig. 804.—Fixing Leg of Washing Tray Stand.

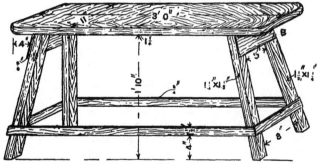

Fig. 806.—Stand for Washing Tray.

operation clearer. One end of the tray is projected in Fig. 800 from the two sections (Figs. 801 and 802), the dotted projectors indicating the various parts. As all the sides are equally inclined, any one may be taken for development. With c (Fig. 802) as a centre, and c A as a radius (this is the sight

the tray be dovetailed at the corners, and its top edge mitred as shown at A (Fig. 800), the bevel for marking the cut on the square edge will be found as shown in Fig. 803. The theory of the operation is that the edge B (Fig. 800), being projected narrow owing to its inclined position, is assumed to have its lower arris lifted up until it is level with the top arris, when the real shape of the end can be seen. Let C A (Fig. 803) represent the top edge; then with C as centre and C A as radius, describe the arc A B; draw a perpendicular line from B into the plan and produce the outer line of the side in plan to meet this perpendicular, and join the

Fig. 807.—Bed-side Table.

intersection to the point c^1, to produce the bevel as shown.

STAND FOR WASHING TRAY.

The stand for this tray (see Figs. 796 and 797) is of white deal $1\frac{3}{4}$ in. thick, the top 9 in. wide and 2 ft. 4 in. long; the legs are 2 in. wide at the top end, tapering to $1\frac{3}{4}$ in. at the bottom, and are notched into the top $\frac{3}{4}$ in. as shown in the isometric sketch (Fig. 804). The bevel for the leg can be found by making on a board or floor a full-size drawing of half the end shown in Fig. 797, and drawing a perpendicular line, $1\frac{1}{4}$ in. from the face of the leg. A bevel set to this can be applied from the face of the leg. Cut the notch in the top, square through, with its end slightly bevelled as shown, to spread the legs lengthways. Two pieces, 4 in. by 1 in., are screwed inside the legs after they are fixed, and a centre rail of like substance is half-notched over them as shown in Fig. 805.

A STRONGER WASHING TRAY STOOL.

A stronger stool for supporting the tray is illustrated by Fig. 806. It should be of sound dry red deal, and requires one top, 3 ft. by 11 in. by $1\frac{1}{4}$ in.; four pieces for the legs, 2 ft. by $1\frac{1}{2}$ in. by $1\frac{1}{4}$ in.; two pieces for the top braces, 9 in. by 4 in. by $\frac{5}{8}$ in.; two pieces for the bottom end braces, 1 ft. by $1\frac{1}{2}$ in. by $\frac{3}{4}$ in.; and two pieces for the side braces, 3 ft. by $1\frac{1}{2}$ in. by $\frac{3}{4}$ in. First prepare the top, which has rounded edges and corners. Then set out and cut the mortises for the leg tenons. The legs are $1\frac{1}{2}$ in. by $1\frac{1}{4}$ in., with the upper ends tenoned square, and wedged into the stool top. They can also be rounded and wedged into holes bored in the stool top. When the legs are fixed, screw the brace B (Fig. 806) immediately under the top, and chamfer the edges. The lower bracing ties the legs together; it is

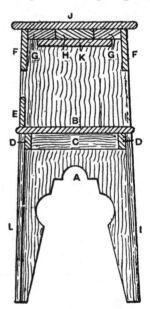

Fig. 808.—Section of Bed-side Table.

screwed on, and the front edges are chamfered.

BED-SIDE TABLE.

For the bed-side table shown by Fig. 807 the first requirement will be two pieces of $\frac{3}{4}$-in. board, 2 ft. 1 in. long, to form the ends,.

which will include the legs. These pieces should be 1 ft. wide at the bottom, tapering to 10 in. at the top. Fig. 808 shows the inner side of one, and the pieces adjacent.

Fig. 809.—Back of Table Shelf.

In the lower part is sawn the opening A, which makes the legs. The end pieces stand 1 ft. 2 in. apart at the bottom and 1 ft. at the top outside, and at the top are joined by the two cross pieces G (Fig. 808), which are of 1-in. board, 2½ in. wide and 1 ft. long, placed 4 in. apart, and screwed down to the end pieces. The ornamental front and back strips F also serve to connect the sides, openings for them, 3 in. long and ½ in. deep, being cut on the edges of the end pieces. These strips, shown clearly in Fig. 807, are of ½-in. stuff, 4 in. wide and 1 ft. 0½ in. long ; they are screwed to the end pieces and to the cross pieces G (Fig. 808). The ledger C is a strip ¾ in. by 1½ in. wide by 8½ in. long ; it is screwed to the end piece, its top being 1 ft. 4 in. from the ground line. To its ends

projects beyond the level of the end pieces by ½ in., and its edges are there rounded off. It is fixed down to the ledgers and strips beneath it, and screws are also driven into it through the end pieces. At the back of this shelf, and fastened to it and to the end pieces, is the ornamental strip E, shown separately by Fig. 809. It is of ½-in. stuff, 3 in. by 11½ in., and prevents articles placed upon the shelf falling off behind. To complete the legs at the front and back are needed four pieces L (Fig. 808) of ½-in.

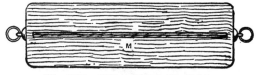

Fig. 810.—Slide of Bed-side Table.

board, 1 ft. 4 in. long, 6¼ in. wide at the bottom, tapering on the outer side only to 5¾ in. at the top. The front pair are shown in Fig. 807 placed together and covering the space between the middle shelf and the ground line. They are screwed to the end pieces and to the cross strips D (Fig. 808) ; it would be well also to unite them by a dowel just above the central opening. The

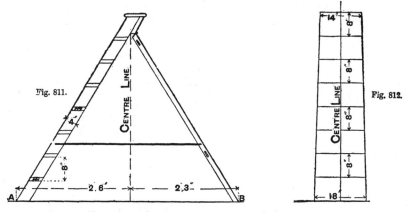

Figs. 811 and 812.—Setting out Stepladder.

and to those of its fellow are screwed at the back and front the two strips D, which are of like thickness and width, but 11¾ in. long. The middle shelf B is of ½-in. board, 11½ in. square. At the front and back it

table top J is of ¾-in. board, 1 ft. wide, the middle part being 1 ft. 3 in. long, and the flaps—hinged to it on the under side—6 in. long each. It is fixed by screws driven through the cross pieces G. Screwed to the under faces of these pieces is the ½-in. board K, 7 in. wide, and reaching from end piece to end piece, which with them forms a sheath for the slide H, the last being shown separately by Fig. 810. It is of 1-in. wood,

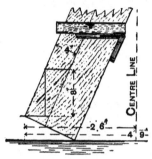

Fig. 813.—Obtaining Length of Stepladder Sides and Pitch.

4 in. wide and 1 ft. 1½ in. long, and must be made to run easily, but not loosely, in its sheath. It projects ¾ in. beyond the end pieces, and the edges of the projections are rounded off. For bed-side purposes both flaps are not likely to be wanted up at the same time, but whichever slide support is required may be drawn out by a ring; an ordinary picture-frame ring will serve the purpose. A groove M (Fig. 810), ½ in. deep, is cut along the middle of its under side, and will run over a metal stud fixed in the

be of lighter construction. Paperhangers, too, do not care for them too heavy. The following list of sizes of steps and timbers required will be found useful to work to:—

Number of Steps, excluding Top.	Width from A to B (Fig. 811).	Width of Sides.	Width of Steps outside Sides at Top (Fig. 812).	Width outside Sides at Bottom (Fig. 813).	Depth of Steps.
	ft. in.	in.	in.	in.	in.
4	3 0	3½	12	16	4½
5	3 6	3½	12	16	4½
6	4 3	4	14	18	5
7	4 9	4	14	18	5
8	5 0	4	14½	18½	5

The stiles and bottom rail of back support should be 2¼ in. or 2½ in. wide, and top rail 4½ in. or 5 in. wide.

Fig. 814.—Stepladder Step.

SETTING OUT HOUSEHOLD STEPLADDER.

Suppose the steps to be made are to have seven steps and a top, making eight rises in all, which, with 8-in. rises, would give a

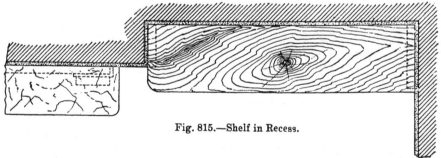

Fig. 815.—Shelf in Recess.

centre of the board K (Fig. 808); the slide cannot then be drawn out too far. The slide must, of course, be put in its sheath before the table top is fixed.

STEPLADDERS.

Builders' stepladders have to be strong, whereas shop and household ladders may

height of 5 ft. 4 in. when the steps are open. The first thing to do is to set out the steps full size on a board, as shown in Figs. 811 and 812, to get the length of sides, steps, etc.; but a good and quicker plan is to take any odd piece of board, about 6 ft. long, run a line down it, 4 in. from the edge, which will correspond with the width of the sides required; then set one end on the floor, and hold it at about the right angle, first measuring the stretch-out on the floor, as shown in Fig. 813. Hold a spirit level across the board, and draw a line under the level when the level is true. Set a bevel to this line, which will be the pitch of the steps. The top of the steps should be a trifle over the centre of the stretch-out, as shown in Fig. 811. Now draw a floor line on the board with a bevel, and measure 8 in. up

Fig. 816.—Shelf Ledge.

at right angles to the line. This will be the top of the first step. Repeat the same for each step; the length of the sides can then be ascertained.

MAKING STEPLADDER.

Cut the material for the stepladder out of 1-in. by 9-in. white deal, that being lighter and generally sounder than red. The pieces required will be two sides 4 in. wide, seven steps 5 in. wide, two stiles for back support 2¼ in. wide, top rail for back sup-

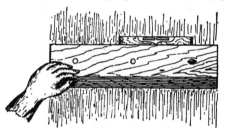

Fig. 817.—Levelling Shelf.

port 5 in. wide, bottom rail for back support 2½ in. wide, back board to which the support is hung 5 in. wide. The top should be wide enough to receive the sides (which should be housed into it ¼ in.) and to project over the front edge of the sides ¾ in. and over the back enough to receive the back board, and project the same over that as over the front edge of the sides. The top

should also hang over the sides 1½ in. at the end, and be rounded all round. Having planed up the stuff, set out one side with the bevel the same as on the board, square over on one edge, and set out the other side by that. Stick a ⅜-in. bead on the front edge of the sides, and cut grooves for the steps ⅜-in. deep in the sides. The bottom and fourth step, in addition to housing, should be tenoned through the sides with a tenon the full thickness of the step and 1¼ in. wide, and wedged both ways as shown in Fig. 811. Put in these two steps temporarily, and then cut in the other steps. Glue and nail the steps together, taking care to have them true. Set out the back by laying it in position on the back of the steps, and frame it together. The steps should be cleaned off level with the edges of sides at the back, but not on the front. As the top front edge of the steps will project in front of the edge of the sides, a piece should be chiselled off at the end of the step after the steps are put together (see Fig. 814). The back can be hung either with butt hinges, flap joints, or a small pair of T-joints, the last-named being the strongest. Put the cord in between the second and third steps, and cut off the back so that the steps are perfectly level when the cord is tight.

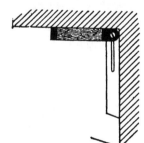

Fig. 818.—Obtaining Angle for Cutting Shelf.

FIXING SHELF IN A RECESS.

In most rooms there are recesses, from 9 in. to 15 in. deep, often utilised for bookshelves, which are made to rest on ledges nailed to the wall. The plan of such a shelf is shown by Fig. 815. In preparing for such a fixture, first ascertain, by tapping with a hammer, whether the shelves will be fixed to a solid wall or to a partition. Proceed to fix the ledge (Fig. 816), using the spirit-level as a guide (see Fig. 817). Nails cannot always be driven exactly into the joints of brickwork, so, if not content to risk

on the line drawn. Transfer this measurement to the shelf. Take the angle of the wall as before, and mark and cut the shelf to the length. Do not make the shelf fit too tightly, and for the sake of the wallpaper

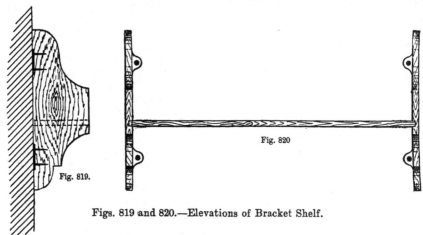

Figs. 819 and 820.—Elevations of Bracket Shelf.

the attempt, drill or chisel a hole in the wall, driving in a wood plug, to which the ledge can then be nailed. (Plugging walls is fully treated in separate paragraphs, later.) Always bore holes in the ledges for the

it is better to have it $\frac{1}{8}$ in. shorter than the extreme width of the recess. Try the shelf in its place, and test it for level or otherwise, before nailing the second ledge. The second ledge must be nailed as before ; and if, as sometimes happens, the ledge shifts in the process of fixing, do not wrench it off, but either raise the low end with a thin slip of wood, or, if possible, correct the slant by careful paring. If several shelves are

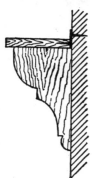

Fig. 821.—Bracket for Suspended Shelf.

Fig. 822.—Brass Plate.

to be fixed, each one may be treated in the same way, as the surface of the wall is not always absolutely true. If the shelves are required to be wider than the depth of the recess, the corners should be rounded as shown in Fig. 815. When one shelf is fitted satisfactorily, measurements can be taken from it, and all the ledges similarly fixed. It will save time if the fitted shelf is tried in each of the other places ; if it fits, it will serve as a template for the rest ; if not, it will give a very good idea of what is required. If, instead of brickwork, one side is a lath-and-plaster partition, find out by

nails, and have these nails of good quality, not too slender. If no spirit-level is at hand, use a square, taking the wall as vertical. Having fixed one ledge, take the angle between the back and the end with a bevel or 2-ft. folding rule (Fig. 818), and cut one end of the shelf to the angle. Mark lightly a horizontal line along the wall to the other end of the recess, and measure the length

tapping with a hammer where the timbers are. The ledges ought then to be made long enough to nail to two of these quarterings. If such length is objected to, the ledge must be well nailed to the timber, and one or two

Fig. 823.
Square and Tapered Plug.

Fig. 824.
Wedge-shaped Plug.

screws inserted into the laths. If the load on the shelf is not to be heavy, this will suffice.

FIXING SHELF WITH BRACKETS, ETC.

Sometimes a shelf is required, not in a recess, and not extending from wall to wall. In such a case it is best to suspend it rather than uphold it (Figs. 819 and 820), the shelf being housed into more or less ornamental ends, which are of the same thickness as the shelf. Another method is shown by the end view (Fig. 821). First find out the kind of wall or partition. If it is lath and plaster, note the places where

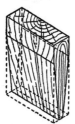

Fig. 825.—Wedge-shaped Plug with Parallel Ends.

the timbers occur, and make two or more neat brackets in wood, afterwards fixing them under the shelf. If preferred, metal brackets, to be bought cheaply, may be used. Fix two or more " glass plates " on the back of the shelf, at the places found suitable. These plates are of sheet metal, having usually three holes, two of which are countersunk for screwing to the back of the article (see Fig. 822). The plates should be

let in, and will leave a projection available for fixing the brackets to the wall. The method of using the brackets is made clear in the illustrations. Sometimes, as has been shown, the brackets supporting a shelf are fixed at the ends, in which case they may be made to serve as ends to the shelf, suspending as well as supporting it, and forming a useful and ornamental finish to the work (see Figs. 819 and 820). In order to fix anything in the middle of a wall, or in the space between the door and a corner, some workers measure the space, halve it, mark the wall at the distance, then measure the shelf, halve the result, mark it on the shelf, and bring the two marks together; but it will save time if the shelf or bracket is placed on the floor or on a table as nearly as the eye can judge in its proper place. If the remaining distance between the shelf and the door and the corner is then measured, the discrepancy will be found to be small. Perhaps it may be 2 in., when, of course, the shelf must be moved 1 in. to be in its correct central position.

WALL PLUGS.

Plugs are pieces of wood or metal, or of wood encased in metal, which are inserted

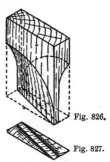

Fig. 826.

Fig. 827.

Figs. 826 and 827.—Twisted Plug.

in the joints of brickwork or stonework, or are driven into holes bored to receive them to afford a hold for nails, etc., which otherwise could not be used. The shapes for inserting into bored holes and into joints between bricks, etc., differ. For the first purpose the usual form is that shown by Fig. 823; this is square, and slightly tapered. To make it, the wood is cut off to 2 in. in length, and cleft into squares of barely ⅝ in.; they can be finished easily and quickly by taking off a thin chip from each side with a chisel. The common wedge-shaped plug for driving into joints is shown by Fig. 824, another

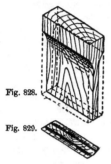

Fig. 828.

Fig. 829.

Figs. 828 and 829.—Plug with Parallel Sides.

and the preferable form being shown by Fig. 825. The so-called twisted plug (Figs. 826 and 827) was no doubt designed to overcome the tendency of a wedge-shaped plug to jump back whilst it is being driven forward. The twisted plug is made from an oblong piece of dry straight-grained pine, from each bottom corner of which a slice of wood is removed, so that the thin or entering edge

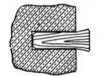

Fig. 830.—Correct Form of Round Plug.

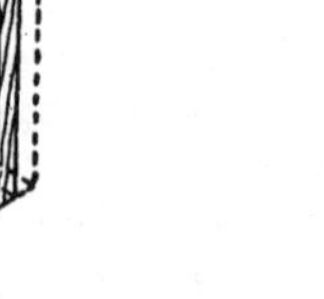

Fig. 831.—Incorrect Form of Round Plug.

of the plug has parallel edges and ends. In Fig. 827, which is a view from underneath, the wood contained in the two triangles is the portion removed. The cutting off of these opposite corners is supposed to give a twist to the cut face of the plug, so that it holds better when driven into the joints of brickwork or stonework. It may be difficult to discover the twist, which is the merit of this plug, except by comparing with an ordinary plug. Actually, the twisted plug is nothing more than the ordinary wedge-shaped kind (Fig. 825) cut slightly across the grain. To make the last named, cut down an oblong piece of wood on each side till it tapers somewhat like a wedge, keeping the

thin edge of the plug of equal thickness along its width, and its edges parallel. On comparing the two plugs it will be seen that as regards slope or angle or thickness there is no difference between the two wedge-shaped pieces of wood, and that one is not any better than the other. As already stated, the twisted plug was designed to counteract the tendency of the ordinary plug to spring back from the joint into which it is being driven; but the facts that all the angles of bricks are right angles, that the joint between two bricks is a joint with

Fig. 832.—Drill.

parallel sides, and that a wedge driven into a joint, the sides of which are parallel, is only in contact with the edges of the joint, were overlooked. The only way, then, of making a serviceable plug is to abandon the wedge shape and make the sides of the plug parallel (Fig. 828 and 829), and to fit each plug to the opening which it is intended to fill.

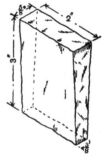

Fig. 833.—Lead Plug.

ROUND PLUGS.

The round wooden plug is used for the same purpose as the square one represented by Fig. 823, that is it is driven into a hole drilled in brick or stone. Often the round plug is made so thick as to be almost useless for the purpose it is intended to serve. The sides of the hole made to receive it are jagged and uneven, and unless the substance of the plug is forced into these indentations, it will, when the wood dries and shrinks, work loose and perhaps fall out. The screw that is driven into the plugs is intended to act as a wedge, so that the fibres of the wood may be forced into and become locked in the rough sides of the

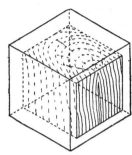

Fig. 834.—Iron-cased Wood Plug.

hole; but if the plug is too thick the force exerted by the screw is effectually resisted, and the plug does not lock, and, moreover, the larger the plug the more in proportion will be the shrinkage in drying. The plug, therefore, should bear an exact relation to the size of the screw. A $\frac{1}{2}$-in. or $\frac{5}{8}$-in. plug is quite large enough for a twelves or fourteens screw. It has already been pointed out that wedge-shaped flat plugs cannot

Fig. 835.—Kitchen Table.

exert any holding power, neither can a tapering round plug. Fig. 830 is a section showing the best form of round plug; Fig. 831 is a bad form, but one that is often ignorantly used.

DRILLING HOLES FOR PLUGS.

For driving wedge-shaped plugs into joints only clearing out is necessary, but for the other kinds the holes must be made carefully. A suitable drill for the job is made of steel to the shape shown in Fig. 832, the stem being $\frac{1}{2}$ in. in diameter, and the point $\frac{5}{8}$ in. wide by $\frac{3}{16}$ in. thick. This drill is used by striking it smartly with the hammer, turning it slightly between the strokes; by its use holes can be made in the bricks in less time than it would take to find a joint. Each hole should be drilled to

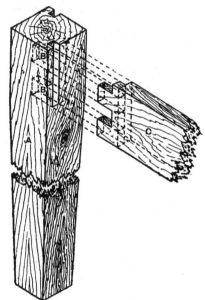

Fig. 836.—Table Leg and Rail.

a depth of about 2 in., so that the plugs have a solid hole in the bricks of $1\frac{1}{2}$ in.

FIXING PLUGS IN CHIMNEY BREASTS, ETC.

All plugs and woodwork should be kept at least 9 in. from fireplaces or flues, and if a plug is required within the prescribed area, it must be made of lead (Fig. 833). If a gas bracket has to be fixed on the chimney breast or opposite a flue, the wood block must be encased tightly in a $\frac{1}{2}$-in. cast-iron box or $4\frac{1}{2}$-in. cube (outside dimensions), the grain of the wood being vertical (see Fig. 834). If these boxes are to be fixed after the walls are up, they must be fastened with iron wedges, then made tight all round with good mortar.

MAKING KITCHEN TABLE FRAMING.

The kitchen table shown in general view by Fig. 835 is 4 ft. 6 in. long by 3 ft. wide,

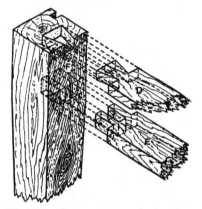

Fig. 837.—Leg and Drawer Framing.

taking the measurements of the top. The top is made by ploughing and cross-tongueing together (see pp. 191 and 192) four or more boards, and whilst the joints are setting in suitable cramps, the framing is prepared of sound yellow pine. The legs are 2 ft. 4 in. long, diminished from 3¾ in. square at the top to 2¾ in. square at the bottom, finished. A distance of 6 in. from the top is left square. Fig. 836 shows a part elevation of one of the legs A, mortised for the rail C. The mortises B B are set in ½ in. from the front edge, and are 1¾ in. long, ⅝ in. wide, and about 2 in. deep. The haunchings are about ⅜ in. deep. The faces where the rails come are also served like this. The face where the drawer comes, really the front of the table, is illustrated in Fig. 837, where D is a dovetail received by a mortise 1¾ in. long, 1⅛ in. wide at its widest portion, 1 in. at the neck, and sunk ¾ in. into the top of the leg, which brings it flush; E goes in a double mortise, 1¼ in. long and ½ in. wide, and 1¾ in. deep, F showing nest space for drawer. The side rails are 5 in. deep and 1¼ in. thick, with barefaced tenons, as shown in the elevation of the rail, C (Fig. 836). When these are

inserted in the mortises, the shoulders are inside. The top and bottom rails for the drawer are 3 in. by ¾ in., and 3 in. by 1¼ in. respectively, and must be dovetailed and double tenoned on both ends, as illustrated in Figs. 837 and 838. The dimensions of all these tenons and dovetails must correspond with those already given for the mortises. In planing up the side rails, only the face and two edges need be tried; the inside faces will do if roughly jack planed over. Prepare the runners and guides as shown in Fig. 839; the runner B is 3 in. wide and 1¼ in. thick, and tenoned and cut to the shape indicated on plan; the guide F is simply a 1-in. square fillet nailed on to the top of the runner as seen in section. Fig. 838 shows clearly the position of these guides, one of which is fixed at each end of the table. The runner is mortised and tenoned into the leg and back rail at one end, and also into the leg and bottom rail of the drawer at the other. In the latter case it is flush at top and bottom. In Fig. 838, A indicates table legs; B, end rail; C, side rail; D, rail over drawer; E, drawer runner; F, drawer guide; G, wooden pins; H, blocks; and J, draw or stop on bottom rail. With brace and bit bore ⅜-in. holes

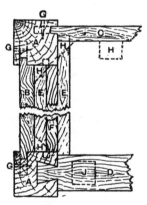

Fig. 838.—Part Plan of Table with Top Removed.

G, G, G (Fig. 838), through the centre of all the side-rail mortises in the legs, to the depth shown. Carefully drive all the side rails into their respective places, and, when the shoulders are up, mark with a lead pencil down the holes their position on each of the tenons. Knock the framing to pieces again, and bore ⅜-in. holes through the tenons where indicated in pencil, but a little out of line with those in the mortises, and

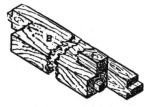

Fig. 839.—Drawer Runner and Guide.

towards the shoulders of the tenons. This draw-boring (see also p. 204) has the effect of pulling up the shoulders when the pins pass through the tenons.

PUTTING TOGETHER KITCHEN TABLE.

After cleaning off, sufficient guidance in putting the framing together may be obtained by consulting Figs. 836 to 839. Care must be taken that the framing is put together square. When this is done, in the angles glue 2-in. blocks of the shape shown by dotted lines at H H H (Fig. 838). The stuff for these blocks must be exceptionally dry and properly squared up, and then ripped down diagonally. Two bits of mahogany about 2 in. square and ¼ in. thick must also be glued and sprigged on to each

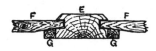

Fig. 840.—Section of Stiffening Rail.

end of the bottom rail of the drawer, to form stops for the latter (see J, Fig. 838, in dotted lines through rail D). The making of the drawer is quite possible to the worker who has mastered the process of dovetailing fully described in pp. 211 to 218; later, more instructions on drawer making will be given in connection with specimens of cabinetwork. For the present, it is necessary only to give the size of drawer, and explain the section represented by Fig. 840. The total width of the table drawer when finished will be 3 ft. 8 in.; front, 3 in. deep by ⅞ in. thick; back, 2¼ in. deep by ⅝ in. thick;

sides, 3 in. deep by ½ in. thick; and bottom, ½ in. thick. The depth from front to back will be about 2 ft. 6 in. In Fig. 840, E is the stiffening rail, F the drawer bot-

Fig. 841.—Table Top, Rail, and Rounded Button.

tom, and G the glued blocks. As this drawer is of an unusual width, the stiffening rail E (Fig. 840) must be introduced in the centre. It is 2¼ in. wide and 1 in. thick full, dovetailed flush under the front of the drawer, and nailed under the back. The drawer bottom will be bevelled, as at F F, into plough grooves on both edges, and also all round the drawer. Blocks, as

Fig. 842.—Table Top, Rail, and Square Button.

shown at G G, will also be glued all round the angles. Now remove the wood cramps off the top and plane it up, first the under side, but only as far from the edges as is necessary to give it a solid bed on the framing. The upper face of the top must be traversed—that is, planed across the grain. When the jack plane, held on its side obliquely across the top, shows no daylight

Fig. 843.—Square Button for Securing Table Top.

under it, that is a fairly satisfactory indication that the top is pretty level. When the traversing is done, try the top up, and cut and shoot the edges to the sizes required —4 ft. 6 in. by 3 ft. This will allow 1¼ in. to overhang the framing all round. Now lay the top on the bench, bottom side upper-most, and reversing the framing (which, of course, has been shot all round at the top), place it in position, and proceed to block and screw the two together. The screws must pass diagonally through the side rails into the top, and the stuff is to be scooped out to form countersinks for their heads.

Fig. 844.—Levelling Table Legs.

The blocks must be glued and rubbed into the angles until they are firm. Turn the table on to its legs, smooth, and then sand-paper the top across the grain, and the table is finished. The corners can be rounded and a thumb mould stuck on the edge if preferred. In Fig. 841 is shown a section of another method of putting on the top ; the oak button C works on a screw pivot that enters the top A, and the rebated portion of the button turns into a plough groove in the

rails B. The same method is shown in the section (Fig. 842), where, however, the but-ton (Fig. 843) is of a different shape, and the screw could with advantage be $\frac{3}{8}$ in. longer.

LEVELLING TABLE LEGS.

Below is described the best method of levelling such pieces of furniture as tables and chairs so that they stand firmly on the floor without rocking. It is almost impos-sible to guarantee that a table shall stand perfectly firm, and in making it is prefer-able to allow a small piece on the end of each leg to provide against any accident prior to gluing up. Fig. 844 shows a plain table packed up to be perfectly level, and ready to be scribed and cut. In the first place the table must stand upon a fairly straight and level surface, and in the case of a large piece of furniture, pieces of board laid on the floor at proper distances, and levelled from one to the other, will be found sufficient. Pack up each leg until a spirit level placed on the table top proves the top to be level. This having been done, a pair of sharp compasses is set to a dis-tance equal to the distance of the bottom of the shortest leg from the floor surface, or from the floor surface to a point found by measuring off the desired height from the top of the table ; with the compass scribe each of the legs plainly, as shown in Fig. 844. Now lay the table in a suitable position to saw off squarely the superfluous material from the bottom of each leg in turn, which will complete the task.

WORKSHOP FURNITURE.

WOODWORKER'S TOOL CHEST.

THE woodworker's first job, when he has attained sufficient skill, should be the construction of a good tool chest. The work

many cases the tool chest is simply a box, with a sliding till or two, into which the tools are thrown anyhow. An ideal tool chest provides a place for everything, and then everything can be in its place. The

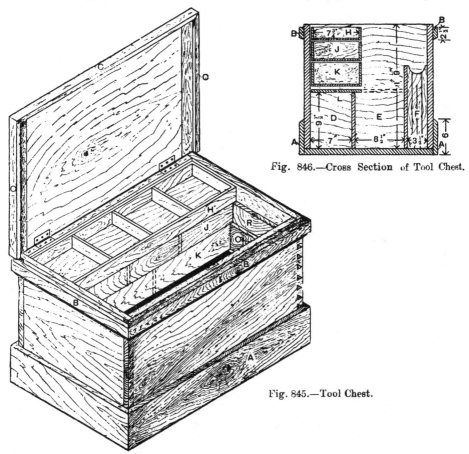

Fig. 846.—Cross Section of Tool Chest.

Fig. 845.—Tool Chest.

will afford him good practice in the use of tools, and the chest, when finished, will enable him to keep them under lock and key when they are not in use. In too

chest illustrated by Fig. 845 will be found to fulfil these conditions, and in this an attempt has been made to eradicate faults common to others. The letter references

17

in Figs. 845 to 847 are : —A, bottom plinth ;
B, top plinth ; C, rim round lid ; D, compartment for bead-planes, plough, etc. ;
E, compartment for various tools, planes,
etc. ; F, compartment for saws ; K, bottom
till ; J, second till ; H, top till ; L, sliding-board to cover compartment E ; M, cleats
to hold division between E and F ; N, cleats
to hold division between D and E ; P, runners for sliding-board L ; R, runners for
tills ; S, runners for tills K. The length of
the chest must be sufficient to accommodate a rip-saw, so the chest is 33 in. long
internally ; and if it is made 20 in. wide by
21 in. deep, it will be found convenient for
all purposes. For the outside case white
deal not less than 1 in. thick is used. In
gluing up the front, back, and ends, to
obtain the necessary width the joints
should be tongued or dowelled, the former
being the better method (see pp. 191 and
192). In dovetailing the framework of the
chest make the pins small, and have them
not more than 1½ in. apart ; take care that
the joints in front and back do not come immediately opposite those in the ends, or
at some future time the chest may break
in two. Fig. 846 is a transverse section through the chest, Figs. 847 to 850
showing details of construction. The
plinths A and B run all round the chest, and
are 6 in. and 2½ in. wide respectively, and
1 in. thick, with the top edge of A and the
bottom of B finished with a plain bevel ;
the top edge of a ¼-in. bead being worked
on it also. The plinths may be mitred at
the corners, but it is better to dovetail
them, and so obtain extra strength and good
appearance. The plinth B is kept down
about ¾ in. from the top of the chest to
form a rebate for the lid to shut upon. The
bottom of the chest is formed with boards
1 in. thick, tongued and grooved, and
nailed on crossways—that is, the grain runs
from front to back of the chest. The lid
also is of 1 in. deal, with the joints tongued
and grooved, and the ends clamped (see
pp. 208 and 209). It overhangs the chest
all round about ⅟₁₆ in., and is hung with a
pair of strong brass butts (see p. 298), and
the self-acting spring lock is put on ; then
the rim C can be dovetailed together at
the corners, and nailed to front and ends.

This should result in a good fit where the
rim of the lid meets the plinth B. This
finishes the skeleton of the chest.

Tool Chest Partitions, Etc.

For the inside fittings of the tool chest
use good yellow deal or pine, which can be
finished by staining, although sometimes a
more fancy wood is used. From Fig. 846
it is seen that the chest is divided in its
width into three parts : —D, for bead-planes,
plough, etc. ; this is 7 in. wide, and is
covered by the sliding tills ; E, for miscellaneous tools, best planes, or anything
which is not in everyday use ; and F (3½ in.
wide inside) is the saw till. These are
divided by the two partitions shown, that
between D and E being 9 in. high, and
that between E and F 14 in. The three tills
H, J, and K slide to and fro to give access
to compartments beneath, and when in
place at the back of the chest form a covering for compartment D ; and a sliding board
beneath the tills, when pulled out as shown
by dotted lines in Fig. 846, covers compartment E. The bench-planes, etc., which are

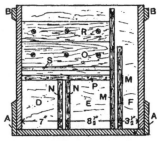

Fig. 847.—End of Tool Chest with Cleats and
Runners.

in everyday use, can be packed away on the
sliding board between the tills and the highest partition. Fig. 847 shows one end of the
chest with the cleats about 1 in. wide by
½ in. thick ; between these the partitions fit.
The cleats holding the partition between E
and F are fixed first, ½ in. apart, and are as
shown at M M (Fig. 847), the one nearer
the back of the chest being continued
nearly to the top, the other, nearer the
front, stopping at the same height as the
partition, namely 14 in. The cleats N must
be 8½ in. high from the bottom of the chest,

and $\frac{3}{4}$ in. apart. The back partitions having been placed in position, fix the ledges P, with their top edges $9\frac{1}{2}$ in. from the bottom of the chest; they run from the back to the long upright cleat M, and on them works the sliding board L, 9 in. by $\frac{3}{4}$ in.; this is clamped at the ends for the sake of strength and to make it slide more easily. It

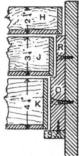

Fig. 848 —Section of Tool Chest Till Runners.

must be a good fit endways to avoid jamming against the ends of the chest. The runners for the tills (see Fig. 848) are made long enough to reach from the back of the chest to the long upright cleat M (Fig. 847), and should be of hard wood. The principal piece R, which forms the runners for the two top tills, is $7\frac{1}{2}$ in. wide by 1 in. thick, rebated to half its thickness at O for a depth of $3\frac{1}{4}$ in. A piece of hard wood S, $1\frac{1}{2}$ in. by $\frac{1}{2}$ in. is screwed on to the thick edge of R, and forms the runner for the bottom till. These runners can be fixed in position one on each end of the chest, leaving about $\frac{1}{8}$ in. clearance between the bottoms and the top of sliding board L. The partition between compartments E and F can be made and fitted between the cleats M M; along its upper side is a strip of $1\frac{1}{2}$ in. by $\frac{1}{2}$ in. deal, cut to fit between the cleats on each end of the chest, fixed level with the top edge on the side nearest the front of the chest and packed off about $\frac{1}{16}$ in. The slot thus formed can be used as a rack for squares, the stocks resting on top of the partition, and the blades hanging down out of the way inside the saw till.

RACKS FOR SAWS AND CHISELS.

The saw racks in the chest, as shown in Figs. 849 and 850, are 14 in. long, $3\frac{1}{2}$ in.

wide, and 1 in. thick, shaped at the top ends. Each has three slots, or, rather, saw kerfs, and in one rack (Fig. 849) the middle kerf runs from the top to within 3 in. of the bottom, the others stopping the same distance from the bottom, and about $1\frac{1}{2}$ in. from the top. In the other rack (Fig. 850) the middle slot is stopped at both top and bottom, the others being open at the top end. These two racks are fixed at about 8 in. from each end by screwing through the horn at the top of each to the front of the chest. The partition being then put into its place, screws can be put through it into each saw-rack, which will hold all in place. When placing the saws in the racks, the points are inserted in the closed slots of racks, and the handle ends dropped into the open slots, two saws pointing one way and one the opposite way. To take chisels, etc., a piece of hard wood, 2 ft. long, 1 in. square, with a series of notches 1 in. apart cut into it wide enough to take the tools, can be screwed to the front of the chest just above the top of the partition; this leaves an equal space at each end to allow the hand to be inserted to remove saws from the rack. The handles of the larger chisels will be just inside the front of the chest, convenient for withdrawal when wanted for use, and the blades will hang out of the way in the saw till.

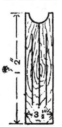

Fig. 849.—Saw Rack.   Fig. 850.—Saw Rack.

TOOL CHEST TILLS, ETC.

The three sliding tills for the inside of the chest only remain. They will all be 9 in. wide outside, but varied in depth, as shown by Fig. 848, on which dimensions are marked. They should be of $\frac{3}{4}$-in. stuff, with $\frac{1}{2}$-in. bottoms and divisions, the rims dovetailed together, and the fronts and back rebated to receive the bottoms, the grain of which should run across the width of tills ; and at each end the bottom should be of hard wood. The divisions should be

pulled forward and its contents exposed without the necessity of touching the others. A strong iron handle on each end of chest will now make it complete.

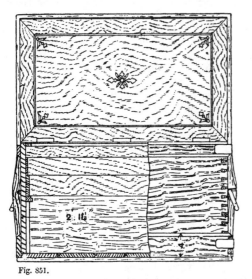

Fig. 851.

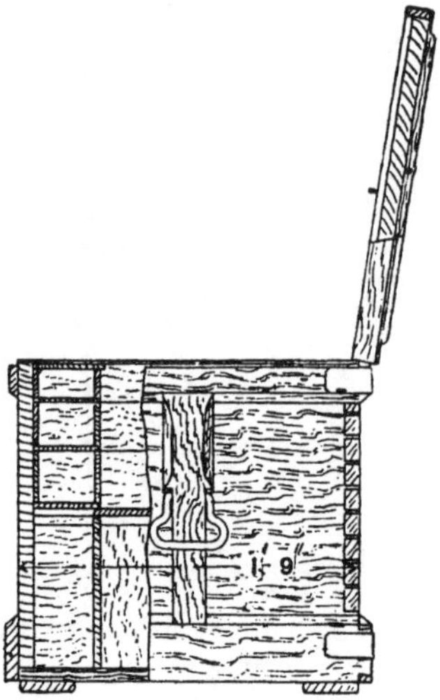

Fig. 852.

Figs. 851 and 852.—Elevation and Sections of Tool Chest.

trenched into the sides, forming in K, J, and H two, three, and four compartments respectively. One of the bottom divisions should be fitted up for the brace and bits, with racks for the bits fitted round the brace. Other divisions can be fitted with racks for small chisels, gouges, gimlets, bradawls, and various other tools, the aim throughout being to have a place for all, so that nothing can roll about and get damaged. Turn-buttons to take the tenon and dovetail saws can be screwed on to the under-side of the lid, so that when it is closed they will be in position between the top till and the front of chest. The purpose of the cleat M, running up higher than its fellow, is to stop the tills from coming into collision with the stocks of squares when in their rack. The sliding-board L can be grasped underneath with the fingers when it is desired to draw it forward, and it should have a couple of thumb-holes cut in its top as a means of pushing it back. Each till should have a pair of flush-rings inserted in the front, so that either can be

ANOTHER TOOL CHEST.

The carcase, plinths, and lid of the chest illustrated by Fig. 851 should be of good

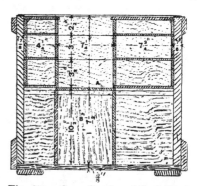

Fig. 853.—Cross Section of Tool Chest.

clean pine, and the fittings may be of mahogany. Fig. 852 is a part end elevation and part cross section. To make the carcase, plane up two pieces of 1-in. pine, 2 ft. 11½ in. by 19½ in., and two pieces, 1 ft. 9 in. by 19½ in., for the sides and ends, glue-jointing if the required width cannot otherwise be obtained. Dovetail together, using rather large pins, and spacing them at about 1½-in. centres. Glue up and screw

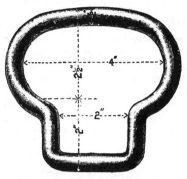

Fig. 854.—Tool Chest Handle.

on the bottom, which is of ¾-in. tongued and grooved matchboarding. Clean up the outside edges of the bottom boards level with the sides and ends, and fix the plinth, which may be dovetailed at the corners the opposite way to the sides. The runners at the ends for the trays are shown on the left-hand half of Fig. 851. At the top for 2½ in. the end is covered with mahogany veneer (veneering will be explained later); below this a piece of 3-in. by ⅜-in. mahogany is fixed to form a runner for the top trays, and under this a piece of 3½-in. by ⅜-in. mahogany is fixed to support the second pair of trays. To carry the bottom trays, a piece of mahogany 1¼ in. square is used, and this also has a ⅜-in. rebate for the board, which slides to cover the well in the centre of the chest A (Fig. 853); this figure shows on a larger scale a section through the chest. The top edge of the chest is next levelled with a plane, toothed, and a ⅞-in. by ¼-in. facing glued on and mitred at the corners. When dry, clean off level inside and outside. The handles are of ½-in. round iron bent to the shape shown by Fig. 854, and welded at the bottom straight part, not butt jointed. The handle carriers are of hard wood, and shaped as in Fig. 855. The safest way of securing the handles is by means of screws, with the heads on the inside of the chest. The ⅝-in. runner pieces inside

may be left loose until the screws have been put in for fixing the handles. Some chests have loops of rope for handles, but the metal ones are better and stronger. The handles should be kept sufficiently high up the ends of the chest to prevent any tendency to turning over if at any time it should be lifted with a crane.

Fig. 855.—Tool Chest Handle Carrier.

TOOL CHEST LID.

For the lid a piece of pine 2 ft. 11½ in. by 1 ft. 9 in. by ⅞ in. must be prepared. In some cases the ends are clamped, but the lid will stand better if properly cross-battened. When the lid has been planed, the inside should be roughed with the toothing plane and two or three battens screwed across the grain on the other side to prevent warping. The inside can then be veneered with a centre panel and a banding about 2½ in. wide, as shown by Fig. 851 (as previously stated, veneering will be explained later). Use Spanish mahogany veneer for the centre panel, and a light or dark fancy wood veneer for the line, which may be about ⅜ in. wide, and for the

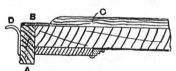

Fig. 856.—Section through Front of Tool Chest Lid.

centre and corner inlays. Some workers veneer the centre, and have a margin about ¼ in. thick, as shown on the underside of Fig. 856, a planted moulding being used for covering the edge of the veneer. When the glue is thoroughly dry the battens may be removed from the back, and the mahogany plinth A (Fig.856) screwed to the front and the ends; the parts seen when the lid is open should be polished.

Pieces of 1¼-in. by ⅛-in. hoop iron B (Fig. 856) can now be screwed round the top of the lid to protect the edges, and the space between filled in with ⅜-in. deal boards C, screwed across the grain of the

Fig. 857.—Top Tray of Tool Chest.

lid; the ends can be rounded down to the hoop iron to strengthen it and also to prevent warping. The lid can now be hung with three 2¾-in. by ¾-in. brass butt hinges (see p. 298) as shown in Fig. 851. A strong lock can then be let in the front, and a sash lift D (Fig. 856) screwed to the plinth at the front. Fig. 852 shows that the top plinth at the back is kept above that of the sides and front to support the lid when open. In addition to the lock, one or two holes should be bored through the lid at both ends and countersunk in the hoop iron, so that the lid can be screwed down for travelling, etc. The outside corners of the chest should be protected with angle plates on the plinth, as shown on the right-hand side of Figs. 851 and 852, and these may be made by bending pieces of 1½-in. No. 16 B.W.G. iron 6 in. long to a right angle, punching the holes and countersinking for No. 10 screws.

Inside Fittings of Tool Chest.

For the interior fittings of the chest a small nest of drawers at the back is sometimes used, but some prefer trays, as shown, as the drawers are liable to stick if a tool gets misplaced. Also they take

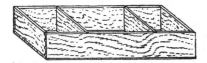

Fig. 858.—Second Tray of Tool Chest.

a lot of material and labour, and the drawers are more difficult to secure than trays when the chest is packed. The arrangement of the interior is shown in section by Fig. 853, which also gives the size of the trays. These should be of ⅜-in. mahogany, dovetailed together like a drawer, the top trays being fitted with lids, as shown by Fig. 857; the total depth over all is 2¼ in. Fig. 858 shows one of the lower trays, and these do not have lids. The cross divisions in the trays may be made to meet requirements, but the following plan of dividing is a good one:— Top tray at the back, space 1 ft. 4 in. long at the centre with divisions about 8 in. at each end; second tray, the same as the top; and the bottom tray, one division in the centre. For the narrow trays, the top

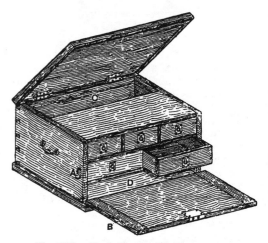

Fig. 859.—Tool Chest with Drawers.

one may be divided the same as the top one at the back; the second tray, with a partition 7½ in. from one end; and the bottom tray, with a division 10½ in. from the opposite end to the tray above. The space in the chest below the trays may be divided longitudinally into three compartments (Fig. 853). The boards to form the divisions are fixed to an upright piece of wood ⅝ in. thick, B, secured to the ends of the chest. This part of the chest is just deep enough to take small planes placed on end. A saw rack may with advantage be fitted in the space under the front trays, and the centre space is covered with a board A, which slides back under the back trays. The inside of the chest should be french-polished, and the outside should have three or four coats of good paint.

PACKING TOOL CHEST FOR TRANSIT.

In packing the chest for travelling, the bottom divisions should be filled first, and the heaviest tools placed in the centre portion: the slide can then be pulled over and fixed with a small screw at one end. The trays can then be filled, and secured either by means of strips fixed across the ends, or by filling the space between them with soft material that will not damage the polish. The lids of the top trays can then be fastened by placing across them at the ends two strips that will just fill up the space between the tops of the trays and

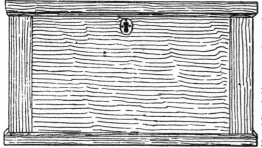

Fig. 860.—Front View of Tool Chest.

the lid, when the latter can be locked and screwed.

SMALL TOOL CHEST WITH DRAWERS.

For the small tool chest with drawers, shown in several views by Fig. 859, a handy size is 1 ft. 9 in. by 1 ft. 2 in. by 1 ft. deep. The sides, ends, bottom, and top are of red deal finishing about ¾ in. thick. The divisions are of ½-in. stuff, and the drawer fronts of ⅝-in. stuff. The sides, backs, and bottoms of the drawers are of ⅜-in. stuff, but of course these dimensions may be varied to meet requirements. Fig. 859 shows that the front is hinged on to the bottom, so as to drop down and allow of ready access to the drawers. To keep the front from twisting and warping, it must be clamped as shown, and when the front is closed up it is secured to the lid by a lock (see also Fig. 860). In addition, a hook A (Figs. 859 and 861) and eye B (Fig.

861) may be used. The bottom is finished off with a plinth, which if rebated as illustrated in the section (Fig. 862) will have extra strength. The lid should be stiffened by a 1¼-in. by ½-in. rim. The

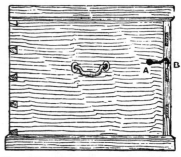

Fig. 861.—End View of Tool Chest.

well C and the space D under the drawers will be found very useful for large tools, etc.

UTILISING TOOL CHEST LIDS.

The insides of tool chest lids are adapted readily to hold hand saws and tenon saws, the ends of which are held in wooden clips as shown at A (Fig. 863). The handle can be fastened by means of a button B, this method being just as suitable for hand saws as for the tenon saw shown. When the button is moved to the position shown by the dotted lines, it will allow of the

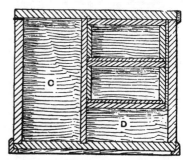

Fig. 862.—Cross Section of Tool Chest.

saw being taken out. Figs. 864 and 865 are enlarged views of the clip and button respectively.

ROOMY TOOL CHEST.

A roomy chest of somewhat different design from any yet illustrated is shown in transverse section by Fig. 866, whilst Fig. 867 is a half longitudinal section. Dimensions are left to the maker. The stuff for the carcase should be ⅝ in. thick,

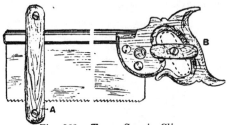

Fig. 863.—Tenon Saw in Clips.

and the corners are dovetailed. At the top a rebate is run round the front edge and the two ends, for the lid to fit over; but for convenience in hingeing, the back

Fig. 864.—Clip for End of Tenon Saw.

edge is left square. Round the bottom edge internally, a plough groove is made to receive the bottom, which is strengthened by a hardwood mitred plinth, 3 in. by ½ in., glued and nailed on. The sides and ends of the lid are ⅞ in. thick, and the top of

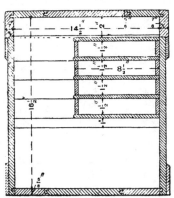

Fig. 866.—Cross Section of Tool Chest.

the chest is thickened up to this extent by pieces glued and nailed on. The top of the lid and the bottom of the chest are framed up with flush panels for strength,

the lid frame being haunch tenoned together. A small quirked bead is run round the inner edge to hide any shrinkage of the panel, which is not glued in; this bead is mitred at the corners, and the tongue on the outside edge is made flush with the under-side. The sides and ends of the lid are dovetailed together, and to prevent the plough groove on the top edge and the rebate on the bottom edge cropping out, it is partly mitred as shown in Fig. 868. Two or three pairs of strong brass hinges attach the lid to the chest, and straps of leather or webbing are fitted to prevent it opening to more than an angle of (say) 10° or 15° beyond the vertical. A good lever box-lock should be fitted to secure the box when shut, and iron or brass lift-

Fig. 865.—Clip for Handle of Tenon Saw.

ing handles should be screwed on at each end. The outside of the chest is usually painted black and varnished, whilst the inside is usually finished with clear shellac varnish.

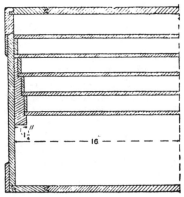

Fig. 867.—Longitudinal Section of Tool Chest.

TOOL CHEST TILLS.

The chest contains small sliding drawers or tills of different lengths to hold gouges, chisels, bits, bradawls, etc. (see Fig. 869). These tills are made of ⅜-in. thick material, the corners are dovetailed, and the fronts are of mahogany or other hard wood, with flush ring handles, or with knobs, or, in rough work, with centre-bit holes.

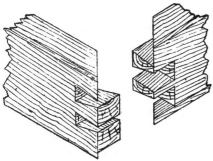

Fig. 868.—Mitred and Dovetailed Joint.

The bottom may be screwed on and worked to a projecting bead in front. The bottom drawers are often deeper than the rest. The top till has a hinged lid. A fastening arrangement for the tills is shown in Figs. 870 and 871. When in the position shown, the till is free, but if it is pushed back and the buttons at the sides are turned to enter slots in the runners, motion is prevented. To hold down the lid of the top till, and to prevent the tills falling from the runners when the chest is inverted, two blocks A B (Fig. 872) are screwed inside the lid of the chest; these just rest on the till lid when the chest is closed. To prevent having gouges rolling or sliding about in the tills, each tool is fitted into a plough groove (see Figs. 869 and 873), and the handles of the tools may point in alternate directions, but

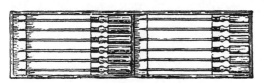

Fig. 869.—Tool Chest Till with Chisels.

the drawback is danger to the fingers when withdrawing a tool, owing to the nearness of the sharp edges of the tools on each side. Other tools may be provided for similarly.

ARRANGEMENT OF TOOLS IN CHEST.

Fig. 872 shows how the lid is utilised for various tools, and Fig. 874 shows a small block screwed to the body of the lid, carrying a boxwood button holding a try square blade in position. The stock of the square is passed under the block A (Fig. 872), and at C one corner of the blade passes into a

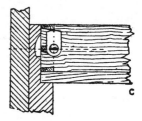

Fig. 870.—Elevation of Till Fastening.

little slot in another block, which also receives the end of the trammel staff. Fig. 875 is a section through the pincer holder. Between the jaws a small block is fixed to prevent movement in the plane of the lid. Other tools that lie flat may be accommodated similarly on the vertical front of the chest, but must be arranged to permit the sliding of the tills. The bigger tools, such as planes, mallet, etc., are secured in the bottom of the chest by means resembling those already described. For instance, Figs. 876 and 877 show plan and elevation of a notched block to hold the mallet, which is indicated by dotted lines; and if shallow partitions are fitted longitudinally along the bottom of the chest, the arrangement is complete. A plane laid between these partitions is fixed in place

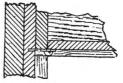

Fig. 871.—Plan of Till Fastening.

if at each end a small cross-partition rises to the height of the plane and has a button attached in the same way as, for instance, in Fig. 874. Before making the fittings for the bottom of the chest, ascertain that the tills above the tool will not prevent its removal.

Fig. 872.—Tool Chest Lid Fitted up.

SIMPLE TOOL CHEST.

The simple chest shown in longitudinal section by Fig. 878 must be long enough to take the rip saw, and it is as light as possible consistent with strength. Fig. 879 is a cross section. The yellow pine is $\frac{7}{8}$ in. thick for the body, 1 in. for the lid, and $\frac{5}{8}$ in. for the outside plinth and facings ; the bottom is of $\frac{3}{4}$-in. red pine. The plinth

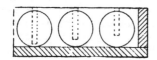

Fig. 873.—Cross Section of Part of Lid.

has an ovolo moulding on it, but an ogee moulding is very common. The top facing is in two parts, one being screwed to the edge of the lid and rounded on the top ; the other one, upon which are run a bead and a chamfer, is merely nailed to the box. The body of the box is dovetailed and glued, but the plinth and top facing are mitred and nailed. The bottom has ploughed and cross-tongued joints water-

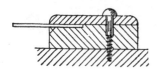

Fig. 874.—Try-square Holder.

proofed by painting with white lead. The top is clamped to prevent warping, and the facings are screwed on after the lid has

been fitted to the size of the box. Battens of red or yellow pine, well painted, are screwed to the under-side of the bottom, to keep the box clear of wet. Fig. 879 shows the inside arrangement. At the back, a space for smoothing planes, rebate planes,

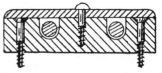

Fig. 875.—Holder for Pincers.

casements, etc., is formed by nailing fillets to the ends of the box, to which the piece of pine A is screwed. Narrow fillets are nailed to the ends of the box outside of the

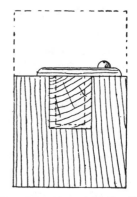

Fig. 876.—Elevation of Mallet Holder.

piece A, and the piece B is screwed to them. A space is thus provided for the tenon saws and hatchet. The method of fixing the hand saws to the inside of the lid is shown by dotted lines in Fig. 878,

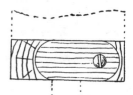

Fig. 877.—Plan of Mallet Holder.

and is on the same principle as that already described. A piece of wood, the thickness of the saw handle, is fitted in the hole, and screwed to the lid. A piece of sheet brass to form a long button then is screwed to the block of wood; this button when turned round as in Fig. 878 prevents the handle of the saw from leaving the lid. The hardwood clip to hold the point of the saw is as seen in Fig. 864, except that there is no recess for the back as there shown. The method of packing the chisels and gouges is seen in Fig. 879.

than mortising the holes. The tray c (Figs. 878 and 879) is a box the whole length of the inside, lap dovetailed at the front and common dovetailed at the back. It is divided into various compartments (two small ones and a large one will be found very handy) by thin pieces of pine, either raggled into the front and back or merely butted and nailed. The bottom, which is $\frac{5}{8}$ in. thick, is screwed up. It is very com-

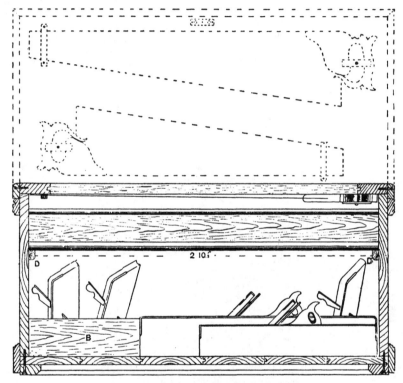

Fig. 878.—Section of Simple Tool Chest.

A small fillet, with a strip of leather glued to the top edge, is nailed to the bottom, and a thin piece of pine, projecting about 1 in. above the leather, is nailed to the fillet. This receives the points of the chisels and gouges. Another piece, with various sizes of holes cut out, is screwed about 3 in. or 4 in. up, to keep the top part steady. Fig. 880 shows the piece with the holes checked out and a thin piece screwed to the front; this is much easier

mon to have a hardwood flap on the tray, as shown, but this can be dispensed with at will. A back stile is screwed to the back of the tray, and the flap is hinged to it. Fillets D are screwed to the ends of the box, on which the tray slides to and fro.

TOOL CABINET.

A useful tool cabinet with panelled doors and three drawers is illustrated by Fig. 881. It would have a neat appearance if made in oak or other hard wood and polished; or even if made of deal, if stained and varnished. The leading dimensions figured in the vertical section (Fig. 882), and in the horizontal section (Fig. 883) are only suggestive. The sides, top, and bottom are of $\frac{3}{4}$-in. material, grooved and tongued together as indicated in Fig. 884. The sides should also be rebated to receive the back, and grooved for shelf as shown in 883 and 884. The two divisions (separating the drawers) should be grooved into the shelf and bottom as shown. The back can be formed of three boards $\frac{5}{8}$ in. thick, its upper part being sawn and smoothed to the shape shown in Fig. 881. The front edges and ends of

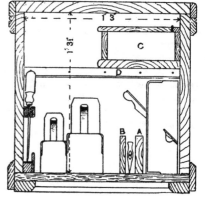

Fig. 879.—Cross Section of Simple Tool Chest

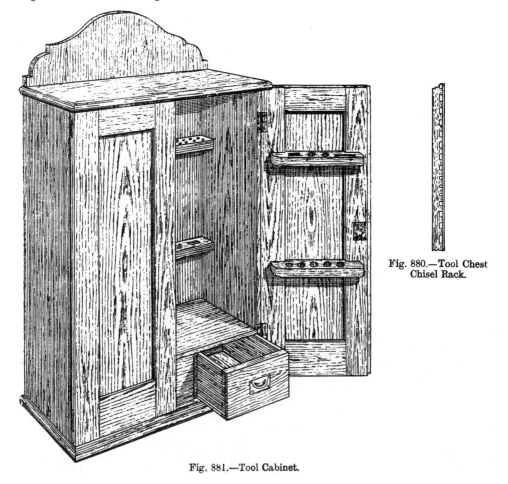

Fig. 881.—Tool Cabinet.

Fig. 880.—Tool Chest Chisel Rack.

the top and bottom may be rounded. Fit all the parts of the case together, and finally secure them by gluing and nailing. Wood about $\frac{7}{8}$ in. thick will be required for the stiles and rails of the doors; the panels may be about $\frac{3}{8}$ in. thick. The doors should be mortised and tenoned together and ploughed to receive panels;

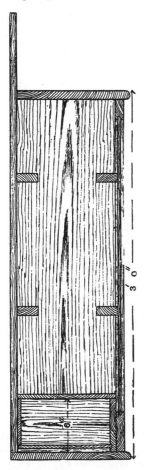

Fig. 882.—Vertical Section of Tool Cabinet.

they should be finished by being glued, wedged, planed off, fitted to the case, and rebated together (see Figs. 881 and 883), after which they can be hung with 3-in. butts. (Instructions on building doors will be given later.) The drawers should be properly dovetailed together; $\frac{3}{4}$-in. stuff

will do for the fronts, and $\frac{1}{2}$-in. for the sides, backs, and bottoms. Brass flush drop handles will be best for the drawer

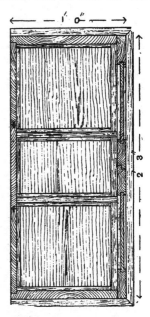

Fig. 883.—Horizontal Section of Tool Cabinet.

fronts. Two small bolts secure the door on the left, and there is a $2\frac{1}{2}$-in. cut cupboard lock on the right-hand door. The cabinet could be fixed to a wall with four holdfasts, or it might rest upon a couple

Fig. 884.—Housing for Sides, etc., of Tool Cabinet.

of brackets or other similar arrangement. The inside can be fitted with racks, etc., according to requirements.

TOOL CUPBOARD.

The tool cupboard illustrated by Fig. 885 is a modification of the cabinet just described. A useful size would be about 2 ft. 6 in. wide, 3 ft. high, and 11 in. deep; but the dimensions may be varied. One-inch material will be suitable for the sides, bottom, and top, and also for the stiles and rails of the doors. The panels of the doors should be of $\frac{1}{2}$-in. stuff, and the back of $\frac{5}{8}$-in. thick boarding, grooved and tongued;

TOOL CABINET AND BENCH COMBINED.

Fig. 886 is a perspective view of a tool cabinet and bench combined, which will be found very useful and convenient by workers in a small way who have not the advantage of a workshop. The suggested dimensions are: Length, 4 ft.; breadth 2 ft.; height to bench top, 2 ft. 7 in. For any bench the height usually remains the same, but length and breadth may both be varied, and where space allows it a larger bench is

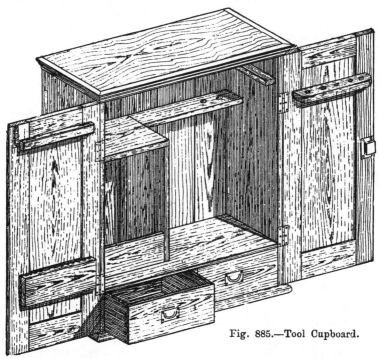

Fig. 885.—Tool Cupboard.

matchboarding will answer the purpose. The shelves and drawer fronts may be of $\frac{3}{4}$-in. stuff, and the sides, back, and bottom of the drawers of $\frac{1}{2}$-in. stuff; these are finished sizes. Forms for racks are shown; these can be fixed where desired. The compartment on the left is for planes, etc. Other arrangements will suggest themselves. Some tool cabinets, made of costly hard woods and excellent examples of high class cabinet makers' work, form furniture of a decorative character which does not suggest their purpose.

generally found more convenient. It is handy to have at each end a shallow cupboard, as shown, and upon the doors are screwed rails and racks for holding tools The cupboard in the front will be found very useful for storing work, materials, and the larger tools; a portion of it might be partitioned off with shelves or drawers. To give the bench stability, four legs, 3 in. by $2\frac{1}{2}$ in., are connected in pairs at each end with cross-rails top and bottom, E and F; these should be dovetailed together. The front framing and doors should be made of

1-in. or 1¼-in. stuff, with panels about ½ in. thick. The two stiles of the front frame go right to the under-side of the bench top, and are fixed to the two front legs by screws from the inside, as indicated in Fig. 887.

end and also to the cheek by screws, as shown in Fig. 889. The bottom of the cupboard may be formed of ¾-in. grooved and cross-tongued boarding nailed to pieces cut just tight between the front and back legs ;

Fig. 886.—Tool Cabinet and Bench Combined.

Figs. 887 and 888 are horizontal sections through the front and back corners respectively. The cheek c (Fig. 886) is

the front pieces can be secured to the bottom rail of the frame as in Fig. 890. The ¾-in. matchboarding is fixed to the back by nailing a fillet to the under-side of

Fig. 887.—Front Corner of Tool Cabinet.

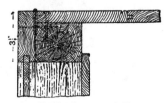

Fig. 888.—Back Corner of Tool Cabinet.

secured by screws passing into the legs. The top is formed with three 9-in. boards, 1½ in. or 2 in. thick, jointed together, and is firmly secured to the cross-rails at each

the top (see Fig. 891), and to the back legs as in Fig. 888. The lower part of the back can be nailed to the fillet fixed to the bottom. The recess at each end is formed by jointing up two 11-in. by ¾-in. boards (or match-boarding will do), and fixing them to the inside of the legs as in Figs. 887 and 888. A cover that can be placed over small work,

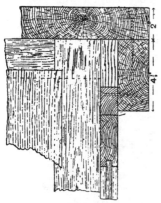

Fig. 889.—Bench Cheek and Top Part of Cabinet Doors and Frame

tools, etc., may be made of 1 in. stuff formed into a rim about 4 in. deep and covering one side of this frame with ¾-in. stuff. The two end doors are hinged to the back legs. The object in having the cheek c projecting beyond the front of the doors is to allow more room for the feet and legs of the operator when working. It will be worth while to procure one of the several good forms of instantaneous grip vices that are now sold. An ordinary wooden stop can be adopted, or perhaps one of the patent

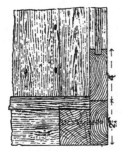

Fig. 890.—Bottom Part of Cabinet Doors, Frame, etc.

iron forms will be found more convenient. A lock can, of course, be added if desired to secure the lid.

CABINET FOR NAILS AND OTHER REQUISITES.

The small cabinet of which Fig. 892 is a front elevation and Fig. 893 a cross-section

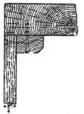

Fig. 891.—Part Back and Top of Tool Cabinet.

on A B is intended for nails, screws, hinges, and other workshop requisites. Its chief feature is the great number of small

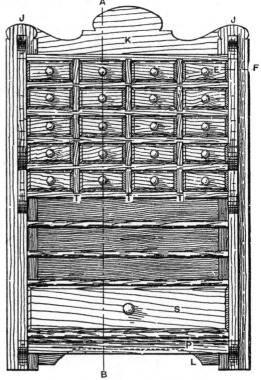

Fig. 892.—Cabinet for Nails, etc.

drawers, the larger one at the bottom being meant for glue, while the intervening shelves are convenient for keeping various grades of glasspaper. The over-all dimensions are 23¼ in. by 15¾ in. by 10⅞ in. Two stiles J are connected by the rails K and L to form a strong frame upon which the rest of the carcase is built. Figs. 894 and 895 show details of the joint between the top rail and stile J, Fig. 894 representing a vertical section showing a tenon on the end of K, and the haunching of K into J. The back edge of J, as shown by the dotted line, is carried up straight, in order to form a close joint with the shoulder at the back of K. Fig. 895 represents a horizontal section through Fig. 894 at C D, and shows K to be thinner than J, so that the tenon is bare-faced. This gives a lighter appearance and a more shapely finish to the end of the stile. The bottom rail L is treated similarly. The backing shown in section

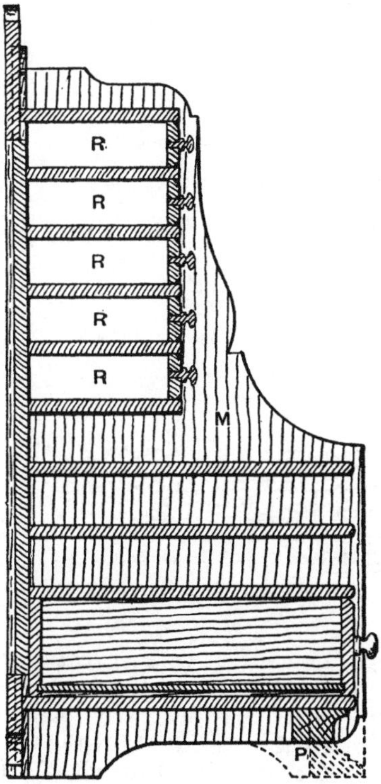

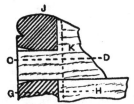

Fig. 894.—Joint between Top Rail and Stile of Nail Cabinet.

First, however, the shelves seen in section in Fig. 893 are fitted into grooves made in the sides. In cutting out these grooves the inexperienced must beware of making them in one piece, so as to be on the outside when placed in position. If the sides are placed with their straight edges abutting, the grooves are correctly marked if

Fig. 895.   Fig. 896.

Figs. 895 and 896.—Joint between Top Rail and Stile of Nail Cabinet.

the lines upon both are all either on the top or the bottom face. It is better to connect the narrow shelves with the vertical partitions T (Fig. 892), and to mark out the grooves to receive them afterwards by scribing the lines directly from the parts which have to fit in the grooves. The partitions T have the grain of the wood vertical. To get them all exactly to one length, plane up a piece of wood 28 in. long, 5 in. wide, and ⅜ in. thick. Square one end with

Fig. 893.—Cross Section of Nail Cabinet.

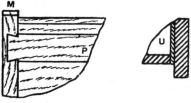

Fig. 897.—Underneath View of Nail Cabinet Front Corner.

Fig. 898.—Joint between Top Rail and Stile of Nail Cabinet.

by Fig. 893 fills in the frame, and is fitted into the grooves on the inner edges of the stiles, as shown in Fig. 896, which is a section at G H (Fig. 894). The backing is

rebated to bring it flush with the face of the frame. Firmly screwed to the frame are the two sides M (Figs. 893 and 897).

plane and shooting-board, and cut off one partition about 1/16 in. longer than the finished size (namely 1⅝ in.). Repeat until

18

the fifteen are done, and then nail a fence on the shooting-board, against which the planed end of each piece is pressed whilst the other end is shot. By "end" is meant the end of the grain, as these pieces are short-grained. The 5 in. allows for cutting the corners off to prevent splitting them when shooting. The partitions are fitted into six grooved shelves, the grooves being marked out by placing all six together and squaring lines across all the edges, from which the lines on the face of each shelf are obtained. By marking

moulded piece P is dovetailed in ; Fig. 897 is a view of one corner as seen from below.

DRAWERS OF CABINET.

Fig. 893 shows the small drawers R. which are merely empty tin tobacco boxes with the lids removed, the fronts being of wood with small knobs inserted. These boxes, each formerly containing $\frac{1}{4}$ lb. of tobacco, are of uniform dimensions (4$\frac{3}{8}$ in. by 3 in. by 1$\frac{3}{8}$ in.), are neatly and strongly made, give a maximum of available space inside for the room they take up, and save

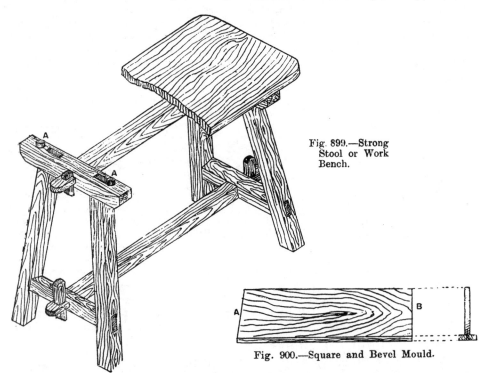

Fig. 899.—Strong Stool or Work Bench.

Fig. 900.—Square and Bevel Mould.

all the front left-hand ends (say) of the shelves before squaring and fitting them up in the same relative positions, the partitions may be kept in perfect alignment. The grooves are brought to a uniform depth by finishing them all with a router, of which the set is not altered for the last cut out of each groove. The extreme top and bottom shelves are wider on account of the thin rails. In order to tie together the front edges of the sides, a

a large amount of work in construction. The hinges are very easily removed. The drawer fronts are made by planing up strips of wood to a width of 1$\frac{3}{8}$ in. and $\frac{3}{8}$ in. thick, and chamfering two edges. These strips are then sawn to the correct length, and, after boring central holes to receive the plugs of the knobs, and chamfering the ends, they are ready to attach to the boxes. This is done by punching holes through which small round-headed screws are passed from the inside and screwed to the wooden front. If any design is embossed on the end of the box, a slight hollow, cut in the wood, will allow the two

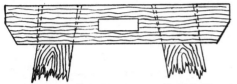

Fig. 901.—Top Bearer of Work Bench.

to bed together. The punching may be done with one of the hollow punches used for making holes in leather straps ; a piece of hard wood sawn to the internal length of the box and placed inside it will support the end whilst the hole is being made. The bottom drawer s (Fig. 892) is made with a plain dovetail joint at the back and a lapped dovetail in front, the bottom being supported by a groove running round the inside. Fig. 898 shows an alternative section at E F (Fig. 892), where the small drawers slide against the projecting sides ; this is intended to prevent any scoring or scratching

 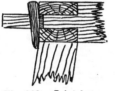

Fig. 902.—Joint between Leg and Bearer.   Fig. 903.—Joint between Bearer and Top Stretcher.

on the projecting part arising from continual withdrawing and replacing of the side drawers, a slip of wood u being placed on the inside of each side piece. This, of course, will necessitate making the whole of the cabinet $\frac{1}{4}$ in. wider, if each slip is $\frac{1}{8}$ in. thick. The dotted lines at the bottom right-hand corner of Fig. 893 show the construction to be followed if the cabinet is to stand upon a shelf or table (it is too small to stand on the floor), and the full lines at the same place indicate the method of finishing if it is desired to hang it upon the wall. In the latter case two strong eye-plates should be well screwed to the top of each

of the stiles J, or the cabinet may be fixed to woodwork by screws passing through the projecting parts of the stiles.

STRONG STOOL OR WORK BENCH.

The stool or bench illustrated by Fig. 899 is useful for various purposes, both in the

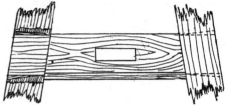

Fig. 904.—Bottom Rail of Work Bench.

household and in the workshop. It can without much trouble be taken to pieces, so that it may be conveniently stowed away when not required for use. When the stool is for domestic use, the sizes of the timber should be about 2 in. by 2 in. for all parts of the frame. The top consists simply of a slab about 1 in. thick, having four holes bored in it to fit over the dowels or pins A. Suitable measurements for the finished article are: Length of top, 2 ft. 9 in. ; width of top, 1 ft. 3 in. ; and height from ground, about 1 ft. 10 in. For a work bench, however, these measurements may be increased, the framework being increased proportionately, and the top, instead of fitting over pins or dowels,

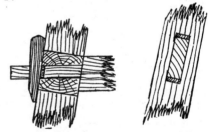

Fig. 905.—Joint between Rail and Bottom Stretcher.   Fig. 906.—End of Rail in Leg.

should be secured with bolts and nuts. The spread of the legs at the bottom should be such that they would occupy the four corners of a rectangle, equal and similar to that of the top; this prevents all tilting, and secures stability for the bench, a point that is often overlooked.

Before marking out the framework, a mould should be made as indicated at Fig. 900; a piece of wood, about ¾ in. thick, is taken, one end of it being squared off, as at B, and the other cut to the desired bevel or in the upper part of the frame; Figs. 904 to 906 show those in the lower part. These figures are sufficiently explanatory in themselves, and need no further comment. All joints should be made by well gluing

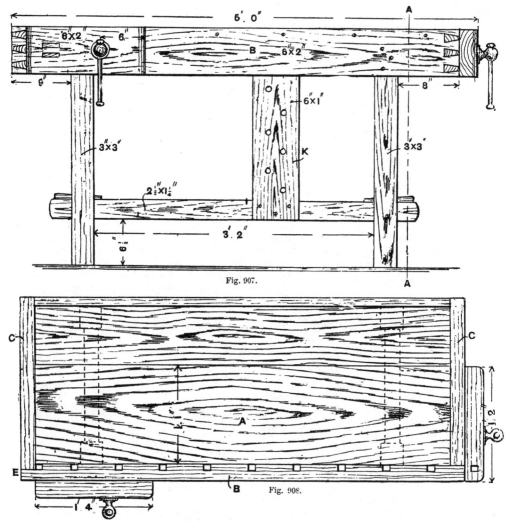

Figs. 907 and 908.—Side Elevation and Plan of Bench with Side and Tail Vices.

splay of the legs, as shown at A; a narrow strip is fastened to the edge, so as to form a fence. With this tool no difficulty should be experienced in marking out in a proper manner the lines for the necessary joints. Figs. 901 to 903 show all the joints and wedging, and the movable key-wedges should be cut from hardwood. A stool or bench made on this principle from good dry wood will stand any amount of rough usage, and should last as long as the timber from which it is made, there being no nails or other source of weakness to lessen its durability.

BENCH WITH SIDE AND TAIL VICES.

The general view of a bench with side

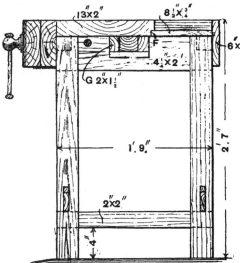

Fig. 909.—Part Elevation and Cross Section of Bench.

and tail vices is given by Fig. 80, p. 22, and the construction of the bench is dealt with below. Fig. 907 is a side elevation, Fig. 908 a plan, and Fig. 909 a section on A A (Fig. 907). Having sawn out the pieces, next plane them true. Then the legs and rails should be set out, the latter for mortising, and the former for tenons. The mortises go right through, producing a much firmer result than when the tenons are only stubbed in half-way. The haunched mortise and tenons between the top rails and legs, with the tenons of the cross rails through the legs, are shown by Fig. 910. The side rails are dovetailed, mortised, and tenoned together as in Figs. 910 and 911 ; the tenon of the rail is firmly held in position by a wedge, which must be released, and the tenon of the rail lifted up, before it can be withdrawn. The side rails have a bare-faced tenon—that is, have a shoulder on the inside only. When these joints fit satisfactorily, the legs and cross rails should be glued together and cramped up, and the tenons fixed by wedges, which

should be glued before insertion. The top should be planed to breadth and thickness, and then the ends cut off and planed square and to length. The front of the back and end cheeks C (Fig. 908) should next be carefully set out and worked. At the front end of the side cheek B, the thickness for dovetailing is not the full 2 in., but is less by $\frac{3}{4}$ in. than the breadth of the pin hole, as shown at E (Fig. 908). After the side cheeks have been dovetailed and fitted together, the front cheek should be grooved on the back for receiving the stop (see Figs. 908 and 912). The inside edge of the top should be rebated as shown at F (Fig. 909) to receive the well board. This should fit just tight between the end cheeks, the front and side back cheeks being firmly secured to the top plank and well board. Four-inch screws may be used for the front and side cheeks, and 2½-in. screws for the back, the heads being sunk

Fig. 910.—Joints of Rails and Legs of Bench.

a little below the surface. The side cheeks should be glued to the main board of the top. The cheeks and ends of the runners should be mortised and tenoned together as in Fig. 913, the top of the runner being kept at the same distance from the top of the cheek as the thickness of the top plank; two tenons may be more troublesome to make, but the result will be stronger than when one tenon only is used. These joints should be firmly glued and

Fig. 911.—Section showing Rail wedged in Bench Leg.

in fixing them into their places the cheek and runner should be pushed in and firmly held in position; then the centre of the hole for the screw in the cheek should be marked, sufficient room being allowed for the flange of the box (or nut) for screwing to the side cheek of the bench (see Fig. 912). The hole should next be bored through the cheeks of the screw and bench with a bit slightly larger than the diameter of the screw. Then the collars and boxes can be fixed in position, and the framework of the legs and top fitted together. The top rail of the back legs should be notched for the runner as shown at H (Fig. 910), and if the work has been done accurately the top will just slide on the upper part of the legs. When the parts are adjusted, the front cheek should be secured to the legs. and the top of the bench to the top rails of the legs with 3½-in. screws. The peg board K (Fig. 907) should be screwed to the front of the bottom rail and to the back of the front cheek. The following are the net

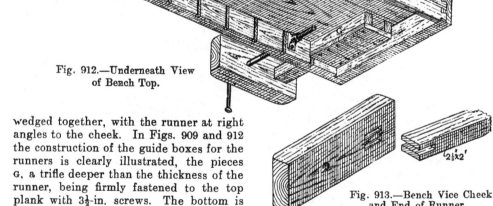

Fig. 912.—Underneath View of Bench Top.

Fig. 913.—Bench Vice Cheek and End of Runner.

wedged together, with the runner at right angles to the cheek. In Figs. 909 and 912 the construction of the guide boxes for the runners is clearly illustrated, the pieces G, a trifle deeper than the thickness of the runner, being firmly fastened to the top plank with 3½-in. screws. The bottom is formed of ¾-in. boarding screwed to the guides. The box for the tail runner extends from the top rail to the inner surface of the end cheek. Wrought-iron bench screws about 18 in. by ⅞ in., having split collars, will be found most satisfactory, and

sizes of the pieces required (a little in excess of these dimensions should be allowed for waste in working): Top board, 2 in. by 13¼ in. by 4 ft. 8 in., ; well board, ¾ in. by 8 in. by 4 ft. 8 in.; peg board,

$\frac{7}{8}$ in. by 6 in. by 1 ft. 9 in. ; runners, 2 in. by 2½ in. by 2 ft. 3 in. ; runner guides, 1½ in. by 2 in. by 3 ft. 2 in. ; guide box bottoms, ¾ in. by 5½ in. by 1 ft. 7 in. ; screw cheeks, 2½ in. by 6 in. by 2 ft. 7 in. ;

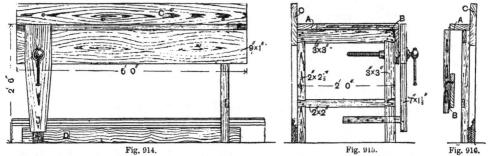

Fig. 914. Fig. 915. Fig. 916.

Figs. 914 and 915.—Elevations of Folding Bench. Fig. 916.—Folding Bench with Flaps Down.

front and end cheek, 2 in. by 6 in. by 9 ft. ; back cheek, 1 in. by 6 in. by 5 ft. ; legs, 3 in. by 3 in. by 9 ft. 8 in. ; top rail (front end), 2 in. by 4 in. by 1 ft. 9 in. ; top rail (back end), 2 in. by 4¼ in. by 1 ft. 9 in. ; bottom rails (ends), 2 in. by 2 in. by 3 ft. 6 in. ; and bottom rails (front and back), 1¼ in. by 2½ in. by 8 ft. 2 in.

PORTABLE FOLDING BENCH.

The portable folding bench shown ready for use by Fig. 82, and with the flap down by Fig. 83, p. 23, is illustrated in side elevation by Fig. 914, and in end elevation by Fig. 915. An end elevation of the bench when folded is given by Fig. 916. Sizes that will meet all ordinary requirements are indicated in the illustrations, which show the construction so clearly that only the leading points need description. The legs and rails are jointed together by plain halving and dovetail-halving. The top is at least 1½ in. thick, and is formed of two boards jointed ; to keep it true it should be clamped. The top should be hinged to the rail marked A, and the side of the bench hinged to the top as represented by B (Figs. 915 and 916), 3-in. butt hinges being used for this purpose. The wall-piece C should be firmly screwed to the rail of the top A. The legs should be hinged at the top to this piece, and also at the bottom to the strip marked D, which should be sufficiently thick to project from the wall to the

thickness of the wall-piece C. The piece C can be attached to the skirting board with a few screws. The wall-piece C, if against a lath-and-plaster partition, can be firmly and very easily fixed to two or three of the studs of the partition with half a dozen screws ; if it is against a brick wall, drill a few holes into the wall and drive in hardwood plugs (see p. 251) ; or, better still, with a long fine bradawl probe the wall until the joints are found (if this is done carefully, little damage will be suffered by the paper), and then with a steel chisel cut some holes about ¾ in. square and about 3 in. or 4 in. deep. These holes may then be fitted with hardwood plugs, into which screws are inserted through the wall-piece. The fitting-up of the screw, cheek, and runner (the last named being of hardwood)

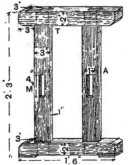

Fig. 917.—End Framework of Cabinet-worker's Bench.

is not difficult. The leg to which the screw is attached is larger than the others. The side and top of the bench when folded up can be kept in position by a hook and eye as shown. The bench may be made additionally firm by inserting a few screws through the side into the legs, and through the top into the rails. When it is required to remove the bench, all that is necessary is to withdraw these screws.

There is also a rack on one side of the 7-in. board cut for the reception of small tools, while underneath it is a band, tacked at short intervals, to hold other tools. If thought desirable, a board similar to the

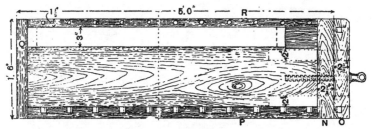

Fig. 918.—Top of Cabinet-worker's Bench.

CABINET-WORKER'S BENCH.

The cabinet-worker's bench illustrated by Fig. 84, p. 24, consists, as has been already stated, of two principal parts, the underneath framework and support, and the top. The underneath framework is made first, and comprises two standards A (Fig. 917) joined by two bars B (Fig. 84). Square up a piece 6 ft. by 3 in. by 2 in., which will cut up into four pieces, each 1 ft. 6 in. long, for the tops and bottoms. Then square up a piece 9 ft. by 3 in. by 1 in., which will cut up into four pieces 2 ft. 3 in. for the uprights. At the ends of the uprights form tenons 2 in. long by cutting a ½-in. shoulder (see T, Fig. 917), and mortise a hole, M, 4 in. by 1 in., about midway between the shoulders. After the top and bottom rails have been mortised to receive the tenons at the ends of the uprights, the frame may be glued up and cramped. A small piece of ½-in. wood should be glued and nailed on to the feet to make the framework firm. Two stays B (Fig. 84) are got out from a board 10 ft. by 7 in. by 1 in. Having planed them up, cut two 1½-in. shoulders at a distance of 4½ in. from each end, thus forming tenons to fit into the mortises M (Fig. 917). At the distance of 1 in. from the shoulder, mortise a ⅜-in. hole to receive the pin P (Fig. 84), and plane up a piece 14 in. by 4 in. by ⅜ in. from which the four wedges can be cut by which the whole framework is held together. A board resting on the feet of the standards will serve to hold heavy tools and other articles.

underneath board can be fitted on the edges of the two stays to hold further tools, thus adding a kind of tool cabinet to the bench. For the bench top (Fig. 918), plane up a piece of oak 3 ft. by 4 in. by 2½ in., and cut it in halves to form the jaws of the vice shown at the right-hand side of Fig. 84. For the parts P, Q, R (Fig. 918) three pieces, respectively 5 ft. by 3 in. by 2 in., 1 ft. 6 in. by 4 in. by 2 in., and 5 ft. by 3 in. by 1½ in., will be required. Cut dovetail tenons on the ends of P and R, and cut the ends of Q and N with open sockets to receive the tenons on P and R. The space between the four rails is filled with a board

Fig. 919.—Section of Part of Bench Top.

4 ft. 6 in. by 11 in. by 1 in., which forms the bench top proper, the remaining space serving as a tray for small tools. The front rail is provided with holes 1 in. by ¾ in., cut about 5 in. apart, on the inner side for holding iron bench pins (Fig. 86, p. 24); while the front face has an inch hole midway between the oblong holes on the edge, to receive a pin 1½ in. square at one end, but made round at the other end to fit tightly into the hole. The pin T (Fig. 84) and the block V (screwed on the end of the movable jaw of the vice) serve to hold wood whilst edge planing. The back rail has ⅝-in. circular holes (made exactly opposite to the

oblong holes in the front rail) to receive the ends of the pins w (Fig. 84), which are convenient for cramping up joints and for other purposes. The 11-in. board should be fitted into the front rail P, and the two end bars provided with tongues. When the various parts have been fitted, they should be glued, cramped up, and left to dry. To form the tray, plane up a piece

mortise made in both blocks to receive them (see Fig. 918). They should be glued and pegged into the movable jaw and made to run evenly through the fixed jaw. A small strip is glued on the under-side of the bench top to act as a guide to keep the vice

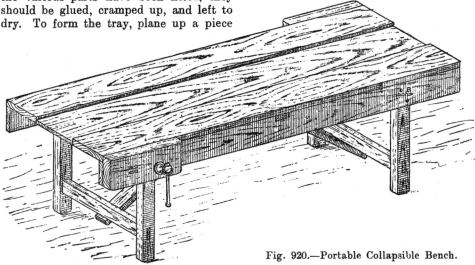

Fig. 920.—Portable Collapsible Bench.

4 ft. 6½ in. by 2 in. by 1 in., and nail it to the under-side of the 11-in. board, then nail to it and to the outer rail a strip 4 ft. 6½ in. by 6 in. by ½ in. The bars forming the jaws of the vice should be worked up in the following manner :—Having procured a 12-in. screw of ⅞ in. diameter, bore a hole

steady when in action. Two oblong holes, as illustrated, are cut to receive pins for cramping. To render the cramping power more effective, these holes are cut slanting

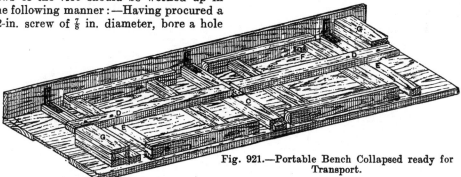

Fig. 921.—Portable Bench Collapsed ready for Transport.

centrally through both pieces at a distance of 7½ in. from the front end, the nut being inserted at the back of the fixed rail to prevent its being drawn out when the vice is screwed up. Then two strips, 15 in. by 2 in. by ¾ in., should be prepared, and a

slightly towards the jaws of the vice (see the section, Fig. 919). It will be found convenient to fill up the tray with blocks of wood about 6 in. from the jaws of the vice, as more room will then be given for sawing up.

PORTABLE COLLAPSIBLE BENCH.

Fig. 920 gives an isometric view showing a good portable bench rigged together ready for working upon, whilst Fig. 921 shows the bench collapsed ready for transit. In the latter figure the nearest side cheek

bearer C; then, when the braces are let down by inserting screws D into the top rail of the legs E, the legs, etc., are held flat as shown. The screws, with the cheek, etc., can be placed inside and secured, with cord or otherwise, to the rails of the legs and the braces. The illustrations show

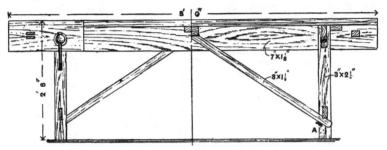

Fig. 922.—Elevation and Section of Portable Bench.

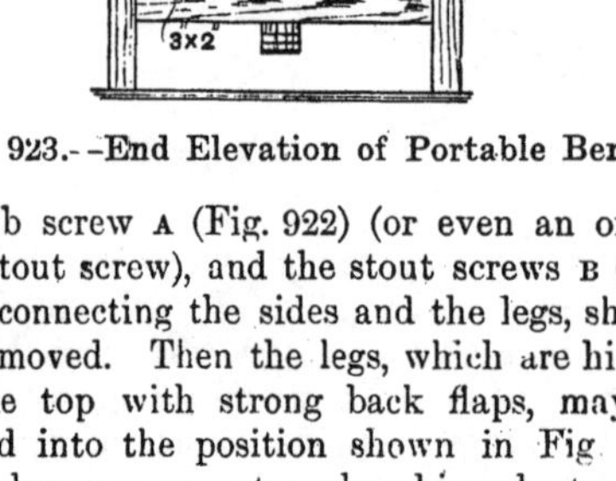

of the bench is omitted merely in order to show the construction more clearly, but it would not be necessary to remove either cheek, as both would remain fixed to the top and bearers of the bench. As things often get roughly handled in transit, it would be a decided advantage further to secure the sides to the bearers by six stout angle brackets as shown by Fig. 921. Assuming the bench made and fixed together, the following is the method of preparing it for transit. Each screw cheek, with screw and runner, should be taken out; then a

clearly the construction, and suggestive sizes are figured on the side view (Fig. 922) and end view (Fig. 923). The legs and lower rails are mortised and tenoned together, whilst the top rails and legs are dovetailed. Of course, it would strengthen the bench if these joints were glued and pinned together. The boxes or nuts for the screws are fixed to the inner sides of the legs as shown at F (Fig. 921). The forms of boxes for the runners are also shown at G G. For a bench of this description, iron screws of about 18 in. by $\frac{7}{8}$ in. will be found of greater service than the clumsy wooden screws. Perhaps the most suitable stop

Fig. 923.--End Elevation of Portable Bench.

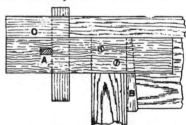

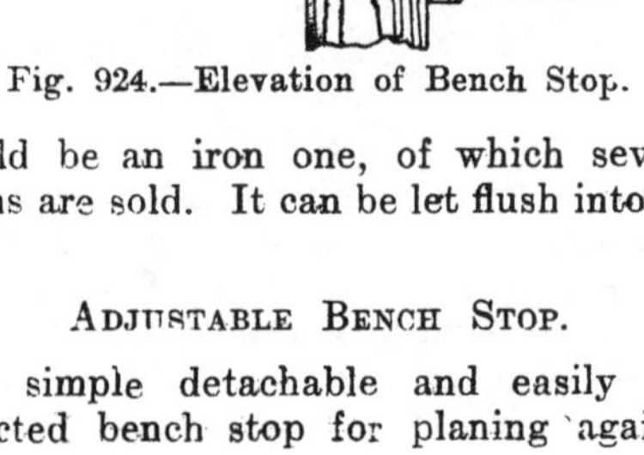

Fig. 924.—Elevation of Bench Stop.

thumb screw A (Fig. 922) (or even an ordinary stout screw), and the stout screws B (Fig. 920) connecting the sides and the legs, should be removed. Then the legs, which are hinged to the top with strong back flaps, may be folded into the position shown in Fig. 921. The braces are strongly hinged to the

would be an iron one, of which several forms are sold. It can be let flush into the top.

ADJUSTABLE BENCH STOP.

A simple detachable and easily constructed bench stop for planing against, which could be quickly and easily attached to an ordinary bench or table, is shown in elevation and plan by Figs. 924 and 925. The piece is illustrated detached by Fig. 926, and as attached by Fig. 927. The bench stop can readily be attached or detached by means of two stout screws and a wedge B. The wedge gives additional firmness. The stop can be adjusted to various heights by the wedge A. The piece shown at C, being level with the top of the table, will be found very convenient, besides forming a good backing for the stop. The piece to clamp on to the leg should be deal, about 15 in. long, 4 in. wide, 3 in. thick; the stop is a piece of hard wood, 2 in. square and 8 in. long.

DISADVANTAGES OF THE ORDINARY SCREW VICE.

The ordinary method of fitting a bench screw vice has already been described (see

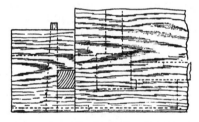

Fig. 925.—Plan of Bench Stop.

pp. 24 to 27), but it is very defective, the movable jaw retaining its parallelism to the bench front for a very short time. In fact, in many respects the old plan of centring the movable jaw near the floor, or of making an iron bar adjustable at certain intervals by means of a series of holes into which a peg can be fitted, is preferable; and when the range of work is limited to two or three thicknesses of boards, this plan works very well. The cabinet-maker's bench, fitted with two screws, is also effective, but the adjustment of two screws takes time that should be devoted to better purpose. The horizontal form of movable jaw, with a sliding wooden bar fixed to it at right angles, the bar moving in a well-made box fixed under the bench top, would be perfect, if the parallelism of the jaw secured by the

squareness of the bar could be permanently maintained. Very rarely indeed is a bench met with in which the adjustment has remained unimpaired for any considerable time. The strain of daily use, and the practice of doing work in the screw that should never be attempted except on the bench, invariably spoil the adjustment very quickly. Perfection is not claimed for the

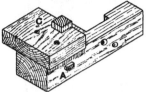

Fig. 926.—Bench Stop Detached.

plan described below, but it offers some advantages over the ordinary type, and is therefore worthy of trial, considering the value of a well-fitting bench screw.

IMPROVED BENCH SCREW VICE.

First, then, if the screw itself could be made to work squarely with the front face of the bench, something would be done towards solving the problem. The use of two nuts would tend to steady the screw, but, unless it were lengthened proportion-

Fig. 927 —Bench Stop in Position.

ately, it would lose in efficiency, so this plan may be dismissed, especially as bench screws are generally purchased ready made, and seldom made to order. A rail can be fitted under the bench top with a semi-cylindrical or segmental groove to catch the screw, and, as the upper part of the bench jaws is most used the rail would be fitted between the screw and bench top. By exercising a little care in designing the bench, a way might be found of making such a rail useful as part of

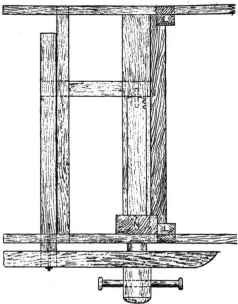

Fig. 928.—Plan of Improved Bench Vice.

the construction. Such a rail might be built up on the nut itself, which too often is fixed merely to the inner side of the vertical front bench, and not connected with the framework. Next, if the inner end of the sliding bar could be

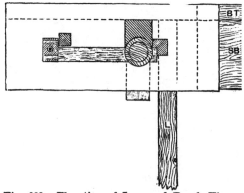

Fig. 929.—Elevation of Improved Bench Vice.

so connected with the inner end of the screw as always to maintain the same distance at the back as at the front, another

important help would be given towards securing the desired result. The upper half of the vice being most used for planing edges of boards, the tendency usually is to raise the inner ends of both bar and screw; but if provision is made to resist such tendency by rails or guides above the screw and bar, guidance below may be neglected. In the same way, when the vice is in use say for sawing tenons, the movable jaw and the fixed jaw of the vice do not lie parallel, the opening at the end nearest the workman soon becoming much wider than that at the other end; it is therefore important to provide some remedy for this. Again, though the bar and the movable jaw have been carefully fitted and glued, the joint is not always strong enough to bear the strain. As a remedy, an iron bolt with a nut let into the bar may be added, so that when glue and wedges fail the screw can be tightened, and fresh wedges inserted at any time. Several ways in which improvements might be made having been thus indicated, it is shown below how these can be embodied, or as much as possible combined in the most simple and practical manner. First take the screw: it will probably be found that it has been turned on a cup centre rather than a cone. Using this ring, or the conical depression, as a guide to centrality, bore a hole about $\frac{5}{8}$ in. diameter, fit a good strong dowel, and glue it in; see that it is true; if not, it must be made so; therefore it will be better to have the dowel large enough to bear a little reduction if needed. The dowel, of course, must project—about 1 in. will be sufficient—and the end will be fitted into a cross-rail, which will be described, and can be seen in the plan (Fig. 929). The sliding bar can next be prepared; it should be as long as the width of the bench will allow. Set out the tenons for insertion into the movable jaw. Two tenons should be made, the outside shoulders being diminished so as to allow room for a screw-bolt to be inserted between them. It is better to have the bar so placed that its top edge is a trifle higher than the top of the screw, so that long boards may rest on the bar rather than on the screw; the dimensions of the bar may be 3 in. by 2 in. or more, at discretion, exact sizes not being important. To this sliding bar a cross-rail is to be fixed by mortise

Fig. 930.—Kitchen Table Narrow-jaw Screw Vice.

and tenon at the distance from the front indicated by the length of the screw. This rail must be kept a little below the top of

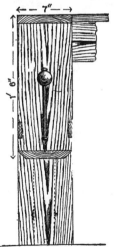

Fig. 931.—Front Elevation of Narrow-jaw Table Vice.

the sliding bar, or part may be cut away at the end behind the screw, if the rail parallel with and above the screw is provided ; the

dowel fixed in the end of the screw will work in a hole in this rail, and the hole will therefore be near its top surface if the rail mentioned at first as a guide to the screw is to be inserted. The position recommended is shown in the elevation (Fig. 929). The end of the rail can be made to slide in contact with another guide if thought necessary. The illustrations show how the whole may be fitted together, and this must be done before the movable jaw is fixed to the tenons of the sliding bar, the screw being inserted last of all. The disadvantage is that, once fixed, it cannot easily be removed like the ordinary screw fitting, but that is a small matter if the result is satisfactory. The mortise and tenon to secure the opening of the vice when the screw is turned is of course necessary. It may be inserted either above or below, but preference should be given to the under-side, especially as the mortise need not then be so deep. The tenon must be of the thickness, and in the position, indicated by a groove which will be found on every bench screw, about 1 in. from the shoulder. For the bolt mentioned a 7-in. bed screw will do, but it should be let in a little, or it may catch the workman's

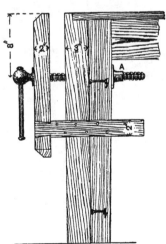

Fig. 932.—Side Elevation of Narrow-jaw Table Vice.

knuckles. The heart side of the beech movable jaw should be outside, as that has a tendency to become convex. The lettering in Figs. 928 and 929 signifies: L, leg; N, nut; B T, bench top; and S B, side board.

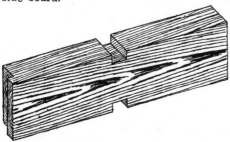

Fig. 933.—Back Cheek of Narrow-jaw Vice.

FITTING DETACHABLE NARROW-JAW SCREW VICE.

Those who have not sufficient room for a proper bench may wish to rig up on their kitchen table a handy attachment which could be easily fixed in a few minutes when required for use, without greatly disfiguring or damaging the table. There are at least two simple forms of screws suitable for this purpose. The attachment of

Fig. 934.—Kitchen Table Wide-jaw Screw Vice.

the screw shown by the general view (Fig. 930) will first be described. For the back cheek E, attached to the table leg, a piece of red or yellow deal 7 in. wide, 3 in. thick, and about 2 ft. 8 in. long (according

to the height of the table) is required. A similar piece about 18 in. long, 7 in. wide, and 2 in. thick will do for the front cheek. Two strips of hard wood, birch or beech, 2 in. by 1 in. and 18 in. long, will do for the two runners, and a 16-in. or 18-in. iron bench screw should be obtained. Four strong hooks and eyes will practically complete the requirements. First truly plane up all the wood to the proper sizes, and mark out and cut the back cheek at the upper end to fit the top of the table; mark and cut out the sockets for runners as shown in Figs. 930 to 933, and when the cheek fits the top, etc., place it in position, and fix hooks and eyes to it and the table leg. Set out and cut the dovetails at

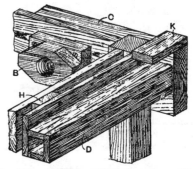

Fig. 935.—Details of Wide-jaw Screw Vice.

one end of each runner; the form of these is shown sufficiently in Fig. 932. Place one of the runners with its dovetailed end on the edge of the front cheek, and mark it, taking care that the pieces are square with each other. The next thing is cutting the socket; make it slightly smaller than the dovetail on the runner, so that the parts may fit tight; this may be done by sawing a little inside the lines. When ready, put these two pieces together, and then place one runner in position so that its edges are in the same planes as the other runner, and then mark and cut out the second dovetail socket. These parts must be so fitted that the runners are quite parallel; they should be secured by glue and two screws. Place the runners and front cheek in their proper positions, and bore the hole for the screw through the two cheeks and leg. The screw is fixed to the front cheek by means of a collar and three or four 1¼-in. screws. Finally the box A (Fig. 932) can be fixed to the leg with two 1½-in. screws, and the holes made in the runners. It will be found better to have a piece of ½-in. round iron about 9 in. long to pass through both runners, instead of two short pieces.

FITTING DETACHABLE WIDE-JAW SCREW VICE.

The attachment illustrated by Figs. 934 to 938 will next be described. For the cheeks, get two pieces of sound deal, 2 in. thick and 7 in. or 9 in. wide; a piece of

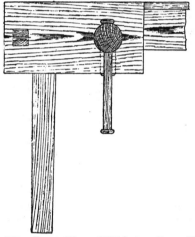

Fig. 936.—Front View of Wide-jaw Screw Vice.

deal, 2½ in. square and 1 ft. 10 in. long, for the runners; and a piece of board 1 in. by 9 in., about 3 ft. long, for the runner-box. Get a 2-in. wooden bench screw complete with nut. Plane the several pieces of wood to their respective dimensions, and carefully cut the back cheek to fit round the table leg, as shown in Figs. 934, 935, and 937; then mortise and tenon together the runner and front cheek; of course two tenons and mortises, as illustrated, will be stronger than only one. These joints should be properly fitted and well glued together, taking care, of course, to keep the runner quite at right angles to the cheek. The box for the runner is clearly illustrated by Figs. 935 and 937; it should so fit that the runner just works freely in it. Having made this,

carefully mark and cut the hole for the runner in the back cheek. It is advisable now to fix the back cheek in position by two screws, as shown, and also the runner-

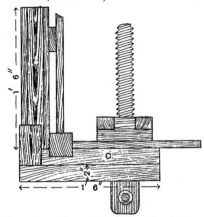

Fig. 937.—Plan of Wide-jaw Screw Vice.

box. Behind the box pack a piece of wood H (Fig. 935), just as thick as the portion of the leg projecting in front of the rail. Mark out accurately, and then make the holes in the cheeks and through the rail of the table. All wooden screws have a groove in the portion working in the front cheek (see Fig. 938), for receiving a piece

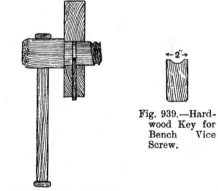

Fig. 938.—Cheek and Handle of Screw Vice.

Fig. 939.—Hardwood Key for Bench Vice Screw.

of hardwood (Fig. 939), in a mortise made in the under edge of the cheek; the hollowed end of the piece of wood fits into the groove of the screw. This contrivance makes the cheek open as the screw is undone. The cheek, with screw and runner, now is placed in position and the nut screwed to the back of the table rail; to avoid using long screws, the corners of the nut B are cut (Fig. 935), short screws being much easier to put in. The piece K (Figs. 934 and 935) is not indispensable, but may be useful for some purposes, as it would be the same thickness as the top, and would piece it out, as it were, to the end of the screw. If this bench screw is carefully made, it will be found to work very satisfactorily, and may be fitted up or detached by five screws. When the wood screws of these two forms of vice are detached, the only part remaining fixed is the box or nut (see A, Fig. 932, and B, Fig. 935); the cheek C and runner-box D of Fig. 935 are meant

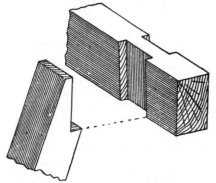

Fig. 940.—Joint for Sawing Stool.

to be detachable. In most of the figures the top of the table or bench is omitted, in order to allow of the details of construction being more clearly shown.

SAWING STOOLS AND WORKSHOP TRESTLES.

Figs. 100 to 105, p. 28, show four kinds of sawing stools, for the making of which there is no need of minute instructions after what has already been said. The joint most generally adopted for connecting the legs to the top beam is shown by Fig. 940. These joints may be fastened with nails, but a stronger method is to glue and screw them together. A serviceable form of trestle for workshop and general use is shown by Fig. 941. Quartering of light or heavy scantling may be used, according to the purpose for which the trestle is required, and the method of

framing together may be varied. It is mortised and tenoned as follows. The four legs A are mortised into the top B, as shown in Figs. 942 and 943. The mortise in B is cut longer than the width a of the

Fig. 941.—Workshop Trestle.

tenon of A, to allow for driving in wedges C. The complete joint thus assumes a dovetailed form, wider at top than at bottom, and the legs, therefore, cannot fall out. The wedges must be driven in as shown, against the ends of the tenon and the end grain of the top B, and not against the flanks b of the tenons. If they were driven against the flanks b, they would split the top B. The short stretchers D (Fig. 941) are mortised into the legs A,

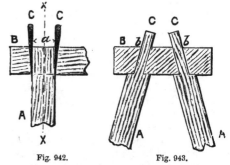

Fig. 942.   Fig. 943.
Figs. 942 and 943.—Legs Mortised and Tenoned into Top of Trestle.

and wedges are driven in against the end grain, as in the previous instance. The long stretcher E (Fig. 941) between the short ones is mortised in the same fashion. A trestle made thus with close joints will stand much rough usage. If the legs were short and the scantling of large section, as in the case of a sawing stool, strutting would not really be necessary. But it is always advisable to strut

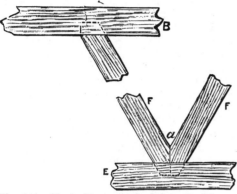

Fig. 944.—Struts Stump-tenoned into Stretcher.

high trestles made of slight scantling, say not exceeding 2 in. by 2 in., or 2 in. by 2½ in. cross section. In Fig. 941 the struts at F F are tenoned into B and E, but the tenons do not pass through, and are not wedged. It is quite enough to stump-tenon the ends of F F (Fig. 944) at top and bottom. The two struts abut at a, and further steady the framing. A simpler method of framing trestles of this type

Fig. 945.—Workshop Trestle.

together is shown in Fig. 945. The only members that are mortised are the legs A, into the top B. The cross stretchers C are simply let for about ½ in. into the legs, and screwed or bolted. The struts D are

19

stump-tenoned into the top, but at the other end they are merely shouldered back to fit over the stretchers C (see also Fig. 946), and screwed or bolted. For a trestle somewhat heavy this simpler method is

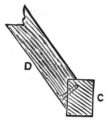

Fig. 946.—Strut Shouldered upon Stretcher.

quite good enough; but for a lighter trestle, like that previously described, the method of framing together with long bottom stretchers and mortised joints throughout makes a firmer job.

SAWING HORSE.

For sawing wood, and more especially for sawing firewood, a horse is a great help. There are more ways than one of making it; but perhaps for ordinary use the best form is that shown by Fig. 106, p. 29, and in end elevation by Fig. 947. This is mainly built of scantling 3 in. square, and is neat, strong, firm, and serviceable. The four pieces forming the legs are about 2½ ft.

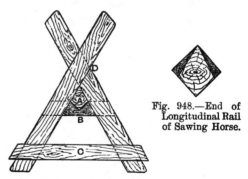

Fig. 948.—End of Longitudinal Rail of Sawing Horse.

Fig. 947.—Sawing Horse.

long, and they are so arranged that the upper limbs of the cross have only half the length of the lower ones; they are halved at the intersection, and strongly nailed together, the nails being driven from the outer side and sent well home ; for, should they project, they would be likely to catch and blunt the teeth of the saw. All the parts have to be so arranged as to leave nothing which can interfere with the free play of the saw, especially no iron. For this reason the central piece A, which chiefly serves to tie the two pairs of legs together, is kept below the intersections, so that it may fit up closely between the legs. Its two ends are, for a length of 3 in., cut as shown in section by Fig. 948. This piece is of the same scantling as the legs to which it is nailed. For ordinary work, 18 in. will be a good length for it. The upper cross rails B B give support to this piece, and are, as is shown, cut away to receive its lower angle at each end. These are of 1-in. wood, 2½ in. wide, and about 1 ft. long, and are nailed to the inner sides of the legs. A part only of one of these rails is seen in Fig. 947, but its extent is indicated by dotted lines. Now nail on the foot-rails C C, 1 in. by 2½ in., to the legs 2 in. from their bottoms. The cross foot-rails are 2 ft. long, and those that run lengthwise 20 in. long. Keep the foot-rails as near the ground as indicated, so that the foot may rest comfortably on them when the horse is in use ; some part of the weight of the person who saws being thus thrown upon the frame will steady it.

PORTABLE SAWING HORSES.

A better portable horse for general purposes than the above can hardly be desired. If less solid, it would be wanting in firmness, and if less strong, it would be liable to be shaken to pieces by the constant jarring to which it is subjected in use. But sometimes a lighter and more portable horse is desirable, and to meet this requirement a shut-up horse may be made as follows : After halving the two pairs of legs as above, mortises should be cut through them at the intersections, say 1 in. wide by 1½ in. high, whilst the central tie-piece must have tenons to pass through and project 1½ in. beyond them. In each tenon will be a hole into which a pin, removable at pleasure, can be driven to fasten the frame together for use. In convenience and stability this horse is of course greatly inferior to that described above.

FIXED SAWING HORSE.

The most simple as well as the firmest of all sawing horses is, however, the primitive fixed one. The legs of this should be about 1 ft. or 15 in. longer than those shown in Fig. 947, and, pointed at the ends like stakes, they are driven into the ground before being nailed together at their intersections. To connect the pairs, all that is wanted is a tie nailed to the legs at the point D (Fig. 947), that is, just below the upper limb and on the side upon which the sawyer will stand. Such a horse has the merit of complete immobility ; but, of course, it will not serve every purpose.

FITTING LOCKS AND HINGES.

The Scope of this Chapter.

Previous chapters have contained examples of articles whose completion involves the fitting of locks and hinges. The thoughtful worker does not need much instruction in this matter, but the work in some cases is not so simple as it looks, and there are a number of special points to which atten-

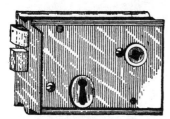

Fig. 949.—Rim Lock.

tion is directed in this chapter. Illustrations and brief particulars of the more important locks and hinges also are given, with the object of assisting the worker in selecting the proper fittings for any job he may have in hand. The value of the information about to be presented will be the more evident when the advanced specimens of joinery and cabinet work come to be described. It hardly needs to be said that the appearance of good work is spoilt if the fittings are chosen badly, and just as badly put on.

Fitting Rim Locks on Doors.

Rim locks are the ordinary cheap locks fixed on bedroom doors, and they are probably the simplest to fix of any. Figs. 949 and 950 show rim locks, the latter having an open cap. The way to fix these is to first let the flange (the projecting lip of the face plate) into the edge of the door, and then, holding the lock in its position, mark through the key-hole and the spindle-hole

with a scribing tool, or bradawl, on to the face of the door. Remove the lock, bore the keyhole top and bottom right through the door with a bit, so that the shoulder of the key passes comfortably through, and finish the work with a keyhole saw or small chisel. The shoulder, or stop, abuts against the lock plate, and keeps the key in its right position to enter and turn. If the keyhole is too large, it does not guide the key exactly to the hole in the lock, but allows the key to strike the lock in a very annoying fashion. Bore the hole for the spindle exactly square with the face of the door; if the hole is out of truth, the worker will find on attempting to screw up the knobs that they bind, and prevent the latch-bolt from springing back freely when the knobs are turned. The holes for the spindle and the key should be bored as nearly to the proper size as the bits can be obtained, and preferably Jennings's bit

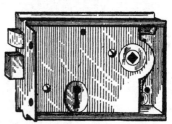

Fig. 950.—Rim Lock with Open Cap.

should be used, care being taken not to force it to cut faster than it is made to do. A ⅜ in. bit answers for an average keyhole, but as these bits are made to every sixteenth from ¼ in. to ¾ in., and every eighth beyond, and as they are useful for so many purposes, as many sizes as possible should be bought. It is essential to the proper entrance of the key and passage of the spindle that the holes for them be square to the surface of the door, when a square is applied with the stock horizontal as well as vertical. A serviceable guide for the boring bit is a turned piece of wood—say, 6 in. long—with a truly central hole from end to end, and a disc

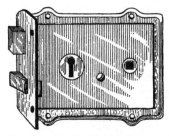

Fig. 951.—Rim Lock with Gothic Steel Case.

shouldered on. But, though such a guide is useful, this refinement of accuracy is not needed for the keyhole of a rim lock. It will be true enough if the precaution is taken to hold the head of the stock at the same height as the point of the bit, and in the other direction as square as the workman can judge. When the bit ceases working, do not force it, but remove the chips if they should be filling the grooves of the bit, and examine the other side of the door to see if the point has got through; if it has, the hole may be completed from that side. Another hole should be made for the bit of the key with a bor-

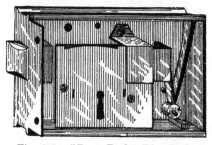

Fig. 952.—"Draw Back" Rim Lock.

ing bit of suitable size, and the two holes cut into one by a keyhole saw. Take care not to cut away too much, which a crooked saw will be almost sure to do; but to avoid this risk cut once only in the middle of the wood between the

holes, and complete the work with a thin chisel. The hole for the spindle can be bored with a $\frac{1}{2}$-in. bit, and if each hole has been made carefully, nothing remains but to screw the lock on and fix the box staple. Round-headed screws are mostly used for rim locks, and ordinary flat-headed screws for the face-plate. Put on the knobs and spindle, and the escutcheon, or keyhole plate; this plate is generally fixed with escutcheon pins. The knobs and spindle, together with the escutcheons and finger-plates, are generally termed lock furniture in the trade; and when ordering, specify rim or mortise lock furniture, as the case may be, as there is a distinct difference between the two. Do not buy the old-fashioned knobs simply secured to the spindles with a screw, a most unsatisfactory arrangement, and one that is bound to give trouble at an early date. There is a great number of patent knobs

Fig. 953.—Night Latch.

in the market, and some of the best of them are the cheapest, and cost very little more than the old-fashioned sort. This matter is returned to later (see p. 294). Cutting in the edge may be needful in the fixing of the box staple; or, on the other hand, the staple may require mounting on a piece of wood. In either case, see that the bolt and latch of the lock have just enough freedom when the door is locked—say, about the thickness of a veneer or stout card. If there is a moulding round the frame, the box staple must be let into it, fitting it very carefully. Fig. 951 shows a rim lock having a Gothic steel case, and this is fixed in just the same way as the others. A further form of rim lock is the draw-back lock shown by Fig. 952, which is also fitted in exactly the same way, except that there is no spindle to be accommodated.

Night latches (Figs. 953 and 954) for street doors are locks that require careful fixing. Measure accurately the distance

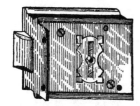

Fig. 954.—Night Latch, Double-handed.

from the edge of the lock to the centre of the key-pin, mark the same on the inside of the door, and bore for the keyhole, cutting for the bit of the key with a small mortise chisel as neatly as possible. Then apply the latch and cut the flange, trying the key before fixing the lock. If the pin on which the key turns projects from the lock, as in Fig. 955, cut in the flange first to the correct size, and then applying the lock and holding it parallel to the door, though it cannot yet be held close to its surface, press enough to imprint the position of the key-pin upon the door. This will at once, if the lock has been carefully adjusted to the position, give the centre of the keyhole. This method is the better plan if the key-pin projects enough, and particularly if it is pointed. The escutcheon

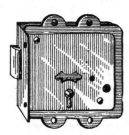

Fig. 955.—Night Latch with Projecting Pin.

for a night latch usually differs a little from that of an ordinary lock. Night latches can be opened with a key only from the outside, there being a knob on the inside for pulling back the latch. Fig. 953 shows a 4-in. two-lever night latch; Fig. 954 a

4-in. two-keyed, double-handed latch ; and Fig. 955 a night latch in a stamped case.

Of the many locks for which mortises have to be cut, the most important is the door mortise lock (Figs. 956 and 957). Generally this has to be let into a finished

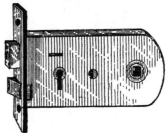

Fig. 956.—Door Mortise Lock.

door, and so the work must not be set out with pencils or gauges. Apply the lock to the door first one side and then the other, similar to the method described for the rim lock, but taking care that the flange is flush with the edge of the door. Then mark the position of the key and spindle-holes with a pointer as was done for rim locks. An essential matter is to see that the edge of the door is square ; if it is not, the marking out, as described, will not agree, but will differ by the amount of variation from the square edge. Usually, truth lies between the extremes, and a compromise must be made. Cut the keyhole and bore for the spindle first, and proceed to mortise for the lock. In this case bore as much of the wood away as possible, and be sure

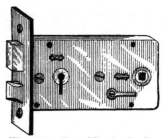

Fig. 957.—Door Mortise Lock.

not to make too tight a fit. Having bored all that is possible, clear out with chisels. A curved mortise lock chisel (Fig. 140,

p. 38) is useful to finish with. When enough has been cut away to let in the lock, the flange may be let in and the lock fixed. For the striking plate, adopt the printing plan used for till locks (see p. 296), and mor-

Fig. 958.—Sash Mortise Lock.

tise for the latch and lock bolts; then when the brass plate is applied at the right height, and just showing the mortise edges coincident with the edges of brass striking plate, it can be marked round, cut in, and fixed. The patent mortise furniture now so much used in preference to the old set-screw fixed knobs (see p. 292) gives trouble, because the screws that fix the rose—in this case not merely an ornament, but a flange, on which the knob can turn, but yet is fixed—are so close to the knob that a tool cannot bore the holes so squarely to the face of the door as is desirable; and if the knob is not fixed correctly it will have to be altered. The best way, probably, is to mark the position of the holes when the knob is in its right place, which can only be ascertained by trial with the square spindle in its place through the lock and

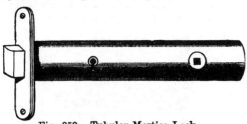

Fig. 959.—Tubular Mortise Lock.

into the knob. Then removing the knob, but noticing the position of the flange, in order to keep the same holes to each other that have been marked, bore the holes, replace the knob, and fix. The reason why the flange must be kept as it was marked is be-

cause the screw holes bored in it are not always equally distant from the centre or from one another.

OTHER MORTISE LOCKS.

Camp-desk locks and pianoforte locks are also fixed in a mortise. For the first, see that the edge has the correct bevel. In the second, see that the mortise is made at the correct angle, for the flange is not generally square to the body of the lock, and pianoforte locks are superior to the desk locks, as, when the former are unlocked, the bolts are flush with the surface, and therefore not in the way. Desk locks are just the reverse of workbox locks, the hooked bolts taking the place of the link-plate. Fig. 958 shows a sash mortise lock fitted in a similar manner to the above.

FITTING TUBULAR MORTISE LOCKS.

The tubular mortise lock (Fig. 959) is quite easy to fix if a certain amount of

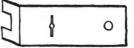

Fig. 960.—Template for use in Fitting Tubular Lock.　　　Fig. 961 — Twist Bit Guide.

care is taken, and the direction and appliances for fixing are supplied with the lock. Fig. 960 shows the template for marking the exact position of the key and spindle holes. Fig. 961 is termed the twist-bit guide; this is screwed temporarily on to the edge of the door, taking care that it stands exactly in a line with the face of the door; then pass the twist-bit through the guide, and bore a hole the exact size of the lock. Remove the guide and push the lock into its place, and by marking the centre of the screw holes in the face-plate on the edge of the door get the exact centre for boring two more holes with the same twist-bit to take the face-plate of the lock; the same twist-bit bores the proper size of sinking for letting in the striking plate. By this method, then, the putting on of a tubular mortise lock is a mere matter of boring a series of holes perfectly true.

How to Order Door Locks.

There are many kinds of locks, known by a variety of names, and great care is necessary in ordering them so that they answer requirements. In ordering a lock for a door, it is a good plan to make a rough sketch, showing how the door is hung, and on which side or hand the lock is to be ; and if there is a latch-bolt, which way this is bevelled. If the rough sketch takes the form of a plan of the door, having the hinges marked, the place of the lock (inside or outside), the thickness of the door, width of stiles, and position of the doorsteps, a mistake is rendered very unlikely, and waste of time avoided. A lock is said to be right-hand when it is on the right-hand edge of the door, viewed in all cases from the outside, and left-hand when it is on the left-hand edge.

Fig. 962.—Till or Drawer Lock.

It is assumed that a door opens inwards. If a door opens outwards, this order is reversed in the case of a rim lock or latch, unless the lock is to be on the inside, and in that case it is called a reverse latch-bolt, either right or left hand. The right-hand lock turns the bolt to the right, the left-hand turns the bolt to the left. In this the lock is supposed to be on the inside. In mortise locks of modern form there is now no difficulty, as the latch-bolt is in most instances reversible, and the striking-plate finished and lacquered both sides ; but as there is often no indication on the outside that the bolt is reversible, inquiry should be made when purchasing. Nearly all mortise and rim locks are now made with reversible bolts. Always tell the ironmonger from whom the lock is obtained the thickness of the door, and see that the key is long enough, especially in rim locks or night latches ; if not, either

a return of the lock, an unnecessary cutting in, or an alteration of the key is required. For a very thick outer door the use of mortise locks is advised whenever the expenditure of a few additional pence is no object.

Fitting Till or Drawer Locks.

A till or drawer lock (Figs. 962 to 964) presents some difficulty to inexperienced

Fig. 963.—Till or Drawer Lock.

workers, but by taking each detail singly, and being careful to do each correctly, a neat job can be made. First ascertain the centre of the drawer front and mark it lightly with a pencil. The length of the flanges of the lock should be measured carefully, and this distance marked off on the top edge of the drawer ; then the lines are squared on the edge and down the inside, as shown at A, B, C, and D (Fig. 965). Take care, of course, that the centre of the keyhole corresponds with the centre of the drawer already determined. With a marking gauge set to the breadth of the top flange, gauge the line E ; set the gauge exactly to the breadth of the wide flange, and make line F. Set out the socket for the body of the lock as shown by G H K L

Fig. 964.—Till or Drawer Lock.

M N, and with a fine saw cut along the lines G N and K L ; of course, these cuts will terminate at the lines H and M, and will therefore be slanting cuts, not being the depth of the lock at the bottom, but being cut to the proper depth by a mallet and chisel. The waste between the lines may be removed by these tools. or by

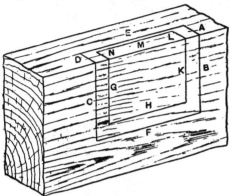

Fig. 965.—Setting out Inside of Drawer for Lock.

simply paring out with a chisel. Next carefully remove the wood for the flanges of the lock as indicated at Fig. 966. If care has been taken, the lock will then be found to fit satisfactorily. The position of the keyhole must now be set out. The pin B usually projects a little beyond the body, and as the lock is pressed into position the end of the pin will make a small indentation. Place the edge of a very fine bradawl directly in the centre of this indentation of the pin, and bore squarely right through to the front of the drawer. With a small centre-bit, or, better still, a

Fig. 966.—Socket for Drawer Lock.

twist-bit, place the point in the hole made by the bradawl and bore right through. To prevent the bit splintering the wood inside,

a piece of waste may be held against it. With a slightly smaller bit, in a similar manner bore through for the hole for the bottom of the keyhole. With a fine keyhole saw remove the wood between these holes, or pare it away with a small chisel. The lock should now be placed in position and the key tried in; if it is satis-

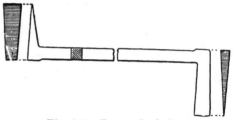

Fig. 967.—Drawer Lock Chisel.

factory, the lock may be fixed by the insertion of two or four screws. An escutcheon may be let in flush on the outside, and it may be necessary to enlarge the keyhole somewhat to fit this in; it must be remembered that this kind of escutcheon must be pressed in sufficiently tight to hold, but at the same time not so tight as to force in the fibres of the surrounding wood. Thread escutcheons may be marked on the work by pressure or a slight tap with a hammer, which will imprint the outline of the escutcheon. To cut the bolt hole in the rail above the drawer, insert the key in the lock (when the drawer is open), turn up the bolt, and smear the end with some black material such as lampblack mixed with a drop of glue or soiled oil from the oilstone; then turn down

Fig. 968.—Box or Chest Lock.

the bolt, shut the drawer, and again turn up the bolt several times so that it strikes against the rail above. After removing the drawer, almost the exact shape of the bolt will be found marked on the rail, and the space thus marked should be chiselled out so that the bolt does not strike against its top. A special tool for cutting out the bolt hole is the drawer lock chisel shown by Fig. 967.

FITTING BOX OR CHEST LOCKS.

The box or chest lock (Figs. 968 and 969) is fixed in exactly the same manner as a drawer lock, but a little care is required

Fig. 969.—Box or Chest Lock.

to fix the link-plate. To do this, lock the link-plate in and slam down the lid of the box sharply. Now unlock it, and the two pins will hold the link-plate in position on the lid, and on carefully opening the lid the link plate will be found ready for marking round exactly over the place where it is to be let in. It is best to let the link-plate remain in the lock while it is cut in, or it may be found that, though space sufficient for the lock has been made, room has not been obtained for the links. The key must be tried before fixing the lock, in order to ensure room for the movement of the bolt. The smallest keyhole that will allow the key to pass is the best, and the hole should be so bored that when the lock is applied the key-pin is in the centre of the hole. This, however, might be said of every keyhole, and of the fixing of every lock. Perhaps it is a lesser evil to slightly

Fig. 970.—Straight Cupboard Lock.

shift the lock to suit a keyhole cut somewhat in error than to destroy the shape and enlarge the keyhole in the attempt to rectify the error, or leave the keyhole so that the key binds in it.

FITTING STRAIGHT CUPBOARD LOCKS.

Straight cupboard locks (Fig. 970) do not need cutting in, but are unsightly. They have an advantage not possessed by a cut cupboard lock, of being equally available

Fig. 971.—Cut Cupboard Lock.

for right or left. Their fixing is very simple, as they are merely screwed flat on the door. The position of the keyhole is got by measurement, and as the bolt shoots out on both sides it is both right- and left-hand, and this advantage, combined with the facility of fixing, makes its use very general.

FITTING CUT CUPBOARD LOCKS.

Cut cupboard locks (Figs. 971 and 972) can be put on in a similar way to drawer locks, except that the hole for the key can, if desired, be bored from the inside, which would be difficult or impossible in a drawer. The cut cupboard lock should be let in flush whenever possible, but sometimes the peculiar fixing of the striking plate prevents this, the back-plate being let in. In fixing, first bore the keyhole, and get this and the keyhole of the lock exactly opposite, and see that the face of the lock is

Fig. 972.—Cut Cupboard Lock.

exactly flush with the edge of the door. Mark with a pencil round the body of the lock and the length of the face-plate, and let these in until the back-plate lies on the back of the door (but not let in); then the key can be tried in the lock, and it must enter readily before the back-plate has been finally let in ; then if the key does not enter exactly, the lock can be shifted a

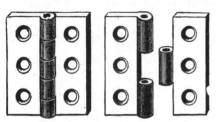

Fig. 973.—Butt Hinge. Fig. 974.—Butt Hinge Divided.

trifle, but to do this after the lock has been let in spoils the job entirely.

Renewing Locks.

Sometimes when a new key is wanted for a lock, the locksmith or ironmonger will advise the purchase of a new lock ; this may be cheaper than having a key cut specially, but the purchaser must be very certain that the proposed new lock is an exact replica of the old one ; otherwise it will be far better to have the old one repaired and a key cut to it, even if it costs more than a new one would, because very often it is much more troublesome to make a new lock fit the place of an old one (unless it has exactly the same shape) than it is to put a lock on a place where there has not been one before. The keyhole often gives most of the trouble, and then there are the screw-holes and the striking plate ; and lastly, modern locks being more compact than the old ones, an ugly mark shows all round them on the

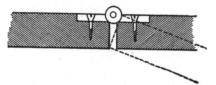

Fig. 975.—Hinge with Centre Outside Door.

door, drawer, etc., as the case may be. If a new lock can be obtained in all respects the same as the old one, its fixing will be a mere matter of screwing it on, as, of course, if the cutting for the old one was correct it must suit the new lock also.

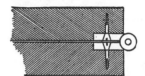

Fig. 976.—Door Hinge Closed.

Butt Hinges.

It would prove interesting to trace the hinge from early ages, when some inventive genius first applied the principle of the hinge by connecting two boards with a flexible joint perhaps of raw hide or twisted fibre, to the ornate metal work of later times, and onward to the more serviceable if more prosaic contrivances of the present day. The modern tendency

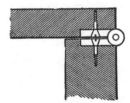

Fig. 977.—Hinge with Centre at Edge of Door.

seems to be towards simplicity, but mediæval hinges are splendid specimens of ornate metal work. The cranked centre hinge which was fastened at the top and bottom of, say, a wardrobe door, is no longer in such general use as it was only a few years ago, having been superseded by the butt hinge. This is the most important hinge

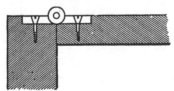

Fig. 978.—Door Hinge Closed.

used in cabinet work, and, indeed, it may be taken as the typical form. Perhaps the butt hinge will be better known as the ordinary door hinge, as shown in Fig. 973.

The general construction can be understood very readily by merely examining a hinge. It consists of two flaps moving on a wire

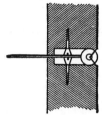

Fig. 979.—Hinge with Centre Inside Flap.

pivot. The side shown in Fig. 973 is known as the front, the reverse as the back. By back, however, is often understood only the rounded part, which is visible when the hinge is fixed and the door, or whatever it may be attached to, is shut. In the finer qualities of hinges the backs are often polished and lacquered; the fronts also may be finished in the same way. The quality varies considerably, both in weight of metal and general style. Roughly speaking, a good hinge is one in which the parts work smoothly against each other without twisting or straining. It is obvious that the joint of a hinge is usually divided unequally; for example, in Fig. 974, where the two flaps of a butt hinge are shown apart, one of them has two projections, and the other only one. However many projections there may be, generally one side has an even number of them, and the other an uneven; thus in Fig. 973 there are three on one and two on the other. The

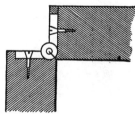

Fig. 980.—Hinge Stopped at 90°.

side with the even number is called the double, and the other the single. The custom is not invariable, as in some hinges each side has the same number; but, not counting "lift-off" hinges, where the reason is obvious, observation shows that the

exceptions are generally of a little lower quality. This remark, however, must not be taken too strictly, and there may be good makes among the exceptions.

PRINCIPLES OF HINGEING.

It will assist the worker to obtain a knowledge of the why and wherefore of

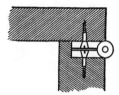

Fig. 981.—Recessed Hinge Closed.

the different methods of hinge fitting if he directs his attention to Figs. 975 to 982. As has been shown, a hinge is a connecting but flexible plate, moving on one or sometimes two centres, which often are of strong wire. When more than one hinge is used on a door, etc., the centres of the hinges must be in one line; and the centre pin should be just outside the flap or door (see Figs. 975 and 976). The flaps there shown will close flat together as in Fig. 976, and will open out as far as the dotted line in Fig. 975, making more than half a revolution. Fig. 977 shows the hinge fixed so that the centre is exactly at the edge of both of the flaps, the possible movement being just a semicircle (see Fig. 978). In Fig. 979 the centre is well within the substances hinged together, and there could not be any movement unless the angle had been removed as shown. If the angle is planed off equally at 45°, and to

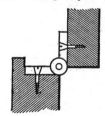

Fig. 982.—Recessed Hinge Open.

the same distance, the movement is limited to 90° (see Fig. 980). But it is not always desirable to cut for hinges in, say, the lid of a box, so the whole substance of the hinge is recessed into the part that will hold the longer screws (see Figs. 981 and 982).

HANGING DOOR WITHIN ENDS.

The easiest way of hanging a door would be to screw the hinges to the outside, but

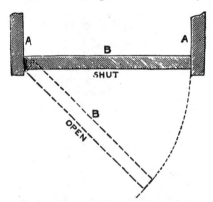

Fig. 983.—Door Hung within Ends.

this would proclaim the novice at once, though it would do for rough-and-ready work. Take for example a door, B, hung within the ends, A, as in Fig. 983, an enlarged detail of the hinge being shown by Fig. 984. The door ought to fill the whole of the opening, so a space must be cut into which the hinge can be sunk. As to whether this recess should be made in the door or in the end, a little consideration will show that it will be far simpler to let the hinge into the door than into the end. Again, it will hardly require a practical trial to convince anyone that it is easier to screw the hinge first to the door, and then to fit the door in its place. For an ordinary butt hinge, a marking gauge is set from the pin in the joint of the hinge to the edge of the flaps; that is to say, the distance between the marking point and the block of the gauge is equal to half the width of the hinge when opened out flat. Gauge this on the edge of the door from its front so as to obtain the width of the recess for the hinge. Its length is easily arrived at by marking direct from the hinge, but it will be well not to trust to this entirely, or at least to take

care that the centre of the knuckle—the pin—of the hinge is exactly true with the edge of the door. Were one hinge of a long door to have its centre not in line with that of the other, instead of both being in line and both being parallel with the edge, there would be an undue strain, and perfect action could not be expected. To avoid risk on this score, however, mark off the ends of the hinges with a square. Cut out the marked out space deeply enough to allow the closed hinge to be laid in it so that no part of it is above the level of the wood. It is customary to cut away the wood a little deeper towards the back, where the joint of the hinge is. This, though flush on the end of the door, projects a little in front. The only reason for letting the hinge in deeper at the back is to provide against any accidental projection of a screw head above the hinge plate, which would prevent the hinge folding close. Of course, proceed the same for the other hinge. The hinges now are screwed to the door, using screws of such a size that their heads can be properly sunk in the hinge countersinks. It is a common practice to knock the screws in with a hammer for a short distance—just far enough in to allow the screwdriver to be used without causing them to wobble. When the hinges have been firmly fixed, the hanging of the door may be proceeded with. In the case of large doors this is a somewhat troublesome operation, but in small work it requires only a little care.

Fig. 984.—Detail of Door Hingeing.

Open out the hinges, and place the door against the ends in the position it is to occupy when the work is completed, holding it partly open, in order that the loose hinge plate may be got at. As a rule, doors in cabinet work are set back from

$\frac{1}{8}$ in. to $\frac{1}{4}$ in. within the ends, according to the size of the article, but there is no real necessity for this; the only reason is that

Fig. 985.—Incorrect Application of Hingeing on Ends.

it looks better. As the door when fixed ought to open and shut freely without scraping against the floor or bottom, the necessary space must be left between the two parts. This should not be great in a well-fitting door. Place a sheet of glass-paper or thin veneer on the floor, and let the door rest on it. The top of the door may be left, for it can be eased off if it fits too close, and till the actual fitting up is all but done it is as well for it to fit tightly. Bore a hole for one screw through the top hinge, and drive in the screw to afford temporary support and allow of adjustment of the door, which can be regulated till it hangs true. Then fasten the other hinge, or, in the case of more than two, the bottom one, with another screw. The door may now be opened and shut, and if it can be moved properly the remaining screws may be driven in. The reason for the temporary fixing with but one screw in each hinge is that, in the event of a misfit, when the door is actually swung, one screw is more easily removed than a greater number, whilst the bite of the

screws is not weakened by unnecessary holes or enlargements of holes which may be required if the position of the door, or rather the hinge, has to be shifted a trifle. One hole to a hinge being a little bit out does not matter, as the other screws will hold well enough, and they can be fitted with certainty.

HANGING DOORS ON ENDS.

Instead of the door being within the ends or framing to which it is attached, it is often found covering these or outside of them. A common example is in an ordinary wardrobe with sliding trays; another is the small drawer pedestals on top of a registered writing table. In the latter the drawers are secured by a narrow hinged wooden pillar, which, for the present purpose, may be regarded as a door. Now it is obvious that were the door in such cases as these fixed within the ends, the trays in the wardrobe and the drawers in the pedestal could not be drawn out, because the hinged edge of the door would stop them.

Fig. 986.—Correct Application of Hingeing on Ends.

Of course, the end by the door may be, and often is, thickened up to allow of the drawers sliding, but then this naturally means that the length of the drawers is shortened by at least the thickness of the door framing. It must not, however, be supposed that hanging the door on the end is applica-

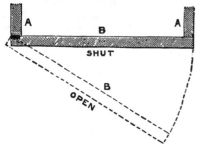

Fig. 987.—Door Hung on Ends.

ble only when there are drawers and trays. However, a general rule is that doors are not hung on the ends when this necessitates cutting away the thickness of the door frames, so as to leave an overhanging part, as, for instance, when there are drawers above the door, as in Fig. 985, which shows

Fig. 988.—Detail of Door Hingeing.

incorrect construction. In this case, and often in sideboards which have drawers above the doors, the doors must be within the ends. When, however, the door goes up to the top, as in Fig. 986, or, as in the case of a wardrobe, runs right up to the frieze or cornice, there is no reason why the door should not be hung on the ends;

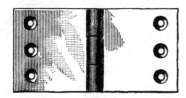

Fig. 989.—Butt Hinge for Carriage Doors, etc.

here it is simply a matter of design. A door is hung on ends much in the way described in the previous paragraph, the chief differ-

ence being that the hinge is sunk in the end with, of course, the joint outside as before; more care is needed to see that the

Fig. 990.—End View of Carriage Door Butt Hinge.

bottom of the door does not drag. The edge of the door frame should be flush with the external surface of the end, and the hinge pin be in the same relative position as before; this is made clear in Fig. 987, the actual hingeing being better shown by Fig. 988. In Fig. 987, A indicates the ends, and B the door.

VARIETIES OF BUTT HINGES.

The many modifications of the ordinary butt hinge are useful at times, but generally they may be dispensed with, and, with a little ingenuity, the ordinary butt substituted, though perhaps at a sacrifice of appearance. Try the effect, for example, of allowing the knuckle of the hinge to project further than mentioned above; then, of course, as the centre or pivot is further from the front, the swing of the door is altered. In many instances, such as with carriage doors, where, owing to their curve, the pivot could not be fixed close up, or when a door must swing clear of a moulding, a hinge allowing of more throw must be used, so as to get all the centres in one straight line. For this purpose some hinges have comparatively wide flanges with screw holes bored near the edges, as in Figs. 989 and 990. Others, as shown in Figs. 991 to 995, are made with the flaps bent, but there is such an immense variety of these cranked hinges that a complete list cannot be given. A few

Fig. 991.   Fig. 992.

Figs. 991 and 992.—Cranked Butt Hinges.

likely to be of more general use may be noted. The heave-off hinge is shown in Fig. 996, from which it will be seen that the flaps are separable easily, and consequently a door or lid fitted with them can be removed without unscrewing the hinges. A

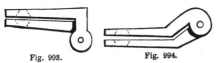

Fig. 993.   Fig. 994.
Figs. 993 and 994.—Cranked Butt Hinges.

familiar example of their use is in Lancaster's old pattern of cheap cameras, in which one half of each hinge is on the bottom board, and the other on the casing of the bellows body. Stop butt hinges (Fig. 997) can be opened only halfway to form a right angle, and are useful for fixing box lids or doors which are not intended to swing far. Sometimes for a heavy door the hinge used has one plate broader than the other, as in

Fig. 995.—Cranked Butt Hinge.

Fig. 998, the extra width of one flap allowing a greater grip to be taken on the wood than when both are narrow or only the width of the thickness of the door frame ; this is known as a wardrobe hinge. It has been mentioned that sometimes each part of a hinge is sunk into the wood, but in furniture this is seldom done except when the weight of the door is so great that additional support is required to relieve the

Fig. 996.—Heave-off Butt Hinge.

downward drag on the screws. Fig. 999 shows a hinge with plates thickened to form a shoulder against the wood, but this is sel-

dom used, although its peculiar construction gives an appearance of massiveness, besides certain other obvious advantages.

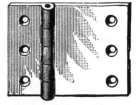

Fig. 997.—Stop   Fig. 998.—Butt Hinge
Butt Hinge.   with Unequal Flaps.

A more usual way of giving a slightly ornamental and finished appearance to the hinge is to have small knobs at the ends of the pins, as in Fig. 1000. Such hinges generally are used in the better class of furniture, and are known as knob hinges or tipped butts. The knobs are made in a large variety of patterns, one catalogue alone giving about thirty of them. As a rule, knob hinges are well made and carefully finished, so their apparent high price is not due solely to the knobs.

BACK-FLAP HINGES.

Next in importance to the butt hinge for general utility is the back-flap, shown by Fig. 1001. In this the proportions are quite

Fig. 999.—Butt   Fig. 1000.—Knob
Hinge with   Hinge or Tipped
Thickened Plates.   Butt Hinge.

different from those of the butt hinge, the plates being wide and short instead of long and narrow. Their function is to connect two flat surfaces which are desired to be hinged in such a way that they may be level when the hinge is opened out. A common application in furniture is in the construction of flap tables ; the hinge plates are

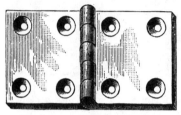

Fig. 1001.—Back-flap Hinge.

let into each piece of the table on the underside with the knuckle downwards—that is, in the reverse way to that illustrated. In old-fashioned bureaux, the back-flap is used to connect the lid or writing table part with the carcase, the hinge being let in on top, with the rounded joint upwards. It is hardly too much to say that the butt and back-flap answer nearly all requirements. All other hinges are modifications of these. For instance, the portable desk or bagatelle hinge, shown in Fig. 1002, is only the back-flap hinge greatly narrowed in the direction of the knuckle with long, projecting plates. This form is used for small writing desks and folding bagatelle tables, the long, narrow plates being sunk into the wood so that only the rounded part projects above the surface. Another shape of these hinges is shown by Fig. 1003.

Card-table or Counter Hinges.

The card-table or counter hinge is a distinct form, and may be used with advantage whenever a projecting knuckle is not desirable. Fig. 1004 is a typical hinge. The

some two, and some more. A card-table or counter hinge of another kind is shown by Fig. 1005. This is used in pairs only ; they are fixed to the ends of the pieces they connect, and not to the surfaces. There is a

Fig. 1003.—Bagatelle Hinge.

hinge similar to this used for attaching the folds of a screen, the plates being sunk in the top and bottom edges of the framing ; also it can be used in other situations.

Screen Hinges.

When a screen is intended to fold in any direction, the proper screen hinge (Figs. 1006 and 1007) must be used. This is the most ingenious of the various kinds of hinges usually met with, and, compared with single-action hinges, it is expensive. They must be very carefully fitted, even more so than ordinary hinges. The ordinary double-action screen hinge is shown open and closed by Figs. 1006 and 1007 respectively ; and there is another important variety somewhat on the principle of the hinge shown by Fig. 1004. It is often difficult to decide which is the best and cheapest way of hanging screen frames. A screen should be hinged so that it will close both ways, but the expense of the special double folding joints already mentioned is too great to admit of their frequent use, and there is a cheap, simple, and efficient

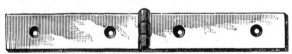

Fig. 1002.—Bagatelle Hinge.

Fig. 1004.—Card-table or Counter Hinge.

flaps are connected, not by a pin running through them, but by a separate plate pivoted to each of them. As with all other hinges, these vary considerably in detail, some having only one connecting piece,

substitute. Assuming that the frames are ready for hanging, and that the screen consists of four frames, there will be three separate hangings, which will require six laths laced together in pairs, as illustrated by Figs. 1008 and 1009. The laths should be sawn out of a ½-in. board the full height of the frames, and if the thickness of them is ⅞ in. the laths should be ¹⁄₁₆ in. wider,

Fig. 1005.—Card-table or Counter Hinge.

to allow the screen to close flat together without any strain. Gauge and plane up the laths both in width and thickness, neatly finish off the ends so that all of them are exactly the same length, and, to prevent the sharp edges cutting the tapes, rub them well off with sandpaper. They are now ready for painting, staining, varnishing, or polishing, as may be preferred. When they are dry, proceed to put on the tape, which may be got in various colours from ¾ in. to 1 in. wide; about 3 yds. will be required for each pair of laths. Mattress binding is good; being made of linen it does not stretch. Begin by tacking the end of the tape to the top end and under-side of one of the laths in an oblique direction; lay the two laths together, pass the tape up between them from the under-side. and lace them together rather loosely, over and under, first left, then right, and leaving a loop as shown in Fig. 1008. When sufficient turns have been put on to reach the

Fig. 1006.—Screen Hinge Open.

bottom, begin again at the top to pull the laths tight together, turn by turn, and regulate the distances; fasten the end off at the bottom to the under-side, as before. It is of

great advantage to hold the two laths edge to edge in the bench vice while pulling the tape tight, as it leaves the two hands at liberty. Proceed now to hang the frames

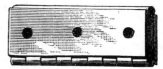

Fig. 1007.—Screen Hinge Closed.

together; bore four holes in each lath, at equal distances between the tapes, neatly countersink for screw-heads, and screw them to the edges of the frames. This joint has a very pleasing effect if it is neatly done and the tape is made to harmonise with the material on the frames. It is durable, draught- and sight-proof, and can, if necessary, be renewed at a very small cost of time and money. Another substitute for the special metal hinge is illustrated by Fig. 1010, though possibly this is not so good as the device just described. The hinge is made on the same method as that of the old-fashioned clothes-horse;

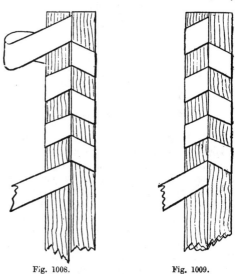

Fig. 1008.   Fig. 1009.

Figs. 1008 and 1009.—Screen Laths Laced Together.

but, instead of a pair of webbings top and bottom, the hinge is continuous and is formed of thin oil-cloth cut to, say, 3 in. or 4 in. wide, as at A (Fig. 1010). Begin

at the top, and tack the strap flush with the
top of the top rail following on to the
bottom, each strap touching the one above.
Such a hinge opens and closes either way,
and costs very little, and the joint is
draught-proof. The hinge should be nailed
on before the screen is covered, so that the
covering hides the tacks and makes a neat
job. The joint is so strong, that thick
calico or black buckram may be used instead of oil-cloth. Webbing would answer
if two widths were put together as at B
(Fig. 1010), but wide strips are less trouble,
taking fewer tacks and less time.

FANCY AND SPECIAL HINGES.

To return to hinges proper, and to fancy
and special hinges in particular, the butler's
tray hinge must be mentioned ; it has what

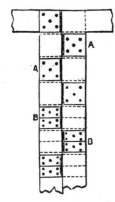

Fig. 1010.—Cloth Screen Hinge.

in default of a better term may be called
a spring stop, by means of which the sides
of a butler's tray are kept upright when
required. The upper surfaces of the hinge
are flush with the wood, without any projecting knuckle. When the tray has square-
ended flaps, this form of hinge is not necessary, as for the spring stop may be substituted a special catch let into the flaps of
the tray. It is, however, advisable to use
a hinge which does not, even at the joint,
project above the wood. Occasionally it is
considered desirable that the hinges should
not be seen, and then is used a secret hinge,
or, to give it its more ordinary name, a
centre hinge ; a plain one is shown by Fig.
1011. These hinges are used for hanging

doors, either within or on the ends, and
their use involves more labour than the
ordinary butt hinge, because either the door

Fig. 1011.—Secret or Centre Hinge.

must be rounded off or a shallow groove for
its edge to turn in must be cut in the piece
against which it works. Centre hinges are
seldom used. Great care must be taken to
get the projecting pin, shown in Fig. 1011,
correctly centred in the door frame. One
part of the hinge is let into this, and the
other into the wood above it. Centre
hinges are to be had cranked or bent in
a variety of ways (Fig. 1012 is an example)
to suit different kinds of doors and to throw
them back as may be desired. Formerly
centre hinges were used for wardrobes, and
occasionally they may be used with advantage ; but the centre hinge is not the proper
thing to use, unless there is a better reason
than the false notion that a hinge is an
ugly thing in itself, and should be kept out
of sight when possible. A hinge may be

Fig. 1012.—Cranked Centre Hinge.

made to serve as an ornament on any piece
of furniture by using a strap hinge, in which
the flap is placed outside. Some made for
this purpose are highly decorative, but the

same effect may be gained by the use of hinge plates, which are mere pieces of ornamental brass. They are screwed on to a door, close up against the hinge, to which they must, of course, be equal in length.

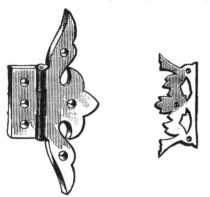

Fig. 1013.—Hinge with Ornamental Flap.　　Fig. 1014. — Ornamental Hinge Plate.

In general design, the hinge plates should correspond with any other brass work, such as handles, about a piece of furniture. Fig. 1013 gives a complete hinge with ornamental flap, and Fig. 1014 shows a separate plate. In addition to the hinges of which mention has been made, there are a large number of others, used principally by builders, and differing in shape as well as in size from those used in cabinet work. For instance, there are the cross-garnet hinge (Fig. 1015) and the tee hinge (Fig. 1016), both employed for heavy and more or less rough work.

Fig. 1015.—Cross-garnet Hinge.

BADLY FITTED HINGES.

Hinges require careful fixing, and may give trouble in three different ways. The spaces may be cut deeper than necessary, causing the door or flap to be hinge-bound; the door may be thicker than expected, and so the back may be too hard

upon the stops—then it is stop-bound; or the screws may not fit into the countersunk holes, but project, causing the work to be screw-bound. This last fault is the worst of all. All these defects produce similar effects, and they are all easily avoided if care is taken.

THE RULE JOINT.

The rule joint is a device used by cabinet-makers and joiners to hide the hinges which connect various parts of table-tops, shutter-flaps, etc., where a neat appearance is desired. It resembles only partly the joint of an ordinary rule (from which it has obtained its name), as the movement of a rule is half a circle, whereas the rule joint used in cabinet work is restricted to but little more than a quadrant. The appearance of the finished work when open is very like an ovolo moulding; when closed, of course, the surface shows only

Fig. 1016.—Tee Hinge.

a joint line. The size of the cylindrical portion of the joint is not important, but it may be about two-thirds of the thickness of the table-top to which the device is to be applied. The tools used for the work are either a pair of hollows and rounds or a pair of planes made for the purpose. These planes closely resemble a hollow and a round, except that they include more of the circle than the general tools. The round has the centre point of arc marked on its ends; and the hollow has a part of the straight abutment, as well as the curved part, included in the operating cutter. A pair of table planes includes also a gauge. There is also an improved rule joint pair of planes, with fence, to be had in various sizes suitable for various thicknesses of wood; these gauge the work from the top side, and it is therefore imperative that the wood be gauged to the proper thickness beforehand, because as the

hinges are let in and fixed on the under-
side, they really form the gauge. A rule
joint made with these planes must have
wood and hinges to agree with the thickness

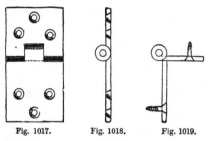

Fig. 1017.   Fig. 1018.   Fig. 1019.

Figs. 1017 to 1019.—Rule Joint Hinge.

of the wood provided for by the planes.
For the present purposes it is assumed that
hollows and rounds and the rebate plane
are the tools used. The edges of the boards
to be joined are shot straight and square.
Supposing that the flush side is the under-
side of the boards, set the gauge to the
radius of the quarter circle, and mark on
the top surface of the fixed flap and the
under-side of the movable board. Make
another gauge line on the edge at a distance
made up of the radius as before, plus the
distance from the surface of the hinge to
the centre of motion. The hinges resemble
a back-flap, but the parts are unequal; the
holes are countersunk on the other side,
and are disposed differently from those
of a back-flap. Further, the hinge has
clearance sufficient to bend back much further than has an ordinary hinge (see Figs.

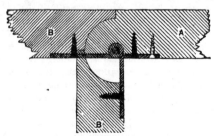

Fig. 1020.—Rule Joint.

1017 to 1019, which show respectively the
face of the hinge, the edge when flat, and
the edge when open at a right angle). The
hinges should be true to gauge, square, and
all alike in thickness and in position of
centre-pin. If the hinges are not good and
true, the job cannot be satisfactory. Fig.
1020 shows a section of a rule joint with
the moving part in two positions. It is
important to notice that the centre of the
hinge-pin must agree with the centre of the
part of circle shown, and that the centre-
pins of all the hinges used must be exactly
on the centre line. Fig. 1021 shows the
wood gauged for working the joint. In
fixing the hinges, help will be given by a
line drawn across the flat surface of the
hinge, indicating the position of the centre,
which, when the hinge is fixed, is out of
sight, especially if a similar line is also
drawn on the under-side of the fixed part
of the table-top. The plate of the hinge
must be let in with special care not to cut
too deep across the joint, though, in order
to allow the brackets or leg rail, or whatever supports the movable flap, to pass
freely, provision must be made, when gauging, for the full distance of the hinge thick-

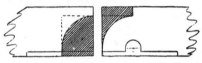

Fig. 1021.—Wood Gauged for Rule Joint.

ness. The knuckle of the hinge is let into
the quarter-cylinder portion of the joint,
and care must be exercised, or the chisel
may cut too deep and show a mark on the
rounded surface, and so spoil the appearance of the joint. It is suggested that the
quarter cylinder should be as much larger
than the knuckle of the hinge as will allow
a reasonable amount of security in this
operation. A small gouge will be of great
service in this work. First fix the hinges
on the fixed part of the work A (Fig. 1020),
and not on the flap B, as is done sometimes.
The screws are to be a good fit in the hinges,
not projecting above the countersink, nor
long enough to push the wood aside on the
visible surface. Beginners will find it an
advantage to use short screws. Fresh holes
in the proper position may be bored much
more easily if short screws have been
wrongly placed, or, at any rate, the error
will be less serious.

HOUSES, RUNS, AND COOPS FOR POULTRY.

Hen Coop with Chicken Run.

The coop shown by Fig. 1022 is intended for use in rearing early chickens. The front has a hinged flap which may rest on the top of the run as shown to shelter it

Fig. 1022.—Hen Coop with Run.

partially during the daytime, or it may be lifted higher and secured with a hook and staple. At night the run may be removed, and the flap let down to keep the brood warm and ward off cats and rats. If the latter are troublesome, the holes over the flap may be covered with wire netting

1½-in. by ¾-in. stuff, as shown at the top and bottom of Fig. 1023. Sound ¾-in. deal should be used throughout, and the joints of the boards should be tongued and grooved for the sheeting. Nail on the boards to form the back, putting a strip up the corners if necessary, and get out a rail A (Fig. 1023), 2 in. by ¾ in., notching it for the front rails to fit in at the bottom, and secure it at the sides. Fit another rail across the top as shown, then put on the roof. Next fit up the front (Fig. 1024), mortising the middle rail A through the roof to allow of its being lifted to release the hen. Make the hinged flap for the front by cutting three or four boards to length and cross-battening them with a couple of ledges; then prepare a rail 2 ft. long by 1½ in. by ¾ in., and secure the flap to this with a pair of butt or tee hinges. This rail should be secured to the front of the coop with screws, so that it can be removed easily with the flap when not required. The run can be made by cutting two 9-in. or 10-in. boards 3 ft. or more

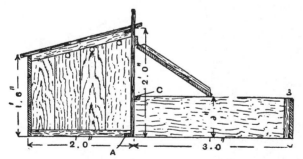 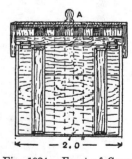

Fig. 1023.—Longitudinal Section of Coop and Run.　　Fig. 1024.—Front of Coop.

The construction is more clearly shown in the longitudinal section (Fig. 1023), and in the view of the front of coop with the run removed (Fig. 1024). To make the coop, first prepare the boards to form the sides; put them together and nail to ledges of

long to form the sides, and a piece 1 ft. 10½ in. by 9 in. wide for the front. Upright pieces may be nailed on to strengthen the corners B (Fig. 1023), and a cross rail C must be used at the side against the front of the coop to carry the wire netting. A hinged flap at the front end of the run will be found useful when supplying soft food and water for the chickens, and the top of the run may be covered with $\frac{3}{4}$-in. or 1-in. mesh

Fig. 1025.—Portable House and Run.

wire netting, secured to the sides and ends with small staples. A few centre-bit holes may be bored in the coop through the top of the sides to ensure thorough ventilation.

PORTABLE FOWL-HOUSE AND RUN.

The house and run illustrated by Fig. 1025 occupies but a small space whilst forming the cheapest possible pen in which fowls may be kept in health and comfort. The house and run are made separately, so that they are easily removable to fresh ground when that on which they are placed becomes foul, and the run is covered with wire netting, which is omitted in Fig. 1025 to prevent confusion. For the house illustrated the run is 8 ft. or 9 ft. long by 5 ft. wide, with a height of 2 ft. 9 in. At the end farther from the house the run is roofed over for a couple of feet, to provide shelter in case of rain at times when it is

not desirable for the birds to crowd into the house. The run is framed together with 1½-in. square deal scantling, with 7-in. by $\frac{3}{4}$-in. boarding round the bottom, and the joints between the uprights and rails may be either half-lapped or mortised and tenoned. In the centre of the back end four or more bars may be framed as shown, to give the birds access to a trough of soft food or clean water, and enable them to take the one or the other without upsetting or fouling it. The two centre bars may be made movable for the purpose of feeding, etc. For a pen for seven or eight birds the dimensions of the house may be 5 ft. long, 3 ft. 6 in. wide, 3 ft. 8 in. high in front, and 2 ft. 10 in. at the back. It may be built throughout with $\frac{3}{4}$-in. matchboarding, strengthened with framing pieces of 2-in. by 1-in. deal. Fig. 1026 is an elevation of the front of the house, the run being removed, and shows the doorway by which the fowls have access from the run. This is cut in the centre, and is fitted with a sliding shutter, which may be closed at night and be held open in the daytime by means of a cord and pulley, or a hole and iron pin. In the top portion a hinged flap is provided for the purpose of ventilation, and this may be opened and closed by means of a common iron stay as used for greenhouse ventilators (see Fig. 1027).

Fig. 1026.—Front of Portable House.

Fig. 1027.—Fowl-house Ventilator.

INTERIOR ARRANGEMENTS OF FOWL-HOUSE.

Fig. 1028 is a longitudinal section of the house, showing the arrangement of the perches, floor, and nesting boxes. The perches are made by sawing a 2½-in. or 3-in. round pole through the centre, or instead a couple of 2½-in. by 1½-in. rails may have the corners rounded off on one side.

removing the eggs, the end of the house behind the nesting boxes is fitted with a ledged door, the outside of which is shown by Fig. 1030. This is hung at the top by

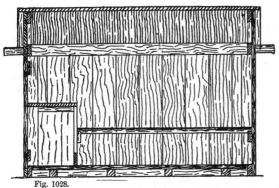

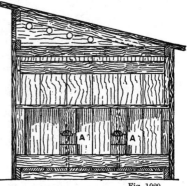

Fig. 1028.

Fig 1029.

Figs. 1028 and 1029.—Sections of Portable House.

For carrying the perches a couple of notched fillets A (Fig. 1029) are nailed to the front of the nesting boxes at one end, and a similar pair may be nailed inside the opposite end of the house; these should be arranged at a height to keep the perches about 1 ft. above the ground. The floor is made by nailing 1-in. boards to three or four 1½-in. square ledges, and it should be well coated with a mixture of hot tar and quicklime sprinkled with as much sand as will lie on it. The floor is simply a platform quite separate from the house, and will fall away when the house is lifted up. Care must be taken that there is not sufficient space between the sides of the house and the floor for the birds to get their feet caught and jammed. At one end, as shown on the left of Fig. 1028, a shelf is fixed across and secured to the sides by means of fillets at about 16 in. or 18 in. above the floor, according to the breed of the birds, and the space under the shelf is divided into three compartments, as shown in Fig. 1029, to serve as nesting boxes. A strip about 2½ in. or 3 in. wide is nailed across the front at the bottom, as shown in Figs. 1028 and 1029, to keep the nesting material in position, and pieces 2 in. wide are nailed up the sides on the outside, pieces 5 in. wide being put on the divisions between the boxes to separate the nests from the rest of the house. For

a couple of cross-garnet hinges, and secured with a turn-button at the bottom, or if necessary by a more secure fastening. For a larger house it may be advisable to have a couple of doors over the boxes. For the purpose of lifting the house, handles (see Figs. 1025 and 1026) are screwed to the top rails, back and front. The roof should be made watertight by nailing strips over the joints or covering with felt, and the house can be painted or tarred outside and well limewashed inside. The woodwork of

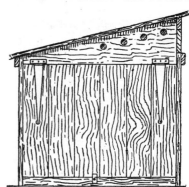

Fig. 1030.—End of Portable House.

the run should also have three coats of paint or a coat of tar. Four ventilation holes are shown at the top of Fig. 1030; these should be bored with a 1-in. centre-bit at each side.

SITTING BOX FOR BROODY HENS.

For rearing chickens under a hen, it is necessary to provide a quiet nest where the mother bird will not be disturbed by the

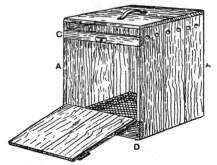

Fig. 1031.—Sitting Box for Broody Hen.

other fowls; and when a special shed would be too expensive, the nesting-box illustrated by Fig. 1031 will be found useful. It may be made of $\frac{3}{4}$-in. deal boarding, or if some sound packing cases can be obtained, Tate's sugar boxes for example, they may be used without much alteration, an inch or so in the dimensions either way not being of much importance. To make the box, first prepare the sides A (Fig. 1031), cutting the boards 1 ft. 4 in. long and making up the width to 1 ft. 4 in., the

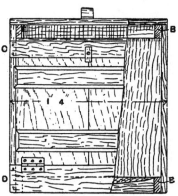

Fig. 1032.—Part Elevation and Section of Box.

strips B (Fig. 1032) being nailed at the top and bottom to hold the sides together. These strips or ledges may be $1\frac{1}{2}$ in. wide by $\frac{3}{4}$ in thick. On the front edges, notch

out a piece at C (Fig. 1032) $1\frac{1}{2}$ in. by $\frac{3}{4}$ in., and $1\frac{1}{2}$ in. from the top, and a piece at the bottom D, $2\frac{1}{2}$ in. by $\frac{3}{4}$ in. Then make up the back E (Fig. 1033) similar to the sides, and nail the back and sides together. Board over the top and prepare for the front a top rail C, $1\frac{1}{2}$ in. wide by $\frac{3}{4}$ in., and nail it in the notches. Prepare the bottom rail D, $2\frac{1}{2}$ in. by $\frac{3}{4}$ in., and on the inside nail a ledge F (Fig. 1033), $1\frac{1}{2}$ in. wide, after which the rail may be fixed in the position shown. Now cut a piece of $\frac{1}{2}$-in. or $\frac{3}{4}$-in. mesh wire netting a little larger than the inside of the box, and secure it to the ledges round the bottom of the box with wire staples, so that it will sag in the middle and nearly touch the ground. Make

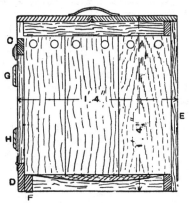

Fig. 1033.—Cross Section of Sitting Box.

a door for the front by nailing ledges G and H (Fig. 1033) across a couple of boards fitted into the opening, the top ledge G being kept a little longer than the width of the door to form a stop. The door may be hung with a pair of butt hinges, or with a couple of pieces of leather fixed to the bottom rail, and secured at the top with a turn-button. To complete the box $\frac{3}{4}$-in. holes should be bored through the sides and back, just below the top ledge, and either a leather strap, as shown, or a common iron handle secured on the top in the centre for carrying the box. Fig. 1031 shows the box with the lid let down to allow the fowl to walk out of the nest; Fig. 1032 is a front view of the box with a portion of the right-hand side in section; and Fig. 1033 is a section of the box from the front to the back, showing the wire netting at the bottom.

LEAN-TO POULTRY HOUSE AND RUN.

Fig. 1034 is a general view of a poultry house and run, Fig. 1035 being a sectional

work, and ¾-in. matchboarding for the roof. As most of the leading dimensions are given on the accompanying illustrations, the sizes and number of the pieces required can be readily seen. The quantity of wood required will be as follows:—For

Fig. 1034.—Poultry House and Run.

plan. Front and end elevations are given by Figs. 1036 and 1037 respectively. The run is continued under the roosting shed, which is an advantage where space is a consideration. The run can be made to any extra length desired, in which case it may be necessary to provide one or more intermediate uprights to the front and cross pieces to the roof to carry the wire netting. Timber about 3 in. by 3 in. will be most suitable for the general frame-

framework, about 80 ft. of 3 in. by 3 in., and 130 ft. of 6 in. by ¾ in., matchboarding for sides and roof; 40 ft. of 6 in. by ⅞ in. grooved and tongued floor boarding for the floor; 10 ft. of 3 in. by 1½ in., and 2 ft. of 4½ in. by 1½ in., for door to run, shown open in Fig. 1034.

ROOSTING SHED OF LEAN-TO HOUSE.

The pieces for the framework of the roosting shed having been cut to length, plane them up and set out the four posts. Mortises are made for the tenons of the bottom rails and the floor, at the same time making mortises for the rails of the run in

posts and the top rail of the front, and top rail of the back, is shown by Fig. 1039. The frame should next be fitted, and the joints nailed together ; a little paint applied to

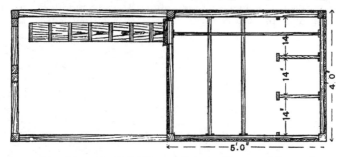

Fig. 1035.—Sectional Plan of Poultry House and Run.

two of the vertical posts. The three rails at the bottom, and the four forming the support for the floor (see also the cross-section, Fig. 1038), now are set out, and the tenons and shoulders cut in the usual way. The mortises in the posts carrying the bottom rails are cut about 2 in. from the bottom, which allows a portion of the posts to go in the ground, and makes the

the parts forming the joints before fastening will add much to their durability. For the floor, tongued and grooved floor boards (or even thick matchlining) is suitable. The floor P R (Fig. 1040) should be nailed to the front and sides, some strips or fillets, about 1¼ in. by 1 in., being nailed to the inside of the posts as shown, care being taken to keep their outer edges flush with

Figs. 1036 and 1037.—Elevations of Poultry House and Run.

structure more rigid. The two top rails A B (Fig. 1038) are planed on the top edge to the slope of the roof. A simple but suitable form of joint for the top of the

those of the floor boards. The match-boarding to the front and sides can then be nailed in position, keeping the frame true while fixing. The door is best formed afterwards by nailing the top of the boards and cutting along the line E F (Fig. 1036). The cut should be started at L before the boards are placed in position. The two

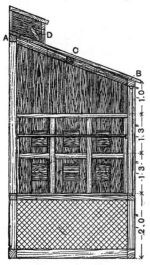

Fig. 1038.—Cross Section of House.

ledges for the back are of the same thickness, and 3½ in. wide, and are secured to the back of the boards by nailing through the front side and clinching the nails on the back of the ledges (see Fig. 1034). The door can be hinged with two 15-in. crossgarnets, as shown in Fig. 1036. To keep out the draught, and also to form stops for the door and support the pieces of board over the top of the door, three strips of wood, about 2 in. wide and ¾ in. thick, should be nailed round the inside of the opening, and should project about ½ in., so that the door shuts against them. Before constructing the roof it will be best to fit up the nests; ¾-in. boarding will do for the purpose. The best means of fixing the shelves and divisions will be to nail fillets to the sides and floor, to which the boarding can be nailed. Matchboarding will be best for the roof, as then rafters will not be required, one bearer, going from side to side c (Fig. 1038), being sufficient to support the roof. The boards in this case run from front to back. The entrance holes for the fowls can now be cut out, and two rebated slides and a sliding door made.

Fig. 1041 shows a portion of a slide made of two strips of wood. A hinged flap is fixed on the outside, covering the holes of the nests, so that eggs can be removed without opening the door of the roost shed (see Figs. 1037 and 1038). A hole is cut in the roof for ventilation, and a ventilator fixed as illustrated. The flap D (Fig. 1038) is hinged to the roof, and can be opened

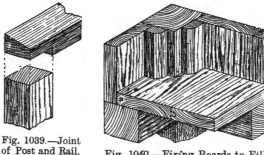

Fig. 1039.—Joint of Post and Rail.

Fig. 1040.—Fixing Boards to Fillets, Floor, etc.

or closed to regulate the ventilation. It is advisable to cover the roof with felt, to make it watertight.

RUN FOR LEAN-TO HOUSE.

The construction of the run for the lean-to poultry house should not present much difficulty. The joints H G O and J (Fig. 1036), and M and N (Fig. 1042), are mortise and tenon. Fig. 1042 is an end elevation of the run. The joints at K and L (Figs. 1036 and 1042) require care in making, the various parts being shown enlarged by Figs. 1039 to 1041,

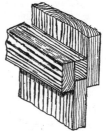

Fig. 1041.—Part of Poultry-house Slide.

and Fig. 1043. Fig. 1043 shows the joint at K (Figs. 1036 and 1038) fixed together, and Fig. 1044 the pieces ready for putting together. The joint at L is illustrated in the same manner by Figs. 1045 and 1046. The door of the run can be constructed of wood about 1½ in. thick, the joints being formed by mortise and tenons, or halving, and should be hinged to the back post with two 3-in. butts. A strip of wood about 1 in.

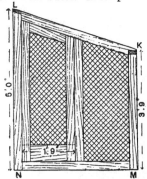

Fig. 1042.—End Elevation of Run.

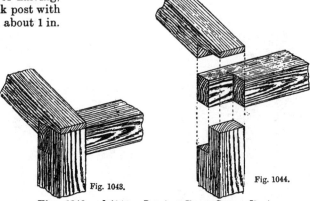

Fig. 1043.   Fig. 1044.

Figs. 1043 and 1044.—Joint at Front Corner Post and Top of Run.

by ¾ in. is nailed to the middle post, so that the door shuts against it. The inclined board, with strips across for the entrance to the roost, should be about 7 in. by 1 in. The fixing of the wire netting and a few fastenings complete the structure.

FATTENING PEN FOR CHICKENS.

Fig. 1047 shows a section and Fig. 1048 a front elevation of a pen or coop for use in fattening chickens or keeping broody hens. The pen is made of ¾-in. matchboarding, and will hold two fowls. The legs and framing may be of 1½-in. by 2-in. deal, and the doors are hinged at the top and secured at the bottom by means of turnbuttons (see Fig. 1048). The doors lift for cleaning, but some pens are made with a barred bottom, and have a drawer underneath to catch the excrement. The roof is of ⅝-in. matchboarding and strips are nailed over the joints to keep them weather-proof. A piece of zinc may be fixed to the wall at the back to prevent the water running down behind, and the roof projects about 6 in. in the front to keep the feeding troughs (Fig. 1049) dry. The compartments, or at least the one to hold water, should be lined with zinc. The troughs are held in position on the doors by brackets made by 1-in. by ⅛-in. hoop-

iron bent to fit (see Fig. 1050). In making the pen, the front and back rails A and B first are framed together with the legs and the end rails C; the last then are nailed to the wall and the bottom is fixed. The front and ends then are framed and nailed in position, and a partition is added to divide the two pens. Next the roof is put on, and the doors are framed together by nailing the ledges across the uprights, and then hung in position, iron hinges screwed on the face being used.

OUTDOOR CHICKEN REARER.

Fig. 1051 shows an outdoor rearer for accommodating fifty chickens. The house

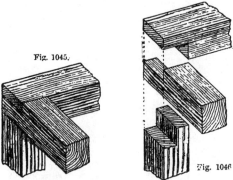

Fig. 1045.

Fig. 1046.

Figs. 1045 and 1046.—Joint at Back Corner Post and Top of Run.

or sleeping compartment A is 2 ft. square, made of ¾-in. floor boards, and is 24 in. high at the front and 18 in. at the back, thus giving a good slope to the roof. Two fillets of wood E (Fig. 1052), 1 in. by ¾ in., are nailed at a distance of 2 in. from the ground, and on this fillet the bottom is fixed. The two sides are shaped at the bottom as shown to allow air to get to the

front of the house at the top. This completes the woodwork for the sleeping compartment.

FITTINGS OF CHICKEN REARER.

The metal fittings of the chicken rearer include the lamp, burning the best crystal

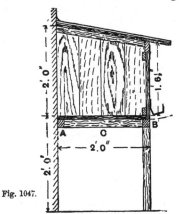

Fig. 1047.

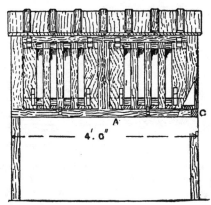

Fig. 1048.

Figs. 1047 and 1048.—Section and Elevation of Fattening Pen for Chickens.

lamp. In the centre of the bottom a 6-in. circular hole is cut to accommodate the lamp reservoir. Two more fillets are nailed as shown at a distance of 10 in. from the inside of the bottom. On these rest the inner lid, made of ¾-in. stuff; it fits easily inside the case, and has handles for convenience in lifting out, and a 3-in. hole should be cut in the middle to allow the waste heat to escape. The four corners should be blocked up with pieces of wood 5 in. wide (not shown), to keep the chicks from overcrowding there, thus making the rearer bottom hexagonal in shape. The outside lid overlaps all round by about 1½ in., and should be hinged by the side. On the front of the house fillets measuring 1½ in. by 1 in. are fixed; they should be 9 in. from the bottom at the ends, and should have a rise of 9 in. at the middle These support one end of the glass run. A small hole is cut in the front of the house for the doorway, and here a ladder is fixed. Another hole D (Fig. 1051), 5 in. by 3 in., is cut in one of the sides midway between the inner lid and the bottom. This hole should be filled with glass, so that the lamp can be inspected without opening the rearer. Four 1-in. holes should be bored in the

oil, fitted with a ⅝-in. "Silver" burner. The reservoir is 5½ in. wide by 3 in. high, and has a concave top, with small holes punched in the flange so that the air can pass to the burner. A shield of coarsely perforated zinc is fixed round the opening cut in the bottom. This shield should be 7 in.

Fig. 1049.—Chicken Feed-   Fig. 1050.—Bracket
ing Trough.   for Feeding Trough.

wide and about 9 in. high, and a piece of fine muslin is tied round the bottom of it to keep the bedding material from falling on the lamp. The flange of the lamp reservoir should be cut so that it passes through this shield easily. The heat, as it rises from the lamp, is thrown down by means of a galvanised tray made in the shape of an oven tin; it is 18 in. square, with sides 2½ in. deep, and is fixed to the under-side of the inner lid, leaving a ¾-in. space between the two. A good way to fasten it to the lid is to make four holes in the corners of the tray to take 1½-in. wood screws and to pack it off with washers to the desired thickness. The heat as it is thrown down by the tray warms the chamber to any degree—90° F. can be attained without any trouble—and the fumes and waste heat escape between the

ing the whole up, hinge together the sides of the glass and wire runs, leaving a ¾-in. space between the two. This space is to support the middle partition, which just slips in. Two pieces of stuff 9 in. by 1½ in. by 1½ in. are nailed at the ends of the wire run, and to these pieces the end is fixed by means of screw-eyes. The sides of the

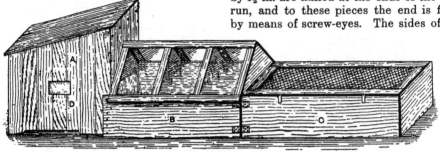

Fig. 1051.—Outdoor Chicken Rearer.

tray and inner lid through the 3-in. central hole, and finally escape through the holes bored in the front of the house.

Runs for Chicken Rearer.

The runs are made to fold up for convenience in packing when the rearer is not in use. For the sides of the runs four pieces will be required, two pieces for the glass run B (Fig. 1051) 2 ft. 8 in. long by 9 in. wide by ⅝ in. thick, and for the wire

glass run overlap the house by 2 in., and are again fastened by means of screw-eyes to the house. One side of the glass lights is fastened to the house by means of brass plates (Fig. 822, p. 250) which are screwed to the frame, one at the top and one at the lower end of the frame. A frame of wood should be made to fit flush on the sides of the wire run, and four pieces of iron 2 in. long by ½ in. wide should be screwed to the sides of this frame to keep it from slipping off. To the under-side of this frame a piece of wire netting, 1 in. mesh, is fixed.

Portable Gable-roof Poultry House.

The gable-roof poultry house (which may or may not be on wheels) illustrated by

Fig. 1052.—Section of Sleeping Compartment of Rearer.

Fig. 1053.—Rearer Partition.

run c two pieces 3 ft. 6 in. by 9 in. by ⅝ in. ; one piece for the end of wire run 2 ft. by 9 in. by ⅝ in. ; and one middle partition (Fig. 1053) made of ¾-in. floor board, which should be cut to the same eave as the fillets on the front of the house. In mak-

Figs. 1054 to 1056 would accommodate about fifteen fowls ; for ten birds, the size may be about 4 ft. 6 in. by 4 ft., for twenty-five birds it should be 7 ft. by 5 ft., and for fifty birds 9 ft. 6 in. by 7 ft. The eaves should be kept to the same height in every case, and the roof should be at the same angle, which will make the centre higher in the larger and lower in the smaller houses. A poultry house as illustrated would be suitable for an orchard or field in which the house can be frequently moved, if it is necessary to

pieces 2 ft.. 8 in. by 2½ in. by 2 in. for the rafters, and one piece 4 ft. 6 in. by 3½ in. by 1 in. for the ledge. The method of securing the ends to the sides is shown by Fig. 1058, notches A being cut in the corner posts, into which the rails are halved as at B, the joints being secured by means of

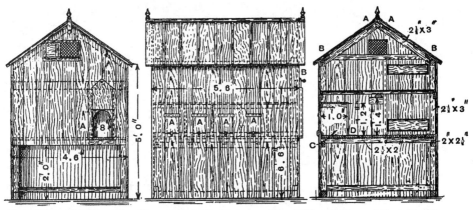

Figs. 1054 and 1055.—Elevation of Portable House.   Fig. 1056.—Section of Portable House.

confine the fowls to a run, thus giving them the advantage of fresh ground. To build the house, prepare four pieces 5 ft. 3 in. by 3 in. by 2½ in. for the corner posts, two pieces 5 ft. 6 in. by 3 in. by 2½ in. for the bottom sills, and four pieces 5 ft. 6 in. by 2½ in. by 2 in. for the rails. Notch the long pieces to the uprights as shown at A in Fig. 1057, which shows the joint between the top rail and the corner post, keeping the top of the middle rail 2 ft. 0½ in. above the bottom, and secure each joint with a couple of 2-in. No. 14 wood screws, or any other approved method can be adopted. See that the frame is square, and nail on the casing, which may be of ¾-in. match-boarding, or preferably, if a little extra expense is not important, 1-in. boarding. On one side, leave four 8-in. spaces in the positions shown at A (Fig. 1055), which may be fitted with doors hinged with a strip of leather at the top and fitted with a button at the bottom, for the purpose of gathering eggs from the nest boxes without entering the house. The timber for the ends may now be prepared; for the front end, one piece 4 ft. 6 in. long by 2½ in.; 2 in. will be required for the bottom rail, two

screws through the outside boards, if it is desirable to take the house to pieces in sections for moving. A doorway 12 in. by 8 in. is cut in the position shown at A (Fig. 1054), and slide pieces are nailed on each side of this to enable the door to be lifted, an iron pin B (Fig. 1055) being used to hold it in position, or it may be hung with

Fig. 1057.—Joint at   Fig. 1058. — Jointing
Corner Post Top.   Side to End of House.

a pulley and cord. At the top, an opening about 12 in. by 8 in. is cut at each end and filled in with ¾-in. mesh wire net, for the purpose of ventilation, a sliding shutter shown at the top of Fig. 1054 being used to regulate the amount of air for cold or warm weather. The method of halving the rafters to the corner posts is shown at B (Fig. 1057), and a recess A (Fig. 1059) is cut at the top of both ends to take the ends of the ridge pole. The inside of the back end is shown in Fig. 1056. A doorway, fitted with a 3 ft. by 1 ft. 8 in. ledged door, which may be hung with cross-garnet

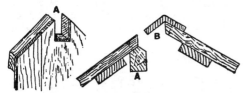

Fig. 1059.—Recess to take Ridge Pole.   Fig. 1060.—Jointing Ridge of House.

hinges and fitted with a hook and staples for a padlock, is provided at this end, the rails being arranged in position for the door to shut against. The boards at this end are brought down to the ground, but the bottom rail is kept up 3½ in. as shown in Figs. 1054 and 1056, so that the notches for this rail and the side sills do not come opposite each other. The object in keeping the front end 2 ft. above the ground, as shown in Fig. 1054, is to provide a dry run for the fowls, and this should have dust baths or should be covered with a few inches of ashes. The floor is covered with 1-in. matchboarding supported on three joists 4 ft. 4 in. long by 2½ in. by 2 in. to which the boards may be nailed. The floor at the ends rests on the end rails, but should not be nailed if the house is built to take apart. The positions of the floor

Fig. 1061.—Chicken Ladder.

joists are shown by dotted lines in Fig. 1055.

Roof of Poultry House.

Sound matchboarding should be used for covering the roof, unless felt or galvanised iron sheets are to be used on the outside. A section of the roof is shown at the top of Fig. 1056; and if the house is to be a fixture, the boards may be nailed to the eaves rails and the ridge pole. But if the house is built in sections, four half boards, as shown at A and B (Fig. 1056), should be nailed to form ledges to keep the boards

together when taken off. One side A (Fig. 1060) may be nailed to the ridge pole, and the crease B, of wood, lead, or zinc, should be nailed to the other side. Then, when the roof is put in position, the ridge pole, with the finials attached to the ends, is simply dropped into the recesses A (Fig. 1059), and the ledge B (Fig. 1056) rests against the eaves rail. The other side is put on, and a few screws through the crease B (Fig. 1060) and at the ends and sides will keep the boards in position. To make the joints of the boards weather proof, strips 1 in. by ½ in. are nailed over them as shown in Fig. 1055.

Interior Fittings of Poultry House.

In fitting up the inside, four nest boxes C (Fig. 1056) are made. To make these,

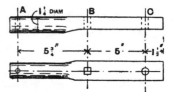

Fig. 1062.—Axle Arm for Portable House.

fillets 1½ in. by 1 in. are nailed to the inside of the house, to which a shelf 1 ft. 2 in. above the floor and the full length of the house is fixed. The space under this is divided into 12-in. compartments, shown by dotted lines in Fig. 1054, an outside door being provided for each at A, and a strip 2½ in. wide D (Fig. 1056) nailed along the front. Three perches are used, two being across the house and one running lengthways in the centre. These may be made by sawing a pole 2½ in. or 3 in. in diameter through the centre, the ends resting on fillets nailed to the ends and sides of the house. The top of the perches should not be more than 1 ft. 6 in. above the floor. A ladder (Fig. 1061), made by nailing strips across a 7-in. by 1-in. board, must be provided to enable the fowls to enter the house from the run.

Mounting Poultry House on Wheels.

When a poultry house of the above description is fitted with iron wheels, a considerable addition is made to cost, but as the wheels are only wanted occasionally, wooden ones will serve the purpose. Two pairs of wheels should be used for a large house, and one pair, fixed in the middle, will be sufficient for a small house. The

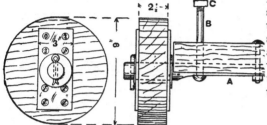

Fig. 1063.—Wheel and Axle Bed.

wheels should be fixed to the house only when required for moving, especially if one pair is used. They should then be taken off and stored in a dry place, and by this means one set of wheels will serve for any number of houses. The axle arms (Fig. 1062) may be of four pieces of $1\frac{1}{4}$-in. round iron about 12 in. long, flattened at one end, with a $\frac{3}{8}$-in. hole drilled at A for a split pin, a $\frac{1}{2}$-in. square hole punched at B, and a $\frac{1}{2}$-in. round hole drilled at C for bolts.

wood $2\frac{1}{2}$ in. thick, sawn or turned to 9 in. in diameter. Two plates, 3 in. by $\frac{1}{4}$ in., are screwed across the grain on each side to prevent splitting and to act as bearings for the axles. A washer is used inside and outside the wheel to prevent the plates rubbing on the end of the bed or on the split pin. When the wheels are not in use, they may be taken off by removing the split pin, and the beds may be left on to act as sleepers for the house, or the bed and wheels may be removed bodily by levering up the ends of the house and taking off the nut C.

Run for Movable Poultry House.

For the house above described, the best way to make a wired run will be in the form of hurdles (Figs. 1064 and 1065), any number from four upwards of that shown by Fig. 1064 being used for the sides, and one like Fig. 1065 for the end farthest from the house. The hurdles shown are intended to form a covered run, 2-in. wire netting being used over the top. This may be fastened to the top rail of the hurdles on one side and tied to the other side with wire. If the run is wide the roofing nets should have a wire reeved through the

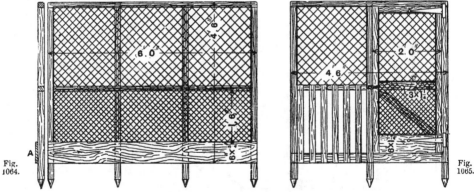

Figs. 1064 and 1065.—Hurdles for Sides and End of Run.

The arms are let into two ash beds $2\frac{1}{2}$ in. square, as shown at A (Fig. 1063). One bolt B should project $3\frac{1}{2}$ in. above the bed to pass through the sill of the house, to which it is secured with a washer and the nut C. The wheels may be of elm or any hard

selvedge edges where they join, and should be supported with a prop placed under the wire in the centre of the run. If a quiet class of fowls is kept, the hurdles may be made 6 ft. high, and it will not be necessary to cover the top of the run with net-

21

ting. To make the hurdles, get out four uprights 5 ft. 2 in. long by 2 in. by 2 in. if deal is used, or 1½ in. square if made of oak. If the latter can be obtained, it will be better

vent splitting the wood. The bottom rail consists of a 6-in. by ¾-in. board nailed to the uprights as shown at A (Fig. 1064). The upper portion of each hurdle is covered

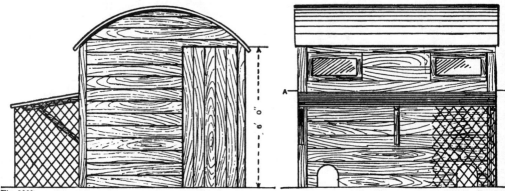

Fig. 1066.
Fig. 1067
Figs. 1066 and 1067.—Side and End Elevations of Fowl House with Semicircular Roof.

to pay the extra cost for this timber on account of its durability, deal posts having a tendency to rot off just above the ground. Next prepare two rails 6 ft. long and of the same size as the uprights. The top rail may be halved to the uprights, and

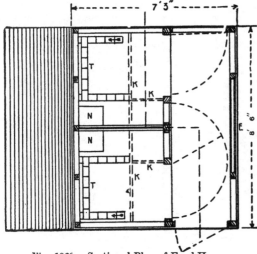

Fig. 1068.—Sectional Plan of Fowl House.

the middle rail tenoned into the outside posts and halved to the middle ones. The joints should be secured with screws, or strong nails driven through and clinched; holes should be bored for the nails to pre-

with wire of 2-in. mesh, and the lower with 1-in. mesh, the object of the latter being to prevent small chickens getting through if the run is used for rearing. In fixing the wire, nail the ends and top of the upper piece, and the ends and bottom of the lower piece, allowing about 1 in. between the upper and lower net; do not stretch too tightly lengthways. The two nets can then be drawn together at the joint with a pair of pliers and wired or nailed to the middle rail; this will stretch the nets tightly on the frame. The construction of the end hurdle (Fig. 1065) is somewhat similar to that of the side hurdle, with the exception that a 2½-in. or 3-in. rail is used at the bottom, and all the joints, except at the top, are mortised and tenoned. A doorway is shown on one side, and the lower netting on the other is superseded by upright bars. A trough for water or soft food may be placed outside this portion, thus preventing the birds getting into the trough and soiling the contents. The door may be of 2½-in. or 3-in. by 1¼-in. stuff, except the bottom rail, which should be wider, and the joints should be mortised and tenoned. A brace is fitted in the corners of the lower portion of the door frame, as shown in Fig. 1065, to keep it square. A pair of cross-garnet or tee hinges may be used for hanging the door, and a hook and staples fitted on the shut side for a padlock. A strip of wood must be nailed on the post against which the door closes, to prevent it falling in beyond the surface of the frame. The house should be given at least three coats of good lead paint on the outside, and the roof may be coated with tar in which a small quantity of quicklime has been stirred. It should be applied hot, and then well sanded. The inside of the house should be limewashed.

FOWL HOUSE WITH SEMICIRCULAR ROOF.

Fig. 1066 shows a side elevation, Fig. 1067 an end elevation, and Fig. 1068 a plan and part section of a simple fowl house with a semicircular roof. Fig. 1068, showing a section on A B (Fig. 1067), makes clear that

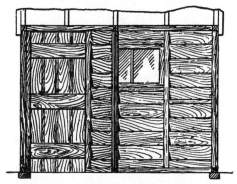
Fig. 1069.—Inside Door of Fowl House.

the house is divided into two compartments, with a passage along the back. The compartments are for the poultry, and might accommodate two kinds separately. Each is complete with nests, roost, and trap, as shown at N, K, T (Fig. 1068). Any suitable boxes will do for nests, and some may be nailed to the sides at convenient heights, instead of being all on the floor. The passage is for attendance, and the fowls should not have access to it. Plain ledged doors are put in the partition between the passage and compartments; there is also a plain ledged door on the passage, the front of which is shown in Fig. 1066. The back of one of the inside doors is shown in Fig. 1069. These inside doors are not boarded close, a space of

1½ in. or so being left between for light and ventilation. A small glazed window is in the front of each compartment, and another in the back of the passage. A covered run stretches along the front, lined up on the side and ends with wire netting.

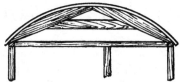
Fig. 1070.—Semicircular Roof.

A semicircular-headed hole at the base of each compartment gives ingress and egress to the run. The roof is, as shown in Figs. 1066 and 1070, semicircular in outline; its boards are ⅝ in. thick, and are covered with felt-cloth tarred. The run is also boarded and similarly covered. The roof ribs or spars will do at 2 ft. centres, one of course to be at each end; 1½ in. thick will be sufficient. The framing is put together with butt joints nailed diagonally. The boarding is rough and laid horizontally, overlapping as shown in Fig. 1071. The window-frames are square arrised, but may be dressed and mortised and tenoned at the joints. The timber may be red or white pine. Corner posts should be 3 in. by 3 in., the rest of the framing 3 in. by 2 in. The posts

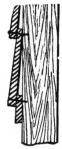
Fig. 1071.—Boarding on Fowl House Framing.

may be let into the ground, but it is best to cut them on the bottom sill, which should be levelled up a few inches. The floor may be simply the ground levelled; but to keep out vermin the floor should be asphalt or concrete, and the netting on the run continued all round.

ACCESSORIES FOR YARD AND GARDEN.

Small and Simple Rabbit Hutch.

A RABBIT hutch may be a very simple construction indeed (see Fig. 1072). Put together a box of suitable size ; or get a common packing-case and remove the lid, if there is one, and one of the long sides. Use this side to heighten the back A, as at E (Fig. 1072), fastening it by wood strips B B. Cut out two pieces C C, and fasten them by strips D to form the body of the

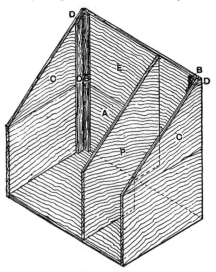

Fig. 1072.—Body of Simple Hutch.

hutch. Cut out a piece to the shape of the sides C (one piece if possible) so as to form partition P (Fig. 1072). Measure one-third the length of hutch from the end. Before inserting the partition, cut out a square of 4 in. or 5 in. from the corner to form the opening shown by dotted lines in Fig. 1072. Insert the partition, and place the lid on the three sloping pieces. Fasten down to form the sloping roof (Fig. 1073), and round the side of the living room L (Fig. 1073) nail

strips S S S S. The framework with wires should form half of the front, leaving a narrow door. The door G, hung with iron

Fig. 1073.—Front Elevation of Hutch.

hinges, covers both the opening O (Fig. 1074) and the sleeping room. On the partition fasten a stout strip, indicated by dotted lines H (Fig. 1073), and hammer a staple to this. Opposite this cut a slit in the door to allow the staple to slip through, as shown in Fig. 1073. A bolt or padlock will easily secure it. The dark or sleeping room should be hidden by a door hung as shown on Fig. 1074, to secure a quiet place while breeding. The roof should be covered with tarred felt. Fig. 1073 shows a front elevation of the complete hutch.

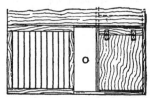

Fig. 1074.—Sleeping-room of Hutch.

Rabbit Hutch with Three Compartments.

In the rabbit hutch with three compartments (Fig. 1075) the sleeping portion can be cut off from the others by a simple slide, as shown at Figs. 1076 and 1077, and the two outer compartments can be opened 1081). For the bottom, use ¾-in. grooved and tongued boards, resting on a fillet as shown by D (Fig. 1078), and on the back rail

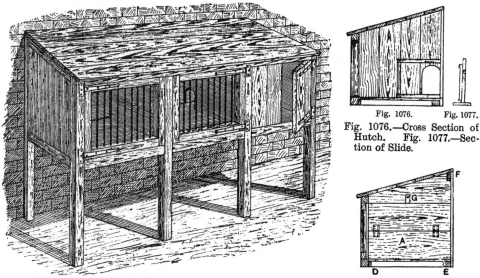

Fig. 1075.—Rabbit Hutch with Three Compartments.

Fig. 1076.   Fig. 1077.

Fig. 1076.—Cross Section of Hutch. Fig. 1077.—Section of Slide.

Fig. 1078.—Cross Section of Hutch.

into one by lifting the board A (Fig. 1078), hinged with two back-flaps and kept up by a button G. The legs and rails of the general framing are of 2-in. by 2-in. stuff. The legs are shown about 2 ft. long, but this is a matter for personal choice.

E. The back is formed of similar boarding running vertical, the bottom ends being nailed to the rail E, and the top ends to the fillet F (Fig. 1078). For the ends, front, and door H (Fig. 1079), use ¾-in. matchboarding, the door having a couple of ledges, about

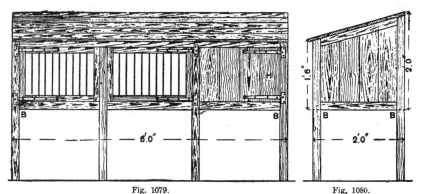

Fig. 1079.   Fig. 1080.

Figs. 1079 and 1080.—Front and End Elevations of Rabbit Hutch.

The pieces should be planed and the joints made, those at B (Figs. 1079 and 1080) being mortised and tenoned together (see Fig. 1½ in. by ¾ in., nailed to the back. Perhaps the best form of roof is boarding covered with felt. The door frames may be of 2-in.

by 1¼-in. material, the open mortise-and-tenon joint for them being illustrated at Fig. 1082. All the doors should be hung with 10-in. cross-garnets. The rails should be bored for the ¼-in. round-iron bars.

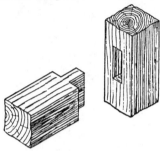

Fig. 1081.—Mortise and Tenon Joint.

GABLE-ROOFED RABBIT HUTCH.

Fig. 1083 shows an easily made rabbit hutch with a gable roof. It is 4 ft. long by 1 ft. 9 in. wide and 1 ft. 9 in. high, exclusive of the roof. Nail the end board to the legs, cut off level, and nail the flat top and the back, and then the bottom, which has a cleat nailed across each pair of legs inside to support it, the boards running length-ways. Nail on the frame of the front, and the middle division of the hutch; make a sliding door in the division so that the hutch will be suitable for breeding. The doors can be halved together, or preferably mortised and tenoned, the grating being formed by ¼-in. iron bars inserted in the top

Fig. 1082.—Open Mortise and Tenon Joint.

and bottom rails of the doors. Bore a few holes in the bottom of the hutch for drainage, and some in the flat top for ventilation. The sloping roof is required only if the hutch has to stand outside. If the ends are

left open as shown, the roof space will be useful as a storage for food and litter. The doors should be hinged on very strongly, and fastened with a padlock by means of two split hasps, which will both fit over one staple in the centre piece of the front frame.

DRAINING A RABBIT HUTCH.

An arrangement for draining a rabbit hutch is suggested in Figs. 1084 and 1085, which show the compartments ranged one over the other. Make the bottoms of the hutches of sound timber, and let them slope slightly to the back corner farthest from the sleeping place. In this corner cut a hole about 6 in. square, and fit in a loose piece of board, through which a few drainage

Fig. 1083.—Gable-roof Rabbit Hutch.

holes may be made with a ½-in. centre-bit. Under this fix a zinc tray, to which a short outlet pipe of the same material may be soldered, leading through the back or side of the box as may be most convenient. Fig. 1084 is a plan of one compartment of the box, with the loose board at A and the outlet pipe at B. Fig. 1085 shows the arrangement in section, A being the zinc trays, B the outlets, and C the loose boards, which can be removed when the hutches are cleaned and the trays swilled out.

SHOW RABBIT HOUSE.

The four houses shown in front and side elevation by Figs. 1086 and 1087 are designed for the reception of fancy rabbits. The framework is 2 in. square oak or ash, and the flooring and sheeting are of $\frac{3}{4}$-in deal, tongued and grooved. The framework is first got ready, the various pieces being mortised and tenoned together, with the exception of the centre posts (back and front) C P (Fig. 1086), which are halved on to the rails. The bottom front rail is 1 ft.

Fig. 1084.—Drain Holes in Hutch.

from the ground, the house being thus kept free from ground moisture and vermin. The height of the doors in the bottom houses is 2 ft. 1¼ in., and only 1 ft. 10¼ in. for the top houses. The front rails F (Fig. 1086) are rebated $\frac{5}{8}$ in. by $\frac{3}{4}$ in., to receive the doors. The middle rail is rebated on each side, as shown in the section (Fig. 1088). The end

top to bottom, and is nailed over them. The inside edges of the whole of the framing pieces should be deeply chamfered (see Fig. 1089). Any square edges which the

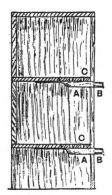

Fig. 1085.—Section of Hutch Floor Drains.

rabbits are likely to gnaw should be taken off. Before fixing, the joints should have a coat of white-lead paint, and the framework can be dowelled together with $\frac{1}{2}$-in. oak dowels. The sheeting is next nailed

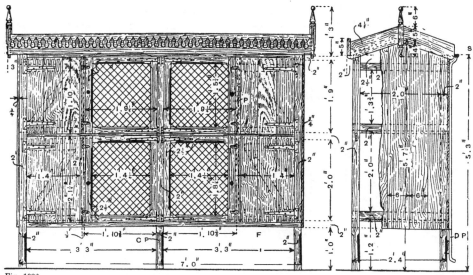

Fig. 1086.

Figs. 1086 and 1087.—Front and End Elevations of Show Rabbit House.

Fig. 1087.

rails are so arranged that the mortises for them come $\frac{3}{4}$ in. above the front rail mortises. It is not necessary to plough either of the back rails, as the sheeting runs from

along the back and each end. The end boards are cut 4½ in. high in the centre, to form the apex of the roof. The ends of the boards are secured together, and strengthened with a batten 2 in. by 1 in. (see B, Fig. 1090). The two floors, the boards of which run from back to front, are now fitted on the

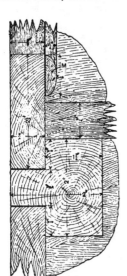

Fig. 1088.—Section of Centre Front Rail and Door Frame.

top side of the front rails, but to the underside of the end rails. This is shown in Fig.

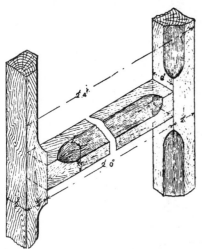

Fig. 1089.—Framing with Stopped Chamfers

1091, in which F B is the floor board, C P corner post, F R front rail, and E R the end rail. Use tongue and groove joints for the

floor-boards, so that when the latter shrink the droppings will not fall through upon the occupants of the lower houses.

CENTRE DIVISIONS OF SHOW RABBIT HOUSE.

To fix the centre divisions D (Fig. 1092) directly above C P (Fig. 1086), screw triangu-

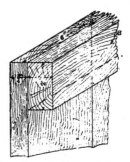

Fig. 1090.—End Board Batten.

lar strips S (Fig. 1092) to the floor and roof boards. Erect a partition 1 ft. 10⅜ in. distant at each side of this division, to enclose the space forming the bed. These partitions are fixed similar to the centre division, and each has a hole 9 in. high by 8 in. wide, through which the rabbit can pass; this hole is seen in the cross section of the upper house (Fig. 1093). A cover piece C P

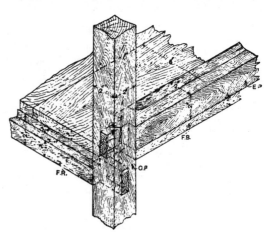

Fig. 1091.—Corner Pillar, Rails, etc.

(Fig. 1093), working upon a button-head screw and washer, fits over this hole. The roof boards R B (Fig. 1093), which run lengthways of the house, are now screwed to the battens of the end boards and to the centre division. Let them overlap at each

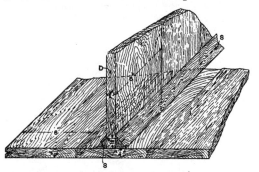

Fig. 1092.—Partition of Show Rabbit House.

end by 3 in., and at the back and front by 2 in. Give them a coat of lead colour paint on the outside, and when it is partly dry, or "tacky," stretch a thick piece of calico or stout canvas over the roof, and, well pressing it, drive in tacks along the ends and back edges. A few tacks can be put along the front edge, but these will afterwards be withdrawn so that it may be turned up the back of the fascia board.

Fascia Boards of Show Rabbit House.

The end fascia boards have square edges, one end of each being shouldered to form a stump tenon, which fits into the end finial, shown in detail by Fig. 1094. The finial is prepared from 2-in. square stuff. The mortises are cut, and the turned part is then set out and worked in the lathe. The fascia boards can now be dowelled, and the whole put up in one piece. To make the front

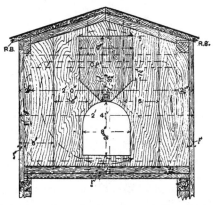

Fig. 1093.—Cross Section through Show Rabbit House.

and another $2\frac{1}{8}$ in. in from the same edge; this last will form the centre line upon which to describe the semicircles. Across the board pencil a series of lines 1 in. apart; these will be alternately the centre line for the circle and the centre line for the pointed piece. Along the line, $1\frac{1}{8}$ in. in, set out each side of the alternate centre line $\frac{11}{16}$ in., and from this point draw the two lines to form the apex. With a 1-in. bit, bore out a row of holes, and pencil a line from the wide part of the pointed piece to form a tangent with the circular hole; and then cut away with a fine tenon saw, the edges being cleaned up with sandpaper. An old round rat-tail file will be found useful for cleaning out the circular work. The edge of the front roof board is planed to an angle to fit the fascia board, which can then be screwed into position. The end fascia

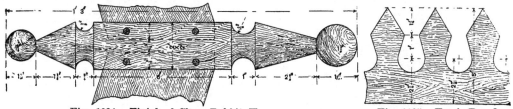

Fig. 1094.—Finial of Show Rabbit House. Fig. 1095.—Fascia Board.

fascia board, set out a board 5 in. wide, 7 ft. $7\frac{1}{2}$ in. long by $\frac{3}{4}$ in. thick, as in Fig. 1095. First pencil a line along its length $1\frac{1}{8}$ in. in,

boards butt behind and support it. Tack the roof canvas R C (Fig. 1096) for about 2 in. up the back of the board. The roof must now have two or three coats of white-lead paint, a liberal coating being given along the canvas gutter, and a watertight

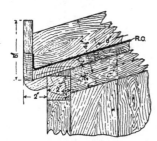

Fig. 1096.—Gutter of Rabbit House.

roof will result. A light zinc spouting s (Fig. 1087), running along the back edge of the roof, is connected with a spout from the front gutter, and conveys rain water to a down pipe D P (Fig. 1087). An alternative method would be to connect the down pipe to the front gutter.

Fronts of Show Rabbit House.

Each of the fronts is composed of two doors, one over the run and another over the bed. That over the bed is made of three widths of board equal to 1 ft. 4 in. wide, fixed together with 2-in. by ¾-in. bat-tens, seen in dotted lines in Fig. 1086. It is hung to the corner posts with strong tee hinges, and fitted with a lock. It is a good plan to bore a few 1-in. or ¾-in. holes to-wards the top of this door for ventilation, taking care to close them up in winter time

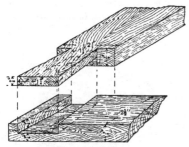

Fig. 1097.—Dovetail Joint for Rabbit House Door.

or on cold nights. A piece of stuff P (Fig. 1086), 1¾ in. by ¾ in., forms a shut piece for each door, and is screwed into the ploughed

grooves in the rails. The openwork door over the run is made of 2½-in. by ¾-in. stuff, dovetail halved together (see Fig. 1097). The pieces forming these doors must be neatly fitted together, and chamfered on the front inside edges as in Fig. 1086. Try them together and put in a screw at each corner, withdrawing it if satisfactory. Glue the joint, and again drive in the screw.

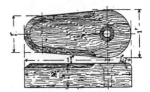

Fig. 1098. | Fig. 1099.—Door
Door Moulding. | Button.

Another screw may be driven in each corner when the glue is dry. The wire netting is fixed with a half-round mould-ing M (Fig. 1088), mitred at the corners. Fig. 1098 is an enlarged section of this moulding, which is prepared by planing two edges off a piece of ⅞-in. by ¼-in. oak or ash, afterwards finishing with a file. This, be-sides giving a finish to the interior of the door, prevents the sharp wire from injuring

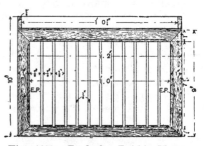

Fig. 1100.—Rack for Rabbit House.

the rabbits. A knob is required for each of the doors; also two wooden buttons, shown by Fig. 1099, fixed with 1-in. No. 14 screws. The doors being the whole length of the house, ample room is afforded for sweeping out or lime-washing.

Interior Fittings of Show Rabbit House.

The interior fitments include a provender rack for green food (see Figs. 1100 and

1101); it is screwed in a convenient position. The rack consists of two end pieces E P (Fig. 1100), the bottom B (Fig. 1101) being nailed to the ends, and the front pieces being mitred and glued on. Before gluing in the end pieces, fit the ⅛-in. iron bars into the top and bottom pieces, boring holes for them about ⅛ in. deep. The whole should fit together without much difficulty. The

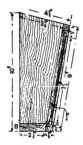

Fig. 1101.—Section through Food Rack.

corn food is placed in an earthen bowl instead of the old-fashioned trough. Placed in the run, upon a layer of sawdust, is a frame (Fig. 1102) of bars ¾ in. by ⅝ in., let into two end pieces 1 in. by 1⅜ in., as shown in Fig. 1103, in which B is the bar and E P the end piece. The droppings from the rabbits fall through the ½-in. spaces, and,

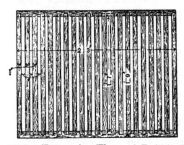

Fig. 1102.—Frame for Floor of Rabbit Run.

together with the urine, are absorbed by the sawdust. This method of littering them down keeps the rabbits dry, and is a safeguard against diseases of the eye, which are prevalent among rabbits where the drainage is not perfect. The interior of the houses should receive two coats of limewash in which glue size has been dissolved. The outside has a coat of priming, the nail holes, etc., being stopped up, and then receives two coats of lead colour and one coat of dark green, or other colour, each coat being glasspapered before the next is ap-

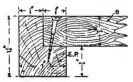

Fig. 1103.—Section through Floor Frame.

plied. When dry, the houses can be moved into position, and when the smell of the paint has disappeared the rabbits can be put in. Where possible, place the houses in a shady position facing the south.

Show Rabbit House in Sections.

After the very full details of a fancy rabbitry just given, it is unnecessary to enter minutely into the construction of the above form of rabbit house. It may be about 14 ft. long by 8 ft. by 7 ft. to eaves. It is made in matchboarding, but should be warm and well ventilated. The framing should be 3¼-in. by 2½-in. deal, and the walls should be double cased, 1-in. boarding being used on the outside and ¾-in. inside. The sections may be fastened together with bolts, and the figures show the arrangement of the joints; A (Fig. 1104) indicates the bottom sill, and B the method of jointing

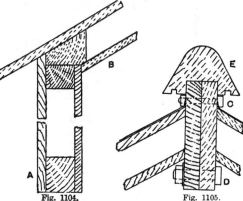

Fig. 1104.   Fig. 1105.
Figs. 1104 and 1105.—Roof Details of Rabbit House in Sections.

on the roof at the eaves. One section is shown shaded with dotted lines, and the other with full lines to distinguish the separate pieces. The method of jointing the roof at the ridge is shown by Fig. 1105. The pole is made in two pieces, which are fastened together with $\frac{3}{8}$-in. bolts c and D,

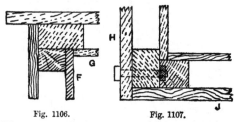

Fig. 1106.   Fig. 1107.

Figs. 1106 and 1107.—Roof Details of Rabbit House in Sections.

and the joint at the top is covered with a cresting-rail E. Fig. 1106 shows the method of framing the roof at the ends, F being the end and G the roof. Fig. 1107 is the joint used at the corners, H showing the side and J the end framing. Two posts are used at each corner, and when the house is put together they are bolted by means of long nuts which have a couple of screw-holes in them (Fig. 1108) and which are let in and screwed to the end posts. The bolts can thus be turned in through the side posts for securing the corners. Three $\frac{1}{2}$-in. bolts

or concrete floor on which the side sills may rest, or one course of blue bricks may be laid on the floor all round to form a foundation for the sides. A small greenhouse hot-water apparatus would be more satisfactory for warming than a stove, as with the former an even temperature may be maintained at a small cost and with little attention.

FERRET HUTCH.

Fig. 1109 shows a front elevation of a ferret hutch, Fig. 1110 a cross section, and

Fig. 1108.—Nut for securing Rabbit House Sections.

Figs. 1111 and 1112 illustrate details of construction. Obviously the difference between this hutch and a rabbit hutch need not be very pronounced. The ends, back, floor, and top may be of 1-in. or $\frac{3}{4}$-in. matchboarding, or a suitable sized packing case may be used instead. The hutch is divided into two compartments by means of a partition with a hole in it, to enable the inmates to be kept to one part whilst the other part is being

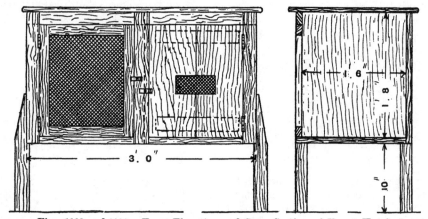

Figs. 1109 and 1110.—Front Elevation and Cross Section of Ferret Hutch.

should be used in each corner. For ventilation, louvres covered with sliding or hinged shutters should be used at the ends, and the skylight should be made to open. It will be a good plan to make an asphalt

cleaned out. The facing on the front may be joined at the corners, as shown in Fig. 1111, and the centre rail as in Fig. 1112, by means of halving them together. The door on the left-hand half of the hutch is made of 1½-in. by 1-in. rails, halved together at the corners as shown in Fig. 1111, and is filled in with fine wire netting and hinged as shown. The door on the right-hand half is made of boarding secured together with a couple of ledges, as shown by the dotted lines, and a small hole is cut in the centre

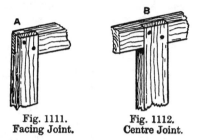

Fig. 1111.
Facing Joint.

Fig. 1112.
Centre Joint.

and covered with fine wire netting. This door is hinged similarly to the other, and both may be fastened with turnbuttons, as shown, or with hooks and eyes. Four legs, which may be cut from 2-in. by 1¼-in. deal, are used to keep the hutch above the floor of the shed in which it may be placed. It is an advantage to have the whole of the front to open as shown, and the doors should be

high as usual, having a total height of only 3 ft. 4 in. ; but special advantage is not claimed for its proportions. Other sizes are given in Fig. 1115. The design can, of course, be easily enlarged or diminished to suit particular requirements. The framing must be cut and jointed accurately at the proper lengths to ensure straightness and parallelism in the several faces and edges. The diagonals of each face should also be made equal in length, to keep the angles or corners right. By attention to these little matters, a job is kept straight and out of twist, whereas neglect of them causes an unworkmanlike appearance, even though the joints are good. Fig. 1115 is a horizontal section on A B (Fig. 1113), and Fig. 1116 indicates that the lower rails are mortised and tenoned into the corner posts. The top sill, or runner, is halved at the back angles and nailed down on all the posts. The timber may be red or white pine, dressed on the exterior of the house, and painted. The sizes of the scantlings for the framing may be : corner-posts 3 in. by 3 in., bottom rail 2 in. by 2 in., top sills and rafters 3 in. by 1½ in.

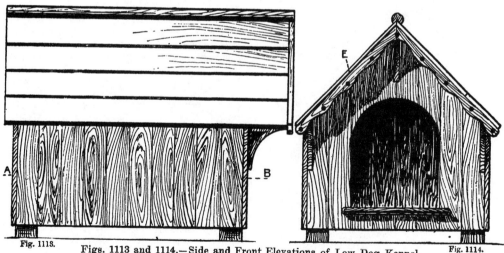

Fig. 1113.

Fig. 1114.

Figs. 1113 and 1114.—Side and Front Elevations of Low Dog Kennel.

brought down to the floor of the hutch, as it is essential to keep a ferret hutch clean.

LOW-BUILT DOG KENNEL.

The dog kennel shown in side and front elevations by Figs. 1113 and 1114 is not so

DOG KENNEL ROOF AND FLOOR.

The roof (see Figs. 1116 and 1117) is formed of three couples, one at each end and one in the middle. The couples are half-cheeked at the crown or apex, nailed at the lower ends or heels to the sill, and covered with ⅝-in. or ¾-in.

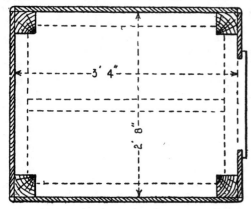

Fig. 1115.—Plan of Low Dog Kennel.

matchboarding. Each board has the outside lip of feathered edge stripped off, to

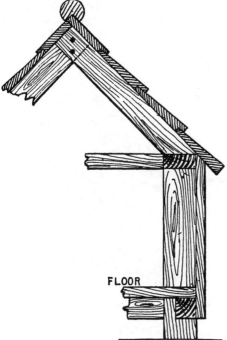

FLOOR

Fig. 1116.—Door Framing of Kennel.

prevent the rain from getting in at the joints. Fig. 1116 makes this clear. The

matchboarding on the sides and ends is of the same thickness as that on the roof, and is put on with vertical joints in the usual manner. The roof has a projection over the front, finished with two light barge boards, as at Fig. 1118, and three brackets, two at the eaves and one at the ridge. The ridge has a rounded batten on the top. The floor is 1⅛ in. thick, and is carried on the lower rails. An additional joist is put in the centre, as shown by dotted lines on plan (Fig. 1115), to stiffen the floor. The board in the door is rounded off on the outside, to finish something like a step.

TALL AND PORTABLE DOG KENNEL.

For the tall dog kennel shown in front and side elevations by Figs. 1119 and 1120, grooved and tongued boarding 6 in. wide and 1 in. thick is a suitable material. The boards of the sides should be nailed to a 1½-in. by 2-in. ledge at the top, and a 3-in. by 1½-in. ledge at the bottom (see K and L, Fig. 1120). The boards of the front and back should be nailed to similar ledges, as shown at E and F (Fig. 1119). The boards forming each side of the roof should be nailed to the three bearers M, N, and O (Figs. 1120). Fig. 1121 shows the construction of the floor. It will be seen that the kennel will be composed of seven main pieces. A fillet about 1½ in. by 1½ in. should be nailed

Fig. 1117.

Fig. 1118.

Fig. 1117.—Part of Kennel Roof. Fig. 1118.— Section of Roof Projection.

to each end of the sides, as shown in the longitudinal section (Fig. 1120), and also by the enlarged section (Fig. 1122); this is taken through A (Fig. 1119). B (Fig. 1122) shows a portion of the boarding of the side with the angle fillet D nailed to it. The front and back can be fixed to the sides by eight 2¼-in. by ⅜-in. bolts and nuts, as shown by Figs. 1119 and 1120, and indicated by the section, Fig. 1122. Each half of the roof can be fixed to the ends by eight bolts and nuts in a similar manner. The floor will rest on the ledges G and H (Fig. 1120)

partment is formed as a door. The dimensions given in Figs. 1124 to 1127 will be found suitable for an ordinary retriever,

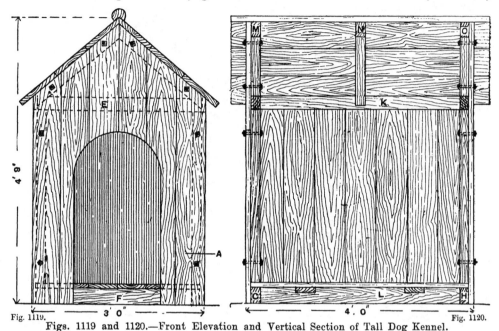

Fig. 1119.
Fig. 1120.

Figs. 1119 and 1120.—Front Elevation and Vertical Section of Tall Dog Kennel.

round the bottom of the boarding. The roof should be covered with felt.

Dog Kennel with Two Compartments.

The dog kennel shown by the general view at Fig. 1123 has two compartments,

but of course the sizes can be increased or decreased as required. The most suitable wood for the kennel is sound red deal, and from the illustrations the lengths and sizes of the various pieces can be ascertained with very little trouble. The several pieces

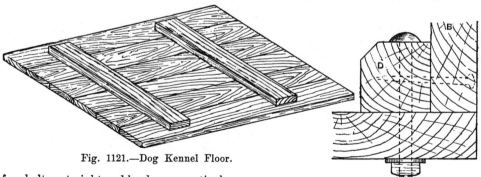

Fig. 1121.—Dog Kennel Floor.

Fig. 1122.—Dog Kennel Joint.

for shelter at night and by day respectively. In addition, one end has a door which is useful in hot weather both by day and night; also one side of the sleeping com-

should be planed up true. Then set out the four vertical posts for mortising, and the bottom rails for tenoning. The intermediate post A (Figs. 1123 and 1124) and the bottom rail should be lap-halved together, as shown at Fig. 1128. The top rail may be ate post A (Fig. 1129) can be notched out at the back C so as to nail on this rail. The

Fig. 1123.—Dog Kennel with Two Compartments.

simply a piece of stuff 1¼ in. by 4½ in., which should be planed to the bevel of the roof, posts and rails should be fitted together, and, when satisfactory, the joints should be

Figs. 1124 and 1125.—Elevations of Dog Kennel with Two Compartments.

as shown at B (Figs. 1126 and 1129). Each end of these rails should be stub-tenoned into the angle posts. Then the intermedi painted, put together, and secured by a few stout screws or nails. The joints must be well made.

Dog Kennel Floor.

For the floor of the kennel, grooved and tongued boards will be satisfactory, and will not require to be specially supported. Ex-

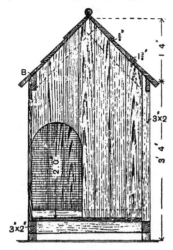

Fig. 1126.—Section of Dog Kennel.

cept the case of the opening at D (Figs. 1123 and 1127), the boards should be kept back from the outer face of the bottom rails by a distance equal to the thickness of the board which is to form the sides (see Fig. 1040, p. 315). Therefore, obtain strips of breadth equal to the thickness of the boarding for the sides, and secure them with three or four small nails to the rails, just

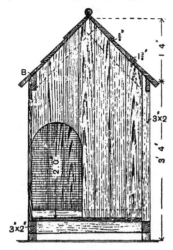

Fig. 1127.—Plan of Dog Kennel with Two Compartments.

flush with the outside. Then the floorboards may be cut to fit between these strips and nailed in position; after which the strips may be taken off and the right

space will be left for the boarding of the sides.

Sides and Roof of Kennel.

Narrow matchboarding, about $\frac{3}{4}$ in. or $\frac{7}{8}$ in. thick, answers well for the sides, and must be cut to fit to the floorboards at the bottom and to the top rail. For the back

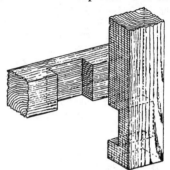

Fig. 1128.—Joint of Intermediate Post and Bottom Rail.

it will be an advantage to cut the boards at a bevel; similarly cut those forming the opening in the front; then, after these boards are nailed in position, parts of the top ends projecting beyond the top rail may be planed flush. The boarding to form both the opening and closed ends should be cut to fit the bottom rail, and also the rake of the roof. The bottom ends, of course, will be secured to the floorboards and bottom rails. The upper ends of the

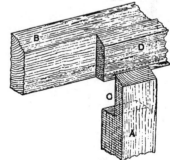

Fig. 1129.—Joint of Intermediate Post and Top Rail.

two ledges F and G (Fig. 1125) should be halved together and fixed to the top rails and angle posts. For the end that opens, the bottom end of the boards should not, of course, be permanently fixed, but should be just tacked in position. Then, with a fine saw, cut along the line H K, and the lower boards will, of course, form the door. This must have two ledges nailed on, and a ledge E (Fig. 1125) should be nailed along the inside of the gable part, its lower edge projecting about ½ in. below the ends of the boarding to answer as a stop. A good method of securing the boards, angle posts, and intermediate posts is to nail on some fillets or beads, as shown by Fig. 1040, p. 315. The partition, shown at Fig. 1126, is simple. The door of the sleeping compartment is fully shown in Figs. 1123 and 1124 ; when this door is closed the top rail will not be flush with it. This may be remedied by

Fig. 1130.—Simple Pole Cote.

nailing on a piece of the same thickness as the door, as indicated at D (Fig. 1129). The door should be hung with 18-in. cross garnets, and at the open end of the kennel five iron bars, about ⅜ in. in diameter, are fitted in holes bored in a fillet at the bottom and in the ledge at the top. For the roof use 11-in. feather-edged boards, that is, 1⅛ in. at the thick edge and ⅝ in. at the thin edge, and rebate them together as indicated in Fig. 1125. This construction is shown more clearly in Fig. 1116, p. 334. The top can be finished with a ridge roll prepared from 1¾-in. square stuff, rounded and V'd so as to fit over the top joint of the boards. To stand the weather well the kennel should have at least four coats of oil and white-lead paint.

SIMPLE POLE COTE FOR DOVES AND PIGEONS.

The simplest form of pole cote is that made from a barrel, as shown by Fig. 1130.

Fig. 1131.—Strutted Base of Cote Pole.

For this get a straight pole 4 in. in diameter and long enough to give it a firm base in the ground. In a fairly open space, 10 ft. above and 3 ft. below the ground will be sufficient. The base should be made of two horizontal pieces halved where they cross each other, and four struts all spiked together (see Fig. 1131). At the top of the pole fix a circular board, strengthened with two cross-pieces. This board should be 6 in. more in diameter than the bottom of the barrel, so as to allow 3 in. all round for the birds to settle on before entering. The top of the pole for about a foot below the cote should be sheathed with zinc, to prevent the entrance of rats and other vermin. The cask should be of sufficient height to admit of three storeys of boxes. To put in the two shelves, the hoops are loosened, and a few staves taken out. Then divide up each floor into four boxes with 1-in. partitions, thus making twelve boxes in all (see Fig. 1132). Now cut holes 6 in. high, in

Fig. 1132.—Section of Pole Cote Barrel.

pairs, with arched heads, and in front of these put little shelves on brackets. Screw the barrel down on the shelf, so that it can be easily removed for cleaning purposes.

To protect the top from rain, a conical roof should be made, with a good projection, so as not to allow rain to drip on the shelves below. The method of making this roof is to fix triangular wood blocks, on which nail boarding, and tack down the zinc on this. Whiten the pigeon cote inside and out on completion.

HEXAGONAL POLE COTE FOR DOVES AND PIGEONS.

The pigeon cote illustrated by Fig. 1133 accommodates four pairs of birds, two pairs

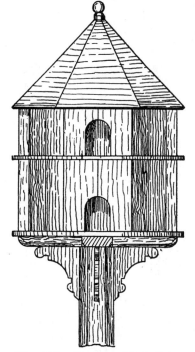

Fig. 1133.—Hexagonal Pole Cote.

in each storey, and, if required, additional tiers may be added. The dimensions are suitable for pigeons of ordinary size, and if the cote is made for larger breeds, such as pouters or runts, a little more room should be given in the lockers. Fig. 1133 is a front elevation looking at the entrance holes. Fig. 1134 is a sectional plan of the cote showing the method of framing the corners and the position of the dividing partitions. Fig. 1135 gives a half roof plan

at A and a half plan of the framing at the top of the pole to carry the baseboard at B. Fig. 1136 is a cross section through the entrances, showing the method of framing

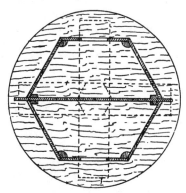

Fig. 1134.—Sectional Plan of Hexagonal Cote.

the cote. To make the cote, procure a pole about 6 in. in diameter, and of the length already stated. Mark a hexagon on both ends, shape it roughly with an axe, and plane as shown by the dotted lines in Fig. 1134. Next prepare two pieces of deal, each 2 ft. 3 in. by 5 in. by 2 in., and halve them together to form a frame for the base of the cote as shown at B (Fig. 1135). Cut a $2\frac{1}{2}$-in. square mortise in the centre, and a tenon on the top of the pole to correspond. Round off the ends and chamfer the under-

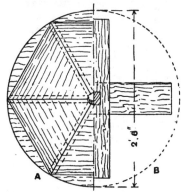

Fig. 1135.—Half Roof and Half Base of Cote.

side as shown in Figs. 1133 and 1136. With sound 1-in. matchboarding, make the bottom of the cote, which is 2 ft. 6 in. in diameter. Nail this to the base pieces, plane it level, and clean up the edges with a spokeshave. Then strike a hexagon with 1-ft. sides, as shown in Fig. 1134. Next prepare the partition between the lockers, as shown in Figs. 1134 and 1136, and fix it in position. Get out the material and make the two half-hexagonal boxes to form the front and back lockers of the lower storey, cutting the pigeon holes in the front and nailing the corners to upright fillets as shown in Fig. 1134. The material for this and the partition may be ¾-in. matchboarding. Now prepare two semicircular boards, 2 ft. 6 in. in diameter, to form a floor for the top lockers and a covering for the lower ones, fixing them to the centre partition by means of fillets (see Fig. 1136). Two boxes, 10½ in. deep, similar to those used for the lower storey, will now be required, and these can be nailed on for the top storey.

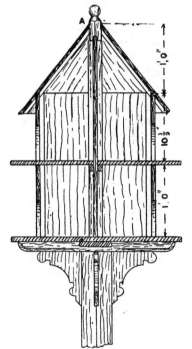

Fig. 1136.—Section showing Interior of Cote.

Roof, etc., of Hexagonal Cote.

For the roof of the cote, the finial A (Fig. 1136), first has to be secured to the central partition. From this are fixed six rafters about 1¼ in. square, reaching to the corners of the lockers and projecting to the outside of the floor circles. The correct angle for

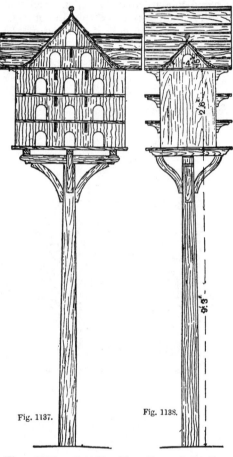

Fig. 1137.   Fig. 1138.

Figs. 1137 and 1138.—Elevations of Another Cote.

bevelling these may be found by trial, the rafters being first put in loosely for this purpose, and then removed and bevelled before finally fixing. The roof may be boarded with ¾-in. matchboarding, and it is a good plan to cover it with sheet zinc. The fronts or one of the sides of the lockers may be hinged, if desirable, for attending to the young birds. The cote should be given three coats of paint, and fixed to the pole, wooden brackets, as shown in Figs. 1133 and 1136, being placed underneath the bottom to improve the appearance and to give greater security, or iron brackets may be screwed on instead. The cote should be

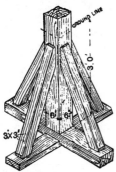

Fig. 1139.—Strutted Base of Cote Pole.

erected in a sheltered position, the pole being let into the ground about 3 ft., and being also strutted to give greater security (see Fig. 1131, and also the next example).

ROOMY POLE COTE FOR DOVES AND PIGEONS.

The cote shown in elevation by Figs. 1137 and 1138 provides accommodation for twenty-six pairs of birds. The over-all dimensions of the house itself are 3 ft. 6 in. by 1 ft. 9 in. by 4 ft. It is mounted on a post standing 9 ft. 3 in. above the ground, and is tenoned into cross pieces and braced on all four sides (as shown in Fig. 1139), and sunk 3 ft. into the ground. The post at the base is 6 in. square, tapering off to 4½ in. square at the top, the reduction beginning 2 ft. 6 in. above the ground line. The head of the post is framed into a 3-in. by 4½-in. cross head supported by curved bracket pieces, and this in turn supports three bearers (Fig. 1140) 2 in. by 2½ in., which are

Fig. 1140.—Bearers of Dove Cote.

screwed to it, the central one being further strengthened with brackets ; on these rests the cote. Its bottom and sides are formed

of 1-in. by 9-in. boards ploughed and tongued together, all the internal divisions being of ¾-in. stuff (see Figs. 1141 and 1142).

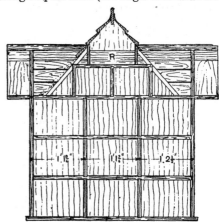

Fig. 1141.—Section of Dove Cote.

The roof is formed of ¾-in. by 4½-in. weather boarding nailed to ¾-in. soffit boards (as shown in Fig. 1137). The main roof is cut where the transverse roof penetrates it, so that square compartments can be obtained for the end boxes ; the ridge piece R (Fig. 1141) runs right through from side to side, and pieces are jointed to it where it passes through the main roof, thus forming a partition between the two sides of the cote. All the internal divisions should be grooved and housed together tightly, this being the best method of keeping out vermin. Each row of boxes is provided with a shelf resting on brackets, and these, if desired, may be

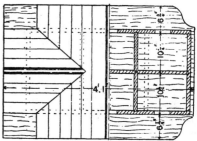

Fig. 1142.—Half Plan and Half Section of Dove Cote.

hinged so that they may be folded over the holes during the night, or at any time when it is desired to imprison the birds, the shelves being lifted by means of cords passing over pulleys let into the fronts. Figs. 1137 to 1140 are to a scale of $\frac{1}{8}$ in. to the foot, and Figs. 1141 and 1142, $\frac{1}{2}$ in. to the foot.

WALL DOVECOT.

The dovecot shown in front and side elevations by Figs. 1143 and 1144 is intended to

in., and rests upon two brackets framed into the back posts, and is supported at the top by iron clips fixed to plugs driven in the brickwork reveal; the clips are made to fit round the plate, which is extended for the purpose. Figs. 1145 and 1146 show sectional plan and transverse section respec-

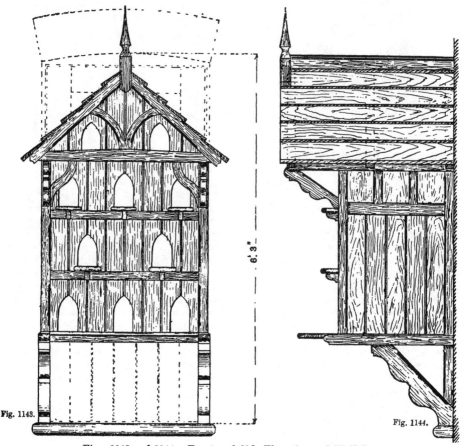

Figs. 1143 and 1144.—Front and Side Elevations of Wall Dovecot.

be made in oak or teak. It provides accommodation for ten pairs of birds at nesting time, and half as many more during flight period, and its dimensions are:— Width, 3 ft. out to out; depth, 2 ft. out to out; and height, 4 ft. 6 in. from sill to crown. The roof extends 1 ft. beyond the front, to prevent rain beating in the boxes. The house is raised above the door sill 16

tively. Each tier of boxes has separate access at the back by means of flaps hinged to the floors, as shown in Fig. 1147, so that the nests, perches, etc., may be cleaned or fixed. If the cot cannot be fixed in a doorway, one of the side panels may be made to open by slightly altering the arrangements. The dimensions of the various parts are given in Figs. 1148 to 1153. It will be noticed that the rails are thinner than the posts—all, however, must finish flush inside, the joints being fitted quite close, so

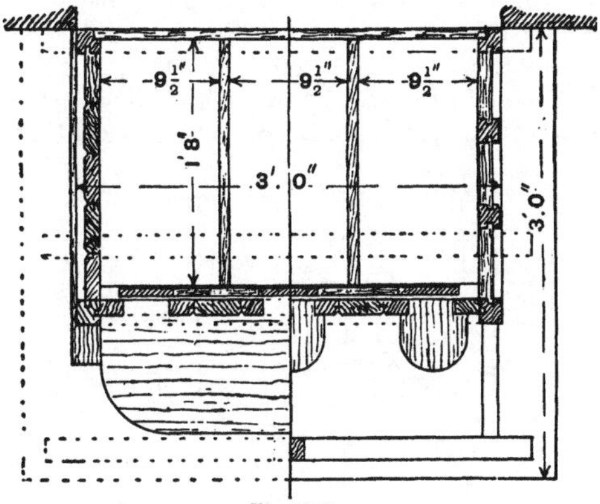

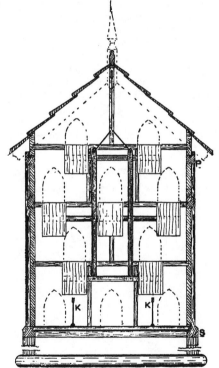

Fig. 1145.

1150) is tenoned into the back post, and being ½ in. thicker is lipped over its face, as shown in Fig. 1144. The lip should be sunk ⅛ in. below the surface. The front post is tenoned through the sill, and the front and back rails stump-tenoned in; the bracket is also tenoned into the sill, as shown in Fig. 1147. At each end the plate P (Fig. 1146) runs 4 in. over the framing at the back in order to form a fixing, as at G (Fig. 1147). All the upright members are tenoned into it, and the small front bracket also. A small fillet is nailed on the outer top edge of the plate to form a stop for the rafters, its end being hidden by the ornamental collar beam. The roof is formed of feather-edged boards nailed to three pairs of rafters. The ridge is merely ornamental,

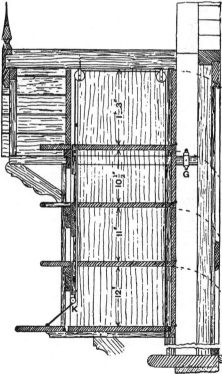

Fig. 1146.

Fig. 1145.—Sectional Plan of Wall Dovecot.

Fig. 1147.

Figs. 1146 and 1147.—Sections of Wall Dovecot.

as not to harbour vermin. The joints are mortised and tenoned through, and are wedged. "Beaumontique" should be used instead of glue. The sill S (Figs. 1146 and

resting on the apex of the rafter, and is ploughed to receive the top edges of the roof boards, and tenoned into the finial, as shown in Fig. 1147. The floors should be housed into the sides of the framing (see Figs. 1146 and 1150), and the division should be removable ; sink them into the floors $\frac{1}{8}$ in. at each end, making an easy fit, and

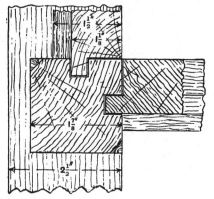

Fig. 1148.—Front Corner Post and Panelling of Dovecote.

stopping the grooves $\frac{3}{8}$ in. from the front edge of the floor to prevent the divisions being pushed too far forward. The floors are kept 1 in. back from the front to provide a space for the shutters to work in (see Figs. 1145 and 1147).

SHUTTERS OF WALL DOVECOTE.

The arrangement of the shutters is shown in Figs. 1146 and 1147, the former showing the house as it would appear if the front panelling were removed, the dotted lines indicating the position of the front, etc. ;

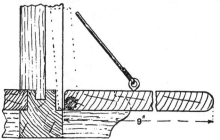

Fig. 1149.—Section of Lower Pitchboard of Dovecot.

the shutters are shown down, and are built of pieces of $\frac{3}{4}$-in. board, slightly larger than the opening, fastened by grooving to a frame of $1\frac{1}{4}$-in. by $\frac{1}{2}$-in. stuff, the whole being

suspended by a cord passing over two pulleys in the roof and down at the back through the bottom to a cleat on the wall. The frame may thus be raised or lowered as desired, being assisted by the weight of the lower pitching board, which is pivoted into the projecting ends of the sill as shown

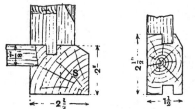

Fig. 1150.—Sill of Dovecot.　　　Fig. 1151.—Side Frame Lower Rail.

in Fig. 1149, and is connected to the shutter frame by two cords passing over pulleys let into the front, as shown at K (Figs. 1146 and 1147). When this board is up, it closes the lower tier of holes, and also removes that which would otherwise become a foothold for cats. A rebate is made in the projecting ends of the sills for the board to rest in when down. Figs. 1143 to 1147 are reproduced to a scale of $\frac{3}{8}$ in. to the foot, Figs. 1149 to 1153 to a scale of 3 in. to the foot, while Fig. 1148 is half full size.

PIGEON HOUSE AND RUN.

The side view of a pigeon house and run

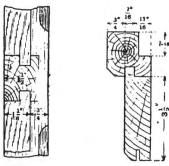

Fig. 1152.—Front Rail of Dovecot Frame.　　Fig. 1153.—Back Corner Post and Panelling.

is shown by Fig. 1154, an end view of the house by Fig. 1155, and an end view of the run by Fig. 1156. This house is for from thirty to forty birds, and it is fitted with twelve nests and the same number of perches on the sides ; a roof perch running the full length is also provided. At the end of the house the roof is continued 3 ft. to this part of the run is covered with wire netting. The house may be built with 2½-in. by 3-in. corner posts and bottom side rails, and the floor joists may be of the same size.

Fig. 1154.—Side Elevation of Pigeon House and Run.

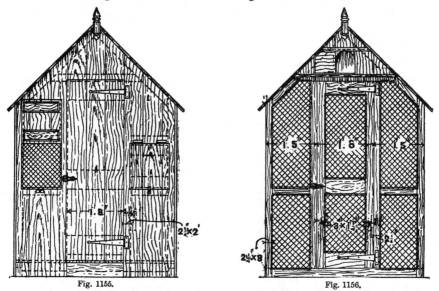

Fig. 1155.

Fig. 1156.

Figs. 1155 and 1156.—End Elevations of Pigeon House and Run.

give the birds a dry run when shut up, and beyond this the ridge pole and eaves plates are carried another 3 ft. to bring the total length of the house to 11 ft. The roof at The remainder of the rails and filling in pieces may be of 2¼-in. by 2-in. scantling. The boarding for the roof and sides may be of ¾-in. matchboarding, and the floor of 1-in.

stuff, red deal being employed for the whole of the timber. Felt may be used for covering the roof, or this may be tarred, covered

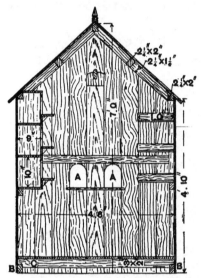

Fig. 1157.—Cross Section of Pigeon House.

with brown paper on the wet tar, tarred over that again, and well sanded.

PIGEON HOUSE DOOR AND WINDOWS.

Fig. 1154 shows the arrangement of the covered and open run of the house, and Fig.

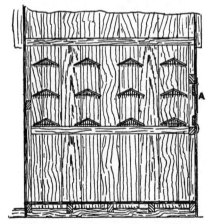

Fig. 1158.—Perches in Pigeon House.

1155 shows the door and the windows. The doorway is 5 ft. by 1 ft. 8 in., and the door

is made of three matchboards ledged with 6-in. by $\frac{7}{8}$-in. deal, and hung with cross-garnet hinges, a loop and staple being provided for fastening. The window openings are filled with wire netting and covered with flap shutters, which may be held up for ventilation and fastened at the top with a hook and eye, as shown on the left-hand side of Fig. 1155. The rebates for the door and flaps are made by keeping the boarding $\frac{1}{2}$-in. back from the framing at the openings. The method of making the flaps will be clear from Fig. 1155, the open one on the left-hand side showing the inside with the ledges, and the flap on the right-hand side showing the hinges and button for fasten-

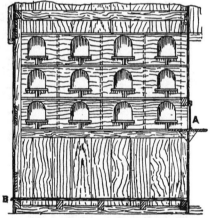

Fig. 1159.—Nesting Boxes in Pigeon House.

ing. Fig. 1156 shows the end of the run. At the top, a flight hole is fitted with a sliding shutter and an alighting board, the opening being about 6 in. by 8 in. The stiles of the door frame are of 3-in. by 1$\frac{1}{4}$-in. deal, and the rails of 6-in. by 1$\frac{1}{4}$-in. deal, the joints being mortised and tenoned together. The hanging is similar to that at the other end, but a strip must be nailed to the framing at the shut side to provide a rebate against which the door can close. The open work of the framing is covered with wire netting of about 1-in. mesh.

INTERIOR, ETC., OF PIGEON HOUSE.

Fig. 1157 gives a cross section through the closed portion of the house, and shows the inside next the run. At the top a perch which runs the full length is shown, and on the right-hand side twelve other perches project 1 ft. from the side of the house. These perches are made by nailing two 1-ft. lengths of 6-in. by ½-in. deal together to form a V, and filling in one end with a piece ¾ in. thick for securing to the side of the house. The arrangement of the perches is made clear by Fig. 1158, the object being to protect the birds roosting on the lower perches, and keep them clean. On the left of Fig.

access from the run to the house are shown at A (Fig. 1157), and a section through one of them is given at A (Fig. 1159). An alighting board is provided on both the inside and outside, and a sliding shutter, which may be closed up at night by means of a couple of cords attached to the sides and brought through the wire to the outside of the house, is fixed outside. From Fig. 1157 it will be seen that the bottom side pieces B are carried the full length of the

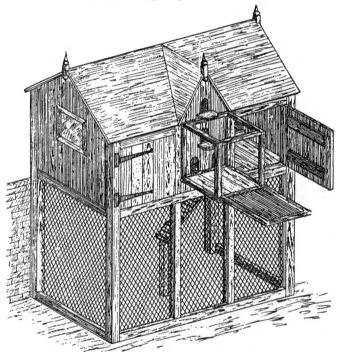

Fig. 1160.—Pigeon House with Loft.

1157 three tiers of nesting boxes are shown, and a front view of these is given by Fig. 1159. These are made by fixing four 9-in. shelves the full length of the house, with 10 in. between them vertically. Each shelf is partitioned into four equal spaces, and a facing piece is put over the front. A pigeon-hole 7 in. by 6 in., about 3 in. above the shelf, and an alighting board about 6 in. wide in the front of each opening, should be provided for each box. For very large birds the boxes, which are for two nests, should be larger. The two holes giving

house, and the joists C are notched to them about 1½ in., the spacing of the joists being shown in Figs. 1158 and 1159. In the former figure a section of one of the window flaps is given at A, and the arrangement of the front framing up to 1 ft. above the eaves is shown. In Fig. 1159 a section through the door is given, showing at B the method of bringing the floor to the outside, with a nosing to keep the wet from penetrating, and also the method of fixing the perch in the centre of the roof. The house should have three coats of good lead paint, both inside and outside, and if possible the bottom should rest on bricks.

PIGEON HOUSE WITH LOFT.

The pigeon house with loft illustrated by Figs. 1160 to 1163 will accommodate about two dozen birds. The sizes and the dimensions of the several timbers are given in the illustrations, which fully show the construc-

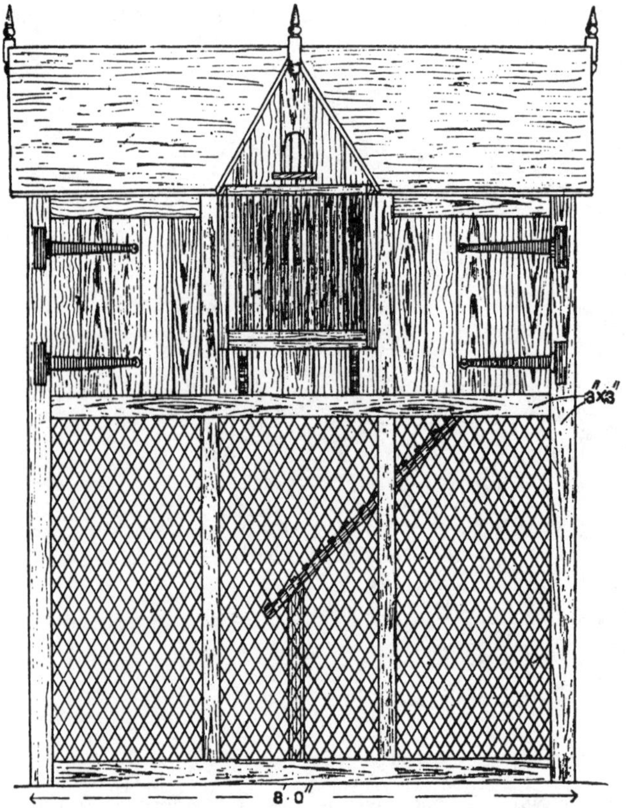

Fig. 1161.—Front Elevation of Pigeon House with Loft.

tion. The general framework should be of 3-in. by 3-in. stuff mortised and tenoned together; ¾-in. matchboarding will be suitable for the spaces between the posts and the rails. At each side of the trap the boarding is nailed to ledges and hung to the posts with cross garnets, thus affording a convenient arrangement for cleaning out and also for access to the nests. The boarding for the

roof should be about ¾-in. thick, supported on two or three intermediate rafters. Sufficient light can be admitted by a small opening filled in with ground glass or wire netting at each end. If desired, the lower part of the house can be enclosed with wire netting to form an aviary. In this case it will be necessary to provide an opening in the floor, and to fix a board, with strips nailed across, as shown in Figs. 1161 and 1162. The higher the loft is from the ground the better will be the protection against cats, etc. The construction of the framework of the trap is clearly shown in Fig. 1160; the bars are left out to prevent confusion in the illustration. The construction of the nests is shown in Fig. 1163. They should be of ¾-in. boards, arranged as in Fig. 1164. Perches about 7 in. long should be fixed to the boarding round the inside, as shown by A and B (Fig. 1163). Fig. 1165 shows an arrangement by which the birds can enter the loft by the top bolt-hole when the trap is closed. A piece of thick wire is bent and secured to the inside by means of two staples, and butts against the small strip of wood A (Fig. 1165), thus preventing the wires being pushed outwards.

VENTILATION OF PIGEON HOUSE.

A roughly made "hit-and-miss" ventilator, fixed in one of the walls at its highest part, will be most effective in a fairly large pigeon house; although if the house is of wood, and not a well-finished affair, plenty of ventilation is provided through the cracks. To form the ventilator, get out two frames, as in Fig. 1166, ¾ in. thick, 7 in. high and 11 in. wide. The upright bars and openings between are 1 in. wide. Fig. 1167 shows the ventilator when closed. Fix one of these grated frames A to a rebated from the outside. In addition, a small air grating should be fixed in the opposite wall.

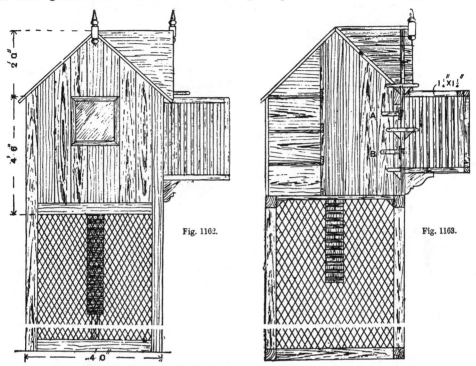

Fig. 1162.

Fig. 1163.

Figs. 1162 and 1163.—Side Elevation and Vertical Section of Pigeon House.

frame B; the outside one C to slide backwards and forwards 1 in., kept in place by strips D nailed to the rebated frame. The best place for the ventilator is just above a doorway, where it could be adjusted

WINDOW BOARD FOR FLOWER POTS.

Fig. 1168 is a section through a window board for flower pots, showing how it is fixed with brackets and screws to the sash frame. The board can be kept level with

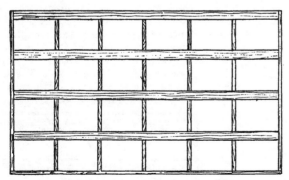

Fig. 1164.—Pigeon House Nests.

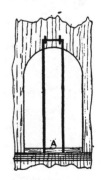

Fig. 1165.—Top Bolt-hole of Pigeon House.

two or three pieces of 1½-in. or 2-in. wood, cut wedge-shape to the splay of the sill, and the outer end can be fitted over the sill and

Fig. 1166.—Pigeon House Ventilator, Open.

the end shaped as shown at A; this will improve the appearance. The board should be about 1 in. thick, and may be of any width from 6 in. to 11 in. It should be cut round to fit the brickwork and just overhang the stone sill, as shown at Fig. 1169; the

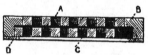

Fig. 1167.—Pigeon House Ventilator, Closed.

bracket pieces should be nailed to the board underneath. A strip of moulding nailed round the edge, so as to project as shown, will prevent the flower pots slipping off.

WINDOW FLOWER BOXES.

Window flower boxes may be made cheaply. A packing-case may be procured for a few pence at almost any grocery or drapery store, and, if of suitable size,

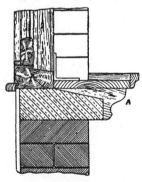

Fig. 1168.—Section of Window Board and Sill.

enough material for one box at least may be obtained from it. Odd lengths of door or small architrave mouldings, with which

to ornament the front, may be purchased at a builder's yard for a trifle. Fig. 1170 shows a box with formal ornamentation,

Fig. 1169.—General View of Window Board.

suited for a stone or stuccoed front; the tiles give a touch of colour which relieves the appearance of the front. The box is about 3 ft. 3 in. long. The mouldings in the box require emphasising by painting them a darker shade of the prevailing tint of the tiles, which should not be so pronounced in colour as to make them unduly assertive; pale tints should be chosen—such as French grey, straw colour, salmon pink, or pale blue. The tiles are intended to cover the whole surface between the mouldings, and a wide rebate or recess is made in the front and ends of the box to receive them. This rebate is made a trifle wider than the tiles, which are usually 6 in. square, the bottom, when screwed on, projecting equal to the depth of the sinking and completing the recess. The length of the box should be an exact multiple of a tile, the front tiles overhanging the edges of the end ones. The sinking at the ends of the box should

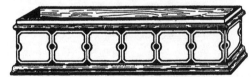

Fig. 1170.—Tiled Window Box.

not run through at the back, but should be made to form a stop for the tiles, as shown by the dotted lines in Fig. 1171. The mouldings, shown enlarged by Figs. 1172 and 1173, are nailed on the face of the box, overlapping the face of the tiles ¼ in. (see

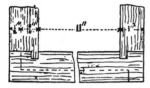

Fig. 1171.—Joints in Window Box.

the section, Fig. 1174). The joints of the tiles may be hidden, if desired, by pointing with appropriate colouring mixed with plaster-of-Paris. In some window boxes a sheet-iron lining is made to fit inside the box to receive the soil. A grip-notch formed in the ends of the boxes, as shown in Fig. 1175, is useful for lifting. Fig. 1176

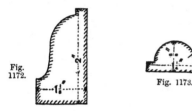

Fig. 1172.

Fig. 1173.

Figs. 1172 and 1173.—Sections of Mouldings.

shows another box, 3 ft. 3 in. long, and this is suitable for windows with overhanging balconies or with wooden bays. If it were 6 in. or 8 in. longer, a second pair of muntins could be introduced with advantage. Fig. 1177 is especially suitable for a window in red brickwork; the ground or panel should be finished in sea green or ivory white enamel, and the hazel twig frame and

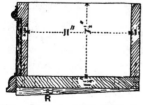

Fig. 1174.—Section of Tiled Window Box.

appliqué work painted a purple-brown or bronze green. Each of the designs given can be extended to meet requirements.

CORK-COVERED FLOWER BOXES.

A material generally used as a rustic overlay on flower boxes is virgin cork, which is

Fig. 1175.—Window Box with Grip-notch.

sold by weight by most horticultural providers. There are various methods of using the cork, the simplest being to nail it on without regular arrangement, the object being simply to cover the front of the box and as much of the ends as shows. A good plan, especially for ferns, is to make the front of the box to represent a rough tree trunk, as shown by Fig. 1178. Horizontal

Fig. 1176.—Framed and Panelled Window Box.

strips A (Fig. 1179) are nailed to the front of the box, the centre one being thicker than those above and below, and the cork is nailed to the strips. Another method is to nail on the pieces of cork vertically, and a novel plan where cork is plentiful is to make the herring-bone pattern (Fig. 1180). In covering window boxes with cork, strive to avoid the formality present in Figs. 1181

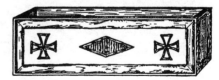

Fig. 1177.—Rustic Panelled Window Box.

and 1182. It is better to aim at a more rustic and far more artistic effect, as in Figs. 1183 and 1184 for instance.

RUSTIC WINDOW FLOWER BOXES.

Rustic work always has a pleasing appearance when suitably set off with foliage

method of using rustic work as an overlay. For this, sticks of hazel, larch, fir, elm, or other suitable woods are cut in the winter and kept until dry, when they are split and

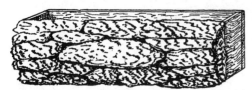

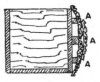

Figs. 1178 and 1179.—Front and End Views of Cork-covered Window Box.

and flowering plants, both in the garden (as will be shown later) and when used as ornamentation on window-boxes, and materials for this purpose can generally be obtained with but little expenditure, as the virgin cork already noted is not by any means the only material available. The boxes should be made the full length of the sills on which they are placed, and the size

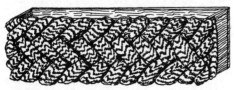

Fig. 1180.—Window Box covered with Herring-boned Cork.

will depend on the kind of plants it is intended to grow in them; for instance, geraniums bloom better if grown in pots, and for these the boxes should be sufficiently large to take at least 6-in. pots with room for a good layer of cocoanut fibre refuse between and around them. Annuals, such as stocks, asters, etc., are best grown with the

laid on as shown. The winter cutting is necessary if the material is to be worked up with the bark on; if cut in the spring or summer when the sap is moving, the bark will peel off, but advantage may be taken of this in making an overlay pattern, where alternate light and dark sticks are used, by cutting the light sticks in the spring and peeling off the bark. Fig. 1186 shows another pattern where the split sticks are used, pieces being first nailed on to form a frame, which is filled in with sticks laid diagonally to form a herring-bone pattern, and the corners are filled in with fir cones sawn in halves. Fig. 1187 shows a more elaborate pattern of a similar nature. The sticks are mitred together at the corners, as shown at A (Fig. 1188), the joints being made by means of a common mitre box and a tenon saw. Where the sticks are jointed together otherwise than at the corners, they may be "mitred" as shown at B, or one piece may be scribed over another as shown at C, to make a good joint by paring the end with a chisel. Pieces of elm bark, or bark of other trees, may often be picked

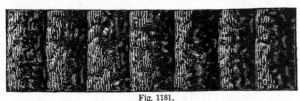

Fig. 1181.

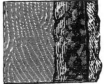

Fig. 1182.

Fig. 1181 and 1182.—Window Box with Formal Cork Decoration.

box filled with soil, and for these the boxes should be about 8 in. deep and from 7 in. to 10 in. wide, according to the size of the window sills. Fig. 1185 shows a common

up in a country timber-yard, and will come in very useful. The rustic form of box shown by Fig. 1189 looks best in windows of brick houses of the cottage type, with gable ends and porched doorways. Fig. 1189 is very effective in a bay window ; the pockets meet across the piers, and so give the whole a continuous appearance. Two rows of

Fig. 1183.   Fig. 1184.
Figs. 1183 and 1184.—Window Box with Artistic Cork Decoration.

segmental ribs, about 8 in. long by 3 in. wide, are nailed to the front of the box, one 1 in. from the bottom, and the other 3 in. from the top. The twigs are nailed to these ribs, thus forming pockets in which

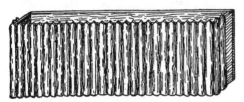

Fig. 1185.—Window Box with Rustic Split Rods

hanging plants may be grown to drape the front of the box.

Constructing Window Flower Boxes.

Various methods may be employed in putting window flower boxes together, and, as they are not required to be watertight, even

Fig. 1186.—Window Box with Rustic Split Rods.

square butt joints secured with wire nails will answer for small sizes ; but this method cannot be recommended for the larger ones, as the weight of the mould is considerable,

23

and the combined effect of the heat of the sun on the outside and the dampness of the soil on the inside soon causes the sides to warp and split if good joinery is not employed in the construction. An easy and efficient mode of jointing up angles of boxes is shown in Fig. 1171, p. 351. The ends should be a little stouter than the sides, but not less than $\frac{7}{8}$ in. thick. A $\frac{1}{4}$-in. or $\frac{3}{8}$-in.

Fig. 1187.—Rustic Window Box of Elaborate Pattern.

tongue is worked on the ends of the back and front, as shown (the grain running lengthwise), and grooves cut to receive them in the two ends. The two ends are nailed to the sides with 2½-in. wire nails, driven in a raking direction with the points inclined to each other, which allows for shrinkage without loosening the joint. Fig.

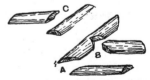

Fig. 1188.—Rods; split and notched.

1190, which shows the joints required for the box illustrated by Fig. 1176, p. 351, is an enlargement of part of Fig. 1191, and shows at M the mortise in the corner post for the front rail, and by dotted lines the tenons and haunching on the front part of the end. No mortises are taken through the posts, which are first fixed on the end, the tenon being screwed from inside and the front glued in. The back is dovetailed to the ends as shown in Fig. 1175, p. 351, which is a sketch of the carcase of the box illustrated by Fig. 1189 turned upside down, the better to show the method of draining and the fixing for the split twigs.

Fig. 1189.—Window Box for Bay Window.

DRAINING FLOWER BOXES.

The wedge-shaped pieces R (Fig. 1175, p. 351) on the bottoms of the boxes allow for the slope of the window sill, and also for ventilation at the bottom. Another method of drainage is shown in Fig. 1192.

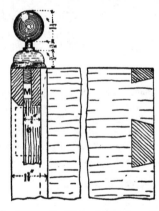

Fig. 1190.—Section of Window Box.

The bottom of the box is formed of narrow battens 3 in. by 1 in., with their edges cut to a bevel and fixed with interstices of ¼ in. between each piece ; a cross batten should be screwed inside at the centre of the length to stiffen them. If the boxes are used for upper windows, some arrangement should be provided to prevent the dirty water running down the face of the window sills or on

to the walls, and for this purpose shallow zinc trays, as shown at A (Fig. 1193), will be found useful. The trays are made the full

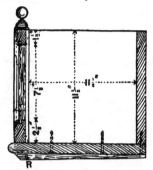

Fig. 1191.—Section of Window Box.

length of the sills, and the boxes are raised on nailed ledges which stand in the trays. The tray and ledges are concealed by bring-

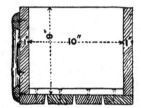

Fig. 1192.—Drainage of Window Box.

ing the cork or rustic work down below the front edge of the box as shown at B, and a short length of pipe C may be fitted in at one corner to run the water away from the sill.

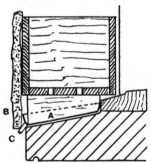

Fig. 1193.—Window Box with Zinc Tray.

PRESERVING FLOWER BOXES.

Paint or tar should not be used on the inside of the box, but to preserve it the wood may be charred in the following way. Well brush the interior of the box with paraffin oil, partly fill with paper or shavings, and set alight and allow to burn until the surfaces are well blackened. It is fair to say, however, that many persons deny that charring acts as a preservative. If the outside is not painted, all nails used should be dipped in linseed oil to prevent rusting.

Fig. 1194.—Ornamental Window Box.

ANOTHER METHOD OF MAKING FLOWER BOXES.

In constructing flower boxes similar to those shown by Figs. 1194 to 1196, it should be remembered that the front boards should stand perpendicular with the sill, and not at right angles to its splay. Were the box made square, or right-angled, it would, when placed on the sill, appear as shown at Fig. 1197, A being the sill, B the bottom, C and D the front and back, respectively, of the box, and E the line of brickwork—that is, if the wedge-shaped pieces shown in Figs. 1174 and 1191 were not used. This, however, may be obviated by making the actual bottom of the box fit the splay of the window-sill. To do this, and assuming that the width from A to B (Fig. 1198) is 7 in., the end pieces must be sawn out less the thickness of the front and back pieces. Therefore, if $\frac{7}{8}$ in. each is allowed for the thickness of the front and back pieces, the required width of the end pieces will be

Fig. 1195.—Ornamental Window Box.

$5\frac{1}{4}$ in., and this will be the width in the clear of the box. Having prepared a piece to this width and of sufficient length for both

ends, stand it on the sill for which the box is intended, and keep one edge flush with the outside of the wall or one edge hard

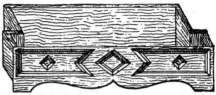

Fig. 1196.—Ornamental Window Box.

against the window frame; in either case the result will be the same. Set a pair of compasses, and scribe the piece parallel to the sill; when sawn off to the scribed line the piece will fit exactly. Square off the top to the depth that the box is to be, and prepare the other end piece similar in size and shape. Next cut off the back to a length which will permit of its being easily removed from within the opening of the brickwork. Nail the back to the ends, keeping the top edges flush; then, with a jack plane, shoot off the bottom of the back piece flush with the bottom of the ends. Nail on the box bottom flush with the back and end pieces, and prepare the front to the required width and long enough to form the ends as shown; an additional 4 in. on each side of the box will be ample. Transfer the

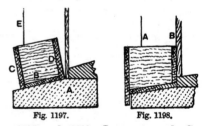

Figs. 1197.   Fig. 1198.

Figs. 1197 and 1198.—Incorrect and Correct Methods of Fitting Window Boxes.

design for the ends from a piece of cardboard or anything suitable, and cut out the pattern with a pad saw, after which the ends must be cleaned up; if a spokeshave is not at hand, a file and glasspaper will answer the purpose. The front may then be nailed on, and the moulding arranged in place. Having decided upon the design, draw its outline, and, parallel to it, the width of the moulding that is to be used; then, from both the external and the internal angles, draw lines, and, when the moulding is cut to these lines, the corners will intersect. All right angles will, of

the box down with glasspaper, and give it, both inside and outside, at least three coats of good oil paint. The front may be finished in two shades of green, or any other tint, according to taste.

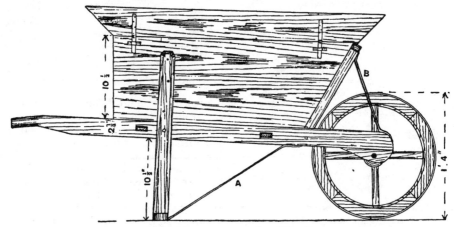

Fig. 1199.—Elevation of Garden Wheelbarrow.

course, be true mitres, and may be cut in a mitre-box. Fit the mouldings carefully, but paint the front of the box before nailing them on. The colour of the paint used will depend on the tint that the box is intended to be finished. If the finishing colour is to be delicate, the first coat may be priming; if dark, a coat of lead colour will be better. When the first coat is suffi-

GARDEN WHEELBARROW.

A garden wheelbarrow is illustrated in elevation by Fig. 1199, and in plan by Fig. 1200, and the best materials for the several parts are:—Shafts and bearers, framework generally, felloes and spokes, of ash; legs and nave of wheel of elm; sides and bottom of elm or birch. The sizes of the various parts are shown in the illustrations. First

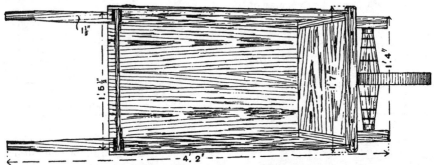

Fig. 1200.—Plan of Garden Wheelbarrow.

ciently dry, the mouldings (the backs of which should also be painted) should be nailed to their respective places. Paint the faces of the mouldings, and, when dry, stop all nail holes and other defects; rub

construct the framework of the bottom. The two shafts should be planed up to $2\frac{1}{2}$ in. wide by $1\frac{1}{2}$ in. thick, and the handles shaped as shown at Figs. 1199 to 1201. Then set them out for the mortises for the two bottom bearers, and also for the slanting front, the positions of which can be seen in Figs. 1199 and 1201. The two mortises for the bearers can be made in the ordinary way, but those for the sloping front stiles must

Prepare the boards for the bottom, $\frac{3}{4}$ in. thick, and fix them to the bearers A and B (Fig. 1201) by means of a few 1½-in. nails. Next prepare the front portion. The two sloping stiles should be tenoned at each end

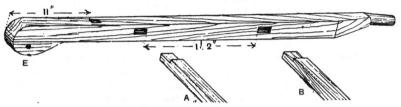

Fig. 1201.—Shaft and Bearers for Wheelbarrow.

be made slightly oblique in two directions. The bearers, 1½ in. wide by 1 in. thick, should next be prepared. To obtain the exact length between the shoulders of these, the shafts should be laid down in position, the distances apart being shown in Fig. 1200. The bearers can then be placed on them directly over the mortises, and the shoulders on the bearers marked. Each end should then be tenoned, as shown

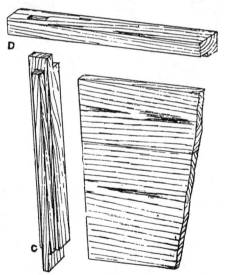

Fig. 1202.—Front Framing, etc., of Wheel-Barrow.

at A and B (Fig. 1201). The bottom framework should now be fitted, and the tenons secured into the mortises by means of hardwood pins driven through the cheeks of the mortises and passing through the tenons.

as shown at C and D (Fig. 1202), the lower end fitting into the mortise in the shaft, and the upper end tenoning into the top rail. The inside shoulder should be longer than the outside, so that it fits into the rebate in the top rail, which also receives the front boards. The stiles will also require rebating on the inside edges for these boards, and on the outer edges for the ends of the side boards. The front framing can now be

Fig. 1203.—Leg of Wheelbarrow.

fitted together, and the tenons fixed into the mortises. The shape of the legs is shown by Fig. 1203, the inner side tapering from the shoulder to the upper end. They should be fixed to the shafts by a couple of bolts. The boards for the sides should be nailed to the front stiles, and screwed to the legs. The legs can be kept rigid by means of two iron rods of the shape shown by Fig. 1204, one end fitting to the leg and the other screwed to the under-side of the shafts (see A, Fig. 1199). The grooves for

Fig. 1204.—Leg and Shaft Connection.

the back sliding piece should be made of a couple of strips ½ in. by ¾ in. nailed to the sides. Seven-inch splayed boards will be wide enough for each slide, which is fixed by means of pieces of iron bent to the required angle, screwed to the side, fitting into eyes fixed on the side of the barrow. Two iron rods (Fig. 1205) to support the front of the barrow should be fixed as shown at B (Fig. 1199).

Fig. 1205.—Front Support for Wheelbarrow.

WHEELBARROW WHEEL.

The wheel is 1 ft. 4 in. in diameter, and 2 in. thick. The nave (Fig. 1206) is 3 in. in diameter in the middle, and $1\frac{1}{2}$ in. at the end, and should be turned and bound by a couple of iron ferrules, as shown. Four mortises should be cut in the middle to admit the tenons of the spokes. The felloes

Fig. 1206.—Nave of Wheel.

should be cut in four pieces out of the solid, the grain of the wood being in the direction shown in Figs. 1199 and 1207. They are square in section, and, after cutting out, plane the ends of each piece carefully true, so that when the four pieces are placed together they fit properly. Then accurately mark out the ends, and bore for $\frac{3}{4}$-in.

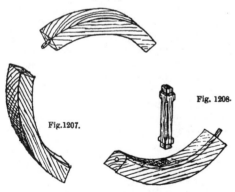

Figs. 1207 and 1208.—Felloes, Spokes, etc., of Wheel.

dowels. The boring must be done at right angles to the surface of the joint in each case. Then prepare the dowels and fit them in the felloes. Next cut the mortises

in the felloes for the spokes (Fig. 1208), and the wheel can then be fitted together. The iron tyre should be made and fitted on by a blacksmith. It is a good plan to paint all the parts of the joints just before putting and wedging them together.

STRONGER WHEELBARROW WHEEL.

A much stouter wheel is shown in elevation by Fig. 1209, the axle with mortise and round rod spoke being shown by Fig. 1210. This is a job that any woodworker may undertake with confidence, especially if he gets a smith to make the ferrules or rings at the ends of the axle, and to tyre the wheel. The axle or spindle may be made

Fig. 1209.—Wheelbarrow Wheel.

square or round; or, preferably, it may be cut out, planed square, set out and mortised, and then turned at each end to fit the rings, which may be previously prepared and given to the turner. The mortise for the cross-rail (Fig. 1211) should, of course, be central both as to length and width, and must be the exact size of the rail; and it is important that the mortise be square. The whole of the wheel may be of oak or ash, the axle 3 in. square, and the cross-rail 3 in. wide by $1\frac{1}{4}$ in. thick. The rail should be gauged and planed to the exact size, and the ends reduced to the desired size to fit the felloes before driving it into the mortise. It is advisable to bore the hole for the round bar from both sides of the axle before the turning is done, as the error which is so easy to make in boring will be much diminished, and, if any discrepancy is found, the holes can be brought in line with

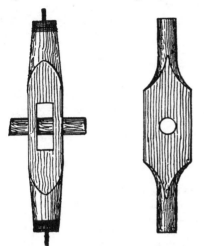

Fig. 1210.—Wheel Axle, Fig. 1211. — Wheel etc. Cross-rail.

very little trouble before the rail is inserted. The worker has also the great advantage of using a gauge which, with a square, will indicate the point for the centre-bit; whereas, if the turning is done first, the application of a square will not be so easy. The hole in the cross-rail, through which the round rod is to be inserted, had better be bored before the rail is driven in the axle. Its central position is thus more correctly determined. The felloes should be cut out of 2-in. ash or oak, free from knots or sap, and quite sound; the radius should be about ½ in. more than half the diameter of the completed wheel, so that the pressure of the tyre may be greatest at the joints, and it will tend to make each quadrant an arc of a smaller circle, as the greatest flexure of a felloe naturally is near the centre, where the grain is straightest. A bow is stouter in the middle for this reason, and those who have tried to describe

an arc of a circle by bending a lath will fully understand what is meant. The joints should be at equal distances from the spokes, which should be the right length for exactly going through the felloes. Each joint should be dowelled, using a card or zinc template to secure correct position of holes; and it is best to keep the holes rather nearer to the outside of the wheel than to the inner surface. The smith should be consulted as to the tyres, rings, and spindles. The dimensions of the wheel depend entirely upon the size of the barrow.

ANOTHER GARDEN WHEELBARROW.

Another wheelbarrow is shown by **Fig.** 1212, and in making this the first job is to get out the shafts, 2 in. square, and preferably of ash. Plane them perfectly straight and true on the outsides, and taper off the ends to about 1¼ in. square on the insides. The tops of the shafts must be made perfectly square with the outsides. **Fig.** 1213 is a plan of the frame and shafts. Mortise in the four cross-pieces (1½ in. by 2 in.) so that the top of each piece is about ½ in. below the tops of the shafts, thus allowing for the thickness of the bottom of the barrow. The front cross-piece, however, 1¼ in. by 1½ in., is let in flush. The piece marked A has its forward side planed to the same bevel as the front, namely, 60°. It will then be an easy matter to screw upon it a couple

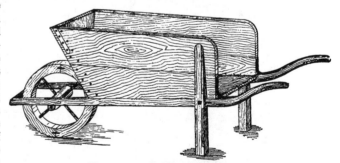

Fig. 1212.—Garden Wheelbarrow.

of battens (see **Fig.** 1214); after which, having put the bottom boards in, nail the front on to the battens. This is not the usual way of putting a front in a barrow, but the method has the merit of being very strong and simple, and the shafts are not weakened with a mortise. The part of a leg is illustrated by Fig. 1215. The notch in the centre is cut to fit tight on to the shaft,

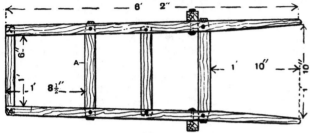 

Fig. 1213.—Wheelbarrow Frame.

Fig. 1214.—Part of Barrow Front.

and will hold it secure while boring the hole for the ½-in. bolt. It is then knocked off, the piece B sawn off, and the leg shaved up before putting it on for good. The side boards are nailed on to the insides of the legs and outside the front board, where a piece of hoop-iron keeps them secure at the top. The barrow is 13 in. deep at the hind

The wheel need not be heavy. The axle piece may be 2½ in. square, with the ends rounded off to 2¼ in. diameter; the taper piece, 2½ in. by 2⅜ in.; the felloes, 1⅝ in.; and the spokes, ⅞ in. in diameter. When completed with the wheel on, the barrow is turned upside down, and the legs are cut off 13 in. underneath by placing a straight-edge on the tyre, marking each leg by this, and then squaring across the front. The tailboard takes in and out. Before fixing

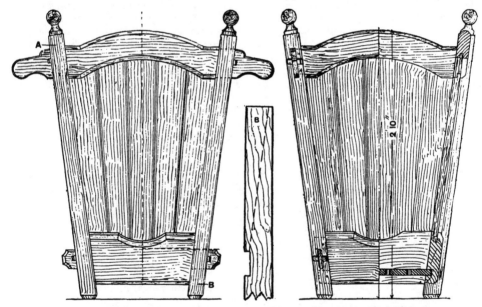

Fig. 1216.—Palm Box. Fig. 1215.—Wheel-barrow Leg. Fig. 1217.—Part Elevation and Section of Palm Box.

part, and 16 in. deep and 22 in. wide at the top of the front; but, if preferred, 6 in. of this depth may consist of a movable frame.

give all the joints of the barrow a good coat of white-lead or other thick oil paint, to keep out the water.

PORTABLE BOX FOR PALMS, ETC.

The portable box shown in Figs. 1216 to 1218 may hold a palm or other ornamental

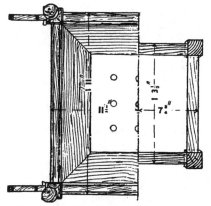

Fig. 1218.—Half-plans of Palm Box.

tree ; it is made of teak or elm, and is well coated with boiled linseed oil. The method of construction is shown in Fig. 1217 ; the tenons of the top rails of the framed sides are brought out through the posts and shaped into handles for convenience in removing. Two of the sides are permanently framed into the posts, but the other two are removable for the purpose of more

Fig. 1219.—Palm Box Handle.

easily introducing and removing the tree ; Figs. 1219 and 1220 show this clearly. The mortises in the posts are made parallel with each other, and consequently pass through the posts at an angle as shown by the dotted line in Fig. 1219, where the post has been drawn upright to

Fig. 1220.—Plan of Palm Box Handle.

make this plain. The tenons must fit tightly, and are kept in place by locking wedges, as shown in Fig. 1220 ; if the post has a small notch cut in the path of the wedge with a slightly curved surface, and the wedge is driven tightly into this, there will be little danger of its working loose. Details of the two sets of bottom rails are given in Figs. 1221 and 1222, which show how the tenons of the adjacent rails miss each other. The tenons in the fixed sides are pinned. The posts are of 2-in. by 2-in. stuff, the rails of 1½ in. by 6½ in. stuff, and the panels (Fig. 1223) are 1 in. thick, the last being flush inside the V-jointed outside. The bottom is of 1-in. slate perforated with ¾-in. holes. The height over all is 3 ft., the width at A (Fig. 1216) 1 ft. 11 in., and at B 1 ft. 3½ in., and the four sides are exactly alike, except for the handles.

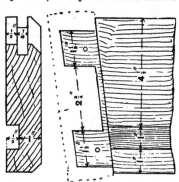

Fig. 1221.—End Bottom Rail of Palm Box.

COAL BUNKER OR BOX.

Fig. 1224 is a general view of a coal bunker or box, which will be found very useful in yards or other places where a coal cellar is not provided ; being portable and unattached, it is a "tenant's fixture." The box is 3 ft. 6 in. long, 2 ft. 6 in. wide, 3 ft. high at the front, and 4 ft. at the back,

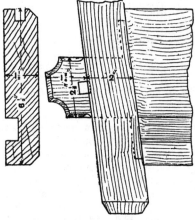

Fig. 1222.—Side Bottom Rail of Palm Box.

and will conveniently hold half a ton of coals, but, of course, the dimensions given may be altered to meet requirements. The angle posts should be 3 in. by 3 in., and the rails 3 in. by 2 in., and the simplest way of joining them is by stub-tenons and mortises, but, for additional strength, iron angle brackets may be let in and screwed to the rails and posts, as illustrated in Fig. 1224. The appearance of the framing will be greatly improved by stop-chamfering. The most serviceable material for the boarding will be $\frac{7}{8}$-in. grooved and tongued matchboards, and, if obtainable, narrow width boards are preferable. They are nailed to the inside of the framework as shown, this preventing the coals pushing them outward. At one end a door should be formed by securing three boards to ledges as indicated at Fig. 1224, and can be hung with 14-in. cross garnets. The lid is made of the same material as the sides, and nailed to ledges, and then hung with 14-in. cross garnets to a board A (Figs. 1225 and 1226, which show front and side elevation), which is about 9 in. wide, and nailed along the top. So that the ledges may be as long as possible, it will be a good plan to notch out the top of the framing as shown in Fig. 1224

ROCKING CINDER-SIFTER.

The cinder-sifter illustrated by Fig. 1227 can be made of red deal, of the following

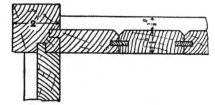

Fig. 1223.—Section through Palm Box Panels.

quantities:—For the back and front, two pieces, each 1 ft. 6 in. by 1 ft. 2 in. by $\frac{5}{8}$ in. ; ends, two pieces, each 1 ft. 2 in. by 1 ft. by $\frac{5}{8}$ in. ; bottom, 1 ft. 6 in. by 1 ft. 1 in. by $\frac{1}{2}$ in. ; corner pieces, 3 ft. by 1 in. by 1 in. ; sliding ; fillets, 3 ft. by 1 in. by 1 in. ; sieve, 4 ft. by 3 in. by $\frac{1}{2}$ in. ; lid sides, 6 ft. by 2 in. by $\frac{1}{2}$ in. ; and top, 1 ft. 6 in. by 1 ft. 2 in. by $\frac{1}{2}$ in. The carcase is of grooved and tongued

Fig. 1224.—Coal Bunker or Box.

boards, nailed or dovetailed together, and strengthened with wooden angle blocks. To form the rockers, the front and back are circular at the bottom, and if the timber at this part is soft, it is advisable to protect it with sheet-iron strips, to take the wear and keep out the damp. Paint the wood before fixing the iron strips. The bottom is ½ in. thick, rebated in the ends,

The second is much the better. In a batten, the grain of the wood is certain to be cut asunder in places, and, in cutting it up to form the sides of a ladder, it is cut again ;

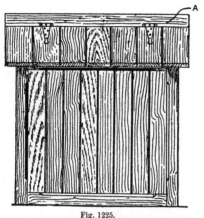

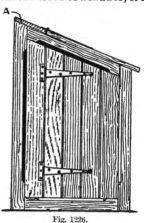

Fig. 1225.   Fig. 1226.

Figs. 1225 and 1226.—Front and Side Elevations of Coal Bunker.

and grooved in the back and front (see B, Fig. 1228). The sieve (Fig. 1229) is 3 in. deep by 1 ft. long by 1 ft. wide, and slides upon the fillets F (Fig. 1228) that are screwed to the carcase. The woodwork of the sieve is nailed or dovetailed together, and must allow at least ⅛-in. play in the width. If suitable wire netting cannot be obtained for the bottom, a sieve can be made by boring holes ⅜-in. from the lower edge of the woodwork, at ⅜-in. or ¼-in. centres, and inserting copper wires, interlacing them where they cross. The lid is of ½-in. stuff, the sides being dovetailed, and the top either rebated as shown in Fig. 1228, or nailed on the sides, and finished with a projecting nosing. Iron flush handles are fixed at the ends, and the corner L-irons shown increase the strength. Give the woodwork two coats of lead-colour paint, and one coat of dark brown. The ironwork should be blacked. With this rocker the ashes can be sifted without the dust flying about.

LADDERS.

Ladders are employed constantly in the yard and garden, and they are of two kinds, the sides of one being an ordinary batten sawn through the middle, and those of the other a pole cut through in the same way.

whereas, in the case of a pole, the saw-cut runs up the pith, and thus follows the grain of the wood instead of crossing it. A pole-sided ladder is stronger than one as stout again made from a batten ; and obviously it is much lighter, a very great advantage. Suitable poles for ladder making and scaf-

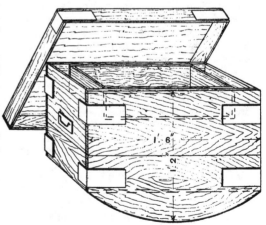

Fig. 1227.—Rocking Cinder-sifter.

folding are sold at all timber-yards ; pick one on which the bark is left, as those which have been peeled are very apt to be partly decayed. Have it cut up the middle

on the saw-bench, as the work is not easy
with the hand-saw.

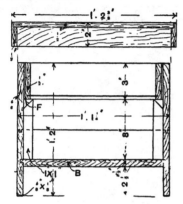

Fig. 1228.—Vertical Section of Cinder-sifter.

MAKING LADDER STAVES OR RUNGS.

Staves or rungs are next required; these
usually can be obtained ready made, and
the best are made of oak, though Spanish
chestnut makes very good ones if they are
cleft out of poles; both kinds are made in
the same way, except that oak staves are
cleft out of larger timber. It is assumed
that chestnut staves are to be used, and that
they are to be made by the worker. For a
ladder 20 ft. long, twenty-five staves are
needed; procure some chestnut poles from
4 in. to 5 in. in diameter, and cut off seven
lengths, varying from 13 in. to 18 in. long,
cutting the largest poles into the longest
lengths; then cleave them through as
shown by lines A A (Fig. 1230). The ring
B represents the sap, which should all be
chopped away, as it soon rots. The four
circles C show the four staves which can be
made out of each length. When all are
cleft out, chop them roughly to shape, first
square, and then taking off the corners, to
make them eight-sided. They should vary
in size from $1\frac{1}{4}$ in. in the middle and $\frac{7}{8}$ in. at
the ends for the longest, to 1 in. in the
middle, and $\frac{5}{8}$ in. at the ends for the shortest. Some make them parallel throughout,
but it is better to have them stouter in the
middle, where the wear comes. The staves
can be finished with the jack plane, and left
eight-sided, or preferably they can be
rounded. A useful tool for this purpose

(assuming a lathe is not available) is a
smoothing plane with a hollow face and
iron. The best way to use it is to drive a
peg into a post diagonally, about 3 ft. from

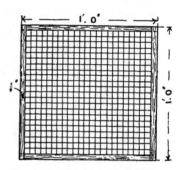

Fig. 1229.—Plan of Cinder-sifter.

the ground, as at D (Fig. 1231), leaving it
projecting about 9 in., and into the end
drive a nail, leaving it about $\frac{1}{2}$ in. out, and
afterwards sharpening it to a point. One
end of the stave is pushed against this
point, and the other held against the breast,
while the stave is rounded, turning the
latter round in the process, and reversing
the ends when necessary. By this means
the staves can be rounded very easily and
quickly, and they look nearly as well as the
turned ones.

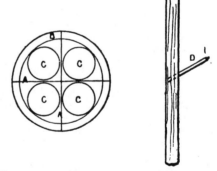

Fig. 1230.—Cleaving Pole   Fig. 1231.—Stop for
to obtain Staves.   use in Rounding
                                              Staves.

SETTING OUT LADDER.

Take a pair of trestles, and lay the
two pole sides on them flat side uppermost, and fix them about 1 ft. apart, so
as to leave room to get between them.

Bore a hole close to the large end of each side, through trestle and all, and insert a pin to hold the sides in position. Pins are shown at E (Figs. 1232 and 1233). Run a plane lightly over the sides, and make a centre line up each one (see Fig. 1232), and then cut a small strip of wood 9 in. long, and

number each stave as it lies, starting at the longest, or bottom, stave, and finishing at the shortest, or top, stave. Fig. 1234 shows the top one, and Fig. 1235 the bottom, the rest lying between them; the marks are shown at F in both figures, one being 12 in. between, and the other 8 in., as marked.

Fig. 1232.—Sides of Ladder Set Out for Boring.

mark the places for the staves, starting just clear of the pins E. Compasses may be used instead of the wood, but practical men appear to prefer the wood, though fixed compasses should be the handier; ordinary compasses are always liable to move. The

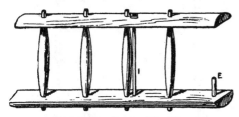

Fig. 1233.—Part of Ladder.

sides now are bored, using a ¾-in. twist-bit for the bottom twelve holes or so, and a ⅝-in. for the remainder. The best way to bore them so as to get the ladder out of twist is to stride the side, and then bore one hole and miss one for the whole length of the side; then, on getting to the other end, turn round, and bore those which were missed, facing the opposite way. By this means, if the worker tends to bore out of upright (and but very few do not, even after long experience), one hole will counteract the other, whereas if all the holes lean one way, the ladder, when put together, will lean one way. Both sides of the ladder being bored, put the staves side by side, graduating them from the longest and stoutest to the smallest and shortest. Then mark 12 in. on the longest, leaving about an equal length at each end, and 8 in. on the shortest, and with a straightedge make marks on the whole lot from one to the other; then, without moving them,

PUTTING TOGETHER LADDER.

A very useful tool for reaming out the holes for the staves or rungs is a bung-borer, which resembles the hollow taper bit (Fig. 379, p. 106); it has a gimlet-type handle. The holes are reamed out with the bung-borer until each stave will fit in its proper place up to the marks F, thus fitting them very easily. But if this tool is not available, employ another method—that is, bore a hole in a waste piece of wood with the same bits as were used for the sides; then cut away the wood of staves from the marks F to the end, as shown by dotted lines at G (Fig. 1235), making a kind of a shoulder until they will fit into the hole the necessary distance. This is done most easily with a drawing-knife, though it can be done with a chisel; they must be made loose enough

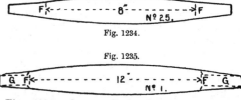

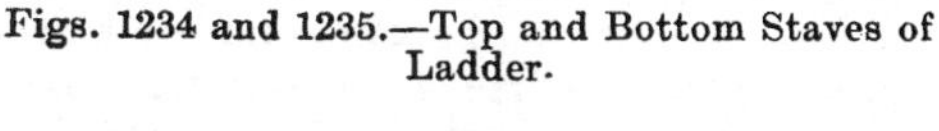

Fig. 1234.

Fig. 1235.

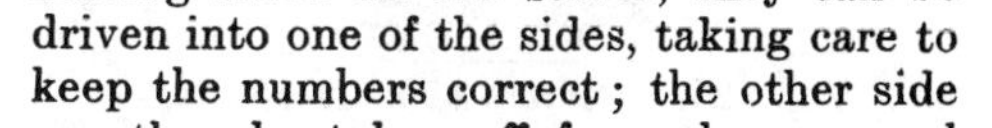

Figs. 1234 and 1235.—Top and Bottom Staves of Ladder.

so that they can be pushed in with the hand, or the sides of the ladder will be split. Having fitted all the staves, they can be driven into one of the sides, taking care to keep the numbers correct; the other side can then be taken off from the peg and placed on the staves, entering them one by one into their holes until all are entered, and then drive it on home, when most likely, if the staves are carefully fitted, both sides will be straight sideways; and if the holes are bored correctly, the ladder will be out of winding; but if it is not so, do not attempt to alter it yet. The sides now re-

Fig. 1236.—Bolt Nut and Wedged Stave of Ladder.

quire to be fastened on in some way, and wedging the staves at both ends is one method. For this the projecting ends of staves are split with a chisel, at right angles to the side of ladder, as at H (Fig. 1236). Do not split them in the same direction as the side runs, or the sides will split when the wedges are inserted; the oak wedges are driven in tightly. Some consider that a better way to fix the ladder together is to bore a ¼-in. hole through the side and stave at intervals of about six staves, and insert a pin; there is no fear of the pins drawing out, but, it is argued, there is a likelihood of the wedges doing so.

FINISHING LADDER.

The ladder can now be taken off the pin E, and turned flat on the trestles, and the ends of staves cut off level with the outside of the sides; the bark can also be taken off, and all knots and other projections trimmed off with the jack-plane, which tool can also be used to chamfer off the sharp edge until the section resembles Fig. 1237. The ends of the sides can also be cut off at both top and bottom, leaving them 9 in. from the centre of top and bottom stave respectively. Three iron bolts must now be inserted as at I (Fig. 1233), one under the next stave but one from the top and bottom, and one half-way between. Quarter-inch bolts are stout enough, and the nuts should be let into the

Fig. 1237.—Section of Ladder Side.

sides so as not to catch the hand when the ladder is in use. The three bolts mentioned are for a 20-ft. ladder. Short ladders would only require two, and longer ones

four or five, or even six, but there should always be one just under the two staves next to the top and bottom, the others being placed between at equal distances, but

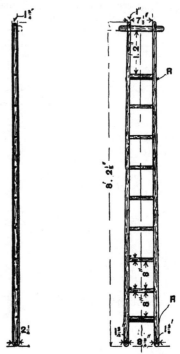

Fig. 1238.—Elevations of Ladder with Top Bar.

always close under a stave. If the ladder is winding or twisting, it must be cramped down at each end, so as to twist it forcibly the opposite way from that which it twists by itself, and after it has been left in this position for a night it will most likely be found all right in the morning. All that

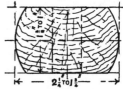

Fig. 1239.—Section of Ladder Side.

now remains is to paint the ladder, and neglect in this particular has caused a great many ladder accidents. A ladder should have at least three coats of good lead paint ; any other is useless. The usual way is to paint the staves about 2 in. from the side, finishing them round neatly. If the staves are, however, of oak, they need not be painted, as it only makes them slippery to walk on, and the oak will last without any painting.

SMALL LADDER.

A light ladder is illustrated by Fig. 1238. The wood used for making it should be dry and sound, and free from any shakes or large knots. The following pieces of timber are required :—Two ash sides, 8 ft. 4 in. by $2\frac{1}{4}$ in. by $1\frac{3}{8}$ in. ; nine oak rungs, 1 ft. by 1 in. by 1 in. ; and one deal bar, 1 ft. by $1\frac{3}{4}$ in. by $\frac{1}{2}$ in. When the sides are planed up, they should, to ensure accuracy, be cramped together, and the holes for the rungs set out and bored without shifting them. The sides should next be shaped as shown in section by Fig. 1239, and the staves or rungs prepared. As before stated, these may be turned in a lathe, or roughly prepared by hand, and finished with sandpaper ; they are of oak, slightly tapering from the middle to each end, and are driven into the sides and wedged as shown in Fig. 1240. Wedging is described above. Second-hand oak wheel-spokes are largely used for ladder rungs. Two iron rivets R (Fig. 1238) are fixed under the top and bottom rungs to keep the sides from drawing. To make the

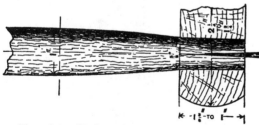

Fig. 1240.—Wedged Stave or Rung of Ladder.

ladder available for inside use, fix a padded bar, as shown in Fig. 1241, to prevent marking the wall-paper, etc. This bar is a piece of wood $1\frac{3}{4}$ in. by $\frac{1}{2}$ in. screwed to the sides, and then covered and padded to form a cloth roll. The outer covering can be baize or washleather, tacked down at the edges.

FOLDING LADDER.

Fig. 1242 is an elevation of a folding ladder closed and open, and Fig. 1243 illus-

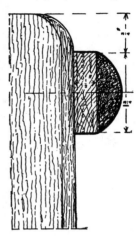

Fig. 1241.—Padded Bar of Small Ladder.

trates a detail of the foot of the ladder. The sides are $2\frac{1}{2}$ in. by $1\frac{3}{4}$ in. sound red deal

Fig. 1242.—Folding Ladder, closed and open.

rounded as shown in section (Fig. 1244), or 3 in. by $1\frac{1}{2}$ in. worked completely round if preferred. Bore $\frac{5}{16}$ in. holes through from front to back on both the sides, 11 in.

from centre to centre, for as many staves or rungs as are required ; they should be $\frac{5}{8}$ in. on from the inside edges to the centre of

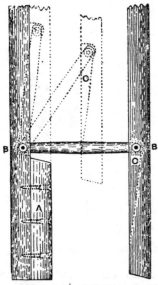

Fig. 1243.—Foot of Folding Ladder.

holes. These holes admit brass pivots $\frac{1}{4}$ in. in diameter that also pass through the ends of the staves, and are riveted front and back over thin copper washers (see B, Fig. 1243). At the top and bottom of the ladder, on opposite sides, pieces of stuff 10 in. long,

Fig. 1244.—Section of Folding Ladder closed.

$2\frac{1}{2}$ in. by $1\frac{3}{4}$ in., bevelled as shown, are screwed on. These pieces produce the alternate sides when the ladder is closed (see A, Figs. 1242 and 1243). Up the centre of each inside face of the sides hollow beds are gouged out for the staves, as shown in dotted lines at C, Fig. 1243. These hollows dip down from a feather-edge to a depth of about 1 in., and correspond with the length (full) and shape of an equal portion of one stave each. The sinkings for a stave in the exact positions they will occupy in either

side of the ladder when it is closed are shown at D D in Fig. 1245. These will be each about 9 in. long, and sufficiently wide to admit its portion of stave easily. The correct shape of the beds is as shown at C, Fig. 1243. The staves are of oak, $10\frac{3}{4}$ in. long over all, $\frac{7}{8}$ in. thick at the ends, and swelling out to 1 in. full in the centre. The ends are bored to correspond with those through the ladder sides after a central space has been marked on them of $8\frac{1}{2}$ in., which will be the inside width of the ladder when it is open. It is desirable to adhere to these dimensions, as the rise from centre to centre of staves for this width will be 11 in. when the ladder is open, and a greater width would, of course, increase the rise to an inconvenient height. It will be noticed that the top and bottom of each bed is dished slightly deeper than the rest of the groove, so as to give free action to the ends of the staves, and to prevent straining the pivots if the ladder skids a little to either side whilst in use. When closed, the ladder

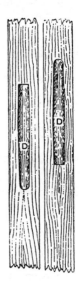

Fig. 1245.—Inner Faces of Folding Ladder Sides.

is fastened together with a hook-and-eye at about the centre of its length. This kind of ladder is specially serviceable for house use, but it is handy for many other purposes.

GATES AND ROUGH FENCING.

FIELD GATE.

WELL-SEASONED oak is the best material for a field gate, but larchwood is cheaper, and is suitable when not too ripe and when felled at the right season. Figs. 1246 and 1247 illustrate one form of braced field gate, 9 ft. long and 4 ft. 6 in. high, the hanging stile being 5 in. by 3 in., the slamming stile 3½ in. by 3 in., the top and bottom rails 3½ in. by 2¼ in., and the intermediate rails and braces 3 in. by 1⅛ in. In making this gate, first cut the different pieces a little larger than the finished sizes, and plane

muntin. As the mortises for this will only be stubbed, lines will only be required on the edge. Each end of the top and bottom rail should have the shoulder lines set out and cut, as shown at Fig. 1251. The three intermediate rails will require the shoulder line to be marked across one face only, as these will be barefaced tenons. The stiles may now be gauged for the mortises, those for the top and bottom rails being in the centre of the stiles, as in Figs. 1249 and 1250, whereas in the intermediate rails one side of each mortise will be in the centre of

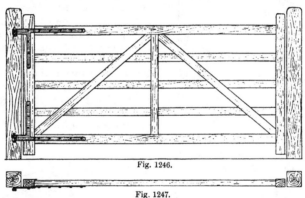

Fig. 1246.

Fig. 1247.

Figs. 1246 and 1247.—Elevation and Plan of Field Gate.

them true to breadth and thickness. The stiles should be set out, and placed with the face sides together and face edges outwards. Then the positions for the mortises should be marked off, and the lines squared down both face edges at once, as shown in Fig. 1248. As all the mortises are to go through, take each stile separately and continue the lines across the face side and down the opposite edge, as in Fig. 1249, which shows the stile set out, Fig. 1250 showing it mortised. All the rails should be placed one on the top of each other and marked off for the shoulders and the centre

the thickness of the stile. Then gauge the rails for the barefaced tenons. The next process will be making the mortise and cutting the tenons and shoulders. The framing thus far prepared should be fitted together, and the whole held square by nailing on a couple of strips. The pieces for the braces should now be laid on and the shoulders accurately marked, the tenons being made as illustrated at Figs. 1252 and 1253. Then, by applying these again to their respective positions the mortises can be marked out. The stiles can now be knocked off and the mortises made

24

in them, and also in the top and bottom rails for the braces. Fig. 1254 shows a post with the rails and brace in position. The mortises and tenons may be coated

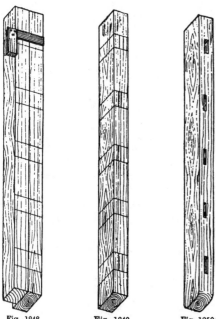

Fig. 1248.   Fig. 1249.   Fig. 1250.

Figs. 1248 and 1249.—Setting out Field Gate Stiles. Fig. 1250.—Field Gate Stile Mortised.

with white-lead paint, and the whole gate put together, cramped, wedged, and pinned. Finally, the intermediate rails, muntin, and braces should be secured together by a few nails, preferably of zinc or copper.

FIELD GATE WITH UPRIGHT BRACES.

A substantial 9 ft. five-bar gate is represented by Fig. 1255, and such a gate, made

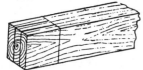

Fig. 1251.—End of Field Gate Rail.

according to the following instructions . and with the best materials, will last in ordinary circumstances for twenty years or more. The harr or back stile, shown by

Fig. 1256, should be 4 in. thick and 6 in. wide, and is mortised through only for the top rail and the fourth rail, as indicated by dotted lines in Fig. 1256. The second, third, and bottom rails are stumped in about 2½ in. All the mortises in the harr should be diminished on the bottom side,

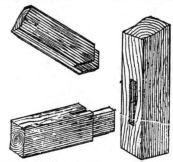

Fig. 1252.—Joints of Stile, Bottom Rail, and Brace.

so that when the draw-bore pin is used each rail fills the space made for it. The old-fashioned way of forming a truss on the harr underneath the top rail, as shown in Fig. 1257, is now obsolete, the truss not being necessary; the head or front stile (3 in. by 3 in.) is generally made of oak, as it is subject to rough usage; this head is mortised in the same manner as described for the harr shown in Fig. 1256. The top rail may be of larch, but oak would better

Fig. 1253.—Joints of Top Rail, Muntin, and Braces.

withstand the liability to fracture. This rail diminishes from 4½ in. by 3½ in. at the harr end to 3¾ in. by 2¾ in. at the head. The bottom rail and the three intermediate rails are of larch, diminishing from 4¼ in. by 1¼ in. at the harr to 3½ in. by 1 in. at the small end. The upright and inclined braces shown in Fig. 1255 are made of

Fig. 1254.—Gate Post with Rails and Brace.

larch, 4 in. wide by 1 in. thick. The bracing is the most important detail of all, for on this the durability of the gate depends. All the braces are secured to the rails by rivets and burrs. Paint should be used for

1258, in which the beam A is 9 ft. 6 in. long, 9½ in. by 3½ in. at the large end, 3½ in. by 2¼ in. at the small end ; the harr B, 4 ft. 6 in. long, 5½ in. by 3½ in. ; the head C, 4 ft. 6 in. long, 3½ in. by 2¼ in. ; the brace D, 5 ft. 6 in. long, 5½ in. by 1⅜ in. ; the rails E, 9 ft. 3 in. long, 3½ in. by ¾ in. ; the downrights F, 3 ft.

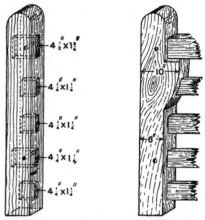

Fig. 1256.—Harr or Back Stile of Field Gate. Fig. 1257.—Trussed Harr of Field Gate.

6 in. long, 3½ in. by ¾ in. The beam A is sawn out with a "frank," as shown, thus adding considerably to the strength without adding much to the weight.

HANGING FIELD GATES.

The majority of field gates are hung with ordinary hooks and rides, and by a little

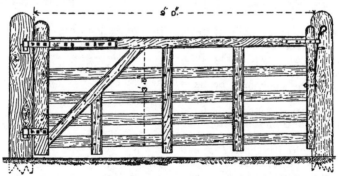

Fig. 1255.—Five-bar Field Gate with Upright Braces.

the mortises, and the rails and braces should have one or two coats where one lies over the other. A gate of very similar design and construction is shown by Fig.

knowledge of certain natural laws these hinges can be so arranged as to give an automatic self-closing power to a gate from any part of the half-circle to which it may be opened. This is a consideration in field gates. Gate posts should be perfectly plumb and in the same vertical plane.

beam of the gate. The neck of the hinge at G should be as short as possible, and the hook should reach through the post and

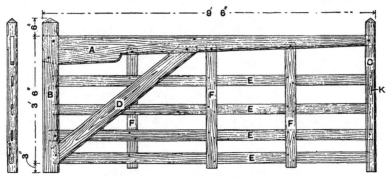

Fig. 1258.—Sussex Field Gate.

When hung, the gate's line of repose should be close to the striking-post. If hung properly this is the only place within the half-circle at which it will remain stationary. In the method of hingeing adopted for the gate shown by Fig. 1255, the top

fasten with nut and screw, as shown. The bottom hinge is short at the sides, and is fixed with two countersunk nails on each side. Its hook should be square and short, as in H, Fig. 1263; the shank being nearly parallel, it then holds tightly and remains

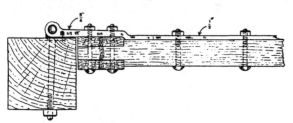

Fig. 1259.—Top Hinge of Field Gate.

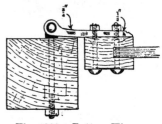

Fig. 1260.—Bottom Hinge.

hinge should be 3 ft. long, made of $2\frac{1}{4}$-in. by $\frac{1}{2}$-in. iron with a gradual thickening over the harr to the eye, as shown in Fig. 1259. This hinge should project about $3\frac{1}{2}$ in. over the harr, so that the hook may be fixed soundly in the post. The bottom hinge is a short one (see Fig. 1260), and is fixed to the harr about 8 in. from the bottom end with two 5-in. by $\frac{1}{2}$-in. bolts. The hooks for the hinges should have screwed and bolted ends. A good form of hook for this class of work is represented in Fig. 1261. A different method of hingeing is shown in Figs. 1262 and 1263, the former showing the top hinge and the latter the bottom. The top hinge is a double strap, and therefore the strain is not put on the bolts or the

firm to the last. Fig. 1264 is a side elevation of a post with a gate hung upon hooks that are in the same vertical and horizontal planes with each other. This method is undesirable for the following reason:—The

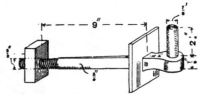

Fig. 1261.—Hinge Hook for Field Gate.

centre of gravitation is always in the same vertical plane, and no matter to what arc of the circle the gate may be moved, there it will remain. The consequence is that it requires the application of the same amount of power to shut it as to open it, whereas the usual requirement is a gate that shuts contact with the striking-post in an oblique position, the top portion of the toe receiving the force of the blow. To avoid this, the striking-post would have to be fixed to

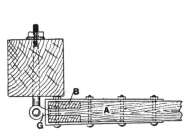

Fig. 1262.—Another Form of Top Hinge. Fig. 1264.—Vertically-hung Field Gate, not Self-closing.

automatically, as discussed in the following paragraph.

HANGING SELF-CLOSING FIELD GATES.

Fig. 1265 is a side elevation of a post with a gate hung upon hooks that are perpendicular with each other, but not in the same horizontal plane—the bottom hook projecting farther from the face of the post than the top one. The result of this is that the gate can clear any rising ground, but its self-closing power is restricted to the quarter-circle either to the right or left. At the quarter-circle, as shown by Fig. 1265, it has reached its highest point, and with a little care will remain stationary and in a vertical position. At this point its fulcrum, or centre of motion, and its line of equi-

the same inclination as the gate. This would be an absurdity, it is true, if carried into practice, but it is the only means whereby a gate so hung may attain its centre of gravitation or line of repose. Fig. 1266 is a front elevation of a gate and posts, in which the former is hung upon hooks that are out of the perpendicular with each other, but in the same horizontal plane. By adopting this method the gate will be self-closing from any point in the half-circle that it may be released from. When opened to the full half-circle, as shown in dotted lines, it will remain in equilibrio at its highest point, and in a vertical position. At this point its centre of gravitation, its fulcrum, and its line of equilibrium are all in the same vertical

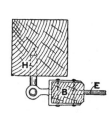

Fig. 1263.—Another Form of
Bottom Hinge.

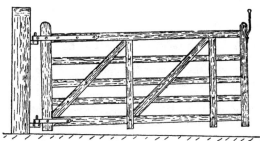

Fig. 1265.—Field Gate, Self-closing within
Quarter-circle.

librium are in the same vertical plane. The moment it loses the latter it falls either to right or left, and either shuts or becomes wide open. If the former, it comes into plane. On leaving this position it at once loses its vertical position, and, on reaching the quarter-circle, has assumed the inclined plane of the hooks. As it approaches the striking-post it gradually loses this oblique plane and again resumes the vertical. Finally it reaches its line of rest against the striking-post in an upright position, but

lating to a gate's line of rest are more clearly demonstrated by Fig. 1267. Let the two small squares shown indicate the hooks, then the actual line of rest for the

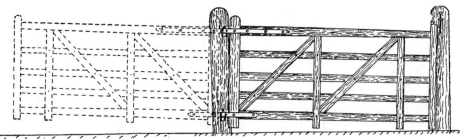

Fig. 1266.—Field Gate, Self-closing within Semi-circle.

with its bars inclined from the horizontal as much as the hooks are apart in the perpendicular. Two points here have to be remembered. (1) The farther the hooks are placed out of the perpendicular with each other, the greater will be the concussion of the gate with the striking-post when re-

gate would be past the striking-post at the point marked A. At the point marked B it would be at its highest altitude in equilibrium, and at these two points only would the gate be in a vertical position. From B it would fall either to right or left. If to the right it would descend direct to its line of

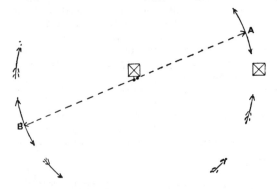

Fig. 1267.—Diagram illustrating Gate's Line of Rest.

leased, and the greater the obliquity of the rails from the horizontal when the gate is at rest. (2) The gate, when it reaches its centre of gravitation at the striking-post, has its toe nearer the ground than at any other portion of the half-circle; therefore the position of the hooks on the hanging-post must be sufficiently high to allow the gate to be well clear of the ground when it reaches this point, being regulated, of course, by the length of the gate and the space that divides the perpendicular planes of the hooks. The foregoing principles re-

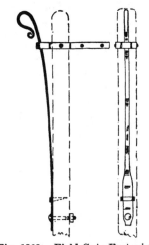

Fig. 1268.—Field Gate Fastening.

gravity at A, acquiring and again losing the inclined plane of the hooks in its descent, and being obstructed by the striking-post before it had either regained its vertical position or its line of repose.

FIELD GATE FASTENINGS.

There are several good forms of fastening for field gates. One is shown by Fig.

1268. It is about 2 ft. long, made of ½-in. square iron with flattened steel spring at the lower end, and bolted to the head as shown. A clip which acts as a guide for

Fig. 1269.—Field Gate Catch.

the fastening is riveted to the gate-head. A catch (Fig. 1269) is fixed in the post for securing the gate. The end is rounded and returned into the post in order to prevent accidents to cattle. The hangings and fastenings should be made to a stock pattern, so that they may be used on any gate. Another fastening is shown by Fig.

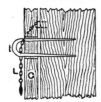

Fig. 1270.—Another Field Gate Fastening.

1270. The large staple I is driven into the post and passes through a mortise K (Fig. 1258, p. 372) in the head of the gate. An iron pin attached to a short piece of chain is then passed through the large staple as shown, thus forming an effective fastening, and one which cannot in any way injure cattle.

Repairing Field Gates.

Fig. 1271 shows an ordinary field gate repaired in all the places where it is likely to

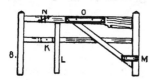

Fig. 1271.—Field Gate Repaired.

require it. Assume a broken rail, which must be spliced, as at K. The old bar or rail is sawn off about a foot from the downright L, as shown by dotted lines. A short

piece of new stuff is then driven into the mortise in the head B, and cut off the right length so that it will fit close up to the downright, the two being then nailed together as shown. Fig. 1272 shows this splicing on plane, the shaded parts being sections of the head and downright. Of course,

Fig. 1272.—Spliced Gate Rail.

longer splicings may be necessary. It is a bad plan to cut the rail halfway on a downright, and butt the other up to it; this may cause the downright to split up the middle. One of the first places for a gate to go rotten is at the junction of the brace and harr. This is caused through the wet lodging there, and eventually finding its way into the mortise, and there being no outlet it has to stay there until it rots its way out. The only way to repair this is, as shown at M (Fig. 1271), by a piece of oak about 4½ in. by 1½ in. nailed firmly to the brace and harr. This should be placed as low down as the bottom ride will allow, unless the wood is

Fig. 1273.—Spliced Gate Beam.

rotten, so that the nails will not hold, in which case it must be placed where the solid wood is; but to be efficient it must be placed low down. At N (Fig. 1271) is shown the beam spliced. This should never be done as shown here, unless it is broken at the small part; if broken farther back, this method of splicing is useless. The splicing on the beam should be cut first, and then the piece to be put on should have the tenon cut to fit in the head; it can then be put in its place and marked exactly by the beam, so that it will fit the first time. The longer the splicing is made the stronger will be the joint; it should never be less

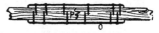

Fig. 1274.—Scarfed Gate Beam.

than 9 in. long, and must be nailed from both bottom and top, and a couple of large nails passed right through and clinched. This splice can be made much stronger by wrapping hoop-iron round it, as shown in Fig. 1273, and nailing well on each side of the splice. The iron can easily be bent round close by fixing one end first and then pulling it over with one hand and tapping it with a hammer at the same time. In the case of a gate beam being broken in the thicker parts, which very frequently happens, the only way to repair it is to scarf it

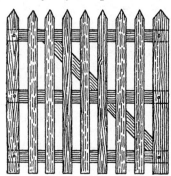

Fig. 1275.—Wicket Gate.

with a piece of oak about 1½ in. thick nailed on each side. This is shown at o (Fig. 1271), and in plan at Fig. 1274. The pieces should have the edges chamfered off, so that they will not injure the cattle, and if nailed on well the gate will be almost, if not quite, as strong as a new one. P (Fig. 1274) shows the fracture of the beam, o being the scarfing pieces, which should be of seasoned oak. The only other repairs likely to be needed to gates are new downrights and heads. The former only require driving in and nailing, and the latter have only to be mortised the same as the old ones and pinned.

Fig. 1276.—Joints in Wicket Gate.

WICKET GATES.

Wickets like that shown in Fig. 1275 are used for entrance courts and gardens. The back stile and the head should be made of oak, the rails, brace, and pales of deal. To frame this wicket, all the rails should be

mortised through the stiles with a bareface tenon, and pinned. Wedging is of no use for this kind of work. The brace (which should never be omitted) should be mortised and pinned into the back stile and the under side of the top rail, as shown at Fig. 1276 and Fig. 1252, p. 370.

SWING WICKETS OR TURNSTILES.

Swing wickets or turnstiles (Fig. 1277) are made in the following manner :—Three oak or larch posts are connected by 1-in. round iron bars, as shown in Figs. 1277 and 1278. The wicket or swing gate should be made as shown in Fig. 1279. Wrought deal boarded hatches are made of 1-in. matched, beaded, or V-jointed boarding, with 7-in. by 1¼-in. wrought chamfered ledges and brace. A deal grooved and weathered capping, to cover the joint between the boarding and the top ledge, is necessary. The ends of ledges and brace should in all cases be secured by rivets, as a preservative measure adding but little to the expense. If the brace is sunk a little into the ledge a better result will be obtained.

TOOLS FOR ROUGH FENCING.

Every kind of fencing which has been prepared by the axe only, the saw not being used except for cross-cutting, is known as rough fencing, and it is surprising what neat work can be turned out by a man who knows how to use the broad axe. The few tools required include an iron socket wedge ; this is a wedge with an easily re-

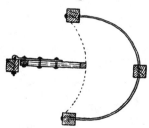

Fig. 1277.—Plan of Turnstile.

movable wooden top to take the force of the hammer blows. A cross-cut saw with two handles, axes, wood wedges, and levers formed by sharpening chestnut poles at one end also are required.

Splitting Logs.

Usually, logs are split in the woods where the trees are cut down; and the following pieces will have to be cleft out:—Rails, 9 ft. long; bars, 10 ft. long; gate-posts,

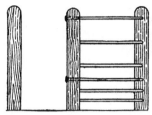

Fig. 1278.—Elevation of Turnstile.

8 ft. long; fence- and bar-posts, 7 ft. long; crib-posts, 5 ft. 6 in. long. In cutting up a tree, it is best to avoid knots as much as possible in the parts intended for rails and bars; for posts it does not matter. For this reason it is usual to cut off a length from the butt end of the trees for rails, as this is generally free from knots; the remainder is then cut up into posts. Fig. 1280 represents a tree as it lies after the bark is taken off and the branches cut away. Cut off a 9 ft. length from the butt with the cross-cut saw, as at I; the knot at K has been purposely introduced to give a better idea how to manage knotty wood. The end of the tree must now be roughly marked out, to see how many rails it will make. If the tree is from 12 in. to 14 in. diameter at the butt, it will make eight rails; if less, only six; and if larger, it is too large to cleave up with advantage. Suppose that the tree is enough for eight rails; to split it up into this number, lay it in the position illustrated, with the knot at the side, and insert a socket wedge at L about half-way between the pith and outside of tree. When this wedge is entered sufficiently to stand by itself, another one must be inserted on the other side of the pith. Then cautiously drive in the two wedges, relieving one after the other, and, most likely, by the time they have quite entered the wood the tree will be in two equal parts; but if the tree has not split, insert a wood

wedge in the end between the two socket wedges so as to release them, and insert them afresh about half-way along the tree (one on each side, if necessary); but keep them in line with the opening cut, and if, instead of splitting clean, the wood hangs

Fig. 1279.—Swing Gate of Turnstile.

together in places by " slivers "—that is, small shreds—these must be cut apart with the broad axe. When the tree has been cleft into two pieces, each must be turned down on the flat sides and cleft again, and where the line of cleavage passes through the knot K particular care is necessary. After inserting one socket wedge at M in the end, and just starting the cut, insert another at N, and guide the cut through the knot with the broad axe. Do not start the cuts at each end, or the whole may be spoilt. Always start at the butt end. The remainder of the tree can be cut up into gate-posts, when it will require no cleaving, or into fence- or bar-posts, which are best made from a round piece cleft through the middle, and the extreme top will do for crib-posts.

Wood for Fencing.

For ordinary fencing, English oak is to be preferred; no other wood lasts so long

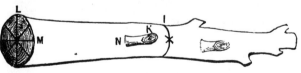

Fig. 1280.—Oak ready for Cross-cutting and Cleaving.

in the ground, with the exception of Spanish chestnut, and this, when grown to a large size, is apt to be brittle, and not suitable for fencing. For pole fencing almost any kind will do for the rails, though chestnut is the best; the stumps should be either chestnut or oak, but oak when small is nearly all sapwood, and rots very quickly. Larch is sometimes used, but it is very poor stuff, and scarcely worth putting up, especially where the fence has any strain to bear, as in fields where the cattle

Fig. 1281.—End of Fence Rail.

rub against it. Wrought-iron rose-head nails should also be used in every case, common cut nails being useless. The length of time that a post will last in the ground depends upon the nature of the wood, and the kind of earth it stands in, sand being the worst, and damp clay the best; some people remove the sand and surround the posts with clay, and this is believed to be the best preservative that can be used. Experience has shown that the use of tar and the practice of charring are quite useless.

Shaping Fence Rails.

For shaping the ends of fence-rails, it is best to have a boy to hold them upright while the end is being chopped, as there is great danger of chopping the hand when a rail is held with one hand and chopped with the other. The part of the rail that was on the outside of the tree must be kept at the bottom, and equal pieces cut from each side, leaving a 1-in. board in the middle, as at o (Fig. 1281). The rail should be turned down flat and cut to 4 in. wide, and the sharp corners taken off. After all the

Fig. 1282.—Notched Fence Post.

rails have been so shaped at one end, take one of the posts, and in the part which will form the bottom cut a notch, or "clave," about 4 in. wide and 3 in. deep, as at P (Fig. 1282). This is to hold the rails in position while they are finished, the shaped end

of the rail being wedged tightly in the "clave," and the sides then trimmed off as straight as the rail will allow; then the other end is cut to match the first. The shaded parts in Fig. 1281 show the parts which are cut away, the clear part showing

Figs. 1283 and 1284.—Rail ends properly and improperly made.

the shape of finished rail. The ends of rails should be shaped with the axe to form a tenon, as in Fig. 1283; for this reason the axe must be ground on both sides, because if it were ground on one side only the tail ends would be shaped as in Fig. 1284, and would split the posts when driven in. The axe-handle should also be held horizontal, and it is made crooked to save the knuckles from being damaged by the wood. In some cases, where the fences are to be boarded, the rails will have to be chopped to the shape shown by Fig. 1285; but this is not often the case, as it is usual to saw them for boarded fences. The bars will require chopping at one end the same as the rails, but the other end must be reduced to about 3½ in. by 2 in. for a length of 2 ft., the middle part being chopped the same as the rails.

Fig. 1285.—End of Rail for Boarded Fence.

Shaping Fence Posts.

The large gate-posts are chopped until they are from 8½ in. to 10 in. square at the top, according to size required; they taper outwards until they are about 1 in. larger at the bottom of the chopped part, which is about 5 ft. from the top ; the bottom goes into the ground just as it is, and does not need chopping. The fence-posts should be chopped on the best side first, then turned down on that side and the edges chopped, and finally the other side. They should in

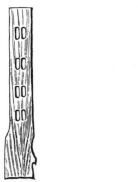

Fig. 1286.—Mortised Fence Rail.   Fig. 1287.—Mortised Crib Post.

all cases be made as wide as possible, but not too thick. A good size is 9 in. by 4½ in., making them nearly parallel in width from top to bottom, but tapering them in thickness by about 1 in. in the 5 ft. R (Fig. 1282) shows a post marked out on the end of a log. The crib- and bar-posts (see p. 380) are chopped up in the same way as are the fence-posts.

PROPER POSITION FOR FENCE POSTS.

Fence-posts often are wrongly put up simply because those engaged in such work have failed to study one important detail. Wood posts should always be inserted in the earth in a natural direction, for when they are placed in the position they would occupy if growing, they do not decay readily at the top. A sound reason for adopting this course has been found by extensive microscopic examinations, which have fully proved that the moisture in wood always passes in the direction of natural growth. For instance, if the top of a post is fixed in the ground, and the butt is allowed to assume a position exactly opposite to that it would occupy if growing, it would decay rapidly, for the reason that the moisture would act in the manner described.

MORTISING FENCE POSTS.

The common fence has usually four rails, and the posts require mortising as shown in Fig. 1286. To set them out, draw a centre line down the side of the post, square across at 6 in. from the top, and again 4 in. lower down—this is for the top mortises. The next mortise is 8 in. from the first, the next 7 in. lower, and the bottom one 6 in. lower still. With a 1¼-in. auger bore two holes on each side of the centre line for each mortise, and cut out the wood between, leaving about ⅜ in. between the mortises, as shown. Also, through the top mortise only, bore a ¾-in. hole for pin. The crib-posts are done in the same way, only there are three rails instead of four. One bar-post in each pair is mortised as the fence-posts, and the other one as in Fig. 1287, the mortises being made 4 in. by 2¼ in., to take the large end of bar before mentioned ; these last will also want a small mortise close to each large one on one side of post only, to take the back rails, as explained later.

ERECTING ROUGH FENCING.

When all the posts are mortised, the holes for them can be dug. Fig. 1288 shows a section of a proper post-hole ; for an ordinary post it should be about 2½ ft. square, and for a gate-post 3 ft. square. Fig. 1289 is a section of the hole dug improperly. To find the places for the holes, the rails should be laid along the ground

Figs. 1288 and 1289.—Section of Post-hole Properly and Improperly Dug.

where the fence has to go, the ends of each overlapping the next about 6 in., the middle of this overlap being the centre of hole. As many holes should be dug as will be required for a day's work—say, about a dozen. Put in the end post and ram the earth to keep it upright, the best tool to ram the earth with being a piece of ash pole about 7 ft. long, with one end reduced to form a handle. Then place the next post in its hole, put in the four rails, crossing them as in the plan (Fig. 1290), and drive the post on so that the rails project

Fig. 1290.—Plan of Rough Fencing.

about 1 in. through the mortises. Put together the whole twelve lengths in this way before ramming any more posts, and prop them up all upright, and adjust the height by lowering them in the holes if too high, or packing them with bricks or tiles if the holes are too deep, until the whole looks right to the eye; they cannot be fixed by a line, as it is necessary to follow the surface of the ground to a certain extent; and by having a number in hand at one time, it is easier to get them right than by doing them singly. Do not be afraid of ramming the earth too tightly, especially at the bottom of the hole. Fig. 1291 shows a section of rough fencing. Cribs are placed in yards, etc., about 3 ft. away from the other fence, and are only 3 ft. high, so that the cattle can reach over the rails to feed. The method of putting them up is exactly the same as described above.

BARWAYS.

Barways are rough fence with movable rails, and are formed simply by cutting gaps in the hedge, and putting up an ordinary fence-post at one side, and a running bar-post at the other, with a distance of 9 ft. between them. The bars are placed

Fig. 1291.—Elevation of Rough Fencing.

in by running the large end through the mortise in the running-post (Fig. 1287), and drawing it back, so that the other end enters the mortise in fence-post, and they are removed in the same way. To prevent

cattle from forcing their way behind the posts, short rails are placed in the remaining mortises, the other ends resting in the hedge. Fig. 1292 shows the barway complete. All the back rails should be pinned in, but, of course, the pins must not be allowed to catch the bars.

POLE FENCING.

The above description applies to the principal kinds of rough fencing; the others do not present great difficulty. Perhaps the most troublesome is the pole fence, formed by stumps driven in the ground and rails nailed on to them. It is used principally for parting fields, etc., and can be put up very cheaply, as it does not require post-holes or mortises. The stumps must be cut from the largest poles, and should not be less than 3 in. in diameter, and for a fence 4 ft. high they should be cut off 5 ft. 6 in. long; the ends should be pointed,

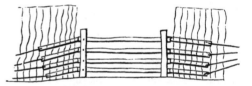

Fig. 1292.—Barway with Back Rails.

as shown in Fig. 1293, but not too sharply, and tapering them on four sides so that the pointed part is of square section. They will drive into the ground comparatively easy, and will hold tight, but if pointed as shown in Fig. 1294 they are driven in with difficulty and do not hold tight for any length of time. The poles which serve as rails are from 12 ft. to 19 ft. long and about 2 in. in diameter at the larger end, which should be chopped flat on one side, where it fits on the stump, as it can then be fixed with shorter nails. In putting up this kind of fence, drive in a row of stumps at the right distance apart to take the ends of the rails—that is, if the rails are 12 ft. long, the stumps should be 11 ft. between; if the lengths vary, as most likely they will, they must be laid out on the ground, and the stumps driven in accordingly, allowing 6 in. at each end for overlapping. When the row of stumps is in, drive in a stump midway between each two, or the fence will be very weak. The rails can then be nailed on, the top one first, and from that gauging with the eye the positions of the others; the stoutest should be at the top, and the larger ends should be kept all one way.

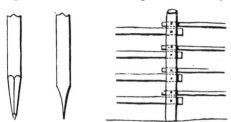

Fig. 1293. Fig. 1294. Fig. 1295.

Figs. 1293 and 1294.—Stumps of Pole Fence, Properly and Improperly Sharpened.
Fig. 1295.—Spliced Rails in Pole Fence.

The splicings are nailed as in Fig. 1295, the thicker end always being under the other.

"Spurring" Fence Posts.

The most common form of repairs needed by post and rail fencing is "spurring," shown in Figs. 1296 and 1297. In the case of good posts the part that is quite covered with earth does not decay for a very long time, but that part at the ground line—neither in the ground nor out of it—decays, in some cases, very quickly, though sometimes many years elapse before the decay is serious. There are many reasons why some posts last longer than others, the principal being, perhaps, the different qualities of timber and the different kinds of earth the posts are embedded in. Posts standing in a dry, hot, sandy soil, even though good timber, will not last so long as those of a worse quality standing in a cool, clayey soil. In such small posts as crib-posts and those used for wire fencing, etc., it may be necessary to spur when the sap only has gone rotten, because the heart is small. If taken in time, a good spur will preserve such a post for a long time. It is doubtful if it pays to spur a post that has decayed through, though it certainly prolongs its life for a year or two. The shape of the spur and the position it occupies when fixed is shown in Fig. 1296, A being the post, decayed at the ground line, and B the spur.

The spurs should reach to a third of the height of the post from the ground line, and should go in the ground nearly, if not quite, as far as the post itself. The spur should be chopped or sawn at the top to form a thin end, as shown in Fig. 1296, for convenience in nailing to the post; the section must not be weakened at the ground line, as it is here that most strength is required. The surplus wood is taken off the round side to make the spur crooked, this keeping the post firmer the further the spur spreads away from it at the bottom, and also clears the bottom of post should the latter happen to run out of plumb under the ground, or, as is often the case, have one or two large knots projecting from it. Fig. 1297 shows the front of spur when fixed. It should be trimmed up to about the width of the post or a little less, and the straighter it is this way the better. A firm abutment for the bottom of spur should be made in the earth, the hole being made large enough for the earth to be well rammed all round the spur, not forgetting the space between spur and post. The spur is nailed to the post before ramming up, and should be placed at the back of the fence. It is at the face of a fence that most pressure is usually applied, and spurs are better able to resist a thrust than the pull caused if they were placed on the face of a fence. This does not apply in some exceptional cases, and it is sometimes thought necessary to spur a post on both sides. In spurring gate-posts, the spur to the hanging-post should be placed

Figs. 1296 and 1297.—" Spurred " Fence Post.

in the gateway, so as to resist the leverage on the post caused by the weight of the gate on it. In the case of the shutting-post, the spur should be put to the side opposite to where the gate slams, the better to resist the jar every time the gate is closed.

REMOVING OLD FENCE POSTS.

It often happens that when most of the posts in some rough fencing will do with spurring, some have to be replaced with new ones. To get out an old post, knock out the pin in the top rails, drive the post to one side until one set of rails will come out; they can then be pulled to one side and the post knocked back again off the other set. The two pins in the adjoining posts at either side must also be knocked

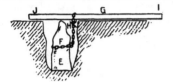

Fig. 1298.—Pulling out Old Post Bottom.

out, and the two lengths of rails taken out and laid by, so that they can be replaced again in their proper order. It is often a difficult matter to get out an old post bottom, especially if it stands in a damp place. In the case of small posts the old bottoms can often be drawn up, after loosening the earth round them, by driving the pick or even the spade into them, and pulling steadily; but if it is the bottom of an old gate-post made from the butt of a tree, all such efforts will be unavailing; and even if the earth is removed entirely, it requires a good amount of bodily strength to lift out a post of this sort. A better and easier plan is that shown in Fig. 1298. The earth is removed all round until about a foot or so of the wood is clear; a chain with a ring at the end is then passed round the wood as low down as possible, the end of chain being passed through the ring and pulled tight. A rail or pole is then laid across the hole, and the end of chain passed over it, and fixed by "shooting a link," that is, one link of the chain is passed through one of the others, and the hook of the chain (if it has one), or a stout nail, passed through it to keep it from drawing out. The whole arrangement is shown in Fig. 1298, in which E is the bottom of post to be lifted out, F the chain round it, G the pole lying on the ground, and H the chain fastening. If the end I of rail be lifted up, it will bring the

post with it, though it may be necessary to obtain more leverage by fixing the chain nearer J; but if this is done the position of the chain must be altered when the post is partly out, as it will not lift it high enough to clear the top of the hole.

RENEWING FENCE POSTS.

The new post having been mortised to agree with the old one, it can be put in. The proper depth can be obtained near enough by taking the length of the new post on a rail, and then placing the latter in the hole and looking along the tops of the other posts from the mark. But remember that it is easier to pack up than to dig deeper after the post is in the hole. Stand the post by the side of the hole, and, putting the two bottom rails into each of the two posts C and D (Fig. 1299), lift up the other ends of the rails, and lean them against the new post, as shown. Fig. 1299 shows only one rail at each side for the sake of clearness, but two should be put in. Most likely the ends of the bottom pair of rails will enter their proper mortises in the new

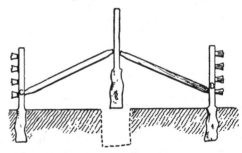

Fig. 1299.—Putting in New Post between Two Old Ones.

post; if not, the post must be lifted up until they will. The bottom of post must now be gently pushed until it slides into the hole, when it will be caught by the two top rails of those entered. The three other rails (assuming it to be a four-rail fence) must now be put in at one end in the same way as the others, and the two which are now holding the post can then be knocked upwards gently until they enter their mortises, and the post hangs by the others, these in their turn being driven upwards until they are all in their proper mortises, when the post will sink gradually to the bottom of the hole. It may be thought that the new post could be inserted in the same way as the old one by driving it on one set of rails, and then back on to the others ; but this would necessitate chopping the ends of the rails much thinner than they should be, and there would be a danger of splitting one or more posts. The method described above is simple, does not involve hard knocking or driving, and does not weaken the rails. After the post is in the hole, it is easy to tell if it is the right height, and if too low it can be lifted by using a pole as a lever under the bottom rail, so that a few pieces of tiles or slates, or a brick if necessary, can be placed under the foot. Do not pack up the post with wood, which will sink into the earth and the post with it. If slates or tiles are not available, a few spadefuls of earth thrown under the bottom of post while it is held up will answer the purpose ; by lifting the post as high as convenient, and allowing it to drop heavily a few times, a solid foundation for it is made, otherwise the post will sink of its own accord in time, and spoil the job.

Renewing Fence Rails.

It is often necessary to put in one or two single rails in a length of rough fencing, and as it would not pay to take up and re-place the posts it is usual to chop one end of the new rail to form a tenon, which, instead of being about $4\frac{1}{2}$ in. long, is about 9 in., and perfectly parallel in both width and thickness. This long tenon allows the rail to be driven into one post until the opposite end is clear of the other post, when the rail can be driven back, and if the long end was chopped parallel, the rail will be tight ; but if it is at all wedge-shaped, it will be loose.

Wattles.

Wattles are long, thin, flexible twigs or boughs of trees, some of the best for use in wattle work being osiers, willows, withes, canes, birch, hazel, oak, ash, furze, broom, and heath or ling. Very thin twigs, up to the thickness of a man's finger, or, say $\frac{1}{2}$ in. in diameter, may be used in their natural condition ; but rods up to 1 in. in diameter even may be used by splitting them. Freshly cut twigs are chiefly to be employed in this work, with the exception of such woods as retain their flexibility several months after being cut, such as osiers, canes, and birch. The best time for cutting twigs for wattles is in the autumn at the fall of the leaf, and in the spring before the sap rises in the wood. Oak, ash, and hazel should be sought for in coppices and spinneys, where there is

Fig. 1300.—Frame for Wattle Hurdles.

generally a good supply of long, thin, and supple saplings, either springing from seed, or the first sproutings from the stumps of recently felled young wood. Suitable wattles may be found sometimes in hedgerows. Furze, broom, and ling should be sought for in dense brakes, where they often run up to a height of from 8 ft. to 12 ft. in long slender rods. Twigs from old trees are usually too brittle, but exceptions may be found in birch and drooping ash.

Tools for Wattle Work.

The tools required in wattle work are very few and inexpensive, consisting chiefly of a heavy bill-hook for cutting the boughs, and a light bill-hook for trimming and splitting the wattles. It is also advisable to have a pair of stout leather gloves to protect the hands from splinters whilst twisting and plaiting the twigs. In making wattle hurdles, it is also advisable to have a frame, as shown in Fig. 1300, to hold the standards whilst the twigs are being plaited in and out between them ; but this frame may be dispensed with if a piece of tough, grassy sward can be used as a working ground.

Wattle Hurdles.

To make a wattle hurdle first select two stout stakes of from $1\frac{1}{4}$ in. to $1\frac{1}{2}$ in. in diameter and 5 ft. in length, to form the end supports. Cut points with the heavy bill-hook on one end of each, and fit them

6 ft. apart in the two end holes of the frame, or in the ground. Select seven stakes of the same length, and from ¾ in. to 1 in. in diameter; point these and put them in the remaining holes in the frame, or at equal distances apart in the ground between the end stakes. Take the long lithe twigs intended for the wattles, and twine them in and out between the standards, as shown in Fig. 1301. Begin with a long, thin rod, grasping its stoutest end tightly in one hand, and gripping it firmly with the other hand at a distance of about a foot or 15 in. from the end. With a dexterous turn of both hands twist this end of the rod, then bend the twisted part around the end stake and fix the end of the rod against

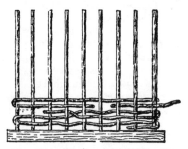

Fig. 1301.—Making Wattle Hurdle.

the next stake, as shown in Fig. 1301. Twine the remainder of the rod in and out between the stakes. If it is long enough to reach the other end, twist that end also as before. But if the rod is not long enough, get another rod and overlap the two ends; then twine this in between the stakes until the end one is reached, when the rod must also be twisted, bent around the stake, and turned back to form the commencement of the next row. The twigs or wattles must be woven in this manner between the stakes, pressing down each layer firmly until the top is reached. The top row must be formed of two long rods interlaced together alternately to form a kind of twisted bar, and the ends must also be tucked back under the row below to keep them from springing out again. These hurdles may be made of any

convenient length and height. They are specially useful in foaling ewes and lambs, as they provide a rough protection for the animals at a time when they need shelter. The hurdles are secured between two rows of stout stakes driven well into the ground, and tied to them by twisted bands of osiers or willows.

WATTLE-WORK HUTS.

Huts for the shelter of sick ewes may be built of wattle hurdles tied to stout poles driven into the ground. If a thoroughly draught-proof hut is required, the poles to form the framework should first be fixed by sinking their lower ends firmly in the ground. Then, two rows of wattle hurdles should be tied to the poles, one on each side, and the space between them packed tightly with straw, fern, or similar litter. Another double row on the tops of these, also well packed with litter, will form the walls of the hut. A flat roof is formed of transverse poles with hurdles tied to them, and a tarpaulin sheet over-all securely tied to the vertical poles. A shepherd's sentry box may be easily constructed by enclosing two-thirds of a circle with light poles, such as hop-poles, driven firmly into the ground and interlacing them with wattle work.

CHICKEN PENS FORMED WITH HURDLES.

It is often advisable to place hens and chickens out on grass land, and in such cases the mother bird is placed in a coop whilst the chicks are allowed to roam about the grass. In order to prevent the young birds becoming lost, a separate pen of wattle work may be made for each family. The hurdles may be made of ling, broom, small brushwood, or even of brambles, and need only be from 1 ft. to 18 in. high. A piece of grass ground 12 ft. by 6 ft. will serve for an enclosure in which the hen coop can be placed; the whole can be moved to a fresh piece in a few minutes when required. It is possible to have these pens in a circular form, all in one piece, about 6 ft. in diameter.

TRELLIS WORK, PORCHES, AND SUMMERHOUSES.

Garden Trellis Work.

Trellis work, or, as it is sometimes called, "lattice work," panels are made in meshes of various sizes, and of square or of diamond pattern, the angles in the latter being 45°, 60°, and 70°. The square mesh shown in Fig. 1302 may be 2 ft. wide and of any length required. The most convenient sizes for the others are as follow :—45°

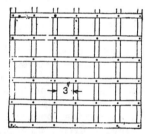

Fig. 1302.—Square Mesh Trellis.

mesh (Fig. 1303), in panels 5 ft. by 2 ft 6 in. ; 60° mesh (Fig. 1304), 4 ft. by 2 ft. 6 in. ; and 70° mesh (Fig. 1305), 6 ft. by 2 ft. 6 in., the longest laths required in each panel being, in order, 3 ft. 6 in., 4 ft. 6 in., and 6 ft. 6 in. The most economical way to purchase the timber is to buy plasterers' sawn laths in bundles of 500 ft. in lengths. In making a trellis, assuming the laths are all of one breadth, prepare a piece of ⅜-in. or ¾-in. board of the same width as the desired distance between the laths, and on one side of the board make grooves to hold five or six laths, the distance apart of the grooves coinciding with the width of the board (see Fig. 1306). Fit a few laths into the grooves in the board, which should be laid over the laths near one end. Then, with the board as a guide, a lath can be placed on and nailed through into the lower laths. At the start, a lath is fixed on each side of the board. The board may then be

25

moved to the other edge of the second lath, when the third lath can be nailed in position. Move the board lengthwise of the under set as laths are added. This process can be repeated until the work is finished. As will be seen, the object of using the board is to keep the lower laths in position whilst the upper laths are being nailed on (see Fig. 1307). The laths should be fixed together with copper nails or small French nails, a piece of iron being placed beneath the lower laths so as to clench the nails by turning them backwards when driven through. If only one nail is used for each joint of the trellis, by merely moving the laths the spaces between them may be either square or diamond shaped. At A (Fig. 1307) a lath is shown broken away in order that it may be seen how the board clips over the under lath.

Making Trellis Work in Quantity.

If a quantity of trellis work is required, the following method of making it should

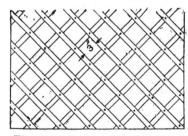

Fig. 1303.—Diamond Mesh Trellis.

be adopted. Get four well-seasoned and thoroughly dry boards the size of the panels and not less than 1½ in. thick. Cut them quite square, and on a 5-ft. by 2-ft. board set out the meshes on the face to Fig. 1302, allowing 3-in. spaces. When all the lines are set out, sink in grooves to the transverse lines $\frac{3}{8}$ in. deep, cutting into the lines, but allowing a little play for the lath. The longitudinal grooves are sunk but $\frac{3}{16}$ in. Fill in the transverse grooves with $\frac{7}{8}$-in.

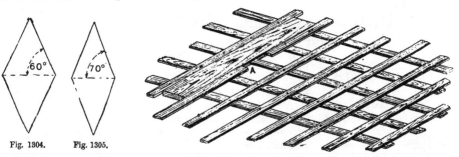

Fig. 1304.   Fig. 1305.

Figs. 1304 and 1305.—Trellis Work Patterns.

Fig. 1307.—Use of Grooved Board in Making Trellis.

hoop-iron, drilled and countersunk and screwed to the woodwork. Then place the laths in the transverse grooves, and follow with the longitudinal ones above them. Nail each centre as shown with $\frac{1}{2}$-in. trellis pins, the hoop-iron underneath the laths clinching each pin as it is driven home. When all the centres are nailed, cut off any projecting laths at the end and side, remove the panel, and fold up. Each of the other panels (Figs. 1303 to 1305) must be set out in a similar manner, care being taken to get the correct bevels.

Fig. 1306.—Grooved Board for Trellis Work.

FIXING TRELLIS WORK TO BAY WINDOW.

For covering the brickwork of a bay window with trellis work, plough grooves to receive the trellis should be made in some 1-in. by $\frac{3}{4}$-in. deal strips; these should be fixed to the angles of the brickwork, as shown in Figs. 1308 and 1309. If the segments of the window heads are sharp, it will be necessary to cut the strips to the curves, as the strips will not bend. The trellis work can next be cut between so as to fit in the plough grooves, and fixed with brads. Fig. 1309 is an enlarged horizontal section through the pier at A A (Fig. 1308).

FIXING TRELLIS WORK FENCE.

The best way to fix a trellis work fence is to drive stumps (A, Fig. 1310) into the ground, and to nail on them a top rail B and a bottom rail C. The trellis can then be nailed to the face of the stumps and rails. The top rail should be 3 in. wide by $2\frac{1}{2}$ in. deep, the top being bevelled off to each side as shown in the section (Fig. 1311), and a 1-in. by $\frac{1}{2}$-in. rebate made on the face side. The stumps should be $2\frac{1}{2}$ in. square, and must be driven into the ground about 18 in., the top then being cut off to the right height. Each stump must be notched to receive the bottom rail, which must also be notched, so that when the two are together they will be level or flush on the face side. The top rail must be notched the depth of the rebate to fit on the top of the stumps, as shown at D D (Fig. 1310), and, in fixing it, the rebate must overhang the face of the stumps; this prevents the wet from getting to the ends of the laths. The end stumps must be rebated in the same way as the top rail, to give a better finish.

GARDEN ARCH WITH TRELLIS WORK GATES.

An arch with gates suitable for the entrance to a garden or for dividing a garden is shown in elevation by Figs. 1312 and 1313. The woodwork is of sound red deal, with elm sweeps for the top rails of the gates. The following quantities of material are required: Four ground posts, 3 ft. 4 in. by 3 in. by 3 in.; four corner posts, 7 ft. by $2\frac{1}{4}$ in. by $2\frac{1}{4}$ in.; two gate stiles, 5 ft. 6 in. by $1\frac{1}{4}$ in. by $\frac{7}{8}$ in.; two gate stiles, 6 ft. 4 in.

by 1¾ in. by ⅞ in. ; two gate sweep rails,
2 ft. by 4 in. by ⅞ in. ; two gate rails, 1 ft.
9 in. by 3 in. by ⅞ in. ; one block, 4 in. by
2 in. by 1 in. ; one block, 1 ft. by 4 in. by

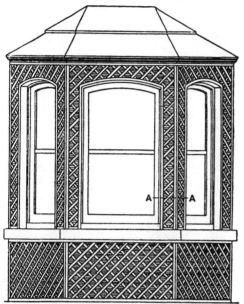

Fig. 1308.—Trellis Work on Bay Window.

4 in. ; 30 ft. of nosing, ¾ in. by ½ in. ; 12 ft.
of lattice, 1 ft. 4¾ in. wide ; two pieces of
iron, 2 in. by ⅛ in. by 6 ft. long ; and 6 yd.
of wire netting, 1 ft. 2 in. wide. Two iron
plates 2 in. by 1¼ in. by ⅛ in., one latch and
flush bolt, a pair of cross-garnet or tee

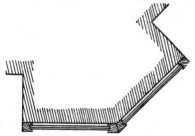

Fig. 1309.—Section of Pier and Trellis.

hinges, half a gross of mixed screws. and
eight bolts, 5¾ in. by ⅜ in., are also required.
First set out the positions of the four corner posts and drive into the ground the four
pieces of 3-in. by 3-in. stuff to which the
corner posts are bolted, as shown in Fig.

1314). In driving in the ground posts, it is
immaterial whether they are perfectly
vertical, as any little inaccuracy can be
remedied when bolting on the corner posts.
Now bore the bolt holes and saw off the
ragged ends caused by driving in the posts.
The 2¼-in. square corner posts are prepared
with ornamental tops, as shown in Figs.
1312 and 1313 ; an enlarged view of these is

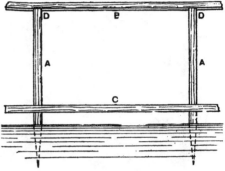

Fig. 1310.—Supports for Trellis Work Fence.

given by Fig. 1315. Obtain two lengths of
hoop-iron 2 in. wide by ⅛ in. thick. to form
the arch ; drill the ends for screws as shown
in Fig. 1316, and bend to shape by hammering the cold iron on a concave block of hardwood (see Fig. 1317). Fasten the top
6 ft. 6 in. from the ground, and over the
whole fix a piece of wire netting of 1-in.
mesh. Wire it to the iron arch, and fix with
staples to the posts.

Fig. 1311.—Top Rail of Trellis Work Fence.

TRELLIS WORK GATES.

The gates are of 1¾-in. by ⅞-in. stiles and
rails, dovetail-halved together, and rebated for the lower half of the lattice work.
The top sweep rails are cut to shape, and
should be of elm or ash. The lattice work
is made as before described, or it can be
bought ready made. Open it to the full
extent, and mark the internal size of the
gate on it ; set out a line ⅜ in. from this,
and saw to size. Then saw the top slats to
the line first made, which allows the lattice work to fit between the edges of the

opening and against the nosing which is screwed on the square edges of the rails and stiles; the back half of the lattice work fits in the rebate. A detail of this is shown by Fig. 1318, in which R is the gate rail, N the nosing, F L the front part of the lattice, and

top they close against a block screwed to the arch (see Fig. 1320). A flush bolt and a latch are provided, and two iron plates (Fig. 1321) are fixed to the gates as shown in Fig. 1322. The whole, when finished, should have three coats of good oil paint.

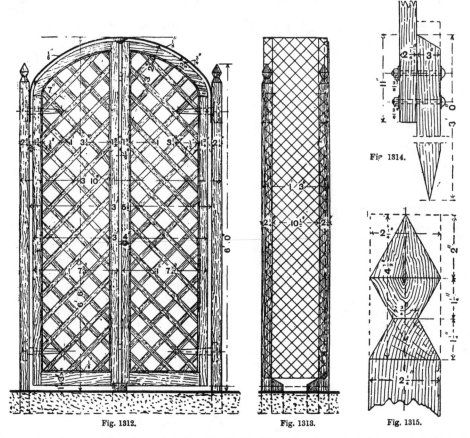

Fig. 1314.

Fig. 1312.

Fig. 1313.

Fig. 1315.

Figs. 1312 and 1313.—Elevations of Arch with Trellis Work Gates. Fig. 1314.—Ground Post, etc. of Garden Arch. Fig. 1315.—Top of Corner Post of Garden Arch.

B L the back part of the lattice. This method does away with a deep rebate, which is necessary if the whole thickness of the lattice is let into the framing. The gates are fixed at the back of the arch with strong cross-garnet or tee hinges 1 in. from the ground, ¾ in. from the posts, and with a space of ½ in. in the centre. Into the ground is let a block (see Fig. 1319) against which the gates close at the bottom; at the

HEATHER-THATCHED LATTICE WORK PORCH.

Any cottage doorway is rendered far more pleasing by the addition of a porch in harmony with the rest of the building. The porch shown by Fig. 1323 is suitable in most circumstances, but is capable of many modifications. For instance, the lattice work may be dispensed with, and the spaces filled in with rustic work; though this involves additional labour and expense. The chief materials are :—Scant-lings, 90 ft. ; slater's laths, 30 ; nails and screws ; coach screws ; small laths, 10 doz. ; a quantity of heather ; 3 red ridge tiles for the roof ; felt, 4 yd. The height of the cottage, of course, must deter-

trellis work, and affording a panel-like appearance. In nailing the laths, it may perhaps be desirable to first cut a template of the desired width and bevelled to the chosen angle, so as to ensure uniformity of angle and space throughout.

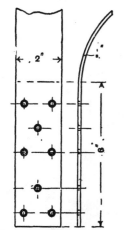

Fig. 1316.—End of Arch Iron.

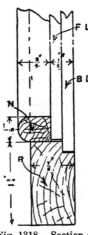

Fig. 1318.—Section of Stile and Nosing.

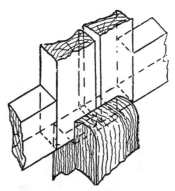

Fig. 1319.—Part of Gates and Ground Block.

mine chiefly the design of the porch. The framework consists of $2\frac{1}{2}$-in. by $2\frac{1}{4}$-in. scant-lings, and to form rebates in which the laths forming the lattice work are fastened, $1\frac{1}{4}$-in. by $\frac{3}{4}$-in. slater's laths are nailed on. The lattice work itself consists of 1-in. by $\frac{1}{4}$-in. plasterer's laths. The framework is mortise-and-tenon-jointed throughout. The sides and front are made first, and pegged together. The front and back gables then are bolted to the uprights, and thus project $2\frac{1}{4}$ in. The finial may be turned, or may be

FIXING PORCH.

The structural work of the porch being completed, the porch is placed in position against the doorway, and two $\frac{1}{2}$-in. holes are bored in the inside uprights about half-way up to take two 8-in. coach screws. The position of the two holes should be chosen opposite two joints in the wall. These joints having been marked and the porch removed, plugs of dry, well-seasoned wood are driven into the joints and bored to a

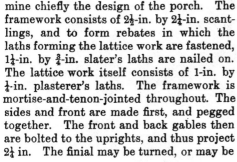

Fig. 1317.—Bending Arch Iron.

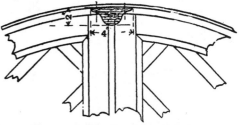

Fig. 1320.—Top Block for Arch Gates.

of rectangular design, as illustrated, and cut with saw and chisel. The laths forming the rebates for the lattice work are inset $\frac{3}{4}$ in., thus giving an inset of $\frac{1}{2}$ in. to the

depth of 4 in. with $\frac{3}{8}$-in. holes. The porch being again placed in position, the screws are driven home to within about half a turn.

Thatching Roof of Porch.

The roof should have back rafters exactly like the front ones illustrated in Fig. 1323. Rough boards about $\frac{1}{4}$ in. to $\frac{1}{2}$ in. thick should be nailed on these rafters as a

Across the shorter width nail slater's laths spaced to about 6 in. or so. To thatch this, about a cartload of heather and six or eight balls of good tar thatching band will be required. The method of procedure is as follows. Take about 3 yd. of the band

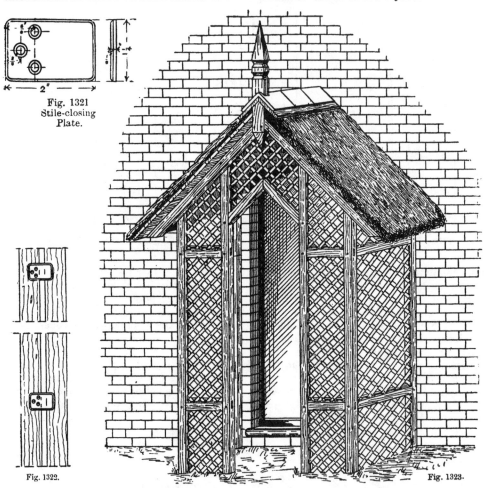

Fig. 1321
Stile-closing
Plate.

Fig. 1322.

Fig. 1322.—Plate Fixed to Arch Gates.

Fig. 1323.

Fig. 1323.—Heather-thatched Porch.

foundation for a covering of good waterproof roofing felt. For thatching, two frames of slater's laths should be made. The length of these frames should equal the distance from centre ridge to outside uprights plus 14 in. or 16 in. for the overhanging eaves. Their width will be the depth from front to back, plus 6 in. for overhang.

and secure one end to the end of the second lath. In the left hand take by the stalks as much heather as can well be grasped. Lay this on the first lath with the bulk of the roots up to the third lath. Bind firmly into position with the string. Proceed thus right across the frame until the second lath is well filled. Secure the end of the string and cut off. Now start again at the same side of the frame as before, but commence at the end of the fourth lath, lay the roots on the fifth, and the twigs and flowers on

Fig. 1324.—Canopied Porch.

the second and third. Work along, alternately using and missing a bar until the frame is quite filled. At the top it will be necessary to use two adjoining laths and a shorter growth of heather. Thatch both frames in this manner, and then secure them to the roof by means of a few good long screws. Do not attempt any regulation of the twigs during the thatching process. When the two frames are in position, crop the heather into correct shape all round with a pair of garden shears or a large pair of scissors, cutting the eaves parallel with the ground. The heather

should appear about twice as thick as that represented in Fig. 1323.

FINISHING PORCH.

Care must be exercised to make a neat job of the ridge. Take two unplaned boards 8 in. wide, ¾ in. thick, and as long as the width of the heather-thatched roof. Screw them firmly together at right angles along their length, and secure them at the ridge of the porch over the bare stalks of the heather. Three bright-red ridge tiles placed along the ridge and secured by two screws in each give a neat finish to the job, the screw-holes and joints being rendered

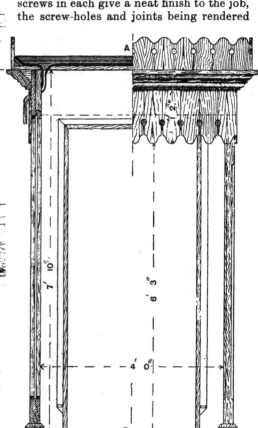

Fig. 1325.—Half Section and Elevation of Canopied Porch.

with good Portland cement coloured with some ground broken tiles. If it is found that the front tile is obstructed by the finial, a hole must be cut into this tile for the finial to pass through. No difficulty will be found in cutting the tile with an old saw and a rough file, removing only small portions at a time. Two seats, about 1 ft. 4 in. high and made of slater's laths, may be fitted within the porch.

Canopied Trellis Work Porch.

A canopied trellis work porch is shown in perspective by Fig. 1324. The height given

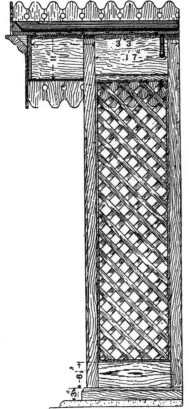

Fig. 1326.—Cross Section of Canopied Porch.

in the front and side elevations (Figs. 1325 and 1326) might be increased advantageously by an additional 6 in. or 9 in., but much depends on the size of the building to which the porch is to be attached. Well-seasoned yellow pine, free from knots, should be used. The four posts having been prepared to the finished size—namely,

1¾ in. by 2½ in.—the bottom rails are tenoned and wedged to the posts 3 in. from the base, the posts being tenoned to the sills.

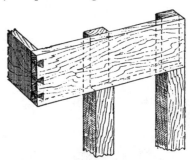

Fig. 1327.—Upper Framework of Canopied Porch.

The ends of the tenons should not come flush by ⅜ in., and the space left is filled with pitch to prevent the end grain rotting. The posts are connected at their top ends with 11-in. by ¾-in. boards 3 ft. 3¾ in. long (housed in flush), and a cross piece 4 ft. 3½ in. long by 11 in. by ¾ in. These three boards form the upper framework (see Figs. 1326 and 1327), to which are attached the ½-in. grooved and tongued boards for the flat roof (Fig. 1328), the cornice and the vertical ornamental boards. To allow the water to drain off, the roof should be made lower at the wall end by

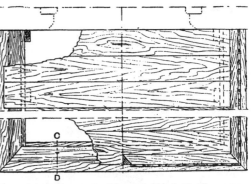

Fig. 1328.—Plan of Porch Roof.

working down the top edges of the two side boards from 11 in. in front to 10½ in. at the back. The lower edge will, of course, be fixed in a horizontal position. The cornice will follow the incline, as it is attached to the roof (see Fig. 1329); but the ½-in. drop will not be perceptible when the porch is in position. The roof is covered with sheet-lead, and a ¾-in. lead pipe is fitted to drain off the water.

FIXING CANOPIED PORCH.

When the posts are framed up, the roofing board is nailed in position next the wall. This will keep the inside top from spreading, and two battens nailed temporarily to the bottom rail will steady the base. Then offer the structure up in its intended position. If there is an existing doorstone, it may be channelled to receive the sills; otherwise a concrete floor can be made, the sill being embedded about ¾ in. in the cement. Pack up the base level, set the frame at an equal distance from each wall jamb, scratch lines on the wall on both

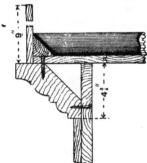

Fig. 1329.—Section of Cornice of Canopied Porch.

sides of the posts, and select three or four suitable places in the wall to receive wood plugs. Square off the positions for plugs on the wall posts while they are still offered up; cut the holes in the wall with a rather long cross-cut or spike chisel, and drive in wooden plugs made from ash or elm. Bore corresponding holes (previously squared off) in the posts, slightly smaller than the nails to be used. Give the back of the post a coat or two of priming before nailing up; next lay the concrete, finishing off the top with a thin layer of neat cement. When the cement has set, nail the roof boards and fix the cornice (Fig. 1329), which is mitred at the angles. Angle blocks are next fixed to support the fencing boards of the attic; the ornamental boards of the

frieze are fixed to the 11-in. by ¾-in. board of the frame. It is advisable to make a template for marking the ornament on the boards, which should, of course, be all of the same width, or the effect will be ludicrous.

Fig. 1330.—Ornamental Boards for Porch Canopy.

Alternative designs for the ornamental boards are presented by Fig. 1330. Boards 5 in. wide by $\frac{7}{16}$ in. thick work in to the correct number, which should be ascertained by actual measurement on the job before the stuff is prepared. A template could be cut from fretboard, or with stout scissors from thin tin-plate. Scribe round the template with a pencil, and cut out with a fine keyhole saw. The lattice work is made from stuff 1½ in. wide by ¼ in. thick when planed, the slats being spaced 3 in. apart; the whole is fixed in position with ⅜-in. by ⅜-in. bead, bradded on (see the section, Fig. 1331). Paint the porch a light tint, as dark colour gives a too heavy appearance.

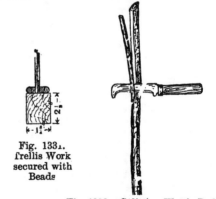

Fig. 1331. Trellis Work secured with Beads

Fig. 1332.—Splitting Wattle Rods.

SUMMERHOUSES.

A summerhouse is well within the scope of the average handyman, because, if desired, it may be so designed that but little constructional ability and skill in using tools need be called into play. The materials may vary from rough rods or wattles to brickwork and well fitted joinery, and in the following pages full instructions on erecting both simple and more or less elaborate structures will be given. Rustic summerhouses are dealt with in the next chapter but one.

WATTLE-WORK SUMMERHOUSES.

Little rustic summerhouses may be made of poles and wattle-work panels, the roof being thatched with straw or with ling. When the rods are large enough and sufficiently free from knots to allow them to be split, another kind of wattle work

Fig. 1333.—Framework of Pitch Roof.

may be introduced by using these split rods for making the panels. The method of splitting is illustrated by Fig. 1332. The workman sits on a low chair or stool, with the rod on his knees and a small bill-hook in his right hand. One end of the rod is sloped off with a stroke of the hook, the edge of the hook is inserted in the middle, and the split is effected by alternate twists of the blade to left and right, as it is pressed into the slit. When long canes, osiers, or willows are employed, the work resembles basket-making, and two rods are often used together, twined one with another alternately above and below as the work proceeds, and thus a different appearance is presented in the finished wattle.

SIMPLE SQUARE ROOFS FOR SUMMERHOUSES.

Generally, there is but little difficulty in erecting the sides of a simple summerhouse. The corner posts may be of stuff 3 in. or 4 in. square, according to the size of the house, and may be tenoned into the sills and plates. Filling up the spaces between with boarding or lattice work is just as easy, but the roof, as a rule, demands more skill. There are two methods of forming the pitch roof of a square summerhouse. It may have a ridge the whole length of the building, or the roof may run up to a point. In the former case the gables are first framed up on the bench, with two raking pieces (A, Fig. 1333), 3 in. by 3 in., halved and spiked together at the top, and cut to correct bevels at the bottom to butt on the plate. The quartering filling up the gable can be tenoned into the plate and raking pieces; or else, to save trouble, they can be put in with square joints, and spiked together when the other timbers are fixed. A notch must be cut at the top of each gable, 1½ in. deep, to receive the ridge B, which may be 1 in. by 5 in. The rafters C should then be cut out; 1½ in. by 3 in. is large enough for a small roof; they must be placed a foot apart, cut to the correct bevel against the ridge, and "haked" or notched to rest on the plates. They may show with cut ends, as

Fig. 1334.—Section of End of Roof Rafters.

at D, in which case they should be planed up; or, if preferred, they may be boxed in with ¾-in. boards. To do this, triangular blocks must be nailed to the feet of the rafters, and the casing should be beaded or moulded at the meeting-angle, and the joint between soffit and plate hidden by a mould (see the section, Fig. 1334). This latter method, however, gives a heavy appearance to a small roof, and does not assist the picturesque effect which it should possess. Supposing the structure is in-

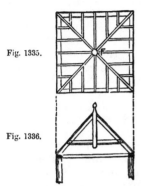

Fig. 1335.

Fig. 1336.

Figs. 1335 and 1336.—Plan and Section of Hip Rafters.

tended to be ceiled, a good plan is to tie in every other rafter with collars : these will form the ceiling joists. They are halved to rafters, dovetail fashion, so as to give them a better pull and prevent their feet from spreading, and are then spiked together.

HEXAGONAL OR OCTAGONAL SUMMERHOUSE ROOF.

There is more work in a hexagonal or an octagonal roof, yet the construction is but little different from that of a square pyramidical roof. First make the hip rafters. These should be 1½ in. by 5 in., and their bevels may be obtained from the sketch plan and section, Figs. 1335 and 1336. Take the length of hip E F from the plan, and set out as in Fig. 1337 ; at F erect the height of the roof F G, obtained from the section ; then draw the hip rafter from E to G, and so obtain its exact length, together with the bevels at top and bottom marked in dark lines. The hip rafters are housed into a 4-in. by 4-in. octagonal post at the apex, and are notched on to the plate at the angle. The end of the post where it projects above the roof may take the form of a finial, or "hip knob," or a weather-vane can be screwed into it ; a piece of 5-lb. lead dressed round and tacked to its base will keep the roof tight at this point. Two

collars are required to tie in the hip rafters ; if a ceiling is proposed, they may cross above each other, but in an open roof they should be halved together in the centre. A good effect is produced by letting the post hang down and cutting it at the bottom to receive the collars ; to give a finish, a turned knob or pendant can be

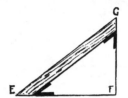

Fig. 1337.—Setting out Hip Rafters.

screwed into them ; all this is illustrated in Fig. 1338. The rafters, although of varying lengths, have all the same bevels, which can be got from the section ; they must be cut to a correct angle where they rest against the hips. All the collars for the ordinary rafters should be on the same level ; where they cross they must be halved out for each other. A ceiling could be formed, one-third up the length of the rafters from the feet, by nailing match-

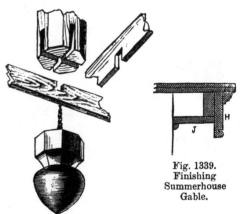

Fig. 1339.
Finishing
Summerhouse
Gable.

Fig. 1338.—Turned Knob screwed into Roof Post.

board to the collars, with a cove moulding at plate-level ; or if an open roof is preferred, the boarding should be nailed to the rafters and a bead stuck in all the hip angles. A common method of finishing the gable is to scribe a mould along under the roof covering, against the end rafter, but it looks rather mean ; a better plan is to fix bargeboards, and for this purpose the ridge and plates should project as a

Fig. 1340.—Gable-roof Summerhouse.

support for the barge rafter, to which are nailed the boards shown in section by H (Fig. 1339). The soffit J between the gable and the barge should be neatly boarded up.

SUMMERHOUSE ROOF COVERINGS.

Slating and tiling work should not be attempted by the inexperienced. Special roofing felt is a suitable covering, and there are several kinds on the market. The rafters must first be rough-boarded to take the felt. Wire-wove roofing and Willesden paper are also much used for such structures, and their pleasing tints accord well with the surroundings, as well as with the filling of the sides, whether it is lattice work, virgin cork, glazed frames, or boarding. A good pitch for a roof thus covered is a third—that is, the height from plate level to apex is one-third the span. Where no hips exist, a sound roof can be formed by means of well-seasoned boards— say ¾ in. thick, cut all to a size, and nailed to battens, similar to slating. The battens should be 1 in. by 2 in., and the distance apart at which they are nailed depends upon the length of the boards. The top

upper surface of each board must be bevelled off evenly with the plane so as to allow the other boards to rest flat upon it. The boards should be laid with the grain, not running horizontally, but in the same direction as the roof slopes ; they will then be less likely to split where nailed, and the exposed ends will not curl upwards and hold the wet, as they are liable to do in the former instance. The application of a few coats of oil paint will greatly increase the durability of this kind of roofing ; the colour of the paint should match, but be some shades darker than the other parts of the house. For instance, the roof may be painted a dark red tile colour and the wood-work a rich brown, with terra-cotta colour panels. Galvanised iron is a very cheap roofing material, and may be used where economy is the main object ; a coat of dark-coloured paint will remove much of its tinny appearance. Lead, zinc, and copper are good coverings if a flat pitch is desired, but they do not look so agreeable as any of the roofs mentioned above. A tarred felt

Fig. 1341.—Side Elevation of Summerhouse.

material is also sometimes used for cover-ing the roof, and resists the rain fairly well for a time.

GABLE-ROOF SUMMERHOUSE OR TEA-HOUSE.

A summerhouse or garden tea house is illustrated by Figs. 1340 to 1343. The di-

mensions given will meet ordinary requirements, but can be altered as desired. The
posts and rails of the framework should be
of 3-in. by 3-in. stuff, and after being planed
to size should be set out and mortised and

Fig. 1342.—End Elevation of Summerhouse.

tenoned together. The upper parts of the
posts and middle rails should be chamfered
to improve the appearance. The lower part
of the framework can be filled in with $\frac{3}{4}$-in.
or 1-in. matchboarding. If machine pre-
pared, the backs of the boards should be
smoothed off. They can be fixed in posi-

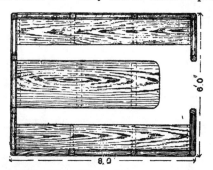

Fig. 1343.—Plan of Summerhouse.

tion with $\frac{5}{8}$-in. machine-prepared guard
beads, such as are used for window frames.
The outer beads should be mitred round
the framework and nailed, and the boarding inserted. The beads can then be mitred

round the inside and fixed; this will be
understood from Fig. 1344, which is a section through the beads, A, and the rail. The
curved pieces at the top of the openings
should be cut to shape and the posts
grooved about $\frac{1}{2}$ in. deep for them, and
secured with a few nails. The rafters should
be of 3-in. by 3-in. stuff; one over each
post will be sufficient if the top ends of the
rafters are fixed to a ridge board about 1 in.
thick. If desired, this ridge may project
above the roof, in which case it can be ornamented. The roof should be $\frac{3}{4}$-in. or 1-in.
matchboarding, the finished side being
fixed downwards. It should be covered
with roofing felt and then tarred and
sanded. Two bargeboards and a finial
should be fixed at each end of the summerhouse. Some light sashes, made to fit the

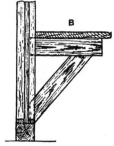

Fig. 1344.—Rail, Beads,
and Boarding.

Fig. 1345.—Bracket for
Summerhouse Seat.

openings and to fasten to the posts, will be
useful in windy weather.

SUMMERHOUSE SEATS AND TABLE.

For the seats, boards 11 in. by 1 in. will
answer, the front edge being rounded very
slightly. They can be fixed at each end
to a 2-in. by 1-in. fillet secured to the
framework. For intermediate support,
brackets can be mortised and tenoned together and to the post, as shown in Fig.
1345. The table should be of boards, $1\frac{1}{4}$ in.
thick, jointed together, the outer corners
being rounded as shown in Fig. 1343. At
one end the table can be supported by
means of a fillet fixed to the framing, and
at the outer end by means of a trestle and
brace illustrated by Figs. 1346 and 1347;
the legs should be halved together. To

prevent the top of the table warping, a
couple of ledges should be fixed underneath

OCTAGONAL SUMMERHOUSE.

The main dimensions of the octagonal

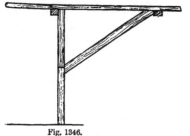

Fig. 1346.

Fig. 1347.

Figs. 1346 and 1347.—Trestle and Brace of Summerhouse Table.

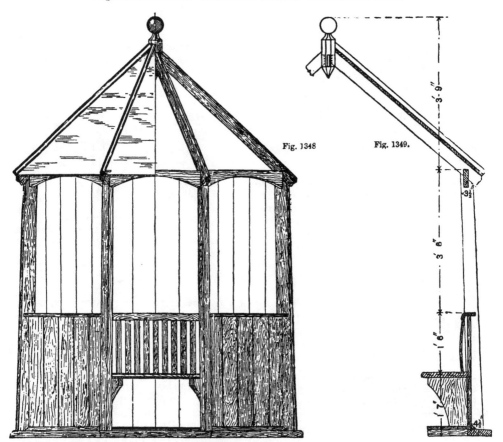

Fig. 1348

Fig. 1349.

Figs. 1348 and 1349.—Elevation and Section of Octagonal Summerhouse.

it. It is a good plan to paint the joints
before nailing or pinning the woodwork
together.

summerhouse about to be described are
given in the illustrations, Fig. 1348 showing an elevation, Fig. 1349 a vertical section

on the line A B (Fig. 1350). The elevation (Fig. 1348) shows in one half the roof covered with zinc laid upon horizontal boarding, in the other half the naked timbers of the roof. The sides of the house

joists. The seat is 12 in. wide, $1\frac{1}{2}$ in. thick, and 16 in. high from the floor; the back is formed with $1\frac{1}{2}$-in. by $\frac{1}{2}$-in. ash laths bent to a sweep and housed into the seat and back rail as shown in Fig. 1353. The back

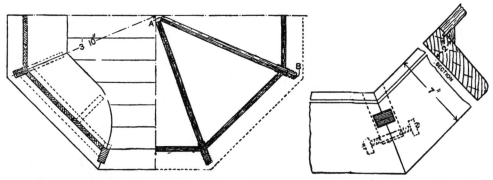

Fig. 1350.—Two Quarter-plans of Summerhouse. Fig. 1351.—Joint at Angles of Summerhouse Sill.

are inclined inwards at the top $2\frac{1}{2}$ in., the two sides next the doorway are boarded half-way up, the remaining sides all the way. The horizontal mid-rail is carried all round, and the boarding below it is placed vertical; the boarding above the rail follows the inclination of the posts. The corner posts are got out of $4\frac{1}{2}$-in. by 2-in. stuff, reduced at the top to $3\frac{1}{2}$ in.; they are boards as shown in the section (Fig. 1351), and are slotted at the top to receive the head rails as shown in Fig. 1352. The sills are out of 7-in. by 2-in. oak, weathered and rounded, and grooved to receive the side boards as shown in the section (Fig. 1351). The joints at the angles are secured with handrail bolts; the dotted outline in Fig. 1351 indicates the foot of the post, and the full line the mortise. The rafters are out of 4-in. by $1\frac{1}{2}$-in. stuff, backed, and bird's-mouthed into the angles, the ends overhanging and being shaped as shown in Fig. 1349, which is a section parallel with the side of the rafter, and therefore shows the latter in true length and inclination. The top end of the rafter is stub-tenoned into the octagonal finial, and the $\frac{3}{4}$-in. boarding is covered on the hips with $1\frac{1}{2}$-in. rolls, the zinc being dressed over these. The floor may be of concrete filled in flush with the sill, or boarded, as shown, on 2-in.

rail is out of $2\frac{1}{2}$-in. by $1\frac{1}{2}$-in. stuff, rounded and rebated to receive the edge of the shelf or rail. A $1\frac{1}{2}$-in. angle fillet is nailed round the bottom of the boarding to throw off the

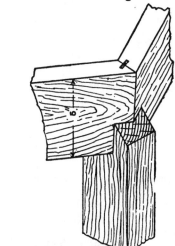

Fig. 1352.—Joint at Head of Summerhouse Posts.

water. This house would look well if executed in pitchpine and varnished.

SUMMERHOUSE WITH BRICKWORK FOOTINGS.

The summerhouses hitherto described have been in the nature of "tenants' fittings," but the last example here to be given is a more ambitious piece of work, and consequently more expensive. Fig. 1354 shows a front elevation, Fig. 1355 a sectional elevation, and Fig. 1356 a sectional plan. The heads, sills, and posts (except the sill for the ventilator, which is 2½ in. thick), are 6-in. by 6-in. angles, cut out of 11-in. by 8-in. stuff, the timber used for these being red deal. The sashes for the windows are 2-in. fixed frames, all glazed in 26-oz. sheet glass. (Glazing is dealt with on p. 434 *et seq.*) The joists are 6½ in.

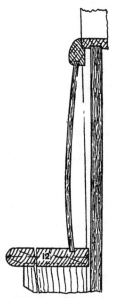

Fig. 1353.—Detail of Summerhouse Seat.

by 2½ in., fixed to 4½-in. by 3-in. wall-plates, and covered with 4-in. by 1⅛-in. grooved and tongued flooring. The panels are filled in with ⅞-in. grooved, tongued, and V-jointed diagonal lining. The roof is constructed as shown in section (Fig. 1355), with centre-post 6 in. square, cut out at the top for the base of the finial, and having a moulded drop at the bottom. The rafters are 4 in. by 2 in., moulded on end as shown, and covered with ⅝-in. sarking. The roof may be slated, or otherwise covered. The ceiling and the pieces down the sides of the interior are lined with 4-in. by ⅜-in. lining. The outside woodwork is painted with

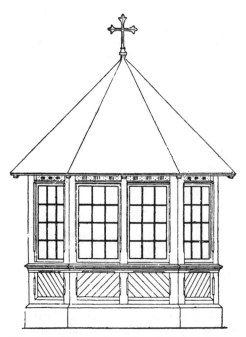

Fig. 1354.—Front Elevation of Summerhouse with Brickwork Footings.

Fig. 1355.—Vertical Section of Summerhouse with Brickwork Footings.

three coats best oil paint. The footings are built of good hard-burnt brick, with

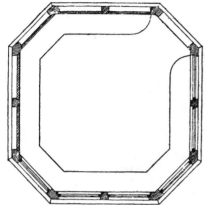

Fig. 1356.—Horizontal Section of Summerhouse with Brickwork Footings.

splayed base all round, and a damp-proof felt course is inserted just under the level of the floors. The seats, 1⅛ in. thick, are constructed as shown by the section (Fig. 1355), with rounded nosing and small cavetto moulding under, and supported on brackets 1½ in. thick, cut or otherwise ornamented. Ventilation is secured with a ventilator placed above the window all round the house, pierced with holes, and fitted with ⅝-in. double covers, so that it can be made to open and shut when required. The iron terminal stands 1 ft. 6 in. high, and is covered with lead at the base. The door is four-panelled, is filled in with diagonal lining, and has a small fanlight over it. The whole interior receives three coats of varnish. It may be mentioned that the construction of a rustic summerhouse is dealt with on pp. 420-22.

GARDEN SEATS.

THE easiest way of putting up a garden seat is illustrated by Fig. 1357, and the work need not occupy more than an hour or two. The seat is perfectly firm, and has a

Fig. 1357.—Fixed Garden Seat.

fairly good appearance, as shown by the perspective view (Fig. 1357). The cross-section (Fig. 1358) will, with a few words, explain the way in which it is put together. The supports A, B, C (Fig. 1358) are merely stakes of any rough wood which may come to hand, their diameter being, say, 2 in. or 2½ in. The upright one A beneath the seat is about 25 in. long; the sloping ones, B and C, are about 3 ft. 9 in. long. These stakes are pointed, let into the ground with a crowbar, and driven with a mallet to the depth of a foot, or nearly so. The sides of these two last, where they come in contact at the top, are cut smooth and fastened together with a nail or two. The cross-piece D, which should have its upper surface tolerably straight, is about 2 ft. long, and is nailed across the supports as shown. As illustrated, the seat board is supposed to be placed 16 in. from the ground, and for most people this is a comfortable

height; but the cross-piece can, of course, be nailed higher or lower. On the above, and on a similar arrangement set up at the proper distance from it, it is only necessary to nail the two boards E for the seat proper, and F for the back, and the seat is complete. These boards as shown are respectively 12 in. and 7 in. wide, but if those which happen to come to hand should not agree with these measurements by 2 or 3 in. it will not greatly matter. The top of the back-board is placed about 18 in. above the seat, but some may prefer to have it a little higher or a little lower. The length of the seat is 3 ft. 3 in., which allows abundant space for two persons to sit comfortably. If the length is increased much beyond this, there must be another support in the middle. A garden seat thus

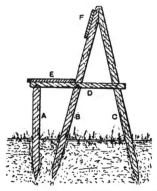

Fig. 1358.—Cross Section of Fixed Garden Seat.

made is a fixture; the ease with which it is set up, and its firmness when built, are in great measure owing to the fact that its legs are driven into the solid ground. This, too, makes possible the use of such rough and light materials. There would be no great difficulty in building a movable seat on similar lines, particularly if sawn stuff were used, and the workmanship were rather more careful. In such a case a second cross-piece would run below D, and

seen from inside. The front and back rails of the seat are fixed 17 in. from the bottom, and are of 2-in. by 2-in. stuff, rounded on the outer edges, and key-tenoned through

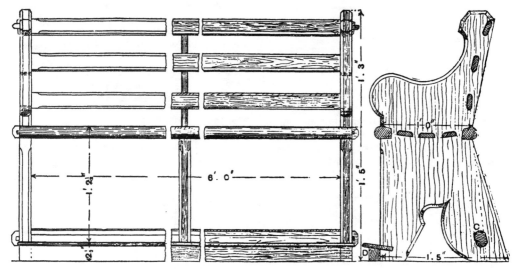

Fig. 1359.—Elevation of Gothic Seat.   Fig. 1360.—Cross Section of Gothic Seat.

some 4 in. or 5 in. from the ground; also a longitudinal bar, of the length of the seat, would be nailed to this piece and its fellow or fellows, and run beneath the seat-board. This second plan, however, cannot be so confidently recommended as the first. The scale of Fig. 1358 is $\frac{1}{2}$ in. to the foot.

the ends; the tenon, which is $\frac{3}{4}$ in. thick and the full width of the stuff, is formed on the back edge as shown in Fig. 1361. The nosing part laps over the edge of the end, finishing flush outside, and the end of the rail is housed $\frac{1}{4}$ in. deep, as shown at A

Fig. 1361.—Tenon on Front Rail of Seat.

GOTHIC GARDEN SEAT.

The garden seat illustrated in elevation by Fig. 1359, and in cross section by Fig. 1360, is Gothic in style, and should be constructed of pitchpine finished in oil and varnish, either pale oak or carriage. The two ends are made in the solid, out of pieces 2 ft. 8 in. long, 1 ft. 5 in. wide, and $1\frac{1}{2}$ in. thick, and are cut to the shape of Fig. 1360, which is an elevation of one end

Fig. 1362.—Housings in Seat End.

(Fig. 1362). The seat battens are of 2-in. by $\frac{3}{4}$-in. stuff, and are housed into the ends as shown at B (Fig. 1362); they are arranged in a curve (see Fig. 1360), the faces being straight. The back is formed in a similar manner, the chamfers in both cases being stopped ¾ in. from the ends (see Fig. 1359). A leg, which is indicated by the dotted line in Fig. 1360, is placed in the centre to stiffen the seat, and a 1-in. by ⅜-in. curved

Fig. 1363.—Tenon or Top Back Batten of Seat.

iron bar supports the back. This is screwed on the outsides of the battens, and the lower end, which is turned up at an angle, is sunk in flush in the back rail. The top back batten and the bottom rail c (Fig. 1360) are both key-tenoned through the ends as shown in the details (Figs. 1363 to 1365),

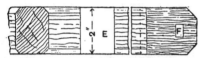

Fig. 1364.—Side View of Bottom Rail of Seat.

and these, with the footrail, form a stiff frame. The footboard is 4 in. by ¾ in., housed at the ends and nailed to the footrail D, which is of 1½-in. by 1¼-in. stuff screwed to the edge of the ends. The bottom rail c is made continuous, and half-notched at the centre leg, as shown at E (Figs. 1364 and 1365), and the keyway in the

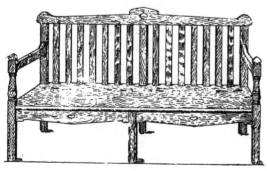

Fig. 1366.—Portable Garden Seat.

tenon is shown at F. These keys should be made slightly tapering in length, and fit tightly in the mortise, which should be so arranged that the key, on being driven in,

will tighten up the shoulder—that is, the shoulder end of the mortise must be kept ⅛ in. within the thickness of the end. To preserve and strengthen the joints, all the tenons, mortises, etc., should be given a coat of litharge of lead mixed with boiled linseed oil, prepared at the time of using, and a couple of coats applied at the bottom of the ends will prevent them rotting.

Fig. 1365.—Edge View of Bottom Rail of Seat.

PORTABLE GARDEN SEAT.

The garden seat illustrated by Fig. 1366 may be constructed of pine. The material required includes two front posts, 2 ft. 7 in. high by 2⅝ in. square, and one front centre leg, 1 ft. 3 in. high by 2⅝ in. square. Three back legs, 3 ft. long by 2⅝ in. square (Fig. 1367), may be marked out with a template side by side on a plank 11 in. wide and 2½ in.

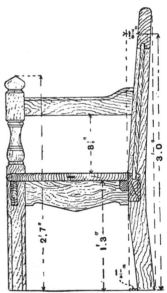

Fig. 1367.—Cross Section of Portable Seat.

thick, and cut at the sawmill; sufficient distance should be allowed between them in marking for the band-saw cut. The front, back, and top rails are continuous.

The front rail is 6 ft. 2 in. long, 4 in. deep by 1 in. ; back rail, 6 ft. 2 in. long, 4 in. deep by 1½ in. ; top rail, 6 ft. 9 in. long, 5 in. greatest width by 1⅛ in. ; two end rails,

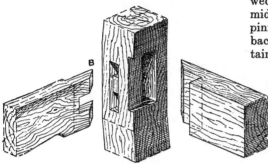

Fig. 1368.—Back Post and Rail Ends of Seat.

1 ft. 8 in. by 4 in. deep by 1 in. ; two arms, 1 ft. 8½ in. by 1½ in. thick by 2½ in. deep at the front and 4 in. at the meeting of the back post. For the seat, two 1-in. planks 6 ft. 3 in. long and 9 in. wide should be dowelled together, a nosing being worked on the front edge and ends. The fourteen balustrades are finished 1 ft. 8 in. long by 1¾ in. wide and ¾ in. thick, slightly rounded on the front and stopped ½ in. from the top and bottom rails ; they are tapered off at the back, and they are pitched at 2 in. Plane the stuff and shape the posts to size, the front rail being shouldered to the intermediate leg (4 in. deep) and also to the

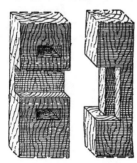

Fig. 1370.—Back Rail and Centre Post of Seat.

end posts. The mortise and tenons are of the same shape as those shown at B (Fig. 1368). The back rail is housed ¼ in. to the posts (see Figs. 1368 to 1370), the top being

1 in. higher than the front rail, or 1 ft. 4 in. from the floor line. The two intermediate rails A and A¹ (Fig. 1369), 1 ft. 5 in. long by 3½ in. deep by ⅞ in. wide, are shouldered and wedged to the back rail and screwed to the middle leg. The arms are stumped and pinned to the front post, and tenoned to the back posts and wedged, the bevel being obtained by fitting a thin wood template after

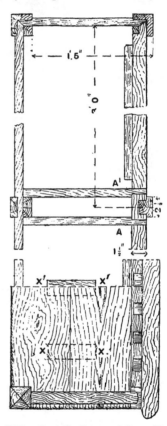

Fig. 1369.—Part Section and Part Plan of Portable Garden Seat

the posts have been driven home temporarily to the shoulders of the end rails ; the arms are then marked from the template. The top rail is mortised to receive the stump tenons of the posts. Try on the rail, then space out the mortises for the balustrades. The seat should be fitted temporarily with the arms out and also in position before the frame is finally jointed up. Instead of dowelling the two boards which form the seat, they could be fitted separately and stiffened with blocks x and x' (Fig. 1369) screwed to the under-side. The mortises and tenons should be given a coat of priming immediately before being put together. The seat can be primed, given a

wood guides which are fixed to the back leg of the seat by means of a bolt and nut. When used as a table top it is lowered and secured by thumbscrews fixed to the front legs, and going through to the wood guides, making it quite secure. In Fig. 1372 the dotted lines show the back of the seat act-

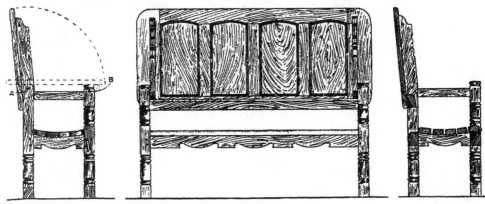

Fig. 1372.   Fig. 1371.   Fig. 1373.

Fig. 1371.—Front Elevation of Garden Table-seat.   Fig. 1372.—End Elevation of Garden Table-seat.   Fig. 1373.—Cross Section of Garden Table-seat.

coat of lead colour, and finished a light green.

GARDEN TABLE-SEAT.

The table-seat illustrated by Figs. 1371 to 1373 is a useful and ornamental addition to a garden or lawn. The figures are to a scale of slightly less than $\frac{1}{2}$ in. to the foot, and show fully the details. (The actual scale is one-twenty-seventh full size.) The table top, which also acts as the back of the seat, is kept in position by the

ing as a table top ; A indicating the position of the bolt and nut, and B the position of the thumbscrew. The back may be panelled, as shown in Fig. 1373, the top of the panel being kept flush with the top of the framing. Plain boarding may be used if desired. The table-seat can be painted, or would look well if stained a green colour. Other seats and tables for the garden are described in the next chapter, which treats on rustic carpentry work.

RUSTIC CARPENTRY.

RUSTIC CARPENTRY WORK FOR THE GARDEN.
GARDEN rustic work, unlike indoor carpentry, does not demand nice skill and a varied assortment of tools. Rustic carpentry uses its materials in a natural state, and endeavours to make them decorative. This, perhaps, is the only style really suitable thatch, and its decorations of moss and fir cones, is in proper keeping with its surroundings. At the same time this style is the least costly and the most simple. There is scarcely any kind of wood which may come to hand in a natural state which is not available for rustic work, though some

Fig. 1374.—Rustic Entrance Gate and Fence.

able for garden purposes. All things in the garden should be in harmony with and suggestive of nature. Glass, metal, and paint are felt to be out of place. Anything of the nature of a greenhouse—whatever efforts may be made to render it ornamental—can scarcely be pretty; whilst the rustic summerhouse, with its wooden walls covered with natural bark, its low roof of sorts lend themselves to the purpose more readily than others. In most country districts there is a wide choice of materials costing little or nothing; but some trouble has to be taken in finding them, as they are not like sawn deals, always to be found in stock at the timber yard, and bought at any time they may be wanted. The example of rustic work shown in Fig. 1374 should be constructed in larch only. Of all common English woods this is the most valuable for rustic carpentry. Its straight growth specially fits it for the carrying out of decorative designs; it lasts longer in exposed situations than any other ordinary wood—heart of oak only excepted—and wearing, perhaps, ten times longer than those portions of the oak which are available for garden purposes; and it is plentiful, for larch plantations now abound in most districts, and when they are thinned the rustic carpenter should look out for his

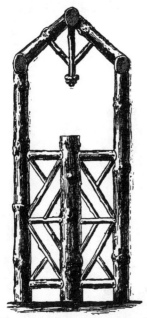

Fig. 1375.—Side of Rustic Arch.

supply. The poles grown in thick plantations are better for rustic work than those that grow singly, as the former taper more gradually and have fewer branches. The wood of spruce and other firs which have the same symmetrical growth have almost as good an appearance, but they do not last like the larch.

Rustic Entrance Gate and Fence.

The fence and wicket entrance shown in Fig. 1374 can be made by anyone capable of using saw and hammer. Rustic work looks none the worse for the workmanship being rough. The general view (Fig. 1374) approximates to a scale of $\frac{1}{2}$ in. to the foot; Fig. 1375 is actually to this

Fig. 1376.—Panel of Rustic Arch.

scale, and the details shown in Figs. 1376 and 1377 are $\frac{3}{4}$ in. to the foot, so the exact dimensions of every part may be easily ascertained. The arch rises to a total height of 6 ft. 8 in.; its width from centre to centre of the side pillars is 3 ft. 6 in. The pillars, exclusive of tenons at their tops, show a height above ground of 5 ft., but another 2 ft. is supposed to be buried in the ground, where it is rammed in with stones and earth like a gate post. It is usual to peel off the bark from those parts which go into the ground, and to give them a good coating of gas tar. Rustic work, in

Fig. 1377.—Rustic Gate.

a general way, is merely nailed together, but in this design the pillars are mortised into the pieces resting on their tops, the bars of the gate into the head and hinge tree, and the rails of the fence into the fencing posts. Fig. 1378 shows how the

Fig. 1378.—Rustic Work Mortise and Tenon.

shoulders of tenons are sawn so as to make them fit best to the rounded wood. A simpler joint, neither quite so strong nor quite so well looking, can be made by halving each piece similarly to the manner indicated in Fig. 1379, and driving a nail. The halving is shown shaded in Fig. 1379. A popular kind of right-angle joint is shown

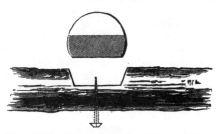

Fig. 1379.—Joint of Rustic Rail and Post.

by Fig. 1380; a V-shaped notch is cut in one stick, and the end of the other shaped to fit. Fig. 1377 shows the side of the gate to which the upright palings are nailed, but on the opposite side the diagonal pieces A and B must not be made of short lengths merely going from bar to bar, but must be

Fig. 1380.—Notched or Mitred Joint.

in one length from top to bottom, to act as braces and give the gate its required strength.

RUSTIC FENCING.

In the example of fencing shown in Fig. 1374, the posts are set 7 ft. 6 in. apart.

Fig. 1381.—Design for Rustic Fence.

Fencing posts are frequently set at wider distances up to 10 ft.; in Figs. 1381 to 1383 they are 8 ft. apart. These posts, as also the gate posts, need to be set as deep in the earth as the pillars. Fig. 1384 illustrates the manner in which the tenons of the rails fit together in the post mortises. The end C is adjusted to the mortise before the post is fixed, the end D afterwards. The slanting braces are let into the earth with a crowbar and then nailed to the rails, and they prevent the latter from having any motion in the mortises. The smaller stuff,

Fig. 1382.—Design for Rustic Fence.

of which the palings and the lighter work generally are made, should properly be of larch as well as the heavier pieces, not only for the sake of appearance, but in order that the whole may wear together. Such stuff may be provided from the tops and branches of the larger poles, and from the

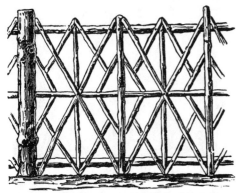

Fig. 1383.—Design for Rustic Fence.

thinnings of young plantations. In Fig. 1374 the palings are nailed about 5 in. distant from centre to centre, so as to keep out most small animals, but if special protection is desired against chickens, etc., the number of palings may be doubled, shorter palings, to rise about 1 in. above the centre rail, being nailed alternately with those illustrated. Common rustic work fences almost invariably are made of oak "bangles" set to cross each other diagonally. Oak bangles are the smaller branches of the oak from which the bark has been stripped for the use of the tanner. Their knotted and twisted forms give them value for rustic carpentry, but for fencing they are not satisfactory, as their crooked and uncertain growth forbids their being worked to any regular design ; but their worst defect is that when exposed they decay very quickly. This is always a serious disadvantage, and especially so when the rustic fence is intended as a support for roses or other climbers ; for by the time the climbers are so grown as to be ornamental the fence is apt to fall to pieces. Few kinds of wood rot more quickly than sap of oak. The smaller branches have little or no heart, and are nearly all sap, and hence their rapid decay. They last best in the dry, but even there they are more subject to suffer from grub than any wood of the

fir kind. One point in their favour is, however, that they are cheap ; for if not used for rustic work, their only value is for firewood. A larch fence will outlast two or three oak bangle fences ; as a safeguard it can be made more secure, and in appearance it will be more artistic. The arrangement of the stuff in ornamental patterns may be varied almost endlessly. Figs. 1381 to 1383 give three additional designs on the ½ in. scale, and these will doubtless suggest still more varieties.

RUSTIC ARCHES.

Fig. 1385 (½ in. to the foot) is an alternative design for the arch over the gate ; or it is a suitable design for use alone. The two supporting pillars could well carry the gate, as any extra strain thus placed upon them would be compensated by the support given by the rails on either side. The bottom struts (F F, Fig. 1385) are necessary ; without them the weight of the upper part of the arch might, if not accurately balanced, tend to pull the structure out of the perpendicular. This arch in its upper part is tied together strongly by the braces G G. This arch is the same width as the one shown by Fig. 1374, and is 7 ft. 6 in. high. In Fig. 1374, every portion of the arch, with the exception of the apple-tree knots with which the lower ends of the pendants are finished, is of larch ; but in Fig. 1385 the

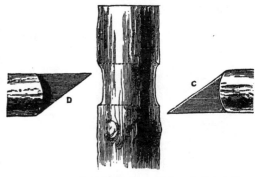

Fig. 1384.—Rail Ends Tenoned and Pointed.

struts at the tops of the pillars and in the ties connecting the two pinnacles with the top of the ridge piece are of apple tree, as here a curved form is more pleasing. Either arch will also do equally well for use within the garden to span a path and serve as a support for climbers.

RUSTIC PEDESTAL FOR SUNDIAL OR FLOWER-VASE.

The pedestal shown in Fig. 1386 is a piece of garden decoration easily made. If a sundial is to be mounted, the top of the pedestal must be a true horizontal plane, and the pedestal itself must be firmly fixed. As the pedestal is a hollow box, the easiest way of fixing will, perhaps, be by letting a piece of wood into the ground like a post, adjusting the pedestal accurately upon it, and then securing it by a screw or two. But if only a vase is to be set on the pedestal

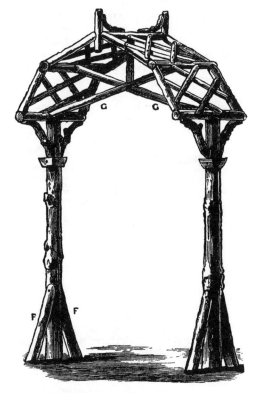

Fig. 1385.—Rustic Arch.

it can be slipped over a stake merely driven into the ground, and this will suffice to keep it from being thrown down. It can then readily be removed at pleasure. Fig. 1386

is a front elevation, Fig. 1387 a vertical section, and Fig. 1388 a horizontal section through the centre ; all these are to a scale of 1 in. to the foot. The body of the pedes-

Fig. 1386.   Fig. 1387.

Figs. 1386 and 1387.—Elevation and Section of Rustic Pedestal.

tal is made of 1 in. elm board, the top being a piece of 2 in. slab. Some fairly large pieces of rough wood, no matter what kind, are required for the base. The split rods used in the rustic mosaic work are about 2 in. in diameter. Wych-elm or maple, with a little mixture of peeled withy, will perhaps look best. A few bits of crooked stuff—say apple tree—will also be wanted. The horizontal section (Fig.

Fig. 1388.—Horizontal Section of Rustic Pedestal.

1388) shows how the carcase, 1 ft. square, is nailed together of 1 in. boards. For the given height (3 ft. 6 in.) these boards must be 3 ft. 4 in. long, which allows 2 in. for the solid piece of slab or plank forming the top. This top is 16 in. square, so that when split rods have been nailed round its edge it may be about 18 in. square. The base is made of four pieces of rough round stuff, 5 in. in diameter by 21 in. long, which should be trimmed a little on that side

Fig. 1389.—Rustic Chair Seat.

which lies against the board. The vertical section (Fig. 1387) shows how these pieces are fixed by nailing through the boards into them; they should also be nailed to each other at the corners. Next above, a 3 in. rod runs round. Two lengths of 2 in. split rod run up each corner, as shown in Fig. 1388, and between these the ends of the small projecting pieces of crooked stuff are fitted in. They should be neatly trimmed for this purpose, and as their position may expose them to accidental knocks, it will be better to screw than to nail them into the board. The arrangement of the rustic mosaic pattern is shown sufficiently clearly by Fig. 1386.

GARDEN RUSTIC SEATS.

Movable garden seats and garden tables can be made well in rustic work, but this style of work has not always been success-

Fig. 1390.—Support for Rustic Seat.

fully employed. Rustic chairs are too often unsightly, uncomfortable, and heavy. For fixed seats, either for the summerhouse or for the open air. rustic work answers ad-

mirably, but for movable furniture great ingenuity is required to get over the difficulties raised above. Larch does not lend itself kindly to chair-making, and in crooked stuff it is a difficult matter to get either an artistic design or a comfortable seat.

RUSTIC CHAIR.

Fig. 1389 is a design for a movable chair in which an attempt has been made to unite comfort, appearance, and reasonable lightness. It is important, in such a piece of furniture as this, that there should be nothing that will hold water. A "gridiron" arrangement of the seat—one, that is, of sticks only—is much to be preferred to one of continuous board. Much of the back and ends is formed of crooked stuff. The three pieces supporting the rods forming the actual seat are, for the sake of comfort, of the form shown in Fig. 1390. Such curves are frequent, and even in a small quantity of crooked stuff it will not be hard to find three pieces of suitable growth; and, of course, their upper sides can be so trimmed as to make them correspond with tolerable correctness. Fig. 1389 is not

Fig. 1391.—Rustic Table with Mosaic Top.

drawn to scale, but the dimensions of the chair are about 4 ft. long, 3 ft. high to top of back, and the actual seat 16 in. high, and the same broad. Whether rough wood with its bark on or peeled wood should be used is much a question of taste; but, in any case, larch will not be suitable for any part of the work. If white peeled wood is preferred—and this will make the lightest chair—it will be well to use withy for the straighter parts of the frame; also for the seat, which should be of withy rods 1 in. or so in thickness, or somewhat thicker if they are used split. The crooked parts would then be of peeled oak bangles. If wood with its natural bark is used, nothing will be better for the straighter parts than small elm saplings, except for the seat, where springy hazel rods should be used.

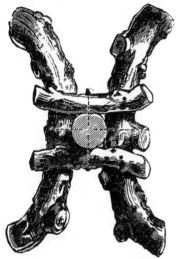

Fig. 1392.—Foot of Rustic Table.

long, and about 3½ in. thick. In some districts the young elms spring up so thickly in the hedgerows that the majority have to be thinned out to allow the others to grow into timber. These young elms have commonly a very ornamental bark—the young wych elm in particular is frequently almost as picturesque in appearance as virgin cork. The foot (see plan, Fig. 1392, drawn to a scale of ¾ in. to the foot) is made of four pieces of rough crooked stuff, the two larger ones not quite so thick as the pillar, but still sufficiently heavy to give the table a solid foundation. These larger pieces are 21 in. long, and the shorter ones about 10 in. Probably no difficulty will be found in obtaining pieces of the curve shown; the curved side is placed downwards and outwards, so as to give the table a firm standing. In the upper and smaller pair the curved form is chosen only for the sake of

Fig. 1393.—Rustic Mosaic Table Top.

Elm or apple-tree branches will in this case serve for the crooked work. The carpentry, as shown by Fig. 1389, is of the most simple kind. There are no mortises, all the pieces being merely nailed together.

RUSTIC TABLE.

Fig. 1391 shows a movable rustic table of a size to be readily lifted from place to place, though so far solid in its lower part as not to be easily upset, which is a point of importance. The dimensions are:— Height, 2 ft. 2 in.; length of top, 2 ft. 2 in.; breadth of top, 1 ft. 1 in. The pillar is an important feature in this table, and should be made of a piece of elm sapling 1 ft. 11 in.

appearance; straight pieces would not look nearly so well. Fig. 1392 shows the foot pieces to be fastened to the pillar and to each other with large nails. These pieces are drawn as of rough and knotted apple-tree wood, and this wood is the most solid and the best looking for the purpose. Failing this, elm would do, or oak still better, provided sticks of the size can be found with the bark on. For the struts that are nailed to the pillar and support the top it will not be difficult to find suitable branches, which, whilst they may differ, perhaps, in their details from those in the drawing and from each other, will yet in a general way agree with both.

RUSTIC MOSAIC TABLE TOP.

The table top (26 in. by 13 in.) is of 1 in. board, and as a safeguard against warping should have a couple of cross-ledgers

Fig. 1394.—Rustic Porch.

screwed underneath. The ends of the struts should be let into mortise holes in these ledgers and firmly fixed there with screws. The struts must be well secured, so that no play of the top may be possible, for the foot is tolerably heavy, and when the table is lifted it is pretty certain to be by its top. The upper surface, with its decoration of rustic mosaic, is shown to scale in Fig. 1393. The dark bands in the present example are supposed to be of split hazel rods, and the filling-up between of peeled withy. The strip running round the edge of the table is also of the latter. Fig. 1393 is drawn to a scale of $\frac{3}{4}$ in. to the foot. Garden furniture should have a coating of inexpensive oak varnish, and an occasional revarnishing is desirable. Movable seats will, of course, be housed during the winter, but through the summer the chances are that they will be left altogether exposed. The chair previously described suffers very little from such exposure ; the table, however, is an article which should be put under cover when not in use. A mere wet-

ting will not hurt it, but if it is left so that the rain water can stand on its top, the bark will, notwithstanding varnish, crack and peel off, and the wood decay.

RUSTIC PORCH.

The porch for which Fig. 1394 gives a design has seats, and is intended for a house standing in its own garden and to some extent secluded from observation. It is built with straight stuff, the heavier parts being of some fir wood, preferably larch. Its dimensions suit a small house. It projects 3 ft. from the wall, is 6 ft. wide, and 6 ft. high to the lintel. The ground plan (Fig. 1395) does not show the actual width of the door opening and porch entrance. It will be seen that the front is supported on four collar-posts, a, a, a, a. These are cut from rough larch poles—say $3\frac{1}{2}$ in. or 4 in. at base, and not much less at top, for plantation-grown larch tapers very gradually. They rise 6 ft. above the ground-line. The best way of setting them is on blocks of stone, an iron dowel being let into the stone and the bottom of the post ; but it will suffice to let them into the ground, like ordinary gate-posts, for a couple of feet, and to well ram them in with stones and earth. If this last plan is adopted, it will be well roughly to shave off the bark from

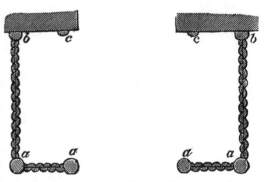

Fig. 1395.—Ground Plan of Rustic Porch.

the part to be buried, and to gas-tar it. Though more liable to rot than when mounted on a stone, a well-seasoned larch-post, thus treated, will last for many years. The back-posts b b are of poles sawn in halves, and nailed to plugs driven into the brickwork. The nails alone will hold them in place, as also the dwarf-posts *c c*, which are 14 in. high, and support the corners of the seats. On the top of the four front collar-posts rests the lintel, which is nailed

Fig. 1396.—Side of Rustic Porch.

down to them, and over the two corner-posts it is cut half through to receive the wall plates *d* (Fig. 1396), which here rest upon it. These wall plates are 3 ft. 3 in. long, and so project 3 in. beyond the collar-posts. This allows the front rafters to be set slightly farther forward than the posts, which will thus be better sheltered by the roof. At top the rafters are cut to clip the rustic ridge-piece, as in Fig. 1397. The back rafters, of course, are of half stuff, and are nailed to the wall. Fig. 1396 is to a scale of $\frac{1}{2}$ in. to the foot.

Filling in Front of Porch.

The main framework of the porch having been put together, the front can be filled in. Between the two collar-posts, at each side, the space is closely filled up half-way —that is, to a height of 3 ft. In the first place, take a piece of quartered stuff and nail it from post to post, one of its sawn

sides being outwards and in a line with the middles of the two posts, and the other sawn side upwards and 14 in. from the ground. To the former side nail the pieces of half stuff seen in Fig. 1394, which form the outer side of the wall, and on the latter will rest the end of the board which forms the seat. The upright pieces of half stuff mentioned above are 2 ft. long, and on their tops another cross-piece of quartered stuff (shown in Fig. 1394) is fixed, and nailed down into them. Other upright pieces of half stuff, so arranged as to break joint, are nailed against these from within, both above and below the seat; and the diagonal pieces seen outside (Fig. 1394) are again nailed against these latter. Above comes some open work, which explains itself, and at top is a little more solid work—namely, four or five horizontal pieces of round stuff, of which the ends are cut to clip the posts somewhat as those shown in Fig. 1397. Above the lintel the gable is filled with open trellis. The little quatrefoils seen in this are made by nailing short bits of rod, with their ends to the front, at the intersections of the smaller members of the trellis.

Ends of Rustic Porch.

The construction of the ends of the porch, as regards their lower and upper parts, is much the same as that of the sides of the front. There is a cross-piece for the seat, and the space beneath is filled by a double row of upright halved stuff; but the closed

Fig. 1397.—Rafters and Ridge-piece of Rustic Porch.

work rises higher than at the front— namely, 4 ft.—in order that the heads of those sitting within may not be exposed to draughts. Fig. 1396 shows the inner side of one end. Here the seat-board, 14 in. wide, is shown fixed, and its edge is ornamented with short strips of split rod. To fix these securely, a slip of lath should be nailed along below the front edge of the seat-board ; the strips can then be bradded to this, as well as to the edge itself. Above the seat, and below the open work, is a large space to be filled with rustic mosaic,

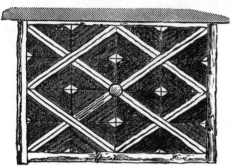

Fig. 1398.—Rustic Mosaic Ceiling of Porch.

to the given design. The cross and upright pieces which form the panels in this serve to keep in place the pieces of half stuff which form the outer wall. In the panels light and dark rods may be used in contrast, the St. Andrew's crosses being of peeled willow, and the filling-in of hazel, birch, or the like, with the bark on. Any chinks that may show should be stuffed with moss.

RUSTIC PORCH ROOF.

The roof has a ceiling of rustic mosaic according to the design given in Fig. 1398. This mosaic is difficult to do overhead. It is better, therefore, to arrange boards to cover one side of the roof, to screw them

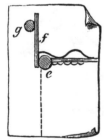

Fig. 1399.—Section showing Trellis on Porch Roof.

temporarily together with ledgers on the off side, and to brad the mosaic upon them before they are fixed up. To the backs of these boards the root proper, which is of

Fig. 1400.—Rustic Dovecote.

zinc or galvanised iron, will be screwed down. A metal roof is easily put on, but it is the reverse of ornamental, and far too effective as a conductor of heat. Therefore, to disguise the roof and to keep it cool, a trellis is thrown over it, so that it may be hidden and shaded by climbing plants. This is made clear in Fig. 1394. If brought close to metal, and the aspect is a warm one, climbing plants will not thrive; the trellis is therefore kept 4 in. or 5 in. above the roof. Fig. 1399 is an oblique section showing how the trellis is fixed over the true roof: *e* indicates the true rafter, *f* one of the short pieces of rod which support the false rafter *g*; and these pieces are nailed to the front of the true rafter and to the back of the false one. The front of the trellis thus projects beyond the roof, and is consequently more effective. At its back the trellis is sup-

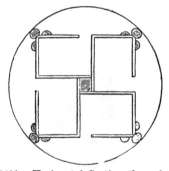

Fig. 1401.—Horizontal Section through Cote.

ported on rafters of half stuff nailed to the wall.

RUSTIC DOVECOTE.

After the instructions on rustic work just given, and the descriptions on pp. 338 to 344 of how dove and pigeon cotes are made, there is no need to enter into a detailed description of the rustic cote shown by Fig. 1400. Suffice it to say that the pole is of larch or other fir wood, and that each tier has four nesting-places (see Fig. 1401). The corners of one tier come over the centres of the sides of the underneath tier. The roof is of zinc or painted sheet-iron, set out as in Fig. 1402, with an allowance A for seaming. The metal is secured with copper nails.

27

RUSTIC GARDEN FLOWER BASKET OR LAWN CENTREPIECE.

Fig. 1403 is a view of a rustic receptacle for flowering plants, which, in plan, is a

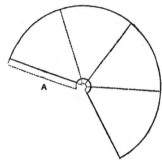

Fig. 1402.—Pattern for Rustic Cote Roof.

plain octagon in its main portion, but on each of its eight sides a shallower triangular box projects, thus bringing its shape more nearly to that of an eight-pointed star. In size it may be varied to suit any particular lawn, but the dimen-

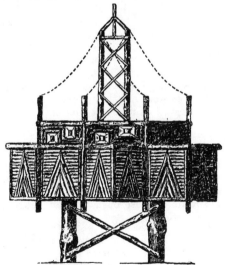

Fig. 1403.—Rustic Garden Flower Basket.

sions recommended are:—Height 5 ft. 6 in., and breadth 4 ft. 6 in. The internal measurements of the large octagonal box (which stands with its top 3 ft. from the ground) are—from side to side 3 ft., and

depth 1 ft. 6 in.   This portion is more
especially intended for climbing plants, for
the support of which a square trellis rises
from its centre, and from this there are also

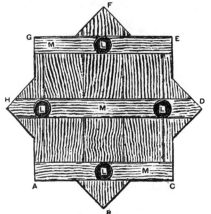

Fig. 1404.—Bottom of Rustic Flower Basket.

flying chains to all the angles.   The eight
smaller boxes, shaped as right-angled triangles, measure internally 1 ft. at base and
7 in. perpendicular; their depth is 1 ft.
They are intended for small, low-growing
plants, such as will afford masses of colour.
For the bottom of the boxes 1-in. board,
and for the sides ¾-in. board, will be required.   Elm is considered to endure best
for such purposes as this.   The four supports may be of any rough and lasting
wood.   The upright sticks which carry the
trellis, as well as those at the angles, will
perhaps look best in maple or wych-elm,
on account of the rough, ornamental bark
on those saplings, but larch or other fir
will look very well.   The rustic mosaic
covering the boxes is partly white, made of
the halves of peeled withy rods, and partly
dark, made of those of hazel, and wearing
their natural covering.

MAKING THE RUSTIC FLOWER BASKET.

Whether the basket is to be a fixture or
removable at pleasure must depend chiefly
on its size.   Shelter during winter will help
to preserve it, but it may suffer damage
from careless moving, and will stand far
more firmly as a fixture.   It is here assumed
that it is to be fixed.   The four supports L
(Fig. 1404) will have to be let into the

ground like so many posts.   They form a
square with 18-in. sides; their diameter is
4 in., and they stand 16 in. above ground,
and go down a foot below.   The bottom of
the boxes, the under-side of which is shown
by Fig. 1404, is nailed together by three
ledgers, M, of the same thickness as the
bottom—1 in.   These ledgers will lie on the
supports, and the box will rest on them
when in position.   The sides are of ¾-in.
stuff, and in order to strengthen them it
is desirable to make the boards cross each
other at the angles.   It will be remembered
that the sides of the large box have to be
boarded to a height of 20 in., and those of
the smaller ones to 14 in.   At the bottom,
a beginning is made with a 9-in. width like
that shown by Fig. 1405; it is 3 ft. long, and
it has to be nailed to the side A C (Fig.
1404).   The opening B is cut slanting as
shown, to admit the angle B in the same
figure.   Strips 2 in. wide are also cut from
its upper edge as shown at I K.   The board
for the side G E is precisely the same, and

Fig. 1405.—Board for Side of Rustic Basket.

those for G A and E C differ only in being
¾ in. longer at each end.   Having placed
these, board up the intermediate angle
boxes B, D, F, H with boards 11 in. long to
the same height as their fellows—namely
7 in.   If for the second course 9-in. widths
are again taken, they can be cut the same
as for the first course, except that the opening at B will not be required.   In this course
nail the first board on the side H B, and so

on round the box, thus making the boards cross those already on, and nail them to the parts of those boards which rise 2 in. above the general level. When this course of boards is nailed on, the angle boxes B, D, F, H will be boarded up to their required height—that is, 14 in.—and the intermediate ones, A, C, E, G, have to be boarded up with short lengths, 7 in. wide, to make their outer sides also complete. What now remains to be done is to complete the deeper octagon box, of which the sides A, C, E, G are at present 16 in. high, whilst the intermediate ones, B, D, F, H, are only 9 in. high. On these last-named fix another 9-in. width, nailing to the rising corners as before, the pieces being 14 in.

Fig. 1406.—Plan of Rustic Flower Basket.

long. Next complete the sides A, C, E, G with pieces of the same length, 4 in. wide. Lastly, 2-in. strips, filling up the sides B, D, F, H, will complete the box. The short 2-in. strips cut from the lower boards will be utilised as ledgers, nailing them vertically up the inner sides of the boxes. The four uprights which support the trellis are kept in place by strips crossing the box near its top, as shown at N N (Fig. 1406). The standards are 4 ft. 11 in. long. The uprights that run up the angles of the octagon should be neatly trimmed with the chisel where they come in contact with the boards. Their tops are connected with those of the trellis by flying chains. These

may be real metal chains, or, what will look more in character, a couple of thin nut rods may be twisted together and placed for the climbers to cling to. The arrange-

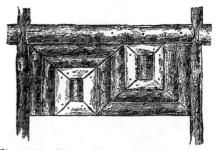

Fig. 1407.—Rustic Mosaic Border on Flower Basket.

ment of these chains is shown by dotted lines in Fig. 1406. The boarding of the boxes is covered with rustic mosaic. The patterns are formed by lengths of split rods bradded to the boards. Of the fret running round the octagon, one of the sides, drawn to a scale of 1½ in. to the foot, appears in Fig. 1407; whilst in Fig. 1408, on the same scale, one of the panels is shown on the line of the shallower boxes. These sixteen panels are all of like dimensions. If it is preferred to have the supports fixed and

Fig. 1408.—Rustic Mosaic Panel.

the basket otherwise movable, iron pins would have to be driven into the supports, and holes for them to fit into bored in the bottom. If the whole thing is to be movable, the supports need only be cut 16 in. long, and they will be nailed to the bottom, but this is at the sacrifice of solidity.

Fig. 1409.—Rustic Summerhouse.

RUSTIC SUMMERHOUSE

The rustic summerhouse illustrated by Fig. 1409 is hexagonal in plan (see Fig. 1410), with open-work front constructed of peeled twigs, the rear sides being filled in with matchboarding; the thatched roof is broken into a gable end over the entrance (see Fig. 1411). The height to the apex of the rafters is 10 ft. 2 in., to the top of the plate 6 ft. 9 in., and the greatest width is 5 ft. 6 in., the sides being each 3 ft. wide from centre to centre of the posts. In work of this class, a high finish to the fitting of shoulders, etc., should not be attempted, as, apart from the great trouble necessary to obtain a fit to an irregularly shaped post, the effect of such fitting when accomplished is not so good as when the

joints are left rough; on the other hand, it is not wise to leave the joints so open that rain gets through and sets up rot in the timber. For forming the corner posts and plates, fairly straight saplings about 3 in. in diameter should be selected. Almost any wood will do, but the previous remarks on the subject should be borne in mind. In trimming the posts, leave a few spurs on, about 2 in. long, as they add to the effect, and are also convenient for suspending flower-pots. The joints for the plates are simply halved and nailed together, the lower half having an inch hole bored through the centre of the joint to receive the pin at the top of the post; all this is shown in Fig. 1412. These pins are sometimes cut in the solid, but more frequently are dowelled in, which is the easier method. In the latter case, fit the plate together, temporarily screwing the joint, turn it upside down, and fit the post at the corner, hollowing it out roughly to shape. Then mark the position of the shoulder on the plate. When the plate is fitted and marked, take it to pieces, bore the holes in the lower half joint, place it in position on its post and turn the auger in through the

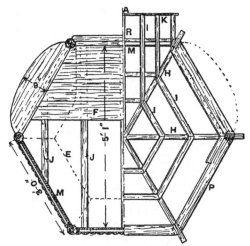

Fig. 1410.—Sectional Plan of Summerhouse.

hole for a depth of 2 in. The dowels should be made of cleft oak or beech. The sills are of wrought deal, 3 in. by 1½ in., and are stump-tenoned into the posts and screwed or pinned inside ; a portion of each post should be cut away to form a flat surface against which the shoulder of the sill bears, but not sufficient to be seen outside. Fig. 1413 is an enlarged section through a sill showing flooring, matchboarding, fixing fillet, and twig plinth. The battens, or rails, upon which the matchboarding is nailed in the middle of the height are

PUTTING UP RUSTIC SUMMERHOUSE.

The best method of constructing the house is to set out upon the ground the complete plan, as shown in the left-hand half of Fig. 1410, first describing a circle of 6-ft. diameter, and setting off the radius around the circumference. This will give the centres of the posts, and lines joining

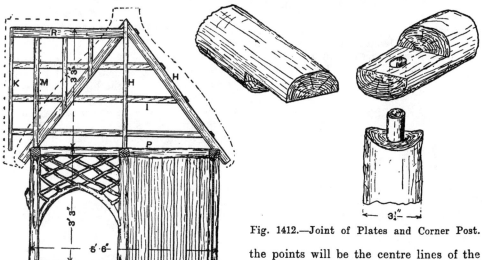

Fig. 1411.—Vertical Section of Summerhouse.

Fig. 1412.—Joint of Plates and Corner Post.

the points will be the centre lines of the plates ; draw in their widths parallel to these ; cut off the pieces roughly to length, place them in position over the lines, and mark their intersections. Form the shoulders and fit the upper ends of the posts and dowel them. Then mark them with a rod 6 ft. 9 in. long whilst in the plates, and remove them and cut off to length. For the

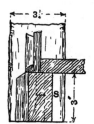

Fig. 1413.—Section of Summerhouse Sill.

mortised for ½ in. into the posts, as shown in Figs. 1414 and 1415, which are respectively a cross section and side elevation of the middle portion of a post. As will be seen, split twigs, roughly scribed, are nailed on each end of the matchboarding to form rebates. The flooring is kept back, as shown in Fig. 1413, to form the inside rebate at the bottom, and the outside fillet should be wide enough to cover the joints of the plinth.

sills to butt against, cut flats about 1½ in. wide and 3 in. long at the bottom end of each post. Then cut off the sills, allowing ¾ in. for tenons at each end, and lay them on the plan, parallel with the plate line but 1 in. further in (see Fig. 1413). Brad slips at the sides of the sills to keep them in place and stand the posts in position on top of them, with the plate above to keep all steady. Correct faults in the position of the posts, and carefully mark their ends on the sills ; this will give the exact shoulder lines. Next draw a pencil line on the ends of the posts along the face of the sills for the direction of mortises, and then upon a rod mark the clear lengths between the posts to get the lengths of the middle battens, which should be cut off 1 in. longer than the gauged lengths. Then take the

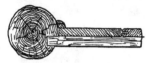

Fig. 1414.—Section of Summerhouse Post and Batten.

posts down, and with a ½-in. chisel mortise in the centre of the thickness of the sill, parallel to a line drawn on the end. Keep the mortise for the battens with its outside face in line with the centre of the sill. Knock together, having first painted the joints, and screw the tenons from the inside. The floor joists, 3 in. by 2 in., are half-notched to the sills, and the flooring, laid crossing the doorway, so cut that the ends lie on the centre of the sills (see Fig. 1413). The matchboarding, which should be 4½-in. by ⅝-in. sound dry yellow wood, may next be fixed, and the arches and lattice work formed. The twigs may be easily bent if green, but if dry should be soaked in boiling water for a short time till pliable. They may be scribed at the ends and nailed, or holes may be bored with a centre-bit and the ends tapered off to fit.

RUSTIC SUMMERHOUSE ROOF.

The roof is formed of six 3-in. by 1¼-in. hip rafters, bird's-mouthed to the plate, six jack rafters for the gable, and three sets

Fig. 1415.—Elevation of Summerhouse Post at Batten Level.

of battens 2 in. by ¾ in. The covering is about 4 in. thick, and formed of wheaten straw, rounded over the hips and laced to the battens. The boarding of the gable is cut to a mitre at each end, and the centre joints are ploughed and tongued, the boards being nailed on the face of the end rafter, which is kept in line with the rebate of the plate for that purpose (see Fig. 1416). The seats are of 10-in. by 1-in. elm boards, resting on bearers at the back screwed to the boarding, the front legs and brackets being housed in at each end. The

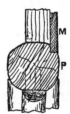

Fig. 1416.—Section of Plate at Summerhouse Doorway.

letter-references in the illustrations (Figs. 1410 to 1416) are :—E seats, F floor, H hip-rafter, I battens, J floor joists, K barge-board, M matchboarding, P plate, R ridge, and S sill.

SHEDS, TOOL HOUSES AND WORKSHOPS.

Open Shed or Hay Barn.

The shed or hay barn described below can be made by any person capable of using axe and saw. Fig. 1417 is an isometric sketch of the frame, and Fig. 1418 is an end view. The posts A go into the ground about 4 ft., project above it about 15 ft.,

deal, should be about 6 in. by 4 in., and be mortised to fit the tenons, allowing them to reach about 6 in. over the end posts. If the proposed building is of such a length that the plates have to be spliced, the splicing should be done by making a halved joint, not less than 1 ft. in length, the joint,

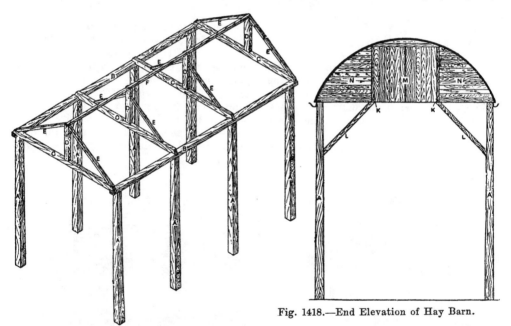

Fig. 1417.—Framing for Hay Barn.

Fig. 1418.—End Elevation of Hay Barn.

and are about 8 in. square at the bottom and taper to 6 in. at the top. They may be either sawn or chopped, or, if timber is scarce, good substitutes may be found in discarded telegraph poles. Each post must have a tenon about 4 in. long, 3 in. wide, and 1½ in. thick, cut on the top end, or the tenon may be left the whole width of the post. Plates B, preferably of yellow

of course, to rest on one of the posts. Ties c should be from 6 in. by 4 in. to 9 in. by 4 in., according to the width of the building. The former dimensions will be stout enough for a structure up to 14 ft. wide, the latter dimensions will do up to 20 ft. wide. Let the king-post D be 6 in. by 4 in., no smaller, whether the building is wide or narrow. It should be tenoned into the centre of the tie, as shown. The braces E, 3 in. square, can be placed as shown in the two end trusses, or the middle ones can be shorter, as illustrated. They need not be mortised or tenoned; if strongly nailed they will answer all re-

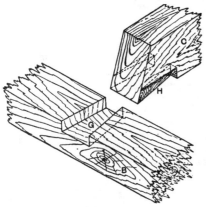

Fig. 1419.—Tie Dovetailed to Plate.

quirements. The ridge F, 3 in. by 3 in., should lie in slots cut in the tops of the king-posts. If it has been spliced, the splicing should be at one end of the posts, as in the case of the plates. The ties c should be dovetailed to the plates B, as in Fig. 1419, which shows the plate cut at G

in their respective places, but as yet nothing should be permanently fixed.

Erecting Hay Barn.

The necessary holes having been dug, the posts should be placed in along one side and propped up to prevent them from falling. The plate for that side can then be put on the tenons at the top and pinned,

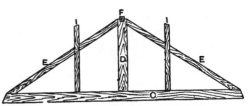

Fig. 1420.—End Truss of Hay Barn.

the pin-holes having been bored beforehand. The two end posts should next be adjusted, so that they stand upright and parallel with each other, also so that the plate is approximately level from end to end. This done, these two posts can be rammed up tightly, and the intermediate ones raised or lowered as required, and adjusted so as to be straight with the end ones, when they can also be rammed. The

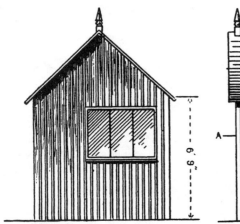

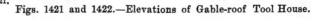

Fig. 1421.

Fig. 1422.

Figs. 1421 and 1422.—Elevations of Gable-roof Tool House.

and the dovetail H on the tie. These should all be fitted and numbered before the posts are put up. The king-post, braces, and ridge should likewise be fitted

other side posts can be erected in the same way, excepting that, as soon as the plate is on and pinned, the ties should be put on as well. It will then be easy to regulate the width, which must be the same at the bottom as at the top. If the ties are fitted as they should be, they will ensure the building being square at the angles when

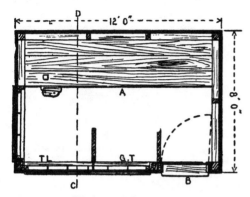

Fig. 1423.—Horizontal Section of Tool House.

finished. After the king-posts, braces, and ridge have been properly adjusted, the structure will be ready for its roof, which should be of corrugated iron, as shown by Fig. 1418, rolled to a segment of a circle. It should be obtained in such lengths as will require three to reach over from eaves to eaves, allowing 6 in. for each of the two laps. These sheets must be fixed together with short bolts while on the ground. They can be placed in position to form the roof by simply nailing or screwing them to the ridge and plates in the ordinary way. Let them overhang 6 in. at each end of the building. When the roof sheets have been put on, two pieces of quartering I (Fig. 1420) must be fixed at each end of the barn. They can be tenoned into the ties, and the braces or rafters cut away so that the upright pieces fit in. On these two pieces are nailed two other pieces, 1¼ in. thick and 1 in. narrower than the quarterings, so as to leave a rebate at the outside, to which the weather-boarding N is subsequently nailed. The 1¼-in. pieces shown at K (Fig. 1418) serve as stops for the ends of boards. Fit the weather-boarding close up to the corrugated-iron sheets—at the top, allowing about two boards to run straight across as shown. The space between the two pieces K is filled in with folding-doors M, made to open outwards. These, when the

barn is full of hay, can be opened to allow a current of air to pass through, and also to ventilate the building. Braces L (Fig. 1418) may next be fixed, not only at the ends but between each pair of posts. Mortise them into the posts with a stub tenon, and nail them to the ties and plates at the top. This method will be stronger and more convenient than nailing at both ends. If a large barn is built, it should be made high enough to admit of loaded waggons being drawn in between the side posts.

GABLE-ROOF TOOL HOUSE, OR SMALL WORKSHOP.

The building shown in Figs. 1421 and 1422 may be used as a garden tool house or workshop. Against the back wall is fitted up a carpenter's bench, on which timber can be wrought, and the tools for the same can be kept dry and clean. The garden implements can be stowed below the bench, and in the space marked G T (Fig. 1423, which is a sectional plan). The space T L could accommodate a turning lathe if desired. The boards forming the divisions for these spaces are fixed to the floor and side framing, and only run up to the window-sill, as shown by the dotted line in Fig. 1424. They

Fig. 1424.—Vertical Section of Tool House.

may be omitted altogether if not required. No notching or mortising and tenoning is used in the framing, except for the top and bottom sills, which are halved at the angles. The posts and rails are cut square and tight-fitting on the joints, and the whole is nailed together diagonally, or cheek-nailed as it is sometimes called, as shown in Fig. 1425. The boarding for the

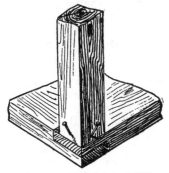

Fig. 1425.—Cheek-nailed Joint of Sill and Post.

sides and ends is ¾ in. thick, and not grooved and feathered on the edges. It is simply set up roughly edge to edge, and well nailed to the framing, and overlaps ½ in. or ⅝ in., covering the joints as at Fig. 1426. The roof consists of couples halved at the crown, and placed at about 2 ft. centres. The end ones serve to carry the boarding on the gables. It is covered with ⅝ in. rough sacking, which again is covered with zinc rolled on the joints. The zinc should be put on by a plumber, to make sure of its being water-tight. If zinc is too expensive, good roofing felt, tarred, may be used. The floor is rough boarding 1 in. thick, carried on sleeper joists spaced at about 18 in. centres, but a concrete or asphalt floor would do as well. The bottom sill is

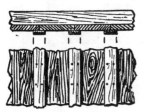 

Fig. 1426.—Tool House   Fig. 1428.—Tool House
Boarding.   Window Section.

laid on a coarse brick or stone foundation, levelled up a few inches above the surface of the ground, to admit of ventilation below the floor. For the same purpose the sleeper

joists should be thin, and have a dwarf wall built underneath to support them in the centre; also suitable air-holes, with small gratings, should be left in the foundation back and front. The window-sashes are dressed and mortised and tenoned; except the glass rebate, the sash stuff is quite plain and square dressed. The door is a ledged one with three bars on the back; it is hung with T-hinges, and should be fur-

Fig. 1427.—Tool House Door Section.

nished with a strong stock or rim lock. To stop it, a ⅝-in. cheek is nailed round the posts and lintel, as at Fig. 1427. The same is also fixed round the windows with the additional bottom one, which forms the projecting and weathered sill shown at Fig. 1428. The bench is constructed of 1¼-in. deals, fixed to strong bearers, one at each end, and one in the centre. In place of a screw, it may be provided with a wedge, as in Fig. 1423, the working of which is simple and easily understood. The timber for the structure may be red or white pine, dressed and painted on the outside of the house; or if this is thought too much expense, the whole may be left rough in shed fashion. For the framing, the corner posts will do at 4 in. by 4 in., or even 3 in.

Fig. 1429.—Portable Span-roof Workshop.

by 3 in.; sills, mid-posts, rails, and rafters 4 in. by 2 in.; sleeper joists and roof collars and bench bearers 3 in. by 2 in.; sash frames 2½ in. by 2 in.; bars for same, 2 in.

by $\frac{7}{8}$ in. The finials on the gables are turned timber, but iron ones, which are very cheap, may be substituted if preferred. A small stone or wooden step is shown in the door.

Fig. 1430.

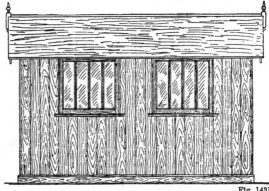

Fig. 1431.

Figs. 1430 and 1431.—Elevations of Span-roof Workshop.

PORTABLE SPAN-ROOF WORKSHOP.

Fig. 1429 is a perspective view of a portable workshop so constructed that the floor

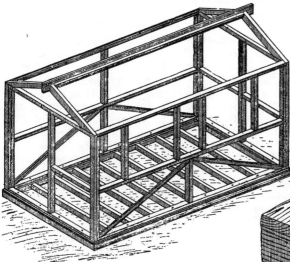

Fig. 1432.—Workshop Framing.

being held together by three $\frac{1}{2}$-in. bolts. For neatness, all the wood should be planed. Figs. 1430 and 1431 are elevational views, and at Fig. 1432 the skeleton framework is shown. The quantities of material required are as follows:—Curb, 38 ft. of $3\frac{1}{4}$-in. by $3\frac{1}{4}$-in. ; joists, 48 ft. of 3-in. by 2-in. ; uprights, 77 ft. of $2\frac{1}{2}$-in. by $1\frac{1}{2}$-in. ; rafters, braces, and bottom rails for window, 41 ft. of $2\frac{1}{2}$-in. by $1\frac{1}{2}$-in.; ridge, 13 ft. of 6-in. by 1-in. ; bargeboards, 16 ft. of $3\frac{1}{2}$-in. by 1-in.; plinth, 38 ft. of 5-in. by $\frac{7}{8}$-in.; floorboarding, 132 ft. of 7-in. by 1-in.; matchboarding, 638 ft. of 6-in. by $\frac{3}{4}$-in.; finials, 3 ft. of $2\frac{1}{2}$-in. by $2\frac{1}{2}$-in.; ridge fillets, 26 ft. of $2\frac{1}{2}$-in. by 1-in. ; roof ledges, 52 ft. of 4-in. by 1-in.; door ledges, 7 ft.

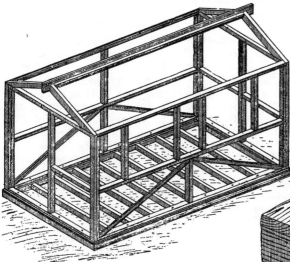

Fig. 1433.—Corner Joint of Curb.

6 in. of 5-in. by 1-in. ; window sills, 7 ft. 6 in. of 4-in. by $1\frac{1}{2}$-in. ; window stiles and top rail, 18 ft. of 2-in. by $1\frac{1}{2}$-in. ; window bars,

with joists and curb forms one piece, the ends and sides each form a section, and each side of the roof can be of one or more pieces as desired. The ends are attached to the sides by the angle posts meeting and

15 ft. of 2-in. by 1¾-in. ; middle rails, 33 ft. of 2½-in. by 2-in. ; bottom and end rails, 48 ft. of 2½-in. by 1½-in. ; side plates, 24 ft. of 3-in. by 2½-in. ; bead (outside), 12 ft. of ¾-in. by ¾-in. ; and bead (inside), 24 ft. of 1-in. by ⅝-in. Beginning with the floor, the curb forming the outside frame should be halved together, this joint being shown at Fig. 1433. The joints should be notched into the curb, and when fitted these parts should be secured by nails. Probably the best material for the floor will be 1-in. grooved and tongued prepared floorboards

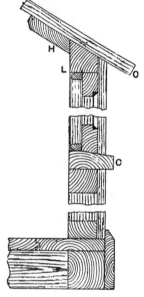

Fig. 1434.—Section of Workshop Window.

cut to length and nailed down with close joints, the boards extending to the outside of the curb all round (see Figs. 1433 and 1434). The framework of each end should be mortised and tenoned together. The top plate of the front and back is splayed off to the same angle as the roof. The outside of the framing should be covered with ¾-in. machine-prepared matchboarding, and to improve the appearance of the inside the backs of the boards should be smoothed over before being fixed to the framing, the beaded sides being outward. Fig. 1435 shows the boards of the sides A and ends B

projecting over the angle posts. The door may be formed of five boards with three ledges nailed across the inside, and can be hung with a pair of 18-in. cross garnets (see

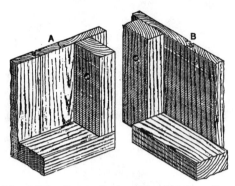

Fig. 1435.—Corner Posts, Sills, and Boarding.

Fig. 1430). Any suitable fastener may be used. Two pieces, 4 in. by 1½ in., should be prepared to the section at c (Fig. 1434) and cut to fit between the window posts, projecting at each end as shown by Figs. 1429 and 1431. Two sashes with three bars may be used ; they are of very simple construction, being mortised and tenoned together, and rebated, either on the inside or on the outside as desired. This kind of sash may be hung to the top of the framework ; it may then be pushed out at the bottom, and held open by means of a small iron stay. To keep out the draught and form a stop to the sashes, pieces of ⅝-in. by 1-in. bead should be mitred round, and fixed to the framing with a few 1½-in. nails. The outside vertical angles of the windows

Fig. 1436.—Part Horizontal Section of Workshop Window.

can be finished with beads as shown at Fig. 1436.

SPAN-ROOF OF PORTABLE WORKSHOP.

The ridge is a piece of 6-in. by 1-in. board sufficiently long to project at each end, and having fillets D and E (Fig. 1437) nailed on its sides with the top edges splayed to the angle of the roof. In preparing for the boarding of the roof, first make the ledges for the top F and G (Fig. 1437) and bottom ends H (Fig. 1434) of the boards. A better job results if the edges of these ledges are

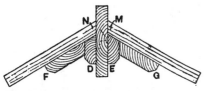

Fig. 1437.—Workshop Ridge and Roof.

splayed, so that the top one fits against the fillet, and the bottom one against the plate L of the sides. The boards should be cut a little longer than the finished length, and the ledges nailed on exactly in position, the face sides of the boards being inside the shop. The top ends M and N (Fig. 1437) should be marked parallel to the ledge, and sawn to the angle required, the bottom ends being marked off with a long straight-edge and cut through square (see O, Fig. 1434). For each side of the roof probably two pieces will be most convenient. The sides and ends may be placed together in position on the floor, and the sills of the framing fastened with a few stout 4-in. screws. The angle posts which meet should be bored right through from the outside of the ends for ½-in. bolts ; one of these holes is shown in Fig. 1435. The bolts should be inserted with their heads on the outside, the nuts being inside. The ridge board should next be placed in position, and then the boarding can be fixed. It will be necessary to cover the outside of the roof with felt, which will be better if tarred and sanded. Each end of the roof may be ornamented with bargeboards and a finial. The plinth round the curb is a piece of 5-in. by ⅞-in. board, with the top edge chambered as shown in Fig. 1434. The woodwork should have two or three coats of oil paint to make it more weather-proof. It will be advantageous to lay down a course of bricks on which the curb may rest, so as to keep the timbers from direct contact with the ground, and it will add greatly to the

durability of the floor if the curb, joists, and under-sides of the boards are given a coat of tar.

PORTABLE WORKSHOP WITH SLANT ROOF.

The workshop illustrated by Fig. 1438 has a boarded floor, and is so arranged as to be a tenant's fixture, and to be easily taken down and re-erected as required. It is constructed of six separable pieces, namely roof, two sides, two ends, and floor ; or in some cases, of course, the wall might serve the purpose of one side, and then there would only be five pieces. The following are the quantities of timber required :—38 ft. of 3-in. by 3-in. for floor frame ; 240 ft. of 3-in. by 2-in. for joists, framing of sides and ends, and rafters ; 156 ft. of 6½-in. by ⅞-in. prepared floor-boards ; 24 ft. of 3-in. by 1½-in. for top horizontal pieces of side frame ; 466 ft. of ¾-in. matchboarding ; about 34 ft. of 1½-in. by 9-in. board will be required for sashes and skylight. As the drawings show the construction very fully and the job is a straightforward one, it has not been considered necessary to give a lengthy or very minute description, but only to give the leading particulars of construction. Fig. 1439 is an inside elevation of one side, Fig.

Fig. 1438.—Portable Slant-roof Workshop.

1440 a section on line A A in the previous figure showing the inside of one end, Fig. 1441 a section on line B B showing the inside of the end containing the door, and

Fig. 1442 shows at A a half-plan with joist and framing of floor, and at B a half-plan of roof with rafters, part of sky-light, and part of boarding. The four out-side pieces of the floor should be formed of 2-in. or 2½-in. floor-brads. The edges of the boards should finish flush with the outside.

SIDES AND ENDS OF WORKSHOP.

The framing of these should be 3 in. by

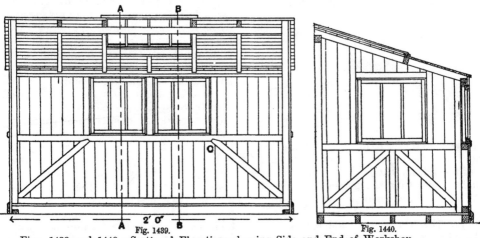

Figs. 1439 and 1440.—Sectional Elevations showing Side and End of Workshop.

3-in. by 3-in. timber, half lapped together at the angles. The joists may be 3 in. by 2 in., notched into the outside pieces. All the joints should be firmly fixed together

2 in., except the top horizontal piece, which may be 3 in. by 1½ in. The pieces should be cut off a little more than the finished lengths, planed up, and set out for mortising, tenoning, etc. The several pieces may then be cut to their respective forms, fitted together, wedged and nailed.

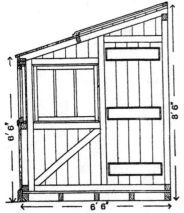

Fig. 1441.—Section showing Workshop Door.

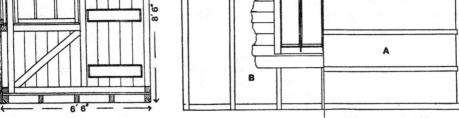

Fig. 1442.—Half-plan of Workshop Roof and Floor.

with 2½-in. nails. Prepared floor-boards will be preferable for the floor, and it is worth the little additional expense to have them grooved and tongued. The boards should be fixed to the joists and sills with

The outsides should be covered with ¾-in. or ⅞-in. prepared matchboarding. The method of arranging the timbers is shown in Figs. 1439 to 1441 and the joints used have already been fully described.

WORKSHOP ROOF.

The rafters may be 3 in. by 2 in., and should be notched at top and bird's-

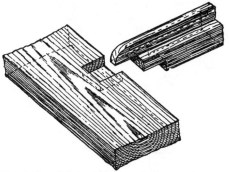

Fig. 1443.—Joint of Bottom Rail and Skylight Bar.

mouthed at the bottom (for the latter see Fig. 1444). If a skylight is required, it will be necessary to prepare for it as shown. The joint of bottom rail and bar of skylight is shown by Fig. 1443; ¾-in. boarding should be fixed to these. Matchboarding, with the best side inside, would look better, but it would be more expensive than plain boards. The roof should be covered with felt, of which about 75 sq. ft. will be required. The object of the plate shown at Fig. 1444 being in two parts is to allow of the roof being easily detached from the long side. Should a back be necessary, it

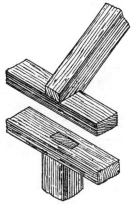

Fig. 1444.—Joint of Upright, Plate, and Rafter.

would be advisable to have this plate in two halves similar to the front one, as shown at Fig. 1444.

WORKSHOP SASHES.

The stiles and rails of these should be prepared of 2¼-in. by 1½-in. stuff, and the bars

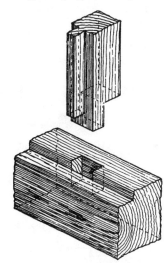

Fig. 1445.—Bar and Rail.

may be 1½ in. by 1 in. The wood should be planed up, set out, mortised, tenoned, and

Fig. 1446.—Skeleton Framing for Shed, Workshop, etc.

rebated. Fig. 1445 illustrates the joint between the bars and rails. The sashes may be made fixtures, or hung at the top so as to open outwards at the bottom; or another good plan would be to make them slide. The two posts at each corner should be fixed

Fig. 1447.—Notched Logs forming Hut Walls.

together with two 6-in. bolts and nuts. The bottom of the outside can be completed by a plinth as shown.

SHED OR WORKSHOP SKELETON FRAMING.

A skeleton framing of a rough shed or barn is given in Fig. 1417, p. 423, and of a

SIDE OF HUT

Fig. 1448.—Section of Log Hut Chimney.

well-built workshop in Fig. 1432, p. 427. The skeleton illustrated by Fig. 1446 would do for a shed, outhouse, workshop, etc.; for

LOG HUTS OR CABINS.

In some districts, log huts or cabins on the American or Canadian system commend themselves, and these should be within the scope of the rough carpenter. In some surroundings, and if rough timber were cheap, such a structure would make

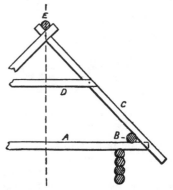

Fig. 1449.—Section of Log Hut Roof.

a strong tool shed and workshop that would look well and be practically everlasting. Log huts are built all the world over in different degrees of finish and comfort, according to their purpose and to the ingenuity of the owner. As a rule, the logs are notched with an axe at a short distance from each end, and built up in alternate

Fig. 1450.

Fig. 1451.

Figs. 1450 and 1451.—Elevations of Log Hut or Cabin.

any of these the slanting members give sufficient strength. Variations on the designs shown will readily suggest themselves.

pairs to form the walls (Fig. 1447), and cut short wherever door- or window-frames occur. The interstices between the logs may be filled up with branches, etc., cemented with clay, and finished with a finer plaster; but in more pretentious buildings the crevices are blocked up neatly with triangular pieces split from logs and nailed to the walls; the inside can then be close-boarded. If a fireplace is required, the best material for it is stone; failing this, earth or bricks. The chimney-

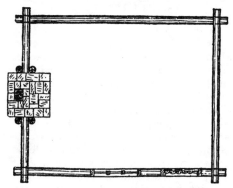

Fig. 1452.—Plan of Log Hut or Cabin.

flue may be formed outside the hut with a wood shaft (see Fig. 1448). In the backwoods the stripped trunk of a tree is used as a core for the flue, inserted temporarily in the centre of the shaft; clay is then rammed in round it, and when the flue is formed the tree trunk is drawn out at the top. The fireplace is made by cut-ting a square hole in the logs just above the floor, forming a wood shaft at the bottom of the flue, and lining inside with clay to a good shape. Then all the clay is coated with a plaster of gravel and clay, cow-dung, and water; but in any ordinary country district in Great Britain this could be improved upon owing to other and better materials being available. As for the roof, it should be high pitched, and have deep eaves. Fig. 1449 shows a section, A indicating tie-beams, 2 ft. or 3 ft. apart; B, wall-plates notched and pinned on to beams; C, rafters, same distance apart as the tie-beams, and secured to them; D, collars spiked to rafters; E, ridge-pole tied with withies to the rafters. Nail battens on the rafters, and cover with shingles. Figs. 1450 and 1451 show a common form of log cabin built up in much the above way. The logs are notched together and further secured by boring with an auger through each log into the last log fixed, and driving in a wooden pin or nail. If a chimney is required, it should be built of some local stone or similar material, but American stoves with piping are often made to serve the purpose. The roof is often formed by splitting the logs in two, as shown, and is covered with some kind of material (handy or easily obtainable) that will render the roof waterproof. Fig. 1452 is a plan of the log hut.

GARDEN FRAMES, WINDOW CONSERVATORIES AND GREENHOUSES

THE SKILL REQUIRED FOR THE WORK.

THIS chapter will deal with examples of work which, in the main, are rather more advanced than any garden fitments yet described. Garden frames, window conservatories, and greenhouses have to be constructed with precision and care, and slovenly work cannot be tolerated. Greenhouses contain much sash work, and the framing of sash-bars, etc., cannot be attempted by anyone who is not fairly proficient in the use of woodworking tools. The work must, as a rule, be watertight, and this, when there is a great number of joints to be made, is only possible when skill and care are exercised.

HORTICULTURAL GLASS.

Glazing is so important a part of the work about to be described that some particular instructions on the glazier's methods and materials appear to be necessary first. Horticultural glass is sold as "fourths" and "thirds" qualities. Cases contain 100 ft. or 200 ft., either 15-oz. or 21-oz.; this is the weight per sq. ft. There are about twenty stock sizes, from 12 in. by 10 in. to 24 in. by 18 in. As the boxes contain all one size, state the dimensions required when ordering. It is sometimes difficult to distinguish between British and foreign glass, but, as all the cheaper qualities on the market are of foreign origin—cheapness in this instance being generally associated with inferiority—it is usually safe to suppose that all low-priced glass, which, being very uneven in surface, produces very bad distortion of any object viewed through it, is foreign; yet, on the other hand, it must be admitted that some of the clearest and best sheet glass made comes from Belgium. It is usual to employ 15-oz. or 21-oz. foreign glass in greenhouses, etc.

GLAZING GARDEN FRAMES.

In glazing garden frames or lights, top as well as bottom putties are preferred almost universally; this is in the same style as ordinary window glazing. The chief disadvantage of this method for what may be termed horizontal work is the tendency of the top putties to come away from the glass (and frequently from the wood), in which case water is drawn in by capillary action, and if the defect is neglected the woodwork soon rots. But if the woodwork received a preliminary coat of paint in addition to the priming, and the edges of the glass were also painted, and if, in addition, the putties were painted as soon as the glazing was completed, and the paint was allowed to extend $\frac{1}{8}$ in. beyond the line of the putty—the work receiving at least two (three would be better) coats of paint—there would be fewer complaints of leaky glazing and of putties stripping. A method employed to a limited extent by market gardeners is to omit the top putties altogether, the back putties being carefully laid, and in more liberal quantity than is usual in ordinary glazing; the glass is then thoroughly bedded, and sprigged or bradded to the sash bars, after which the putty is levelled off to the surface of the glass; a line of thick paint, extending $\frac{1}{2}$ in. or so over the glass, is then applied on each side of the bar. This makes a good watertight job, and, as compared with the prevailing method, breakages are more easily repaired, considerably less putty is used, and the rebates in the bars—for new work—need not be so deep. Between the two systems, both thoroughly done, there would be little to choose, from a utilitarian point of view—appearance being beside the question—but the gardeners' system should be considerably the cheaper.

GLAZING GREENHOUSE.

In glazing a greenhouse it is advisable that the glass should only be bedded in putty, front putty being entirely dispensed with ; this is found by practical experience

Fig. 1453.—Glazier's Knife.

to be the better plan. Well paint the rebate with lead and oil, then run a layer of putty made from whiting and boiled oil, to which a little red lead may be added. Cut the glass in tight to size, well rub down into the putty, and force in sprigs along the edges, after which give the edges and rebate three coats of good oil colour. A

Fig. 1454.—Painter's Stopping Knife.

glazier's knife—the " putty knife "—is illustrated by Fig. 1453, and an old strong table-knife ground down to serve as a hack knife is indispensable when repairing. A painter's stopping knife (Fig. 1454) also comes in useful. When front putties are used, the work is done as follows ; to save space the process of re-glazing is described, though, of course, the work is the same in

window frame and hit it with a hammer. Work all round the frame in this manner until all the old putty is removed, care being taken not to chip the window frame by driving the knife in too far. The putty being removed, get a little paint, and apply it all round the rebate of the frame, and, after it has dried a little, take some fresh putty in the right hand and press a thin layer round the frame with the thumb. Put in the pane of glass, press it evenly all

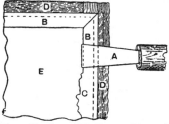

Fig. 1455.—Glazing with Top or Front Putties

round to bed it in the putty, and fix it on each side with two small tacks driven into the window frame with a light hammer, allowing the heads of the tacks to protrude about $\frac{1}{8}$ in. Putty the outside of the pane all round and bevel it with a sharp knife, resting against the edge of the window frame and on the glass in the manner shown by Fig. 1455, pressing the thumb against the side A. The figure also shows the cut putty at B, the uncut putty at C, a portion of the framing at D, and the win-

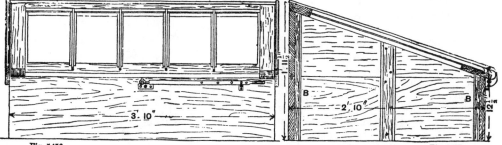

Fig. 1456.

Figs. 1456 and 1457.—Elevations of Garden Frame and Light.

Fig. 1457.

each case. First knock out the old glass and putty. This can be done with an old knife worn down to about 2 in. or 3 in. from the handle. When the knife has made its way into the putty, keep it flat against the

dow-pane at E. The glazing is completed when the surplus putty on the inside has been removed. Putty can be softened with linseed oil, and is best kept in a can immersed in that oil.

PORTABLE GARDEN FRAME AND LIGHT.

The frame illustrated in front elevation by Fig. 1456, and in cross-section by Fig. 1457, is useful for growing melons, cucumbers, etc., in the summer, and for storing plants during the winter. It consists of a rectangular box of 1-in. red deal, with sloping ends, without a bottom, and with a glazed top-light, hinged, and capable of being thrown right back, or set open at any distance by the casement stay shown in Fig. 1456. It has a 1½-in. light and 3-in. by ¾-in. wind-guards. The height is suitable for 11-in. boards, but if these are

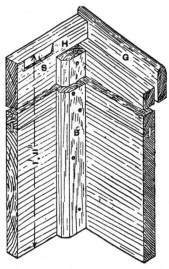

Fig. 1458.—Back Corner of Garden Frame.

not procurable 9-in. will do nearly as well. Fig. 1458 shows a back corner of the frame; block pieces B (Figs. 1457 and 1458) are screwed to the back and front on the insides 1 in. from the ends after they are squared off. This forms a rebate in which the ends of the frame are screwed or nailed to the blocks. The front and back are nailed to them, thus getting a fixing both ways; wire nails should be used. The boards should be tongued, using ⅛-in. straight-grained tongues to prevent the admission of wind. The tongue and joint should be painted, the intermediate battens being nailed on as shown in the cross section

tion (Fig. 1457). With 11-in. boards a 1½-in. piece must be nailed at the back for hanging the light, and this joint need not be ploughed. When the frame is fixed to-

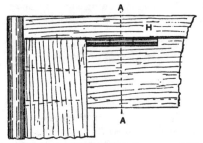

Fig. 1459.—Plan of Corner of Frame and Light.

gether, nail on the two wind-guards G (Fig. 1458) outside, so that the nosing projects ½ in. above the hanging piece H (Figs. 1458 to 1460), thus forming rebates for the light.

LIGHT FOR GARDEN FRAME.

The light is made simply "rebate and square," as the under-side is not seen, and the stuff may be purchased, if desired, ready worked from any horticultural builder. The sections of timber required in the construction are shown in Figs. 1461 to 1464. Procure two stiles 3 ft. 3 in. long by 3 in. by 1½ in.; one top rail 3 ft. 10 in. by 3 in. by 1½ in.; one bottom rail 3 ft. 10 in. by 5¼ in. by ¾ in.; four bars 2 ft. 9 in. by 1½ in. by 1 in.; and set out the stiles, by marking on their face edges the outside

Fig. 1460.—Section of Corner of Frame and Light.

dimensions of the light. This will be the distance down the slope of the frame from H to the front, plus 1 in. for overhang; square within these lines the width of the two rails, and set off half of each width for the mortise. Gauge the top rail mortise to a $\frac{1}{2}$-in. chisel in the centre, and the bottom mortise to a $\frac{3}{8}$-in. chisel, in line with the rebate, that is $\frac{3}{4}$ in. on. To set out the width of the top light, place the top rail on the frame, and mark the clear length between the wind-guards, set off the width of the stiles within these lines, and beyond these sight lines; shoulder lines $\frac{5}{16}$ in. on; these will be the outside shoulders, the sight lines giving the inside one. Space the mortises for the bars $\frac{7}{8}$ in. wide, and at equal distances apart, and mark with the gauge used for the tenons. Pair the bottom rail with the top, and square the lines over; the back shoulder line will not be required, as the tenon has only one shoulder (see Fig. 1465); square over the notches for the bars on the outside of the rail; gauge them 2 in. on, and set a gauge full $\frac{3}{8}$ in. for the depth, which will also answer for the tenon. The gauging on the bottom rail is all to be done from the back

Fig. 1461.—Top Rail of Light.

Fig. 1462.—Stile of Light.

or outside, the rest of the stuff being gauged from the inside. The bars may be set out from the stiles, drawing on the sight lines, and two others at the bottom end at 2 in. and $4\frac{1}{2}$ in. respectively for the tusk and the tail, and at the top end 1 in. for stub tenon (see Fig. 1464). Use the top rail gauge for the top end; at the bottom end gauge $\frac{3}{8}$ in. for the tusk and $\frac{3}{4}$ in. for the tail. Cut the tenons and mortises with taper haunches as shown in Fig. 1459, plough the top rail with a $\frac{1}{4}$-in. groove $\frac{3}{4}$ in. on, and bevel it to Fig. 1461. Gauge and rebate the stiles and bars, if not obtained ready worked, the rebates to be $\frac{3}{4}$ in. on and $\frac{5}{16}$ in. deep; knock together with red-lead paint, and wedge up. Nail the tails of the bars as in Fig. 1465, and round them off with the chisel; cut off the stiles flush at the top, and $\frac{3}{4}$ in. longer than the rail at the bottom, and round them with a smoothing plane.

Then shoot the light to fit easily between the guards, with a joint $\frac{1}{8}$ in. all round.

HANGING TOP LIGHT OF GARDEN FRAME.

To hang the light, a pair of 3-in. wrought-iron butts will be required; sink the knuckle into the top rail as in Figs. 1459

Figs. 1463 and 1464.—Section and Elevation of Bar of Light.

and 1460, so as not to reduce the strength of the hanging piece. Put the butts on the light first, keeping them in line with the stile, with the centre of the knuckle flush with the top side; then lay the light in position with the butts closed, and on the frame mark their ends with a chisel. Square down the points and set a gauge to the distance between the crosses in Fig. 1460, and run it on between the lines. Cut out the pieces wedge shape, tapering to $\frac{1}{8}$ in. deep at the bottom, as at s (Fig. 1458). Then screw up and try the working; should there be binding anywhere, either pack out the hinge nearer the tight place or sink the other a trifle further. A 22-in. casement stay fixed to the under-side of the light, with the plates let in flush, will complete the fitting. Give two coats of paint all over, and glaze with 21-oz. sheet-glass, using plenty of oil in the putty, and driving a brad at the tail of each sheet to prevent slipping.

Fig. 1465.—Bottom Rail of Light.

ANOTHER KIND OF GARDEN FRAME AND LIGHT.

The proposed size of the frame shown in plan by Fig. 1466 and in side elevation by

Fig. 1467 is 4 ft. long by 3 ft. wide, outside measurement, and the material is 1½-in. red deal. The sizes of stuff required will be as follows:—Four pieces 4 ft. 7 in. by 9 in. for sides; two pieces 2 ft. 10 in. by

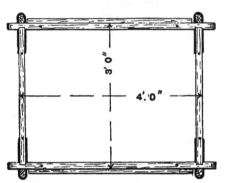

Fig. 1466.—Plan of Garden Frame.

9 in. for top end; two pieces 2 ft. 10 in. by 7 in. for bottom end. These are net sizes, and sufficient should be allowed for squaring up. Fig. 1468 is a plan of the light, and Fig. 1469 a cross-section through light and frame. The stuff, after being gone over with a jack plane, should be tried up, but not too elaborately, one side of each piece being marked for the face. As the joints are not to be glued, extreme care need not be exercised in shooting them. As will be seen by reference to the illustrations, the joints are held together by means of ⅜-in. square iron dowels and ¾-in. round-iron pins. The distances for which these should be set out are as follows:—On the sides, pins 9 in. from each end and dowels 18 in.;

being left on for guidance in boring through. The holes for the pins should be bored with a ⅜-in. twist bit, and from each edge of each piece, a gauge line having been run through the centre of the pencil

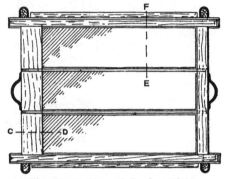

Fig. 1468.—Plan of Garden Light.

mark. The holes for the dowels should be bored with a $\frac{5}{16}$-in. twist bit. The joints may now be knocked together on the dowels and levelled off, and the sides tapered and set out for grooving for the ends. The sides should run beyond the grooves 3½ in. The ends are then squared and traversed to the width of the grooves, which for 1½-in. stuff would probably not be more than 1⅜ in., and the grooving and squaring up should be done. By reference to Figs. 1466, 1467, 1470, and 1471 it will be seen that 3 in. from top and bottom of each groove a mortise is required, which should be $\frac{9}{16}$ in. wide, and the length $\frac{9}{16}$ in. beyond each side of the groove; this will require setting out for and gauging as a matter of

Fig. 1467.—Side Elevation of Frame and Light.

Fig. 1469.—Section through Frame and Light.

on the ends, pins 6 in. from each end and dowels 12 in. The joints should be brought together in pairs face to face, and from the points found lines should be squared across; those for the pins require squaring over to the other edge, the pencil marks

course. The use of this mortise is explained later.

PINS AND BOWS OF GARDEN FRAME.

The pins should be cut from ⅜-in. round-iron to the exact length of the holes through the different pieces, and iron washers with $\frac{3}{8}$-in. holes should be riveted on each end after the pins have been driven through, the edges having been sunk slightly for them on the top and bottom; $\frac{3}{8}$-in. iron pins made in the ordinary way

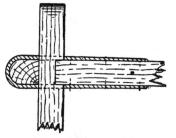

Fig. 1470.—Pin and Bow of Garden Frame.

with heads and nuts may be used if preferred, but the former method can be carried out with ease. Having proceeded thus far, it will be necessary to have eight bows made out of $\frac{1}{2}$-in. round-iron; these will be about 12 in. long, flattened at each end, and having three countersunk screw holes made in them (see Figs. 1470 and 1471) by which they are fixed. The frame should be knocked together and held by means of a cramp, and the bows having been previously slipped through the mortises already referred to, the top ones should be

Fig. 1471.—Pin and Bow of Garden Frame.

adjusted to stand out 2 in. inside measurement, and the bottom ones $1\frac{1}{2}$ in. Four tapered wood pins or wedges with circular backs (see Fig. 1470) will be required, and these should be made to fill up the spaces in the bows when driven down them (see

Figs. 1470 and 1471). A strip of wood $4\frac{1}{2}$ in. by 1 in. requires screwing along each of the sides at the top on the outside to form a rebate for the light (see Figs. 1467, 1471, and 1472); previous to this, however, the frame should be knocked apart, and roughly smoothed up, the size of the light having been taken previously, allowing $\frac{1}{4}$-in. clearance on each side.

LIGHT FOR GARDEN FRAME.

The light may be constructed by the simplest possible method. The sizes of the stuff may be as follows:—Stiles, 2 in. by 2 in.; top rail, 3 in. by 2 in.; bottom rail, $5\frac{1}{2}$ in. by $1\frac{1}{8}$ in.; and bars, 2 in. by 1 in.; $\frac{1}{2}$-in. tenons on the top rail (Fig. 1472), $\frac{5}{16}$-in. tenons on the bottom rail (Fig. 1473), and a good rebate for glass (say $\frac{7}{8}$ in. by $\frac{1}{4}$ in.); this and a reference to the illustrations will no doubt afford all the informa-

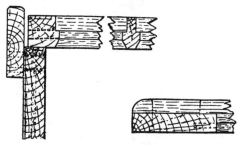

Fig. 1472.—Cross Section of Part of Frame.   Fig. 1473.—Bar Tenoned into Bottom Rail.

tion required. The light when finished should have a handle attached at top and bottom, as shown in Fig. 1468; these handles should be bowed sufficiently to allow a person's hand to be inserted freely; they should be made of $\frac{1}{2}$-in. round-iron, and flattened for screws. The frame and light when finished should be painted white, but the ironwork while hot should have been dipped in tar by the smith.

PLANT PROPAGATOR.

For a propagator suitable for raising early batches of seeds and striking cuttings, etc., a lamp A (Fig. 1474) must be made or procured first, as on it depends the height of the frame, etc. For a large propagator a duplex burner may be used, and the oil reservoir should hold about 1 qt., but for a small propagator with a glass frame measuring, say, 2 ft. 6 in. by 2 ft., a single-burner lamp will be sufficient. Next make

Fig. 1474.—Cross Section of Propagator.

a rough stand as shown in Fig. 1475, with 1½-in. square legs and 2½-in. by ¾-in. rails. The top of this should be about 1½ in. above the lamp chimney. On the top of the stand is placed a shallow tank B (Fig. 1474) to contain water. This may be about 18 in. square by from 2½ in. to 3 in. deep, and can be made of sheet copper, or, as a substitute, a square tin baking dish may be used. The case can be made of 1-in. matchboarding; a section of this is shown in Fig. 1474, and a

Fig. 1475.—Frame for Propagator Tank.

general view of the outside by Fig. 1476. A ledge c (Fig. 1474) is nailed round the inside with the top level with the top of the

tank, and on this a sheet of iron is placed to form a bottom for the propagating chamber and a cover for the tank. The depth of the propagating chamber should be about 14 in. at the back and 9 in. at the front, which will make a total depth for the case of 18½ in. above the lamp chimney at the back, and 13½ in. at the front. A doorway D may be cut through the bottom of the case on the side that may be most convenient, and can be fitted with a hinged shutter and with a turnbutton or hook and eye, for the purpose of attending to the lamp. A few holes should be bored in the side of the case to allow the fumes from the

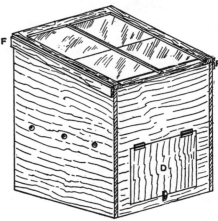

Fig. 1476.—Plant Propagator.

lamp to escape, and it would be a good plan to let a small sheet of glass into the side, so that the lamp may be seen without opening the shutter. A layer of cocoanut fibre refuse E should be spread over the bottom of the propagating chamber, and into this the pots containing the cuttings or the seed pans are plunged. A couple of runners F (Fig. 1476) are nailed to the sides of the case, and the top is covered with a sash such as has been described in detail for an ordinary garden frame.

WARDIAN CASE OR WINDOW CONSERVATORY.

The wardian case or window conservatory illustrated in vertical section by Fig. 1477, in front elevation by Fig. 1478, and in horizontal section by Fig. 1479, is light in appearance, but substantial if well constructed, the shaped top adding much to its effect; but a flat slope may easily be substituted if preferred. The case is composed of four upright rounded bars, 1 in. in diameter, each with its upper portion bent to a quarter-circle sweep, the two outside bars being continuous, and the inside two cut and mitred to a horizontal bar and tenoned at the ends into a solid top and bottom. The

frame. It is hung to the side piece, and kept in any position by a drop hook fitted inside the bottom rail and engaging in a series of holes in the margin of the bottom. The case is supported upon two wrought-iron brackets fixed to the sash frame and face of the wall. It is fitted with a wrought-iron or zinc tray, which should be 3 in. deep if pots are to be used, and

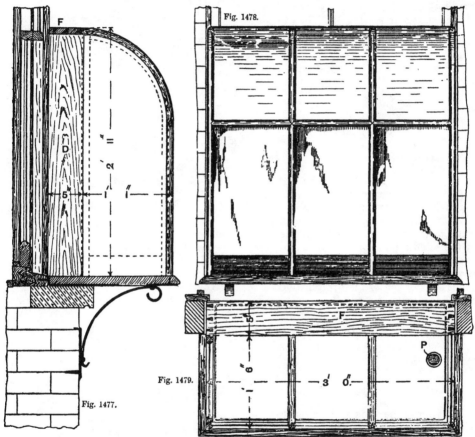

Figs. 1477 to 1479.—Vertical Section, Front Elevation, and Horizontal Section of Wardian Case.

top or flat is of 1-in. deal, secured to similar side pieces by dovetails, and is a little wider than the depth of the window reveal. The sides are also dovetailed into the bottom, which is of 1½-in. stuff notched out to fit the window opening, as shown in Fig. 1479. A door is provided at the left for ventilation, and is made to the same sweep as the end, fitting into a ¼-in. rebate in the

6 in. deep if the plants are to be placed direct into the mould. The illustrations show the former arrangement, but, in both cases, the glass must be painted on the inside to the same depth as the tray used.

WARDIAN CASE ILLUSTRATIONS EXPLAINED.

Before giving the details of construction of the wardian case, it will make the in-

structions clearer to explain the illustrations. As already stated, Fig. 1478 is a front
elevation of the case complete, Fig. 1477 is
a vertical sectional elevation, showing how
the case is fixed, the dotted lines indicating
the door in the end; and Fig. 1479 is a sectional plan, the parts below the cross-bar
being in section, the flat, the rim of the
bottom, and two inner bars being in plan;
the black line shows the tray, and a waste
pipe is shown at P. Fig. 1480 is a full-size

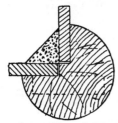

Fig. 1480.—Corner Bar of Wardian Case.

section of the corner bar to the right, the
dotted line indicating the tenon at its end.
Fig. 1481 is a portion of the top end of an
interior bar, showing the method of jointing it to the flat. Fig. 1482 is an elevation
of the middle joint of the same bar. Fig.
1483 is a plan of the same; M is the mortise
in the cross-bar, and the section is that of
the lower portion of the upright bar. Fig.
1484 is the elevation, and Fig. 1485 the plan

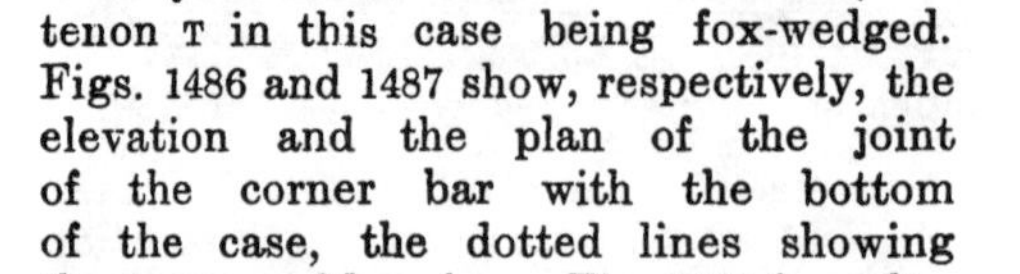

Fig. 1481.—Inside Bar of Wardian Case.

of the joint at the ends of the cross-bar, the
tenon T in this case being fox-wedged.
Figs. 1486 and 1487 show, respectively, the
elevation and the plan of the joint
of the corner bar with the bottom
of the case, the dotted lines showing
the tenon and housing. Fig. 1488 is a plan
of the inner corner of the bottom, with the
sockets F for the dovetails of the side piece.
Fig. 1489 shows a longitudinal section of the
lower part of the case, with the method
of tilting and draining the tray; Fig. 1490
an elevation of the upper corner of the

door, etc., showing the joint; Fig. 1491
a section through the stile; Figs. 1492 and
1493 show part elevation and plan at the
front bottom corner of the door; Fig. 1494
shows a section of the bottom rail; Fig.

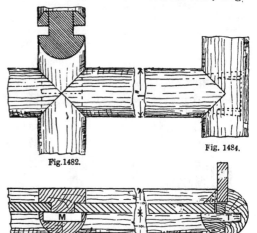

Fig. 1484.

Fig.1482.

Fig. 1483.   Fig. 1485.

Figs. 1482 to 1485.—Joints in Cross-bar of
Wardian Case.

1495 a section of the cross-bar; Fig. 1496 a
section of one of the upright bars.

BENDING BARS OF WARDIAN CASE.

The bars (Fig. 1496) are made of tough
wood, such as ash or oak, and the re-

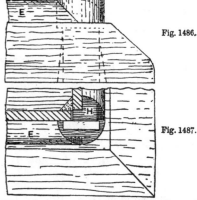

Fig. 1486.

Fig. 1487.

Figs. 1486 and 1487. Joint in Corner Bar of
Wardian Case.

mainder of the case of yellow deal. The
bars are shaped by steaming and fastening

them to a mould made of 2-in. deal, shaped to the required inside curve of the bar. This has a number of holes in it about 6 in

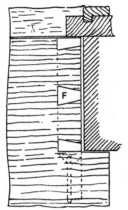

Fig. 1488.—Inner Corner of Wardian Case Bottom.

apart, and 2 in. from the edge, into which the jaws of the handscrews fit and pinch the bar to the mould. Square the bar to size, and steam it for a quarter of an hour.

Fig. 1489.—Section of Wardian Case showing Tray.

Then fasten the top end to the mould, and gradually bend down the tail until the next hole is reached, when a hand screw is fixed. Continue until the bottom end is reached, tapping the bar gently with a mallet to bed

Fig. 1490.—Elevation of Top Corner of Door.

it to the mould. It must be left on the mould until thoroughly dry. It may then be removed, set out, and worked. To

facilitate the working of the rebates, a small plough groove may be made at the rebate line whilst the bar is straight, but it must be sunk from the inside, and not on the edge, as the latter would cause the bar to break in bending.

TENONING AND FITTING WARDIAN CASE BARS.

Arrange the tenons on the outside of rebates, as shown in Figs. 1480 and 1481 ; cut

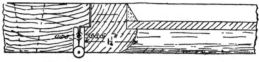

Fig. 1491.—Plan of Top Corner of Door.

the shoulders at the bottom end $\frac{1}{8}$ in. longer than the sight line, and house the whole bar to that depth. The tenons at the top end are stumped in $\frac{3}{4}$ in. and screwed (see Fig. 1481). The shoulders should be cut to the depth of rebate and rounded. The tenons

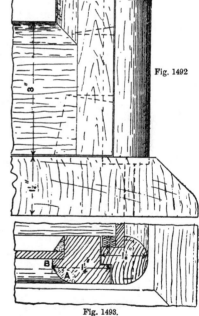

Fig. 1492.

Fig. 1493.

Figs. 1492 and 1493.—Bottom Corner of Door.

should be cut right down, and the shoulders half-way, before rounding, or the lines will be lost. Make a template to the section of the bars, etc., and apply it at each end; prepare the rebates first, the rounding last, and make the mortises before rounding, but cut the mitres afterwards. Work the

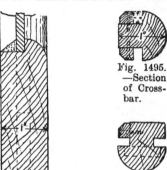

Fig. 1495.
—Section
of Cross-
bar.

Fig. 1494.—Bottom Rail
of Wardian Case.

Fig. 1496.—Inner
Upright Bar.

interior bars before cutting them in two, and $\frac{1}{8}$ in. should be allowed between the sight lines of the cross-bar for the saw cut. Cut the mitres about $\frac{1}{4}$ in. deep, and scribe over the remainder. This will strengthen the bars, as shown in Fig. 1493, A being the portion mitred and B the portion scribed. The front edge of the flat is rounded and rebated. Where possible, fillets should be used in preference to putty for fixing the glass, as they are removed easier. Quarter-

solid, as shown at H (Fig. 1487), levelling the bottom of the housing with a router. Make the mortises parallel with the front, and cut back the margin to the depth of the reveal, and cut the sockets for the dovetails as at F (Fig. 1488); the pins must come on the sides D (Figs. 1477 and 1490), otherwise the bars will be strained in putting together. The sockets in the flat F (Figs. 1477 and 1479) require setting further back to provide a mortise for the end bars.

PUTTING TOGETHER WARDIAN CASE.

To put together, begin by entering the bars into the bottom dry, glue the upper tenons, etc., and drive in the cross-bar and cramp it up, leaving the cramp or cleat on. Next glue together the sides and flat, then the top ends of the bars; these may be brought up tight to the shoulders by notching a saddle piece over the bar, screwing it into the rebate, and turning a handscrew against it and the edge of the flat. When tight, turn in the screws as shown in Fig.

Fig. 1498.—End Elevation of Greenhouse.

Fig. 1497.—Lean-to Greenhouse.

round rim fillets are bradded round the front and closed end, as shown at E (Figs. 1486 and 1487), and are mitre-scribed to the bars. Prepare the bottom as shown in the details, setting out the positions of the bars by aid of the cross-bar; house all in

1481; the end ones must be put in from the top. When all are in, knock off the bottom, glue the tenons and dovetails, and finally wedge up. The door is mortised and tenoned together as shown in Figs. 1490 and 1492. The glass rebate should be stopped at the mortises, and the haunching bevelled as shown. Mitre-scribe the shoulders as above described; glue a rough block on the back of the sweep rail to cramp against. Work the outside rebate after the door is glued up, and hang with a pair of 2½-in. brass butts. The glass should be fixed with putty, as the inside may be exposed to rain. Fix a tapering piece of stuff in the bottom of the case to give a fall to the tray (see Fig. 1489). Paint the inside with two coats of zinc white, and stain the outside black and varnish it. Coat the iron or zinc tray with Brunswick black.

Lean-to Greenhouse.

The lean-to is the form of greenhouse that is most popular; and such a house, constructed as described below, will be a tenant's fixture, readily erected and easily

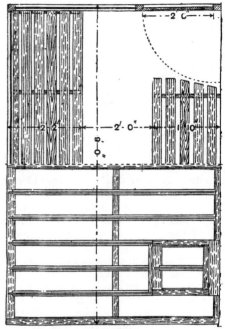

Fig. 1500.—Plan of Greenhouse.

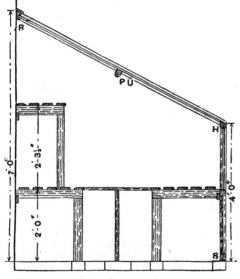

Fig. 1499.—Cross Section of Greenhouse.

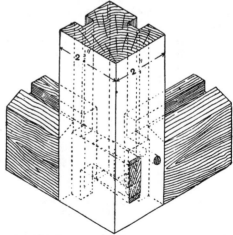

Fig. 1501.—Corner Post and Sill of Greenhouse.

taken to pieces for removal, and will remain serviceable for many years. Fig. 1497 is a perspective view, showing the house fixed against a wall and resting on a row of loose bricks laid on the surface of the ground; this provision constitutes the structure a "tenant's fixture." Fig. 1498 is an end elevation, Fig. 1499 a cross-section, and Fig. 1500 a plan. The outside dimensions of the house are—9 ft. long, 6 ft. wide, 7 ft. high to the ridge, 4 ft. high to the eaves, with a 5-ft. 6-in. by 2-ft. by 1¼-in. glazed and flush panelled door, a roof ventilator 1 ft. 9 in. by 1 ft. 6½ in. by 1¼ in., and a spandrel ventilator 2 ft. by 1 ft. This is a very useful size of house for a small garden, but, of course, the size may be increased without altering the method of construction.

Fig. 1502.—Section through Front Head. Fig. 1503.—Section of Plate. Fig. 1504.—Section of Sill.

FRAMING ENDS OF LEAN-TO GREENHOUSE.

The end shown in Fig. 1498 is framed up complete, with mortise-and-tenon joints, including the door-sill, which should preferably be of hard wood, say oak or elm. The transom T is stump-tenoned into the striking jamb J ¾ in. deep, and screwed from inside; the jamb also is stump-tenoned into the head H and screwed. The plate P and sill S are tenoned through the jamb and corner post, and wedged as shown in Fig. 1501. A barefaced tenon is cut on the lower end of the jamb J, to secure it to the door-sill; this is to avoid the mortise that is cut in the main sill. The hanging jamb W is tenoned and wedged to the other ends of the rails, and thus frames up the end complete, the matchboarding M being treated as a panel, and framed up within the framing. The opposite end is treated in a similar manner, being, of course, simpler to construct, as it contains no doorway. It will be seen from Fig. 1498 that the lower end of the head H runs, or lips, over the top of the post; this is to prevent

Fig. 1505.—Side Bar of Greenhouse. Fig. 1506.—Ridge of Greenhouse.

the end grain of the post being exposed to wet, which would soon cause decay. There is no necessity to treat the wall posts in the same way, because the flashing fillet F runs over them.

FRONT OF LEAN-TO GREENHOUSE.

The front—consisting of the head (Fig. 1502), plate (Fig. 1503), and sill (Fig. 1504), matchboarding and bars (Fig. 1505)—has its rails stump-tenoned into the corner posts and pinned, as shown in Fig. 1501, which indicates how the two sills are fixed to the corner post, the dotted lines showing the position of the tenons. The front mortise runs into the end mortise, and the tenon of the former is put on dry and drawbore pinned, the hole for the pin being bored completely through the post, and thus at any time the pins may be driven out and the rails released.

ROOF OF LEAN-TO GREENHOUSE.

The construction of the roof will be gathered from the cross section (Fig. 1499), and from the enlarged details (Figs. 1502, 1506, and 1507); it consists of a number of

Fig. 1507.—Elevation of Front Head. Fig. 1508.—Section of End Head.

bars stump-tenoned into a ridge-piece R (Fig. 1499) at their upper ends, and notched at their lower ends into the head H, as shown in Figs. 1506 and 1507, and supported in the middle by a purlin P U, which is notched out to receive them (Fig. 1499). The centre bar is made of extra width to strengthen the roof and carry the purlin, and a short trimming bar is framed between the two end bars to form an opening for the ventilator. Fig. 1500 shows a general plan, the left-hand half showing the lower part of the framing and the right-hand half the roof.

SETTING OUT END OF LEAN-TO GREENHOUSE.

Nearly all the sections here given are stock sizes, and may be obtained ready worked from horticultural builders; but those who determine to work the sections themselves will find that it saves time and labour to set out all the various mortises, tenons, rebates, etc., whilst the stuff is in the square. In the absence of a suitable floor on which to set out the end, a method that, if carried out carefully, will give satisfactory results, may be here described.

Fig. 1509.—Joint in Greenhouse Plate.

Having planed the various pieces straight and square, and cut them, with a little to spare in length, say 1½ in. on pieces to be mortised at the ends and ½ in. on those to be tenoned, begin with the end containing the doorway. Take the post G (Fig. 1498) and square over two lines on its outer face, representing the bottom of the sill and the top of the head. In this case they will be 4 ft. apart. Exactly midway between these, square another line on the inner edge, representing the top of the plate P. Set off from these the widths of sill and plate. Treat the size of the stuff as wrought, say 2⅞ in. ; the head is left for the moment. Draw on lines for the sinkings, namely ⅜ in. for rebate in plate and ½ in. for plough-groove in the under edge of the plate and the top of the sill (see sections, Figs. 1503 and 1508). From these lines set off the mortises, the lower one 1½ in. wide, the upper 2 in., then square the lines over the contiguous edge. As the front rails are of the same size, set a mortise gauge to a ⅝-in. chisel, and run it ⅝ in. from the outside face, so as to bring the tenon in the centre of the 2-in. rails. Place the wall post W and the jamb J edge up in their relative positions by the side of the post set out, and square across the lowest line over the three, and all the remaining lines on the jamb J only. Separate and gauge the jamb on the edge opposite the post G. A ⅝-in. barefaced tenon is to be gauged from the face at the bottom end of the jamb, for going in the sill ; the shoulder lines with the under side of the main sill.

Now lay the three posts on the floor at their respective distances apart—that is, 6 ft. out to out and 1 ft. 11 in. between the edges of the door jambs. Make them quite parallel to each other, and, with a straightedge, make the lowest or sill line range on the three. Test with a rod to see if they are lying square—that is, see that the diagonal lengths between the two rail lines on the jambs are equal—then lay the head H in position on the jamb and post, and also the plate, sill, and transom, just as they are shown in Fig. 1498, except that the rails will be lying on the upper faces of the posts. The head must be laid to the extreme marks previously made, and the sight lines of the post and jamb squared up across its edge ; a pencil line drawn along its edge on the face of the posts will give the required bevels for shoulders and the direction of the mortises. The sight lines of the posts should be squared on the other rails, and these will give the inside shoulders. The outside shoulder of the plate will require bevelling to fit the rebate (see Fig. 1509). Set off the depth of this on the edge,

Fig. 1510.—Greenhouse Transom.　　Fig. 1511.—Greenhouse Roof Bar.

namely ⅜ in., and square it down to meet a ⅝-in. gauge line run on the face from the upper edge. The shoulder will be drawn from the intersection to the sight line, and the same process must be gone through on the post (see Fig. 1498). The transom and door sill will have the sight lines placed on them in the same manner, the former having square shoulders ½ in. longer than the sight lines, because the jambs are re-

bated ½ in. for the door on the inside, and
have a ½-in. bead stuck all round outside.
(Fig. 1510 is a vertical section of the transom.) The door sill will be kept flush inside, and project about 2 in. outside, and
run over the posts as shown. The setting-

Fig. 1512.—Plan of Ventilator Bottom Rail.

out of the head mortise in the corner post
can now be finished. This will be about
1¼ in. wide, consequent on the end of the
post standing down ⅜ in. to allow for the
overlapping of the head (see Fig. 1498).
Square the mortise over for the front head,
and make the edge A (Fig. 1502) of this
member range with the cut-off end of the
post. Pair and set out the opposite post
by this. The wall post at the opposite end
may be set out from and in pair with its
own corner post, so far as the lower rails
are concerned, the height for the head being obtained from the post w, so as to
ensure both ends being alike. The lengths
of these rails may be better left until the
first end is knocked together, when they
may be arranged over it and the lengths of
the various shoulders obtained accurately.

SASH BARS OF LEAN-TO GREENHOUSE.

Now space out the bars on the top edges
of the plates. To get these all alike (which
is advisable for the easier fitting of the
glass), take the total length in inches, between the sight lines of the posts, plus the
thickness of a bar, and divide it by the
number of openings required, which will
always be one more than the bars; the
quotient will be the distance from the side
of one bar to the same side of the next.
For example, say the clear span to be
divided is 3 ft. 4 in. plus 1 in. for bar equals
41 in.; say four bars are required, $41 \div 5$
$= 8\frac{3}{16}$ in. full. Space this from the sight
line, then 1 in. more; this will be the
mortise for the first bar. Then set off the
same distance from each side of that mortise, and so on, when all the spaces will be
found equal. The head should not be set
out until the frame is knocked together,

when the bars may be placed, either with
one end tenoned and inserted in the
mortises, or laid over the face and spaced
parallel, when their lengths and the position of the head mortises may be determined with accuracy. Gauge the mortises
for the bars to fit a $\frac{5}{16}$-in. chisel in a line
with the glass rebate, and run it from the
outside, the mortises to be 1 in. deep. The
front rails will be set out by squaring on
the sight line of the posts on the sill—that
is, 9 ft., less the thickness of the two posts.
Pair the other rails with it in consecutive
order, and mark over the sight lines on
their edges, then set ⅜ in. beyond the sight
lines on the head and plate; square this
over the outside of the head for the
shoulder line, and make the bevel shoulders
on the plate, as advised for the ends. Set
out the bars in a similar manner, except
that, in this case, the rails being parallel,
both may be marked at once. The position of the notches for the roof bars (Fig.
1511) may be marked on the inner face of
the head, but should not be cut until the
piece is bevelled and otherwise wrought
to section, when they will be cut in as
shown in Figs. 1502 and 1507, the tails of
the bars running over the top edge and not
being sunk. The mortises in the ridge may
be set off from the head, and will be cut
as shown in Fig. 1506. A ¼-in. plough
groove is run on the face of the ridge in a
line with the rebate of the bars; work this
from the top side, after bevelling. To
obtain the bevel for the top shoulder of the
bars, draw Fig. 1512 full size and set the

Fig. 1513.—Section of   Fig. 1514.—Section of
Ventilator Bottom Rail.   Ventilator Top Rail.

bevel to it; this will be the shoulder line
before the bars are chamfered, and the saw
should be run in before the chamfering is
done. (Fig. 1512 is the plan, and Fig. 1513
the section of the bottom rail of ventilator.)
Complete each operation—for instance, all
the ploughing, rebating, gauging, etc., that
are alike—before shifting the tools. Cut
off the matchboards so that they will just
go easy in the grooves, and paint the

grooves and the edges of the boards before putting the work together. The two end frames, when worked and fitted, may be glued up and cleaned off. The front may now be fitted into each end piece by piece.

Fig. 1515.   Fig. 1516.

Figs. 1515 and 1516.—Horizontal Sections of Lower and Upper Part of Door.

Ventilators of Lean-to Greenhouse.

The ventilators should not be made until the openings to receive them are finished, when the exact shape and size may be ascertained by laying the pieces over the opening. The bars forming the sides of the roof ventilator opening will only require to be worked up to the trimmer ; and this piece, tenoned through and wedged, will also not be worked on the upper side, and will be ploughed, not rebated, on the lower. Fig. 1514 is a section of the top rail of the ventilator. The spandrel ventilator can be hung either to the wall jamb or to the transom.

Erecting Lean-to Greenhouse.

In erecting the greenhouse, level the ground and lay a brick at each corner of the site. See that these lie in the same horizontal plane, then stand up one end of the structure, securing it with temporary braces. Insert the front sill, then the matchboarding in the groove ; next the plate, then the bars and head—first, however, painting the mortises and tenons. (Glue must not be used on the work.) To insert the tenons in the head, lift up the free end, push it home into the post, and, as bar after bar enters its mortise, drive it well home with a mallet. Then the other end may be stood up, entered, and knocked home. The shoulders may be brought up close either with drawbore pins or by means of a long wood cleat and wedges. Then paint the hardwood pins and drive them, leaving the end projecting slightly. Next cut the ridge off to the clear length between the end heads at the front. Test the house diagonally to see if it is square,

29

and fix the ridge to the wall with a couple of wall cliphooks so that its top edge is flush with the heads. Drive wallhooks against each wall post, as shown in Fig. 1515, to secure the ends, and then the purlins will require to be fitted. (Figs. 1515 and 1516 are horizontal sections of lower and upper part of door.) Locate the position of the post by temporarily inserting the two end roof bars, entering the purlins in the notches ; mark its length, cut a short dovetail at each end, and notch it in the ends ; paint and insert it, screwing it down ; then the bars can be fixed, entering them in the ridge first, sliding them into place at the lower end sideways, and driving them home in the notches, into which they should fit tightly, but it is not necessary to nail them. Of the exterior fitting nothing remains to be done but the flashing piece at the ridge, which should be scribed to the wall, well painted underneath, and nailed on. The house will then be ready for priming and glazing. Fill in the bricks tightly under the sills, also insert one where a stage standard is intended to be placed, and fill the interior with gravel. The stages can then be erected. The brackets are formed as shown in Fig. 1517, by halving standard and bearer together and dovetail-notching the back end of the bearer into fillets nailed to the plate and wall (see Fig. 1518). Figs. 1498 to 1500 are reproduced to a scale of ⅜ in. to the foot, and have figured dimensions. The other illustrations are to a scale of 2 in. to the foot.

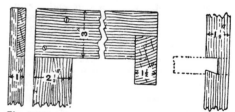

Fig. 1517.—Part of Stage Bracket.   Fig. 1518.—Wall End Bracket.

Materials for Span-roof Greenhouse.

The portable greenhouse about to be described (see the half elevations and sections, Figs. 1519 and 1520) may be erected as a span-roof structure, or may be divided into two smaller structures having lean-to roofs. The sides and ends consist of six complete frames, which are held together with bolts. Sashes form the roof, and are fixed with screws. The leading dimensions are given in Figs. 1519 and 1520. The

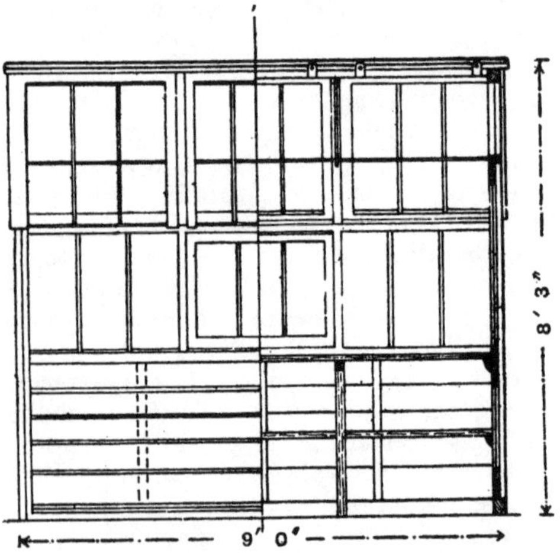

Fig. 1519.—Half Side Elevation and Section of Span-roof Greenhouse.

materials required are as follows:—Timber (finished sizes): Oak.—Bottom rails: Two pieces, 9 ft. by 2¾ in. by 2¾ in.; four pieces, 4 ft. 8 in. by 2¾ in. by 2¾ in. Deal.—Plates and middle rails: Four pieces, 9 ft. by 2¾ in. by 2¾ in.; two pieces, 2 ft. 2 in. by 2¾ in. by 2¾ in.; two pieces, 4 ft. 8 in. by 2¾ in. by 2¾ in. Door frames: Four pieces, 8 ft. 3 in. by 2¾ in. by 1¾ in.; four pieces, 6 ft. 6 in. by 2¾ in. by 1¾ in.; two pieces, 2 ft. 9 in. by 2¾ in. by 1¾ in. Top rails of end: Four pieces, 5 ft. 6 in. by 2¾ in. by 1⅜ in. Rafters: Four pieces, 5 ft. 4 in. by 2¾ in. by 1¾ in. End bars: Four pieces, 3 ft. by 1⅞ in. by 1¼ in.; two pieces, 3 ft. 9 in. by 1⅞ in. by 1¼ in.; two pieces, 5 ft. by 1⅞ in. by 1¼ in. Angle-posts: eight pieces, 5 ft. 6 in. by 2¾ in. by 1⅜ in. Doors: Four pieces 6 ft. 8 in. by 4¼ in. by 1⅜ in.; two pieces, 2 ft. 7 in. by 4¼ in. by 1⅜ in.; two pieces, 1 ft. 9 in. by 4¼ in. by 1⅜ in.; four pieces, 2 ft. 7 in. by 9 in. by 1⅜ in.; two pieces, 3 ft. 3 in. by ⅞ in. by 1⅜ in.; four pieces, 1 ft. 8 in. by 9½ in. by ⅞ in. Ridge capping: One piece, 9 ft. 4 in. by 3¾ in. by 1¾ in. Fillets: Twelve pieces, 2 ft. 8 in. by 2½ in. by ¾ in. Studs: Eight pieces, 2 ft. 8 in. by 1¾ in. by 1¾ in. Weather-board (prepared): 190 ft. by 6 in. by 1 in. Mullions: Four pieces, 2 ft. 6 in. by 2¼ in. by 1¾ in. Side bars: Eight pieces, 2 ft. 4 in. by 1⅞ in. by 1¼ in. Side sashes: Four pieces, 2 ft. 4 in. by 2 in. by 1⅜ in.; two pieces, 3 ft. by 2 in. by 1⅜ in.; two pieces, 3 ft. by 3¼ in. by 1⅜ in.; four pieces, 2 ft. 2 in. by ⅞ in. by 1⅜ in. Roof sashes: Four pieces, 5 ft. 8 in. by 3¼ in. by 1⅜ in.; eight pieces, 5 ft. 8 in. by 2¾ in. by 1⅜ in.; six pieces, 3 ft. 3 in. by 2¾ in. by 1⅜ in.; six pieces, 3 ft. 3 in. by 2¾ in. by ⅞ in.; twelve pieces, 5 ft. 6 in. by 1⅜ in. by 1⅜ in. Chamfered fillets: Four pieces, 5 ft. 8 in. by 2 in. by ⅝ in. Stops: Three pieces, 6 ft. by 1⅜ in. by ½ in.; four pieces, 6 ft. 8 in. by 1⅜ in. by ½ in. Flower stage: Twenty-two pieces, 8 ft. 8 in. by 2 in. by 1 in.; eight pieces, 1 ft. 10 in. by 2½ in. by ¾ in.; six pieces, 1 ft. 9 in. by 2½ in. by ¾ in.; four pieces, 3 ft. by 1¾ in. by 1¾ in.; four pieces, 2 ft. by 1¾ in. by 1¾ in.; four pieces, 1 ft. 9 in. by 1¾ in. by 1¾ in.; six pieces, 1 ft. 6 in. by 2½ in. by ¾ in. Ironwork as follows:—Tie rod: One 8 ft. 6½ in. long by ½ in. wrought-iron. Suspending rods: Two 2 ft. long by ½ in. wrought-iron, with hooked ends, nuts, and

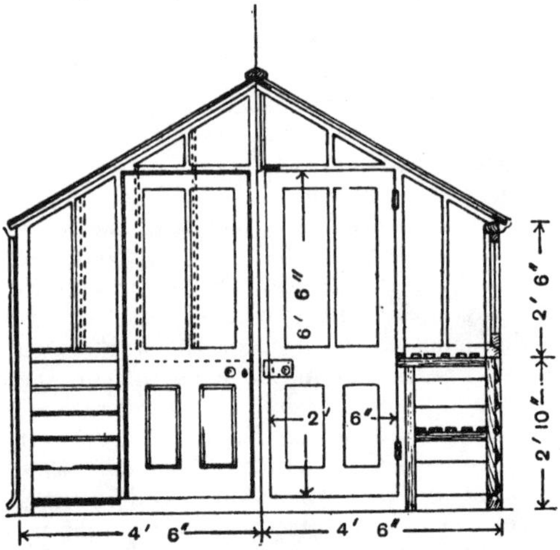

Fig. 1520.—Half End Elevation and Section of Span-roof Greenhouse.

plates. Wrought-iron ridge plates: Twelve 2½ in. by 1½ in. by ¼ in., drilled for screws and bolts. Bolts: Eight 4½ in. by ½ in.; twelve 4 in. by ½ in. Two pairs of

3-in. butts, two pairs of 2½-in. butts, two 10-in. casement stays, two rim locks, six gutter bolts, quantity of screws and nails. Glass and paint: One 100-ft. box 21-oz., one 100-ft. box 15-oz. horticultural glass; 15 lb. of putty; 20 lb. of paint.

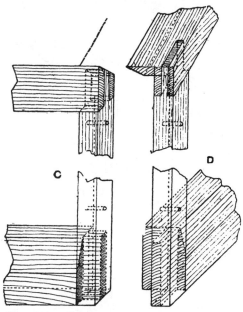

Fig. 1521.—Joints at Angle-post and Bottom Rail.

SIDE FRAMES OF SPAN-ROOF GREENHOUSE.

The side frames should be constructed first, the long rails and posts being made to form joints at angles, as shown in Fig. 1521; C shows the side and D the end posts. The distance between the shoulders of the rail should be 8 ft. 6½ in.; that from under the bottom rail to the middle rail, 2 ft. 10 in.; and that from the under-side of the middle rail to the top angle of the plate, 2 ft. 6 in. When setting out for space between the bars, keep the glass as near as possible to the same size. Mortise the rail for bars, studs, and rebated mullions. Omit the bars where side sashes occur. Weather the rails and plate to their respective sections (shown in Figs. 1521 and 1522), and groove and rebate them for glass. A rebate ⅜ in. by $\frac{5}{16}$ in. will be sufficient in all cases. Before putting the frames together, paint the mortises and tenons, then wedge and pin up tightly. Great care is essential to the production of weather-proof work.

ENDS OF SPAN-ROOF GREENHOUSE.

The rails and posts forming the ends should next be taken. Begin by marking, from a square end of the bottom rail, the position and exact size of the longer door-post. From this measure 2 ft. 6 in., the width of the door. Then mark the position and size of the other post. From this take 1 ft. 5¾ in. for the shoulder line at the angle-post. The same measurement is the length between the shoulders of the short middle rail. The total length of the rail from mortise to shoulder should be 4 ft. 3¼ in., which length applies to other bottom rails of the end frames. Prepare one end of the doorposts and angle-post for joint with the bottom rail, also the mortises for the door

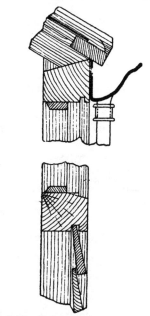

Fig. 1522.—Head and Sill of Greenhouse.

head and the short middle rail. The pieces so prepared to form the end frame should now be placed together on a flat surface, and, where practicable, temporarily secured with pins or a few wedges at the mortises. When the frame has been squared and held to the required position, proceed in the following manner to find the angle made by the top rail: Cut the door head 2 ft. 6 in. from the shoulder, and let the squared end butt against the shorter doorpost. See that the other shoulders are close up to the bottom rail; then measure up the doorposts from the under-side of the rail 8 ft., and up the angle-post 5 ft. 4 in. These are the outside points of the frame, and the thickness of the top rail of the end frame must be marked inside of these for the shoulder line. Lay the rail edgeways on the frame and mark for mortises and a splayed joint at the angle-post, as shown in

Fig. 1523.—Details of Greenhouse Doorpost.

rod passes (Fig. 1525). The bevels and lengths of the rafters can be obtained from the top rail of one of the framed ends. The

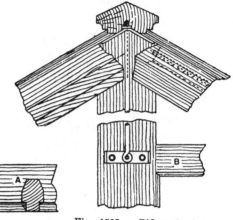

Fig. 1525. — Ridge Section showing Suspending Rod.

Fig. 1521. The short doorpost and end bars A (Fig. 1523) must be tenoned to the top rail, but the door head needs only a splay-cut and screws. The parts of this frame should be fixed together, and another frame, to pair, made from it. The remaining two end frames are similar, with the exception of the doors, and are fitted with bars, indicated by the dotted lines on the left of Fig. 1520.

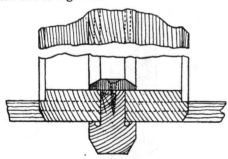

Fig. 1524.—Rafter Jointed to Roof Sash.

ERECTING SPAN-ROOF GREENHOUSE.

The rafters, after being rebated to receive the roof sashes (Fig. 1524), are cut and screwed at foot as shown in Fig. 1522. The top ends meet, and are held together with a plate through which the suspending

six frames forming the sides and ends should be bored for bolts and erected in a level position on a few bricks or other suitable blocks. In bolting together, use three 4-in. bolts in each angle-post, and four 4½-in. bolts in the doorpost. The bolt for the doorpost is shown in Fig. 1523, that for the angle-post in Fig. 1526. The framework should have a coat of paint as it stands. The tie-rod must have plates, drilled for screws, and riveted on at each end as shown at the door head B (Fig. 1525). The suspending rod is turned up at the lower end as in Fig. 1527 to allow the tie-rod to drop in. The other end passes through the plate (let into the rafter) at the top, and is provided with a thread and nut for screwing up. These rods may be fixed with the rafters in position, and the whole structure held square and rigid with braces. Afterwards prepare the roof sashes with mortise and tenon joints to cover the spaces between the rafters and the ends. The outside sashes have a wide stile to cover and project over the top rail of the end. The rebated portion of the bars should be taken across the bottom rail. Rebate the stiles and groove the top rails for glass. When the sashes are wedged together, fit and bevel them at the ridge, and let in plates opposite each other as shown in Fig. 1528. Hold each pair of plates together with a gutter bolt, which should make a fairly close joint. The projecting part of the plates and bolts must be let into the under-

3-in. butts and stopped by $\frac{1}{2}$-in. beaded pieces fixed on the outside of the door frame (see Fig. 1523). Cut one edge of the fillets step fashion to fit the back of the weather boarding (Fig. 1522) and fix to the posts. Provided the weather boarding has been well painted, it may be nailed to the

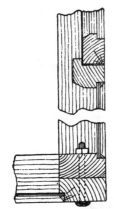

Fig. 1526.—Greenhouse Angle-post.

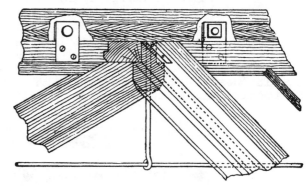

Fig. 1528.—Roof Sashes Jointed to Ridge.

side of the ridge capping. Prepare the ridge capping to section, fit it over sashes and plates, and fix with screws. The bottom rail of the sashes should be screwed to the plate, on side framing, and the wide stiles should be screwed from the inside to the top rail of the end frames. Complete the fixing of the sashes by screwing the

Fig. 1527.—End of Suspending Rod with Tie-rod.

chamfered fillets to the top of the rafters as shown in Fig. 1524. The side sashes should be made to fill the space between the rebates of the mullions. The rebates at head and sill are formed by nailing on $\frac{1}{2}$-in. stops (Fig. 1522). Mortise the bars through both rails. When the sashes are wedged together, fit and hang them to open outside on $2\frac{1}{2}$-in. butts. If it is preferable to purchase the doors ready made, the material in the quantities for this purpose should be deducted. They should, however, be well framed and put together with thin white-lead, and afterwards hung to open inside on

fillets and studs. The zinc gutter is shown in Fig. 1522.

GREENHOUSE FLOWER STAGE, GLAZING, ETC.

The legs and rails of the bearers for the flower stage should be framed together (see Fig. 1520). To fix them, cut the back legs of the bearers to fit tightly between bottom and middle ribs. The battens forming the shelves lie loose upon the bearers, and are held together with ledges screwed on the under-side. Fillets fixed on the ends of the greenhouse support the ends of the shelves (see Fig. 1519). As regards painting, every part should have at least one coat. Two coats must be given to the whole structure before the glass is put in. The glazing of the roof sashes would be more easily performed on a bench, the sashes being re-placed when the bed putty is hard. As outside putty is not recommended for a roof, the glass must be well secured with sprigs of zinc, afterwards the rebates should be well painted. Put outside putty to the upright glazing, and give a finishing coat to all parts, fixing the locks and other fastenings when the work is dry. The ridge plates on the roof sashes allow of fixing to the wall, so as to use the structure as a lean-to melon house or tomato house.

LATHES, TURNING, AND TURNERY.

THE SCOPE OF TURNING.

THE woodworker who adds a lathe to his outfit of tools extends the scope of his work very largely and in quite a new direction. The lathe has been aptly called the father of mechanism, and although its application is here considered only in connection with woodwork, yet the beauty and variety of its productions, even in this branch, make it distinctly desirable. The modern lathe ranges from the tiny tool used by the watchmaker, worked by a slip of whalebone for a bow and a horsehair for a cord, to machines weighing scores of tons and large enough to take in work weighing many hundredweights. Turning is one of the earliest handicrafts, and commenced with the potter's wheel, used hundreds of years before the Christian era.

Fig. 1529.—Plain Turning Lathe.

A PLAIN LATHE DESCRIBED.

A wood-turning lathe is the simplest of all lathes. It consists essentially of standards, bed, headstock, tailstock, T-rest and socket, with fly-wheel or driving wheel crank shaft and treadle to give the motion. The headstock in which the mandrel runs is called the mandrel headstock, or fast head-stock, to distinguish it from the movable or poppit headstock, which takes the back centre. Fig. 1529 will enable every reader to distinguish the various parts of a lathe ; A indicates the headstock, B the poppit, or loose headstock ; A and B, respectively the fast and loose headstocks, are often called the lathe heads, or simply " the heads." Between A and B is the hand-rest socket E, holding the rest T for the tool. The headstock A carries the mandrel with

visable to hold it down by two bolts, one near each end. The headstock A is firmly fixed upon the bed G, whilst the tailstock B and the hand-rest socket E are movable, and can be secured upon the bed in any position by screw handles F F below, as may best suit the dimensions of the work marked W, which is held between the forked chuck C and the cone centre D. The treadle K rocks on the treadle-bar L. The weight or power of the foot on the treadle K is communicated to the crank by the

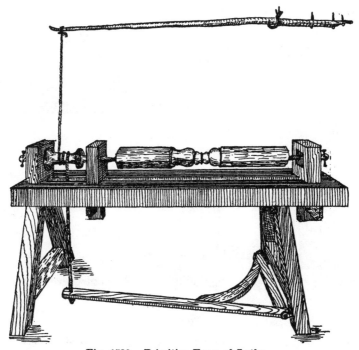

Fig. 1530.—Primitive Form of Lathe.

the pulley, which receives motion from the fly-wheel I by means of the band N. The headstock, with its mandrel, is the most important part of the lathe, and it is essential that the headstock casting shall fit the bed properly. In many cases it will be found that the casting gets bent when the holding-down bolt has been screwed tight, thus throwing the boring of the collar-hole and the tail-pin hole out of continuity. A direct pull by one bolt near the centre so often bends the headstock casting that it is ad-

hook. It will take a little while to get quite accustomed to working a treadle. It is worked backwards and forwards, fast and slow, the worker's body being kept quite steady ; the leg only is moved, and the body must not move up and down with the foot. Two standards H H support the bed, and a diagonal brace or stay M adds very much to the rigidity of the whole machine. The fly-wheel of such a lathe should have a series of grooves in steps corresponding to those of the mandrel pulley, so that the band may be shifted to any pair of the series, and fit taut without any readjustment of length; there should be two series of grooves, and a special length of band is necessary for each. The extreme diameter of the fly-wheel may be 2 ft. to 2 ft. 2 in., with a series of three or four grooves graduated from the largest possible size. The second series would be about half that diameter, and have but two grooves. Fly-wheels are generally too light; $\frac{3}{4}$ cwt. is not at all too heavy for one

shape. Still, it does very satisfactory work within the limits of its capacity. The illustration sufficiently shows the construction, which is obviously inexpensive.

Wood Turner's Lathe.

Fig. 1531 gives a front view of a good type of lathe for general wood turning suited for professional use. The frame may be 6 ft. to 7 ft. long, and the headstocks 5 in. to 7 in. above the bed. The mandrel headstock may be reversed on the bed as

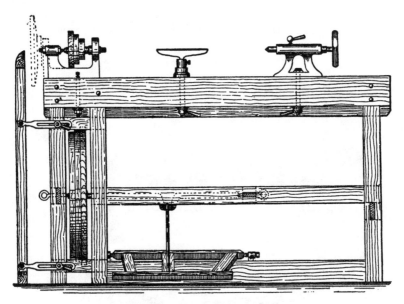

Fig. 1531.—Wood Turner's Lathe.

2 ft. 1 in. in diameter. The lathe here described is very suitable for beginners.

Primitive Form of Lathe.

Fig. 1530 shows a lathe which, in a modified form, is still extensively used in some parts of France and elsewhere. The design is supposed to be of Persian origin. The cutting takes place only as the foot is being pressed down, for as the treadle rises the wood rotates the wrong way. This type of lathe is now being superseded by lathes of the ordinary type, and by those specially constructed for the production of large quantities of articles uniform in size and

shown by the dotted lines, so that the chuck overhangs the frame. In this way work of large diameter may be swung on the lathe, and though a foot lathe is not sufficiently powerful for such a purpose, yet work 6 ft. in diameter may be swung overhanging the left-hand end. A rest on which to support the turning tool is shown supported by the floor; it is fixed where required by means of two slotted stays and handled nuts. The details of construction of this lathe will be better understood after reading the following particulars of the various parts, but it is shown here as a specimen of the kind of lathe used by professionals.

WOODEN LATHE STAND AND BED.

The woodworker who has mastered the previous chapters of this book can now make his own lathe stand. Fig. 1532 shows

Fig. 1532.—Frame of Lathe.

a wooden stand, bed, footboard, wheel, etc., ready for the headstocks and the hand-rest. Sound red deal will be suitable material of which to make it ; but if beech, birch, or similar hard wood is used the dimensions

standards are tenoned and fitted into the mortises in the sole-piece as at B (Fig. 1535). To keep the standards firm, braces should be cut with splayed shoulders and tenons fitting into mortises made in the sole-piece and standards, as shown at C and D (Fig. 1535). When these joints are fitted satisfactorily they should be fixed by ½-in. iron bolts and nuts. Next make the footboard ; for this, the three cross rails have end tenons which fit into mortises made in the back rail. The front ends are notched for the front rail to fit, as illustrated at E (Fig. 1536). The joints of the footboard framing should be well glued and screwed. A simple means of hingeing the footboard to the back rail is by a couple of strong brass backflap hinges, one flap of the hinge being screwed to the back rail of the footboard and the other flap fixed to the stretcher bar G (Figs. 1533 and 1536) ; or, if desired, the footboard may be held at each end between centres. The stretcher bar is cut out to fit over the sole-piece, as shown at Fig. 1536, and should be screwed to it. To prevent the standards spreading at the bottom, the sole-pieces should be fastened to

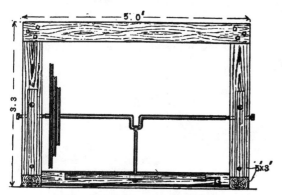

Fig. 1533.—Front View of Lathe.

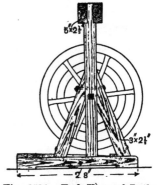

Fig. 1534.—End View of Lathe.

could be decreased by about one-quarter or one-third. Figs. 1533 and 1534 are fully dimensioned, and it is only necessary to mention the leading points in the construction. First plane the timbers to size. Then the upper parts of the standards are notched on each side, and the inner sides of the bed pieces are also notched, as shown at A (Fig. 1535). The bottoms of the

the floor by bolts or screws ; or a ½-in. iron rod with a nut on each end may be used, as shown in Figs. 1532, 1533, and 1534. The frame is now ready for the wheel, crank shaft, etc., to be fixed in position.

WOODEN LATHE DRIVING WHEEL.

Difficulty is sometimes experienced in procuring a suitable cast-iron turned driving wheel, and in such a case a wheel in hard wood, as shown in front elevation by Fig. 1537 and section by Fig. 1538, may be made. It may be from 1 ft. 8 in. to 2 ft. 6 in.

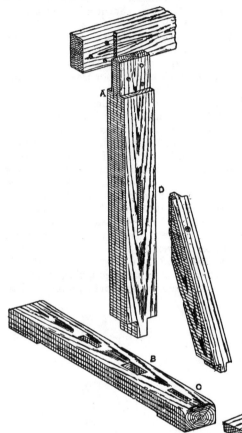

Fig. 1535.—Standard for Lathe.

in diameter. The arms are made of stuff 2½ in. wide by 1 in. thick, and may be housed together by the method shown at Fig. 1539, each of the three pieces used for arms being long enough to cross the full diameter of the wheel. Each arm is cut away to fit the others, leaving one-third of the total thickness in each piece. One piece is shown lifted out of place at Fig. 1540. An easier method is shown at Fig. 1541, where the ends of the six arms are merely butted together. In either case a hardwood boss, about 4½ in. in diameter and ⅜ in. thick, is

glued and screwed on each side of the arm centre, and ⅛ in. is gauged and planed off each side of the thickness of the arm ends, thus tapering them to ¾ in. thick. The arms are also tapered down to 2 in. wide inside the rim, as shown at Fig. 1537. Eighteen segments of hard wood ¾ in. thick are cut to form the rim. The middle layer has each segment fitted between two arms, as shown at A (Fig. 1537). The top and bottom layers have the joints lapped, and are glued and screwed in position as shown at A, where one top segment has been removed. The wheel should now be placed in a lathe large enough to swing it, and the rim turned to the section shown at Fig. 1538, thus providing three speeds. The centre hole should also be bored in the lathe, after which the two ¼-in. iron plates shown in Figs. 1537 and 1538 should be screwed over the wooden bosses, the centre holes having been previously drilled to fit the crank shaft, and a keyway cut. The crank shaft is next inserted and keyed up, and if the wheel does not run quite evenly, it may be turned true in its place.

THE MANDREL HEADSTOCK.

It has been mentioned already that the headstock (Fig. 1542), which carries the revolving mandrel, is the most important

Fig. 1536.—Details of Lathe Footboard.

part of a lathe ; it is a strong casting, which is planed and fitted to the bed and bolted hard down. A section of this headstock is shown in Fig. 1542, with the mandrel in place. The mandrel, made of hardened steel, runs in a coned collar fitting into the casting ; this collar is generally made of steel, but in the illustration it is shown with a flange, as it would have if made of brass, which fits close inside the head, and the mandrel is fed up by a hardened steel cone-pointed tail screw having

Fig. 1537.—Elevation of Wooden Driving Wheel.

two adjustment nuts as shown. The shape shown is one of the best for a high speed lathe, and high speed is essential in woodturning. The mandrel is 1⅛ in. diam. on the parallel part, and 1⅜ in. to 1¼ in. diam. at the tapered bearing part, the bearing being 1¾ in. long. The mandrel nose is 1 in. diam., and screwed eight threads to an inch. The nose is bored centrally and tapering for a distance of 1½ in., from ½ in. to ⅜ in. at the back. This serves to receive the fork chuck, etc. Fig. 1542 shows the cone pulley in section ; it is keyed to the mandrel as shown.

Fig. 1538.—Section of Driving Wheel.

THE MANDREL TAILSTOCK, ETC.

The tailstock has a sliding barrel, 7 in. long and 1 in. diam. Fig. 1543 is a section showing the various parts in position. The barrel is actuated by an internal screw,

turned by the hand-wheel, which is 6 in. in diam., and fitted with a small handle, as shown. The casting is bored right through to admit the barrel, which is tubular, being bored ¼ in. short of through with a ⅝-in. drill,

Fig. 1539.—Two Arms Housed Together.

and the remaining ½ in. being tapped for the ½-in. traversing screw ; the other end is coned to take the back centre. The internal screw, 7 in. long, has 5 in. screwed ½ in. ; then a collar ¼ in. thick, and beyond the collar 2 in. left plain to receive the handwheel. To prevent the barrel turning round, a long shallow groove is made in it, and a small screw passing through at the

Fig. 1540.—Arm Cut for Housing.

back of the casting enters the groove ; the barrel is thus free to slide, but not to revolve. The tailstock, which must slide along the bed as required, is fixed down by a ⅝-in. bolt having a wing nut. A similar wing nut screwed on a ⅝-in. bolt fixes down the hand-rest socket, and two bolts, with ordinary nuts and clamping plates under the bed, fix down the mandrel headstock.

Fig. 1541.—Six Arms Butted Together.

The hand-rest socket is a casting 10 in. long, with the sole planed true, and a T-groove cored to receive the head of holding-down bolt (see section, Fig. 1544). On the near end is an upright boss 3½ in. high, having a 1⅛-in. vertical hole to receive the T, which is fixed by a ½-in. pinching screw, its head having ⅜-in. holes, crossing diameterwise, to receive a lever by which the

scale figures, provided that all the measurements are enlarged or diminished in the same ratio. For a 5½-in. lathe, the headstock casting (Fig. 1547) would be 10 in.

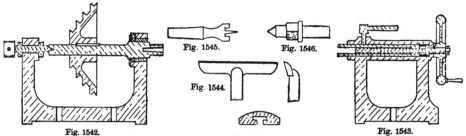

Fig. 1542—Mandrel Headstock.   Fig. 1543.—Mandrel Tailstock.   Fig. 1544.—T-rest.
Fig. 1545.—Forked Chuck.   Fig. 1546.—Tailstock Cone Centre.

screw is turned. The T is a casting, two views of which are shown in Fig. 1544. The rest leans forward towards the lathe centres, as shown in Fig. 1544.   Fig. 1545 shows the forked chuck for wood-turning; it fits in the nose of the running mandrel.

long at the base, with a portion of the boss which holds the tail-pin projecting about ½ in. to the rear, the total length of the hole in which the tail-pin fits being fully 2 in. The tail-pin should be cylindrical, perfectly true, and fit the hole tightly.

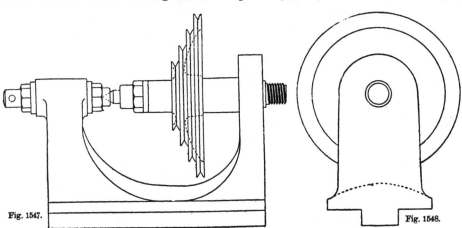

Figs. 1547 and 1548.—Plain Mandrel Headstock.

Fig. 1546 shows the cone centre that fits in the barrel of the tailstock.

THE PLAIN MANDREL HEADSTOCK.

The illustrations (Figs. 1547 and 1548) show the construction of a very simple, yet very good, mandrel headstock, especially suited for a light running foot-lathe. The dimensions being proportionate, a headstock of any size may be made from these

being held by a nut on each end. Tail-pins which are themselves threaded and screwed through the casting and fixed with a locknut, as shown in Fig. 1542, should be avoided, as with such the cone point of the screw is sure to be eccentric when turned in the thread, and thus the axial line of the mandrel would be continually altered. Fig. 1548 shows the face end of the casting and the circumference of the pulley.

The upright of the casting which holds the steel collar has its upper part rounded by a semicircle struck from the centre of the mandrel. The tenon projecting below is intended to fit between the cheeks of the lathe bed.

chuck is bored with a ⅜-in. hole, and into this hole the shank of the steel fork is firmly driven. The cone point is brought true, so that it revolves on the centre line of the mandrel. The notches filed on each side of it are unequal in size, so as to make one

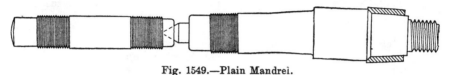

Fig. 1549.—Plain Mandrel.

THE PLAIN MANDREL.

The length of the running mandrel adds much to the steadiness of the lathe in turning, provided always that only the smallest possible amount projects from the collar at the nose end. Fig. 1549 shows a mandrel suited to the headstock illustrated by Fig. 1547. It is 8 in. long, and to be in good proportion would be spaced thus: The screw of the nose, ¾ in. long, cut with a ¾-in. Whitworth thread; cone for front bearing, 1 in. long, the diameter being about 1⅛ in., tapering about 1° ; plain part, 1¼ in. long, 1⅜ in. diameter; pulley, 2¼ in. ; washer, nut, and plain part behind pulley, 2 in., with a small part ¾ in. long terminating in a cone point. It is rather unusual to make the male cone on the end of the mandrel and the female cone in the tailpin as shown in the illustration (Fig. 1549). Generally the cones are in reversed positions; but the method last shown is the better.

FORK CHUCK.

A chuck screws upon the mandrel so as to turn with it; it holds the work, causing it to turn, whilst the turner applies the tool to it. The chucks employed by turners are of almost limitless variety. When a comparatively long piece of wood has to be turned, it is so fixed in the lathe that the revolutions of the mandrel shall be communicated to it. This is done by means of the fork chuck shown at Fig. 1550, which is one of the simplest as well as one of the most useful of chucks. The body of the chuck screws on to the nose of the mandrel by a thread which is shown dotted. The

chisel edge longer than the other ; that is done so that the wood may be replaced correctly after removal, when the longer chisel edge is put into the longer cut, and this ensures that the work shall again run true. These chisel edges are bevelled so that the driving edge is the flat one, and the two edges being out of line, the liability of the fork to split the wood is lessened. The

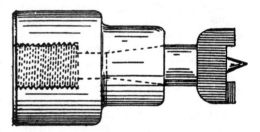

Fig. 1550.—Fork Chuck.

wood is often driven upon the fork with a hammer.

FLANGED TAPER SCREW CHUCK.

Of the vast number of chucks used for holding work by one end only, one of the most useful is the taper screw chuck, which may be made in two forms : with a flange as in Fig. 1551, or without as in Fig. 1552. The former is the more usual form ; it consists of a boss A, which screws upon the mandrel nose ; its front forms a flange or face-plate B, usually about 2¼ in. in diameter. From the centre of this plate projects a taper screw with a thread like that of a joiner's wood screw ; this is about ⅝ in. long, and from ⁵⁄₁₆ in. to ⅜ in. diameter at the large end. There is a hole c into which an iron or steel rod, called a "tommy," can be put, to unscrew the chuck and take it off. Such a point is often formed as a tail to the handle of a spanner used about the lathe. When a piece of

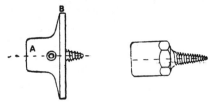

Fig. 1551.—Flanged Taper Screw Chuck.　　Fig. 1552.—Plain Taper Screw Chuck.

wood is to be fixed upon the taper screw chuck, it is first turned true between the centres by aid of the fork chuck; the right-hand end is turned flat, or a little hollow. The wood is taken off the lathe, and a gimlet screwed into the centre of the wood for about ¾ in. The hole is next coned out equally all round, which is easily done with a shell gimlet. The wood should be screwed on the taper screw of the chuck, and, to enable both hands to be used, the tommy, or spanner tail, may be put into the hole c, and then rested on the lathe board, so as to hold the chuck while the wood is screwed on tight against the face-plate of the chuck. This plate assists to hold the wood firmly, and also causes it to shoulder up fairly true; however, the gimlet is sure to draw a little to one side, though started truly central by means of the little indent of the back-centre point, and the wood should be turned true in its place.

Plain Taper Screw Chuck.

Fig. 1552 shows a form of the plain taper screw chuck with no face-plate against which to screw the work. The screw for the first ⅝ in. may be considered to be the same as that shown in Fig. 1551; then, in place of the flange or face-plate, the taper screw is continued till it is about 1½ in. long and ¾ in. in diameter. Procedure with these two forms of chuck differs thus: With Fig. 1551 it is necessary to square the end of the work to be screwed against the flange of the chuck; with Fig. 1552 a rough chopped block may

be selected, a hole bored in it by the gimlet, and then, without further preparation, it may be screwed upon the taper screw chuck and turned as desired. For this reason this chuck is for some purposes preferred to that shown in Fig. 1551. A piece of work must not be taken off the taper screw when partly done, because it cannot be replaced so as to run perfectly true. Work taken off the screw of the chuck, when replaced, must be re-turned with the tool over all the finished part to true it up. When the turning is finished the work may be taken off; and if it be required to repolish a day or two afterwards, as is generally done, it can be replaced quite true enough for that purpose.

Cup Chuck.

Fig. 1553 shows a cup chuck, usually made of brass or of cast-iron; it screws upon the mandrel nose in the ordinary way. Cup chucks are inexpensive, and a turner may have a dozen of them of different sizes, ranging from 1½ in. to about 4 in. diam. inside. The wood to be turned is fitted by chopping or rasping it till it can be driven into the chuck, which is turned out slightly coned, so as to be a trifle larger at the mouth. If a piece of wood that is too small for the chuck is to be fitted in, the chuck can be filled by driving in any suitable short piece of waste wood, which can then be faced off square, and bored out to suit the size of the work. A fairly long rod

Fig. 1553.—Cup Chuck.

of soft deal, screwed endwise of the grain upon the taper screw chuck, would soon work loose, because a screw holds badly in end wood; but the same piece driven into a cup chuck would hold very well. A piece of soft deal plank could, however, be screwed flatwise upon the taper screw, and would hold well, especially upon the chuck shown in Fig. 1551. The taper screw is useful for flat work of large diameter, and it is therefore of wider application and more generally useful than the cup chuck.

FACE-PLATE CHUCK.

For turned work of large diameter, turned without the support of the back-centre, the face-plate chuck is used. This is shown screwed at Fig. 1554 front view and Fig. 1555 side view. Fig. 1555 shows the usual boss with internal thread to screw upon the mandrel nose, cast solid with a disc bored with holes, to allow of wood screws being passed through from the back, to hold wood close against the face of the chuck. The face-plate is much used in pattern making. A board is screwed to the front of it; this may project beyond its edge, and is faced up in the lathe, care being taken not to cut into the points of the screws; then, with glue, or otherwise, the work is fixed upon a level and true surface. In this way large rings, wheel patterns, etc., are turned. Fig. 1554 shows the front of the face-plate turned true and flat, and bored with holes for screws. There is a strengthening rim cast round the edge (shown also in Fig. 1555), and the chuck, though made of gun-metal on expensive lathes, is better of cast-iron, as the softer metal is apt to get indented and bruised,

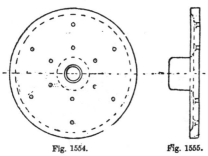

Fig. 1554.   Fig. 1555.

Figs. 1554 and 1555.—Front and Side Views of Face-plate Chuck.

though it has the advantage over iron of not rusting.

TURNING LONG, SLENDER WORK.

It is not possible to turn a very long piece of work unless it is supported at both ends. Generally an ordinary foot lathe cannot manage a greater length than 5 in. or 6 in. when the work is held at one end only; but the length will depend upon the steadiness of the mandrel, the firmness with which the work is screwed

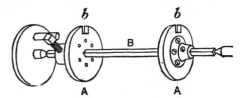

Fig. 1556.—Chuck for Square Turning.

upon the chuck, and the strength of the work itself. The beginner is advised at first not to exceed a length of 4 in. for work held by one end only; by attempting longer work he will encounter difficulties in a tendency to "chatter" or tremble. For hollowing out long work, such as the nozzle of a candlestick, an appliance called a boring collar is used to support the end. In turning slender rods in the lathe the expert turner keeps it running true to the tool with his left hand only, but it takes considerable practice to do this. In turning wooden rods all of one thickness, such as broom handles, a hole is bored through a block of hard wood, and a cutter similar to a plane iron is fixed in the hole in such a way that it will take off a shaving. The wood to be turned is first made eight-sided by plane or saw, then a short length at the end is turned down to the size wanted. The block is put on to this turned part, and, the work being revolved in the lathe, the block is pushed along with both hands, and thus the rod is reduced uniformly to the size allowed by the cutter.

CHUCK FOR SQUARE TURNING.

Though called square, the work produced is not strictly so, as each side of the quasi-square is part of a circle of large diameter. The process will be understood by reference to Fig. 1556. This shows two discs mounted on a square shaft, and notched at b, b. The pieces to be turned would be planed square, so as to fit these notches, in which they would be secured. A number of pieces to be turned would be placed in notches and so form a kind of barrel. These would then be turned as one large cylinder. Each piece has then to be unfixed and turned

chisel (Figs. 1557 and 1558), and excellent work may be done by the gouge alone. The tools must be kept sharp. The method

Fig. 1557.—Wood-turner's Gouge in Handle.

quarter round and again turned. The first three sides can be turned so that the edge of the work will have the support of the side of the groove; but precautions must be

of doing this has been fully described in the earlier pages. Two views of the end of a small gouge are given in Fig. 1559, and similar views of a large gouge are given in

Fig. 1558.—Wood-turner's Chisel in Handle.

taken to prevent breaking down the last edge. The foregoing brief description is intended only to explain how square turn-

Fig. 1560. These enlarged views show the shape to which these tools should be ground. Fig. 1561 shows two views of a

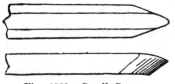

Fig. 1559.—Small Gouge.

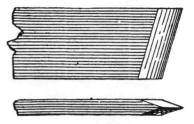

Fig. 1561.—Narrow Chisel.

ing is done, as the process is a mystery to many. In Fig. 1556, A A are the discs, and B is the shaft on which they are fixed.

narrow chisel and Fig. 1562 two views of a broad chisel, which obviously differ from the carpenter's chisels.

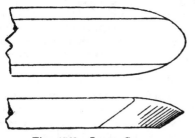

Fig. 1560.—Large Gouge.

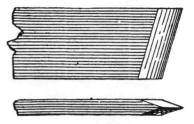

Fig. 1562.—Broad Chisel.

TURNER'S CHISELS AND GOUGES.

Wood-turning tools for special purposes are many and various, but for soft woods nothing is required but the gouge and

PARTING TOOLS.

There are several ways of cutting off work in the lathe; it may be sawn, or it may be cut off with the acute corner of the flat chisel. This allows of a little under-cutting, but it wastes some of the wood. The best way is to use a parting tool, shown

Fig. 1563.—Parting Tool.

handled complete by Fig. 1563. The side of the parting tool, and the plan of it as it lies upon the rest, are shown on a larger

Fig. 1564.—Two Views of Parting Tool.

scale in Fig. 1564. The blade at A is rather thinner than the edge B; the tool may be

Fig. 1565.—Right and Left Side Tools.

$\frac{1}{16}$ in. thick at A, and $\frac{1}{32}$ in. more at B. It is sometimes thrust into the wood for $1\frac{1}{2}$ in.; and this thinning of the blade is necessary to prevent its jambing in its own cut.

Fig. 1566.—Double Side Tool.

MISCELLANEOUS TOOLS.

There are, of course, a number of other tools that are commonly found amongst

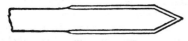

Fig. 1567.—Point Tool.

a woodturner's outfit, as they are handy for various purposes. For instance, Fig. 1565 shows a pair of right and left side tools.

Fig. 1566 shows a side tool which combines the last two illustrated. Fig. 1567 shows a point tool which is similar to the last except that one has a flat and the other an acute point. Fig. 1568 shows a round-nose tool, and Fig. 1569 a pair of half-round

Fig. 1568.—Round-nose Tool.

tools. Figs. 1570 and 1571 show bead tools. Figs. 1572 and 1573 show a pair of comb screw chasers, one being for cutting outside or male threads, the other for inside or female threads.

Fig. 1569.—A Pair of Half-round Tools.

HOOK TOOLS.

Hook tools (Fig. 1574 gives two views), when properly made, are easily used, and will cut rapidly even into hard African black wood. Before using a hook tool,

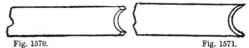

Fig. 1570.   Fig. 1571.

Figs. 1570 and 1571.—Bead Tools.

bore a hole to nearly the full depth to be hollowed, and begin at the edge of the hole with a light cut, the edge of the tool being

Fig. 1572.   Fig. 1573.

Figs. 1572 and 1573.—Comb Screw Chasers.

almost horizontal. The hook tool must be well sharpened before using. The slips for whetting the tool are made from pieces of

30

ragstone ; these are bought in rough splinters, which require to be dressed to the proper shape. Water is the lubricant used

Fig. 1574.—Hook Tool.

when sharpening the tool. Fix the T-rest close to the work so that the arm-rest will have as little overhang as possible. The handle of the arm-rest is held under the left arm, whilst the hand takes a firm grip of the shank close up to the T-rest. Lay the hook tool across the bend of the arm-rest and start the cut. If the tool is found to be cutting too deep, it should be held on its side in a scraping position until the cut is felt, and its cutting edge can then be raised

Fig. 1575.—Arm-rest.

to an angle of about 45°, at the same time drawing both arm-rest and hook tool outwards and towards the turner.

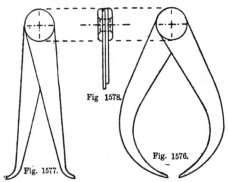

Fig. 1576.—Outside Callipers. Fig. 1577.—Inside Callipers. Fig. 1578.—Calliper Joint.

TURNER'S ARM-REST.

The arm-rest (Fig. 1575) is a tool used in conjunction with the hook tool and several others. Time is economised by its use, as

it enables the operator to turn inside work without setting the T-rest at right angles to the lathe, as he would otherwise have to do. It also gives the turner greater control over the tool. The arm-rest is made from $\frac{3}{8}$-in. square iron about $10\frac{1}{2}$ in. long ; one

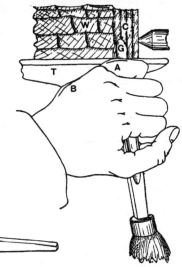

Fig. 1579.—Holding Gouge.

end of the rod is bent upward to form the rest for the hook tool, the other end is forged into a tang and driven into a suitable handle, often measuring 2 ft. long.

CALLIPERS.

The use of callipers has already been mentioned (see p. 12) in connection with the tools used by the carpenter, but the turner uses them almost constantly for some jobs, whereas in ordinary carpentry they are used but seldom. Outside callipers (Fig. 1576) are used for measuring solid cylindrical work, whereas the inside callipers (Fig. 1577) are used for taking the diameters of turned recesses. hollow cylinders, etc. Figs. 1576 and 1577 are half full size. Fig. 1578 is an end elevation of the top of both forms of tool. For small callipers with which to measure up to a diameter of $2\frac{1}{4}$ in., the mild steel should be at least $\frac{3}{4}$ in. wide and $\frac{1}{16}$ in. thick ; a length of $5\frac{1}{4}$ in. is sufficient for outside callipers, and $4\frac{1}{2}$ in. for inside ones. The washers may be $\frac{11}{16}$ in. in diameter.

HOLDING A GOUGE.

Fig. 1579 is intended to show how the wood-turning tool is held upon the rest. The wood, roughly chopped to shape, and cut by the tool at one end, is marked w, the top of the rest is marked T, and the point of the tool G. Wood-turning tools have long handles, to give more power to the turner, who grasps the middle or end of the handle with his right hand. The position of the left hand is important, and that is clearly shown in Fig. 1579; it is with the left hand that the tool is chiefly held and guided. The little finger presses firmly upon the tool at A, and holds it upon the T-rest, whilst the side of the hand at B is supported by the T-rest. The rest at B acts very much as the little finger does in writing; it steadies the hand, and enables it to have a more perfect control over the

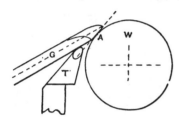

Fig. 1580.—Gouge with Cutting Edge too High.

instrument with which it works. In turning, as well as in carpentering, care must be taken to cut wood with the grain. If in Fig. 1579 the cut were made to the left from the position shown, it would be against the grain, lifting up the fibres of the wood. To avoid this, in turning wood always begin from the highest point—that is, commence on the large diameter, and cut towards the smaller. To do this, draw back the tool to clear the work, then move it to the left, advance it cautiously forward into cut, and then let it slant a little to the right; this produces the series of rings seen at c on the turned part in Fig. 1579. When the work is turned true it will not jerk the tool back, nor touch it intermittently, but evenly. To bring work true in turning requires a steady hand, and it cannot be accomplished if the right hand and body follow the motion of the leg, as is commonly

the case with a beginner; but this difficulty will disappear with practice.

CORRECT HEIGHT FOR TURNING TOOLS.

It is important to hold the tool at the right height upon the rest, and, as the posi-

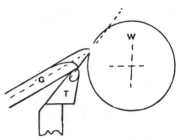

Fig. 1581.—Gouge with Cutting Edge too Low.

tion of the tool depends on the height of the rest, the two should be considered together. Grasp the handle of the tool in the right hand, and hold it close to the right side of the body, a little above the hip; this is the right position for that hand. Place the tool on the rest, as shown in Fig. 1579, approaching it to the work. An inspection of Fig. 1580 will show that, as there held, the tool could not possibly cut. In Figs. 1580, 1581, and 1582, G is the gouge, T the rest, and w is the work; the only difference in these three figures is in the height of the tool and rest. As before remarked, in Fig. 1580 the tool is evidently too high; its point is in the air, and the work simply rubs against the part which has been ground at A. In Fig. 1581 the rest is shown put down too low; here the dotted line from the

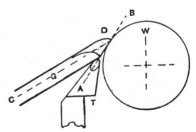

Fig. 1582.—Correct Height for Cutting Edge.

tool edge cuts off too deep a cut from the circumference. In Fig. 1582 the tool is placed at the correct height, and the dotted line in continuation of the tool face appears almost as a tangent to the circle representing the wood. It would be easy to turn with the rest as high as in Fig. 1580 by holding the right hand higher ; also turning could be done with the rest as low as in Fig. 1581 by lowering the tool handle ; but the workman would feel the position awk-

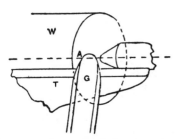

Fig. 1583.—Gouge Applied to End Grain.

ward. The dotted line A B in Fig. 1582 follows the line of the front face of the tool, and must be nearly a tangent to the circle representing the work ; the line C D represents the upper surface of the tool at the middle of the gouge, so that the angle C D A is the cutting angle of the tool. The tool should always be placed so that the front face shall form a tangent to the work, and in grinding the tool the cutting angle C D A must be greater according to the hardness of the material. Soft woods can best be turned by a tool ground to an angle of about 30° If the material to be turned were hard, such as boxwood or cocus, an angle of 45° to 60° would be right ; for brass, as when turning up the ferrule on a tool handle, an angle of 90° is suitable. If the foregoing directions have been understood, a beginner should be able to reduce the rough billet w in Fig. 1579 to circular form as marked at C ; care should be taken not to get depressions, or grooves, through allowing the tool to remain too long in one place ; the tool must be continually moved, so as to cut away the ridges.

GOUGE CATCHING IN THE WORK.

How to manage the gouge so as to cut necks may next be practised, and here the young turner is likely to have a " catch-

in " ; which means that the tool has been presented to the wood so as to draw into it, and, as the wood is in rapid revolution, there is an unpleasant jerk of the tool handle, and often a piece is chipped out of the work. Fig. 1583 shows how a " catch-in " is produced with the gouge : w is the wood in revolution, G is the gouge laid on the rest T. If the gouge is moved up to touch the wood with the side of its edge at A, immediately the edge touches the wood it is drawn into cut ; the pressure on the left side of the gouge causes it to twist in the workman's hand, in spite of his grasp of the handle, and something has to give way. To understand more clearly what happens, stop the lathe, lay the gouge as in Fig. 1583, pressing it into the wood whilst at rest ; with the left hand on the top of the mandrel pulley turn it slowly towards the worker ; the

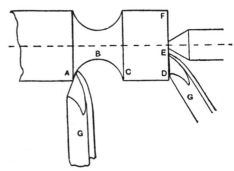

Fig. 1584.—Gouge Applied Correctly.

gouge will twist in the hand, and will not take a proper shaving. The same effect would have been produced had the other side of the gouge been brought up to cut the other end of the work. There are two reasons why a gouge cannot be used in the way shown in Fig. 1583 ; the first is that the hand is not able to prevent its twisting ; and the second, that the edge at A does not form a tangent to the work. If the gouge were flat underneath and ground less acutely, it would be possible so to cut with it ; and this is done with the round-nose tool shown by Fig. 1568, p. 465. This tool, being flat at the bottom, does not twist on the rest, and its edge is not formed so as to draw into the wood. The beginner should remember to cut with the middle of the edge of the gouge; in attempting to cut with the side, as shown in Fig. 1583, he will cause the tool to catch in.

TURNING WITH A GOUGE.

Fig. 1584 shows how a hollow may be cut in the work without applying the sides of the gouge to cut the sides of the groove. The gouge G is laid on its side, in such a way that it is the point, or rounded end, of the gouge which cuts the wood. The gouge is twisted over a little towards its back, because the hollow at A slants; and as the gouge cuts down the rounded side from A to B, it is twisted over still more, till, when it reaches B, it lies on its back. In cutting down the other side of the hollow

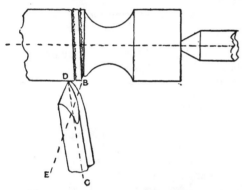

Fig. 1585.—Gouge Applied Incorrectly.

from C, the gouge must be twisted over on its other side, and worked to the middle of the hollow at B; twisting gradually till, when it reaches B, the gouge lies again upon its back. To cut down the end of the wood, as at D E F, then, to begin the cut, the gouge must be laid so that the edge shall be vertical; if not, it will slide away to the left, cutting a spiral line; having cut in about ⅓ in., the gouge will be slightly turned as at G, and the cutting continued to the cone centre. Suppose that the edge of the hollow was somewhat rounded off, and, rounded edges looking slovenly, the gouge is applied at B (Fig. 1585), and turned on its side, so that the edge is not quite vertical. The result will be as shown; the gouge will slide away to the left, making

a spiral cut, and quite spoiling the corner. To avoid this accident, take care that the edge is quite vertical at the point when commencing to cut; as soon as the edge

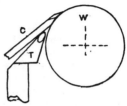

Fig. 1586.—End View of Chisel cutting towards the Right.

has got in about ⅛ in. it may be twisted a little without doing any harm. Also the gouge should not be laid as shown by the solid lines D C, but it should be in the direction of the dotted line B E.

TURNING WITH A CHISEL.

The turning chisel is not shaped at its cutting edge like the carpenter's, but it is ground on both sides. The chisel is not ground square, but slanting, one corner being acute and the other obtuse. The prominent corner will catch in, if allowed to get near enough to the wood. The turner's chisel can be used in two ways: for cutting and for scraping. Soft woods should be worked by cutting, the shavings coming off in strips, and the edge of the tool being presented as shown in Figs. 1586 and 1587. Fig. 1586 shows that, as in the

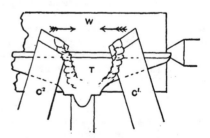

Fig. 1587.—Front Views of Chisels cutting towards Right and Left.

case of the gouge, the under face of the chisel must be presented to the work almost at a tangent; it is well first to lay the tools a little too high, and then draw them down till they cut. Fig. 1587 shows the two positions in which the tool is held. That on the left is the most convenient to a beginner, as the right hand comes close to the right hip, the body facing the lathe. When the position shown on the left is adopted, to finish the right-hand end of the work, the left side of the body is brought close to the lathe-bed. If the chisel were held so that its edge were level, its entire edge would cut if it were possible to keep one corner from getting in deeper than the other. The chisel being twisted so that the edge is slantways on the work, touches only at a point in its width, as shown in Fig. 1587, where the tool edge touches in the middle, and both the corners are free, the edge being near to the horizontal position. The path left by the tool is almost flat—in fact, if the edge were

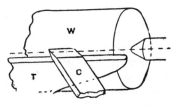

Fig. 1588.—Chisel Applied as a Scraping Tool.

held still, it would cut a very shallow groove. The tool is moved slowly forward as shown by the arrows, in the direction of the obtuse angle, and it should leave a smooth surface, free from ridges. Suppose the learner has used the gouge to true up a piece of wood; he then takes the ¾-in. chisel, and, laying it as shown in Fig. 1587, he cuts carefully along both ways, smoothing off the ridges left by the gouge.

Scraping with a Chisel.

Though a distinct cutting action should always be aimed at, it is perhaps permissible where a very true cylinder is required, and when only a thin shaving is to be removed, to lay the chisel flat on the rest, then, raising the handle or lowering the rest till the chisel edge is in a line with the centre of the work, to scrape lightly the high points. Fig. 1588 shows the chisel as held for scraping. This way of working

suits beginners because they do not have slips and catches-in; it is not a proper way to turn soft wood, as it produces dust and not shavings. In turning hard woods, such as rosewood, cocus, etc., scraping may be proper, but not for oak, beech, etc., which are only hard by comparison with deals. The gouge is never used to scrape; even on the hardest woods it is used as on soft wood; the round-nose tool (Fig. 1568, p. 465) is used where a rounded neck is to be scraped out clean and smooth.

Hollowing with a Gouge.

The way to hold the gouge, when hollowing, is shown in plan at Fig. 1589, where the wood is marked A; the rest, turned round to an angle of about 45°, is marked B; G is the gouge, the ¼-in. one by preference. Fig. 1590 is a front view of the same three parts marked with the same letters; the rest is a little above the centre, and the gouge points downwards. By pressing the point of the gouge into the wood, it would form a slight central cavity; then, by raising the point a little, the side of the edge above the point will begin to cut. The pressure of the cut tends to push the gouge back into the turner's hands; he resists this pressure, and, by continuing to depress the handle, causes the point still to rise and at the same time to move a little forward along the dotted line till it arrives at C (Fig. 1590). The gouge slides forward a little on the rest, and follows the dotted line to C; when it has reached this point, another cut is begun from the centre as before. By this method of hollowing, the wood is really cut away in real curls of wood, and the work proceeds very rapidly. By this method the hollow can be made about 1 in. deep, after which another means of cutting must be adopted. When the hollow is about 1 in. deep, it will be found that, in spite of all one's care, the tool will chatter and produce rough work.

Hollowing a Bowl with a Gouge.

To hollow a bowl, turn the face smooth. Turn a hollow in the centre to give the ⅝-in. boring bit a true start; but, before boring the hole, a mark should be made on the bit to prevent it from boring too deep. **Knock** the bit into a tool handle, and bore the hole, taking care that it is not bored deeper than the mark. When turning the inside of the bowl, the gouge should be held on its side, with its back towards the turner, the thumb of the left hand supporting the

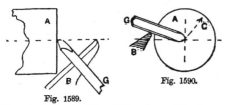

Fig. 1589.

Fig. 1590.

Figs. 1589 and 1590.—Hollowing with Gouge.

back of the gouge, whilst the forefinger takes a firm grip of the T-rest underneath. The actual cuts of the gouge are made towards the central hole, the back of the gouge pressing lightly on the edge from which it is cutting, the edge serving for a fulcrum, from which it makes a steady, sweeping cut. In the hands of a beginner, the turning gouge has a strong tendency to run away from the cut. To overcome this tendency, hold the gouge firm and steady, especially when starting a fresh cut.

DEEP HOLLOWING WITH A GOUGE.

The method of turning a deep hollow with a gouge is shown in Figs. 1591 and 1592, where the wood is supposed to be cut through the centre horizontally, so as to show the action of the tool. In Fig. 1591 the hollowing is supposed to have been begun by the method before described, and carried about 1 in. deep. The rest is now refixed, as in Figs. 1591 and 1592, placing it about ⅛ in. below the centre, so that when the gouge is laid level upon it, its point will come to the centre of the hollow. Begin by pressing the gouge forward into the wood ; if it be held exactly upon the centre, it will bore its way steadily in. By holding it firmly on the rest the centre can be found, and the gouge will become steady in the position shown at Fig. 1591. It should now be turned half over on its left side, as in Fig. 1592 ; this put the left edge of the point in the right position for cutting. The side of the edge by this method is in a fairly advantageous position for cutting,

but the point scrapes. Deal cannot be cut very smoothly thus ; apple, pear, etc., which are much easier woods to turn, come fairly smooth with a sharp tool. A hole 3 in. deep can easily be turned out in the way last described, but at greater depths the work becomes rather difficult. If the hole is large, it is often possible to get the T of the rest into the hole, so as to support the gouge. The position shown in Fig. 1591 is quite correct when turning the bottom of the hole, but when the side of the point is cutting the gouge must be turned as shown in Fig. 1592.

DEEP HOLLOWING WITH A HOOK TOOL.

Suppose it is required to hollow a deep flower vase, the wood should be cut 1½ in. longer than the vase, to allow for chucking. Fix the piece of wood between the lathe centres and turn it roughly, and turn one end of it the size to suit. Drive it into the cup chuck firm and true ; then turn down the end, and bore a hole in it with a nose-bit to facilitate turning inside the vase ; a ⅜-in. or ⅝-in. bit will be best to use. The hole should be bored as deep as the hollow is meant to be. The inside of the vase is

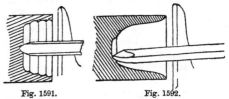

Fig. 1591.

Fig. 1592.

Figs. 1591 and 1592.—Deep Hollowing with Gouge.

turned in the reverse way that the inside of the bowl was done—that is to say, the cuts are made from the central hole, and towards the lip of the vase ; and, as it is too deep and narrow to finish with the gouge, it will afford practice for the hook tool. This is a tool that very few know how to use properly ; and it is little wonder that this is so, as the tool usually sold for this purpose is anything but pleasant to use, being generally far too slim and springy. The hook tool, which is illustrated by Fig. 1574, p. 466, should be 1 ft. 6 in. long, exclusive of the handle, and the shank of the tool should have a section of not less than $\frac{1}{2}$ in. square. The end of the steel rod should be drawn out for about 2 in. in length, and bent to form the hook, which should not be more than $\frac{6}{16}$ in. across the bend, and the end of the hook must be

avoided if the cutting is done with the point only of the chisel. Having the work turned parallel, and cut to length at both ends, A and D (Fig. 1593), mark the distance A B on the wood; then mark the diameter of the

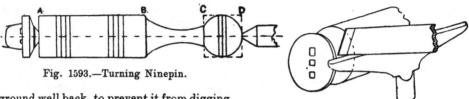

Fig. 1593.—Turning Ninepin.

ground well back, to prevent it from digging into the wood when the tool is in use. The other end of the rod is drawn out and slightly tapered, to form a tang, and the tool is provided with a good stout handle 1 ft. in length. This length of tool and handle may seem excessive, but it is necessary, as the handle of the tool when in use must be held firmly under the armpit, to give the worker a good command over the tool.

Turning a Ninepin.

A ninepin, as shown in Fig. 1593, forms an example that will furnish useful practice to a beginner in turning. The size of the work is of little importance; about 7 in. long and 1½ in. diameter will suit. The method of roughing out with the gouge has been described; the wood should be reduced at both ends to about $\frac{1}{16}$ in. more than 1½ in. diameter, measuring with the callipers, then the whole piece should be turned parallel from end to end, the eye being guided by the sized parts. Then with the large chisel smooth the whole from end to end, reducing it to 1½ in., and cut the ends square, making the wood 7 in. long. The bottom of the ninepin must be cut in with the chisel, so as not to waste a long piece of wood. Fig. 1593 shows the fork-chuck driving the wood. The marks of this chuck must not appear in the finished work as they do in Fig. 1594; the wood is therefore selected longer than required for the ninepin, and the bottom can then be turned true with the long corner of the chisel. To ensure its standing firm, the bottom would be under-cut. The position of the chisel when doing this work is as shown in Fig. 1594, and it easily catches in. This will be

Fig. 1594.—Undercutting Bottom of Ninepin.

work, 1½ in., from D to C, and draw circles at B and C. To turn the neck first, cut straight in at C, leaving the head as dotted; the neck is then brought to size and shape with the gouge and smoothed with the chisel, which, as already explained, can be made to cut flat curves. A practised turner would quickly form the head spherical with no other guidance than that of his trained eye, but the beginner had better cut a 1½-in. circle in a bit of card, and use about one-third of this as a template, applying it to the work to test its shape. Most of the shaping will, of course, be done with the gouge, but the smoothing must be done with the chisel.

Turning the Ballhead of Ninepin.

The reader has already been warned not to cut with that part of the chisel's edge nearest to the acute corner, otherwise a

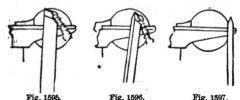

Fig. 1595.   Fig. 1596.   Fig. 1597.

Figs. 1595 to 1597.—Turning Ninepin Ballhead.

catch-in will result. In rounding a sphere the warning is still more important; that part of the edge close to the obtuse corner must be used, and the handle must be held to the left when cutting down the right side of the ball, and to the right when cutting down the left side of it. An inspection of Fig. 1595 shows the tool laid on as it would be for a cylinder; it begins to cut upon the top of the round. In Fig. 1596 the tool handle has been twisted over by the right

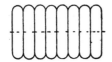

Fig. 1598.—Bead Turning.

hand, and has been moved towards the left. To continue the work, the tool is twisted over still more by the right hand, the handle is gradually raised so as to lower the point, and is also moved towards the right, till it reaches the position shown in Fig. 1597, and stands at right angles to the lathe-bed, the acute corner being uppermost: the obtuse corner, with which the cutting has been done, having reached the centre. The left side of the ball will be treated in a similar way, except that the tool will be reversed. Testing with the card template and observation of the profile will show where the wood needs to be removed, and the cutting is continued till the head is fairly spherical. The production of a really true sphere will require very much more care. The four black lines near the top and bottom of the body, and the three on the head, improve the appearance, if they are uniform in depth and equally spaced; but if unequal, they will look bad. They

gives a polish sufficient for such work as this. The ninepin may now be separated at A (Fig. 1593), by a last cut with the long corner of the chisel, from the little bit which the fork-chuck holds.

BEAD TURNING.

When the directions for turning the ball-head have been mastered, work like that shown by Fig. 1598 may be proceeded with. It is difficult for a beginner to turn a series of beads and have them all alike. A pair of compasses used on the rest will scratch a succession of lines all the same distance apart; then, with the chisel held pointing squarely to the lathe-bed, these marks are cut straight in with the acute corner of the chisel. The right side of each bead is then rounded off with the obtuse corner, after the manner just described; then the chisel is reversed, so as to round off the left side of each bead. Probably the acute corner will be again used to deepen the notches between the beads, and then every bead will require rounding off again on both sides. This work is very good practice for cutting mouldings that have to be uniform.

TURNING TOOL HANDLES.

The many kinds of handles suitable for different kinds of tools afford very good practice. Fig. 1599 shows a handle for a wood-turning tool. It may be of beech or ash. Such tools range from about 10 in. to 2 ft. long, the smaller being 1½ in.

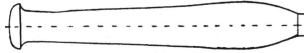

Fig. 1599.—Handle for Wood-turning Tool.

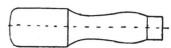

Fig. 1600.—Handle for Chisel and Gouge.

should be **V**-grooves, each made by two cuts with the chisel. The ninepin being finished, it may be smoothed with glass-paper, which is constantly shifted length-ways; if held motionless on the revolving work, it is apt to scratch rings. The lathe may be revolved forwards and back-wards, and, when the work is quite smooth, a handful of turnings held against it removes any grit from the glasspaper, and

diameter at the largest part and 1 in. at the smallest, the ferrule being ¾ in. diameter and about ½ in. long. The enlargement at the small end is intended to support the tool when it is resting in the rack, in which it hangs blade downwards. Fig. 1600 shows one shape of handle used for the numerous chisels and gouges of the carpenter. These handles are about 5 in. long, 1¼ in. diameter at the largest part, and the ferrule is ¾ in. diameter by ½ in. long. This shape may be made rather smaller in diameter, with a ⅝-in. ferrule for tools ½ in. wide and under, and again still smaller, with ½-in. ferrule, for very small

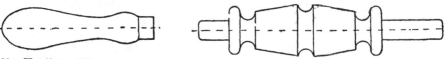

Fig. 1601.—Handle for Files and Metal working Tools.

chisels and gouges. Fig. 1601 shows the shape of handle for files and other tools for hard wood and metals. These handles are about 5 in. long, 1¼ in. diameter at the largest part, and have ferrules ¾ in. diameter by ½ in. long. For the small gravers and small files, such as saw-files, etc., the ferrule may be ½ in. diameter, with a corresponding reduction in the diameter of the handle. In the earlier pages of this book will be found many examples of handles suited for various tools. It is a mistake to introduce beads and mouldings, or to adorn the handles with fancy patterns, etc., as they hurt the hands. To make tool handles, wood should be sawn square, cut into lengths as required, and a number of handles made at once. In making the handles, the part of the wood nearest the lathe centre would be turned down to fit the ferrule first, as shown in Fig. 1602, the callipers being set to the size of the wood.

rosewood would do well—and turn it true at one end. Before fitting it into the ferrules, see that each one is free from roughness inside, and slightly coned out, so that it will tend to compress and not cut the wood

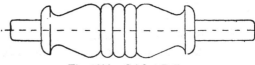

Fig. 1603.—Cricket Bail.

when driven on. This can be done by scraping round the inside edge with the side of a turning tool. Next turn the wood to a slight cone, as in Fig. 1602, till a ferrule can be driven on, and see whether the cylindrical part of the ferrule runs true. The edges will be turned. Fig. 1602 shows how they may be done with a tool like Fig. 1565, p. 465; it is that part marked A which is cutting the edge of the ferrule. The tool needs to be pressed firmly on the rest, that it may not be pushed away from its work, and it will be found that the brass tube is soft, and the edge will come true easily. The other edge and the cylindrical part do not require to be touched now, as they will be done when the ferrule is on its own handle. The corner of the tool should be put inside the ferrule, and the inner arris taken off; it is this trued-up edge which is intended to go on to the handle first. Knock the ferrule off and drive on another, and thus do all

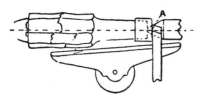

Fig. 1602.—Turning Edge of Ferrule.

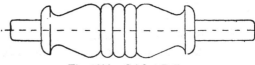

Fig. 1604.—Cricket Bail.

Putting Ferrules on Tool Handles.

Brass ferrules can be bought at the ironmongers', but it is easy to cut them in the lathe from a piece of brass tube. If they have been roughly cut off with a hack-saw, they will be improved by having their edges turned true. To do this, prepare a piece of hard wood like Fig. 1602—boxwood or

the ferrules quickly one after another. The fit of the ferrule on its handle must be tight, so the ferrules will require driving on hard; the trued edge will come up against the turned wood shoulder, and fit neatly, which it could hardly do if not turned or filed fairly square. The outer edge of the ferrule can, when on its own handle, be turned true, as before described. The cylindrical part can be cleaned up with a file applied to it as it revolves in the lathe ; or it could be turned true.

DUPLICATING TURNED WORK.

At Figs. 1603 and 1604 are drawings of cricket bails, the former being rather the easier pattern to turn. Bails may be made

ner, however, will have to spend much time in measurement.

PATTERNS FOR FINIALS AND SPINDLES.

The accompanying illustrations (Figs. 1605 to 1609) show patterns for finials, and Figs. 1610 to 1616 show patterns for spindles suitable for small cabinet work, for

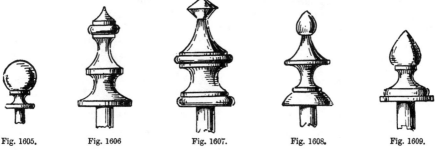

Fig. 1605. Fig. 1606 Fig. 1607. Fig. 1608. Fig. 1609.

Figs. 1605 to 1609.—Patterns for Finials.

of any tolerably hard English wood, such as oak, beech, etc. ; and it is very good practice to turn them, because they must be alike, and both sides of each bail must

supporting shelves, etc. They can be turned by the reader who has learned to do the work already described. The wood to be employed depends, of course, on the mate-

Fig. 1610. Fig. 1611. Fig 1612. Fig. 1613. Fig. 1614. Fig. 1615. Fig. 1616.

Figs. 1610 to 1616.—Patterns for Spindles.

be uniform in pattern. This introduces the next step in turning—the copying or the exact repetition of a pattern A practised turner does this with the guidance of his trained eye alone, or with very slight assistance from rule and callipers ; the begin-

rial used for the rest of the article, but a pattern should be selected which will not easily break if it has any force to withstand. The mouldings must be cut clean, so that the edges be well defined, or the pattern will be lost and the lines will not look firm.

TURNING A HOLLOW VASE.

The reader is now ready to undertake a piece of hollow work; it may as well be a cup, like Fig. 1617. This may be about 3½ in. high and 2 in. in diameter. Choose a sound piece of wood, carefully ascertaining that there are no shakes in it; sound wood is always important, but especially so for work which is to be turned thin. If the chuck to be used is a flanged taper screw

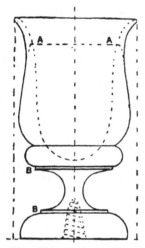

Fig. 1617.— Hollow Vase.

chuck, as shown in Fig. 1551, the wood must be begun upon the fork chuck; but with the plain taper screw chuck shown in Fig. 1552 (p. 462) to work with, a hole may at once be bored in the centre of one end of the wood with the gimlet, and the wood screwed on the chuck for about ½ in. The wood having been thus firmly fixed upon either of the taper screw chucks, first true it up all over with gouge and chisel, and then proceed to the hollowing out. The cup having been hollowed out by one of the processes already described, as shown by dotted lines in Fig. 1617, the outside will be turned according to the directions already given; but the thin stem must be left till last, as it is too weak to support the cup while being turned. Great care must be exercised in cutting the outside of the lip, as the slightest catch-in here, where it is so thin, will spoil the form, and the

cup must be made of a different shape: as, for instance, that dotted at A A. The outside should be finished with very sharp tools, and requires only the finest glass-

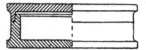

Fig. 1618.—Simple Wooden Box.

paper. In using this it is easy to spoil the work by rubbing down the corners at B B; these should be left quite square and sharp, by folding the glasspaper and applying it carefully, so as not to touch the corner.

BOXES MADE ON THE LATHE.

Wooden boxes may be turned out of two circular discs cut from a plank; but then the fit will not long remain perfect: the top and bottom will shrink crossways of the grain, and both top and bottom will become oval, so that the lid can only go on when the ovals coincide, and cannot be rotated on the bottom. In making boxes with lids, which must fit, a high degree of exactness is required. The quarterings of a tree may be sawn into, say, 6-in. lengths, and chopped into round billets ready for the lathe. These are very suitable for turning boxes, spill cases, cups, etc. etc.; smaller timber, not above 3 in. diameter, may be used whole, only chopping away the bark and the sapwood next to it. Boxes made of the whole round in this way are rather apt to have a little pith in the centre, and to develop radial cracks, so that for turning it is better to cut a piece out of a large tree. It is of great importance that wood intended for a box should be properly seasoned. However dry it is, when cut to form the box it will dry a little more, contracting slightly; this will not matter if the

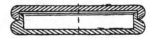

Fig. 1619.—Shallow Wooden Box.

box and lid contract equally, but if the lid be made first and left for a few days (during which it contracts), then if the bottom be made and the lip turned to fit the lid, however well the fit may be made, the result must be disappointing, because the lid has done most of its shrinking when the fit is made, but the box has not; it must follow from this that in a few days the fit will be-

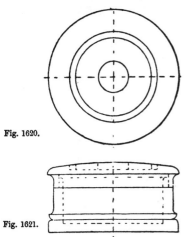

Fig. 1620.

Fig. 1621.

Figs. 1620 and 1621.—Plan and Elevation of Deeper Box.

come loose. If the lid were made, and immediately afterwards the box, then both would shrink together, and the fit would not be disturbed so much. The sun, too, greatly affects such work as this; it is apt to bleach and split the wood; while a hot place on the chimney-piece will often cause such boxes to crack.

DESIGNS FOR BOXES.

Figs. 1618 to 1622 show several designs for boxes, the first four being of shallow type. Fig. 1618 is the simplest, and it only differs from a chemist's wooden tooth-powder box

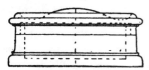

Fig. 1622.—Ornamented Box.

in having a little rim round the top and bottom to assist the fingers when opening it; half of the illustration is in section, to show how the lid is fitted on. Fig. 1619 is all in section; it represents a suitable shape to

contain a photograph, and to go in the pocket. Fig. 1620 is a plan and Fig. 1621 an elevation of a deeper box. It may have rings inlaid in the lid, as dotted; these rings are best shown in Fig. 1620, which is

Fig. 1623.—Cutting Square Side.

a plan view of the top of the lid. The box shown by Fig. 1622 is to be made of hard dark wood; the pattern is more elaborate, and the lid has a returned curve, shown dotted. This shape looks very well at first, but, as dust will always collect in the hollow in the lid, it is better not to adopt it unless the box is to be kept out of the dust. If it be desired to inlay rings of different woods in Fig. 1621, the rings will be prepared as discs about $\frac{1}{16}$ in. thick, as large as the outside of the rings; one side of each disc must be turned flat and the edge turned true. Then, when turning the top of the box, a shallow recess will be made to contain the largest disc, which will be fitted and secured with glue, and squeezed rough side out into its place by the screw of the back-centre, a little bit of flat wood being interposed between the cone point and the disc to distribute the pressure and prevent injury. The glued joint being left under pressure for an hour or so, will be set enough to bear cautious turning, to remove the centre of the first disc for the insertion of the second, which will be fixed in a way

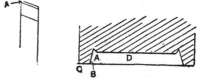

Fig. 1624.—Cutting Point.　　Fig. 1625.—Faulty Cutting.

similar to the first. When the last disc has been inserted, the whole may be smoothed and polished. Holly is the whitest wood, and makes a good contrast with darker kinds. Pieces of holly cut from a tree will do, but they should be barked and boiled, and then piled under cover for from six to twelve months, according to size.

TURNING A BOX.

To make any of the boxes already illustrated, chuck a piece of wood on the taper screw chuck, true it up, and hollow out the end to the depth of the lid. Take care to cut in quite straight with the side of the acute corner of a chisel (see Fig. 1623); the side of the point at A (Fig. 1624) smooths the side. Do not push the chisel too far, or the corner will look like A (Fig. 1625); and do not let the side slant in, as B, or the lid will not hold on. A tin template, like Fig. 1626, will help a beginner; after a while the cut will be made square enough without any guide. The side should be turned very true as well as square; and the shoulder at C, which will become the fitting edge, must be very true and a little lower at the inner edge than the outer, to ensure a good fit. The bottom of the inside of the lid at D can be smoothed by the turner's chisel (Fig. 1624), or an ordinary carpenter's chisel may be used. When the lid is hollowed out, measure its height, and, allowing $\frac{1}{16}$ in. for finishing, make a nick with the chisel where it is to be cut off; then with a tenon-saw placed in the nick, the left hand being laid on the pulley to hold the work from

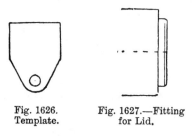

Fig. 1626.
Template.

Fig. 1627.—Fitting
for Lid.

turning, saw a few strokes, and, with the left hand, turn the wood round a little way and saw again; continue thus, sawing gently, so as not to disturb the chucking, till the lid drops off. It will be quite rough from the saw outside. Only the hollowing is done, at B, D D, and the shoulder at C; these parts cannot be touched again, so they must be left smooth and true; a little glasspaper will be applied to D D before it

is cut off, and, having done this, the lid may be laid aside.

COMPLETING TURNED BOX.

Now proceed with the box itself. Turn up the end of the wood, and turn down a short piece to form the lip or fitting on

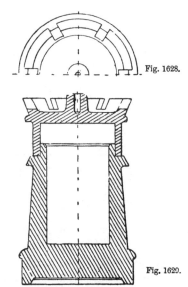

Fig. 1628.

Fig. 1629.

Figs. 1628 and 1629.—Box for Matches.

which the lid is to go (Fig. 1627). This is to be parallel, except at the outer edge where it is bevelled off; this makes it easier to put on the lid, and also facilitates the fitting. The size of the inside of the lid can be taken very exactly with ordinary outside callipers (Fig. 1576, p. 466), by laying them across the mouth of the opening and setting them a trifle too large; the fitting will be turned to this, and when the bevel is made, the lid can be tried upon it—it will enable the turner to judge how much more he has to take off. The shoulder must be cut down perfectly true and rather undercut, to ensure a good joint; then, when the fitting is still a little too large, it is well to hollow out the box, because this sometimes slightly disturbs the fit. Having hollowed the box, complete the lip so that the lid can be pressed on; it must not require much force or it will split, nor must it be too slack or it will come off when its outside is turned, as can now be done. The box and its lid are now so held that all but the bottom of the box can be worked upon; the outside can thus be finished, bringing it to the shape shown in the simple wooden box (Fig. 1618, p. 476); then glasspaper, rub with shavings, polish, and proceed to cut off. In cutting off the box with the parting tool, the handle must be held in close enough to the side to slightly under-cut the bottom, when the cutting off can be quickly performed at one operation, leaving the bottom fairly flat, and sufficiently smooth and even to not need further turning.

plan would facilitate the cutting of the turrets, of which there are six, shown in half-plan at Fig. 1628. These can be cut with a chisel by hand, or by a flat file which may be run through two notches at once, if the central socket be afterwards inserted. The shallow recess turned in the bottom of the box contains a piece of sand-paper on which to strike the matches. This recess cannot be formed with the parting tool when cutting off the box; and to make it, the box must be re-chucked by turning a wooden plug on the taper screw chuck to fit its interior, and pressing the box upon

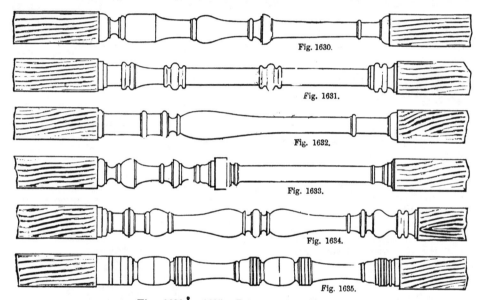

Fig. 1630.

Fig. 1631.

Fig. 1632.

Fig. 1633.

Fig. 1634.

Fig. 1635.

Figs. 1630 to 1635.—Patterns for Balusters.

TURNED BOX FOR MATCHES.

Figs. 1628 and 1629 is a match-box, its form resembling a castle used in the game of chess. Its depth and size would be made to suit any matches it is intended to hold. There is a little socket in the top of the lid intended to hold a lighted wax match while sealing a letter. The hole is easily bored with a bradawl while the lid is revolving in the lathe; by holding the bradawl on the rest, the hole is properly centred. This little socket may be made of a bit of darker and harder wood inserted in the lid, and then turned and bored; that

it. In this position it will be easy to turn the recess. The inside of the box, if properly turned, will be true with the rest; if the plug has also been turned about 1 in. long with a steady hand, and the box is pressed firmly upon it, it will again run true after this re-chucking. Then the bottom can be faced off true and the recess turned. Work of this kind is often required, and will prove a by no means light test of the skill of the turner; for if the box is not hollowed out with a steady hand, it cannot be expected to run true in the lathe when re-chucked.

Figs. 1630 to 1641 are baluster patterns, description of which is not now necessary.

are two ways of tracing a spiral round a cylinder: (*a*) to cause the work to move lengthways on the line of centres—this is done in a lathe with a traversing mandrel;

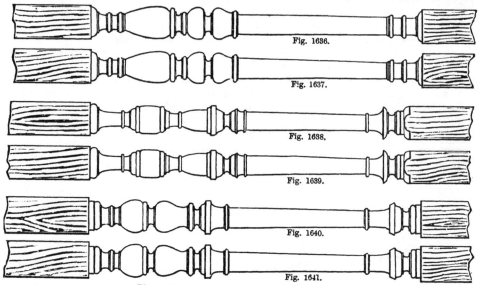

Figs. 1636 to 1641.—Patterns for Balusters.

FACE WORK TURNED ECCENTRICALLY.

Fig. 1642 shows a quatrefoil made by first turning a disc of wood plankways and then re-chucking it eccentrically in four positions, and in each position turning one of the four arcs as shown. A similar plan may be adopted for trefoils and cinquefoils, or for any other number of divisions.

TURNED RING CUT AND REVERSED.

Fig. 1643 shows how a ring may be turned, divided, reversed, and re-joined to form curves of various kinds. For this kind of work the section of the ring must be symmetrical, the inner surface and the outer surface must be alike in pattern, and both sides of the ring must also be alike.

TURNED NEWEL.

Fig. 1644 shows a specimen of turning which in size reaches about the limit of work that can be done on a foot lathe.

CUTTING SPIRALS IN WOOD.

The spirals often seen in wood-turning are seldom done simply by turning. There

(*b*) to cause the tool to move lengthways as the work revolves between fixed centres. In the first case, the screw or spiral is of the pitch of the guide screws fitted to the

Fig. 1642.—Turned Quatrefoil.

lathe mandrel; in the second case, the pitch of screw or spiral depends on the relative speed of the traverse of the tool and of the rotation of the work. For example, 1 in. travel of tool from right to left, to each rotation of the work in the lathe, will give a pitch of 1 in. from centre of each cut to centre of next; the relative speed of movement is determined by change wheels.

The spirals cut by these two methods and others of similar nature are usually of too fine a pitch to be useful in such articles as pillars for whatnots, balusters, candlesticks, and stands. Usually a process of hand-cutting is adopted, which, though not turning, is yet done while the work which has been turned remains on the lathe. A strip of paper the width of the desired thread is wound round the work in a spiral direction, leaving the wood between each turn of the paper uncovered the width the groove is intended to be ; a little gum or glue will fix the paper temporarily, and, the band being removed from the driving wheel, the left hand can govern the mandrel while the right cuts to the desired

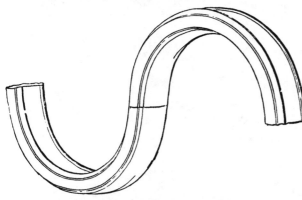

Fig. 1643.—Turned Ring Reversed.

depth in the uncovered space between the coils of paper ; first with a saw, then with gouges, and lastly with rasps and glasspaper. This is easier to do than would appear from the description. If a double twist is desired, two strips of paper are used, both the same width, but of different colours, a space being left for the cut-out portion, and the two spirals are begun exactly opposite each other.

A HANGING CABINET IN TURNERY.

The illustrations (Figs. 1645 to 1647) show a hanging cabinet in turnery or mouche work, which is easily made. This style of turnery has been introduced in many varieties in furniture, screens, stair balusters, etc. Fig. 1645 shows the front of the cabinet, and Figs. 1646 and 1647 show parts

31

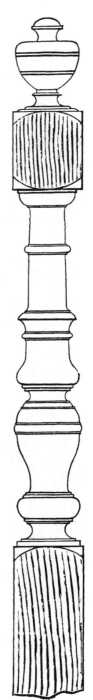

Fig. 1644.—Turned Newel.

of the turnery full size, from which it will be easy to copy.   All instructions necessary

wholly of turned work is shown by Fig. 1648, and as it is fairly elaborate it gives an op-

Fig. 1645.—Hanging Cabinet with Turned Work.

to enable this kind of work to be executed arc given in the preceding pages.

WALL CABINET IN TURNED WORK.

A cabinet which is composed almost

portunity for displaying good workmanship in the turning of the various parts.   The wood to be used may be of any hard, clean, close-grained kind, such as birch, mahogany, walnut, or satinwood—any wood that will allow of the most delicate members in the turned parts being cleanly cut. Such

Fig. 1646.—Detail of Turned Work in Cabinet.

an article as this can be made up almost entirely of scrap wood. Most of the pieces are so small that in any large cabinet-maker's shop abundance of wood is burned that would do for this work. Even if every piece required has to be bought, there is not very much of it to cost much money. Those who have the opportunity of selecting the wood they require out of what they have on hand may begin at once on some of the

Fig. 1647.—Detail of Turned Work in Cabinet.

smaller pieces, such as the short spindles, circles, etc. The only portions of the entire article which are not turned are the two shelves. These form the bottom and the top of the cupboard, and its sides, back, and front, which are placed inside the turned work. The sides and front are not absolutely necessary, as the turned spindles are placed so close together that they themselves are almost sufficient. But dust would get inside the cupboard unless some backing were put behind the spindles; and a thin wood board, covered with silk, cretonne, or any simple material, is the best for this purpose.

How the Cabinet is Built.

In this cabinet there is one principal shelf with rounded ends, and in the centre of it the cupboard is placed. The top of the cupboard forms another shelf. The back frame is fixed up all in one piece, and the

Working Drawings.

It will be as well before commencing the work to have a full-sized drawing of the cabinet, so that the various pieces may be got exactly right. For this purpose drawings should be made as shown in Fig. 1649 the front view, Fig. 1650 the side view, and Fig. 1651 the plan. The illustrations will

Fig. 1648 —Wall Cabinet in Turned Work.

shelves are placed against this. with two quarter-circle brackets supporting the under one. The door to the cupboard is formed of spindle-work all fitted together, and one of the end spindles is made long enough to enter into both shelves, and this forms the hinge by which the door opens. The pillars at the extreme corners of the cupboard, as well as the spindles forming the ends, are let into the two shelves in the same way, but they have to be glued fast and firm.

enable all the sizes to be obtained, as they are printed to scale, and the various parts, dimensions of which are given, conform to these sizes. It may be well to note here that the space between the two principal posts at the back is 10½ in., and the space clear between the two shelves is 8 in. The doorway is therefore 10½ in. by 8 in. clear, and the size over front and back posts is 8 in. These sizes are the principal ones, and should be adhered to ; the others are not so important. The full-size drawing need not be elaborate. Fig. 1652 shows how it may be done; it is sufficient to show the thickness of the wood and the size of the parts. Half of the front view (Fig. 1649)

five finials as shown in Fig. 1654. The three circles are turned as shown in Fig. 1655, the section being shown at A. Every spindle and pillar should be left so that it

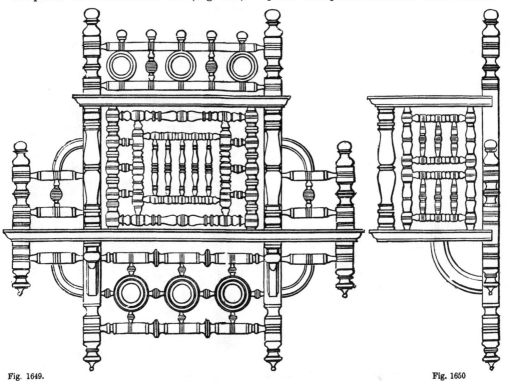

Fig. 1649.   Fig. 1650

Figs. 1649 and 1650.—Front and Side Views of Wall Cabinet.

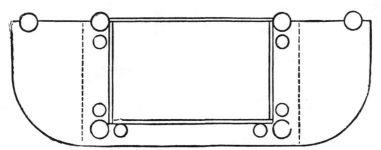

Fig. 1651.—Plan of Wall Cabinet.

and the whole of the end view (Fig. 1650) should be so drawn.

TURNING THE COMPONENTS.

To begin with, four spindles may be turned as sketched in Fig. 1653, and the

may be put in the lathe again to polish after all the turning has been completed. The parts forming the back of the cabinet may next be turned. Fig. 1652 shows the main pieces in the back, several spindles and circles, etc., being afterwards added. The short posts are turned as shown in Fig. 1656, where the dotted lines show the position of the shelf which fits in the cheek formed for

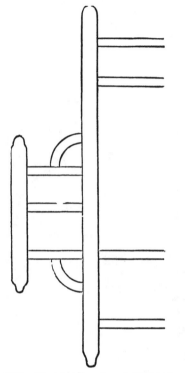

Fig. 1652.—Working Drawing of Wall Cabinet.

it in the post. The long posts (Fig. 1657) have their members exactly the same as the short ones, but there are long plain portions in their centres. The small sketch given shows how the various members are distributed. Two necks will be observed here for the two shelves. The two top rails, which are 1 ft. 2 in. long, are turned as shown in Fig. 1658. The dotted line in the left hand of the illustration represents the

Fig. 1653.—Spindle.

Fig. 1654.—Finial.

distance the rail will enter the post, and the dotted line on the right hand shows the centre of the circle which is to be fixed at

that place. At each point where the centre of a spindle or the centre of a circle comes in the length of the rail, the three beads are turned as here shown. There are six rails, each 6 in. long, for the wings. They are

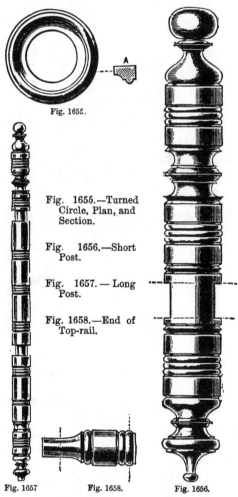

Fig. 1655.

Fig. 1655.—Turned Circle, Plan, and Section.

Fig. 1656.—Short Post.

Fig. 1657. — Long Post.

Fig. 1658.—End of Top-rail.

Fig. 1657.　　Fig. 1658.　　Fig. 1656.

turned as shown in Fig. 1658. The two lower rails, 1 ft. 2 in. long, are turned as shown in Fig. 1659, which illustrates all the different members used in its entire length. The arrangement of circles and spindles between these two rails is shown in Fig. 1660, the section of the circle being given at A. These circles are turned out of pieces 3 in. by 3 in. by $\frac{5}{8}$ in. thick, and the spindles out of pieces 3 in. by $\frac{3}{4}$ in. square. The only other portions of the back are the four quarter circles in the wings, shown in Fig. 1652. These are turned from a piece of wood 5 in.

Fig. 1659.—Half of Lower Rail.

by 5 in. by ½ in. in one circular ring, and this is cut in four and fastened with pins inserted in their ends.

THE SHELVES.

The shelves are next to be prepared. The plans of the two shelves are given in Fig. 1651, that of the lower shelf by a firm

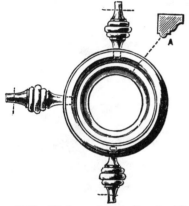

Fig. 1660.—Circle and Spindles in Plan, and Section of Circle.

line, and that of the top shelf by a dotted one. The shelves should be dressed up cleanly and to the exact size required. In doing this, allow for the shelves going

Fig. 1661.—Back Edge of Shelf showing post fitted.

Fig. 1662. — Edge Moulding for Lower Shelf.

halfway back or to the centre of the back posts, as shown in Fig. 1661. The firm line there shows the back edge of the shelf, the

dotted circle the circumference of the post immediately above and below the shelf, and the inner dotted curve the thickness of the

Fig. 1663.—Half of Corner Pillar.

post just where the shelf abuts on it. Along the front and ends an ogee moulding is worked, as shown in Fig. 1662. The cupboard sides and door are next attended to. The two shelves are held together by means of the spindle arrangements forming the gables or sides of the cupboard and the two corner pillars.

Fig. 1664.—Drop Finial to Lower Shelf.

THE CORNER PILLARS, ETC.

The two corner pillars are turned from pieces 10 in. by 1⅜ in. square; Fig. 1663 shows half the pattern on its side. The dotted line is the centre line. The pin at one end must fit tightly into the under side of the upper shelf, which must be bored to

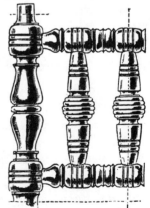

Fig. 1665.—Quarter of Gable Spindleade.

receive them. The pin at the other end may be of the same size to fit tightly into the drop underneath the lower shelf. Fig. 1664 shows this drop, which is turned from wood 4 in. by $1\frac{3}{8}$ in. square, and it has a stouter pin than usual in order to be capable of receiving within it the pin of the corner pillar above. The shelf must, of course,

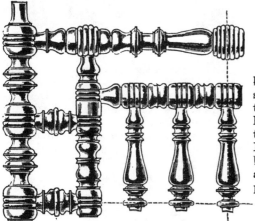

Fig. 1666.—Quarter of Wall Cabinet Door.

be bored to receive the pin of the drop. One quarter only of the gable spindleade is given in Fig. 1665, the other three quarters are repetitions of this one. It is fixed between the shelves by means of the long upright at either end.

The Door Spindleade.

In Fig. 1666 is shown a quarter of the door. The left-hand pillar of the door is the full length between the shelves, but the right-hand pillar is $\frac{1}{2}$ in. longer, and is inserted moderately tightly into the

Fig. 1667.—Section of Quarter Circle Brackets to Lower Shelf.

shelves, but left unglued so that the door may turn on it as on a hinge. The quarter-circle brackets supporting the lower shelf (see Fig. 1650) are turned out of wood 8 in. by 8 in. by $\frac{7}{8}$ in. thick. The circle is 8 in. in diameter outside and $6\frac{7}{8}$ in. inside; its section is as shown in Fig. 1667. Only two quarters are required of this circle, the other half may be laid aside.

Completing Wall Cabinet.

The pine boards are next to be fitted inside the cupboard. The door has its back fitted to it, one size being exactly the space

Fig. 1668.—Plan showing how Door is Hinged.

between the two shelves; the other size should be rather less than the distance between the two corner pillars. The right-hand end piece should be allowed to come to the front, so that the door may open (see Fig. 1668), the left-hand piece standing in behind the door, as shown. It will require a little manipulation to fix these two side pieces properly. The back piece is taken

Fig. 1669.—Specimen of Quasi-square Turning.

over the edges of both shelves, and fits between the posts; a few sprigs into each shelf fix it securely. All the turning should be polished in the lathe; such a plan gives the best result, and at the least expenditure of labour. After that, all the parts should be fixed together firmly and securely. The door should open freely, yet not too easily, as there is no handy method of fastening it when closed. The pine boards

shown at an annual exhibition of the Turners' Company. This was produced by a modification of the method described and illustrated on pp. 463 and 464. The faces of the work are curved, and more nearly approach a straight line as the diameter of

Fig. 1670.—Geometrical Facework Turnery in Soft Wood.

may be covered outside with silk or other material; it might also be advantageous to line the inside as well, using a different coloured material. Since so much time is devoted to the woodwork, it is worth while devoting considerable care to the finishing of the cabinet.

SPECIMEN OF QUASI-SQUARE TURNING.

The illustration shown at Fig. 1669 is reproduced from a photograph of a specimen of so-called square turning which was

the ring increases. The short arcs as shown in the illustration are often hard to distinguish from straight lines, but the difference becomes more noticeable as the arcs are longer. The base of the candlestick illustrated has its curved sides reversed.

GEOMETRICAL PATTERN TURNED IN SOFT WOOD.

The illustration shown at Fig. 1670 shows a specimen of turnery that was awarded a first prize by the Turners' Company. It consists of a centre flower and ornament for a ceiling, turned with ordinary tools out

four blocks forming the primary parts, with paper between them so that they may be

Fig. 1673.—Section of Spindle.

Fig. 1672.—Section of Moulding

Fig. 1671.—Circular Bracket.

of plain deal, and in point of general excellence of workmanship, fitness of design, and symmetry of shape, could hardly be surpassed.

CIRCULAR BRACKET IN TURNERY.

The circular bracket illustrated by Fig. 1671 was awarded a first prize by the Turners' Company. The bracket consists of ordinary turning, some done between centres, some on the face-plate, and some on the oval lathe. Fig. 1671 gives a general view of the bracket; Fig. 1672 is a section of the oval moulding; and Fig. 1673 is a section of one of the spindles on the top of the bracket. First glue together the

easily separated. These blocks are turned between centres. The circular front moulding and the oval side moulding are next turned. The lower part is finished by fixing the turned drop piece (also glued up in halves). The mouldings spring from this drop piece, and at the top butt against squares on which are placed oval rosettes. The top consists of a circular moulding with gallery of spindles, and finished with moulding on top.

VENEERING.

VENEERING is the process by which wooden furniture, fittings, etc., are covered with a very thin layer (the "veneer") of a choicer wood than that employed in the body of the article. The objections to

Fig. 1674.—Veneering Hammer.

veneered furniture—the principal of which is that it is a sham—cannot be entered into here, and the fact remains that if veneering is done well it will last as long as the article it adorns, whilst its decorative effect cannot be gainsaid, and its popularity increases constantly. In the following description of the methods of veneering, the endeavour has been to meet the requirements of those having little experience and few appliances. The broad outlines are those of the processes carried out in cabinet-makers' workshops, but variations in detail are rendered necessary by the absence of a complete veneering plant.

KNIFE-CUT AND SAW-CUT VENEERS.

Veneers are of two kinds—knife-cut and saw-cut; the knife-cut are the thinner, ranging from the thickness of notepaper up to $\frac{1}{16}$ in., the average thickness of the usual woods being thirty-six leaves to 1 in. This kind of veneer is turned off the log in a veneer-cutting machine, similar to a lathe, the wood being fed up to the edge of a long fixed knife, and the veneer coming off as a continuous shaving from 3 ft. to 8 ft. wide, according to the length of

the log. There is little or no waste by this method, and a much handsomer figure is obtained than would be displayed if the veneer were cut off the side of the log. Saw-cut veneers range from 5 and 14 to 1 in., and are cut off the sides of square balks with a thin circular saw about 20 ft. in diameter. Saw-cut veneers are more expensive, wear longer, and are more difficult to lay.

VENEERING HAMMER AND CAULS.

The veneering hammer, Figs. 1674 and 1675, is used, not as a hammer, but as a scraper, and consists of a piece of hardwood about 4 in. by 5 in. by 1 in., with a piece of stout hoop-iron or steel fitted tightly into a saw-cut in its lower edge. The iron has its working edge rounded with a file and rubbed bright on an oilstone to make it slip easily. A handle about 9 in. long is wedged into the head at an angle of about 95° with the face. Knife-cut veneers are laid generally by the aid of this hammer, whereas saw-cut veneers are laid with

Fig. 1675.—Head of Veneering Hammer.

cauls and clamps. Cauls are blocks of wood or thin pieces of wood faced with zinc and made the exact reverse of the surface to be veneered. For flat surfaces the caul is about 1 in. thick and is planed up true and gauged to uniform thickness; this is heated and laid on the veneer, then both caul and work are clamped together with such appliances as are available and are left to cool.

PREPARING GROUND OR CORE FOR VENEERING.

The tools required for hammer veneering with mahogany the end of a cabinet or sideboard are a veneering hammer, toothing plane, large pot of glue, large glue brush, sponge, flat-iron, piece of soap, veneer knife, and a few pins. The wood to be veneered, called the ground or core, should be soft, thoroughly dry, and free from knots and sapwood; if there are knots, these must be cut out and the holes filled in with a freshly made mixture of glue and plaster-of-Paris. The ground should be cut to its finished size, planed quite true with the trying plane, but not smoothed, and the heart side of the wood used for the face side, as in Fig. 1676, where the top side A is the surface to be veneered. The other side would cast hollow on the

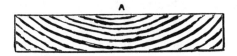

Fig. 1676.—Side of Board to be Veneered.

face. Joints in the ground or core should be well made, or the veneer will break them when shrinking, and all imperfections will show through the veneer. Well tooth the ground the way of the grain, and if a toothing plane is not at hand a fairly good makeshift is a piece of No. 2 glasspaper held tightly over a planed wood block; this must be rubbed in long strokes from end to end of the work without crossing. About twenty minutes before glueing on the veneer, slightly damp the face of the ground with warm water and stand the piece with its back towards a fire, which will cause the face to cast round, and so compensate for the hollowing occasioned by the shrinkage of the veneer. When sufficiently cast, brush some thin glue in the face, and when this is dry the ground will be ready for applying the veneer.

PREPARING VENEER.

Examine the leaf of veneer for splits or other faults, and if any are found glue over them on the face side a piece of thin strong paper, first bringing the edges of the shake or split close together. With a knife cut the veneer to size, using a straightedge, and being careful to have it lying solid on a clean bench or board; its size should slightly exceed that of the ground, say $\frac{1}{16}$ in. all round. Next turn the veneer over and well tooth the back, working the plane in long parallel strokes equally all over to produce a uniform roughened surface which will hold the glue. To hold the veneer whilst toothing, with a strip of wood across it gripped firmly with handscrews, fasten it down at the tail of the bench by the end, so that in planing the pull will be away from the fixing.

VENEER PINS.

Veneer pins are made of very fine wire, from $\frac{1}{4}$ in. to $\frac{3}{4}$ in. long, and without heads; they are used for temporarily fastening the veneer in place, the shorter ones being finally punched through the veneer into the ground, and the longer ones being turned over when driven sufficiently and eventually pulled out again.

LAYING VENEER.

Fix the ground or core to the bench by securing slips around it with brads. Have the glue boiling hot and of a consistency to run from the brush freely. It must be just so thin that it can be spread easily with the brush in a film like paint, but not so thin that it sinks directly into the wood, leaving the surface dry. A good method of testing its consistency is to take a pinch from the brush with thumb and finger; at first these should rub over each other easily, but after a couple of seconds a distinct pull should be required to separate them. Have also at hand an ordinary laundry flat-iron, either made black hot on a stove, in which case a damp linen rag must be interposed between the iron and veneer when using, or, better, have it standing in a bowl of boiling water.

Take the veneer and lightly sponge the face side with hot water, thus making it curl up, then rub a little yellow soap on the surface. Turn it over, and quickly glue the back, dipping the brush alternately in the glue and the boiling water; this will cause the veneer to go flat again. Then proceed rapidly to coat the ground likewise with glue, but more freely, care being taken that the ground is fixed securely to the bench. Lift the veneer by the two ends, place it in position, letting the middle touch the ground first. With the hands spread it out flat, slide it in its right position; then drive in two short veneer pins near the middle to keep it from moving. With the left hand take the head of the veneering hammer with the handle turned away (see Fig. 1677); commence in the middle of the veneer, and scrape towards each end in straight overlapping strokes so as to cause the veneer to lie close and expel the air. A quantity of the glue beneath the veneer should be got away; rub the face of the hot flat-iron with soap, and pass it quickly all over the veneer to melt the glue; again, commencing in the middle, with the head of the hammer in the left hand and the handle in the right, work it with a wriggling motion towards the edges, driving the glue before it. Keep it well soaped, or the veneer will be torn up; and if at any place the glue does not run freely, apply the hot iron for a moment, and follow up with the hammer immediately. Having got rid of the superfluous glue, with the hammer handle tap the veneer all over to test if it is down all over; if not, the faulty places or blisters, when struck, will be betrayed by the hollow sound.

BLISTERS IN VENEER.

Blisters may generally be laid by placing a wet rag on the spot, and resting the hot iron on this for a short time; the steam generated will be driven through the veneer and soften the glue, a few vigorous rubs with the hammer completing the operation. Occasionally blistering arises through insufficient glue having been laid on the ground, or through using

sapwood insufficiently sized; such blisters are difficult to lay, and in bad cases a piece of the veneer may have to be carefully cut out with a knife, glued, and replaced; such a cut should be in the shape of an irregular oval, the end of the cut finishing neatly into the commencement. Having laid the veneer, remove all glue from the surface and edges. To do this go over it lightly and quickly with a sponge damped in hot water, the object being to remove the glue with as little water as possible. Then turn the veneered surface down on the bench top or other flat surface with a piece of paper between the two, and weight down for twelve hours; or put the work into a press.

LAYING AND PATCHING FANCY VENEERS.

Mahogany, wainscot oak, Hungarian ash, Italian walnut, and amboyna veneers may all be laid as described; but pollard oak,

Fig. 1677.—Method of Using Veneering Hammer.

burr walnut, and bird's eye maple require previous damping and placing between two flat boards either weighted down or hand-screwed together for several hours to flatten the veneer. Any faulty places in the burr or pollard oak veneers can be made good by cutting in pieces with a fine fret or marqueterie saw and pasting or glueing strips of paper over the faces of the joints. When cutting in these pieces, lay the repairing piece on top of the place to be filled, mark round a line sufficient to cover the fault, endeavouring to make the line coincide with any marking in the figure, bore a hole with a fine bradawl, and insert the saw; then cut through both veneers with an inclined cut, so that the patch will be larger than the hole; round the edges rub some glue coloured to match the wood, and place the patch in position, rubbing it down with the bench hammer face; then paste on the paper, and when dry the veneer will be ready for laying.

Veneering Tops of Sideboards, etc.

Sideboard and cabinet tops whose edges as well as the surface require veneering should have these edges veneered first, and, when dry, cleaned off flush and then the upper surface veneered. The end grain wood in the ground should be rubbed over with thick glue to fill up the pores, and, when dry, toothed before laying the veneer. It is customary in the cheap cabinet trade to cross-band all edges—that is, to lay the veneer with the grain running across the edge instead of with it, thus falsifying the

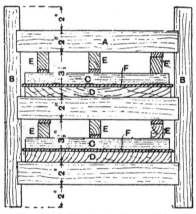

Fig. 1678.—Veneerer's Frame Cleat.

construction. In such instances the veneer is more liable to rise than when straight-banded.

Laying Veneers with Sandbag.

Ogee and other intricate curved surfaces, such as moulded work, shaped drawer fronts, console table legs, etc., cannot be veneered with the hammer, and are usually laid with the sandbag. This is a thin canvas or stout calico bag or pillow, filled with silver sand, large enough to reach over all the turns in the wood; it is used with a rough caul—that is, a block of wood straight on one side and cut on the other to a rough approximation of the curves of the work; sometimes it is necessary to have several

cauls on one piece of work. The sand is made as hot as possible in an oven or on a hot plate, then poured into the bag, the open end of which is afterwards turned over into a hem and pinned. The ground and veneer being glued, the latter is gently pushed down into the hollows with a stick laid crossways. The veneer is covered with paper and the sandbag placed on it, the sand being worked into all the turns, so that it everywhere covers the veneer; then the cauls are brought into the most suitable positions and screwed down tight with handscrews until the glue runs out at the edges. The bag should be left on at least twelve hours; then the veneer is cleaned off with the scraper and glasspaper.

Veneering Round Work.

Having made, say, a drawer and prepared its swelling front true to the sweep and straight across, size it as previously described, then tooth the ground and veneer; next damp the veneer well on the face side, which will cause it to curl round. Bed it well down on the front, turn both over, and mark the outline of the front on the back of the veneer. With the veneer knife cut the latter off, a shade full to the lines; then take a strip of calico the width of the drawer front, turn in one end double, and tack it down on the drawer side near the end. Glue and place the veneer in position, and stretch the calico over it, tacking the loose end down on the drawer side; damp the calico with hot water, which will cause it to shrink and pull tight, then go over the calico with the veneering hammer, squeezing out all the superfluous glue as previously described.

Laying Saw-cut Veneer with Cauls.

This method of veneering is more suitable for shaped work than the hammer method, and is imperative in the case of sawn veneers. The caul is a block or slab (whichever is more convenient) of pine shaped accurately to fit the surface to be veneered; in the case of a flat surface such as a pilaster, which has afterwards to be carved or fluted, the caul is made quite true on the face, and when the veneer is glued and laid on the ground, the caul, after being heated at a clear fire, has its surface rubbed with soap, and is laid in place and nipped tight to the work with as many handscrews as are available. Fig. 1678 shows a useful cleat for tightening the caul c when the surface is too wide to be covered with handscrews. It is made of 2-in. by 3-in. stuff, and the bars A, against which

Fig. 1679.—Veneerer's Frame Cleat.

the wedges E press, are housed into the side pieces B, and the latter are fastened with wire nails. The cleat is shown with a central bar, making it available to wedge up two veneers F at a time; further, when the veneers are not very large, two may be laid at once in each opening if a sheet of paper is placed between them. These cleats are placed from 12 in. to 15 in. apart, and Fig. 1679 illustrates a cleat to be used when the surface to be veneered is not large, such as the end of a sideboard; in this case, no caul is used, but the veneer and ground, after being made very hot, are glued and placed in the cleats, and cross bearers, planed hollow in their length, are laid on the veneer and wedged tightly down as shown. The cleats should not be more than 1 ft. apart, and between them handscrews should be placed round the edges.

THE VENEERING BOX.

Another contrivance which an amateur will find very handy in veneering small surfaces is shown in Fig. 1680. This is a pack-ing-case or cube-sugar box with the top and bottom removed, and the sides strengthened by lengths of hoop-iron bound round and fixed with short "town clouts." The holes in the iron to receive these may be made with a small nail punch or a broken bradawl, the iron being bedded upon a block of wood endways of the grain. To veneer with the box, having glued and fixed the veneer with four pins at the corners as described previously, place the work in the box, resting the ground on two or three narrow strips, as shown in Fig. 1680, the strips being planed straight and packed out of winding; then place similar strips on the veneer, but crossing the lower ones, and cut struts between them and the top of the box, driving these in tightly and commencing at the middle, so that the glue may be forced out towards the sides. The struts should be moved a few inches at a time until the glue is worked out, when they can be left as shown. If the piece is too long to be covered at once by the box, it may be moved forward as the

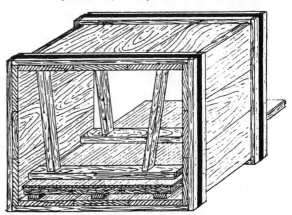

Fig. 1680.—Veneering Box.

glue is worked out, but the advanced part should have a handscrew placed at each end of a cross strip, to prevent the veneer rising again.

LAYING KNIFE-CUT VENEER WITH CAULS.

Fig. 1681 illustrates the method of laying a knife-cut veneer with a zinc-faced caul on an ogee truss. The core G is shaped and checked out for the veneer, and the top edge of the veneer is fixed with veneer pins, and

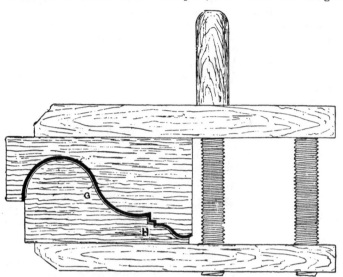

Fig. 1681.—Veneering Shaped Work with Caul.

the remainder worked down into the sweep and pinned at the bottom. The cross strip of veneer at H is next rubbed on, and the smaller ogee covered, no veneer being placed on the lower horizontal edges. Then the zinc-faced wood caul, made very hot and soaped, is laid in place and nipped with the handscrew. When the caul method is used for knife-cut veneer the glue should be stained to match the veneer, because by the pressure it is forced through the substance, and if different coloured will spoil the appearance, especially in the light-coloured woods. A suitable glue for these can be made by mixing flake white or powdered chalk with the ordinary glue until it becomes cream colour; for red woods use alkanet root or red ochre as a stain, and for yellow woods such as oak or ash use yellow ochre.

Cleaning Off Veneered Work.

For this purpose, a metal smoothing plane set very "fine" may be used for sawn veneers; for knife-cut veneers no planing

should be attempted; merely go over the work with the toothing plane to level it, and then bring it to a smooth surface with a sharp scraper, finishing off with fine glass-paper.

Veneering Picture Frames.

The kind of picture frame illustrated by Fig. 1682 is known as a plain chamfer, and there is quite a simple method by which such a frame may be veneered without the necessity of taking it to pieces. Veneer $\frac{1}{8}$ in. thick can only be laid with cauls; and a suitable one is shown, and also the method of fixing it. The dotted outline of the caul is shown in section in Fig. 1683, with the veneer between it and the base. If the frames are polished, remove the polish carefully with a sharp scraper; avoid working the surface into holes, but leave it rough from the scraper. Cut the veneer to a

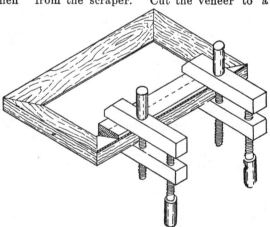

Fig. 1682.—Veneering Picture Frame.

width that will allow sufficient margin for bevelling, as shown in Fig. 1682, and tooth or scratch the under face with a saw. Shoot the inside edge to a correct bevel, cut to a mitre and shoot the ends in a mitre shoot, bedding the veneer either on a piece of the moulding or on a waste piece chamfered to the same angle ; this is to obtain a vertical face to the mitre. Next prepare the caul

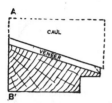

Fig. 1683.—Section of Frame, Veneer, and Caul.

(as shown in Fig. 1683) out of a piece of deal. The caul should be ¼ in. shorter than the veneer, and mitred at each end, not cut square as shown in Fig. 1683, which is drawn thus for clearness. Make the caul slightly round in length and bevelled, so that the two surfaces marked A B are quite parallel. Well glue the veneer and the frame, lay the veneer in the proper position, place a strip of paper on the surface of the veneer, and lay the caul (preferably hot) upon this paper and fix with handscrews as shown ; the more screws the better. Take care that the inside edge of the veneer is flush with the edges of the frame. Proceed to fix the opposite side in like manner ; then wipe off the superfluous glue with a rag dipped in hot water, and wash the mitres clean ; then fit in the two end pieces, which can be fixed in the manner described for the sides. Allow twelve hours to dry, then clean off the back edges and scrape up the faces. The in-

side edges may be gilded or stained black, or a small chamfer might be worked as shown by the dotted line in Fig. 1682.

RENOVATING VENEERED FURNITURE.

Unless veneer is very badly damaged it is better to replace defective portions with new veneer ; small places can be filled in with a mixture of equal parts of beeswax and resin melted in an old iron spoon or ladle ; to it should be added a little dry colour—Venetian red for mahogany, and umber for walnut. Press it with a slip of wood, level off with a knife or chisel, and finally smooth down with glasspaper. The old veneer may be removed by heating a flat-iron and pressing it well against the veneer ; the latter can then be readily prised up by means of a stout knife or chisel. The old glue can be removed with hot water and rag. If fresh veneer has to be relaid, prepare a piece of wood as large as the damaged surface, and heat it in an oven to make a caul. Remove the old veneer, and coat both the new veneer and woodwork with thin glue sparingly applied ; then secure the veneer to the work and hot wood caul with handscrews. A piece of paper should be placed between the veneer and the hot caul, so that no glue will reach the caul, or the work will be spoilt. Repairs to veneer are best done with V-shaped or oval-shaped pieces, making the grain agree as nearly as possible. A piece of paper glued over the repair will exclude the air and improve the joint. Scrape off all grease and dirt wherever veneer is to be applied.

OFFICE, LIBRARY, AND STUDY FURNITURE.

HANGING NEWSPAPER RACK.

NOT much skill is required to make the newspaper rack shown by Fig. 1684, as all the joints are plain butt joints, with the front I to the shelf F should be as strong as possible, and it is for this reason that the brackets are dovetailed into I, as shown in Fig. 1686. When the shelf and brackets are

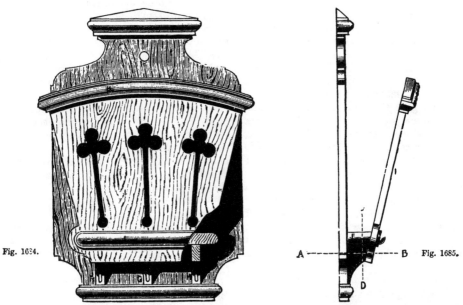

Fig. 1684.　　Fig. 1685.

Figs. 1684 and 1685.—Front and Side Elevations of Hanging Newspaper Rack.

exception of the dovetailing of the brackets into the front, and even here butt joints can be used if wished. The shelf E (Fig. 1685) and brackets F, G, H (Fig. 1684) should

all fixed to the front, their edges, which butt against the back, may be planed up together. The cocked bead J is for the purpose of concealing the screws which fasten

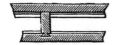

Fig. 1686.—Dovetailing of Brackets.

Fig. 1687.—Successive Sections of Moulding.

be made of thicker stuff than the back and front pieces, as they have to receive screws in their edges. The attachment of the

I to the shelf E. J is dowelled on after the screws are driven in, but the corresponding holes for the dowels are best bored by putting J into place and boring through I into J before the shelf is attached; care must, of course, be taken that the holes do not pierce J. In making this bead, the neatest

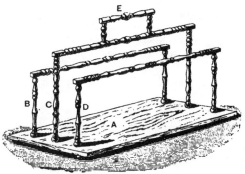

Fig. 1688.—Newspaper Rack in Turned Wood.

result is obtained by shaping and glass-papering the two parts separately, and then gluing them together. The radius of the curved moulding K is 2 ft., and this may be made without a template by reducing it into the successive sections shown in Fig. 1687. This is done with chisel and gouge, finishing with a bull-nose plane. To mark out the centres of the dowels for fastening the curved moulding, lay on the curved edge of I ordinary pins with their heads situated where dowels are required. K being put in place, a smart knock on the top will impress the heads of the pins in both pieces. The straight mouldings may be made and attached in the same way as the curved one, and this will ensure sound-

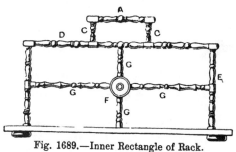

Fig. 1689.—Inner Rectangle of Rack.

:ness af the returns, which are worked out of the solid. In marking out the trefoils on the front, note that, on account of the radial slot running into the trefoil, the

lower lobes have their centres a little higher than they would be if the three were equidistant. The trefoils are made entirely with the centre-bit.

NEWSPAPER RACK IN TURNED WOOD.

A general perspective view of a newspaper rack in turned woodwork is shown in Fig. 1688; the rectangles are filled in as in Fig. 1689, the filling being omitted from Fig. 1688 for the sake of clearness. It consists of a baseboard A, on which are fastened three rectangles B, C, D. The centre one of these is taller than the rest, and has a handle. The baseboard has a turned foot at each corner, secured by a screw passing through its centre. The baseboard is about 1 in. thick, and its edge is moulded all round. It may be made of polished wood, or of deal covered with plush; if of the latter, the holes are bored for the reception

Fig. 1690.—Outer Rectangle of Rack.

of the uprights before covering. The rectangles may be made of any pattern, Fig. 1688 being a suggestion. Of the middle one (Fig. 1689), A is the turned wood handle, fastened on by two short pieces C; D is the horizontal; E, two side pieces; F, a rosette fastened on centrally to four pieces G. The exact length and diameter of each piece must be determined upon before any rectangle can be made. All the pieces are connected together by means of tenons, $\frac{1}{4}$ in. in diameter, at the ends. The distance between the axes of the side pieces is, say, exactly 1 ft., the rosette is 2 in. in diameter, and the uprights E are 1 in. in diameter where the horizontals G meet them; then the length of the horizontal pieces G, exclusive of the tenons, will be $4\frac{1}{2}$ in. In the same manner, if the length of each of the pieces E from the point where they meet D to the baseboard is 8 in., the length of each of the vertical pieces G will be 3 in. When the exact length of each piece has been settled, they may all be turned, and should be neatly finished and highly polished. The lower ends of the vertical pieces should have tenons, so that they can be fastened to the baseboard. The two outer rectangles are constructed in the same manner, and are glued into the baseboard, as

HANGING THREE-DIVISION MAGAZINE OR NEWSPAPER RACK.

The magazine rack illustrated by Fig. 1691 is designed to hold nine ordinary sized magazines with the title pages in front, thus enabling a person to see at a glance the magazine required. Fig. 1691 shows a front view, Fig. 1692 a side view, and Fig. 1693 a

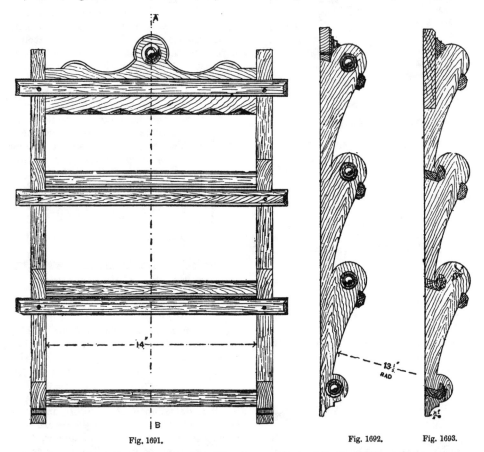

Fig. 1691.   Fig. 1692.   Fig. 1693.

Figs. 1691 to 1693.—Front Elevation, Side Elevation, and Vertical Section of Three-Division Rack.

little glue as possible being used; otherwise the excess will ooze out, and spoil the appearance of the work. Fig. 1690 shows another design for the rectangles, or it may be taken as the design for the outer rectangles, whilst Fig. 1689 serves for the middle one.

vertical section of the rack, which can be made in oak, walnut, or mahogany, and polished, or in one of the pines (pitchpine would look well) varnished. The sizes of the material required when planed up are : One piece for the back, 1 ft. 4½ in. by 5¼ in. by ¾ in. ; two pieces for the sides, 2 ft. ¾ in.

by 3⅛ in. by 1 in. ; three pieces for the shelves, 1 ft. 4½ in. by ½ in. by 1 in. ; three pieces for the back rails, 1 ft. 3½ in. by ½ in.

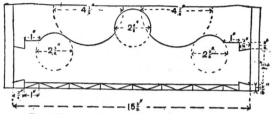

Fig. 1694.—Setting out Back of Rack.

by 1 in. ; three pieces for the front rails, 1 ft. 5 in. by ½ in. by 1 in. Each length is 1 in. more than the finished size. Set out the piece for the back as shown in Fig. 1694 ; cut the curved parts with a bow saw, and finish with a spokeshave, afterwards working a chamfer ¼ in. wide round a part,

4 in., while the other three will be 1 ft. 2½ in. long. Next set out the two sides as shown in Figs. 1698 and 1699, the latter showing

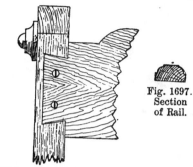

Fig. 1697.
Section
of Rail.

Fig. 1696.—Joint of Back to Side of Rack.

the back edge. Cut the curved parts with a bow saw, and finish with a spokeshave and wood file. Then place the dovetailed

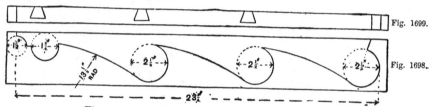

Figs. 1698 and 1699.—Setting out Side of Rack.

as shown in Fig. 1694. Next on the lower edge work the stop-chamfer mould, an enlarged detail of which is given by Fig. 1695. It is worked for ⅜ in. on both the face and lower edge. The back is connected to the sides by means of a dovetail on each end, as shown in Fig. 1696.

MAKING THE RACK.

Next prepare the three shelves—the full length is 1 ft. 3½ in.—dovetailing both ends of each for ¾ in. Work the ovolo mould on the edges of the six rails, as shown in the

Fig. 1695.—Stop-chamfer Mould.

sections (Figs. 1693 and 1694); return the mould across the ends of the three long rails, the full length of which will be 1 ft.

ends of the shelves in position on the back edge of the sides ; mark the outline of the dovetails, sloping the shelves ¼ in., as shown in Fig. 1693. Cut the slots with a saw and chisel, and fix the shelves temporarily, one

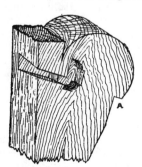

Fig. 1700.—Part of Side ready for Shelf and Rail.

side at a time. Apply the ends of the short rails to the sides, the backs of the rails fitting close to the front edge of the shelves.

Mark round the ends of the rails on the sides, and, taking out the shelves, cut the housings as marked ¼ in. deep, as shown in

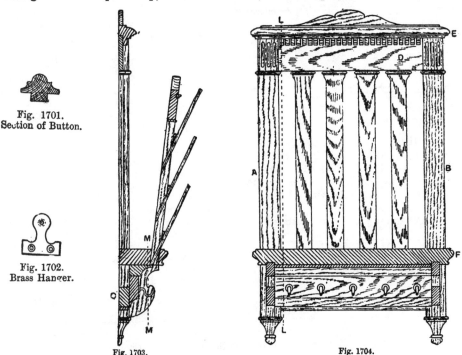

Fig. 1701.
Section of Button.

Fig. 1702.
Brass Hanger.

Fig. 1703.

Fig. 1704.

Figs. 1703 and 1704.—Sections and Back Elevation of Combination Rack.

Fig. 1700. Next cut out the notch A (Fig. 1700) on the front edge of the sides for the front rails, the depth being equal to the width of the square left on the top edge of the rail after the mould is stuck. Place the back on the edge of the sides, mark, and cut out for the dovetail. After cleaning up the pieces, put them together, first placing the short rails into the housings on the sides; then fix the shelves into the sides, and secure the rail to the front edge of the shelf by screwing from the back edge with 1¼-in. screws. Secure the back to the sides with 1½-in. screws, as shown in Fig. 1696, and the front rails to the sides with 1-in. round-headed brass screws. The buttons (as shown in section by Fig. 1701) for ornamenting the sides can be turned in the lathe. Holes to receive the dowels should be bored with a centre-bit, and the buttons glued in. The rack can be hung

with small brass hangers, as shown by Fig. 1702; or the shape shown by Fig. 822, p. 250, can be employed. It should be understood that Fig. 1693 is a vertical section taken on the line A B (Fig. 1691).

COMBINATION RACK FOR NEWSPAPERS, LETTERS, AND KEYS.

A vertical section of a rack to receive letters, newspapers, and keys is shown by

Fig. 1705.—Joints at   Fig. 1706.—Horizontal
Top Corner.   Section of Top of Rack.

Fig. 1703; Fig. 1704 shows the back portion, and is a section taken on M M (Fig. 1703). The back consists of a frame fitted with vertical bars. The side pieces A and B and the horizontal bar C are each about

1¼ in. wide by ⅜ in. thick, and c is connected by a stopped dovetail halving or mortise-and-tenon joint. The lower ends of A and B are cut to the ornamental shape

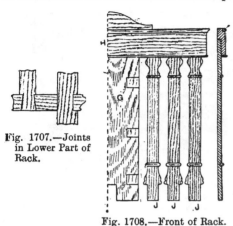

Fig. 1707.—Joints in Lower Part of Rack.

Fig. 1708.—Front of Rack.

shown. The top rail D (Fig. 1704), with curved top, is made thinner and connected to the other parts by a joint shown in Fig. 1705, which is a view from the back. Fig. 1703 is a section on L L (Fig. 1704). A solid strip of wood E is attached as shown in Figs. 1705 and 1706, the latter being a horizontal section taken through the centre of this strip; A and B are cut back and have dovetail pins at their top ends, which are let into the piece E. Fig. 1706 also shows the section of D where it passes through E.

slats or bars which fill in this frame are about ¼ in. thick, and are attached easily by means of dovetail joints (see Figs. 1705 and 1706). Their lower ends are fastened to a cross-piece F (Fig. 1704), which is screwed to A and B from the back; A and B are notched as shown in Fig. 1706. Below F is a cavetto moulding, extending between the two brackets, which are housed into F. Below this moulding is a strip, which carries a number of hooks for hanging keys upon, and this may be secured by screws passing through c (Fig. 1703). The inclined front (half shown by Fig. 1708) consists of a nearly vertical part G let into a horizontal part H (as shown in Fig. 1703), the two forming a T-shaped piece. Three pieces, as shown in Fig. 1709, and carried by G, form the letter rack. A sort of oblique bridle joint is shown in Figs. 1703, 1708, and 1709, as the means of uniting the letter-rack fronts to G; and in Fig. 1703 are seen little fillets glued in the angles in order to strengthen the joints. Six shaped slats J (Fig. 1708) are dovetailed into H and pass through F. A little beaded strip is glued to the bottom edge of H, and a small moulding is attached to the top.

NEST OF PIGEONHOLES.

A nest of pigeonholes for ordinary office use should contain at least twenty-six holes, one for each letter of the alphabet, though

Fig. 1709.—Design for Letter Rack.

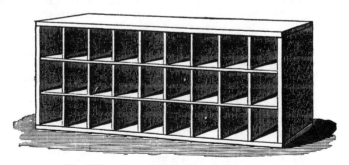

Fig. 1710.—Nest of Plain Pigeonholes.

The lowest member of E is cut away at each end to fit the side pieces, and the intermediate part is formed into dentils with saw and chisel. The four vertical

as that number is an inconvenient one to deal with, it is usual to have twenty-seven (as in Fig. 1710), or only twenty-four. The material may be pine, clean and free from knots; the thickness may be ⅜ in., though the case may be ½ in. thick if thought advisable. The depth from back to front is not important; it may be just the width of

Fig. 1711.—Joint of Partition and Shelf.

Fig. 1714.—Nest of Ornamental Pigeonholes.

the board from which the job is to be made. As the wood will probably have an irregular edge, it must be set out from the narrowest part, and this should not be much less than 9 in. After the wood is planed smooth, with the aid of the square cut off two pieces 2 ft. 3 in. long, and two 1 ft. long. These form the top, bottom, and ends of the case, and are nailed or otherwise jointed together. The shelves are now cut to fit tightly within the ends. They are the same width as the top and bottom, and should be cut with perfectly square corners. Do not fasten them in until the partitions are ready and the grooves are cut for their reception. The joint of the shelves and the partitions is shown nearly full size by Fig. 1711; the edge of the partition is sunk in a groove cut for it in the

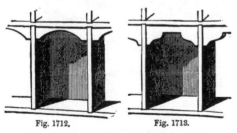

Fig. 1712.   Fig. 1713.

Figs. 1712 and 1713.—Pigeonholes with Ornamental Brackets.

shelf. This is quite strong enough for the purpose. The width of the grooves is just enough to allow of the partitions fitting

tightly into them. To mark and cut these grooves, at equal distances from each other, mark out, either with compasses or by other convenient means, the positions of the divisions, remembering that at the ends of the shelves the spaces must be shorter by half the thickness of the partitions than the others. The reason for this is that there are no partitions at the ends, but just the actual casing. Square lines across, representing the width of the grooves, and cut these lines down to a uniform depth with a wide chisel, or, guided by a straight-edge, draw the chisel along so that it cuts into the wood. Remove the waste wood with a ⅜-in. chisel. The cuts at the sides of the grooves allow the wood between them to be removed without disturbing the surfaces of the shelves. The shelves now may be fitted in their places and the upright partitions forced in. The grooves will hold those between the shelves, while those above the top and below the bottom shelf will be held partly by the grooves and partly by a few nails through the top and bottom. It only remains to fasten thin wood on the back, and the nest of pigeonholes is complete, as far as actual construction is concerned. It is a good plan to mark each hole with a letter of the alphabet, according to the documents it is intended to hold.

FINISHING NEST OF PIGEONHOLES.

An excellent finish, relieving the stiff, straight lines, may be easily formed by putting thin pieces of wood at the top of each hole. They are cut with a fret-saw, and fastened by small blocks of wood glued in behind them. Figs. 1712 and 1713 will give suggestions. Fig. 1714 shows a nest of pigeonholes, virtually the same as that made, may be stained and polished or painted, according to fancy.

Fig. 1715.—Nest of Pigeonholes with Two Doors.

described above, but ornamented with the bracket pieces and with top and bottom mouldings. The ends are thicker, and their front edges are ornamented by scratching with a cutting gauge or scratch beading router (described later). The top moulding is of pine. The bottom is thickened up, and the appearance of moulding given to it by three pieces of stuff, 1 in. thick and, say, 2 in. wide, being fastened on to the bottom board by means of screws driven through from below. The front piece should be the whole length of the job and the end pieces shouldered up behind it, so that they need not be mitred at the corners. If these end pieces are cut off across the

PIGEONHOLES WITH DOORS.

Doors may be added to the nest of holes made as previously described. The hinges could be fastened on the front edges; but this would not be so neat as hingeing the doors within the ends (see pp. 300 to 302), the fronts of the doors then being flush with, or a trifle back from, the edges of the ends, top, and bottom. It is necessary to have the partitions and shelves less by the thickness of the door—say $\frac{3}{4}$ in.—than the depth of the casing. On the left-hand door a bolt is fitted to shoot into either the top or bottom of the case, or, if preferred, two bolts, one at top and one at bottom. On the right-hand door a cupboard lock (see

Fig. 1716.—Nest of Pigeonholes with Writing Flap.

grain of the wood, instead of with it, they will look better. The edges can easily be rounded off, as shown, with the plane, and finished with glasspaper. The job, when

p. 297) with bolt shooting to the left will be fixed. The nest of pigeonholes so made will resemble Fig. 1715. Ornamentation in the way of mouldings, beadings, etc., can be added as desired. For a small nest, possibly one door may be preferable to two. In a long, low nest, if one door is preferred, it should be hinged at the top or bottom

Fig. 1717.—Nest of Pigeonholes with Revolving Shutter.

rather than at the end. If hinged at the top, a stay of some kind will be advisable to keep it open when the contents are being got at, but this arrangement will be more awkward generally than if the door is hinged at the bottom. In the latter case the door remains open by its own weight. and, if not allowed to hang down, forms a convenient table on which to sort or look over any of the contents of the holes.

PIGEONHOLES WITH WRITING FLAP.

The door hinged at the bottom may be used easily as a writing flap, in which case, of course, the panel and framing must be flush on the inside, and will be pleasanter if lined with cloth or leather. To prevent the flap falling further than required, a pivoted brass stay may be used, or instead a simple chain or cord fastened to the insides of the flap and ends. If the flap is to be used for writing purposes, part of the space occupied by the pigeonholes may be devoted to stationery—such as notepaper, envelopes, ink, pens, etc., and Fig. 1716 is suggestive in this connection. This illus-

tration gives an idea as to how the article may easily have a more ornamental appearance given to it. The pigeonholes are now a sightly piece of furniture, which, if carefully made, would not be out of place in any library. It is worthy of being made in better wood than pine, which, however, will do very well for the shelves and partitions.

PIGEONHOLES WITH SHUTTER OR REVOLVING FRONT.

The construction of a nest of pigeonholes with shutter or revolving front may now be described. The doors or shutters slide, and, in order to turn corners, are flexible. They are formed of narrow strips of wood, fastened close together on a canvas or other

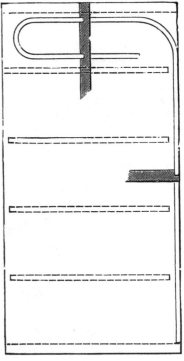

Fig. 1718.—Side of Nest, showing Provision for Shutter.

suitable backing, and slide in grooves prepared for them. A nest of pigeonholes, smaller than has yet been described, is illustrated by Fig. 1717. It is rather taller than it is wide, and is divided into sixteen holes, four in each row. The extra height allows of the shape of each hole being rect-angular, and is caused by the fact of there being two tops to the case—the outer one,

Fig. 1719.—Shutter Strip with Rounded Edge.   Fig. 1720.—Shutter Strip with Bevelled Edge.

and the other immediately above the pigeonholes. Between the two is a 3-in. space to hold the shutter when it is raised, as it is shown to be partly in Fig. 1717. A suitable size for the nest is 1 ft. 8 in. high, 1 ft. 4 in. wide, and 10 in. deep, outside measurements. These may be varied to suit particular purposes ; but note that as the pigeonholes must be set back to allow of the shutter working in front of them, there is a risk of their not being deep enough to hold papers, which must be cleared by the shutter. The shutter slides in grooves in the sides or ends of the case, so that, in setting out these, both the thickness of the wood forming the sliding front and the width of the groove will have to be considered with regard to each other. For a small nest, ordinary ¼-in. stuff will be thick enough for the front, although, as even the veriest tyro will know, its thick-ness will be considerably less than ¼ in. when smoothed and worked down. It will hardly be too thin if ⅛ in. thick. The groove should be a trifle wider, so that the shutter moves easily and freely in it, though not loosely. From lack of tools or other reasons, it may not be convenient to make the grooves just the right width, so the shutters themselves may be adapted, as shown later, to fit in slightly narrower grooves. At present it is assumed that these are made exactly of the required width. Fig. 1718 represents the inside of the right-hand end of the case. These ends should be of ¾-in. stuff. Along the front edge cut a rebate the width of the thickness of the shutter, and about half the thickness of the end in depth. The rebate merges into a groove between the two tops, and in

order that the shutter may work freely, fol-lows a circular line. The length of the groove may be determined by actual mea-surement, but it will be as well in the first place to make it excessive, and to stop up the excess after fitting the shutter. The groove should be cut as cleanly as possible, to assist the free action of the shutter, which should run as smoothly as a well-made drawer. The two ends of the casing, of course, are made to correspond.

FLEXIBLE ROLL SHUTTER FOR PIGEONHOLES.

The shutter itself is composed of narrow strips of wood. The case should be fitted together, if only temporarily, before the shutter is made, so as to get the exact length of the strips. Each piece must be narrow enough to pass the rounded corners without jamming ; and to avoid any risk of this defect, the groove at the corners may be slightly widened. The shutter strips should not be more than ¾ in. wide, but they may be as much narrower as de-sired ; but the narrower they are the more work there will be—½ in. may be assumed as the medium. Each strip may be per-fectly plain and flat, with square edges, but it is better to break the joints by round-ing off each edge to the section shown in Fig. 1719. Two of these being placed close together, the actual line of the joint is hidden ; a shutter formed of several pieces shaped thus presenting the appearance of a series of wide beads. The edges may be simply bevelled, as in Fig. 1720 ; or the pieces may be of any section desired. Thus the shutter may be made to resemble a series of small half-round beads, as in Fig. 1721 ; it might be made up of a number of pieces, each the size of the beadings shown,

Fig. 1721.—Three Beaded Strips of Shutter.

but the only advantage of this would be a slight saving in the waste space between the outer and the inner top, caused by the rounded corners having a sharper curve.

Alternative designs for the strips are given by Fig. 1722. The case being together, begin to make the shutter by cutting a board of the required thickness, of any convenient width, and of such a length that it just fits within the rebates in the two ends. Square the edges, and proceed to work

Fig. 1722.—Alternative Designs for Shutter Strips.

beads across from one edge to the other. A handy tool for this purpose is the scratch or beading router. Fig. 1723 shows this tool; the stock is formed of two pieces of hard wood, 8 in. to 1 ft. long, and ½ in. thick. The narrow part may be 1 in. wide, and the wider part—the shoulder or fence—is from 1½ in. to 2 in. The fence must not be thicker than the board to be worked. Three or four screws hold the two parts together, and clamp in place the steel scraper, which is as thick as an ordinary scraper (p. 114), and ½ in. or so wide. The position of the scraper longitudinally of the tool is altered easily. The right hand grasps the fence, the left the other end of the stock, and the fence is pressed against the edge of the board and the scraper worked with pressure backwards and forwards until the beading is formed. The scraper should not project from the stock more than is absolutely necessary; it is shaped by filing. After the beads have all been worked, widths can be cut off easily with a fine saw without injury to the beads between which it cuts. If a fine saw is not available, leave a slight space when setting the iron between each two or three beads, so that the saw kerf, by removing this excess, will allow each piece to be fitted closely together. If preferred, the pieces may be cut before the beadings are formed, but this will probably be found more troublesome and tedious than the way suggested. Another way is to have a piece much longer, and only 3 in. or 4 in. wide; run the beads upon this for its entire length, and then cut pieces from it to just fit within the rebates.

GLUING AND FITTING FLEXIBLE SHUTTER.

Were the shutter strips to be fastened together by gluing the edges to each other, the shutter would be rigid, and for the present purpose useless. They must, therefore, be glued on to a flexible backing of canvas, calico, or some similar suitable material. Hessian canvas used by upholsterers is admirable. Glue alone, or a mixture of glue and good strong flour paste, is a suitable adhesive. The canvas may cover the whole of the back of the shutter, though it will be better to leave the portion which fits in the groove bare, or it may be in strips from top to bottom. All that is needed is that the pieces shall be hinged to each other. If, as is very possible, some glue gets between the pieces, be careful to remove it before it has set; to do this, bend the shutter backwards at each joint. To allow of a lock being fastened to the shutter, have for its bottom strip a wider and thicker one, which need only work up and down in the rebate or straight part of the groove, and will not have to be worked round the corners; it should be plain instead of beaded. Reduce the thickness of the ends of the bottom piece sufficiently for them to fit within the grooves. It is better to have the extra thickness at the back of the door, so that the front of the piece is flush with the remainder. This, of course, is managed by removing whatever wood may be necessary from the back only. The size of the bottom piece will be determined by the kind and dimensions of the lock. After the glue is dry, try the shutter to see if it fits and runs well. The top strip

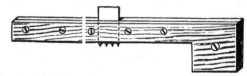

Fig. 1723.—Scratch or Beading Router.

should be high enough to enter the rounded groove while the bottom one is in its normal position, so that when all is finished the front will be quite closed. When it has been opened till the bottom of the lowest slip is on a level with, or a little below, the inner top, the remainder of the groove, if any, may be filled up by gluing a piece of wood in it, to act as a stop; for, of

piece of moulding may be planted on it and carried round the ends. In order to raise and lower the shutter, a couple of

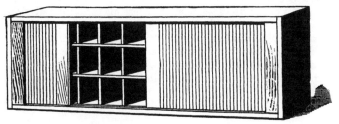

Fig. 1724.—Nest of Pigeonholes with Double Shutter.

course, the shutter will never have to be pushed further than the position named. Now, should the wood of the shutter be too thick to fit easily within the grooves, just bevel it off until it is sufficiently thin. If much has to be removed, take it from the back; but if only a little, it may be taken from either back or front. Possibly a little rubbing down with glasspaper may be sufficient. Up till now the shutter hangs in the front rebates curtainwise, so that it can be lifted forwards, instead of merely sliding up and down. To make grooves of the rebates so as to enclose the sides of the shutter, glue thin slips of wood on the front edges. The shutter, being in its place before these pieces are glued on, is now

knobs should be fastened to the bottom piece.

PIGEONHOLES WITH DOUBLE SHUTTERS.

A nest of pigeonholes similar to Fig. 1710 (p. 503) may have, instead of one shutter sliding up and down, two shutters, opening sideways from the centre, as illustrated by Fig. 1724. In this case no double top will be wanted, as the shutters will turn into the ends, each of which, therefore, must be made double. The rebates must be on the edges of the top and bottom, and the grooves, of course, will be in the same pieces. To prevent the doors when locked from being pushed on one side, and so allowing of access to any of the pigeon-

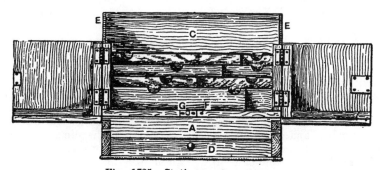

Fig. 1725.—Stationery Box, Open.

securely fastened, so that it can only move up or down. To bring up the edge of the bottom flush with the ends, a similar piece must now be glued on to it. The same must be done at the top, but the piece there must be of a suitable width: and a

holes, and to prevent either door being drawn too far, a stop should be placed at the centre in the rebated groove. This can easily be managed by cutting a small corner out of the doors, just where they come in contact with the stop. Instead of the shutters when opened being folded entirely by the ends and top, they may simply pass through the space and in behind. In this case naturally two backs will have to be made. When the height or length of the nest is great in proportion to the depth from back to front, it will be plain that this form of construction is better than the former, and may be the only one possible. In large work, when the shutters are heavy and open sideways, it is sometimes advisable for them to run on rollers.

from front to back at an angle of about 38° measured from the horizontal. The particular angle is determined by the proportions of the box ; but there is an advantage in letting the angle of slope approach the horizontal rather than the perpendicular, as the weight of the lids then acts to better advantage in keeping them in position when the case is in use. The material used in the construction may be oak, mahogany, or other suitable wood, planed to $\frac{7}{16}$ in., and for the inside divisions to about $\frac{1}{8}$ in.

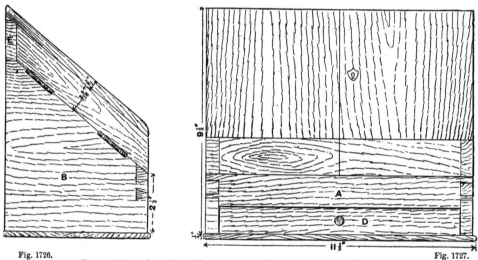

Fig. 1726.   Fig. 1727.

Figs. 1726 and 1727.—Side and Front Elevations of Stationery Box.

STATIONERY BOX WITH HINGED LIDS.

The stationery box, case, or cabinet shown by Fig. 1725 is intended to stand on a writing-table or desk. When not in use the lids are closed, to protect the contents from dust. The inside is divided into compartments to contain different sizes of writing paper and envelopes. In the lower part there is a small drawer for pens, pencils, sealing-wax, and other requisites. A space is also provided for an inkpot, but opinions may vary as to the advisability of bringing the paper and the inkpot into close proximity. The general construction of the article may be gathered by an inspection of the end and front elevations (Figs. 1726 and 1727), and section (Fig. 1728). The top of the box slopes upwards

thickness. The requirements of the user best determine the size ; that given in the figures will probably be found generally useful. The principal dimensions may be : Length, $11\frac{1}{2}$ in. ; width, $6\frac{1}{4}$ in. ; height at back, $9\frac{3}{4}$ in., from which other measurements may be scaled off on the figures, observing that the dimensions of the lids, and other sloping parts, must be taken for lengths from Figs. 1725 and 1727 ; widths and depths from Fig. 1726, and the cross section (Fig. 1728), as, in consequence of these parts being oblique to the plane of the paper in the first-named figures, the same scale is not applicable to them. The inside fittings are made to fit. The piece of wood A forming the front of the box, above the drawer D, and the sides B are dovetailed together as shown. The back piece c, 11⅜ in. by 9 in., is let into rebates in the sides B. Two small pieces of wood E are glued on the upper parts of its ends; these conceal the end grain of the wood, and fill up the space that would otherwise be left in consequence of the back piece c not being the full length of the box.

STATIONERY BOX LIDS.

The lids, made in one piece to fit the box, are afterwards divided down the centre with a fine-toothed saw. They are hinged to the sloping edges of the box, and furnished with lock, as shown. In the edge

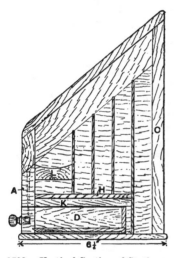

Fig. 1728.—Vertical Section of Stationery Box.

of that part of the left-hand lid which forms a part of the box front when closed there is a spring catch made of brass; when the lid is closed this catch hooks into a hole in the brass plate G, which is fixed in the centre of the bevelled edge of A, and so holds the lid down. The other lid being turned in and locked, all is securely covered. Fig. 1729 is an enlarged view of the edge of the left-hand door where the spring catch is fixed. The spring is let into a slight hollow cut to receive it, which, of course, must be made deeper where the free end of the spring is than where it is secured by the screw shown in the figure.

The small peg shown at the back of the spring falls into a hole bored to receive it easily. This peg may, if thought fit, be dispensed with. The hook end of the spring is shaped to catch into the hole G on closing the lid. Viewed as at Fig. 1729, the hook is of triangular form, with a bevel from the longer side to the opposite corner. The lock shown in Fig. 1725 measures 1¾ in. by 1¼ in., and is let into the door. If thought desirable, the edges of the box may be rounded off, which rather improves the appearance.

STATIONERY·BOX DRAWER AND DIVISIONS.

The little drawer D measures 10⅜ in. by 4⅝ in. by 1¼ in.; it is of simple construction,

Fig. 1729.—Spring Catch.

and the sides join the front in a rebate cut in its ends. It is secured by a brass pin, shown in dotted outline in Fig. 1728, the pin passing through a vertical hole F (Fig. 1725) bored through A into the drawer front, as is commonly done with drawers in small boxes. The head of the pin which secures the drawer when closed, projecting above the bevelled edge of A, would prevent the left-hand door from closing, so that a cavity must be cut in the door at the place where the pin-head touches it. The divisions inside the box slip into V-shaped grooves cut in the side pieces, and the cross divisions are held in place in the same manner. The division at the back goes the full depth of the box, as shown in the section (Fig. 1728); the three other divisions for paper rest upon a bottom H, which is supported upon slips κ, sprigged to the box ends. The distance between the divisions is ¾ in., and a wider space, 1⅞ in., at the front is for a pen-rest towards the left hand ; the smaller space to the right (see Fig. 1725) is for an inkbottle. That the pens may be easily picked up, the left-hand space is filled up by a slightly hollowed slip L (Fig. 1728), which, if not made of stuff thick enough to

the last measurement including the projecting knobs of the horizontal drawers. Its carcase consists of two curved sides joined together by the shelves immediately above and below the small horizontal drawers, and a frame at the back. The shelves and the sides may be screwed together, and the heads of the screws concealed by the small cocked bead and fillet H (Fig. 1730), which

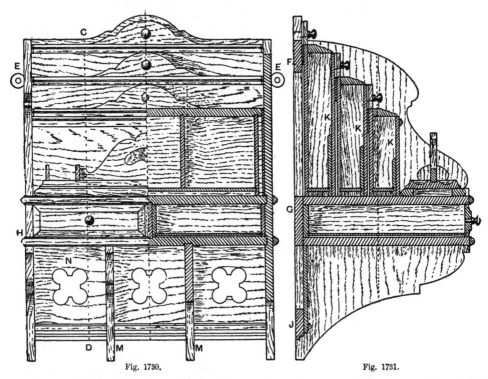

Fig. 1730.

Fig. 1731.

Fig. 1730.—Front and Sectional Elevation of Bracket Cabinet.

Fig. 1731.—Cross and Vertical Section of Bracket Cabinet.

rest upon H, is supported by little blocks of wood glued to its under side.

BRACKET CABINET FOR STATIONERY.

Fig. 1730 illustrates part front elevation and part sectional elevation, and Fig. 1731 shows transverse section on C D (Fig. 1730) of a stationery cabinet to hang upon a wall by means of brass eye-plates E E. The total height of the cabinet is 1 ft. 9¾ in., the extreme width 1 ft. 4⅞ in., and the depth from front to back 1 ft. ⅛ in.,

is planted on the front edges of the shelves and returned along the sides. The frame at the back is formed with two stiles and three rails F, G, J, whose sections are seen in Fig. 1731. The middle rail G may be tenoned on, but to avoid unsightliness a halving dovetail joint may be used for the other two at each of the corners, the dovetail being formed on the stile. Along the edges of the stiles, tongues are made which fit into grooves at the back edges of the side pieces. These grooves must be stopped towards the bottom, because the frame does not extend completely along the side pieces, as may be seen in the lower part of Fig. 1731. κ (Fig. 1731) shows three

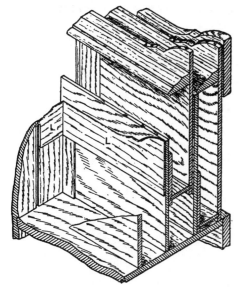

Fig. 1732.—Vertical Drawers of Bracket Cabinet.

vertical partitions, also represented in the isometric projection (Fig. 1732). These are housed into the sides, and serve to separate three vertical drawers (which are shown in the same figures, and which may also be housed into the shelf below them).

Bracket Cabinet Drawers.

In Fig. 1732 the middle drawer is raised from its lowest position, and the front one is removed entirely in order to show the thin beaded slips L, which are fixed on the front of each partition and on the sides to prevent the drawers rubbing on an exposed part as they are moved in or out. These drawers have each a shallow front (Fig. 1731), which is sufficient to prevent their contents from falling out when the drawer is lifted up, but is not deep enough to impede their removal when required. The lifting is effected by means of small knobs, shown in Figs. 1730 and 1731, but omitted from Fig. 1732. The largest of these drawers will accommodate foolscap paper and a

33

blotting-pad, the middle one notepaper and envelopes, this drawer being divided by a partition shown by vertical dotted lines towards the right hand of Fig. 1730. The smallest drawer, in front also divided by a partition, will hold postcards and foolscap envelopes, and in the case of each drawer a sufficient amount of free room is left at the top to facilitate removal of contents.

Stationery Cabinet Bracket and Pen-tray.

The two brackets M M (Fig. 1730) have the same contour as the lower part of each side, and they are housed into the lower shelf, and further secured by screws which come through from the upper part of the shelf to which they are attached. These brackets are cut away at the back to allow the transverse piece N to take its position. This piece is housed into the sides and screwed to the back edges of the brackets, which are thus fixed more firmly. The three perforated quatrefoils in N may be made entirely by using brace- and centre-bits. A small moulding is shown along the bottom edge of N. Standing on the shelf in front of the vertical drawers is a pen-tray, which is, of course, removable. Views of this pen-tray are given in Figs. 1730, 1731, 1733, and 1734. In Fig. 1733 is seen the method of fitting in the small curved pieces which retain the inkpots in place. The ends of the part upon which the handle is formed should be housed into the small

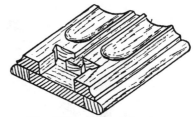

Fig. 1733.—Part of Pen-tray.

pieces just mentioned, and screws entering from below the pen-tray will firmly fix the handle piece. Fig. 1734 is a half plan of the pen-tray.

Book Racks.

Books which are frequently in use are best accommodated in book racks, and a useful design with simple cut-through work is shown in Fig. 1735. Fretworkers could

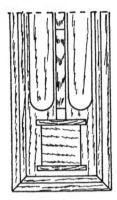

Fig. 1734.—Half-plan of Pen-tray.

combine the side and back as shown by Figs. 1736 and 1737, while Fig. 1738 gives a design suitable for carving. Fig. 1739 would make a suitable back if, instead of removing the wood round the centre leaf with a saw, the ground were removed to a depth of $\frac{1}{8}$ in. by a carving tool and afterwards stippled with a matting tool. The racks could be made up in whitewood, satin-walnut, or mahogany, and the dimensions given in Figs. 1736, 1738, and 1739 can readily be

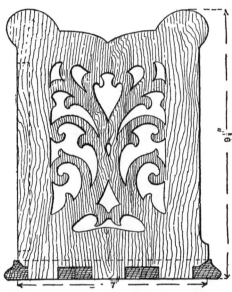

Fig. 1736.—Fretwork Book Rack Side.

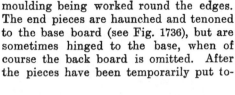

Fig. 1735.—Book Rack.

altered to suit special requirements. The base may be prepared from stuff 9 in. wide that will clean up $\frac{5}{8}$ in. thick, a suitable

moulding being worked round the edges. The end pieces are haunched and tenoned to the base board (see Fig. 1736), but are sometimes hinged to the base, when of course the back board is omitted. After the pieces have been temporarily put to-

gether, the fretwork or carving should be done. Fig. 1740 shows a rack with cut-through work and sloping shelf, the ends being somewhat unusual. This is known as a seat rack. Fig. 1741 gives the principal dimensions. The shelf is planed from stuff $\frac{5}{8}$ in. thick, cleaning up to $\frac{9}{16}$ in. thick, and is half-dovetailed to the ends. The back board is rebated to the ends and screwed to the back edge of the shelf. If the book rack is much longer than 1 ft. 10 in., a support in the centre will be required. When soft wood is used, the racks can be given a priming coat of glue and whiting, which is rubbed down. Then, when it has set hard, apply two coats of enamel paint. For hard wood, staining and polishing will be the best finish.

SLIDING BOOK RACK.

Fig. 1742 shows a sliding book rack or book slide which may be made in any of

this may be done conveniently by placing a feather-edge strip of wood on a shooting block and shooting the edges of the sliding board and slides. While shooting, the face

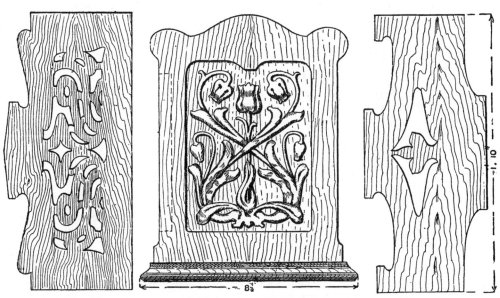

Fig. 1737.—Back of Fretwork Book Rack.　Fig. 1738.—Carved Side of Book Rack.　Fig. 1739.—Back of Fretwork Book Rack.

the ordinary hard woods. The different pieces should be cut out a little larger than finally required, and then planed down to the dimensions shown in Figs. 1743 and 1744. The base (Fig. 1745) is of framework, the three cross rails A, B, and C being carefully stub-tenoned into the stiles and glued. After the glue has set, the framework should be cleaned off flush on each side. The pieces D and E (Figs. 1742 and 1745) should fit just tight between the stiles, the best result being obtained by shooting the ends of the pieces ; the outer edge should be rounded as shown. The sliding board H (Fig. 1742) and the slides F and G should next be prepared, the sliding board including at first the piece shown at K. Care must be taken to plane the sides and the sliding board at the same angle, and

side of the sliding board will be upwards, but the face side of the slides must be down-

Fig. 1740.—Seat Rack for Books.

wards. The sliding board and slides should next be shot to lengths and placed in position on the base framing. Next each slide should be attached to the framing by three or four screws inserted from the under side of the stiles of the base. The sliding board may then be slipped out, and the portion

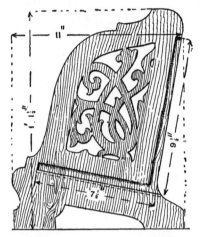

Fig. 1741.—Fretwork Side of Seat Rack.

K separated from it by a fine saw. This piece and E should be glued together and to the framing, D being glued to the under

board. To prevent the sliding board being pulled right out, a small round-headed screw can be inserted from the under side near the inner end, in which case it will be necessary to cut a small groove in the rail B, to allow the screw head to pass; this head will stop against the rail A (Fig. 1745). It is much simpler to make a rack with a

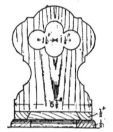

Fig. 1744.—End Elevation of Sliding Rack.

solid base instead of framing, but the working is not so satisfactory, for if the base warps or becomes slightly concave on the top, the slides bind against the sliding board; or, on the other hand, if it becomes concave on the lower side, the slides recede from the sliding board, and thus become loose.

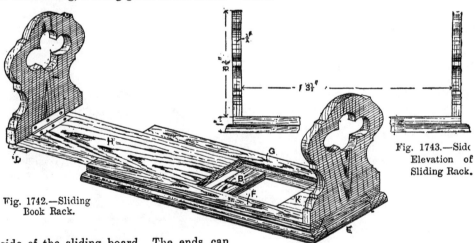

Fig. 1742.—Sliding Book Rack.

Fig. 1743.—Side Elevation of Sliding Rack.

side of the sliding board. The ends can next be prepared. The quatrefoiling should be bored with a brace and bit, and the curves can be worked by means of bow-sawing, paring, and filing. The ends should be hinged by narrow brass butts let in flush with the surfaces of the end and sliding

SLIDING BOOK-RACK WITH FRETWORK ENDS.

The book slide here described may be of oak, walnut, or mahogany, but the timber should be thoroughly dry. Fig. 1746 is a side elevation, and gives a fretwork design for the end, but this may be plain or carved

to prevent warping. When dry, the pattern shown in Fig. 1746 may be marked out and cut with a frame- or pad-saw. Clean up

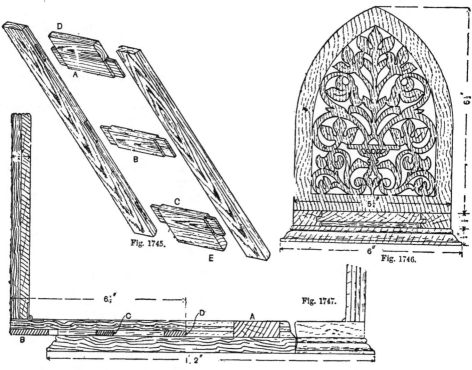

Fig. 1745.—Framed Base of Sliding Rack. Figs. 1746 and 1747.—End and Side Elevations of Sliding Rack with Fretwork Ends.

as desired. Fig. 1747 shows rather more than half of the stand in section on the left-hand side, and a part side elevation of the other end on the right-hand side of the figure. Fig. 1748 is a cross section of the stand with the slides removed. To make the stand, prepare a piece of stuff 1 ft. 2 in. by 6 in. by ½ in. for the bottom, plane it, and mould the edges, or bevel them. Next prepare two pieces A (Fig. 1748), 1 ft. 1¼ in. by 1 in. by ½ in., and groove them as shown. Then get out a piece A (Fig. 1747), 5 in. by 1½ in. by ½ in., and tenon it in the centre between the two long pieces. Fix it to the bottom, and prepare two pieces for the ends, each of which should be made by gluing together two pieces of $\frac{5}{16}$-in. stuff, with the grain of one across that of the other

and work a couple of beads on the edges to break the joint where the two pieces have been glued (see Fig. 1747). Two pieces, 6⅞ in. by 3⅞ in. by ¾ in., must now be prepared for the slides. These are tongued and fitted into the grooves at each end, and a piece of stuff B (Fig. 1747) is glued across the outer end of each one to make the

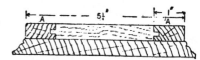

Fig. 1748.—Cross Section of Sliding Rack.

thickness ½ in. The ends are fixed to the slides with a pair of 2½-in. by ⅝-in. brass butt hinges, as shown in Fig. 1747. Before putting together, the pieces should be polished. After the polish is hard, the slide may be put together, the piece C (Fig. 1747) being fixed to the bottom before the slide is added. D is slipped underneath and secured with a couple of fine screws to the slide after it is in position; this prevents

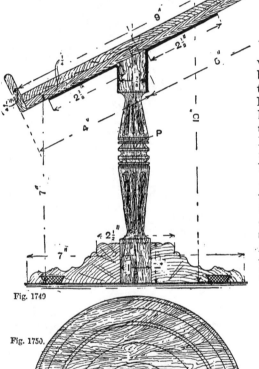

Fig. 1749.

Fig. 1750.

Fig. 1749.—Sectional Elevation of Table Reading Stand. Fig. 1750.—Half-plan of Stand Base.

the slides being drawn out too far. A piece of green baize or cloth glued underneath the bottom completes the slide.

TABLE READING STAND OR BOOK REST.

The small reading stand or book rest illustrated in Fig. 1749 will be found con-

venient for supporting a book or newspaper when reading at a table. Any of the hard woods is suitable for use in its construction. The bottom of the stand (see Fig. 1750) is a heavy-turned piece with a lead-filled recess; the pillar mortise hole is cut first, and must be quite square and true, as upon the fit of the pillar depends the stability of the stand. The upright pillar P (Fig. 1749) is of square section, being first cut and planed down to 1 in. square, the ornament being then set out and chiselled. It should now be driven into the bottom stand, using a little hot thin glue, and the wedge inserted as shown in Fig. 1749. The book rest (Fig. 1751) is made from stuff $\frac{1}{4}$ in. thick, shaped at the ends as illustrated. Pieces, 2 in. by $\frac{1}{4}$ in., as shown by the dotted lines in Fig. 1751, are glued and screwed on the back, to prevent the top piece twisting. Fix these battens before cutting the ends to shape, so that the top board and end batten may be cut at the same operation. Along the near edge a moulding, $1\frac{1}{4}$ in. by $\frac{1}{4}$ in. (Fig. 1749), is fixed, to prevent the book or paper slipping off. To fix the rest on the pillar head, cut a mortise hole in the centre 2-in. piece P (Fig. 1752) exactly to fit the pillar head; glue them together, and, when dry, fit the brass plates B P (Fig. 1752). It will be seen from Fig. 1752 that the head

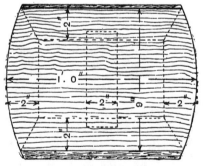

Fig. 1751.—Book Rest.

of the pillar is reduced to $\frac{7}{8}$ in. thick to allow these brass strengthening plates to be let in with the outline of the lower part of the pillar. The plates (Fig. 1753 gives three views of one) are made from 2-in.

by $\frac{3}{32}$-in. brass. The corners are turned by heating the brass to dull red, slowly cooling it, and, when cold, putting it in a vice and bending it over with a pair of tongs or

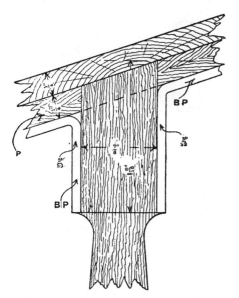

Fig. 1752.—Book Rest fixed on Pillar.

pliers. A sharp corner is not essential. The screws must well fit the holes in the plates, and, when fixed, there will be no fear of the book rest getting loose. The stand should now be cleaned off and polished, or, if desired, it can be left in the natural colour, giving it a rub over with

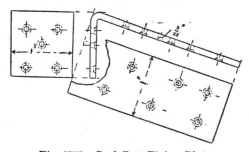

Fig. 1753.—Book Rest Fixing Plate.

wax to prevent the dust adhering; a piece of thick cloth or baize should be glued to the under side of the turned bottom, the edges being trimmed off when dry.

ADJUSTABLE READING STAND OR BOOK REST.

The book rest illustrated in section by Fig. 1754 looks well if made in walnut or mahogany, which should be well seasoned and free from knots and shakes. It has an adjustable joint, which allows the book board to be placed at any angle. The following pieces of wood will be required for making the stand: One piece $9\frac{1}{2}$ in. in diameter by 2 in. thick for the base; one for the pillar $10\frac{1}{2}$ in. long by $2\frac{1}{2}$ in. square; one

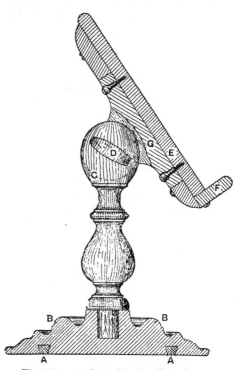

Fig. 1754.—Adjustable Reading Stand.

for the book board 1 ft. 3 in. long by 10 in. wide by $\frac{5}{8}$ in. thick; one for the ledge board 1 ft. 3 in. long by 2 in. wide by $\frac{5}{8}$ in. thick; one strengthening piece for the back of the book board 10 in. long by $2\frac{1}{2}$ in. wide by $\frac{3}{4}$ in. thick; and one for the hinge 6 in. long by $3\frac{1}{2}$ in. wide by $\frac{5}{8}$ in. thick. The adjusting screw should be made from a piece of boxwood 5 in. long by 2 in. wide by $\frac{5}{8}$ in. thick. First make the base of the stand. Fix the necessary piece of wood on the screw chuck and strip the under side, leaving it slightly hollow towards the centre, which will make it stand steady. Turn a recess in the under

Fig. 1755.—Plug-pointed Centre-bit.

side as at A (Fig. 1754), which can be filled with lead to make the stand solid. Reverse the base on the screw chuck and turn the upper side. B (Fig. 1754) gives a section of the base. For boring the hole for the pillar tenon, use a centre-bit as illustrated by Fig. 1755, which shows that, instead of the ordinary cutting point, the bit has a plug point which guides it into the small hole bored in the upper side of the base. If a bit as illustrated is not obtainable, use the ordinary centre-bit, plugging the small hole made by the screw chuck, and then nicking the centre with the corner of the turning chisel. A hole for the point of the bit should first be bored through the plug with a small shell-bit or a bradawl, to prevent the point of the centre-bit running off the centre.

PILLAR OF ADJUSTABLE READING STAND.

The pillar is shown with a plain turned tenon, but, if preferred, the base and pillar could be tapped and threaded respectively,

The slot in which the hinge-piece G (Figs. 1754 and 1756) works should be sawn and the hole for the thumbscrew bored and tapped before turning the pillar. The slot

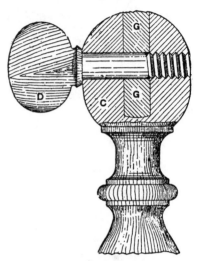

Fig. 1756.—Book Rest Pillar.

is $\frac{5}{8}$ in. wide, and is cut 2 in. deep (from the top) in front and $1\frac{1}{2}$ in. at the back. Before sawing the slot, it is best to bore the hole and tap it to receive the thumbscrew. The hole is at right angles to the slot, $1\frac{1}{4}$ in. from the top, and is bored halfway through with a $\frac{3}{8}$-in. centre-bit, the other half being bored to tapping size ($\frac{1}{2}$ in.) for a $\frac{5}{8}$-in. wood screwing tap, which should be run through from the wide end of the hole. Then fix the pillar in the lathe with the top end towards the poppet head, and turn it to the pattern

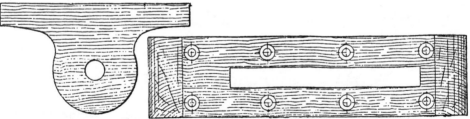

Fig. 1757.—Hinge Piece.   Fig. 1758.—Strengthening Piece for Book Rest.

so that they could be taken apart for packing. To proceed with the pillar, set the marking gauge to half its thickness, and mark the centre on both ends for turning.

shown at C (Figs. 1754 and 1756). The thumbscrew can next be fixed. The pin for the screw should be turned $\frac{1}{4}$ in. longer than the finished size, and the point chamfered with the gouge to start the thread. After cutting the screw, refix it in the lathe and turn the head as shown by D (Figs. 1754 and 1756), and cut off the screw to the required length. The hinge-piece (Fig. 1757) should fit tightly in the slot so that the joint works stiffly. It should be just deep enough to let the strengthening piece, into which it is mortised, swing clear of the

from each end, and the other two 4 in. apart. The screw holes in the strengthening piece and the ledge board should be countersunk to receive the small turned buttons.

PUTTING TOGETHER READING STAND.

The stand can now be fixed together. First fix the parts with screws, and then

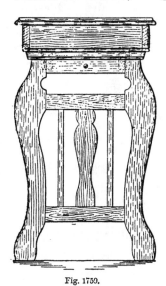

Fig. 1759.

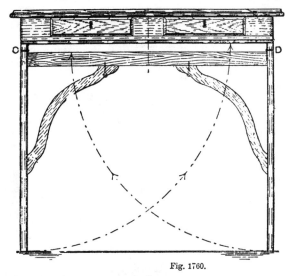

Fig. 1760.

Figs. 1759 and 1760.—Elevations of American Typewriter Table.

Fig. 1761.—Plan of Table with and without Top.

Fig. 1761.

head of the pillar. The hole in the centre should be large enough to receive the thumbscrew. The strengthening piece is shown by Fig. 1758 with the mortise cut for the hinge-piece, and the holes bored for the screws. The book board is shown in section by E (Fig. 1754). A ledge board F is fastened to the lower edge of the book board by means of four screws, one 1½ in.

take apart again and apply glue to the hinge piece, strengthening piece, and ledge board, and secure with the screws. The pillar should be glued to the base of the stand. The buttons for covering the screw holes, fourteen of which will be required, can be made from any small pieces of wood to the shape shown in Fig. 1754. After the buttons are fixed, the stand should be sandpapered and polished. If necessary, a piece of dark-coloured baize can be glued to the under side of the base, to prevent it scratching the table top.

AMERICAN TYPEWRITER TABLE.

There are advantages in having a special table or desk for a typewriter, which may weigh from 20 lb. to 35 lb., and which therefore is not very portable. Moreover, ordinary tables and writing-desks are too high for use as typewriter stands, if the operator is seated on a chair of the ordinary height. A suitable table or desk is shown

comparatively small space. It will be seen from the front elevation (Fig. 1760) that the leg C is hinged to the top of the desk, whereas the leg D is hinged at a distance from the top equal to the thickness of C, so that when folded it lies horizontally underneath the leg C; the dotted lines in Fig. 1760 indicate the way the legs fold together. Fig. 1761 is a plan of the desk, A showing the top in position, and B showing the runners for the drawers, the top being removed. The drawers will be found very convenient for keeping typewriting paper and the various accessories of the

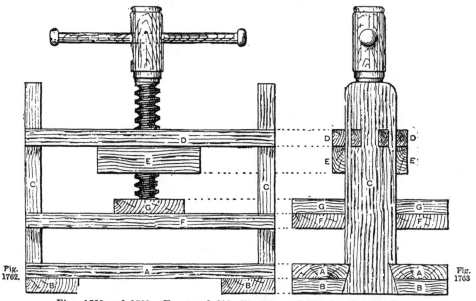

Figs. 1762 and 1763.—Front and Side Elevations of Wooden Copying Press.

by Figs. 1759 to 1761. Its height is 2 ft. 4 in., which is about sufficient to allow the fore-arm of the operator, when seated on an ordinary chair, to be level with the keyboard. The other dimensions are, to a great extent, a matter of convenience, but the top may measure 2 ft. 9 in. long by 1 ft. 5 in. wide, and the body of the desk 2 ft. 6 in. long by 1 ft. 3 in. wide. Oak, walnut, and mahogany are equally suitable. The side legs are hinged as shown in Figs. 1759 and 1760, so that they may be folded together under the top of the desk, thus enabling the desk to be packed into a

typewriter—such as brush, indiarubber, oil-can, etc. The addition of mouldings, turned work, or carving would add to the appearance.

WOODEN COPYING PRESS.

Copying presses are usually of iron and steel, but the press about to be described is wholly of wood, the screw being a wooden bench screw. The press is shown in front elevation by Fig. 1762, and in end elevation by Fig. 1763. It is made of pine, as free from knots as possible, though a harder wood would be more suitable. Wood, 1 in.

thick, planed down to a trifle over ¾ in., does very well. Beech would answer well; while a really handsome press might be made by using mahogany or walnut, the cost of which is not great. It will be seen that the only pretension to ornamental finish is in the rounded tops of the standards, the remainder being quite plain. There will be no difficulty in introducing suitable ornament if the press is required for study use. For example, a moulding may be planted on the edges all round the bottom, and a small moulding may be worked on others. Chamfered edges would also be effective and not difficult. The length is 1 ft. 2½ in., and the width 9 in., which allows of the ordinary quarto copying book being used. The bottom piece A, or bed of the press, is 1 ft. 2½ in. long by 9 in. wide. On the under side are screwed two ledges B, one at each end, serving to give rigidity to the bottom. In the event of the press being screwed to the top of a dwarf piece of furniture, perhaps the ledges may be dispensed with. The two standards C are 1 ft. long by 3 in. wide, fitted to the bottom with a plain single dovetail joint. The top crosspiece D is 4 in. wide, the same length as the bed, and is 2½ in. from the top of the standards C, through each of which a couple of mortises are cut for corresponding stout tenons in D. Through this a hole is cut to allow the screw to pass freely, and on the under side is fastened the threaded block E, in which the screw works. If the block were placed above D, the thrust of the screw would force it off; naturally, the tendency of the screw, when using the press for copying, is to force the block E upwards. The cover board F is exactly the same size as the bed, which it resembles in every respect, except that at each end spaces are cut away to allow of the standards fitting loosely into them; and only one piece G, instead of two, is fixed across. Now these parts and the screw could be fitted up, and the press would be effective as far as copying is concerned; but there is the objection that the loose board F would not rise with the motion of the screw, and so would have to be lifted each time the book was put in the press. The end of the screw generally is tapered beyond the thread, and should be

sawn off, leaving the bottom end of the screw perfectly flat. Get a piece of brass or zinc plate, about $\frac{1}{16}$ in. thick, and screw it to the under side of the cross piece G about the centre; have this metal large enough to allow of it being properly fastened with two or three screws, and to have a hole about $\frac{3}{16}$ in. bored through it. The metal might be dispensed with altogether perhaps if the piece G is of some hard wood. This hole is bored through both metal plate and crosspiece G, and is big enough to allow a large screw nail to revolve freely within it. This screw is run through the hole and driven into the bottom of the wood screw, so that the metal turns round easily on the screw nail as an axis. Fig. 1764 shows in section the metal plate at the bottom, the wooden piece G above, with

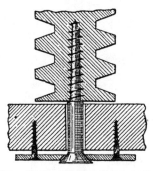

Fig. 1764.—Fixing Wooden Screw to Copying Press Cover Board.

the nail passing through them into the screw. The spaces round the nail and between the bottom of the screw and G are slightly exaggerated for the sake of clearness. In order that G may be screwed down closely to the piece F, the latter is slightly scooped out to receive the metal plate and screw head.

PUTTING TOGETHER WOODEN COPYING PRESS.

The parts are now ready for fixing together, and, when done, the press is complete. Screw the two pieces B to A, if this has not been done when cutting the sockets for the dovetails at the end of C. Pass the wooden screw through D and then through E. Fasten D and E together, taking care that the wooden screw does not jam in the hole through D, in which it should revolve freely. Then attach G to the end of the wooden screw. Fix one of the standards C

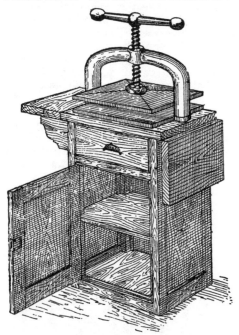

Fig. 1765.—Copying Press and Stand.

to the bottom, when F may be placed in position. The tenons at the end of D, corresponding with the mortises in the piece C, already fitted, may then be inserted, and finally the remaining standard C be fastened. Glue should be used at the mortise and tenon and dovetail joints, but it will be better to screw the other parts together. It now only remains to screw G to F, and the press is complete. The handle by which the screw is turned is the ordinary one supplied with it for bench purposes. Any tough stick would, however, do as well; and instead of leaving it loose, as it generally is in bench screws, it is well to fasten it in by a couple of brads—

one on each side—so as to keep the handle immovable longitudinally. An iron handle may better suit the purpose.

LINEN PRESS, VENEERER'S PRESS, ETC.

Wooden linen presses are a convenient means of keeping such things as table-cloths, etc., nicely pressed. They very much resemble in construction the copying press just described. The linen press, however, is larger, and its handle, instead of being at the top, is placed between the parts D and F (Fig. 1762). In the copying press this would have been awkward owing to the small space between the standards. Either position will suit either purpose, though undoubtedly the better position for a copying press is the one illustrated. It will be perceived that such a press may be turned to a variety of uses. For example, it will be found handy in laying small veneers with a caul, and in mounting and pressing photographic prints, etc.

COPYING PRESS STAND WITH DRAWER AND CUPBOARD.

Fig. 1765 gives a general view of a drawer and cupboard forming the stand for the usual kind of iron and steel copying press. Fig. 1766 is a front elevation, Fig. 1767 a

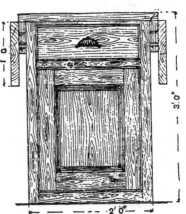

Fig. 1766.—Front Elevation of Copying Press Stand.

Fig. 1767.—Cross Section of Copying Press Stand.

cross section, and Fig. 1768 shows the framework. Assuming the parts to be planed to dimensions, the leading points in the construction are as follow: From Fig. 1768 it will be seen that there are four posts or legs, and to these the lower rails are stub-mortised and tenoned, the top rails being dovetailed into the legs. The front of the framing round the door and drawer is beaded (see Figs. 1766 and 1768). This should be specially noted when making the joints, because the front shoulders require to be made longer than the back ones. The sides and back may be formed of a single panel—that is, boards glued up to form the requisite widths—and then these can be secured between beads fixed inside and out, as illustrated in Fig. 1769. The bottom rails and those under the drawer are rebated, so as to receive the boards forming

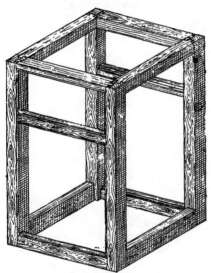

Fig. 1768.—Framework of Copying Press Stand.

the bottoms. The drawer is of the ordinary dovetail construction, and the door is haunched and mortised and tenoned, the panel fitting into plough grooves. In Fig. 1765 is shown a shelf, which is supported on bearers screwed to each side of the frame. If the top is formed of two pieces, the joint should be ploughed, tongued, and glued, and secured by screwing up through the top rails. The leaves are hinged to the top with back flap hinges, and the brackets are hinged to the legs, Fig. 1770 illustrating a bracket supporting one of the flaps.

CHAIR STEPS.

The chair steps illustrated by Fig. 1771 have many domestic uses, and would be handy in a small library. Suitable woods would be oak, mahogany, walnut, teak, or

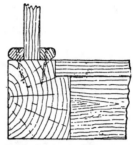

Fig. 1769.—Method of Fixing Panel.

any other hard wood. Figs. 1772 and 1773 are front and side elevations of the chair, and Fig. 1774 is a side elevation as extended

Fig. 1770.
Bracket supporting
Press Stand Flap.

Fig. 1771.—Chair Steps, Open.

for use as steps. The leading points in the construction are as follow: The pieces forming the hind legs and the back should be cut to the shape shown in Fig.

1774, and the lower rail of the top and four vertical rails should be mortised and brass butt hinges, let in flush, being suitable for this purpose. The seat should be

Fig. 1772.   Fig. 1773.   Fig. 1774.

Figs. 1772 and 1773.—Elevations of Chair Steps used as Chair.   Fig. 1774.—Elevation of Chair Steps used as Steps.

tenoned together. Then the front rail B (Fig. 1772) and the side rail A (Fig. 1773) are mortised and tenoned into the back leg and sloping rail L (Fig. 1774). The special form of joint at C (Figs. 1773 and 1774) is shown in detail at Fig. 1775, and the small gusset piece C should be dowelled and glued to both the sloping rail and the back leg. Then the board forming the top step when the chair is open should be dovetailed to the legs and gusset piece as at D, Fig. 1775. The steps are housed into the sides and front legs, as shown at E and F (Fig. 1776). A short piece of rail G (Figs. 1773 and 1774) should be haunched and tenoned into the rail H (Fig. 1776), and the other end dovetailed into the legs, as at K. The upper and lower rails of the back are mortised and tenoned into the sides, and the vertical rails at the back fit into mortises made in the rails. The seat is formed of two pieces, whose appearance will be greatly improved by moulding the edges. The two parts will require hingeing together, a pair of 2½-in.

fastened with brass screws driven down from the top or through the rails into the

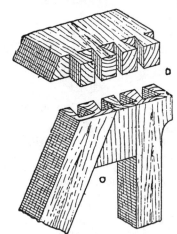

Fig. 1775.—Special Dovetail Joint.

seat. Of course, additional security will be gained by gluing the joints together.

Fig. 1777 gives a perspective view of the washstand closed, showing a sloping top,

mirror, and room for all the necessary accessories to a washstand. Fig. 1779 shows the stand in section, A being the upright division, B the projection to which to fasten

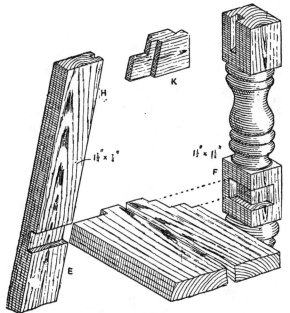

Fig. 1776.—Joints in Chair Steps.

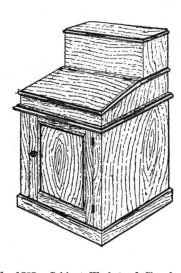

Fig. 1777.—Cabinet Washstand Closed.

the plinth, C the ledge to which the sloping top is hinged, D the space for the water

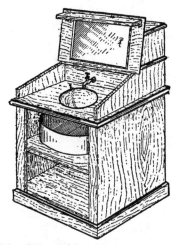

Fig. 1778.—Cabinet Washstand Open.

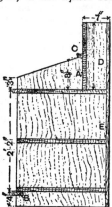

Fig. 1779.—Section of Cabinet Washstand.

which may be used as a writing flap. Fig. 1778 is a sketch of the washstand open, showing cupboard, with door removed, tap,

tank, and E the back. Fig. 1780 shows how to cut the top, F being the hole for the circular washing basin. The first parts required are two ends 3 ft. 11 in. long, 1 ft. 10 in. wide, and 1 in. thick; a bottom and shelf 2 ft. 2 in. long, 1 ft. 9½ in. wide, and 1 in. thick; and a top 2 ft. 4 in. long, 1 ft. 10½ in. wide, and 1 in. thick. The ends must be shaped as in Fig. 1779 to the dimensions there shown, and the whole nailed together as shown. The top must be cut to fit to the outside of the ends, and stand out 1 in. to cover the top of the pilasters and the door, as illustrated in Fig. 1780. The shelf and the bottom must stand in ½ in. at the back so as to allow the back to fit in flush with the ends. The upright division A (Fig. 1779) and the back should

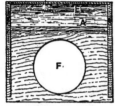

Fig. 1780.—Plan of Cabinet Washstand.

now be put in, and the pilasters, which are 2½ in. wide and 1 in. thick, nailed on. Then fasten a piece of wood 2½ in. wide and 1 in. thick to the under side of the bottom, with the front edge flush with the front of the pilasters B (Fig. 1779). To this the plinth is secured. The plinth should be 4 in. deep, mitred round, and secured by glue and nails. Mitre the moulding along the front edge of the top, and continue it round the ends.

SLOPING TOP, DOOR, ETC., OF CABINET WASHSTAND.

To make the sloping top, take a piece of wood 2 ft. 4 in. long, 1½ in. wide, and 1 in. thick, bevel it as shown at C (Fig. 1779), and nail it down to the ends. Fit a piece 2 ft. 6 in. long on to the slope of the ends, allowing it to extend over each end 1 in. Lay this in its position, and fit a front piece, 1 in. thick, on to the front of the ends, and bevel it on its top edge to fit against the top. As can be seen from Fig. 1778, this piece will be fastened to the top and will open with it. The top should extend over this front 1 in. Mould the front

and ends of the top and hinge it to the piece marked C (Fig. 1779). Take a piece of moulding of the same section as that worked round the top, fit it to the top, and nail it square across the ends. Fasten a piece of silvered plate, 1 ft. 6 in. by 1 ft.

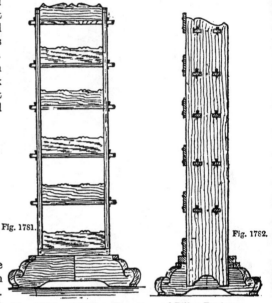

Figs. 1781 and 1782.—Elevations of Pillar Bookcase.

1 in., to the under side of the top with strips of rebated moulding. The flat top over the water tank is not hinged. It is 1¼ in. thick, and is rebated on the under side so that the projecting portion will fit between the ends, division, and back,

Fig. 1783.—Foot of Pillar Bookcase

and prevent it from being knocked off. To make the door—which should now be put together—it will be necessary to have two stiles 2 ft. 3 in. long, and two rails 1 ft. 8 in. long, all 2½ in. wide and 1 in. thick. These must be mortised and tenoned together, and grooved on the inside edges to receive a panel ⅜ in. thick. A moulding may or may not be mitred round the panel, this being left to the discretion of the maker. The thickness of the hinges may be sunk into the door. A knob or handle, with a turn-buckle to turn behind the pilaster, will be the only fitting required. The tank

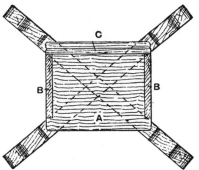

Fig. 1784.—Base of Pillar Bookcase.

should be 2 ft. 2 in. by 1 ft. 4 in. by 5½ in., and should have a tap screwed in about 1 in. from the bottom. Bore the hole for the tap

PILLAR BOOKCASE.

The tall, narrow form of the pillar book-case shown by Figs. 1781 and 1782 renders a comparatively heavy base desirable; the diagonal pieces which form its feet should therefore be cut from 2-in. plank. They are 2 ft. 6 in. long by 6 in. high, and are halved in the middle, as shown in Fig.

Fig. 1785.—Pillar Bookcase Shelf.

1783. For each of the two sides use $\frac{3}{4}$-in. board, 8 in. wide and 4 ft. 3 in. high; the shape of their tops is shown sufficiently in Fig. 1782. The sides are mortised for the tenons of the top and four shelves, and their lower ends are shaped as seen in Fig. 1782. Also, below the bookcase bottom

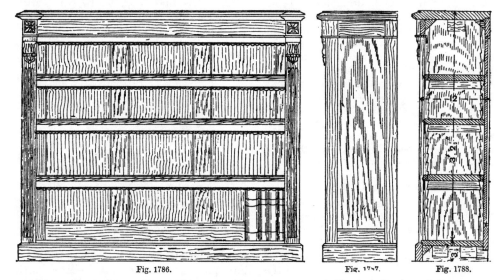

Fig. 1786.

Fig. 1787.

Fig. 1788.

Figs. 1786 to 1788.—Front Elevation, End Elevation, and Vertical Section of Dwarf Bookcase.

through the division, and put the tank in the recess. Screw the tap into position, put the circular washing basin in the hole, and the washstand is complete.

their inner edges have to be chamfered to fit against the feet, to which, as well as to the bottom piece, they are firmly fixed with round-headed screws. The bottom A

(Fig. 1784) is of 1-in. board, 1 ft. 1½ in. by 11 in. In its ends B (Fig. 1784) are cut openings, 8 in. by ¾ in., to admit the sides. The corners are slightly rounded, and the bottom is screwed to the feet. Fig. 1785

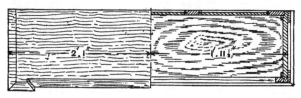

Fig. 1789.—Half Plan and Section of Dwarf Bookcase.

shows one of the four shelves. These are of ¾-in. board, 7½ in. wide and 1 ft. 4 in. long, each tenon being 2 in. long, and pegged outside a standard. The top resembles the shelves, but is 8 in. wide, its front edge coming flush with the sides, whereas the front edges of the shelves stand back ½ in. Strips of wood, ½ in. thick, prevent the books going too far back; they are 4 in. wide and 1 ft. 1½ in. long, and their shape is suggested in Fig. 1781. The back strip C (Fig. 1784) of the bottom is only 3¼ in. wide, but it is ¾ in. thick. Screws driven into it through the bottom piece fix it in place; it is also screwed to the backs of the standards like the strips. This case is not intended for heavy volumes, and the space between the shelves is only sufficient to admit octavos and smaller sizes of books, the three lower compartments being 8¼ in., and the two upper 7¼ in., high.

MATERIALS, ETC., FOR DWARF BOOKCASE.

The dwarf bookcase illustrated by Figs. 1786 to 1789 is intended to be executed in mahogany. The length is 4 ft., height 3 ft. 6 in., and depth 1 ft. The construction is simple but strong. The ends are formed of a plain ¾-in. board, rebated to receive the framed back, and tongued into the front pilaster. The top rail, which forms a frieze under the moulded top, is dovetailed into the front pilaster. The bottom, a ¾-in. plain board, is housed ¼ in. into the ends, as shown at Fig. 1790, and rebated over the plinth in front. The end pilasters are

mitred to the front ones and glued upon the ends of the case, as shown in section by Fig. 1791. A bottom rail with moulded edge is planted on the ends and finishes flush with the pilasters, the return plinth

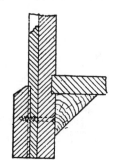

Fig. 1790.—Section through Bookcase End and Plinth.

sitting upon this. The whole is screwed from the inside of the end (see Fig. 1790). The shelves are movable, resting on bearers that sit in the rack shown enlarged in Fig. 1792. The rack is 3/16 in. by ¾ in., with notches 1¼ in. apart, and it is screwed to the ends. The top is 1½ in. thick, moulded in the solid and broken round the pilasters in front; the back is a ¾-in. panelled frame,

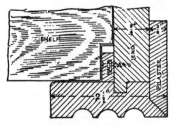

Fig. 1791.—Section through Pilaster, etc.

with two muntins and ½-in. bead butt panels. Leather edging is fixed to the shelves by means of fillets fitted tightly into plough grooves, and secured with sprigs as shown in Fig. 1793. The stuff required, rough sizes, includes: Top, 4 ft. 2½ in. by 1 ft. 2 in. by 1½ in.; bottom, 3 ft. 10 in. by 11 in. by ¾ in.; two ends, 3 ft. 5 in. by 11¾ in. by ¾ in.; three shelves, 3 ft. 9½ in. by 10½ in. by ¾ in.; front plinth, 4 ft. 2 in. by 3 in. by 1¼ in.; end plinth, 2 ft. 2 in. by 3 in.

by $\frac{3}{4}$ in.; frieze rail, 3 ft. 9 in. by $2\frac{1}{2}$ in. by $\frac{3}{4}$ in.; bottom rail, 1 ft. 5 in. by $2\frac{1}{2}$ in. by $\frac{3}{4}$ in.; necking moulds, 4 ft. 6 in. by 2 in. by $\frac{3}{4}$ in., and 2 ft. 6 in. by $\frac{1}{2}$ in. by $\frac{3}{8}$ in.; two front pilasters, 3 ft. 2 in. by $2\frac{5}{8}$ in. by $\frac{3}{4}$ in.; four end pilasters, 3 ft. $4\frac{1}{2}$ in. by $2\frac{1}{8}$ in. by $\frac{3}{8}$ in.; two trusses, $7\frac{1}{2}$ in. by $2\frac{1}{2}$ in. by $\frac{3}{4}$ in.; racks, 12 ft. 6 in. by $\frac{3}{4}$ in. by $\frac{3}{8}$ in.; bearers, 3 ft. 4 in. by $1\frac{5}{8}$ in. by $\frac{3}{8}$ in.; back top rail, 3 ft. 10 in. by $3\frac{1}{2}$ in. by $\frac{7}{8}$ in.; back bottom rail, 3 ft. 10 in. by $4\frac{1}{2}$ in. by $\frac{7}{8}$ in.; two stiles, 3 ft. 5 in. by $3\frac{1}{4}$ in. by $\frac{7}{8}$ in.; two muntins, 3 ft. by $3\frac{1}{8}$ in. by $\frac{7}{8}$ in.; and three panels, 2 ft. $8\frac{1}{2}$ in. by 1 ft. by $\frac{1}{2}$ in.

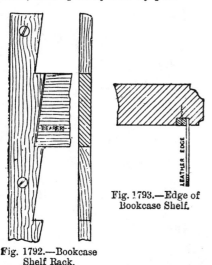

Fig. 1793.—Edge of Bookcase Shelf.

Fig. 1792.—Bookcase Shelf Rack.

MAKING DWARF BOOKCASE.

In the construction the ends should be rebated out $\frac{3}{8}$ in. for the back, and the front tongue fitted into the pilasters, a housing being sunk across the inside for the bottom, and another across the top and outside for the necking bead. The top end should be squared off to the length; then clean off both sides and paper up the outside. Next set out the two front pilasters, and work the fluting; this may be done with a scratch, a piece of steel filed to shape and fixed into a stock or handle, with a face cut on one side of it to preserve the distance of the cutters from the edge (see p. 508). It is rubbed up and down until the flutes are worked to the required depth, the finishing

of the ends being done with gouges and chisels. Plough the front pilasters on the back for the tongue from the outside edge, and arrange the groove so that the edge overhangs the end a trifle more than the thickness of the end pilaster; scribe a line on it from the face of the end, and gauge

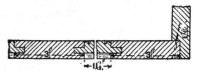

Fig. 1794.—Part Section of Bookcase Back.

another line on the edge $\frac{3}{8}$ in. from the face, and work out the rebate; then mark a mitre on each end, and with a rebate plane or shoulder plane work to a mitre the piece left on. Next glue on the pilasters, and when these are dry, fit and glue the end pilasters also, fixing them with a few screws from the inside. Square a line on each face $\frac{1}{2}$ in. below the top of the bottom housing for the plinth sinking, and work this down $\frac{1}{16}$ in. thick; then glue in the

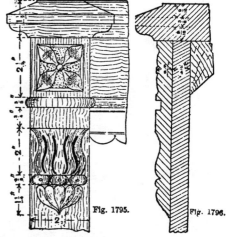

Figs. 1795 and 1796.—Elevation and Section of Truss.

bottom, nailing it through the ends. Nail a stretcher across the top end, square the front of the case, and block the bottom. Fit the plinth round and block the front piece, and screw the end pieces as shown in Fig. 1790. Set out the shoulders of the frieze rail between the pilasters at the bottom, cut dovetails at the ends, and fit

rebates. Carve the trusses (Figs. 1795 and 1796) and fix them to the pilasters, turn

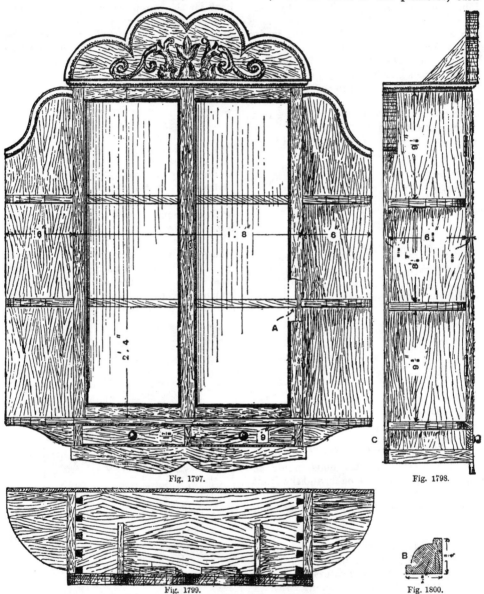

Fig. 1797.

Fig. 1798.

Fig. 1799.

Fig. 1800.

Figs. 1797 and 1798.—Front and Side Elevations of Hanging Bookcase. Fig. 1799.—Plan of Hanging Bookcase. Fig. 1800.—Section of Moulding.

these into the top of the pilasters; then clean the face off and glue in. Glue up the back (Fig. 1794) and fit and screw it to the

the carcase upside down on the top, and keep it flush at the back, and, with an inch block, mark round the outline of the front and ends. Cut the top carefully to the lines, and gauge round from the edge a 1¼-in. line, and work the moulding to this; a plough groove along the front, and a tenon saw-cut across the ends ⅛ in. deep,

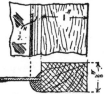

Fig. 1801.—Glass fastened in Door Frame.

will be the best way to commence. Gauge lines for the various members on the edge, and work the chamfer and the moulding down to these. Work across the ends first,

in thickness to that of the truss) upon the edge from the seat of the moulding, and mitre a loose piece of moulding around the break and across the ends. The last piece should be tongued on. Next fit the top, which, being narrow, may be screwed and blocked on.

RACKS AND SHELVES OF DWARF BOOKCASE.

Prepare the racks of oak or beech, cut them to the length, brad them all together, and set out the notches, starting 6 in. from each end. Run a pencil line down each side ¼ in. on, and down to this make a series of cuts with the saw. Pare with firmer or paring chisel from the top of one cut to the bottom of the next, being careful not to split the succeeding piece off; this

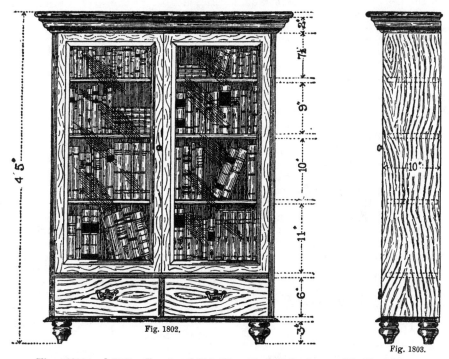

Fig. 1802.

Fig. 1803.

Figs. 1802 and 1803.—Front and Side Elevations of Bookcase with Glass Doors.

then the projection over the pilasters, and, finally, the run on the front edge. An easier, but inferior, way is to run the front edge through, mitre the moulding back at the break, glue a ⅝-in. piece (a piece equal

method of cutting ensures that the bearers will be interchangeable. Bore half a dozen holes through the lot for screws, separate them, and smooth and fix them. Fit in the bearers and shelves; the latter should be notched at the ends to pass easily over the racks as shown in Fig. 1791. Finally, plough the under edges of the shelves, and fit the edging slips and mould. The case will then be ready for polishing, but to

Fig. 1804.—Bookcase Cornice.

obtain the best finish all the parts should be fitted together accurately when dry: then each should be polished or bodied in, and the whole glued up, when the finishing coat of polish may be applied.

Hanging Bookcase.

The bookcase shown in Figs. 1797 to 1799 requires 10 ft. of $\frac{3}{8}$-in. by $6\frac{3}{4}$-in. mahogany or walnut for the rectangular frame. The two side pieces C (Fig. 1798) are continued downwards for 3 in., and on the inside of these, and 2 in. below the bottom shelf, two strips of wood are tacked or glued on. Another piece of wood, $\frac{3}{8}$ in. by $6\frac{3}{4}$ in. by 3 in., is also nailed to the centre of the shelf underneath, and projects downwards to correspond with the sides. Two strips of wood are likewise fastened on each side of this, and on them

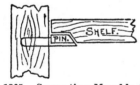

Fig. 1805.—Supporting Movable Shelf.

slide the two drawers, which are 9 in. by 7 in. by $1\frac{3}{4}$ in. deep, with a small bead running along the front at the top and bottom. The two middle shelves are let into the sides as at A (Fig. 1797), and may be spaced out as seen in Fig. 1798, or as re-

quired. The two doors are made from 1-in. by $\frac{5}{8}$-in. stuff. They are 10 in. wide by 2 ft. 4 in. in length, and each is fastened by two hinges. A small catch should be screwed inside the left-hand door and made to engage with a hole drilled in a brass plate, sunk into the shelf. A narrow strip of $\frac{1}{4}$-in. round beading should be glued round the inside of the doors, as shown in Fig. 1800, or the frame may be rebated and a fancy moulding run along the outside. The glass for the doors is held in position as shown in Fig. 1801, by gluing a few strips of wood along the inside of the frame. The moulding B (Fig. 1800) for the top and sides can be turned in the lathe in the form of a ring, cut up, and glued to the top of the board, and to fill in the space in the top of the case a little fretwork or carving may be

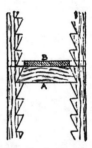

Fig. 1806.—Double Rack for Bookcase Shelves.

introduced. The three shelves on the sides are all of one size, or the bottom one may be larger and the other two made smaller. They are fastened to the sides of the frame as indicated at A (Fig. 1797), and should be of the same thickness as those on the inside. The back of the case is $\frac{3}{8}$ in. thick (see Fig. 1799), and the three shelves on the inside should be covered with green baize. The whole can then be finished off and french-polished.

Bookcase with Glass Doors.

Mahogany is a suitable wood for the bookcase shown in front elevation in Fig. 1802 and side elevation in Fig. 1803, but if this is too expensive pine or cherry may be used. The actual size of the bookcase depends entirely upon the requirements of the worker. Having decided upon the size and material, get the quantities required for the work run out at the timber yard, always allowing, of course, a working margin. Care must be taken that the wood is thoroughly seasoned and perfectly dry, otherwise it will give endless trouble. These preliminaries over, proceed to the construction of the carcase. This consists of the gables, carcase top, carcase bottom,

Fig. 1807.—Fixing Bookcase Back.

and back. An ordinary moulded beading may be fixed to the top of the carcase (as in Fig. 1804). The shelves in a bookcase of this size are 3 ft. 4 in. long, 8½ in. wide, and ¾ in. thick. They should be fixtures, as, unless a bookcase is very solidly built, movable shelves cause much trouble. One plan, should adjustable shelves be preferred, is to bore two parallel rows of holes, on the inside of the gables. These are fitted with brass pins (see Fig. 1805), and the shelves are countersunk so that the pins may be flush. Another method is that known as the double rack (see Fig. 1806) already mentioned. In this the movable slip A gives a firm support to the end of the shelf B, which is cut to fit upon it. The slip and rack should be about ½ in. thick. Having got so far, fix in the upright that divides the drawers at the bottom of the case. The back, which consists of 6-in. by ⅝-in. lining, may now be fixed (see Fig. 1807). Next come the doors. The strips of wood intended for this purpose must be tenoned and mortised as shown in Fig. 1808. The inside edges of these pieces must also be rebated, so that the glass can be let in. Having fixed the glass in its proper position, fasten the doors in their respective places. On the inside and at the bottom of one of these doors fasten a small bolt. On the other door fix a small knob similar to that shown in Fig. 1809, which will serve both as handle and fastener.

The drawers should be made next. The front, ends, and back of each drawer are dovetailed to each other. In fitting the sides to the front, use the lap dovetail (p. 216). With this the ends are sunk in the drawer front, so that when looking at it from the front no joint is perceptible. Fit the back with the ordinary dovetails into the sides. These drawers must be cut to fit very tightly; if they do not run easily enough, a rub with glasspaper will soon ease them sufficiently afterwards. Fasten two handles to the fronts of the drawers, and they are then complete. The feet are turned from 2¾-in. wood. The best method is to fix them by means of two strong oak dowels in each foot. If the wall against which the bookcase is to be placed is inclined to be damp, a space should be left between the back of the case and the wall, through which the air can circulate freely; or, if it is known that the wall is damp, a better method is to make the back of the bookcase of zinc. To protect the edges of books placed on the shelves, cover the shelf with baize, over which is placed another covering of smooth American cloth.

BOOKCASE WITH LOWER CUPBOARDS AND GLAZED DOORS.

The bookcase of which Fig. 1810 shows the front elevation, Fig. 1811 shows side

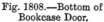
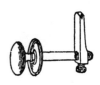

Fig. 1808.—Bottom of Bookcase Door.

Fig. 1809.—Door Knob.

elevation, and Fig. 1812 shows a vertical section and front elevation, should be constructed in mahogany. It is made up in two carcases. The lower part is enclosed by two doors with veneered panels, as shown in Fig. 1810, and supported by a base, consisting of a pine frame mortised and tenoned together, with a moulding mitred round the edges of the front and the ends. Four tapered feet are fixed to the frame at the corners. The upper part is enclosed by two glass doors, divided by astragals in the positions indicated at Fig. 1810. An astragal is a rebated bar

1814. The top and bottom, of ⅝-in. pine, are dovetailed to the gables. They should be flush at the front edges, and kept in at the back to allow the back to overlap. The back consists of three muntins, 3 in. wide, and two panels which are tongued to the

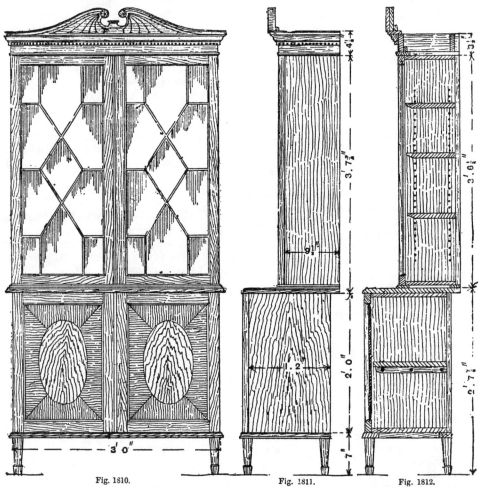

Fig. 1810. Fig. 1811. Fig. 1812.

Figs. 1810 to 1812.—Front Elevation, Side Elevation, and Cross Section of Bookcase.

used in glass door or window construction. A loose cornice and pediment complete the upper part. Commencing with the lower part, plane up the two gables, and square them to 2 ft. long, by 1 ft. 2 in. wide, by ⅝ in. thick. Rebate the back edges to receive the back, which is ⅝ in. thick, and tongued and grooved as shown in Figs. 1813 and

muntins; the joints are broken with a bead. A shelf, ⅞ in. thick, rests on fillets screwed to the gables. The shelf may be bevelled away on the under side at the front to give it a thinner appearance. The two doors are mortised and tenoned together, the stiles and rails being 2 in. wide, except the two meeting stiles, which should be kept ¼ in.

wider for the rebates and bead A (Fig. 1815). A moulding is run on inside the edges, and a rebate made for the panel, which is fixed with a bead on the inside (see Fig. 1815).

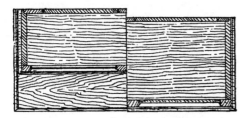

Fig. 1813.   Fig. 1814.

Figs. 1813 and 1814.—Half-plans of Upper and Lower Parts of Bookcase.

The panels are veneered, as shown in Fig. 1810. Sound African mahogany, $\frac{1}{2}$ in. thick, should be used for a foundation for the veneer, and the surface gone over with a toothing plane before veneering. Commence by laying the piece for the oval, allowing a good margin, which can be afterwards cut off by placing a thin pine mould cut to the size over the veneer, and drawing a sharp chisel round the edge. A showy curl veneer should be used for the oval, the two axes of which may be 1 ft. 2 in. and $8\frac{1}{2}$ in. It can be rubbed down with a hammer, as fully described on pp. 491 to 497. The veneer round the edges of the oval should be straight grained to show a contrast, and should be mitred at the corners, with the grain running in the direction shown in Fig. 1810. Mortise and tenon a frame together for the base $\frac{7}{8}$ in. thick. Then mitre and glue a moulding round the edges of the front and ends. The shaped feet are screwed to the frame. The top of the lower part is $\frac{7}{8}$ in. thick, and projects

Fig. 1815.—Section of Bookcase Door.

over the gables at the front to cover in the doors; it also projects $1\frac{1}{4}$ in. over the back. The two gables of the upper part should be squared up to 3 ft. 6 in. long by $9\frac{1}{2}$ in. wide by $\frac{7}{8}$ in. thick, and rebated on the back edges for the back, similar to the lower

gables. The top and bottom are dovetailed to the gables as already described for the lower carcase.

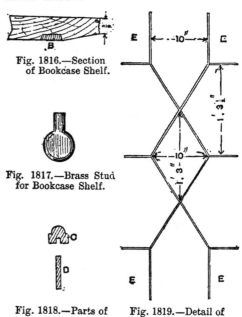

Fig. 1816.—Section of Bookcase Shelf.

Fig. 1817.—Brass Stud for Bookcase Shelf.

Fig. 1818.—Parts of Astragal.   Fig. 1819.—Detail of Glass Door.

COMPLETING BOOKCASE.

The three movable shelves are $\frac{7}{8}$ in. thick, and are bevelled on the under side, and a moulding is run on the edge (see Fig. 1816). Bore holes on the inside of the gables 1 in. apart for the brass studs (Fig. 1817), which

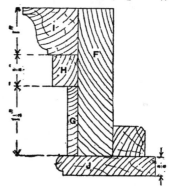

Fig. 1820.—Cross Section of Cornice.

support the shelves. Sink the studs into the shelves at B (Fig. 1816). The stiles and

rails of the astragal doors are 1¾ in. wide
by 1 in. thick. Frame up the doors before
fixing in the astragals, which are made up
in two pieces, c and d (Fig. 1818). The

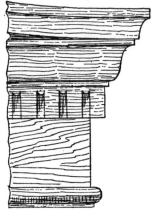

Fig. 1821.—Detail of Cornice.

moulded piece c can be bought ready made
from any dealer. Draw the design on a
board, and make up the four corners e
(Fig. 1819) with the pieces d (Fig. 1818),
dovetailing them together at the corners.
The other pieces are next glued in position.
All the joints should be strengthened by
gluing on pieces of strong tape. The
corners and middle pieces should be mortised to the edges of the stiles and rails.
The moulded pieces are glued to the
pieces d (Fig. 1818), mitring them at the
corners, and to the sash moulding on the
stiles and rails. The glass is bedded in
with putty, the latter being coloured to
match the wood. A plain moulding, 2½ in.
wide by ½ in. thick, is mitred and glued to
the top of the lower part of the bookcase to
form a base for the upper carcase. Fig. 1820

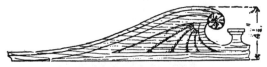

Fig. 1822.—Detail of Pediment.

is an enlarged view of an angle piece joined
to a square corner. The cornice consists of a
separate frame of pine to which the various
mouldings are glued. The front and ends

of the frame f (Fig. 1820) are 3⅛ in. wide
by ¾ in. thick, and are dovetailed at the
corners. The back of the frame is kept
1 in. in from the back, and is fixed with a

Fig. 1823.—Section of Glass Door.

dovetailed groove. The frieze g (Fig. 1820)
is 1½ in. wide by ¼ in. thick, glued and
mitred at the corners. The piece for the
dentils h is next glued to the top edge of
the frieze, the dentils being cut with a

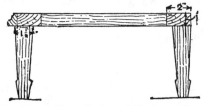

Fig. 1824.—Cross Section of Bookcase Base.

gouge as shown in Fig. 1821. The top
moulding i comes next, and the bottom
piece j is glued to the edges of the frieze.
The pediment is ⅝ in. thick, and is shaped
as shown in Fig. 1822. The hollow moulding is shaped and glued to the face of the
pediment, one end running into the carved
patera, the outer end being mitred to a

Fig. 1825.—Dwarf Revolving Bookcase.

straight piece of the same moulding at the
ends. The pediment is screwed to the top
of the cornice ; a few blocks are glued to the
back. Flush bolts should be fitted to the

edges of the left-hand doors at the top and bottom. Fig. 1823 shows an enlarged section of glass doors, and Fig. 1824 illustrates

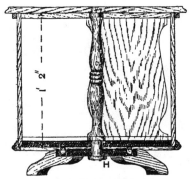

Fig. 1826.—Vertical Section of Revolving Bookcase.

a cross section of the base. Brass locks and hinges complete the fittings for the bookcase.

DWARF REVOLVING BOOKCASE.

The bookcase shown by Fig. 1825 may be constructed from American satin-walnut. Fig. 1826 shows a vertical section on A B (Fig. 1827). The top and bottom boards are connected by four fretted banisters and by the centre turned column, which is tenoned about two-thirds into the top shelf and fitted snugly to the lower shelf to project through a clearing hole in the base or turntable. A disc of hard wood H (Fig. 1826) is screwed

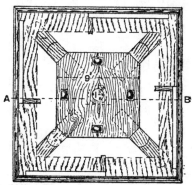

Fig. 1827.—Plan of Lower Part of Revolving Bookcase.

on the pivot to retain the base in position when lifting the bookcase. Fig. 1828 shows the under side of the top board, and the

method of striking the curves. The segment D E is struck with a radius C D; then with centres on the lines C D and C E pro-

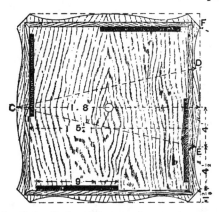

Fig. 1828.—Under-side of Top Board of Revolving Bookcase.

duced, and with a 7-in. radius, mark the curve D F. A template should be made of Bristol board or thick paper, when the four sides can be marked off by it with a pencil. A moulding is worked round the edges, and fillets are glued and screwed to the under

Fig. 1829.—Fretwork Banister of Revolving Bookcase.

side to prevent warping. The banisters (see Fig. 1829) are housed to the bottom shelf (Fig. 1830) and screwed to the fillets on the top (Fig. 1831). A moulding mitred at the corners is planted on the edges of the lower shelf, thus concealing the screw heads and end grain, and giving a better

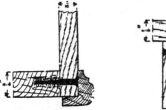

Fig. 1830.—Detail of Lower Shelf.

Fig. 1831.—Detail of Top.

finish generally. The base is of deal, 9 in. by 9 in. by ⅞ in., and is shown in plan by Fig. 1827, part of the lower shelf being omitted for the sake of clearness. Procure four castor rollers (Fig. 1832), 1 in. in diameter, and sink them in their slots, leaving ¼ in. clearance between the base and the shelf. Their pivots should fit tightly in grooves. The pivot ends pointing to the centre column may be slightly depressed, this will counteract the tendency of the rollers to work outwards when the case is revolving. The feet are made from birch, the method of securing them to the base being shown at Fig. 1833. Fit up the case temporarily and try it on the rollers, adjusting them by lowering the higher ones to the plane of the lowest roller till each has an equal bearing. Then cut off the projecting pivot of column, and fix the disc H in position to clear the baseboard in revolving. The lower shelf is divided by four fillets (see Figs. 1825 and 1327) to keep the books in their proper spaces. The case may be disconnected, the fretwork cut, and the various parts thoroughly glasspapered, stained, and polished. Prepare a full-size drawing of the fretwork on cartridge paper,

Fig. 1832.—Roller.

and cut out the spaces on the drawing, which will then form a stencil plate; fix

the plate on the wood, taking care to get it central, fasten it down with four drawing pins, and dab over the design with a sponge, using umber mixed rather thick with tur-

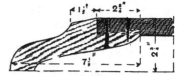

Fig. 1833.—Side View of Foot.

pentine. The same plate will do for the four banisters, but it is usual to give the stencil plate a coat of knotting on each side when many duplicates are required. The surplus wood may be removed with a brace and bits and a keyhole saw. The end grain of the top board will require extra filling before polishing. Give it a coat of size or very thin glue, allow it to dry thoroughly,

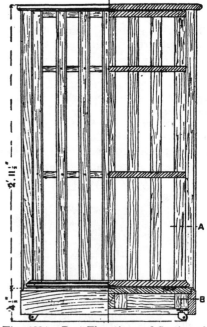

Fig. 1834.—Part Elevation and Section of Revolving Bookcase.

then rub down carefully with fine glass-paper; repeat this operation till the grain ceases to rise, when it will be found to take the polish without sinking in.

3-FT. REVOLVING BOOKCASE.

Fig. 1834 is a half elevation and half vertical section on the centre line of a revolving bookcase. In some instances, the actual

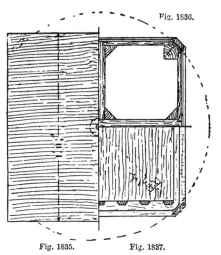

Figs. 1835 to 1837.—Half Top Plan and Two Quarter Sections of Revolving Bookcase.

case revolves on an iron standard mounted on cross legs, but here it is pivoted between a square plinth and a solid top, the latter being fixed on four corner pilasters. Two pairs of circular pivot plates are used, fixed centrally in the top and case, as indicated by the dotted lines in the half plan of the top (Fig. 1835). Figs. 1836 and 1837 are respectively quarter horizontal sections at B and A (Fig. 1834). The iron pivot plates, 2 in. in diameter, are shown in plan and elevation in Fig. 1838. Fig. 1839 is an enlarged broken section through the middle of the top of the case, showing the method

Fig. 1838.—Pivot Plates.

of fixing the pivots and the necessary clearance ; the bottom pair may be fixed similarly. After what has been said, only a few particulars as to how the bookcase is

constructed need be given. The corners of the base mould are rounded, not square. The corner pilasters are of 3-in. by $\frac{1}{2}$-in. stuff, moulded to match the case. The moulding is stopped at the bottom end, and

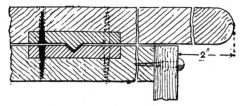

Fig. 1839.—Pivot at Top of Revolving Case.

the pilasters are sunk flush with the faces of the plinth ; at the upper ends they are housed $\frac{3}{8}$ in. into the top. The bookcase, when revolving, must just clear the corners of the outer case ; and the size will be best found by making the case first, mounting the pivots, and revolving the bookcase on a drawing board, when its path, as shown by the dotted lines in Figs. 1836 and 1837, will indicate the size of the plinth and top. Four drawer rollers (Fig. 1840) should be sunk flush into the upper side of the plinth to take the bearing of the case, which is otherwise liable to rub on the bottom when unequally loaded ; they should be mounted as shown in Fig. 1837, with the axis of the roller lying in a line radiating from the centre. It would be a further advantage to insert in the bottom of the case an annular band of metal, over which the rollers might travel. An alternative fitting is shown in Fig. 1841, which is known as a dumb-waiter pivot pin. If these are

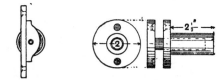

Fig. 1840.—Friction Roller.   Fig. 1841.—Dumb-waiter Pivot Pin.

used with the rollers described above, a pivot will not be required at the top, and the pilasters may be dispensed with ; then the top will be fixed direct to the case. But by this method a central standard, about 2 in. square, will be required, into the lower end of which the sleeve, shown partly up in Fig. 1841, must be sunk, the pivot

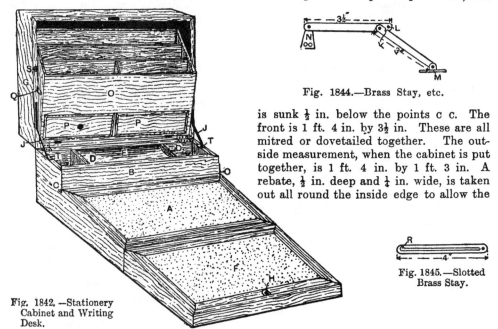

Fig. 1842. —Stationery Cabinet and Writing Desk.

plate being fixed in the top of the plinth. The iron standard may be enclosed within a square shaft, to prevent the books rubbing against the standard, and so in time suffering more or less damage to their covers; this shaft may be about 4 in. square, built up with ⅜-in. linings, and housed into the top and bottom shelves.

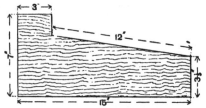

Fig. 1843.—Side of Writing Desk.

STATIONERY CABINET AND WRITING-DESK.

This cabinet (see Fig. 1842) can be made of any kind of wood, but walnut is preferable. The sides (or ends), back, and front of the foundation part A are of ⅜-in. stuff;

the size and shape of the ends are given in Fig. 1843. The back part is 1 ft. 4 in. by 7 in. deep. The strip B is 2½ in. wide, and

Fig. 1844.—Brass Stay, etc.

is sunk ½ in. below the points C C. The front is 1 ft. 4 in. by 3½ in. These are all mitred or dovetailed together. The outside measurement, when the cabinet is put together, is 1 ft. 4 in. by 1 ft. 3 in. A rebate, ½ in. deep and ¼ in. wide, is taken out all round the inside edge to allow the

Fig. 1845.—Slotted Brass Stay.

bottom (which measures 1 ft. 3¼ in. by 1 ft. 2¼ in. by ½ in.) to be glued in. A piece of ¼-in. stuff is glued between B and the back to form the bottom of the pen-rack; this is shown by a dotted line. Two little partitions are fitted across at D D. The pen-tray E, which is hollowed out, rests on two small ledges glued on to D D. Narrow strips of wood are also glued all round the part A, ¼ in. from the top, so as to form a ledge for the lid to rest upon. The part F is made in a similar manner, and measures 1 ft. 4 in. by 1 ft. It is 3½ in. deep where it is hinged on to A, and 2 in. deep at the narrowest part. The size of the desk proper, when folded, is 1 ft. 4 in. by 1 ft. 3 in. by 7 in. The lids A and F are made of ¼-in. stuff, planed up smooth, and with a frame of the same thickness glued round them. Both lids have a piece of velvet or fine leather let in to form the writing surface. A small flush-bolt or catch is fitted to F at H. A catch is not necessary on A. The framework of the lid G is made of ⅜-in.

stuff and the top of ¼-in. ; this lid is 5 in. deep. The brass stays J (Fig. 1842), also shown in Fig. 1844, are made of $\frac{1}{16}$-in. brass, ¼ in. wide. A little peg L is riveted at one end, and projects $\frac{1}{10}$ in., so as to fit in the slot K when the stay is open. The part M (Fig. 1844) is screwed down to T, and N is screwed to G from the inside, a recess 4 in. long, ⅜ in. wide, and ½ in. deep being cut up the edges of G to allow the stays to fold in when the desk is closed.

THE STATIONERY CABINET.

The stationery cabinet O is 1 ft. 2¾ in. long, and should just fit in the lid G. It is 1 ft. ½ in. high at the back, 10 in. at the front, and 4½ in. deep from back to front. The sides and back are of ¼-in. stuff ; the rest is $\frac{1}{16}$ in. thick. Two small drawers are fitted at P P. The exact height of these drawers does not matter, but 2½ in. to 3 in. will be found about right. Other divisions besides those shown can be fitted to the cabinet if desired. Cut two pieces of $\frac{1}{16}$-in. brass to the shape shown in Fig. 1845 ; one has a small hollow filed at the end of the slot, as at R ; the slot in the other stay is quite straight. Fit one of these inside each

end of the lid (the wood of which will want cutting slightly away) by passing a screw through the slot into the wood. The hollow R must be nearest the top of the cabinet. The cabinet is next hinged to the lid, and the stays Q are fastened to it so as to allow it to be pulled out about 3 in. ; the hollow R then drops over the screw and keeps the cabinet in position until the stay is lifted up with the finger. A small turn-button S is fitted to each side to keep the cabinet from falling forward when the desk is closed. Small locks or catches should be fitted to the drawers for a like purpose, and a lock can also be fitted to the desk. The cabinet and writing-desk can now be completed by french-polishing, or staining and varnishing if common wood be used.

DAVENPORT WRITING CABINET.

The top part of this writing cabinet is closed with a hinged flap, which, folding down on the top of the table, is inclined at the angle of an ordinary writing-desk. This angle can be altered in the construction by either reducing or enlarging the depth of the bottom drawer. Immediately at the back of the flap, and on the divisional shelf

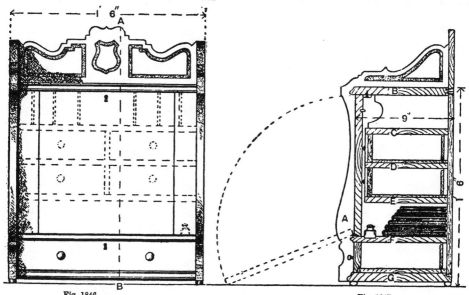

Figs. 1846 and 1847.—Front Elevation and Cross Section of Davenport Writing Cabinet.

to which it is hinged, are placed two ink-bottles, and midway between them is a channel for receiving pens and pencils. On

Fig. 1848.—Desk Flap Up.

this shelf, note-books, etc., may be placed. There are also four drawers sliding on shelves and separated by divisions. Immediately above the drawers are pigeonholes for note-paper, old letters, accounts, etc. The top of the cabinet can be used for either books or ornaments. The cabinet is intended to stand on a side table with its back to the wall. Fig. 1846 is a front elevation of the cabinet, the dotted lines showing the arrangement of the interior. Fig. 1847 represents a vertical section on A B, showing the construction, A indicating a design to which the gables may be cut out. Above the top, and following the design, is a small channel cut in with a gauge and chisel, then punched with a tool that carvers use for that purpose. The top B and shelves C, D, E, F are dovetail raggled to the gables. The bottom G is lap-dovetailed to the gables. The gables are checked to receive the back, which is nailed to them and to the shelves. The bottom part (see Fig. 1847) has its grain running up and down, and the grain of the top part running across. The top part is shaped out as shown in Fig. 1846, and channelled out and punched in the same manner as the gables. Four turned balls are screwed

to the bottom to raise the cabinet off the table.

DESK FLAP.

The desk flap shown by Figs. 1847 and 1848 can be made either to fit into a recess or to fix against a wall. Wood about $\frac{7}{8}$ in. thick will be most suitable for all the parts. To keep the top true it should be clamped as shown. When the bracket is glued together, the top joint should be further secured by a couple of screws. The brackets should be hinged to the side pieces, or they can be made with pins at each end fitting into sockets in the top piece or lower rail. The framing can be secured by two hold-fasts driven into the wall underneath the top piece, and the bottom of the side pieces can be nailed to the floor or skirting.

Fig. 1849.—Desk Flap Down.

CONVERTING KITCHEN TABLE INTO KNEE-HOLE WRITING TABLE.

The pedestal writing table illustrated by Fig. 1850 is an ordinary square-legged kitchen table fitted with a cupboard and drawer carcase at each end, and a desk on top. Fig. 1850 shows a very small table, it being only 3 ft. 6 in. by 1 ft. 8 in., but any size of table can be fitted up on the same principle. The knee-hole is 1 ft. 6 in. broad, and, being in the middle, governs the size of the drawers and cupboard at each end. The drawers are locked secretly, and underneath the desk is a semi-secret receptacle for papers, etc. Fig. 1851 is a longitudinal section of the table, showing giving a side view of the locking arrangement; Fig. 1853 is a section through the

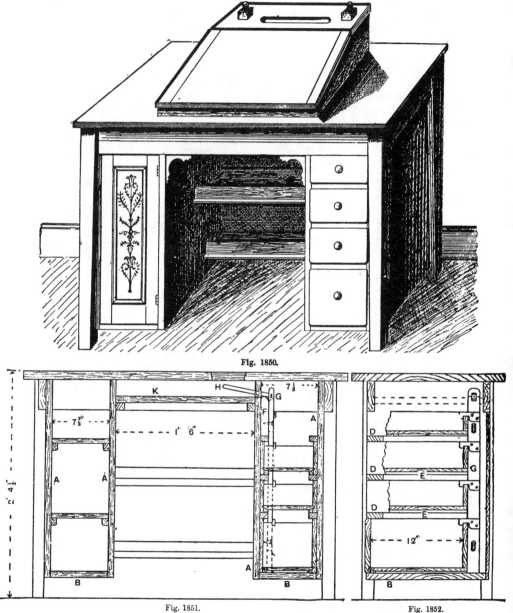

Fig. 1850.

Fig. 1851.

Fig. 1852.

Figs. 1850 to 1852.—General View, Longitudinal Section, and Horizontal Section of Knee-hole Writing Table Converted from Kitchen Table.

the general construction; Fig. 1852 is a cross section through the drawer space, desk, showing the shelves in the knee-hole, and a series of flaps cut out of the solid top

35

to give access to the space below the desk ;
Fig. 1854 is a section on the line A B (Fig.
1853), showing the pigeonholes in the interior of the desk ; Fig. 1855 is a part plan
of the table with the top part of the desk
taken away, showing the position of the
flaps ; Fig. 1856 is an enlarged section
through a table leg and gable, the dotted
lines representing the front and end rails.
The gables A, which are ½ in. less in width
than the over-all width of the front and
back rails of the table, are checked at the
top to fit inside the rails to which they are
screwed, the bottom B being dovetailed to

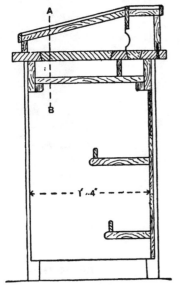

Fig. 1853.—Section through Desk and Table.

the gables. As the legs of a kitchen table
are tapered inside, they require to be
checked to allow the outside gables to stand
plumb. It may happen that the table which
is to be converted has very small legs, and,
when they are checked, the gable lies hard
against the end rails ; but when this cannot be the case owing to the size of the leg
and the position of the rails, a block can be
fixed to the gables to close up the space
which is shown in Fig. 1856. The drawer
divisions D are raggle-dovetailed to the
gables, and fillets E are screwed at the back
of them. Before fixing the drawer carcase

together, put on the locks. Blocks F (Fig.
1851) are fixed to the gables to carry the
locking part G, which has two screw slots
cut out of it to allow it to slide up and down.

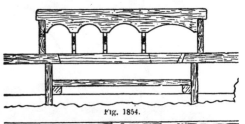

Fig. 1854.

Fig. 1855.

Figs. 1854 and 1855.—Section and Part Plan of
Table Top.

At the top end a mortise is cut, into which
is inserted a small lever H, fixed with an
iron pin. When the lever is depressed, it
raises the part G high enough to allow the
back of the drawers to clear the small brass
plates which hold them in. When the
drawers are pushed hard back and the
lever is raised, the sliding part G is lowered,
and the plates fit over the drawer backs.
The lever is of sufficient length to give the
necessary power. The gable requires to be
mortised also. The shelves in the knee-

Fig. 1856.—Section through Table Leg and
Gable.

hole should be raggle-dovetailed to the
gables to bind the two ends together. The
legs should not be checked at the back of
the rails, as that would weaken the table ;

it is better to check the gable at that part. After the carcases are fixed to the table, the shelves in the knee-hole glued in, and off as shown in Fig. 1852. The desk, the bottom of which is formed by the table top, is secret-dovetailed in front, and the drawer

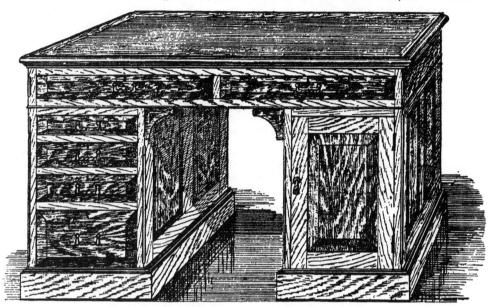

Fig. 1857.—Pedestal Knee-hole Writing Table.

the back nailed on, the false bottom K should be fitted, and fixed to the fillets after they are screwed on. Fillets are also screwed to the inside of the cupboard to carry the shelves. The cupboard door. dovetailed at the back. The divisions are raggled into the top part of the desk, which is nailed down to the sides and back. The bead, shown in elevation in Fig. 1854, is let into the desk sides, and projects above

Fig. 1858.   Fig. 1859.   Fig. 1860.

Figs. 1858 to 1860.—Half Back Elevation. Side Elevation, and Cross Section through Pedestal of Knee-hole Desk.

which is mortised and tenoned, is hung $\frac{1}{8}$ in. inside to break the joint. The fronts of the drawers project $\frac{1}{8}$ in. or so, and are rounded the top the same distance as the back one. It also projects out from the sides the thickness of itself to mitre with the side bead on the top. The flap is clamped at each end with 2-in. pieces to keep it from warping, the bead being returned on the front

work. The panels and drawer fronts could be veneered with burr walnut, but as this is a somewhat difficult veneer with which

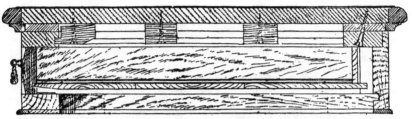

Fig. 1861.—Cross Section of Knee-hole Table Top.

and ends, and rounded at the top end. The flap is hung with brass butts, the ball being sunk into the bead. The desk is fixed by means of screws from below, as shown by Fig. 1853. To facilitate the raising of the flaps under the desk, two holes should be countersunk in them, and screws inserted. The edges of the screw heads should be slightly rounded, otherwise they may cut the fingers. The countersink must also be large enough to allow of the finger-nail being inserted below the head of the

to make a good job, it is advisable to form them of solid walnut. The material should be obtained as dry as possible, and free from shakes and blemishes. The length of the table is 4 ft., the width of the framework from back to front 2 ft., and the height 2 ft. 9 in. ; and before proceeding with its construction working drawings should be prepared. Fig. 1858 shows a half elevation of the back, Fig. 1859 a complete side elevation, Fig. 1860 a vertical section, Fig. 1861 an enlarged section through the table

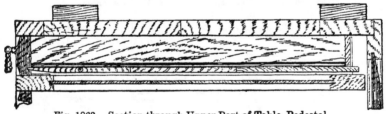

Fig. 1862.—Section through Upper Part of Table Pedestal.

screw. Small brackets may be fixed at the corner of the knee-hole for ornamentation. When completed, the table may be either painted or stained.

PEDESTAL KNEE-HOLE WRITING TABLE.

This pedestal writing table, as illustrated by Fig. 1857, can be made externally of pitchpine and walnut, the inside fittings being of American whitewood. Pitchpine, however, although it looks well in combination with walnut, is, unless thoroughly dry, a treacherous material to deal with ; therefore it is advisable to make the visible parts entirely of walnut, using whitewood (or mahogany for preference) for the inside

top, and Fig. 1862 an enlarged section through the top of one of the pedestals.

WRITING TABLE PEDESTALS.

The pedestals may be taken in hand first. In each there are three pieces of framework—namely, two sides and one back ; and in size they are exactly the same, the only difference being in the fitting up. The bottom rails should be 6½ in. wide, this width being a convenient one to fix the skirting to. Walnut need not be used throughout; for the sake of economy a strip 3 in. wide may be glued to another 3½ in. wide of pine or any cheaper wood. Four bottom rails 2 ft. long and two

1 ft. 3 in. long will be required, the same number of top rails 2½ in. wide, twelve stiles 2 ft. 1½ in. by 2½ in. (four of these are for the backs), and four muntins 1 ft. 6 in. by 2½ in. The door in the right-hand pedestal will require two rails 1 ft. 1 in. by 2½ in. and two stiles 1 ft. 9 in. by 2½ in. All the foregoing will be 1 in. in thickness, and the stuff should be got out and prepared straight and perfectly out of winding, and should then be set out, not forgetting to set back the ½ in. allowed for the panels. The setting out being completed, the requisite mortising, tenoning, shouldering, and ploughing can be proceeded with. It should be noticed that the mortises in the stiles of the pedestal sides, also of the door, do not go right through, as the end grain of the tenons, if allowed to show, would make the work look unsightly; to obviate this, the tenons are stumped and fox-wedged. The mortises for the back frames, being hidden, may go right through. The framing may be knocked together, care being taken that the shoulders come up well. The pedestal framing is rebated round the upper inner edges to receive the tops, except in the front, where it is dovetailed; and the rails should be rebated before the framing is glued up. The bottoms of the pedestals, as shown by Fig. 1860, are housed ¼ in. deep into the rails and stiles all round, and it will be easier to plough the rails before gluing up, and to run saw-cuts in the stiles afterwards, the intervening wood being then taken out with a sharp chisel. The groove should be small enough to ensure a tight fit for the bottom. The panels will be of ⅝ in. finished thickness, and the sizes for these can be obtained from the framework already prepared; eleven panels will be required, five for each pedestal and one for the door. These having been faced up, thicknessed, and accurately squared, set a cutting gauge to 2 in., and cut all round the panels on the face to the depth of ⅛ in.; this will allow a 1½-in. margin to show, as seen in Fig. 1859. Set another gauge to the width of the plough groove, and mark the edges of all the panels from the back, and sink them to the gauge marks.

GLUING UP WRITING TABLE PEDESTALS.

For gluing up, place a couple of strips on the bench, perfectly out of winding, and be sure that the glue is hot and sufficiently liquid. (For the making of glued joints see p. 183). Bring the joints well up with cramps, and see that the framing is perfectly square and out of winding. The best thing to do with the framing for the present is to pack it away in a dry place, with strips laid between each portion so that the air may get all round them. If laid out of winding, a weight placed on the top of the lot will keep them from casting. In order that the glued joints of any material which has to be jointed may have a good chance

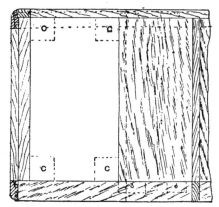

Fig. 1863.—Plan of Table Top Framework.

to get hard before being required for use, attention should now be given in this direction. Commence with the pedestal drawer bottoms, of which four are required; as the drawers are 1 ft. 1 in. wide and the grain runs across them, four bottoms must be prepared 1 ft. 1 in. long and about 1 ft. 10 in. wide, to make which eight pieces 9 in. by ½ in., and four pieces 4½ in. by ½ in., all 1 ft. 1 in. long, will be required, two of the 9-in. pieces and one of 4½ in. width making one bottom. There are also two drawers in the table, for which two bottoms 1 ft. 11 in. wide by 1 ft. 10 in. will be wanted; these may also be built up of two 9-in. and one 4½-in. boards 1 ft. 11 in. long. For dust-boards between the drawers in the pedestal—three in number, and about 1 ft. long by 1 ft 7 in. wide—⅜-in. stuff may be jointed up as before. The tops and bottoms of the pedestals are of 1-in. stuff, and measure 2 ft. bv 1 ft. 3 in. in size, and to the largest, must be of hard wood, or they will probably snap off. See that the mortises are free from stray chips, and that the glue is hot. The joints may be made and cramped, and placed aside to dry.

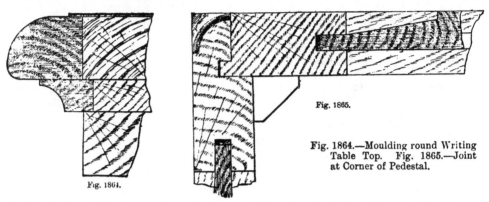

Fig. 1865.

Fig. 1864.—Moulding round Writing Table Top. Fig. 1865.—Joint at Corner of Pedestal.

Fig. 1864.

the front edges of the tops a piece of walnut about 2 in. wide is jointed.

TOP FRAMING, ETC., OF WRITING TABLE.

For the table top, a piece of good sound dry yellow pine will suffice, the moulding, etc., being planted on. The size being 4 ft. by 2 ft., three 1-in. boards, 9 in. wide and 4 ft. long, will be required, and it will be advisable to cross-tongue the joints. A piece of 1-in. stuff will also be required to cover over the knee-hole under the drawers, as shown in plan (see Fig. 1863); this will be 1 ft. 8 in. wide and 2 ft. long. The framework of the table top, which is 5 in. wide, may next be taken in hand. It is shown in the figures with the corners framed up to carry the same line as the framing of the pedestals; this looks much better than the plain mitre, but the latter is much the quicker to do. Presuming that framing is decided upon, clamp the ends of the two sides and back. The sides will have to be stump-tenoned and fox-wedged, but the back may have its mortises run through, as the rebate will cover them. Cut the tenons of the former ⅛ in. less in length than the depth of the mortises, and slightly undercut the mortises, so that there will be room for the tenon to spread out when wedged. The wedges, of which four will he sufficient, the two outside ones being

When the glue is hard, the top framing can be taken in hand again; and after facing and thicknessing the two sides and back of the frame, the board that is to go in the bottom, the three rails and pieces to go between the drawers, and the two narrow bearers, the sides and back may be rebated, grooved, and tongued together. The ovolo mouldings may be worked now, or when the frame is glued up. Place the back and ends together on the bench, and draw the joints up with a cramp. The exact width for the front rails can now be got; on each end of these rails (see Fig. 1863) are two dovetails. Having cut these, lay the rails in position on the sides and mark and cut the sockets. The rails being in position, the centre of the front may be marked for the piece between the drawers, and this piece may be prepared and dovetailed (as shown in Fig. 1868). The dovetail groove must be diminished ¼ in. on the back, so as to make it fit like a wedge. Fig. 1861 shows in section a rail, with a screw passing through it into the top; this rail runs right across at the back (see dotted line in Fig. 1863), the ends are dovetailed into the sides, and the back edge fits into a rebate in the rail. The cover board and the bearers for the drawers, coming flush with the top of the bottom rail, can be tenoned into it as shown in Fig. 1863, and either dovetailed or grooved and tongued into the back; dovetails will make a much firmer job and keep the back from springing much better than the other method. The bottom will act as two of the drawer bearers, and a rail will be required to divide the two drawers; this may be of 2-in. by 1-in. section, and it can be grooved into the bottom and back about ¼ in. and tenoned into the division in front. After ploughing ⅜-in. grooves in the two sides and top front rail, to accommodate the holding clips of the top, as shown in Fig. 1861, the whole may be fitted together to see that all joints are satisfactory; and if so, gluing up may be proceeded with. Place a couple of strips of wood—out of winding, and about 4 ft. 6 in. long—on the bench, leaving them about 1 ft. 9 in. apart; and then, having the glue quite hot, proceed to glue all parts into their places, using a cramp where necessary to draw the joints close up, and making sure that everything is square. Under the table top, as shown in Fig. 1861, a fillet with a scotia worked on its front edge is fixed; this is formed by jointing a strip of walnut to a wider strip of pine; jointing is, of course,

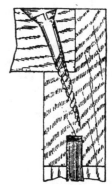

Fig. 1867.—Method of Fixing Top.

(see Fig. 1864), and have an ⅛-in. groove ploughed all round in the centre to accommodate a loose tongue. The nosing may now be prepared, and should be squared and thicknessed both ways, and grooved on the jointing face, to match that ploughed around the edge of the top. This done, it may be mitred around the top and glued, using cross tongues in the grooves, and fixing temporary wooden cramps across till the glue is dry. The nosing should be

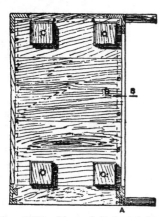

Fig. 1866.—Plan of Pedestal Top.

unnecessary if a piece of walnut sufficiently wide is to hand. The top may now be taken in hand and planed up perfectly straight and out of winding, and also to a uniform thickness of 1 in., and cut to the proper length and width. The edges must be carefully squared for jointing with the nosing

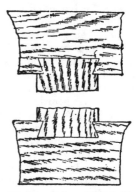

Fig. 1868.—Division between Table Top Drawers.

worked up after the glue is hard, but if preferred it can be worked previous to jointing. When the glue has hardened, the scotia may be glued and screwed around underneath as shown, and the veneer edging laid on the top. This latter should be about 2 in. wide, but its width may be governed by the size of the leather which it is desired to work in.

COMPLETING PEDESTALS OF TABLE.

The pedestals, the framing of which is already glued up, may now be completed by cleaning it off on the face, fitting all the corners together—for details, see Fig. 1865—first working and stopping the ovolo moulding on the angles as shown. Care should be taken to see that the work is quite square and that the corners come well together. The bottoms will be fitted into the grooves already ploughed in the sides and back, and secured in them by screws passing through the sides and back from the outside ; the heads will be covered by the skirting. The tops will be fixed in the rebates and dovetails provided by brass screws and cups placed round the edges, as shown in Figs. 1866 and 1867. The divisions between the drawers consist of front and back rails, dovetailed into the sides of the pedestals in the same manner as shown in Fig. 1868. The side rails or runners should fit close up to the panels, and in order that they may do so the muntins must be notched and the ends must be tenoned to fit into mortises cut into the front and back rails. All being ready for gluing up, take the left hand pedestal and first glue the back and sides together. Put the cramps on, then glue in the top and drive all the screws home ; slide the bottom in and similarly secure it, and well glue-block it underneath. Next glue in the back division rails, place the bearers in position, then slide in the dust-boards, and lastly fix the front rails. A few angle-blocks glued in the back corners of the pedestals, as shown by Fig. 1865, will give additional strength, but they must be small or they will prevent the drawers from quite closing. To ensure that the drawers will slide properly, narrow strips of wood should be glued in the panels just above the bearers. The right-hand pedestal will be treated in the same manner, but, there being no drawers, it will be easier to do. The skirting, a section of the moulding of which is shown in Fig. 1869, can then be mitred round the base of the pedestals, glued on, and secured by screws from the back.

KNEE-HOLE BRACKETS AND OTHER DETAILS.

The brackets, which fit in the upper corners of the knee-hole, are slightly sunk on the face (this sinking can be left plain, or chequered with a carver's punch), and are dovetailed to the sides of the pedestals as shown by Fig. 1870. Four blocks c (see Figs. 1863 and 1866) are now glued and bradded to the tops of the pedestals, so that when the top framework is placed over them it will be held in its proper position. The table top will be secured to the top framing by eight hardwood clips (see Fig. 1861, p. 548) ; the screw holes should be bored to give the screws plenty of room, so as to prevent splitting the wood when they are screwed home. A bead to break the

Fig. 1869.—Moulding on Writing Table Plinth.

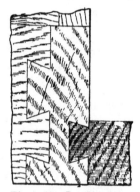

Fig. 1870.—Brackets Dovetailed to Pedestal Sides.

joint must be fixed round the bottom of the top framing, as shown in Fig. 1861, and the drawers made and fitted. The table top is now complete, with the exception of the leather covering. The right-hand pedestal can now have its door fitted and hung, and the drawers can be made and fitted to the other. The drawer fronts are 1 in. thick, and the sides and back $\frac{1}{2}$ in. Locks and drop handles are fitted to the drawers and also to the door. Castors can be fixed to blocks arranged at each corner of the pedestals inside the skirting, and of such thickness that the skirting will just clear the ground. It should be finished by french-polishing.

KITCHEN FURNITURE.

MINCING OR CHOPPING BLOCK.

A BLOCK (as illustrated by Figs. 1871 and 1872) on which meat, vegetables, etc., can be minced with an upright chopper, can be

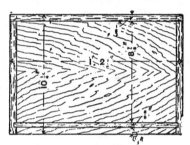

Fig. 1871.—Plan of Mincing Block.

made with a piece of ash 1 ft. 1½ in. by 9⅞ in. by 2 in., two ends of deal 11 in. by 6 in. by ½ in., one side of deal 1 ft. 3 in. by 6 in. by ½ in., and one side of birch 1 ft. 2 in. by 4 in. by ⅜ in. Plane the block to thickness, and square the sides and ends. The fence above the block, 1 ft. 1¼ in. long by 9¼ in. wide, inside measurement, should first be dovetailed together. Then separate the three pieces and rebate them to a depth of ⅛ in., so as to fit over the block.

Fig. 1872.—Side View of Mincing Block.

This forms a close joint, and prevents the minced stuff working down between block and fence. The two end pieces are grooved for a loose side of ⅜-in. thick birch (see s, Fig. 1873); this lifts out to enable the minced contents to be readily removed from the block. The inside of the block should be glasspapered clean, and the outside sized and varnished.

‑ KITCHEN CORNER CUPBOARD

A small corner cupboard as illustrated in Fig. 1874 will be found very useful, and can be quickly constructed. The body, outer frame, and door frame can be made from ¾-in. prepared stuff, to save planing up. No mortises, grooves, or rebates will be required. Fig. 1874 gives a general view of the cupboard, and Fig. 1875 a general view of the body. To make the body, cut from some 8-in. by ¾-in. prepared stuff four 2-ft. 6-in. lengths. Nail small cleats or battens across them (see c, Fig. 1875); these will make the two parts that form the back of the cupboard. Fig. 1876 shows a plan of top and bottom; these should be cut from ¾-in. stuff. Two shelves must be cut from ½-in. or ⅝-in. prepared material to the shape of the top and bottom, but 1/16 in. less from front to back. This will allow the door frame to come flush with the outer frame when the door is closed. The four pieces referred to being cleated, and the top, bottom, and shelves cut to their proper shape and size, nail the two parts that form

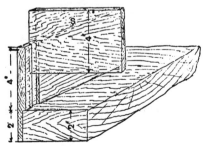

Fig. 1873.—Loose Side of Mincing Block.

the back to the top and bottom; then place the shelves on the cleats c c, nail with small wire nails, and the body is finished, except for planing the front edges of the back a little, so that the outer frame may lie flat and even against it.

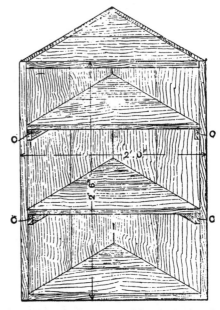

Fig. 1875.—Shelves, etc., of Corner Cupboard.

Fig. 1874.—Kitchen Corner Cupboard.

OUTER FRAME OF CORNER CUPBOARD.

The outer frame is made from ¾-in. stuff as follows: Cut off two 2-ft. 6-in. lengths, and two 2-ft. ½-in. lengths; these should be 2½ in. wide. Halve the ends, and nail these

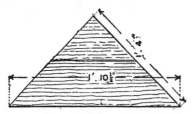

Fig. 1876.—Top or Bottom of Corner Cupboard.

together, and the frame F (Fig. 1874) is made. A small portion of the frame is cut away with a chisel to receive two butt hinges. This frame is nailed against the front of the body, and the outer edges of the frame are planed to correspond with the angle of the back of the cupboard. The door frame is made from stuff 2 in. wide, and the ends are halved and put together as the outer frame, which should thus fit nicely within the outer frame. On the inside of the door frame a piece of pine of suitable length and width, and about $\frac{5}{16}$ in.

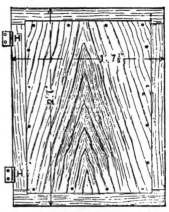

Fig. 1877.—Corner Cupboard Door.

thick, nicely planed up, is nailed or screwed to the frame, as shown in Fig. 1877; this piece forms the door-panel, and at the same time tends to strengthen the door frame, and looks as well from the outside as if the frame had been mortised and tenoned together, and the panel let into a rebate in

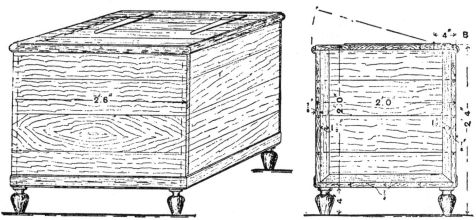

Fig. 1878.—Flour Bin.

the frame. Secure two 1½-in. butt hinges, as shown. Hang the door D (Fig. 1874) to the outer frame by securing the hinges H H. Fix a knob and fastener as shown in Fig. 1874, then fill in the nail-holes with putty, and rub up the outer frame, door frame, and panel with glasspaper; then the cupboard may be stained, sized, and varnished, or painted.

Flour Bin.

A serviceable flour bin, as shown by Fig. 1878, and in vertical section by Fig. 1879, can be made of dry pine, of which the following quantities are necessary. For the front and back, eight pieces 2 ft. 7 in. by 7 in. by ⅞ in.; ends, eight pieces, 2 ft. 1 in. by 7 in. by ⅞ in.; bottom, four pieces, 2 ft. 7 in. by 7 in. by ⅞ in.; top or lid, four pieces, 2 ft. 7 in. by 7 in. by ¾ in.; half-round moulding, 10 ft. by 1½ in. by ¾ in.; plinth, 10 ft. by 2 in. by ⅜ in.; corner angle-pieces, six pieces, 2 ft. by 1½ in. by 1½ in., and two pieces, 2 ft. 6 in. by 1½ in. by 1½ in. For the turned feet, 2 ft. by 3¼ in. by 3¼ in. of ash will be required. The front, back, and ends are of 7-in. by ⅞-in. grooved and tongued boards, glued together, and when dry, planed and cleaned off. The vertical corner joints are dovetailed, and when finally fixed an

angle-piece is screwed in each corner (see Fig. 1880). The bottom is of ⅞-in. thick grooved and tongued boards, grooved into the surround with angle-pieces placed along

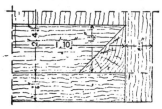

Fig. 1879.—Vertical Section of Flour Bin.

the inside, and mitred and fitted over the vertical angle-pieces as in Fig. 1881. The lid is of ¾-in. thick grooved and tongued boards, glued together, with two battens screwed on the underside, or the ends of the boards can be tongued and tenoned for a clamp. It is then hinged with strong T-hinges to a board B (Fig. 1879), 4 in. wide, which is screwed to the top edges of the ends and the back. The

Fig. 1880.—Corner of Flour Bin.

screws are recessed, and driven from the inside. A half-round moulding M (Fig. 1882) is bradded to the edge of the lid to form a folding joint, and carried round the hinge piece (see Fig. 1878). A plinth P (Fig.1881) 2 in. by ⅜ in. is fixed at the bottom. Then mount the bin on four turned feet with dowelled ends to fit into the bottom of the bin. They should also be glued and further fixed with a small hardwood wedge; see Fig. 1881, in which w is the wedge, F the turned foot, B the bottom, and E the end. The bin should then be sandpapered and cleaned inside and out, and

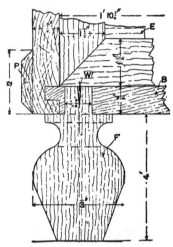

Fig. 1881.—Flour Bin Foot.

the exterior painted and varnished, or oak grained. Cover the inside with strong, clean white paper, such as cartridge drawing-paper, fixed with good flour paste. This prevents the flour getting darkened by contact with the wood. The paper should be renewed from time to time.

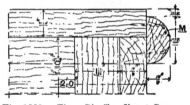

Fig. 1882.—Flour Bin Top Front Corner.

HOUSEHOLD TIDY.

A small cabinet, made as shown in the accompanying drawings, should prove most useful. Fig. 1883 is part front elevation, part section. In Fig. 1884, which is a section on N N (Fig. 1883), A is one of a pair of vertical side pieces, into each of which a shelf B is housed. A top C is jointed as shown in Fig. 1883. A back may be fitted in by grooving the inner edges of the sides, or by rebating and screwing on a strip as

in Fig. 1885. Two small doors hinged to the sides are framed up and panelled flush on the inside. Fig. 1886 shows a section of them at the meeting stiles. The piece D (Fig. 1884) should be screwed from behind. E (Fig. 1883) is a strip to carry hooks for the reception of keys, etc, and F (Fig. 1884), to which this strip is fastened, is screwed to the shelf. A space G (Fig. 1883) is divided centrally, and is useful for the reception of small books, etc. The spaces H (Fig. 1883) may receive small drawers, which may be made of tobacco boxes with the lids removed, and with wooden fronts L (Fig. 1884) screwed through holes punched in the fronts of the boxes. Small compartments J

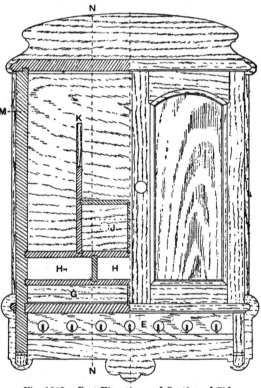

Fig. 1883.—Part Elevation and Section of Tidy.

(Fig. 1883) are closed by sliding fronts pierced by centre-bit holes, as indicated by the dotted circle. Each space may contain a ball of string, the hole being used to facilitate the removal of the front and to admit one end of the string. The vertical partition K is carried well up so that a gum- or paste-pot with a protruding brush may be protected if placed in the recess at the side. The inside of each door has a strip of leather near the top fastened transversely (as in Fig. 1887), and in the loops formed some such article as a hammer, screwdriver, or sardine-tin opener may be placed. This will be found very handy for a number of household tools, etc. The cabinet may be hung to the wall by eye-plates, attached one on each side at about the level of M (Fig. 1883). The total width of the article is 17 in., the height is 23¼ in., and the depth is 6 in.

Fig. 1885. — Back of Tidy Jointed to Side.

Fig. 1886.—Section through Door Meeting Stiles.

Fig 1887.—Looped Leather Strip.

Fig. 1884. — Cross Section of Tidy.

SPICE BOX WITH DRAWERS.

To make a spice box as illustrated by Fig. 1888, yellow pine or deal is the best material, but, in any case. the wood must be thoroughly dry. The following pieces

will be required : One piece 7¾ in. by 6½ in. by ¼ in. for back of case ; two 7¾ in. by 3 in. by ¼ in. for sides ; two 7¾ in. by 3¼ in. by ¼ in. for top and bottom ; four 6½ in. by

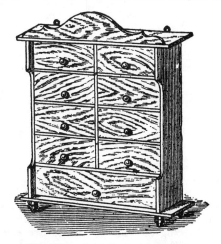

Fig. 1888.—Spice Box with Drawers.

2⅝ in. by $\frac{3}{16}$ in. for shelves ; one 6⅛ in. by 1 in. by ¼ in. for partition ; one 7¼ in. by 1¼ in. by ¼ in. for ornament ; eighteen 2⅝ in. by 1⅜ in. by $\frac{3}{16}$ in. for sides of drawers ; eight 2⅝ in. by 1⅜ in. by $\frac{3}{16}$ in. for backs, and eight 3 in. by 1⅜ in. by ¼ in. for the fronts of small drawers ; eight 3 in. by 2⅜ in. by $\frac{3}{16}$ in. for bottom of small drawers ; one 5⅞ in. by 1⅜ in. by $\frac{3}{16}$ in. for back of bottom drawer ; one 6¼ in. by 1⅜ in. by ¼ in. for front of bottom drawer ; and one 6¼ in. by 2⅜ in. by

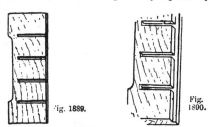

Fig. 1889.

Fig. 1890.

Figs. 1889 and 1890.—Spice Box Sides.

$\frac{3}{16}$ in. for bottom of drawer. These are all finished sizes. The other materials required are nine small brass knobs, two bracket eyes, four wooden feet, and a handful of small nails. To make the case, cut the two side pieces to the shape shown by

Fig. 1889. Cut four grooves (see Figs. 1889 and 1890) ⅛ in. deep and 2½ in. long, in which to fit the shelves, and treat the back edge

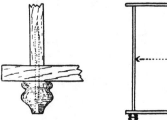

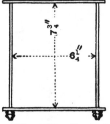

Fig. 1891.—Spice Box Foot.

Fig. 1892.—Vertical Outline of Spice Box.

of these pieces in the same manner. The width of the grooves is just sufficient to allow the shelves to fit tightly into them. At equal distances from each other carefully mark out the positions for the grooves by dividing the side piece into five equal parts. The places for the grooves being ascertained, draw lines across representing

they are not seen when the parts are fitted together. Nail the top and bottom on to the sides. The feet can be put on at the same time by driving the nail first through the foot (see Fig. 1891). The case when fixed (see Fig. 1892) should measure, inside, 7¾ in. by 6¼ in. Next take three of the four shelves and cut them as shown by Fig. 1893.

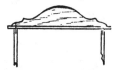

Fig. 1895.—Part of Spice Box Drawer.

Fig. 1896.—Top of Spice Box.

The piece cut from the middle is 1 in. long and ¼ in. wide. The pieces cut from the sides are ⅜ in. long, and ⅛ in. wide. The fourth and bottom shelf is cut similarly, only the middle piece is left in. Fit the shelves and partition into their respective places, the partition being nailed to the top of the case and to the

Fig. 1893.—Spice Box Shelf.

Fig. 1894.—Spice Box Case.

Fig. 1897.—Plate Rack.

the widths of the grooves; then cut these lines down to a uniform depth with a chisel, cutting downwards, or, guided by a straightedge, draw it along so that it cuts into the wood. The bottoms of the grooves need not be absolutely smooth, as

bottom shelf. If the back is now fixed in its place, the case (see Fig. 1894) may be considered complete. All that remains to be done is to make the drawers. The "fronts" (so called for convenience) should be cut so that the sides will fit into them as in Fig. 1895. After making the drawers, fix a knob on each to serve as a handle for pulling them out. If the remaining piece is cut to the shape shown by Fig. 1896, a passable ornament will be the result. It is fixed to the top by nails driven down into the two side pieces. By fixing two bracket eyes to the back, the box can either be hung against the wall or stood in any convenient place. In order to add a finish to the box, it can either be stained and polished, or painted—according to taste.

make the mortise-and-tenon joints. Set out the centres of the holes for the bars. The distance apart of the centres for the plate portion should be about 2 in., and for the dish part about 3 in. The holes can then be bored right through, or partly, as preferred ; the two middle rails should be bored right through. Care must be taken to bore these holes true with a twist bit. The bars, which should be about $\frac{3}{16}$ in. in diameter, can be prepared by hand as follows : Cut strips of wood about $\frac{3}{4}$ in. square,

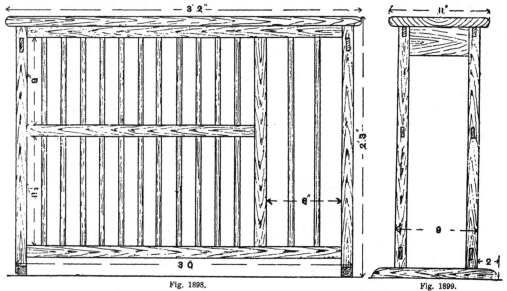

Fig. 1898.

Fig. 1899.

Figs. 1898 and 1899.—Front and End Elevations of Plate Rack.

TWO-TIER STANDING PLATE RACK.

The plate rack illustrated by Figs. 1897, 1898, and 1899 should be made of good red deal. For the rails and stiles of the framework, wood $1\frac{1}{4}$ in. thick and $1\frac{1}{4}$ in. or $1\frac{1}{2}$ in. wide will be suitable, except for the two top rails at the ends, which should be twice the breadth of the other rails, in order to allow the tenons to pass over each other. The lengths of the various parts and the number of pieces required can be obtained from Figs. 1897 to 1899. First saw off the pieces about $\frac{1}{2}$ in. longer than the finished lengths, and plane the face side and face edges square. Gauge them to thickness and breadth, and plane. Next set out and

and of the full length required, and plane up to $\frac{5}{8}$ in. square. Then plane off each corner so as to form an octagon in section, and next plane the resultant corners so as to form sixteen sides. The strips can then be made almost round with a smoothing plane set fine, or with a hollow or bead plane. Finish the bars with glasspaper. A simple apparatus for holding the bars whilst planing (see Fig. 1900) is made by chamfering one edge of two pieces of wood and nailing them together. A piece of wood should be nailed at one end to form a stop (see B, Fig. 1900). Now fit the plate rack together and wedge the tenons into the mortises, or fasten them with hardwood pins. The joints should be painted with a mixture of white-lead, red-lead, and a little oil before fastening together ; this preserves the joints, and is better than glue. Any projecting parts at the joints should be smoothed off and the two parts connected to the feet pieces and top rails. The top is made of a 1-in. board, with the edges rounded as shown in Fig. 1897, and should be secured to the top rails by means of a few nails or screws.

THREE-TIER HANGING PLATE RACK.

The plate rack or drainer, shown in half front elevation by Fig. 1901 and in vertical section by Fig. 1902, is made almost entirely of $\frac{1}{2}$-in. wood, and holds three dozen plates in three sizes ; a special place has not been made for dishes, but the top is made full,

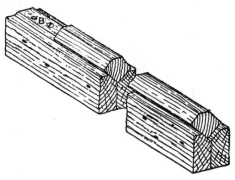

Fig. 1900.—Appliance for Holding Bars whilst Planing.

so that they rest on it, leaning against the wall. The two side pieces are prepared first, the curved brackets at the bottom being cut out with a bow-saw, and finished with gouge, chisel, and spokeshave. The shape of these brackets may be varied, and the total length between them is 3 ft. 5 in. To form the bars or uprights which keep the plates in their places, rip two boards, 2 ft. 8½ in. by 11 in. by $\frac{1}{2}$ in., each into eleven equal strips, which must then be planed down to $\frac{3}{4}$ in. wide. The four thicker horizontal pieces are prepared about 1 in. thick and exactly 2 ft. 1 in. long ; three of them are 1¼ in. wide, and the fourth is 2¼ in. The two bottom pieces should have the top inside corner bevelled off. Take two of the narrower pieces, and, starting 1⅜ in.

from one end, screw at even distances along them eleven of the $\frac{3}{4}$-in. strips, whose ends finish flush with the top piece, and lap over the other slightly. The two thicker pieces from outside to outside, if made 1 in. thick, should be 2 ft. 8 in. apart. Before screwing

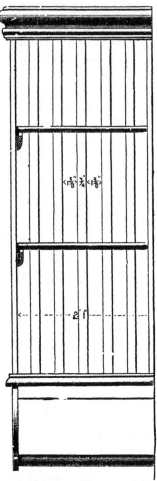

Fig. 1901.—Half Front Elevation of Hanging Plate Rack.

on the other eleven strips, slightly bevel one edge of the horizontal pieces, and so compensate for the rake of the upright pieces, as seen in the side view (Fig. 1902). Now get out the thinner horizontal strips, and slightly bevel off the inside top corner ; fasten with brads and screws to the upright piece. There are now two grids, which can be connected by attaching the four battens, $\frac{3}{4}$ in. thick, which support them in position, two at each end. In attaching these, work from the inside end, and the rake of the back grid will come as required. Place the double grid on the floor, resting it on one end; lay one side piece carefully in its

but this is rather awkward to do. To complete the plate rack, two mouldings should be mitred at the ends, and glued and bradded in position. A piece of broomhandle will serve for the dish-cloth rod at the bottom.

PANTRY SAFE OR CUPBOARD PANTRY.

Fig. 1903 is a front elevation of a pantry safe which is rectangular in plan, and Fig. 1904 shows the end elevation. For the three pieces of framing, six stiles, 2 ft. 8 in. by 2 in. by 1 in.; three rails for the door, 1 ft. 10 in. by 2 in. by 1 in.; and six rails for the ends, 1 ft. 6 in. by 2 in. by 1 in.

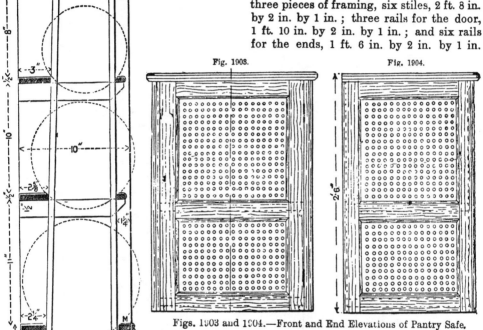

Fig. 1903.   Fig. 1904.

Figs. 1903 and 1904.—Front and End Elevations of Pantry Safe.

Fig. 1902.—Section of Hanging Plate Rack.

place on top, set off screw-holes accurately, and from the outside screw the battens in position; also put screws into the ends of the thick horizontal pieces. Turn it over, and, if all is square, screw on the other side in the same manner. It is quite possible to screw the battens on from the inside, by which method the screw-heads are hidden,

36

will be required. These pieces are mortised and tenoned together, the six top and bottom rails having haunched tenons, as shown in Fig. 1905. The other three rails have tenons as shown in Fig. 1906, and the pieces of framing are glued and wedged together. The two framings for the ends are rebated $\frac{1}{2}$ in. each way on the back edges to receive the back, which is formed of 3-in. by $\frac{1}{2}$-in. tongue and groove-jointed matchboarding. The front edge of the ends has a $\frac{3}{4}$-in. chamfer on the outside corners. The shelves and top should be got out of a wide board of pine or whitewood. The top, when finished, is 1 ft. $10\frac{1}{2}$ in. long and 1 ft. 6 in. wide, which allows it to project

¼ in. over the front and ends. The projection should either have a nosing worked on,

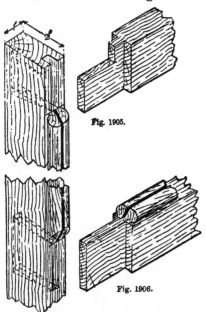

Fig. 1905.

Fig. 1906.

Fig. 1905.—Top and Bottom Rail Joint.
Fig. 1906.—Middle Rail Joint.

as shown in Figs. 1903 and 1904, or a chamfer. The shelves are 1 ft. 3¾ in. wide by

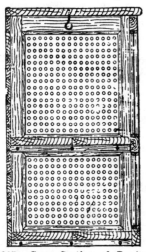

Fig. 1907.—Cross Section of Pantry Safe.

1 in. thick, supported by four fillets, 1 ft. 3¾ in. by ¾ in. by ½ in., screwed to the sides

of the safe as shown in Figs. 1907 and 1908. In fixing together, the top may be secured to the ends with 1½-in. screws, three through each top rail. The bottom shelf is fixed

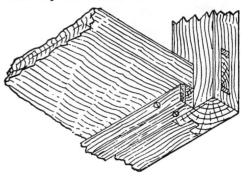

Fig. 1908.—Bottom Shelf of Pantry Safe.

with screws to the fillets, thus securing the lower ends of the sides as shown in Fig. 1908.

FITTING TOGETHER PANTRY SAFE.

Before fixing the back, the framing should be squared, and a temporary lath fastened diagonally across the front to hold it square until the back is completed. Fit in the boards for the back and fasten with 1½-in. oval wire nails. Fig. 1909 shows the end rebated to receive the back. A 1½-in. screw through the top into the edge of the back will stiffen it considerably. Two or three hooks should be screwed into the top for

Fig. 1909.—Back Corner of Pantry Safe.

meat to hang from (see Fig. 1907), and the middle shelf should be left loose, so that it can be removed when the hooks are used. The door may next be fitted in, and a ⅜-in. bead, worked down each side, will prevent the butt hinges looking unsightly on the hanging side ; 2-in. butt hinges are used, and are fixed 3 in. from each end, the whole of the hinge being let into the door stile.

at the corners, and fastened with 1-in. brads. The door may be fastened either with an ordinary turnbutton or lock, or with a special catch.

Fig. 1910.   Fig. 1911.

Figs. 1910 and 1911.—Front Elevation and Section of Tall Cupboard Pantry.

The spaces are covered with perforated zinc, which may be fastened on the inside of the safe with tacks, or may be secured by beads (as shown in Figs. 1903 and 1904), which is a neater and better method. About 60 ft. of ½-in. beading will be required for the latter method, the beads being mitred

MATERIALS FOR MAKING TALL CUPBOARD PANTRY.

A cupboard pantry (see illustration of front elevation and vertical section, Figs. 1910 and 1911) can be made with some clean, sound, and dry yellow pine, prepared in the following sizes : Two ends, 7 ft. by 1 ft.

$2\frac{1}{8}$ in. by $\frac{3}{4}$ in. ; two front corner stiles, 7 ft. by 4 in. by $\frac{7}{8}$ in. For the back frame, two rails, 3 ft. 6 in. by 4 in. by $\frac{3}{4}$ in., and two stiles, 7 ft. by 4 in. by $\frac{3}{4}$ in. ; one panel,

ing grooves in the sides, s indicating the side, and c s the corner stile of the back frame. The sides are $\frac{3}{4}$ in. thick, and are dovetailed to the carcase at the top and the bottom. An examination of the dovetailing found in drawer fronts and sides will be of assistance in understanding how to arrange the jointing so that it is not apparent on the face view. The division above the drawer is $\frac{3}{4}$ in. thick, grooved in the side pieces, and extends between the front corner stiles to the level of the door front, as shown in Figs. 1911 and 1913. The drawer is made with a $\frac{3}{4}$-in. thick front, dovetailed to the ends $\frac{1}{2}$ in.

Fig. 1912.—Part Horizontal Section of Cupboard Pantry.

2 ft. 10 in. by 6 ft. 4 in. by $\frac{3}{8}$ in. For the door, two stiles, 5 ft. 6 in. by 4 in. by $\frac{7}{8}$ in., two rails, 3 ft. by 5 in. by $\frac{7}{8}$ in., one rail, 3 ft. by 4 in. by $\frac{7}{8}$ in., and one panel, 3 ft. 6 in. by 2 ft. 4 in. by $\frac{7}{16}$ in. ; fillets for zinc panel, 7 ft. by $\frac{7}{16}$ in. by $\frac{1}{4}$ in. One top, 3 ft. 6 in. by 1 ft. 3 in. by $\frac{3}{4}$ in. ; one bottom, 3 ft. 6 in. by 1 ft. 3 in. by $\frac{3}{4}$ in. ; one division, 3 ft. 6 in. by 1 ft. 3 in. by $\frac{3}{4}$ in. ; four shelves, 3 ft. 6 in. by 1 ft. 1 in. by $\frac{1}{2}$ in. For the drawer, one front, 3 ft. by 1 ft. by $\frac{3}{4}$ in., one back, 3 ft. by $11\frac{1}{8}$ in. by $\frac{1}{2}$ in., two ends, 1 ft. 2 in. by $11\frac{3}{4}$ in. by $\frac{1}{2}$ in., and one bottom, 3 ft. by $11\frac{3}{4}$ in. by $\frac{3}{8}$ in.. Two fillets, 2 ft. by 1 in. by $\frac{3}{4}$ in. ; two folding rebate slips, 5 ft. 6 in. by $\frac{7}{8}$ in. by $\frac{1}{4}$ in., and two ditto, 3 ft. by $\frac{7}{8}$ in. by $\frac{1}{4}$ in. ; one moulding, 6 ft. 6 in. by $\frac{3}{8}$ in. by $\frac{3}{8}$ in. ; one frieze panel, 6 ft. 6 in. by 2 in. by $\frac{3}{8}$ in. ; one cornice moulding 7 ft. by $1\frac{3}{4}$ in. by $\frac{3}{4}$ in. ; and four turned feet, 6 in. by 4 in. in diameter.

thick, and back $\frac{1}{2}$ in. thick. The bottom is $\frac{3}{8}$ in. thick, grooved in the ends and front, and fitted with glued blocks. To enable the drawer to work easily, fillets

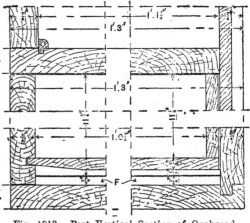

Fig. 1913.—Part Vertical Section of Cupboard Pantry Drawer.

CONSTRUCTING TALL CUPBOARD PANTRY.

The framework for the back is put together first ; it consists of 4-in. by $\frac{3}{4}$-in. framing filled with a $\frac{3}{8}$-in. thick panel made up of several widths of stuff, butt-jointed and glued together. A section of the back is shown in Fig. 1912 ; the edges of the framework are tongued to fit in corresponding

or runners on which the drawer rides are placed as shown at F in Figs. 1913 and 1914. The front of the drawer must project $\frac{1}{4}$ in. below the bottom to hide these runners. Two wooden knobs or brass handles are fixed to the drawer, and the drawer can be provided with divi-

sions and light trays as necessary. Pine
¼ in. thick for the main divisions and ⅛ in.
or $\frac{3}{16}$ in. for the smaller ones should be
used.

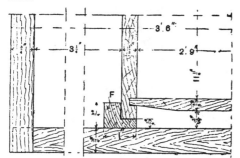

Fig. 1914 —Part Section of Cupboard Pantry
Drawer, etc.

' CUPBOARD PANTRY DOOR.

The door is ⅞ in. thick, with stiles and
rails mortised, tenoned, and wedged together. The edges of the framing are
moulded and grooved for a panel as shown
in Fig. 1912. Square-edged framing may be
substituted and a moulding afterwards
pinned in the opening, but this is not re-

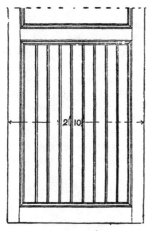

Fig. 1915.—Door with Vertical Panelling.

commended. The panel should be made up
of two or three widths of timber, butt-
jointed and glued, or the framework may
be filled as shown in Fig. 1915, where
grooved, tongued, and beaded boards 3 in.
by ⅜ in. are used, placed vertically. An-

other method is shown in Fig. 1916, the
boards being placed diagonally. The other
panel consists of perforated zinc or fine

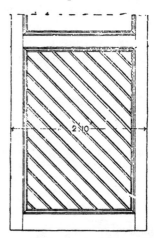

Fig. 1916.—Door with Diagonal Panelling.

gauze, and fits in the rebate of the door
framing, a moulded slip s keeping the
zinc z in position, as shown in Fig. 1917.
The rebate in this part of the door stile

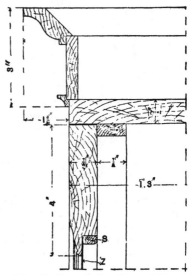

Fig. 1917.—Section of Cornice and Door Rail.

is made by cutting away the inside piece
left after the panel grooving has been run.
The front corner stiles are grooved to the

sides as shown in Fig. 1912, and mortised
into the top and bottom. The folded edges
are beaded to relieve the joint. Hang the
door with strong brass butts, and furnish
it with a knob, lock, and key.

• CUPBOARD PANTRY INTERIOR, ETC.

The interior of the cupboard is provided
with four shelves, 1 ft. 1 in. wide and $\frac{1}{2}$ in.
thick. The top shelf should be fixed near
the centre of the perforated zinc, so that
the two top spaces can be used for fresh
meat, etc. The lower shelves can be fitted
as required. The cornice has a small
moulding to cover the joint with the top
(see Fig. 1917), and is rebated for a frieze
panel $\frac{3}{8}$ in. thick, surmounted by a cornice
moulding. The mouldings and panel are
mitred and keyed at the corners, and

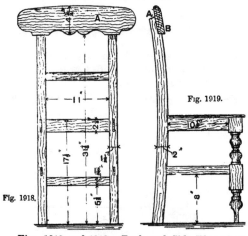

Figs. 1918 and 1919.—Back and Side Elevations
of Kitchen Chair.

strengthened with blocks glued at the
angles. When finished, the cornice forms
a separate piece from the carcase, so that
it can be moved when desired. The four
feet are turned in the lathe, and have dowel
ends fitting into the carcase bottom and
fixed with wedges. A plinth finish can
readily be adapted if preferred. This cupboard pantry can easily be converted to a
wardrobe if desired by removing the zinc
panel and inserting a bevel panel corresponding with the lower one, so that it is
desirable to finish the interior in a neat
manner.

• WOODEN CHAIRS.

A serviceable chair is shown in elevation
by Figs. 1918 and 1919. To make a chair of
this description, obtain a piece of board

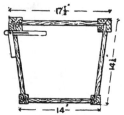

Fig. 1920.—Chair Seat Framework.

about 1 ft. 6 in. by 1 ft. 3 in.—any thickness will do—and strike out the plan of the
seat to the shape shown at Fig. 1920. This
will be a guide in getting out the rails,
and from this the correct bevel to make
the blocks (Figs. 1921 and 1922) for mortising the front and back legs to receive the
side rails will be arrived at. The material
required for making two chairs is 2 ft. 10 in.
by 9 in. by 1½ in. for back legs, 6 ft. by
2¼ in. by 2¼ in. for front legs, 12 ft. by 9 in.
by ¾ in. for seats and rails, and three
pieces of hardwood of the shape shown in
Fig. 1923, each measuring about 1 ft. 8 in.
or 1 ft. 9 in. long by 4½ in. or 5 in. broad
by ⅞ in. thick, for top rails and slats.
Now cut out the back legs; make a pattern
(Fig. 1924) and mark out the board (2 ft.
10 in. by 9 in. by 1½ in.) with it, as at Fig.
1925. The pattern is made of a piece of
½-in. stuff, and is 2 in. broad; when finished, it is simply an arc or piece cut out
of a large circle, and has about 1 in. of
sweep. The lines on the side (see Fig.

Fig. 1921.—Block for Mortising Front Legs
of Chair.

1924) show where the mortises are required
to be for the back rails; the mortise at A
is for the slat rail. Having planed and
marked out the board, take a narrow rip
saw and cut carefully to the lines, keeping

the saw perfectly straight. After sawing out the pieces for the legs, place two together, and plane the round and hollow edge so that they are both alike in shape ;

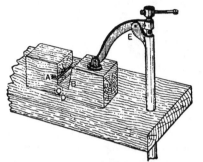

Fig. 1922.—Block and Bench Holdfast used in Mortising Back Legs of Chair.

then put a mark on each to indicate the outside or inside edge of each pair of legs, and number them so that they may not get mixed. Having planed and paired the legs, mark on lines for the mortises for the back rails, the position of which is shown in Fig. 1924. The mortise A requires to be done on the bevel block (Fig. 1921) for the slat rail, on account of its being curved ; the other mortises B and C are made straight. In marking the lines for the mortises on the round edge to receive the side rails, it will be observed that the narrow side rail is directly above the back rail. In gauging for the mortises (which, by the way, are all made with a $\frac{3}{8}$-in. mortise chisel), the narrow rail may be kept in the centre ; but the broad rail should be kept flush with the outside face of the leg, so as to be the farther removed from the broad back rail, and consequently give a longer tenon and make a stronger job. A

Fig. 1923.—Chair Top Rail.

saw-kerf should be put in the line at D (Fig. 1924) from the outside corner to $\frac{3}{8}$ in. past the inside corner on the front edge— that is, where the top rail shoulders against the back leg (see Fig. 1926). Now get the

pieces of stuff for the front feet, $2\frac{1}{4}$ in. by $2\frac{1}{4}$ in., cut in lengths of 1 ft. 6 in., and square up ; then mark lines for the front and side rails off the back legs that have

Fig. 1924.—Pattern of Back Leg of Chair

already been marked, the narrow front rail being the same distance from the ground as the narrow back rail. The plan (Fig. 1920) shows where to place the mortises. Before commencing to mortise, make two blocks as shown in Figs. 1921 and 1922. To make the block shown in Fig. 1921, get a piece of hardwood 1 ft. 2 in. by 4 in. by $1\frac{1}{2}$ in. Set the bevel as shown in Fig. 1920,

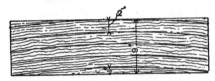

Fig. 1925.—Marking out Back Legs of Chair.

and bevel the piece of wood as at Fig. 1927, which is a sectional view of Fig. 1921. The wood being truly bevelled, put in two $\frac{3}{8}$-in. dowel pins, allowing them to project 1 in. These pins should be square with the bevelled face ; they keep the legs from slipping off the block when mortising. The mortise-block, shown at Fig. 1922 fixed to the bench by the holdfast, is a bit of hardwood about 1 ft. by 4 in. by 3 in., with a recess cut across it about $2\frac{1}{2}$ in. deep and

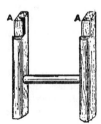

Fig. 1927.—Section of Block for Mortising Front Legs of Chair.

Fig. 1926.—Back Legs of   Fig. 1928.—Rider for
Chair to receive Top Rail. Holding Down Chair Leg.

2 in. wide to allow the back leg to lie across it when mortising ; lines B C, Fig. 1922, are square with each other, the line B getting

the same bevel from D as at Fig. 1927. A slot is made at A to receive a wedge or key, which tightens up the leg against the face B when mortising. Having made these blocks, proceed to mortise the legs, taking

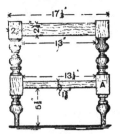

Fig. 1929.— Front Legs of Chair Framed.

Fig. 1930.—Marking Tenon Lines on Seat Rail.

the front legs first, and mortising for the front rails perfectly straight; then, to mortise for the side rails, lay the leg on the block (Fig. 1921) with the outside of the leg resting against the dowel pins. Lay the rider (Fig. 1928) on top of the leg, and fasten with the holdfast to the bench. When mortising, hold the chisel perfectly straight; this will give the correct bevel in the mortise for the side rail. Having mortised the front legs, turn them to the shape required. It would be better to have the portions of legs A (Fig. 1929), where the mortises are for narrow rails, rounded in the lathe, and not kept square as at the top. Next take up the back legs, and mortise perfectly straight B and C (Fig. 1924). To mortise A (Fig. 1924), lay the leg on the block (Fig. 1921) with round edge to dowel pins, and mortise straight; this will give the bevel in mortise to allow for the sweep of the slat rail. Then, to mortise for the side rails, lay the leg in the recess of the block (Fig. 1922), with the side already mortised against face B; put a wedge in slot A, tighten up, and fasten with holdfast E to bench, then hold the chisel perfectly straight, and begin cutting. Having finished mortising, get out the rails. Figs. 1918, 1919, and 1929 will show the length and breadth to make them, making allowance for tenons. Four broad and six narrow rails should be got out of a 9-in. board, but the rails should be ⅛ in. broader than the length of the mortise, and a nice easy fit, just rubbing against the sides of the mortise the narrow way; for if the tenon is made thicker than the mortise it is apt to split the legs when cramping together. Now proceed to fit up the front legs and cramp home as at Fig. 1918. It will be observed that the leg projects about ½ in. above the broad rail. This is as it should be; it is what is called the joggle, and is cut off later on. Now take up the back legs, and smooth out with the smoothing plane the lines that were used when marking for mortises. With a round-sole plane clean up the back edge, taking off a chamfer from 1 in. above the broad or seat rail to the top of the leg on both corners; also on the front edge, from 1 in. above the seat rail to the top round the edge, with the smoothing plane inclining more to the inner or mortised side. The slat rails with halved ends should now be made, after which the legs can be fitted up. These rails are made from one of the top rails (see Fig. 1923). It is divided into three, and, if only two chairs are made, the third piece is not required. Plane up the edges with the trying plane and bring them to the right breadth; then with the narrow back rail mark lines for the shoulder, as at Fig. 1930, and square across the face. Then gauge the thickness of the mortise for the tenon from the back side, and, with a dovetail saw, make a squared line on the face down to the gauge lines for the tenon, then with a spokeshave nicely thumb over the front edge, and glasspaper; saw down lines for the tenon, and the slat is complete.

Fig. 1931.—Dovetail Gauge.

Fig. 1932.—Half Pattern of Chair Top Rail.

Now fit the slats into the back legs, together with the other rails, and cramp home. Next take up the top rails (Fig. 1923) and plane up the round side A, also the edges; then lay the planed side, with edge to saw kerf, on top of the back legs, and with a sharp chisel nicely bed it to the leg; then, keeping the top rail in position, mark a line on the inside of the leg for the depth of dovetail, $\frac{5}{16}$ in., using a gauge as shown in Fig. 1931. This gauge is simply a piece of wood about 4 in. by $1\frac{1}{2}$ in. by $\frac{3}{4}$ in., with the point of a wire nail project-

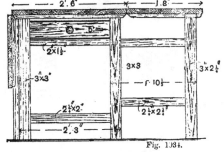

Figs. 1933 and 1934.—Side and Front Elevations of Gate-legged Table.

ing on the end to mark the line with. Next lift off the top rail and make a dovetail on the end of the leg, as shown at A (Fig. 1926); then lay the top rail with under edge up-

Fig. 1935.—Underneath Plan of Gate-legged Table.

wards on the bench, and place the end A to the edge of the top rail, and mark the dovetail on the edge with a fine point. Continue these lines up the top rail the same distance as the sunk portion of the leg; then saw the lines and chisel out carefully, and the finished appearance will be as in Fig. 1923. Hammer the top rail on the legs about 1 in. or so down, and with a piece of cardboard cut to the pattern

shown in Fig. 1932, mark one end, then reverse the pattern and mark the other end; take the top rail off the legs, and with a bow saw cut to the lines and trim up any inequalities made in sawing. Then

put the top rail on the legs again, and with the holdfast E (Fig. 1922) fasten it to the bench. With the round-sole plane clean up the face, thumbing over the upper edge and round the ends. As these top rails are generally made from sycamore, birch, beech, or other hard wood, they will bear scraping up, which should be done with a

Fig. 1936.—Gate-legged Table Framing.

sharp scraper. After well glasspapering, take off the top rail and lay it aside. Next, the side rails should be fitted up and cramped home, after which the seats should

be jointed and glued ; the plan of the seat
will give an idea of its size, or the already
framed up chair will be a guide. When
cutting out the seat, allow about ¾ in. pro-

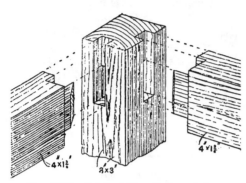

Fig. 1937.—Joint of Top Rails and Leg.

jection all round ; this will give plenty
when fitting on. Having jointed the seat,
take up the chair, cut off the joggles of
the front feet, and level up with a plane,
so that the seat will lie on nicely. Clean
and glasspaper all round the chair ; then
plane up the seats if the joints will bear
it, and fit them into the back legs, so that
the edge of the seat will be flush with them.
Then mark the projection of the seat over
the frame, which should be about ½ in.
on the front edge and ¾ in. on the ends at
front ; cut to lines, then with the smoothing
plane clean up, and thumb over the front
edge and ends. Round the corners at the
front with compasses set to 1½ in., then
glasspaper, and sprig or brad the seat down
to the frame. After nailing, make some
square blocks about 1½ in. by 1¼ in. by 1¼ in.,
split in two from corner to corner with a
chisel, and glue to seat and rail on the
inside. This is called blocking, and should
be done carefully, taking care that the
blocks lie close to the seat and the rail.
After blocking, bevel the end of the leg
from the dovetail, as at A (Fig. 1919). Glue
the top rail, and hammer home, using a bit
of wood on the top edge to prevent marking. The chairs should now be complete,
and ready for staining and polishing. It is
usual for a chair of this description to be
polished a dark red, using plenty of Bis-

marck brown in the polish ; but a walnut or
oak colour may be used if preferred.

GATE-LEGGED KITCHEN TABLE.

Figs. 1933 to 1936 illustrate a gate-legged
kitchen table which, when closed, is 2 ft.
6 in. wide by 4 ft. 4 in. long. The leading
points in the making are as follow :—The
legs and rails should be planed up square
to sizes, and the legs set out for mortising.
The mortises for the lower rails are of a
simple character, the tenons being stubbed
in. For the long top rails the mortises and
tenons at one end should be as shown at A
(Fig. 1937) and at the other end as shown at
B (Fig. 1938). Each end of the top rail C
(Fig. 1936) is of the form shown at C (Fig.
1937). The two rails F (Fig. 1936) for the
drawer have the joints illustrated at D and
E (Fig. 1938), the upper rail being dovetailed in the top of the legs. The two gate
legs and their rails are stub-mortised and
tenoned together. Figs. 1939 and 1940 show

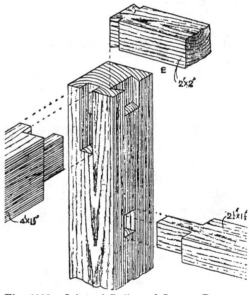

Fig. 1938.—Joint of Rails and Leg at Drawer
End.

how the gate-leg stile is jointed to rails.
After the joints are made the whole of the
framing should be carefully fitted, and the
joints numbered ; then the framing should
be separated, and the internal parts

smoothed off. After the joints are glued and fitted, they should be cramped in position until the glue is dry; odd strips of wood, with a block nailed on each end and a wedge inserted, may be used for this purpose. The top, including the flaps, should be formed of 1½-in. boards, ploughed, tongued, grooved, and glued together. The top and flaps should be planed off true, and the top secured to the

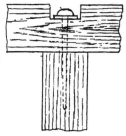

Fig. 1939.—Jointing Gate Leg Stile and Rail.

rails of the framing by 2½-in. screws driven obliquely from the inside of the rails. The flaps may be attached to the top by 2½-in. wrought-iron back-flap hinges as illustrated at Fig. 1935. The top and flaps should be strengthened by 2-in. by 1-in. thicknessing fillets, which are screwed on as indicated at Figs. 1934 and 1935. The stiles of the

through the top rail as in Fig. 1939. As the depth of the side rails will not be sufficient for fixing the runners of the drawer, pieces

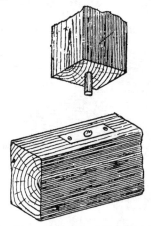

Fig. 1940.—Pin and Socket of Gate Leg Stile and Rail.

G (Figs. 1933 and 1936) should be added, and to these two runners can be fixed, and also a cross rail; see H and K (Fig. 1936). The drawer front should be carefully fitted between the rails and legs, and the sides and back prepared, the back being made wide enough to extend only as far as the plough groove to receive the bottom. The dove-

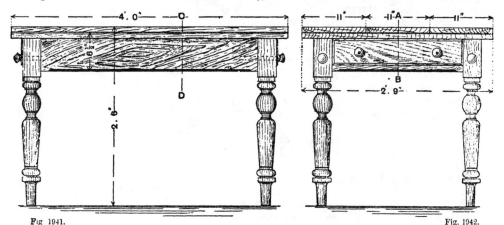

Fig 1941.   Fig. 1942.

Figs. 1941 and 1942.—Side and End Elevations of Table with Turned Legs.

gate legs should be fixed at the bottom end by a pin working in a socket (Fig. 1940), the upper end being secured by a screw sunk

tailing can then be set out and made. After this the plough grooves for the bottom should be made. Next some ½-in. boards should be glued up for the bottom, the edges being chamfered to fit into the plough grooves. To secure the bottom it should be nailed into the lower edge of the back, and have strips underneath fixed to the bottom and the sides, these being

appearance of solidity (see Figs. 1943 and 1944). The legs may be constructed of white or yellow deal, and they can be turned in accordance with instructions given on pp. 450 to 490, and should be about 3 in. by 3 in. in section. Fig. 1945

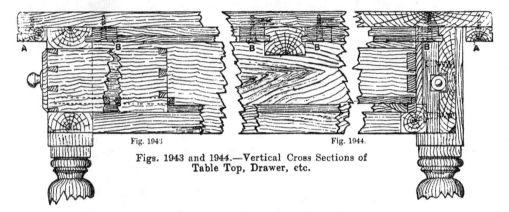

Figs. 1943 and 1944.—Vertical Cross Sections of
Table Top, Drawer, etc.

secured with glue and planed off flush. A knob or handle should be provided and fixed to the front of the drawer.

DETACHABLE KITCHEN TABLE WITH TURNED LEGS.

The kitchen table illustrated in Figs. 1941 and 1942, showing side and end views, can be taken apart in several sections. The dimensions given in Figs. 1941 and 1942 are suitable for an ordinary cottage kitchen, but need not be adhered to, as the same construction and dimensions of the several parts are applicable to tables up to 9 ft. by 5 ft. top surface, with the one exception of the legs, which should be increased in size sectionally when the length of the table exceeds 5 ft. The top can be made from sycamore wood, good white deal, or fir, free from knots, sap, and shakes, and can be got in 11-in. widths. White deal or fir is preferable to yellow deal or pine, as it always scrubs clean and white, and does not become discoloured. The wood should be 1 in. in thickness. A fillet 2 in. by 1 in. is mitred at the angles, and screwed on the under side of the top all round the edges, the joint being broken by a bead worked on the fillet. This not only serves to protect the edges of the top, but gives it an

shows the mortise and dovetail notch to receive the rails (Fig. 1946). There are four bolts (one in each leg), which should be about 8 in. long and $\frac{1}{2}$ in. in diameter; they should have snap-heads, having a slot cut

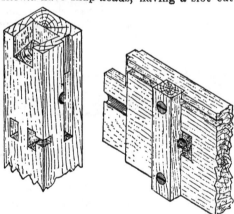

Fig. 1945.—Mortises   Fig. 1946.—Rail with Slot
in Table Leg.   for Bolt and Cleat.

across them with a file, for the purpose of inserting the blade of a screwdriver when turning them either in or out. The long-side rails are also of deal 6½ in. wide and 1 in. thick, grooved on the inside for the buttons for attachment to the top; a hard-wood cleat is fitted into a notch, and well glued and fixed with screws, a hole being bored through it to accommodate the bolt (Figs. 1946 to 1948). The tenon at the end, which is about $1\frac{1}{4}$ in. long by $\frac{5}{8}$ in., should fit easily into the leg. The upper cross-rail

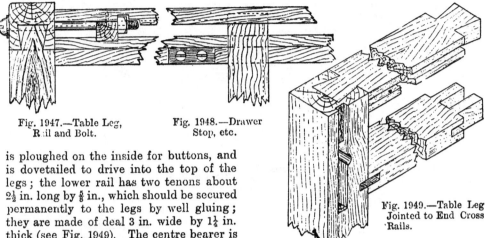

Fig. 1947.—Table Leg, Rail and Bolt.

Fig. 1948.—Drawer Stop, etc.

is ploughed on the inside for buttons, and is dovetailed to drive into the top of the legs; the lower rail has two tenons about $2\frac{1}{2}$ in. long by $\frac{5}{8}$ in., which should be secured permanently to the legs by well gluing; they are made of deal 3 in. wide by $1\frac{1}{4}$ in. thick (see Fig. 1949). The centre bearer is about 2 in. by 2 in. in section, and has a lip tenon to fit into the mortise in the long rails at the middle of their lengths, and should be grooved for buttons and made of deal (see Figs. 1944 and 1948).

KITCHEN TABLE DRAWERS, ETC.

The runners are 2 in. by 2 in. in section, and are rebated to form a guide for the drawers (Fig. 1944); they are notched to fit over the cleat for the bolt (see Figs. 1947 and 1950). A hard-wood drawer stop, about $\frac{3}{4}$ in. by 1 in., is screwed into the rebate, as shown in Fig. 1948. The front of the drawer measures 4 in. by 1 in., each side 4 in. by $\frac{5}{8}$ in., and the back 3 in. by $\frac{5}{8}$ in.; they are dovetailed together. The bottoms, which are $\frac{1}{2}$ in. thick, are fitted into grooves in the front and sides, and are nailed on to the back. The sides and front should be secured to the bottom by glued blocks underneath, as shown in Figs. 1943 and 1944, and the buttons should be of hard wood (oak, beech, or ash), 2 in. long by $1\frac{1}{2}$ in. by 1 in., with lip to fit into grooves in rails; they should be secured to the top with stout brass screws to prevent rusting in, which would occur if iron were used (see

B, Figs. 1943 and 1944). The side rails should be fitted into their respective legs, and marked by cutting Roman numbers on the inside with a chisel to correspond, and the holes for the bolts should now be bored. All that is necessary in taking

Fig. 1949.—Table Leg Jointed to End Cross Rails.

the table apart is to slack the screws with a screwdriver, and, turning the buttons round, disengage them from the rails, lift off the top, take out the bolts, and draw off the united pairs of legs at the ends, leaving the long rails, centre bearer, and runners in separate pieces. The reverse method is adopted in re-erecting the table. The method of jointing here described might also be adopted in making dining tables, kitchen dressers, etc.; the diffi-

Fig. 1950.—Drawer Runner.

culties of moving such articles from house to house would thus be greatly lessened.

FITTING ADDITIONAL DRAWER TO TABLE.

The method described below of fitting an extra drawer to a table can be undertaken without any structural alteration, and the extra drawers can be removed at any future time without showing any disfigurement.

The drawer passes in and out under the existing rail of the table instead of cutting through it, the runners being fixed sloping inside the rails (see Figs. 1951 and 1952). Of course, there are a few cases where this

which are sections taken respectively at B B (Fig. 1952) and C C (Fig. 1953). The screws in the runners and strips must be well sunk to avoid trouble in the running of the drawer.

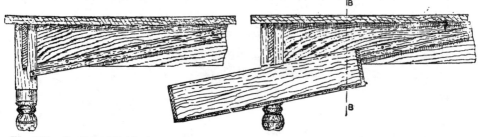

Fig. 1951.—Section of Table showing Drawer Runners.

Fig. 1952.—Section of Table with Drawer partly Opened.

inclined condition would be wholly unsuitable. When the drawer has been pushed in, the front end is raised behind the rail of the table until the drawer is level (see Fig. 1953), and held in that position by some simple device, which may take the form of a button or bolt; in any case, the fastening must be strong, as a large proportion of the weight of the drawer and its contents falls on it. When thus closed, the drawer is out

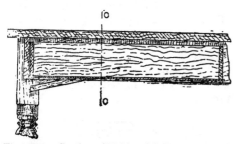

Fig. 1953.—Section of Table with Drawer closed.

of sight, and its privacy can be increased, if desired, by arranging the fastening in a secret manner. The runners can either be made solid by rebating a piece of stuff, or can be formed by screwing two plain pieces together, but the top surfaces must be sufficiently wide to allow the drawer to pass between the legs of the table. Strips, which fit in the rebates of the runners, are screwed on each side of the drawer at the upper edge, as shown in Figs. 1954 and 1955,

KITCHEN TABLE WITH PORTABLE LEAF.

The table shown in front elevation by Fig. 1956 and in cross-section by Fig. 1957 is a departure from ordinary practice. In many instances the hinged leaf of an ordinary kitchen table, when down, is in the way of anyone sitting at that side of the table. To obviate this difficulty, a new method of using the leaf and of stowing it is here described. The table is constructed in the usual manner, with the rail at the back and ends, and the

Figs. 1954 and 1955.—Sections of Drawer and Runner.

drawer stretchers at the front. The drawer fronts are, however, raised, which gives them a better appearance. Figs. 1958 and 1959 show the plates required to carry the leaf. The plate, with a slight hook A (Figs. 1958 and 1959), is screwed to the underside of the leaf, and fits into a piece of bent brass B. By pulling out the table brackets the leaf is rendered immovable. To support the leaf when not in use, another pair of brass plates is screwed to the underside of the drawer slides, and a wooden button is fixed to the drawer or stretcher to secure it firmly.   Fig. 1957

top edge of the side rails in which the ⅜-in. tongues A (see Fig. 1962) of the four oak buttons run along when the top of the table,

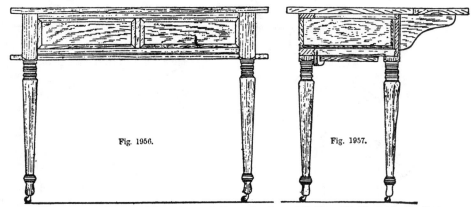

Fig. 1956.

Fig. 1957.

Figs. 1956 and 1957.—Elevation and Cross Section of Table with Portable Leaf.

shows the method of securing the leaf beneath the table, and also its position when in use.

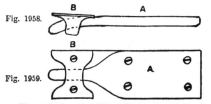

Fig. 1958.

Fig. 1959.

Figs. 1958 and 1959.—Plates for Table Leaf.

EXTENDING KITCHEN TABLE.

The top of this extending kitchen table (see Fig. 1960) is 4 ft. 6 in. by 4 ft. ; and a

which is in two divisions, is pulled apart. The buttons are glued and screwed to the underside of the table top, and their positions are shown in Fig. 1963, which is a plan of the underside of the table. Also, on the underside of each half of the top, two oak runners worked on the dovetail are glued and screwed (see B, Figs. 1961, 1962, 1963, and 1964). These runners slide along slots cut in the top edge of the end rails. The two halves of the table top are held together by brass clips that slide into sockets fixed on each side of the joint C (Figs. 1963 and 1965) ; Figs. 1965 to 1967 show the socket and clip. In the edge of one half of the table three ⅜-in. oak dowels D, Fig.

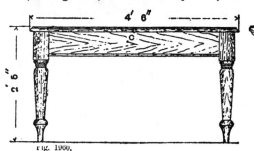

Fig. 1960.

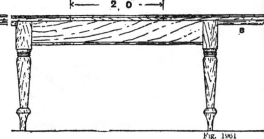

Fig. 1961.

Figs. 1960 and 1961.—Elevations of Extending Table without and with Leaf.

2-ft. leaf can be added (see Fig. 1961). The frame of the table is made in the usual way, but a plough groove is made on the inside

1963, are glued and fit dry into the edge of the other half.   The leaf is held in place in the same way, three dowels being glued into one of its edges to correspond with holes in one of the top halves, and three holes being bored in its other edge to correspond with

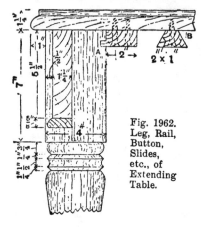

Fig. 1962. Leg, Rail, Button, Slides, etc., of Extending Table.

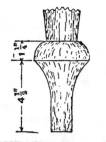

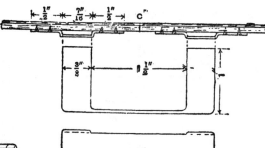

Fig. 1963.—Underside of Extending Table.

dowels fixed in the other half of the table. Two additional clips are necessary to secure the joint when the leaf is inserted. A stop 1½ in. by 1 in. should be fixed on the underside of each half of the table and cut

in between the oak runners (see E, Fig. 1963) to prevent either half being overdrawn. If these stops are fixed with a

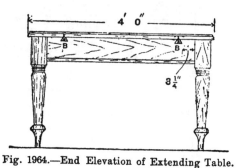

Fig. 1964.—End Elevation of Extending Table.

space of 13 in. between them and the inside of the rail, it will allow the dowels to clear themselves before the joints are closed.

Fig. 1965.—Brass Clip and Socket.

The frame and legs may be made of pitch-pine varnished, and the top of whitewood; or yellow pine, stained and dull polished, can be used throughout.

Fig. 1966.—Plan of Socket.

Fig. 1967.—Section of Clip.

LONDON DRESSER WORKING DRAWINGS EXPLAINED.

In regard to the dresser shown in Fig. 1968, Fig. 1969 is a section through the centre showing the general construction and the shape of the shelf brackets. Fig. 1970 shows two half plans, that on the left being above the top drawer rail, and that and the top rail c with dovetail. The dotted lines indicate the tenons and haunching of the end rails D. Fig. 1972 is an isometric drawing of the top of a back leg, full lines

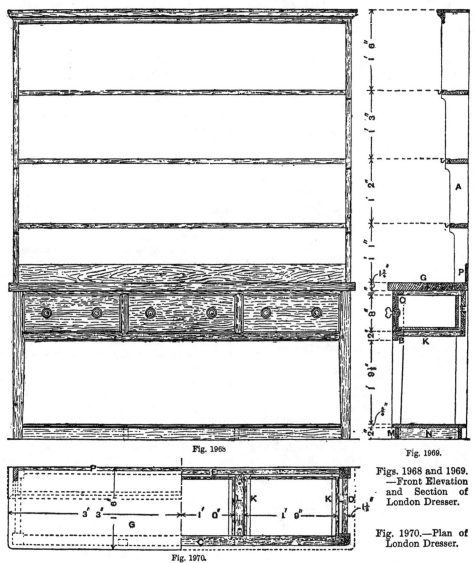

Fig. 1968.

Fig. 1969.

Figs. 1968 and 1969.—Front Elevation and Section of London Dresser.

Fig. 1970.—Plan of London Dresser.

Fig. 1970.

on the right above the lower drawer rail, the cross rail over the drawers being omitted to show the runner, etc., beneath. Fig. 1971 is an enlarged detail of the upper end of the front legs, showing in full lines the lower drawer rail B and edge of runner indicating the back rail E, and the drawer runner and guide, and dotted lines the end rail and the various mortises and tenons. Fig. 1973 is a cross section through one of the bearers F and top G showing the method of fixing the latter by buttons H. Fig. 1974

37

illustrates the usual manner of cutting two brackets from a 10-in. board. The dimensions given can of course be varied to suit circumstances, but 7 ft. 9 in. is the usual height of dressers for ordinary kitchens, and 6 ft. 6 in. a suitable width. Spruce deal is employed throughout, except for the drawer knobs, which are of mahogany.

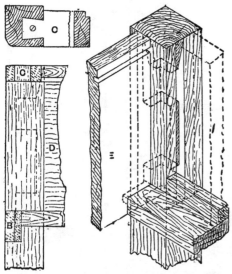

Fig.1971.—Front Leg of London Dresser.

Fig. 1972.—Back Leg of London Dresser.

MAKING LONDON DRESSER.

This dresser is usually made in two parts —the bottom containing the drawers and cupboards, and the top holding the shelves, which are made to fit tightly between the top of the dresser and the ceiling, being housed ¼ in. into the former. A wall hook is fixed under the centre of each shelf, two hooks being fixed above the cover boards, should it not reach to the ceiling. The two back legs are square, and the two front ones tapered as shown. The top rail is dovetailed into the legs as at o (Fig. 1971), and

the drawer rail framed with a bare-face stump tenon and bevel shoulder as at B. The end rails D are stump-tenoned into the front legs, and mitre tenoned with the back rail into the back legs; the tenons are barefaced, with the shoulders inside. The

Fig. 1973.—Securing Dresser Top.

drawer runners K (Fig. 1969) are made wide enough to overhang the drawer sides ¾ in., and are tenoned into the front and back rails as shown in Figs. 1969 and 1972, the guide pieces L (Fig. 1970) being screwed on square with the front after putting together the carcase. The cross bearers, rebated for buttons (see Fig. 1973), are dovetailed into the top and back rails, while the potboard rails M are mitre tenoned in a similar manner to the top rails, the cross bearers N being housed and secured by nails. The two end rails and the back should have a ⅜-in. groove cut on the inside, ¾ in. from the top edge, for buttons. The division rails between the drawers are tenoned through the front rails and wedged. The ends are put together first, and when set the division rails are glued square into the lower front rail, which latter is inserted into the end leg square. The runners are next put in and glued, then the back and potboard rails are fixed in position. Close up by driving on the other framed end, after which attach the cramps and leave them on until the work is dry. The top rail is inserted in the dovetails and the divisions

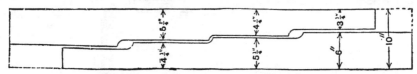

Fig. 1974.—Cutting out Dresser Brackets.

is fixed under the centre of each shelf, two hooks being fixed above the cover boards, should it not reach to the ceiling. The two back legs are square, and the two front ones tapered as shown. The top rail is dovetailed into the legs as at o (Fig. 1971), and

are wedged in tight, the cross and potboard bearers being cut in, after which the carcase is cleaned off, the drawers are fitted, and the guides screwed on. The drawers must be made ½ in. less in depth than the carcase, ½-in. blocks being glued in at the backs to act as stops. The top is made of two 9-in. by 1¾-in. boards tongued and glued, tried up on the top side, traversed for the bearers, and gauged to the proper thickness at the front and for 4 in. at the

in place and the exact length of the bevel part marked off. Cut tight and enter one end at a time. The brackets A for the shelves are cut to the shape shown in Fig. 1974. If many are to be done, one should be care-

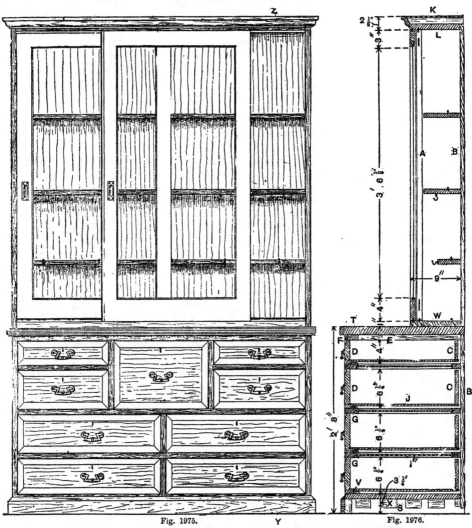

Fig. 1975.   Y   Fig. 1976.

Figs. 1975 and 1976.—Front Elevation and Section of Scotch Dresser.

ends. The front edge is screwed to the top rail and the remainder buttoned. The potboard is cut in and nailed to the bearers, the size being found by standing the dresser on the board and marking round the legs, after which the front edge is put to the legs

fully marked and cut out first and used as a template to mark the remainder. The cut is sawn down each end with a half-rip saw, and the turns with a compass saw which is afterwards run down the other cuts. Fig. 1974 shows for clearness two distinct cuts, but one only is necessary. The plate grooves in the shelves are $1\frac{1}{2}$ in. from the front edge, and are made with a rebate

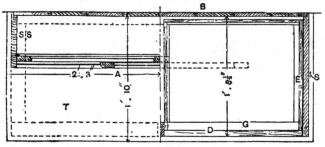

Fig. 1977.—Horizontal Sections of Scotch Dresser.

plane, the ends of the shelves being housed $\frac{3}{8}$ in. into the brackets, notched back $\frac{1}{4}$ in., and nailed through. The skirting P and the cornice rail are let in solid, and nailed on. The cover board may be simply cut over the top ends and nailed, or it may be dovetailed, the ends being covered by the return cornice, which is not attached until the dresser is fixed. The shelves are next placed on the top, and the ends of the brackets marked around, and after the housing is cut it is ready for fixing.

Scotch Dresser Working Drawings Explained.

Figs. 1975, 1976, and 1977 show the elevation, vertical section, and sectional plan, to a scale of $\frac{3}{4}$ in. to a foot, of a closed Scotch dresser, consisting of two separate and complete pieces of framing, the upper part comprising a plain cupboard 9 in. deep, with matchlined back, three shelves, and a pair of glazed sliding doors surmounted by an ogee cornice; the lower part being a chest of nine varied drawers, with flush chamfered fronts, locks, and drop brass handles, a planted plinth, a matchboard back, and a $1\frac{1}{2}$-in. solid top 22 in. wide reeded on the edge. The plan (Fig. 1977) is divided into two halves, that on the right hand being a section through the lower drawers, that on the left a section through the cupboard above. The dotted lines show the parts above and below the planes of section, and the top and plinth are indicated by the outer full line. Fig. 1978 is

an enlarged detail at the top end of the chest, showing the method of fixing the front rail, the drawer tilter, and the but-

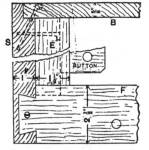

Fig. 1978.—Framework under Dresser Top.

ton for fastening the top. Fig. 1979 is a sketch of the same parts, and shows also how the drawer divisions are fixed by means of a dovetail tapered groove; the dotted lines indicate the framed division.

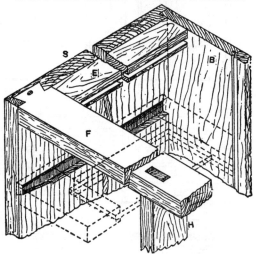

Fig. 1979.—Carcase of Scotch Dresser.

Fig. 1980 is the end of one of the divisions, showing the tapered dovetail. Fig. 1981 is a sketch of the lower end of the cupboard, showing door and slider beads, which are of $\frac{5}{16}$-in. oak. A dust fillet is grooved in each side. Fig. 1982 shows the upper end of the side, and indicates how the top of the case is dovetailed to the side. Fig. 1983 shows a portion of the edge of the dresser top, and Fig. 1984 shows a section of the cornice and cover board. The same letters are used to indicate the same parts throughout, and are thus explained: A doors, B the back, C drawer backs, D drawer

Fig. 1980.—End of Dresser Division.

fronts, E tilting fillet, F top rail, G drawer divisions, H vertical divisions, I dust board, J drawer bottom, K cover board, L top of cupboard, S side of chest, S S side of cupboard, T the dresser top, W bottom of cupboard, X angle blocks, V drawer stops.

MAKING SCOTCH DRESSER.

A few hints as to the construction may not be out of place, but quantities need not be given, as these will be learned readily from the full-sized drawings that will have to be made from the accompanying scale drawings. It is assumed that all stuff is

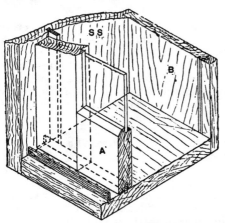

Fig. 1981.—Corner of Dresser Cupboard.

jointed up, planed, and gauged to a thickness, with the exception of dust boards, drawer bottoms, and matchlining, which need only be planed on one side and mul-

shelves, in both cases, are of one length between the shoulders; therefore they can all be struck over at once. Set out a pair from the rod or drawing, allowing the extra

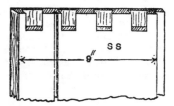

Fig. 1982.—Top End of Cupboard Side.

for sinking at each end. Place one at the bottom, arrange all the divisions G—the two tops, two bottoms, and shelves—in consecutive order, lay the other above all, and square the shoulder lines over; remove the shelves and square over a line $\frac{1}{4}$ in. farther out at each end for the housing; gauge to a width, the lowest shelf being kept narrower to allow of cups hanging, with a quarter notch at each front, and they will be finished.

CUPBOARD, ETC., OF SCOTCH DRESSER.

The top and bottom of the cupboard will require $\frac{3}{4}$ in. extra at each end for dovetails, which should be marked as shown at Fig. 1982; gauge to width of sides less $\frac{3}{8}$ in. for back, with two grooves for sliders, and one other in the bottom, $1\frac{1}{2}$ in. from back edge, for plate strip; this will complete the upper carcase. The cupboard sides are squared off to length, rebated for the back, and

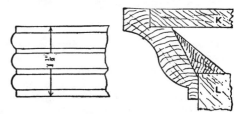

Fig. 1983.—Moulded Edge of Dresser Top.   Fig. 1984.—Section of Dresser Cornice.

housed $\frac{1}{4}$ in. deep, stopped in front; dovetail the ends as shown at Fig. 1982, plough for the dust fillets, plough the shelves for plate slips, and knock together; square sides, clean off, and fix the cornice. Then all is ready for fitting the doors. These are made of full 1-in. stuff, stiles and top rails 3 in. wide, bottom rails 4 in., rebated $\frac{1}{4}$ in. for glass, chamfered and put together with mortise and tenon. The top and bottom edges are ploughed with $\frac{5}{16}$-in. groove for the sliders, and the doors are arranged to slide with $\frac{1}{8}$-in. clearance between them ; a $\frac{1}{8}$-in. bead glued on the back of the outside meeting stile fills the void when closed. For the lower one, mark the dovetails on the top rail F and mortises for vertical divi-

Fig. 1985.—Sideboard Dresser.

sions, as at H (Fig. 1979) ; pair with second and third long divisions, and square them over. Square these divisions $\frac{5}{16}$ in. longer at each end, and mark for $\frac{3}{8}$-in. plough groove at inside edge. The length of the cut division is taken between the mortises, the inner ends are tenoned to upright divisions, the outer ends housed $\frac{5}{16}$ in. into sides. The bottom is housed in solid $\frac{5}{16}$ in. and nailed through the sides. The back division rails are cut off to the same neat length as the front. The sides s are set out

in pairs, the divisions, etc., marked on front edges in pencil, top and floor line squared off ; the housings struck over from front edge, with scriber, stopping them $2\frac{1}{2}$ in. back to form the dovetail (see Fig. 1979) ; gauge the rebate for the back lining, sink the housings, and fit the runners in ; cut the dovetail socket slightly tapering, as shown, then drive each division into its place, and mark the dovetail and cut as at Fig. 1980. When all are cut, drive in, enter the back divisions flush with rebate, and mark shoulders of drawer runners E, which should be of oak or beech ; cut a tenon at each end of these to fit plough groove, knock all in, take length of dust-boards and cut in tight. Fit dovetail of top rail, knock asunder, take a smooth shaving off each part, and glue division ends, first inserting intermediate divisions ; enter the bottom and the top rail, nail and square front, brace it, drive in runners, dustboards, and back divisions, and skew-nail the latter to sides ; flush off shoulders of runners, nail on the back, square the carcase. Flush off the front, and fix the drawer guides square from it and parallel to each other ; mitre round the plinth and fix with angle blocks.

SCOTCH DRESSER DRAWER FRONTS AND OTHER DETAILS.

Next fit in the drawer fronts, letting them finish hand-tight ; number and cut backs to match, cut off square, and plough sides and fronts, the sides $\frac{1}{4}$ in. deep, fronts $\frac{5}{16}$ in. ; cut sides for dovetail sockets in pairs and fit to fronts, glue up, insert the bottoms, and block square. When the glue is dry, fit in, stop as shown at v (Fig. 1976) with oak stops, end grain to the front, and flush off fronts ; pencil a line 1 in. on face and $\frac{7}{16}$ in. on edge, and chamfer all round. Fit locks and handles. Fasten on the top by screwing front rail and buttoning all round inside, and clean off top side and reed the edges. Secure the two parts together with three $1\frac{1}{2}$-in. No. 12 screws through the bottom w.

SIDEBOARD DRESSER WITH TURNED LEGS.

The leading dimensions of the sideboard dresser shown in Fig. 1985 are given in

Figs. 1986 to 1988, and the main features of the construction are as follow: Having cut the pieces to dimensions, they should

fashion. Reference to the illustrations given on p. 133 will show clearly what is meant by this. Next prepare the top, which

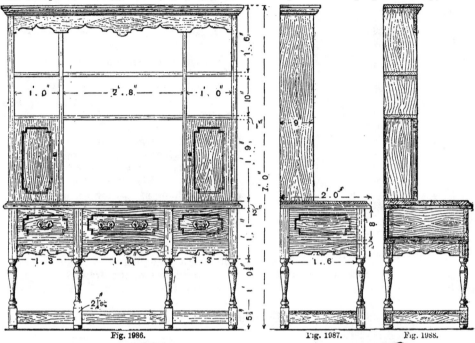

Fig. 1986.

Figs. 1986 to 1988.—Elevations and Vertical Section of Sideboard Dresser.

all be planed true. Then the legs should be turned to pattern and set out for mortising, the rails being marked for the tenons. The housings in the legs should be made to receive the ends of the curved rails, but need only be about ⅜ in. deep. When all the joints are made, the whole framework should be fitted together. Then the curved rails should be prepared and fitted, and the joints of the rails and legs can be glued together and further secured by a few screws or nails inserted obliquely from the inside. The nosing N (Fig. 1989) should next be prepared, and should be mitred at each front corner M. Where the back rail o meets N, it may be stop-halved, and the cross bearers, one of which is shown at P, can be dovetail-halved. The whole of these parts should next be nailed into the top of the legs, driving the nails in obliquely so that they hold in dovetail

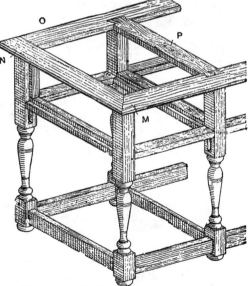

Fig. 1989.—Sideboard Dresser Framework.

can be secured by screwing upwards from the under side of the bearers and rails. The

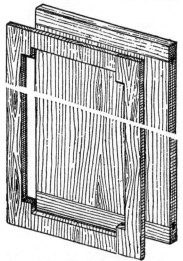

Fig. 1990.—Sideboard Dresser Door.

pot-board must be marked out and cut so as to fit accurately round the legs. The

and ends, so as to form a member of the cornice moulding (see Fig. 1988). This moulding must be mitred and fixed after the top is secured.

DOORS AND DRAWERS OF SIDEBOARD DRESSER.

The two doors should be made of pieces of board sufficiently wide, and clamped at each end as shown at Fig. 1990, the clamps being secured by grooving, tonguing, and gluing. When the glue is dry the surfaces should be planed off true. Then the pieces forming the marginal parts should be prepared and glued on to the boards. The two main parts forming the door are shown separately at Fig. 1990. The two doors should be hung in position with $2\frac{1}{4}$-in. brass butt hinges. In constructing the drawers, the front, two sides, and back can all be dovetailed together. The sides and front will require ploughing to receive the bottom, or a ploughed fillet may be used. After the joints of the drawers have been glued together, the parts forming the mar-

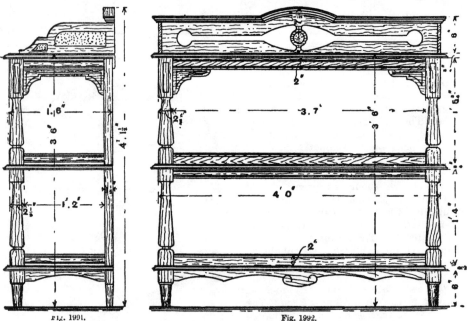

Fig. 1991.

Fig. 1992.

Figs. 1991 and 1992.—Side and Front Elevations of Kitchen Waggon.

sides and shelves are grooved together, the top being allowed to project over the front

gin may be glued on in a similar manner to that adopted when preparing the door.

MATERIALS FOR MAKING KITCHEN WAGGON.

Figs. 1991 and 1992 show in elevation a useful kitchen waggon, which can be made

rails, 1 ft. 4 in. by 2 in. by 1 in. ; two front corner brackets, 7 in. by $3\frac{1}{2}$ in. by $\frac{3}{8}$ in. ; two end brackets or supports to back panel, 1 ft. 5 in. by 5 in. by $\frac{1}{2}$ in. ; one front span

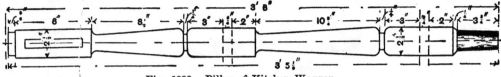

Fig. 1993.—Pillar of Kitchen Waggon.

of common mahogany and polished, or of pine and deal stained and varnished, or painted and grained. The following quantity of timber is required : Two front pillars, 3 ft. 7 in. by $2\frac{1}{2}$ in. by $2\frac{1}{2}$ in. ; two

rail, 3 ft. 9 in. by 3 in. by $\frac{3}{8}$ in. ; two end span rails, 1 ft. 3 in. by 2 in. by $\frac{3}{8}$ in., and two 1 ft. 3 in. by 4 in. by $\frac{3}{8}$ in.

MAKING KITCHEN WAGGON.

The two front corner pillars are turned from a square section to Fig. 1993. Mortises to take the several rails, and a stump tenon at the top, are provided. The lower ends are rounded, and, if desired, castors can be added. The bottom and central

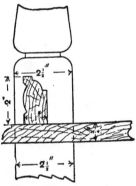

Fig. 1994.—Centre Shelf at Side of Waggon.

back pillars, 3 ft. 7 in. by $2\frac{1}{2}$ in. by $1\frac{1}{2}$ in. ; two shelves, 4 ft. 3 in. by 1 ft. 7 in. by $\frac{3}{4}$ in. ; one top, 4 ft. 3 in. by 1 ft. 7 in. by $\frac{3}{4}$ in. ; one back top panel, 4 ft. by 11 in.

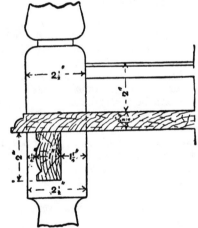

Fig. 1996.—Centre Shelf at Front of Waggon.

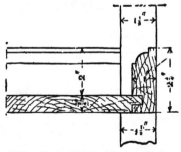

Fig. 1995.—Back Bottom Part of Waggon.

by $\frac{1}{2}$ in. ; one moulding, 5 ft. 6 in. by $1\frac{1}{2}$ in. by 1 in. ; three back rails and two front rails, 3 ft. 10 in. by 2 in. by 1 in. ; six end

shelves are supported by the end and back rails (see Figs. 1994, 1995, and 1996), and are also tenoned into the pillars. The face edges of the rails and shelves are moulded as in Fig. 1994. The back rails are moulded on the front side, as shown in Fig. 1995, and for the end rails a corresponding moulding is worked. A span rail, finished with sweep work, is fixed under the lowest shelf, both at the front and back. This is cut in and fixed with glued blocks. The waggon top is $\frac{3}{4}$ in. thick, and has a moulded edge to correspond with the shelves. At the back, it fits flush with the back top rail (see Fig. 1997), so that the panel can be screwed to the rail. The panel is fret

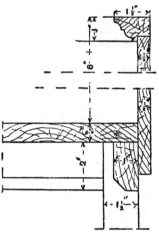

Fig. 1997.—Back Top Part of Waggon.

cut (see Fig. 1992), and is supported by two end brackets, or supports, dowelled and glued to the top. A moulding, $1\frac{1}{2}$ in. by 1 in., rebated to the panel, gives the necessary finish, the overhang at each end being the same as for the shelves. Ornamented corner brackets may be fixed to the front and ends, below the top rails. The shelves and tops are best made by glue-jointing several narrow widths of timber together, and, when dry, cleaning up the whole width at one operation. They are then cut to size, and the article is complete.

CEILING CLOTHES-RACK.

A simple clothes-rack is made with two end pieces as shown in Fig. 1998, each of which is formed of two pieces of 3-in. by 1-in. deal halved together at right angles to one another. The horizontal piece should be about 2 ft. 3 in. long, and the upright one 1 ft. 9 in. long. Four 1-in. holes are bored through these end pieces (see Fig. 1998), and round rods fitting into these holes form the rack; the length of the rods is regulated by the length of rack required. To fix this kind of rack, two single-sheave pulleys are screwed into the

ceiling, care being taken to ensure that they have a good hold in the joists. The pulleys should be in a line running parallel with the fireplace, and at such a distance from it as to lie in the centre line of the rack. They should also be at such a distance apart as to well balance the rack when it is loaded. If the rack or the rods of the rack are 10 ft. long, the pulleys should be about 6 ft. apart, or as near to that as the joists will permit, because it is necessary that the pulleys should be screwed into the joists, or the rack, when loaded with clothes, will fall. A double-sheave pulley must be screwed into the joist near that side or corner of the room which it is most convenient to work the rack from, and a cleat hook plugged to the wall immediately under it.

PUTTING TOGETHER CEILING CLOTHES-RACK.

Put the rack together by placing the rods in the holes in the end pieces, then pass the ends of some fairly strong sashcord through the double-sheave pulley, one end over each wheel, and also over the single pulleys. Fix one end of the cord round the top rod (in the top hole) close to the end piece, and the other end round the same rod, but close to the opposite end piece; and end pieces must be so arranged on the rods as to make the cords hang vertically when

Fig. 1998.—End Piece of Clothes-rack.

the rack is down. The cord can then be cut off to the right length so that the rack will always wind up parallel. A knot is tied at the end of the cord, and the job is finished. The single pulleys should be screwed in so that the wheels are on the same plane as the double pulley; if this is not done, the cord will be constantly break ing, besides being apt to run off the wheels. The rack, if made 10 ft. long, will give a hanging space of nearly 40 ft., and if the end pieces are 6 ft. apart the clothes may

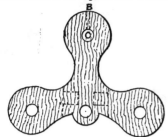

Fig. 1999.—Ornamental End Piece.

be hung on each side of them, thus preventing undue strain on the rods.

Improved Ceiling Clothes-rack.

An end piece of a more elaborate pattern is shown in Fig. 1999; it looks well if made of 1½-in. pitchpine, the grain of the centre piece running vertically and of the two wings horizontally, the latter being fixed to the former with mortise and tenon as shown by dotted lines. It can be made of any size required, but the top rod should not be more than 2 ft. over the three rods at the bottom. This rack is fixed in the same manner as the first, but the cord is passed through a hole bored for the purpose down through the top of the end piece at B (see Fig. 1999). This hole is countersunk inside the hole C to receive the knotted end of the cord, so that when the top rod is in position the knot of the cord is out of sight, this being a much neater arrangement than that previously described.

Larger Ceiling Clothes-rack.

The larger rack illustrated in Fig. 2000 consists of two side pieces D, 4 in. by 1½ in., two end pieces F, 4 in. by 1¼ in., and the necessary number of round rods E, each 1 in. in diameter. In the diagram (Fig. 2000) seven rods are shown, and these rods, with the two sides D, give a hanging space of 72 ft. if the rack is 8 ft. long. To fix such a rack, screw four single-sheave pulleys into the joists, as at G¹, G², G³, and G⁴ (Fig.

2001); these pulleys must form a parallelogram of such a size that the cords can be brought down vertically from each pulley and fixed either to the sides D or to the ends F of the rack: either sides or ends will do. In the centre of this parallelogram two double-sheave horizontal pulleys must be screwed on, as at H (Fig. 2001), and in the corner or side of the room from which the rack has to be worked an ordinary double-sheave pulley must be screwed, as at J (Fig. 2001). Pass a length of cord through the single pulley G¹, round both of the wheels in the nearest horizontal pulley H, down over the pulley G², and fix the ends to one end of the rack, one at each side. Pass a second length of cord up over pulley G³, down through pulley G⁴, and fix it to the other ends of the rack. A third length of cord must now be passed up through the double pulley J, one end through each wheel, and the several ends tied one to each loop at K and L, formed by the first two cords. The two cords first inserted are then adjusted for length, so that the rack may hang level and draw up straight. It must not be forgotten that the pulleys G¹, etc., must all

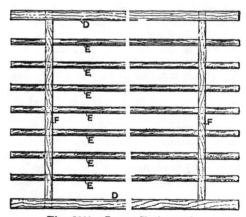

Fig. 2000.—Large Clothes-rack.

line towards the centre pulleys H, and that the cords must all drop to the rack from the outside of the pulleys G¹, etc. Instead of using the two pulleys H, a four-sheave pulley may be used; but the method already described is simpler to rig up, and makes a stronger job. A double-sheave pulley, as used at J, and a single two-wheel horizontal pulley, as used at H, are shown

as before ; the cords T are then taken direct to the barrel, where their free ends are now securely nailed, the rack being adjusted by

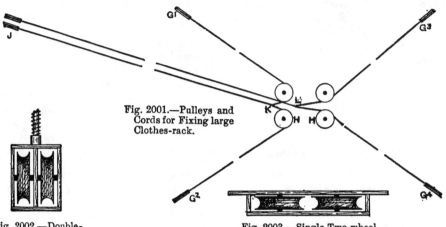

Fig. 2001.—Pulleys and Cords for Fixing large Clothes-rack.

Fig. 2002.—Double-sheave Pulley.

Fig. 2003.—Single Two-wheel Horizontal Pulley.

in Figs. 2002 and 2003 ; the one screws into the ceiling and the other is screwed not into but upon the ceiling.

Working and Fixing Ceiling Clothes-rack.

A good method of working a heavy rack is by a windlass (Fig. 2004). This consists of an iron rod M fixed vertically in suitable bearings in one corner of the room, the top end being as close to the ceiling as possible. A barrel N, made of wood, about 1 ft. long by 6 in. in diameter, is fixed on this bar near the top, and on the bottom of the bar, which should be about 3 ft. 6 in. from the floor, is fixed a cog-wheel O of about the same diameter as the barrel. A short spindle P, with worm wheel R (Fig. 2005), is fixed so as to engage with the cog-wheel O. The pulleys H (Fig. 2001) are not required if the rack is to be worked by a windlass. One end of each of the four cords is fixed to the rack, one under each pulley G¹, etc.,

means of the cords supporting it, as before described. In this arrangement the cords will pass over the pulleys all in one direction, and the pulleys must stand in a straight line towards the windlass. The advantages gained by this method of fixing a large rack are that it can be wound up or left at any intermediate height, and it does not require fastening ; there are no loose ends of cords hanging about, whether

Fig. 2004.—Windlass for Working Clothes-rack.

Fig. 2005.—Spindle and Worm of Windlass.

the rack is up or down ; and the heaviest rack will work easily if the bearings of the windlass are kept properly oiled.

HALL FURNITURE.

SHELF BRACKET FOR ENTRANCE HALL.
THE dimensions of the shelf bracket illustrated in elevation and plan by Figs. 2006 to 2008 are: Length, 2 ft. 10 in.; supports, being let into them and fixed with 1-in. No. 10 screws. The shelf is finished to 9 in. by ⅝ in. and fixed to each support with 1¼-in. No. 10 screws, and surrounded

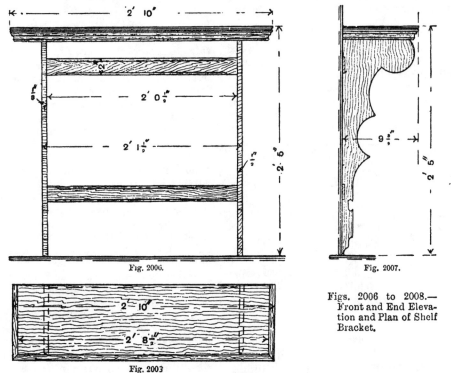

Fig. 2006.

Fig. 2007.

Fig. 2003

Figs. 2006 to 2008.—Front and End Elevation and Plan of Shelf Bracket.

width, 9¾ in.; and height, 2 ft. 5 in. The two supports, seen in Figs. 2006 and 2007, are cut from ⅝-in. stuff and finished to ½ in. thick, and set out as shown in Fig. 2009. The scrollwork is cut with a band saw, the rough edges being afterwards cleaned with a spokeshave, file, and sandpaper. Alternative designs for the supports are given in Figs. 2010 to 2012. Two rails, 2 in. by ½ in., with chamfered edges, connect the by a moulding, shown in section in Fig. 2013. The moulding is fixed with cut brads, and mitred at the corner joint to return the shelf ends. The top is covered with fancy oilcloth, fixed with thin glue. The shelf bracket is fixed to the wall by screws driven through the rails into wooden plugs fixed in the wall, the support being cut away to fit over the skirting. The following wood is required: 5 ft. 6 in. by 2 in.

by ½ in. ; 2 ft. 10 in. by 9 in. by ¾ in. (to finish ⅝ in.) ; and 2 ft. 10 in. by 9 in. by ⅝ in. (to finish ½ in.). Pine is a suitable wood to use, and looks well if finished by staining

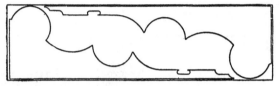

Fig. 2009.—Marking out Shelf Bracket Supports.

in imitation of walnut. Fig. 2008 is a plan of the bracket complete.

Hall Mirror with Hat and Coat Rail.

Mahogany or oak is a suitable wood with which to construct the hat- and coat-rail mirror illustrated by Fig. 2014, care being taken to select dry material. The two rails R (Fig. 2014) are 3 ft. by 3 in. by 1 in., with chamfered edges. The two uprights U (Fig. 2014) are 1 ft. 6 in. by 3 in.

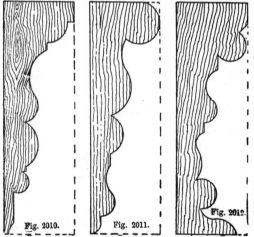

Figs. 2010 to 2012.—Shelf Bracket and Supports.

by 1 in. over the shoulders, and are tenoned and wedged into the two rails, the edges being chamfered to match the rails. In the opening thus formed, a piece of silvered plate glass, which should have bevelled edges, is now placed, the rebate to receive this being formed by gluing and bradding a strip of wood 1 in. wide (S, Fig. 2015) along

the uprights and rails ; the thickness of the strip must be determined by the thickness of the glass used, ⅜ in. additional being allowed to take a board B (Fig. 2015) ¼ in.

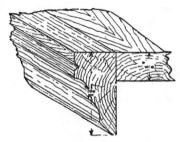

Fig. 2013.—Edge Moulding on Shelf Bracket.

thick to protect the glass. Instead of using these strips, the rebate may be ploughed out of the rails and uprights ; but the former method is easier, and quite as effective. The four corner ornaments C O (Fig. 2014) are used to strengthen and finish the outer corners, and are set ⅜ in. on from the face edge ; cut them with a band saw, glue in position, and afterwards screw them from the back. The top ornament T O (Fig. 2014) is ⅝ in. thick, set back from the face edge, and may be of any desired shape ; a piece of carving may with advantage be substituted. Five pegs for hats and seven hooks for coats are to be screwed to the rails ; good strong brass hooks and pegs should be used, as they last longer and afford a good support. The hat pegs H P (Fig. 2015) are put along the top rail at 8-in. centres, the coat hooks P (Fig. 2015) being placed along the bottom rail at 5½-in. centres. The screw-holes for the pegs and hooks having been set out, the woodwork should be polished before the article is fixed. Four strong brass plates B P (Fig. 2014) are used to fix it to the wall. These should be cut out of 1/16-in. sheet brass. The wall must be plugged for the fixing screws or nails (see p. 251). If mahogany has been used, the work should be french-polished ; but if made of oak, it would look well cleaned up, rubbed over with wax, and left dull. The glass for the mirror had better be bought, of the required size, ready silvered and bevelled.

SMALL HALL TABLE.

The small hall table shown by Fig. 2016 may be made of bass wood or American whitewood, or any similar soft wood. The number and size of pieces required can be ascertained from Figs. 2017 and 2018. They should be faced true, and gauged and planed to thickness, after which the curves should be marked out. The most satisfactory way to do this is to make templates worked by overhand paring with a keen chisel and finishing with No. 1 glasspaper. The thumb moulding shown round the edge of the top (see Figs. 2017 and 2018) may be worked by means of a scratch tool.

HALL TABLE STANDARDS, ETC.

The two standards are connected by means of a rail, and have mortises that allow a whole-thickness tenon to pass through, and they are finally secured by

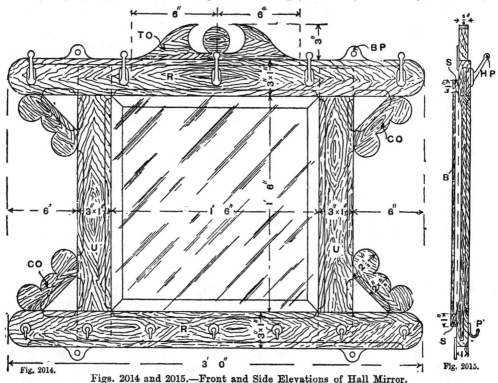

Figs. 2014 and 2015.—Front and Side Elevations of Hall Mirror.

of stout paper or thin cardboard, because, as the parts of the table are symmetrical, a template made for one half would suffice for the other half. The curved parts should next be sawn out. Some of the straight parts which join the curves should be finished with the chisel and a small thumb-plane or spokeshave; generally this will be found more satisfactory than trying to finish with a file. The large curves can be finished with a spokeshave, and some of the small curves with a file, or these may be

wedges. The top on its under-side is grooved to a depth of about $\frac{1}{4}$ in., so as to receive the top ends of the standards. The top and the standards can be fixed rigidly together by gluing a few angle blocks to them. The back piece and the top are secured by glue, and by inserting a few screws from the under-side of the top. The two pieces marked A (Fig. 2017) should be fixed to the standards and top by angle blocks glued in the inner angles, and by driving in a few small sprigs or screws after the glue has set. If there is a skirting or plinth projecting beyond the wall where the

Fig. 2016.—Hall Table.

A small bevelled mirror can be fixed to the back either by recessing the latter or cutting a hole right through and fixing a piece of moulding round. A simpler and

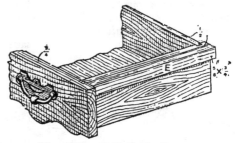

Fig. 2020.—Hall Table Drawer.

quite as effective a method is to obtain the glass mirror with bevelled edge and buy a piece of moulding c (Fig. 2019) ready prepared. This can be rebated at the back, mitred round, and fixed in position with a

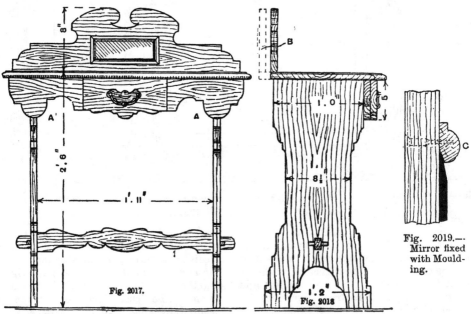

Fig. 2017.

Fig. 2018.

Fig. 2019.—Mirror fixed with Moulding.

Figs. 2017 and 2018.—Front and Side Elevations of Hall Table.

table has to stand, the top should overhang at the back a little more than the thickness of the skirting, as shown by the dotted lines at B (Fig. 2018).

few round-headed brass screws, or the screws may be inserted from the back, as shown in Fig. 2019. The drawer (Fig. 2020) has the front side and back dovetail-grooved together, the bottom fitting into plough grooves in the sides and front or

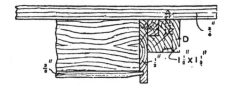

Fig. 2021.—Hall Table Drawer Runner.

into a ploughed fillet. The latter should be grooved and sprigged to the sides and front. The runner D (Fig. 2021) is rebated so as to receive the fillet, which is glued and sprigged on to the sides of the drawer, as shown at E (Fig. 2020). Fig. 2022 shows a plan of the table. A suitable brass handle

HALL TABLE WITH SHELVES.

The hall table shown in elevation by Figs. 2023 and 2024 may be constructed in black walnut or mahogany. The legs are of 1½-in. square stuff, tapered off equally all round, above and below the drawer

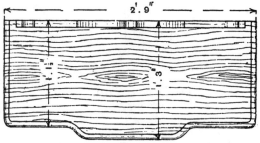

Fig. 2022.—Plan of Hall Table.

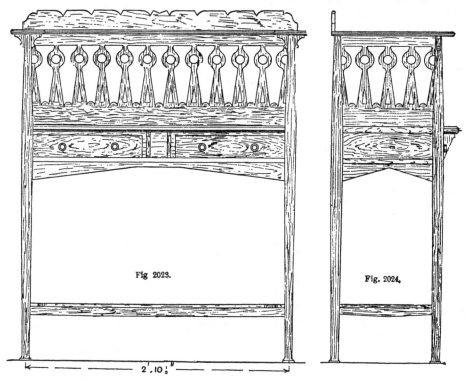

Figs. 2023 and 2024.—Elevations of Hall Table with Shelves.

should be obtained and screwed on, and the table may be finished either by simply varnishing, or by staining and varnishing.

rails, the reduction being to ¾ in. square at the top, and to 1 in. at the neck of the foot (see Fig. 2025). The table top, which is shaped as shown in the half plan (Fig. 2026), is of 1-in. stuff. Fig. 2027 is a half horizontal section with the top removed ; the table top is simply cut around the legs

small brackets are glued to it underneath the overhanging part of the table top. A cross rail T (Fig. 2030) is dovetailed into the back and front rails, and prevents the

Fig. 2025.—Bottom of Hall Table Leg.

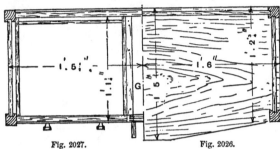

Fig. 2027.   Fig. 2026.

Figs. 2026 and 2027.—Section and Half Plan of Hall Table.

and notched into them $\frac{1}{4}$ in., as shown in Figs. 2028 and 2029. The front edge is double chamfered, but the ends, which finish flush with the legs, are left square. The bottom, of $\frac{3}{4}$-in. stuff, is treated similarly, except that it is finished flush and square all round. The back rail, $\frac{3}{4}$ in. thick, is stub-tenoned into the legs as shown in Fig. 2028, and the end rails, $\frac{1}{2}$ in. thick, are grooved in $\frac{5}{16}$ in. all round as shown in Figs. 2027, 2028, and 2029. The front rail is cut away to provide openings for the drawers, from the bottom edge to within

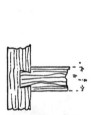

Fig. 2031.—Dovetail Joint for Stretcher.

Fig. 2028.—Back Leg Joints.

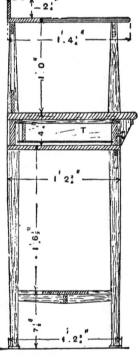

Fig. 2029.—Detail of Hall Table Front Leg.

Fig. 2030.—Vertical Section of Hall Table

$\frac{1}{2}$ in. of the top edge; this portion is checked into the legs $\frac{1}{4}$ in. at the ends, and glued and screwed to the top. The central part is tongued into the bottom, and two

drawers tilting up when drawn out. Guides for the drawers, shown at G (Figs. 2027, 2028 and 2029) are nailed to the bottom, and should be fixed square with the front, the drawers being made $\frac{1}{16}$ in. narrower at the back than at the front.

SHELVES OF HALL TABLE

The shelf rails, of $\frac{5}{8}$-in. stuff, are stub-tenoned into the legs, the stretcher being

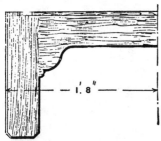

Fig. 2032.—Half Plan of Table Top Shelf.

dovetailed as illustrated in Fig. 2031. The shelf (shown in half plan in Fig. 2039) is cut tight in between the legs and cleaned off flush with the outside. A small shelf, $4\frac{1}{2}$ in. wide and $\frac{1}{2}$ in. thick, runs round the back and ends of the table, resting on brackets sunk into the legs. A half plan of this shelf is shown in Fig. 2032, and details of the shaped rail are given in Fig. 2033. The chamfer on the edge is worked into a solid mitre at c (Fig. 2033). · In making this joint it will be best to work the rebate in the end pieces, and fix first by dowelling on to the legs; then shoot the back piece tightly between the shoulders whilst it is in the

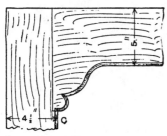

Fig. 2033.—Part of Shelf showing Joint Line.

square, cut the rebate, and cut and shape the edge.

OTHER DETAILS OF HALL TABLE.

The perforated panels in the back and ends are best constructed as shown in Figs.

2034 and 2035, using a straight top rail $1\frac{1}{2}$ in. wide and a straight bottom rail 3 in. wide, cut out with a series of 2-in. seats for the pillars and mortised with a $\frac{1}{8}$-in. chisel. The pillars are cut out separately to a pattern, and a tenon is formed on

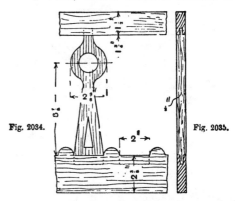

Figs. 2034 and 2035.—Elevation and Section of Perforated Panel.

each end. They may of course be cut out of the solid with a fret-saw, but will then be much weaker. If constructed as described here they should be glued up and treated as a solid panel, being grooved into the legs, and glued to the table top at the back, while the ends are tongued into a $\frac{3}{16}$-in. groove across the top. The plinth, first shaped and finished off, is glued and screwed to the shelf, and the knee-rails, of $\frac{1}{2}$-in. by $2\frac{1}{2}$-in. stuff, are glued and blocked to the bottom, and sunk $\frac{1}{4}$ in. into the legs. The drawers (Fig. 2036) are dovetailed, the fronts being of $\frac{3}{4}$-in. stuff, and the backs

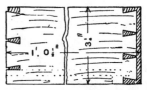

Fig. 2036.—Side Elevation of Drawer.

and sides of $\frac{1}{2}$-in. and the bottoms of $\frac{3}{8}$-in. stuff; these are grooved in and blocked. The fronts are sunk $\frac{1}{4}$ in. below the face of the legs and $\frac{1}{8}$ in. below the face edge of the bottom. Fig. 2037 gives an enlarged view of the front leg and drawer rails, Fig. 2038 a section of the table top, and Fig. 2039 a half plan of the bottom shelf. All the parts should be fitted together complete, then taken to pieces, and all except the outside surfaces of the legs bodied in with polish,

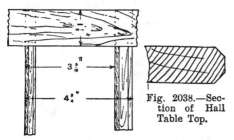

Fig. 2038.—Section of Hall Table Top.

Fig. 2037.—Hall Table Drawer Rails, etc.

glued up, cleaned off where necessary, and the polishing finished.

Artistic Umbrella Stands with Turned Work.

The umbrella stands shown by Figs. 2040 to 2043 may be effectively made of light oak stained brown. The front and back A (Fig. 2044) should be $\frac{3}{4}$-in. stuff, preferably without joint. They should be fastened together with four fine panel pins, before cutting to get them both the same size. The plinth is in two parts, B and C. The part B should be of $\frac{7}{8}$-in. stuff, cut to the size required, gauged on $2\frac{1}{2}$ in. all round, and cut out in the centre part to receive the zinc drip pan. This drip pan is shown in section at D. Now work the mould round. The piece C, of $\frac{7}{8}$-in. stuff, is

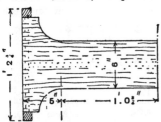

Fig. 2039.—Half Plan of Bottom Shelf.

got out in two lengths; after working the mould, mitre it round, and screw and glue it fast to the piece B. Then set out the front and back, bore for spindles E and buttons F, and put these parts together.

The front and back are fixed to the plinth by screws, but boring through the plinth into the front and back for three or four dowels will make the job much stronger. The turned buttons hide the screws that

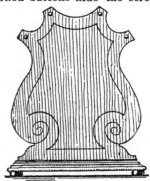

Fig. 2040.—Front Elevation of Umbrella Stand.

fasten the spindles. A V-line at G (Fig. 2043) is cut to continue the line of the shield. Fix the turned crush balls H (Fig. 2044) with two screws in the plinth.

Umbrella Stand in Turned Wood.

The size of the umbrella stand shown by Figs. 2045 and 2046 is 2 ft. by 1 ft. It is preferably made of ash and varnished, but may be of oak, mahogany, beech, or any hard wood. The materials required are four pieces for the legs, each 2 ft. 6 in.

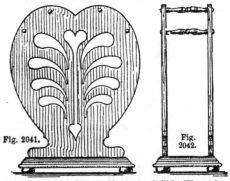

Figs. 2041 and 2042.—Front and Side Elevations of Umbrella Stand.

long and $1\frac{3}{4}$ in. square when trued up, which should be turned to the pattern given in Fig. 2045. Get two pieces 1 ft. 11 in. long, and true up to $1\frac{1}{4}$ in. square; these are for the longer bars, as shown in Fig.

2046. For the smaller bars (Fig. 2047) three pieces 10½ in. long each and of the same scantling as the longer bars will be required. Turn all these to the de-

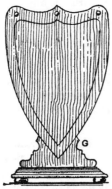

Fig. 2043.—Front Elevation of Umbrella Stand.

sign illustrated, making sure the shoulders are left the proper length, and taking care to turn ¾-in. lugs on to each end of sufficient length that, when cut to a mitre as in Fig. 2048, they will meet and form the joint in the holes that are to be bored in the legs to receive them, as will be afterwards explained. It is perhaps better to turn these lugs a trifle too long— say, fully 2 in.—and trim them to fit afterwards. The shoulders of the centre bar must be rather longer than those of the

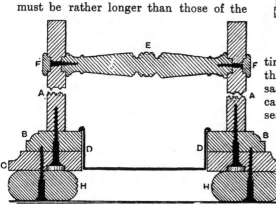

Fig. 2044.—Cross Section of Umbrella Stand.

end bars. This completes the turning portion. Next get four pieces for the bottom; two of them will be 1 ft. 11 in. long (Fig. 2045) and two of them 10½ in. long: they

will be 3½ in. deep and 1 in. thick. On the ends of these must be cut the lugs that are to go into the holes as before mentioned. The holes in the legs are made with a ¾-in.

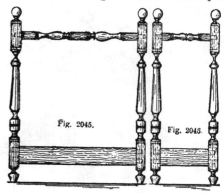

Figs. 2045 and 2046.—Elevations of Umbrella Stand in Turned Work.

bit, and the lugs that go into them are turned on to the ends of the turned pieces and driven into them. The lugs on the bottom pieces will have to be done by hand, as they cannot be easily turned. In put-

Fig. 2047.—Plan of Umbrella Stand.   Fig. 2048.—Joint in Umbrella Stand.

ting the parts together, care must be taken that corresponding parts are exactly the same size, so as to have symmetry. In the case of the bottom pieces, sink a shallow seat in the legs for about ⅛ in., in order

Fig. 2049.—Zinc Drip Tray.

that the piece may sit in it to that depth, and so make a cleaner joint with less danger of warping; but care must be taken to allow ¼ in. on each length extra. When all the parts are made and fitted properly, they may be glued up into position. All that now remains to be made is the tray for the bottom, which should be a plain, square,

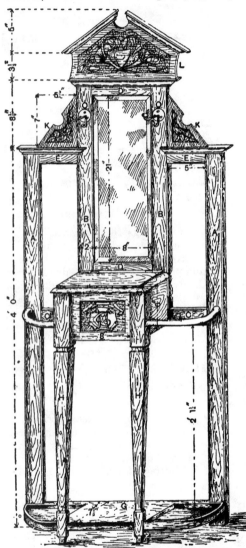

Fig. 2050.—Hat and Umbrella Stand with Mirror and Brush Box.

shallow tray of zinc (Fig. 2049), with a wire edge. This is merely laid into the bottom, and is supported on small bits of wood nailed on to the insides near the bottom. The projecting cheeks of the legs inside

will not allow the tray to be made quite square, but the bottom of the tray, by being made slightly slanting, will cause it to fit down without any trouble. To obtain a perfect fit without any trouble, a tray should be made with double corners to fit the legs exactly. There being no wooden bottom, nothing remains but to varnish the stand. First give the whole work two coats of good glue size, which will give a solid appearance to the varnish. When the size is properly dry, the work should be sandpapered, and then two coats of varnish will finish all.

HAT AND UMBRELLA STAND WITH MIRROR AND BRUSH BOX.

The hat and umbrella stand shown by Fig. 2050 is made in dark oak. It has two parts, the upright frame A at the back, and a box to hold brushes, etc., supported by two legs H H. These two parts are connected by a curved brass rod for holding umbrellas, and a board at the bottom (see Fig. 2050). The stand is 5 ft. 5 in. high, and projects only 8 in. from back to front. To construct the stand, begin with the back framework. This consists of two upright bars A A, each 4 ft. by 2 in. by 1 in. ; two smaller uprights B B, each 2 ft. 1½ in. long, with a tenon 1 in., making 2 ft. 2½ in. by 2 in. by 1 in. ; with a middle rail C 1 ft. 10 in., with a tenon at each end of 1 in., making in all 2 ft. by 2 in. by 1 in. ; two smaller rails E E, each 5 in., with a tenon of 1 in. at each end, making in all 7 in. by 2 in. by 1 in. ; and two central rails D D, each 8 in., with tenon of 1 in. at each end, making in all 10 in. by 2 in. by 1 in. Plane up the wood to the correct width and thickness, and saw to length, allowing 1 in. more to all the uprights to ensure firm mortises in the top ; this spare inch may be sawn off when the rails are all glued in. Cut the tenons of all the rails, and, having mortised the uprights and the middle rail (which is to receive the two middle uprights), put all together and see that every joint is good. In order to get neat and close joints the tenons should be marked with a chisel held obliquely, and run along the blade of the square before sawing off. If all fit well, take apart, and mark all the chamfers according to plan ;

the chamfers giving a lighter and more finished appearance to the work. The central portion, consisting of two uprights and two rails, is to receive a bevelled mirror F, Fig. 2051, so the inner edges must be rebated $\frac{1}{2}$ in. by $\frac{3}{4}$ in., as shown in Fig. 2051. The two outside uprights A A must

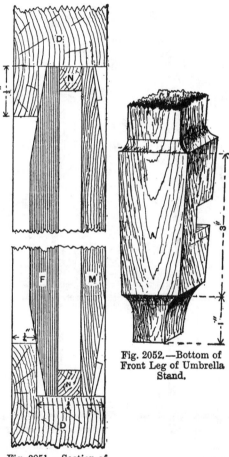

Fig. 2052.—Bottom of Front Leg of Umbrella Stand.

Fig. 2051. —Section of Mirror Frame.

also be cut at the distance of 2 in. from the bottom, to receive the bottom board G. When all are cut and fitted glue up the central portion, which is to receive the mirror ; then add the midrail C and two smaller rails E with the two uprights A, and cramp up. Whilst the stand as far as it is made is drying, other parts can be prepared.

UMBRELLA STAND BRUSH BOX, AND LEGS.

Now prepare the box, which consists of a front panel 8 in., with a tenon of 1 in. at each end, making in all 10 in. by 6 in. by $\frac{1}{2}$ in. ; two sides 5 in., with a tenon of 1 in. at one end, making in all 6 in. by 6 in. by $\frac{1}{2}$ in. ; a back $10\frac{1}{2}$ in. by $5\frac{1}{2}$ in. by $\frac{1}{2}$ in. ; two legs H H, each 2 ft. 8 in. by 2 in. by 2 in. ; a bottom piece to fit into a groove of $\frac{3}{8}$-in. stuff ; and a lid 1 ft. 1 in. by 7 in. by 1 in. The legs should be cut according to plan, with mortises made at the upper part to receive the box sides, and cut to receive a dovetail tenon to hold the board at the bottom. The front panel may be carved in low relief, and should have a tenon of 1 in. at each end to fit into the legs, and also a groove $\frac{1}{4}$ in. to receive the bottom of the box ; the top edge of this groove should be $\frac{1}{2}$ in. from the bottom edge. The two side panels should have a tenon of 1 in. at one end to fit into the legs, and the other end should be mortised for stopped lap-dovetail, as well as a groove $\frac{1}{4}$ in. to receive the bottom. The back should be dovetailed at both ends ; the bottom should be of $\frac{3}{8}$-in. stuff, bevelled at three edges to fit the groove, and nailed to the back. The top should be cut with a quarter round and fillet on three sides, and when this is done a 1-in. strip should be cut off from the unmoulded edge, fastened on the box by means of dowels, and hinged to the other part of the lid. When all is fitted, glue the tenons of the four sides into the legs and into one another, and cramp up square. When the glue is dry, fix the 1-in. piece of lid with dowel pins, and, the bottom being let in, the box is complete.

DRIP PAN AND BRASS RAILS OF UMBRELLA STAND.

The board for the bottom should be 2 ft. 2 in. by $7\frac{1}{2}$ in. by 1 in. ; the two ends are rounded, and hollows sunk $\frac{3}{4}$ in. to receive pans for drips. The front leg is cut away as in Fig. 2052 to receive the pan. Board G is let into the back legs $\frac{3}{8}$ in., and into the front legs by hidden dovetail. A $\frac{5}{8}$-in. hole should be bored $\frac{7}{8}$ in. deep into the sides of the front legs and front part of the back legs to receive the brass rail ; the centre of this bore should be $\frac{9}{16}$ in. from the outside edge of legs, and on a level with the top edge of back rail c. The curved brass tube may be obtained from an ironmonger, to whom a pattern drawn full size should be supplied. Let the centre of the curved tube

Fig. 2053.—Umbrella Stand Moulding.

be drawn from a $6\frac{1}{2}$-in. radius, and allow $\frac{3}{4}$ in. at each end beyond the quadrant for insertion. Now drive the brass rail into the front legs, and cramp up the front part, consisting of box and legs, with the back frame and bottom board. Secure the bottom board to the back legs, as well as the box to the rails, by screws from the back.

COMPLETING THE UMBRELLA STAND.

The moulding (Fig. 2053) should be fitted by being glued on the face at the top of the back framework; the triangular spandril K (Fig. 2050) may be fastened with screws, and the top piece L when carved may be affixed with two dowel pins. The mirror should be affixed by the method shown in Fig. 2051 after the whole has been polished. The daylight size being 1 ft. 9 in. by 8 in., a plate 1 ft. $9\frac{1}{2}$ in. by $8\frac{1}{2}$ in., bevelled 1 in., should be procured; M indicates the back panel and N the block. Two brass hooks O (Fig. 2050) for caps may be screwed on as shown. Cut a paper pattern of sunk hollows in the bottom board, and get an ironmonger to make two zinc trays standing 1 in. high, with a beading on the top, and the stand is complete.

HAT AND UMBRELLA STAND FOR LARGE HALL.

This hat and umbrella stand (see the elevation, Fig. 2054, and sectional plan, Fig. 2055) should be constructed in oak. The following specification gives the amount

of timber required at finished sizes, the allowance for tenons being reckoned in: For two back stiles, 11 ft. 6 in. by $2\frac{1}{2}$ in. by 1 in.; two intermediate stiles, 7 ft. 2 in. by $2\frac{1}{4}$ in. by 1 in.; one rail, 2 ft. by $1\frac{1}{2}$ in. by 1 in.; one rail, 3 ft. 7 in. by $2\frac{1}{4}$ in. by 1 in.; two rails, 1 ft. $7\frac{1}{2}$ in. by 1 in.

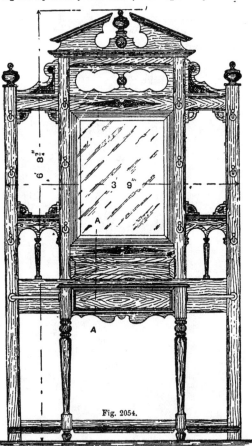

Fig. 2054.

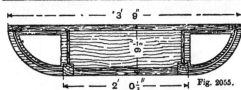

Figs. 2054 and 2055.—Elevation and Sectional Plan of Umbrella Stand.

by 1 in.; one rail, 3 ft. 7 in. by $6\frac{1}{2}$ in. by 1 in.; one rail, 3 ft. 7 in. by $1\frac{1}{4}$ in. by 1 in.; two turned legs, 4 ft. $9\frac{3}{4}$ in. by 2 in. by

2 in. ; two box ends, 1 ft. 4 in. by $4\frac{7}{8}$ in. by $\frac{7}{16}$ in. ; one box front, 1 ft. 11 in. by $4\frac{7}{8}$ in. by $\frac{7}{16}$ in. ; one box bottom, 1 ft. $10\frac{5}{8}$ in. by

by $1\frac{1}{4}$ in., and 2 ft. 4 in. by 2 in. by 1 in. ; three finials, 7 in. by $2\frac{1}{2}$ in. by $\frac{5}{8}$ in. ; one drip-tray board, 3 ft. 9 in. by $9\frac{1}{2}$ in. by $\frac{3}{8}$ in. ; and mirror backing, 4 ft. super. at $\frac{1}{4}$ in. thick.

CONSTRUCTING HAT AND UMBRELLA STAND.

The back scantling is framed as shown in Fig. 2056, the various pieces being mortised and tenoned, except the $2\frac{1}{2}$-in. top rail, which is dovetail-halved over the intermediate stiles. The chamfering for the

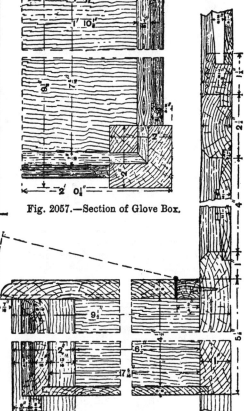

Fig. 2057.—Section of Glove Box.

Fig. 2056.—Back Framework of Umbrella Stand.

$7\frac{7}{8}$ in. by $\frac{3}{8}$ in. ; one box top, 2 ft. $1\frac{1}{2}$ in. by $8\frac{1}{4}$ in. by $\frac{5}{8}$ in. ; one fillet for box top, 2 ft. $1\frac{1}{2}$ in. by $\frac{3}{4}$ in. by $\frac{5}{8}$ in. ; one sunk panel, 1 ft. $8\frac{1}{2}$ in. by $4\frac{1}{2}$ in. by $\frac{1}{2}$ in. ; one scroll panel, 1 ft. $8\frac{1}{2}$ in. by $6\frac{1}{4}$ in. $\frac{1}{2}$ in. ; one frieze panel, 2 ft. $2\frac{1}{4}$ in. by $5\frac{1}{2}$ in. by $\frac{1}{2}$ in. ; one scroll between the turned legs, 1 ft. 9 in. by 2 in. by $\frac{3}{8}$ in. ; two corner ornaments, 1 ft. $3\frac{1}{2}$ in. by $6\frac{3}{4}$ in. by $\frac{1}{2}$ in. ; eight corner blocks, 1 ft. 8 in. by $2\frac{1}{2}$ in. by $\frac{1}{2}$ in. ; four capital blocks, 4 in. by $1\frac{1}{8}$ in. by 1 in. ; two shafts, 1 ft. $4\frac{1}{2}$ in. by 1 in. by 1 in. ; two arched panels, 1 ft. 4 in. by $3\frac{1}{2}$ in. by $\frac{1}{4}$ in. ; two fillets for arched panels, 1 ft. 4 in. by $\frac{3}{8}$ in. by $\frac{1}{4}$ in. ; 8 ft. of mirror moulding, $1\frac{5}{8}$ in. by $\frac{7}{8}$ in. ; 4 ft. of plinth moulding, 1 in. by $\frac{1}{2}$ in. ; $8\frac{1}{2}$ ft. of box front and ends moulding ; cornice mouldings, 2 ft. $4\frac{1}{2}$ in. by $1\frac{7}{8}$ in.

Fig. 2058.—Vertical Section of Glove Box, Mirror Frame, etc.

whole framing is seen in the elevation. Figs. 2057 and 2058 show the glove-box sides dovetail-tenoned into the wide rail and mortised into the squares of the front turned legs. The front is similarly fixed, and the

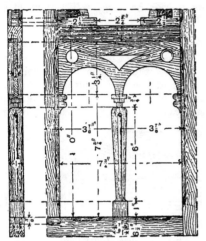

Fig. 2059.—Shaft and Arched Panel of Umbrella Stand.

tenons plugged with small dowels from the inner side. The front and ends are surrounded with a small moulding. The lid has its edges relieved with an ovolo moulding, and is hung to a fillet, screwed to the back rail, with two 2-in. by ⅜-in. brass butts. The front and ends are rebated to receive the bottom. The shaft is square, with fluted sides, and is tenoned into the top edge of the framing rail (see Fig. 2059). The arch panel rises from two capital blocks tenoned into the framing, the panel being let into these blocks and the top of the shaft for

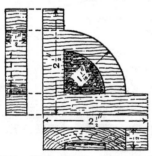

Fig. 2060.—Umbrella Stand Corner Block.

about ¼ in. deep, as shown in Fig. 2059. It is also rebated into the framing and fixed with a small fillet. The corner blocks for

the side openings are glued in position, and a few small pins driven in from the rear side (see Fig. 2060). The panelling is about

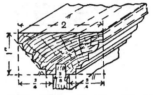

Fig. 2061.—Upper Cornice Moulding.

¼ in. deep, and slightly scored or picked with the corner of a chisel. The two side top corner ornaments are ½ in. thick, with low relief panels. The cornice moulding is rebated on the frieze panel, as shown in

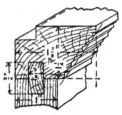

Fig. 2062.—Lower Cornice Moulding.

Fig. 2061, which is rebated into the moulding below, fitting on the top framing with a dowel slip. Figs. 2061 and 2062 show the upper and lower cornice mouldings respectively. The finials (see Fig. 2063) are held in position by dowels into the stiles

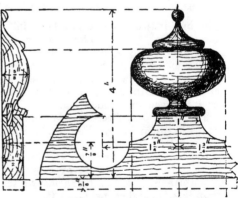

Fig. 2063.—Umbrella Stand Finial.

and a dowel slip in the central finial, which is slightly larger than the two side ones. The scroll panel is rebated in the framing.

MIRROR, SCROLLWORK, AND OTHER DETAILS.

The mirror has a bevel edge, and is framed in a reeded moulding, the outer edge

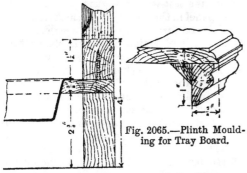

Fig. 2065.—Plinth Mould-ing for Tray Board.

Fig. 2064.—Drip Tray and Board.

of which is ploughed to fit the rebate in the framing, the stiles of which should be 2¼ in. wide, not 2½ in. as shown. The glass is protected at the back by a thin board, which should be fixed with a small fillet between it

below the glove-box and between the two front turned legs, glue being sufficient to hold it in position. The bottom board carrying the tin-plate or enamelled drip-trays (see Fig. 2064) is fixed to the legs and under the bottom edge of the lower back rail in the framing. The front edges are moulded and fitted with a plinth moulding (Fig. 2065). A rest for umbrellas and walking-sticks is formed with ⅝-in. diameter brass tube, passing from the glove-box to the back framing. The tube is fitted with flanged collars to receive the screws for fixing it. After the stand has been polished, twelve brass hooks for hats and coats should be fitted. The wood can be polished in its natural light colour, or darkened.

HALL CHAIR.

A hall chair for execution in wainscot oak or walnut is shown in side elevation by Fig. 2066, and in front elevation by Fig. 2067. Whatever material is used, if polished, it should be finished with a dull

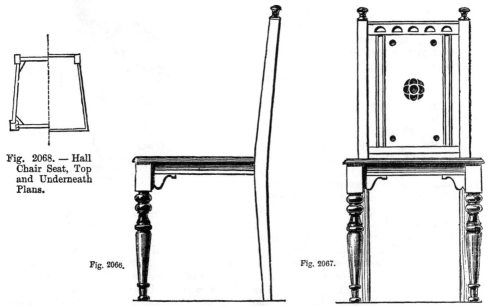

Fig. 2068. — Hall Chair Seat, Top and Underneath Plans.

Fig. 2066.

Fig. 2067.

Figs. 2066 and 2067.—Elevations of Hall Chair.

and the glass to prevent the board scrubbing the silvering. The opening below the mirror is filled with a fielded panel fitting in rebates. A piece of scrollwork is fixed

surface. This chair is 3 ft. 1 in. in height, 1 ft. 4¾ in. from back edge of seat to front edge, which is 1 ft. 6 in. long, extreme measurement, and the width of the back edge is governed by the legs, which measure 1 ft. 2¼ in. out to out (see Fig. 2068). The front legs are turned out of 2 in. square stuff. The rails are either dovetailed into the legs, or mortised and tenoned, as the back rails and back ends of

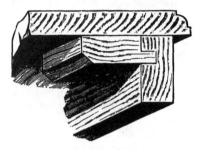

Fig. 2069.—Hall Chair Seat Buttoned to Frame.

side rails must go into the back legs. Any pegs used to secure the tenons in the mortises should not penetrate the outer face of the stuff, but be carefully made and fitted so as to fill properly the tenon without its being necessary to drive them right through in the ordinary way; but screws, fairly stout, and carefully put in, will answer, although they do not draw up the shoulders on the rails in the same way as pegs. Inside the frame, just under the seat, must be fitted angle brackets. It is preferable that they should be fitted and screwed on dry in the first instance, and then removed and glued well before finally fixing. Run a plough groove in the rails to receive the lip of the buttons which will secure the seat to the frame. The lip of the button is cut to fit the plough groove in the rails. This is made clear in Fig. 2069. The back is fitted together before the remaining portion of the framing is glued up; in fact, the back portion must be taken up and finished off completely. The back legs are 1¼ in. square when finished; the lines to which they must be cut are shown in the side elevation (Fig. 2066). The distance between the inner faces of the legs is 11¾ in. Semicircular sinkings in the top rail die away into the face of the stuff;

these are best cut in with a scribing gouge and round-nosed chisel, after having been marked out with a sharp pair of compasses. The reeding in the rails under the seat will be worked with a router. The panel in the back is $\frac{4}{16}$ in. thick finished, and is perforated by a geometrical pattern; half elevation of this is shown full size at Fig. 2070. This may be cut out with a fret-saw; a keyhole saw is likely to splinter the back. The four corner holes are simply ⅝ in. centre-bit holes carefully cleaned out. The seat is ⅝ in. in thickness finished, and has an ovolo moulding on the edges. The top is finished quite flat, and is 1 ft. 6¼ in. from the floor. After the top is fitted between the back legs, it should be securely fixed by the aid of the buttons already described. The two knobs surmounting the back legs are turned separ-

Fig. 2071.

Fig. 2070.

Fig. 2070.—Fretwork in Hall Chair Back.
Fig. 2071.—Hall Chair Knob.

ately, and fixed with glue; a half elevation is given by Fig. 2071. The brackets in front and at side underneath rails are ⅝ in. thick when finished, and are fixed with screws. The front angles of the seat should be slightly rounded, and the sharpness of the arrises generally eased.

BEDROOM FURNITURE.

SHAVING CABINET.

THE shaving cabinet illustrated by Fig. 2072 is so arranged that when the doors are open, as shown at the left hand of Fig. 2072, the light is reflected on each side of the face. The back of the cabinet should be made first. It is of ½-in. stuff, 2 ft. 7 in. ½ in. thick and 2 ft. 6½ in. by 7½ in. The ends form an angle of 45° with the back. The front edge has a length of 1 ft. 3½ in. These boards are 1 ft. apart, and are fixed with screws through the back as at A (Fig. 2074). Frame up the front 1 ft. 3 in. by 1 ft., the rails and stiles being 1¼ in. by

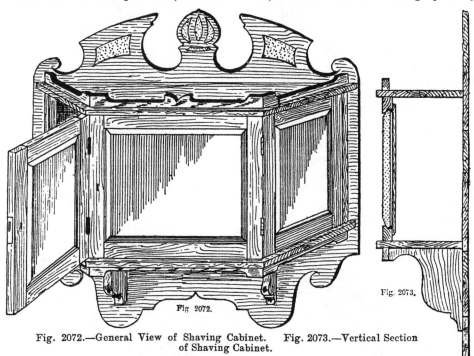

Fig. 2072.—General View of Shaving Cabinet.
of Shaving Cabinet.

Fig. 2073.—Vertical Section

by 2 ft. 5 in., and is either jointed up, as shown in section by Fig. 2073, or framed, a ¼-in. board forming its centre. Cut it out with a bow-saw ; the ornamental panels at the top have the outlines cut in about ⅛ in., the centres being bevelled down and punched with the point of a wire nail. The top and bottom boards at the back are ¾ in., rebated for the glass, and the back edge of the stiles being bevelled off at an angle of 67½°. Cut and fit the brackets as shown in Fig. 2073. They are glued and screwed through the bottom board and back. Get out the ornamental rails at top and bottom, mitre them, and glue and brad them in place, ½ in. within each edge, and they will then cover up the screws used to secure the front, as at c (Fig. 2074). Fasten a slip cut to the section of B (Fig. 2075) in each angle at the back; with these slips

Fig. 2074.—Joints of Shaving Cabinet.

the doors will come flush. Frame the doors 1 ft. by 9½ in. of similar section to the front, with the hinge stile bevelled to 67½°, and hang the door in place. This can be fitted either with locks or with hanging handles and catches. Stain and polish, or otherwise finish to taste, and, lastly, insert the mirrors. These should be securely wedged as at D (Fig. 2074), and covered at the back with thin wood to protect them from scratches.

Fancy Matchbox for Bedroom.

A fancy matchbox is shown in oblique perspective by Fig. 2076, end and side views

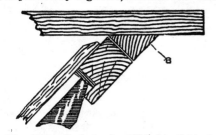

Fig. 2075.—Back Angle of Shaving Cabinet.

are given by Figs. 2077 and 2078 respectively, and Fig. 2079 is a cross section. The box consists of two principal parts— the foot A into which is mortised the flat

upright pillar B, and the box or match container, which slides upon the pillar, and is supported by it. The box may be made of mahogany, walnut, or other fancy wood, dressed to $\frac{3}{16}$ in. in thickness, with the exception of the foot, which should be cut from thicker wood or built up. The pillar is 3 in. wide, and the length rather less than 7 in., being exactly determined after all the parts of the box are put together. A slot is cut in the centre of the broad face of the pillar (see dotted outline in Fig. 2078). The end view (Fig. 2077) shows the form of the two end pieces of the box, with the

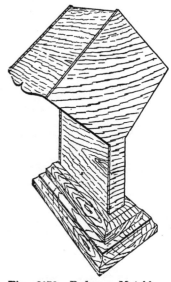

Fig. 2076.—Bedroom Matchbox.

several dimensions indicated. The side pieces D and H that lie between the end pieces just described will hardly require further description than what the figures themselves afford. They are plain, rectangular pieces, with one of each of their edges bevelled, in order that they may fit together as shown.

Matchbox Lids and Pillar.

The two lids F (Fig. 2079) of the box are bevelled on their upper edges to meet the flat sides of the pillar B, and the lower edges have an ornamentation cut upon them. These lids turn upon pivots G (Fig. 2077), which are plain brass pins or fine round nails driven through the top edges of the box sides c (Fig. 2079) into holes bored into the ends of the lids. The lids cannot be lifted up unless the whole box is slid up the pillar B, so that the top edges of the lids can pass inwards (see the dotted lines in Fig. 2078). The peg E passes through two holes opposite each other in the side H in line with the slot in the pillar before mentioned. Its use is to hold the box to the supporting foot. In the figure this peg is touching the lower end of the slot, the

exactly determined by trial when the parts are fitted together.

PUTTING TOGETHER MATCHBOX.

The several parts of the box are fastened together with fine nails or screws, with a little glue applied to the joints. On sliding the box up the pillar, one of the matches contained in the receptacle drops into the groove on the top of the pillar B, and, on sliding the box back into the position, the match is brought to the apex of the box,

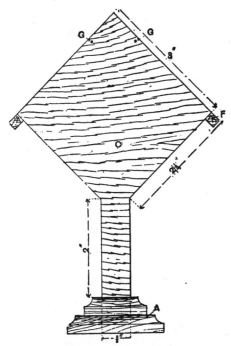

Fig. 2077.—End View of Bedroom Matchbox.

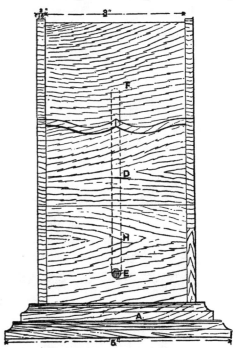

Fig. 2078.—Side View of Bedroom Matchbox.

usual position ; and it will be seen that, in sliding the box up the pillar, the pin traverses the slot until it meets the upper end of it, further motion of the box being then stopped. A V-shaped groove, which is cut upon the top edge of the pillar at B (Fig. 2079), should then fill in the angle made by the lower sloping sides D D of the box. The maker must get the several parts into adjustment so that this may happen— that is to say, the height of the pillar and the length of the slot should first be made approximately correct, and afterwards

from which it may be easily picked up, even in the dark.

BOOT AND SHOE RACK.

Figs. 2080 and 2081 illustrate a rack for boots, shoes, and slippers, which would be useful in almost any part of the house. It can be made of ¾-in. yellow pine or sound red deal, and requires two ends, 2 ft. 9 in. by 11 in. by ¾ in. ; one top, 4 ft. by 11¾ in. by ¾ in. ; two braces, 3 ft. 6 in. by 3 in. by ½ in. ; six rails for shelves, 3 ft. 7 in. by 2 in. by 1 in. ; and one moulding, 6 ft. by

$1\frac{1}{2}$ in. by $\frac{7}{8}$ in. First prepare the rails. Plane them square, and take off the sharp corner to form a slight chamfer. Shoulder

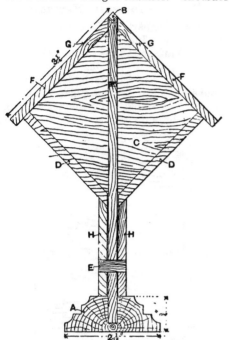

Fig. 2079.—Section of Bedroom Matchbox.

and tenon each end ready for the ends, which can then be prepared with the mortises. Space them out as shown in Fig. 2082, the two top rails for children's boots

and slippers being closer together than the others. When the mortises are cut, gently drive on the ends and wedge the rail tenons. Across the back, screw two braces B (Fig. 2082), and then screw on the top from the under-side. The ends and braces should be gouged for the screws. At the front, immediately below the top, place a $\frac{5}{16}$ in. diameter iron rod I R (Fig. 2082) suspended by brass hooks, on which to fix a curtain C (Figs. 2080 and 2082) to cover the boots. The finishing moulding along the top can next be fixed, and the rack is then ready for painting, or staining and varnishing. Rails are preferable to solid shelves, as they admit of a free current of air to dry the soles of the boots.

BED REST.

For the bed rest illustrated by Fig. 2083 the following materials will be required: For the frame A (Fig. 2083) two pieces 2 ft. 1 in. by 3 in. by 1 in., planed to $2\frac{3}{4}$ in. by $\frac{7}{8}$ in.; two pieces 1 ft. 4 in. by 3 in. by 1 in., planed to $2\frac{3}{4}$ in. by $\frac{7}{8}$ in. For the frame B, two pieces 1 ft. $4\frac{1}{2}$ in. by 2 in. by $1\frac{1}{4}$ in., planed to $1\frac{3}{4}$ in. by $1\frac{1}{8}$ in.; one piece $11\frac{1}{2}$ in. by 2 in. by $1\frac{1}{4}$ in., planed to $1\frac{3}{4}$ in. by $1\frac{1}{8}$ in. For the frame C, two pieces $10\frac{1}{2}$ in. by $1\frac{3}{4}$ in. by $1\frac{1}{4}$ in., planed to $1\frac{1}{2}$ in. by 1 in.; and one piece $11\frac{1}{2}$ in. by $1\frac{3}{4}$ in. by $1\frac{1}{4}$ in., planed to $1\frac{1}{2}$ in. by 1 in. There will also be required between 5 yd. and 6 yd. of webbing, one pair of $1\frac{1}{4}$-in. back flaps, some $\frac{3}{4}$-in.

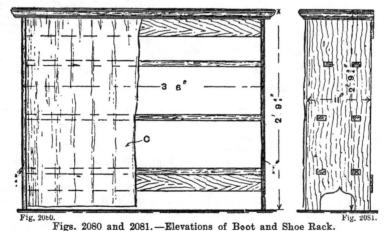

Figs. 2080 and 2081.—Elevations of Boot and Shoe Rack.

screws, and two coach-screws, 3 in. by $\frac{1}{4}$ in. The wood must first be planed up true.

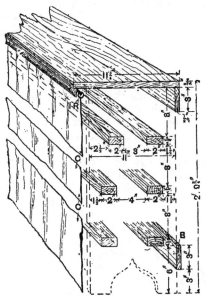

Fig. 2082.—General Sectional View of Boot Rack.

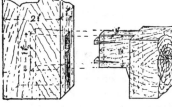

Fig. 2083.—Bed Rest.

Commence by planing true the face side and face edge of each piece of wood, afterwards gauging to the several widths and thicknesses, taking care that in each measurement the gauge is set quite $\frac{1}{32}$ in. full to allow for smoothing off when glued up. When this is quite true, lay it on the bench face side uppermost, and as the other pieces are planed lay them on the prepared piece, and if each piece does not lie perfectly flat plane off the part where it touches, that being the highest part. The face edge of each piece can be done in a similar manner. To test with the eye alone, hold up a piece of wood in the line of sight, then slowly turn up the further edge into the line of sight. Note which corner comes into view first—that will be the high part; plane this down, also the opposite corner of the diagonal. The reason for this is that if one corner curls up $\frac{1}{8}$ in., taking $\frac{1}{16}$ in. off the opposite corner will make it equally true, and the stuff will hold thicker than if the $\frac{1}{8}$ in. was planed off one corner. Having planed all the material on the face sides and face edges, set the gauge to the width. As each piece is gauged, plane down to the line, taking care that the edge is exactly square before the line is reached; if two gauges are to hand, then the other gauge can be set to the thickness, and the planing of each piece of wood finished. Care must be taken in planing the last side of each piece; plane down to the gauge line on each edge, testing for level by placing the back edge of the try-square across the grain.

Fig. 2084.—Joint at Corner of Bed Rest Frame.

SETTING OUT BED REST.

Now proceed to set out, remembering that in setting out work the face sides and face edges must always pair. For example, take the frame marked A (Fig. 2083). Take one of the sides, 2 ft. 1 in. long, 2¾ in. by ⅞ in., and, keeping the face side to the worker and the face edge uppermost, find the centre of length; mark off 1 ft. (half the height) on each side of this, and square

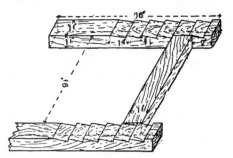

Fig. 2085.—Horizontal Frame of Bed Rest.

lines across the edge. Then from these lines mark 2¾ in. inwards, being the width of rail at top and bottom of frame, and set out 1⅝ in. width of tenon. Note that the tenon does not go through, only entering 1⅝ in., which is quite sufficient, the joint being fastened by fox-wedging, which is here shown by Fig. 2084, but which has already been described (see p. 207). Thus, setting-out lines will only be needed on the face edge. Having set out one side of frame A, take the other side and place it beside the one set out, so that the two sides pair—that is, both face sides are outside and both face edges uppermost. Having squared lines across, set the mortise gauge to the chisel that is nearest one-third the thickness of stuff, adjusting the teeth of the mortise gauge so that the chisel just rests comfortably between the points of the teeth, then set the gauge head so that the teeth are exactly in the centre, trying first one side and then the other by pricking in the points of the teeth until the points coincide; then tighten up, and, holding the stock of the gauge close to the face side, mark the mortises and continue gauge lines for the haunching, running the lines on to the end. Next proceed to set out top and bottom rail of frame A (Fig. 2083). Take one rail, find the centre of its length, and set off half-width of frame less 2¾ in. (width

of stile) on each side of centre. Square all these lines, taking great care, for it is very important that these, being shoulder lines, should be marked true. Note that the try-square should always be applied to either a face side or face edge. The lines must next be squared to the other rail, it having been first noted in placing the rails together that they pair; then with the mortise gauge mark the tenons all round the end from shoulder to shoulder. Now set out frame B (Fig. 2083). The stuff is ½ in. longer than the finished lengths. Set out one side, starting ¼ in. from one end, and marking off 1 ft. 4 in., thus leaving a little waste to be sawn off, and enabling a square end to be cut, which can also be shot just before gluing together. From the first line set off 2 in. (see Fig. 2085), the distance the rail is from the end, then 1¾ in. width of rail. As none of the tenons goes through, the gauging is confined to the face edge only. Set out the other side so that it pairs with the first one, and then gauge. Before leaving it will be well to set out the notches (see Fig. 2085). On the face side of one of the 1-ft. 6-in. pieces, commencing ¾ in. from the rail end, set out successively six spaces of 1½ in. each; place the other side so that they pair. Square lines across the two pieces by means of the

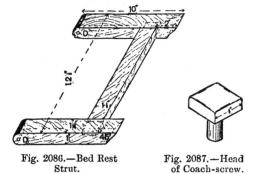

Fig. 2086.—Bed Rest Strut.   Fig. 2087.—Head of Coach-screw.

try-square; square also down each edge a little way, and with a marking gauge set to ¼ in. just make a mark on the line; mark the slope with a striking knife, using the edge of the try-square as a straight-edge; then set out the rails 9½ in. between shoulders, the tenons 1 in. longer, prepared for fox-wedging, as in frame A. Frame C (Fig. 2083) comes next, taking one side and proceeding to set it out as in the case of frame B. For dimensions of C, see Fig. 2086. Note that one end of frame C is semicircular, and that at the centre of this portion a $\frac{5}{16}$-in. hole must be bored through each piece (see D D, Fig. 2086), so as to

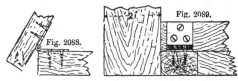

Figs. 2088 and 2089.—Side and Back Views of Corner of Bed Rest Frame.

enable the coach-screw (the head of which is shown at Fig. 2087) to pass through for the purpose of hanging frame C to frame A, and allowing it to hinge easily. The other ends of the frame C must be cut at an angle of 45°, to obtain which it is not necessary to have a bevel, for if the thickness of the stuff is set off from the end and a line joined diagonally from this point to the top edge, the angle will be 45°. The cross-rail is set out similarly to frame B; it is 9½ in. between the shoulders, and the tenons are 1 in. longer. The setting-out is now complete.

MAKING BED REST.

Commence actual work by mortising the sides for frame A (Fig. 2083). The mortises are 1⅝ in., and are widest at bottom for fox-wedging (see Fig. 2084); note also that the haunching (Fig. 2084) tapers from nothing at the end to ⅜ in. at the tenon. Great care must be used in mortising, for if the hole is not perpendicular it will cause the frames to twist, as the tenons will follow the holes, and so tend to take the stuff with it. After mortising, cut the tenons, ripping down first, then sawing the shoulders, afterwards marking width of tenons 1⅝ in. from face edges, and the haunched part of tenon ⅜ in. to nothing (see Fig. 2084). Next make two cuts in each tenon about ¼ in. from the side and 1 in. long, and prepare and insert in each cut a small wedge of the same thickness as the tenon, ¾ in. long, and tapered $\frac{1}{16}$ in. to nothing, leaving the wedge pro-

jecting at the tenon end. On driving or cramping the frame together the wedges are driven in, and the end of each tenon is widened so that, with the glue, it is impossible to pull it out. A hole should now be bored in the centre of each face edge of stiles 9 in. from the bottom, the hole to be a little less than ¼ in. diameter for the coach-screw to fasten in tight when hanging. It is best done before gluing up, for when together it would be found awkward to bore except with a rather large gimlet. Smooth the edges of the frame so as to leave it clean, and the frame is ready for gluing. The frames B and C can be served in a similar manner. In gluing up the frames, be sure the glue is hot. Get the cramp or cramps at hand before commencing, and see that the fox-wedges are right. When the frames are glued up, test them with a large square whilst applying the cramp; a slight movement of the cramp will correct any error. In frame A, if the diagonals are the same length it is square. If an iron cramp is not to hand, a wooden one can be constructed by screwing cleats of wood on a piece of board, 2 in. or 3 in. wide, and allowing for a pair of folding wedges. Always use a piece of wood between the frame and the hammer to avoid dents. When the glue

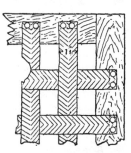

Fig. 2090.—Webbing on Bed Rest Frame.

is set, the frames can be smoothed over and the fixing together proceeded with. A pair of 1¼-in. back flaps and ¾-in. screws will be required to hinge frame B to A (see Figs. 2088 and 2089); about half the knuckle of the hinge projects. The drawings will fully explain the position of the hinges. Two coach-screws, 3 in. by ¼ in., are required to hang frame c in position in frame A (see Fig. 2083); these can be turned in with a pair of pincers. The front should be now covered with webbing. The lengths

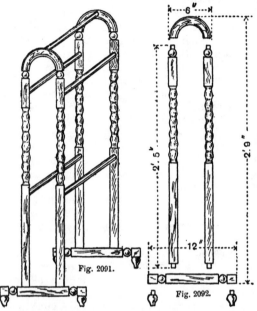

Fig. 2091.

Fig. 2092.

Figs. 2091 and 2092.—Ordinary Towel Rail.

are cut to the dimensions of frame A, about ¾ in. at each end being turned under and fastened by two ¾-in. clout nails at each end. The spaces between webs should be no more than the width of the webbing, as shown in Fig. 2090, where it will be noticed that the webbing is interlaced; 5 yd. will suffice, though a little more would certainly make the whole a little stiffer. Finish with a light stain and a coat of varnish.

Towel Rail.

Fig. 2091 gives a view of the common form of towel rail. Four pieces of wood are required for the sides, each 2 ft. 5 in. long; five pieces for the rails, each 2 ft. 7 in. long, ½ in. being allowed at each end for pins; two pieces 1 ft. long for cross-pieces; four small sections for feet; and one circular piece about 6¼ in. in diameter and 1⅛ in. thick. The cross-pieces and uprights are all 1 in. square, whilst the rails are ¾ in. in diameter. These latter

may be octagonal in section if preferred, but all the ends must be shouldered down to fit tightly in centre-bit holes previously made in the uprights. Fig. 2092 illustrates the end elevation of the towel rail (disjointed), and shows some details of construction. The uprights are represented as having a certain portion of their length turned, but if preferred the entire length may be left square. Pins are formed on the ends of these uprights, and these fit into ½-in. holes which have been previously bored in the cross-pieces and the half rings which "head" the sides. The rails are wedged to the sides first. The holes to receive these pins are, of course, "blind," and the wedges are therefore inserted in the pins before the latter are driven home. To some this may appear a difficult job, but the neatness of the joints thus made fully compensates for the trouble they necessitate. Fig. 2093 is part of a front elevation

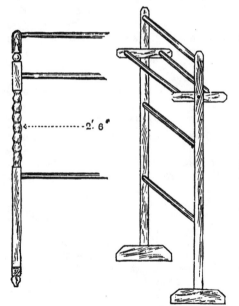

Fig. 2093.—Part Front Elevation of Towel Rail.

Fig. 2094.—Another Form of Towel Rail.

of the article. The feet may be of almost any shape, and are simply pinned to the cross-pieces (see Fig. 2092). The tops of the sides are turned in the lathe from a circular piece of wood, the ring thus produced being afterwards cut into two equal parts.

THREE OTHER TOWEL RAILS.

Fig. 2094 illustrates a towel rail made principally from square-sectioned wood. The cross-pieces which support the two side rails are fixed to the uprights by means of ordinary halving joints, whilst the uprights are united to the feet by means of tenons and mortises (see Fig. 2095). In this case it will be found advisable to make the feet from wood nearly double the thickness of the uprights, as greater stability is then obtained. Fig. 2096 shows another form of towel rail, which, like the one just described, can be cut from plain pieces of

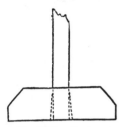

Fig. 2095.—Foot and Upright of Towel Rail.

Fig. 2097.—Ornamental Top for Towel Rail.

wood. The uprights are square, and on the top of each of them an ornamental section is securely fixed. An alternative design for the top is given at Fig. 2097. If the wood for the feet is cut 1 in. longer than is necessary, the superfluous ½ in. at each end can easily be sawn off. To construct the towel rail shown in Fig. 2098, a lathe is needed, as both the uprights and the feet are turned. Side pieces are fixed into the uprights to carry the upper rails, which enter those pieces at their broadest parts.

RACK OR SCREEN FOR CLOTHES AND TOWELS.

A useful rack or screen for clothes, heavy towels, etc., is shown with the "spokes" down in the position of disuse by Fig. 2099, whilst Fig. 2100 shows the body with the spokes removed, and Fig. 2101 the top of the screen when the spokes are in the position for use. The wood required to make

the body is a piece of ¾-in. pine board, 3 ft. 6 in. long and 10 in. broad; the eight rods or spokes can be made of wood of any other colour, according to taste. Measure off 2 ft. 10 in., which is the extreme length, and saw the board across, keeping the smaller piece for brackets, shelves, etc. Plane it smooth on both sides. Mark off 2 in. on each side at the extreme end of the board, and from this pencil mark draw another (using a straight-edge) exactly to the corner at the other end. Do the same to the other edge. This done, saw off this portion, keeping as close to the pencil line as possible. Now plane both edges smooth; draw the design as shown in Fig. 2100, the width at the top being 6⅝ in., and the width at the bottom

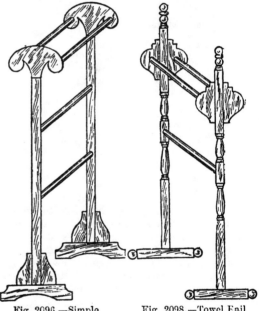

Fig. 2096.—Simple Towel Rail.

Fig. 2098.—Towel Rail in Turned Wood.

9 in., and cut it out. Then give it ½-in. bevel all round. Next take up the other part of the board, and cut the brackets, etc., to the following measurements. The shelf shown in Fig. 2102 is 5¾ in. long and 2⅞ in. broad; the slots shown at A are ⅜ in. wide and 1⅛ in. long, and are eight in number; they can be cut out easily with a saw. The shelf B (Fig. 2100) is 3½ in. long and

1¾ in. broad, and is semicircular. The shelf c is also of this shape, and is 7¾ in. long and 4 in. broad. The eight rods or spokes are ¼ in. thick, 1 in. broad, and 2½ ft.

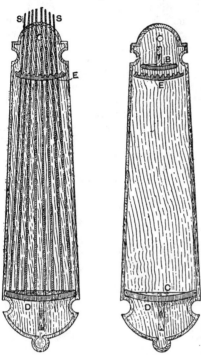

Fig. 2099.—Clothes Rack or Screen.   Fig. 2100.—Rack with Spokes Removed.

long. A piece of brass or stout zinc (Fig. 2103), 10¼ in. long, 1¾ in. broad, with slots or notches, eight in number, ⅜ in. wide, cut in it, is fastened with screws to the edge of the shelf shown by Fig. 2102, each notch being placed opposite each slot (see E, Figs. 2100 and 2101); another piece of brass or zinc D, 1 ft. 1½ in. long and

their place. The whole thing should be put together with screws. The bevel round the edge should be painted black, and the whole may then be varnished. When in use the spokes should be drawn up and slipped into their respective notches. The brackets securing the shelves B and c (Fig. 2100) are triangular with a slight curve.

WALL RACK FOR CLOTHES AND TOWELS.

Fig. 2104 shows a wall rack for use in drying clothes. The rack has a base 2 ft. 6 in. by 8 in. by 1 in., with five rods 3 ft.

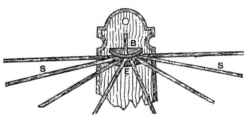

Fig. 2101.—Rack with Spokes Extended.

by 1 in. by ⅝ in. These are mortised in, and glued and wedged. Fig. 2105 shows a method of cutting out the rods with economy. As this contrivance may have to support considerable weight, it will be necessary to plug the wall from which it is suspended, as described on p. 251. Therefore mark off on the wall the positions of the screws, cut the paper in the form of the letter **H**, and gently raise the two flaps. With a cold chisel, chop out two holes of a rectangular shape about 1½ in. by 1 in., and fit in each hole two taper plugs with the broad ends inside; then, after gluing the centre wedge, drive it in, and, when set, cut it off flush to the wall. The paper may now be pasted back in place and the screws

Fig. 2102.—Upper Shelf of Clothes Rack.

Fig. 2104.—Wall Clothes Rack.

Fig. 2103.— Notched Brass Strip.

1¾ in. broad, being fastened with screws or ornamental nails to the edge of the shelf c. This keeps the bottom ends of spokes in

inserted, as in Fig. 2106. Cut the holes and slots in the base as in Fig. 2107, and place the base, etc., in position; the appliance will be perfectly secure, but easily removed when not required for use.

Fixing Temporary Mantelboards.

Fig. 2108 illustrates the method of fixing a temporary mantelshelf when the existing one is of wood and too small. To the under-side of the temporary board A pieces of wood B, about 2 in. thick and 3 in. wide, are screwed about 1 ft. 3 in. apart; they

Fig. 2105.—Cutting out Wall Rack Rods.

are ripped out, as shown, to fit over the existing board C, to which they are screwed. When the existing shelf is of iron, as in Fig. 2109, it will be necessary, in order to avoid driving nails into the wall, to get a black-

Fig. 2106.—Wall Plug with Screw.

Fig. 2107.—Method of Hanging Clothes Rack.

smith to make some lugs D of about $\frac{3}{16}$-in. by $\frac{3}{8}$-in. mild steel, well tempered. They are let in and screwed to the under-side of the shelf as shown, and a fly bolt E is passed through a hole in the lug and then through the nut F. If the nut is held in the hand and the bolt screwed up, the nut will force

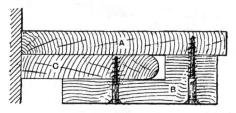

Fig. 2108.—Fixing Temporary Board on Wooden Mantel Shelf.

the lugs out and sufficient pressure will be exerted to establish a firm fixing; the bolt should catch against the front of the iron shelf as shown, and the lugs should be

about 1 ft. to 1 ft. 6 in. apart. Iron shelves generally slope to the front, but the inclination is often not enough to affect articles

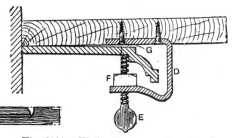

Fig. 2109.—Fixing Temporary Board on Iron Mantel Shelf.

standing on the slope; and if it is much, the upper shelf will be brought right by inserting some wedge-shaped chips of wood at G.

Unwarpable Mantelboards with Dovetail Keys.

The usual shapes of mantelboards are shown by Figs. 2110 to 2112, in all of which

Fig. 2110.—Bedroom Mantelboard.

a dovetail key is illustrated; this is the feature that prevents the boards from warping. An extra key inserted from the opposite edge is shown in Fig. 2113. In this method the shelf is grooved out as shown in Fig. 2114. A simple method of cutting the sides of all the grooves at one angle is to have a piece of wood about 3 in. by 2 in. with one end cut to the angle required; then the side of the saw

Fig. 2111.—Sitting-room Mantelboard.

may be kept to this slope, as indicated in Fig. 2115. After the superfluous wood is removed, the bottom of the groove should be made even in depth by a router or "old woman's tooth." When making the keys, the bevels can be set to the angle of the piece of wood against which the saw rested, and can be applied to the edges of the keys when planing them. The keys may be

Fig. 2112.—Sitting-room Mantelboard.

made of hardwood if desired, and finished flush with the under-side of the shelf, or they may be thicker and allowed to project, this method giving greater strength. The keys must fit accurately, and must not be driven in too tight, or they will bend the shelf, making it hollow in its length. They can be glued in position. The whole process of cutting the keys and the sockets for the dovetail keys will be better understood if the instructions given on pp. 211 to 222 are referred to.

Fig. 2113.—Mantelboard, Dovetail Keyed.

UNWARPABLE MANTELBOARDS WITH METAL TUBING.

In the second method, illustrated at Figs. 2116, 2117, and 2118, the board is planed true and shaped, and is then bored nearly through, so as to receive three gas pipes, as shown by Fig. 2116. With care, in a shelf $\frac{7}{8}$ in. thick, a piece of gas pipe $\frac{1}{2}$ in. in outside diameter can be inserted. A simple means of making the auger bit bore truly is illustrated by Fig. 2118. At one end of a piece of wood about $1\frac{1}{2}$ in. square and 1 ft. 6 in. long, fix a block. In this make a groove with the gouge so that the upper part of the bit fits in it, arranging so that when the upper part of the bit rests in the groove, and the point of the bit is in the centre of the thickness of the shelf, the bit is quite parallel to the under surface of the longer piece of wood (see A, Fig. 2118). Thus, when boring, by pressing with the left hand on this piece, it will travel across

the upper surface of the shelf, and the bit, by being kept against the block B (Fig. 2118), will work truly through the thickness. The most suitable material for mantelboards is pine, which must be very dry, otherwise it will warp and twist.

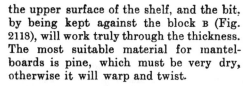

Fig. 2114.—Dovetail Key and Mantelboard Socket.

• CLOTHES BOX WITH TRAYS.

A clothes box, 3 ft. 6 in. long, 2 ft. 3 in.

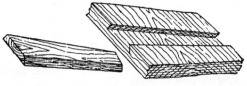

Fig. 2115.—Sawing out Dovetail Key Socket.

high, and 2 ft. from the back to the front, is shown in conventional sectional view by Fig. 2119, whilst Figs. 2120 and 2121 are front and sectional elevations, and Figs.

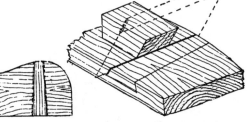

Fig. 2116.—Mantelboard Stiffened with Metal Tubing.

2122 and 2123 end elevation and cross section respectively. The material used may be good pine, red deal, or white deal, according to choice ; red deal would stand the most wear. The boards for the sides, ends, bottom, and top should be about $\frac{7}{8}$ in. thick after being planed, and should be carefully jointed and ploughed and cross-tongued and glued. An important matter when jointing up for a box is not to have the glued joints of the front and back in the same plane as those of the ends. Fig. 2120 shows the front formed of two pieces

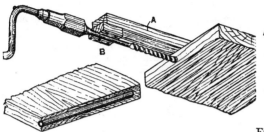

Fig. 2117.—Metal Tubing in Mantelboard.   Fig. 2118.—Boring Mantelboard.

jointed, and Fig. 2122 shows the end formed of three pieces. It is a good plan to make the rim of the lid and the sides and the ends all in one; then, when the top and bottom are fixed on, the part to form the rim is separated from the sides and ends by sawing along the lines as shown at A A (Fig. 2120) and B B (Fig. 2122). The sides and ends should be dovetailed together as shown. The lid being curved on the top, it will be necessary to form it of strips

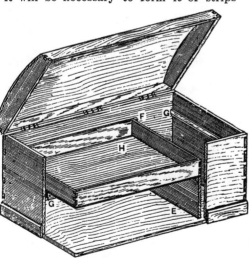

Fig. 2119.—Clothes Box with Trays.

about 4 in. wide, which should be carefully jointed and ploughed and tongued together as shown at D (Fig. 2123). The bottom can be formed of three boards jointed and

tongued together. By referring to the illustrations, it will be seen that the bottom is nailed direct to the lower edges of the sides and the ends; it will be much

Fig. 2120.—Front Elevation of Clothes Box.

stronger if glued to them before nailing. The plinth round the lower part of the box should be about 3½ in. wide and ⅝ in. thick, and chamfered as shown; it should be fixed

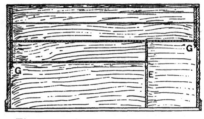

Fig. 2121.—Section of Clothes Box.

with glue and a few small nails. The division E (Figs. 2119 and 2121) should be about ½ in. or ⅝ in. thick, and may be slightly housed into the sides. The trays should be made of wood about ⅝ in. thick, the corners

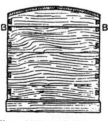 

Figs. 2122 and 2123.—End Elevation and Cross Section of Clothes Box.

being dovetailed together as shown in Figs. 2119, 2124, and 2125; the bottoms of the trays may be thin boarding about ⅜ in. thick, jointed together. For most purposes it will be better for the top tray to have a bottom formed of webbing interlaced as shown in Fig. 2125. Two fillets of wood about 1¼ in. by ¾ in. (G, Figs. 2119 and 2121) should be fixed to the ends to support the trays. Two small fillets will also be required to keep the lower tray H (Fig. 2119) in position as shown at F. The box, having been fitted with three hinges and a lock, is then complete.

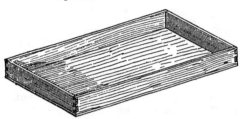

Fig. 2124.—Clothes Box Tray with Wooden Bottom.

LINEN CHEST.

Deal is the best material probably with which to make the linen chest illustrated by Fig. 2126. The elevations and inside view of the chest, which is 2 ft. 3 in. high, 4 ft. long, and 1 ft. 10 in. wide, are represented by Figs. 2126 to 2128. The two uprights at the front corners are strips of 1½-in. stuff, 2 ft. 3 in. long by 4 in. wide. Fig. 2129 shows a front and Fig. 2130 a side view of that to the right hand. In both figures, A denotes where the upper 4 in. is cut away from the front to a depth of ½ in. to receive the end of the upper front rail; whilst at

of ¾-in. board only; 1½-in. wood may be used, to make the job stronger, but one half will have to be sawn away as far as E to receive the ends of the back-boards. Below E, where the double thickness is needed to form the leg, a second piece of ¾-in. stuff should be screwed on. At F and G this upright is cut away ½ in. to receive the ends of the rails. The rails are all of ¾-in. board and 4 in. wide. The front ones are 4 ft. long. The ends of these are cut away behind for a distance of 4 in. and to the depth of ¼ in. to fit the corresponding

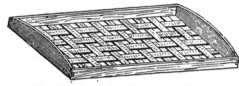

Fig. 2125.—Clothes Box Tray, Webbed.

cuts in the uprights. To these they are fastened with round-headed screws, as shown. The stiles are also of ¾-in. stuff, 1 ft. 4 in. long and 3 in. wide, with the exception of the middle one of the front, which is 4 in. Their tops and bottoms are halved in front for 1½ in. (see H H, Fig. 2132), corresponding cuts being made in the rails above and below to receive them. Their front edges, as well as those of the rails against the panels, are chamfered off. The panelling of the front is done with ½-in.

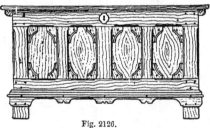

Fig. 2126.

Fig. 2127.

Figs. 2126 and 2127.—Elevations of Linen Chest.

Fig. 2128.

Fig. 2128.—Inside View of Chest Front.

B is a similar cut to take the end of the lower front rail. At C and D are other cuts for the end rails, all being ½ in. deep. A side view of the right-hand back upright is shown by Fig. 2131. Its length and breadth are those of its fellow at the front, but it is

board, cut to 1-ft. 7-in. lengths. These reach from the bottom of the lower rail to the middle of the upper one, above which is a longitudinal strip of the same board. This may be seen in Fig. 2128, which shows the inner side of the chest front. This arrangement will make a neater finish than could be gained by carrying the upright boards to the top. In Fig. 2128 the position of the stiles is shown by dotted lines, and the joints of the panelling should be so arranged as to be covered by them.

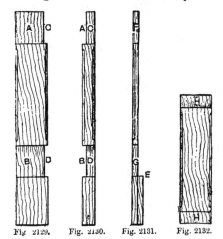

Fig 2129.   Fig. 2130.   Fig. 2131.   Fig. 2132.

Figs. 2129 and 2130.—Front Corner Upright of Linen Chest. Fig. 2131.—Back Corner Upright. Fig. 2132.—Front Middle Stile.

The panels which have been thus made are 1 ft. 1 in. by 7½ in. at sight; and, before leaving them, it will be well to finish them by adding the small ornamental spandrils, one of which is illustrated by Fig. 2133. These are of ¼-in. board, and the curved edge of each is worked to a hollow moulding with the gouge. The length of the end rails is 1 ft. 9½ in. The backs of their ends are cut away ¼ in. deep to fit the openings

Fig. 2133.—Spandril for Linen Chest Panels.

in the uprights—the front end for 1 in. and the back end for 1½ in. The end of the chest (Fig. 2127) has a 3-in. stile, and is panelled like the front. The back is of ¾-in. boarding, the pieces being 4 ft. long and (together) 1 ft. 9 in. wide. At the corners openings will have to be cut, 4 in. by ½ in., to admit the ends of the rails. The back-boards are screwed to the uprights, and should also be

dowelled together. For the bottom ½-in. matchboarding will be best, the pieces being 4 ft. long and (together) 1 ft. 10 in. wide. Openings are cut at the corners, 4 in. by 1½ in., to admit the uprights. These boards are screwed to the lower end rails, also to the lower front rail and to the back-board. For their further support, three ledgers (L L L, Fig. 2128), 2 in. by 1½ in., are placed beneath them and screwed to the back and front rail. The ledgers are placed in line with the middle of the stiles. This completes the carcase of the chest.

Fig. 2134.—Pedestal Cupboard.

LINEN CHEST BASE-BOARDS, LID, ETC.

It is necessary to add to the carcase the ornamental base-boards and mouldings shown in Figs. 2126 and 2127, running along the front and ends. These boards are ¾ in. thick and 4 in. wide. The front one is 4 ft. 1½ in. long; those at the ends are 1 ft. 10¾ in. long. They are mitred where they meet at the corners, and their lower edges are so shaped as to hide the ends of the ledgers. Their tops overlap the lower rails 1 in., and they are screwed to the uprights, etc. Upon these is placed a strip of mould-ing, $\frac{3}{4}$ in. square, with its front edges simply rounded off. These strips, like the boards below, are mitred at the corners ; the front strip is 4 ft. 3 in. long, the end strips 1 ft. 11$\frac{1}{2}$ in. The lid is formed of $\frac{3}{4}$-in. boards, 4 ft. 6 in. long and (together) 2 ft. wide. These boards are screwed down to four ledgers, two of which appear in Figs. 2126 and 2127 ; the others are within the chest, and are placed at equal distances from the outer ones and from each other. As a prop for the lid, have a lath about

back consists of spars fixed in notches cut in the top and bottom, thus providing a means of ventilation. The two gables, of $\frac{7}{8}$-in. stuff, are planed and squared to 2 ft. 4$\frac{1}{4}$ in. in length by 1 ft. in width. The carcase top, of pine $\frac{5}{8}$ in. thick, is lap-dovetailed into the gables, and is of the same width as the latter. The bottom, of $\frac{3}{4}$-in. pine, is fixed to the gables by a sliding dovetail joint. A 1-in. piece is glued to the front edge of the bottom to take in the thickness of the door. It is kept on a level with the base moulding, 3$\frac{1}{2}$ in. from

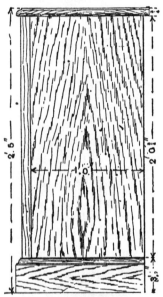

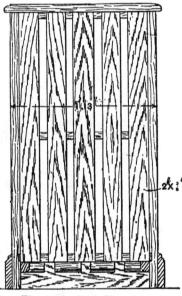

Fig. 2137.—Detail of Plinth.

Fig. 2138.—Part Section through Door.

Fig. 2135.—End Elevation of Pedestal Cupboard.

Fig. 2136.—Back Elevation of Pedestal Cupboard.

1 ft. 4 in. long, working on a screw driven into the inner side of one of the end rails near the front. The chest may be stained to a dark oak colour. It may be said that whilst staining, varnishing, and polishing are outside the present scope, they are dealt with fully in the *Work* Handbook "Wood Finishing."

PEDESTAL CUPBOARD.

The pedestal cupboard illustrated by Figs. 2134, 2135, and 2136 may be con-structed in ash or any other light wood. It is enclosed by a door, with a shelf on fillets dividing the space in two. The

the floor, and blocks glued on the under-side of the bottom help to strengthen the joint. The five spars of the back are of pine, 2 in. wide by $\frac{3}{8}$ in. thick ; the two end spars are butted against the gables, the others being spaced about $\frac{3}{4}$ in. apart. Notches are cut in the top and bottom of the pedestal, and the spars laid in and sprigged on (see Fig. 2136). The shelf, $\frac{5}{8}$ in. thick, is supported by two fillets screwed to the gables. The plinth consists of a piece $\frac{5}{8}$ in. thick, with a moulding worked on the top edge, and mitred round the front and ends. At the front it is glued to the edge of the bottom, and further secured by blocks on the inside as shown in Fig. 2137. The ends should be glued at the mitres, and

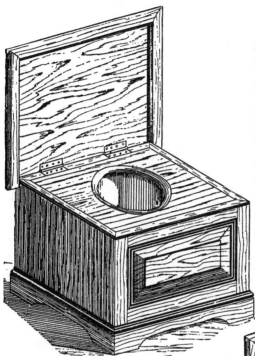

Fig. 2139.—Panelled Front Night Commode.

screwed to the gables from the inside, thus preventing the gables shrinking or swelling and loosening the moulding. The top is $\frac{3}{4}$ in. thick, with a moulding on the front and ends; the back part projects $\frac{3}{4}$ in. over the gables. At the front it has a projection of $1\frac{1}{2}$ in. to cover in the door, which is of 1-in. stuff, mortised and tenoned together, the stiles and rails being $2\frac{1}{2}$ in. wide, including the $\frac{1}{2}$-in. rebate for the moulding. The panel is $\frac{1}{2}$ in. thick, and chamfered on the inside and beaded in (see Fig. 2138). The door should project slightly over the gables, sufficient to break the joint. It is hung with two brass butt hinges, and a wooden knob is fitted on the left-hand stile. To keep the door shut, a wedge-shaped piece of thin wood about 2 in. long is glued to the under-side of the top. When the door shuts, the top edge presses against the wedge-shaped piece.

PANELLED-FRONT NIGHT COMMODE.

The panelled-front night commode illustrated by Fig. 2139 looks well if constructed of mahogany, walnut, satin walnut, or pitchpine. The sizes and numbers of pieces for the various parts can be obtained from the illustrations, which are, practically, fully dimensioned. Fig. 2140 is a sectional view with front removed, whilst Figs. 2141 and 2142 are respectively front and side elevation. The front framing should be $\frac{7}{8}$ in. thick, and the stiles and top rail $2\frac{1}{4}$ in. wide. The stiles extend to the floor, forming a fixing for the plinth; the bottom rail should be about $3\frac{7}{8}$ in. wide. The rails and stiles should be mortised and tenoned together, and the moulding is stuck on the solid and mitred at the junction of the stiles and rails as shown in Fig. 2143. In setting out, allow the shoulders for the rails on the front to project beyond those at the back by the breadth of the moulding, as shown in

Fig. 2140.—Commode shown Partly in Section.

Fig. 2143. The panel (Fig. 2144) is of $\frac{5}{8}$-in. stuff, gauged all round on the face side and on the edges for the sinking. This can be done with a wide rebate plane, panel plane, or even with a smoothing plane having a

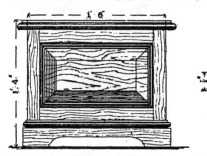

Fig. 2141.—Front Elevation of Night Commode.

movable slip. In working the two end sinkings (across the grain), take care to plane just to the lines and make the sinking parallel to the flat face of the panel. The top and bottom sinkings of the panel can then be worked to the same level as the ends. The splays with the grain and across the grain should meet in a true mitre. The joints of the framing and panel should be glued and cramped together, and the tenons can be further secured by a screw inserted from the back. The front, sides, and back should be grooved and tongued together as shown in Figs. 2140, 2141, and 2145. A satisfactory job will be made if the sides, front, and back are grooved, as shown in Figs. 2140 and 2146, to receive the bottom,

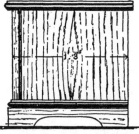

Fig. 2142.—Side Elevation of Night Commode.

which is of $\frac{1}{2}$-in. pine. The sides and back should be of $\frac{3}{4}$-in. board, the grain of the sides being vertical, as shown in Fig. 2146, and the grain of the back horizontal. The front and sides and the back and sides

can be held firmly together by triangular blocks glued on as shown in Fig. 2145. The plinth should be about $2\frac{1}{2}$ in. wide, with a torus mould, and should be mitred at the two front angles and hollowed on the lower edge. It should be glued to the front and sides, and secured by a few screws from the back. The top of the framework should be finished with a strip having a beaded edge

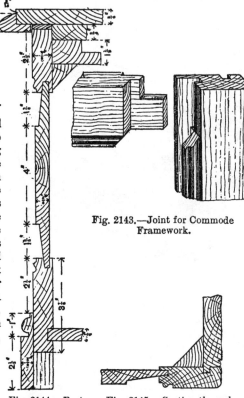

Fig. 2143.—Joint for Commode Framework.

Fig. 2144.—Part Vertical Section of Commode Front.

Fig. 2145.—Section through Stile and Panel.

about $\frac{7}{8}$ in. wide and $\frac{1}{4}$ in. thick, fixed with glue and a few fine sprigs. The top should be $\frac{3}{4}$ in. thick and wide enough to project at the back so as to keep the lid nearly vertical when open. The front and side edges of the top are finished with a thumb moulding, which is rebated so that it can be securely fixed and project below the under-side of the lid. The lid should be fixed with a pair of 3-in. brass butt hinges let in as shown. The board to support the pan should be of pine, the hole being recessed for the rim; this support should be fixed to the front, sides, and back by gluing blocks as shown in Fig. 2146, keeping the

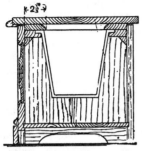

Fig. 2146.—Cross Section of Commode.

pan at a distance from the top equal to the thickness of the seat.

SEAT OF NIGHT COMMODE.

The seat of the commode can next be fitted. The hole should be cut with a pad saw, and the edge rounded. To prevent the seat warping, a couple of dovetailed hardwood keys should be glued in as shown in Figs. 2140 and 2147. To cut out the hole in the seat, first mark its centre, and then with a fine bradawl bore a hole right through. Next with a pair of compasses strike out the curve on the top side. With the compasses set to a radius of about $\frac{3}{8}$ in. less, describe the curve on the under-side,

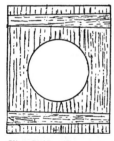

Fig. 2147.—Commode Seat Dovetail Keyed.

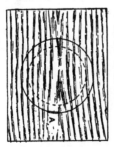

Fig. 2148.—Commode Seat Set out.

as indicated by the dotted line in Fig. 2148. With a fine bradawl make two or three holes very close together, so that they touch the lines on the upper and bottom surfaces. Care must be taken to hold the

bradawl at the proper angle. The wood between the holes should be cleared out with the bradawl, thus making an entrance for a pad saw, as shown at A (Fig. 2148).

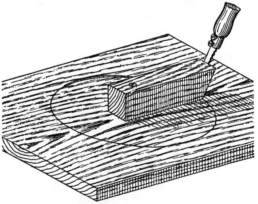

Fig. 2149.—Cutting out Hole in Commode Seat.

Place the saw in the hole, keeping it at the same angle while sawing all the way round the curve, as at Fig. 2149 (as will be seen, this only represents part of the seat), carefully noticing that the saw is following both lines. Fig. 2150 shows a method that will better ensure keeping the saw at the proper angle. Cut one end of a piece of wood to the angle at which the saw is to be held and insert a screw near the other end, so that it will go into the centre of what is going to be the lid. The piece of wood can then

Fig. 2150.—Cutting out Hole with Guide.

be made to go round with the saw. Having cut the piece out, the hole should be rounded.

CLOCK BRACKET.

Fig. 2151 is a front elevation of a bracket case to contain a cylindrical clock. Oak is the best material with which to construct the bracket. Fig. 2152 is a transverse vertical section, showing a curved pediment at the top which is fixed to a frame moulded on the front and the two ends. Figs. 2153 and 2154 show how this frame is made by mitring and halving at the corners. Figs. 2152, 2154, and 2155 show the sides A of the

lower moulding, as shown in Fig. 2157. It can also be screwed from behind. In Fig. 2151 the lower moulding is shown decorated by radiating flutes, but if desired it can be left plain, as shown in Fig. 2152. Two turned pillars are fixed at the front by a small plug on the top end of each fitting into holes bored in the corners of the frame.

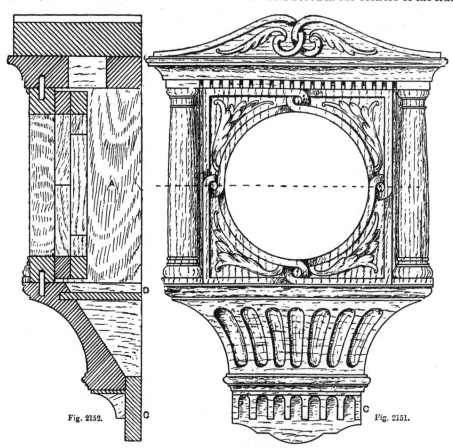

Fig. 2152.　　Fig. 2151.

Figs. 2151 and 2152.—Front Elevation and Vertical Section of Clock Bracket.

main part of the bracket; these are tongued into the end portions of the moulded frame. The lower part of each side is tongued into the large moulding forming the bottom of the bracket in Fig. 2156. D (Fig. 2152) is a slip of wood glued into grooves in the lower moulding to keep the sides of the bracket together. The extreme bottom part c (Figs. 2151 and 2152) is attached to the

At the lower end the pillar should have a tongue cut to fit into the groove made in the end portions of the lower moulding, as shown in Fig. 2156. The circular hole in the front piece (Fig. 2151) is cut to a size that just enables the clock to pass through (see Figs. 2152 and 2155). The centre portion is swivelled centrally at top and bottom, so that the clock may be turned round for the purpose of winding. Two fillets are shown in section by B B in Fig. 2155. The one on the right-hand is wider than the

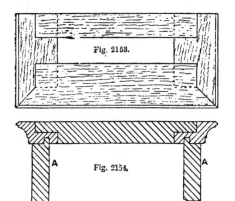

Fig. 2153.

Fig. 2154.

Figs. 2153 and 2154.—Moulded Frame beneath Pediment of Clock Bracket.

other, and has a small rebate into which the front fits. If the front is pressed on the left-hand side it will swing round so that

that on the right-hand side the ring and part of the fillet must be cut away, in order that the former may swing outward. Two eye-plates should be screwed on the back edges of the side pieces, and, if placed to point inwards, will not be visible when the bracket is hung.

TOILET GLASS.

The toilet glass illustrated by Figs. 2159 and 2160 is constructed of polished oak, and requires the following quantities of wood : For the mouldings, 7 ft. by $1\frac{1}{2}$ in. by $\frac{3}{4}$ in. ; pediment, 1 ft. 2 in. by $3\frac{1}{2}$ in. by $\frac{3}{8}$ in. ; box ends, 1 ft. by 8 in. by $\frac{3}{8}$ in. ; box back, 2 ft. by 3 in. by $\frac{3}{8}$ in. ; hinge fillet, 2 ft. by 1 in. by $\frac{3}{8}$ in. ; lid, 2 ft. by $4\frac{1}{2}$ in. by $\frac{3}{8}$ in. ; front, 2 ft. by $1\frac{3}{4}$ in. by $\frac{3}{8}$ in. ; bottom, 2 ft. by 6 in. by $\frac{3}{8}$ in. ; towel rail, 2 ft. by $\frac{1}{2}$ in. in diameter ; and four knobs or turned ends, each $1\frac{1}{4}$ in. in diameter by 1 in. long. First make the mirror frame, which consists of four lengths of moulding worked to the section shown in Fig. 2161 and mitred together.

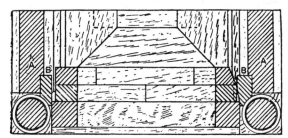

Fig. 2155.—Horizontal Section through Clock Bracket.

Fig. 2156.—Joint of Side and Lower Moulding.

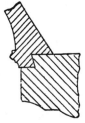

Fig. 2157.—Section of Neck Moulding.

the back of the clock is exposed. When the motion is reversed the face comes outward, the rebated fillet preventing the front being pressed in too far. A very slight easing of the square base of the pillar will enable the front to swing past it. A wooden ring built up of two courses of segments, to strengthen the front and to support the clock, is shown in section in Figs. 2152 and 2155, and in part plan in Fig. 2158. To fix the clock in position, small recesses should be cut in the ring to receive the pegs on the bottom of the clock, which enables it to stand by itself. These recesses should be arranged for at one of the joints of the ring. In Fig. 2155, it will be seen

40

Strengthen the corners with hardwood keys put in on the inner side before the mitre

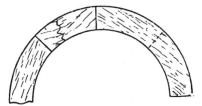

Fig. 2158.—Ring behind Front Piece of Clock Bracket.

is glued and cramped together ; picture-frame moulding may be used if desired. Fit a bevel-plate mirror, $\frac{3}{16}$ in. thick, into the frame, and fix it in the rebate with small fillets. The back of the glass should be protected with a cover board $\frac{1}{8}$ in. thick, as shown in Fig. 2161. The pediment may be

to match the bottom. Hang it with $1\frac{1}{2}$-in. brass butt hinges to the fillet so that it fits between the end pieces with a projection above of about $\frac{1}{4}$ in. The hingeing of the lid is better accomplished if the box bottom is

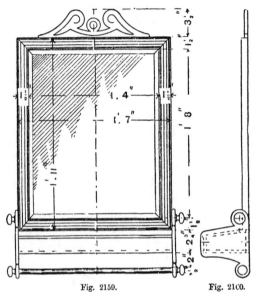

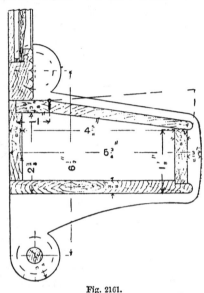

Fig. 2159.   Fig. 2160.   Fig. 2161.

Figs. 2159 and 2160.—Front and Side Elevations of Toilet Glass. Fig. 2161.—Enlarged Section of Toilet Glass Box.

$\frac{3}{8}$ in. thick. The design should be first pencilled on the wood, then cut out with a band saw or hand pad saw. Clean the edges with a file and some No. 1 glasspaper. The ornamentation consists of a V-cut groove following the outer line of the curves, or a single line may be scribed on about $\frac{1}{16}$ in. deep.

Box of Toilet Glass.

Below the mirror a box for brushes and combs and a towel rail are provided. The box ends are of oak $\frac{3}{8}$ in. thick; a rebate at the back edges receives the box back, the face edges being rounded as shown. The ends are pinned and glued to the mirror frame, and the box back is fixed in. Next fit the hinge fillet, which is 1 in. wide and $\frac{3}{8}$ in. thick. It is rebated to the back and pinned to the framing. The lid and front should next be fitted. The lid of the box is $\frac{3}{8}$ in. thick at the hinge edge, and $\frac{1}{4}$ in. thick at the front edge, which is rounded

fitted last. The front piece is $1\frac{5}{8}$ in. deep and $\frac{3}{8}$ in. thick, pinned to each end and the bottom. In making the bottom, run a rebate $\frac{1}{8}$ in. deep along the front, and round the edge of the remaining thickness (see Fig. 2161).

Toilet Glass Towel Rail.

The bottom should now be fixed over the front and flush with the back. The towel

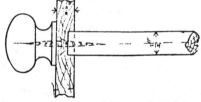

Fig. 2162.—Towel Rail and Finial.

rail is $\frac{1}{2}$ in. in diameter, and should be let into each end $\frac{1}{8}$ in. deep (see Fig. 2162), being placed in position before the second end is finally fixed. A turned oak knob is screwed into each end of the rail, and another knob screwed into the centre of the top piece of the box completes the making. Glasspaper the work, and stop all nail and pin holes. Then darken the wood and finish by polishing or varnishing. The mirror can be fixed to the wall with three

tended to be constructed in mahogany. Fig. 2165 is a plan of the base. For the frame, which measures 1 ft. 8 in. long by 1 ft. 4 in. wide, plane up two stiles 1 ft. 8 in. by 1½ in. by ⅞ in. thick. The top rail is of the same width and thickness as the stiles, but the bottom rail is only 1 in. wide to allow the back to pass it (see Fig. 2166).

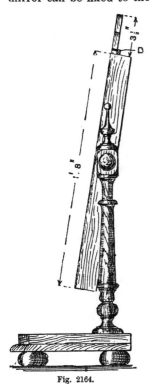

Fig. 2164.

Figs. 2163 and 2164.—Front and Side Elevations of Dressing Glass. Fig. 2165. —Plan of Dressing Glass Base.

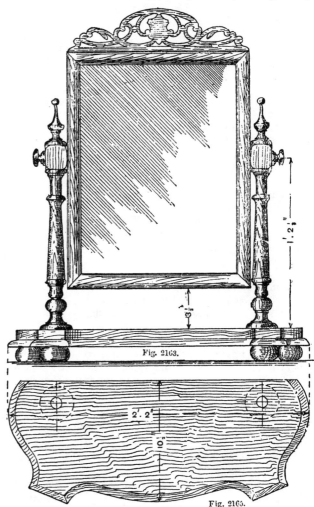

Fig. 2163.

Fig. 2165.

or four strong eye-plates, arranged to suit the joints in the brickwork.

DRESSING GLASS.

Figs. 2163 and 2164 are front and side views respectively of a dressing glass in-

The top and bottom rails are lap-dovetailed to the stiles. The two stiles and top rail are grooved for the pine back, which is ½ in. thick, chamfered to fit the groove, and slid up from the bottom (see Figs. 2166 and 2167). Two screws secure it to the bottom rail. For the face moulding, plane up sufficient lengths to go round the frame, 1¼ in. wide by ⅜ in. thick, and rounded as in A (Fig. 2167); then mitre and glue the lengths to the frame, thus forming the

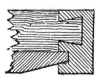

Fig. 2166.—Bottom Rail and Back of Dressing Glass.

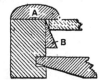

Fig. 2167.—Part Section of Dressing Glass Frame.

rebate for the mirror plate, which shows a sight size of 1 ft. 5½ in. by 1 ft. 1½ in. The plate itself should be ½ in. more in length and width to give ¼ in. cover all round. Before fixing in the mirror, go round the inside of the rebate with a small brush and some black varnish, to prevent the bright edge being shown on the outside. Fix the plate to the frame by small wedges B, glued at intervals round the edges. The base (Fig. 2165) for the dressing glass should be of ⅞-in. stuff, cut and shaped to the sizes given, a moulding c (Fig. 2168), ⅜ in. thick, being clamped to the under-side at the front and ends, and projecting ⅜ in. over the edges. The clamps should be 3½ in. wide ; glue and screw them to the bed. Four flat balls for the feet, 2½ in. in diameter, are fixed at the corners with a strong screw and a touch of glue. Each turned standard should have a pin 1 in. in diameter at the end glued into the bed. The pediment is fretted out of ½-in. stuff, and a small fillet D, as shown at Fig. 2164, is glued to the back at the bottom for fixing the pediment to the top of the frame.

Fig. 2168.—Section of Dressing Glass Base.

PIVOTING MIRROR OF DRESSING GLASS.

The method of swinging the glass is shown in Fig. 2169. A long screw is inserted in the knob, and a plate with a corresponding thread is screwed to the inside of the mirror frame. A hole is bored through the standard and frame, wide enough to allow the screw to pass through easily till it reaches the plate.

PORTABLE BUNK BED.

Fig. 2170 gives a general view of the portable bunk bed. Fig. 2171 is a cross section through one of the posts, showing the method of construction. A represents the post, turned at the top and having its inside and outside edges rounded. A groove is run to receive a feather which is worked on the haffits B. These latter are screwed to the posts, and the holes dowelled. The shaped rails c are tenoned to the haffits, and the blocks D screwed to the inside of the rails. The bolt catches both the rail and the block, and draws them firmly up to the haffit. An ornamental dowel is shown in the section at Fig. 2171, filling up the hole bored for the bolt-head. The dowel should be of an easy tightness, so that it can be taken out when required

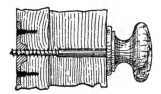

Fig. 2169.—Pivot for Dressing Glass.

to get at the bolt. The front and back rails are shown in two pieces—a broad piece at the top, and a narrow one, having a bead on both edges, at the bottom. These two pieces should be dowelled together ; but a better job would be made if the rails were all in one, and the beads run with a handbeader. Fillets are screwed to the inside of the rails to carry the bottom F. The latter, as shown by Fig. 2170, is made up of narrow strips having a piece taken out of each edge for ventilation. Fig. 2172 represents separately the post A, haffit B, and rail c, to show, as far as possible, the method of putting them together.

DOUBLE BUNK BED.

Fig. 2173 is a vertical section of a bed frame having two beds in the height. The construction is the same, but it would be rather top-heavy for house use unless plates were screwed to the posts and floor. The inside dimensions of the bed should be at least 6 ft. 3 in. by 2 ft. 2 in. The height from floor to the straight part of the rails is 2 ft. 10 in. The scantlings of the

$1\frac{1}{2}$ in., and should be well screwed. The bottom should be at least $\frac{3}{4}$ in. thick; the width may vary from 4 in. to 7 in.

CHILD'S WOODEN COT WITH MOVABLE SIDES.

The cot shown in general view by Fig.

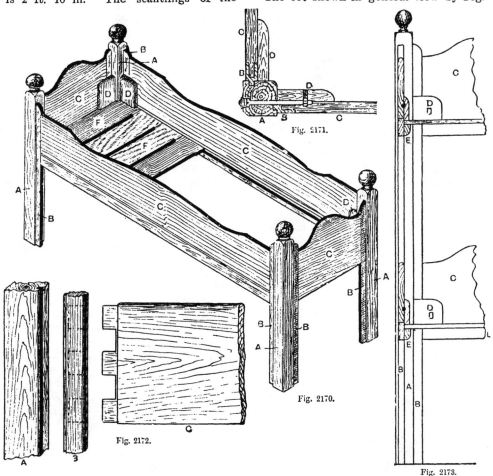

Fig. 2170.—Portable Bunk Bed. Fig. 2171.—Section through Post and Rails. Fig. 2172.—Post, Haffit and Rail of Bunk Bed. Fig. 2173.—Vertical Section through Double Bunk Bed

various pieces may be : Posts, 3 in. by 3 in. ; haffits, 2 in. by $1\frac{1}{8}$ in. The front and back rails should be 1 ft. 1 in. broad by $1\frac{1}{8}$ in. The end rails usually rise higher in the crown, varying from 3 in. to 6 in. The blocks should be about 4 in. or 5 in. broad and $1\frac{1}{8}$ in. thick. The fillets are 2 in. by

2174 is so arranged that the whole or part of the sides can be removed. As illustrated, the head piece and the foot piece can be made movable if required. Fig. 2175 illustrates side elevation and Fig. 2176 end elevation. Almost any kind of wood, from ordinary deal, which can be stained and varnished, to oak or mahogany, which can be polished, will be suitable for making the cot. The following are the particulars of the different pieces of wood required:

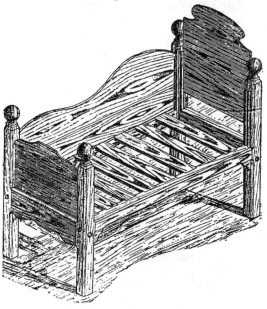

Fig. 2174.—Child's Wooden Cot.

Two posts for the head, 3 ft. 10 in. long and 3 in. square, and two posts for the

thick; two short rails—one for the head and the other for the foot—each 2 ft. long, 6 in. wide, and 1½ in. thick. The two lower boards for the sides should be 6 in. wide and 4 ft. 2 in. long, and the corresponding board for the foot 6 in. wide and 1 ft. 7 in. long. The two upper curved boards for the sides can be got out of boards 11 in. wide and the curved boards for the foot out of 9-in. boards. The head board can be made by jointing three pieces of 9-in. board. All the above-mentioned boards should be ⅞-in. stuff, so that when they are planed on each side they will be ¾ in. thick. Eight pieces 3 in. wide, ¾ in. thick, and 1 ft. 10 in. long will be required for the laths. Reference to the dimensions on the drawings will show that sufficient has been allowed to each piece for waste. In making the cot, first plane up all the pieces of wood to their proper breadth and thickness, after which the mortises in the legs and the tenons of the rails should be set out; the shapes of these are shown by Fig. 2177, where A is the tenon at the end of a side rail, and B that of a short rail. It will be seen that the mortises are not at the same level, which allows of the tenons going in farther, and that the bolts are not sufficiently near each other to weaken the post. The mortises and tenons should fit properly,

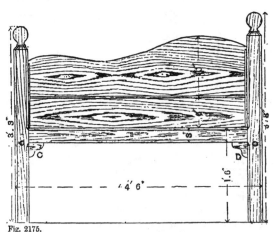

Fig. 2175.

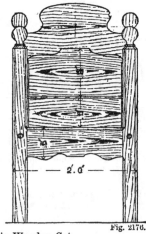

Fig. 2176.

Figs. 2175 and 2176.—Elevations of Child's Wooden Cot.

foot, 3 ft. 5 in. long; two long rails for the sides, 4 ft. 6 in. long, 3 in. wide, and 2 in.

the shoulders on the rails butting against the post, thus making the cot rigid. Eight

¾-in. bed screws and nuts will be required for the rails and legs. Mortises should be made in the rails for the nuts, as shown in Figs. 2177 and 2178, holes being bored in the legs for the heads of the bolts, as shown

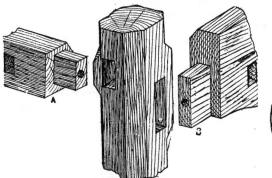

Fig. 2177.—Joints between Rails and Leg of Cot.

in the section (Fig. 2178). Care must be taken to mark out for the mortises for nuts and holes, and for the heads of bolts, in the same straight line. Next bore the holes for the bolts through the posts into the tenons while the joints are together, keeping the parts square to each other while doing so. The bolts and nuts should now be fitted into their respective places and tightened up with a bed key. Then fix the nuts by means of a few small wedges and fill the holes in the rails with pieces of wood so that the grain of the rail appears to be continuous. This will keep the nuts

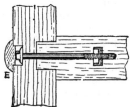

Fig. 2178.—Section through Part of Leg and Rail.

in their proper positions when it is necessary to take the cot to pieces. Next take the legs and rails apart, and mark each tenon and mortise with a distinguishing mark, so that the same can be put together again, and cut out the sockets for the ends

of the laths in the sides, the shape of these being as shown in Figs. 2174 and 2179. The rails at the head and foot can now be cut with a bow saw to the curved form shown, and smoothed with a spokeshave.

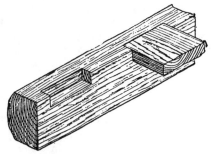

Fig. 2179.—Sockets for Ends of Laths.

The chamfering to the legs and rails should next be done, and round knobs fixed at the top of the post, as shown in Fig. 2174.

PUTTING COT TOGETHER.

Now put the framework together, and fit in the laths as shown at Fig. 2174. The boards for the head, foot, and sides should be carefully fitted in between the posts only just hand-tight, so as not to force off the legs from the shoulders of the rails. A simple and effective way to keep these boards in position is by means of ½-in. by

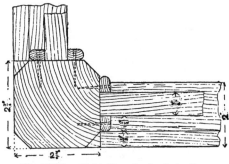

Fig. 2180.—Side Boards fixed to Leg.

¾-in. beads, as shown in the illustrations. These beads are strips of wood with a rounded edge, as shown by the section in Fig. 2180. Fix the outside beads first with glue and a few sprigs; then place the boards in position and fix the inside beads in a similar manner close up to the boards. The curving to the top of the boards can now be marked and cut with a bow saw and smoothed. Two wooden brackets, glued and screwed to the under-side of the side rails, as shown at c and d (Fig. 2175), will make the cot more rigid. The heads of the bed screws can be concealed by a turned wooden button fitting tightly into the hole, a section of which is shown at e (Fig. 2178). The shape of the movable sides is shown sufficiently in Figs. 2174 to 2176.

CHILD'S FOLDING BED.

The folding bed, shown closed in Fig. 2181 and open in Fig. 2182, is made in $\frac{3}{4}$-in. stuff; the sides are 3 ft. 4 in. long and 2 ft. wide, a strip being fastened crosswise 10 in. to its top edge from the bottom of sides on the inside. The top will be 3 ft. 1 in. long and 1 ft. wide. The bed, when closed, as in Fig. 2181, greatly resembles an old-fashioned chest of drawers. The bevelled part can either be made as a panel, as shown in Fig. 2181, or an ordinary board 3 ft. 1 in. long and 1 ft. 3 in. wide. The front is made up in separate pieces. To do this, fasten a three-cornered piece on the sides $\frac{3}{4}$ in. from the front edge, and nail the boards to this from the inside. Start at the bottom with a strip 2 in. wide and 2 ft. 10$\frac{1}{2}$ in. long. Next comes a piece 6 in. wide, then a strip 1 in., another 6 in.,

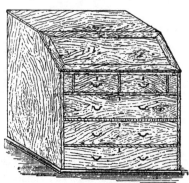

Fig. 2181.—Child's Folding Bed, Closed.

The small imitation drawers are made by a slight saw-cut across the boards 1$\frac{1}{2}$ in. from each end, with 1 in. between cuts and

again exactly in the centre. The bottom is $\frac{1}{2}$ in. thick, with moulding 1$\frac{1}{2}$ in. deep running round the front and sides. Now make a frame 2 ft. 10$\frac{1}{2}$ in. long and 1 ft. 9 in. wide. This should be of ash or elm 2 in. square, firmly mortised at the joints. Before fitting together, however, cut pieces out for the laths; there will be five of these, 2 in. wide, $\frac{1}{2}$ in. thick, and 5$\frac{3}{4}$ in. apart. Now make another similar frame, but 2 ft. 10$\frac{1}{2}$ in. wide and 2 ft. 2 in. long. Two legs 10$\frac{1}{2}$ in. long will be fastened on its rear end with hinges, so that they fold beneath the bed. A small rail 6 in. deep is now put along the bottom and 1 ft. 6 in. up each

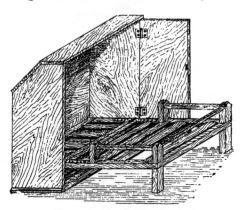

Fig. 2182.—Child's Folding Bed, Open.

side. Put the frame made first into the chest on to the cross-pieces and firmly fasten. A good way is to run a couple of small pins through each side, the heads being sunk flush with the outside, and screw tightly together. Place the larger frame into position and fasten together with long hinges. Two doors are wanted for the back, each 1 ft. 5$\frac{1}{4}$ in. wide; these may be made of $\frac{1}{2}$-in. matchboard. The bedstead is now complete as far as woodwork is concerned. When not in use, the bed can be stowed away in the front of the chest, the legs being pushed down and the frame tilted up against the bed. The doors are closed and the chest is placed against the wall. Only one door instead of two is shown in Fig. 2182. The handles and brass keyholes can be put on last; the latter are bored about halfway through

Oak Bedstead.

Fig. 2183 illustrates a bedstead that presents a very good appearance if made of

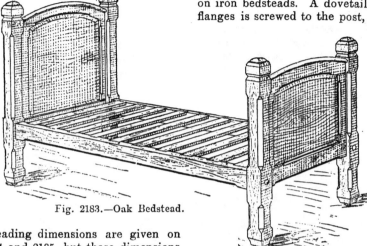

Fig. 2183.—Oak Bedstead.

oak. Leading dimensions are given on Figs. 2184 and 2185, but these dimensions can be varied to the requirements. Alternative methods of connecting the sides to the foot and head are shown, Figs. 2186 and 2187 illustrating the old bed-screw method of connecting by means of a bolt and nut.

of the rail, and a nut B (Fig. 2187) is inserted, the bolt-head being hidden by the turned wooden button C. A method that is now being generally used is illustrated at Fig. 2188, the principle being that used on iron bedsteads. A dovetail piece with flanges is screwed to the post, the flanges being let in, and a corresponding dovetail socket piece is fitted and screwed to each end of the rails. The illustrations show the construction fully. The pieces of tim-

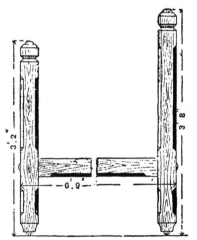

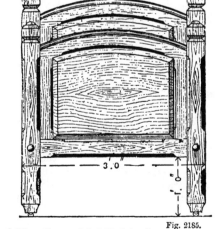

Fig. 2184.

Fig. 2185.

Figs. 2184 and 2185.—Side and End Elevations of Oak Bedstead.

In this case a hole A (Fig. 2186) is bored from the end of the tenon longitudinally in the rail; a mortise is made from the inside

ber having been cut to their several sizes, each should be planed to finished dimensions. Then the posts and rails should be set out and the mortising and tenoning done. The forms of joints for connecting the stiles and rails of the head and foot are clearly shown at D and E (Fig. 2189), and the top rails are curved to improve the appearance. It will make a stronger job to house the posts to a depth of about ¼ in. so as to receive the stiles of the framing, as indicated at Fig. 2189. The curved top rail has a stub-tenon at each end to enter corresponding mortises in each post. The stiles and rails are ploughed to receive a panel, which is shown in Figs. 2186 and 2189, with splayed margins. Cut an oval-sectioned piece F (Fig. 2189) to the proper

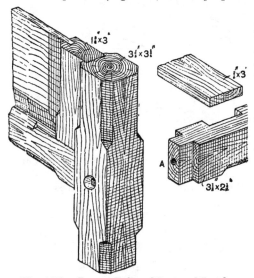

Fig. 2186.—Part of Bedstead Post and Panel.

sweep and sink out the under-side to fit on to the curved rail, the posts being recessed so as to receive the ends of the capping. After the joints fit satisfactorily, the posts, rails, and stiles should be stop-chamfered and the tops and bottoms of the posts worked to shape. The joints of the head and foot framings can then be glued together, and when the glue is dry the stiles and rails can be smoothed off. Then the top and bottom rails and stiles can be finally fitted into the posts, and then these can be glued together also. Four castors can be fixed on the bottoms of the posts to complete the bedstead.

A CORNER WASHSTAND.

The corner washstand illustrated by Fig. 2190 should be made of mahogany. Fig. 2191 is a plan of the top, and Fig. 2192 is a

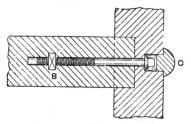

Fig. 2187.—Bed-screw Joint.

plan of drawer, etc., with shelf removed. The two parts of the splashboard are dovetailed at the angle and housed and glued to the top ; the board is also screwed from beneath near each end and about halfway on each side (see Fig. 2193), but before this is done the quadrant shelf should be glued into its housing, and further secured with a couple of well-sunk brads. The holes for the basin, soap-dish, etc. (see Fig. 2191), should be cut with a keyhole- or bow-saw, and the edges smoothed and rounded with a spokeshave. The piece removed for the basin-hole can be used in turning the

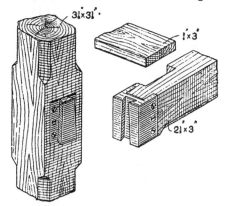

Fig. 2188.—Metal Dovetail for Bed Rails.

ring for the jug stand (Figs. 2193 and 2194). The front rails, etc., are of ⅝-in. stuff, and a piece 2 ft. long by 7 in. wide will be sufficient. This should be curved by means of saw-kerfing to a radius of 1 ft. 3½ in.

When the saw-cuts are made and the glue is well rubbed in, the curve may be formed, and a piece of canvas or strong muslin

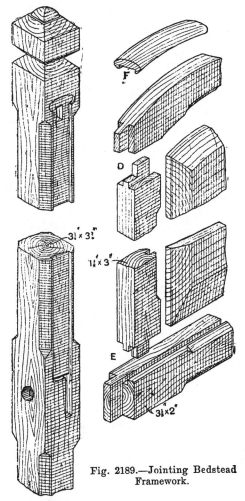

Fig. 2189.—Jointing Bedstead Framework.

method of securing the tenons into the legs is shown by Figs. 2193 and 2194. The stiffening or supporting bracket (Fig. 2195) is housed into the under surface of the shelf and glued. The ring, which should be turned in a lathe, is fitted into a groove, glued, and further secured by means of a few thin screws inserted from below. An easy way to cut this circular groove is to drive a steel pin into the stock of the cutting gauge and file the end to a sharp point projecting about $\frac{3}{16}$ in. Then, with the

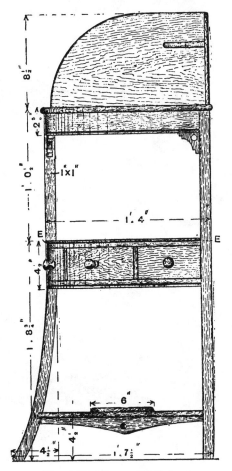

Fig. 2190.—Corner Washstand.

should be glued to the concave side and allowed to remain for at least twenty-four hours. The jug shelf (Figs. 2193 and 2194) is in five parts, the arm reaching to the corner leg being joined to the front portion by a straight tongue-and-groove joint as illustrated. A stronger method is by making a mitred joint as indicated by dotted lines in Fig. 2193, in which case the supporting piece extending to the back leg may be omitted, as it is not seen. The

blade set out sufficiently, adjust the distance to half the diameter required and cut a circle about $\frac{3}{32}$ in. deep. Then cut another one inside at the proper distance and remove the intervening portion with a chisel. The side rails in the centre and at the top are mortised into the legs, as shown in Fig. 2192, which is a section at E E (Fig. 2190) taken at a level just above the drawer. The legs, 1 in. square in section, may be steamed and bent or cut from the

Fig. 2191.

D

Fig. 2193.

B

D

Fig. 2192.

Fig. 2191.—Plan of Corner Washstand Top.
Fig. 2192.—Plan of Washstand Drawer, etc.
Fig. 2193.—Plan of Jug Shelf.

solid. The spring of the curve is just below the drawer shelf, but if it be desired to put brackets in these angles, as in the angles under the top, the curve should commence 2 in. lower.

CURVED RAILS AND DRAWER FRONT OF CORNER WASHSTAND.

Fig. 2196 is a section on B B (Fig. 2192), and shows the fitting of the guides and

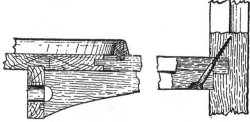

Fig. 2194.—Section of Jug Shelf.

bearers of the drawer, the bottom piece being of pine rebated into the sides and bradded or screwed in last. A section through the drawer in the opposite direction D D (Fig. 2192) is shown by Fig. 2197. Fig. 2198 is a section through the top on C C (Fig. 2191), and shows the housing of the splashboard and the fixing of the top to the front and side rails by glued angle blocks. The curved front rails, drawer front, etc., are constructed as follows: A piece of wood, kerfed to the required curve, should when dry be cut with a fine tenon saw to the following sizes: for the top rail, have one piece $1\frac{3}{4}$ in. wide and one $\frac{3}{8}$ in. wide. The sawn surfaces may be smoothed

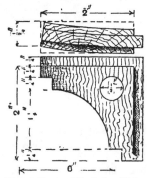

Fig. 2195.—Corner Washstand Brackets.

with a piece of coarse glasspaper and glued. A thin piece of ebony, or a piece of ebony and another of white holly or chestnut (also glued), should then be inserted, and the whole cramped up tightly till dry.

The projecting edges of the "inlaid" wood should then be removed, and the surface glasspapered flush. The rail into which the drawer is fitted is worked in a some-

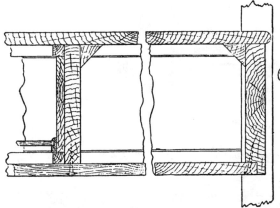

Fig. 2196.—Section of Corner Washstand Drawer.

what similar way. A piece 3 in. wide is sawn off and its edges are faced with ebony, or ebony and white wood. When dry the drawer front must be cut from the centre, and the vertical edges veneered to match the top and the bottom. The remaining parts should then be cut to the exact length, and the mock drawer fronts arranged by vertical slips of veneer carefully recessed and glued into position. Two

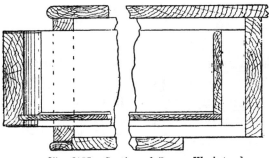

Fig. 2197.—Section of Corner Washstand Drawer.

strips of the curve, $\frac{3}{8}$ in. and $\frac{1}{2}$ in. wide respectively, will be required for the portions above and below the drawer, and also a $\frac{1}{4}$-in. nosing for the bottom (Fig. 2197). The upper and lower edges of the dummy

drawers may then be glued, the various parts arranged in their respective positions and cramped together until dry, when the projections should be removed.

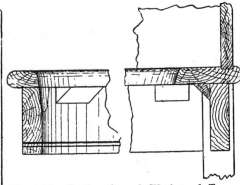

Fig. 2198.—Section through Washstand Top.

CORNER WASHSTAND DRAWER, ETC.

The drawer is constructed as shown in Figs. 2192, 2196, and 2197, and may be furnished with a turned wooden knob, shown enlarged in Fig. 2199, or a lacquered brass knob may be used. Similar knobs should be fitted to the mock fronts. If the knobs are glued in they should be fixed after the polishing is completed. The canvas or muslin on the inside of the curved drawer front should be removed and the inside worked to a smooth surface before the sides are fixed. The washstand, when ready for polishing, will be improved by staining a Chippendale colour, or stained oil may be used before bodying in; the whitewood slips should, in any case, be slightly

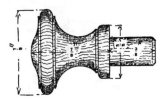

Fig. 2199.—Drawer Knob.

stained. The under surface of the top and the inside of the top rails should be given a few coats of polish applied with a brush, this preventing any possible loosening of glued parts by spilled water.

WASHSTAND WITH TILED BACK.

The washstand of which Fig. 2200 is a front elevation, and Figs. 2201 and 2202 are stretchers, tenoned to the legs at each end. A shaped shelf (see Fig. 2203) above the tiled back rests on end brackets. The four legs are $1\frac{1}{2}$ in. square. Plane them up true

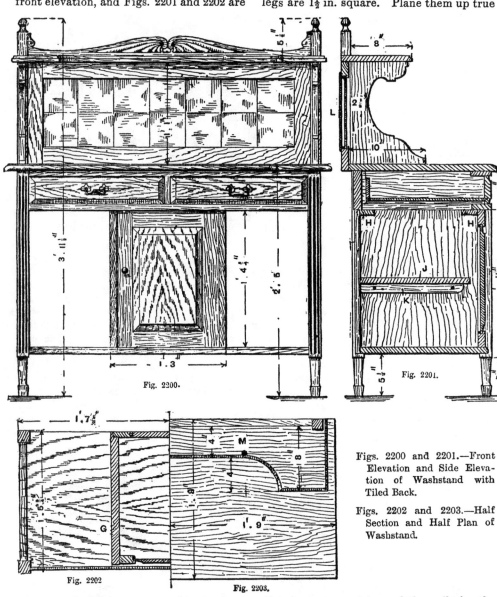

Fig. 2200.

Fig. 2201.

Fig. 2202

Fig. 2203.

Figs. 2200 and 2201.—Front Elevation and Side Elevation of Washstand with Tiled Back.

Figs. 2202 and 2203.—Half Section and Half Plan of Washstand.

sections, should be constructed of ash or birch. It contains two drawers and also a pedestal cupboard enclosed by a door, and supported by a shelf which is screwed to and mark the positions of the rails for the mortises. The end rails A (Fig. 2204) and back rail B are 5 in. deep by $\frac{7}{8}$ in. thick, and are stub-tenoned to the legs, keeping the rails $\frac{1}{8}$ in. back from the outside. The rails are rebated at the top, and two stretchers, $1\frac{1}{8}$ in. by $\frac{3}{4}$ in., are tenoned to the legs. The ends of the shelf are screwed to the under-sides of the stretchers. The construction of the frame is shown in detail by Fig. 2204. The rail c below the drawers

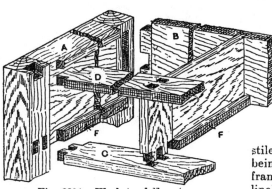

Fig. 2204.—Washstand Framing.

is double tenoned to the leg, the top rail D being dovetailed at the ends. The division between the drawers is fixed to the top and bottom rails by cutting square pins at the front and fitting them into corresponding mortises in the rails. The division extends to the back rail, where it is housed in a dovetail groove. The division is made up in two pieces. At the front the grain runs in a perpendicular direction, the inside piece lying horizontally, and the two pieces are fixed together by a tongue joint. The drawer bearers F (Fig. 2204) are glued and sprigged to the inside of each end rail and at each side of the division. The two ends of the cupboard G (Fig. 2202) are $\frac{7}{8}$ in. thick, and are housed into the shelf, which is grooved to receive them, the grooves being stopped at the front edges. Make a slight taper on the grooves, and bevel one side to make a dovetail joint, to ensure the cupboard ends being tight when driven in from the back. The edges are rebated to receive the back. Two rails H (Fig. 2201) are dovetailed to the ends at the back and front, the one at the front being kept back the thickness of the door from the front edges of the cupboard ends, and the back rail set in $\frac{3}{8}$ in., to allow the tongued and grooved back to overlap. The shelf J, inside the

cupboard, rests on two fillets K. The stiles and rails of the door are 2 in. wide by $\frac{7}{8}$ in. thick, and should be rebated at the back for the panel, which is bevelled $1\frac{1}{4}$ in. deep all round the edges, and beaded in from the back. The door should be fitted with a pair of 2-in. brass butt hinges on the right-hand side, and secured by a latch. The top, $\frac{7}{8}$ in. thick, has a moulding on the front and ends, and projects $\frac{3}{4}$ in. at the front, and $1\frac{1}{2}$ in. at the back and ends. The two drawers are $3\frac{1}{2}$ in. deep, with a $\frac{3}{4}$-in. bevel round the front edges. The four feet are shaped as shown in Fig. 2200, the two front legs being also fluted. The back consists of a frame (Fig. 2205) stub-tenoned together, the stiles and rails, 2 in. wide by $\frac{7}{8}$ in. thick, being rebated. A vertical section of the frame is shown in Fig. 2201. Tile pattern linoleum can be substituted for a tile back if desired. A thin pine board L (Fig. 2201) is sprigged to the back of the frame, while the edges are rounded over. Leave the bottom rail of the back about 1 in. wider for screwing to the back edge of the top. The two end posts, $1\frac{1}{4}$ in. square, are dowelled to the edges of the frame, their top ends being either turned or moulded square. The two end brackets, $\frac{7}{8}$ in. thick, shaped as shown in Fig. 2201, are screwed to the posts at the back, and two dowels in the bottom edge secure them to the top.

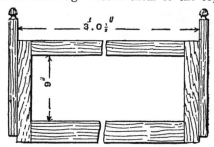

Fig. 2205.—Frame for Washstand Back.

The shaped shelf M (Fig. 2203), $\frac{3}{4}$ in. thick, is screwed to the top edge of the back, and dowelled to the top edges of the brackets. The carved pediment, $\frac{3}{4}$ in. thick, is screwed to the shelf ; Fig. 2206 shows an enlarged detail of the carving.

COMBINED WASHSTAND AND DRESSING TABLE.

Fig. 2207 illustrates a washstand and dressing table combined which would look

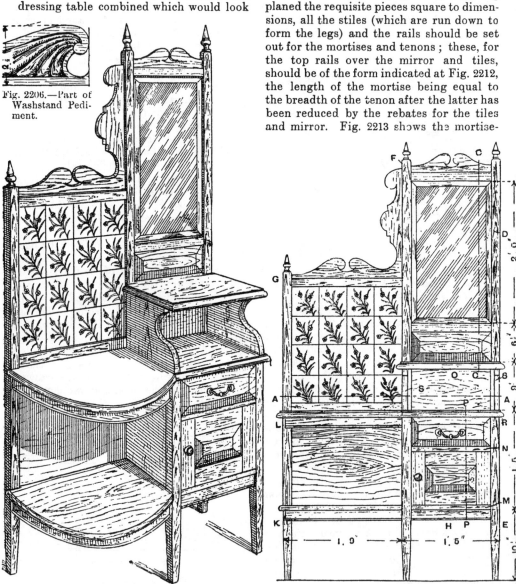

Fig. 2206.—Part of Washstand Pediment.

Fig. 2207.—Combined Washstand and Dressing Table.

Fig. 2208.—Front Elevation of Washstand and Dressing Table.

are dimensioned, so only the chief points in the making need be described. Fig. 2210 is a section at A A (Fig. 2208). Having planed the requisite pieces square to dimensions, all the stiles (which are run down to form the legs) and the rails should be set out for the mortises and tenons ; these, for the top rails over the mirror and tiles, should be of the form indicated at Fig. 2212, the length of the mortise being equal to the breadth of the tenon after the latter has been reduced by the rebates for the tiles and mirror. Fig. 2213 shows the mortise-

well if made of mahogany, walnut, oak, birch, ash, or even red deal stained and varnished. Figs. 2208, 2209, 2210, and 2211

and-tenon joints required for the rails beneath the mirror and tiles, B (Fig. 2214) showing the same. Next rebate the rails, allowing the rebates to run right through. The long back stile D (Fig. 2208) is rebated from the top down to the under-side of the shelf E. Stile F is rebated the same distance on each edge, and stile G is rebated on the inner edge to within the same distance of the lower end as the others. The two front legs and stile G require mortising

Fig. 2210.

Fig. 2209.   Fig. 2211.

Fig. 2209.—Side Elevation of Washstand and Dressing Table. Fig. 2210.—Horizontal Section of Washstand, etc. Fig. 2211.—Section of Drawer and Cupboard.

for the tenons of the rail H and curved rails K and L. These two rails will be best cut out of the solid. The two narrow rails M and N (Figs. 2208 and 2211) should be rebated for the horizontal divisions O and P (Fig. 2211), and then stop-housed into

41

the two front legs. The framework may next be fitted together, and, if satisfactory, the joints may be glued up. Then prepare the shelves O (Fig. 2208) and R (Figs. 2208 and 2214); these are $\frac{7}{8}$ in. thick, and are

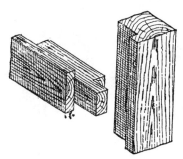

Fig. 2212.—Joint in Framing.

rebated at the back edge on the upper and lower surfaces. Two bracket pieces S (Figs. 2208 and 2209) should be prepared, being housed a little way into the shelf O, but secured to the shelf R by screwing from the under-side. The panels for the back and sides should be fitted and fixed into their respective rebates, being held in position by beads, mitred and nailed round as in Fig. 2211. A drawer is shown with a splayed marginal front, the sides, back, and front being dovetailed together in the usual manner, and the bottom fitting in plough grooves made in the front and sides, as

Fig. 2213.—Joint in Framing.

indicated at Fig. 2211. The door is of simple construction, the stiles and rails, $2\frac{1}{4}$ in. by $\frac{3}{4}$ in., being stub-tenoned and mortised together as illustrated at Fig. 2215; they have rebates in which a splayed marginal panel is secured by beads, mitred and nailed; see Fig. 2211, which is a section at P P (Fig. 2208).

TOP AND BACK OF WASHSTAND.

The top of the washstand would of course

prevent the marble sliding off, a few small blocks of stone should be secured with plaster-of-Paris to the under-side, against the inside of the curved rail, or a few dowels (brass screws with the heads filed

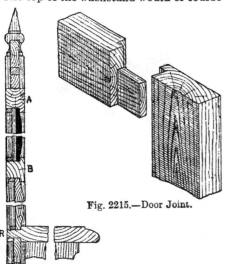

Fig. 2215.—Door Joint.

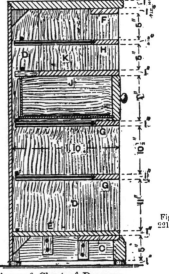

Fig. 2214.—Section through Mirror.

Fig. 2216.—Chest of Drawers.

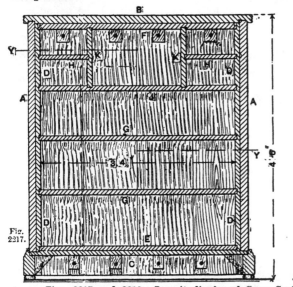

Figs. 2217 and 2218.—Longitudinal and Cross Sections of Chest of Drawers.

be better if made of marble, and would not be costly; it would rest on the front curved rail, fillets being screwed underneath. To

off) may be screwed into the rail to fit in holes on the under-side of the marble. The lower shelf is of wood, having the edge rounded, and is secured by screws inserted from the under-side of the rail, and from the back. The curved boarding forming the ornamentation at the top should next be cut out and fixed in position. Tile-

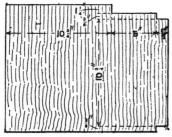

Fig. 2219.—Vertical Partition for Chest of Drawers.

pattern linoleum will make a cheap back, or tiles may be used if desired. The doors may be hinged with a pair of 1½-in. brass butts, and a lock or fastener and a brass handle for the drawer may be obtained of a pattern to suit personal taste. Finally, the mirror should be procured and fixed in position by backboarding and beads, as at A in Fig. 2214, which is a section at C C (Fig. 2208).

Framework of Chest of Drawers.

The chest of drawers illustrated by Fig. 2216 is 4 ft. wide, 4 ft. 6 in. high, and 2 ft. deep outside. The two sides A, 1½ in. thick,

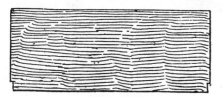

Fig. 2220.—Horizontal Partition for Chest of Drawers.

1 ft. 10¾ in. wide, and 3 ft. 11½ in. high, support the top B, which is 1½ in. thick, 2 ft. wide, and 4 ft. long, the grooves being ½ in. deep. Two inner pieces D, 1 ft. 10¼ in. wide, and 3 ft. 10⅝ in. long, and a bottom E, 1 ft. 10¼ in. wide and 3 ft. 5¼ in. long, rest on the piece C (see Figs. 2217 and 2218). The top piece F and the two lower partitions G are 5½ in. wide and 3 ft. 5¼ in. long,

the shorter partitions H being 5½ in. wide and 10½ in. long. The partition J is 1 ft. 4¾ in. wide and 3 ft. 5¼ in. long, and the vertical partitions K are 1 ft. 0¾ in. deep by 1 ft. 4¾ in. long, cut to the shape shown

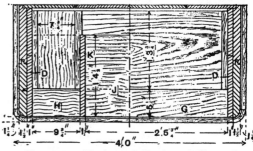

Fig. 2221.—Horizontal Section of Chest of Drawers.

by Fig. 2219, to rest in ⅜-in. grooves in the pieces B, F, and J. All the partitions, including F and bottom E, are cut out as shown by Fig. 2220, and rest, as shown in Fig. 2217, in ⅜-in. grooves. Fig. 2220 is a plan of the broad partition J. All partitions in the sides, top, and bottom of the inner framework are 1 in. thick. Side rails 1½ in. wide and 1 ft. 3¾ in. long, and resting in ⅜-in. grooves in the partitions D and K, are put in at each side of the drawer spaces for the drawers to run on (see Figs. 2218 and 2221). A ¼-in. boarding separates the drawers, as indicated by the black lines in

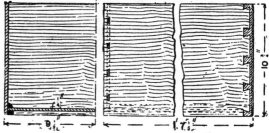

Figs. 2222 and 2223.—Drawer Details.

Fig. 2218. The plinth is 2½ in. thick and 5 in. deep, and should be cut out to receive the bottom and sides, as shown. The whole is raised slightly from the ground by means of buttons, 1 in. thick, screwed to the plinth. The framework should be strengthened where necessary by triangular blocks.

THE DRAWERS.

The drawers are fitted together as shown in Figs. 2222 and 2223, but the bottoms of the long drawers are strengthened with two battens. The drawer fronts are 1 in. thick, the sides ⅜ in. thick, and the bottom 1 ft. 7 in. wide, by 1 ft. 7½ in. ; the four short drawers are 5 in. deep, 9¾ in. wide, by 1 ft. 7½ in. Drawer stops should be fixed on the runners. The handles may be of either wood or brass. The back is ½ in. thick, and is strengthened vertically by two battens, and rests in a groove in the top B

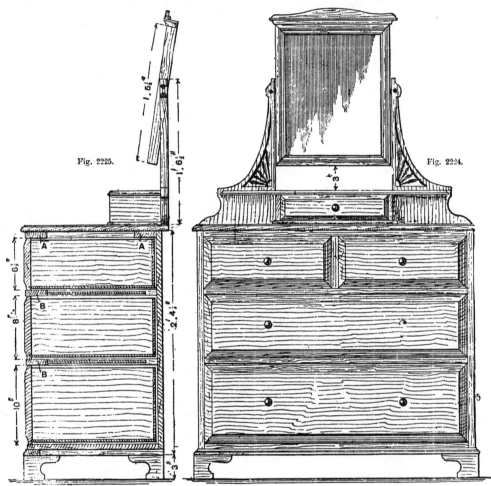

Figs. 2224 and 2225.—Section and Elevation of Chest of Drawers and Dressing Glass.

and back ¼ in. thick ; the smaller drawers may be of thinner stuff. The clear spaces for the drawers are as follow : Bottom drawer, 11 in. deep, 3 ft. 4½ in. wide, by 1 ft. 9¾ in. ; the two other long drawers are similar, but 9 in. and 10½ in. deep. The bonnet drawer is 1 ft. 10¾ in. deep, (see Fig. 2218). The top should be reed moulded. The bottom long drawer can be made deeper, and, instead of the four small drawers and centre bonnet drawer, two short drawers can be substituted if found desirable. Fig. 2221 is a section on Y Y (Fig. 2217).

Chest of Drawers and Dressing Glass.

Fig. 2224 shows the front elevation of a chest of drawers, with a dressing glass and jewel drawer fitted to the top. The chest contains four drawers, one 10 in. deep, one 8 in. deep, and two short drawers 6½ in. deep. The chest measures 3 ft. over the gables. The two gables should be planed and squared up to 2 ft. 3½ in. in length by 1 ft. 6 in. in width by ⅞ in. thick. The back edges are rebated to receive the back, which consists of ⅜-in. matchboarding. The bottom, of pine ¾ in. thick, is lap-dovetailed to the gable ends. Two pieces A (Fig. 2225), 3 in. wide by ¾ in. thick, are fixed to the gable ends in the same manner as the bottom, the object of one being to

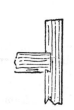

Fig. 2226.—Dovetail Joint in Gable.

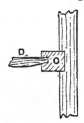

Fig. 2227.—Drawer Bearer.

allow the back to overlap. The front piece may be of pine, with a thin slip of walnut glued to the edge. The two fore-edges B are also 3 in. wide by ¾ in. thick, and are fixed to the gables by grooving the latter to form a dovetail (Fig. 2226). The fore-edges are slid in from the back. Stop the grooves at the front, and rebate the fore-edges to bring them flush there.

Drawers and Bearers.

The drawer bearers are housed in grooves c (Fig. 2227) in the gables, and should be 1¼ in. wide, and grooved to receive the dust-board D. A small tenon may be cut on the front end of the bearer and fitted into the groove in the fore-edge. Screw the bearers to the gables. The division between the two short drawers is the same width and thickness as the fore-edges, and is tenoned at the top and bottom as shown at E (Fig. 2228). A broad bearer, 3 in. wide by ¾ in. thick, has a small tenon at the front, and is

dovetailed at the back to the upright piece G, which in turn is dovetailed to the horizontal piece H. The guide I is glued and sprigged to the bearer. This should be grooved on the edges for the dustboard,

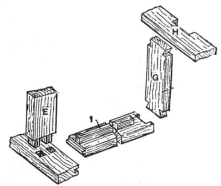

Fig. 2228.—Drawer Bearers and Divisions.

which may be of ⅜-in. stuff slid in from the back, the object being to keep the dust from the contents of the drawer below. The base moulding J (Fig. 2229), 2½ in. wide by ¾ in. thick, is screwed to the bottom and mitred at the corners. The shaped feet are mitred and glued to a block of pine, as in Fig. 2230, and are then screwed up to the moulding, and the drawer fronts, ⅞ in. thick, are fitted tightly in their places. Next fit the drawer backs in the same way, making them 1 in. narrower than the fronts. The sides are lap-dovetailed to the fronts. The top edge of the back is ¼ in. below the edges of the sides, and the bottom edge is kept up ¾ in. Grooved slips K (Fig. 2231)

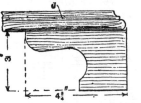

Fig. 2229.—Foot, etc., of Chest of Drawers. Fig. 2230.—Section of Base.

are glued to the sides to carry the drawer bottom, and are rounded on the top edges. The bottoms of the long drawers are in two, and are supported by a muntin L grooved on the edges similar to the slips at the sides. It is sunk into the bottom edge of the drawer front to bring it in line with the groove in the latter, and is secured with screws. The bottoms should be ⅛ in.

Fig. 2231.—Section through Drawer.

thick, with the grain of the wood parallel to the fronts. All the drawer fronts are chamfered at the edges, as shown in section by Fig. 2225. Fit the drawers before fixing the carcase back. The drawers are set back ⅛ in. from the outside, and are stopped by gluing and sprigging to the fore-edges small pieces of hardwood M (Fig. 2232), 2 in. square by ⅛ in. thick. The top, ¾ in.

Fig. 2232.—Drawer Stop.

thick, projects ¾ in. over the front and ends, but at the back it should project at least 1 in.

JEWEL BOX OF DRESSING CHEST.

The box for the jewel drawer consists of the shaped shelf (Fig. 2233), ⅝ in. thick, into which the two ends N (Fig. 2234) are housed with a dovetail groove, stopped at the front. The ends are ⅝ in. thick, and the bottom O is ½ in. thick, and fixed to the

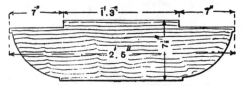

Fig. 2233.—Dressing Glass Shelf.

ends by screws. The two side brackets P (Fig. 2235), 1 in. thick, may be relieved by flat carving, and are screwed to the back edge of the shelf. Two screws may also be

put into the edge of the bracket which butts against the side of the box. The whole is then secured to the top of the chest by screws through the top into the brackets.

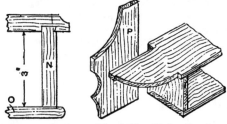

Fig. 2234.—Section of Jewel Box.   Fig. 2235.—Fixing Bracket to Jewel Box.

Two screws should be driven through the bottom of the box at the front edge into the top. A thin piece of pine is sprigged to the back of the jewel box.

MIRROR OF DRESSING CHEST.

The mirror frame shown in section by Fig. 2236 is made by dovetailing together a frame ⅞ in. wide by ¾ in. thick, the outside dimensions being 1 ft. 5½ in. by 1 ft. 2½ in. The top and bottom pieces of the frame are lap-dovetailed to the sides. The moulding R, 1¼ in. by ⅜ in., is mitred and glued on the face of the frame, and forms the rebate for the mirror plate, which is fixed by wedge-shaped blocks glued round the edges. A pine back S is rebated and screwed to the back of the frame. A plate ⅝ in. thick, with a hollow moulding worked on the edges, is screwed to the top of the frame, and the pediment is glued to the

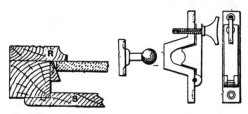

Fig. 2236.—Section of Mirror Frame.   Fig. 2237.—Mirror Pivoting Arrangement.

plate. The mirror frame is hung about 1 in. above its centre with a pair of brass catches, shown in Fig. 2237. The sockets are sunk flush with the edges of the frame, and the pivots are fixed to the brackets. Brass till locks should be fitted to the drawers, which are also provided with

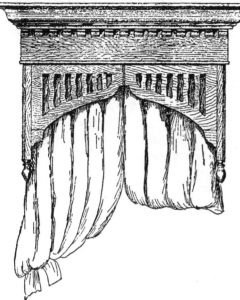

Fig. 2238.—Corner Wardrobe.

turned knobs. All the parts shown may be in walnut, or the whole could be in pine, which should be stained a suitable colour and polished.

CORNER WARDROBE.

A corner wardrobe as shown by Figs. 2238 to 2240 is provided with hinged shut-

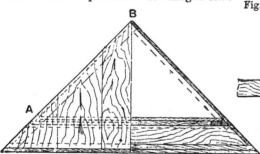

Fig. 2240.—Plan of Corner Wardrobe.

ters, to which are attached curtains reaching to the floor; Fig. 2241 illustrates the curtain rod. In a low room the cornice

(Fig. 2242) might be fitted close up to the ceiling, then the necessity for dustboards would be obviated. Also, when the ceiling

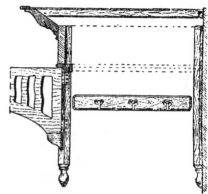

Fig. 2239.—Section of Corner Wardrobe.

is unusually high, the top of the shutters may be fixed at the same height as the bedroom door. First prepare two posts (Figs. 2239 and 2243) 2 ft. 9 in. long; these can be sawn diagonally from stuff 3 in. square. Fix the posts to the walls, the top of each being 9 in. higher than the shutters, and 2 ft. 6 in. from the corner of the room—

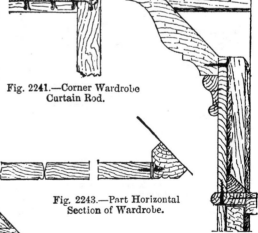

Fig. 2241.—Corner Wardrobe Curtain Rod.

Fig. 2243.—Part Horizontal Section of Wardrobe.

Fig. 2242.—Section of Wardrobe Cornice.

that is, from A to B (Fig. 2240). Next nail on the frieze board. The ends should mitre to the walls, and on the under edge is fixed a fillet with a nosing worked on its outer edge; on the back edge is nailed a stop fillet to prevent the shutters swinging inside. About 5 ft. of cornice moulding is

Fig. 2244.—Fixing End of Cornice.   Fig. 2245 —Shutter Terminal.

required, and it mitres to the walls, the lower edge being fixed to the frieze with screws, and the upper ends being nailed to 2-in. by 1-in. battens. The dustboards are bradded to cornice and battens (see Figs. 2240, 2242, and 2244). Fig. 2245 shows the end of the shutter. Figs. 2246 and 2247 show alternative designs for shutters fitted with fretwork panels and for the cornice frieze, the fret-board being $\frac{1}{2}$ in. thick by 1 ft. 2 in. wide. The shutters of Fig. 2238 are cut from stuff $\frac{7}{8}$ in. thick by 1 ft. 2 in. wide, the bottom-shaped piece being tongued and glued on after the fretting is finished. Two battens provided with hooks (Fig. 2239) are nailed to the walls at a convenient height. The woodwork should be primed and painted or enamelled.

wall. The drawers are of the usual pattern and make. A wooden back would strengthen the bookshelf, but for ordinary use the ornamental top A and the piece of backing B behind the drawers is sufficient. Fig. 2250 shows a larger and more highly ornamented set of small shelves with lockers beneath. The shelves and sides may be

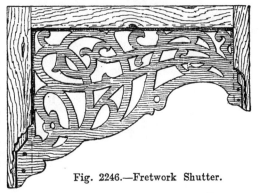

Fig. 2246.—Fretwork Shutter.

made of $\frac{5}{8}$-in. deal, the outer frame being 3 ft. 4 in. by 2 ft. 4 in. by 6 in. deep, and the pieces may be screwed together for simplicity of construction. The back and top should be of well-seasoned $\frac{1}{2}$-in. boards, glued and clamped up together. The out-

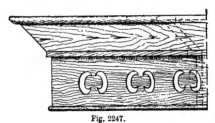

Fig. 2247.

Fig. 2247.—Corner Wardrobe Fretted Cornice. Figs. 2248 and 2249.— Front and Side Elevations of Simple Bedroom Bookshelf.

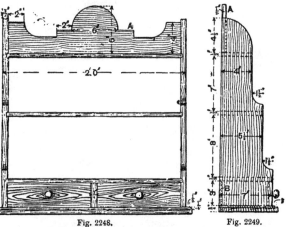

Fig. 2248.   Fig. 2249.

BEDROOM BOOKSHELVES.

Fig. 2248 shows the front view and Fig. 2249 the side elevation of a bookshelf which may stand on a table or be hung on the

lines of the ornament at the top (Fig. 2251) and at the lower ends of the side pieces (Fig. 2252) should be roughly shaped out, and the ornament applied in gesso. The whole of the ornament may be applied in this way, or, of course, may be carved. The doors of the lockers should be panelled, and hinged at the bottom to open downwards. A coat of white enamel, and, if desired, a judicious application of gold paint or leaf will add a finish to the work.

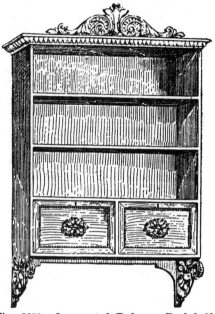

Fig. 2250.—Ornamented Bedroom Bookshelf.

Fig. 2252.   Figs. 2251 and 2252.—Gesso Ornaments for Bookshelf.   Fig. 2251.

WARDROBE IN PARTS.

The wardrobe shown complete in Fig. 2253 is made in four parts—the top two presses and the bottom with drawer—so that it may be quickly taken to pieces. It stands about 6 ft. 6 in. high, 4 ft. wide, and 1 ft. 6 in. from back to front. The top, bottom, and outer sides of the presses are made of 1-in. wood, and the two inner sides

Fig. 2253.—Wardrobe made in Parts.

of $\frac{5}{8}$-in. wood. The top and bottom parts are dovetailed into the outer sides for $\frac{1}{2}$ in. of their thickness, and are glued and screwed (see Figs. 2254 and 2255). The inner sides of the presses are made only 1 ft. $5\frac{3}{8}$ in. wide, and are kept back $\frac{5}{8}$ in. from the front edges; they are nailed to the edge of the top, bottom, and back pieces. On the front edge of one of these is fixed a piece, $\frac{5}{8}$ in. thick, $1\frac{1}{4}$ in. wide, and 4 ft. $8\frac{1}{4}$ in. long, to overlap the edge of the other press when the two are close together. The two are fixed in position by three screws. A similar piece, $2\frac{1}{4}$ in. wide, is fixed to the back linings, to overlap and, with screws, fasten the presses together at the back. The backing of $\frac{5}{8}$-in. stuff is fixed in the ordinary way, a $\frac{5}{8}$-in. rebate being cut in the top, bottom, and side pieces to let it go in flush; the inner side piece is nailed to the edge of it. The

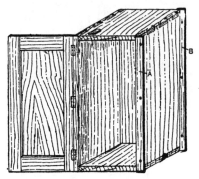

Fig. 2254.—Wardrobe Press.

top (see Fig. 2253) is made in the shape of a frame of wood about 6 in. deep, and having a moulding about 3 in. deep, mitred and glued at the corners, fixed at an angle to the upper part of the front and ends. The top should be about 4 ft. 1$\frac{1}{2}$ in. long and 1 ft. 8 in. wide at the bottom edge; while at the top the projecting moulding will be about 4 ft. 4 in. by 1 ft. 9$\frac{1}{2}$ in. Blocks are fixed on top of the presses near the outside corners to register the top part. The top projects over each end and at the front about $\frac{3}{4}$ in. over the doors. The doors of the presses are of 1$\frac{1}{4}$-in. stuff, with stiles 4 in. wide, which have a bead run in the centre of each and have sunk panels. They are hung with three 2-in. brass hinges to each door. The doors should be rebated to overlap at the centre, or should have a $\frac{3}{4}$-in. half-round piece of wood fixed on one of them for that purpose. A brass pendant on each door, a top and bottom catch on one and a lock on the other, complete them. The sides of the bottom part (Fig. 2256) are pieces of 1-in. wood thickened at front to 1$\frac{1}{4}$ in., 1 ft. 3 in. high and 1 ft. 7$\frac{1}{4}$ in. wide, with a framework at top and bottom as shown, and a plinth $\frac{3}{4}$ in. thick and 3$\frac{1}{2}$ in. deep. The back has $\frac{1}{2}$-in. linings fixed to the top and bottom frames, which only go within $\frac{1}{2}$ in. of the back. These frames are

10 in. apart. Pieces 4 in. wide and 1 in. thick, cut to lengths and mitred and glued at the corners, are fixed to the top of the bottom part so as to project $\frac{3}{4}$ in. at the sides and front. The recess made by these is used to keep the two presses in place, blocks of wood being fixed on the bottoms of the presses to fit tightly inside the recesses. The drawer is made in the usual way, 10 in. deep, 1 ft. 6$\frac{1}{2}$ in. back to front, and 3 ft. 9$\frac{1}{2}$ in. long. The two presses are kept together when in position by screws passing through the back and front overlapping pieces. The wardrobe can easily and readily be taken down by removing the screws. The wardrobe may be made of yellow pine, with red wood panels to doors and drawer front.

6-FT. WARDROBE WITH FULL-LENGTH MIRROR.

The wardrobe of which Fig. 2257 illustrates the front elevation is 6 ft. 9 in. high, 6 ft. wide, and 1 ft. 9 in. deep. There are three doors, that on the right hand opening outwards, the centre one opening in the same direction, whilst the left-hand one opens also outwards—that is, in a reverse direction from the other two, so that the two left-hand doors meet when closing. Fig. 2258, which is drawn to a scale of $\frac{3}{4}$ in.

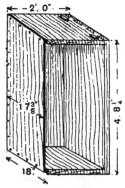

Fig. 2255.—Wardrobe Press.

to the foot, is a front elevation of the wardrobe complete, with the doors removed, and showing the interior. At the right-hand side will be seen the hooks for suspending clothes, with a sliding tray underneath, which covers a space for soiled linen, etc., suitably covered in front by a board B. The drawers and sliding trays shown at the left are useful, but should more hanging accommodation be required,

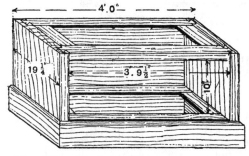

Fig. 2256.—Wardrobe Bottom Framework.

a similar space can be reserved at the left (behind the other end door) for the purpose by shortening the length of trays and drawers. Fig. 2259 shows a vertical section of the wardrobe.

Body of Wardrobe.

In constructing this wardrobe the body should be made first. As seen in Fig. 2258, it consists of a top C, bottom D, and back E. The thickness of the sides is $\frac{3}{4}$ in., whilst the top and bottom need only be $\frac{1}{2}$ in., and the back only $\frac{3}{8}$ in. The back E should be made up of boards, which should be tongued and grooved together to give a more satisfactory result, and to prevent the dust from entering. The right-hand side is divided from the rest by means of two partitions, F and G, arranged as shown in the horizontal section (Fig. 2260) and enlarged in Fig. 2261. These partitions should be $\frac{1}{2}$ in. thick, and made up of boards tongued and grooved together. A piece H, 3 in. wide, is fixed to these two partitions F and G in the position shown in Fig. 2261, thus leaving a space between F and G. Before, however, these partitions are fixed in position, the various grooves for the sliding trays should be made. The ornamental moulding at the top is made in three pieces, J, K, and L (Figs. 2262 and 2263). The top pieces L are jointed at the side as shown in the plan in Fig. 2264, a small piece M being fixed at each end so as to keep the ends rigid.

The pieces K are made with a front and two sides, the round corners being filled in to the required curvature by means of three or four separate pieces cut out of a solid piece and glued together, a stiffener or batten being fixed at the back for strength if desired. The pieces J are made with a front and two side pieces, the two front corners being fitted in with wedge-shaped pieces with a rounded front, so as to conform to the curvature of the body. Two beads are shown (see Fig. 2263), the top one being a small strip semicircular in section, the bottom one being much wider. Either or both forms may be used if desired. Running from front to back at the top is a stiffener, as shown in Fig. 2257. A skirting piece O, with a beaded top, runs round the bottom and supports the body.

Fig. 2257.—Wardrobe with Full-length Mirror.

Wardrobe Trays and Drawers.

Fig. 2265 shows an isometric view of one of the longer trays, which measure 3 ft. 10 in. long by 1 ft. 5 in. wide, all the parts of which may be made of pine or other cheap wood if desired. Strips R are fixed at the sides as shown, which slide in grooves provided for them in the partition and side. The sides of the trays are shaped as shown,

side to stiffen it. This may be secured in position by means of screws from the side

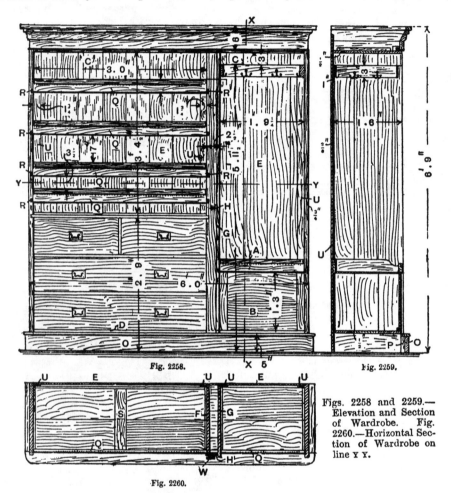

Fig. 2258.

Fig. 2259.

Fig. 2260.

Figs. 2258 and 2259.—Elevation and Section of Wardrobe. Fig. 2260.—Horizontal Section of Wardrobe on line Y Y.

the front Q being rounded for convenience in handling. No knobs or handles are shown fixed on the front, but these may be used if desired. As the trays are rather long, and the bottom is only thin ($\frac{1}{4}$ in.), stiffeners S are used, one at the top as shown and one underneath. Two long drawers and two short drawers are shown, the depth of each being 7 in. And there are four trays. The front B, which covers the receptacle for soiled linen, is made up of two boards 1 ft. $9\frac{1}{2}$ in. long, with two additional pieces, 1 ft. 3 in. long, at each

and partition. The six clothes hooks are

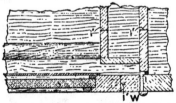

Fig. 2261.—Part Section of Wardrobe Door.

fixed to a rail running round the side, back, and partition. This rail consists of three pieces 1 in. thick, one piece for the back 1 ft. 9½ in. long, and the other two 1 ft. 4 in. long, and all 3 in. wide. Fastened to the back are three battens U, running from top to bottom, which act as a stopper to prevent the trays and drawers from going back too far.

Fig. 2261, by means of a strip running round the back edge, and finally a backboard, also a beading in front. When the doors are closed, the left-hand door is locked by means of two small bolts let in flush at top

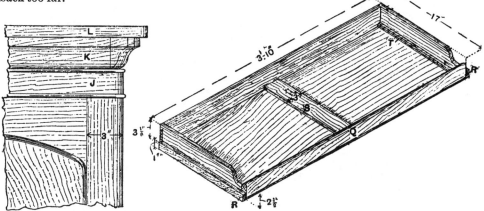

Fig. 2262.—Top Corner of Wardrobe.

Fig. 2265.—Wardrobe Tray.

WARDROBE DOORS.

The two outside doors are hinged at the side, the front edges nearest the hinge being rounded as shown in Fig. 2266. The outer doors are simply panelled with a semicircular beading running round the edge,

and bottom, and the centre one closes and locks into it, whilst the right-hand door locks in a catch provided for that purpose in partition G. The centre door is not hinged, but has a plate V (Fig. 2267) fixed at the top and bottom with a pin that fits and works in a hole in a plate W that is screwed to skirting and top piece J. The

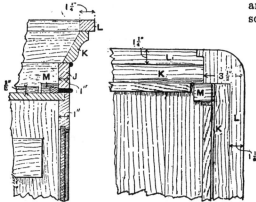

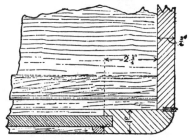

Fig. 2266.—Section of Wardrobe Outer Doors.

Fig. 2263.—Section of Cornice, etc.

Fig. 2264.—Plan of Cornice Moulding.

which can be glued on. To finish elaborately, the panels may be carved. The middle door contains a mirror which is let in a recess and fixed in position, as shown in

position which this plate occupies is shown dotted at W in Fig. 2261.

6-FT. 6-IN. WARDROBE WITH SIDE MIRROR.

Figs. 2268 and 2269 illustrate a wardrobe 4 ft. 6 in. wide by 1 ft. 7 in. deep, which can be constructed in birch or ash. Fig. 2269 is a vertical section, showing the in-

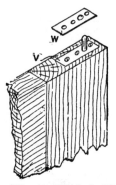

Fig. 2267.—Hingeing Wardrobe Middle Door.

tion. First prepare the two outside gables of ⅞-in. stuff. Square them to 5 ft. 10 in. by 1 ft. 5½ in., and rebate the back edges for the back ¾ in. thick. After the gables are cleaned on the outside, the pilasters should be dowel-jointed to the front edges of the gables, projecting slightly over the outside to break the joint. Two flutes are worked on the face of the pilasters, stopping at the top and the bottom. The carcase bottom of ¾-in. pine, with a strip of ash glued to the front edge, is flush with the pilasters at the front and lap-dovetailed into the gable ends. The top, of pine of the same thickness, is fixed in the same manner as the bottom, but is kept back at the front so that the doors overlap. The bottom

Fig. 2268.

Fig. 2269.

Figs. 2268 and 2269.—Front Elevation and Section of Wardrobe with Side Mirror.

ternal arrangement of the drawers, tray, and shelves in the left-hand side of the wardrobe, and Fig. 2270 is a horizontal sec-

shelf A (Fig. 2269) is of pine, ⅞ in. thick, slipped with ash on the front edge. The ends are let into the gables, the under-side forming a dovetail. The shelf is inserted from the back and glued. The grooves in the gables should have a gradual taper from back to front. They are stopped ½ in. at the front, and the shelf is rebated to bring it flat with the pilasters. The centre

to the ends, and kept 1 in. back from the end. It can be veneered, or clamped with thin ash and mitred at the corners. Pieces of pine 1¼ in. by ⅞ in. are glued along the inside of the plinth at the top to form a bed for the moulding (see A, Fig. 2272).

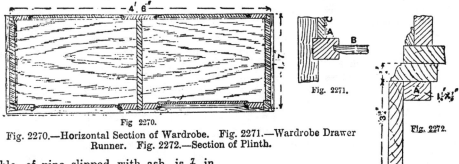

Fig 2270.

Fig. 2270.—Horizontal Section of Wardrobe.   Fig. 2271.—Wardrobe Drawer Runner.   Fig. 2272.—Section of Plinth.

gable, of pine slipped with ash, is ⅞ in. thick. Square pins are cut on the ends, and let into the bottom shelf and carcase top. A diagonal saw-cut is made in each pin, and a wedge inserted and driven in tightly. The drawer fore-edge B (Fig. 2269), 3 in. by ⅞ in., is fixed to the centre and left-hand gables by means of the sliding dove-tail in the same manner as the bottom shelf. Grooves ⅞ in. wide are cut in the gables to receive the drawer bearers A (Fig. 2271), which are 1¼ in. by ⅞ in., and grooved to house the dustboard. The back edge of the fore-edge is also grooved. The dustboard B (Fig. 2271) is a piece of ⅜-in. pine with the edges bevelled and slipped into the grooves in the bearers to keep the dust from the contents of the drawer beneath it. The top shelf C (Fig. 2269) is of the same thickness as the fore-edge, and is fixed in the same manner as the bottom shelf. The pine back is framed up of ¾-in. stuff, the stiles and rails being 3½ in. wide. A rail 3 in. wide divides the length of the back, while a centre muntin 7 in. wide divides the width. The stiles, rails, and muntin are grooved ½ in. to receive the four panels. If preferred, the back could be made in two and joined at the centre gable.

WARDROBE PLINTH AND CORNICE.

The plinth, without the moulding, is 3¾ in. deep. The two ends are dovetailed to the front, the back being slip-dovetailed

For the cornice, a frame 3 in. deep by ¾ in. thick is dovetailed together in the same manner as the plinth A (Fig. 2273). Fig. 2274 is an elevation of the cornice. It has a filling of pine along the bottom on the inside, forming a bed for the bottom moulding (see Fig. 2273). All the other mouldings are planted on the face, sections being given in Fig. 2273. A dustboard ½ in. thick is fitted in the rebate formed by the top

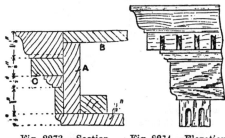

Fig. 2273.—Section of Cornice.   Fig. 2274.—Elevation of Cornice.

moulding projecting above the pine frame (see B, Fig. 2273). The dentils C (Fig. 2273) are cut out of the solid with a gouge. The bottom moulding of the cornice is 2½ in. wide for fixing to the carcase top.

DOORS OF THE WARDROBE.

The mirror and cupboard doors are framed up of 1-in. stuff, the stiles and rails for each door being $3\frac{5}{8}$ in. in width, and a $\frac{5}{8}$-in. rebate is worked on the edges. The mirror door (Fig. 2275) is fitted with a bevelled plate in the following manner. When the moulding is mitred and glued in the rebate, put the door face downwards on the bench, place the plate in position, taking care to have an equal margin all round ($\frac{3}{16}$ in. is sufficient), and glue wedge-shaped pieces of pine A (Fig. 2275), about 2 in. long, at short intervals all round the edges. A pine back B (Fig. 2275) $\frac{3}{8}$ in. thick, rebated on the edges and screwed to the door, secures the plate from damage on the inside. The cupboard door is fitted with a $\frac{1}{2}$-in. panel, chamfered on the back, and secured on the inside by beads mitred and sprigged to the edge of the door.

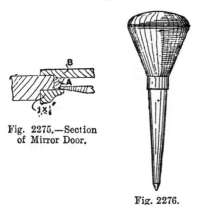

Fig. 2275.—Section of Mirror Door.

Fig. 2276. Chair-caner's Reamer.

WARDROBE TRAYS AND DRAWERS.

The tray D (Fig. 2269) is dovetailed together like a drawer, the sides being shaped to meet the front, which is rounded on the top edge. It runs on the shelf beneath it. The two upper shelves are laid on fillets screwed to the gables. The fillets of the shelf above the tray are fixed immediately above the sides of the latter, with just sufficient clearance for the tray to slide easily. The drawer fronts have a moulding mitred round the edges. A thin piece of pine about $1\frac{1}{2}$ in. wide is fixed inside the gable to make up the thickness of the pilaster, and to allow the drawers to run smoothly; C (Fig. 2271) shows this guide in the short drawer.

COMPLETING WARDROBE.

The hook plate E (Fig. 2269) is $2\frac{1}{2}$ in. wide by $\frac{5}{8}$ in. thick, the two ends being dovetailed to the back; it stops 1 in. from the mirror door, and is fitted in the hanging space. After the hooks are screwed to the plate the latter is fixed to the gables and back. The doors and drawers are fitted with brass locks and handles, and the doors are hung with brass butt hinges, three for the mirror door and two for the cupboard door. Stops for the doors are glued and sprigged to the centre gable; they are of the same length as the doors. The plinth is screwed from the carcase bottom. When the plinth is fixed in position, tilt back the wardrobe, and fix blocks in the corners of the carcase bottom, so that the carcase can be dropped into its place without any trouble. The same plan can be adopted with the cornice before fixing the dustboard. The mirror plate should not be fixed to the door until the latter is polished.

BEDROOM CHAIRS.

The style of chair for use in bedrooms is generally light and simple, and there is a marked preference for those with caned seats. The construction of a bedroom chair will not present any difficulty to the worker who has mastered the details of the simple wooden chair described so fully on pp. 566 to 570, except with regard to the caning of the seat. This, however, is not a difficult task, and the following instructions on the subject will be found sufficient.

CANE FOR CHAIR SEATS.

The caning or re-caning of chairs is generally done with a species of split rattan cane, varying in lengths from 10 ft. to 15 ft.; it is sold by weight and is of two qualities, known as No. 1 and No. 2. The No. 1 cane measures approximately $\frac{1}{8}$ in. in width, and the No. 2 cane $\frac{3}{32}$ in. The quantity required will depend on the pattern adopted, and the ordinary six-strand diamond lacing will take about $\frac{1}{4}$ lb. for two bedroom-chair seats of the ordinary crown-back, ladder-back, or Oxford-back patterns.

Preparing for Caning.

Before caning can be commenced, $\frac{3}{16}$-in. (full) holes must be bored all round the seat frame with a brace and bit or a boring machine. These holes should be $\frac{5}{8}$ in. apart, and $\frac{5}{8}$ in. from the inner edges. Any

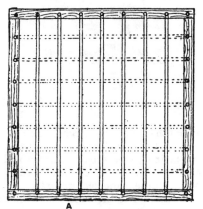

Fig. 2277.—First Stage for Diamond Pattern Caning.

staining and polishing of the frames should be done before the caning is begun. The special tool required is a reamer (Fig. 2276), a smooth steel spike, $2\frac{1}{2}$ in. long, tapering from a blunt point to $\frac{5}{16}$ in. at the tang, and firmly secured in a short hardwood handle. A few hardwood pegs shaved from $\frac{1}{2}$-in. stuff and about 2 in. long will also be wanted. Soak the cane for twelve hours in a tub of clean cold water, rainwater being preferable; this makes the cane pliable and also prevents cracking and splitting when lacing. The cane will also contract on drying and make a firm, tight job.

Caning Chair Seats Diamond Pattern.

In the diamond lacing the strands of cane square with the frame are of No. 2 stuff, and those running diagonally are of No. 1 cane. In Figs. 2277 and 2278 each separate line represents a strand, making six in all. In commencing work, place the chair on a bench or table, and pass up a strand of No. 2 cane through the centre hole on the chair front; then pass the other end of the cane up through the next hole, pull up both strands, and get them equal in length.

42

Then cross the seat to the opposite holes and pass the cane down, pull it quite tight, and hold it with the left hand; insert the reamer with the right hand and press down. This effectually prevents the cane slipping until it has been laced to the opposite side, when the reamer should be transferred. Continue the single lacing to the last hole but one, then secure the cane with a hardwood peg and follow the same procedure with the other half of the cane, putting this through the same hole, thus making a double strand to each hole (see A, Fig. 2277). The same operation is then done on the right until the seat is laced from front to back. The second lacing is across the seat from side to side, and is interlaced as shown in Fig. 2279. In doing any lacing, always commence in the centre of the seat frame, as this ensures the strongest part of the cane being in the middle of the seat. Secure a loose end with a hardwood peg temporarily, as the next strand of cane passed through the hole will fasten it. The third lacing A (Fig. 2278) is done with No. 1 cane, the lacing going from corner to corner across the centre of the

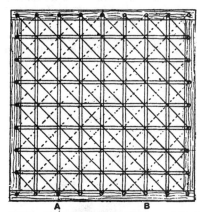

Fig. 2278.—Second Stage for Diamond Pattern Caning.

seat, and being interlaced through the squares of double cane as Fig. 2280. Next follows the fourth lacing as B (Fig. 2278); this is in the opposite direction to the third lacing (see Fig. 2281), and, if the caning has been properly done, will form the diamond pattern.

BORDER CANING.

The unsightly appearance round the holes is remedied by putting on a border cane. Select a stout No. 1 cane for the border

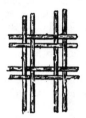

Fig. 2279.—Simple Interlacing of Eight Canes.

and tie down with a piece of No. 2; double this in the centre and pass through the right-hand corner hole, double together, open the eye and slip the end of the border cane through, then pull down until tight. Pass one end of the tying-down cane up through the next hole but one, then over the border cane and down through the hole again, the border cane being kept straight and free from puckers. Continue tying down at each alternate hole as shown by the dotted lines in Fig. 2282. In Fig. 2283 is shown a section of the frame with the tying-down cane over the border. When the whole is laced, allow it to dry slowly, then brush up with a hard bristle furniture brush.

OTHER PATTERNS OF CANING.

Another pattern, called the "cross-square," and shown in Figs. 2284 and 2285,

Fig. 2280.—Caning Interlaced by Diagonals.

is very useful for nurse-chair seats, mail-cart sides, etc., as it makes a very close pattern, and is done entirely with No. 1 cane. It can be worked quicker than the

diamond pattern, as the strands are not interlaced so much, and this will plainly be seen on referring to Fig. 2284, which shows the patterns for the first and second lacing. Six strands are used as before.

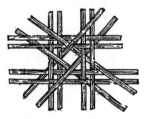

Fig. 2281.—Caning Interlaced by Diagonals.

Should other designs suggest themselves, they must be carried right through the different lacings, or a broken pattern will result. No varnish or polish is needed for finishing these cane chair seats, as the natural enamel of the cane would be difficult to improve.

RE-CANING AND RENOVATING CHAIR SEATS.

These instructions also apply to re-caning old work, as the whole of the cane must be removed and the holes cleaned out before caning can be done. Discoloured

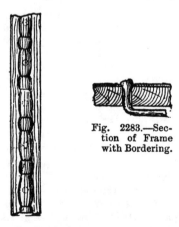

Fig. 2283.—Section of Frame with Bordering.

Fig. 2282.—Bordering.

and baggy seats can be renovated by well swilling with boiling hot water until the cane is thoroughly wet; then place the work in a strong draught of air to dry, and the subsequent contraction will bring up the seats tight and level. Do not use soda or soap in the water.

Fig. 2284.—Cross-square Lacing; First and Second Stages.

RE-SEATING CHAIRS WITH RUSH OR CORD BOTTOMS.

Chairs with rush or cord bottoms may need to be re-seated. To do this, first carefully remove the four thin battens which are nailed on the edges of the seat, and pull off the old rush, dust, etc. The sides of the seat frame are sunk slightly below the corners, so that the

Fig. 2285.—Cross-square Lacing; Finished.

work will be flush with the latter when finished. The work is very simple, and pro-

ceeds from one corner regularly round to others in succession, terminating in the centre, so that all four sides are worked together, as shown in Fig. 2286. A, B, C, D, are the sides of the seat frame. Have a good coil of cord on a stick, and make the end fast to the leg E (right-hand back corner), pass the coil up and out over A, then up and out over B, over C and up and out over A, then over D and up and out over C, etc. This will be quite clear from the

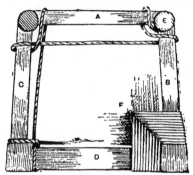

Fig. 2286.—Re-seating Chair with Rush or Cord Bottom.

cord shown loose in the illustration. When pulled up snug and tight and as the work proceeds it will have the appearance at each corner of that at the corner F. Any joining of the cord or rushes must, of course, be done after a back turn, so that it will come underneath. Stuffing can be pushed in between the upper and lower layers of cord as the work proceeds, and the end which is first hitched to the leg can be knotted and afterwards cut off.

DINING-ROOM FURNITURE.

The Scope of this Chapter.

HOUSEHOLD furniture in great variety has already been treated, and the two remaining chapters will deal with examples of skilled work especially adapted for use in the dining- and drawing-rooms. In many of the examples previously described, glass, plain or silvered, was a feature, and instructions were given at the time for its proper fitting. An opportunity will now be taken to deal with this matter more fully. It is obvious that the particular method employed of fitting glass panes and panels exercises the greatest influence for good or ill on the ultimate appearance of the finished article of furniture. Diagrams which may be studied in this connection appear on pp. 533, 538, 606, 626, 628, 642, 646, 652, and 656. This chapter will also

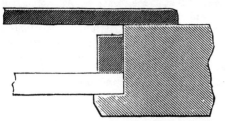

Fig. 2287.—Square-edged Silvered Glass in Deep Rebate.

discuss briefly the repairing of furniture. Four styles of glass are fitted into furniture : they are (1) plain with square edges ; (2) silvered with square edges ; (3) plain with bevelled edges ; and (4) silvered with bevelled edges.

Fitting Square-edged Silvered Glass.

In fitting a piece of square-edged silvered plate—that is, an ordinary mirror—first turn the framing to be glazed face downwards on a table, taking care to have a piece of baize or similar material under

the frame. The backboard then must be removed, and in doing so it should be noted whether this is laid on the back or fitted within the rebate. Fig. 2287 shows a deep rebate of a convenient size for silvered glass. Measure the full size of the

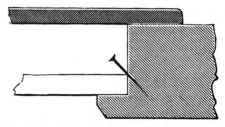

Fig. 2288.—Bad Method of Securing Silvered Glass.

rebate and have the glass cut accordingly. It should just fill the space comfortably, so that there can be no movement laterally or perpendicularly when the frame is in position, which may be taken as upright. There is, however, nothing to prevent the plate moving backwards and forwards between the backboard and the front, and so blocks or strips of wood must be glued behind the glass to the framing ; provided they do not interfere with the backing board, their shape and size are unimportant, and they may be placed a few inches apart. Do not try to fasten the plate down with brads or nails as illustrated by Fig. 2288, as that method is very likely to injure the glass. But there is no harm in driving a small brad or wire nail in a similar manner through the glued block. Care must be taken not to let the nail come in contact with the glass. Fig. 2289 represents a shallower rebate than that shown in Fig. 2287, being just deep enough to receive the glass without any space for the blocks. If the plates are small, it will be only necessary to fasten the back down. But it would be better to put a layer of soft flannel or a sheet or two of soft paper by way of padding between the glass and the back. If the glass is silvered by the

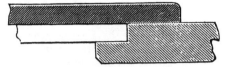

Fig. 2289.—Square-edged Silvered Glass in Shallow Rebate.

old process, some such precaution is absolutely necessary to prevent the silvering being damaged. The newer process does not require such delicate handling, but the silvering might get injured by contact with the backing board, especially if this is either rough or panelled. Fig. 2290 shows a rebate both wide and deep. As there is no occasion for so wide a margin of glass as there would be were the space to be filled, it is optional whether the glass be cut to fit exactly or not. There is no need to make the glass fit to the fractional part of an inch, but just leave a vacant space both at the edge and behind the glass, which is free to be moved in any direction. Therefore, fasten it in by blocks, as shown in Fig. 2290, which bind in both directions. If the space is too wide for the triangular-shaped block to wedge the glass down, the section of the block can easily be altered to that shown in Fig. 2291. Fig. 2292 shows

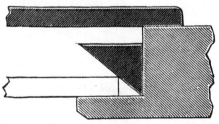

Fig. 2290.—Square-edged Silvered Glass in Wide Deep Rebate.

a wide but shallow rebate in which the wedge-shaped blocks cannot well be used. It is therefore necessary to use those of rectangular section, which possibly may not require any gluing in, as the glass and

backing board will hold them. Fig. 2293 shows the backboard fitted within the rebate, and so the available depth for the

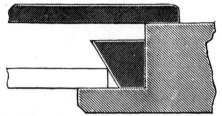

Fig. 2291.—Securing Silvered Glass with Differently Shaped Block.

wedges is much curtailed. The methods adopted for fixing are, however, the same as given in previous instances.

PUTTING IN SILVERED GLASS.

The following directions should be observed. Blacken the inside of the rebate against which the face of the glass rests,

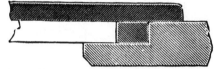

Fig. 2292.—Square-edged Silvered Glass in Shallow Wide Rebate.

and also blacken the edges of the glass, which will be more or less rough. If the blacking be omitted, the reflection of the wood will be visible, and the rough edges of the glass will reflect in an unsightly manner, unless they are an unusually long way within the rebate. A mixture of size or weak glue with some gas-black is the

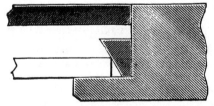

Fig. 2293.—Framed Glass with Backing Board within Rebate.

best thing that can be used for blacking. Care should be taken to prevent any glue getting on to the back of the plate, for, if allowed to harden, it might, in drying, pull the silvering under it away from the glass, and leave an unsightly blemish.

FITTING SQUARE-EDGED PLAIN GLASS.

In fitting square-edged plain glass, such as is used in bookcase doors, wedges or

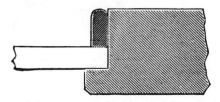

Fig. 2294.—Square-edged Plain Glass Beaded in.

blocks cannot be used, as there is no back panel with which to hide them. The glass, therefore, must fit as accurately as possible within the rebate, where it is held by strips of beading, as shown in Fig. 2294. If the glass does not fit quite so tightly as it should, thin strips of wood should be placed in a somewhat similar fashion to that shown by Fig. 2295, taking care that they are covered by the beading, which should be neatly fitted and mitred at the corners. The strips should be long enough not to require jointing except at the mitred corners. The beads may be secured with wire nails, brads, or small brass screws with rounded heads. Fastening the beads with glue is a method not to be recommended, as it prevents a broken glass being removed without destroying the beading. Instead of beads, the glass may be fastened in with putty (see pp. 434 and 435), a method which cannot be recommended for cabinet work.

FITTING BEVEL-EDGED SILVERED GLASS.

In fitting bevel-edged silvered plates, there should be sufficient glass behind the rebate to hold the plate securely, without too much of the bevel being hidden. It is sometimes argued that the more glass there is behind the rebate, the more secure the plate will be; but this is not correct, as Figs. 2296 and 2297 show. In Fig. 2296 a bevelled plate with a very narrow margin behind the rebate is illustrated, and in Fig.

2297 a bevelled plate with a very much wider margin. It is evident that the glass, being bevelled, is in contact only with the extreme edge of the rebate, and does not lie flat against the bottom, as in the case of square-edged plates. It is therefore unnecessary to have more than just enough glass to hold within the rebate, and ½ in. is generally sufficient. Less may do occasionally, but cannot be recommended, and it is safest to order the plate ⅜ in. larger than "sight" size. Thus, if the "sight" size is 1 ft. 11⅝ in. by 1 ft. 8⅛ in., order a plate 2 ft. by 1 ft. 8½ in. This allows $\frac{1}{16}$ in. surplus at each edge. The edge is seldom perfectly regular, and this extra $\frac{1}{16}$ in. must be allowed as a waste margin for irregularities in cutting the glass. The term "sight" size, or light size, means the surface of glass visible from the front when the plate is fixed, as contrasted with the rebate or actual size as seen from the back. For irregular or fancy-shaped plates, it is best to get the glass cut from a template, which is made by cutting a thin board, or several joined together, to fit in the rebate, and marking the sight size with a pencil. If the backing board is made to fit within the rebate, draw the template on a sheet of paper, which can easily be stretched on the board. Such templates will give exact sight size, but, when sending them to the glass-cutter, it is best to state on them distinctly that the lines give "sight." When

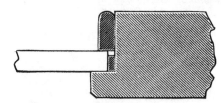

Fig. 2295.—Square-edged Plain Glass Blocked and Beaded in.

it is practicable, frames to be glazed with bevelled silvered plates should, instead of being laid on a table or bench, be supported on trestles, so that the worker by looking underneath can see that the glass shows an equal width of bevel all round, and that the mitres fit accurately to the corners of the framing. Do not attempt to alter the position of a plate by forcing it with a chisel, screwdriver, or other tool used as a lever, as damage to the plate will most likely result. To get a plate into its right position, a few light blows with the hand on the edge of the framing will be sufficient. The directions regarding plain-edged plates are, on the whole, applicable to those with bevelled edges. When fitting these in, however, it will be found in the majority of cases that blocks, as shown in Figs. 2290, 2291, and 2293 are the most suitable. The best method is, first, to get the plate into proper position, then, being careful not to disturb it, fit the blocks in dry—that is, without glue—and then, seeing that the position of the glass has not been accidentally altered, glue down the blocks. It is not always necessary to blacken the edges and inside of the rebate in the case of bevelled plates as in plain ones, but no harm can result from doing so. The blocks

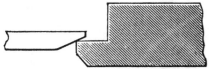

Fig. 2296.—Bevelled Glass with Narrow Margin Hidden.

do not require a high finish; to make them, take a board of 1-in. pine of straight, even grain, and saw a piece about 2 in. wide from one end across the grain. From this shape the blocks by splitting it up into square pieces first, and then diagonally with a knife or chisel. These are good enough for their purpose.

FITTING BEVEL-EDGED PLAIN GLASS.

Bevelled transparent plates are fixed in a similar manner to those with plain edges, but the rebate should be narrow. This can easily be arranged when making the frame, if it is then known that the plate is to be bevelled. If the rebate is too wide it will be better to reduce it to the proper dimensions by gluing on continuous strips of wood, as suggested by Fig. 2298.

FITTING GLASS: FINAL HINTS.

When through some irregularity at the edge a plate will not quite fit, a little judicious paring away of the obstructing wood with a chisel will often do all that is necessary, and is much more satisfactory than trying to chip the glass itself. Careful

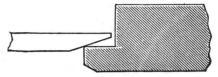

Fig. 2297.—Bevelled Glass with too Wide Margin Hidden.

choice should be made as to which, when fixed, shall be the top or bottom of a piece of glass. For example, in the case of an oblong piece, one end of which will be high up, where it cannot be closely inspected, while the other will be where every defect is conspicuous, it is better to fix the glass so that its worst end, if there is any difference, will be at the top. The chief blemishes found on silvered plates are scratches on the metal or glass, water stains caused during the silvering, and small round bubbles or seeds in the glass itself. But it may be remarked that it is impossible to get an absolutely perfect piece of glass of any size, though it may be sufficiently good for all purposes of the cabinet-maker.

MATERIALS FOR DINNER WAGGON.

The dinner waggon illustrated by Fig. 2299 is very simple, and, when finished, should form a handsome and useful piece of furniture, standing 3 ft. 5 in. long, 1 ft. 5 in. wide, and 3 ft. 8½ in. high from floor to top of pediment when castored. These are the extreme outside measurements. The waggon can be made in mahogany,

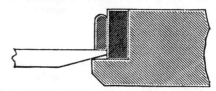

Fig. 2298.—Framed Bevelled Plain Glass with Rebate Filled up.

oak, or walnut, and requires the following pieces of timber: Four 2½-in. pillars, turned to sizes and design in Fig. 2300; six short rails, 2¼ in. by 1 in., for side rails (C, D, E,

Fig. 2300); six long rails, $2\frac{1}{4}$ in. by 1 in., for front and back rails under shelves; three $\frac{3}{4}$-in. shelf boards, 1 ft. $4\frac{1}{2}$ in. by 3 ft. 4 in.; one piece, $1\frac{1}{4}$ in. by 1 in. by 3 ft. long, for

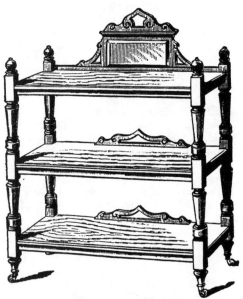

Fig. 2299.—Dinner Waggon.

rail A (Fig. 2301), on which the pediment rests; three pieces of 1-in. stuff for frame of glass back (E D, Fig. 2301); two fret-cut brackets (F, Fig. 2301); one piece for moulding (C, Fig. 2301); one piece for fret for pediment (B, Fig. 2301); two pieces for fret galleries (Fig. 2302); one piece of $\frac{3}{4}$-in. bevelled plate (silvered), 1 ft. by 7 in., and some $\frac{3}{8}$-in. dowel pins. The materials, cut to the desired sizes and glasspapered down, having been obtained, the construction of the waggon can be commenced.

MAKING DINNER WAGGON.

In the two pillars shown in Fig. 2300 where the rails or stretchers come, on which the shelves rest, the wood has been left in the square (5 in. long)—that is, not turned away. On these mark out the position the rails will occupy, starting about $\frac{1}{2}$ in. from the bottom of the square (Fig. 2300), and seeing that they come in the same place on both the pillars. Next take three of the short arms (C, D, E, Fig. 2300), and on both

ends of these mark out the places where the dowels will come, taking care to place them across the wood diagonally, and not in the same straight line; this gives greater strength to the joint. Two dowels will be sufficient, but three would add to the stability of the job. Within the space marked out on the two pillars for the side arms carefully mark the places with a gauge where the other ends of the dowel pins will come, to correspond exactly with those on the end of the arms. With a twist-bit bore a $\frac{3}{8}$-in. hole in each of the spaces marked on the arms and pillars, and glue them afterwards. Into these holes on each end of the arms drive a dowel pin with a mallet, till it stands $\frac{3}{4}$ in. in and $\frac{3}{4}$ in. out. Then fit the outstanding ends into the holes on the side pillars, cramping the whole up tightly, leaving them so for some little time till the glue has set. Now see that the dowels

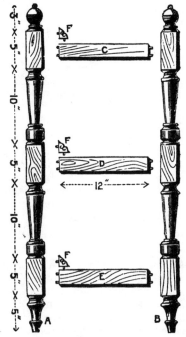

Fig. 2300.—End Framing of Dinner Waggon.

correspond exactly in arms and pillars; if carefully done they should fit firm and square. Proceed to do exactly the same with the other two pillars and three short rails, then the two ends of the waggon are ready. See that the rails are the same height from the ground in both sets, or the shelves will be slanting down on one side or the other. The same instructions with regard to the three front and three back rails can be observed as with the side ones, taking care that all the rails are in the same plane as those at the side. Cramp all up tightly as before. The framework is now complete, and it should stand firm and square.

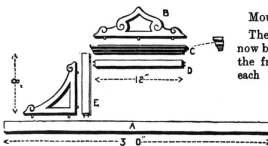

Fig. 2301.—Pediment in Pieces.

on to the rail A in the centre, thus forming the fourth side of the frame. As all this stuff is 1 in., these should be fitted up flush back and front. Now fix rail A (Fig. 2301) in position, fastening it on with screws from under the back rail and through the top board, or as before from above, sinking the heads, filling up those which are exposed afterwards with turned buttons. Be careful to have this fixed square and firm, or the glass when put in will cause it to tilt forward.

MOULDING AND FRETWORK PEDIMENT.

The piece of moulding (C, Fig. 2301) can now be planted on, and on to the top of that the fretwork pediment B. Also fasten at each side a fret-cut bracket (F, Fig. 2301).

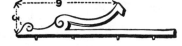

Fig. 2302.—Fret Back or Gallery.

FITTING ON DINNER WAGGON SHELVES.

To fit on the three shelf boards, first cut out from each corner squares, where the pillars will come, and mould or cant off the top edges of the sides and front, as this will much improve the finish and appearance. Having done this, lay the shelves in position, screwing them firmly down with a $2\frac{3}{4}$-in. screw from under the rails, or screw them down from above, sinking the screw-heads, and afterwards fixing in buttons over them to hide the heads.

COMPLETING DINNER WAGGON.

Now commence to build the pediment back and fit it on. This is not a necessary feature, and could be left out if desired. Fig. 2301 clearly shows how it is built up. Let the rail A be $1\frac{1}{4}$ in. by 1 in., and cut to fit exactly between the pillars along the back of the job, as shown in Fig. 2299. Now take two pieces of 1-in. stuff 8 in. long, as shown at E, and one piece 1 ft. long for D (Fig. 2301), and dowel them together as in Fig. 2301, thus forming three sides of an oblong frame, the whole to be dowelled

At the back of the middle and bottom shelf fasten on a piece of $\frac{1}{2}$-in. fret 1 ft. 6 in. long, as shown in Fig. 2302, to form a sort of rail or gallery; this will improve the appearance of the waggon. (See Fig. 2299.) Now put in the glass plate, which should be a $\frac{3}{4}$-in. bevelled plate, and, to prevent its falling through, glue inside the frame, all round, a small bead, and at the back of this put in the plate, fastening it in with pieces of wood glued to the sides of the frame. Then fasten on a backboard, and all is complete. The appearance of the waggon can be still further improved by fastening small brackets at the back pillars on top of the shelf, as shown at F (Fig. 2300). Now thoroughly glasspaper up all joints, and clean up generally. A set of $1\frac{1}{4}$-in. socket or ring castors should be provided. The waggon is completed by polishing.

CHIPPENDALE CABINET.

The cabinet illustrated in front elevation by Fig. 2303, in horizontal section by Fig. 2304, and in vertical section by Fig. 2305, is 3 ft. high to the top of the sash by 2 ft. wide and 1 ft. deep. Shelves can be arranged to suit taste or requirements. The sash is made $\frac{3}{4}$ in. thick, finished, and the bars are $\frac{7}{8}$ in. thick. To set out the bars properly,

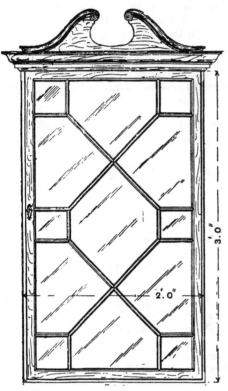

Fig. 2303.—Chippendale Cabinet.

the size of the corner squares must first be decided, and in this case they are 4 in., sight size. Allowing for the bars $\frac{1}{2}$ in. thick, finished, the distance left will be the distance from A to B (Fig. 2305). The cross bars intersect at right angles, and are at an angle of 45° with the horizontal. The two centre squares in the margin work out in size according to the height of the sash, the centre panel being extended or shortened similarly. The sash is set out on a rod and the bars are mitred, being held together by putting a dovetail cut close up to the square of the rebate as at A (Fig. 2306) and gluing in a thin veneer, forming a key. The bars are glued together and dropped into the sash after the latter has

been glued up and cleaned off. The case is formed of $\frac{3}{4}$-in. stuff dovetailed together, the back being tongued and fitted to grooves in the sides and bottom. The top is not dovetailed, but is fitted into a groove prepared in the side and glued and nailed. The fixing will be covered by the cornice, which is mitred round the case, the fixing being obtained by inserting screws from the inside. Figs. 2307 and 2308 illustrate details of cornice. Round the inside of the case on the back is fixed a $\frac{3}{4}$-in. by $\frac{1}{2}$-in. rebated and rounded fillet, which holds a piece of silvered plate glass. The sash is glazed with selected sheet glass or patent plate, and if the work is executed in mahogany it should be stained to imitate rosewood before being polished; if to be ebonised, it may be made in mahogany or basswood.

HANGING CUPBOARD WITH SHELVES.

The hanging cupboard, of which Fig. 2309 shows the front elevation, Fig. 2310 sectional plan, and Fig. 2311 sectional elevation, looks best when made of polished mahogany or walnut, with the raised portions of the panels veneered with walnut burr. A softer wood may, however, be used, such as satin-walnut, or the cupboard may be made of whitewood and enamelled. The sides, two lower shelves, and door framing may be worked out of $\frac{3}{4}$-in. stuff, which, when cleaned up, will finish $\frac{5}{8}$ in.

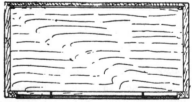

Fig. 2304.—Horizontal Section of Chippendale Cabinet.

The back hanging pieces, brackets, and top shelves may be cut out of $\frac{5}{8}$-in. wood, and the nosings in front of the shelves of stuff that will clean up to $\frac{5}{8}$ in. thick. It is advisable to provide a deal or pine backing for the lock-up portion of the cupboard, as the dust will get in if it depends upon the wall for a back.

MAKING THE HANGING CUPBOARD.

In making the cupboard, the first thing is to prepare the sides, for which two pieces

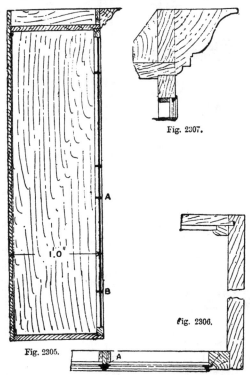

Fig. 2307.

Fig. 2306.

Fig. 2305.

Fig. 2305.—Vertical Section of Chippendale Cabinet. Fig. 2306.—Sash and Side of Cabinet. Fig. 2307.—Cabinet Cornice.

3 ft. by 9½ in. are required. On these mark the positions of the shelves, the top of the lower shelf being 5½ in. from the bottom, the top of the second shelf 11 in. above the top of the lower one, the third shelf 8½ in. above the second, and the top one 6 in. higher than the one below. The ends of the shelves should be sunk into the sides about ¼ in., or, if the two lower shelves are brought forward flush with the front, the sinking should be only as deep as the bead in the front, so that the two beads may be mitred as shown in the front elevation in Fig. 2309. The pattern may be drawn on the sides (see sectional elevation, Fig. 2311) and cut out with the bow or pad saw. The setting-out may be facilitated by covering the side with 1-in. squares.

THE SHELVES OF HANGING CUPBOARD.

The shelves should be 2 ft. 2 in. long, the back of the lower one being rebated ⅜ in. and the second one reduced ⅜ in. in width for the cupboard backing. In addition, pieces 4½ in. by ½ in. should be cut out at the ends of all the shelves at the back to receive the hanging pieces and bottom brackets. To make a good job, the hanging pieces should be rebated into the sides as shown in the sectional plan and detail, and, of course, it will be necessary to get out the rebates with the fillister plane before putting together. Some good glue may now be prepared and the shelves and sides driven together, cramped up, and placed on one side for the glue to set thoroughly. The hanging pieces and brackets are set out in a similar manner to the sides. They should be fixed to the back of the shelves and in the side rebates with glue and 1-in. No. 6 screws. A reference to Fig. 2309 will show that hanging pieces are provided in the lock-up portion for the cupboard doors. These may be ⅞ in. wide, and it is a good plan to let them into the sides and frame them into the shelves when

Fig. 2308.—Elevation of Cabinet Cornice, etc.

putting the cupboard together. The cupboard door panels may be carved to the design shown in Fig. 2312, a section of the carved panel being shown by Fig. 2313. Of course, any suitable design may be adapted for the carving; it should be quite simple, and executed in only slight relief. The stiles and rails of the doors should be 1⅛ in. wide and mortised and tenoned at the corners with the panels grooved in. The method of panelling is shown in the

Fig. 2314 shows the front elevation of an

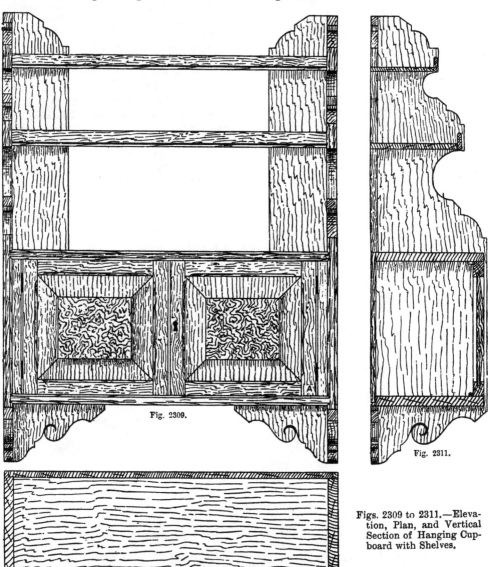

Fig. 2309.

Fig. 2310.

Fig. 2311.

Figs. 2309 to 2311.—Elevation, Plan, and Vertical Section of Hanging Cupboard with Shelves.

sectional plan. The doors should be hung with 1¼-in. by ½-in. brass butt hinges, and a small flush bolt and a lock and key provided to complete the fittings.

oak corner cupboard. The extreme width from angle to angle, measured across the front, is 2 ft. 6 in., and the total height is 6 ft. In Fig. 2315 an outside angle post is shown which may be either turned or worked square as shown, and square parts are left into which the rails are framed. The face parts of these posts may be relieved with carving. Fig. 2316 is a cross section of the cupboard. The doors are hung folding, with dust-proof joints, on brass ornamental hinges which are screwed on the face of the door. The back post is of the bottom of the cupboard showing the joint between the door and the framing. The rail will need no relief in the way of carving, but should only be moulded as shown. Fig. 2318 shows the pot-board, or shelf suitable for a large vase. This shelf is supported on 2-in. by 1½-in. cross rails framed into the legs or posts. In Fig. 2319 is shown a section through the pediment.

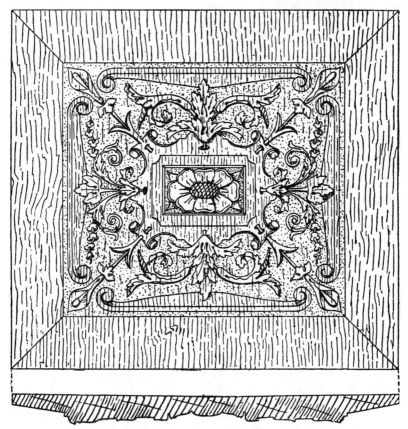

Figs. 2312 and 2313.—Elevation and Section of Carved Panel.

shown rebated to receive the framing of the two sides which face the wall. The outside edges of the shelves are shaped to an easy line, which will take away the stiffness produced by straight lines. The two sides are shown framed in Fig. 2316, and are better than solid sides, preventing cracking, and reducing the weight of the cupboard a little. Fig. 2317 gives a detail These tops may be purchased already worked. The glass fronts of the doors may be formed out into squares or diagonals. The cross bars should be scribed together as shown in Fig. 2320, with a beaded fillet in the back. Bevel-edged plate, if used in the doors, will improve the appearance; it is fitted as previously described. The folding joint of the doors is shown at Fig. 2321;

for hanging joints see Fig. 2322, and for joints at the top and bottom rails see Figs. 2323 and 2324. If an antique appearance is required, the cupboard may be fumigated with ammonia, or it may be washed over

Fig. 2315.   Fig. 2314.

Fig. 2314.—Elevation of Corner Cupboard.
Fig. 2315.—Elevation of Cupboard Angle Post.

with a solution of carbonate of potash, and then polished.

PLATE AND CUTLERY CABINET.

Good, dry walnut or mahogany should be used in the construction of the cabinet of which Fig. 2325 shows the front elevation with one door removed, Fig. 2326 shows end

elevation, and Fig. 2327 shows sectional elevation. The inside dimensions are as follow: Length, 1 ft. 11⅞ in.; width, 1 ft. 3⅜ in.; and height, 1 ft. 1⅜ in. The following quantities of timber are required: For

Fig. 2316.—Horizontal Section of Corner Cupboard.

the top, 2 ft. 3⅜ in. by 1 ft. 6⅞ in. by 1 in.; bottom, 1 ft. 11⅞ in. by 1 ft. 3⅜ in. by 1 in.; moulding, 7 ft. 9 in. by 1 in. by ⅞ in.; framing, 27 ft. 5 in. by 2 in. by 1 in.; panels, 4 ft. 6 in. by 1 ft. 0¾ in. by ½ in., and 1 ft. 9 in. by 11⅜ in. by ½ in.; drawer bottoms, 10 ft. by 1 ft. 2 in. by ⅜ in.; sides, 6 ft. 5 in. by 1 ft. 2 in. by ⅝ in.; drawer fillets, or runners, 10 ft. by ½ in. by ¼ in., and 2 ft. 6 in. by ¾ in. by ¼ in.; dust fillets, 2 ft. by ¾ in. by ⅝ in., and 2 ft. by ⅝ in. by ¼ in. In making, the bottom piece should first be got out square and true, and rebated into the rails of the end and back panel framing, as shown in the enlarged sectional view (Fig. 2328). When that is fixed, a moulding worked to the section is fastened along the bottom

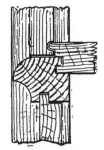

Fig. 2317.—Bottom Rail of Cupboard.   Fig. 2318.—Section of Bottom Shelf.

edges and hides the screw heads. The back is of 2-in. by 1-in. framing, with a ½-in. plain surface panel rebated in. The inner face edges of the framing are relieved with chamfers. The ends are formed of

2-in. by 1-in. stuff, mortised together, and rebated for a ½-in. sunk panel. A moulding is worked on the edges of the end framing.

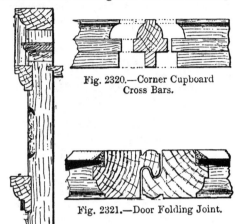

Fig. 2320.—Corner Cupboard Cross Bars.

Fig. 2321.—Door Folding Joint.

Fig. 2319.—Vertical Section through Pediment.

The corners of the panel squares are cut ⅛ in. down, and slightly scored. The back corner stiles are jointed together as shown in the enlarged view, Fig. 2328, which illustrates a part horizontal section of the cabinet. The cabinet top is a plain surface piece of 1-in. stuff, with moulded edges all round, as shown in section by Fig. 2329, and it is secured to the top rails of the ends and back with screws driven from the under-

DOORS OF PLATE AND CUTLERY CABINET.

The doors are hung with 3-in. brass butts, and fitted with a lever lock and flush bolts.

Fig. 2322.—Corner Cupboard Hanging Joint.

The dust fillets along the top and bottom edges of the doors form the rebate in which they close, and the thickness of the ends

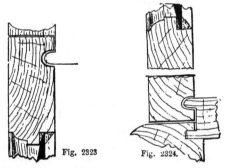

Fig. 2323   Fig. 2324.

Figs. 2323 and 2324.—Sections of Corner Cupboard Top and Bottom Rails.

answers the same purpose. The face of the fillets and ends, and the top and bottom edges of the door, are covered with felt of a sufficient thickness just to bind the doors,

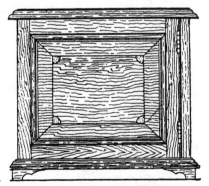

Figs. 2325 and 2326.—Front and End Elevations of Plate and Cutlery Cabinet.

side. The doors are framed from 2-in. by 1-in. stuff, with a ½-in. panel rebated in, the ornamentation being similar to that of the end panels.

thus making the interior air-proof. An enlarged detail of these lined edges is shown by Fig. 2330, the felt being shown by thick black lines.

DRAWERS AND TRAYS OF PLATE AND CUTLERY CABINET.

The cabinet is fitted with five drawers or trays, 1 ft. 11¾ in. long by 1 ft. 2¼ in.

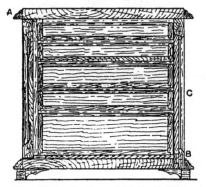

Fig. 2327.—Section of Plate Cabinet.

wide over all. The sides are ⅜ in. thick, dovetailed to the ends, and the bottom is rebated in as indicated in Fig. 2330. The trays are illustrated in plan, which shows how they are spaced out for the various sets. Each article rests in two racks cut to fit the handle and reverse end. These racks are covered with green baize or felt and glued into the tray, any exposed portion of the tray bottom being lined afterwards. The knife tray (Fig. 2331) is 1¾ in. deep, and divided for twelve large knives, twelve small knives, one bread knife, and one butter knife. The fork tray (Fig. 2332) is 1¾ in. deep, and divided for twelve large forks, twelve small forks, one bread fork, two pickle forks, one jam spade, one pair

twelve teaspoons, four knife-rests, four salt-spoons, and a row of serviette rings. The next tray (Fig. 2334) is 1⅞ in. deep, spaced out for carvers, salad servers, nut crackers, and corkscrew, leaving a space 5 in. wide,

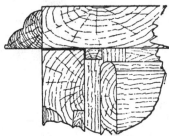

Fig. 2329.—Moulded Edge of Plate Cabinet Top.

which can be used for fish knives and forks, or other articles. The bottom tray, 4 in. deep, requires no divisions, but should be lined with green baize for entrée dishes, soup ladles, grape scissors, salt cellars, etc. The bottom of each drawer should be covered with baize to prevent injury to polished surfaces. Two handles or knobs are required for each drawer, and it is convenient to have small ivory labels screwed on indicating the contents of each tray. Fillets, ½ in. by ¼ in., are grooved into each end of the cabinet; on these the drawers slide (see Fig. 2335). The fillets should be fixed with screws. A detailed view of the fillets is given. The cabinet is mounted upon four feet (Fig. 2336), the bottoms of which are covered with felt. When constructed, the cabinet should be glass-papered, any nail or screw holes stopped, and the whole polished.

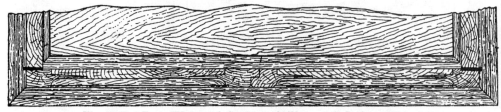

Fig. 2328.—Part Horizontal Section of Plate and Cutlery Cabinet.

of sugar tongs, and one sugar sifter. The spoon drawer (Fig. 2333) is 2¾ in. deep, spaced out for six large tablespoons, twelve small tablespoons, twelve egg-spoons,

COMBINED SIDEBOARD AND BOOKCASE.

The construction of the combined sideboard and bookcase illustrated by Fig. 2337 should be carried out in hard wood as far as concerns all parts that show, but the inside parts may be of pine, as free from knots and shakes as possible; American

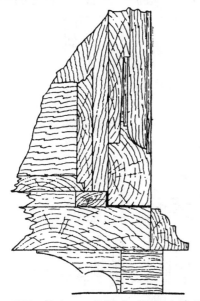

Fig. 2330.—Bottom of Plate Cabinet Bottom Rail.

walnut is very suitable. The top over all is 4 ft. 8 in. by 1 ft. 8 in., and is of ¾-in. stuff. All measurements given are for finished work. This must be remembered

Figs. 2331 and 2332.—Knife Tray and Fork Tray.

Figs. 2333 and 2334.—Spoon Tray and Carver Tray.

when cutting out the various parts. For the base, two pieces are required for front and back uprights, one 4 ft. 7 in. by 4 in.

by ¾ in. for the front, and one 4 ft. 5½ in. by ¾ in. for the back, the latter being of pine. Have also two hardwood sides 1 ft.

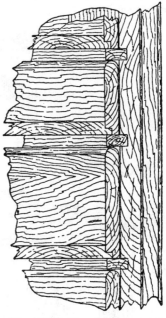

Fig. 2335.—Tray Runners, etc.

6½ in. by 4 in. by ¾ in. The two front corners are mitred, and secured by blocks inside the corners. The two sides run right back

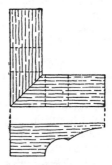

Fig. 2336.—Plate Cabinet Corner Support.

over the ends of the back piece, and two pieces, 1 ft. 5 in. long, 4 in. deep, by ¾ in., run on the edge from front to back, and the front top piece is 4 ft. 6½ in. by 3 in. by ¾ in. The sides are 1 ft. 6 in. by 3 in. by

¾ in., the back being 4 ft. 2½ in. by 3 in. by ¾ in., including 1 in. on each end for the dovetail joint into the sides. The two stretchers are 1 ft. 2 in. by 2½ in., 2 in. of the length also being for dovetails. All

running a piece across the top back as in front. The door frames are 11½ in. wide, 1 ft. 10 in. high, and ¾ in. thick, and are made from stuff 2 in. wide, rebated ⅜ in. to take the panels, which are thus 8½ in. wide

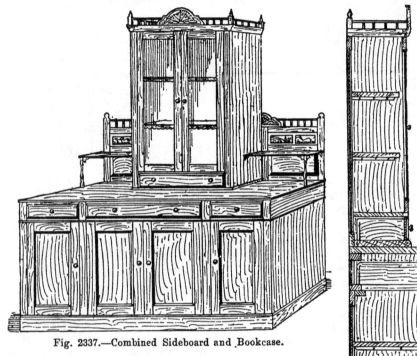

Fig. 2337.—Combined Sideboard and Bookcase.

this top frame may be pine, but the front and sides must have a slip of hardwood, ¾ in. by 1 in. wide, glued along the outside edge, and rounded off as shown in Fig. 2338.

CONSTRUCTION OF THE BASE.

Fig. 2339 fully shows the construction of the base. The sides of the cupboards are 1 ft. 4½ in. wide, 1 ft. 10½ in. high, and ¾ in. thick, the two centre ones being of pine. The uprights carrying the doors are 1 ft. 10½ in. high, 2½ in. wide, and ¾ in. thick; across the top inside is carried a piece of pine, 2½ in. wide by ¾ in., on which the doors butt, and to carry which a piece is cut out of the top front corner of the two inside divisions. When these are in place, cover in the bottom with ½-in. pine, and frame in the back in the ordinary manner,

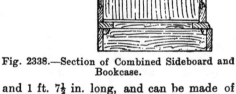

Fig. 2338.—Section of Combined Sideboard and Bookcase.

and 1 ft. 7½ in. long, and can be made of pine, veneered with a figured wood. This improves the appearance, and enhances the value of the finished article. The cupboards and base are now in one solid piece, the sides being screwed on from underneath by a dozen 2½-in. screws, three to each division; and the drawers and bookcase are made complete in themselves. This detachability will be found a great convenience in moving the furniture, and in other ways.

In proceeding with the upper part (Fig. 2340) the four long pieces are got out 4 ft. 4½ in. by 3 in. by ¾ in., the two front edges being faced with strips of hardwood ½ in.

The bookcase side (Fig. 2341) is 3 ft. 8 in. high, 9 in. wide, by ¾ in. The base (pine, with hardwood edge and mitred corners) is 2 ft. 3½ in. by 9¾ in., and ¾ in. thick, with

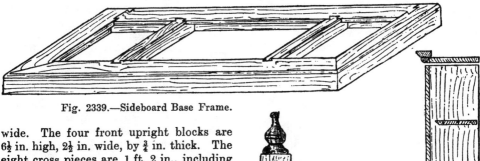

Fig. 2339.—Sideboard Base Frame.

wide. The four front upright blocks are 6½ in. high, 2½ in. wide, by ¾ in. thick. The eight cross pieces are 1 ft. 2 in., including 2 in. for joints, by 3 in. by ¾ in. The two centre uprights are of ½-in. pine, 1 ft. 4½ in. long by 5 in. high, but the two ends are carried right back from the front blocks over all, and are thus 1 ft. 5¼ in. long and 6½ in. wide by ¾ in. The back is closed in with ⅜-in. pine as shown in Fig. 2338. The dimensions of the two small drawers are: Fronts, 11½ in. wide, 5 in. deep, of ¾-in. stuff; sides, 1 ft. 3 in. long, 4¾ in. deep, by ⅜ in.; back, 11½ in. wide, 4 in. deep, by ⅜ in., the front and sides being rebated to take the bottom. The centre drawer dimensions are the same except in regard to the

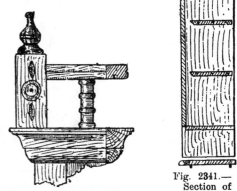

Fig. 2342.—Bookcase Top.

Fig. 2341.— Section of Bookcase.

a rounded edge. The top is the same size, and carries a projecting piece 3 in. wide, with moulded edge. The carved centre

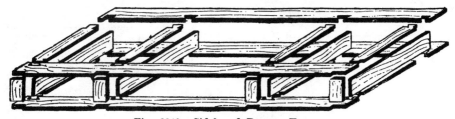

Fig. 2340.—Sideboard Drawer Frame.

width, which is 1 ft. 11 in. When made, insert the drawers in their places, allowing them to go in ½ in., and mark the positions of the guides and stop blocks at the back. A slip of ½-in. quarter-round moulding is placed round the drawer fronts and under the top above the drawers, and also round the door panels; it must be neatly mitred at the corners.

piece and rail round the cornice are shown in Figs. 2342 and 2343, the turned pillars being 1½ in. high, and the corner pieces 1 in. square and 2 in. high, with 1½-in. turned knobs on top. The reeded rail is 1 in. wide and ¼ in. thick. The centre is 5 in. high and 1 ft. long, and the carving can be done with the gouge. The side is rebated to take the bottom shelf of the bookcase, 4½ in. from the bottom, the rebate being $\frac{3}{4}$ in. wide, and stopped 1 in. from the front edge; above this shelf the side is only $8\frac{1}{4}$ in. wide to

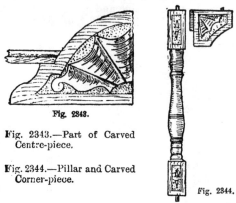

Fig. 2343.

Fig. 2343.—Part of Carved Centre-piece.

Fig. 2344.—Pillar and Carved Corner-piece.

Fig. 2344.

drawer are: Front, 2 ft. $0\frac{1}{2}$ in. long, $4\frac{1}{2}$ in. deep, by $\frac{3}{4}$ in.; sides, $7\frac{1}{2}$ in. long, $4\frac{1}{4}$ in. deep, by $\frac{3}{8}$ in.; back, 2 ft. $0\frac{1}{2}$ in. long, 4 in. deep, by $\frac{3}{8}$ in. The side frames for the panels are 1 ft. $2\frac{1}{2}$ in. long, $1\frac{1}{4}$ in. at each end being for the mortises, $1\frac{1}{2}$ in. wide by $\frac{3}{4}$ in., and the inside upright is 1 ft. 2 in. high, $1\frac{1}{2}$ in. wide, by $\frac{3}{4}$ in., the outside upright being 1 ft. 6 in. (allowing $1\frac{1}{2}$ in. for the rounded top), $1\frac{1}{2}$ in. wide by $\frac{3}{4}$ in. Before finally fixing, put the frames in position and mark off a rebate for the panel, $\frac{1}{4}$ in. deep, all round the bottom part, and also one the same depth round the top to take the glass, mount, and photos, or another panel if preferred. The panels are 6 in. high and 1 ft. $0\frac{1}{2}$ in. long. The shelves

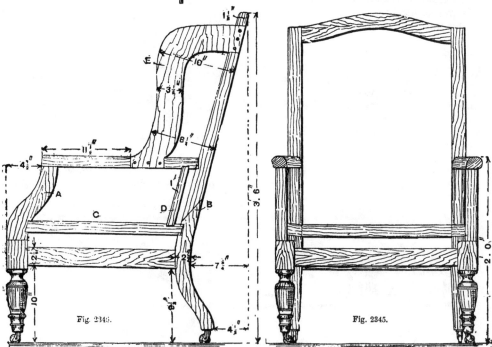

Fig. 2346.

Fig. 2345.

Figs. 2345 and 2346.—Front and Side Elevations of Grandfather or "Cheek" Easy-chair Frame.

allow the doors to come flush. The doors are 3 ft. 2 in. long, 1 ft. 1 in. wide, by $\frac{3}{4}$ in., and are framed of stuff 2 in. wide, and rebated to take the glass panels, which fit in from the back, and are held by slips all round. The dimensions of the stationery

are 1 ft. $2\frac{3}{4}$ in. long, 5 in. wide, by $\frac{1}{2}$ in., and are screwed through from the back, and through the side of the bookcase, being carried by turned pillars (Fig. 2344). The pillars are $1\frac{1}{4}$ in. square and $7\frac{3}{4}$ in. high, and are dowelled at the top and bottom.

There are eight of the small corner pieces (see Fig. 2344), two from the bookcase, two from the back frame, and two from each pillar.

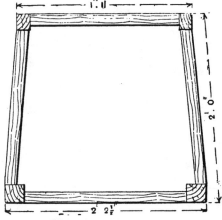

Fig. 2347.—Seat Frame.

GRANDFATHER OR " CHEEK " EASY-CHAIR FRAME.

The frame illustrated by Fig. 2345, showing front elevation without " cheek," and

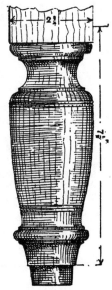

Fig. 2348.—Front Leg of Easy-chair.

by Fig. 2346, showing side elevation, is for what is generally known as a " cheek,"

or " grandfather " easy chair. It is stuffed all over, the only parts of the framework seen being the legs. Mahogany or walnut is suitable for the legs, and birch could be used for the other parts of the frame. Fig. 2347 shows a plan of the seat frame, and Fig. 2348 shows the pattern of the front legs, which are $2\frac{3}{4}$ in. thick, and are turned to fit cup castors at the bottom, and mortised for the front and side rails, keeping them flush on the outside. The ends of the front legs should be kept 1 in. above the top edges of the rails, where the stumps A (Fig. 2346) meet them. The back legs are made up in two pieces spliced at B by means of glue and screws. Make a mould of thin pine for the back leg, line out on wood $1\frac{3}{4}$ in. thick, and cut out to the shape. After dressing up to the size, grip the back legs

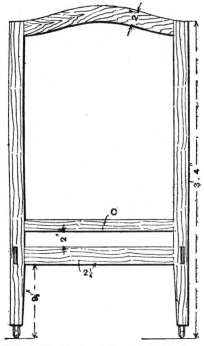

Fig. 2349.—Back of Easy-chair Frame.

together and mark them for the mortises, the positions of which are shown in Fig. 2349. The front rail, side rails, and back rail are $2\frac{1}{4}$ in. wide by $1\frac{1}{2}$ in. thick. The back stuffing rail c (Fig. 2349), $1\frac{1}{2}$ in. wide by 1¼ in. thick, is tenoned to the back legs ; it should be flush on the inside. Allow a space of 2 in. between the top edge of the bottom rail and the bottom edge of the

back leg in the same manner, and should be 2 in. away from the top edge of the seat rail. The arm rail is 2 in. wide by 1½ in. thick, and is dowelled to the stump and

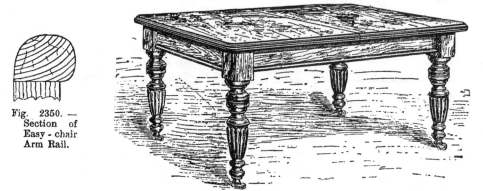

Fig. 2351.—Extending Dining Table.

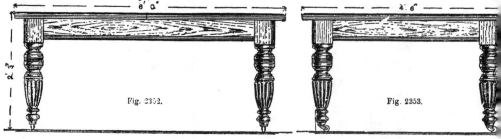

Fig. 2350. — Section of Easy - chair Arm Rail.

stuffing rail. The shaped top rail is 1½ in. thick, tenoned to the back legs, with a rebate on the top. The top edge should be well rounded over. The back legs are tapered on the inside to 1½ in. at the bottom. The back may be cramped together after mortising for the side rails. The front legs and rail should next be fixed together. A half-plan of the seat should be drawn full size to obtain the shoulders for the side rails. Set a bevel stock to the required bevel for marking the shoulders.

back leg. The upright stuffing rail D (Fig. 2346) is housed into the bottom stuffing rail and arm rail, and cheek-nailed ; it is ¾ in. distant from the back leg. The cheeks E (Fig. 2346) are cut out of 1-in. stuff, and shaped to the sizes given in Fig. 2346. It is let into a rebate cut in the arm rail and screwed. The top of the back leg is also rebated to receive the cheek. The inside edge of each cheek should be well rounded over. Fig. 2350 shows a section of the arm rail. The seat of the frame is ½ in. higher

Figs. 2352 and 2353.—Side and End Elevations of Extending Dining Table.

The tenons are square with the shoulders, and the rails should be made flush on the outside. The shaped stumps A (Fig. 2346), cut out of 1½-in. wood, are dowelled to the top of the front legs. The stuffing rail C (Fig. 2346) is housed into the stump, and glued and cheek-nailed ; it is fixed to the

at the front than the back. The frame is now in a condition for upholstering.

UPHOLSTERY.

It is outside the scope of this book to give detailed instruction on upholsterer's work. A special treatise is necessary to deal with this branch profitably, and nothing more than a few hints on the work can be given here (see p. 703). But readers desirous of doing their own upholstery will learn all they require to know on the subject from a handbook which the Editor of THE HANDYMAN'S BOOK has now in course of preparation.

stuff glued to a backing as shown. The inner rails or slides and the two cross rails should be of hardwood, such as beech or birch. The screw can be obtained from any large furnishing ironmonger. In constructing the framework, first plane the stuff to the sizes given, and then set out the mortises of the legs and the tenons of the rails,

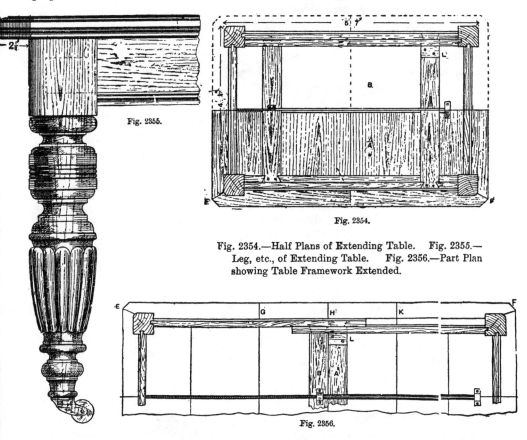

Fig. 2355.

Fig. 2354.

Fig. 2354.—Half Plans of Extending Table. Fig. 2355.—Leg, etc., of Extending Table. Fig. 2356.—Part Plan showing Table Framework Extended.

Fig. 2356.

EXTENDING DINING TABLE.

The extending dining table shown by Fig. 2351, and of which Figs. 2352 and 2353 illustrate side and end elevations respectively (Fig. 2354 is a half plan of table), is simple in construction, and should be of mahogany, oak, or walnut. The legs can be obtained ready turned, or, if preferred, can be turned from stuff about 5 in. square. The outer rails for the framework may be solid, or the outside portion may be of $\frac{1}{2}$-in.

as shown in Fig. 2355. The mortises for the inner sliding rails are farther from the front edge of the legs than those for the outer rails, as shown in Figs. 2354, 2356, and 2357. The slides should be ploughed from their top edges, 1 in. wide and $\frac{1}{2}$ in. deep. This groove can be made with a $\frac{1}{2}$-in. plough-iron, or with a rebate plane by fixing a piece of wood at the right distance parallel to the top edge. A piece of hardwood should be planed so as just to fit in the grooves, and should then be firmly glued into the groove of the inner rail. The moulding on the bottom of the outer rails o (Figs. 2357 and 2358) should next be fixed with glue and screws. The cross rails A and B (Figs. 2356 and 2357) should be dove-

The top should be dowelled and glued, and the under-sides of the top and leaves trued up. Next join together the two portions of the permanent top and the two leaves, and dowel them with hardwood pins about $\frac{3}{8}$ in. in diameter, projecting about $\frac{5}{8}$ in. (see Fig. 2360). The whole top should then be turned bottom side up and the framework

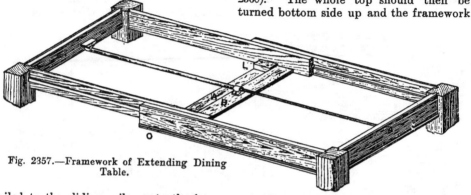

Fig. 2357.—Framework of Extending Dining Table.

tailed to the sliding rails; B to the inner rails, and A into the projecting moulding, as shown in Figs. 2354 and 2359. Care must be taken in making these dovetails, or the rails, not being parallel, will prevent proper working. When all the joints fit

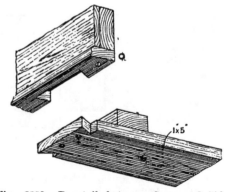

Fig. 2358.—Section of Sliding Rails.

properly, those between the legs and the rails, and between the cross rails and the latter, should be glued together, keeping the legs and rail square. The cross rails should also have a couple of screws inserted, as shown in Fig. 2359.

Top of Extending Table.

The top must be of well-seasoned material. If it can be obtained in about 1-ft. 6-in. widths, each half will require only one joint. The leaves are also 1 ft. 6 in. wide.

stretched out to its full length, as shown in Fig. 2356, and fastened to the two permanent parts of the top by screws inserted obliquely, as shown in Fig. 2358.

Fixing the Screw and Barrel.

The screw and barrel should now be fixed, the handle end of the screw being secured

Fig. 2359.—Dovetail between Cross and Side Rails.

to the end rail of the table. The box in which the screw works, and which holds one end of the barrel, can be fixed to the cross rail B (Figs. 2356 and 2357), the other end of the barrel being secured to the under-side of the top; it may be necessary to fix a wood block to the under-side of the top for this purpose. Next tighten the screw a

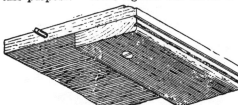

Fig. 2360.—Corner of Table Leaf

COMPLETING THE EXTENDING TABLE.

The thicknessing fillet shown in section by D (Fig. 2358), with a small bead worked on one edge and the other rounded, should next be prepared. It should be mitred at the angles E and F (Figs. 2354 and 2356) and fixed with glue and screws. It is best to have the two side pieces long enough to reach from end to end, thus taking in the

Fig. 2361.—Chiffonier Sideboard.

little so as to hold the top firmly together, plane the top and leaves, and work the moulding round the edges.

two leaves; then cut with a fine saw where the joints of the leaves should occur, as shown by G, H, and K (Fig. 2356). A stop

L (Figs. 2354, 2356, and 2357) prevents the framework moving too far. The table when closed is 6 ft. long, and will extend to 9 ft. with two 1-ft. 6-in. leaves. It would be firmer if it extended to 8 ft. 6 in. only, the leaves being 1 ft. 3 in. wide. This would give the sliding rails a lap of 2 ft. (Fig. 2362), the cupboards B, the drawers C, and the glass back and cornice D. The extreme height from floor to top of centre ornament is 7 ft., and extreme width over nosing of sideboard top 4 ft. 7 in. Fig. 2362 is a side elevation, and Fig. 2363 half front elevation; these are to a scale of

Fig. 2362.   Fig. 2363.   Fig. 2364.

Figs. 2362 and 2363.—Side and Half Front Elevations of Chiffonier Sideboard.
Fig. 2364.—Section of Bottom of Chiffonier Sideboard.

instead of 1 ft. 6 in. In Fig. 2354, A is a half plan looking up, and B an ordinary half plan with the top removed.

CHIFFONIER SIDEBOARD BUILT IN SECTIONS.

The chiffonier sideboard illustrated in Fig. 2361 is designed with a view to portability. It is made in five parts : the stand A

1 in. to a foot. Fig. 2364 is a section of the bottom part of sideboard, showing moulding of doors, panels, etc., drawn quarter full size. Fig. 2365 gives half plan of bottom, showing the deal framing, also the method of attaching the legs. The scale of this figure is 1½ in. to the foot. To construct the sideboard, make a frame of

2-in. by 1¾-in. deal as A (Figs. 2364 and 2365), 4 ft. 4¾ in. long by 1 ft. 6 in. wide, with cross-rails in the position shown. From centre to centre of the cross-rails, and from the front to within ¾ in. of the back edge of the frame, must be covered with mahogany ¼ in. thick, as shown in Figs. 2364 and 2365. A strip of mahogany, 1½ in. wide, is planted on the remaining part of the front rails of the frame. The rest of the frame is made up level with strips of deal 2 in. wide, with the exception of the ¾ in. left at the centre of the back. The edge of the front and ends of the frame should be made straight and square.

Legs of Sideboard.

The legs are 6 in. long, 3½ in. wide, and 1¼ in. thick. The front corner legs are

Fig. 2365.—Half Plan of Bottom Framing.

mitred lengthways, and a tongue is grooved into them. Fig. 2365 shows how the legs are connected to the frame by shouldering and screwing. The legs should project ⅝ in. from the frame when fixed, and the space between them should be filled up with ⅝-in. mahogany, with two reeds as shown at c (Fig. 2364). The brackets (see Fig. 2363) are then screwed into the frame and leg. They are made from ⅝-in. mahogany, and are kept back ¼ in. from the face of the legs.

Sideboard Cupboards and Shelves.

The two cupboards are next taken in hand. The framing of the end and door is of 3½-in. by 1¼-in. mahogany, moulded as shown at D (Fig. 2364). The panels a are of ⅞-in. mahogany, moulded and raised;

the width of the side frame is 1 ft. 5 in., and of the door 1 ft. 6½ in.; the height of both is 2 ft. The side of the cupboard towards the centre of the sideboard is formed of ⅞-in. mahogany, or of yellow pine veneered. This side is to be ¾ in. narrower than the panelled end. The back stile of the panelled end should be rebated out ¾ in. square to take the back. The top and bottom are of ½-in. pine dovetailed into the plain side and stiles of the panelled side, while the rails of the panelled side are rebated to suit. The door is hung on the panelled side; and an ordinary box lock on the plain side, with the catch fixed to the door, will prevent disfigurement with a keyhole. Four small corner pieces are nailed on the bottom of the cupboard to fit exactly in the space F (Fig. 2365), to prevent the cupboard moving when placed on the stand. The back, which is of ½-in. matchboard, should cover only half of the plain side edge to form a rebate for the back of the centre opening. The shelves may be to suit the maker's fancy; three in the left cupboard and one in the right, high enough to take a bottle underneath, will be found convenient. They are of ½-in. pine. Ledges must be screwed across the cupboard inside to carry the shelves.

Frames of Chiffonier Sideboard.

The back of the centre opening consists of a frame of 3½-in. by ¾-in. mahogany, rebated to receive a plain panel of ½-in. mahogany. This fits into the ¾-in. rebate left in the bottom and plain sides of the cupboard, and is kept in place by two brads on each side at the back. Another frame, similar in external dimensions to the one made for the bottom, but of 2-in. by 1¼-in. deal, with two cross-rails of 3-in. by 1¼-in. deal, 1 ft. 5⅓ in. from outsides of frame to centre of rail, is shown in part section at G (Fig. 2364); also a top frame of the same external size, but of 2-in. by 1½-in. deal, with one cross-rail in the centre, is shown at H (Fig. 2364). These two frames are connected on the front edge by the uprights, 1¼ in. by 1½ in., a mahogany strip between the drawers being mortised into them, keeping the frames 4¼ in. apart inside. The faces of the uprights are kept 3/16 in. in front of the deal framing, and flush with the drawer fronts, to avoid showing the joint of deal and mahogany strip carried round under the drawers. Matchboard ½ in. thick is nailed on the back of the frames to keep them at the right distance apart, and also to form a finish for the back. A strip of mahogany, 1¼ in. by ⅝ in., with one reed, is carried round the front and two ends of the bottom frame, as shown at K (Fig. 2364).

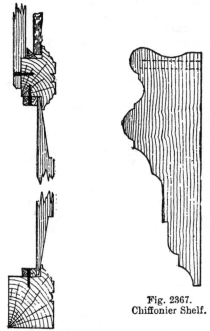

Fig. 2366.—Section of Side Glass and Panel

Fig. 2367. Chiffonier Shelf.

Pieces to the width of centre uprights, and of a width to fill the remainder of the space at the ends, and ¾ in. thick, are nailed to the four cross-rails of the bottom frame, and form guides for the drawers.

SOME DETAILS OF THE CHIFFONIER SIDEBOARD.

The cornice moulding is mitred round the top frame front and each end (M, Fig. 2364). The drawer fronts are of ⅞-in. mahogany; the sides, back, and bottom are ½-in. yellow pine. The top of the sideboard is of mahogany, 1 ft. 7 in. wide and ½ in. thick, moulded as shown at N (Fig. 2364); it is fixed by screws along the front edge, and by buttons at each end, and to the cross-rail and back. Nail corner pieces on top of the cupboards to fit openings in the frame, in the same way as for the bottom frames. The two brackets in the centre opening are screwed in flush with the inner sides of the cupboard when the doors are opened. Fig. 2366 gives a section of the glass back (half size). The brackets and shelves are attached by screws through the back. The brackets are fixed on centre stiles only. Fig. 2367 gives a pattern for the shelf. If desired, a second shelf might be fixed over the side mirrors, the bracket being put on the outside stiles only.

THE SIDEBOARD PEDIMENT.

The pediment may be made separately, and attached by screws to the frame over the centre glass. Two wire dowels are driven in the bottom rail of the back, and fit into two holes bored in the sideboard top. Two brass "ears" are attached to the back of the frame, between the top of side brackets and cornice, to form a means of fixing the back to the wall. The side brackets are of ¾-in. mahogany, and are kept ¼ in. back from the face of the framing, into which they are fixed by screws. As the moulding and general style of this sideboard are of an old massive type, it will be inadvisable to use bevelled silvered glass. The following would be more suitable: One best silvered plate, 2 ft. 8 in. by 1 ft. 10½ in., and two, 1 ft. by 1 ft. 2 in. These sizes allow a margin all round the rebate, which should be fitted with several wedge-shaped pieces glued in as shown at Fig. 2366. A thin back is then screwed over all to keep out dust, etc.

REPAIRING FURNITURE.

In the repairing of broken furniture, first examine thoroughly the article, and, having decided how it is to be dealt with, get all tools and materials ready before beginning operations. If the article is to be glued and screwed, bore the holes and turn the screws into their places before any glue is put on; if handscrews or clamps are to be used, see that suitable ones are provided, and try them in the places they are intended to occupy ; and, if wedges or bevel blocks are required, have them in readiness. Take the article to pieces, glue up with hot thin glue, and put together again, and the result should be satisfactory. It must not be forgotten that glue will not hold unless the surfaces of the wood are in contact.

SCREWING UP BROKEN WORK.

A well-fitting screw, wherever possible, is the best thing with which to mend broken work. But dowels, or nails and screws, are sometimes used. When driving in dowels, there is always a tendency to drive the joined surfaces apart, however well they may be secured, and this accident is inevitable if the dowels touch the bottom of the holes ; while on the other hand a screw is always pulling the surfaces together. Care, however, should be taken to use screws of a size proportionate to the work, and, within reason, the finer the screws are the better ; because the larger the number of threads that are forced into the wood the better will the screw hold.

REPAIRING CHAIR BACKS.

The method of repairing the backs of the old-fashioned dining-room chairs, that have a broad flat back fitted by a dovetail on the top of the sides, is an illustration of the use of unsuitable screws. When these backs work loose, they are usually repaired with glue and with a screw driven through the back of the upright ; generally about a $\frac{3}{4}$-in. No. 9 or No. 10 screw is used. When the backs work loose again and are taken off, it is found that the screw has penetrated the back for about $\frac{1}{4}$ in. and is holding with only two or three threads ; these break out with such little force that they are practically useless. If, however, a No. 5 or No. 6 1-in. screw is used, and is bored carefully in, coming as near the front as safety will allow, it will be found that there is a $\frac{5}{8}$-in. hold instead of $\frac{1}{4}$ in., with perhaps seven or eight threads instead of two ; and a much neater as well as stronger job is the result, the small head of the screw being carefully countersunk and neatly filled up. Again,

screw-holes should be bored so as to fit the neck as well as the thread of the screw, for if this is not done the screw will always have a tendency to work loose ; the same care should be taken in making holes for nails. For work of this kind small half-twist bits are very useful.

REPAIRING CURVED FRAMINGS, ETC.

If the article to be mended has any curved framing, such as easy-chair seat frames, etc., care must be taken to get them well up at the joints. Pieces are very frequently found glued in where cramping nicks have been cut when the frame was made ; these should be knocked out, and the cramp put in the nicks to draw them well up. Many

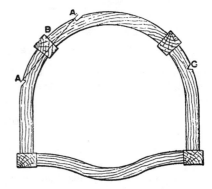

Fig. 2368.—Chair Seat Frame.

frames are, however, framed up with a band cramp, no nicks being required. In such cases some frames are cut when repairing. Strike a line across the joint, and cut two pieces out of the rails in such a position that the pull of the cramp will be directly through the middle of the joint (see Fig. 2368). The letter references in this figure are : A A, position of nicks to cramp on back foot B ; C, position of nick to cramp front foot to side rail.

DOWEL HOLES IN RE-FRAMING WORK.

In re-framing work of this class, take care that the dowel holes are deep enough, and that the dowels are not too long, for in the cheap goods now so common it will frequently be found that the dowels touch the bottom of the holes, and prevent the joint going up close. If after every effort the joint still gapes somewhere (which it frequently will through not being properly cut at first), fit a small wedge and glue it tightly in, so as to prevent any working of the joint, for it is the presence of these little

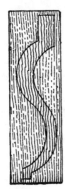

Fig. 2369.—Marking out Cabriole Leg.

spaces that causes the frames to twist about, leading ultimately to broken dowels and similar accidents.

Substitutes for Plates in Furniture Repairing.

Occasionally in a very bad case a well-fitting plate or square may be necessary as an auxiliary to other methods, but the common plan of screwing a plate that does not fit over a joint that does not touch and filling up the rest with glue is worse than useless. If the fracture is concealed from sight, as in a stuffing frame, a better plan than using a plate is, after gluing and screwing, to well glue the joint, and wrap it round with a piece of strong canvas saturated with hot thin glue, and well rub down with the hand. This will dry nearly as hard as the wood, and will defy almost every effort to get it off again. In splicing, or otherwise fitting on pieces, it is an excellent plan, after doing as much as possible with the chisel, etc., to scrape the surfaces the way of the grain with a fine sharp toothing iron. This not only roughens the surface and gives the glue a better hold, but if carefully done removes ridges and humps and gives a truer and more even face to the joint, care being taken, of course, not to

work it out of truth. For holding pieces on while the glue is drying, handscrews of various sizes are generally used, but for small work a handier tool is a small thumb-cramp, of the same shape as the G-cramp illustrated by Fig. 109, p. 29.

Cutting out Chair Cabriole Legs.

Among the jobs that are often considered difficult are the cutting out and fitting of new cabriole legs to chairs, etc. (see Fig. 2369). The job is not nearly so difficult as it looks, though much care is required, and the details of the operation must be well mastered before any beginning is made, or good stuff may be wasted. The first thing required is a correct mould. To make this, procure a good clean picture-frame backboard, free from knots and shakes. Lay the chair on its side, or in the most convenient position, and carefully-trace on the board the line of the existing leg, testing it by setting up the square against the leg in several places, and seeing that it comes down on to the line of the pattern. Then cut out the pattern with a sharp chisel or knife, and trim up neatly. It is a good plan to glue a piece of fine canvas over one side of the mould, and trim it off when dry; this will allow it to be bent into hollows and curves without fear of snapping. A waste strip of blind union will answer the

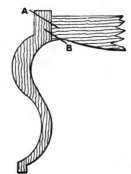

Fig. 2370.—Cabriole Leg Dowelled on.

purpose. A front leg, being the simplest, as only one mould is required, may be first taken as an example. Having got out the mould, select a square piece of scantling of the required size, or a piece of plank of the necessary thickness, remembering that one angle of the square will form the front, and the other the back of the leg, and arranging any flaws, etc., accordingly. Then place the mould on one side of the piece, strike it out, and saw out with band-

Fig. 2371.—Angle-iron and Chair Cross-bar.

saw or frame-saw. If the latter is used, it is well to square a line over and mark it out again on the bottom side to ensure square sawing. Then place the pattern on the other (cut) side and mark out the other lines, making sure that the same angle is kept for the back; a mistake is very easily made here by taking one of the outside edges. This, when sawn out, will give a leg in the rough. The back angle will now, with perhaps a little planing, fit into the space between the ends of the front and side rails.

FITTING ON CHAIR CABRIOLE LEG.

It is by far the better plan in putting on a new front leg to cut away the old tenons, fit the leg into the angle, and then dowel in, springing the frame open to allow the dowels to enter. The leg should be cut (carved and shaped) and nearly finished before being put in, leaving only a little cleaning off to be done last. A back leg is, of course, more difficult, as two moulds are required, one for each face, and the stay and top must be arranged for; but the principle is the same. The seat rails should be fitted first, then the stay, and the height cut off last. Care must also be taken to get the leg upright, which can be tested by measuring from back foot to front, etc., trying the new one by the old. This

remark applies also to the front legs. A method of procedure of putting on a cabriole leg when the chair is well made and properly blocked is as follows: The broken leg and tenons may be cut away, leaving the rails held in position by the block. The leg is then fitted into its place, and two dowels are bored into the end of the front rail, and a dowel hole downward and backward through the lower part of the side rail and out on the under edge of the rail at the curve just behind the leg. The holes in the foot are next bored, and the leg is cramped on to the front rail; then, with the cramp on from back to front, a dowel is bored at A (Fig. 2370) through the stuffing square above the carving into the side rail, the hole in the bottom edge of the rail being continued into the leg with a ratchet brace, and a dowel at B driven through the rail into the leg, making a sound and neat job, without any difficulty. If a ratchet brace is not available for jobs of this kind, and an ordinary brace cannot be used, a handy substitute may be made by fitting a hardwood cross-handle on to the top of the twist-bit and converting it into a temporary worm auger, a bit of twine being twisted over the handle and round the neck of the bit to assist in drawing the bit out.

Fig. 2372.—Chair Ball Foot.

REPAIRING CHAIR CROSS-BARS.

Up to somewhat later than the middle of the seventeenth century it was the rule that chairs should be tied by cross-bars mortised into the legs near the ground; and rough usage and exposure will often cause these mortises to work loose. Provided the wood is sound, the joint may again be made firm by driving in one or more thin glued wedges. If moisture has lodged in the joint, and tenon and mortise are alike tender, still drive in wedges to tighten the joint, but in addition screw an angle-iron (Fig. 2371) be-

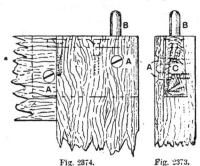

Fig. 2374.   Fig. 2373.

Figs. 2373 and 2374.—Chiffonier Door Stud Hinge, etc.

neath the cross-bar; this, if let into the wood, will scarcely be seen, especially as it must be painted to match. Such irons may be used with advantage for strengthening other work, as the upper frames of tables, etc.

RENEWING BALL FEET OF CHAIRS AND TABLES.

The smaller tables, as well as chairs, joint-stools, etc., commonly stand on ball feet, and these may become defective. To substitute new feet is, however, a simple matter. The original limbs are sawn off, as in Fig. 2372, and holes are bored as shown, and in them the shanks of new ball feet, turned to match the old, are glued.

TREATMENT OF RUSTED-IN NAILS.

Nails are sometimes thoroughly rusted into the wood. Should the nail come out leaving a clean hole, a mere stopping of coloured putty—putty kneaded with van-dyke brown or burnt umber—may suffice. If it is difficult to get a good grip on these old nails without bruising and disfiguring the surface, it is better to sink a hole round the head with the gouge till a firm hold can be obtained. The hole so made can be readily trimmed to shape, and a fresh piece of wood let in and glued, due care being

given to direction of grain, etc. Indeed, when a screw from the front seems desirable to strengthen any crazy piece of old work, it will be found that to countersink deeply, and to hide the head in this manner, is the best thing.

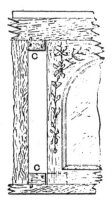

Fig. 2375.—Part of Chiffonier Door.

REPAIRING CHIFFONIER OR SIDEBOARD DOOR.

Repairing a chiffonier door where the stud hinges have been broken off, and there is a difficulty in removing the upper part, is a rather awkward job, though it may be accomplished in the following manner: Fit two pieces of well-seasoned English elm at the upper and lower corners of the door; these should be slightly dovetailed as shown

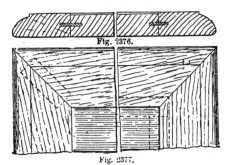

Fig. 2376.

Fig. 2377.

Figs. 2376 and 2377.—Part of Leather-covered Table Top.

in end view at C (Fig. 2373). Each piece is secured with two screws A (Figs. 2373 and 2374) from the inside. The new studs B are then let in and screwed to these pieces, but they must occupy the original position. The screws are next taken out and the dovetailed pieces withdrawn and slipped in their positions c (Fig. 2375) in the chiffonier frame, hot glue being applied to the joining parts, and the door is slid over the dovetails. The screws will then house in well, and this completes the job.

RE-COVERING WRITING TABLE TOP.

In re-covering a writing table top, first clean off the old leather covers and well smooth the surface with glasspaper. For roans, moroccos, and leather cloths, make a paste of rye-flour and boiling water, stirring well to keep it free from lumps, and for oilcloths use hot, thin glue. Cut the leather rather larger than the space to be covered, then paste the top, rubbing well in with a stiff brush and picking out lumps. Next warm the leather before a fire or stove, place it on the table top, and, commencing in the centre, with a cork pad work out the wrinkles and puckers to the ends and side. Continue stroking until the leather lies quite flat, then dress it off with a sharp, thin-bladed knife and lay down the edges. For thin leather cloth a rubber-covered squeegee is even better than the cork pad. For oilcloth the process is the same, but hot thin glue is used as the sticking medium. Start smoothing in the centre and keep the hands clean. No advantage will be gained in wetting the cloth, and if paste is used it should be as thick as starch. Writing table tops having leather centres usually are constructed as in Figs. 2376 and 2377, which show a section and plan respectively, the moulded rim being mitred round the centre and fixed with a ploughed and tongued joint. The rim stands $\frac{1}{16}$ in. bare above the centre, so that when the leather is laid it will lie flush. The rim is cleaned off flush with a small piece of the leather to be used in covering. The best covering is tanned sheepskin (levant is the trade term), but for common work good American oilcloth can be employed, this having a linen back and being capable of folding without cracking; a cracked material could not be tolerated.

STRAIGHTENING WARPED TABLE TOP.

To straighten a round table top that is warped across the centre, first remove the top from the pillar, turn it face downwards, and sponge several times with clean water. Then apply heavy weights or pressure at its highest points for several days, frequently damping the unpolished part. Water should not be allowed to remain on the polished portion. To prevent the top going back again, glue and screw several strengthening bars across.

44

DRAWING ROOM FURNITURE.

INTRODUCTORY REMARKS.

THIS chapter will give designs and instructions for making many of the more important articles of furniture that find their place in the sitting-room, parlour, and drawing room. Taken as a whole, they are not difficult examples of work, while in most cases their design is pleasing and appropriate, and their construction will be found a pleasure by the handyman who has

mahogany, and is shown to be made in the solid. The shelves are quadrant-cornered with breaks, and may be left plain, or inlaid

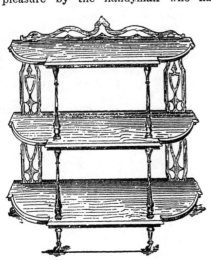

Fig. 2378.—Centre Whatnot.

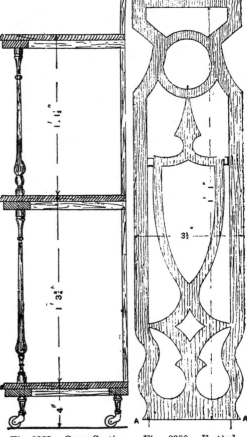

Fig. 2379.—Cross Section of Whatnot.

Fig. 2380.—Fretted Back Pillar of Whatnot.

worked through such a graduated course as this book has endeavoured to present.

CENTRE WHATNOT.

Fig. 2378 is a general view in perspective, Fig. 2379 a vertical section, and Fig. 2380 an illustration of a back pillar of a large centre whatnot of light appearance but strong construction. The design is suitable for execution either in walnut or

to either of the alternative designs shown in the two half plans (Fig. 2381). The height to the top shelf is 2 ft. 9¼ in., the length over all 2 ft. 6 in., and the width 11 in. The shelves are of ⅝-in. stuff, and are lined up underneath with rails of ¾-in. by 2¼-in. section, which give an appearance

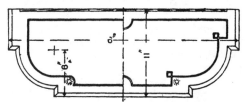

Fig. 2381.—Half Plans of Whatnot Shelves.

of solidity and also prevent the shelves warping. The end pieces which run across the grain in the shelves should be slot-screwed—that is, after the holes are bored through the lining piece for the screws, a small slot or mortise is made across the hole in the direction of shrinkage of the stuff, and the edges of the slot should be slightly chamfered to allow the head of the screw to slip easily. No glue should be employed with the end pieces, but the front lining may be glued as well as screwed on, as shown in Fig. 2382. The quadrant corner of the lining should have the grain running as shown in Fig. 2383, when its shrinkage will not affect the joints; nor will it prevent the top shrinking. These pieces also may be glued on. A full-size drawing similar to Fig. 2379 should be set out as a preliminary to the construction; it is unnecessary to draw in the details of the pillars, as a pattern of these must be prepared separately for the turner, unless a

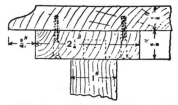

Fig. 2382.—Front Edge of Whatnot Shelf.

stock pattern is used, in which case the pillars should be obtained first, and the rod set out to suit. The shelves are spaced differently in Fig. 2379 to give more accommodation for various sized vases, etc., and

also improve the appearance. The expense will be a little more, as pillars of different length are required. If the shelves are to be inlaid, the stringings should also be obtained before beginning, as they vary in width, and a suitable scratch must be made for the grooves. It will not be necessary to set out a plan, as one shelf may be prepared and used as a pattern for marking the others.

MAKING WHATNOT SHELVES.

The procedure in making the shelves may be as follows: Cut off, and with a trying plane true up the shelves and various pieces to the given dimensions, gauging all

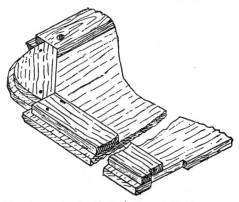

Fig. 2383.—Underneath View of Shelf Corner.

to thickness; then, taking one of the shelves, shoot its best edge and plane the ends square to the given length; then gauge to width. Next strike out the quadrant corners with a 6-in. radius, at 7 in. from the end and front, to give a 1-in. break. This marking should be done on the under-side so as not to damage the face. Then cut off to the line with a bow saw, and clean up with a chisel and spokeshave square. Mark the centres for the pillars at 2 in. from the edges, and square the point over to the front edge. Also mark on the back edge equidistant from the ends a 3-in. slot or recess for the back pillars. Of these an upper one (Fig. 2380) is cut out of ½-in. stuff, finishing about ⅜ in., and this amount should be gauged on each face between the marks on the shelf. Then place the shelf in order, face up on the others, mark the lines on their edges, and successively the outlines of the first on the other two; treat these like the former,

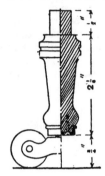

Fig. 2384.—Foot of Whatnot.

and, if the shelves are to be inlaid, prepare a scratch tool of suitable width and run it round the edges as far as the design permits, finishing the remainder, after it has been set out, with chisels or gouges as may be most convenient. The grooves should be a shaving less in depth than the thick-

the round corners, and finally the breaks, the latter being worked with gouges into mitres with the running moulds, as shown in Fig. 2381. The strings may now be grooved in; fill the grooves with glue, and rub in the string with the face of a hammer. The curves, squares, etc., are best inlaid first, and the straight lengths made good to them when the glue is dry. The faces may be smoothed up, but not papered for the present; but the face must not be damaged in the subsequent operations. Next prepare the linings, glue on the corner pieces at the proper distances from the edge, cut the other pieces between, and fix them. Cut out the back end for the fretted pillars, as shown in Fig. 2383, and bore $\frac{3}{8}$-in. holes for the front pillars, obtaining the position by squaring the marks over from the shelf.

WHATNOT PILLARS.

The pillars may next be fitted, the dowels of the turned ones being cut to length; see that they go down to the shoulder

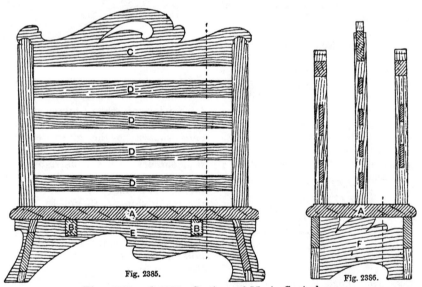

Fig. 2385.

Fig. 2386.

Figs. 2385 and 2386.—Sections of Music Canterbury.

ness of the strings. Having completed the stringing grooves, mould the edges, a plane or a scratch being used for this. The front edge should be treated first, then the ends,

square. The back pillars must now be prepared, and a drawing may be made and a tracing taken of it and transferred to the wood, first chalking the latter, and then going over the tracing, reversed, with a lead pencil. The design being repeated, all that is necessary is to set out on the stuff the thickness of the three shelves, as shown in Fig. 2379, testing the distances by means of the length between the turned ends of the front pillars, keeping the line A A (Fig. 2380) on the tracing to the top side of the shelves. The back pillars are continuous from top to bottom. A deeper square will be shown on the top end of the fret in the lower shelf, but as this cannot be seen in the ordinary position it will not matter. The frets being prepared, notch them out to fit the shelves and fix them with screws. The top fret, which is shown sufficiently in Fig. 2378, may now be prepared, and can be fixed with three screws from underneath.

PUTTING WHATNOT TOGETHER.

All should be fitted together dry, and when correct knocked apart, glasspapered up, and french-polished. When dry, scrape off any polish that may be on parts to be glued, and glue all together, commencing at the bottom; glue in the turned pillars, lay the carcase on its face, and glue in the fretted pillars. Try the back for squareness, and then turn it upside down and fix in the castor pillars. When these are dry, glue and fix the fret rail on the top, and fit on the castors (Fig. 2384), when the article will be complete.

MUSIC CANTERBURY.

The wood required for making a music canterbury, as shown in section and front elevation by Fig. 2385, is: One piece, 17 in. by 8½ in. by ¾ in., for the base A and the two ledges B B, in Fig. 2385; one piece, 12 in. by 8 in. by ¾ in., for the six stiles; one piece, 16 in. by 4 in. by ½ in., for the middle rail C (Fig. 2385); one piece, 14 in. by 5 in. by ¼ in., for the four rails D, in Fig. 2385; two pieces, 17½ in. by 4 in. by ½ in., for the two base supports E; one piece, 12 in. by 4 in. by ½ in., for the two end pieces F (Fig. 2386); and one piece, 57 in. by 3 in. by ¼ in., for the slanting crossbars G, in Fig. 2387. This last piece is estimated on the supposition that two bars are got out of one width, the curved parts

of one bar coming opposite to the straight part of the other. This principle has already been discussed. All the dimensions given (except thicknesses) allow a margin for working. Fig. 2385 is a section through the base A, showing the middle leaf, but omitting the framed side leaf beyond. In constructing the middle leaf the part C is tenoned into the ends of the stiles, the curved terminals of the stiles being notched to allow the ends of C to pass through. A much neater appearance will be secured if the mortises are made blind, so that C does not completely pass through them. The ends of the rails D are let into mortises

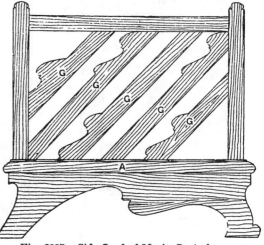

Fig. 2387.—Side Leaf of Music Canterbury.

about ⅛ in. deep. When this leaf is framed up it is ready to fix to the base A; this is best done by making double bare-faced tenons at the lower end of each stile, as the joints should be as strong as possible. The side leaves may be dealt with in a similar manner. To find the position for the pieces G, it will be best to mark out full size the rectangular area bounded by the inside of the frame. A vertical line is then drawn through the centre and bisected. The point so found is the centre of the middle bar, and through it a line is drawn at 45°, which will be at right angles to the direction of the bars. The width of the middle bar is laid off on the slanting line, half on each side of the central point first found.

From each edge of the middle bar, distances of 1 in. are marked off—four on each side, to give widths of spaces and remaining bars. Lines drawn at 45° through these points will mark out the straight parts of the bars. In working the curved parts they may all be clamped together and worked through as a whole. The two ledges B (Fig. 2385) are screwed on the bottom of the base A to strengthen it, and are

got rid of altogether by tonguing cleats on the ends of A. The ends F should be housed into the side pieces E and strengthened by glued blocks inside. A firmer base may be secured by splaying the pieces E outward to about the same extent as the pieces F. In fixing the parts together the bars in the side leaves should slant in opposite directions, and the curves of the pieces E and F should be placed in opposi-

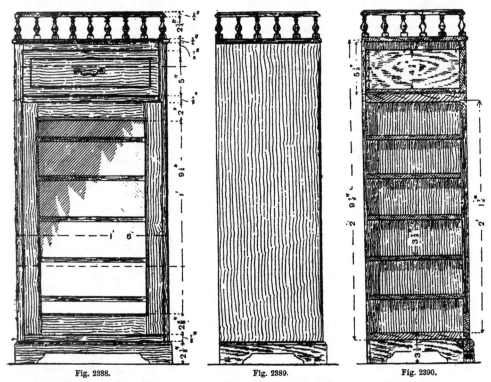

Fig. 2388. Fig. 2389. Fig. 2390.

Figs. 2388 to 2390.—Front and End Elevations and Vertical Section of Music Cabinet.

placed where they are invisible. If preferred the ledges may be fixed as dovetailed keys, but in this case the moulding on the edges of the base would need to be planted on afterwards. As shown in Fig. 2385, the moulding is stuck on the base. If, however, the moulding is planted, it would be better to tongue the side pieces E into the base A rather than make the plain butt joints shown where the connection to A is made by dowels. The ledges B may be

tion to each other. The kind of wood to be used may be settled according to taste; but if the cabinet is made of ash, stained green and polished, a good effect would be obtained. The curves may be marked by ruling lines across the printed figures at even distances apart, and measuring on the scale the lengths of the portions cutting the curves. These being set out full size will indicate the course of the curves, which then may be cut.

Materials for Music Cabinet.

The music cabinet of which Fig. 2388 shows front elevation, Fig. 2389 end elevation, and Fig. 2390 vertical section, is 3 ft. 4 in. high, 1 ft. 6 in. wide, by 1 ft. deep. The lower part has a sashed door, the part above being fitted with a drawer. The top is moulded along the front edge and ends, and is surmounted by a dwarf balustrading forming a gallery; at the bottom is a plinth cut and shaped to form four feet. The interior is fitted with five shelves, and the work may be executed in wainscot-mahog-

Fig. 2391.—Rebate and Grooves in Top and Side.

any, walnut, birch, or ash. The material required, with allowances for tooling, is as follows:—Two ends, 3 ft. 1 in. by 1 ft. by $\frac{7}{8}$ in.; bottom, 1 ft. 5½ in. by 11 in. by 1 in.; top, 1 ft. 7 in. by 1 ft. 0½ in. by $\frac{3}{4}$ in.; five shelves, 1 ft. 5 in. by 10½ in. by ½ in.; one division, 1 ft. 5½ in. by 11½ in. by 1 in.; back, 2 ft. 8 in. by 1 ft. 5 in. by ½ in.; bottom rail, 1 ft. 5 in. by 3⅜ in. by $\frac{7}{8}$ in.; top rail, 1 ft. 5 in. by 1 in. by $\frac{7}{8}$ in.; plinth (one), 1 ft. 7 in. by 2½ in. by ½ in., and (two) 1 ft. 1 in. by 2½ in. by ½ in.; drawer fronts, one, 1 ft. 4½ in. by 5 in. by $\frac{3}{4}$ in., and another, 3 ft. 9 in. by 1¼ in. by $\frac{5}{16}$ in.; drawer bot-

tom, 1 ft. 4 in. by 11½ in. by ½ in.; two drawer sides, 11 in. by 5 in. by ½ in.; drawer back, 1 ft. 4½ in. by 4½ in. by ½ in.; drawer blocks, one 1 ft. 4 in. by $\frac{3}{4}$ in. by ½ in., and two 11 in. by $\frac{3}{4}$ in. by ½ in.; two fillets, 11 in. by $\frac{7}{8}$ in. by $\frac{3}{4}$ in.; two sash stiles, 2 ft. 3 in. by 2 in. by $\frac{7}{8}$ in.; sash rails, one 1 ft. 4 in. by 2 in. by $\frac{7}{8}$ in. and another 1 ft. 4 in. by 2⅝ in. by $\frac{7}{8}$ in.; gallery rail, 3 ft. 6 in. by 1 in. by $\frac{3}{4}$ in.; nineteen balusters, 3 in. by $\frac{7}{8}$ in. by $\frac{7}{8}$ in.; two glazing slips, 1 ft. 11 in. by $\frac{3}{8}$ in. by ¼ in., and two 1 ft. 1½ in. by $\frac{3}{8}$ in. by ¼ in.; twelve glue blocks, 2 in. by 1½ in. by 1½ in.; and a piece of clear sheet-glass, 1 ft. 10 in. by 1 ft. 1½ in. by 32 oz. Also one 3½ in. brass drop drawer handle; one pair of 3-in. machine-made brass butts; one 2½-in. brass cut cupboard lock (left hand); one fancy brass escutcheon plate; 1½ doz. 1¼-in. No. 8 screws; and ½ doz. 1-in. No. 7 screws.

Making the Music Cabinet.

Fig. 2391 is an enlarged detail of rebate and grooves in top and side. Fig. 2392 shows a part inner view of side, and Fig. 2393 gives an enlarged part vertical section. First prepare the two ends. Face these and thicken them to $\frac{7}{8}$ in., shoot the best edge for the front, and gauge to 12 in. wide, then cut off one end square, and shoot it perfectly straight. Set a gauge to $\frac{3}{8}$ in., and mark it on both sides to form a shoulder to the dovetail $\frac{3}{8}$ in. long on the end. Form a groove 1 in. wide on the inside face of the end, this groove being stopped $\frac{7}{8}$ in. from the front edge. Now set off from the shoulder line a distance of 2 ft. 8½ in. and form a groove here, stopping it from the front edge $\frac{7}{8}$ in. Now set a gauge ½ in., and mark down the back edge and on the inner face, and rebate out for the back. On the front edge gauge ¼ in., the depth of the rebate, and $\frac{7}{8}$ in. on the inner face to receive the sashed door; the rebate will stop at the under-side of the division. Stick a $\frac{1}{8}$-in. bead on the inside edge as shown, and chamfer the outer edge, stopping it at the ends. These must be worked exactly alike, but right- and left-handed. Next face up the bottom, and shoot the best edge; thickness it to 1 in.

Gauge it to width, cut each end square to length, and form a tongue on the front edge from the lower face.

MUSIC CABINET DIVISION, ETC.

The piece for the division is faced up and gauged to 1 in. thick. The shoulder on the end of the division is diminished, the longest point being on the under-side, where the rebate occurs. Details show the groove in which the division must fit, and the bottom tongued to the riser or bottom rail; the latter is mitred to the bead on the rebate of the end, and is held in position by the tongue on the bottom and by screws driven through the lower part of the end, the screws being covered by the plinth. Before fixing the bottom rail it should be cut to shape. The top rail over the drawer

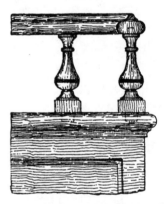

Fig. 2394.—Music Cabinet Balustrading.

is mitred and fixed between the ends. Next prepare the top and gauge it to $\frac{3}{4}$ in. thick, shoot the front edge, and get it to width; cut the ends square, and on the under-side set out two dovetailed grooves. The grooves must be stopped $\frac{1}{2}$ in. from the front edge. Rebate out the back edge to receive the back, stopping the rebate at the groove at each end. The top may next be moulded on the front edge and ends. Then set out and cut the grooves $\frac{1}{4}$ in. deep for the shelves on the inner face of the ends. When the shelves are prepared, clean up the work, glue it together, and let it stand while the sash and drawer are being made.

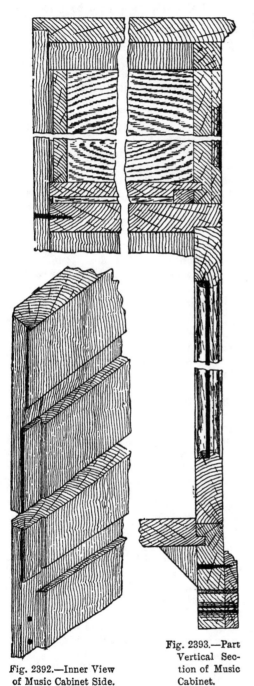

Fig. 2392.—Inner View of Music Cabinet Side.

Fig. 2393.—Part Vertical Section of Music Cabinet.

MUSIC CABINET SASH.

For the sash, face the two stiles and rails. Get them to size, and set out the stiles for the mortises and the rails for the tenons, the sight line between the mortises being 1 ft. $9\frac{1}{2}$ in., allowing $\frac{1}{4}$ in. at each end for the depth of the rebate and sticking of mould-

MUSIC CABINET DRAWER AND FINAL DETAILS.

Prepare the front of the drawer as shown with a moulded margin planted on the face to form a sunk and moulded panel. The front itself will be $\frac{5}{8}$ in. thick when finished. Fit it into the opening, and take the sides

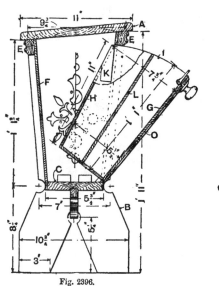

Fig. 2396.

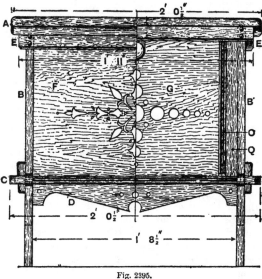

Fig. 2395.

Figs. 2395 to 2397.—Front and Back Elevations, Cross Section, and Plan of Combined Organ Bench and Music Cabinet.

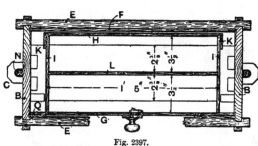

Fig. 2397.

ing on the stiles. Allow $\frac{7}{8}$ in. for width of tenon, and splay the haunching as shown; the length between the shoulders on the rails is 1 ft. $1\frac{1}{4}$ in., that including the depth of the rebate at each end. Fit the sash and glue it, and fit it, when dry, into place. Hang it with brass butt-hinges, and put on the cupboard lock. Particulars of the way in which the joints are made and stiles and rails prepared need not be given here, these matters having already been described.

and gauge them 5 in. wide and $\frac{1}{2}$ in. thick. Cut them square at each end, the back being of the same length as the front. Cut dovetails in the sides and pin on the front and back as shown. Plough the lower inner edge of the drawer front and side $\frac{5}{8}$ in. up, and make a $\frac{3}{16}$-in. groove to receive the bottom, which will be $\frac{1}{2}$ in. thick. Form the tongue on its front edge and ends as shown, and glue the drawer together, sliding-in the bottom. Put three screws along the back edge of the bottom into the back and glue in the blocks. Now clean off the face of the drawer, and mitre round the 1¼-in. by ¼-in. margin which has been prepared. It must be glued on and held in

COMBINED ORGAN BENCH AND MUSIC CABINET.

An organ bench with a separate music cabinet that can be opened without requir-

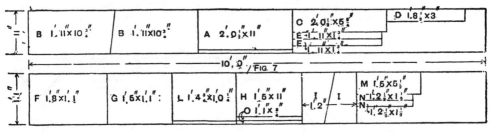

Figs. 2398 and 2399.—Cutting Wood for Organ Bench Cabinet.

position by hand-screws until thoroughly dry, when it may be cleaned off and finished. Next put on the handle and prepare the boards for the back. Plough the two edges which come together, and put in a small tongue which, in case of shrinkage, will keep out the dust. Screw the boards into the rebate and prepare the plinth. Work the moulding on the edge as shown, and cut it to shape, mitring the two front angles. These may be glued on, and extra fixing obtained by screws through the in-

ing the performer to rise from his seat is shown in back and front elevations by Fig. 2395, in cross section by Fig. 2396, and in plan with the seat removed by Fig. 2397. The wood should be of the same kind as

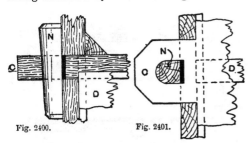

Fig. 2400.   Fig. 2401.

Figs. 2400 and 2401.—Fixing Brace Rail of Organ Bench Cabinet.

side of bottom rail. For balustrading, an enlarged detail of which is shown by Fig. 2394, get the capping to the required width and thickness, and work the moulding on both edges. Mitre this together to fit the top exactly to the square of the moulding, and return the two ends in front. Get the balusters with pins on both ends turned and polished in the lathe. The cabinet should be finished by french-polishing.

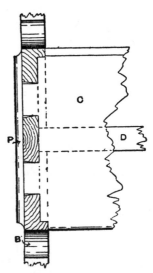

Fig. 2402.—Fixing Brace Rail of Organ Bench Cabinet.

that used for the organ or harmonium; about 10 ft. each of ¾-in. by 11-in. and ¼-in. by 13-in. will be required, and the most economical method of cutting it is shown by Figs. 2398 and 2399 for the ¾-in. and ¼-in. stuff respectively. The two ends or standards B may be screwed together and cut out simultaneously, the screws being inserted in the waste portions. The centre-bit holes should first be made, and by reversing and cutting from the opposite side as soon as the spur of the bit penetrates, all splintering is avoided and a smooth hole results. Before sawing out and, consequently, separating the sides, the position of the mortises for the tenoned rail c must be marked on each outside surface. Two methods of fixing this rail are shown in Figs. 2400, 2401, and 2402, one needing a wedge or cotter N through the projecting

end. The perpendicular strips Q on each side of the cabinet are glued in the rebate and fixed by angle-blocks. The music cabinet is made entirely of $\frac{1}{4}$-in. stuff, the front being fretted to the same pattern as the bench panel. All corners to H, I, and G are mitre dovetailed, the division L being housed into the ends, the reeded strips O on the front effectually concealing the dovetail joint. A cupboard turn should now be fitted, and the cabinet hinged to the rail c, after which the stops K should be glued to its sides.

Figs. 2403 and 2404.—Front and End Elevations of Music Stool.

tusk tenon, and the other having glued and wedged tenons, their flush ends being concealed by a $\frac{3}{4}$-in. by $\frac{1}{4}$-in. reeded strip P (Fig. 2402) planted afterwards. Both the rail c and the bracket D are housed $\frac{1}{8}$ in. into the standards and fixed by glue. The front panel F of the bench is housed, but not glued, into the standards, and is rebated into the brace rail c, to which it is glued and sprigged. It is secured to a top rail by a couple of screws in slotted holes, to allow for contraction. The two $1\frac{3}{4}$-in. rails E, on which the seat rests, are checked out, the tops of the standards being suitably recessed, and then secured by glue and a couple of round-headed iron screws at each

COMPLETING BENCH AND CABINET.

When the polishing is completed, pieces of sateen or other suitable material should be fastened inside the frets, and the seat A screwed to the rails. If, however, it is not intended to upholster the seat, the appearance of these screws would be objectionable, and if only to allow for subsequent access to the interior, a preferable method would be to secure the seat by four picture plates sunk in and screwed to the ends of the rails E. To provide an alternative design for the panels, etc., where a fret-saw is not available, centre-bits may be usefully employed, as shown to the right of Fig. 2395. All parts in the illustrations are similarly lettered, and Figs. 2395 to 2397 are to a scale of 2 in. to 1 ft., Figs. 2398 and 2399 being $\frac{1}{2}$ in. to 1 ft., and Figs. 2400 to 2402 4 in. to 1 ft.

top, and omitting the tenons. On this half-inch glue a strip of wood on each side to act as a stop. To obtain the correct angle for the end, drop a perpendicular line $16\frac{3}{4}$

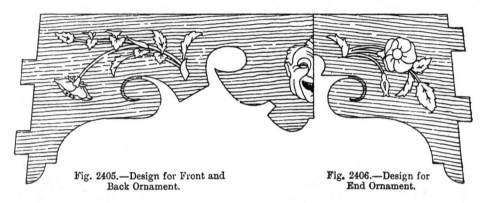

Fig. 2405.—Design for Front and
Back Ornament.

Fig. 2406.—Design for
End Ornament.

MUSIC STOOL WITH IMITATION INLAID WORK.

The material used for making this music stool, of which Figs. 2403 and 2404 are front

in. in length, as the dotted line shown in Fig. 2403, then 1 in., measured at right angles, will give the point where the end of the leg will come. This template will be

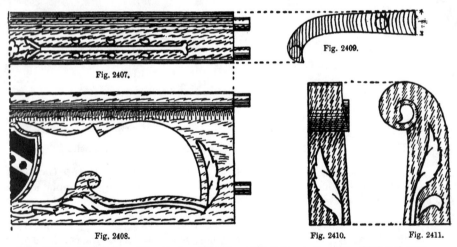

Fig. 2407.

Fig. 2409.

Fig. 2408.

Fig. 2410.   Fig. 2411.

Figs. 2407 to 2409.—Plan, Elevation, and Section of Half Handrail. Figs. 2410 and 2411.—
Corner Pillar.

and end elevations respectively, is clean kauri pine. For the sides and ends of the frame, plane up two pieces 22 in. by 6 in. by $\frac{1}{2}$ in., and two $11\frac{3}{4}$ in. by 6 in. by $\frac{1}{2}$ in. Next make a template, by drawing the outline of Fig. 2405 on stout cardboard, and cut out, allowing an extra half-inch at the

found to give the pattern for the whole of the outline of the frames, except the centres of the ends, which can be drawn with compass and straightedge. Cut the outline with a bow saw, but notice that parts of the scrolls are merely incised so that they may not be weakened unduly. The tenons are cut $\frac{1}{2}$ in. long, $\frac{7}{8}$ in. wide, and $\frac{1}{4}$ in. thick, flush with the front surface of the frame. All the tenons on the front and back are cut as in Fig. 2405, and those on the ends as in Fig. 2406. By this means the mortises do not run into one another, and it is possible to give more length to the tenons than otherwise. Get out the legs

Fig. 2412.—Music Stool Seat Frame.

17 in. by 1 in. by $\frac{7}{8}$ in., tapering to $\frac{3}{4}$ in. by $\frac{5}{8}$ in. at the bottom; set the gauge to mark the mortises $\frac{1}{4}$ in. from the outside faces, so that the surfaces of the frame will be $\frac{1}{4}$ in. back from those of the legs. The joints should be a tight fit.

MUSIC STOOL HANDRAILS, ETC.

The two handrails (Figs. 2407, 2408, and 2409) are $9\frac{3}{4}$ in. by $2\frac{3}{4}$ in., and as the dowels

marked from a tin template similar to Fig. 2411, to get them all four alike; the carving required is very simple. The stool top is $23\frac{1}{4}$ in. by $12\frac{3}{4}$ in. by $\frac{5}{8}$ in., with an ogee moulding run round $\frac{5}{8}$ in. from the edge.

MUSIC STOOL SEAT, ETC.

From beech or ash, $1\frac{1}{4}$ in. by $\frac{3}{4}$ in., construct a frame upon which to build the stuffing, having outside measurements of $19\frac{1}{2}$ in. by 11 in. (Fig. 2412). Put the frame and legs together to ensure a correct fit, and plane off the edges to get a flat surface for the seat to rest upon. The handrails are dowelled to the end pillars, as shown in Figs. 2408 and 2410; then a dowel is fixed in the base of each pillar, put through a slot cut in the stool top, and finally sunk into the top of the leg. Further fix the seat by screwing ledges inside the front, back, and ends, and attaching L-shaped buttons to the seat to engage them. Fig. 2413 is a detail of music stool leg with inlay. Take all apart, and stain and polish. A thin wash of indigo, when the colour of the wood is brought out by the polish, will give a satisfactory green for the leaves. Make all the colours used a trifle brighter and more intense than required, as the subsequent operations tone them down. Glue and cramp up, and give an extra polish with the spirit rubber. On the frame (Fig. 2412) build up a double-stuffed seat 4 in. high in the centre, with a firm smooth roll $2\frac{3}{4}$ in. high at the edges and hanging over $\frac{1}{2}$ in. Cover with any of the ordinary materials, such as tapestry, Roman satin, etc., of a shade to harmonise with the other furniture

Fig. 2413.—Inlaid Leg of Music Stool.

are cut on the ends, $10\frac{1}{2}$ in. will be the length required for each. They can be got out of $\frac{7}{8}$-in. wood, worked to the section shown in Fig. 2409. Figs. 2410 and 2411 show end and front details of corner pillars. The pillars at the ends of the rails are 1 in. by $\frac{7}{8}$ in. at their bases, and should be

and draperies. Fix this stuffed part on by four screws with washers under them, working in slots cut in the stool top, and the stool is finished. Figs. 2407 to 2411 and Fig. 2413 are drawn to half-size; Figs. 2403, 2404, and 2412 are drawn to a scale of $1\frac{1}{2}$ in. to 1 ft.

MUSIC STOOL WITH TURNED RAILS.

Figs. 2414 and 2415 show front and end elevation of music stool respectively. The stool should be made of mahogany, hard straight-grained stuff being necessary for the legs, which should not be less than 1 in. thick when finished, and must be free from shakes. They must be cut so as to bring the top edge of the rail 1 ft. 5 in. from the floor, and when they are finished the front and back rails, also of 1-in. board, should be got out. They are first cut 1 ft. 6 in. long, 1½ in. at each end being tenoned into

the ends of the rails for 1½ in., and into the legs for ¾ in., thus doubly securing the long rails. (Dowel making and the process of fitting dowelled joints are described on pp. 185 to 188). Two turned rails are required, also 11 in. long, not including the ¾-in. by ⅜-in. pins left at each end to be fitted into the centre of the scroll-shaped tops of the legs (see Fig. 2415). After gluing and cramping, a bottom may be fitted into the box opening, which is 1 ft. 3 in. by 11 in., this being the size suitable for ordinary sheet music. The

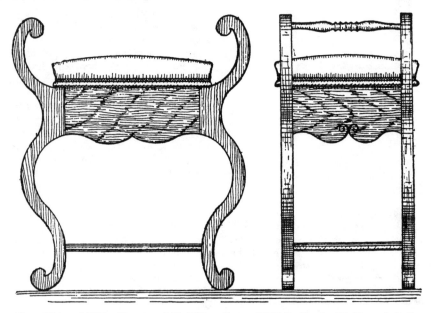

Figs. 2414 and 2415.—Front and End Elevations of Music Stool with Turned Rails

the mortise of the legs (see Fig. 2416, A being a section of the long rail, and B a section of the leg). The rails are then 1 ft. 3 in. long, and when cut to shape, the front and back may be glued and cramped up. The short rails are 11 in. long, and the same thickness as the other rails. If mortised and tenoned, they would cut the tenon of the long rails, besides weakening the joint materially. It is best, therefore, to use dowels, as shown at c (Fig. 2416). Beech dowels can be purchased in 3-ft. lengths at 6d. per dozen, and those used in this case should be ½ in. thick. They should go into

bottom is of ½-in. board, neatly fitted and secured with a few sprigs, then glue-blocked underneath. Scrolls are carved in the centre of the lower edge of the short rails, as shown in Fig. 2415. The shelf is of ¾-in. board cut to the shape shown by Fig. 2417, a thumb mould being worked on all four edges. It is then fitted to the legs, 4 in. from the floor, by being cut out at the corners 1 in. by 1 in., and secured by screws through the legs. The screw heads should be sunk ¼ in. below the surface, and the hole filled with wood. Glue should also be used to steady the joint.

MUSIC STOOL SEAT.

The seat frame is next made of white-wood or pine, or if hard wood is preferred, birch or beech is most suitable. It is of

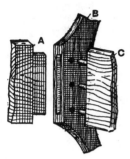

Fig. 2416.—Rail and Leg Joint.

2-in. wide by ¾-in. thick material, the size being 1 ft. 6 in. by 1 ft. 2 in. The joints are halved, glued, and screwed. English webbing should be stretched as tight as possible, and tacked on the upper side, as shown in Fig. 2418. A good quality canvas is then tightly stretched and tacked over the webbing, and a rib of 1-in. square wood screwed on all round for the padding. This is done by tacking a strip of canvas, 4 in. wide, round the outside of the frame, putting flocks on the rib, and covering with the canvas. This should be tacked to the inside of the rib, and stitched round with a 6-in. double-pointed upholsterer's needle, using

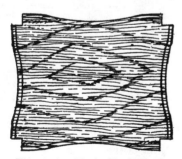

Fig. 2417.—Music Stool Shelf.

a suitable twine that can be obtained for the purpose. Fig. 2419 shows the method of stitching. Hair should be used for stuffing. It should be first well teased out, as it will then retain its spring, and keep the

cushion soft, and it will not get flat as when flocks are used. The hair is then covered with strong calico or canvas, tacked to the edges of the frame, and when this is done, a sheet of wadding must be laid over, and

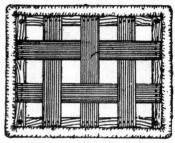

Fig. 2418.—Seat Frame Webbed and Padded.

the final covering put on. Crimson silk plush or Utrecht velvet is suitable for this. The tack heads are then covered with a gimp to match, small-headed gimp pins being used for securing the gimp. The underside of the seat should be covered with a twill lining material of suitable colour, which is stretched tightly and tacked on. A strip of mahogany 5 ft. long by 1½ in. wide by ½ in. thick, with one edge rounded, should be worked on round the under-side of the seat. It is mitred at the corners, and screwed on, but should first be polished, as this is not conveniently done when fixed, and the stool is handier for polishing with the seat off. It will look best if finished a

Fig. 2419.—Stitching Seat Padding.

dark colour and polished. When the polishing is finished, the moulding can be put on the seat, which is fixed to the back long rail with brass butt hinges.

ROUND MUSIC STOOL WITH TURNED LEGS.

Fig. 2420 shows an elevation of an ordinary music stool with a rising top A. The stool itself consists of a circular top B 1 in. thick, 12⅜ in. in diameter at the top, and 13¼ in. at the bottom. Its central hole is

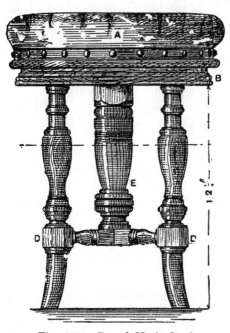

Fig. 2420.—Round Music Stool.

1¹⁄₁₆ in. in diameter. This top is supported by four 2-in. legs, 1 ft. 2⅜ in. long, exclud-

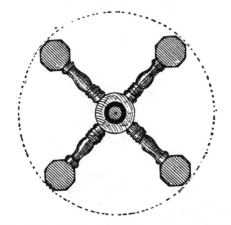

Fig. 2421.—Horizontal Section of Music Stool.

ing the tenon shown in Fig. 2421. The circle containing the centres of the holes

for the legs is 10¾ in. in diameter, the tops of the holes being covered by buttons, as shown at C. The legs, which are octagonal at D, are connected by two spindles (see Fig. 2422) 8¾ in. long, excluding tenons. They are halved together where they cross (see Fig. 2423), and form a support for the centre column E. This column is about 9½ in. long and 2½ in. in diameter, and is fixed by a long stout screw underneath, and at the top by three screws passing through the flange of a brass socket piece F, which is fitted through the central hole (see Fig.

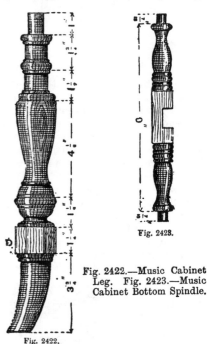

Fig. 2423.

Fig. 2422.—Music Cabinet Leg. Fig. 2423.—Music Cabinet Bottom Spindle.

Fig. 2422.

2424). Fig. 2425 is an enlarged section showing the flange (2 in. in diameter) of the socket resting in a slight recess in the top B of the stool, E being the centre column. The centre of this column is hollowed to within 2½ in. of the bottom to take the nut (see Fig. 2426), the bore being about 1 in. full. The square-threaded screw is ⅞ in. bare in diameter, the shank, 3¾ in. long, being encircled by a brass tube. At the top of the spindle is an oblong plate 2½ in. by 3 in., to which the spindle top is riveted. This plate is secured to the under-side of the rising top by four screws. A section of the rising top is shown by Fig. 2427, and an underneath plan by Fig. 2428. This top

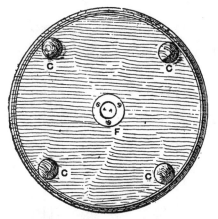

Fig. 2424.—Plan of Music Stool Top.

consists of five pieces J, 1 in. thick, tenoned together, the rivet head of the screw resting in a recess provided for the purpose. At the bottom of these pieces are six curved pieces forming a circle. The top is stuffed with flock and covered with leather. The buttoning comes through the under canvas L, and is tacked to the sides of the pieces J. The length of the screw should

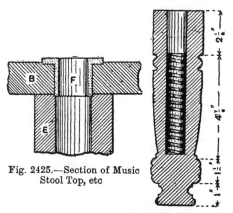

Fig. 2425.—Section of Music Stool Top, etc

Fig. 2426.—Music Stool Centre Column.

be adjusted so that when the top is screwed right down the bottom of the screw just clears the bottom of the hole, and when the

45

top is raised only the brass part N should be seen.

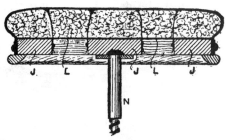

Fig. 2427.—Section of Music Stool Rising Top.

HAMLET SEAT.

The hamlet seat of which Fig. 2429 is a front elevation and Fig. 2430 a side elevation of frame may be made of walnut or some other dark-coloured wood, or of birch or beech stained dark or ebonised; soft woods, such as pine or whitewood, are unsuitable. The four legs are each $1\frac{1}{4}$ in. by 1 in. in section when finished; therefore, in marking out, allow $\frac{1}{8}$ in. each way for dressing and smoothing. A pair of legs can be sawn from a sound board 3 ft. 3 in. long by 8 in. wide, as shown in Fig. 2431. Dress the legs with a spokeshave and smooth them

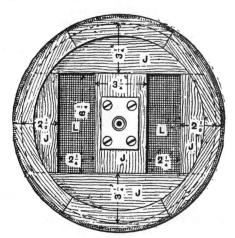

Fig. 2428.—Underneath Plan of Music Stool Top.

with a scraper and glasspaper. The legs are fastened in the centre with brass chair-rivets, $2\frac{3}{8}$ in. long by $\frac{3}{8}$ in. thick, and each pair is stretched by a turned spindle about 1 ft. 9 in. long by 1¼ in. thick, a hole being bored in the inside of each leg 6 in. from

but much more difficult to make. The seat frame side rails are 1 ft. 8 in. long by 1½ in. wide, and the end rails are 1 ft. 6 in. long

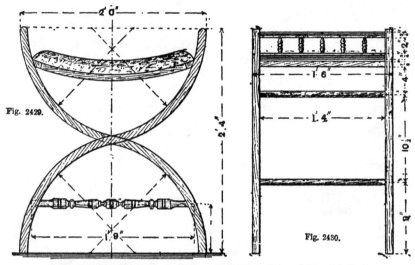

Figs. 2429 and 2430.—Front and Side Elevations of Hamlet Seat.

the bottom to receive the spindle end, which is secured by gluing. The cross framing (see Fig. 2430) consists of two plain spindles of rounded dowel wood, ½ in. thick and 1 ft. 5½ in. long, and two centre-beaded rails ¾ in. by ½ in. thick; between these two rails four or five wood spindles, 2 in. long by ⅜ in. thick, are spaced equally, and are secured by turned tenons at each end, fitting into holes bored in the inside edges of the beaded rails. These rails are

by 2 in. wide, all being cut from 1-in. stuff, rough sawn. The four pieces are framed up with dowel joints, and all the edges are rounded. The dimensions given will also apply to a curved seat frame, the dip of the curve being 2 in., measured at the centre.

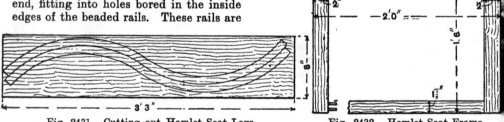

Fig. 2431.—Cutting out Hamlet Seat Legs. Fig. 2432.—Hamlet Seat Frame.

stump-tenoned into the legs; when a good fit has been obtained glue them up and cramp till dry.

SEAT FRAME OF HAMLET SEAT.

The seat frame (Fig. 2432) can be made either straight or curved, the latter shape being more in harmony with the design,

The seat will be much better handled if, before it is fixed in the frame, the top is up-holstered; to do this, cross-web the open space in the centre with grey webbing, the webs being 4 in. apart both in the length and width, and laced under and over as usual. Then cover with hessian, tacking this on the extreme inside edges.

About 5 lb. of curled horsehair will be required for stuffing the seat, which will look much better if tufted. The outside the edges being finished off with a coloured gimp to match the cover. Obviously such matters must be decided by individual

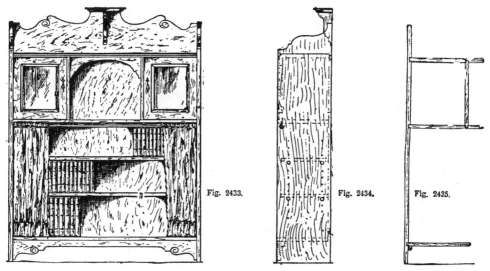

Figs. 2433 to 2435.—Elevations and Part Section of Bookshelves

cover should not be put on until the whole of the staining and polishing is done, and taste. The seat can be fastened to the frame either by 1½-in. brass angle brackets

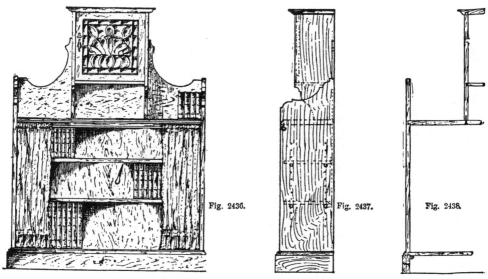

Figs. 2436 to 2438.—Elevations and Part Section of Bookshelves.

may be of crimson moquette; or a rich-coloured printed velveteen will be suitable, or by 2-in. round-headed brass screws put right through the legs.

Four designs of artistic bookshelves are

case ends, and the cupboard ends into the tops and bottoms as illustrated. The cup-

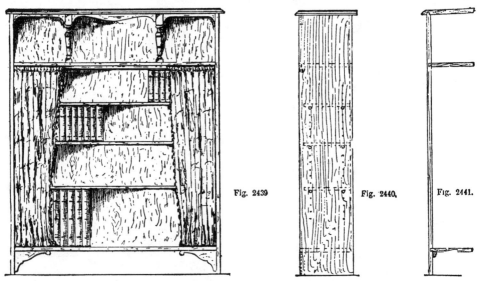

Fig. 2439.   Fig. 2440.   Fig. 2441.

Figs. 2439 to 2441.—Elevations and Part Section of Bookshelves.

shown by Figs. 2433 to 2435, 2436 to 2438, 2439 to 2441, and 2442 to 2444 respectively.

board doors in Figs. 2433 and 2442 have transparent glass panels, and the cupboard

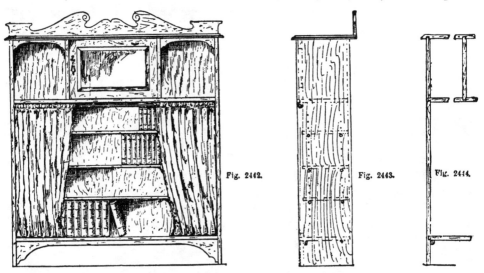

Fig. 2442.   Fig. 2443.   Fig. 2444.

Figs. 2442 to 2444.—Elevations and Part Section of Bookshelves.

The shelves may be made either in hardwood or in pine, for enamelling. The tops and bottoms are all dovetailed into the car-

door in Fig. 2436 is a leadlight panel. The shelves are movable, and rest on turned wood pins or on the ordinary iron bookcase studs. The holes for the pins should be bored about 1½ in. apart and 2 in. from the front edge of the end, and 1¼ in. from inside the carcase back. The curtains will hang on ½-in. brass rods resting on two cup-hooks screwed under the top. The plinth in Fig. 2436 is mitred round the carcase and screwed through the carcase end. Other details of construction are unnecessary, the construction of bookcases and bookshelves being treated so fully on pp. 528 to 541, whilst some dining-room bookcases are described in the preceding chapter.

bars 1 in. wide. It is best to obtain the moulding ready cut. It must be of solid oak and not a veneer, and is, of course, rebated. Two 12-ft. lengths of each width will make the whole framework. The eight cross-bars are all cut 1 ft. 5 in. long, which allows 1 in. at each end for the tenon. Two of the uprights are 3 ft. long each, and the two others 2 ft. 10 in. each. These lengths being cut, the four inside cross-pieces will each require a second rebate to be cut opposite to the one which will be cut when the moulding is bought, as shown by the

Fig. 2446.—Section of Screen Cross-bar.

Fig. 2445.—Dwarf Folding Screen.

ORNAMENTAL DWARF FOLDING SCREEN.

The framework of the dwarf folding screen, a general view of which is shown in Fig. 2445, may be made of oak stained to a dark shade. The screen stands 3 ft. high, and each fold is 1 ft. 6 in. wide. The moulding used for the framework should be reeded as shown at Fig. 2446, which is a full-sized section of one of the cross-bars. Fig. 2447 is a plan of one of the folds, and is drawn to a scale of one-eighth the full size. The uprights are 1½ in. wide, and the cross-

dotted lines in Fig. 2446. The framework must be carefully mortised together, the mortises, of course, not being cut completely through the uprights; if cut 1 in. deep—the length allowed for the tenons—and good joints are made, the whole will be quite rigid, and when completed the two folds should be perfectly square, and should lie quite flat when placed together. Be careful in cutting the tenons not to cut the shoulder so as to leave a gap at the back where rebated. The rebates in all the projecting ends of the framework will have to be filled up neatly by gluing in pieces of oak, and the angle-brackets can then be glued in their places. They are best fixed in position by a peg through each extremity, and should be cut out of ½-in. oak. Fig. 2448 suggests how the bottom one may be shaped; the top one would be almost the same, only inverted and larger.

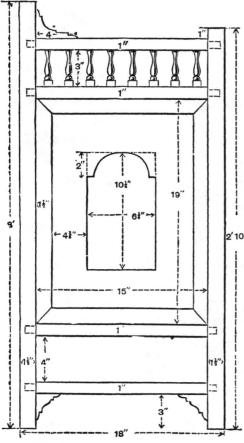

Fig. 2447.—One Fold of Screen.

BALUSTRADE OF SCREEN.

The balustrade is formed of pillars (see Fig. 2449). They are turned, and will necessitate the use of a lathe, but a part design for a fretwork panel in place of a balustrade is given at Fig. 2450. If this be used, it can easily be fitted into the rebate and held in its place by strips of wood. The pillars

used are fixed between two strips of oak, which are bored to receive the pegs left at the ends of the pillars, taking care to have them coincide, otherwise the pillars will not stand upright. It is a good plan to hold the two strips together, and so bore the two at the same time. The strips should exactly fit and fill up the rebate. The pillars can then be placed in a row between them, and the whole will fit in place, the rebates at the two sides being filled up with small strips in the same way as the projecting ends were treated. The balustrade should not be permanently fixed until the staining has been done.

SCREEN PANELS, ETC.

The two bottom panels may be of plush of a golden-green shade. This is mounted upon a piece of thin wood the size of the panel, using a little glue and paste mixed together, so as when cold to be about the consistency of a stiff jelly. A flat ½-in. gold slip should go round these panels, which can be mitred and glued upon the plush, or a slip frame made separately. For panel centrepieces, two sepia-tinted autotypes or a couple of etchings, in oak mounts, would look very well. The material used for the autotype mounts is a veneer of oak upon a card foundation. (Do not attempt to use solid oak.) They must have a gilt edge, and can either be cut to the shape shown in Figs. 2445 and 2447, or can be cut square. The strips round the outer edge of the large panels should be of plush the same shade as that used for the lower panels. It will be best to cut eight strips of thin wood and mitre them, covering each piece separately with a strip of plush; they should then be firmly glued to the outside of the glass, which will be placed in front of the mounts.

BACK OF SCREEN.

To make the back of the panels, cut from some backing boards pieces that will fit not too tightly into the rebates. The large ones will have to be joined, as a single width of a plank will not be wide enough; but a joint can be easily made by pasting a strip of brown paper on each side of it. These backs are to be covered with a brocade or other suitable material, fixed with the paste and glue, and turned over at the edges all round ; they will then be ready for fitting in. Now cut some strips of thin

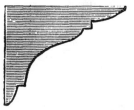

Fig. 2448.—Screen Bracket.

brass about ¼ in. wide and ¼ in. longer than the depth of the rebate. These are to be fixed inside the rebate with a small tack, as shown in Fig. 2448, so that when the panels, glass, and backs have been put in, the projecting ends can be turned down and will keep them in place ; three of these clips on each side will be found sufficient. It will be as well before placing the glass and autotypes in position to bind them together by pasting a strip of thin paper over the edges, so as to prevent any dust

Fig. 2450.—Fretwork Screen Panel.

from working in between them. The glasses and large panels should be fixed in the frame with a few brads ; the other panels and the backs can then be put in their places and the brass clips turned down. To hinge the folds together, use a couple of good strong 2½-in. butt hinges.

SCREEN FOR HOLDING PHOTOGRAPHS.

The screen for holding photographs shown by Fig. 2451 is made of picture-frame moulding, which can be obtained

Fig. 2449.—Balustrade Pillar.

from any dealer. Old negative glasses are cleaned and immersed one at a time, with a photograph of corresponding size, in a bath of warm gelatine (1 part gelatine in 20 parts water). When thoroughly dry, the paper of the print is rubbed away from the back with glasspaper (No. 0), leaving the picture thin and transparent. The pictures may now be coloured roughly with oil colours from the back, as in the crystoleum

Fig. 2451.—Photograph Screen.

process, and when viewed from the front will be effective, always provided, of course, that the colourist possesses artistic taste. The pictures are then fitted into the frames

margin of gold may be put inside the frames either as a slip, or painted on the glass before mounting the photographs. If the worker has not the necessary artistic skill, the picture may simply be mounted in optical contact in the manner described, and the colouring omitted.

FIRE-SCREEN.

The fire-screen of which a general view is given in Fig. 2452 can be made of almost

The stiles are mortised to a depth of about $\frac{7}{8}$ in., and the rails tenoned correspondingly, as shown in Fig. 2455. The four pieces forming the legs should be cut out the way of the grain, and their appearance will be much improved by carving, as shown. The flatness on the outer edges will be relieved by working a single reed on them. Shallow mortises are made in the stiles to receive stub tenons formed at the upper ends of the legs. The curved ornamental pieces at the top and bottom are also stub-tenoned at each end into the

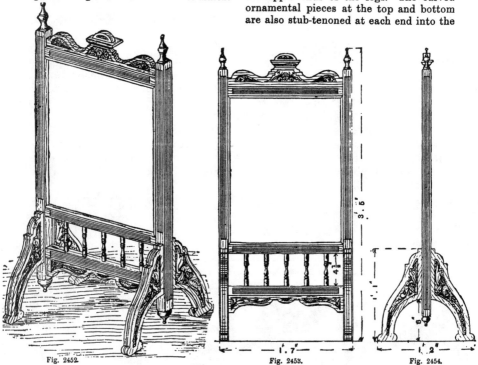

Fig. 2452.   Fig. 2453.   Fig. 2454.

Figs. 2452 to 2454.—General View and Elevations of Fire-screen.

any kind of wood to match other furniture. Leading dimensions are given in Figs. 2453 and 2454. The two stiles and three rails are about $1\frac{1}{4}$ in. square, and the finial and drops at the top and bottom of the stiles may be turned on the solid or may be turned separately with dowels on them, and the top and bottom of the stiles can be bored and the dowels glued and inserted.

stiles to a depth of $\frac{7}{8}$ in. These pieces also would be improved by carving. As will be seen, the stiles and rails are reeded, which may be done in the usual manner with a scratch. The five spindles shown should be turned with projecting pins; then holes should be bored in the two rails to receive them. The small pedimental feature at the top is made of $\frac{3}{4}$-in. stuff, with a moulding worked on the lower edge as shown, and the upper piece is ornamented with a little detail of carving on each side. The panel may be of stained glass, needlework, etc., and can be secured in position by beads.

FIRE-SCREEN WITH TURNERY AND FRETWORK.

The fire-screen illustrated by Fig. 2456 may be made of fretwork, turnery, or cabinet work. The size may be varied to suit the fireplace in which the screen is to stand, but about 2 ft. 6 in. high, with an extreme width of 2 ft., is very suitable. Fig. 2457 shows (out of scale) the upper shelf with the sides moulded; a similar shelf, but longer, forms the bottom part of the framework. These shelves should be 3 in. wide and $\frac{3}{4}$ in. thick; they are connected by two turned pillars with turned knobs at the top. An enlarged section of a pillar and knob is shown by Figs. 2458 and 2459. The panel is of wood $\frac{3}{4}$ in. thick, moulded at the sides, the central portion being cut out to oval shape, and having a moulding to form the rebate to take a mirror. If preferred, two sheets of glass with fern leaves or wild flowers pressed between them may be substituted for the mirror, or a piece of ornamental painted velvet or crewel work may be adopted. In any case, a back board of thin wood will be necessary. If desired, the top of the screen may be ornamented with a fretwork scroll as shown; but the screen looks well without it. Fretwork spandrels are inserted in the corners of the panel round the mirror, the spaces for them being previously cut. Figs. 2460 and 2461 show alternative designs for the fretwork.

FEET OF FIRE-SCREEN.

The feet to support the screen are formed of four brackets of wood, 1 in. thick, cut as shown, and carried on flat balls of wood. The square blocks to which these brackets are fixed are screwed to the under-side of the bottom shelf, to which also is screwed a strip to give a more solid effect to the feet. This strip may be ornamented by small turned pateræ, as shown in Fig. 2456, or cut out with the fretsaw to any suitable design. This screen may be made of good red wood, but would look better in mahogany or American walnut. When completed it should be french-polished.

FANCY ARCH, SHELVES, AND HANGINGS FOR MANTELPIECE.

This method of improving a plain mantelpiece consists mainly in encasing the sides

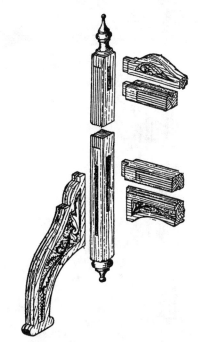

Fig. 2455.—Fire-screen Joints.

with two artistic covers, these being surmounted by a fancy arch and two upper shelves or rails (see Fig. 2462). The wood employed is yellow pine, and the two covers are made, in the ordinary way, to fit tightly over the side pillars or supports from the hearth right up to the under-side of the mantelpiece itself, no gap being left at any corner or angle which would be deleterious to the general effect, and, if properly fitted, the covers will remain upright unsupported by any catch or fastening. The front of each has two panels, one small one near the top and a larger one below, the latter having a lincrusta design let into it, whilst the front edges of the covers are moulded or reeded.

FANCY ARCH IN TURNED WORK.

Lying flat on the top and projecting from the edges of the mantelpiece is a board

(of 1 in. largest diameter) of the followi lengths: Two 1 ft. 2 in. over all (being t long end pillars at each side), each havi two small squares ⅜ in. deep, one at a d tance of 6 in. from the top of the pillar the top of the square, and the other at t

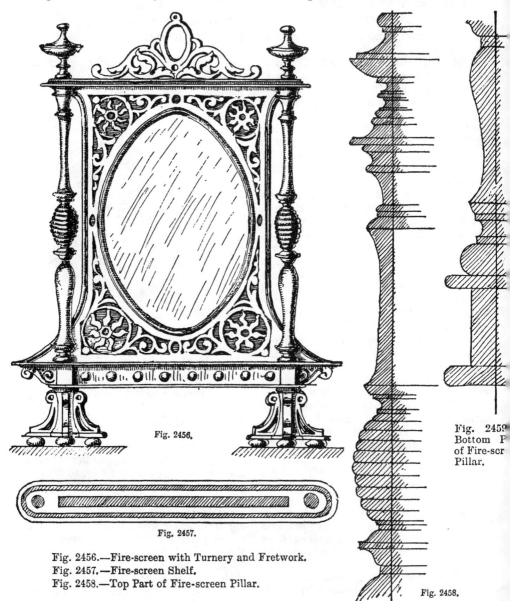

Fig. 2456.

Fig. 2457.

Fig. 2459 Bottom P of Fire-scr Pillar.

Fig. 2458.

Fig. 2456.—Fire-screen with Turnery and Fretwork.
Fig. 2457.—Fire-screen Shelf.
Fig. 2458.—Top Part of Fire-screen Pillar.

4 in. (these last six being the remaining pillars in the arch above the flat strip); two 3½ in. ; and two 1¼ in. (these being the small pillars at each side of the arch below

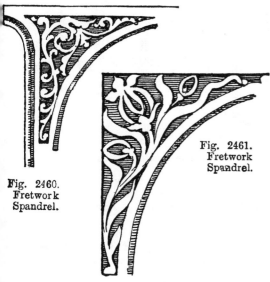

Fig. 2461.
Fretwork
Spandrel.

Fig. 2460.
Fretwork
Spandrel.

the flat strip). A shoulder of ½ in. diameter and ½ in. long is turned at the top of all those pillars which fit into the piece of wood affixed to the under-side of the board on the mantelpiece, ½-in. holes being bored to take their ends. To the under-side of the board on the mantelpiece, at a distance of 1 in. from the edge, is fixed a piece of wood 1 in. thick and 1¼ in. deep, cut to the shape shown in Figs. 2462, 2463, and 2464, into which the tops of the several pillars are sunk. The piece of wood forming the arch itself is 1 in. wide and ⅜ in. thick, and is attached to the bottom ends of the pillars, these latter being cut to suit it, whilst the ends of the arch are neatly joined on to one side of the small square at the bottom of each end pillar. A piece of wood similar in size to the arch is inserted between the side pillars, as shown in Figs. 2462 and 2464, one end being fixed to the centre square on each end pillar, and the other to the arch. Both of these two thin strips have their front edges reeded to improve their appearance. The small pillars at either side of the arch below the flat strip can also be suitably cut and

secured in their places. To maintain the arch in a regular curve, it is better to attach it first at the centre and then work outwards to the two end pillars. The side arches are completed in a similar manner to the front one, the piece of wood to which the pillars are fixed at the top being mitred at its front corners. The back pillar of each side arch is 7½ in. long over all, and has a small square, similar to the front end pillar, at the bottom, whilst the middle pillar is made to suit the curve of the arch, which is secured as before described (see Fig. 2463). The letter references in Fig. 2464 are as follow: A, under-piece and pillar supports; B, strip of arch; C, side strip.

Fig. 2462.—Mantelpiece with Fancy Arch, Shelves, and Hangings.

MANTELPIECE SHELVES AND HANGINGS

The two upper shelves or rails are each 3 ft. 6 in. long, 5 in. wide, and ¾ in. thick, and have a ⅞ in. wide piece cut out inwards

from the front edge from 5 in. from one end
to 5 in. from the other. The top of Fig.
2462 shows what is meant. The rail over
the shelf is $\frac{1}{2}$ in. thick and 1 in. wide, and
is supported by thirteen small pillars 1$\frac{1}{2}$ in.

from the front and $\frac{1}{4}$ in. deep. The face
sides should then be fluted, the flutes in the
top rail running right out at the ends,
whilst those of the uprights terminate 1 in.
from the base rail and from the moulding at

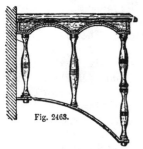

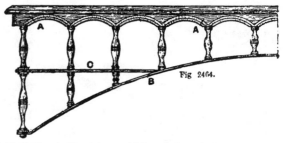

Fig. 2463 and 2464.—Side and Half Front Elevations of Mantelpiece Arch.

high, eleven of which are in the front and
one at each side. Fig. 2465 shows the form
of these pillars. The front edges of both
shelf and rail are bevelled, and the whole
is supported by a fancy wooden angle (Fig.
2466) about $\frac{1}{2}$ in. thick and 5 in. deep. The
two shelves are fixed 1 ft. 4 in. apart, and
a piece of silk is artistically pleated and
stretched behind them, being attached to
the back of the top shelf with a piece of
tape and some small nails, and to the wall
at the top of the mantelpiece. A similar
piece of silk is also hung behind the arches
to relieve their bareness and throw up the
pillars. The wood (and Lincrusta design) is
first given three coats of thin cream paint,
each coat being allowed to dry and being
sandpapered before applying the next; a
finishing coat of hard cream enamel is then
given to the whole. The measurements
here mentioned are suitable only for an
ordinary sized mantelpiece with the centres
of the pillars in the front arch 6 in. apart.

Framing a Pier-glass.

The pier-glass of which a front elevation
is shown in Fig. 2467 is 5 ft. 9 in. high by
5 ft. 6 in. wide over all, and should be made
in solid oak. The framework consists of
one base rail 5 ft. 6 in., one top rail 3 ft.
9 in., and two uprights each 5 ft. 2 in., all
2 in. wide by 1$\frac{1}{4}$ in. thick. When these
are planed and squared up, a rebate must
be run along one edge of each, $\frac{1}{4}$ in. back

the top. They need not be more than $\frac{1}{4}$ in.
wide, and should finish round. On the base
rail they also finish 1 in. from the ends,
running into a cross-flute, as in Fig. 2468.
The top rail must be tenoned 1$\frac{1}{2}$ in. at each
end on the face side, and 1$\frac{1}{4}$ in. at the back
on account of the rebate, and then mor-
tised into the uprights 1$\frac{1}{2}$ in. from the ends.
The lower ends of the uprights are tenoned
2 in. at the face side and 1$\frac{3}{4}$ in. at the
back, and are let into mortises right

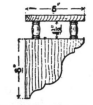

Fig. 2465.—Mantel-
piece Shelf Pillar.

Fig. 2466.—Side Eleva-
tion of Mantelpiece
Top Shelf.

through the base rail, at equal distances
from the end.

Pier-glass Curved Oak Rail.

Before the joints are fixed, the curved
oak rail (Fig. 2469) must be got out. This,
if in one piece, would require to be cut out
of a 10-in. board 1$\frac{1}{4}$ in. thick, but for
economy two pieces of $\frac{1}{2}$-in. oak, 1 ft. by
5 in., may be jointed to a piece 2 ft. 6 in.
by 5 in. in a manner to give space for the
curved rail, a template for which should

have previously been made in cardboard or stiff paper. This will make the oak facing, and the back .part of the rail may be made of deal or white wood 1 in. thick, but the joints must not come directly behind those in the oak. What time may appear to be lost in doing this is saved by cutting the deal $\frac{1}{2}$ in. narrower than the facing, so that, when glued together the

The frame may now be taken to pieces, and the curved rail dowel-jointed to the uprights, and then finally put together with glue, the tenons of the top rail being sawn and "blind-wedged," so as to tighten them inside the mortises (see Fig. 2469). These joints and those of the curved rail are made first, and it will be necessary to cramp them up immediately; then the base rail

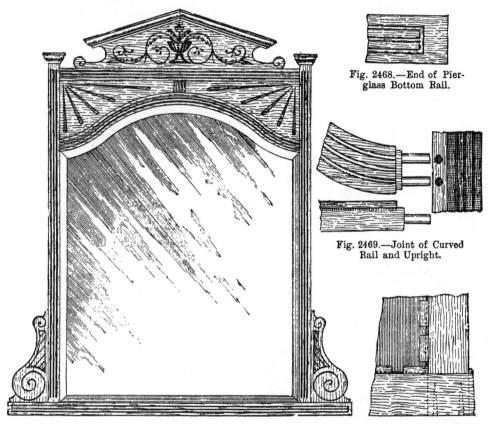

Fig. 2468.—End of Pier-glass Bottom Rail.

Fig. 2469.—Joint of Curved Rail and Upright.

Fig. 2467.—Pier-glass.

Fig. 2470.—Back Lower Corner of Pier-glass.

curved rail is rebated at both edges, thus saving the difficult task of rebating the solid oak. In fastening the facing, hot glue should be used on both pieces, which should be pressed well together with several handscrews until thoroughly set. The rail is then fitted, and also the piece, 2 in. in length, which divides the two panels, and which is fluted like the top rail.

is jointed on, the wedges being driven in from the outside (see Fig. 2470). The short piece is secured with screws through the curved rail and top rail, the heads being countersunk well below the surface of the wood, so as not to come in contact with the glass. It is most important to see that the frame is quite square, and out of winding, before it has had time to set.

PIER-GLASS PANELS, PEDIMENT, ETC.

The two panels are of ½-in. oak board, simply carved with a gouge in the form of flutes ⅜ in. wide, tapering to a point in the

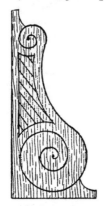

Fig. 2471.—Pier-glass Side Bracket.

corners; they are neatly fitted and kept in place by a slight beading at the back. The brackets (Fig. 2471) should be of ¾-in. oak, and the pediment (Fig. 2472) of ½-in. oak; they must have the design drawn in pencil, which should then be cleanly cut in with a very small carver's gouge, say about $\frac{1}{16}$ in. The line of the scrolls is continued along the edge of the brackets, which are then fixed in place with glue behind the rebate of the base rail, and against the uprights, a few small blocks being also glued behind. Fig. 2473 shows the moulding on the front of the pediment, the same

Fig. 2472.—Pier-glass Pediment.

moulding being used for the small cornices at the top end of the uprights. A simple and efficient detachable method of fixing the pediment is to fix a strip of wood about 1 ft. 6 in. long by ¾ in. by ¼ in. with three

screws flush with the lower edge of the pediment; it can then be screwed from behind to the top rail. When ordering the mirror (see Fig. 2474), send a template (Fig. 2475) in any dry thin board nailed and

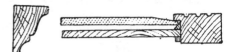

Fig. 2473.—Sec-   Fig. 2474.—Fixing Pier-
tion of Pediment   glass Mirror.
Moulding.

glued, to ensure its not being put out of square. It should fit loosely, yet evenly, and, in fact, it will be well to allow ⅛ in. play all round. The frame, now complete, is ready for polishing, and should be toned medium, and in order to make the job look well the fluting and carving should be gilded. The template with more timber fixed across makes the backboard. The frame is placed face downwards, and the mirror put gently in; then small three-cornered blocks are glued round to regulate it to show the bevel evenly, and when these are sufficiently set the backboard may be put in, and a square beading put round and fixed with fine sprigs.

TWO SIMPLE ARTISTIC OVERMANTELS.

This overmantel, a design for which is shown by Fig. 2476, looks well if made in mahogany, rosewood, oak, or American walnut. If it is desired to ebonise the

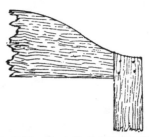

Fig. 2475.—Part Template for Glass.

finished overmantel, oak should not be used; the other woods are suited for the purpose. A very good effect can be produced by staining mahogany to "Chippendale colour." which is virtually an imi-

tation of rosewood. The size of the overmantel should depend upon requirements,
but the measurements given will be found
generally useful. If it is advisable to make

overmantel chiefly depends on the height of
the room; but it should not be out of proportion with the width. The proper width
can be judged from the distance between

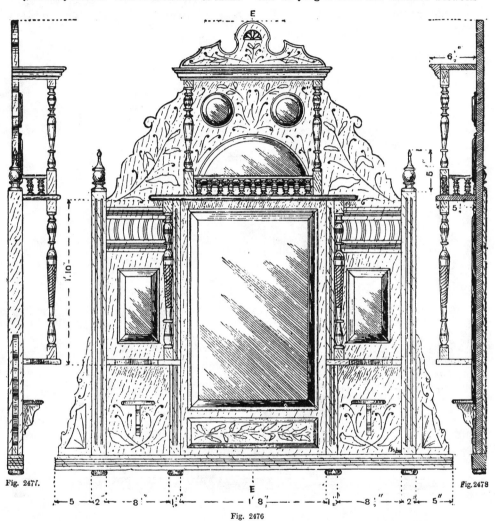

Fig. 2477.　　　　　　　　　　　　　　　　　　　　Fig. 2478.

Fig. 2476

Figs. 2476 to 2478.—Front and Side Elevation and Section of Artistic Overmantel.

the bottom of the overmantel larger than
the mantel-shelf, fix a mantel-board of the
required size on the top of the latter, and
then cover its edge with art muslin or
other suitable material. The height of the

the outer edges of the fireplace jambs,
as these are usually in a line with the outer
uprights of the overmantel. In constructing overmantels, every joint should be
neatly and carefully made; and it is advis-

able that the mortise-and-tenon method be adopted whenever possible. Fig. 2477 is an end elevation of the overmantel illustrated by Fig. 2476, and Fig. 2478 is a vertical section on the line E E (Fig. 2476). The the lengths of A and B, and ⅜ in. to C, which will enable the uprights, etc., to be let into grooves in the adjoining sections, thus strengthening the whole structure. The boards used are of ¾-in. stuff, the lengths of

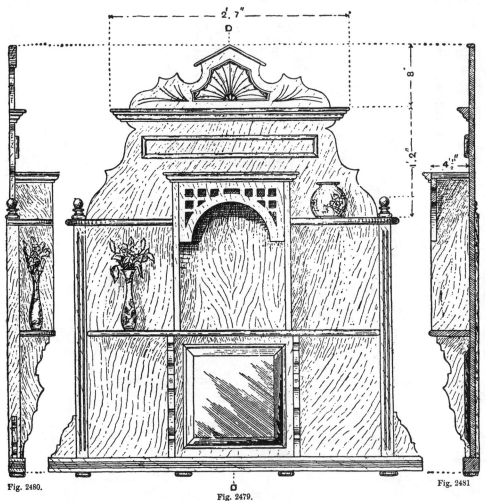

Fig. 2480.

Fig. 2479.

Fig. 2481.

Figs. 2479 to 2481.—Front and Side Elevations and Section of Artistic Overmantel.

overmantel has four turned feet. The overmantel shown by Fig. 2479, of which Fig. 2480 shows an end elevation, and Fig. 2481 a vertical section of the same on the line D D (Fig. 2479), may be made of walnut, or, if a cheaper wood be desired, deal. First put the frame together as shown in Fig. 2432. An extra ¾ in. may be added to which can be obtained from the sizes of the various compartments given in Fig. 2482. The head of this overmantel has ornamental edges and a decorated (carved) face, but some other design may be substituted if preferred. On the top of each of the two outside posts is a turned knob, which can easily be fastened in position by means of a dowel. A piece of moulding is tacked on the backboard right along the base of the head-piece, and a similar moulding is

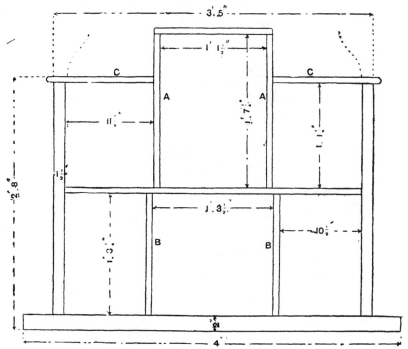

Fig. 2482.—Overmantel Framework.

fixed round the top of the central compartment. A gallery of spindles, similar to that shown above the square mirror in Fig. 2476, can be placed along the front edge at the bottom of this compartment. The spindles should be turned in a lathe, and holes bored in the shelf to receive the bottom dowels. A strip of wood, 1 in. square and about 1 ft. 2 in. long, is fixed to the tops of the spindles, and the whole fixed in position. The central compartment is still further improved by fixing at the top the simple fret shown by Fig. 2483. If desired, two reeds can be marked on the outside posts, as shown in Fig. 2479. Bevelled glass mirrors add greatly to the richness of overmantels. In the simple form shown by Fig. 2479 one piece of plate, 1 ft. 1 in. long by 1 ft. 1 in., is used ; and in the other overmantel (Fig. 2476) six bevelled plates of the following measure-

ments : Central plate, 1 ft. 6 in. by 2 ft. 3 in. ; side plates, 10 in. by 6 in. ; and the semicircular plate, 1 ft. 4 in. (along its straight edge) by 7 in. ; the circular plates are about 5 in. in diameter. Each piece of

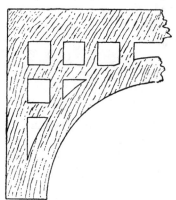

Fig. 2483.—Ornamental Fretwork.

glass must be measured $\frac{3}{8}$ in. longer and wider than sight size. The cost of the overmantel shown by Fig. 2476 can be reduced by substituting wood panels for some of the mirrors. If enamelling the overmantel, instead of polishing, first give it a coat of size, and when dry a couple of coats of enamel.

rail D, 3 ft. 3 in. long, crosses the stiles B and connects the stiles A. The bottom rail E is 4 ft. long. All the rails, including F, and stiles are halved together. A beading strip, $\frac{3}{16}$ in. thick, $1\frac{3}{4}$ in. wide, and 1 ft. 8 in. long, is let into the rails C, and a strip $\frac{9}{10}$ in.

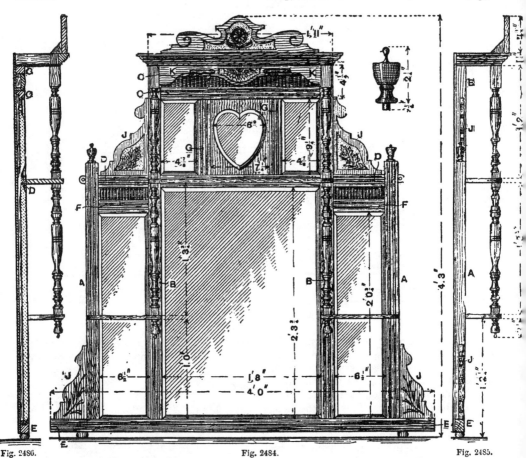

Fig. 2486.   Fig. 2484.   Fig. 2485.

Figs. 2484 to 2486.—Front and Side Elevations and Section of Overmantel.

ANOTHER OVERMANTEL.

The overmantel illustrated in front and side elevation by Figs. 2484 and 2485 is made chiefly of $1\frac{1}{2}$-in. by $1\frac{1}{8}$-in. stuff, with two beads run on the face. The two outer stiles A are 2 ft. $8\frac{1}{4}$ in. long, and the two inner stiles B are 3 ft. $8\frac{1}{4}$ in. long. The stiles B are joined together at the top by two rails C, which are 1 ft. 11 in. long and $1\frac{1}{4}$ in. apart; see Fig. 2486, which is a vertical section through the middle. The

thick, 2 in. wide, and $6\frac{1}{2}$ in. long, into the rails D and F in $\frac{1}{4}$-in. rebates. Two stiles G (Fig. 2484), $11\frac{1}{2}$ in. long, are halved to the lower rail C and the rail D. The lower shelves are $9\frac{1}{2}$ in. long, $4\frac{1}{2}$ in. wide, and $\frac{1}{2}$ in. thick, the outer corners being rounded; they also have a dowel hole for the pillar. The top shelf is 1 ft. 11 in. long, with its ends left square. The shelves are fixed from behind by means of screws. The pillars and finials are dowelled into the shelves and top. This top is $\frac{3}{16}$ in. thick, $5\frac{5}{8}$ in. wide, and 1 ft. $11\frac{1}{2}$ in. long. It is fixed to the top of the stiles B and the pillars, and on the top is a cornice $1\frac{5}{16}$ in.

Fig. 2487.—Simple Overmantel in White Enamel.

deep and $1\frac{1}{2}$ in. wide. The ornamental pieces J (Figs. 2484 and 2485) are let into the rails and stiles for $\frac{1}{8}$ in. The piece K is let into the tops of the pillars, and fixed to the top by means of small blocks. The mirrors are inserted in the usual manner, and for the one that is heart-shaped a panel $\frac{3}{16}$ in. thick is let into a rebate in the stiles G and the rails C and D. The feet for supporting the overmantel are $\frac{3}{4}$ in. thick and $1\frac{1}{2}$ in. in diameter. A pediment $4\frac{1}{2}$ in. deep, 1 ft. $6\frac{1}{2}$ in. long, and $\frac{5}{8}$ in. thick, is fixed to the top. A $\frac{1}{4}$-in. boarding should be fixed all over the back. The two side mirrors extend from the rails F to the rail E. Two eyes for fastening should be fixed to the top of the rails A.

SIMPLE OVERMANTEL IN WHITE ENAMEL.

The overmantel illustrated by Fig. 2487 looks well if constructed of good pine or American whitewood and finished in white enamel, with a gilt frame for the mirror, and a gilt slip or bead (not shown) on the margin where the shelf and the side brackets join. If oak or walnut is used, select moulding for the mirror with carved

egg-and-tongue ornament, and finish by french-polishing. The framework is for a bevelled mirror 2 ft. by 1 ft. 6 in. Prepare two stiles, 3 ft. by $1\frac{3}{4}$ in. by 1 in.; two inner stiles, 2 ft. 4 in. by $1\frac{1}{4}$ in. by 1 in.; one bottom rail, 3 ft. 9 in. by $1\frac{1}{4}$ in. by $1\frac{1}{4}$ in.; two inner rails, halved to the inner stiles and flush with them at the back, 2 ft. $1\frac{1}{2}$ in. by $1\frac{1}{4}$ in. by $\frac{5}{8}$ in.; and a shelf notched to fit the outer stiles and mortised for the ends of the inner stiles, 3 ft. 5 in. by $6\frac{1}{2}$ in. by $\frac{3}{4}$ in. The top rail is 3 ft. 7 in. by $2\frac{1}{4}$ in. by $1\frac{1}{4}$ in., and mortises should be cut at each end to fit over the outer stiles, and a rebate to receive the frieze panel. Work the moulding round the edges, and attach a beaded slip to form a guard for china plates, etc. Rebate the stiles and the rails, as shown in Fig. 2488, to receive a $\frac{5}{8}$-in. board; the mirror frame and side brackets should just lap the joints of the $\frac{5}{8}$-in. stuff. Then form a rebate, 3 ft. $1\frac{1}{2}$ in., on the front of the bottom rail, and a $\frac{1}{4}$-in. chamfer below. Next prepare two brackets, 6 in. by $5\frac{1}{2}$ in. by $\frac{3}{4}$ in., and two lower brackets, 2 ft. $2\frac{1}{2}$ in. by $9\frac{1}{2}$ in. by $\frac{3}{4}$ in. Cut the fretwork and the mortises for the stump tenons of the small shelves, 8 in. from the base, and trim. The bevelled pieces under the brackets are halved to the lower rail. The frieze panel is 3 ft. $1\frac{1}{2}$ in.

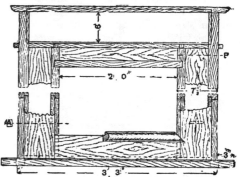

Fig. 2488.— Overmantel Frame Back and Front.

long by $6\frac{1}{2}$ in. by $\frac{5}{8}$ in., and is rebated to the top rail, and butts against a fillet glued to the top shelf. The parts should be fitted temporarily with screws before filling and polishing. Fig. 2488 is a diagram of the

framework, the top part showing the back
and the bottom part the front.

EASILY MADE PEDIMENTS.

The pediment or top-finish to an overmantel, or over-door, or to various articles

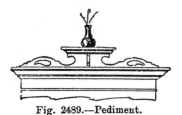

Fig. 2489.—Pediment.

of furniture, such as cabinets, sideboards,
and wardrobes, is capable of a great variety
of forms, as already illustrated on many
previous pages. The pediments shown in
Figs. 2489 to 2493 are simple outlines,
showing how easily the design can be
altered by following new curves and different arrangements of mouldings. An otherwise handsome piece of furniture, a sideboard, for instance, may be disfigured by
an ugly pediment. All the pediments
shown in the figures just referred to are
detachable. When designing, first firmly
decide on the ornament and draw the whole
out on stiff cardboard to full size. Cut
this out with a strong pair of scissors and
try it in position. This, when judged to be
correct, can be used as a template. The

Fig. 2490.—Pediment.

job will then not fail to be satisfactory,
and valuable timber will not be wasted, as
might be the case if a template were not
employed.

ORNAMENTAL CHIMNEY-PIECE AND OVER-MANTEL.

The chimney-piece shown in elevation in
Fig. 2494 is designed for a tenant's fixture,
is easily removed, and is capable of re-
adjustment to similar openings with little

trouble. It may be constructed of yellow
deal or basswood, which may be stained an
olive green or a ruby red, to harmonise

Fig. 2491.—Pediment.

with the surrounding furniture. An original novelty in the shape of two small
cupboards under the mantel has been introduced; these will be found very handy
receptacles for miscellaneous articles such
as pipes, match-boxes, etc. Fig. 2494 is
an elevation of the chimney-piece and
mantel-board complete, and Fig. 2495 is a
sectional plan of it, the left-hand half
being a section about 1 ft. above the floor,
and showing the arrangement of the jamb

Fig. 2492.—Pediment.

casing, etc., the parts above being indicated by dotted lines. The right half is a
section through the cupboards, immediately under the mantel-board, the dotted
lines showing the jamb beneath; the pieces
marked C C are the two ends of one of the
aforementioned cupboards, D is the sliding
door passing in front of the enclosed space
B, of which no further use is made in the
present instance than to strengthen the
bottom of the cupboards. F is a quadrant

Fig. 2493.—Pediment.

corner piece to cover the end of the slate
head, the line G being the plan of the
mantel-board. Fig. 2496 is a front elevation of the overmantel, which consists of

a plain back with three shelves supported by shaped brackets and a central mirror

figure shows parts above the top shelf, and the other side parts above the lower

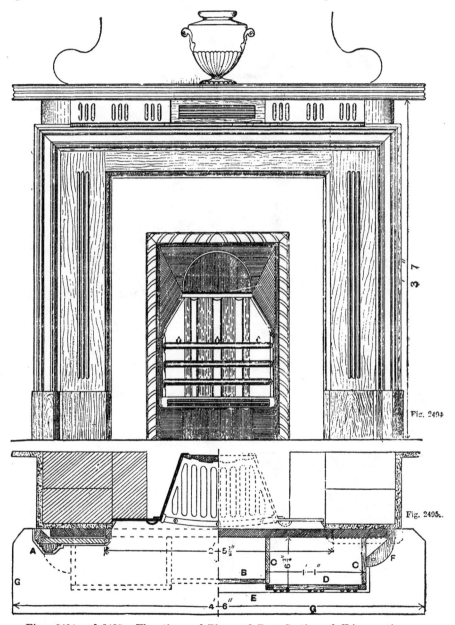

Figs. 2494 and 2495.—Elevation and Plan and Part Section of Chimney-piece.

with sprung head. Fig. 2497 is a plan of the overmantel. The portion on the left of

shelves. H is the back and I a cross batten. Fig. 2498 is a section, half full size, of the mirror frame. Fig. 2499 is a broken section, half full size through the jamb on case, showing its construction. The mar-

working between two $\frac{3}{16}$-in. fillets at top, and on a tongue and groove in the bottom E; at K is shown a dowel for fixing the

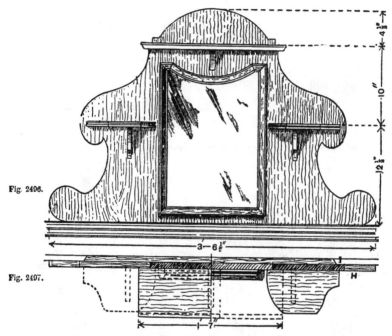

Fig. 2496.

Fig. 2497.

Figs. 2496 and 2497.—Elevation and Plan of Overmantel.

ginal line is the plan of the base block. Fig. 2500 is a detail of mantel cupboard, one quarter full size, and from this it will be seen that the old mantel-shelf is boxed

bottom to the moulded head. B is the front of the fixed compartment in the centre of the chimney-piece. Figs. 2501 and 2502 show the method of fixing the base blocks

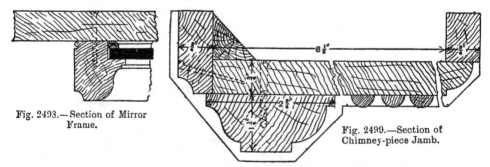

Fig. 2493.—Section of Mirror Frame.

Fig. 2499.—Section of Chimney-piece Jamb.

in by a thin casing, so arranged that by screwing up the soffit J the whole thing is fixed securely without any need of an attachment to the walls. D is the sliding door

to the jamb by means of dowel and dovetail; Fig. 2503 is a sketch of part of a door, showing its construction. Fig. 2504 shows an end view of the top shelf and bracket, and Fig. 2505 gives an end view of the bottom shelf, also with bracket.

JAMBS, ETC., OF CHIMNEY-PIECE

Assuming that a full-size plan has been set out, as shown in Fig. 2495, showing all the parts, and working from the actual fire-place, set about the construction of the jambs first. These consist of one wide and two narrow pieces of $\frac{3}{4}$-in. board, planed both sides, moulded as shown with ovolo and cove, and nailed and glued together.

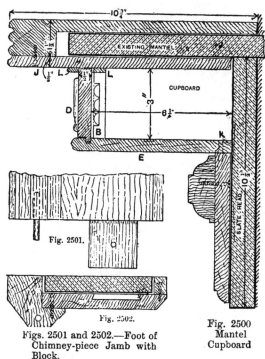

Fig. 2501.

Fig. 2502.

Figs. 2501 and 2502.—Foot of Chimney-piece Jamb with Block.

Fig. 2500 Mantel Cupboard

Before, however, fixing on the edge pieces, cut a barefaced dovetail at the lower end, as shown in Fig. 2501, shoulder back the top end to the moulding line, and plough a $\frac{1}{8}$-in. groove for a cross tongue. Treat the head in the same manner, and fasten it with a raking screw through the top edge. It will be noticed that it does not require edging except at the ends beyond the cupboards. This method of construction is adopted for convenience of re-adjustment after removal, and for the same reason the jambs are made wider than is quite necessary (see A, Fig. 2495). Glue the cross tongues in the jamb shoulders, screw the

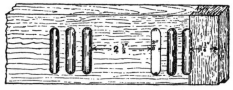

Fig. 2503.—Mantel Cupboard Slide Door.

head up, but do not glue it, put a stretcher at the bottom, and clean off. Brad on the reeds, rounding their ends with a file, and then fix the edging and mitre up the moulding. Make a square shoulder at the bottom

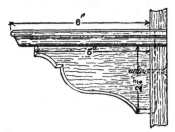

Fig. 2504.—Overmantel Top Shelf

flush with the jamb shoulder, and screw on from the back. The bases are built up of two pieces, one 6 in. long and 1 in. thick, and the other $3\frac{1}{8}$ in. by $3\frac{3}{4}$ in. by 6 in., fixed together as shown in Fig. 2502. When the dovetail has been fitted, the centre for the dowel holes may be found by driving into

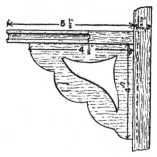

Fig. 2505.—Overmantel Bottom Shelf.

the shoulder the short end of a needle point, and tapping the block up until the point is indented, when it may be removed with the pincers, and the holes bored with a twist-bit.

CHIMNEY-PIECE MANTEL-BOARD, ETC.

For the mantel-board, a piece of pine 11 in. by 1½ in. by 4 ft. 6 in. is required, rebated out to fit easily over the existing shelf. The necessity of having the rebating stopped at each end may be avoided, if desired, by substituting a ½-in. board for

Fig. 2506.—Combined Overmantel and Bookcase.

the top, and gluing a fillet equal in thickness to the shelf along the front edge and at each end. The soffit board is fitted and screwed to the same, so that it may grip the shelf tightly and prevent the board slipping off. The edges may now be moulded, and, if the use of a plane of the right section cannot be had, the beads may be planted on. Next prepare the piece E of ½-in. stuff, plough a ¼-in. groove $\frac{3}{16}$ in. deep and ¾ in. from the front edge; it should be

stopped 1 in. from each end. Bore two $\frac{3}{8}$-in. dowel holes near the back edge, and prepare the five pieces marked B and C, which are each 3 in. wide; square them off $\frac{1}{16}$ in. short of the groove in the piece E, and fix with brads and glue. Make the two doors 3¼ in. wide, clamping them as shown in Fig. 2503; brad on the reeds and fit the tongue to slide easily in the groove, and notch back the tongue from the end to form a stop. Fit this case to the head of the chimney-piece, arranging it exactly in the centre, and mark the holes for the dowels K (Fig. 2500). Now take off the soffit board, erect the frame in position again, slip in the soffit, and mark around the divisions with a pencil; it can now be taken down and fixed with brads or screws in the proper position as indicated by the pencil marks. The fillets L L must then be bradded on to form guides for the doors, and the quadrants P F screwed from the inside of C and the top of the soffit. The chimney-piece is now completed, and it is fixed by entering the dowels at the bottom of the blocks into the floor, bringing the jamb frame up to the wall, pushing into place the cupboard, dropping in the two pins K, which keep the top end in position, and then re-screwing the soffit to the mantel-board.

OVERMANTEL TO GO WITH CHIMNEY-PIECE.

The back of the overmantel is formed of five lengths of $\frac{3}{8}$-in. by 9-in. board, glued together, and then cut to shape. Care should be taken that the heart sides of all the pieces are arranged in one direction— toward the back for preference. To obtain an approximate reproduction of the curve of the back, draw a number of parallel horizontal lines across the sketch, make a similar number of lines at corresponding distances to scale upon the stuff, and measure the distance from a centre line; each line passes through the curve, and these lengths should be pricked off upon the stuff, thereby obtaining points through which to draw the curve full size. The shape may be cut out with a bow-saw, and worked with spokeshave and file. Next set out and sink the housings ¼ in. deep for

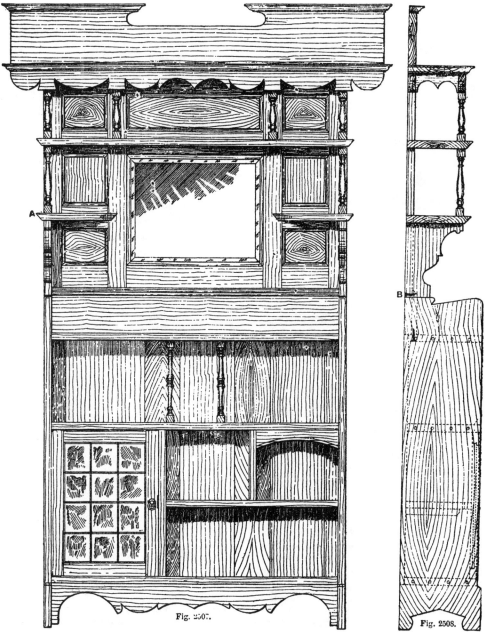

Figs. 2507 and 2508.—Front and Side Elevations of Combined Overmantel and Bookcase.

the shelves; square with the centre line. The top shelf groove can be run through, as it will be covered by the return end of the shelf (see the plan, Fig. 2497), but the others must be stopped at the length of the shelves. In the preliminary housing, the lines should be left in, so that they may be worked up to when the shelves are cleaned off, and left tight. The shelves and brackets should now be prepared, the former with the grain running parallel to the front edge and the latter with the grain crossing the shelves, into which they should be housed ⅛ in., but not so tight as not to allow

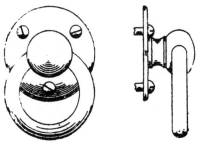

Fig. 2509.—Cupboard Door Ring.

for shrinkage. A 3-in. by ½-in. batten should be fitted to the back at its widest part with slotted screws, and the mirror frame proceeded with. It is as well to procure the glass first, in case of mistakes, though these should be avoided if a template of thin stuff is cut to the shape required and less ⅛ in. all round in size; this allowance is for the diamond. Figure on the dimensions, or the glazier may cut off an additional ⅛ in. The moulding may be purchased ready stuck at a sawmill; and if a piece is worked square for the head to the right sweep, it will be run through the machine to the same section for a few pence. Mitre up the four square mitres first, leaving the short pieces at the top longer than required. Then set a bevel and work the mitres on the sprung-piece; bore holes for fine screws square with the mitres, and screw all up. See that the sides are parallel; lay the sprung-piece on top and scribe over the mitre lines; unscrew, cut off and shoot, glue, and screw up again. The whole may now be cleaned off and stained. The mirror fillets may then be bradded in as shown in Fig. 2498, and the frame screwed to the back. A pair of brass "glass plates" (Fig. 822, p. 250, or Fig. 1702, p. 502), screwed to the back of the wings for securing it to the wall, complete the mirror.

COMBINED OVERMANTEL AND BOOKCASE.

This combined overmantel and bookcase, of which Fig. 2506 is a general view, Fig. 2507 the front elevation, and Fig. 2508 a side elevation, is composed of two main parts, which can either be made to form one article, or constructed to be taken apart for the purpose of forming two articles, the upper part as a mantel and the bottom part as a bookcase. Hard wood— such as walnut, mahogany, or oak—is required, the boards being preferably not less than 11 in. wide and 1 in. thick.

MAKING THE BOOKCASE.

The bookcase part should be first made. Cut off two lengths 3 ft. 9 in. by 11 in. (for the sides or ends), three lengths 3 ft. 4 in.

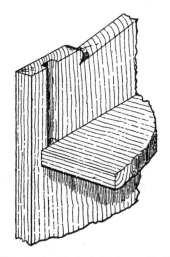

Fig. 2510.—Part of Bookcase Shelf.

by 10⅝ in. (for the three long shelves), one length 2 ft. by 10⅝ in. (for the short shelf), one length 1 ft. 8 in. by 10⅝ in. (for the long division next to the door), and one length 9½ in. by 10⅝ in. (for the short division between the shelves). These are the net sizes, so that some allowance must be made for squaring and trimming. The door is made when the rest of the bookcase has been put together. Take the two end pieces and cut them out to the shape shown in Fig. 2508, the small bevelled piece at the front bottom edge of each being glued on. On the inner faces of the end pieces, in the positions shown in Fig. 2508, bore holes ⅝ in. deep for the dowels which hold the ends and the shelves together. To ensure a good fit, great care must be taken in marking off the positions of these dowel holes, which is best done in the following manner: First run a gauge line through the centre of the ends of the shelves, and square lines across for the centres of the dowel holes; lay the shelves in position on the end pieces, and mark off both the positions of the four dowel holes and the centre gauge line. If the holes are not marked off perfectly true with one another, the dowels will not fit properly. The depth of the dowel holes in the ends of the shelves is 1½ in. and the diameter ½ in., if in an inch board. Having glued the holes in the ends of the shelves, drive in the dowels and cut them off to the required length by measuring off the depths of the holes in the ends, care being taken not to make the dowels too long, or the joints will not close up. Smooth up the surfaces of the end pieces and shelves with a fine-set smoothing plane, scrape them well with a scraper, and finish off with glasspaper, using first fairly coarse and then fine paper. Glue the joints well with thin, hot glue, and set to dry; with cramps, better and closer joints will be made. The upright stiles of the door are 1 ft. 8 in. by 1¾ in. by 1 in., and the rails 1 ft. 2½ in. by 1¼ in. by 1 in. At each end of the rails cut a tenon $\frac{5}{16}$ in. thick and 1½ in. long, which will give a width of 11½ in. between the shoulders. The stiles and rails are rebated ⅜ in. in the thickness of the wood and $\frac{5}{16}$ in. in the width, to receive the leaded light, which is secured by a narrow bead at the back fastened with brads. It is intended that there should be a removable shelf inside the cupboard, resting on two strips fastened to the sides, in the position indicated by dotted lines on the side elevation (Fig. 2508). The cupboard door ring is shown by Fig. 2509.

OTHER DETAILS OF THE BOOKCASE.

The two pieces of fretwork over the short shelf and under the long bottom shelf are made from 1-in. stuff, and are glued in place and held at the back by small glued blocks. The two fancy centre pillars are fixed at the top by means of dowels, and screwed at the bottom. The top shelf of the bookcase (Fig. 2510) is surmounted by a beaded back-piece, fitting into grooves cut on the insides of the end pieces, the purpose of which is to cover the joint between the two parts of the fitment. The

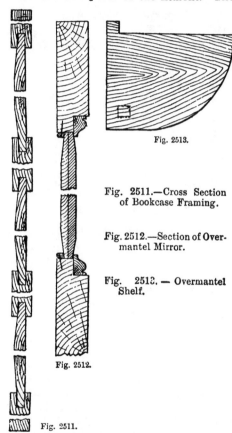

Fig. 2513.

Fig. 2511.—Cross Section of Bookcase Framing.

Fig. 2512.—Section of Overmantel Mirror.

Fig. 2513. — Overmantel Shelf.

Fig. 2512.

Fig. 2511.

back of the bookcase is made of pine, and is put together with muntins ⅝ in. thick, of which four will be required, two for the outside and two for the inside. Fig. 2511 is a cross section of the bookcase framing. The outside muntins fitting against the inner faces of the ends are 2 in. wide, and are grooved on one edge, while the inside muntins are 5 in wide and grooved on both edges. The spaces between the muntins are filled with panels ⅜ in. thick bevelled at the back as shown, to fit easily into the grooves in the muntins. The completed back is held securely by screwing it to the shelves, the outside muntins being also glued to the end pieces. The muntins will require to be notched out ¼ in. to allow the shelves to fit flush with the face of the bookcase.

Fig. 2514.—Folding Card-table Closed.

MAKING THE OVERMANTEL.

In making the overmantel part, which should be done next, first cut out the framing, which is of ¾-in. pine, halved at the joints, and faced with ¼-in. wood similar to that used for the bookcase. The facings are best put on after the framing has been joined up ¼ in. less at the inner sides, so as to form a rebate for the ½-in. mould which surrounds the panel openings. The rebate formed by the facing will only be ¼ in. deep; as it is necessary that it should be ½ in. deep to take the mould, the pine framing will need to be rebated ¼ in. in order to obtain the required depth. The wood panels, which may be either plain or carved, are put in from the back, and fastened by beads in the same manner as the leaded light in the door. The mirror is secured as shown in Fig. 2512. The pediment, shelves, and fretwork of the overmantel are 1 in. thick, the shelves being screwed from the back. The pillars are turned with a small pin at each end, holes being bored in the shelves to receive them. It will be seen that the bracket which supports the half-

round shelf (Fig. 2513) is not fixed against the face of the framing, but against the edge, so as not to show a joint. It is then necessary to cut out a piece of the framing to receive the bracket, which is held by screws passed through the framing from the panel openings before the panel is placed in position. The edge of the top shelf is moulded, while the edges of the other shelves are bevelled; with the exception of the top shelf, all are returned past the edge of the framing. The four top pillars have a longer square portion at their upper ends than the others; this extra piece is halved into the fretwork, so that the pillars may lie flush with the face side. The fretwork is fastened with screws put in from the back by means of pocket holes.

FIXING COMBINED OVERMANTEL AND BOOKCASE.

The overmantel is fixed on top of the bookcase by screws passing through the overmantel framing into the beaded back-piece on the bookcase; if this construction is to be used as two articles, the overmantel should be provided with dowels fitting into holes bored in the top of the sides of the bookcase. When completed, all the woodwork is french-polished. The front and side elevations are drawn to a scale of 1½ in. to the foot; the shelf plan, the elevation showing the method of jointing door framework, and the inside view of bookcase end at B, to a scale of 3 in. to the foot; the transverse section of bookcase framing, the elevation showing the method of fixing bookcase shelves, and that showing the method of fixing the mirror, to a scale of 6 in. to the foot; while the door ring is two-thirds full size.

MATERIALS FOR INLAID FOLDING CARD-TABLE.

The card-table shown open by Fig. 2514, and closed by Fig. 2515, is made so that when the top is folded the whole answers as a side table. The wood for the top should be well seasoned, as, being connected to the table frame by a centre only, it is liable to warp if not thoroughly dry; mahogany is suitable. The ornamental lines are inlaid with satinwood or boxwood stringing, which can be obtained from most cabinet-makers or veneer merchants. Instead of the inlaying, the lines can be incised with a tool shaped like a **V**, or a

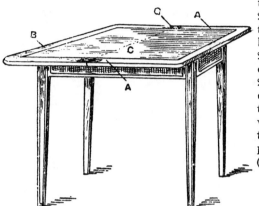

Fig. 2515.—Folding Card-table Open.

small gouge. If not to be inlaid, the table could be made of pine, with birch legs, and afterwards stained, painted, or enamelled. The following are the dimensions of the stuff required, allowing a little for working : Two pieces for the top, 3 ft. by 1 ft. 6 in. by 1 in. ; four legs, 2 ft. 5 in. by 1¾ in. by 1¾ in. ; two side rails, 2 ft. 9 in. by 4¼ in. by 1 in. ; two end rails, 1 ft. 4 in. by 4¼ in. by 1 in. ; two strips of veneer for the top (A, Fig. 2515), 3 ft. by 2 in. ; strips for gluing round the inside of the tops to form a recess for the cloth (B, Fig. 2515), 1 ft. 3 in. by 2 in. (endway of grain) ; one cross-rail on which the top revolves (D, Fig. 2516), 1 ft. 4 in. by 3 in. by 1 in. ; one inside rail (E, Fig. 2516), which forms the inside end of the box for holding cards, etc., 1 ft. 4 in. by 3½ in. by 1 in. ; and one piece for the bottom of the box (F, Fig. 2516), 1 ft. 4 in. by 1 ft. 5 in. by ½ in. The bottom F can be kept in position by ½-in. strips nailed or screwed to the side and end rails.

MAKING CARD-TABLE.

To proceed with the making, plane the top to thickness and take to length and width. Next mark, with a toothing plane,

the inside face of the top, which makes the cloth and the veneer borders stick better. The veneer (A and B, Fig. 2515) can then be laid, the end pieces being endways, and the grain running the same way as that of the top. Then insert the stringing H (Fig. 2514) in the uppermost side of the top when the table is closed ; the outer line should be 1½ in. from the edge and the inner line 2 in. from the edge. If desired, the corners of the top may be rounded as shown in Fig. 2515. When the veneer and stringing are dry, the two outside edges and ends of the top can be rounded, the two inside edges, which are hinged, being left square. The top should then be cleaned up and sand-papered ready for hingeing, as shown at G (Fig. 2515).

LEGS AND FRAME OF CARD-TABLE.

The legs should be squared up to 1¾ in., and the side and end rails planed and taken to width. Before tapering the legs, they should be mortised to receive the tenons on the ends of the rails. Allowing for the legs to stand in underneath the top 1¼ in. at the ends and ½ in. at the sides, the length from shoulder to shoulder of the side rails will be 2 ft. 6 in., and of the end rails 1 ft. 1½ in. The legs should be tapered to 1¼ in. square at the bottom, commencing the taper 4¼ in. from the top. The stringing is inlaid in the legs ¼ in. from the edge, and in the rails ½ in. from the edge. Before gluing the frame together, the inside rail E (Fig. 2516)

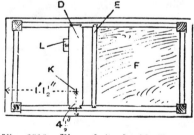

Fig. 2516.—Plan of Card-table Frame.

should be fitted either with stump tenons or dovetails 1 ft. 5 in. from the end rail. The latter rail is ¾ in. narrower than the other rails, which allows the bottom of the card-box to be screwed underneath it.

The cross rail D (Fig. 2516) can be dovetailed into the side rails when the frame is together.

CARD-TABLE TOP.

When the frame is together, the top should be hinged and the centre may be fixed. The hinges (see Fig. 2415) and the revolving centre can be obtained of most 2515, a piece of wood L (Fig. 2516) about 1 in. wide is screwed to the under-side of the top. The baize or cloth c (Fig. 2515) should be pasted down after the table has been polished.

CHESS AND DRAUGHTS TABLE.

A side elevation of the chess table is shown by Fig. 2517. Fig. 2518 is an end

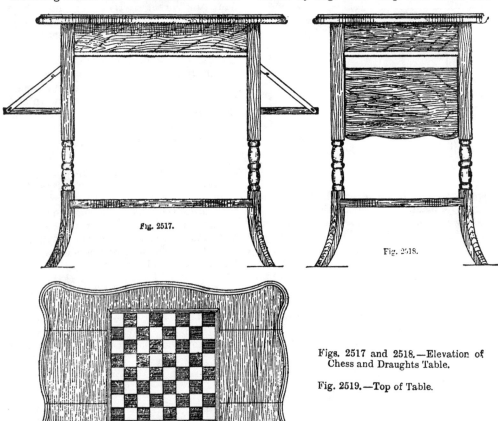

Fig. 2517.

Fig. 2518.

Figs. 2517 and 2518.—Elevation of Chess and Draughts Table.

Fig. 2519.—Top of Table.

Fig. 2519.

ironmongers. The position for the revolving centre is shown at K (Fig. 2516), 1 ft. 1½ in. from the end of the top and 4½ in. from the side. The large plate is screwed to the under-side of the top, the bolt goes through the rail D (Fig. 2516), and the nut screws up underneath. To prevent the top turning too far when opened, as in Fig. elevation, and the top of the table is shown in Fig. 2519. It will look best if made in Spanish mahogany. The four legs are 2 ft. 3 in. long, and are marked out on a piece of 1½-in. plank. The cutting out, however, is not finished till they have been turned in the lathe (see Fig. 2520). A length of 1 ft. 1 in. of the upper part of the leg is 1½ in.

square, then 6 in. is turned, the remaining 8 in. being cut to the curved shape shown, and tapering from $1\frac{1}{4}$ in. square to 1 in. square at the foot. Figs. 2517 and 2518 show that the lower parts of the legs point direct towards the corners, and also that the angle of the upper part is in line with the centre of the flat of the lower part; this is illustrated in Fig. 2521, which also shows the leg cut out $\frac{1}{4}$ in. deep by $\frac{3}{4}$ in. wide for the shelf. Two rails must be got out 1 ft. 10 in. long by 3 in. wide by $\frac{3}{4}$ in. thick, and two of the same section cut 1 ft. 3 in. long. These are tenoned 1 in. at each end into the legs, and mitred; they are then rebated on the lower edge inside, to receive the box

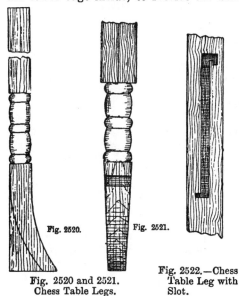

Fig. 2520. Fig. 2521.

Fig. 2520 and 2521. Chess Table Legs.

Fig. 2522.—Chess Table Leg with Slot.

bottoms, which are of $\frac{1}{2}$-in. board. Each leg is mortised, and the corner cut out as a continuation of the rebates in the rails.

CHESS TABLE FLAPS.

Before gluing up the legs and rails, the slots for the flaps should be made; they should not be more than $\frac{1}{4}$ in. wide by $\frac{3}{8}$ in. deep, and 4 in. long. Fig. 2522 shows a slot, the lower end having a little retreat backwards to receive the pin, which is put towards the back edge of the flap, so that when it is in use (see Fig. 2517) it will not tip up at the back when weight is put near the front. To put the flap out of use, as shown by Fig. 2518, it is moved forwards, the back edge being pushed upwards, and

Fig. 2523.—Metal Arm for Chess Table Shelf.

the pin slides to the top of the slot and, slightly moved forward, falls into the recess made for it. To ascertain the exact position of the slot, make one of the arms of a strip of brass $9\frac{1}{2}$ in. long by $\frac{1}{2}$ in. wide by $\frac{1}{10}$ in. thick. A hole to take a No. 8 screw is then drilled $\frac{3}{8}$ in. from one end, and countersunk on one side, then a hole is drilled $\frac{3}{8}$ in. from the other end, and another so close to it as almost to run into it. These holes are both countersunk on the other side, and then should be filed into each other, using a ward file and forming a slot about $\frac{3}{8}$ in. long by $\frac{9}{16}$ in. wide. The flap itself is of $\frac{1}{2}$-in. board 1 ft. $0\frac{3}{4}$ in. long by 8 in. wide. The arms are screwed through the slot to the side edges 1 in. from the front edge, but the screw should move freely in the slot, and 1-in. No. 8 screws, with the heads filed flush with the necks, are screwed in $\frac{1}{2}$ in. from the back edge, and stand up $\frac{5}{16}$ in. These are the flap pins which work in the leg slots. The recess

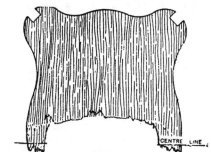

Fig. 2524.—Part Plan of Chess Table Shelf.

(see Fig. 2523) must be filed at the position where the arm falls against the back screw, when the screw in the slot is farthest from the end. When the arm is screwed in its place on the leg, the top end of the leg slot is marked from the recess in the arm, and the lower end 4 in. below it. All four legs must be treated in this manner, there being four arms, two for each flap (see Fig. 2517).

CHESS TABLE SHELF.

The shelf (Fig. 2524) is next taken in hand. The corners are cut out to the legs, which should fit tightly, and then the legs, rails, and shelf are glued up at the same time, the shelf being further secured by screws driven in on the slant from underneath into the back of the legs. Two rails are now required, each 1 ft. 2½ in. long by 2½ in. wide by ¾ in. thick; they must be half dovetailed (see Fig. 2525) into the long rails 5 in. from the end rails, and thus form the inner sides of the boxes. They must stop at the corner of the rebate, and be flush at the top.

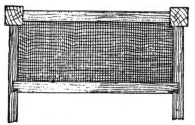

Fig. 2525.—Horizontal Section of Chess Table Frame.

CHESS TABLE TOP, BOXES, ETC.

The table top is made of two thicknesses of timber, the first being ⅝ in. thick with the grain running lengthwise. It measures 2 ft. 4 in. by 1 ft. 8 in., and is cut to the shape shown by Fig. 2519, a 1-ft. square being marked on the upper side exactly central. To make the checker-board, a piece of sycamore board 1 ft. 2 in. long by 7 in. wide by ¾ in. thick must be planed quite flat and square, and a piece of dark, straight-grained mahogany is likewise prepared, the thicknessing and squaring being important. The second piece must be stained with Stephens' ebony stain, which is allowed to penetrate into the wood as much as possible. The sixty-four check squares measure 1½ in., and should be cut from the two boards, on a fine-toothed, hollow-ground circular saw, such as is employed by camera makers, pattern makers, and toy manufacturers; this will cut them accurately, and almost as smoothly as if they were planed. Thirty-two black and white squares will be wanted, and they are fastened with thin glue. There must be a black square at the left-hand corner when the player is sitting in position, and the

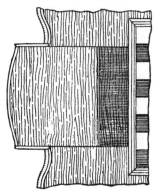

Fig. 2526.—Sliding Lid of Chess Table Box.

worker, when standing by the side of the top, should commence by laying the line nearest him, having a black at the left-hand corner first. Another item is to put the grain of the whites running one way, and of the blacks the other. A surround of ½-in. by ⅜-in. oak is then put in, the oak contrasting with both black and white, and the end pieces should be grooved on the outside $\frac{3}{16}$ in. deep and $\frac{3}{16}$ in. wide to admit the tongue of the box lid. Two rectangular holes, 8 in. by 3½ in., must now be cut through the top, commencing from the surround piece. The remainder of the top is next covered with ⅜-in. board, the grain running crosswise, and to do this two pieces are made first to cover the ends which are cut for the sliding lids of the boxes (see Figs. 2519 and 2526). The lids are grooved on the back and end edges ½ in. deep by $\frac{3}{16}$ in. wide. Tongues of boxwood must be fitted in these, standing out ¼ in. on the end edges and ⅛ in. at the back (see Fig.

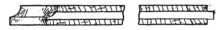

Fig. 2527.—Edge of Sliding Lid.

2527). The lids will not then have a tendency to warp, or get easily broken, the tongues acting as clamps. Corresponding grooves must be made in the top parts, which are then glued on, and the remainder of the top is covered. If the wood is kept of one thickness, the top should require little else than glasspapering, especially the checker-board, or perhaps a little use of the scraper, but if any of the blacks should require touching up, a marquetry stain will be best. The thicknessing and fitting of the sixty-four squares forming the checker-board are matters requiring

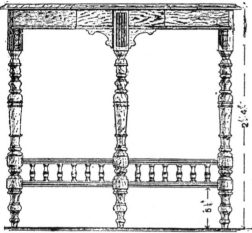

Fig. 2528.—Octagonal Occasional Table.

great care. The box lids should be left fitting rather tightly till the top has been moulded, or they can be made tight by wetting the tongues and grooves, and closing the lids immediately; this causes them to swell, making it almost impossible to move them until they have become quite dry again. The top is fixed on by being screwed through the upper edge of the rails, which must be thumb-notched with a gouge inside, blocks being glued round it. The box bottoms may then be secured in place, and a thumb-mould, of $1\frac{1}{4}$-in. by $\frac{1}{2}$-in. material, put under the rails, and fixed with screws. The flaps are made of $\frac{1}{2}$-in. board to the shape shown by Fig. 2518, but the arms are again detached, for convenience in polishing both table and flaps. The lids should be eased sufficiently to enable them to be drawn by pressure of the thumb; and the space between the boxes may be utilised for a drawer. The table, with a cover on the top, can be used as a window table or for afternoon tea.

47

OCTAGONAL OCCASIONAL TABLE WITH TURNED LEGS.

Mahogany, walnut, or any other fancy wood will be suitable for making the octagonal table of which Fig. 2528 is an elevation; Fig. 2529 is a half plan looking up and a half plan looking down. The form and construction of the different joints and connections are clearly shown in the figures. The top should be in one piece, if wood sufficiently wide can be obtained, or it may be in two pieces jointed in the middle. To make a strong joint, the pieces should be dowelled and glued, and the joint held by a couple of cramps until the glue is thoroughly dry. Next true the top, then mark out and cut it to shape, and plane the edges true. The moulding can next be worked on the edges. The legs should be turned to the pattern shown in wood about $1\frac{3}{4}$ in. square. The upper ends of the legs will be improved if they are reeded as shown in Figs. 2528, 2530, and

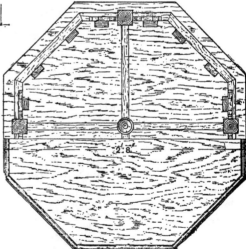

Fig. 2529.—Top and Underneath Plans of Table.

2531. The rails should be trued, and the ends carefully mitred and grooved for a cross-tongue, or they may be dowelled. The pieces can then be placed in position on the top and fitted together. Four of the rails and legs can next be jointed and fitted together, the joint being shown by

Fig. 2531. The top of the leg is forked to go over the rail, and the rail is notched on the inner side to keep the leg more rigid. A shallow groove should be made on each side of the leg for the bracket (see A, Fig. 2531). Then make the cross-rails connecting the leg, as shown in section by Fig.

Fig. 2530

Fig. 2531.

Fig. 2530. — Part of Table Leg, Bracket, etc.

Fig. 2531.—Joint between Table Leg and Rail.

2532. The small balusters and centre-piece connecting the rails (see Fig. 2532) should be obtained, and care must be taken to make the mortises in their true positions in the centre-piece. The rails are stub-tenoned into this piece, and also into the legs. The rails should now be bored for the pins on the ends of the small balusters.

When the parts have been carefully fitted, the joints should be glued together. The rails are secured to the top by means of angle blocks fixed with glue (see Fig. 2529). The moulded fillet B (Fig. 2530) should next be mitred round and fixed to the rail with glue and a few fine sprigs. The brackets are fixed to the legs and fillet with glue. The table should be finished with the scraper (if necessary), and rubbed with fine glasspaper in the direction of the grain of the wood.

EASY LOUNGE CHAIR.

The chair shown in Fig. 2533 as an easy chair and in Fig. 2534 as a lounge chair may be made of dark mahogany, American walnut, or oak. By means of the spring

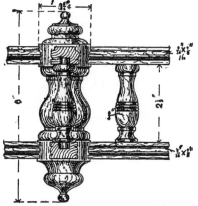

Fig. 2532.—Centre-piece Balusters, etc.

and stop-rack (Fig. 2535), the seat and back can be made to form almost any inclined lounge. Pressing the button B (Figs. 2533 and 2534) liberates the seat, which can be drawn along the cradle. The cradle (Fig. 2536) consists of two sides joined by three rails, A, B, and C; each side has two rails D and E, D being 2 ft. 6 in. by 2 in. by 2 in., and E 2 ft. 4 in. by 2 in. by 2 in., with a tenon to fit into the leg F. The rails D and E are connected by four small turned pillars and a large one at one end, all being 7 in. long. The legs should all be turned similar to F (Fig. 2536), the rail E being inserted into the leg F by means of a tenon, and the leg G let into the rail E. The dimensions of the legs allow the lower portion marked P to be inserted into the socket of the castor. A bead should be run along the top and bottom edges and joined with a similar bead at the ends on the outside of the rails, as shown. When the two sides are so far constructed, glue and screw at the bottom of the inside of the lower rail a bearer

are each 1 ft. 8 in. long and 1½ in. in diameter. One inch should be allowed at either end for the tenon. The seat and back are shown in Fig. 2537. The dimensions of all the parts are shown, and the material may be 1 in. thick.

COMPLETING THE EASY LOUNGE CHAIR.

When the framework is completed, join in the centre with two brass butt hinges as shown, and in the part intended for the seat insert the stop-rack R (Fig. 2535), on the edge of the rail in the position marked X Y in Fig. 2537, and also as shown in Fig. 2534. The front plate M (Fig. 2537) is

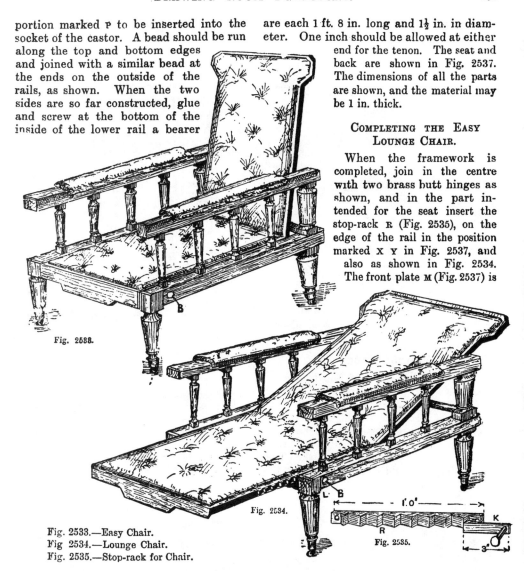

Fig. 2533.—Easy Chair.
Fig 2534.—Lounge Chair.
Fig. 2535.—Stop-rack for Chair.

H (Fig. 2536), projecting 1 in. and level with the front rail—that is, 1 in. from the top of the rail. Also insert the spring catch K (Fig. 2535) as shown at S in Fig. 2536) with the button B projecting as shown in Figs. 2533 and 2534. The two sides being completed, join them by the three rails A, B, and C (Fig. 2536). A is 1 ft. 8 in. by 2 in. by 1 in., and is flush with the front, and 1 in. from the top of the legs. B and C

screwed and glued to the front edge of the frame, and can be ornamented if desired ; if cut as shown in Figs. 2533 and 2534, it will be found convenient for drawing out the seat when required for a lounge, and for preventing the seat going too far back when required for an easy chair. A margin of 1 in. should be allowed all round the inside of the frame for attaching the webbing and canvas for the upholstery. The framework and the two arms should be upholstered as shown in Figs. 2533 and 2534, and finished

by 2-in. pine, lap-jointed at the square end and dowelled at the round end, or foot,

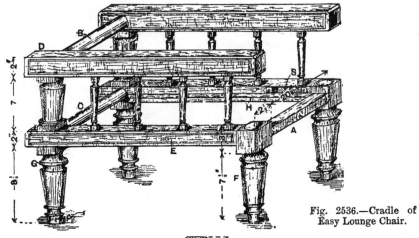

Fig. 2536.—Cradle of Easy Lounge Chair.

with a covering on the back. The whole of the woodwork should be glasspapered and polished.

PARLOUR COUCH.

The show wood parts of the couch, of which Fig. 2538 is a general view, should preferably be made of hard wood, the choice of which will depend on the surrounding furniture, but sound clean pine will be quite suitable for all the inside framework. Fig. 2539 shows a leg. The bottom frame should be made first of 3-in.

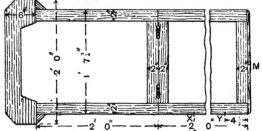

Fig. 2537.—Seat and Back of Lounge Chair.

which can be sawn from a piece 4 in. wide, 3 in. thick, and 2 ft. long. The bottom

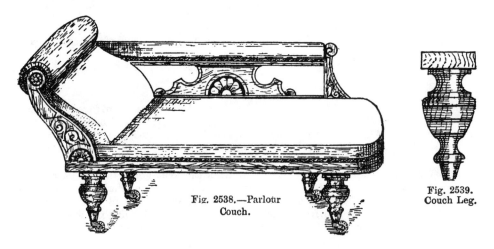

Fig. 2538.—Parlour Couch.

Fig. 2539. Couch Leg.

frame is 5 ft. long by 2 ft. wide outside. The two cross-rails are housed into the side stuff, and the show-wood scroll of $\frac{5}{8}$-in. hardwood, with the edges beaded, and the face

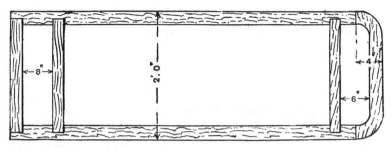

Fig. 2540.—Bottom Frame of Parlour Couch.

rails to a depth of $\frac{3}{4}$ in., and dressed flush with the top and bottom. Particular care should be taken to avoid any twist in the frame when put together. Fig. 2540 shows the bottom frame. The legs (Fig. 2539) are turned from wood blocks 10 in. long by $4\frac{1}{2}$ in. square, and the castors to be used should be given to the turner, Fig. 2539 being suited to socket castors. The side rail has a moulding attached to it, the latter being $1\frac{3}{8}$ in. wide by $\frac{1}{2}$ in. thick, and decorated by a centre bead. At the foot the moulding will require kerfing or steaming to the sweep.

is decorated to pattern with incised carving, the petals of the rosettes being worked slightly in low relief. The stuffing scrolls are framed up with two cross-rails, the top rail being 6 in. wide and housed into the scrolls, and the bottom rail 2 in. square and shoulder tenoned. The finished head should be exactly 2 ft. wide, and is secured to the bottom frame by three dowels at each side, glued and cramped. The show-wood scroll butts against the moulding.

BACK OF COUCH.

The couch back, with the exception of the baluster, is shown in Fig. 2543, the finial A being 1 ft. 4 in. long by 5 in. wide, and

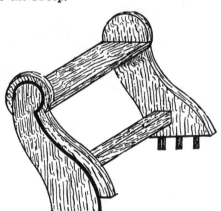

Fig. 2541.—Couch Head Frame.

HEAD OF COUCH.

A general view of the couch head is shown in Fig. 2541, and patterns of the stuffing scrolls and show-wood scrolls are given in Fig. 2542. The stuffing scrolls are of 1-in.

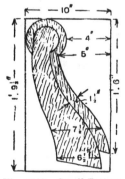

Fig. 2542.—Scroll Pattern.

$1\frac{1}{2}$ in. thick, carved to pattern on the face side only, and centre-beaded on the outside edge. The top rail is $2\frac{1}{2}$ in. wide by $\frac{3}{4}$ in. thick, and has attached on the top a pine stuffing rail 2 in. by $\frac{1}{2}$ in., on which the covers are tacked. The bottom rail is 1½ in. wide by ¾ in. thick, both rails being

cient for the bolster head, each being fastened to the rail with wire staples. The

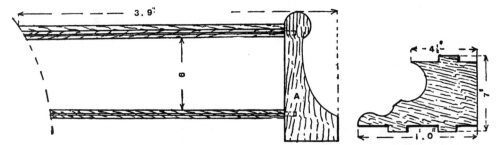

Fig. 2543.—Back of Couch. Fig. 2544.—Half Pattern of Baluster.

beaded on the face and tenoned into the finial. The baluster, a half pattern of which is shown in Fig. 2544, is of 1-in. hardwood sawn out to pattern and carved on the face; it is fixed by stub tenons to the top and bottom rails. The back rails are half jointed and screwed into the back of the couch head, and the legs are secured by three dowels to each, two being let into the side rail and the centre dowel into the cross-rail.

COMPLETING THE COUCH.

The couch above described is intended to be upholstered with a spring seat, spring swell, and spring bolster head, the bolster arm at the back being stuffed up firm. In Fig. 2545 is shown a part view of the swell and bolster head before the first stuffing is commenced. Five springs are required for the swell, and are sewn to the webs, and four springs will be suffi-

parts which require stitching up to a square edge are both sides of the swell, each

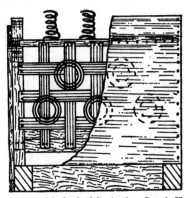

Fig. 2545.—Method of Springing Couch Head.

end of the bolster head, and the back and front edges of the bottom, and also the round foot.

INDEX.

(Illustrated subjects are denoted by asterisks.)